Lecture Notes in Artificial Intelligence 13721

Subseries of Lecture Notes in Computer Science

Series Editors

Randy Goebel
University of Alberta, Edmonton, Canada

Wolfgang Wahlster
DFKI, Berlin, Germany

Zhi-Hua Zhou
Nanjing University, Nanjing, China

Founding Editor

Jörg Siekmann
DFKI and Saarland University, Saarbrücken, Germany

More information about this subseries at https://link.springer.com/bookseries/1244

S. R. Mahadeva Prasanna · Alexey Karpov ·
K. Samudravijaya · Shyam S. Agrawal (Eds.)

Speech and Computer

24th International Conference, SPECOM 2022
Gurugram, India, November 14–16, 2022
Proceedings

 Springer

Editors
S. R. Mahadeva Prasanna ⓘ
Indian Institute of Technology Dharwad
Dharwad, India

K. Samudravijaya ⓘ
Koneru Lakshmaiah Education Foundation
Vaddeswaram, India

Alexey Karpov ⓘ
St. Petersburg Federal Research Center
of the Russian Academy of Sciences
St. Petersburg, Russia

Shyam S. Agrawal
KIIT Group of Colleges
Gurugram, India

ISSN 0302-9743   ISSN 1611-3349 (electronic)
Lecture Notes in Artificial Intelligence
ISBN 978-3-031-20979-6   ISBN 978-3-031-20980-2 (eBook)
https://doi.org/10.1007/978-3-031-20980-2

LNCS Sublibrary: SL7 – Artificial Intelligence

This Springer imprint is published by the registered company Springer Nature Switzerland AG
The registered company address is: Gewerbestrasse 11, 6330 Cham, Switzerland

SPECOM 2022 Preface

The International Conference on Speech and Computer (SPECOM) has become a regular event since the first SPECOM held in St. Petersburg, Russia, in October 1996. SPECOM was established 26 years ago by the St. Petersburg Institute for Informatics and Automation of the Russian Academy of Sciences (SPIIRAS).

SPECOM is a conference with a long tradition that attracts researchers in the area of speech technology, including automatic speech recognition and understanding, text–to–speech synthesis, and speaker and language recognition, as well as related domains like digital speech processing, natural language processing, text analysis, computational paralinguistics, multi–modal speech, and data processing or human–computer interaction. The SPECOM conference is an ideal platform for know–how exchange – especially for experts working on Slavic or other highly inflectional languages – including both under–resourced and regular well–resourced languages.

In its long history, the SPECOM conference was organized alternately by the St. Petersburg Institute for Informatics and Automation of the Russian Academy of Sciences and by the Moscow State Linguistic University (MSLU) in their home towns. Furthermore, in 1997 it was organized by the Cluj-Napoca subsidiary of the Research Institute for Computer Technique (Romania), in 2005 and 2015 by the University of Patras (in Patras and Athens, Greece), in 2011 by the Kazan Federal University (in Kazan, Russia), in 2013 by the University of West Bohemia (in Pilsen, Czech Republic), in 2014 by the University of Novi Sad (in Novi Sad, Serbia), in 2016 by the Budapest University of Technology and Economics (in Budapest, Hungary), in 2017 by the University of Hertfordshire (in Hatfield, UK), in 2018 by the Leipzig University of Telecommunications (in Leipzig, Germany), in 2019 by Bogaziçi University (in Istanbul, Turkey), in 2020 and 2021 by SPIIRAS/SPC RAS (fully online).

SPECOM 2022 was the 24th event in the series, and this time it was organized by the KIIT College of Engineering, Gurugram, India, and held during November 14–16, 2022, in a hybrid format, both physically in Gurugram and online via video conferencing. SPECOM 2022 was supported by the International Speech Communication Association (ISCA).

During SPECOM 2022, three keynote lectures were given by Hema A. Murthy (Department of CSE, IIT, Madras, India), Shrikanth (Shri) Narayanan (University of Southern California, Los Angeles, USA), and Gérard Bailly (GIPSA-Lab, CNRS, Grenoble Alpes University, and INP Grenoble, France).

This volume contains a collection of submitted papers presented at SPECOM 2022 which were thoroughly reviewed by members of the Program Committee and additional reviewers consisting of more than 80 specialists in the conference topic areas. In total, 51 full papers and nine short papers out of 99 papers submitted for SPECOM 2022 were selected by the Program Committee for presentation at the conference and inclusion in this book. Theoretical and more general contributions were presented in common plenary sessions. Problem-oriented sessions as well as panel discussions brought together specialists in niche problem areas with the aim of exchanging knowledge and skills resulting from research projects of all kinds.

We would like to express our gratitude to all authors for providing their papers on time, to the members of the Program Committee for their careful reviews and paper selection, and to the editors and correctors for their hard work in preparing this volume. Special thanks are due to the members of the Organizing Committee for their tireless effort and enthusiasm during the conference organization. We are also grateful to KIIT and its management for hosting SPECOM 2022 in Gurugram, India.

November 2022

S. R. Mahadeva Prasanna
Alexey Karpov
K. Samudravijaya
Shyam S. Agrawal

Organization

The 24th International Conference on Speech and Computer (SPECOM 2022) was organized by the KIIT College of Engineering Gurugram, India. The conference website is https://www.specom.co.in.

General Chairs

Shyam S. Agrawal	KIIT Group of Colleges, India
Amita Dev	IGDTUW, Delhi, India

Program Committee Chairs

S. R. Mahadeva Prasanna	Indian Institute of Technology, Dharwad, India
Alexey Karpov	St. Petersburg Federal Research Center of RAS, Russia
K. Samudravijaya	Koneru Lakshmaiah Education Foundation, India

Program Committee

Shyam S. Agrawal	KIIT Group of Colleges, India
Paavo Alku	Aalto University, Finland
Elias Azarov	Belarusian State University of Informatics and Radioelectronics, Belarus
Shikha Baghel	Indian Institute of Science Bangalore, India
Gerard Bailly	GIPSA-Lab, CNRS, Grenoble Alpes University, and INP Grenoble, France
Mrinmoy Bhattacharjee	Indian Institute of Technology, Guwahati, India
Milana Bojanić	University of Novi Sad, Serbia
Jean-Francois Bonastre	Université d'Avignon, France
Nick Campbell	Trinity College Dublin, Ireland
Eric Castelli	International Research Center MICA, Vietnam
Vladimir Chuchupal	Federal Research Center "Computer Science and Control" of RAS, Russia
Andrea Corradini	Design School Kolding, Denmark
Rohan Kumar Das	Fortemedia, India
Vlado Delic	University of Novi Sad, Serbia
Olivier Deroo	Acapela Group, Belgium
Govind Divakaran	K L University, India

Akhilesh Dubey	K L University, India
Vera Evdokimova	St. Petersburg State University, Russia
Nikos Fakotakis	University of Patras, Greece
Todor Ganchev	Technical University of Varna, Bulgaria
Philip N. Garner	Idiap Research Institute, Switzerland
Gábor Gosztolya	University of Szeged, Hungary
Chandrashekar H. M.	Siddaganga Institute of Technology, India
Abualseoud Hanani	Birzeit University, Palestine
Sarmad Hussain	CLE, Pakistan
Denis Ivanko	St. Petersburg Federal Research Center of RAS, Russia
Denis Jouvet	INRIA - LORIA, France
Samudravijaya K.	Koneru Lakshmaiah Education Foundation, India
Ildar Kagirov	St. Petersburg Federal Research Center of RAS, Russia
Sishir Kalita	Armsoftech.AIR, India
Veena Karjigi	Siddaganga Institute of Technology, India
Alexey Karpov	St. Petersburg Federal Research Center of RAS, Russia
Heysem Kaya	Utrecht University, The Netherlands
Irina Kipyatkova	St. Petersburg Federal Research Center of RAS, Russia
Daniil Kocharov	St. Petersburg State University, Russia
Liliya Komalova	Moscow State Linguistic University, Russia
Sunil Kumar Kopparapu	Tata Consultancy Services Ltd., India
Evgeny Kostyuchenko	TUSUR University, Russia
Benjamin Lecouteux	LIG, Grenoble Alpes University, France
Natalia Loukachevitch	Moscow State University, Russia
Elena Lyakso	St. Petersburg State University, Russia
Konstantin Markov	University of Aizu, Japan
Yuri Matveev	ITMO University, Russia
Peter Mihajlik	Budapest University of Technology and Economics, Hungary
Nobuaki Minematsu	University of Tokyo, Japan
Jagabandhu Mishra	IIT Dharwad, India
Bernd Möbius	Saarland University, Germany
Sebastian Möller	Technische Universität Berlin and DFKI Berlin, Germany
Ruban Nersisson	VIT University, India
Oliver Niebuhr	University of Southern Denmark, Denmark
Stavros Ntalampiras	University of Milan, Italy
Géza Németh	Budapest University of Technology and Economics, Hungary

Win Pa	University of Computer Studies Yangon, Myanmar
Sandeep Pandey	Indian Institute of Technology, Guwahati, India
Nickolay Petrovsky	Belarusian State University of Informatics and Radioelectronics, Belarus
Branislav Popović	University of Novi Sad, Serbia
Rodmonga Potapova	Moscow State Linguistic University, Russia
Vsevolod Potapov	Moscow State Linguistic University, Russia
Mahadeva Prasanna	IIT Dharwad, India
Sergey Rybin	ITMO University, Russia
Dmitry Ryumin	St. Petersburg Federal Research Center of RAS, Russia
Priyankoo Sarmah	Indian Institute of Technology, Guwahati, India
Andrey Savchenko	HSE University, Russia
Maximilian Schmitt	Independent Researcher, Germany
Björn Schuller	University of Augsburg, Germany
Friedhelm Schwenker	Ulm University, Germany
Milan Sečujski	University of Novi Sad, Serbia
Rajib Sharma	Indian Institute of Information Technology, Dharwad, India
Tatiana Sherstinova	HSE University, Russia
Nickolay Shmyrev	Alpha Cephei Inc., Russia
Vered Silber-Varod	The Open University of Israel, Israel
Ivan Tashev	Microsoft, USA
Deepak Thotappa	Indian Institute of Information Technology, Dharwad, India
Isabel Trancoso	INESC-ID Lisboa/IST, Portugal
Jan Trmal	Johns Hopkins University, USA
Liliya Tsirulnik	Stenograph LLC, USA
Vasilisa Verkhodanova	University of Groningen, The Netherlands
Klara Vicsi	Budapest University of Technology and Economics, Hungary
Andreas Wendemuth	Otto-von-Guericke Universitaet, Germany
Chai Wutiwiwatchai	NECTEC, Thailand
Zeynep Yucel	Okayama University, Japan
Milos Zelezny	University of West Bohemia, Czech Republic

Organizing Committee

Shyam S. Agrawal (Chair)	KIIT Group of Colleges, India
Neelima Kamrah	KIIT Group of Colleges, India
Kanika Kaur	KIIT Group of Colleges, India
Anshuman Kamrah	KIIT Group of Colleges, India

Kartikay Sharma	KIIT Group of Colleges, India
Atul Kumar	KIIT Group of Colleges, India
Alexey Karpov	St. Petersburg Federal Research Center of RAS, Russia
Irina Kipyatkova	St. Petersburg Federal Research Center of RAS, Russia
Ildar Kagirov	St. Petersburg Federal Research Center of RAS, Russia
Dmitry Ryumin	St. Petersburg Federal Research Center of RAS, Russia

Additional Reviewers

Ayush Agarwal
Gerasimos Arvanitis
Mrinmoy Bhattacharjee
Rohan Kumar Das
Denis Dresvyanskiy
Ivan Gruber
Nikša Jakovljević
Roman Korostik
Danila Mamontov

Jagabandhu Mishra
Branislav Popović
Amartya Roy Chowdhury
Somnath Roy
Yang Saring
Milan Sečujski
Nikola Simić
Siniša Suzić

Contents

Thematic Diversity of Everyday Russian Discourse: A Case Study Based on the ORD Corpus

Eleonora Akinshina[1] and Tatiana Sherstinova[1,2]

[1] National Research University Higher School of Economics, St. Petersburg, 123 Griboyedova Canal Emb., 190068 St Petersburg, Russia
evakinshina@edu.hse.ru, tsherstinova@hse.ru
[2] St. Petersburg State University, 7/9 Universitetskaya emb., 199034 St. Petersburg, Russia

Abstract. The paper is devoted to the study of thematic diversity of Russian oral discourse. It examines and analyzes the real-life episodes taken from the corpus of everyday spoken communication "One Day of Speech". In the course of the study the main hyper-themes of Russian everyday communication have been identified. Each hyper-theme consists of several micro-themes. Based on these empiric data, the frequency of occurrence of various hyper-themes in everyday communication was obtained. For example, it was found that the most frequent themes of the empirical sample turned out to be "work", "past and future", "health", and "household issues". Statistical data on the duration of conversations on each particular theme have been obtained as well. The results of the study can be used in further studies of Russian oral discourse and for solving a number of practical tasks related with spontaneous conversation understanding, spoken speech topic modelling, as well as creating chatbots for everyday casual conversations.

Keywords: Everyday communication · Russian everyday speech · Thematic diversity · Pragmatics · Dialogue studies · Corpus linguistics

1 Introduction

Recently, the research on thematic organization of speech has become increasingly popular. The relevance of this topic can be noted in many linguistical studies [1–7]. Themes of Russian spoken speech have been discussed to some extent in a number of publications [8–22]. However, despite the fact that we use everyday speech on a daily basis, its statistical characteristics fall out of the field of current linguists due to the fact that it is very difficult to obtain reliable statistics and calculate even just the total number of words spoken by some person during one day. An even more difficult point is to obtain statistics on thematic diversity of everyday conversations. Nevertheless, these data are extremely important for many interdisciplinary studies (linguistics, anthropology, sociology, communication studies, language teaching, etc.), in the center of which there is a person, his/her actual interests and communication skills. In addition, information about the distribution of everyday communication themes is quite necessary to solve many

© Springer Nature Switzerland AG 2022
S. R. M. Prasanna et al. (Eds.): SPECOM 2022, LNAI 13721, pp. 1–9, 2022.
https://doi.org/10.1007/978-3-031-20980-2_1

practical tasks related to understanding spontaneous conversation, modeling the conversation of colloquial speech, and creating chatbots for everyday casual communication. In this paper, for the first time in the Russian language, the empirical diversity of themes of everyday discourse is analyzed.

2 Data and Method

The study of oral discourse thematic diversity was carried out on the basis of speech data taken from the corpus of everyday spoken speech "One Day of Speech", also known as the ORD corpus [23, 24, 25]. It contains natural speech of Russian people recorded in the conditions of their daily life and provides valuable data to study speech in its most natural settings and in the rhythm of life which is casual and familiar to the informants. When selecting volunteers to participate in recordings for this corpus, their gender and age, as well as their professions and belonging to different social groups were taken into account. This selection helps to take into account various categories that make the analysis of the themes of everyday communication the most accurate and complete.

Initially, about one hundred macroepisodes were selected for expert analysis. Macroepisodes are "major episodes united by the place of communication, its conditions, and participants" [26]. The example of macroepisodes are "university gathering", "afternoon tea", "work meeting" or "a date with a young man". The participants of these macroepisodes were informants and their interlocuters whose age ranged from very young children to the elderly. Thus, the next selection criteria were gender and age of the speakers. The ORD database contains information about the informants themselves and the main interlocutors—database fields "Gender", "Prof" and "EWho" were used to select these categories [23]. For other participants the expert estimation of these parameters was used. Thus, with the help of professional identifications like "housewife", "plumber" it was possible to draw a conclusion about gender (in rare cases, exclusively by voice), and with the help of identifications like "pensioner", "child" / "daughter"/"son", "girl-employee", the conclusion about age of interlocuters was made [27].

However, in the process of expert listening and analyzing the selected recordings, it was decided to exclude from consideration a number of macroepisodes, which either contained mostly silence, or too much noise making it impossible to determine the topic, or consisted of a very small number of utterances that could not be considered as a full-fledged dialogue (e. g., aimed only at indicating objects that were in the speaker's field of vision or focusing at an action that he/she commits/plans to commit at the moment of speaking like "I go to the store. Bye", "Take the package", "Hello, how are you?—Thank you, fine". The decision to exclude these episodes from the analysis was made to prevent affecting the statistics that is the aim of this study.

In the result of such preselection, about 60 macroepisodes were selected for the study, in which the informants belong to different social groups. The categories of those who took part in the communication (where it was possible) were also taken into account. Thus, the group of elderly people (55–70 years old) makes up 13% of the total number of speakers in the sample of episodes, men and women of middle age (35–55 years old) number 47%, whereas young people (17–35 years old) make up 35%. Children interlocuters (0–17), occupy the smallest number in the study (4.2%), and it was decided not to take their speech fragments into account.

With regard to gender, it turned out that women "talk" a little more often than men do: the number of macroepisodes in which the female speech predominates turned out to be slightly larger than those in which the male one is involved. In the sample, having excluded children's speech, the percentage ratio turned out to be as follows: women — 50%, men — 45.8%.

The areas of speakers' activity, the place of communication and the type of conversational topics change were taken into account when compiling the sample of macroepisodes.

The information on all macroepisodes from the sample was entered into the database, which contains the following categories for each of them:

- code of the macroepisode in the ORD corpus;
- place of communication;
- the beginning of the micro-theme (in minutes);
- the end of the micro-theme (in minutes);
- micro-theme;
- type of micro-theme change;
- age categories of speakers.

Basing on this data the following quantitative data describes below have been obtained.

3 Thematic Diversity of the Test Sample: Hyper-themes and Micro-themes

In our study, when developing a system for classifying themes of everyday communication, we based on the system proposed by Kositsina [21], which has been significantly revised. In the process of expert manual analysis of the selected macroepisodes, the following sixteen hyper-themes have been identified:

1. Science/Knowledge.
2. Art.
3. Nature.
4. Household issues.
5. Past and future.
6. Food.
7. Health.
8. Work.
9. Family and friends.
10. Shopping.
11. Social Issues.
12. State And Politics.
13. Education.

14. Hobby.
15. Weather.
16. Cars.

This classification of hyper-themes has become the result of expert analysis of micro-themes found in macroepisodes. Their distribution was as follows: each episode of a sample was divided into segments, which are different in thematic organization. For each of such segments, correspondent micro-themes have been identified. Further, these micro-themes were grouped into hyper-themes.

For example, the hyper-theme of "Science/knowledge" can include the following micro-themes found in macroepisodes: astrology, mythology, cultural studies, evolutionary theories, corpus linguistics, philosophy, medicine, osteopathy, as well as not quite scientific knowledge like reincarnation, coaches and their teachings. The "Art" hyper-theme contains such micro-themes as photographs, literature, reading, films, cartoons, performances, music, singers, series, history of performance, paintings, etc. When talking about "Nature", people often discuss animals, pets, zoos, flowers, fish, etc. "Household issues" is a very big hyper-theme category, which includes various issues: repairs, clutter, home appliances and computer equipment, gas in the apartment, as well as discussions about who should go to the store, how one should pay for the phone, what kind of audibility the apartment has, and so on. The "Past and Future" is a large independent category, which has an indefinite number of micro-themes due to the breadth of its concept. In the analyzed sample, there are "plans for the weekend", "vacation plans", "discussing trips to St. Petersburg", "news of the week", "summer hikes", "a friend's birthday", "memories", including that of a military service.

The "Food" hyper-theme contains talking about groceries, product availability in stores, discounts on groceries, drinks, wines, cakes, recipes, etc. The "Health" category may be divided into the following micro-topics: well-being, visiting the doctor, problems with teeth, appearance, physical activity, solarium, fitness rooms, sleep, swimming pool, treatment, vitamins, etc.

"Work" as a hyper-theme consists of discussions about new hires, team relationships, work environment, money, wages, past job challenges, building a business, bonuses, schedules, interviews, etc. "Family and friends" theme includes in particular micro-themes of a grandmother's anniversary, a friend's pregnancy, spending time with a young man, a romantic relationship, a meeting at a child's school, etc. Discussing "Purchases" relates to clothing, discounts, sales, and shops. The hyper-theme of "Social issues" breaks down into a number of the following micro-themes: the influence of television, bad habits, parenting, resentment against friends, housing, nationalities, quarrels with a girl, types of girls, waste recycling, etc. The "State and politics" include aspects such as the work of state lawyers, laws, utility prices, exports and imports of products, salaries, elections.

The "Education" hyper-theme is not represented well enough in the analyzed selection of macroepisodes. It relates to the study of English, translation courses, education at the university and at school. "Hobby" can also have no boundaries as a hyper-theme, but in our research data it is limited to talking about hobbies, extreme types of recreation, playing football, traveling, and dancing. "Cars" relate to the traffic laws, driving, types of cars, car behavior on the road, car power, pedestrian behavior on the road. The "Weather" hyper-theme is the most independent and has no micro-themes.

Evidently, in common everyday communication, more hyper-themes can be found, therefore an infinite number of micro-themes can be involved, but the list presented above reflects the topics that occurred in the sample selection of recordings.

4 Frequency of Themes in Russian Everyday Discourse

All the themes of the selected macroepisodes were divided into micro-themes, which, in turn, were assigned to one of 16 hyper-themes (see previous section). Evidently, each hyper-theme was discussed in conversations with different frequency. In order to determine the most and least common topics of oral discourse, quantitative analysis was made. It turned out that there occurred 355 different micro-themes in the sample. According to this number the following percentage data were calculated (see Fig. 1).

Thus, it turned out that hyper-themes "Work" and "Past and Future" have the same frequency of occurrence and take 12.5% of the total number of themes. The next most popular theme is "Health", which is used in 11.5% of cases. "Art" occupies 10% of our conversations, "Household issues" cover 9.6%, whereas "Social issues" make 8.4% of all conversational themes.

The least popular theme is "Family and friends", which has the seventh rank and occupies 6.7%. Themes "Food" and "Science/Knowledge" have almost the same percentage of occurrence — 5.6% and 5.2%, respectively. Less popular is the topic of "State and politics", which, according to the results of calculations, is gaining only 3.8%. Even less people discuss "Nature" — it amounted to 3.6% of the total. Next comes "Education", the frequency of which is 3.4%. The last ranks are occupied by the themes "Cars" (2.8%), "Purchases" (2.2%), and "Hobbies" (2%).

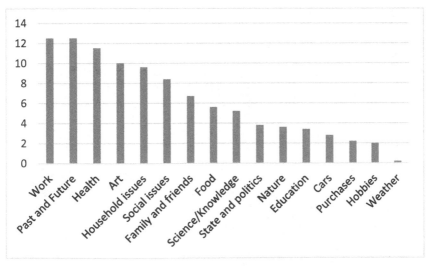

Fig. 1. Frequency of hyper-themes in Russian everyday discourse.

Surprisingly, the least common topic in Russian everyday discourse turned out to be the "Weather", which did not gain even one percent (0.2%).

Thus, the frequency of occurrence of identified hyper-themes varies from 0.2% to 12.5%.

5 Relative Duration of Themes in Russian Everyday Discourse

Analyzing frequency of occurrence of various themes in real-life spoken discourse, one should take into account not only which themes are discussed more or less often, but also how much time is spent for each theme.

In our research, when calculating frequencies of micro-themes occurrences, the duration of each thematic fragment was also measured, i. e. how many seconds the interlocutors talk on a certain micro-theme.

To make this analysis, it was necessary to calculate the sum of the time of all micro-themes of each hyper-theme and make the corresponding statistics. The pure duration of speech in macroepisodes excluding pauses is 5.6 h. According to that number the following percentages were calculated.

The results of the analysis show that the theme which is the longest one is "Work". We have already seen that this theme is also the leading one in terms of its frequency of occurrence. In relation to its temporal context, this topic occupies 13.9% of everyday conversation time. "Health" takes the second place here taking 11.7% in average. This theme also occupies a high position in frequency, but not as much as in duration. In the third rank there is the theme of "Past and Future" with 10.2%, and the next is theme "Household issues" which takes a close value of 10.1%.

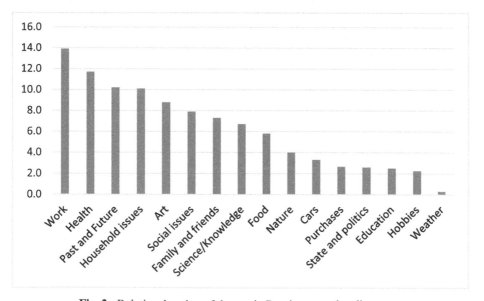

Fig. 2. Relative duration of themes in Russian everyday discourse.

Further on the rank list there is the theme of "Art". It occupies a middle position, as well as in the frequency of occurrence, and covers 8.8% of the total duration. "Social issues" is close to it. This theme was supposed to occupy more time and we could expect that discussions on this subject should last longer. However, empirical research revealed that this topic occupies on our data just 7.9%. It is followed by "Food", "Family and friends", and "Science" making 5.8%, 7.3%, and 6.7% correspondently.

Less than five percent of our conversations are about "Nature" (3.4%), "Cars" (3.3%), "Shopping" (2.65%), "Government and politics" (2.6%). In the bottom of the rank list there are themes of "Education" and "Hobby" having 2.5% and 2.25% correspondently. And the last place is occupied by the "Weather" (as well as in the frequency of occurrence). It gets the least amount of time and attention. The duration of discussions about weather is 0.3% of the total time.

6   Conclusion

The significance of the presented study is justified by the fact that it presents statistical data on thematic distribution in real-life everyday communication of Russian-speaking interlocutors. Due to the limited sample size, the data obtained should be considered preliminary. Obtaining more meaningful statistics is difficult because speech recognition systems still perform poorly on audio recordings of everyday speech making it impossible to obtain large amount of real speech transcripts. Moreover, segmentation of speech into micro-themes is an expert manual work as well as assigning thematic tag to each speech fragment, since systems of automatic classification of texts by themes (topic modeling) also do not work well on such complex data as everyday spontaneous speech, in which a large number of unrelated themes may be mixed in a quite fancy way. In this article we do not present information on thematic distribution depending on gender and age of the informants and their interlocutors. This data deserves more space and will be published later.

Further, it should be taken into account that the recordings of the ORD were made in 2007–2016, therefore they represent the thematic distribution of speech for that period. Evidently, each historical period may be characterized by a certain shift of priorities, which may be determined by some external causes, for example, social changes or significant events. For example, during the Olympic Games, an increase in the share of sports conversation may be expected. However, as there is no statistics on thematic distribution in different time periods, this hypothesis cannot be tested.

In addition, it should be borne in mind that the resulting distribution is largely determined by the classification of hyper-themes, which underlies the research. Obviously, the proposed classification scheme — like any other — is not the only one and, perhaps, is not the most optimal one. Nevertheless, the data obtained are of considerable interest and can be used to solve a number of practical issues related to modeling and understanding real-life speech communication.

Acknowledgements. The study was financially supported by the grant from St. Petersburg State University (project No. 75254082 "Modeling the communicative behavior of Russian metropolis residents in the social, speech and pragmatic aspects using artificial intelligence methods").

References

1. Van Dijk, T.A.: Voprosy pragmatiki teksta [Questions of text pragmatics]. In: New in foreign linguistics. Issue VIII. Moscow: Progress, pp. 259–336 (1980)
2. Van Dijk, T.A.: Yazyk. Poznaniye. Kommunikatsiya [Language. Cognition. Communication]. Moscow: Progress, p. 312 (1989)
3. Kozhevnikova, K.: O smyslovom stroyenii spontannoy ustnoy rechi [On the semantic structure of spontaneous oral speech]. In: New in foreign linguistics. Issue 15. Moscow: Progress, pp. 512–523 (1985)
4. Novikov, A.Yu.: Angliyskiy rok-diskurs: tematicheskiy aspekt [English rock discourse: thematic aspect]. In: Chelovek v kommunikatsii: aspekty issledovaniy [Man in society: aspects of research: a collection of scientific papers] Volgograd: Change, pp. 147–157 (2005)
5. Skirdach, O.M.: Lingvisticheskiye printsipy tematicheskoy organizatsii teksta: K probleme dinamiki tekstovykh struktur [Linguistic studies of thematic organization of text: On the problem of the dynamics of text structures] PhD in Philology dissertation abstract, 10.02.19. Moscow, p. 24 (1985)
6. Smith, J.B.: Tematicheskaya struktura i tematicheskaya slozhnost [Thematic structure and complexity]. In: New in foreign linguistics. Iss. IX. Moscow: Progress, pp. 333–355 (1980)
7. Schutz, A.: Smyslovaya struktura povsednevnogo mira: ocherki po fenomenologicheskoy sotsiologii [Semantic structure of the everyday world: essays on phenomenological sociology] Moscow, p. 336 (2003)
8. Baranov, A.N., Mikhailova, O.V., Satarov, G.A., Shipova, E.A.: Politicheskiy diskurs: metody analiza tematicheskoy struktury i metaforiki [Political discourse: methods of analysis of thematic structure and metaphors]. In: Baranov, A.N. (ed). Fund INDEM, p. 94 (2004)
9. Borisova, I.N.: Russkiy razgovornyy dialog: Struktura i dinamika [Russian colloquial dialogue: Structure and dynamics] Moscow, LIBROKOM, p. 320 (2009)
10. Kobozeva, M.A.: Kognitivnyye i rechevyye strategii vvoda temy v nauchno-populyarnom diskurse [Cognitive and speech strategies for topic introduction in popular science discourse] PhD in Philology dissertation abstract, 10.02.19. Stavropol, p. 24 (2011)
11. Kolesnikova, N.A.: O roli leksiko-tematicheskikh liniy v vyrazhenii referentsii teksta [On the role of lexical-thematic lines in the expression of text reference]. In: Problems of the meaning of a linguistic sign. Kyiv: KSPIIA, pp. 117–121 (1982)
12. Kormilitsyna, M.A., Sirotinina, O.B.: Yeshche raz o strukture razgovornogo teksta [Once again about the structure of a spoken text]. In: Kormilitsyna, M.A., Sirotinina, O.B. (eds.) Traditional and New in Russian Grammar: Collection of Articles in Memory of V. A. Beloshapkova. M.: Indrik, pp. 312–321 (2001)
13. Matveeva, T.V.: Tematicheskoye razvertyvaniye razgovornogo teksta [Thematic deployment of a spoken text]. In: Matveeva, T.V. (ed.) Yazykovoy oblik ural'skogo goroda [Linguistic appearance of an Ural city: a collection of scientific papers]. Sverdlovsk: Ural State University, pp. 46–54 (1990)
14. Novikov, A.I., Chistyakova, G.D.: K voprosu o teme i denotate teksta [On the issue of the theme and denotation of the text]. In: Proceedings of the Academy of Sciences of the USSR, pp. 48–56 (1981)
15. Rizun, V.V.: O teme teksta i tematicheskoy gruppe slov [On the theme of the text and the thematic group of words]. In: Language and Composition of the Newspaper Text: Theory and Practice. Sverdlovsk, pp. 35–37 (1987)
16. Sibiryakova, I.G.: O gruppirovke tematicheskikh fragmentov v razgovornom tekste [On the grouping of thematic fragments in a colloquial text]. In: Sibiryakova, I.G. (ed.) Semanticheskiye protsessy na raznykh urovnyakh yazykovoy sistemy [Semantic processes at different levels of the language system] Saratov, pp. 118–126 (1994)

17. Sibiryakova, I.G.: Opyt tematicheskogo analiza dialogicheskogo razgovornogo teksta [Experience in thematic analysis of a dialogic conversational text]. In: Yazykovoy oblik ural'skogo goroda: sbornik nauchnykh trudov [Linguistic appearance of an Ural city: a collection of scientific papers] Sverdlovsk: UrGU, pp. 61–71 (1990)
18. Sibiryakova, I.G.: Tema i zhanr razgovornoy rechi [Theme and genre of colloquial speech]. In: Goldin, V.E. (ed.). Genres of speech: collection of articles. Saratov, pp. 57–65 (1997)
19. Sibiryakova, I.G.: Tematicheskoye strukturirovaniye razgovornogo dialoga [Thematic structuring of conversational dialogue] PhD in Philology dissertation abstract, 10.02.01. Ekaterinburg, p. 19 (1996)
20. Grudeva, E.V.: Sposoby vvedeniya i opredeleniya temy v russkom yazyke i strategii nositeley yazyka v yeye opredelenii (eksperimental'noye issledovaniye) [Ways of introducing and defining a topic in the Russian language and the strategy of native speakers in its definition (an experimental study)]. In: Proceeding of the Russian State Pedagogical University named after A. I. Herzen: Social and Human Sciencesl. No. 11(71), pp. 36–44 (2008)
21. Kositsina, Y.: Tekushcheye tematicheskoye razvitiye: kogerentnyy i kogezivnyy aspekty [Current thematic development: coherent and cohesive aspects]. Bull. Kemerovo State Univ. 4(52), 281–284 (2012)
22. Saakyan,V.L.: K voprosu opredeleniya temy ustno-rechevogo diskursa [On the issue of determining the topic of oral speech discourse]. In: Scientific Bulletin of the Voronezh State University of Architecture and Civil Engineering, pp. 11–17 (2016)
23. Asinovsky, A., Bogdanova, N., Rusakova, M., Ryko, A., Stepanova, S., Sherstinova, T.: The ORD speech corpus of russian everyday communication "One Speaker's Day": creation principles and annotation. In: Matoušek, V., Mautner, P. (eds.) TSD 2009. LNCS (LNAI), vol. 5729, pp. 250–257. Springer, Heidelberg (2009). https://doi.org/10.1007/978-3-642-04208-9_36
24. Sherstinova, T.: The structure of the ORD speech corpus of Russian everyday communication. In: Matoušek, V., Mautner, P. (eds.) TSD 2009. LNCS (LNAI), vol. 5729, pp. 258–265. Springer, Heidelberg (2009). https://doi.org/10.1007/978-3-642-04208-9_37
25. Bogdanova-Beglarian, N., et al.: Sociolinguistic extension of the ORD corpus of Russian everyday speech. In: Ronzhin, A., Potapova, R., Németh, G. (eds.) SPECOM 2016. LNCS (LNAI), vol. 9811, pp. 659–666. Springer, Cham (2016). https://doi.org/10.1007/978-3-319-43958-7_80
26. Sherstinova, T.: Macro episodes of Russian everyday oral communication: towards pragmatic annotation of the ORD speech corpus. In: Ronzhin, A., Potapova, R., Fakotakis, N. (eds.) SPECOM 2015. LNCS (LNAI), vol. 9319, pp. 268–276. Springer, Cham (2015). https://doi.org/10.1007/978-3-319-23132-7_33
27. Bogdanova-Beglaryan, N.V., Blinova, O.V., Zaides, K.D., Sherstirova, T.: Corpus of the Russian language of everyday communication "One day of speech" (ORD corpus): current state and prospects. In: Proceeding of the Institute of the Russian language named after V. V. Vinogradov Russian Academy of Sciences. – Moscow, pp. 100–110 (2019)

Neural Embedding Extractors for Text-Independent Speaker Verification

Jahangir Alam$^{(\boxtimes)}$, Woohyun Kang, and Abderrahim Fathan

Computer Research Institute of Montreal, Montreal, Quebec H3N 1M3, Canada
{jahangir.alam,woohyun.kang,abderrahim.fathan}@crim.ca
https://www.crim.ca/en/

Abstract. In neural network-based speaker verification tasks, extraction of speaker embeddings plays a vital role. In this work, in order to extract speaker discriminant utterance level representations, we propose to employ two neural speaker embedding extractors that incorporate multi-stream hybrid neural network (MSHNN) and ensemble of neural speaker embedding networks. In the proposed MSHNN approach, an input acoustic feature frame is processed in multiple parallel hybrid neural network (HNN) pipelines where each stream has a unique dilation rate for incorporating diversified temporal resolution in embedding processing. The proposed ensemble neural speaker embedding extractor employs a hybrid neural network, a Time Delay Neural Network - Long Short-Term Memory (TDNN-LSTM) hybrid network and a time delay neural network (TDNN) in parallel manner for including diversified temporal resolution as well as for capturing the complementarity exists in different architectures. A set of speaker verification experiments were carried out on the CNCeleb and VoxCeleb corpora for evaluating the performances of the proposed systems. The proposed multi-stream hybrid neural network performs better than the conventional approaches trained on the same dataset. The ensemble approach is found to yield the best performance in terms of equal error rates (EER) and minimum detection cost function (minDCF) evaluation metrics.

Keywords: Speaker verification · Neural embeddings extractor · Hybrid neural networks · TDNN · PLDA

1 Introduction

Automatic verification of the claimed speaker identity based on the given speech signal has become a key technology for personal authentication in various applications such as contact centers, smart home, mobile banking, device login etc. In a speaker verification system, utterance-level fixed-dimensional embedding vectors are normally extracted from the enrollment and test recordings using a frontend feature extractor (e.g., i-vector [6]) and then fed into a backend (e.g., cosine similarity) to measure their similarity. In the last few years, with the advent of deep learning, the neural speaker verification approaches have shown

© Springer Nature Switzerland AG 2022
S. R. M. Prasanna et al. (Eds.): SPECOM 2022, LNAI 13721, pp. 10–23, 2022.
https://doi.org/10.1007/978-3-031-20980-2_2

great success and demonstrated significant improvement over the conventional i-vector [6]) based methods.

In this direction, one of the most popular methods is the x-vector paradigm [3,24], which uses a time-delay neural network (TDNN) architecture and statistics pooling for extracting a speaker discriminant utterance-level embedding. This framework has shown great performance in text-independent speaker verification [24]. The Extended TDNN (ETDNN) [25] and Factored TDNN (FTDNN) [27] architectures are the two extensions of x-vector framework proposed to boost the performance. For the past several years, there have been many attempts on employing the residual network (ResNet) architecture for speaker embedding extraction [4,32], which have proven to be the dominant approach in the image classification field [12]. Moreover, to exploit the speaker-dependent information within the temporal variability of the speech sequence, many researches also focused on employing a recurrent neural network such as the long short-term network (LSTM) for speaker embedding extraction [13,28]. Since different network architectures (e.g., convolutional neural network, TDNN, LSTM) are known to learn complementary information about the input representation [1,14,26] various hybrid approaches were proposed which employ non-TDNN modules such as LSTM or convolutional neural network (CNN) to the x-vector framework, and showed noticeable performance enhancement.

Especially in [9,20,22], it was observed that the robustness of x-vectors can be improved by adding residual connections between the frame-level layers. Moreover, [26] proposed a multi-level pooling scheme for considering the statistics from different modules (e.g., TDNN, LSTM), and showed promising performance in speaker verification. The ECAPA-TDNN architecture introduced in [7], has shown state-of-the-art performance by introducing residual and squeeze-and-excitation (SE) components to the widely used TDNN-based embedding system. Recently, the hybrid neural network (HNN) was introduced in [1,14] for speaker embedding extraction, which not only employs different types of network architectures (i.e., 2D-CNN, TDNN, LSTM) but also exploits the short-durational statistics of the hidden representations for bagging the instantaneous speaker-dependent information.

Attributed to these characteristics, the HNN system provided promising results across various challenging datasets [1,14]. In [11], a multi-stream CNN architecture was introduced for automatic speech recognition (ASR) task, where the network processes the input speech with multiple temporal resolutions by applying different dilation rates to the CNN. Since the speaker-dependent information can be latent in different temporal contexts, we can assume that the speaker embedding extraction network can greatly benefit from analyzing the multiple resolutions of the given speech.

Motivated by the aforementioned, in this work, we focus on further extending the HNN framework to fully extract the speaker information latent in the input speech and propose two novel neural speaker embedding extractors that utilize multi-stream hybrid neural network (MSHNN) and ensemble of neural speaker embedding networks. Our proposed approaches not only take advantage of the complementary speaker information encoded by different network architectures but also greatly benefit from the multi-resolution analysis of the input signal. In order to evaluate the speaker verification performance of our proposed systems, we conduct a set of experiments on the most challenging multi-genre CNCeleb dataset [17].

In this work, our contributions are as follows:

- We propose a novel embedding architecture for speaker verification, which incorporates the multi-streaming scheme into the HNN embedding extractor and here, we denote this extractor as MSHNN.
- In order to include diversified temporal resolution and complementary information we also propose an ENSEMBLE neural speaker embedding extractor which employs a HNN, a TDNN-LSTM and a TDNN architectures in a parallel fashion.
- We report the performance of the HNN approach on the multi-genre CNCeleb corpus.
- We evaluate the performance of the proposed approaches on the challenging multi-genre CNCeleb corpus as well as on the widely used VoxCeleb dataset.

2   Hybrid Neural Network (HNN) Embeddings Extractor

An overview of the HNN embedding extractor is presented in Fig. 1 which is composed of 2D-CNN-based feature extraction module, TDNN-LSTM-based frame-level network and multi-level global-local statistics pooling mechanism [1,14]. In Fig. 1, the HNN backbone architecture is depicted inside the red dotted rectangle.

2.1   2D-CNN-Based Feature Extraction Module

At first, SpecAugment [29] is applied on-the-fly over the input Mel-FilterBank (MFB) features, where both time and frequency masking are performed. After that, the input augmented MFB features are passed through a stack of five 2D-CNN layers to obtain frame-level representations with information on both spectral and temporal correlations within the input features.

2.2   TDNN-LSTM-Based Frame-Level Network

The 2D-CNN module is then followed by a frame-level network which is made up of TDNN and LSTM layers, to extract local descriptors with sufficient temporal information for speaker discrimination. In Fig. 1, the TDNN-LSTM-based frame-level network is shown inside the black dotted rectangle.

2.3   Multi-level Global-Local Statistics Pooling

A multi-level statistics pooling (MLSP) [26] is employed for aggregating statistics from the last layers of CNN, LSTM and TDNN blocks to capture speaker-specific information from different spaces and learn more discriminative utterance level representations by taking advantage of the complementary speaker information encoded by different individual networks.

Similar to the standard x-vector, the HNN extracts the first- and second-order statistics. However, unlike the conventional x-vector, the HNN extracts the statistics not only globally, but also locally within a short durational moving window to exploit the short-durational correlation. Each module (i.e., TDNN, LSTM) takes both the frame-level outputs from the previous layer, and the local statistics extracted from them as input. During the local statistics pooling operation, the input sequences are resampled and the pooling window shift rates are adjusted to match the sequence length with the frame-level features.

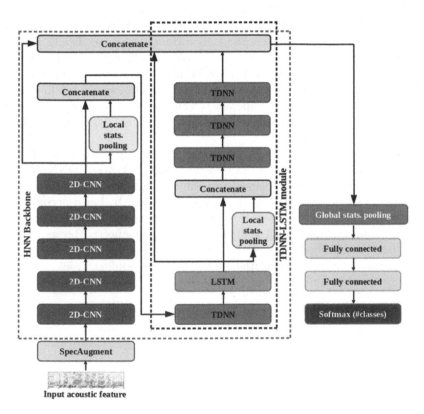

Fig. 1. Schematic diagram of the hybrid neural network (HNN) architecture as embeddings extractor for speaker verification task [1,14].

After propagating the input features to the frame-level network, a global statistics pooling is performed to aggregate the local descriptors obtained from the CNN, LSTM and TDNN blocks. The global first- and second- order statistics are concatenated to form a fixed-dimensional utterance-level representation which is then projected into a 512-dimensional embedding vector via two fully-connected layers. Once the training is completed, the embeddings are extracted from the fully-connected layer close to the global statistics pooling layer.

3   Proposed Neural Embedding Extractors

This section provides a detailed description of the proposed embedding extraction frameworks for text-independent speaker verification task.

3.1   Multi-stream Hybrid Neural Network (MSHNN) Embeddings Extractor

Unlike the standard HNN, which only consists of one TDNN-LSTM block, the proposed MSHNN employs multiple TDNN-LSTM blocks to capture the speaker information latent in different temporal resolutions. More specifically, after processing the input acoustic feature with 5 layers of 2D-CNN layers, the CNN output along with its local statistics are branched out to 3 different streams, where each stream process consists of a TDNN-LSTM block with a unique dilation rate. The outputs from the different streams are then concatenated to each other, and then fed into the following TDNN layers as in the standard HNN framework.

Like the HNN architecture, a multi-level statistics pooling (MLSP) [26] is employed for pooling statistics from the last layers of CNN, TDNN blocks, as shown in Fig. 2, to capture speaker-specific information from different spaces and learn more discriminative utterance level representations by bagging complementarity available in different networks. The global first- and second- order statistics are concatenated and passed through two fully-connected layers to obtain a 512-dimensional embedding vector. The embeddings are extracted from the fully-connected layer adjacent to the global statistics pooling layer.

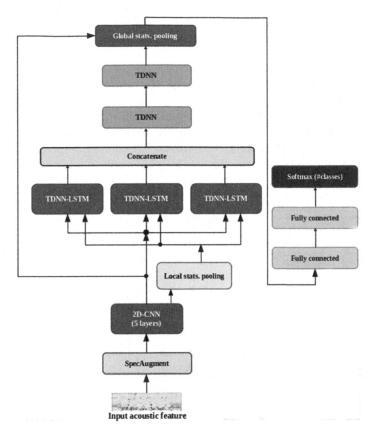

Fig. 2. Block diagram of the proposed Multi-Stream Hybrid Neural Network (MSHNN)-based embeddings extractor for speaker verification task [2].

3.2 The Ensemble Neural Embeddings Extractor

Our proposed ensemble neural embedding extractor, denoted as ENSEMBLE, incorporates two hybrid (the HNN described in Sect. 2 and the TDNN-LSTM) and one single (TDNN) backbone networks, in parallel manner, the description of which are presented below:

– The Standard HNN: This is the conventional HNN backbone architecture, the description of which is already presented in Sect. 2. In Fig. 3, this standard HNN backbone is highlighted using a red dashed rectangle.
– The TDNN-LSTM: This hybrid backbone, highlighted using a black dashed rectangle, is similar to the standard HNN but does not employ any 2D-CNN layers. As presented in the Fig. 3, this TDNN-LSTM hybrid module is similar to the x-vector architecture but the second TDNN layer was replaced with the LSTM layer and the local statistics are appended as in the HNN.

Moreover, unlike the standard HNN which applies SpecAugment to the Mel FilterBank (MFB) features, the TDNN-LSTM applies masking directly to the Mel-frequency cepstral coefficient (MFCC) features and we denote this augmentation as CepAugment.

- The TDNN: The third parallel backbone network of the proposed ENSEMBLE embedding extractor is highlighted in Fig. 3 using a gray dashed rectangle. This is similar to the backbone network of the popular x-vector paradigm but employs local statistics pooling as in the other two parallel backbone networks (i.e., HNN & TDNN-LSTM). Like the TDNN-LSTM module, on-the-fly data augmentation is performed using CepAugment.

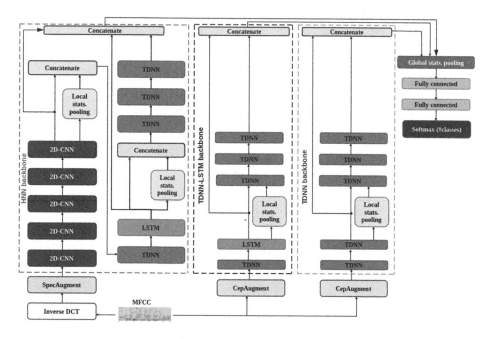

Fig. 3. Schematic diagram showing various steps of the proposed ensemble neural speaker embeddings extractor for speaker verification task.

While the standard HNN can capture the time-frequency correlation via the 2D-CNN module, the TDNN-LSTM and TDNN are expected to focus more on the temporal information attributed to the large number of TDNN layers. Therefore, the proposed ensemble architecture may exploit the complementary information captured by these three different backbone networks.

As shown in Fig. 3, in order for the proposed ensemble approach to learn more discriminative and relevant utterance level representations the global multi-level statistics pooling (MLSP) is carried out from the last layers of these three backbone architectures to capture speaker-specific information from different modules as well as complementarity exists in these three parallel backbone networks.

The temporal pooling layer, also known as global statistics pooling, concatenates element-wise estimates of first- and second-order statistics of the set of local descriptors over the time axis and yields fixed-dimensional utterance-level representations. The outputs of the pooling layer are finally passed through two fully-connected layers to yield outputs corresponding to conditional log-probabilities over the set of training speakers. Once training is done, 512-dimensional embeddings are normally extracted from the fully-connected layer near the global statistics pooling layer.

Following the same general framework with ENSEMBLE, we also build ENSEMBLE2 and ENSEMBLE3 embedding extractors:

- ENSEMBLE2: This framework ensembles the HNN and the extended TDNN-LSTM (ETDNN-LSTM) architectures [2].
- ENSEMBLE3: This is similar to ENSEMBLE (as shown in Fig. 3) but combines the HNN, the ETDNN-LSTM, and extended TDNN (ETDNN) configurations.

4   Experiments

4.1   CNCeleb Corpus and Evaluation Metrics

The multi-genre CNCeleb corpus [8,16], comprised of CN-Celeb 1 [8] and CN-Celeb 2 [16] corpora, is used to carry out text-independent speaker verification experiments. Statistics of CNCeleb corpus is presented in Table 1 in terms train - eval splits, number of speakers, recordings and evaluation trials. Training data consists of approximately 2,800 speakers in 11 different genres (i.e., advertisement, drama, entertainment, interview, live broadcast, movie, play, recitation, singing, speech, vlog) [17].

Standard Kaldi recipe is used to perform offline data augmentation (i.e., on waveform-level) over the training data using the MUSAN noise [23] and the RIRs [15] datasets.

Speaker verification results are reported on the evaluation subset of the CN-Celeb 1 [8] dataset (as mentioned in Table 1) in terms of EER (equal error rate) and the minimum detection cost functions minDCF01 minDCF001 computed for p-target = 0.01 & p-target = 0.001, respectively.

Table 1. Statistics of CNCeleb 1 & 2 data in terms of numbers of speakers, recordings, total number of trials and target trials.

Train/Test sets	# Speakers	# Recordings	# Trials	# Target trials
CNCeleb1_train	797	107953	N/A	N/A
CNCeleb2_train	1996	524787	N/A	N/A
CNCeleb_train (1 & 2)	2793	632740	N/A	N/A
CNCeleb1_Eval	200	17973	3484292	17755

4.2   Frontend and Backend

As a frontend, 40-dimensional Mel-Frequency Cepstral Coefficients (MFCC) are extracted using an analysis window of 25 ms with a frame shift of 10 ms. The MFCC features are normalized using cepstral mean normalization over a window of 300 frames. Energy-based speech activity detector (SAD) is used to remove non-speech frames and a Probabilistic linear discriminant analysis (PLDA) back-end is used for verification scoring after reducing the embeddings' dimension to 150 using a linear discriminative analysis (LDA).

4.3   Experimental Setup

All our developed systems apply offline data augmentation to the input speech prior to the MFCC extraction process. In addition to the typical additive and reverberant noise augmentation, we have explored the use of the SpecAugment technique [29], which has shown great performance in speech recognition.

Since SpecAugment is applicable on the Mel-Filterbank (MFB) features, for the case of extractors with 2D-CNN the MFCC features are passed through the IDCT-layer (inverse discrete cosine transform) to obtain d-dimensional MFB features. Here $d = 40$. Over the MFB features, SpecAugment is applied on the fly, where both time and frequency masking are performed. For an MFB feature sequence with n frames, the policy for time and frequency masking are as follows:

- Frequency masking: for a randomly sampled $f{\sim}unif(\ 0, F)$ and $f_0{\sim}unif(0, d - f)$, the Mel-frequency channels $[f_0, f_0 + f)$ are masked, where F is the frequency mask parameter.
- Time masking: for a randomly sampled $t{\sim}unif(0, T)$ and $t_0{\sim}unif(0, n - t)$, the time steps $[t_0, t_0 + t)$ are masked, where T is the time mask parameter.

Though SpecAugment augmentation is normally applied on spectral features (e.g, MFB) the ETDNN_CA, ETDNN-LSTM_CA, FTDNN_CA, ENSEMBLE, ENSEMBLE2 and ENSEMBLE3 systems apply masking directly to the MFCC features and in this work, we denote this augmentation as CepAugment. Our developed systems ETDNN_CA, ETDNN-LSTM_CA, FTDNN_CA, HNN, MSHNN, ENSEMBLE, ENSEMBLE2 and ENSEMBLE (as presented in Table 2) use both offline augmentation and on-the-fly data augmentation using SpecAugment and/or CepAugment techniques. Systems named using *_CA indicate that CepAugment is used for on-the-fly data augmentation where masking is applied directly to the cepstral features. Implementation of all experimented systems was done using the Kaldi toolkit [21] following the egs/cnceleb/v2 speaker verification recipe.

4.4   Experimental Results on the CNCeleb Corpus

In this experiment, we compare the speaker verification performance of the proposed neural embedding extractor including the HNN (hybrid neural network)-based embeddings extractor and the other conventional speaker embeddings

Table 2. The experimental results of the proposed Hybrid Neural Network (HNN) -based systems and conventional methods on the CNCeleb1 evaluation sets in terms of EER and minimum detection cost functions minDCF01 & minDCF001. The best results in each evaluation metrics are highlighted in bold font.

System	Backend	EER	minDCF01	minDCF001
TDNN [17]	PLDA	12.39	0.6011	0.7353
ResNet34	Cosine similarity	11.71	0.6692	0.7562
ResNet34	PLDA	10.71	0.5840	0.7281
ECAPA-TDNN	Cosine similarity	11.84	0.4955	0.6501
TDNN	PLDA	11.33	0.5704	0.7200
ETDNN	PLDA	11.09	0.5626	0.7190
ETDNN_CA	PLDA	10.88	0.5588	0.7105
FTDNN	PLDA	11.00	0.5546	0.7134
FTDNN_CA	PLDA	10.58	0.5461	0.7127
ETDNN-LSTM_CA	PLDA	10.30	0.5459	0.6828
HNN	PLDA	9.175	0.4994	0.6441
MSHNN	PLDA	**9.05**	**0.4874**	**0.6425**
ENSEMBLE	PLDA	**8.752**	**0.4721**	**0.6314**
ENSEMBLE2	PLDA	**8.938**	**0.4822**	**0.6389**
ENSEMBLE3	PLDA	**8.786**	**0.4722**	**0.6316**

extraction frameworks such as ResNet34, ECAPA-TDNN, TDNN, ETDNN, FTDNN, ETDNN_CA, FTDNN_CA, and ETDNN-LSTM_CA.

We introduced the HNN for speaker verification with promising results in [1] for the first time, later in [14], we demonstrated an extensive analysis of the performance of HNN including the ablation study.

Table 2 shows the results of the experimented systems. As shown in the results from ETDNN, FTDNN and TDNN, increasing the temporal context (ETDNN, FTDNN), factorizing the weight matrix and adding skip connections (FTDNN) can help to improve the performance significantly. Using CepAugment with the ETDNN (i.e., ETDNN_CA) further improved the performance, which achieved an EER of 11.09%. We discovered a similar trend when comparing the performances between FTDNN and FTDNN_CA.

The HNN and the ETDNN-LSTM_CA hybrid systems outperformed the conventional TDNN-based architectures (i.e., TDNN, ETDNN, FTDNN). Especially the standard HNN outperformed the conventional TDNN with a relative improvement of 25.95% in terms of EER. This may be attributed to the complementary information learned by different network architectures (e.g., LSTM, TDNN, CNN). Moreover, from these results, we can assume that capturing the time-frequency correlation and increasing the temporal context can both improve the embedding networks ability to capture the speaker discriminative footprints.

The third best performance was observed from the ENSEMBLE2 system, which outperformed the standard HNN with a relative improvement of 2.58% in terms of EER. This indicates that the standard HNN and the ETDNN-LSTM_CA can learn complementary speaker-dependent information to each other.

The proposed ENSEMBLE system demonstrated the best verification performance, which provided a relative improvement of 4.24% over the HNN system in terms of EER metric. The gain in performance achieved by the ENSEMBLE3 system over ENSEMBLE2 may be attributed to the multi-resolution and complementarity provided by the additional ETDNN architecture. Observing the results of TDNN, ETDNN and FTDNN systems from Table 2 depth seems to play a key role in building good embedding extractor networks and helps to improve the performance of the authentication system. Again, by comparing the results attained by the ENSEMBLE and ENSEMBLE3 systems it can be stated that emsembling of lighter embedding extractor networks is helpful for boosting speaker verification performance.

Table 3. Speaker verification performances of the proposed embedding extractors on the VoxCeleb1_O test partition of Voxceleb 1 corpus. Here, AMS stands for additive margin softmax.

	Backend	EER (%)
Chung et al. [5]	Cosine	3.95
Xie et al. [31]	Cosine	3.22
Hajavi et al. [10]	Cosine	4.26
Xiang et al. [30]	Cosine	2.69
Monteiro et al. [18]	Learned sim.	2.51
SpecAugment+TDNN [29]	PLDA	2.59
SpecAugment+TDNN+AMS [29]	Cosine	1.96
SpecAugment+ResNet34 [29]	PLDA	1.68
HNN	PLDA	**1.55**
MSHNN	PLDA	**1.49**
ENSEMBLE	PLDA	**1.43**

Interestingly, although the proposed MSHNN is not ensembled with other network architectures, it was also able to achieve comparable performance to the ensembled systems. By only adding a multi-streaming scheme, the MSHNN was able to outperform the HNN with a relative improvement of 1.36% in terms of EER. Such performance improvement may be attributed to the capability of the MSHNN to extract the speaker information latent in different temporal resolutions.

4.5   Experiments on VoxCeleb Corpus

In the VoxCeleb experiments, only the Voxceleb2 [5] development set that contains only 5,994 speakers with 1,092,009 utterances was used for training the embedding extractors. Similar data augmentation was performed as done in the experiments for CNCeleb but PLDA backend was trained on the original portion of training data. Results are reported on the original Voxceleb 1 test set (VoxCeleb1_O) [19] in terms of EER(%) only.

Speaker verification performances of the proposed neural embedding extractors and the considered baseline systems are reported in Table 3. Like the CNCeleb, on the Voxceleb dataset the proposed approaches outperformed the baselines with significant margin and the proposed ENSEMBLE neural embedding extractor demonstrated the best verification performance in terms of EER.

5   Conclusion

In this work, we introduced two novel neural speaker embedding extraction schemes for effectively extracting the speaker-dependent information from the input speech signal. We first proposed a MSHNN, which processes the input speech in multiple streams of TDNN-LSTM blocks to capture the speaker information latent in different temporal resolutions. Additionally, we proposed an ensemble embedding extractor, which combines two different hybrid backbone architectures (HNN and TDNN-LSTM) with the TDNN-based x-vector architecture to exploit the complementary information learned by them.

Our experimental results on the CNCeleb and VoxCeleb datasets demonstrated that both our proposed methods can outperform the considered conventional methods. Instead of multi-streaming similar architectures with different dilation rate, ensembling of more than one heterogeneous backbone architectures helped to attain the best performance by capturing both the diversified temporal resolution and the complementarity available in different architectures.

Acknowledgments. The authors wish to acknowledge the funding from the Government of Canada's New Frontiers in Research Fund (NFRF) through grant NFRFR-2021-00338 and Natural Sciences and Engineering Research Council of Canada (NSERC) through grant RGPIN-2019-05381 and Ministry of Economy and Innovation (MEI) of the Government of Quebec for the continued support.

References

1. Alam, J., Fathan, A., Kang, W.H.: Text-independent speaker verification employing CNN-LSTM-TDNN hybrid networks. In: Karpov, A., Potapova, R. (eds.) 23rd International Conference on Speech and Computer (SPECOM), LNCS, Springer, Cham. vol. 12997, pp. 1–13 (2021). https://doi.org/10.1007/978-3-030-87802-3_1
2. Alam, J., Kang, W.H., Fathan, A.: Hybrid neural network-based deep embedding extractors for text-independent speaker verification. In: Proceedings of Odyssey (2022)

3. Cai, Y., Li, L., Wang, D., Abel, A.: Deep speaker vector normalization with maximum gaussianality training (2020)
4. Chung, J.S., et al.: In defence of metric learning for speaker recognition. In: Interspeech (2020)
5. Chung, J.S., Nagrani, A., Zisserman, A.: Voxceleb2: deep speaker recognition. arXiv preprint arXiv:1806.05622 (2018)
6. Dehak, N., Kenny, P.J., Dehak, R., Dumouchel, P., Ouellet, P.: Front-end factor analysis for speaker verification. IEEE Trans. Audio Speech Lang. Process. **19**(4), 788–798 (2011). https://doi.org/10.1109/TASL.2010.2064307
7. Desplanques, B., Thienpondt, J., Demuynck, K.: ECAPA-TDNN: emphasized channel attention, propagation and aggregation in TDNN based speaker verification. In: Meng, H., Xu, B., Zheng, T.F. (eds.) Interspeech, pp. 3830–3834. ISCA (2020)
8. Fan, Y., et al.: Cn-celeb: a challenging chinese speaker recognition dataset. In: IEEE International Conference on Acoustics, Speech and Signal Processing (ICASSP), pp. 7604–7608. IEEE (2020)
9. Gusev, A., et al.: Deep speaker embeddings for far-field speaker recognition on short utterances (2020)
10. Hajavi, A., Etemad, A.: A deep neural network for short-segment speaker recognition. Proc. Interspeech **2019**, 2878–2882 (2019)
11. Han, K.J., Pan, J., Tadala, V.K.N., Ma, T., Povey, D.: Multistream CNN for robust acoustic modeling. In: IEEE International Conference on Acoustics, Speech and Signal Processing (ICASSP), pp. 6873–6877 (2021)
12. He, K., Zhang, X., Ren, S., Sun, J.: Deep residual learning for image recognition. In: IEEE Conference on Computer Vision and Pattern Recognition (CVPR), pp. 770–778 (2016). https://doi.org/10.1109/CVPR.2016.90
13. Heigold, G., Moreno, I., Bengio, S., Shazeer, N.: End-to-end text-dependent speaker verification. In: 2016 IEEE International Conference on Acoustics, Speech and Signal Processing (ICASSP), pp. 5115–5119. IEEE Press (2016). https://doi.org/10.1109/ICASSP.2016.7472652
14. Kang, W.H., Alam, J., Fathan, A.: Hybrid network with multi-level global-local statistics pooling for robust text-independent speaker recognition. In: IEEE Automatic Speech Recognition and Understanding Workshop (ASRU) (2021)
15. Ko, T., Peddinti, V., Povey, D., Seltzer, M.L., Khudanpur, S.: A study on data augmentation of reverberant speech for robust speech recognition. In: Proceedings of IEEE ICASSP, pp. 5220–5224 (2017). https://doi.org/10.1109/ICASSP.2017.7953152
16. Li, L., et al.: Cn-celeb: multi-genre speaker recognition (2020)
17. Li, L., et al.: CN-celeb: multi-genre speaker recognition (2021)
18. Monteiro, J., Albuquerque, I., Alam, J., Hjelm, R.D., Falk, T.: An end-to-end approach for the verification problem: learning the right distance. In: International Conference on Machine Learning (2020)
19. Nagrani, A., Chung, J.S., Zisserman, A.: Voxceleb: a large-scale speaker identification dataset. arXiv preprint arXiv:1706.08612 (2017)
20. Novoselov, S., Shulipa, A., Kremnev, I., Kozlov, A., Shchemelinin, V.: On deep speaker embeddings for text-independent speaker recognition. CoRR abs/1804.10080 (2018). https://arxiv.org/abs/1804.10080
21. Povey, D., et al.: The kaldi speech recognition toolkit (2011)
22. Zhang, R., et al.: Aret: aggregated residual extended time-delay neural networks for speaker verification. In: Proceedings of Interspeech, pp. 946–950 (2020)

23. Snyder, D., Chen, G., Povey, D.: MUSAN: A Music, Speech, and Noise Corpus (2015). arXiv:1510.08484v1

24. Snyder, D., Garcia-Romero, D., Sell, G., Povey, D., Khudanpur, S.: X-vectors: robust DNN embeddings for speaker recognition. In: 2018 IEEE International Conference on Acoustics, Speech and Signal Processing (ICASSP), pp. 5329–5333. IEEE (2018)

25. Snyder, D., et al.: The JHU Speaker Recognition System for the VOiCES 2019 Challenge. In: Proceedings of the Interspeech, pp. 2468–2472 (2019). https://doi.org/10.21437/Interspeech.2019-2979

26. Tang, Y., Ding, G., Huang, J., He, X., Zhou, B.: Deep speaker embedding learning with multi-level pooling for text-independent speaker verification. In: IEEE International Conference on Acoustics, Speech and Signal Processing (ICASSP), pp. 6116–6120 (2019)

27. Villalba, J., et al.: State-of-the-art speaker recognition for telephone and video speech: The JHU-MIT submission for NIST SRE18. In: Proceedings of the Interspeech, pp. 1488–1492 (2019). https://dx.doi.org/10.21437/Interspeech.2019-2713

28. Wan, L., Wang, Q., Papir, A., Moreno, I.L.: Generalized end-to-end loss for speaker verification. In: IEEE International Conference on Acoustics, Speech and Signal Processing (ICASSP), pp. 4879–4883 (2018)

29. Wang, S., Rohdin, J., Plchot, O., Burget, L., Yu, K., Černocký, J.: Investigation of specaugment for deep speaker embedding learning. In: IEEE International Conference on Acoustics, Speech and Signal Processing (ICASSP), pp. 7139–7143 (2020)

30. Xiang, X., Wang, S., Huang, H., Qian, Y., Yu, K.: Margin matters: towards more discriminative deep neural network embeddings for speaker recognition. arXiv preprint arXiv:1906.07317 (2019)

31. Xie, W., Nagrani, A., Chung, J.S., Zisserman, A.: Utterance-level aggregation for speaker recognition in the wild. In: ICASSP 2019–2019 IEEE International Conference on Acoustics, Speech and Signal Processing (ICASSP), pp. 5791–5795. IEEE (2019)

32. Zhou, T., Zhao, Y., Wu, J.: Resnext and res2net structures for speaker verification. In: IEEE Spoken Language Technology Workshop (SLT), pp. 301–307 (2021). https://doi.org/10.1109/SLT48900.2021.9383531

Deep Speaker Embeddings Based Online Diarization

Anastasia Avdeeva[1]([⊠]) and Sergey Novoselov[2]

[1] ITMO University, St. Petersburg, Russia
ananaskelly@mail.ru
[2] STC Ltd., St. Petersburg, Russia

Abstract. This paper describes our experiments with the Unbounded Interleaved-State Recurrent Neural Network (UIS-RNN) model for development of an online diarization system. For this task several UIS-RNN models based on different speaker embeddings extractors were trained. These systems were evaluated in terms of Diarization Error Rate (DER) metric on public and private test datasets. Also systems were tested on real dialogue data recorded in a bank office. Proposed online models outperform standard offline Agglomerative Hierarchical Clustering (AHC) approach and are compatible with the state-of-the-art Bayesian HMM (VBx) offline method.

Keywords: Deep learning · Diarization · Online diarization

1 Introduction

Speaker diarization is a process of labeling segments of audio recording with classes that correspond to unique speaker identity or in other words it is a task of determining "who spoke when". Historically, it comes along with tasks of speaker identification and speech recognition and used as a preprocessing step [12]. Diarization is a complicated task due to the necessity of determining speaker identity on extremely short segments. In spite of the recent success of deep learning approaches, getting robust embedding from short duration speech segments is still a tricky task. And it is a more complicated problem in online settings where the number of speakers is not known and must be estimated on the fly.

In this research we explore the UIS-RNN approach for an online diarization system development. Our aim was to elaborate an universal model and to compare performance of such an online method with offline approaches on different datasets.

2 Related Work

All diarization algorithms, regardless if it was developed for working offline or online, can be divided into two groups: cascaded approach and end-to-end models. Cascaded approach appears to be more widespread. These methods usually consist of several blocks such as feature extraction, Voice Activity Detector

© Springer Nature Switzerland AG 2022
S. R. M. Prasanna et al. (Eds.): SPECOM 2022, LNAI 13721, pp. 24–32, 2022.
https://doi.org/10.1007/978-3-031-20980-2_3

(VAD), segmentation and clusterization (Fig. 1). It is common practice to use speaker embeddings extracted from speech segments as input features for clusterization.

Currently, main investigations in cascaded approach rely on better embedding extractors and development of clusterization methods. For instance, in [4] the ECAPA-TDNN model which earlier has shown impressive results in a speaker verification task used for diarization. According to the authors results, such a diarization system outperforms systems based on x-vector Time Delay Neural Network (TDNN) and ResNet101 models. While meaning clusterization approaches there are AHC and k-means algorithms which are commonly used for this task. However, there remained room for improvement. In [20] proposed spectral clustering framework adopted for the diarization problem. In [5,14] proposed a VBx diarization method based on AHC clusterization followed by a clustering based on Bayesian Hidden Markov Model (HMM). In compliance with the authors results given in [14], VBx based system shows state-of-the-art results on such popular evaluation protocols as well-known CALLHOME, AMI [3] and DIHARD II [23].

Fig. 1. Diarization pipeline.

Overall review of diarization methods can be found in [21]. Whereas in this research we are more interested in online diarization studies. Commonly offline approaches propagated to online settings with some additions. In [27] authors replace the clusterization module with an online generative process described by Recurrent Neural Network (RNN) model. Then a distant dependent Chinese process used for working with an unknown number of speakers. This model works with speaker embeddings as input features. In [7] authors propose modifications to this approach introducing new loss function and slightly different formulae for modeling of the speaker turn behavior. Whereas in [8] suggested end-to-end model. Authors formulate a diarization problem as a multi-label classification task. Despite of convenience of end-to-end approach such model has some drawbacks: it can deal only with number of speaker it was trained and can not be used in online fashion due to fact it was trained with Permutation Invariant Training (PIT) [26]. Thus labels between iterations are not unique. To solve the problem with a fixed number of speakers, an attractor-based model is suggested in [9]. In [25] buffer-tracing suggested to solve the problem with label permutations for a flexible number of speakers and match labels between different chunks. In [10] authors come with a block-wise approach to work with an unlimited number of speakers. Thus the final solution is not elegant: it has local attractors for chunks, global attractors for final decision and buffer for labels mapping between chunks.

Alternatively, in [24] recently proposed Target Speaker Voice Activity Detection (TS-VAD) approach [17] adopted to an online diarization task.

There are also online methods based on simple clusterization algorithms. One of the important drawbacks of such popular methods as AHC and k-means is the necessity of determining threshold for stopping criteria in case of AHC or number of speakers in case of k-means respectively. In [28] introduced an approach based on AHC. For running in an online manner authors suggest a label matching algorithm. Also speaker embedding graph proposed for re-clusterization.

In addition, there is a group of alternative methods in this field based on source separation algorithms development. This approach is commonly aimed to solve such problems as denoising or separate signals of different nature but it also can be applied for diarization. Typically such models take as input feature signal with a mix of speakers and predict a separate signal for every speaker found in the mix. So, it can easily handle overlapped speech which is a weak point for the majority of diarization algorithms. In [11] authors use Deep Clustering (DC) architecture for a speaker separation task. Also there are examples of using speaker separation approaches in an online manner [18]. But the main drawback of such methods is it usually works with a fixed number of speakers and for working with another one a separate model must be trained.

3   Experimental Setup

3.1   Speaker Encoder Networks

For training UIS-RNN model speaker embeddings must be extracted and then used as input features. In this research we compare several deep speaker embeddings extractors for the task: RepVGG [6], ResNet34, wav2vec 2.0 based model [19]. All these extractors share the same training dataset and strategy of training. Training dataset contains a wide variety of different telephone and media sets both available online and private.

- Switchboard2 Phases 1, 2 and 3
- Switchboard Cellular
- Mixer 6 Speech
- NIST SREs 2004 - 2010
- NIST SRE 2018 (eval set)
- concatenated VoxCeleb 1 and 2
- RusTelecom
- RusIVR corpus.

RusTelecom is a private Russian corpus of telephone speech, collected by call-centers in Russia. RusIVR is a private Russian corpus with telephone and media data, collected in various scenarios and recorded by different types of devices (telephone, headset, far-field microphone, etc.).

Wav2vec 2.0 based model was trained on raw wav data whereas RepVGG and ResNet34 models were trained on Mel-filter bank (MFB) energies with the following settings:

- frame-length – 25 ms;
- frame-shift – 10 ms;
- low frequency – 20 Hz;
- high frequency – 3900 Hz;
- number of mel bins – 64.

For detecting speech region Unet-based VAD [15] was used.

Table 1 demonstrates results of described extractors on well-known protocols for speaker verification system evaluation. We also take into account FFSVC2020 and CommonVoice protocols as far as these protocols formed from short duration enrolls and tests. Such conditions correlate with a diarization task where we need to compare speaker models obtained from short speech segments. FFSVC2020 protocol was realised as an evaluation protocol in The Far-Field Speaker Verification (FFSVC) challenge 2020 [22]. CommonVoice is test set generated from Russian language data getting from [1].

Our intuition for such a model's architecture choice was as follows. RepVGG and ResNet34 are relatively fast models showing acceptable quality on different test datasets. While wav2vec 2.0 based model is significantly (approximately 10 times) slower architecture but providing better results. So one of our investigations in this research was to compare the impact of extractors performance on the final diarization system performance. Also all of these models try to be universal in some senses due to the training on a set of data from different domains – microphone, telephone, augmented with different kinds of noises, signal-to-noise ratio settings, etc. These models are optimized for working with various speech duration as well.

Table 1. Comparison of extractors used for diarization model training in terms of EER (%) metric.

	Voxceleb1 (cleaned)	SRE16 eval	SRE19 eval	FFSVC2020	CommonVoice
repVGG	1.96	5.43	3.07	16.74	4.46
resnet34	2.13	6.25	3.13	14.20	2.55
wav2vec	0.47	3.82	1.88	13.04	1.12

3.2 Training Dataset

Models were trained on a subset from private corpora consisting of telephone and microphone data collected in different conditions such as silence indoor, noisy indoor and noisy street with various signal-to-noise ratio and reverberation time. It contains 800 speakers. Speakers mixes for training were generated synthetically. For training UIS-RNN model data needs to be packed into an array of sequences. One such sequence consists of segments with speech of several speakers. Duration of segments and number of speakers was chosen randomly in ranges from 30 to 45 s and 1 to 5 speakers correspondingly. Duration of single speaker utterance in sequence was fixed to 1.5 s.

3.3   Testing Datasets

Trained models were tested on both private and publicly available datasets for diarization system evaluation:

- RusIVR_test
- NIST 2008
- DIHARD II

RusIVR_test and NIST 2008 subsets contain mixes only of two speakers whereas DIHARD II consists of sessions with variable number of speakers: from 1 to 10.

RusIVR_test is a subset of corpora described earlier (RusIVR) excluded from training.

NIST 2008 is a test subset composed from the NIST SRE 2008 evaluation set [16] which consist of telephone speech. Ideal markup was generated from Automatic Speech Recognition (ASR) transcriptions supplied with an evaluation set.

The second DIHARD challenge dataset [23] was released as the second in series of DIHARD speech diarization challenges. For this evaluation data corresponding to track 2 of this challenge was used. This set consists of single channel recordings with duration of 5 to 10 min drawn from different domains such as interviews, audiobooks, meeting speech, YouTube videos, etc.

Also models were tested on a small subset (called Bank_office) of real data recorded in a bank office. It consists of several sessions of dialogues between operator and client recorded on a small microphone array from 2 microphones with total duration 2 h and 30 min (for an evaluation only one channel was used). VAD markup was received from words bounds obtained with the ASR system.

4   Results and Discussion

4.1   Diarization Performance

DER metric was obtained with a pyannote software [2]. Table 2 shows results of trained UIS-RNN models based on different speaker embedding extractors. It also compares such online systems with offline AHC clusterization. AHC clusterization in all our experiments based on RepVGG embeddings. We specify a speaker confusion error in this table since we don't use oracle VAD markup in this case. Tests were running in an online manner: if for a given chunk of audio (1,5 s) duration of clear speech bigger the threshold speaker embedding for this was extracted and then passed to UIS-RNN model. It can be seen that in our experiments the UIS-RNN model trained on embeddings from RepVGG shows better quality whereas in verification tests (see Table 1) wav2vec extractor significantly outperforms RepVGG. Although, to our assumption there is no considerable difference between these speaker embeddings extractors for a diarization task. It can be found that the online UIS-RNN approach performs better on DIHARD

II and NIST 2008 datasets, but slightly worse on our test set. Studying this case more carefully we found out that recordings from RusIVR_test contain a lot of loud background speech not included in our ideal markup as separate classes and sometimes contained in target intervals. While UIS-RNN is able to handle this and separate such speech in new clusters. If we lower *crp_alpha* value, which corresponds to probability of new cluster creation, during UIS-RNN inference we get 7.90% on this test subset (this constraint will lead the model to find only 1–3 clusters). Detailed information about the purpose of this parameter can be found in the original paper [27].

Table 3 describes results on a real data subset. It is noticeable that the UIS-RNN model based on RepVGG extractor significantly outperforms offline AHC clusterization performance. Surprisingly it even outperforms the VBx approach [14] in this case. Markup for the VBx method was obtained with open source software which can be found in [13].

Table 2. Speaker confusion (%) on trained UIS-RNN models based on different extractors and using AHC.

	RusIVR_test	DIHARD II (single channel)	NIST 2008
repVGG	**13.43**	**12.11**	9.28
resnet34	15.07	13.57	**9.03**
wav2vec 2.0	14.92	13.60	10.90
AHC (with threshold)	10.79	16.09	9.92

Table 3. DERs (%) on trained UIS-RNN models based on different extractors on real data.

	Bank_office
repVGG	12.97
resnet34	19.54
wav2vec 2.0	22.70
AHC (with threshold)	20.74
VBX [14]	34.45

Also results obtained in experiments were compared with one given in [14]. Table 4 demonstrates comparison between VBx approach and UIS-RNN based on RepVGG extractor on DIHARD II dataset. DERs metric for VBx method derived directly from [14] and for UIS-RNN computed as described in reference paper: using oracle VAD and dscore software. "Full" means scoring DER without any collar while "fair" with 250 ms collar and "forgiving" with 250 ms collar and ignoring overlapped speech. Evidently, VBx method outperforms UIS-RNN but online approaches usually perform worse than offline models thus we found our results satisfactory and still compatible with [14].

Table 4. DERs (%) comparison of VBx approach and UIS-RNN on DIHARD II.

	Full	Fair	Forgiving
VBx	18.19	12.23	–
UIS-RNN	21.91	16.55	10.90

4.2 Diarization in Verification Task

Developed diarization system was also tested in a verification task. In practice we can face a situation in which test recording for verification contains speech of not only a single speaker but a mix of several speakers. In this case diarization preprocessing is useful for separate speakers to get better speaker models. To emulate these conditions we build an evaluation protocol from the RusIVR_test subset. Enroll files contain speech only of the target speaker whereas test files are mixed speech of two speakers with background noise. We evaluate verification performance in an ideal case – getting test embedding from segments corresponding to the target speaker according to ideal markup. And then we compare this result with verification using AHC offline clusterization for test recording, UIS-RNN online approach and with any diarization at all. In case of employing diarization as some kind of preprocessing step for a test file this procedure was organized as follows. After diarization of test recording segments corresponding to the same speaker concatenated in a single one for embedding extraction. Then all received models compared with the enroll model and maximum of scores returned as final decision. Table 5 shows significant improvement when using diarization before verification. It is also noticeable that the online approach performs approximately the same as offline AHC clusterization. Such preprocessing can be used in real applications when we need to extract the target speaker from streaming audio and verify him/her after getting enough clear speech.

Table 5. Verification tests with diarization based on repVGG extractor.

	EER (%)
Without diarization	14.04
UIS-RNN	7.84
AHC offline	7.70
Ideal case (taget rttm)	5.95

5 Conclusion

In this paper we compare diarization performance of several UIS-RNN models trained on embeddings from different speaker encoder networks. Proposed online models outperform standard offline AHC approach and are compatible with the state-of-the-art VBx offline method. Described approach is applicable in the task of the verification with diarization and gives acceptable results on the real data.

Surprisingly, in our experiments using a better embedding extractor in verification sense does not lead to improvements in the diarization task. Thus future work could investigate training of more specific speaker embeddings extractors – performing better on short duration segments and in noisy conditions.

References

1. Ardila, R., et al.: Common voice: a massively-multilingual speech corpus. In: LREC (2020)
2. Bredin, H., et al.: Pyannote.audio: neural building blocks for speaker diarization. In: ICASSP 2020–2020 IEEE International Conference on Acoustics, Speech and Signal Processing (ICASSP), pp. 7124–7128 (2020)
3. Carletta, J., et al.: The ami meeting corpus: a pre-announcement. In: MLMI (2005)
4. Dawalatabad, N., Ravanelli, M., Grondin, F., Thienpondt, J., Desplanques, B., Na, H.: Ecapa-tdnn embeddings for speaker diarization. In: Interspeech (2021)
5. Díez, M., Burget, L., Landini, F., Wang, S., Černocký, J.H.: Optimizing bayesian hmm based x-vector clustering for the second dihard speech diarization challenge. In: ICASSP 2020–2020 IEEE International Conference on Acoustics, Speech and Signal Processing (ICASSP), pp. 6519–6523 (2020)
6. Ding, X., Zhang, X., Ma, N., Han, J., Ding, G., Sun, J.: Repvgg: making vgg-style convnets great again. In: 2021 IEEE/CVF Conference on Computer Vision and Pattern Recognition (CVPR), pp. 13728–13737 (2021)
7. Fini, E., Brutti, A.: Supervised online diarization with sample mean loss for multi-domain data. In: ICASSP 2020–2020 IEEE International Conference on Acoustics, Speech and Signal Processing (ICASSP), pp. 7134–7138 (2020)
8. Fujita, Y., Kanda, N., Horiguchi, S., Nagamatsu, K., Watanabe, S.: End-to-end neural speaker diarization with permutation-free objectives. In: INTERSPEECH (2019)
9. Horiguchi, S., Fujita, Y., Watanabe, S., Xue, Y., Nagamatsu, K.: End-to-end speaker diarization for an unknown number of speakers with encoder-decoder based attractors. ArXiv abs/2005.09921 (2020)
10. Horiguchi, S., Watanabe, S., García, P., Takashima, Y., Kawaguchi, Y.: Online neural diarization of unlimited numbers of speakers. ArXiv abs/2206.02432 (2022)
11. Isik, Y.Z., Roux, J.L., Chen, Z., Watanabe, S., Hershey, J.R.: Single-channel multi-speaker separation using deep clustering. In: INTERSPEECH (2016)
12. Kanda, N., et al.: Guided source separation meets a strong ASR backend: hitachi/paderborn university joint investigation for dinner party ASR. In: Proceedings of Interspeech 2019, pp. 1248–1252 (2019). https://doi.org/10.21437/Interspeech.2019-1167
13. Landini, F., Profant, J., Diez, M., Burget, L.: Bayesian hmm clustering of x-vector sequences (vbx) in speaker diarization: theory, implementation and analysis on standard tasks. Comput. Speech Lang. **71**, 101254 (2022)
14. Landini, F., Profant, J., Díez, M., Burget, L.: Bayesian hmm clustering of x-vector sequences (vbx) in speaker diarization: theory, implementation and analysis on standard tasks. ArXiv abs/2012.14952 (2020)
15. Lavrentyeva, G., et al.: Blind speech signal quality estimation for speaker verification systems. In: INTERSPEECH (2020)

16. Martin, A.F., Greenberg, C.S.: Nist 2008 speaker recognition evaluation: performance across telephone and room microphone channels. In: INTERSPEECH (2009)
17. Medennikov, I., et al.: Target-speaker voice activity detection: a novel approach for multi-speaker diarization in a dinner party scenario. ArXiv abs/2005.07272 (2020)
18. Morrone, G., Cornell, S., Raj, D., Zovato, E., Brutti, A., Squartini, S.: Leveraging speech separation for conversational telephone speaker diarization (2022)
19. Novoselov, S., Lavrentyeva, G., Avdeeva, A., Volokhov, V., Gusev, A.: Robust speaker recognition with transformers using wav2vec 2.0. ArXiv abs/2203.15095 (2022)
20. Park, T.J., Han, K.J., Kumar, M., Narayanan, S.S.: Auto-tuning spectral clustering for speaker diarization using normalized maximum eigengap. IEEE Signal Process. Lett. **27**, 381–385 (2020)
21. Park, T.J., Kanda, N., Dimitriadis, D., Han, K.J., Watanabe, S., Narayanan, S.S.: A review of speaker diarization: recent advances with deep learning. Comput. Speech Lang. **72**, 101317 (2022)
22. Qin, X., et al.: The ffsvc 2020 evaluation plan. ArXiv abs/2002.00387 (2020)
23. Ryant, N., et al.: The second dihard diarization challenge: dataset, task, and baselines. In: INTERSPEECH (2019)
24. Wang, W., Lin, Q., Li, M.: Online target speaker voice activity detection for speaker diarization. ArXiv abs/2207.05920 (2022)
25. Xue, Y., et al.: Online end-to-end neural diarization handling overlapping speech and flexible numbers of speakers. ArXiv abs/2101.08473 (2021)
26. Yu, D., Kolbæk, M., Tan, Z., Jensen, J.H.: Permutation invariant training of deep models for speaker-independent multi-talker speech separation. In: 2017 IEEE International Conference on Acoustics, Speech and Signal Processing (ICASSP), pp. 241–245 (2017)
27. Zhang, A., Wang, Q., Zhu, Z., Paisley, J.W., Wang, C.: Fully supervised speaker diarization. In: ICASSP 2019–2019 IEEE International Conference on Acoustics, Speech and Signal Processing (ICASSP), pp. 6301–6305 (2019)
28. Zhang, Y., et al.: Online speaker diarization with graph-based label generation. In: Odyssey (2022)

Overlapped Speech Detection Using AM-FM Based Time-Frequency Representations

Shikha Baghel[1]($\boxtimes$), S. R. M. Prasanna[2], and Prithwijit Guha[1]

[1] Department of Electronics and Electrical Engineering,
Indian Institute of Technology Guwahati, Guwahati 781039, Assam, India
{shikha.baghel,pguha}@iitg.ac.in

[2] Department of Electrical Engineering, Indian Institute of Technology Dharwad,
Dharwad 580011, India
prasanna@iitdh.ac.in

Abstract. Overlapped speech contains simultaneous speech of multiple speakers. The presence of overlapped speech is one of the main sources of error for speaker diarization, speech, and speaker recognition systems. Most of the existing works used magnitude spectrum based features for overlap detection. This work focuses on detecting overlapped speech by exploring instantaneous phase and amplitude information of speech signal. Phase characteristics are captured by the Instantaneous Frequency Spectrogram (IFSpec), while Teager-Kaiser Energy Operator (TEO) based pyknograms are used for representing instantaneous amplitude. Features are learned from the IF spectrogram and TEO-based pyknogram automatically using Fully-Convolutional Neural Network (F-CNN). This work is evaluated on the SSC corpus, which has been previously used in this task. Significant performance improvement is observed when both representations are combined in an early fusion framework. The performance improvement upon combination indicates the presence of complementary information in the feature representations. Classification is performed over three different segment durations, i.e., 1 s, 500 ms, and 250 ms, to analyze the effect of segment duration over overlap detection. The effect of speaker gender present in overlapped speech is also studied in this work.

Keywords: Overlapped speech · Instantaneous frequency · Instantaneous amplitude · Pyknogram · CNN · Gender effect

1 Introduction

Overlapped Speech is produced when two or more speakers speak simultaneously. It is frequently present in spontaneous conversations like meetings, interviews, debates, etc. However, most conventional speech processing systems expect speech from a single speaker. Thus, the performance of these systems degrades

© Springer Nature Switzerland AG 2022
S. R. M. Prasanna et al. (Eds.): SPECOM 2022, LNAI 13721, pp. 33–43, 2022.
https://doi.org/10.1007/978-3-031-20980-2_4

in the presence of overlapped speech [12, 13]. The presence of overlapped speech is one of the main challenges for conventional speech processing applications such as speaker diariazation [13], speech recognition [12], conversational speech analysis [7, 16], to name a few. Ryant et al. [11] also discussed the importance of overlapped speech detection for speaker diarization systems. Therefore, this work aims to classify overlapped speech from single speaker's speech.

Signal characteristics of overlapped speech are significantly different from single speaker's speech. These differences are reflected in time domain characteristics as well as in spectral-domain features. Due to the superimposition of two or more speakers' speech, the spectral harmonicity decreases in the case of overlapped speech. Additionally, the temporal variation of pitch period increases for overlapped speech [10].

In literature, overlapped speech has been widely studied to improve the performance of speaker diarization systems. In this regard, Boakye et al. [4] studied Mel-Frequency Cepstral Coefficients (MFCC, henceforth), Root Mean Square (RMS), and Linear Predictive Coding (LPC, henceforth) coefficients. These features were used to learn the Hidden Markov Model (HMM, henceforth), where the states were modeled using Gaussian Mixture Models (GMM, henceforth). The HMM-GMM model was used for detecting overlap speech to improve diarization error [4]. The same research group [5] extended their previous work [4] by expanding the feature set with kurtosis, zero-crossing rate, residual energy, modulation spectrogram, and spectral features.

Features related to prosody, voice-quality, MFCC, energy, and spectral characteristics have been studied for detecting the competition in overlap speech [6]. Authors of [16] claim that the occurrence of overlapped speech is correlated with conversational features, and hence they explored silence patterns and speaker change statistics along with acoustic features. Mel-filter bank based features have also been used to detect overlapped speech for improving speaker diarization system [12]. Recently, Andrei et al. [1] have studied MFCC, signal envelope, FFT, AR coefficients, and squared features for overlap detection and speaker counting application. Shokouhi et al. [13, 14] have proposed a pyknogram based distance measure to identify overlapped speech. Convolutive Non-negative Matrix Factorization (CNMF) has also been studied and compared with Pyknogram based distance measure [18]. Yousefi et al. [18] showed that pyknogram works well in real scenarios than CNMF. Some works have also explored deep learning based approaches for the current task. A $1 - D$ Convolutional Neural Network (CNN, henceforth) has been learned from the magnitude frequency spectrum, MFCC, log energy, signal envelope computed with Hilbert Transform, and 12th order Auto-Regressive Model Coefficients [2]. Geiger et al. [9] proposed an overlapped speech detection system based on Long Short-Term Memory (LSTM) Recurrent Neural Network (RNN) learned over MFCC and LPC.

1.1   Motivation

Existing studies have mainly explored magnitude spectral features in combination with HMM, SVM, or GMM based classifiers. Especially, MFCC is the most widely used feature. Few works have also used deep learning based approaches for automatic feature learning from spectral features. However, phase information, being an important part of the speech signal, has not been explored much in the literature. To the best of the author's knowledge, our previous work [3] established the significance of phase information in the overlapped speech detection task. This work is the continuation of the earlier work by exploring the instantaneous frequency and amplitude components of the speech signal. The instantaneous frequency and amplitude can be obtained by Amplitude Modulation and Frequency Modulation (AM-FM) decomposition.

Instantaneous Frequency (IF) spectrum [15] represents the time varying phase characteristics. In our earlier work [3], cosine coefficients of IF were used. However, the current work utilizes the raw representation of the IF spectrogram with the motive of automatic feature learning. Additionally, instantaneous amplitude information is represented in terms of TEO-based pyknogram [13,18] which has already been studied in the context of overlapped speech. TEO-based pyknogram is more robust for real noisy (noisy) scenarios like news debates. Authors of [13] proposed a distance measure between consecutive frames of pyknogram and used these distances as features for overlap detection. However, we believe that automatic feature learning from pyknogram would capture more relevant information for the current task. The same research group [17] also explored the usefulness of pyknogram for frame-level (25 ms) overlapped speech detection using CNN based architecture. A frame-level feature representation might not capture sufficient overlapped speech information. Therefore, the present work uses a segment duration (longer than a frame) for detecting overlapped speech. A Fully- Convolutional Neural Network (F-CNN) based architecture is used to learn relevant features automatically from the raw feature representations. The F-CNN architecture was learned over IF spectrograms and TEO-based pyknograms for classifying overlapped and single speaker's speech. The main contributions of the work are as follows.

1. The present work uses AM and FM components of speech signal for single and overlapped speech classification. The raw IF-spectrogram and TEO-pyknogram are considered as the AM and FM representatives, respectively.
2. Automatic feature learning is performed using F-CNN based architecture.
3. Effect of three different segment durations, viz., 1 s, 500 ms, and 250 ms, is studied for the current task.
4. Effect of gender on the overlapped speech detection task is also studied.

The rest of the paper is organized as follows. Section 2 briefly discusses the AM-FM based time-frequency representations. The F-CNN architecture is described in Sect. 3. Experimental setup and classification results are presented in Sect. 4. Finally, the work is concluded in Sect. 5 with possible future directions.

2   Features for Overlapped Speech Detection

The decomposition of a speech signal into its Amplitude Modulated (AM) and Frequency Modulated (FM) components is an alternative approach for studying

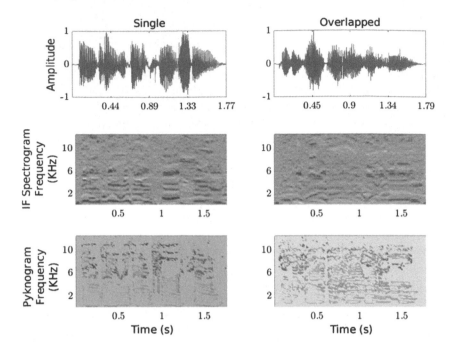

Fig. 1. Illustration of Instantaneous Frequency (IF) spectrogram (second row) and TEO-based pyknogram (third row) for single speaker and overlapped speech.

time-varying frequency information of the signal. The AM-FM analysis decomposes a Narrow Band (NB, henceforth) signal into its instantaneous amplitude and instantaneous phase part. Due to the phase wrapping problem, the FM component has gained lesser attention in speech related applications than AM component [15]. However, some studies have shown the importance of the FM component in speech applications. This work studies the relatively less explored phase component along with instantaneous amplitude information for the overlap detection task. The IF spectrogram is used to represent FM information. The TEO-pyknogram is explored as a representative of AM information. These features are briefly discussed next.

2.1 Instantaneous Frequency (IF) Spectrogram

In the current work, Instantaneous Frequency (IF, henceforth) is used as the phase representation of the speech signal. The IF [15] is defined as the time derivative of the analytic phase. The IF extraction procedure utilizes the properties of Fourier Transform and thus avoids the phase wrapping issue. The feature extraction of IF is discussed next.

The pre-emphasized speech signal $s_e[n]$ is passed through a filter bank containing L narrow band overlapping filters. The filters are bell-shaped and linearly spaced. Narrowband components of the speech signal, i.e., $s_e^i[n]$, $i = 0, \ldots L - 1$

are obtained from the filter bank. Each narrowband component $(s_e^i[n], i = 0, \ldots L-1)$ is decomposed into the corresponding analytic phase $\theta[n]$. The $\theta[n]$ is considered an FM component of the speech signal. The IF is represented as the time derivative of the analytic phase $\theta[n]$. The IF feature extraction for a $s_e^i[n]$ is given below:

$$\theta_i^{(1)}[n] = \frac{2\pi}{N} \Re \left\{ \frac{\mathcal{F}^{-1}(kZ_i[k])}{\mathcal{F}^{-1}(Z_i[k])} \right\} \tag{1}$$

where, inverse Fourier transform is represented by $\mathcal{F}^{-1}$. The $Z_i[k]$ denotes the FT of analytic signal $z_i[n]$ obtained from the narrowband component of speech signal $s_i[n]$. Next, the deviation of each IF is computed from the center frequency of the corresponding filter. The IF deviations across multiple frames are considered as the IF spectrogram. For the current work, $L = 80$ narrow band filters are used.

Figure 1 illustrates the IF spectrogram (second row) for single speaker and overlapped speech. Regular patterns can be observed from the IF spectrogram of the single speaker's speech. However, distorted patterns can be seen in the IF spectrogram of overlapped speech. Therefore, the different patterns present in IF spectrograms can be utilized for the classification of single speaker's and overlapped speech.

2.2 TEO-Based Pyknogram

TEO-based pyknogram preserves the harmonic patterns present in speech signals by suppressing non-harmonic components [13]. However, it is expected that these patterns will be disturbed in overlapped speech due to the presence of more than one speaker's speech. The pyknogram feature is extracted as follows.

Speech signal $s[n]$ is passed through a Gamma-tone filterbank to obtain bandpass speech signals $(s_j[n], j = 1 \ldots L_g)$. The Gamma-tone filterbank contains logarithmically spaced L_g number of overlapping filters. Each bandpass signal $(s_j[n])$ is further decomposed into its instantaneous amplitude $(a_j[n])$ and frequency $(f_j[n])$ component using an energy separation algorithm. Teager-Kaiser Energy Operator (TEO) is used to find the energy of each bandpass signal $(s_j[n])$. The instantaneous frequency $f_j[n]$ is computed as

$$f_j[n] = \frac{1}{2\pi} \arccos \left(1 - \frac{E_{teo}(s_j[n] - s_j[n-1])}{2E_{teo}(s_j[n])} \right) \tag{2}$$

where, the Teager-Kaiser energy operator E_{teo} is defined as

$$E_{teo}(s[n]) = s^2[n] - s[n-1]s[n+1] \tag{3}$$

The instantaneous amplitude of each $s_j[n]$ is computed as follows

$$a_j[n] = \sqrt{\frac{E_{teo}(s_j[n])}{sin^2(2\pi f_j[n])}} \tag{4}$$

Further, a weighted Frequency ($F_w[j,t]$) is computed by taking a weighted average of instantaneous frequency over a frame duration of 20ms. Here, t denotes frame index. Instantaneous amplitude ($a_j[n]$) is used as weight for extracting F_w. Similarly, an averaged amplitude ($A[j,t]$) is computed over a frame duration of 20ms.

Next, frequency candidates corresponding to spectrogram peaks are selected based on some criteria. Only those frequency candidates are retained which are aligned with the center frequency of corresponding filters. Let $F_w^s[t]$ be the list of selected frequency candidates in a frame. Finally, the TEO-based pyknogram $P[j,t]$ contains average amplitude $A[j,t]$ values corresponding to retained frequency candidates.

$$P[j,t] = \begin{cases} A[j,t], & \text{if } j \in F_w^s[t] \\ 0, & \text{otherwise} \end{cases} \tag{5}$$

In this work, the $L_g = 120$ number of filters is used to compute TEO-based pyknograms. Figure 1 shows pyknograms (third row) for single speaker's and overlapped speech. Pyknogram for overlapped speech has a distinct pattern in comparison to a single speaker. In the case of single speaker's speech, regular and parallel harmonic tracks are observed in the pyknogram (especially in the lower frequency range). In contrast, such patterns get disturbed in overlapped speech. Such variations present in the pyknogram can be automatically learned using neural networks.

3 Feature Learning Using Fully-Convolutional Neural Network (F-CNN)

This work proposes a Fully Convolutional Neural Network (F-CNN, henceforth) architecture for automatically learning features from the raw IF spectrograms and TEO-based pyknograms. The architecture of the F-CNN is illustrated in Fig. 2. The F-CNN architecture contains two Convolutional Blocks (Conv-Block), *Batch Normalization* (BN), *Flatten* and output layer. Each Conv-Block comprises one convolutional, drop-out, and *LeakyReLU* activation layer. A drop-out rate of 0.4 is used. All the details of both the Conv-Blocks are given in

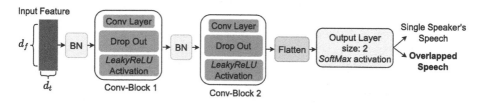

Fig. 2. Illustrating Fully-Convolutional Neural Network (F-CNN) architecture. The size of the input feature is $d_f \times d_t$, where d_f and d_t denote feature and time dimension, respectively.

Table 1. Convolutional layer's specifications used in each Conv-Block of F-CNN architecture.

	Convolutional layer specifications		
	# Kernels	Kernel size	Stride
Conv-Block 1	128	13×9	$(13, 2)$
Conv-Block 2	64	6×3	$(2, 2)$

Table 1. Padding is used in all the Conv-Blocks so that the input and output size of the convolutional layer remain the same.

The network is trained for 50 epochs with a mini-batch size of 64. Each batch is normalized prior to network training. A binary cross-entropy loss is minimized using $ADAM$ optimizer with an initial learning rate of 0.0001.

4 Experiments and Results

This section presents and discusses the experimental results for evaluating the proposed work. For the current work, speech signals (sampling frequency, $F_s =$ 16 kHz) are processed with a frame duration of 20 ms and a shift of 10 ms. The experimental setup of the present work is described next.

4.1 Dataset

This work is evaluated on the speech separation challenge (SSC) corpus [8]. It contains speech data of 34 speakers (16 females and 18 males). Each speaker speaks 500 utterances in the English language. This corpus has been used in earlier works related to overlapped speech [13]. It contains overlapped speech that is synthetically generated by mixing two single speakers' speech at six different dB levels. However, the overlapped data available in this corpus is too small for learning a neural network. Hence, the overlapped speech used in this work is generated synthetically by mixing two speakers' speech at 0dB. Such synthetic generation of overlapped data is also used in earlier works. This study only considers overlapped speech of two speakers.

For the evaluation of this work, single speaker data of the SSC corpus is split into train and test sets based on speakers. The test set contains speech data of randomly chosen 6 speakers (3 females and 3 males), and the remaining speakers' data is considered as the train set. Overlapped speech, used to train the FCNN architecture, is generated by mixing single speaker data from the train set only. Similarly, overlapped testing data is generated using single speakers' speech from the test set. This policy ensures that the test results are speaker independent and the learned models are more generic.

4.2 Classification Performance

Classification performance for a segment duration of 1 s is reported in Table 2. Results are evaluated in terms of the F1-score of individual classes and their average F1-score as well. For IF Spectrogram (IFSpec), the F1-score of overlapped speech is higher in comparison to the single speaker's speech. A decent overall performance is observed for IFSpec. However, the performance of IFSpec is lower than the TEO-based pyknogram, indicating the success of TEO-based pyknograms for overlap detection. TEO-based pyknogram also shows a higher performance for overlap class than that of single speaker's speech. This indicates that the features learned for overlap class might capture sufficient class-specific information.

Table 2. Classification performance for a segment duration of 1 s.

Features	F1-score (%)		
	Single	Overlap	Average
IF Spectrogram (IFSpec)	81.29	85.16	83.22
TEO-based Pyknogram (Pyk)	82.42	89.72	86.07
IFSpec + Pyk	95.88	97.25	96.56

The IF spectrograms and TEO-based pyknograms represent different characteristics of the speech signal. The utilization of their complementary information together might enhance the overall performance of the current task. In this context, classification is also performed with an early fusion of IF spectrogram and TEO-based pyknogram (IFSpec+Pyk). A notable improvement of $\approx$ 10% in F1-Score is observed for the combined feature, i.e., IFSpec+Pyk, compared to the individual features. This improvement suggests that the IF spectrogram carries some additional information that is not captured by TEO-based pyknograms. It can thus be said that the combination of IF spectrogram and TEO-based pyknogram can be used to obtain an enhanced overlapped speech detection.

4.3 Effect of Segment Duration

Overlapped speech detection might be sensitive to segment duration used for classification. Therefore, this work further analyses the effect of segment duration on the current task. Classification decision of overlap or single speaker speech is provided for different segment durations. In this work, three different segment durations, i.e., 1 s, 500 ms, and 250 ms, are considered. The choice of these segment durations is motivated by the literature. The performance of the proposed approach is reported in Table 3 in terms of the mean F1-score of both the classes.

It can be observed from Table 3 that performance decreases as the segment duration reduce from 1 s to 250 ms. This trend is consistent across the individual features and their combination. However, a lower decrement is observed for

Table 3. Classification results using F-CNN for three different segment durations.

Features	F1-score (%)		
	1 s	500 ms	250 ms
IF Spectrogram (IFSpec)	83.22	75.92	62.58
TEO-based Pyknogram (Pyk)	86.07	83.48	74.31
IFSpec + Pyk	96.56	84.6	78.64

TEO-based pyknogram in comparison to IF spectrogram. The best classification performance is observed for the combination feature, i.e., IFSpec+Pyk, across all three segment durations. This further justifies that the combination of IF spectrogram and TEO-based pyknogram provides a better overlapped speech detection system.

4.4   Effect of Gender Combinations Present in Overlap Speech

Gender of speakers, present in overlapped speech, might affect classification performance. Therefore, this work studies the effect of gender on the current task. In this work, overlapped speech of two speakers are used. Hence, there are three possible combinations of genders present in overlapped speech, viz., male-male (M-M), female-female (F-F), and male-female (M-F). The learned models (used to produce the results of Table 2) are tested for all three gender combinations separately. Single speaker data is the same in all three combinations. Table 4 reports classification results for gender combinations in terms of accuracy.

It is observed that M-F has higher performance in comparison to M-M and F-F in most cases. TEO-based pyknogram has better performances for both M-F and F-F combinations. The commonality between M-F and F-F is the presence of female speaker data. Speech produced by a female speaker is expected to be more non-stationary compared to a male speaker. This non-stationarity further increases in F-F and M-F overlapped speech. This might lead to more disturbance in the time-frequency representations of F-F and M-F overlapped speech than that of M-M speech. This could be the reason for the lower performance

Table 4. Effect of gender combinations present in overlapped speech for the classification task. Classification performances (in terms of accuracy) are reported for three possible gender combinations, viz., male-male (M-M), female-female (F-F), and male-female (M-F) are studied.

Features	Accuracy (%)		
	M-M	F-F	M-F
IF Spectrogram (IFSpec)	87.01	83.6	85.12
TEO-based Pyknogram (Pyk)	77.57	82.26	82.96
IFSpec + Pyk	94.72	95.03	95.60

of M-M speech in the case of TEO-based pyknogram. However, such a specific trend is not observed in the IF spectrogram. It can be observed that the combined feature IFSpec+Pyk follows the same trend as that of the TEO-based pyknogram. Thus, it can be said that detecting overlapped speech containing the opposite gender is easier to detect than the same gender combination.

5 Conclusion

This work explores the instantaneous amplitude and phase information of speech signals for overlapped speech detection. Phase information is captured by the Instantaneous Frequency (IF) spectrogram. At the same time, TEO-based pyknograms are used to represent instantaneous amplitude information. The present work is evaluated on the SSC corpus. The classification performance has supported the significance of raw phase information for the current task. TEO-based pyknogram shows better performance than IF spectrograms. However, significant performance improvement has been observed for the combination of IF spectrogram and TEO-based pyknogram. The effect of segment duration on classification performance is also studied for three different durations, i.e., 1 s, 500 ms, and 250 ms. The combined feature IFSpec+Pyk shows a better classification performance across all three segment durations. The effect of different genders present in overlapped speech is also analyzed for three gender combinations, viz., male-male, female-female, and male-female. It is observed that TEO-based pyknogram and IFSpec+Pyk have higher performance for male-female combinations followed by female-female. The lowest performance is obtained for the male-male combination. However, the IF spectrogram feature shows better results for the male-male combination.

The present work can be extended in the following directions. First, it is observed that the IF spectrogram plays an important role, but its performance degrades with reducing segment duration. Hence, the phase representation can be explored further for operation with smaller intervals. Second, this work reported results with the early fusion of pyknogram and IF spectrogram. Possibilities of classification performance enhancement can be explored through intermediate and late feature fusion frameworks.

References

1. Andrei, V., Cucu, H., Burileanu, C.: Overlapped speech detection and competing speaker counting-humans versus deep learning. IEEE J. Select. Top. Sig. Process. **13**(4), 850–862 (2019)
2. Andrei, V., Cucu, H., Burileanu, C.: Detecting overlapped speech on short time-frames using deep learning. In: INTERSPEECH, pp. 1198–1202 (2017)
3. Baghel, S., Prasanna, S.R.M., Guha, P.: Overlapped speech detection using phase features. J. Acoust. Soc. Am. **150**(4), 2770–2781 (2021)
4. Boakye, K., Trueba-Hornero, B., Vinyals, O., Friedland, G.: Overlapped speech detection for improved speaker diarization in multiparty meetings. In: 2008 IEEE International Conference on Acoustics, Speech and Signal Processing, pp. 4353–4356 (2008)

5. Boakye, K., Vinyals, O., Friedland, G.: Improved overlapped speech handling for speaker diarization. In: Twelfth Annual Conference of the International Speech Communication Association (2011)
6. Chowdhury, S.A., Danieli, M., Riccardi, G.: Annotating and categorizing competition in overlap speech. In: 2015 IEEE International Conference on Acoustics, Speech and Signal Processing (ICASSP), pp. 5316–5320 (2015)
7. Chowdhury, S.A., Riccardi, G.: A deep learning approach to modeling competitiveness in spoken conversations. In: Proceedings of the IEEE International Conference on Acoustics, Speech and Signal Processing (ICASSP), pp. 5680–5684 (2017)
8. Cooke, M., Hershey, J.R., Rennie, S.J.: Monaural speech separation and recognition challenge. Comput. Speech Lang. **24**(1), 1–15 (2010)
9. Geiger, J.T., Eyben, F., Schuller, B., Rigoll, G.: Detecting overlapping speech with long short-term memory recurrent neural networks. In: Proceedings INTERSPEECH 2013, 14th Annual Conference of the International Speech Communication Association, Lyon, France (2013)
10. Lovekin, J., Krishnamachari, K.R., Yantorno, R.E., Benincasa, D.S., Wenndt, S.J.: Adjacent Pitch Period Comparison (APPC) as a usability measure of speech segments under co-channel conditions. In: IEEE International Symposium on Intelligent Signal Processing and Communication Systems, pp. 139–142 (2001)
11. Ryant, N., et al.: First dihard challenge evaluation plan. 2018, Technical Report (2018)
12. Ryanta, N., et al.: Enhancement and analysis of conversational speech: JSALT 2017. In: Proceedings of the IEEE International Conference on Acoustics, Speech and Signal Processing (ICASSP), pp. 5154–5158 (2018)
13. Shokouhi, N., Hansen, J.H.L.: Teager-Kaiser energy operators for overlapped speech detection. IEEE/ACM Trans. Audio Speech Lang. Process. **25**(5), 1035–1047 (2017)
14. Shokouhi, N., Ziaei, A., Sangwan, A., Hansen, J.H.L.: Robust overlapped speech detection and its application in word-count estimation for prof-life-log data. In: 2015 IEEE International Conference on Acoustics, Speech and Signal Processing (ICASSP), pp. 4724–4728 (2015)
15. Vijayan, K., Reddy, P.R., Murty, K.S.R.: Significance of analytic phase of speech signals in speaker verification. Speech Commun. **81**, 54–71 (2016)
16. Yella, S.H., Bourlard, H.: Overlapping speech detection using long-term conversational features for speaker diarization in meeting room conversations. IEEE/ACM Trans. Audio Speech Lang. Process. **22**(12), 1688–1700 (2014)
17. Yousefi, M., Hansen, J.H.L.: Frame-based overlapping speech detection using convolutional neural networks. In: Proceedings of the IEEE International Conference on Acoustics, Speech and Signal Processing (ICASSP), pp. 6744–6748 (2020)
18. Yousefi, M., Shokouhi, N., Hansen, J.H.: Assessing speaker engagement in 2-person debates: overlap detection in united states presidential debates. In: INTERSPEECH, pp. 2117–2121 (2018)

Significance of Dimensionality Reduction in CNN-Based Vowel Classification from Imagined Speech Using Electroencephalogram Signals

Oindrila Banerjee, D. Govind[✉], Akhilesh Kumar Dubey,
and Suryakanth V. Gangashetty

Speech Research Group, Department of Computer Science and Engineering,
Koneru Lakshamaiah Education Foundation, Vaddeswaram, Guntur 522502,
Andhra Pradesh, India
{2102030002,d_govind,dubey18oct,svg}@klunivesity.in

Abstract. The work presented in this paper aims to show the effectiveness of dimensionality reduction in convolutional neural network (CNN) based vowel classification from covert/imagined speech. Imagined speech is referred to as phonological classes, words or sentences pronounced internally. It is acquired in a non-invasive manner by placing Electroencephalogram (EEG) sensors over the cerebral cortex region of the head. Covert speech is a spontaneous imagination or active thoughts of speaking of a human being without any articulatory movements. Therefore, identifying phonological classification attracted many applications for those who have the inability to speak due to lock-in syndrome or motor muscular impairments. The present study develops a CNN-based vowel classification system by processing EEG representing the imagined speech. In the proposed methodology, the CNN features extracted from the spectrograms (Time-Frequency) representation of each EEG channel data have been subjected to dimensionality reduction using principal component analysis (PCA). Dimensionally reduced CNN features are further subjected to linear discriminant analysis for transformation and classification. A significant improvement in the imaginary vowel classification performance is confirmed for linear discriminant analysis (LDA) based classification of dimensionality reduced CNN feature vectors. The CNN-based vowel classification performance is just above the chance level. The variational mode decomposition (VMD) based preprocessing of the EEG channels prior to classification further improved the performance of vowel recognition. The performances are observed to be consistent on all 15 subjects in the open access Coretto DB EEG database where each imagined utterance has been acquired using 6 EEG Channels.

Keywords: Imagined speech · Covert speech · Electroencephalogram · Coretto database

S. R. M. Prasanna et al. (Eds.): SPECOM 2022, LNAI 13721, pp. 44–55, 2022.
https://doi.org/10.1007/978-3-031-20980-2_5

1   Introduction

Speech is the most common form of communication among human beings. During the speech communication, a thought process is generated in the brain before the articulatory muscle movements which results in the production of speech [18]. The notion of imaginary speech or covert speech is referred to as the neural stimuli evoked at the cerebral cortex of the brain due to thought process generated for producing a speech utterance. Decoding the imagined speech finds important assistive technological applications for the speakers having speech disorders such as lock-in syndrome, motor muscular impairments and so on [14]. The objective of the present work is to develop a vowel classification system by processing the imagined speech acquired using electroencephalogram (EEG).

EEG is one of the most commonly used approaches for the non-invasive acquisition of imagined speech utterances using a wearable sensor cap. The sensor cap is kept around head covering the cerebral cortex region of the brain. The number of sensors used for acquiring the brain activity varies from 6 - 256 channels. In the current study, imagined speech collected using 6 channel EEG device is used. The focus of the present work is to decode the vowel classes from a 6 channel EEG utterance. The present work explores the open access EEG database consisting of imagined and pronounced utterances developed by Coretto et al. (Coretto DB) [4].

There are a few studies reported for the task of vowel and command recognition from imagined speech obtained from EEG [1–3, 9, 12, 13, 15]. In [9] authors targeted to classify six imagined speech command words (e.g., Arriba (up), Abajo (down), derecha (right), izquierda (left), Adelante (forward) and atras (backward)) from raw EEG signals. They used Siamese neural network encoder for the feature extractor and k-nearest neighbors for the classification of the commands. In another work, Sukanya et al., also focused on covert speech classification [2]. Here, the EEG utterances were decomposed into five basic EEG rhythmic distinct bands (alpha, beta, delta, gamma, theta) using discrete wavelet transform (DWT). Common spatial patterns were extracted from each band to use as features for the modeling of the vowel classes using support vector machines (SVM). The reported vowel and command recognition accuracies were well above the chance level (over 40.59%) for the open access Coretto DB. In another work, the same authors tried for 6 Spanish command word classification in imagined speech [2]. Here, the authors focused on the brain's lateralization during imagined vowel classification. In particular, authors have shown that the sensors kept on the right side of the cerebral cortex were contributing more towards the vowel recognition performance as compared to EEG sensors kept at the left part.

The overall reported vowel recognition performances were slightly above the chance level for five vowel classes available in the Coretto DB. DWT based coefficients are used as the features from the signal which was subjected to EMD and VMD based decompositions. Further, the features were modeled using SVMs. In [12] authors used a CNN based Siamese neural network for feature extraction and then KNN algorithms for classifying covert speech commands. Panachakel et al., reported a DNN based novel approach for imagined speech classification [16]. They worked in the Kara One dataset containing 11 channels of data [19]. In their work, authors used DB4 wavelet for feature extraction and a 2 layer based DNN model for classification. In another recent work [3] used transfer Learning (TL) approach for classifying EEG data correspond to imagined speech. They used two different TL methodologies based on deep CNN model for classifying vowels correspond to imagined speech. Lee et al., also tried a command classification on EEG signal corresponding to imagined speech in the Coretto DB [13]. The command recognition system was proposed in two steps, both of the steps perform feature extraction and classification using a KNN classifier. In step 1, a pre-trained CNN-based Siamese neural network is used and performed base class classification. In step 2, the network weights were fine tuned by adding a fine tuning layer.

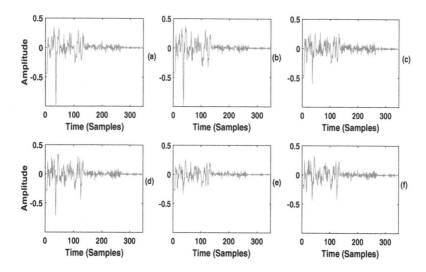

Fig. 1. EEG utterance of an imagined speech for 6 channels. The subplots of signals in (a), (b), (c), (d), (e) and (f) represent the channels F3, F4, C3, C4, P3 and P4, respectively. The notations of the channels are used in accordance with the Correto Db' [4].

Based on the review article by Panachakel et al., the challenges in decoding the imagined speech from are (1) firstly, the low SNR of the EEG data and (2) secondly the poor time and frequency resolution of the signal. Figure 1 shows an example of a 6-channel EEG data collected for an imagined speech utterance. From the Fig. 1, signals collected by all the 6 channels are noisy in nature. Compared to vowel characteristics of speech signals, there are difficulties in observing common periodic patterns in EEG.

To alleviate the problem of low SNR in the present work we first checked the effect of conventional variational mode decomposition (VMD) based signal denoising in the vowel recognition performance from imagined EEG utterances

[5,17]. High dimensional CNN based features are extracted for modeling the vowel classes. The effect of dimensionality reduction on the CNN features is then tested for decoding the vowels from the EEG. Further, to increase vowel inter class variabilities and reduce the intra class variabilities, linear discriminant analysis has been used for transforming the CNN features. Accordingly, the paper is organized as follows: The details of the imagined speech EEG database are provided in Sect. 2. Section 3 describes the CNN architecture used for the feature extraction. The detailed explanation of the proposed methodology is given in Sect. 4. The experimental results are presented in Sect. 5. Finally, Sect. 6 concludes with the scope for future work.

2   Description of the Imagined Speech Database

For the experimental studies, we have used Coretto DB for the imagined speech vowel classification. There are 15 volunteers (speakers) in age group between 24 and 27 (with 7 women and 8 men) present in Coretto DB. Imagined and pronounced speech of about 5 vowels and 6 command words were recorded from the speakers. In the database, one among the 15 subjects is left handed and remaining are right handed.

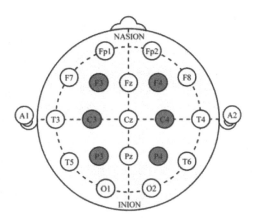

Fig. 2. Six Channel EEG sensor used for the acquisition of EEG data in Coretto DB. (Courtesy: Coretto et al. [4]).

The EEG utterances are acquired from each volunteer through 6 channels. The positions and labels of the EEG sensors are depicted in Fig. 2. The order of the channel data present in each trail is according to Channel F3 (from Samples 1,4096), Channel F4 (from Samples 4097, 8192), Channel P3(from Samples 8193 to 12288), Channel P4 (from Samples 12289, 16384) and Channel C3 (from Samples 16385, 20480), Channel C4 (from Samples 20481 to 24576), respectively. Each channel data is acquired with sampling rate of 1024 samples/sec. In the Coretto DB, the vowel classification experiments are conducted only for the imagined speech utterances. Among the 9315 total utterances, 6871 utterances trails belong to imagined speech category and remaining 1848 trails are pronounced speech utterances. From 6871 imagined speech utterances, 3101 utterances are vowels. For experiments presented in the paper we have used 3101 vowel imagined speech utterances of the Coretto DB. Vowel imagined speech utterances belong to each speaker are further split into 75% and 25% for training and testing, respectively. The train and test utterances were kept the same throughout the conduction all the studies carried in this paper.

3 Convolutional Neural Networks Based Feature Extraction

The spectrograms of the EEG utterances of each channel are generated. The spectrogram images are given as the input to the convolution layer of the CNN [10, 11]. Figure 3, shows the architecture of CNN used in the present work. The embeddings obtained as the output of the flatten layer is used as the features for modeling the imagined vowel classes. The dimensions of the each of the layers in the 4 layer CNN is also indicated in Fig. 3. Each EEG channel data of an imagined utterance provide a 4096 dimensional feature vector.

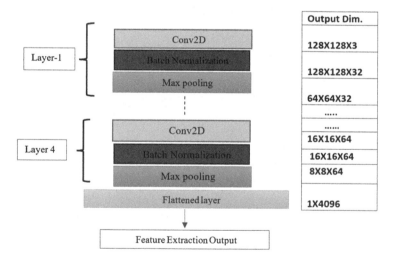

Fig. 3. CNN architecture used for feature extraction from imagined speech EEG utterances. The output dimension of each layer is given on the right side.

4   Proposed Methodology for Vowel Classification from Imagined Speech

In the proposed approach, a VMD based signal denoising is proposed as a pre-processing step before generating the spectrograms of the EEG utterances. As a post processing step the CNN feature extracted are subjected to dimensionality reduction using PCA. The intra class variabilities are then reduced by transforming the dimensionally reduced CNN features using LDA. Figure 4 shows the schematic block diagram of the proposed method for improving the vowel recognition from imagined speech EEG utterances.

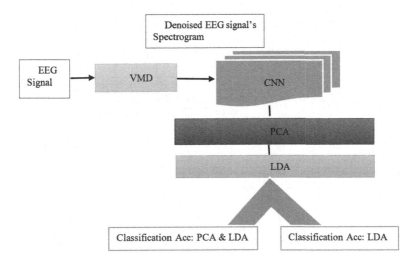

Fig. 4. Block diagram of the proposed methodology for vowel recognition from imagined speech EEG utterances.

4.1   Variational Mode Decomposition Based EEG Signal Denoising

Due to low SNR, denoising is essential prior to the decoding of information carried by the EEG signal. In the VMD based signal denoising, the signal is decomposed to a finite number of intrinsic functions such that the summation of the intrinsic functions gives back the original signal [5,17]. These intrinsic functions are known as the modes. Each mode captures, the variation of the signal around the central frequency (most significant mono component). Generally, in VMD based enhancement applications, the higher decomposed modes are discarded which is assumed to contain noise characteristics during the reconstruction of the signal. The decomposition of the given signal into different intrinsic modes is formulated as an optimization problem as given in (1) [7].

$$\min_{\{u_k\},\{\omega_k\}} \left\{ \sum_{k=1}^{K} \left\| \partial_t \left[\left(\delta(t) + \frac{j}{\pi t} \right) * u_k(t) \right] e^{-j\omega_k t} \right\|_2^2 \right\}, \tag{1}$$

$$s.t. \quad \sum_{k=1}^{K} u_k = s(t)$$

where $s(t)$ is the signal to be decomposed, $u_k(t)$ represents k^{th} intrinsic mode around central frequency ω_k such that K is the total number of modes. For the present work, the number intrinsic modes for VMD is fixed as $K = 3$.

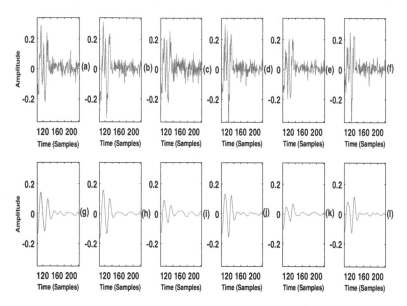

Fig. 5. VMD Based Denoising. (a–f) EEG utterance from F3, F4, C3, C4, P3 and P4 channels, respectively. (g–l) The corresponding VMD mod 1 signals.

Figure 5 compares the noise levels in the original EEG utterance in each channel and significant improvement in the SNR by using VMD based denoising. The denoising is achieved by keeping the first intrinsic mode and discarding all other higher intrinsic modes obtained during reconstruction of the signal in each channel.

4.2   PCA Based Dimensionality Reduction

Visual inspection of these higher dimensional CNN features indicated redundancies. Therefore, each CNN features are subjected to PCA based dimensionality reduction for removing the redundancy and thereby improving the between class discrimination [8].

In the present work, length of the CNN feature vectors are reduced using PCA. In the PCA, the N dimensional feature vectors are projected onto K eigen vectors corresponding to K maximum eigen values. The Eigen values and eigen vectors are computed from the covariance matrix generated from the set of feature vectors [6]. Since eigen vector corresponding to the maximum eigen value provides the direction of the prominent spread in the data, by projecting feature vectors on the K eigen vectors reduces the N dimensional features to K dimensions where $K << N$. For the dimensionality reduction, the CNN embedding obtained from the flatten layer of CNN are subjected for dimensionality reduction.

4.3   Linear Discriminant Analysis

In addition to PCA, linear discriminant analysis based classifiers are used for discriminating the CNN features into five vowel classes [6,8]. Prior to classification/transformation, LDA increases the inter-class variability and reduces the intra-class variability among the features. The feature transformation using LDA is based on the eigen decomposition of $W = eig\{S_w^{-1}S_b\}$, Where S_w and S_b are the within class scatter matrix and between class scatter matrix, respectively.

For classification, the posterior probability of feature vectors for each class is computed using Bayes' theorem. Based on the following expression:

$$Argmax\, P(Y = k|X = x) = \frac{p_k P(X = x|Y = k)}{\sum_{k=1}^{K} p_k P(X = x|Y = k)}, x\epsilon R^d \qquad (2)$$

where p_k is the prior probability of kth class and $P(X = x|Y = k)$ is the likelihood computed for the feature vector, x with respect to the Gaussian density functions for the kth class. The parameters of the multivariate Gaussian density is computed from the LDA transformed features, $x\epsilon R^d$ where d is the dimension. The $argmax$ of the posterior probabilities as shown in (2) of the feature vectors obtained for various classes gives the predicted class.

5   Experimental Results

As mentioned in Sect. 2, from a total of 6871 imagined EEG utterances 3101 imagined vowel utterances of Coretto DB were used for the experimental studies presented in the paper. The spectrograms of EEG utterances were generated by fixing a frame rate of 100 frames per second. The spectrogram images generated for each of the imagined EEG utterances were given as to CNN as input to extract 4096 dimensional CNN feature as embedding at the flatten layer.

The CNN features are then subjected to dimensionality reduction using PCA. The performances were computed for 5 class vowel recognition by varying number of principal components. Figure 6 plots the average performance obtained for various subjects in the Coretto DB. The vowel recognition performance for each subject is obtained by varying CNN feature dimension from 100 to 4096. Keeping 4096 feature length indicates no dimensionality reduction performed in the CNN feature vectors. After dimensionality reduction using PCA, the vowel recognition accuracies are obtained from the LDA based classifier. From Fig. 6, most of the subjects in Coretto DB showed higher recognition rate for reduced

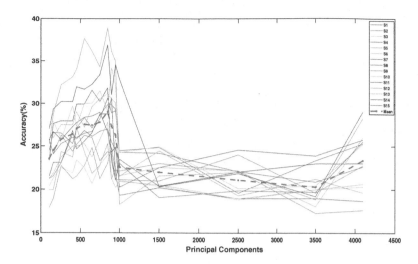

Fig. 6. Vowel Recognition accuracies (in%) for all the subjects the database for various feature dimensions using PCA. Red colored bold plot shows the average performance obtained. (Color figure online)

feature dimension between 800 and 950 as compared to using CNN features without dimensionality reduction. From the mean performance (indicated by the red bold plot), a feature dimension of 850 provided the best performance. Table 1 provides a comparison between the vowel recognition rates obtained for each subject without dimensionality reduction and with dimensionality reduction achieved using PCA. Vowel recognition performances of dimensionality reduction achieved using 850 principal components are tabulated in Table 1. From the Table 1, 850 dimensional feature vectors showed a significant improvement in the vowel recognition performance for all the subjects in the database. Therefore, in the rest of the experiments we used 850 as the default dimension for the CNN features extracted from imagined speech EEG utterances.

Table 1. Comparison of the imagined speech vowel recognition accuracies (%) with dimensionality reduction for 850 principal components and no dimensionality reduction in Coretto DB.

Subject	S1	S2	S3	S4	S5	S6	S7	S8	S9	S10	S11	S12	S13	S14	S15	Mean
Vow.Recog(No PCA)	22.62	17.61	20.3	18.67	19.62	20.62	23.02	25.3	22.76	25.25	25.76	28.26	25.99	29.03	25.53	**23.36**
Vow.Recog(PCA)	30.65	23.03	24.01	28.79	25.31	27.81	31.87	29.89	24.39	29.12	26.68	38.9	31.19	36.91	27.02	**29.04**

For the VMD based denoising, each utterance is decomposed into three modes. In VMD based denoising, each EEG signal is reconstructed only from the first VMD mode and discarding the remaining two VMD modes. While decomposing the given utterance using VMD, bandwidth constraints parameter, $\alpha = 2000$ and noise tolerance fidelity parameter, $\tau = 0$ were set as the default parameter values. Figure 7 shows the effect of VMD based denoising in the vowel recognition performance. There is a significant improvement in vowel recognition rate when the EEG utterances are denoised using VMD prior to CNN feature extraction. The average vowel recognition rate obtained in the case of VMD based denoising is 48.95% and 43.99% in absence of any denoising performed on the signal.

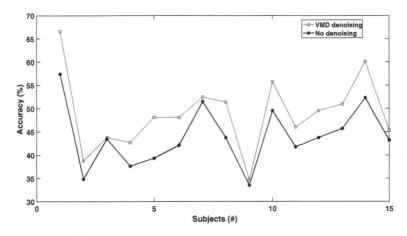

Fig. 7. Comparison of VMD based denoising in vowel recognition accuracies (in %) from imagined speech.

6   Summary and Conclusion

The work presented in the paper was focussed on the vowel classification from imagined speech utterances acquired from EEG signals. The CNN features are extracted initially for the classification using LDA. Based experiments, it was observed that, the reducing the dimensionality of CNN features found to improve the vowel recognition accuracy. A well known PCA based dimensionality reduction method was used for the dimensionality reduction presented in the paper. As EEG signals are acquired by placing sensors around the cerebral cortex regions over the skull, the EEG signals are found to be noisy. The second part of the study was focussed on the denoising the EEG utterances as a preprocessing step to improve the recognition. The VMD based denoising approach used in the present work found to show significant improvement in the vowel recognition rates from imagined speech.

Even though, by denoising and dimensionality reduction, the performance where raised well above the chance level performance (which is 20% for a 5 category classification problem), techniques at the feature level and modeling level have to be adopted to raise the performance at par with speech based isolated vowel recognition performance. Further, to achieve acceptable levels of word and sentence level recognition performance, the sequence learning of different phonological classes from imagined speech EEG utterances have to be explored.

7   Data Availability and Conflict of Interest Statements from Authors

Authors have used the open source EEG database consisting imagined and pronounced utterances for all the studies presented in the paper. The programs will be made available on a reasonable request to the authors. Further, authors declare that there are no conflict of interests with any academic institutes/research organizations or individual researchers in the context of the work presented in the paper.

Acknowledgments. The presente work is funded by the ongoing MEITY, Govt. of India, funded NLTM-BHASHINI consortium project titled "Speech technologies in Indian languages: speech quality control". The authors were motivated to work in the decoding of imagined speech from the Global Initiative for Academic Networks (GIAN) course on Cognitive Speech Processing conducted by Prof. H. L. Rufiner, Research Institute for Signals, Systems and Computational Intelligence, National University of Litoral (UNL), Santa Fe, Argentina and Prof. S. R Mahadeva Prasanna. Department of Electrical Engineering, IIT Dharwad, INDIA. GIAN course was organized in April 2022.

References

1. Biswas, S., Sinha, R.: Lateralization of brain during EEG based covert speech classification. In: Proceedings of 15th IEEE India Council International Conference (INDICON), pp. 1–5 (2018)
2. Biswas, S., Sinha, R.: Wavelet filterbank-based EEG rhythm-specific spatial features for covert speech classification. IET Sig. Process. **16**(1), 92–105 (2022)
3. Cooney, C., Folli, R., Coyle, D.: Optimizing layers improves CNN generalization and transfer learning for imagined speech decoding from EEG. In: Proceedings of the IEEE International Conference on Systems, Man and Cybernetics (SMC), pp. 1311–1316 (2019)
4. Coretto, G.A.P., Gareis, I.E., Rufiner, H.L.: Open access database of EEG signals recorded during imagined speech. In: Proceedings of the 12th International Symposium on Medical Information Processing and Analysis, vol. 10160, p. 1016002 (2017)
5. Dragomiretskiy, K., Zosso, D.: Variational mode decomposition. IEEE Trans. Sig. Process. **62**(3), 531–544 (2014)
6. Duda, R.O., Hart, P.E., Stork, D.G.: Pattern Classification. wiley, New York (2001)
7. Govind, D., Pravena, D., Ajay, S.G.: Improved epoch extraction using variational mode decomposition based spectral smoothing of zero frequency filtered emotive speech signals. In: Proceedings of the National Conference on Communications (NCC) (2018)

8. James, G., Witten, D., Hastie, T., Tibshirani, R.: An introduction to statistical learning with applications in R. Springer (2014)
9. Lawhern, V.J., Solon, A.J., Waytowich, N.R., Gordon, S.M., Hung, C.P., Lance, B.J.: Eegnet: a compact convolutional neural network for EEG-based brain-computer interfaces. J. Neural Eng. 15(5),(2018)
10. LeCun, Y., Huang, F.J., Bottou, L.: Learning methods for generic object recognition with invariance topose and lighting. In: Proceedings of the IEEE International Conference on Computer Vision and Pattern Recognition (2004)
11. LeCun, Y., Kavukcuoglu, K., Farabet, C.: Convolutional neural networks and applications in vision. In: Proceedings of the IEEE International Symposium on Circuits and Systems (ISCAS) (2010)
12. Lee, D.Y., Lee, M., Lee, S.W.: Decoding imagined speech based on deep metric learning for intuitive BCI communication. IEEE Trans. Neural Syst. Rehab. Eng. 29, 1363–1374 (2021)
13. Lee, D.Y., Lee, M., Lee, S.W.: Decoding imagined speech based on deep metric learning for intuitive. BCI Commun. 29, 1363–1374 (2021)
14. Nicolas-Alonso, L.F., Gomez-Gil, J.: Brain computer interfaces, a review. Sensors. 12(2), 1211–1279 (2012)
15. Panachakel, J.T., Ramakrishnan, A.: Decoding covert speech from EEG-a comprehensive review. Front. NeuroSci. (2021). https://doi.org/10.3389/fnins.2021.642251
16. Panachakel, J.T., Ramakrishnan, A., Ananthapadmanabha, T.: Decoding imagined speech using wavelet features and deep neural networks. In: Proceedings of the IEEE 16th India Council International Conference (INDICON), pp. 1–4 (2019)
17. Pankaj, D., Govind, D., Narayanankutty, K.A.: A novel method for removing RICIAN noise from MRI based on variational mode decomposition. Biomed. Sig. Process. Control 69,(2021)
18. Rabiner, L.R., Juang, B.H.: Fundamentals of Speech Recognition. PTR Prentice Hall,Englewood Cliffs, N.J. (1993)
19. Zhao, S., Rudzicz, F.: Classifying phonological categories in imagined and articulated speech. In: Proceedings of the International Conference on Acoustics, Speech and Signal Processing (ICASSP) (2015)

Study of Speech Recognition System Based on Transformer and Connectionist Temporal Classification Models for Low Resource Language

Shweta Bansal[1]([✉]), Shambhu Sharan[2], and Shyam S. Agrawal[3]

[1] K R Mangalam University, Gurugram, India
s.bansal6281@gmail.com
[2] Indira Gandhi Delhi Technical University for Women, Delhi, India
[3] KIIT Group of Colleges, Gurugram, India

Abstract. Sequence-to-sequence methods have been extensively used in end-to-end (E2E) speech processing for recognition, translation, and synthesis work. In speech recognition, the Transformer model, which supports parallel computation and has intrinsic attention, is frequently used nowadays. This technology's primary aspects are its quick learning efficiency and absence of sequential operation, unlike Deep Neural Networks (DNN). This study concentrated on Transformer, an emergent sequential model that excels in applications for natural language processing (NLP) and neural machine translation (NMT) applications. To create a framework for the automated recognition of spoken Hindi utterances, an end-to-end and Transformer based model to understand the phenomenon classification was considered. Hindi is one of several agglutinative languages, and there isn't much information available for speech/voice recognition algorithms. According to several research, the Transformer approach enhances the performance of the system for languages with limited resources. As per the analyses done by us, it was found that the Hindi-based speech recognition system performed better when Transformers were used along with the Connectionist Temporal Classification (CTC) models altogether. Further, when a language model was included, the Word Error Rate (WER) on a clean dataset was at its lowest i.e., 3.2% .

Keywords: Connectionist Temporal Classification · CTC model · Low-resource language · Speech recognition · Transformer

1 Introduction

People are integrating cutting-edge information and digital technology more and more into their daily lives [1]. Such technologies include automatic speech recognition (ASR), pictures recognition, and speech synthesis. In particular, voice-based solutions seem to be frequently employed in robotics, telecommunications, as well as other industrial fields [2, 3]. One approach to communicating with technology is through speech recognition.

© Springer Nature Switzerland AG 2022
S. R. M. Prasanna et al. (Eds.): SPECOM 2022, LNAI 13721, pp. 56–63, 2022.
https://doi.org/10.1007/978-3-031-20980-2_6

With speech recognition technology, single words or text passages may be recognized and converted into instructions or word sequences.

Traditional speech recognition technologies rely on lexicons, linguistic models, and acoustics, as depicted in Fig. 1 [4]. These systems' components were trained independently, making it difficult to configure them. This decreased the effectiveness of employing these systems. Deep learning has increased the efficacy of speech-to-text systems. GMM was replaced by artificial neural networks for acoustic modelling, which enhanced the outcomes of several research projects [5–7]. However, one amongst the widely used and popular model for continuous speech recognition is the HMM-DNN architecture.

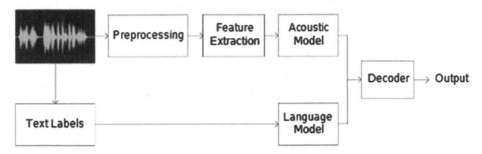

Fig. 1. The traditional ASR architecture [8].

The end-to-end (E2E) system offers knowledge of auditory signals mostly as label sequences with no intermediary stages, necessitating no further output processing, making it simple to implement. The primary issues associated with the description of such approaches, the gathering of a reasonably big database of speech with proper transcription, and the accessibility of highly efficient machinery must be resolved to improve the performance of E2E systems [9]. These problems must be determined to deploy speech recognition systems and other deep learning systems successfully. E2E methods may also significantly boost recognition quality by learning or training from a lot of training data. The Convolutional Neural Network (CNN) as well as improved Recurrent Neural Networks (RNNs) are used in aforementioned E2E models. The RNN models that are used produce a hidden state series with respect to network's prior hidden state by performing computations on position of characters of input as well as output data. With more extended input data sequence and a longer training time, the technique doesn't enable parallelisation of learning in training instances. Another Transformer-based approach that parallelises the learning process and eliminates repeats was suggested in [10]. This model also leverages internal attention to find relationships between the input and output data. Combining an E2E model, such as CTC, along with the Transformer model improved performance of the English and Chinese ASR system to a greater extent, according to earlier studies [11, 12]. It is very much important to mention that the attention mechanism is a typical technique which significantly raises effectiveness of proposed system in speech recognition and NMT domain. Furthermore, the Transformer model speeds up learning by using this attention mechanism. This model has internal alignment that finds an alignment-free representation of the set by aligning every location in the input sequence. Moreover, large amounts of speech data are needed for training to build such models, that in itself likely to be a challenge for language families with little datasets, such as low-resourced languages including Hindi [13, 14].

The primary objective of our work is to apply models based on Transformer & CTC for Hindi language recognition to increase training data and enhance the accurateness of the ASR for continuous spoken Hindi utterances. The Transformer model was initially developed by the Google Brain team for NMT tasks, later taking the place of RNNs in NLP applications. Recurrence was abolished in this model; instead, signals were created for each statement to indicate the relevance of other sequences for this speech utilising the internal attention process (self-attention mechanism). As a result, the characteristics created for certain assertion are outcome of many sequence-feature linear modifications. The Transformer model is made up of a single massive block that is made up of blocks of encoders and decoders, as shown in Fig. 2. Here, the encoder generates a series of intermediate representations after receiving the feature vectors from the audio signal as input, i.e. $Y = (y_1,..., y_T)$. Furthermore, the decoder duplicates the output sequence $Z = (z_1,..., z_M)$ using the incoming representations. Because the model is autoregressive, each stage outputs the previous symbols before moving on to the next.

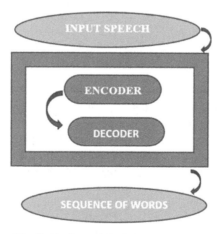

Fig. 2. Basic model of transformer [15].

The overall structure of the paper is presented in different sections, wherein the proposed model is explained in Sect 2, whereas overall experiment and results are presented in Sect 3, where the outcomes are also evaluated. The final section comprises the discussion and conclusions.

2   Proposed Model

Without even pre-aligning the input & output data, recurrent neural networks (RNN) may be trained to identify input voice. The Connectionist Temporal Classification (CTC) is typically utilized for the same [11]. Since straight decoding will not function well, it's very much required to employ a language model (LM) i.e., an external model comprising probability of different word sequences, in order to get the CTC model to execute well. The method by which words are formed in the Hindi language is also rather varied, which makes it easier to recognise Hindi speech when it is spoken. In this study, the Transformer and CTC models with LM will be used in tandem. When LM CTC is used for decoding, the model converges quickly, cutting down on decoding time and enhancing system performance. When LM CTC is used for decoding, the model converges quickly, drastically reducing on decoding time and enhancing system performance. After receiving the encoder output, the CTC function determines the likelihood of random arrangement among output of the encoder & the output symbol sequence using the formula 1. Here, y is the encoder's output vector, R is a further operator for eliminating repeated symbols and empty spaces, and z is a sequence of anticipated symbols. The formula aids in training the neural network on unlabelled input by utilising dynamic programming to calculate the total of all alignments.

$$P_{CTC}(Z|Encoder(y)) = \sum_{Z \in R} p(z|y)$$

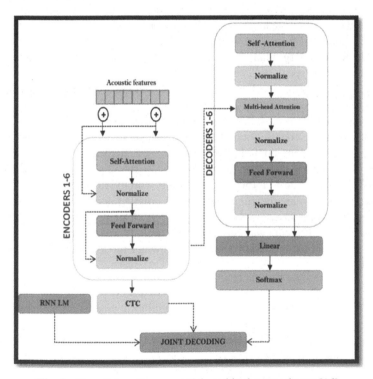

Fig. 3. Overall transformer model used in the experiment [16].

While training with the approach involving multi-task loss, the mathematical expression for combination probabilities based on the negative logarithm was introduced, as described in [16]. The model that results may be described by the expression 2 where θ is the variable parameter, whose values lies between 0 and 1. Figure 3 depicts the suggested model's structure.

$$P(z|y) = \theta\, P_{Transformer} + (1 - \theta)\, P_{CTC}$$

The two criteria were applied to measure the recognition rate of the system for the Hindi language i.e., character error rate (CER), which measures the improperly detected characters, and word error rate (WER) that measures the improperly detected words.

3 Experiment and Results

To train the Transformer model, Transformer model with CTC not having the language model in first case and having the language model in second case, it was ascertained to consider the 300 h of spoken utterance database. This corpus was assembled in the laboratory. The audio files of the spoken utterance database are separated into train and test sections, which are 85% and 15%, correspondingly. The spoken utterance corpus comprises recordings of 200 native Hindi speakers of diverse age groups & genders (Male and Female). The voice recording of the individual speaker took approximately 1 h. Whereas for the text data, sentences containing words of rich phonemes were selected. Text data was collected from various domains like news, defence, general etc. in Hindi language. Students, undergraduates, institute staff members, as well as friends and family members to record the speakers. The voiceovers were recorded over the course of around six months, and to ensure excellent quality, Hindi linguists and linguistics specialists were brought in to examine and review the corpus.

It was important to verify both the accuracy of the transcription of the data as well as the speech data. The construction of a phoneme-level lexicon is not necessary for the speech recognition system; audio and text data are sufficient. After the aforementioned effort, one of the crucial components—a vocabulary foundation for the speech recognition system—was made (11,150 non-repeating words). Repeated words have been eliminated and all recorded messages have been compiled into a single file. After being alphabetized. Wav format was used for the audio data. A single channel has been created out of all audio data. The data was converted into digital form using the PCM technique. 44.1 kHz discrete frequency, 16 bits. The Transformer models were created using the PyTorch toolset.

Table 1. Results obtained for different models.

Models	Character Error Rate (CER)	Word Error Rate (WER)
CTC LM	9.5	18.1
Transformer	8.8	16.7
Transformer + CTC	6.3	12.8
Transformer + CTC LM	3.2	7.9

The Transformer model with CTC produced a CER of 6.3% and a WER of 12.8%, as shown in Table1. The Transformer model with CTC performs well both with and without the usage of the language model. The system became heavier as a result of the incorporation of an external language model, however the CER and WER rates were dramatically decreased by 3.2 and 7.9%, respectively. The directional six-layer Bi-Directional long short term memory is used for the CTC has 256 cells per layer and an interpolation weight of 0.2. At the decode stage, the beam research width is 18. The language model was trained using a created vocabulary base for a speech recognition system and has two 1024-unit LSTM layers. The model has undergone 40 iterations of training.Different models were used in experiments to identify Hindi speech.

As we can see from Table 1, the Transformer and CTC LM model tends to produce optimum results with respect to current database. Furthermore, when compared to other models, as depicted in Fig. 4, the Transformer model with CTC trained and converged considerably faster.

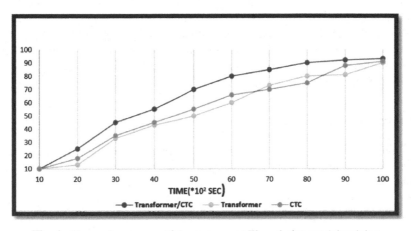

Fig. 4. Comparing curves of Accuracy w.r.t Time during model training.

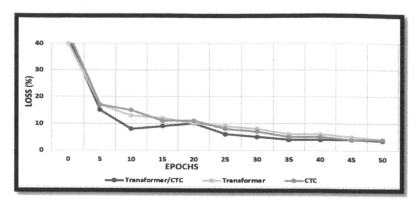

Fig. 5. Loss vs Epoch graph of different models.

Additionally, it was simpler to integrate the final model with LM. The acquired data were aligned with the aid of the CTC. The experiment's findings demonstrate the value of combining the CTC with the E2E language model, and the greatest performance on Hindi dataset was attained. Additionally, our model's performance is often enhanced with the addition of a CTC. In the future, we must increase the size of our speech corpus and enhance CER and WER.

4   Discussion and Conclusion

A DNN-based language model was incorporated into the model to enhance the performance of these measures. In our situation, there is no other option to get decent outcomes than this. Additionally, the quality of recognition can be impacted by adding more trials to a corpus that has a larger volume. However, it's unlikely that just adding more data to the training set would address the issue. The Hindi language has several different accents and dialects. It is impossible to gather adequate information for every situation. Transformer trains the language model better and takes into consideration the complete context, and CTC aids in the model's learning to generate recognition that is best matched with the recording. Further modifications to this architecture are possible for streaming speech recognition.

In this research, the self-attention components of the Transformer architecture for automated identification of Hindi continuous speech were taken into consideration. Although there are many model parameters that need to be adjusted, parallelizing the procedures helps speed up the training process. In terms of character and word recognition accuracy, the combined Transformer + CTC LM model produced an excellent performance in Hindi speech recognition and decreased these numbers by 3.2 and 7.9%, respectively, then utilising them independently. This demonstrates the model's applicability to various low-resource languages.

In order to test the model that has been constructed, it is intended to expand the speech corpus for the Hindi language. Additionally, the Transformer model will need to undergo major changes in order to eliminate word and symbol mistakes in recognition of Hindi continuous speech.

References

1. Anderson, J., Rainie, L.: The positives of digital life (2018), https://www.pewresearch.org/internet/2018/07/03/the-positives-of-digital-life/. Accessed 15 May 2022
2. Deuerlein, C., Langer, M., Seßner, J., Heß, P., Franke, J.: Human-robot-interaction using cloud-based speech recognition systems. Procedia CIRP **97**, 130–135 (2021). https://doi.org/10.1016/j.procir.2020.05.214
3. Rogowski, A., Bieliszczuk, K., Rapcewicz, J.: Integration of industrially-oriented human-robot speech communication and vision-based object recognition. Sensors **20**(24), 7287 (2020). https://doi.org/10.3390/s20247287
4. Sharan, S., Bansal, S., Agrawal, S.S.: Speaker-independent recognition system for continuous hindi speech using probabilistic model. In: Agrawal, S.S., Dev, A., Wason, R., Bansal, P. (eds.) Speech and Language Processing for Human-Machine Communications. AISC, vol. 664, pp. 91–97. Springer, Singapore (2018). https://doi.org/10.1007/978-981-10-6626-9_10
5. Seide, F., Li, G., Yu, D.: Conversational speech transcription using Context-Dependent Deep. Neural Netw. (2011). https://doi.org/10.21437/interspeech.2011-169
6. Bourlard, H.A., Morgan, N.: Connectionist Speech Recognition. Springer, Boston, MA (1994). https://doi.org/10.1007/978-1-4615-3210-1
7. Smit, P., Virpioja, S., Kurimo, M.: Advances in subword-based HMM-DNN speech recognition across languages. Comput. Speech Lang. **66**, 101158 (2021). https://doi.org/10.1016/j.csl.2020.101158
8. Yu, C., Kang, M., Chen, Y., Wu, J., Zhao, X.: Acoustic modeling based on deep learning for low-resource speech recognition: an overview. IEEE Access (2020). https://doi.org/10.1109/ACCESS.2020.3020421
9. Perero-Codosero, J.M., Espinoza-Cuadros, F.M., Hernández-Gómez, L.A.: A comparison of hybrid and end-to-end ASR systems for the IberSpeech-RTVE 2020 speech-to-text transcription challenge. Appl. Sci. (2022). https://doi.org/10.3390/app12020903
10. Wang, D., Wang, X., Lv, S.: An overview of end-to-end automatic speech recognition. Symmetry (2019). https://doi.org/10.3390/sym11081018
11. Karita, S., Soplin, N.E.Y., Watanabe, S., Delcroix, M., Ogawa, A., Nakatani, T.: Improving transformer-based end-to-end speech recognition with connectionist temporal classification and language model integration. In: Interspeech-2019, pp. 1408–1412 (2019). https://doi.org/10.21437/Interspeech.2019-1938
12. Miao, H., Cheng, G., Gao, C., Zhang, P., Yan, Y.: Transformer-based online ctc/attention end-to-end speech recognition architecture. In: IEEE International Conference on Acoustics, Speech and Signal Processing (ICASSP), pp. 6084–6088 (2020). https://doi.org/10.1109/ICASSP40776.2020.9053165
13. Bansal, S., Agrawal, S.S., Kumar, A.: Acoustic analysis and perception of emotions in Hindi speech using words and sentences. Int. J. Inf. Technol. **11**(4), 807–812 (2018). https://doi.org/10.1007/s41870-017-0081-0
14. Agrawal, S.S., Bansal, S., Sharan, S., Mahajan, M.: Acoustic analysis of oral and nasal Hindi vowels spoken by native and non-native speakers. J. Acoust. Soc. Am. **140**(4), 3338 (2016). https://doi.org/10.1121/1.4970648
15. Bie, A., Venkitesh, B., Monteiro, J., Haidar, M.A., Rezagholizadeh, M.: A Simplified Fully Quantized Transformer for End-to-end Speech Recognition (2019). https://doi.org/10.48550/arXiv.1911.03604
16. Orken, M., Dina, O., Keylan, A., Tolganay, T., Mohamed, O.: A study of transformer-based end-to-end speech recognition system for Kazakh language. Sci. Rep. **12**(1), 8337 (2022). https://doi.org/10.1038/s41598-022-12260-y

An Initial Study on Birdsong Re-synthesis Using Neural Vocoders

Rhythm Rajiv Bhatia$^{(\boxtimes)}$ and Tomi H. Kinnunen

University of Eastern Finland, Kuopio, Finland
{rhythm.bhatia,tkinnu}@cs.uef.fi

Abstract. Modern speech synthesis uses neural vocoders to model raw waveform samples directly. This increased versatility has expanded the scope of vocoders from speech to other domains, such as music. We address another interesting domain of bio-acoustics. We provide initial comparative analysis-resynthesis experiments of birdsong using traditional (WORLD) and two neural (WaveNet autoencoder, parallel Wave-GAN) vocoders. Our subjective results indicate no difference in the three vocoders in terms of species discrimination (ABX test). Nonetheless, the WORLD vocoder samples were rated higher in terms of retaining bird-like qualities (MOS test). All vocoders faced issues with pitch and voicing. Our results indicate some of the challenges in processing low-quality wildlife audio data.

Keywords: Bioacoustics · Neural vocoding · Birdsong

1 Introduction

Birdsong is a subject of intensive research. Richness and variety of birdsong has intrigued basic research into the communicative function of birdsong. Besides ecology, birdsong has raised interest within the signal processing and machine learning communities too. This includes tasks such as species recognition [19] and locating active bird segments (akin to speech activity detection) [21].

While a number of recognition, segmentation and labeling approaches has been proposed, *generation* of birdsong has received less attention. There are, however, many potential applications ranging from games, movies and virtual reality to education and robotics where flexible generation of birdsong (and other animal vocalizations) could be useful.

Most prior work considers specialized physical models (e.g. [2,12]) or adapts speech vocoders to birdsong (e.g. [16]). A limited number of studies also use *text-to-speech* (TTS) techniques to synthesize birdsong [3,7]. An obvious difficulty is that, even if birdsong and speech both serve a communicative function, 'bird language' lacks a commonly-agreed, standard written form (ortography). Human language exists both in written and spoken forms and the statistical association between the two enable tasks such as TTS or automatic speech recognition. In the limited number of 'bird TTS' studies, the problem has been addressed using

© Springer Nature Switzerland AG 2022
S. R. M. Prasanna et al. (Eds.): SPECOM 2022, LNAI 13721, pp. 64–74, 2022.
https://doi.org/10.1007/978-3-031-20980-2_7

acoustic units learnt using unsupervised techniques. Similar approaches have recently been addressed by the speech community [4,22].

We address birdsong generation using **neural waveform models**. Traditional TTS methods use fixed (signal processing based) operations to represent speech waveforms using a small number of parameters—such as spectral envelope, fundamental frequency and aperiodicity. A major breakthrough was brought in 2016 by the introduction of *WaveNet* [15], an approach to model raw waveform samples directly. WaveNet and other neural waveform models have provided excellent results in modeling other acoustic signals beyond speech—such as music. However, unlike physical models and traditional vocoders, the neural models require (often time-consuming) training and, similar to any machine learning task, can be sensitive to choice of training data, architectures and control parameters.

As far as the authors are aware, our work is the first to address birdsong generation using neural waveform models. We purposefully limit our focus to the **vocoder** part only, which is a key component of complete synthesizers. Given limited work in this domain, we feel the selected focus is justified. To this end, we have chosen three modern vocoders—WORLD [14], WaveNet Autoencoder [5] and Parallel WaveGAN [23]. We compare them through analysis-resynthesis experiments, including objective and subjective evaluation.

2 Selected Vocoders

Our aim is to compare traditional and neural vocoders in their ability to re-synthesize birdsong. We consider three popular vocoders using architectures and parameter settings from the original code repositories (WORLD[1], WaveNet AE[2], Parallel WaveGAN[3]). The neural vocoders are retrained on birdsong (detailed below) without further parameter tuning. While the main reason is computational, we also want to find out how well the architectures designed for speech cope with birdsong 'off-the-shelf'.

WORLD [14] is a signal processing based vocoder without trainable components. It decomposes a waveform into fundamental frequency (F0), spectral envelope, and aperiodicity parameters. Being an alternative to classic vocoders such as STRAIGHT [11] and TANDEM-STRAIGHT [10], WORLD is adopted in many text-to-speech and voice conversion studies. We use D4C edition [13] of WORLD.

WaveNet autoencoder [5] is a data-driven model that learns temporal hidden codes from training data and models long-term information using an *encoder-decoder* structure. The encoder infers hidden embeddings distributed in time which the decoder uses to reconstruct the input. The temporal encoder has the same dilation block as WaveNet but uses *non-causal* convolutions by considering the entire input context. The model consists of 30 convolutional

---

[1] https://github.com/JeremyCCHsu/Python-Wrapper-for-World-Vocoder.
[2] https://github.com/magenta/magenta/tree/master/magenta/models/nsynth.
[3] https://github.com/kan-bayashi/ParallelWaveGAN.

layers followed by an average pooling layer to create a temporal embedding of 16 dimensions every 512 samples. The vanilla WaveNet decoder with 30 layers (each layer being 1×1 convolution along with a bias) is used to upsample the embedding back to the original time resolution. The model is trained for 100k iterations with a batch size of 32.

Parallel WaveGAN [23] is a small footprint waveform generation method based on *generative adversarial network* (GAN) [6]. It is trained jointly on multi resolution short-time Fourier transform loss and waveform domain adverserial loss. The model consists of 30 convolutionally dilated layers with exponentially increasing 3 dilation cycles with 64 residual and skip channels and filter size of 3. The discriminator consists of 10 non-causal dilated 1-D convolutions with leaky ReLU activation. Linearly increasing dilations in the range of one to eight along with the stride of 1 are applied for the 1D convolutions apart from the first and the last layer. Weight normalization is applied to all the convolutional layers for both the generator and the discriminator [18]. The model is trained for 100k steps using RAdam optimizer. The discriminator was fixed for first 50k steps after which both the models were trained jointly. The minibatch size was set to eight along with the 24k timesamples audioclip i.e. length of each audio clip was 1.0 s. The initial learning rate for generator is 0.0001 and for discriminator 0.00005.

3   Experimental Set-Up

3.1   Dataset

We use a subset of *xccoverbl* dataset [20] in our experiments. It contains vocalizations of 88 bird species commonly observed in the UK, gathered from the large *Xeno Canto* collection [1].The sampling rate is 44.1kHz. For all the 88 species, 3 audio files (each 30 s of total audio) are used for training and 2 other files (each 20 s) are held out for testing purposes. Our experiments include both objective and subjective evaluation. Given the time-consuming nature of the latter, we limit the experiments reported to 10 bird species in total, selected randomly out from the 88.

3.2   Objective Evaluation

We use *root mean square error* (RMSE) to measure distance of the mel cepstra of the original and resynthesized birdsong as our objective quality measure. The lower the RMSE, the higher the (objective) quality [8]. The MFCCs used in RMSE computation are calculated using the speech signal processing tool kit (SPTK) [9].

3.3   Subjective Evaluation - Species Discrimination (ABX)

Our subjective experiments serve to address two questions: how much vocoding influences (1) bird species discrimination; and (2) preservation of bird-related traits. We adopt an ABX test and a quality rating experiment to address these questions, respectively. In practice, we gather the responses to both simultaneously.

For the ABX test, each listener is provided with triplets (trials) of audio files. A and B correspond to natural audio of two different species, and X represents either a natural or a resynthesized sample of one of the species. The listeners are asked to choose whether X resembles more A or B. We prepare a total of 10 trials (ABX triplets) per each of the three vocoders. Along with the additional case of natural audio (no vocoding) this yields a total of 40 ABX trials per subject.

The A and B samples in a given trial are selected from the training set of the vocoders. X is always selected from a *different* audio file corresponding to species of either A or B; this way, the subject cannot do trivial 'content-matched' comparison of original-vs-resynthesized file, but will have to pay attention to the general properties of the two species. We summarize the results of the ABX test as percent-correct identification rate (from pooled listener responses) broken down according to the vocoder.

In preparing the listening test, the order of the trials is randomized, with different order for each subject. The duration of each of the 40 samples was fixed to 10 s (of total audio). All files prepared for the subjective test were additionally normalized using `ffmpeg-normalize` tool [17].

3.4 Subjective Evaluation - Bird-Related Cues (MOS)

Evaluation of bird-related cues, in turn, is based on 5-point mean opinion (MOS) score ratings. The subject is asked to rate the X sample in each of the ABX trials in an ordinal scale [1 ... 5], where 1 means that X does not resemble bird sounds at all while 5 means X resembles perfectly bird sound.

The samples were presented through a PHP-based web-forms. The subjects were free to listen to the samples as many times as needed with their own pace. The subjects took part voluntarily and were informed about the study aims, with standard consent forms provided by the authors' institution in place. No compensations were provided.

We recruited an initial pool of 17 subjects. We excluded afterwards two subjects who obtained, respectively, only 2 and 3 correct responses in the ABX test on the 10 natural samples. The results summarized below correspond to the responses of the remaining 15 subjects, all who obtained at least 5/10 correct on the natural samples.

4   Experimental Results

4.1 Objective Evaluation Results

The RMSE results shown in Table 1 are computed from the same audio files presented to the listeners in the next subsection (10 audio files per method). The results indicate the lowest and highest values for WORLD and WaveNet autoencoder, respectively, with parallel WaveGAN between the two. The higher RMSE values for the two neural approaches suggest issues in generalization from training set to the test data.

Table 1. Average root mean square error (RMSE) along with 95% confidence range from standard error of mean (SEM).

Model	RMSE
WORLD	0.6879 ± 0.41
WaveNet Autoencoder	3.2047 ± 1.20
Parallel WaveGAN	1.82647 ± 0.67

4.2   Subjective Results: Species Discrimination (ABX)

The ABX results summarized in Fig. 1 indicate the following:

- results for all the four cases exceed 50%;
- there are no significant differences between the three vocoders, or between natural vs. vocoded samples.

The first result suggests that naive listeners are able to identify X more accurately than by guessing, on average. The average values suggest that natural samples might be classified more accurately (73.53%) than any of the re-synthesized samples. Due to limited sample size, however, this effect cannot be firmly confirmed.

The overall species discrimination is obviously far from perfect. There are a number of possible reasons. First, most of our subjects are non-experts who might not be exposed to birdsong on a regular basis; they may not know to which cues to pay attention to. Second, the audio samples are short. Third, originating from field recordings, some of the samples are noisy (including sounds of other birds in background).

A look at listener-specific accuracies (not shown due to lack of space) revealed that the individually most accurate listener had 38 (out of 40) correct cases overall. This was the only subject who obtained perfect result on *two* vocoders—parallel WaveGAN and wavenet autoencoder. For the rest of the subjects, there were always at least one classification error on the vocoder samples.

4.3   Subjective Results: Bird-Related Cues (MOS)

The results from our second experiment are summarized in Fig. 2. We observe the following:

- natural samples and WORLD vocoder yield the highest MOS values with the overall range around $4.12 - 4.44$;
- the two neural vocoders yield lower MOS, WaveNet autoencoder samples being rated least 'bird-like'.

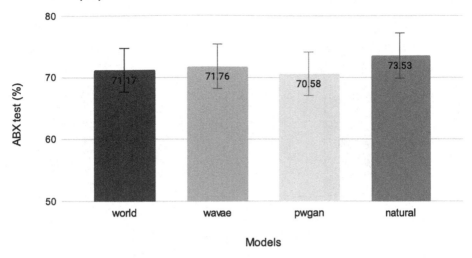

ABX test (%) vs. Models

Fig. 1. Summary of ABX (species recognition) results.

The WORLD vocoder was deemed to retaining bird-related acoustic cues better than the two neural vocoders. The relative order of the mean responses aligns with the broad order given by the objective results (Table 1). For completeness, RMSE vs. MOS scatterplot for individual files is displayed in Fig. 4. The subjective and objective measures are only weakly correlated. There is generally less RMSE variation for WORLD samples.

5   Discussion

Informal listening reveals strong artifacts or noisy quality in many of the re-synthesized samples. Thus, we looked further into the individually most challenging ABX trials and lowest-rated files. For the former, we simply count the percentage of subjects who responded correctly. What constitutes a difficult trial was found to depend on the vocoder. The species pairs in the hardest trials, per vocoder, are

- Natural (60% correct): *Red-throated loon* vs. *European herring gull*, **and** *Eurasian blackcap* vs. *Marsh warbler*
- WORLD (60% correct): *European goldfinch* vs. *Western yellow wagtail*
- WaveNet Autoencoder (53% correct): *European goldfinch* vs. *Western yellow wagtail*
- Parallel WaveGAN (53% correct): *Eurasian reed warbler* vs. *European golden plover*, **and** *European goldfinch* vs *Western yellow wagtail*

One particular case—*European goldfinch* vs *western yellow wagtail*—is shared across the three vocoders. The authors believe that the difficulty does not actually relate to the species in question but to general audio properties: one of the

MOS vs. Models

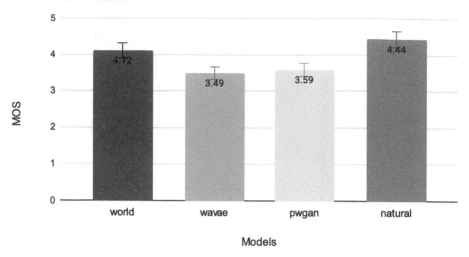

Fig. 2. Summary of bird-related cue evaluation using 5-point mean opinion score (MOS) rating.

reference samples (A or B) in these trials has very little active bird audio (but instead contains a loud splash of water, which may confuse listeners). Additionally, for all the vocoders in their respective hardest trials we noted systematic problems in reproducing voicing: the vocoders appeared to replace clear F0 trajectories in the original audio with broadband noise.

Concerning the species pairs in *easiest* cases per vocoder, two are common to all the vocoders (accuracy $\geq 80\%$ correct)—*European nightjar* vs *redwing*, **and** *common moorhen* vs *willow tit*. These cases might be easy because there is a continuous birdsong in the audio and the pairs have easily distinguishable characteristics. Additionally, some of the easy trials contain common species that might be *familiar* even to naive listeners. For instance, 86.7% on all trials containing *northern raven* were responded correctly.

As for MOS, the lowest-rated (least bird-like) sample is curiously the same for all the methods (including natural sample). The species in the said sample is *red-throated loon*, with a peculiar finding: it sounds there are *two* birds singing in unison but with different pitch values. The spectrograms are displayed in Fig. 3. For the birdsong generated by wavenet autoencoder there is silence for approximately initial 3 s. Comparing each of the vocoders with the natural vocalization, WaveNet AE fails to generate harmonics. Even if WORLD and parallel WaveGAN may look better on spectrograms, listening reveals noisy and inharmonic characteristics.

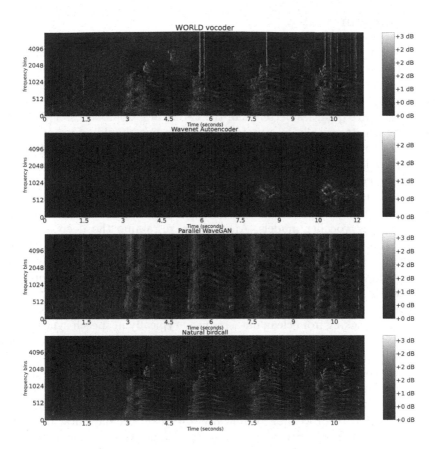

Fig. 3. Natural birdcall (bottom) along with its resynthesized versions with WORLD, Wavenet AE and Parallel WaveGAN.

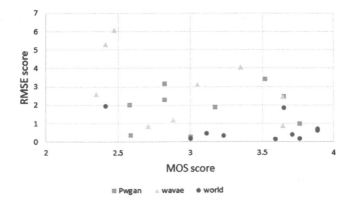

Fig. 4. Scatter plot of 5-point mean opinion score (MOS) rating and root mean squared error (RMSE).

6   Conclusion

We presented an initial study on bird vocalization resynthesis using neural vocoders. The subjective evaluation—the main part of our study—reveals that cues relevant for species identification are retained similarly by the three vocoders. The traditional WORLD vocoder samples, however, were rated as retaining bird-like qualities better than the two neural approaches. This finding should *not* be categorically interpreted to suggest one should adopt non-neural vocoders. Since our study includes only three vocoders and one dataset, the findings should indeed be considered 'initial' as suggested by the title. Future work should therefore expand the battery of vocoders and datasets.

It should be emphasized that our aim was *not* to optimize a state-of-the-art birdsong resynthesis results but, rather, to carry out an out-of-the-box evaluation of existing vocoder models. Apart from retraining the deep models on bird audio, we did not consider architectural modifications, data cleaning or control parameter tuning. We expect better results to be obtained with higher-quality—and larger amounts of—training data. We also expect noise suppression pre-processing and different treatment of bird-present and bird-absent regions to be helpful. Overall, synthesis of acoustic wildlife data represents new challenges that are lacking from clean datasets used typically in speech synthesis and voice conversion research. The above data-engineering related questions requires detailed investigation.

For the most part, the resynthesized samples retain the important audio qualities. But it is also apparent that in a number of cases the selected vocoders struggled in reproducing correct pitch and voicing information. Apart from the challenges related to processing technically low-quality audio data, it must be kept in mind that birdsong is not the same as human voice. Thus, rather than enforcing existing *voice* coders to handle bird vocalizations, in the long term it might be more beneficial to address combinations of physics-inspired and learnable models.

Acknowledgments. The work was partially sponsored by Academy of Finland. The authors express their gratitude to the subjects and to Dr. Rosa González Hautamäki for her help with the PHP-forms.

References

1. xeno-canto – sharing bird sounds from around the world (2017). www.xeno-canto.org/. Accessed 11 Mar 2021
2. Amador, A., Mindlin, G.B.: Synthetic birdsongs as a tool to induce, and listen to, replay activity in sleeping birds. Front. Neurosci. **15**, 835 (2021)
3. Bonada, J., Lachlan, R., Blaauw, M.: Bird song synthesis based on hidden Markov models. In: Interspeech 2016, pp. 2582–2586 (2016). https://doi.org/10.21437/Interspeech.2016-1110

4. Dunbar, E., Algayres, R., Karadayi, J., Bernard, et al.: The zero resource speech challenge 2019: TTS without T. arXiv preprint arXiv:1904.11469 (2019)
5. Engel, J., Resnick, C., Roberts, A., Dieleman, et al.: Neural audio synthesis of musical notes with wavenet autoencoders. In: International Conference on Machine Learning, pp. 1068–1077. PMLR (2017)
6. Goodfellow, I.J., et al.: Generative adversarial nets. In: Proceedings of the NIPS. pp. 2672–2680 (2014). http://proceedings.neurips.cc/paper/2014/hash/5ca3e9b122f61f8f06494c97b1afccf3-Abstract.html
7. Gutscher, L., Pucher, M., Lozo, C., Hoeschele, M., C. Mann, D.: Statistical parametric synthesis of budgerigar songs. In: Proceedings of the 10th ISCA Speech Synthesis Workshop, pp. 127–131 (2019). https://doi.org/10.21437/SSW.2019-23
8. Haque, A., Guo, M., Verma, P.: Conditional end-to-end audio transforms. arXiv preprint arXiv:1804.00047 (2018)
9. Imai, S., et al.: Speech signal processing toolkit (sptk) (2009)
10. Kawahara, H., Morise, M., Takahashi, T., Nisimura, R., Irino, T., Banno, H.: Tandem-STRAIGHT: a temporally stable power spectral representation for periodic signals and applications to interference-free spectrum, f0, and aperiodicity estimation. In: Proceedings of the IEEE ICASSP, pp. 3933–3936 (2008). https://doi.org/10.1109/ICASSP.2008.4518514
11. Kawahara, H., Masuda-Katsuse, I., de Cheveigné, A.: Restructuring speech representations using a pitch-adaptive time-frequency smoothing and an instantaneous-frequency-based F0 extraction: possible role of a repetitive structure in sounds. Speech Commun. 27(3–4), 187–207 (1999)
12. Moore, R.K.: A real-time parametric general-purpose mammalian vocal synthesiser. In: Interspeech 2016, pp. 2636–2640. ISCA (2016). https://doi.org/10.21437/Interspeech.2016-841
13. Morise, M.: D4C, a band-aperiodicity estimator for high-quality speech synthesis. Speech Commun. 84, 57–65 (2016)
14. Morise, M., Yokomori, F., Ozawa, K.: WORLD: a vocoder-based high-quality speech synthesis system for real-time applications. IEICE Trans. Inf. Syst. 99-D(7), 1877–1884 (2016). https://doi.org/10.1587/transinf.2015EDP7457
15. van den Oord, A., et al.: Wavenet: a generative model for raw audio. In: The 9th ISCA Speech Synthesis Workshop. Sunnyvale, CA, USA (2016)
16. O'Reilly, C., Marples, N.M., Kelly, D.J., Harte, N.: YIN-bird: improved pitch tracking for bird vocalisations. In: Interspeech, pp. 2641–2645. ISCA (2016). https://doi.org/10.21437/Interspeech.2016-90
17. Robitza, W.: ffmpeg tool (2015). https://github.com/slhck/ffmpeg-normalize. Accessed 11 March 2021
18. Salimans, T., Kingma, D.P.: Weight normalization: a simple reparameterization to accelerate training of deep neural networks. arXiv preprint arXiv:1602.07868 (2016)
19. Somervuo, P., Härmä, A., Fagerlund, S.: Parametric representations of bird sounds for automatic species recognition. IEEE Trans. Speech Audio Process. 14(6), 2252–2263 (2006)
20. Stowell, D., Plumbley, M.D.: Automatic large-scale classification of bird sounds is strongly improved by unsupervised feature learning. PeerJ 2, e488 (2014)
21. Stowell, D., Wood, M., Stylianou, Y., Glotin, H.: Bird detection in audio: a survey and a challenge. In: IEEE International Workshop on MLSP, pp. 1–6 (2016). https://doi.org/10.1109/MLSP.2016.7738875

22. Tjandra, A., Sisman, B., Zhang, M., Sakti, S., Li, H., Nakamura, S.: VQVAE unsupervised unit discovery and multi-scale code2spec inverter for zerospeech challenge 2019. arXiv preprint arXiv:1905.11449 (2019)
23. Yamamoto, R., Song, E., Kim, J.M.: Parallel WaveGAN: a fast waveform generation model based on generative adversarial networks with multi-resolution spectrogram. In: Proceedings of the IEEE ICASSP, pp. 6199–6203 (2020)

Speech Music Overlap Detection Using Spectral Peak Evolutions

Mrinmoy Bhattacharjee[1]([⊠]) [iD], S. R. Mahadeva Prasanna[2] [iD],
and Prithwijit Guha[1] [iD]

[1] Indian Institute of Technology Guwahati, Guwahati 781039, Assam, India
{mrinmoy.bhattacharjee,pguha}@iitg.ac.in
[2] Indian Institute of Technology Dharwad, Dharwad 580011, Karnataka, India
prasanna@iitdh.ac.in

Abstract. Speech-music overlap detection in audio signals is an essential preprocessing step for many high-level audio processing applications. Speech and music spectrograms exhibit characteristic harmonic striations that can be used as a feature for detecting their overlap. Hence, this work proposes two features generated using a spectral peak tracking algorithm to capture prominent harmonic patterns in spectrograms. One feature consists of the spectral peak amplitude evolutions in an audio interval. The second feature is designed as a Mel-scaled spectrogram obtained by suppressing non-peak spectral components. In addition, a one-dimensional convolutional neural network architecture is proposed to learn the temporal evolution of spectral peaks. Mel-spectrogram is used as a baseline feature to compare performances. A popular public dataset MUSAN with 102 h of data has been used to perform experiments. A late fusion of the proposed features with baseline is observed to provide better performance.

Keywords: Speech overlapped with music · 1D Convolutional Neural Networks · Spectral peak tracking

1 Introduction

Speech and music are two audio categories frequently occurring in movie and television audio. Often these signals are encountered in overlapped conditions. Music in TV programs is mostly overlapped by speech or other sounds [8]. The performance of high-level audio-based applications like Music Information Retrieval (MIR) and Automatic Speech Recognition (ASR) may be hugely affected by overlapping sounds. It is essential to detect and enhance overlapped audio segments before using them for MIR or ASR applications. Thus, efficient discrimination of overlapped speech and music signals (*SpMu*) from clean speech (*ClSp*) and clean music (*ClMu*) is a pertinent task. However, this task becomes challenging when the signals are mixed at high SNR [15]. High homogeneity in the acoustic properties of some overlapped signals with other clean signals makes their detection difficult [5]. This work attempts the task of discriminating *ClSp* and *ClMu* from *SpMu* mixed at varying SNR.

© Springer Nature Switzerland AG 2022
S. R. M. Prasanna et al. (Eds.): SPECOM 2022, LNAI 13721, pp. 75–86, 2022.
https://doi.org/10.1007/978-3-031-20980-2_8

1.1   Related Work

Researchers have previously explored various audio classification techniques. Zhang et al. [26] performed segmentation and classification of the audio signal from movies or TV programs into basic categories such as speech, music, song, environmental sound, speech with music background, environmental sound with background music, and silence. The authors employed various spectral and temporal audio features like energy and fundamental frequency to perform the task. Taniguchi et al. [20] performed sound source classification into speech, musical instrument, singing voice, and instrumental with singing. The authors proposed a dynamic-programming based spectral tracking method to generate features that performed well with a Gaussian Mixture Model (GMM) classifier in detecting speech with background music. Vavrek et al. [24] adopted a hierarchical strategy to classify broadcast news audio into pure speech, speech with music, speech with environmental sound, pure music, and environmental sound. The authors used various temporal and spectral features with Support Vector Machine (SVM) based classifiers at split nodes of binary decision trees. Castán et al. [5] classified audio into speech, music, speech with music, speech with noise, and others using a Hidden Markov Model classifier. The authors used factor analysis over GMM-UBM super vectors trained using Mel-frequency Cepstral Coefficient (MFCC) feature blocks to compensate for within-class variability. The authors used an HMM backend for the segmentation and classification system. Lopez-Otero et al. [11] showed an improvement in the performance of a similar task posed in the Albayzin 2010 audio segmentation evaluation [4] using an ensemble of various state-of-the-art classifiers. In a similar task, Vavrek et al. [23] observed that the highest miss-classification occurred for music and environmental sound.

In a slightly different approach to the audio classification task, some works detect the presence of speech or its lack thereof in any audio signal. Anemuller et al. [1] targetted the detection of speech embedded in a natural acoustic background. They obtained decent results using features from an amplitude modulated spectrogram (AMS). Bach et al. [2] hierarchically detected speech in the presence of strongly varying acoustic background using AMS based feature with an SVM classifier. The authors detected background sounds in the first step, followed by discrimination of speech vs. non-speech. Weninger et al. [25] proposed a semi-supervised music suppression algorithm. Their approach used the Non-negative Matrix Factorization method. The approach of Weninger et al. [25] was effective in high-noise environments. Mohammed et al. [14] analyzed overlapping audio content using Singular Spectrum Analysis. Authors separated the signal into components of reduced overlap to identify their class using a random forest classifier.

Music detection is another audio classification task that many researchers have explored. Raj et al. [15] studied the extent of performance degradation introduced in Automatic Speech Recognition (ASR) due to the presence of background music. The authors observed that enhancing regions with high signal-to-noise ratios is challenging due to the nonstationarity of music signals. Vanroose et al. [22] used Independent Component Analysis to separate overlapping speech

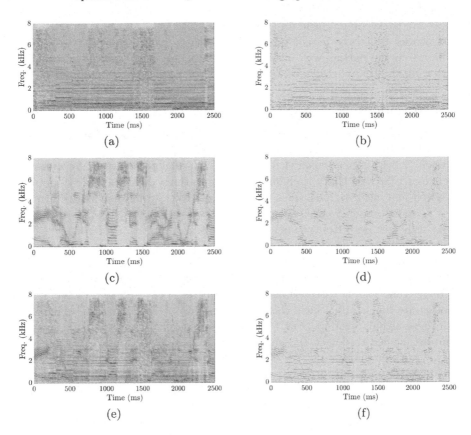

Fig. 1. Illustrating DFT spectrograms of (a) *ClMu*, (c) *ClSp*, (e) *SpMu*, and SPT spectrograms of (b) *ClMu*, (d) *ClSp*, (f) *SpMu*. For illustration purposes, *SpMu* signal is generated by mixing *ClMu* and *ClSp* at 0 dB SNR.

and music signals for improving ASR performance. In another work [16], authors automatically detected the foreground or background music in TV audio. In their proposal, the authors used a continuous frequency activation feature and other standard audio features, with various classifiers like SVM. Lee et al. [10] detected music in real-world ambient sounds. Authors found that sporadic or partial music, singing voice, and other high-energy sounds created the most confusion. MFCC and other spectral and empirical features were used by Izumitani et al. [8] for detecting background music. The authors performed dimension reduction using Principal Component Analysis and classification using GMM and k-Nearest Neighbor classifiers.

Recently, music detection has been explored using various deep-learning-based approaches. Jia et al. 2020 [9] attempted the joint task of music detection and music relative loudness estimation. The authors proposed a Hierarchical Regulated Iterative Network classifier that performed the joint task in two steps. First, music vs. non-music classification is performed, followed by detecting foreground and background music. In another work [6], authors used Recurrent Neural Networks (RNN) to detect music. The authors demonstrated that using a loss based on the partial area under the receiver operating characteristic curve for training the RNN performed better in this task than cross-entropy loss.

1.2 Motivation

In most of the previous works, *SpMu* signals have been considered either as an independent category [4,5,11,23,24,26], or as overlapping signals in the detection of speech [1,2,14,25] or music [6,8–10,15,16,22]. The detection of *SpMu* in the presence of *ClSp* and *ClMu* is challenging due to the acoustic similarity between the mixed and clean signals. This work addresses a common scenario in movie and TV audio where *SpMu* segments are embedded between *ClSp* and *ClMu* signals. Efficient detection of such segments and application of required compensations might be necessary to improve the performance of high-level audio applications.

The spectro-temporal properties of music (Fig. 1a) and speech (Fig. 1b) signals have some visible distinctions. Harmonics in speech are wavy, while that in music are linear [10]. Such class-specific characteristics are preserved even when these signals overlap (Fig. 1c). Detection of such characteristics may be an important cue to detect speech or music in any given signal. In a previous work [3], authors proposed a spectral peak tracking (SPT) algorithm. This work uses the SPT algorithm of [3] to track the evolution of signal harmonics and use that with a 1-dimensional Convolutional Neural Network (CNN) classifier to distinguish between *SpMu*, *ClSp* and *ClMu* signals.

This paper is organized as follows. Section 2.1 discusses the SPT algorithm in brief. The proposed 1-dimensional CNN classifier architecture is described in Sect. 2.2. The experiments performed are discussed in Sect. 3. The paper is concluded in Sect. 4 with a few directions for extension of this work in the future.

2   Proposed Work

This work proposes that the distinct harmonic patterns of speech and music can be used as evidence for detecting the overlap of these signals. The harmonic patterns of a signal can be captured by tracking prominent spectral peak evolution across short-term audio frame spectra. A Discrete Fourier Transform (DFT) based magnitude spectrogram contains all harmonic information in the signal. However, it also holds other features that might create confusion while differentiating a clean signal from a mixed one. If the DFT-based spectrogram is pre-processed in a manner that reduces the misdetection of *ClSp* and *ClMu* signal as *SpMu*, the overall system performance may be improved. In this context, it would be beneficial if the harmonic patterns in the DFT spectrogram of the signal could be isolated. Hence, this work proposes to use the SPT algorithm [3] to identify the prominent spectral peaks in a signal's spectrogram and use their evolution over time as a feature to detect *SpMu* signals. In the following subsection, the SPT algorithm and the features used in this work are discussed.

2.1   Feature Computation

Let, $\mathbf{S}_{n_f \times n_t}$ be the DFT magnitude spectrogram with n_f frequency bins and n_t frames of a signal sampled at s_r. The location of p highest spectral peaks for each frame spectra are identified. These frequency locations are stored in a matrix $\mathbf{L}$ in the following manner.

$$\mathbf{L}[k,j] = \{i : (\mathbf{S}[i,j] > \mathbf{S}[i-1,j]) \wedge (\mathbf{S}[i,j] > \mathbf{S}[i+1,j])\} \tag{1}$$

where $i = 1 \ldots n_f$, $j = 1 \ldots n_t$ and $k = 1 \ldots p$. In frames with less than p spectral peaks, the highest frequency peak location is repeated in the blank places to maintain cardinality. Using the peak location matrix $\mathbf{L}$, a $p \times n_t$ peak amplitude matrix $\mathbf{V}_{SPT}$ is computed as follows.

$$\mathbf{V}_{SPT}[k,j] = \mathbf{S}\left[\mathbf{L}[k,j],j\right] \tag{2}$$

where $j = 1 \ldots n_t$ and $k = 1 \ldots p$. The columns in $\mathbf{L}$ and $\mathbf{V}_{SPT}$ are arranged by their corresponding frequency value. The rth row in $\mathbf{L}$ (and $\mathbf{V}_{SPT}$) contains the spectral peak locations (or peak amplitudes) of the rth peak in consecutive frames of $\|S\|$. Many of these rows would contain traces of various harmonics in the signal. For a detailed discussion on the SPT algorithm, the reader is encouraged to refer to the original paper [3]. This work uses these peak traces to detect the *SpMu* signals.

The peak location matrix $\mathbf{L}$ is used in this work to generate another spectrogram $\mathbf{S}_{SPT}$. Every spectrum content other than the peaks selected in $\mathbf{L}$ is suppressed in $\mathbf{S}_{SPT}$. This spectrogram has the same shape as $\mathbf{S}$ and is defined as follows.

$$\mathbf{S}_{SPT}[i,j] = \begin{cases} \mathbf{S}[i,j] & \text{if, } i \in \mathbf{L}_j \\ 0 & \text{if, otherwise} \end{cases} \tag{3}$$

where, $i = 1 \ldots n_f$ and $j = 1 \ldots n_t$. Examples of $\mathbf{S}_{SPT}$ spectrograms for music and speech are shown in Fig. 1(d) and Fig. 1(e), respectively. It can be observed that the $\mathbf{S}_{SPT}$ captures most of the prominent harmonic patterns present in $\mathbf{S}$. The $\mathbf{S}_{SPT}$ matrix may thus be viewed as a cleaner version of $\mathbf{S}$. The $\mathbf{S}_{SPT}$ spectrogram of *SpMu* (Fig. 1f) captures the important harmonics of both the classes. This work hypothesizes that training models using the spectral peak evolution patterns extracted in $\mathbf{L}$ and the clean spectrogram $\mathbf{S}_{SPT}$ would aid in the better detection of *SpMu* signals. The features used in this work are described next.

One of the most widely used feature in recent audio classification works [7, 13, 18] is the Mel-scaled spectrogram $\mathbf{MS}$. The Mel-scale relates natural frequency with human perceived frequency [21] and is popularly used to compute features for audio analysis. The Mel filter-bank $\mathbf{H}_{n_m \times n_f}$ composed of n_m filters is defined as [17]

$$\mathbf{H}[m,i] = \begin{cases} 0, & \text{if } f_i < \omega^c_{m-1} \\ \dfrac{f_i - \omega^c_{m-1}}{\omega^c_m - \omega^c_{m-1}}, & \text{if } \omega^c_{m-1} \le f_i < \omega^c_m \\ \dfrac{f_i - \omega^c_{m+1}}{\omega^c_m - \omega^c_{m+1}}, & \text{if } \omega^c_m \le f_i < \omega^c_{m+1} \\ 0, & \text{if } f_i \ge \omega^c_{m+1} \end{cases} \tag{4}$$

where, $m = 1 \ldots n_m$, $i = 1 \ldots n_f$, $n_m \ll n_f$, f_i are the Hertz-scale frequencies, and ω^c are the Mel-scale center-frequencies of the n_m filters. Hertz-scale frequencies in the range $\left[0, \dfrac{s_r}{2}\right]$ are converted to Mel-scale using the following relation.

$$\omega = 2595 \log_{10}\left(1 + \frac{f}{700}\right) \tag{5}$$

Subsequently, n_m equally spaced frequencies in the Mel-scale are selected as center frequencies for the Mel filter-bank. Then, Mel-scaled spectrogram $\mathbf{MS}$ of size $n_m \times n_t$ is computed as follows.

$$\mathbf{MS} = \mathbf{H} \cdot \mathbf{S} \tag{6}$$

Similarly, the $\mathbf{S}_{SPT}$ spectrogram is Mel-scaled to obtain $\mathbf{MS}_{SPT}$. This work proposes the use of $\mathbf{V}_{SPT}$ and $\mathbf{MS}_{SPT}$ as features for detection of $SpMu$ signals. A block diagram of the feature extraction process is illustrated in Fig. 2. The $\mathbf{MS}$ feature is considered a baseline feature in this work to compare with the performance of proposed features.

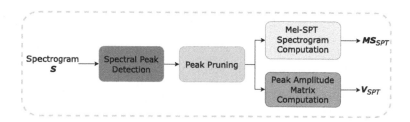

Fig. 2. Block diagram of the feature computation process.

2.2   Classifier Design

Authors in [3] trained GMMs over the spectral peak traces to generate features that were used with various classifiers. This work proposes to use a 1-dimensional CNN ($SpMu\text{-}1DCNN$) as an automatic feature learning algorithm to model the class-specific temporal evolution of spectral peaks directly from the Mel-scaled

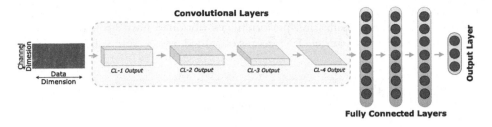

Fig. 3. Illustrating the architecture of *SpMu-1DCNN* classifier proposed in this work.

spectrograms. The proposed classifier architecture is shown in Fig. 3. The input feature matrices (like **MS** or **MS**$_{SPT}$) are fed in such a manner that each row in the matrix is considered a separate channel of data. The *SpMu-1DCNN* model consists of four convolutional layers CL-1 to CL-4 with 64, 128, 256 and 512 convolutional kernels, respectively. CL-1 uses kernels of size 5×1 to span over ≈ 50 ms of the input signal at once. This duration is chosen since it is believed to be the maximum pitch period observed in human speech. The remaining convolutional layers use kernels of size 3×1. Each convolution layer uses *ReLU* activation followed by a *BatchNormalization* layer. The output of each convolution layer is max-pooled to half. After CL-4, a flattening operation is performed, followed by three fully connected (FC) layers. All *FC* layers have 512 neurons and are activated with *ReLU*. The output of each *FC* layer is batch-normalized, followed by a *Dropout* of 40% of the layer activations. Output layer consists of 3 neurons with a *Softmax* activation. The *SpMu-1DCNN* model is trained with a categorical cross-entropy loss and a *Nadam* optimizer with an initial learning rate of 10^{-4}. The weights of all the layers in *SpMu-1DCNN* are l_2 regularized.

3   Experiments and Results

The experimental setup used to validate the current proposal is discussed here. A widely used public dataset - MUSAN - A Music, Speech, and Noise corpus [19] (≈ 102 h) have been used to validate the performances of proposed and baseline features in the current task. Only the speech and music classes of the MUSAN dataset have been considered in this work. For generating the *SpMu* signals, randomly selected speech and music files have been mixed. The mixing SNR level is chosen uniformly from $\{-5, 0, 5\}$ (in dB). The audio signals used in this work are resampled to 16000 Hz and pre-emphasized with a pre-emphasis factor of 0.97. Short-term processing of the audio signals is performed with a frame size of 25 ms and a frame shift of 10 ms. Silence regions longer than 100 ms are removed. Parameters used for feature computation are $p = 21$, $n_f = 201$, $n_t = 68$ and $n_m = 21$. The number of spectral peaks (p) picked using the SPT algorithm is kept the same as the number of Mel filters (n_m). Such a choice helped keep the same shape of proposed features ($\mathbf{V}_{SPT}$ and $\mathbf{MS}_{SPT}$) and baseline feature (**MS**). The number of *SpMu-1DCNN* parameters remained consistent with similar input shapes that allowed direct comparison between the feature performances. The classification performances obtained have been reported as the *mean±standard-deviation* of $F1$-scores obtained over 3 cross-validation folds.

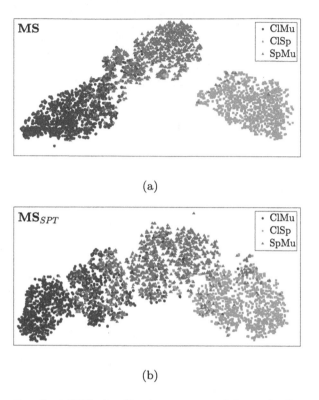

(a)

(b)

Fig. 4. Illustrating the t-SNE visualizations generated from the flattened output of CL-4 layer of *SpMu-1DCNN* classifier trained on (a) **MS** and (b) **MS**$_{SPT}$ features, respectively. Training with MS seems to bias the classifier to confuse between $SpMu$ and $ClMu$. Training with MS_{SPT} avoids such a bias.

3.1   Performance Analysis

Table 1 lists the performances obtained using the proposed features ($\mathbf{V}_{SPT}$ and $\mathbf{MS}_{SPT}$) and baseline feature (**MS**) using the *SpMu-1DCNN* classifier. Taken individually, the features $\mathbf{V}_{SPT}$ (86.18±2.20) and $\mathbf{MS}_{SPT}$ (81.12±0.77) perform well, while **MS** gives the best performance (91.26 ± 0.87). However, improved performances are observed when the proposed and baseline features are combined in a late-fusion framework. Classifiers trained on different features are used in a late-fusion framework to obtain prediction scores for the same test signal. The mean computed from individual classifier scores is used to obtain

Table 1. This table lists the classification performances of **MS**, $\mathbf{V}_{SPT}$, and $\mathbf{MS}_{SPT}$ features with *SpMu-1DCNN* classifier over the MUSAN dataset. F1-scores are shown in percentages, in the form of mean±standard deviation of 3 cross-validation folds. The best performance is highlighted with a ▲, while the second-best is indicated using a •.

Features	F1-score			
	Music	Speech	Speech+Music	Average
MS	92.51 ± 1.70	97.54 ± 0.47	83.73 ± 1.14	91.26 ± 0.87
V_{SPT}	87.14 ± 3.81	95.51 ± 1.03	75.90 ± 2.81	86.18 ± 2.20
MS_{SPT}	84.59 ± 0.61	92.53 ± 1.62	66.25 ± 0.64	81.12 ± 0.77
$MS + MS_{SPT}$	93.54 ± 1.96	97.93 ± 0.40	83.73 ± 0.92	91.73 ± 0.85 •
$MS + V_{SPT}$	93.89 ± 1.25	98.36 ± 0.50	84.31 ± 1.69	92.18 ± 0.92 ▲

the final prediction. The combination of $\mathbf{MS} + \mathbf{V}_{SPT}$ provides the best performance (92.18 ± 0.92), while $\mathbf{MS} + \mathbf{MS}_{SPT}$ provides the second-best performance (91.73 ± 0.85). Such improvements obtained after combining the proposed and baseline features justify the current proposal's efficacy in this task.

3.2 Discussions

The t-SNE algorithm is widely used for high-dimensional data visualizations [12]. This work uses the t-SNE algorithm to generate a class-wise distribution of the flattened output obtained from the CL-4 layer of the *SpMu-1DCNN* classifier. Fig. 4(a) is generated from the outputs obtained from the classifier trained using **MS**. Similarly, Fig. 4(b) is generated from the outputs obtained from the classifier trained using $\mathbf{MS}_{SPT}$. The t-SNE algorithm attempts to preserve the inter-class separability and intra-class similarity present in the data while generating the lower dimensional embeddings. However, the distances observed in the visualizations may not represent the actual distances in the original data. Here, the CL-4 layer output generates these visualizations to gauge the class separability learned by the *SpMu-1DCNN* classifier. It can be observed from Fig. 4(a) that the classifier trained using **MS** seems to find the mixed signals (*SpMu*) more similar to *ClMu* than *ClSp*. Whereas the classifier trained using $\mathbf{MS}_{SPT}$ appears to have no such bias (Fig. 4b). However, the comparatively poor performance of $\mathbf{MS}_{SPT}$ is indicated by the increased overlap between the classes (Fig. 4b). It may thus be argued that the classifier trained with **MS** may sometimes detect *SpMu* as *ClMu* or vice-versa. In such cases, the lack of such a bias in the classifier training with $\mathbf{MS}_{SPT}$ might help to improve the performance in combination with the classifier trained with **MS**.

Although the proposed features performed decently, they cannot improve upon the performance of the **MS** feature. Such a result may be reasoned by acknowledging the information loss occurring while the generation of $\mathbf{V}_{SPT}$ and $\mathbf{MS}_{SPT}$ features. The SPT algorithm picks only a fixed number of prominent spectral peaks from the spectrogram. This process ignores other spectrum components that may carry important class-specific information. Thus, the proposed features' performances are lower than the baseline **MS** feature. However, the features obtained from the peak picking process can be observed to aid the baseline feature in the late-fusion framework. A couple of reasons may be attributed to such a performance. First, the SPT algorithm tends to focus on the prominent harmonic patterns in the spectrogram. This results in improved detection of *ClSp* and *ClMu* classes using the proposed features in combination with **MS**. Second, not all information in the DFT-based spectrogram may be useful in the current task. *SpMu-1DCNN* trained on the *MS* feature has to identify the relevant class-specific information and learn the discrimination. However, the *SpMu-1DCNN* classifier is presented with the class-specific harmonic information when trained on $\mathbf{V}_{SPT}$ or $\mathbf{MS}_{SPT}$. Thus, the proposed approach allows the classifier to focus on learning mostly prominent class-specific patterns. Hence, the SPT algorithm based proposed features can be useful in the current task of discriminating *SpMu* signals from *ClSp* and *ClMu* signals.

4   Conclusion

This work uses spectral peak tracking to compute new feature representations that can improve the detection of speech overlapped with music signals. A 1-dimensional CNN architecture that learns the temporal evolution of captured spectral peaks is also proposed. Peak picking is a lossy approach that results in individual performances of the proposed features being lower than the baseline Mel-spectrogram feature. However, extracting signals' prominent harmonic information enabled the proposed features to improve baseline features' performance in a late-fusion combination framework.

Some future extensions of the current proposal may be explored. First, the number of peaks parameter used in the SPT algorithm may be optimized for the current task. Second, Long-Short Term Memory based classifier may be used for better modeling of the temporal evolution of the spectral peaks. Third, other feature combination strategies like early-fusion and intermediate-fusion of the proposed features may also be explored.

Acknowledgments. Supported by Visvesvaraya PhD Scheme, MeitY, Govt. of India - MEITY-PHD-1230.

References

1. Anemüller, J., Schmidt, D., Bach, J.H.: Detection of speech embedded in real acoustic background based on amplitude modulation spectrogram features. In: Proceedings of the 9th Annual Conference of the International Speech Communication Association (2008)
2. Bach, J.H., Anemüller, J., Kollmeier, B.: Robust speech detection in real acoustic backgrounds with perceptually motivated features. Speech Commun. **53**(5), 690–706 (2011)

3. Bhattacharjee, M., Prasanna, S.R.M., Guha, P.: Speech/music classification using features from spectral peaks. IEEE/ACM Trans. Audio Speech Lang. Process. **28**, 1549–1559 (2020)
4. Butko, T., Nadeu, C.: Audio segmentation of broadcast news in the Albayzin-2010 evaluation: overview, results, and discussion. EURASIP J. Audio Speech Music Process. **2011**(1), 1–10 (2011)
5. Castán, D., Ortega, A., Miguel, A., Lleida, E.: Audio segmentation-by-classification approach based on factor analysis in broadcast news domain. EURASIP J. Audio Speech Music Process. **2014**(1), 34 (2014)
6. Gimeno, P., Mingote, V., Ortega, A., Miguel, A., Lleida, E.: Partial AUC Optimisation using Recurrent Neural Networks for Music Detection with Limited Training Data. Proceedings. Interspeech, pp. 3067–3071 (2020)
7. Hershey, S., et al.: CNN architectures for large-scale audio classification. In: Proceedings of the IEEE International Conference on Acoustics, Speech, and Signal Processing, pp. 131–135 (2017)
8. Izumitani, T., Mukai, R., Kashino, K.: A background music detection method based on robust feature extraction. In: Proceedings of the IEEE International Conference on Acoustics, Speech, and Signal Processing, pp. 13–16 (2008)
9. Jia, B., Lv, J., Peng, X., Chen, Y., Yang, S.: Hierarchical regulated iterative network for joint task of music detection and music relative loudness estimation. IEEE/ACM Trans. Audio Speech Lang. Process. (2020)
10. Lee, K., Ellis, D.P.: Detecting music in ambient audio by long-window autocorrelation. In: Proceedings of the IEEE International Conference on Acoustics, Speech, and Signal Processing, pp. 9–12 (2008)
11. Lopez-Otero, P., Docio-Fernandez, L., Garcia-Mateo, C.: Ensemble audio segmentation for radio and television programmes. Multimedia Tools Appl. **76**(5), 7421–7444 (2017)
12. Maaten, L.V.D., Hinton, G.: Visualizing data using t-SNE. J. Mach. Learn. Res. **9**(Nov), 2579–2605 (2008)
13. Meng, H., Yan, T., Yuan, F., Wei, H.: Speech emotion recognition from 3D log-mel spectrograms with deep learning network. IEEE Access **7**, 125868–125881 (2019)
14. Mohammed, D.Y., Li, F.F.: Overlapped soundtracks segmentation using singular spectrum analysis and random forests. In: Proceedings of the 2nd International Conference on Knowledge Discovery and Data Mining, pp. 49–54 (2017)
15. Raj, B., Parikh, V.N., Stern, R.M.: The effects of background music on speech recognition accuracy. In: Proceedings of the IEEE International Conference on Acoustics, Speech, and Signal Processing, vol. 2, pp. 851–854 (1997)
16. Seyerlehner, K., Pohle, T., Schedl, M., Widmer, G.: Automatic music detection in television productions. In: Proceedings of the 10th International Conference on Digital Audio Effects (DAFx 2007). Citeseer (2007)
17. Sigurdsson, S., Petersen, K.B., Lehn-Schiøler, T.: Mel Frequency Cepstral Coefficients: An Evaluation of Robustness of MP3 Encoded Music. In: ISMIR, pp. 286–289 (2006)
18. Sinha, H., Awasthi, V., Ajmera, P.K.: Audio classification using braided convolutional neural networks (2020)
19. Snyder, D., Chen, G., Povey, D.: Musan: a music, speech, and noise corpus. arXiv preprint arXiv:1510.08484 (2015)
20. Taniguchi, T., Tohyama, M., Shirai, K.: Detection of speech and music based on spectral tracking. Speech Commun. **50**(7), 547–563 (2008)

21. Umesh, S., Cohen, L., Nelson, D.: Fitting the Mel scale. In: Proceedings of the IEEE International Conference on Acoustics, Speech, and Signal Processing, vol. 1, pp. 217–220 (1999)
22. Vanroose, P.: Blind source separation of speech and background music for improved speech recognition. In: Proceedings of the 24th Symposium on Information Theory, pp. 103–108 (2003)
23. Vavrek, J., Fecil'ak, P., Juhár, J., Čižmár, A.: Classification of broadcast news audio data employing binary decision architecture. Comput. Inform. 36(4), 857–886 (2017)
24. Vavrek, J., Vozáriková, E., Pleva, M., Juhár, J.: Broadcast news audio classification using SVM binary trees. In: Proceedings of the 35th International Conference on Telecommunications and Signal Processing, pp. 469–473 (2012)
25. Weninger, F., Feliu, J., Schuller, B.: Supervised and semi-supervised suppression of background music in monaural speech recordings. In: Proceedings of the IEEE International Conference on Acoustics, Speech, and Signal Processing, pp. 61–64 (2012)
26. Zhang, T., Kuo, C.C.J.: Audio content analysis for online audiovisual data segmentation and classification. IEEE Trans. Speech Audio Process. 9(4), 441–457 (2001)

Influence of Accented Speech in Automatic Speech Recognition: A Case Study on Assamese L1 Speakers Speaking Code Switched Hindi-English

Joyshree Chakraborty[(✉)] , Rohit Sinha , and Priyankoo Sarmah

Centre for Linguistic Science and Technology, Indian Institute of Technology Guwahati, Guwahati 781039, India
{jchakraborty,rsinha,priyankoo}@iitg.ac.in

Abstract. The goal of this work is to show the influence of accented speech on state-of-the-art speech-to-text (S2T) systems. In the current study, Assamese accented Hindi-English (AAHE) code-switched speech samples and Native Hindi-English (NHE) code-switched speech samples are subjected to four commercial S2T systems. The results of this study found that the word error rate averaged across the four systems is found to be 27.33% and 38.35% for the NHE and AAHE groups, respectively. This performance gap is mainly attributed to substitution errors. On further analysis, it was found that those errors resulted from the distinct phonetic and phonological properties of the Assamese language. Thus, there is a scope for accent adaptation even in concurrent S2T systems supporting Indian languages.

Keywords: Non-native ASR · Accent mismatch · Robustness and inclusiveness

1 Introduction

An inclusive speech-to-text (S2T) system implies that it is able to handle sociolinguistic variations gracefully. It has been noticed that such an inclusive system becomes more important in a multilingual country like India, where depending on the first language (L1) of the speakers, several accents of the dominant lingua-franca exist. In the case of Indian English, which is spoken by about 10% [9] of the population, several studies have been undertaken, and it has been reported that depending on the L1 of the Indian speakers, various Indian Englishes have emerged [18]. However, even though Hindi is spoken by about 14% [9] of the Indian population as a second (L2) and third (L3) language [9], not much is known about the Hindi accents arising due to L1 influences. Hence, in the case of S2T systems, the issue of incorporating various Hindi accents has not gathered due attention. Motivated by that, in the current work, we perform a preliminary study to measure the influence of L1 on L2 in the context of state-of-the-art S2T systems.

© Springer Nature Switzerland AG 2022
S. R. M. Prasanna et al. (Eds.): SPECOM 2022, LNAI 13721, pp. 87–98, 2022.
https://doi.org/10.1007/978-3-031-20980-2_9

There are noticeable phonetic influences of the L1 on L2, in terms of both segmental and suprasegmental features. For example, the phonological influence of L1 on L2 can be perceived in terms of stress [8] and intonation patterns [6]. While using L2, speakers often try to use the stress and intonation patterns of their L1 [12]. In terms of segmental features, the L2 phonemes that are absent in L1 may not be produced by the speakers, and they may be either deleted or replaced by acoustically most similar phonemes in the L1. Such segmental or suprasegmental changes may result in an L2 variation that may sound 'accented' by the L1 of the speakers [8,15].

In the case of Indian English, the local accents primarily emerge due to the transfer from the speakers' L1s. One such transfer effect is reported for the English spoken by Assamese speakers, where, a study on the influence of the Assamese language on stops of English revealed that it is the effect of voicing instead of aspiration that marks a distinction between English spoken by Assamese speakers with American/British English [16]. Deterioration in the recognition performance from native to non-native ASR resulted due to phonetic mismatch [15]. The errors due to discrepancies in the phonetic realizations can be handled using lexical adaptation [14] and cross-lingual accent adaptation [15]. From our assessment, we can claim that there is a gap in the literature in the study when an L1 speaker speaks Hindi-English as L2. There are 15.3 million Assamese speakers in India, out of which 2.45 million speak Hindi as their second subsidiary language as per the 2011 census [9]. This motivated us to explore the influence of Assamese accented Hindi-English (AAHE) spoken by Assamese L1 speakers on popular commercial S2T APIs.

The S2T is a quite mature technology and finds application in our daily life. A typical S2T system is developed using deep learning techniques on a large corpus of data [13]. Currently, a number of S2T application purpose interfaces (APIs) are available, supporting many languages across the globe that including some Indian languages. India is a multilingual country that has 22 scheduled and several non-scheduled languages [10]. In India, English is studied as a second or foreign language that is widely followed in business and formal communications. Indians are usually multilingual and they speak Hindi and English apart from their native languages. As a result of that, people involuntarily switch between languages. The code-switching between languages is quite common and Hindi-English forms a dominant variant.

The study aims at assessing the influence of L1 on L2 speech in the context of S2T systems. For the same, we first extracted some native Hindi-English (NHE) speech samples from an existing speech corpus. Following that native Assamese speakers were asked to read out the transcripts of the NHE speech data in order to collect corresponding Assamese accented Hindi-English (AAHE) speech data. So collected NHE and AAHE speech data is then subjected to four popular S2T APIs supporting Indian languages developed by Amazon, Google, IBM, and Microsoft. These S2T APIs don't explicitly include Hindi-English in their language settings. But in our observation we found them to produce reasonably well transcription for Hindi-English code-switching input speech. From the evaluation of the hypotheses produced by all four S2T APIs, we found a significant degradation in the recognition performance for the AAHE speech when compared with that of NHE speech. This degradation is attributed to a possible acoustic mismatch due to L1 influence on L2. We further analyzed the errors in the hypotheses to correlate them with the phonetic and phonological properties of the Assamese language.

The rest of the paper is organized in a way such that Sect. 2 deals with the data collection procedure of the NHE and AAHE groups with its description. Section 3 talks about the commercial S2T APIs used in this study. It also talks about the mixed scripting in the NHE transcript and its normalization. In Sect. 4 we convey the results of the recognition performance of the NHE and AAHE speech averaged over the four popular S2T APIs with a discussion of the errors.

2   Data Collection

In this section, we describe different kinds of data sets involved in this study. For assessing the influence of L1 over L2, we could have used any monolingual L2 context. To capture the multilingual scenario, we performed this study in the code-switching domain. For logistic ease, we chose the Assamese language for L1 and code-switched Hindi-English for L2. The following subsections provide the relevant details of the native and non-native accented Hindi-English code-switching speech data.

2.1   Native Hindi-English Speech Data

The native Hindi-English (NHE) speech data and its transcripts have been derived from the Microsoft-sponsored challenge at Interspeech-2021 titled "Multilingual and Code-Switching ASR Challenges for Low Resource Indian Languages" [3]. Out of the code-switching ASR task, we accessed the Hindi-English code-switching test speech data and extracted 10 speech files from it in a gender-balanced manner. Since the said Microsoft Challenge speech data did not come with any metadata, the gender of the speakers was determined by listening. The speech files are in WAV format, sampled at 16 kHz with 16-bit encoding. The total duration of the speech data is 1.6 h. The reference transcripts of the NHE group speech data comprise 12252 words with a vocabulary of 1540 unique Hindi-English words. A rough estimate of the rate of code-switching is about 50%. This set is referred to as NHE group data henceforth.

2.2   Assamese Accented Hindi-English Speech Data

The Assamese accented Hindi-English speech data was collected by the authors from 10 native Assamese speakers. The speakers were instructed to read the code-switched transcript derived from the NHE group data. The Assamese speakers could speak both Hindi and English as their second or third languages. Speech data were collected from 5 male and 5 female speakers reading Hindi-English text transcripts of NHE group data ensuring mostly identical code-switching instances. Data was collected by instructing each speaker to record his/her data using their mobile phone.

To be consistent with the NHE group data, gender was matched for each reference transcript. All the Assamese speakers were residing in Guwahati city while recording the speech data. All speakers have bachelor's degrees in various domains, and their ages range between 25 to 35 years. The total duration of the collected speech data is 1.94 h. In order to be consistent with NHE data, the collected speech data was converted to WAV format with a 16 kHz sampling rate and 16-bit encoding. This set of data is referred to as the AAHE group data henceforth.

Care was taken to keep the fluency level of Hindi of the AAHE speakers as consistent as possible. Even though some AAHE speakers sounded more proficient than the others, overall, it was observed that the AAHE speakers were significantly less fluent than the NHE speakers. In order to confirm that, we performed a fluency judgment test on both groups by native speakers of Hindi. We extracted sentences produced by native and non-native audio files and embedded them in a webpage[1]. We provided the website link to five native speakers of Hindi and requested them to rate the audio files on a scale from 1 to 5, 1 when perceived as the least fluent and 5 when perceived as the most fluent. The average fluency of the NHE and AAHE speakers obtained was 4.94 (SD = 0.31) and 4.14 (SD = 0.82), respectively. As the scores are quite close and standard deviations are high, we decided to subject the fluency judgment scores of the evaluators to a Linear Mixed Effects (LME) test. For the LME test, scores were considered dependent variable, the two groups of speakers (NHE vs AAHE) were considered fixed effects, and evaluators and individual speakers were considered random effects. The resulting LME model was constructed on R [11] using the package $lme4$ [2]. Subjecting the model to a Type-II Wald χ^2 test for the Analysis of Deviance (Anova) test, it was seen that the evaluators' ratings for the two groups, NHE and AAHE, were significantly different ($\chi^2 = 7.2, df = 1, p < 0.001$). The estimates of the intercept and difference from the AAHE group are provided in Table 1.

Table 1. Estimates of the LME models for fluency judgment scores

	Estimate	Std. error	df	t-value	p-value
Intercept	4.94	0.25	7.58	19.87	0
AAHE	−0.80	0.29	6.96	−2.78	<0.05

---

[1] https://sites.google.com/view/testoffluency/home.

3   Speech-to-Text Setup

In order to assess the robustness of the current S2T systems in accommodating the said accent mismatch, we chose the following four popular commercial S2T APIs for decoding the task-specific speech data:

- Amazon Transcribe [1]
- Google Cloud Speech to Text API [4]
- IBM Watson Speech to Text service [5] and
- Microsoft speech-to-text service built on their JavaScript SDK [7]

As the above S2T systems are commercial systems, details about their acoustic and language models are not available in the public domain. Therefore, the purpose of this study is not to comment on any individual S2T system, but to make a robust assessment of the targeted accent mismatch. While submitting the speech data to each of the S2T APIs for transcription, the language is set to Hindi. All S2T systems produce the transcript in Devanagari script for the input Hindi-English code-switched speech data.

3.1   Normalization of Reference Transcription

The hypothesized transcriptions were produced by the considered S2T APIs in Devanagari script. On the other hand, the reference transcripts of the NHE group speech data consisted of English words or phrases written in both Devanagari and Latin scripts. A snippet of the transcription of the NHE group data is provided in Fig. 1 (a). It is seen that the words 'thunderbird' and 'transitions' are written in both Devanagari and Roman script. For normalizing the inconsistency, the transcriptions of the NHE group data have been manually corrected, and an example of the corrected snippet is shown in Fig. 1 (b).

The speech recognition performance is measured using the word error rate (WER), defined as:

$$\text{WER (in \%)} = 100 * (D + S + I)/N \tag{1}$$

where D is the total number of deletions, S is the total number of substitutions, I is the total number of insertions and N is the total number of words in the reference transcription. For this purpose, a python script[2] was used. The results of the S2T experiments are discussed in the following section.

4   Results and Discussion

For studying the impact of L1 influences on L2, we decoded the NHE and AAHE group speech data with each of the chosen S2T APIs. The resulting hypotheses are then evaluated against the normalized reference transcription. Figure 2 shows the overall recognition performances for native (NHE) and non-native accent

---

[2] http://progfruits.blogspot.com/2014/02/word-error-rate-wer-and-word.html.

(a)

H: इसी के साथ हम **thunderbird** के इस ट्यूटोरियल के अंत में आ गये हैं P: isi ke sath hum thunderbird ke is tutorial ke ant me aa gaye hain E: With this we come to the end of the thunderbird tutorial
H: थंडरबर्ड में एक ईमेल अकाउंट कन्फिगर करें P: thunderbird me ek email account configure kare E: Configure an email account in thunderbird
H: आगे **slide transitions** के बारे में सीखते हैं P: aage slide transitions ke baare me sikhte hain E: Let us learn about slide transitions further on
H: ट्रांजिशनस्स वो प्रभाव हैं जो **slides** पर लागू किये जाते हैं जब हम प्रस्तुति में एक **slides** से दूसरी **slides** पर स्थानांतरण या **transitions** करते हैं P: transitions prabhav hain jo slides par lagu kiye jaate hain jab hum prastuti me ek slides se dusari slides par sthanantaran ya transitions karte hain E: transitions are those effect that are applied to slides when during presentation we transit from one slide to another

(b)

H: इसी के साथ हम थंडरबर्ड के इस ट्यूटोरियल के अंत में आ गये हैं P: isi ke sath hum thunderbird ke is tutorial ke ant me aa gaye hain E: With this we come to the end of the thunderbird tutorial
H: थंडरबर्ड में एक ईमेल अकाउंट कन्फिगर करें P: thunderbird me ek email account configure kare E: Configure an email account in thunderbird
H: आगे **स्लाइड ट्रांज़िशन्स** के बारे में सीखते हैं P: aage slide transitions ke baare me sikhte hain E: Let us learn about slide transitions further on
H: ट्रांज़िशन्स प्रभाव हैं जो स्लाइड्स पर लागू किये जाते हैं जब हम प्रस्तुति में एक स्लाइड्स से दूसरी स्लाइड्स पर स्थानांतरण या ट्रांज़िशन्स करते हैं P: transitions prabhav hain jo slides par lagu kiye jaate hain jab hum prastuti me ek slides se dusari slides par sthanantaran ya transitions karte hain E: transitions are those effect that are applied to slides when during presentation we transit from one slide to another

Fig. 1. A snippet of the reference transcript of NHE group data where H represents the transcript in Hindi, P represents the phonetic transcription of H, and E represents the translation of H in English, showing (a) inconsistent scripting of English words in blue, red, and purple colour in reference transcript (H) and (b) transcription obtained after normalizing the inconsistency in scripting. (Color figure online)

(AAHE) cases yielded by each of the S2T APIs in terms of WER. The average WER across all the four S2T systems comes out as 27.32% and 38.33% for the NHE and AAHE groups, respectively. Evidently, a systematic increase in WER is noticed for the AAHE group.

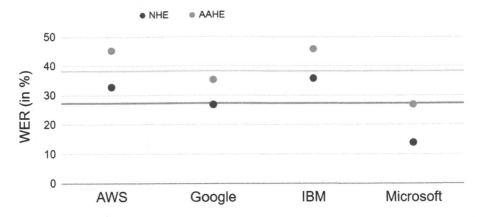

Fig. 2. Plot showing the WERs when NHE and AAHE group speech data corresponding to identical text is decoded separately with four popular S2T systems. For each
group of data, the horizontal line shows the WER averaged over all four S2T systems.

In order to reveal the sources of the errors, we looked into the constituents
of the WER in each case, as shown in Fig. 3. All the S2T systems have shown
a similar trend in all three constituents of errors. The gap in the recognition
performance between NHE and AAHE can be attributed to the increased substitution errors. It is worth highlighting that the NHE and AAHE speech data
are collected independently, hence the background conditions in the two are not
identical. In contrast to the NHE data, some of the files in the AAHE data carry
significant background noises like recording hums, ambient sounds, traffic noise,
etc. In order to assess the impact of such background differences on the WERs
obtained for the corresponding test sets, we manually extracted the beginning,
end, and inter-word silences from 5 speech files corresponding to 5 speakers
from both NHE and AAHE test datasets. These extracted silence portions were
concatenated and then decoded with each of the APIs. Despite varying background acoustic events in the said silence portions, we did not find any textual
output being produced by the APIs. This allows us to argue that the different
background conditions in the two test sets do not contribute significantly to the
WERs and therefore, the said differences are hypothesized to be caused solely
due to the acoustics differences between the native and non-native groups of
speakers.

As mentioned earlier, our intention is not to compare the recognition performance across the considered S2T systems. Yet we wish to clarify that the high
WERs yielded by the IBM system are partly attributed to the reduction of the
sampling rate of the input speech data from 16 kHz to 8 kHz as IBM supports
only the 8 kHz model for Hindi which is also known as the Telephony model[3].

---

[3] https://cloud.ibm.com/docs/speech-to-text?topic=speech-to-text-models-ng.

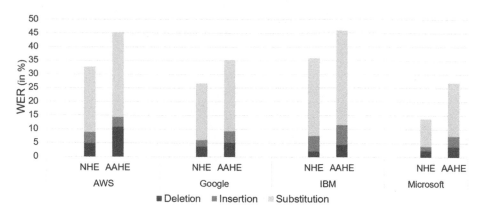

Fig. 3. Breakup of the WER for NHE and AAHE speech data for a better understanding of the sources of errors.

The Microsoft system has yielded the least errors. Since we have taken the NHE group of data from the Microsoft challenge itself, this could be a possible reason why the Microsoft API is outperforming the others. Our objective is not to highlight the inter-API performance comparisons but to emphasize the gap in the performance of NHE and AAHE speech which is consistent across the two groups for the four S2T APIs.

In this work, we have shown that the S2T APIs perform less efficiently when non-native Hindi-English speech is given as input. This shows that the state-of-the-art S2Ts are not completely able to accommodate the accented varieties of Hindi-English. Even though our study is restricted to Assamese accented Hindi-English speech, we postulate that the same may be true for other Hindi accents. As mentioned earlier, in a multilingual country like India, accommodating accented varieties of lingua-franca ensures better inclusiveness in S2T systems.

The WER gap noticed between the native and non-native transcriptions in this study motivates us to look into the possible causes of such differences. It is argued that the accented L2 speech is often coloured by the L1 speech characteristics [18]. It is also seen that at times, L2 speech features are atypical of both L1 and L2 characteristics.

A look into the error patterns of the AAHE group, performed on the Microsoft API output, as it is the least erroneous hypothesis, revealed some recurring patterns. Some of those patterns are summarized in Table 2. As seen in the table, Assamese speakers' production of the /tʃ/ is consistently recognized as /s/. Similarly, the long vowel /iː/ in /kiː/ is recognised as /i/. The word /kəmanɖ/ ending with a complex coda /nɖ/ is recognized as /kəman/. We can also see that the voicing in word final bilabial plosive /b/ in /tɛːb/ changes to a voiceless plosive /p/ in /tɛːp/ in the decoded speech.

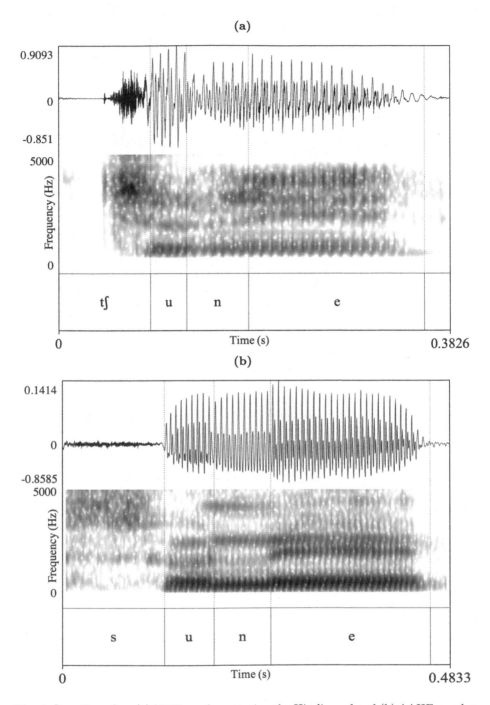

Fig. 4. Iteration of an (a) NHE speaker uttering the Hindi word and (b) AAHE speaker uttering the phoneme /tʃ/ of as /s/.

Table 2. Highly substituted words from AAHE speech showing Assamese L1 influence on Hindi-English L2

Words	Reference	Hypothesis	Words	Reference	Hypothesis
चुनें	tʃune	sune	यह	jəh	je
save	sew	sirf	प्रविष्ट	prəwiʃt	prəweʃ
save	sew	sef	की	ki:	ki
keyword	ki:wərd	ki:bord	command	kəmand	kəman
libre	libər	liwər	tab	tɛb	tɛp
sorter	sɔrtər	ʃətər			

These errors confirm that these are indeed induced by the L1 influence of the Assamese speakers. Assamese phonology differs from Hindi phonology in several respects, despite both languages being from the same language family. For instance, Assamese does not have any affricates in the language and hence, any affricate present in the loan words is pronounced as a fricative by Assamese L1 speakers. From Fig. 4 (a) and (b), which belongs to NHE and AAHE group respectively, we can see that the word /tʃune/ is actually pronounced as /sune/ by the Assamese speaker. Similarly, unlike many other Indian languages, Assamese does not have any phonological length distinction in the vowels. Hence, the long vowels in the L2s (English or Hindi) are often mispronounced as shorter vowels by Assamese speakers. This must have resulted in the misrecognition of the /i:/ vowel as /i/, as shown in Table 2.

When we look into the errors in the words such as /prəwiʃt/ and /kəmand/ are concerned, an interesting pattern emerges. In these words, which are loan words from English, the Assamese speakers have resorted to cluster simplification of the word final coda reducing the final /ʃt/ and /nd/ to /ʃ/ and /n/, respectively. In the case of Indian English, it has been noticed that /s/ + stop (e.g. ask), stop + stop (e.g. project), liquid + nasal (e.g. film), etc. are some of the clusters that are usually mispronounced and difficult for Tibeto-Burman speakers to produce [17]. The Assamese speakers, in a similar way, find it difficult to produce the consonant clusters, resorting to cluster simplification by means of deletion of consonants. Another dominant error is the word final devoicing of the voiced coda in the Hindi produced by Assamese speakers. As seen in Table 2, the coda in the word /tɛ:b/ is produced as a voiceless plosive /p/. This devoicing pattern is also noticed in the loan words of Assamese (e.g. the Arabic word for book /kita:b/ becoming /kitap/ in Assamese). Again, it is also observed that in the English produced by the speakers of Tibeto-Burman languages, such devoicing is dominant [17].

The discussion above is provided in order to argue that the errors noticed in the S2T system in decoding Hindi speech by Assamese speakers are not random. Rather, these errors are systematic and induced by the native phonology of the Assamese speakers. Considering that, it is imperative that S2T systems address the predictable errors in the developed systems which will ensure enhanced inclusiveness in the systems.

5   Conclusion

In this paper, we have studied the influence of Assamese L1 on Hindi-English L2. For the same, a few commercial S2T systems were used to decode the task-specific data in order to estimate the accent mismatch. Our study finds a significant influence of L1 on current S2T systems. On further analysis of the error patterns of the Assamese accented speech, it is shown that they happen to correlate with the L1 phonology and phonotactics.

References

1. Amazon Transcribe: Speech to Text - AWS. https://aws.amazon.com/transcribe. Accessed 14 Mar 2022
2. Bates, D., Mächler, M., Bolker, B., Walker, S.: Fitting linear mixed-effects models using LME4. J. Stat. Softw. **67**(1), 1–48 (2015). https://doi.org/10.18637/jss.v067.i01
3. Diwan, A., et al.: Multilingual and code-switching ASR challenges for low resource Indian languages. In: Proceedings of Interspeech (2021)
4. Google Cloud: Speech-to-Text: Automatic Speech Recognition. https://cloud.google.com/speech-to-text. Accessed 04 Mar 2022
5. IBM Watson: Watson Speech to Text. https://www.ibm.com/cloud/watson-speech-to-text. Accessed 09 Mar 2022
6. Mennen, I.: Phonological and phonetic influences in non-native intonation. Trends Linguist. Stud. Monogr. **186**, 53 (2007)
7. Microsoft Azure: Speech-to-Text. https://azure.microsoft.com/en-us/services/cognitive-services/speech-to-text. Accessed 01 Mar 2022
8. Mishra, S., Mishra, A.: Linguistic Interference from Hindi in Indian English. Int. J. Stud. Engl. Langu. Lit. **4**(1), 29–38 (2016)
9. Office of the Registrar & General Census Commissioner, India: C-17 population by bilingualism and trilingualism (2011). https://censusindia.gov.in/2011census/C-17.html. Accessed 24 Mar 2022
10. Office of the Registrar General & Census Commissioner, India: Family-wise grouping of scheduled and non-scheduled languages (2011). https://censusindia.gov.in/2011Census/Language-2011/Statement-9.pdf. Accessed 24 Mar 2022
11. R Core Team: R: A Language and Environment for Statistical Computing. R Foundation for Statistical Computing, Vienna, Austria (2019). https://www.R-project.org/
12. Rasier, L., Hiligsmann, P.: Prosodic transfer from L1 to L2. Theoretical and methodological issues. Nouveaux cahiers de linguistique française (New Noteb. French Linguist.) **28**, 41–66 (2007)
13. Seide, F., Li, G., Yu, D.: Conversational speech transcription using context-dependent deep neural networks. In: Proceedings of Twelfth Annual Conference of the International Speech Communication Association (2011)
14. Tomokiyo, L.M.: Lexical and acoustic modeling of non-native speech in LVSCR. In: Proceedings of Sixth International Conference on Spoken Language Processing (2000)
15. Vu, N.T., Wang, Y., Klose, M., Mihaylova, Z., Schultz, T.: Improving ASR performance on non-native speech using multilingual and crosslingual information. In: Proceedings of Fifteenth Annual Conference of the International Speech Communication Association (2014)

16. Wiltshire, C., Sarmah, P.: Voicing contrasts in the stops of Indian English produced by Assamese speakers. Proc. Meet. Acoust. **42**(1), 060003 (2020)
17. Wiltshire, C.R.: The "Indian English" of Tibeto-Burman language speakers. Engl. World Wide **26**(3), 275–300 (2005)
18. Wiltshire, C.R.: Uniformity and Variability in the Indian English Accent. Elements in World Englishes. Cambridge University Press (2020). https://doi.org/10.1017/9781108913768

ClusterVote: Automatic Summarization Dataset Construction with Document Clusters

Daniil Chernyshev[✉] and Boris Dobrov

Research Computing Center, Lomonosov Moscow State University, Moscow, Russia
chdanorbis@yandex.ru

Abstract. Creating a summarization dataset is a costly task due to the amount of expertise and human work required to compose quality summaries. To alleviate the issue, several pseudo-summary approaches were developed, but due to a lack of domain adaptation mechanism, they were not applied beyond language model pretraining. We find that this shortcoming can be overcome by leveraging document clusters. We propose ClusterVote, a pseudo-summarization approach that accounts for domain summarization patterns by studying links between related documents. The method can be configured for different levels of granularity and produce both extractive and abstractive summaries. We evaluate the approach by collecting Telegram news summarization dataset and testing state-of-the-art models. The experimental results show that the most refined variant of ClusterVote has similar extractive properties to CNN/Daily Mail dataset and proves to be challenging for summarization systems.

Keywords: Abstractive summarization · Dataset for summarization · Clustering

1 Introduction

Text summarization is one of the most challenging and demanded domains of Natural Language Processing. The task can be conceptualized as text compression which has two approaches: extractive and abstractive. Extractive summarization leverages existing text fragments to produce a compression that would retain all necessary information. Abstractive summarization expands the extractive approach with additional language resources to paraphrase the extractive fragments into the most concise summary. Training an abstractive summarization system requires a collection of examples with quality summaries. The most common approach to obtaining such data is hiring human experts. However, the amount of work and expertise required to compose quality summaries impose high costs on the procedure. A cheaper alternative would be leveraging resources with prewritten summaries, but such solution is feasible only for a limited selection of domains. Furthermore, significant stylistic and layout differences between subdomains exacerbate

© Springer Nature Switzerland AG 2022
S. R. M. Prasanna et al. (Eds.): SPECOM 2022, LNAI 13721, pp. 99–113, 2022.
https://doi.org/10.1007/978-3-031-20980-2_10

the situation due to strong pattern bias which later dominates the training signal of the summarization systems [9], making them unsuitable for transfer learning.

To alleviate the issue, several universal automatic dataset construction procedures have been proposed [19–21,23]. The idea is to exploit sentence-wise statistics to determine extraction patterns and use the selected sentence subset as a pseudo-summary. This approach proved to be efficient for pretraining language models for abstractive summarization that produce current state-of-the-art results in both supervised and unsupervised settings, such as Pegasus [21] and PRIMERA [19]. However, the heuristics used in existing pseudo-summary methods are human-agnostic and, thus, the extracted sentence subset may significantly differ from the real summary.

Given the source document only, we are limited to the author's viewpoint and cannot derive an unbiased pseudo-summary that would align with the average reader's perception. However, a global salience of source content can be approximated by studying connections with related documents. By selecting the most cited/mentioned sentences we can obtain an objective extractive pattern that would reflect community interest. Following that idea, we propose a new method for pseudo-summary construction - ClusterVote. Unlike previous approaches, our method can produce both extractive and abstractive summaries of variable granularity and accounts for domain on the community level. Using this method, we build Telegram News dataset for abstractive summarization based on data for Telegram Data Clustering Contest 2020[1]. We evaluate different variations of the method by comparing them with the previously proposed pseudo-summary baseline [2] in terms of task complexity and factuality. The results show that the most refined version of ClusterVote has similar extractive properties to popular CNN/Daily Mail dataset [13] and poses the most challenge to state-of-the-art models.

2 Related Work

2.1 News Summarization Datasets

Datasets were always the cornerstone of abstractive summarization research. Historically the first large-scale dataset for mixed summarization was The New York Times Annotated Corpus [18] with several hundred thousand articles written between 1987–2007 that have paired summaries composed by library scientists. However, due to low accessibility and lack of attention in the scientific community that dataset was overshadowed by CNN/Daily Mail [13]. Originally introduced for question answering by Herman et al. [7], CNN/Daily Mail was adapted for abstractive summarization by Nallapati et al. [13] and since then it served as the standard for abstractive summarization evaluation. Due to low abstractiveness of this dataset Narayan et al. [14] later proposed Xsum dataset with extremely compressed summaries for BBC articles. At the same time, Grusky et al. [6] addressed the lack of publisher diversity by scraping HTML metatags from web articles of 38 publishers and constructing Newsroom dataset.

---

[1] https://contest.com/docs/data_clustering2.

2.2 Pseudo-summary Methods

Summarization datasets contain layout and stylistic biases that differ between sub-domains [9]. This makes knowledge transfer inefficient and implies that the dataset should be constructed exclusively for the domain. But due to high costs of manual obtainment researchers sought to develop a universal automatic solution. Several pseudo-summary dataset construction methods were proposed but they were generally employed in pretraining. One of the first to apply the idea to train the language model for summarization was Yang et al. [20]. In their TED model, they exploited the inverted pyramid[2] concept and used the leading sentences of the article as a summary. Zhang et al. [21] showed that this strategy performed worse than random sampling and proposed Pegasus model that utilizes ROUGE [10] score to find the most representative sentences as a proxy summary for summarization pretraining. Xiao et al. [19] followed pyramid evaluation method [15] to expand Pegasus approach to multi-document summarization and use it to pretrain PRIMERA summarization model. Zhong et al. [23] introduced event-based summarization pretraining that aims to recover randomly masked sentences given their event descriptions as a prefix for the input text and, thus, train the language model for controlled summary generation.

3 Constructing Dataset with ClusterVote

As the basis for our experiments, we chose data provided for Data Clustering Contest 2020 hosted by Telegram. The goal of the contest was to cluster news articles based on various features: language, categories, and topics. The result of this process are news threads which essentially should contain only contextually similar documents. Based on the contextual similarity assumption, we develop a Cluster-Vote method that ranks sentences based on popularity of presented information.

3.1 Telegram Data Clustering Contest 2020 Dataset

There are multiple languages in Telegram Data Clustering Contest dataset, however, we processed only the English part. This part has more than 560 000 articles from 1346 publishers covering a time span of 52 days. Since Telegram did not provide ground truth labels for the contest data, the clusters were collected manually[3] To ensure coherence, we filtered out all data that had less than 50 words in the main body and had more than 30% of numeric characters. Afterward, we followed a simple iterative clustering procedure.

To optimize clustering performance, all data was split into 72-hour buckets with 24-hour overlap to take into account the possible 48-hour lag that is typical for analytical articles. Each bucket was clusterized in two steps using DBSCAN [4] algorithm with cosine distance. First, all articles in the bucket were clusterized

---

[2] https://en.wikipedia.org/wiki/Inverted_pyramid_(journalism).
[3] All scripts used for dataset collection are available at: https://github.com/dciresearch/ClusterVote.

according to mentioned named entities to isolate different subjects. Then, these clusters were broken down into smaller event-wise subclusters with standard tf-idf vectors on leading 4 sentences of the article. At this stage recall is more important than precision as our method will further refine the clusters.

3.2 ClusterVote Method

The document context can be described as a set of textual facts. This means that contextual similarity can be interpreted as similarity of presented fact sets. Following that logic, the document clusters are formed around some factual core that remains constant regardless of document. The distance of individual fact to this core reflects how interested is the community. The closest (zero-distance) facts were ranked as salient by majority of authors and can be considered as the basis for objective document-wise summary, while the farthest facts were omitted in most documents likely due to their supplementary nature.

Given that facts are naturally grouped into sentences, the cluster's factual core can be represented as the most common similar sentence subset. This subset can be identified by pairing each sentence with sentences of all other documents in the cluster and then calculating the relative number of support the sentence received:

$$vote(s_i) = |\{D_k \mid s_i \notin D_k, \exists s_j \in D_k : s_j \equiv s_i\}| \tag{1}$$

where D_k is k-th document of cluster and s_i is sentence. By selecting sentences that received support over some threshold we can obtain a cluster summary from document's viewpoint. Varying the sentence selection threshold would yield summaries of different levels of granularity. Naturally, sampling sentences over the same document would yield an extractive summary. To obtain an abstractive summary we can sample the sentences from any other document in the cluster. As a side effect, this process identifies cluster outliers and identical articles, dropping which will improve overall clustering quality and will ensure contextual similarity. In some sense, the documents are voting for sentences from other documents in the cluster, hence the name of our method, ClusterVote.

To pair sentences, we used DBSCAN algorithm with cosine distance and sentence embeddings obtained by paraphrase-mpnet-base-v2 model from Sentence-Transformers [17]. To avoid redundancy, connections within the same document were blocked by setting distances to ∞. Since both total number and diversity of cluster sentences can vary, we dynamically set the neighborhood threshold ε with grid search to guarantee that the maximum distance within the cluster would not exceed the paraphrase threshold $d_{par} = 0.2$. We classified as outliers all articles in which sentences had been paired only with articles that had more than 60% of zero vote sentences and as identical which had more than 80% of similarly paired sentences. We produced two variants of summaries:

- CV-full – vote threshold $t_{vote} = 1$
- CV-max – vote threshold $t_{vote} = \max(\{vote(s_i) \mid s_i \in \text{Article}\})$

In each clustering pair the article to serve as a source of summary sentences was chosen according to the ratio of paired sentences.

Comparison with LexRank. The ClusterVote method can be thought of as a specific variant of unweighted LexRank [3] with additional edge filtering. Such filtering can be conceptualized as a reduction of a sentence similarity graph to a cluster graph where the only remaining connected components are cliques. Since each node's degree centrality scores cannot be influenced by nodes other than those in clique, LexRank is guaranteed to preserve clique-wise centrality and, thus, produce the same ranking as ClusterVote.

3.3   Dataset Statistics

After all clustering and filtering procedures, we were left with 110 713 source-summary pairs. For convenience, we name the resulting dataset Telegram News. We split our summarization dataset into training (80%, 88 573), validation (10%, 11 070), and test (10%, 11 070) sets. Since our dataset uses artificial summaries, their human-likeliness should be evaluated. The simplest way to address that is to compare to existing human collected datasets. Table 2 compares our dataset to popular summarization datasets. We chose CNN/Daily Mail since it is the standard for testing single document summarization systems. Additionally, we compare with Newsroom as its automatic HTML metatag scraping approach is a direct alternative for our ClusterVote method in the internet news domain. Besides ClusterVote summaries, we compare a simple pseudo-summary baseline obtained by taking leading 3 sentences from a paired summary article (denoted as Pseudo Lead). In previous work, this approach proved to be eligible for training abstractive summarization models [2]. Example of pseudo-summaries is provided in Table 1.

In addition to length statistics, we report extractive metrics [6] to give some insights into the abstractiveness of automatic cluster-based summaries. Extractive fragment coverage is a percentage of words in the summary that were retained during the summarization process:

$$\text{Coverage}(A, S) = \frac{1}{|S|} \sum_{f \in F(A,S)} |f| \tag{2}$$

where A is an article text, S is a summary text, $F(A, S)$ is a set of summary fragments that were extracted from the article and $|t|$ is number of words in text t. This metric demonstrates vocabulary similarity and, thus, word-substitution paraphrases. Extractive fragment density is the average length of extractive fragment f to which each word in the summary belongs:

$$\text{Density}(A, S) = \frac{1}{|S|} \sum_{f \in F(A,S)} \sum_{w \in f} w \cdot |f| = \frac{1}{|S|} \sum_{f \in F(A,S)} |f|^2 \tag{3}$$

while density looks similar to coverage it is sensitive to the number of extractive fragments. For instance, if we have a summary of length of 60 and the total length of extractive fragments of 42, we will have a density of 29.4 in case of only one extractive fragment and of 14.7 if there are two equally sized fragments while

Table 1. Example of pseudo-summary strategies. ClusterVote variants provide more information than Pseudo Lead, but CV-max completely filters out the citations.

Source URL: https://www.vanguardngr.com/2020/04/ronaldinho-says-arrest-and-confinement-has-been-hard/
Pseudo Lead: Kindly Share This Story: Former Brazilian football star Ronaldinho said on Monday that his arrest and subsequent house arrest in Paraguay for using a false passport was "a very hard blow". "I would never have imagined myself in such a situation," said the former Barcelona and Paris Saint-Germain striker in an interview with the Paraguayan newspaper ABC
CV-full: Former Brazilian football star Ronaldinho said on Monday that his arrest and sub-sequent house arrest in Paraguay for using a false passport was "a very hard blow". Ronaldinho and his brother Roberto de Assis Moreira are accused of entering Paraguay in possession of false passports. "I was completely caught off guard when I found out that these passports were not valid," Ronaldinho said in his first public statement since his arrest two days after arriving in Asuncion at the beginning of March. Since April 7 they have been under house arrest at the Palmaroga Hotel in the historic centre of the Paraguayan capital. Ronaldinho said he hopes to be released "as soon as possible" after cooperating with the Paraguayan police investigation. Ronaldinho and his brother face up to five years in prison if found guilty
CV-max: Ronaldinho and his brother Roberto de Assis Moreira are accused of entering Paraguay in possession of false passports. Since April 7 they have been under house arrest at the Palmaroga Hotel in the historic centre of the Paraguayan capital. Ronaldinho and his brother face up to five years in prison if found guilty

coverage will be 0.7 regardless of fragment partition. The maximum value of extractive density is equal to the length of the summary, thus, to negate dataset summary length distribution effect it should be normalized. The normalized density indicates the proportion of whole sentence paraphrases.

Table 2. Comparison of different automatic summary construction approaches to popular abstractive summarization datasets. "norm." is length normalized values.

Dataset	Source # words	Summary # words	Coverage	Density	
				raw	norm.
CNN/DM [13]	781	56	89%	3.87	0.07
Newsroom [6]	659	27	83%	9.51	0.36
Telegram news					
Pseudo Lead	438	88	87%	26.10	0.29
CV-full		237	91%	43.43	0.18
CV-max		95	92%	28.81	0.30

The first noticeable trait is that our dataset has generally shorter source articles, while summaries are at least two times longer on average than summaries of CNN/Daily Mail and Newsroom. Nevertheless, Newsroom has the highest length normalized average density while CNN/Daily Mail has the lowest. Among our summaries, CV-full has the lowest density but it is more than two times larger than of CNN/Daily Mail and CV-max has the same density as Pseudo Lead. This indicates that lower vote sentences are likely to contain more full-phrase paraphrases. On the other hand, the average coverage is around 90% for all summaries but Newsroom which has 83%. This implies that most paraphrasing in summaries is based on word reordering.

The next question is how faithful is paraphrasing? Factual mistakes are common in abstractive summarization models, and it has been shown that training dataset plays a major role in erroneous text hallucinations [11]. Since summary is a text compression it must contain no other information than the source article. Therefore, factual correctness must have a higher priority than abstractiveness. Currently, there is no universal measure for factuality since fact definition heavily relies on the extracted context. To address different factual aspects, we measure multiple summary-source precision metrics. Phrasal Accuracy complements extractive fragment coverage reflecting a phrase extraction ratio:

$$phrase_{acc}(A, S) = \text{ROUGE-}2_{prec}(S, A) \tag{4}$$

High phrasal extractiveness guarantees that summary sentences align with text's content, while low values indicate excessive paraphrasing or unrelated external information. Named entity overlap (NEO) is a percentage of named entities that have been correctly reproduced in summary:

$$NEO(A, S) = \frac{|NE(A) \cap NE(S)|}{|NE(S)|} \tag{5}$$

where $NE(T)$ is named entities of text T. Named entities define the contextual core and, thus, do not tolerate any distortions in most cases. Factual accuracy is a percentage of summary subject-relation-object fact triplets supported by the source article:

$$fact_{acc}(A, S) = \frac{|Facts(A) \cap Facts(S)|}{|Facts(S)|} \tag{6}$$

$fact_{acc}$ is the basic way to measure factuality in summarization [5]. We use Spacy[4] to extract named entities and OpenIE[5] to extract fact triples for metrics.

The common problem with mentioned metrics is that they are not robust to synonymous substitutions. This renders them misleading in extreme paraphrasing scenarios. To accommodate this case, we report BERTScore [22] summary-article precision which has been shown to have a better correlation with human judgement in FRANK factuality metric benchmark[6] [16].

---

[4] https://spacy.io/.

[5] https://nlp.stanford.edu/software/openie.html.

[6] https://frank-benchmark.herokuapp.com/.

Table 3 compares datasets in terms of factuality. First of all, our automatic summaries have a significantly higher percentage of extracted phrases than summaries from popular datasets. This means that our summaries are less likely to contain unsupported content. But, despite higher extractiveness, Pseudo Lead is more erroneous in terms of named entity reproduction than more abstractive counterparts, being the most inaccurate in the comparison set. Since NEO and $fact_{acc}$ require exact matches, it was expected that the most extractive approach, CV-max, demonstrates the highest results. However, according to $fact_{acc}$ CNN/Daily Mail has the most unfaithful summaries. This is the result of metric strictness that penalizes any paraphrasing. Since CNN/Daily Mail has the lowest extractiveness metrics, with a normalized average density of 0.07, n-gram-based measures are ineffective. Therefore, auxiliary embedding-based metrics are essential. According to BERTScore CNN/Daily Mail still has the lowest factuality, though it is marginally lower than Newsroom. Unexpectedly, CV-full method exhibits the highest BERTScore factuality almost twice of CNN/Daily Mail and 6% more than Pseudo Lead and CV-max. Considering lower extractiveness and $fact_{acc}$ values, this result reaffirms the hypothesis that lower voted sentences are likely to be more paraphrased.

Table 3. Factuality statistics for datasets.

Dataset	$phrase_{acc}$	NEO	$fact_{acc}$	BERTScore
CNN/DM [13]	49.78%	78.12%	9.39%	36.28%
Newsroom [6]	53.89%	76.42%	38.39%	38.42%
Telegram news				
Pseudo Lead	72.10%	75.53%	44.57%	63.41%
CV-full	79.28%	80.18%	54.57%	**69.77%**
CV-max	**83.09%**	**84.38%**	**61.90%**	63.15%

4   Evaluation

The main concern about any dataset is "how eligible it is for the task?" or "how trivial is the solution pattern?" Answering that question requires experimenting with systems of various complexity. A good dataset should avoid two extremes: a low performance of the most advanced approaches would indicate inconsistency in solution patterns that is likely to be attributed to noisy examples [8], while high performance of the simplest strategies will reveal strong pattern bias [14]. Additionally, since our summaries were obtained automatically by leveraging external information (cluster of related documents), by benchmarking solutions we are also studying how efficiently this information can be derived from the source document only. We evaluate the performance of state-of-the-art abstractive summarization models in both supervised and unsupervised settings and compare them to extractive baselines.

4.1   Extractive Baselines

Lead-k. The most common baseline in text summarization is taking k leading sentences of the source document as a summary. Usually, those sentences introduce facts essential for document context comprehension. However, in the news domain leading sentences can cover the whole summary. This is due to the widespread inverted pyramid news writing scheme, that ensures that the information is presented in the order of salience. According to the scheme, the first paragraph must contain the minimum information set to give the reader idea of the story. The first paragraph usually consists of 2–4 sentences, hence the common value $k = 3$. This strategy is considered to be a lower performance bound for news summarization.

Oracle. The popular method for approximating an upper performance bound for text summarization is the greedy oracle. The idea is to iteratively sample source sentences to maximize the reference summary similarity metric.

TextRank. TextRank is a sentence-level extractive summarization system proposed by Mihalcea et al. [12]. TextRank was proposed at the same time as LexRank and is based on the same PageRank [1] algorithm but was designed for single document summarization. TextRank defines the lower performance bound for extractive summarization systems.

Table 4. Model performance comparison for Pseudo Lead summaries.

Model	ROUGE-1	ROUGE-2	ROUGE-L	# words
Extractive baselines				
Lead-3	74.41%	64.31%	68.57%	84
Oracle	80.16%	70.67%	74.40%	85
TextRank	47.46%	30.89%	37.81%	92
Unsupervised				
PRIMERA	36.49%	19.33%	25.63%	146
Pegasus	42.68%	28.23%	34.62%	79
Supervised				
PRIMERA	72.13%	62.66%	66.43%	102
Pegasus	76.17%	66.53%	70.68%	90

4.2   Abstractive Summarization Models

At the moment of writing this article, Pegasus [21] and PRIMERA [19] models achieve state-of-the-art results in unsupervised abstractive summarization. Both models were specifically pretrained for abstractive summarization, but

PRIMERA specializes in multi-document setting and has four times larger input limit thanks to sparse attention. In a supervised setting both models achieve the same or comparable results to state-of-the-art methods. Fine-tuning these models will provide insights into similarity of automatic summarization dataset construction approaches and the effects of pretraining biases.

4.3   Setup

In the Oracle baseline we maximize the average of ROUGE-1 and ROUGE-2 F1 scores. In Lead-k we choose $k = 3$ for Pseudo Lead and CV-max and $k = 6$ for CV-full. TextRank number of extracted sentences is controlled by desired summary length which we configured to the average length of reference summaries. For a fair comparison of abstractive summarization models, we limit input text to Pegasus maximum input length of 1024 tokens. To generate summaries, we use beam search with beam size 5 and trigram blocking. We report ROUGE F1 scores and prediction-source precision factuality metrics: $phrase_{acc}$, NEO, $fact_{acc}$, and BERTScore.

4.4   Summarization Metrics

Table 4 reports Pseudo Lead reference summaries results on test set. As expected, Lead-3 baseline performs better than more complex non-Oracle methods. However, only 64% of phrases come from article lead and the best extractive strategy won't cover more than 70%. Due to strong extractive positional bias, universal unsupervised methods will significantly underperform. Since PRIMERA was trained for multi-document summarization it is biased towards longer summaries and produces more irrelevant content than Pegasus in unsupervised setting. Even though fine-tuning improves the performance, the length bias is still strong, preventing the PRIMERA from surpassing the Lead-3 baseline.

Table 5. Model performance comparison for CV-full summaries.

Model	ROUGE-1	ROUGE-2	ROUGE-L	# words
Extractive baselines				
Lead-6	56.96%	47.49%	50.24%	176
Oracle	86.15%	78.70%	80.87%	227
TextRank	58.28%	44.60%	47.77%	218
Unsupervised				
PRIMERA	45.60%	30.25%	32.81%	146
Pegasus	38.00%	28.01%	31.95%	79
Supervised				
PRIMERA	66.91%	57.24%	60.02%	162
Pegasus	65.47%	56.29%	58.80%	160

The results for CV-full evaluation are presented in Table 5. Despite longer summaries, the upper bound for extractive method performance is significantly higher with Oracle average ROUGE-2 score of 79%. Lead baseline is noticeably less efficient in this case which indicates a more uniform salient sentence distribution. PRIMERA outperforms Pegasus in both supervised and unsupervised settings, however, the difference for fine-tuned models is marginal. This suggests that lower PRIMERA performance on Pseudo Lead summaries was attributed to the model's length bias.

CV-max performance is reported in Table 6. Despite similar average reference summary length, Lead-3 baseline has the worst performance in this case, covering only 39% of summary phrases. In contrast, Oracle achieves the maximum extractive phrase coverage of 81%. These two facts combined mean that CV-max summaries are indeed extractive but require complex strategies for sentence sampling. For PRIMERA this type of reference is slightly more familiar than Pseudo Lead, meanwhile Pegasus summaries differ the most. However, just like with Pseudo Lead, Pegasus outperforms PRIMERA in both supervised and unsupervised settings due to the same length bias persistence of the latter. Overall performance of fine-tuned abstractive summarization model in CV-max scenario is similar to CV-full which indicates the consistency of extractive patterns during vote threshold reduction.

Table 6. Model performance comparison for CV-max summaries.

Model	ROUGE-1	ROUGE-2	ROUGE-L	# words
Extractive baselines				
Lead-3	52.07%	38.60%	43.56%	84
Oracle	87.00%	81.14%	83.72%	85
TextRank	43.04%	26.73%	33.70%	92
Unsupervised				
PRIMERA	37.03%	21.60%	27.32%	146
Pegasus	39.12%	23.71%	30.87%	79
Supervised				
PRIMERA	60.92%	51.36%	54.87%	114
Pegasus	64.91%	55.33%	59.09%	88

To study the extractive patterns, we report Oracle extracted sentence relative distribution in Fig. 1. As it can be seen, Pseudo Lead is extremely skewed towards the first sentences of the article which explains extraordinary Lead-3 performance. As was noted earlier, CV-full is significantly more balanced, showing almost uniform distribution for the first half of the source sentences, however, the probability of sampling sentences after that point falls sharply. CV-max summaries are the most natural of all, bearing the most extractive pattern similarity to CNN/Daily Mail. Considering that CV-max is a more refined version of CV-full, we can conclude that lower voted sentences are sentences that were frequently filtered out from the original material or rarely placed at the top of inverted pyramid. The inverted pyramid scheme also explains the undersampling of concluding sentences as those are used to provide optional comments or background information about subjects and events. This does not imply that this information cannot be salient, as CNN/Daily Mail distribution demonstrates the otherwise, however, the relevance of this content is strictly dependent on the reader's knowledge.

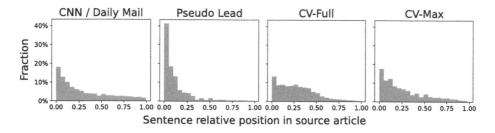

Fig. 1. Oracle extracted sentence relative position distribution for each summary type. We use CNN/Daily Mail as the baseline for comparison since most previous work on dataset biases studied the effect of that dataset on summarization model performance.

4.5   Factuality Metrics

To assess dataset factuality bias, we compare factuality metrics before and after finetuning. If examples in the training set promote extrinsic hallucinations (not directly deducible from the source text), we will observe token-wise factuality degradation for models that were specifically pretrained to leverage source text facts only. Pegasus was trained to recover sentences that had the most common extractive fragments with a text remainder. Given that these extractive fragments contain the same phrasal form of facts and entities, Pegasus is expected to have high NEO and $fact_{acc}$ values. Since PRIMERA expands Pegasus approach for multi-document clusters and prioritizes named entity frequency over extractive density and does not employ any source-summary fact connection verification procedures, the model is likely to be pretrained on both more abstractive and noisier summaries and, therefore, produce less faithful texts.

Table 7. Factuality scores for abstractive summarization models.

Model	$phrase_{acc}$	NEO	$fact_{acc}$	BERTScore
Unsupervised				
PRIMERA	86.74%	90.69%	76.47%	54.65%
Pegasus	98.13%	98.74%	93.42%	70.16%
Supervised - Pseudo Lead				
PRIMERA	87.97%	85.74%	64.83%	73.10%
Pegasus	93.74%	90.12%	74.82%	74.62%
Supervised - CV-full				
PRIMERA	91.61%	88.64%	69.76%	79.78%
Pegasus	95.99%	93.26%	80.35%	84.58%
Supervised - CV-max				
PRIMERA	96.02%	95.04%	82.51%	75.95%
Pegasus	96.44%	95.49%	83.10%	79.71%

Table 7 provides the results of our factuality measurements. Just as hypothesized, PRIMERA has a lower factuality than Pegasus. However, its lower NEO was not expected as the model was trained specifically to consider named entities in cases where Pegasus would underestimate their importance. Unsupervised Pegasus has an almost 100% named entity reproduction rate and over 93% fact triplet overlap which is explained by 98% phrasal overlap. However, BERTScore at 70% suggests that summaries have altered context meaning likely due to phrase permutation or omitted words.

Fine-tuning models on our datasets shifts the extractive behavior. In all cases, PRIMERA learns to follow the text more carefully, while Pegasus starts to paraphrase. Despite the positional bias, the least extractive summaries are produced after fine-tuning on Pseudo Lead summaries. On the other hand, with this type of summary we observe the strongest factuality decline for both models. Considering that CV-max reference summaries promote the most extractive behavior and yet have higher BERTScore, Pseudo Lead summaries are likely to be inconsistent with the source article. CV-full holds the middle ground, having the best BERTScore and more abstractive models than CV-max which again confirms "lower vote - more abstractive" hypothesis. Interestingly, all generated summaries have substantially higher factuality and extractiveness than references they were learning to replicate. This hints an existence of strong extractive bias in pretrained summarization models that prevents them from learning abstractive patterns.

5   Conclusion

In this work, we proposed ClusterVote, a new method for automatic construction of a summarization dataset that, in contrast to previous approaches, produces pseudo-summaries with objective extractive patterns by leveraging document cluster connections. Using the method, we construct a Telegram News dataset. We evaluated two extreme cases of ClusterVote granularity: CV-full – sentences with at least one vote, and CV-max - the most refined version with maximum cluster support. We compared these pseudo-summaries to our previous Pseudo Lead baseline that exploits inverted pyramid news structure and alternative publishers. According to statistics, CV-max is the most extractive of all yet has the closest resemblance to human-annotated datasets like CNN/Daily Mail in terms of sentence extraction pattern. CV-max summaries also show the highest factuality, however, CV-full lower measurements are likely attributed to higher abstractiveness which was consistently suggested during our experiments. Despite that, both strategies were found fairly difficult for state-of-the-art abstractive summarization models, achieving only 66% ROUGE-1 after fine-tuning. The equivalence of extreme cases suggests that max-full interpolation will be also eligible for summary proxy. The models themselves have demonstrated a biased behavior during the fine-tuning process with PRIMERA failing to abolish summary length bias and Pegasus hardly deviating from familiar from pre-training extractive strategy. We believe that both bias and low abstractiveness issues can be overcome by data scaling as larger clusters will have more diverse voting patterns as well as better paraphrase ranking.

Acknowledgments. The work of Daniil Chernyshev (experiments, survey) was supported by Non-commercial Foundation for Support of Science and Education "INTELLECT". The work of Boris Dobrov (general concept, interpretation of results) was supported by the Russian Science Foundation (project 21-71-30003).

References

1. Brin, S., Page, L.: The anatomy of a large-scale hypertextual web search engine. Comput. Netw. ISDN Syst. **30**, 107–117 (1998)
2. Chernyshev, D., Dobrov, B.: Abstractive summarization of Russian news learning on quality media. In: van der Aalst, W.M.P., et al. (eds.) AIST 2020. LNCS, vol. 12602, pp. 96–104. Springer, Cham (2021). https://doi.org/10.1007/978-3-030-72610-2_7
3. Erkan, G., Radev, D.R.: LexRank: graph-based lexical centrality as salience in text summarization. J. Artif. Int. Res. **22**(1), 457–479 (2004)
4. Ester, M., Kriegel, H.P., Sander, J., Xu, X.: A density-based algorithm for discovering clusters in large spatial databases with noise. In: Proceedings of the Second International Conference on Knowledge Discovery and Data Mining (1996)
5. Goodrich, B., Rao, V., Liu, P.J., Saleh, M.: Assessing the factual accuracy of generated text. In: proceedings of the 25th ACM SIGKDD International Conference on Knowledge Discovery and Data Mining, pp. 166–175 (2019)
6. Grusky, M., Naaman, M., Artzi, Y.: Newsroom: a dataset of 1.3 million summaries with diverse extractive strategies. In: Proceedings of the 2018 Conference of the North American Chapter of the Association for Computational Linguistics: Human Language Technologies, Volume 1 (Long Papers), pp. 708–719 (2018)
7. Hermann, K.M., et al.: Teaching machines to read and comprehend. In: Advances in Neural Information Processing Systems 28 (2015)

8. Kang, D., Hashimoto, T.B.: Improved natural language generation via loss truncation. In: Proceedings of the 58th Annual Meeting of the Association for Computational Linguistics, pp. 718–731. Association for Computational Linguistics (2020)
9. Kryściński, W., Rajani, N., Agarwal, D., Xiong, C., Radev, D.: BookSum: a collection of datasets for long-form narrative summarization. arXiv:2105.08209 (2021)
10. Lin, C.Y.: ROUGE: a package for automatic evaluation of summaries. In: Text Summarization Branches Out, pp. 74–81 (2004)
11. Maynez, J., Narayan, S., Bohnet, B., McDonald, R.: On faithfulness and factuality in abstractive summarization. In: Proceedings of the 58th Annual Meeting of the Association for Computational Linguistics, pp. 1906–1919 (2020)
12. Mihalcea, R., Tarau, P.: TextRank: bringing order into text. In: Proceedings of the 2004 Conference on Empirical Methods in Natural Language Processing (2004)
13. Nallapati, R., et al.: Abstractive text summarization using sequence-to-sequence RNNs and beyond. In: Proceedings of The 20th SIGNLL Conference on Computational Natural Language Learning, pp. 280–290 (2016)
14. Narayan, S., Cohen, S.B., Lapata, M.: Don't give me the details, just the summary! topic-aware convolutional neural networks for extreme summarization. In: Proceedings of the 2018 Conference on Empirical Methods in Natural Language Processing, pp. 1797–1807 (2018)
15. Nenkova, A., Passonneau, R.: Evaluating content selection in summarization: the pyramid method. In: Proceedings of the Human Language Technology Conference of the North American Chapter of the Association for Computational Linguistics: HLT-NAACL 2004, pp. 145–152 (2004)
16. Pagnoni, A., Balachandran, V., Tsvetkov, Y.: Understanding factuality in abstractive summarization with FRANK: a benchmark for factuality metrics. In: Proceedings of the 2021 Conference of the North American Chapter of the Association for Computational Linguistics: Human Language Technologies, pp. 4812–4829. Association for Computational Linguistics (2021)
17. Reimers, N., Gurevych, I.: Sentence-BERT: Sentence embeddings using Siamese BERT-networks. In: Proceedings of the 2019 Conference on Empirical Methods in Natural Language Processing and the 9th International Joint Conference on Natural Language Processing (EMNLP-IJCNLP), pp. 3982–3992 (2019)
18. Sandhaus, E.: The New York times annotated corpus (2008)
19. Xiao, W., Beltagy, I., Carenini, G., Cohan, A.: PRIMERA: pyramid-based masked sentence pre-training for multi-document summarization. In: Proceedings of the 60th Annual Meeting of the Association for Computational Linguistics (Volume 1: Long Papers), pp. 5245–5263 (2022)
20. Yang, Z., et al.: TED: a pretrained unsupervised summarization model with theme modeling and denoising. In: Findings of the Association for Computational Linguistics: EMNLP 2020, pp. 1865–1874 (2020)
21. Zhang, J., Zhao, Y., Saleh, M., Liu, P.: PEGASUS: pre-training with extracted gap-sentences for abstractive summarization. In: International Conference on Machine Learning, pp. 11328–11339. PMLR (2020)
22. Zhang, T., Kishore, V., Wu, F., Weinberger, K.Q., Artzi, Y.: BERTScore: evaluating text generation with BERT. arXiv preprint arXiv:1904.09675 (2019)
23. Zhong, M., et al.: Unsupervised summarization with customized granularities. arXiv preprint arXiv:2201.12502 (2022)

Comparing Unsupervised Detection Algorithms for Audio Adversarial Examples

Shanatip Choosaksakunwiboon[1], Karla Pizzi[1,2], and Ching-Yu Kao[1,2(✉)]

[1] Technical University Munich, Garching, Germany
`shanatip.choosaksakunwiboon@tum.de`
[2] Fraunhofer Institute for Applied and Integrated Security, Garching, Germany
{`karla.pizzi,ching-yu.kao`}`@aisec.fraunhofer.de`

Abstract. Recent works on automatic speech recognition (ASR) systems have shown that the underlying neural networks are vulnerable to so-called adversarial examples. In order to avoid these attacks, different defense mechanisms have been proposed. Most defense mechanisms discussed so far are based on supervised learning, which requires a lot of resources. In this research, we present and compare various unsupervised learning methods for the detection of audio adversarial examples (including autoencoder, VAE, OCSVM, and isolation forest), requiring no adversarial examples in the training data. Our experimental results show that some of the considered methods successfully defend against a simple adversarial attack, e.g., with isolation forest. Even in a more elaborate attack scenario that considers human psychoacoustics, we still achieve a high detection rate with the cost of slightly increased false positive rate, e.g., with an autoencoder. We expect our detailed analysis to be a helpful baseline for further research in the area of defense methods against audio adversarial examples.

Keywords: Speech recognition · Adversarial examples · Adversarial detection

1 Introduction

Voice-based AI or virtual assistants are more and more part of safety-critical technologies including smart homes, vehicles or even medical tools [19]. Already a slight speech-to-text transcription error in these technologies can lead to unexpected behaviour, potentially posing a danger to the users. This can, e.g., be enforced with so-called adversarial examples. These instances contain noise that is manipulated in such a way that it can fool the neural network-based systems into a misclassification. Recent findings have proven the existence of adversarial examples in the audio domain [5], creating noise that allows an audio file to be transcribed to any chosen target transcription. Some methods even allow to create noise that is imperceptible to human ears and remains robust when played over-the-air [20,23].

© Springer Nature Switzerland AG 2022
S. R. M. Prasanna et al. (Eds.): SPECOM 2022, LNAI 13721, pp. 114–127, 2022.
https://doi.org/10.1007/978-3-031-20980-2_11

Due to the relative complexity of these attacks, there are not many published works on effective defenses against these attacks yet, which greatly motivates our work. In this work, we mainly build on [24]. Here, the authors presented an approach to analyse how an input propagates through a neural network in order to detect whether it is adversarial or not. When classifying adversarial examples, the neural network may exhibit noticeably higher-than-expected activations at some subset of neurons which differ from when classifying benign examples. Hence, the authors propose to extract hidden activations from the model under adversarial attack and train a second neural network to distinguish between benign and adversarial inputs to the first model. As this approach requires analysing the hidden layers, they call it dense layer analysis (DLA). DLA in its original version is based on supervised training. Inspired by DLA, we work in an unsupervised training setup that neither requires labeled data nor adversarial examples for training. Our research leverages this idea by employing the DLA approach in an unsupervised manner to detect audio adversarial examples. This makes it much easier to apply in a real-world setting, as the costly calculation of adversarial examples is not needed anymore. We show that our detection model trained with a two-stage training framework achieves an accuracy of up to 0.962 and a recall of 1.0 against a simple audio attack; and an accuracy of up to 0.845 and recall of 0.87 against a psychoacoustic-based adversarial attack.

2 Related Work and Background

In this section, we present some background in automatic speech recognition and state-of-the-art works on adversarial attacks and defenses with a special focus on the audio domain.

2.1 Automatic Speech Recognition

Automatic speech recognition (ASR) is the ability of a computer program to transcribe spoken words to text. Let $f(\cdot)$ be the ASR system. Then, $f(x) = y$ denotes the output transcription y for a given audio input x. An ASR system usually consists of two parts: an acoustic model and a decoder (often with a language model). The acoustic model receives audio as input and yields the probabilities over letters in the alphabet as output. An approximate search algorithm (also called decoder) is used in combination with the language model to further convert these probabilities into sequences of words. The language model is used to resolve linguistic ambiguity such as homophones and select the most likely sequences of words to form a sentence. Among the common deep learning-based open-source ASR systems are Mozilla DeepSpeech, Lingvo, Kaldi, and SpeechBrain. In this research, we focus on Mozilla DeepSpeech [14] and Speech-Brain [21]. We build our detection framework based on the English pre-trained DeepSpeech model version 0.9.3 and an English CRDNN-based SpeechBrain model[1].

---

[1] https://huggingface.co/speechbrain/asr-crdnn-transformerlm-librispeech.

2.2   Adversarial Examples in General

Modern ASR systems are susceptible to adversarial examples [1]. Adversarial examples are manipulated inputs that cause the models to produce incorrect outputs. Let $f(\cdot)$ denote a trained model (e.g., an ASR system). Let $h(\cdot)$ be a human judgement. For a given benign example x and corresponding ground-truth output y, an adversary can create an adversarial example x' by adding a small adversarial perturbation δ, i.e., $x' = x + \delta$ (where $\|\delta\| < \epsilon$ for some small $\epsilon \in \mathbb{R}^+$), while $h(x) = h(x')$ and $f(x) \neq f(x')$. An attacker may create an adversarial example that forces the ML model to misclassify the input as a specific target output. This is called a targeted adversarial example. In this work, we focus on targeted adversarial examples.

2.3   Adversarial Examples in Audio

Following Mendes and Hogan [12], we categorize the attacks into two groups, namely norm-bounded audio attacks and psychoacoustic-based audio attacks.

Norm-Bounded Audio Attacks. Many publications on adversarial attacks rely on the L_p norm (denoted as $\|\cdot\|_p$) to restrict the magnitude of the adversarial perturbation. Norm-bounded attacks (especially L_2 and L_∞-based) are very common in the image domain, while some powerful attacks in the audio domain also employ these norms to ensure the perturbation is small enough to be inaudible by humans. CW attack presented by Carlini and Wagner [5], which proposes a white-box attack to generate targeted audio adversarial examples based on optimizing the Connectionist Temporal Classification (CTC) loss, while using the L_∞ norm to constrain the amount of adversarial perturbation to be added. CommanderSong [31] and Yakura [29] attempt to generate robust over-the-air audio adversarial examples targeting the Kaldi and DeepSpeech model, respectively.

Psychoacoustic-Based Audio Attacks. A light mutation on the audio may already be easily detected by the human ear, whereas bigger mutations may remain undetected. As a result, crafting imperceptible audios using L_p norms can be quite challenging at times. The Dolphinattack [32] by Zhang et al. is one example of an untargeted, imperceptible, and robust audio adversarial attack that targets traditional, non-deep-learning-based ASR models. Their approach adds ultrasonic adversarial perturbations which have a frequency beyond 20 kHz (the upper bound of human-audible range).

The more novel approaches leverage the frequency masking phenomenon of the psychoacoustic principle. Frequency masking takes place when a louder sound (masker) causes the softer sounds at nearby frequencies (maskees) to be inaudible [13]. In other words, the masker (or the original audio signal) is creating a "frequency masking threshold", in which any signals (i.e., the adversarial perturbations) that fall below this threshold will be imperceptible. Qin et al. [20] gives for a detailed explanation on how to calculate the frequency masking threshold and how to compute the targeted imperceptible adversarial example. More examples of a masking threshold approach are the work by Schönherr et al. [23] and Szurley and Kolter [26]. The attack by Schönherr et al. creates an imperceptible audio adversarial example that successfully fools the Kaldi ASR system up to 98% of the time in a non-over-the-air scenario. Qin et al.'s imperceptible adversarial examples successfully fool the Lingvo model with 100% accuracy. When tested with imperceptible and simulated over-the-air adversarial examples, the attack success rate is approximately 50% (and 23% WER). Similarly, Szurley and Kolter succeed in attacking the DeepSpeech model with 100% success rate. However, in the over-the-air scenario, the attack succeeds with a word error rate of zero for three out of the four trials.

2.4   Audio Adversarial Defenses

With the increasing number of audio adversarial attacks, audio adversarial defenses also came into focus. Mendes and Hogan [12] categorize the defenses into two main categories, namely *mitigation methods* and *detection methods*.

Mitigation Methods. To mitigate the effects of adversarial examples, different pre-processing techniques can be applied to remove the adversarial perturbations and receive the correct results. Das et al. [6] and Andronic et al. [3] propose a mitigation method by applying MP3 compression to the audio adversarial examples to remove all signals below the human hearing range. The method works well in eliminating imperceptible adversarial examples, but results in performance degradation on benign examples. Subramanian et al. [25] showed that their method of additive white noise outperforms the MP3 compression defense method. There have also been proposed several mitigation methods using self-supervised learning. Wu et al. [28] uses the self-supervised learning based model "the Mockingjay" [9] as a feature extractor before the features are passed on to the anti-spoofing model to detect the fake voice. [10] proposed the Transformer Encoder Representations from Alteration (TERA) model, representing a more advanced self-supervised learning based denoising model than Mockingjay. Wu et al. [27] makes use of the benefit of the TERA model by proposing an attack-agnostic mitigation method that places K cascaded TERA models in front of the automatic speech verification (ASV) system as a first line of defense. In this work, however, we focus on detection methods.

Detection Methods. Instead of fixing the adversarial noise, another approach is to detect it and exclude it from being classified. Yang et al. [30], e.g., take advantage of the audio's temporal dependency property (i.e., the correlation between consecutive audio frames) to detect audio adversarial examples. The WaveGuard defense framework [7] aims to detect audio adversarial examples by looking out for a huge difference (measured by character error rate) between the transcriptions of the input audio x and the transformed input audio $g(x)$.

Further, Park et al. [17] are able to detect audio adversarial examples by adding noise to the outputs of the acoustic model (i.e., logits) before they are passed on to the decoder of the ASR.

The detection methods we have discussed so far only rely on the audio features extracted through some signal pre-processing methods (e.g., MFCC). Sperl et al. [24] and Paul [18] diverge from the above approaches, as they take advantage of the dense layer analysis (DLA) for adversarial example detection. They propose an adversarial detection with the assumption that dense layers in the neural network (NN) may carry security-sensitive information that can be used as features to train the alarm NN (the model used for detection). The DLA architecture from [18] is shown in Fig. 1. Akinwande et al. [2] utilize a similar method called "subset scanning", in which they observe strange spikes in the activations of some subset of neurons in specific layers in order to detect audio adversarial examples (generated by CW attack).

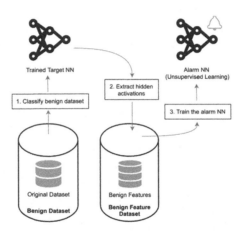

Fig. 1. Unsupervised DLA architecture used by Paul [18]. The benign hidden activations are extracted from the pre-trained target model (i.e., ASR system) during the classification of the benign dataset, the alarm model is trained using those benign hidden activations in an unsupervised setting in order to distinguish between benign and adversarial examples.

3   Methodology

Our work is inspired by the DLA technique. We further improve this approach by extracting activations from a different layer and exploring various unsupervised (or self-supervised) learning methods to detect audio adversarial examples. The DLA architecture [18,24] is displayed in Fig. 1. With our approach, we focus specifically on unsupervised-based adversarial detection in the audio domain.

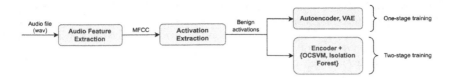

Fig. 2. Overview of the training process. (1) MFCCs are extracted from a clean audio file (wav format), (2) MFCCs are fed into the target model for activation extraction (3) the alarm models are trained using the extracted benign activations.

3.1   Target Model

Our target model is an ASR neural network used for transcribing speech to text. The goal is to defend the target model from adversarial attacks. In this research, we use the latest version of the DeepSpeech pre-trained model (version 0.9.3) as our main target model. We also conduct an extra experiment using SpeechBrain based on a CRDNN architecture.

3.2   Alarm Model

An alarm model is a model that aims to detect adversarial examples. It is trained to receive the extracted hidden activations as inputs and produce binary outputs (normal or adversarial). We experimented with multiple types of unsupervised alarm model, namely autoencoder, variational autoencoder (VAE) [8], one-class support vector machine (OCSVM) [22] and isolation forest [11]. The details of each of the models can be found in Table 1.

Our **autoencoder** consists of five layers. The autoencoder receives an array of benign activations as input, compresses it to a lower dimension of size 64, decompresses it back to their original size as output, and then calculates the reconstruction error (i.e., mean squared error) between the input and the output to determine if the input is benign or adversarial. A variant of an autoencoder is **VAE** [8]. Instead of mapping the input into a discrete latent vector, VAE maps the input to a distribution from which the latent vector is sampled. Unlike in autoencoder, the loss function in VAE consists of two components: reconstruction loss (i.e., mean squared error) and Kullback-Leibler (KL) divergence loss. The KL divergence loss ensures the distribution generated by the encoder is similar to the prior probability distribution of the input (which is assumed to be a Gaussian distribution by default). Our VAE consists of five layers (one input layer, three hidden layers, one output layer) and the same number of nodes in each layer.

An **OCSVM** [22] learns to profile the benign training samples by fitting a hypersphere to the training data. Then, new unseen examples are classified as adversarial if they lay outside of the hypersphere. The hypersphere is influenced by a choice of hyperparameters such as the kernel, ν, and γ. The parameter ν refers to the maximum fraction of outliers in the training set and minimum

Table 1. Alarm models used during experiments with CommonVoice dataset and Mozilla DeepSpeech as target model. The table shows the details of their architectures or hyperparameter settings that are selected through grid search. Note that for an extra experiment conducted with LibriSpeech dataset and SpeechBrain as target model, the hyperparameters of OCSVM and isolation forest are adjusted due to change in data distribution and a smaller dataset size.

Model name	Model details
Autoencoder VAE	– five layers
	– layer 1 (#neurons = input_size)
	– layer 2 (#neurons = 128, dense+ReLU)
	– layer 3 (#neurons = 64, dense+ReLU)
	– layer 4 (#neurons = 128, dense+ReLU)
	– layer 5 (#neurons = input_size, dense)
OCSVM	– kernel = rbf (radial basis function)
	– ν (nu) = 0.05[a]
	– γ (gamma) = 0.1[a]
Isolation forest	– n (training samples) = 1000[b]
	– m (isolation trees) = 100

[a] $\nu = 0.0001$ and $\gamma = 10.0$ for LibriSpeech dataset and SpeechBrain as target model.

[b] n (the number of randomly selected training samples for isolation tree construction) is scaled down to 300 for LibriSpeech dataset and SpeechBrain as target model due to smaller training set size.

fraction of support vectors. The parameter γ defines how far the influence of a single training example reaches which affects the broadness and curvature of the hypersphere. In our work, we use kernel = rbf (radial basis function) then set $\nu = 0.05$ and $\gamma = 0.1$ based on the hyperparameter tuning by applying grid search on the validation set consisting of both benign and adversarial activations. We usually keep the value of ν low to avoid too many misclassifications on benign examples. The value of γ totally depends on the data. In this case, we use a low γ which implies that the data are highly spread.

A variation of random forest, called **isolation forest** [11], is used for anomaly detection in an unsupervised setting. The algorithm assumes that anomalous instance is much easier to 'isolate' than a benign instance. In other words, it would take much fewer random partitions to isolate an anomalous data point when constructing an isolation tree compared to a benign data point. To construct an isolation tree, the algorithm sub-selects n samples from the training set and isolates them (i.e., applies random partitions) until each data point in the subset is isolated. We repeat the above steps in order to build a forest of m isolation trees. In our experiment, we set $n = 1000$ training samples based on the hyperparameter tuning by applying grid search on the validation set consisting of both benign and adversarial activations. We set $m = 100$ isolation trees based on the original paper [11], in which they empirically found that the optimal value for m is 100. According to [11], a small sample size n produces better isolation trees because the swamping and masking effects are reduced. Therefore, we try to keep a low value of n relative to the actual benign dataset size.

Table 2. Overview of the three experiments conducted.

Exp.	Dataset	Target model	Alarm model
1	**CommonVoice** (9000 benign train, 1000 benign test, 1000 adversarial test)	DeepSpeech v0.9.3	Autoencoder, VAE, OCSVM, isolation forest
2	Case 1: **CommonVoice** as training set (9000 benign train) and **LibriSpeech** as test set (100 benign test, 100 adversarial test) Case 2: **Mixed** training set and test set (combination of both CommonVoice and LibriSpeech	DeepSpeech v0.9.3	Autoencoder, VAE, OCSVM, isolation forest
3	**LibriSpeech** (3000 benign train, 100 benign test, 100 adversarial test)	SpeechBrain	Autoencoder, OCSVM, isolation forest

3.3 Training Process

Our training process consists of three major steps: audio feature extraction, activation extraction and alarm model training. The block diagram in Fig. 2 summarizes the flow of our training process. For activation extraction, we chose to extract from layer 2 of the DeepSpeech target model as [2] reports it to be the layer with most discriminative activations. For training of the autoencoder and VAE (deep-learning-based alarm models), we need one step which is feeding the model with the training set (i.e., the extracted benign activations). We denote this as one-stage training. For training of the OCSVM and isolation forest that may potentially suffer from curse of dimensionality, we solve this by applying a two-stage unsupervised training. In the first stage, we train an autoencoder with the extracted benign activations. We then discard the decoder and use the trained encoder as dimensionality reduction method to produce the learned representations of the benign activations. In the second stage, we adopt an unsupervised ML model (i.e., OCSVM or isolation forest) using the learned representations from the first stage as our training set.

4   Experiments

In this section, we explore the effects of different unsupervised learning algorithms on the performance of audio adversarial detection. The experiments we conducted are summarized in Table 2. In the following, we provide more details on the datasets and methods used.

4.1   Datasets

We use the English audio files of the Mozilla CommonVoice dataset [4]. To generate the corresponding adversarial examples with Mozilla DeepSpeech as the target model, we use an updated implementation of the CW attack[2] and an adapted version for the Qin attack. In addition, we use SpeechBrain as target model in combination with the LibriSpeech dataset [16]. To generate the corresponding adversarial examples, we use [15] for both the CW the Qin attack.

4.2   Evaluation Methods

To evaluate the performance of our approaches, we use accuracy, recall, and f1 score. For the evaluation of the autoencoder and the VAE, the mean squared error is used to calculate the adversarial score (i.e., a score that measures how much the observation deviates from the normality), while the classification decision is made based on a quantile-based adversarial threshold. In our work, we chose the quantile $q = 0.90$. The value of the threshold is calculated using the benign validation set. From the list of adversarial scores obtained from the benign validation set, the score on the 0.90-quantile of the list is set as the adversarial threshold. Setting the quantile to 0.90 implies that we are likely to misclassify around 10% of the benign test samples, but as a trade-off we are able to detect more adversarial test samples. Decreasing the quantile any further would result in too many misclassifications on the benign examples. Empirically, we believe a 0.90-quantile is the optimal threshold as it allows us to detect most of the adversarial examples while avoiding misclassifying too many benign examples. For the evaluation of the OCSVM, we learn a decision boundary (hypersphere) for the benign training set. Any test data points that lie outside of the hypersphere are considered adversarial. The generalization power and the broadness of the decision region are determined by the hyperparameters ν and γ. For the evaluation of the isolation forest, we calculate the adversarial score according to [11]. In our experiment, the classification is based on the following threshold according to [11]: If $s(x, n) > 0.5$, we consider it as adversarial, otherwise as an benign sample.

5   Results and Discussion

Table 3 summarizes the experimental results of our defense systems from experiment 1 in which we use the CommonVoice dataset as input and DeepSpeech

---

[2] https://github.com/timherng/audio_adversarial_examples.

as the target model. For defenses against the CW attack, two-stage training methods (i.e., OCSVM and isolation forest) significantly outperform the one-stage training methods (i.e., autoencoder and VAE) by achieving near-perfect performances. We propose the two-stage training with isolation forest as the better method to defend against the CW attack because of its great detection performance and faster training in comparison to OCSVM.

Table 3. Summary of results from **experiment 1** on DeepSpeech. OCSVM and isolation forest yield the best results on CW attack. The autoencoder trained with sub-selected features yields satisfactory results on Qin attack.

Attack method	Alarm model	Accuracy	Recall	F1 score
CW attack	Autoencoder[a]	0.8475	0.797	0.839
	VAE[a]	0.8555	0.818	0.850
	OCSVM	0.9655	0.994	0.966
	Isolation forest	0.9620	1.000	0.963
Qin attack	Autoencoder[b]	0.8430	0.797	0.835

[a] Autoencoder and VAE are trained and evaluated on sub-selected features (first half of the features) since we observe that they are potentially the most discriminative features.
[b] Similarly, this autoencoder is trained and evaluated on sub-selected features but only the first 2048 features (i.e., activations of the first audio frame).

The adversarial audio crafted by the CW attack is only quasi-imperceptible and still leaves many traces that are detectable by both the human ears and our autoencoder. An adversary can exploit this knowledge of our defense mechanisms to reduce those traces in the adversarial example by employing the Qin attack which tries to inject the perturbation with appropriate frequency into certain regions of the audio. Under the Qin attack, all methods considered lose in accuracy. As a workaround, we sub-select features that are believed to be potentially discriminative and use them for training to improve the detection performance. The autoencoder trained with 2048 sub-selected features achieves satisfactory results against Qin attack, see Table 3.

The results for experiment 2 are summarized in Table 4. In the first case of experiment 2, when trained with CommonVoice and tested with LibriSpeech, the one-stage training performance slightly drops for the CW attack, while the two-stage training misclassifies all LibriSpeech benign examples as adversarial. When evaluated on Qin attack using LibriSpeech test set, the performance of our autoencoder trained with sub-selected 2048 features drops (achieving a recall as low as 0.37). This empirically proves that 2048 feature sub-selection approach does not generalize well as it only works with CommonVoice. In the second case of experiment 2 we re-train the alarm models with mixed dataset. Here, the benign accuracy remains above 90% but adversarial accuracy drops by 20%.

Table 4. Summary of results from **experiment 2** on DeepSpeech trained with Common Voice training set and tested on CW attack with LibriSpeech test set.

Alarm model	Accuracy	Recall	F1 score	AUC
Autoencoder[a]	0.810	0.75	0.798	0.901
VAE[a]	0.745	0.87	0.773	0.803
OCSVM	0.500	1.00	0.666	–
Isolation forest	0.500	1.00	0.666	–

[a] Autoencoder and VAE are trained and evaluated on sub-selected features (first half of the features) since we observe that they are potentially the most discriminative features.

Hence, re-training with a mixed dataset does not solve the problem. According to the results, our two hypotheses are either: (1) layer 2 in DeepSpeech model holds poor discriminative power for LibriSpeech or (2) LibriSpeech might just not work well with DeepSpeech as target model. These hypotheses encourage us to conduct an experiment 3 in order to investigate a different target model, namely SpeechBrain.

Table 5. Summary of results of **experiment 3** on SpeechBrain. The autoencoder (AE) maintains benign accuracy over 90%, but detects CW/Qin-based adversarial examples poorly, hence the overall balanced accuracy is close to 0.50. OCSVM significantly improves the adversarial detection rate, with the expense of benign accuracy dropping to 82%, hence the overall balanced accuracy increases to over 0.80.

Method	CW attack (Qin attack)			
	Accuracy	Recall	F1 score	AUC
AE (full features)	0.585 (0.530)	0.22 (0.11)	0.346 (0.190)	0.824 (0.777)
AE (1st half features)	0.500 (0.500)	0.04 (0.04)	0.074 (0.074)	0.760 (0.760)
AE (2nd half features)	0.515 (0.495)	0.11 (0.07)	0.185 (0.122)	0.661 (0.540)
OCSVM	0.910 (0.845)	1.00 (0.87)	0.917 (0.849)	–
Isolation forest	0.550 (0.515)	1.00 (1.00)	0.687 (0.673)	–

According to the experiment results, the success of the approach depends on the target model and dataset. Using SpeechBrain as target model instead and two-stage training with OCSVM as alarm model gives us promising results against both CW attack and Qin attack, see Table 5 for the results of experiment 3. Here, OCSVM provides a good adversarial detection rate for both the CW and the Qin attack. Thus, empirically, it seems better to have separate target and alarm model for different datasets. For the CommonVoice dataset, Mozilla DeepSpeech as target model and two-stage training with isolation forest as alarm model are preferred to defend against the CW attack (but not Qin attack). For

LibriSpeech dataset, SpeechBrain as target model and two-stage training with OCSVM as alarm model are preferred to defend against both CW attack and Qin attack.

Table 6. Comparison with state-of-the-art adversarial detection methods against CW attack and Qin attack. On CW attack, our method significantly outperforms existing DLA approaches and performs comparably to other existing methods. On Qin attack, the input transformation method significantly outperforms our autoencoder trained with sub-selected features.

Attack	Method	Target model	Accuracy	Recall	F1 score	AUC
CW attack	Temporal dependency [30]	DS v0.4.1	–	–	–	0.936
	Input transformation [7]	DS v0.4.1	1.0	–	–	1.0
	Logit noising [17]	DS v0.1.0	–	1.0	–	–
	DLA by Sperl et al. [24]	DS v0.4.1	–	–	0.820	–
	DLA by Paul [18]	DS v0.9.3	0.891[a]	0	0	–
	Subset scanning [2]	DS v0.4.1	–	–	–	0.973
	Our DLA (isolation forest)	**DS v0.9.3**	**0.962**	**1.0**	**0.963**	–
Qin attack	Input transformation [7]	DS v0.4.1	1.0	–	–	1.0
	Our DLA (autoencoder)	**DS v0.9.3**	**0.843**	**0.797**	**0.835**	–

[a] The high accuracy of 0.891 is due to strongly imbalanced adversarial-benign test set.

We compare our adversarial detection methods with several state-of-the-art methods. In Table 6, we present our best methods with some cutting-edge pre-processing-based methods, non-machine-learning methods and original DLA-based methods. Note that [2] uses a similar approach to ours, hence the performance is similar to our method, though expressed through other measures.

6   Conclusion

In this paper, we implemented an unsupervised adversarial detection system for audio. We extended the DLA framework by Sperl et al. [24] by demonstrating the use of two-stage unsupervised training for the alarm model in order to improve the performance of our adversarial detection system. We showed that (1) our proposed methods are able to accurately distinguish between benign and adversarial audios generated by the CW attack. Our best detection model based on a trained encoder and isolation forest demonstrates the most effective performance achieving a high accuracy of 0.962, recall of 1.0 and f1 score of 0.963. The results show that we are able to outperform several modern defense systems. We also showed that (2) using an appropriate target and alarm model for different datasets can improve the adversarial detection performance. According to the experimental results, we could successfully identify the CW attack on the CommonVoice dataset using Mozilla DeepSpeech as the target model and two-stage training with isolation forest as the alarm model. For both the CW and the Qin attack, a successfull approach on the LibriSpeech dataset was SpeechBrain as target model and two-stage training with OCSVM as alarm model.

Acknowledgment. This research was supported by the Bavarian Ministry of Economic Affairs, Regional Development and Energy.

References

1. Abdullah, H., Warren, K., Bindschaedler, V., Papernot, N., Traynor, P.: SoK: the faults in our ASRs: an overview of attacks against automatic speech recognition and speaker identification systems. In: 2021 IEEE Symposium on Security and Privacy (SP), pp. 730–747. IEEE (2021)
2. Akinwande, V., Cintas, C., Speakman, S., Sridharan, S.: Identifying audio adversarial examples via anomalous pattern detection (2020)
3. Andronic, I., Kürzinger, L., Chavez Rosas, E.R., Rigoll, G., Seeber, B.U.: MP3 compression to diminish adversarial noise in end-to-end speech recognition. In: Karpov, A., Potapova, R. (eds.) SPECOM 2020. LNCS (LNAI), vol. 12335, pp. 22–34. Springer, Cham (2020). https://doi.org/10.1007/978-3-030-60276-5_3
4. Ardila, R., et al.: Common voice: a massively-multilingual speech corpus. In: LREC 2020 (2020)
5. Carlini, N., Wagner, D.: Audio adversarial examples: targeted attacks on speech-to-text. In: 2018 IEEE Security and Privacy Workshops (SPW), pp. 1–7. IEEE (2018)
6. Das, N., et al.: Compression to the rescue: defending from adversarial attacks across modalities. In: KDD Project Showcase (2018)
7. Hussain, S., Neekhara, P., Dubnov, S., McAuley, J., Koushanfar, F.: WaveGuard: understanding and mitigating audio adversarial examples. In: USENIX Security 2021 (2021)
8. Kingma, D.P., Welling, M.: Auto-encoding variational Bayes (2013). https://doi.org/10.48550/arxiv.1312.6114. https://arxiv.org/abs/1312.6114
9. Liu, A., Yang, S., Chi, P.H., Hsu, P., Lee, H.: Mockingjay: unsupervised speech representation learning with deep bidirectional transformer encoders. In: ICASSP 2020–2020 IEEE International Conference on Acoustics, Speech and Signal Processing (ICASSP) (2020)
10. Liu, A.T., Li, S.W., Lee, H.: TERA: self-supervised learning of transformer encoder representation for speech. IEEE/ACM Trans. Audio Speech Lang. Process. **29**, 2351–2366 (2021)
11. Liu, F.T., Ting, K.M., Zhou, Z.H.: Isolation forest. In: 2008 Eighth IEEE International Conference on Data Mining, pp. 413–422 (2008)
12. Mendes, E., Hogan, K.: Defending against imperceptible audio adversarial examples using proportional additive Gaussian noise (2020)
13. Mitchell, J.L.: Introduction to digital audio coding and standards. J. Electron. Imaging **13**, 399 (2004)
14. Mozilla: Project DeepSpeech (2021). https://github.com/mozilla/DeepSpeech
15. Olivier, R., Raj, B.: Recent improvements of ASR models in the face of adversarial attacks (2022). https://doi.org/10.48550/ARXIV.2203.16536. https://arxiv.org/abs/2203.16536
16. Panayotov, V., Chen, G., Povey, D., Khudanpur, S.: LibriSpeech: an ASR corpus based on public domain audio books. In: 2015 IEEE International Conference on Acoustics, Speech and Signal Processing (ICASSP), pp. 5206–5210 (2015). https://doi.org/10.1109/ICASSP.2015.7178964

17. Park, N., Ji, S., Kim, J.: Detecting audio adversarial examples with logit noising. In: Proceedings of the 37th Annual Computer Security Applications Conference (ACSAC 2021) (2021)
18. Paul, M.: An adversarial detection model for different data types. Master's thesis, Technical University of Munich (2021)
19. Pereira, A., Thomas, C.: Challenges of machine learning applied to safety-critical cyber-physical systems. Mach. Learn. Knowl. Extract. **2**, 579–602 (2020)
20. Qin, Y., Carlini, N., Cottrell, G., Goodfellow, I., Raffel, C.: Imperceptible, robust, and targeted adversarial examples for automatic speech recognition. In: International Conference on Machine Learning, pp. 5231–5240. PMLR (2019)
21. Ravanelli, M., et al.: SpeechBrain: a general-purpose speech toolkit (2021). arXiv:2106.04624
22. Schölkopf, B., Williamson, R., Smola, A., Shawe-Taylor, J., Platt, J.: Support vector method for novelty detection. In: Neural Information Processing Systems 12 (NIPS 1999), vol. 12, pp. 582–588 (1999)
23. Schönherr, L., Kohls, K., Zeiler, S., Holz, T., Kolossa, D.: Adversarial attacks against automatic speech recognition systems via psychoacoustic hiding (2018)
24. Sperl, P., Kao, C., Chen, P., Böttinger, K.: DLA: dense-layer-analysis for adversarial example detection. CoRR abs/1911.01921 (2019). https://arxiv.org/abs/1911.01921
25. Subramanian, V., Benetos, E., Sandler, M.B.: Robustness of adversarial attacks in sound event classification. In: Proceedings of the Detection and Classification of Acoustic Scenes and Events 2019 Workshop (DCASE 2019), pp. 239–243 (2019)
26. Szurley, J., Kolter, J.Z.: Perceptual based adversarial audio attacks (2019)
27. Wu, H., Li, X., Liu, A.T., Wu, Z., Meng, H., Lee, H.: Adversarial defense for automatic speaker verification by cascaded self-supervised learning models. In: ICASSP 2021 (2021)
28. Wu, H., Liu, A., Lee, H.: Defense for black-box attacks on anti-spoofing models by self-supervised learning (2020)
29. Yakura, H., Sakuma, J.: Robust audio adversarial example for a physical attack. In: Proceedings of the Twenty-Eighth International Joint Conference on Artificial Intelligence (2018)
30. Yang, Z., Li, B., Chen, P.Y., Song, D.: Characterizing audio adversarial examples using temporal dependency (2019)
31. Yuan, X., et al.: CommanderSong: a systematic approach for practical adversarial voice recognition. In: USENIX Security 2018 (2018)
32. Zhang, G., Yan, C., Ji, X., Zhang, T., Zhang, T., Xu, W.: DolphinAttack: inaudible voice commands. In: Proceedings of the 2017 ACM SIGSAC Conference on Computer and Communications Security (2017)

Celtic English Continuum in Pitch Patterns of Spontaneous Talk: Evidence of Long-Term Contacts

Maria Chubarova[✉] and Tatiana Shevchenko

Moscow State Linguistic University, 38 Ostozhenka St., Moscow 119034, RF, Russia
maryglazunova@yandex.ru, tatashevchenko@mail.ru

Abstract. The present study addresses the issue of national identities of young urban citizens in Celtic regions (Irish, Welsh, Scottish) manifested by pitch patterns in their spontaneous English speech. We believe that intonation may be an identifying factor due to the specific shape, distribution, frequency of usage of pitch patterns and their association with duration and pitch span. Corpora data of 36 adolescents from five British and Irish cities, equally balanced for gender, engaged in interactive tasks which elicited unprepared talk, were processed audio-visually, measured for FO, duration and pitch span and statistically tested. Our goal is to shift emphasis from variation which previous research on reading context-free sentences found "a potential for miscommunication' to common Celtic features in actual communication. The results suggest that residents of the areas which are known for long-term language contacts and common history are more likely to preserve their common pitch patterns. The overall picture of Celtic pitch patterns' continuum with typical rises, levels and rise-falls suggests that long-term contacts created long-standing patterns which might provide for successful across-dialect communication.

Keywords: Celtic English (Welsh, Irish, Scottish) · Spontaneous speech · Pitch patterns · Continuum

1 Background

The growing prestige of regional varieties of English in the British Isles claimed by David Crystal is supported by research in the field, and corpora data provide statistically verified comparisons.

Cross-dialect comparison of discriminating pitch patterns includes their shape, distribution, frequency of usage and association with duration, pitch span and intensity. Our early studies [1–3] were particularly focused on the role of pitch range variation of regional English in the British Isles: Welsh English proved to display the widest pitch range, while Irish English had the narrowest one. Recent research on Welsh English identification corroborated our finding on pitch span distinction [4].

Concerning specific Celtic pitch patterns shapes we found that rises, rise-falls and level tones were most common but they are used in varying proportions, their frequency

© Springer Nature Switzerland AG 2022
S. R. M. Prasanna et al. (Eds.): SPECOM 2022, LNAI 13721, pp. 128–138, 2022.
https://doi.org/10.1007/978-3-031-20980-2_12

of occurrence being geographically and socially determined [3]. The IViE corpus authors also found great variance in the British adolescents' reading of context-free sentences (declaratives, WH-questions, polar questions, echo-questions) as regards nuclear tones, which, the authors suggested, might be potentially the cause of miscommunication [5]. The basic finding in syntactical types distinctions consisted in the well-known principle that lexical-grammatical and intonation means were in trading relations, which resulted in the highest pitch of echo-questions, a feature common for all British dialects but displayed in varying degrees. The salient feature of rising patterns dominance in Belfast, predicted by previous research [6], appeared to have no analogy in other urban varieties of Irish English [7].

In search of rhythm patterns in the British Isles certain expectations to find common syllable-based patterns of Caribbean English in London, Punjabi English in Bradford and Welsh English in Cardiff failed. Grouping of dialects on geographical proximity principle was successful in case of two northern cities, Newcastle and Leeds, and, paradoxically, the Irish city of Dublin and Cambridge. The other Irish city, Belfast in Ulster, could not be coupled with Dublin Irish on account of their duration patterns. There was also evidence of considerable overlap between dialects which allows discrimination only at 0.3–0.35 levels. An important comment was that grouping of dialects on duration measurements did not coincide with those made on pitch and loudness [8].

The limitations of most previous work on cross-dialect comparisons consisted in the fact that it was based on reading sentences, identical texts or retelling a familiar fairy tale. The actual use of pitch patterns and the specific features of their configurations associated with duration, pitch span and intensity were to be found in spontaneous talk. Another point to consider was history of language contacts in each particular area which could account for certain paradoxical findings in digital analysis whose relevance we cannot doubt [8]. Celtic regions, for instance, present particular interest as specific for their pitch patterns and history of language contacts whose traces could be still noticeable in young people's speech. Describing cross-dialect variance as an aggravating condition in discourse and presenting the varieties as a patchwork of unrelated entities does not help to account for their differences and similarities; we have to look at the history of language contacts to understand and accept variation.

The present research is aimed at finding specific spontaneous talk pitch patterns characteristics typical of Irish, Welsh and Scottish English varieties compared to Cambridge English.

2   Methods

2.1   Material

The corpus: samples of unprepared speech of 36 British adolescents, 28 from the three Celtic areas (Irish, Welsh and Scottish) and 8 from Cambridge, aged 16–19, equally balanced for gender, were selected from the following sources:

a)The IViE Corpus [9]. The corpus compiles samples of adolescent speech collected between 1997 and 2000 in nine urban centers of the UK. For the current study we selected dialogue recordings of 32 students (16 girls and 16 boys) aged 16 at the time of the data collecting, coming from Belfast, Dublin, Cardiff, and Cambridge. The conversations covered the non-linguistic topic of teenage smoking and were conducted unsupervised, in friendly settings. The slightly tilted balance should be acknowledged: the group of the respondents from Cardiff is smaller than the other groups (two girls and two boys), which can be accounted for by lack of data taken from our earlier study [3].

b)The HCRC Map Task Corpus [10]. The corpus, collected in the 1990s at the University of Edinburgh for Human Communication Research Centre to fit the objectives of computational linguistics, provided samples of dialogues between teenagers aged 16–19 from Glasgow (four girls and four boys).

The corpus can be considered representative: it is balanced for gender and region; the respondents share the same occupation; pragmatically, the corpus meets the demands of style homogeneity as all the adolescents used their casual register for a friendly informal impromptu conversation; as regards speech acts, representatives by far prevail in all the samples. All the samples present a dialogue spontaneous speech about a predetermined subject; thus, they may be considered comparable.

The choice of the cities was guided by the study of the historical and geographic factors of the linguistic situation in the region, and the prosodic trends previously discovered in the studies of urban British intonation [6, 11, 13, 14]. Cambridge dialect was selected as a reference for comparing the Celtic areas speech with southern standard English [11].

Thus, the total corpus comprises samples of 36 speakers: four boys and four girls from each urban center (Belfast, Dublin, Glasgow, and Cambridge), and two boys and two girls from Cardiff.

2.2 Methods of Analysis

In order to assess the frequency and the structure of nuclear tones auditory and acoustic analyses were conducted.

At the stage of the auditory analysis the boundaries of intonation phrases were marked; in each intonation phrase a terminal nuclear tone was identified; nuclear tones were described and classified by a trained labeler as: simple tones (rise, fall, level) and complex tones (fall-rise, rise-fall). Statistical and comparative analyses followed.

Measurements

Out of 1288 nuclear tones marked at the stage of auditory analysis 1242 were handpicked for further acoustic analysis which could be accounted for by the quality of the recordings. The mean time of a dialogue is 120 s and the total duration of the selected recordings is 36 min.

The acoustic analysis was to verify the results of auditory analysis and identify the acoustic structure of nuclear tones. The samples were processed with Praat, v.6.1.13 [12] to determine the following pitch and temporal measurements:

Fundamental frequency measurements (F0): F0 max (Hz), F0 min (Hz) in a tone; F0 range of the rising element (st), F0 range (F0-span) of the falling element (st).

Duration measurements (T): duration of the falling element (ms), duration of the rising element (ms), duration of the level element (ms) in a nuclear tone.

Statistical Analysis

In order to verify the significance of the results obtained during the auditory and acoustic analyses and earmark significant principles of intergroup variation, a three-stage statistical analysis was carried out using the statistic toolbox of the computing environment MATLAB (MATrix LABoratory). The analysis was performed in three stages: 1) multivariate analysis of variance (MANOVA); 2) one-way analysis of variance (ANOVA); 3) comparative analysis of median values. The transition to the later stages of analysis was conditioned by the positive result at the previous stages.

The independent variables were specified as: 'city' ('Dublin', 'Belfast', 'Glasgow', 'Cambridge'); 'gender' ('male', 'female'); the dependent variables at the stage of nuclear tone frequency analysis were constituted by the quantity of nuclear tones of the following types: 'L' (level tones), 'F' (falling tones), 'R' (rising tones), 'FR' (falling-rising tones), 'RF' (rising-falling tones), and at the stage of tone duration analysis by the values of the tone duration: 'L duration' (level tone duration), 'R duration' (rising tone duration), 'F duration' (falling tone duration).

The null hypothesis suggested the absence of a significant variance between the groups motivated by the regional and gender factors. The hypothesis was considered true if the result of the analysis of variance exceeded the P-value preset as 0.05.

It should be acknowledged that the results of the acoustic analysis of Cardiff speech were not statistically verified for lack of sample data, so all the conclusions concerning this dialect are presumptive. Furthermore, the statistical analysis of the F0 range characteristics could not be conclusive, as the samples lacked normal distribution.

3   Results

3.1   Tone Frequencies in the Speech of Adolescents from the Five Cities

The first stage of MANOVA statistical analysis revealed significant intergroup variance. Hence, further analysis to find which factors determine the variance was required.

At the stage of ANOVA the significance of geographic variance between the groups determined by the geographic factor stood true for the rising tones (P-value $= 0.01 \leq 0.05$), the falling tones (P-value $= 0.0218 \leq 0.05$), and the rising-falling tones (P-value $= 0,0286 \leq 0,05$), while for the level tones (P-value $= 0.1208 \geq 0.05$) and the falling-rising tones (P-value $= 0.0671 \geq 0.05$) the intergroup variance was proved insignificant.

In the Fig. 1 below the distribution of tone frequencies in the speech of the adolescents from the five cities is presented.

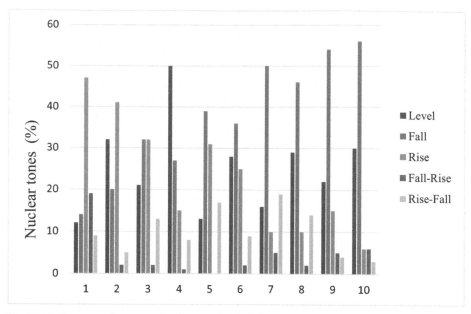

Fig. 1. Nuclear tone frequency in the speech of adolescents from the five cities (1 – Belfast, f; 2 – Belfast, m; 3 – Glasgow, f; 4 – Glasgow, m; 5 – Cardiff, f; 6 – Cardiff, m; 7 – Dublin, f; 8 – Dublin, m; 9 – Cambridge, f; 10 – Cambridge, m).

The tone frequency distribution analysis starkly illustrates geographic variance and transmits the idea of a melodic continuum primarily in the proportions of rising and falling tones. The Celtic dialects could be lined up from the most regionally marked Belfast dialect to Dublin which is the closest to southern standard dialect of Cambridge.

The speech of Dublin and Cambridge speakers is characterized by a dominant use of falling tones (Dublin: 50% f, 46% m; Cambridge: 54% f, 56% m). Glasgow and Cardiff tone frequency analysis showed similar shares of falling patterns (Glasgow: 32% f, 27% m; Cardiff: 39% f, 36% m), while Belfast speech is marked by the smallest share of falling tones (14% f, 2% m). The comparative analysis of the median values showed significant intergroup variance in falling tone frequencies between Belfast and Cambridge, as well as between Belfast and Dublin.

Rising tones are predominant in Belfast speech (47% f, 41% m). They make up a significant share of the total number of nuclear tones in Glasgow and Cardiff speech (Glasgow: 32% f, 15% m; Cardiff: 31% f, 25% m). The smallest proportion of rising tones was found in Dublin (10% f, 10% m) and Cambridge (15% f, 6% m). As demonstrated at the stage of the statistical analysis (2.2), Dublin and Cambridge rising tone frequencies are significantly different from Belfast and Glasgow.

Rising-falling tones are typical of all the Celtic varieties (Dublin: 19% f, 14% m; Cardiff: 17% f, 9% m; Glasgow: 13% f, 8% m; Belfast: 9% f, 5% m), while they are scarce in Cambridge tone repertoire (4% f, 3% m). The intergroup variance is significant between Cambridge and Glasgow, and Cambridge and Dublin values.

As regards gender variance we may suggest that the use of level tones is defined by gender factor rather than by regional variance: level tones prevail in the speech of males from all the five cities (Glasgow: 21% f, 50% m; Cardiff: 13% f, 28% m; Belfast: 12% f, 32% m; Dublin: 16 f, 29% m; Cambridge: 22% f, 30% m). Rising tones are prevalent in female speech, excluding females from Dublin. Complex tones are generally predominant in the speech of females; RFT are more common in the speech of female speakers from all the five cities.

3.2 The Acoustic Structure of Nuclear Tones

In our research we have aimed to define specific melodic features of the Celtic dialects both in tone frequencies and shapes. To outline the structure of a certain tone we collected data on fundamental frequency and duration.

Nuclear Tone Duration

Significant intergroup variance was confirmed at the stage of MANOVA. ANOVA allowed us to narrow down the variance to the following factors: "rising tone duration" (P-value = 0.01), and "falling tone duration" (P-value = 0.015), while the factor "level tone duration" does hot command variance between groups (P-value = 0.173).

The Table 1 below presents median values of falling and rising tone duration. No conclusive evidence of gender variance was found, so the table presents only data for joint city samples.

Table 1. Median values of falling (FTD) and rising tone duration (RTD) for joint city samples (ms).

	Belfast	Glasgow	Cardiff	Dublin	Cambridge
FTD	322	289	327	305	341
RTD	332	281	309	328	286

Cambridge adolescents' falling tones are longer in duration (341 ms), while Glasgow speech is characterized by the shortest falling tones (289 ms); the intergroup variance is significant as shown at the third stage of statistical analysis. By this parameter, Cambridge speech is more similar to Dublin, Cardiff, and Belfast.

Rising tone duration is a significant distinctive feature for Belfast and Glasgow; Belfast rising tones (332 ms) are maximal, whereas Glasgow ones are minimal in duration (281 ms).

Longer falling and rising tones are typical of Belfast speech, which makes it similar to Cardiff and Dublin data, while the tones are generally shorter in Glasgow.

Based on a number of relevant features and their clusters, such as both duration and frequency, Belfast pitch pattens are contrasted with Cambridge. Dublin and Cambridge tone duration values, however, are close for falling tones but not for rising tones. Glasgow tones are distinct in duration compared to all the other Celtic varieties.

As far as the structure of the complex rise-falling tone is concerned, we may suggest that Celtic RFT tends to have rising and falling elements of equal length, which makes it distinctive from the pattern previously reported for southern standard, in which the falling element is twice as long. The graph below shows the average ratios of the rising element duration to the falling element duration in rising-falling tones (RFT) (Fig. 2).

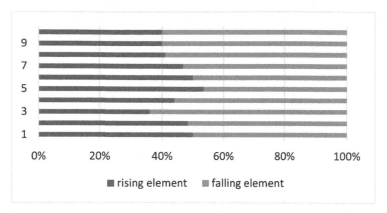

Fig. 2. Average ratios of the rising to the falling element duration in RFT (%).

Fundamental Frequency Range

Due to the lack of normal distribution the results of the range characteristics analysis are not statistically verified (Fig. 3).

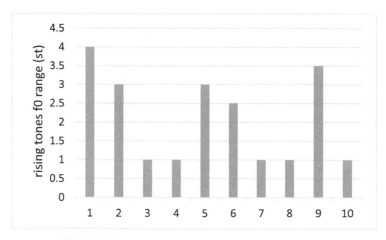

Fig. 3. Rising tones fundamental frequency range (st).

Rising tones in the speech of adolescents from Belfast (4 st f; 3 st m) and Cardiff (3 st f; 2.5 st m), and females from Cambridge (3.5 st) are wider (Fig. 4).

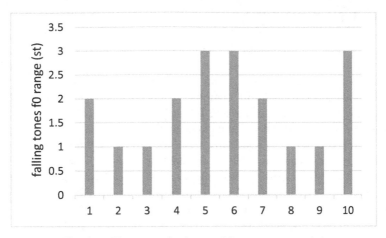

Fig. 4. Falling tones fundamental frequency range (st).

The data of the falling tones f0 range analysis defy any conclusive interpretation concerning the influence of the factors of geographic or gender variance. We may suggest that falling tones in the Celtic dialects, with the exception of Cardiff, are characterized by a narrow f0 range (Belfast: 2 st f, 1 st m; Glasgow: 1 st f, 2 st m; Cardiff: 3 st f, 3 st m; Dublin: 2 st f,1 st m; Cambridge: 1 st f,3 st m).

The graph below demonstrates the average ratios of F0-spans of rising element to F0-spans of the falling element in RFT. The common tendency is a wider F0-span in the falling element of the complex tone (Fig. 5).

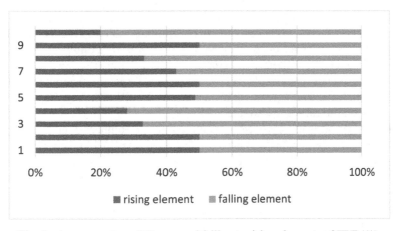

Fig. 5. Average ratios of F0 spans of falling to rising elements of FRT (%).

F0 spans of rising and falling elements of the other complex tone, FRT, are nearly equal in the speech of adolescents from Belfast (0.95 f /1 m) and Glasgow (1 f / 1 m). Cardiff (0.49 f / 0.34 m) and Dublin (0.75 f / 0.5 m) have a narrower rising element. The Cambridge data on the tone are scarce.

4 Discussion

By establishing correlation between the factor of region and pitch patterns characteristics of nuclear tones frequency, their acoustic structure determined by duration and pitch span, in spontaneous conversation of adolescents from five cities of Great Britain and Ireland we may conclude that Celtic-specific regional variance can, above all, be inferred from the frequencies of rising, falling, and rising-falling tones. The analysis of tone frequencies allows us to suggest the existence of a melodic continuum of Celtic city dialects.

Belfast dialect shows more regionally specific features than the other city dialects; rising tones are predominant, and falling tones are less frequent in the dialect. This result corroborates observations made in previous research by E. Jarman and A. Cruttenden [1976], as well as E. Grabe [2004]. In the current study we also found that rising tones in Belfast dialect are characterized by greater duration and FO span. The speech of adolescents from Glasgow and Cardiff also reveals a comparatively high percentage of rising tones. The Cardiff rising tones are similar in acoustic structure to the Belfast ones, while the Glasgow rising tones are shorter in duration and narrower in f0 range.

The rising tone is known as a feature typical of the Urban Northern British intonation from a number of studies: it is systemically present in declaratives in Ulster dialect in Belfast [6], Glasgow dialect [13, 14], Liverpool dialect [15], Manchester dialect [16]. The studies mentioned above, however, were based on the analyses of speech samples in reading. The study of Glasgow dialect conducted by A. Cruttenden [14], in which two speech styles were produced by one speaker who found herself in the situation of diglossia, evidenced that the choice of intonation patterns was style-dependent: reading was characterized by fewer regional traits than unprepared conversation. In the current study based on the two corpora of unprepared talks we were bound to find more regionally-specific features typical of Celtic urban dialects.

The proximity of Belfast dialect to the Scottish variant can be accounted for by the presence of "Ulster Scots" in the area after the plantations in the XVII c. [17]; R. Hickey talks about Scottish influence on the segmental system of Belfast English [18]. We found pitch patterns common for Belfast and Glasgow.

The RFT frequency analysis also allows us to draw a conclusion about the similarity of the Celtic dialects. The tone is comparatively frequent in the Celtic speech, which goes in tune with the earlier research [6, 19].

Dublin dialect intonation proved to be closest to the southern standard. The result is concordant with the conclusion based on reading by A. Loukina and G. Kochanski who considered both varieties to be equally "conservative" [11]. We found that falling tones prevail in Dublin and Cambridge dialects; they are also similar in duration. Rising tones, on the contrary, are scarce. Our results of unprepared talks analysis confirms earlier research data on Dublin English statements which were mainly pronounced with a falling intonation [20]. However, a number of features, such as the frequency and the acoustic structure of RFT, show that Dublin dialect preserves regional Irish features as well. The similarity of Dublin dialect to southern standard English can be explained by long-term contacts with England. Besides, the southern standard English has always been considered highly prestigious in the Irish capital being associated with success and enhanced social opportunities [18].

We are thankful to the first reviewer for reminding about the complexity of the phenomenon of pitch pattern variation. We understand that patterns of variation do not simply fall out from pre-existing social structures or a place of origin: locally-relevant factors, such as pertaining to a student clique, and an individual's linguistic behavior targeted at constructing a speaker persona may be accountant for accent peculiarities. As the Third Wave variationists emphasize, there are no binding links between social factors and an individual's linguistic behaviour [21]. Besides, as shown in studies [4, 14], other than regional social factors may appear more relevant for defining a chosen representative group.

5   Conclusion

We may conclude that the pitch patterns' shapes, frequency of usage, association with duration and pitch span proved to be important clues to Irish, Welsh and Scottish national identities preserved in the speech of young generation. The analysis of pitch patterns in Celtic urban dialects based on unprepared talk of young people evidenced dialect-specific and gender-specific variation, but it also confirmed a considerable overlap of common Celtic features that developed as a result of long-term contacts in common history, specified for particular regions.

References

1. Shevchenko, T.I.: An analysis of regional variation in english intonation. In: Van den Broeke, M.P.R., Cohen, A. (eds). ICPhS 1983. Proceedings of the Tenth International Congress of Phonetic Sciences. Foris Publications, pp. 586–582 (1983)
2. Shevchenko, T.: What's in a voice: a system of regional and social acoustic characteristics based on the analysis of 100 British English voices. In: Tubach, J.P., Mariani, J.J. (eds). Eurospeech 89. European Conference on Speech Communication and Technology, vol. 2, pp. 131–134 (1989)
3. Shevchenko, T., Buraya, E., Fedotova, M., Sadovnikova, M.: Welsh English intonation and social identity. Socioling. Stud. 11(1), 153–174 (2017)
4. Mayr, R., Morris, J., Roberts, L.: Can you tell by their English if they can speak Welsh? Accent perception in a language contact situation. Int. J. Bilingualism, 2–50 (2019)
5. Grabe, E., Kochanski, G., Coleman, J.: the intonation of native accent varieties in the british isles: potential for miscommunication?. English Pronunciation Mod. Changing Scene, 311–338 (2005)
6. Jarman, E., Cruttenden, A.: Belfast intonation and the myth of the fall. J. Int. Phon. Assoc. 6(1), 4–12 (1976)
7. Grabe, E.: Intonational variation in urban dialects of English spoken in the British Isles. In: Gilles, P., Peters, J. (eds.) Regional Variation in Intonation. Linguistische Arbeiten, Tuebingen, Niemeyer, pp. 9–31 (2004)
8. Loukina, A., Kochanski, G.: Patterns of durational variation in British dialects. In: PAC Workshop in Montpellier, pp. 1–49 (2010)
9. Grabe, E., Post, B., Nolan, F.: Modelling intonational Variation in English. The IViE system. In: Puppel, S., Demenko, G. (eds). Proceedings of Prosody 2000. Adam Mickiewitz University, Poznan, Poland (2001)

10. Anderson, A.H., Bader, M., Bard, E.G., Boyle, E.A., et al.: The HCRC map task corpus. Lang. Speech **34**(4), 351–366 (1991)
11. Loukina, A., Kochanski, G., Rosner, B., Keane, E.: Rhythm measures and dimensions of durational variation in speech. J. Acoustical Soc. Am. **129**(5), 3258–3270 (2011)
12. Boersma, P., Weenink, D.: Praat: doing phonetics by computer [Computer program], Version 6.1.13 Retrieved on 25 July 2021. http://www.praat.org/ (2012)
13. Mayo, C., Aylett, M., Ladd, D.R.: Prosodic transcription of Glasgow English: an evaluation study of GlaToBi. In: Proceedings of the ESCA Workshop on Intonation: Theory, Models and Applications, Athens, Greece, 18–20 September 1997, pp. 231–234 (1997)
14. Cruttenden, A.: Intonational diglossia: a case study of Glasgow. J. Int. Phon. Assoc. **37**(03), 257–274 (2007)
15. Nance, C., Kirkham, S., Groarke, E.: Intonational variation in Liverpool English. In: Proceedings of the XVIII International Congress of Phonetic Sciences, pp. 14–18 (2015)
16. Cruttenden, A.: Gimson's Pronunciation of English, 6th edn. Edward Arnold, London (2001)
17. Britain, D.: Language in the British Isles. Cambridge University Press, Cambridge (2007)
18. Hickey, R.: The Handbook of Language Contact. John Wiley & Sons, Chichester (2012)
19. Coupland, N.: English in Wales: Diversity, Conflict and Change, A. R. Thomas ed., Avon (1990)
20. Dalton, M., Ni Chasaide, A.: Tonal alignment in Irish dialects. Lang. Speech **43**, 441-464 (2006)
21. Eckert, P.: Three waves of variation study: the emergence of meaning in the study of sociolinguistic variation. Annu. Rev. Anthropol. **41**, 87–100 (2012)

Coherence Based Automatic Essay Scoring Using Sentence Embedding and Recurrent Neural Networks

Dadi Ramesh[1](✉) and Suresh Kumar Sanampudi[2]

[1] Computer Science and Engineering, S R Engineering College, Warangal, India
dadiramesh44@gmail.com
[2] Department of Information Technology, JNTUH College of Engineering Jagitial, Nachupally (Kondagattu), Jagtial Dist, Telangana, India
sureshsanampudi@jntuh.ac.in

Abstract. Automatic essay scoring (AES) is an essential educational application using natural language processing and deep learning. However, enacting advanced deep learning models and natural language processing has improved AES systems' accuracy and performance. Though the current AES systems failed in certain areas like content-based assessment, the models are not tested on adversarial responses and giving feedback on the essay. In this paper, we proposed a sentence-based embedding to capture text's coherence and cohesion into a vector. Then, we trained these vectors on LSTM and Bi-LSTM to find the sentence connectivity internally and externally to check the sentence framing, its association with other sentences, and its relevance to the prompt. Finally, we tested our trained model on different adversarial responses and observed decent outcomes. We used two different data sets: one is the standard ASAP Kaggle dataset, and another is a collection of responses from the operating system domain.

The result shows that the LSTM model outperformed with baseline model quadratic weighted Kappa (QWK) by 0.76. Moreover, the testing on adversarial responses enhances the efficiency of the proposed model in different domains.

Keywords: Essay scoring · Sentence embedding · Bi-directional long short-term memory · Adversarial responses · Relevance-based scoring

1 Introduction

An automated essay scoring system evaluates student responses and gives the final score. Unlike one-word answers and multiple-choice questions, essay evaluation has many challenges and is an essential task in today's education system. With the increase in the student-teacher ratio, there is a need for a reliable automated assessment system to evaluate essays by considering linguistic consistency and context to assign a final score. But evaluating student responses by considering cohesion, coherence, and relevance to the prompt is challenging. In addition, assessing and handling adversarial responses is tedious with the black box type of deep learning model. These models automatically extract features from essay vectors, unlike machine learning models.

© Springer Nature Switzerland AG 2022
S. R. M. Prasanna et al. (Eds.): SPECOM 2022, LNAI 13721, pp. 139–154, 2022.
https://doi.org/10.1007/978-3-031-20980-2_13

The AES system introduced by [1], called project essay grading, evaluates essays based on statistical features. After this, many researchers worked on AES systems and implemented systems like Intelligent Essay Assessor (IEA) by [15]. E-rater by [5], C-rater by [8], but all these systems from 1973 to 2003 have extracted statistical features from essays and used machine learning algorithms to predict scores. But statistical features and machine learning model combinations have not provided an optimal evaluation system.

The rapid evolution of NLP and Deep learning models since 2010 has facilitated the researchers to extract context-based features from an essay. The features extracted are [27], a bag of words, TF-IDF (term frequency, inverse document frequency), parts of speech, etc., and trained deep learning algorithms like CNN and RNN. However, with these approaches, the system's accuracy has been improved but failed in context-based assessment and cannot capture features like cohesion, coherence, and relevance from an essay.

Advanced text embedding techniques like Word2vec [25], and Glove [19] have extracted context-based features from the essay and achieved good results. But these embedding techniques cannot differentiate the semantics of a word concerning its adjacent terms. It creates the same vector for an expression involved in various sentences with a separate meaning.

Researchers extracted sentence-level embedding differently with hierarchical, integrated neural networks like CNN + LSTM and CNN + Bi-LSTM approaches. First, they have embedded words by word embedding techniques. Later, they used the skip flow layer or CNN layer to sum up, individual word embeddings to create a sentence, but these approaches are missing semantics from an essay while connecting word embeddings. On the other hand, a system developed with black box models like deep learning models automatically extracts features from essay vectors prone to adversarial responses. However, [17, 20, 28] proved that these systems are more prone to adversarial responses. It is challenging to handle repeated sentences, prompts, and irrelevant responses.

The main challenges of AES systems that use word embeddings are cohesion and coherence-based text embeddings into a vector. In addition, they need a deep learning model to train sequences to sequence relevant patterns from essay vectors to give a final score by handling adversarial responses.

Contributions

Our proposed AES system mainly focused on sentence-based text embedding to capture sequential patterns without splitting the sentence.

- We used a universal sentence encoder to capture sentence-level sequential patterns without splitting the sentence.
- We trained sequential neural networks, LSTM, and Bi-LSTM, to traverse dependency paths and learn relevant representations to assign a final score for the essay.
- We trained and tested our model on two data sets, standard and domain-specific, to know the robustness of the model.
- And we tested our model on different types of adversarial responses.

The remainder of the paper is organized as follows. In Sect. 2, the related work about text embeddings and machine learning models used for AES systems and their challenges. Section 3 presents the proposed method of the AES system on different datasets and sentence embeddings. Section 4 discusses the implemented models, their architectures, and the hyperparameters used during training. Section 5 discusses the experimental results compared with other models and presents the model's performance on adversarial responses. Finally, Sect. 6 discusses the conclusion and future work.

2 Related Work

Research on AES systems was started in 1973, but from 2010 actual goals of AES systems were advancing with advanced natural language processing and deep learning models. The main challenges of AES systems are text embedding that retrieves semantic and linguistic features from text into a vector, training a proper deep learning model to learn the connectivity of sentences internally and externally, and handling irrelevant responses.

In natural language processing, text embedding is a significant challenge, such as converting all text into a vector with context. The first AES system by [1] used handpicked features from an essay like the number of words, sentence length, etc. E-rater, C-rater, and Intelimetric are other AES systems that worked on handpicked statistical features [2, 3, 9, 13, 26, 31] extracted features like a bag of words, one-hot encoding, n-gram, word frequency, and Inverse document frequency. However, the systems evaluated essays with statistical features blindly missing the sentence connectivity.

Word2vec [25] and Glove [19] are pre-trained text embedding NLP libraries that convert a word into a vector. Most of the publications like [14, 21, 29, 36, 37] used word2vec and Glove pre-trained models in text embedding and achieved good results in essay scoring. However, these approaches extract semantics from an essay but fail to extract unique vectors with semantics while embedding polysemous words.

The essay is a sequence of sentences that are connected internally and externally. Therefore, we need a recurrent neural network to capture sequence features from an essay [30, 32] used machine learning models to predict an essay score but failed to capture sequence patterns from an essay and failed to get immeasurable accuracy. On the other hand, [21, 22, 28, 35–37] all implemented LSTM, CNN-LSTM deep learning models to capture the sequence patterns from an essay. These models performed well in the Quadratic weighted Kappa (QWK) score. On the other hand, [23, 24, 39] models embedded the essay word by word and converted these word vectors to a sentence vector with an extra layer like lookup layer, skip flow layer, CNN layer. Still, the vectors do not capture an essay's semantics when embedding word by word. Table 1 illustrates possible combinations of feature extraction methods and machine learning models.

On the other hand, irrelevant responses and adversarial answers like repeated sentences, the question as a response, and random words will challenge AES systems. However, based on the observations of [6, 7, 17] when a student submits irrelevant responses or adversarial responses, the automated scoring systems outperform.

Table 1. Comparison of machine learning models and features extraction methods.

	BoW/Tf-Idf	Word2vec/Glove
Regression models/classification models	The system implemented with Bow features and regression or classification algorithms will have low cohesion and coherence	The system implemented with Word2vec features and regression or classification algorithms will have low to medium cohesion and coherence
Neural Networks (LSTM)	The system implemented with BoW features and neural network models will have low cohesion and coherence	The system implemented with Word2vec features and neural network model (LSTM) will have medium to high cohesion and coherence

3 Method

Unlike previous work for AES systems, we proposed a different approach that implements sentence-level embedding and trained on neural network models like LSTM, Bi-LSTM [18] and CNN-Bi-LSTM, including a prompt to capture relevance between essay to prompt. We used two datasets to train and test our models and compare the results. The overview of implemented AES system with a Bi-LSTM neural network is shown in Fig. 1.

3.1 Data Set

The data set we used in our AES model is the standard dataset from Kaggle ASAP, consisting of 12,978 responses with eight different prompts, and all the prompts are on various topics. Prompts 3,4,5,6 are source-dependent essays, and the remaining are others. The detailed description of the ASAP dataset is presented in Table 2. In addition, we created new data set on the domain operating system (OS) to test the performance of AES systems on domain-specific essays. We collected 2390 responses from 626 undergraduate students on five prompts for the OS data set. Two subject experts scored the new dataset on 0- 5, the minimum score is 0, and the maximum score is 5. We used the QWK score to measure the agreement between the two raters. The resulting score is 0.842(QWK). A detailed description of the OS dataset is presented in Table 3.

Table 2. Kaggle ASAP data set for essay scoring.

Essay set	No. of essays	Average length of essays	Rating range
1	1783	350	2–12
2	1800	350	1–6

(continued)

Table 2. (*continued*)

Essay set	No. of essays	Average length of essays	Rating range
3	1726	150	0–3
4	1772	150	0–3
5	1805	150	0–4
6	1800	150	0–4
7	1569	250	0–30
8	723	650	0–60

Table 3. Operating System data set (https://github.com/RAMESHDADI/OS-data_1-set-for-AES)

Essay id	No. of essays	Length of essays	Rating range (min to max)
1	516	1–21	0–5
2	596	1–21	0–5
3	312	1–21	0–5
4	513	1–21	0–5
5	453	1–21	0–5

3.2 Sentence Level Embedding

In the proposed AES system, first, we removed all special symbols like @, #, etc., from essays and tokenized all the essays into sentences. Then we converted all sentences into a vector with a Universal Sentence Encoder (USE) [11]. of dimension 512. USE converts all sentences of an essay into individual words, bi-grams words, and embeds all these combinations to vector, then averages all word vectors together to form a sentence and passes to the feedforward deep neural networks to give sentence embedding. Unlike other models, [23, 24, 39] first embedded all the words, then averaged all word embeddings into sentences with an additional neural network layer. However, this averaging of word embeddings has limitations like the inability to capture the actual semantics of the sentences.

We have not used a word vector for embeddings like word2vec, Glove. Because these word embeddings techniques convert each word into a vector, they do not consider the semantics when the word's meaning depends on its adjacent words, especially polysemous words. So, cohesion can be missed when a word has two meanings that concur with adjacent terms.

We vectorized all the essay sentences with USE and converted all sentences into a unique dimension of 512. So, for all the sentences, whatever the number of words, the vector size is 512. But the number of sentences is different in an essay, so we performed

Table 4. ASAP dataset, OS data set essay vector after padding.

Dataset	Essay vector	Dimension
ASAP	[[0.01377844 -0.09247074 0.01014971... -0.01349053 -0.04146808 0.05626552] [-0.01370333 -0.0240192 -0.03880018... -0.05234249 -0.06115109 0.05296136] [-0.05529318 -0.02587196 -0.00212097... 0.02701825 0.02506788 0.00300164] ... [0. 0. 0.... 0. 0. 0.] [0. 0. 0.... 0. 0. 0.] [0. 0. 0.... 0. 0. 0.]]	96 * 512
OS	[[-0.04040171 0.00535519 -0.02015072... -0.07707731 -0.07179338 0.05336216] [-0.00677465 0.01085155 0.03253689... -0.07136418 -0.05266594 -0.01695863] [0.03762686 0.02985795 -0.05078415... -0.05361476 -0.02895073 0.04693419] ... [0. 0. 0.... 0. 0. 0.] [0. 0. 0.... 0. 0. 0.] [0. 0. 0.... 0. 0. 0.]]	21*512

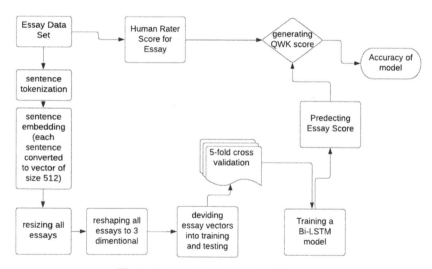

Fig. 1. Overview of proposed AES system

padding to equalize all essays. So that we have all essays in the form of 96* 512 size. 96 is the maximum number of sentences, and 512 is the sentence dimension.

In our approach, we did not extract any word from a sentence separately, like removing stop words, and collecting a bag of words, because the stop words will connect the words and sentences in an essay. Instead, we embedded sentence by sentence so that the model can easily capture the cohesion and coherence of the essay in training.

4   Model

The essay is a sequence of internally connected sentences concerning the prompt. Therefore, the model should consider and capture an essay's linguistic sequences, coherence, and cohesion to assess an essay and assign a final score. Because sentence coherence depends on its adjacent and connecting words, and essay cohesion depends on the flow of sentences, the model should capture information recurrently. We individually used recurrent neural network models like LSTM and Bi-LSTM to capture linguistic sequences and coherence from an essay vector. On the other side, we used one layer of a conventional neural network to capture the N-gram features on top of the recurrent neural network. For all neural network models, the dense layer with activation layer ReLu will predict the final score of the essay. The architecture of LSTM, Bi-LSTM, and CNN-LSTM for the AES system is shown in Fig. 2.

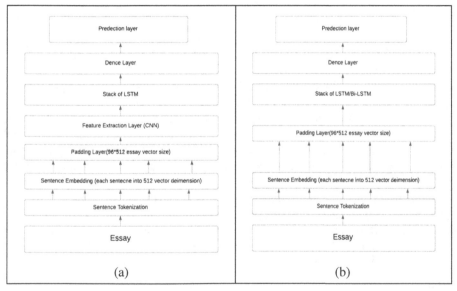

Fig. 2. The AES model (a). CNN with recurrent neural network for AES system. (b) LSTM/Bi-LSTM model for AES system.

LSTM is a recurrent neural network that can process a sequence of information with its memory cell. The memory cell consists of input gate (2), forgot gate (1), output gate (3), and context gate (4) to process the information and store the long-term dependency information required for feature use, and that is passed to the next cell input gate. The following equations explain LSTM units.

$$f_t = \sigma g(w_f x_t + u_f h_{(t-1)} + b_f) \tag{1}$$

$$i_t = \sigma g(w_i x_t + u_i h_{(t-1)} + b_i) \tag{2}$$

$$o_t = \sigma g(w_o x_t + u_o h_{(t-1)} + b_o) \tag{3}$$

$$C_t = tanh(w_c x_t + u_c h_{(t-1)} + b_c) \tag{4}$$

where w_f, w_i, w_o, w_c are weights of respective gates, b_f, b_i, b_o, b_c are bias vectors, x_t, h_t is input sentences for the time t. Then, each sentence vector is passed to the input gate containing the sigmoid function, tanh function, and sigmoid function will decide which data should capture in the cell, and the tanh function will extract features. Finally, both outputs are multiplied and passed to the context gate.

Bi-LSTM is a recurrent neural network; unlike LSTM, the input is passed to the input gate in both directions. Bi-LSTM also contains three gates, input gate with the sigmoid function will decide which information to forget and what to forward to the next cell.

$$H(forward) = \sigma(w_1 x_1 + w_2 x_2 + w_3 x_3 + \ldots + w_t x_t + b) \tag{5}$$

$$H(backward) = \sigma(w_1 x_1 + w_2 x_2 + w_3 x_3 + \ldots + w_t x_t + b) \tag{6}$$

where w_1, w_2, w_3 ..... w_t weights, b is bias, σ is activation function, y is output, and t is the number of sentences in the essay.

The sentence vectors are transformed to these Bi-LSTM recurrent networks to the forward (5) and the backward (6) layers. From each sentence, context information will be stored and attached to the following sentence from these combined sentences; again, some info is stored like that all sentences will summarize and predict the final score for the essay.

Integrating deep learning model (CNN + recurrent neural network). We also implemented an integrated neural network model with one layer of CNN on top of LSTM, Bi-LSTM, to capture features from the embedded vector, flatten the vector, and pass to a recurrent neural network. The function (7) is used in the CNN layer to capture N-gram features from the sentence vector.

$$S_i = \sigma(x_i : x_{(i+k-1)}) w_s b_s \tag{7}$$

where x_i is the sentence vector, w_s is the weight matrix, b_s is the bias vector, k is the kernel size of the CNN layer, and σ is the ReLu as the nonlinear activation function. Finally, Si is the output of the feature vector.

4.1 Experiment Setup and Training

We used USE to embed each sentence into 512 vector sizes transformed to the neural network input layer in the embedding process. Then, an integrated approach CNN + Recurrent neural network 96*512 matrices are given to CNN layer input, using kernel size of 3, number of filters 128, and added 1-dimensional max-pooling layer to extract features. Finally, all extracted features are flattened and passed to LSTM/Bi-LSTM input gate.

In LSTM, we stacked five layers of LSTM; each unit has an input gate, output gate, and context gate. RMSprop as optimizer used mean square error to calculate loss like [13] drop rate as 0.5, assigned initial learning rate as 0.001, activation function as ReLU. The hyperparameters of our models are shown in Table 5.

In the training phase, we used 5-fold cross-validation to split the essay vectors into training and testing for both data sets, each fold trained for 10,15,20,35 epochs to fix hyperparameters. We also trained the essay vector on the integrated and recurrent neural network models and captured the results. We use QWK as an evaluation metric in our models to find the agreement between the human and system rater. In each fold, we calculated the QWK score. Finally, we use the model that achieves the best performance on training data to predict the test data. Figure 3 illustrates the training and validation loss of the proposed model, and it portrays that our proposed model is neither overfitted nor under fitted.

We used the same hyperparameters and 5-fold cross-validation to train sentence-LSTM and sentence-Bi-LSTM on the OS dataset. OS data set input dimension is 23*512 for each essay; 23 is the maximum number of sentences, and 512 is the sentence vector.

Table 5. Neural network parameters and values

Layer	Parameter	Value
Embedding	Sentence embedding	512 size vectors for each sentence
CNN layer	Input size	(1,96,512), (1, 23,512)
LSTM layers	No of layers	5
LSTM units	LSTM units	300
Hidden	Hidden units	200,100
Drop out	Dropout rate	0.4
	Recurrent drop out	0.5
Others	Epochs	35
	Batch size	32
	Learning rate	0.001

5 Result Analysis

The results show that our proposed models outperformed and equally performed with other models. The comparison of all baseline models on the ASAP dataset and our proposed models on average QWK score is shown in Table 6. We found that sentence embedding-LSTM and sentence embedding-Bi-LSTM models performed well compared to other models and were consistent with the human rater score. Furthermore, it observed that Sentence Embedding-LSTM and Bi-LSTM performed better than models like [4, 24, 33], LSTM-MOT model of and CNN + LSTM integrating deep learning model (2021). Though SKIPFLOW-LSTM (2017), [13] and CNN-LSTM Attention [23]. Models performed equally with sentence embedding-LSTM and Bi-LSTM; these integrated models did not capture sentence coherence and formed a sentence from word vectors.

Table 8 shows that all AES models poorly performed on prompt-8. However, like other models, our model also consistently performed on source-dependent essay traits like prompt 3,4,5,6; these essay traits' rating range is between 1 and 6. Furthermore, based on the QWK score, the performance of our models and other baseline models on persuasive, narrative, and expository essay traits is the same and a little bit high. However, the performance was reduced when we used the CNN layer on the Sentence Embedding-LSTM, Bi-LSTM neural networks model.

The models trained on the ASAP dataset were also used on the OS dataset with the same hyperparameters, and it is performed with an average QWK score of 0.744, 0.740 by Bi-LSTM, LSTM models. Table 7 illustrates the prompt-wise QWK score and average QWK score of the Sentence Embedding-LSTM, Sentence Embedding-Bi-LSTM model on the OS dataset.

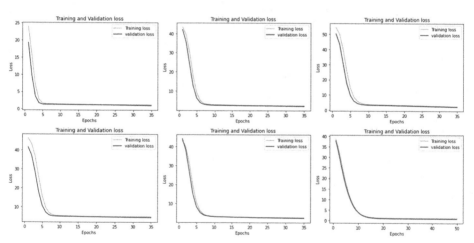

Fig. 3. Training and validation loss of prompts 1,4,6 of ASAP dataset (top row) and prompts 1,2,4 of OS data set (bottom row).

Table 6. Prompt wise QWK score with LSTM and Bi-LSTM on ASAP dataset.

Models	1	2	3	4	5	6	7	8	Avg
Rater1 to Rater 2 agreement	0.721	0.812	0.769	0.851	0.753	0.776	0.720	0.627	0.754
Multi-task (word&sentence sentiment) [Muangkammuen, Fukumoto 2020]	0.803	0.658	0.664	0.772	0.799	0.816	0.787	0.644	0.743
EASE	0.76	0.61	0.62	0.74	0.78	0.78	0.73	0.62	0.71
LSTM-MoT model [Taghipour, Ng 2016]	0.775	0.687	0.683	0.795	0.818	0.813	0.805	0.594	0.746
SKIPFLOW-LSTM model [Tay et al. 2018]	0.832	0.684	0.695	0.788	0.815	0.810	0.800	0.697	0.764
TSLF-ALL [Liu et al. 2019]	0.852	0.736	0.731	0.801	0.823	0.792	0.762	0.684	0.773
CNN + LSTM integrating deep learning model	0.87	0.64	0.63	0.83	0.86	0.85	0.79	0.53	0.73
LSTM-CNN attention [Dong et al. 2017]	0.822	0.682	0.672	0.814	0.803	0.811	0.801	0.705	0.764
Sentence Embedding-LSTM*	0.812	0.708	0.709	0.816	0.812	0.809	0.798	0.656	0.765
Sentence Embedding-Bi-LSTM*	0.809	0.698	0.698	0.812	0.810	0.808	0.794	0.651	0.760
Sentence Embedding-CNN-LSTM*	0.794	0.675	0.685	0.812	0.81	0.801	0.781	0.643	0.750
Sentence Embedding-CNN-Bi-LSTM*	0.791	0.667	0.672	0.807	0.805	0.799	0.764	0.634	0.742

Table 7. Average QWK score of word embedding and sentence embedding models on OS dataset

Model	P-1	P-2	P-3	P-4	P-5	QWK score
Word embedding models	0.745	0.738	0.634	0.722	0.742	7.16
Sentence Embedding -LSTM	0.762	0.759	0.696	0.748	0.756	0.744
Sentence Embedding-Bi-LSTM	0.761	0.758	0.688	0.742	0.752	0.740

Table 8. Testing and comparing results of proposed model and word embedding model on adversarial responses

Test case	Adversarial responses	Actual score (human rater score)	Predicted score of proposed models (Sentence embedding with LSTM)	Predicted score of Word embedding model (GP2 + LSTM)
1	Essay from Prompt -1 which is relevant to the response	9	9.5	7.7
2	One sentence response for prompt-1	2	2.2	1.5
3	Essay from Prompt-1 which is relevant to the response	7	7.1	5.2
4	Prompt as response	1	1.02	2.1
5	Irrelevance response to the prompt-1(where few words are matching to the prompt)	0	0.89	2.90
6	Response with repeated sentences (where 50% of the answer is correct)	5	4.82	7.6
7	One word response	0	0	0.4
8	Response with 50% relevant answer and remaining 50% is irrelevant	6	5.88	7.2

5.1 Testing on Adversarial Responses

To know how models perform on adversarial responses and to know whether the essays are evaluated based on the semantics or not. We prepared eight test cases on adversarial responses like irrelevant, relevant responses, prompt as response, and repeated sentences.

Table 8 compares actual and predicted scores of word embedding and sentence embedding models on all eight test cases. From test cases 1,2,3, the difference between the actual and predicted scores of the word embedding model is high. On the other hand, the sentence embedding model performed well.

In tests cse-5 and 6, the word embedding model is underperformed when we tested irrelevant responses with few words matched with content. On the other hand, in sentence repeated responses test cases-5 and 6, it captures the semantics of the essay and does not consider duplicate sentences while providing the final score.

We observed that the word embedding model is underperformed and does not capture semantics from essays. In contrast, Sentence Embedding with LSTM performed well on irrelevant responses, given a final score based on relevance.

We strongly argue that our model captures coherence and cohesion from essays while evaluating and assigning a score. We used sentence-to-sentence embedding and trained neural networks to capture sequence-to-sequence patterns from the essay. However, our model's average QWK score is greater than or equal to other baseline models, but our model assesses essays based on coherence and cohesion. And our model performance is consistent in semantics and relevance while testing on adversarial responses.

6 Conclusion

In this paper, we proposed and implemented a novel approach for an AES system with a combination of sentence embedding with a recurrent neural network and added a CNN layer on LSTM and Bi-LSTM. All four models are trained and tested on the Kaggle ASAP and OS datasets. In this approach, we embedded the essay sentence by sentence after preprocessing to capture sequence-to-sequence coherence patterns and trained on recurrent neural networks. Specifically, we compared these four models: Sentence embedding-LSTM, Sentence Embedding-Bi-LSTM, Sentence Embedding- CNN-LSTM, and Embedding-CNN-Bi-LSTM. It's observed that Sentence Embedding-LSTM and Bi-LSTM performed well among all four models. Moreover, our proposed models outperformed other baseline models.

We tested our proposed models on adversarial responses and compared the actual and predicted scores. While testing on adversarial responses, our model assigned scores for essays based on coherence and cohesion; when we were given irrelevant responses and repeated sentence essays, our model captured content and assigned scores. From the results, it's proved that our models are performing consistently. Furthermore, we also trained our models on different datasets like OS and observed consistent performance.

In the future, we will continue our study on AES systems to improve the QWK score and test more adversarial responses to test the robustness of the model. We also concentrate on feedback generation for the essay. To handle Out of Vocabulary (OOV) words, we are creating a separate corpus related to the OS dataset domain with that we can handle OOV words.

References

1. Ajay, H.B., Tillett, P.I., Page, E.B.: Analysis of essays by computer (AEC-II) (No. 8–0102). Washington, DC: U.S. Department of Health, Education, and Welfare, Office of Education, National Center for Educational Research and Development (1973)
2. Adamson, A., Lamb, A., Ma, R.: Automated Essay Grading (2014)
3. Ajetunmobi, S.A., Daramola, O.: Ontology-based information extraction for subject-focussed automatic essay evaluation. In: 2017 International Conference on Computing Networking and Informatics (ICCNI), pp. 1–6. IEEE (2017)
4. Agrawal, A., Agrawal, S.: Debunking Neural Essay Scoring (2018)
5. Burstein, J.: The E-rater® scoring engine: automated essay scoring with natural language processing. In: Shermis, M.D., Burstein, J. (eds.) Automated essay scoring: A cross-disciplinary perspective, pp. 113–121. Lawrence Erlbaum Associates Publishers (2003)
6. Bejar, I.I., Flor, M., Futagi, Y., Ramineni, C.: On the vulnerability of automated scoring to construct-irrelevant response strategies (CIRS): an illustration. Assess. Writ. **22**, 48–59 (2014)
7. Bejar, I.I., VanWinkle, W., Madnani, N., Lewis, W., Steier, M.: Length of textual response as a construct-irrelevant response strategy: the case of shell language. ETS Res. Rep. Ser. **2013**(1), i–39 (2013)
8. Claudia, L., CC-rater, M.A.R.T.I.N.: Automated scoring of short-answer questions. Comput. Human. **37**, 92-96 (2003)
9. Cummins, R., Zhang, M., Briscoe, T.: Constrained multi-task learning for automated essay scoring. ACL (2016)
10. Chen, M., Li, X.: Relevance-based automated essay scoring via hierarchical recurrent model. In: 2018 International Conference on Asian Language Processing (IALP), pp. 378–383. IEEE, November 2018
11. Cer, D., et al.: Universal sentence encoder. arXiv preprint arXiv:1803.11175(2018)
12. Ding, Y., Riordan, B., Horbach, A., Cahill, A., Zesch, T.: Don't take "nswvtnvakgxpm" for an answer–The surprising vulnerability of automatic content scoring systems to adversarial input. In: Proceedings of the 28th International Conference on Computational Linguistics, pp. 882–892, December 2020
13. Dong, F., Zhang, Y., Yang, J.: Attention-based recurrent convolutional neural network for automatic essay scoring. In: Proceedings of the 21st Conference on Computational Natural Language Learning (CoNLL 2017), pp. 153–162 (2017)
14. Darwish, S.M., Mohamed, S.K.: Automated essay evaluation based on fusion of fuzzy ontology and latent semantic analysis. In: Hassanien, A., Azar, A., Gaber, T., Bhatnagar, R., Tolba M. (eds) The International Conference on Advanced Machine Learning Technologies and Applications (2020)
15. Foltz, P.W., Laham, D., Landauer, T.K.: The intelligent essay assessor: applications to educational technology. Interactive Multimedia Electron. J. Comput. Enhanced Learn. **1**(2), 939–944 (1999)
16. Horbach, A., Zesch, T.: The influence of variance in learner answers on automatic content scoring. Front. Educ. **4**, 28 (2019). https://doi.org/10.3389/feduc.2019.00028
17. Higgins, D., Heilman, M.: Managing what we can measure: quantifying the susceptibility of automated scoring systems to gaming behavior. Educ. Meas. Issues Pract. **33**(3), 36–46 (2014)
18. Huang, Z., Xu, W., Yu, K.: Bidirectional LSTM-CRF models for sequence tagging. arXiv preprint arXiv:1508.01991(2015)
19. Jeffrey Pennington, Richard Socher, and Christopher D. Manning. GloVe: Global Vectors for Word Representation (2014)

20. Kumar, Y., et al.: "Calling Out Bluff: Attacking the Robustness of Automatic Scoring Systems with Simple Adversarial Testing." ArXiv abs/2007.06796 (2020)
21. Kumar, Y., Aggarwal, S., Mahata, D., Shah, R.R., Kumaraguru, P., Zimmermann, R.: Get IT Scored Using AutoSAS - An Automated System for Scoring Short Answers. AAAI (2019)
22. Kopparapu, S.K., De, A.: Automatic ranking of essays using structural and semantic features. In: 2016 International Conference on Advances in Computing, Communications and Informatics (ICACCI), pp. 519–523 (2016)
23. Liu, J., Xu, Y., Zhu, Y.: Automated essay scoring based on two-stage learning. arXiv preprint arXiv:1901.07744(2019)
24. Muangkammuen, P., Fukumoto, F.: Multi-task learning for automated essay scoring with sentiment analysis. In: Proceedings of the 1st Conference of the Asia-Pacific Chapter of the Association for Computational Linguistics and the 10th International Joint Conference on Natural Language Processing: Student Research Workshop, pp. 116–123, December 2020
25. Mikolov, T., Chen, K., Corrado, G., Dean, J.: Efficient estimation of word representations in vector space. arXiv preprint arXiv:1301.3781(2013)
26. Nguyen, H., Dery, L.: Neural networks for automated essay grading (2018)
27. Ramesh, D., Sanampudi, S.K.: An automated essay scoring systems: a systematic literature review. Artif. Intell. Rev. **55**(3), 2495–2527 (2021). https://doi.org/10.1007/s10462-021-100 68-2
28. Riordan, B., Flor, M., Pugh, R.: How to account for mispellings: quantifying the benefit of character representations in neural content scoring models. In: Proceedings of the Fourteenth Workshop on Innovative Use of NLP for Building Educational Applications, pp. 116–126, August 2019
29. Ruseti, S., et al.: Scoring summaries using recurrent neural networks. In: International Conference on Intelligent Tutoring Systems, pp. 191–201. Springer, Cham, June 2018
30. Ramachandran, L., Cheng, J., Foltz, P.: Identifying patterns for short answer scoring using graph-based lexico-semantic text matching. In: Proceedings of the Tenth Workshop on Innovative Use of NLP for Building Educational Applications, pp. 97–106, June 2015
31. Sultan, M.A., Salazar, C., Sumner, T.: Fast and easy short answer grading with high accuracy. In: Proceedings of the 2016 Conference of the North American Chapter of the Association for Computational Linguistics: Human Language Technologies, pp. 1070–1075, June 2016
32. Sakaguchi, K., Heilman, M., Madnani, N.: Effective feature integration for automated short answer scoring. In: Proceedings of the 2015 Conference of the North American Chapter of the Association for Computational Linguistics: Human Language Technologies, pp. 1049–1054 (2015)
33. Taghipour, K., Ng, H.T.: A neural approach to automated essay scoring. In: Proceedings of the 2016 Conference on Empirical Methods in Natural Language Processing, pp. 1882–1891, November 2016
34. Tay, Y., Phan, M., Tuan, L.A., Hui, S.C.: SkipFlow: incorporating neural coherence features for end-to-end automatic text scoring. In: Proceedings of the AAAI Conference on Artificial Intelligence, vol. 32, No. (1), April 2018
35. Bittencourt, I.I., Cukurova, M., Muldner, K., Luckin, R., Millán, E. (eds.): AIED 2020. LNCS (LNAI), vol. 12164. Springer, Cham (2020). https://doi.org/10.1007/978-3-030-52240-7
36. Wang, Z., Liu, J., Dong, R.: Intelligent auto-grading system. In: 2018 5th IEEE International Conference on Cloud Computing and Intelligence Systems (CCIS), pp. 430–435. IEEE, November 2018

37. Zhu, W., Sun, Y.: Automated essay scoring system using multi-model Machine Learning, david c. wyld et al. (eds): mlnlp, bdiot, itccma, csity, dtmn, aifz, sigpro – 2020 (2020)
38. Zhao, S., Zhang, Y., Xiong, X., Botelho, A., Heffernan, N.: A memory-augmented neural model for automated grading. In: Proceedings of the Fourth (2017) ACM Conference on Learning@ Scale, pp. 189–192, April 2017
39. Zhang, H., Litman, D.: Co-attention based neural network for source-dependent essay scoring. arXiv preprint arXiv:1908.01993(2019)

Analysis of Automatic Evaluation Metric on Low-Resourced Language: BERTScore vs BLEU Score

Goutam Datta[1,2]([⊠]) [iD], Nisheeth Joshi[1], and Kusum Gupta[1]

[1] School of Mathematical and Computer Science, Banasthali Vidyapeeth, Rajasthan, India
gdatta1@yahoo.com, jnisheeth@banasthali.in, gupta_kusum@yahoo.com
[2] Informatics, School of Computer Science, University of Petroleum and Energy Studies,
Dehradun, India

Abstract. The accurate evaluation of machine translation (MT) is a difficult task. Human evaluation (judgment) is considered to be the best, but it is time-consuming. Hence, the importance of developing an automatic evaluation metric got researchers' attention. In this paper, we have done an in-depth analysis of the performance of the MT engine on low-resourced Bengali to English translations. We analyzed the scores generated by automatic metrics such as BLEU and BERTscore. We have computed the scores of the translation engine manually also based on the parameters used in the human evaluation. Finally, we have measured the correlation of BLEU and BERTScore with human judgment and found that BERTScore has a higher correlation with human judgment for our English to Bangla language pair.

Keywords: BLEU · BERT score · Human evaluation · Machine translation

1 Introduction

MT which automates the conversion of one natural language to other with the help of a sufficient parallel corpus has witnessed a tremendous paradigm shift.

MT started its journey from a dictionary-based, rule-based, statistical MT, phrase-based and most recently MT industry exploits artificial neural network (ANN) in its implementation called Neural Machine Translation (NMT). NMT has its various frameworks with their own merits and demerits [1–4].

MT evaluation is a challenging task when designing a translation system [3, 5, 6]. An evaluation is essential for determining how effective the current model is, estimating how much post-editing is required, and accordingly, the model can be improved during its design phase. MT evaluation is a challenging task since natural language is highly ambiguous. The same sentence can be interpreted differently by two different persons. In MT evaluation it compares translated text i.e. candidate text sometimes also called hypothesis text with the gold standard reference text. There may be single or multiple reference texts that can be produced by human or translation systems. When evaluating MT systems, it can either be done manually or automatically. Sometimes it demands

© Springer Nature Switzerland AG 2022
S. R. M. Prasanna et al. (Eds.): SPECOM 2022, LNAI 13721, pp. 155–162, 2022.
https://doi.org/10.1007/978-3-031-20980-2_14

both. Human evaluation is best but it is time-consuming, costly, and can't be reused. In human evaluation, a quality measure scale of 1 to 5 is given accordingly the translated text is scored based on its adequacy and fluency. Adequacy refers to the completeness of the translated text. Fluency ensures the grammatical correctness of the translated text.

There are numerous automatic evaluation metrics available in the MT evaluation process. Bilingual Evaluation Understudy (BLEU) is one of the popular evaluation metrics based on precision [7]. There is another metric METEOR (Metric for Evaluation of Translation with Explicit ORdering) which is based on both precision and recall. However, more weightage is given to recall than precision. Some other automatic metrics such as precision, recall, F-measure, ROUGE (Recall-Oriented Understudy for Gisting Evaluation), etc. are available. The most recent automatic metric is BERTScore which captures semantic similarity between reference and translated text.

In this paper, we have attempted to evaluate the accuracy of BERTScore and BLEU scores with the help of a gold standard human score while translating Bangla to English sentences.

The rest of the paper is structured as follows: Sect. 2 highlights some previous work on MT evaluation. Section 3 briefs about our methodology and experimentation. We have analyzed and discussed the results in Sect. 4. Finally, we have presented a brief conclusion and future direction in Sect. 5.

2 Some Previous Work in MT Evaluation

Human evaluation is assumed to be the best in MT evaluation but sometimes it lacks agreement among inter annotators. Also, reusability is a challenge in human evaluation. The authors addressed these two problems with human evaluation in their paper [8].

BLEU is one of the popular automatic evaluation metrics based on precision. BLEU's precision-based computation is based on token matching between a hypothesis text and one or more reference texts. Depending on how many tokens are considered i.e. n = 1,2, or 3 it is called uni-gram, bi-gram, or tri-gram. It has been found that lower grams always have a higher score than a higher gram due to their exact token matching criteria.

Another popular automatic evaluation metric is METEOR. METEOR also exploits unigram matching criteria between candidate and reference text at their surface level, and semantic level and it is based on the combination of precision and recall [9].

In Chrf, which is a language-independent, n-gram-based automatic evaluation metric where character level n-gram is exploited to compute F-score to evaluate MT performance. Chrf has shown a better correlation with a human score [10].

ROUGE (Recall-oriented Understudy for Gisting Evaluation) is a recall-based automatic evaluation metric. ROUGE has also different variants. ROUGE-N is like BLEU with multiple n-grams [11].

BERTScore is an embedded-based automatic evaluation metric.BERTScore generates a score with the help of semantic similarity between candidate and reference text, hence its accuracy during evaluation is higher than n-gram-based metrics [12]. BERTScore metric exploits BERT which is a pretrained language model [13, 14].

3 Methodology and Experimentation

In this section, we discuss our methodology used to measure the effectiveness of two popular automatic evaluation metrics: BLEU which is n-gram based, and BERTScore which is embedded based in Bangla to English translation. Our primary objective is to evaluate how well these two automatic evaluation metrics correlate with gold standard human evaluation (human score). The better one will be having a higher correlation with the human score (human judgment). To find the correlation we have used one of the commonly used correlation metrics i.e. Pearson correlation. The Pearson correlation coefficient measures the linear relationship between two variables.

Its value ranges from -1 to $+1$. -1 indicates there is a complete negative correlation and $+1$ indicates a complete positive correlation. 0 indicates no correlation. The values 0.8 and 0.6 indicate strong and moderate positive correlations respectively. The values -0.8 and -0.6 represent strong and moderate negative correlations. The methodology is represented in Fig. 1.

We used the English to Bangla tourism data set collected from TDIL (https://www.tdil-dc.in/index.php?lang=en). It contains English to Bangla Parallel sentences total of 11976. We have randomly picked a couple of Bangla sentences from this data set. The corresponding English sentences have been considered reference texts. These selected Bangla sentences are passed to Google translate to translate them into English.

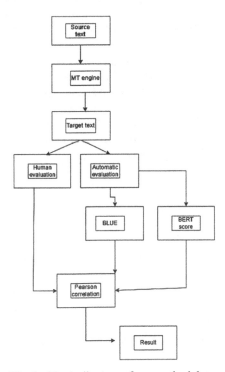

Fig. 1. Block diagram of our methodology.

The randomly picked sentences from 1 to 5 are represented in Table 1.

Table 1. Randomly picked Bangla sentences, their ground truth, and translated texts.

No.	Source Sentence	Reference Sentence (Ground Truth)	Hypothesis Sentence (Translated sentence)
1	সে মে মাসের প্রথম সপ্তাহ থেকে আমাদের সাথে দেখা করেনি।	He has not visited us since the first week of May.	He has not seen us since the first week of May.
2	তিনশো বছরেরও কম পুরনো নবীন শহর জয়পুর ঘুরে দেখ।	Take a tour of Jaipur to know the city which is fairly young, less than three centuries old.	Explore the new city of Jaipur, which is less than three hundred years old.
3	পান্ধারপুর শোলাপুর থেকে ৬৫ কিমি দূরে ভীমরথী নদীর তীরে অবস্থিত।	Pandharpur is located in a place, which is 65 km away from Sholapur, on the banks of river Bhimarathi.	Pandharpur is located on the banks of the Bhimrathi River at a distance of 65 km from Sholapur.
4	হিমাচল প্রদেশে পর্যটনের সেরা সময় অক্টোবর মাস, যখন বহুল প্রচলিত কুল্লু দাশের অনুষ্ঠান পালিত হয় সমগ্র রাজ্যে।	The best time to take up Himachal Pradesh tours is during the month of October, when the popular Kullu Dussehra is being celebrated in the state.	The best time to visit Himachal Pradesh is the month of October, when the popular festival of Kullu Das is celebrated across the state.
5	কেরালার সবথেকে আধুনিক শহর হল কোচি যেখানে সবথেকে ভাল দোকান,বাজার অবস্থিত।	Kochi is the most modern city of Kerala where the best shopping, markets and bazaars are located.	The most modern city in Kerala is Kochi where the best shops and markets are located.

3.1 Manual Score (Human Judgment)

We computed the BLEU score and BERTScore of all these translated texts. For manual score generation, had created a questionnaire that asks for some predefined questions having scales ranging from 0 to 5 to capture the adequacy and fluency of the translated sentences that we had supplied to 10 different human experts having linguistic expertise in these two languages such as Bangla and English. The human experts were given translated versions and reference texts to assign their scores. Finally, we have taken the average of all these scores given by ten different human judges. The adequacy scale has a value of 5 if all meaning is correct, most meaning has a value of 4, and much meaning, a little meaning, and none have the values 3,2 and 1 respectively. Adequacy is used to ensure the completeness of the translated text. Fluency ensures the grammatical correctness of the translated text. The fluency scale is as follows: the highest score of 5 is assigned to flawless English, good English has a score of 4, and non-native, disfluent, and incomprehensible English have scores of 3,2, and 1 respectively [15].

3.2 BERTScore

BERTScore is computed by feeding ground truth (reference sentence) and candidate sentence into the pre-trained BERT model. The BERT model has words that are contextually embedded. It tries to match tokens of hypothesis and reference texts with cosine similarity. The BERTScore produces the following output values: precision, recall, and F1-score whose range varies from 0.0 to 1.0.

BLEU

BLEU is a precision-based metric since during its computation it does not consider whether all the words in the reference texts are covered in the hypothesis text or not. BLEU tries to match the MT engine-generated text with one or more reference texts based on how many tokens are considered at a time. That is based on the number of tokens selected for matching it can be 1-g, 2-g, etc.

The computed automatic and manual scores are presented in Table 2. Its diagrammatic representation is given in Fig. 2. The BERT score and human judgment (human score) correlation is given in Table 3.

The BLEU score and human score (human judgment) correlation is presented in Table 4. The observed pattern between two different automatic evaluation metrics and Human scores is discussed in Sect. 4 (Result Analysis and Discussion).

Table 2. Automatic and human scores of the translated texts.

Sentence no	MT Engine	BLEU score(n = 3)	BERTScore	Human judgment
1	Google Translate	0.66	0.93	0.95
2	Google Translate	0.16	0.66	0.85
3	Google Translate	0.17	0.68	0.95
4	Google Translate	0.29	0.73	0.96
5	Google Translate	0.13	0.78	0.94

Table 3. Pearson Correlation between BERTScore and Human Score

BERTScore	Human judgment	Pearson correlation
0.93	0.95	0.46
0.66	0.85	0.46
0.68	0.95	0.46
0.73	0.96	0.46
0.78	0.94	0.46

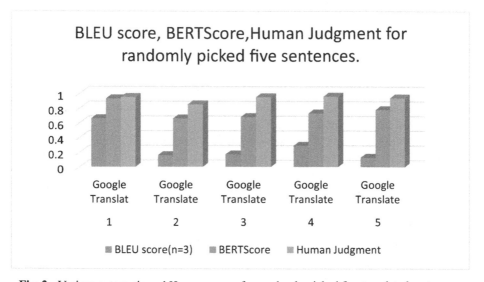

Fig. 2. Various automatic and Human scores for randomly picked five translated sentences.

Table 4. Pearson correlation between BLEU score and human judgment (human score)

BLEU Score	Human judgment	Pearson correlation
0.66	0.95	0.34
0.16	0.85	0.34
0.17	0.95	0.34
0.29	0.96	0.34
0.13	0.94	0.34

4   Result Analysis and Discussion

Analyzing the results, we obtained in Sect. 3, we can see that the automatic evaluation metric BERTScore exhibits a higher correlation with human **judgment** compared to the n-gram-based BLEU metric (Table 3). The Pearson correlation coefficient has been computed separately between these two automatic metrics and human **judgment** (Human score), i.e., the BERT score vs human score and the BLEU score vs human score. As per the correlation values in Tables 3 and 4, BERTScore always has a higher correlation value with human scores because of its ability to capture a contextual representation of reference and hypothesis texts. Since BLEU tries to match exact tokens between candidate and reference sentences, it fails to generate an authentic score since the word may have its synonym. Further, when we analyze the BLEU score and BERTScore of all these five sentences, it has been found that sentence 1 has the highest score in both the automatic metrics compared to the rest of the sentences (Table 2). The reason for this is reference text and hypothesis text both have maximum token matching in this sentence (Table 1). Hence BLEU and BERTScore both have generated the highest score for this sentence based on their own measuring criteria.

5   Conclusion and Future Work

MT is a fast-growing field. Researchers are continuously working in this domain to upgrade the model to achieve higher accuracy. However, during model design, automatic performance evaluation of the model plays a vital role. Designing an automatic evaluation metric is a challenging task because of its inherent linguistic, syntactic, and semantic intricacies that need to be checked in the hypothesis and reference texts while evaluating the generated (hypothesis) text. Hence, using appropriate evaluation metrics is important. We have understood the patterns of BLEU and BERTScore with gold standard human judgment. For this, we have used appropriate correlation i.e. Pearson correlation. Pearson correlation is suitable when we want to find a linear correlation between the two variables. Based on the patterns of correlation with the human score one can select the appropriate evaluation metric.

However, based on this study, we can say that we still have to go far in the MT automatic evaluation metric. Designing interpretable automatic evaluation metrics which is context-oriented is essential to achieving higher accuracy. However, to design such an evaluation metric creating a domain-specific reference corpus is equally important to achieve the task.

References

1. Stahlberg, F.: Neural machine translation: a review. J. Artif. Intell. Res. **69**, 343–418 (2020)
2. Bahdanau, D., Cho, K.H., Bengio, Y.: Neural machine translation by jointly learning to align and translate. In: 3rd Int. Conf. Learn. Represent. ICLR 2015 - Conf. Track Proc. 1–15 (2015)
3. Ramesh, A., Parthasarathy, V.B., Haque, R., Way, A.: Comparing statistical and neural machine translation performance on Hindi-To-Tamil and English-To-Tamil. Digital **1**, 86–102 (2021)
4. Zhang, Z., Liu, S., Li, M., Zhou, M., Chen, E.: Bidirectional generative adversari-al networks for neural machine translation. CoNLL 2018 - 22nd Conf. Comput. Nat. Lang. Learn. Proc. 190–199 (2018) https://doi.org/10.18653/v1/k18-1019
5. Lankford, S., Afli, H., Way, A.: Human evaluation of english-irish transform-er-based NMT. Information **13**, 309 (2022)

6. Fomicheva, M., Specia, L.: Taking MT evaluation metrics to extremes: beyond correlation with human judgments. Comput. Linguist. **45**, 515–558 (2019)

7. Papineni, K., Roukos, S., Ward, T., Zhu, W.-J.: Bleu: a method for automatic evaluation of machine translation. In: Proceedings of the 40th Annual Meeting of the Association for Computational Linguistics 311–318 (Association for Computational Linguistics) (2002). https://doi.org/10.3115/1073083.1073135

8. Joshi, N., Mathur, I., Darbari, H., Kumar, A.: HEVAL: yet another human evaluation metric. Int. J. Nat. Lang. Comput. 2 (2013)

9. Banerjee, S., Lavie, A.: METEOR: an automatic metric for MT evaluation with improved correlation with human judgments. Intrinsic Extrinsic Eval. Meas. Mach. Transl. and/or Summ. Proc. Work. ACL 2005 65–72 (2005)

10. Popović, M.: CHRF: character n-gram f-score for automatic MT evaluation. 10th Work. Stat. Mach. Transl. WMT 2015 2015 Conf. Empir. Methods Nat. Lang. Process. EMNLP 2015 - Proc. 392–395 (2015) https://doi.org/10.18653/v1/w15-3049

11. Lin, C.-Y.: ROUGE: a package for automatic evaluation of summaries. In: Text Summarization Branches Out 74–81 (Association for Computational Linguistics, 2004) (2004)

12. Zhang, T., Kishore, V., Wu, F., Weinberger, K.Q., Artzi, Y.: BERTScore: evaluating text generation with BERT. 1–43 (2019)

13. Devlin, J., Chang, M.W., Lee, K., Toutanova, K.: BERT: pre-training of deep bi-directional transformers for language understanding. NAACL HLT 2019 - 2019 Conf. North Am. Chapter Assoc. Comput. Linguist. Hum. Lang. Technol. - Proc. Conf. **1**, 4171–4186 (2019)

14. Hanna, M., Bojar, O.: A Fine-Grained Analysis of BERTScore. WMT 2021 - 6th Conf. Mach. Transl. Proc. 507–517 (2021)

15. Koehn, P., Och, F.J., Marcu, D.: Statistical Phrase-Based Translation. 48–54 (2003)

DyCoDa: A Multi-modal Data Collection of Multi-user Remote Survival Game Recordings

Denis Dresvyanskiy[1,2]([✉])[iD], Yamini Sinha[3][iD], Matthias Busch[3][iD],
Ingo Siegert[3][iD], Alexey Karpov[4][iD], and Wolfgang Minker[1][iD]

[1] Ulm University, Albert-Einstein-Allee 43, 89081 Ulm, Germany
{denis.dresvyanskiy,wolfgang.minker}@uni-ulm.de
[2] ITMO University, Kronverksky Pr. 49, bldg. A, 197101 St. Petersburg, Russia
[3] Otto von Guericke University, Universitätsplatz 2, Magdeburg, Germany
{yamini.sinha,matthias.busch,siegert}@ovgu.de
[4] St. Petersburg Federal Research Center of the Russian Academy of Sciences
(SPC RAS), 14th Line V.O. 39, 199178 St. Petersburg, Russia
karpov@iias.spb.su

Abstract. In this paper, we present a novel multi-modal multi-party conversation corpus called DyCoDa (Dynamic Conversational Dataset). It consists of remote intensive conversations among three interaction partners within a collaborative problem-solving scenario. The fundamental aim of building up this corpus is to investigate how humans interact with each other online via a video conferencing tool in a cooperation setting and which audio-visual cues are conveyed and perceived during this interaction. Apart from the high-quality audio and video recordings, the depth and infrared information recorded using the Microsoft Azure Kinect is also provided. Furthermore, various self-evaluation questionnaires are used to get socio-demographic information as well as the personality structure and the individual team role. In total, 30 native German-speaking participants have taken part in the experiment carried out at Magdeburg University. Overall, the DyCoDa consists of 10 h of recorded interactions and will be beneficial for researchers in the field of human-computer interaction.

Keywords: Group interaction · Multi-party interaction · Remote meetings · Paralinguistics · Affective computing · Online conversations · Engagement · Dominance

1 Introduction

Spoken/written language is not the only channel humans use to transmit information to each other. According to the A. Mehrabian [24], during human-human conversations, people convey only 7% of the information through words, while the largest part of communicative information is transmitted via non-verbal (55%) and vocal (38%) cues. Thereby, humans can express additional information such as emotions, engagement, dominance, etc.

© Springer Nature Switzerland AG 2022
S. R. M. Prasanna et al. (Eds.): SPECOM 2022, LNAI 13721, pp. 163–177, 2022.
https://doi.org/10.1007/978-3-031-20980-2_15

Despite some progress in detecting and interpreting non-verbal cues in dyadic conversations [5,37], the research community is still far away from a whole understanding and interpretation of paralinguistic, extralinguistic, and non-verbal signals. However, by learning how to exploit all conveyed by humans' information, technical systems will be able to embed in human society and become natural agents in human-computer interactions.

One of the bottlenecks in development of such systems is still a lack of data. Among all datasets available today, there are many laboratory-controlled ones [23,29]. Moreover, the fast-growing digitalization, speeded-up by the COVID pandemic, embraces more and more use cases, and nowadays, online meetings have become common. Such conversations differ from the personal ones [22,35]. However, for conducting research in this domain, there are not many corpora to provide the researchers with enough amount of data and diversity.

In this work, we introduce a novel corpus *DyCoDa (Dynamic Conversational Dataset)*, which represents intensive online collaborative conversations among a group of three people. The participants interact with each other to jointly solve a gamified task, expressing a huge amount of affective information and conversational dynamics. Apart from the standard audio and video data, we provide depth and infrared channel information, which can serve as a good basis for gesture and posture recognition.

The DyCoDa corpus has been designed to connect such individual and group dynamics as *Emotions*, *Engagement*, and *Dominance*. This is feasible due to the fact that *Emotions* by definition are affective information, while *Engagement* and *Dominance* include an affective component [8,20]. Although there are several corpora with similar conditions (e.g. [23,32]), none of them combine multi-party online settings with aforementioned annotations.

Thus, the main contributions of the paper are as follows. First, we provide a new multi-party multi-modal corpus with fully online conversations. The dataset offers 10 h of recorded data for the analysis of conversational dynamics in a problem-solving setting. Second, all experiments are done with native German speakers, giving the opportunity to investigate the peculiarities of social cues in the German culture. Third, the DyCoDa serves to fill the gap in the analysis of conversational dynamics within an online environment, which differs from broadly presented in-person interactions.

The rest of the paper is organized as follows: we analyze the current available group conversational datasets in Sect. 2. Afterwards, Sect. 3 presents a corpus design and the equipment we have used. Next, Sect. 4 specifies the collected data. The description of the main and supplement annotations is given in Sect. 5. In Sect. 6, we provide the opportunities to obtain data. Lastly, Sect. 7 summarizes the performed work.

2   Related Work

So far, several corpora have been collected to analyze social behavior in small groups.

One of the most well-known corpora dedicated to the analysis of multi-party interactions is the AMI meeting corpus [23]. In this database, the participants played the roles of employees in an electronic company, developing a new product for the market. One of the key features of these corpora is that they are decently structured: the role of each participant and the structure of the interactions are pre-determined. The DOME corpus [1] is a subset of the AMI meeting dataset, which investigates the dominance aspects of the multi-party interactions.

In the Mission Survival Corpus 2 [27], developers have collected multi-modal small group interactions within the Survival Task scenario. As it was done in the AMI meeting corpus, the functional roles of every participant were predefined before the experiment, thus setting the task to automatically predict these roles from multi-modal social cues. However, the angle of the video camera does not allow for analysis of the facial expressions of all participants.

In the Idiap Wolf Corpus [15], authors have collected an audio-visual corpus of big group interactions (eight to twelve people) based on the competitive role-playing scenario. Although the roles were predefined, participants did not know the role of others, giving room for conversations oriented to guessing *who is who?*

In [32], authors have published the ELEA corpus dedicated to the emergent leadership phenomenon. During every session, four participants have played the Survival Task (as in [27]), showing valuable conversational information and dominance cues, which are supposed to be used for the automatic identification of an emergent leader in a group of unfamiliar persons.

Similar to the ELEA [32] setting, the GAP corpus [4] was designed to study the group cohesion, leadership, post-meeting satisfaction, and group member influence. Analyzing collected data, authors found a significant connection between task performance, post-task satisfaction rating, and group characteristics.

M. Koutsombogera and C. Vogel in [19] have presented the MULTISIMO corpus, which is intended to study collaborative aspects in task-performing small groups. The dataset has multi-modal rich annotated data, including affective information, dominance, lexical markers, and other information.

Regarding the online setting, several datasets were introduced so far. F. Ringeval et al. [29] have presented the multi-modal corpus of dyadic spontaneous interactions called RECOLA. During experiments, participants should have done a collaborative task remotely, while their mood was manipulated. The dataset contains a variety of annotations, including emotions, engagement, and dominance. However, the two latter are provided only for the whole video.

In [9], authors have collected an audio corpus of cooperative dyadic interactions called CReST. The participants were involved in the remote collaborations in a way that one participant cannot resolve a problem without getting help from another one. The dataset contains speech signals and dialogue transcriptions, while the dialog structure, disfluencies, constituent, and dependency syntax were additionally annotated. However, this corpus has no video modality.

Although many of the aforementioned corpora have rich multi-modal group interactions and are annotated in terms of different dynamic conversational attributes, they are highly structured (controlled). Because of predefined roles and interaction structure, the participants are not free to act as they want to, while the role pre-definition itself influences the naturalness of the conversation. Moreover, the most of considered datasets have no online interaction settings, while those, which have it, contain only dyadic conversations. Besides, only RECOLA contains emotions, engagement, and dominance annotation simultaneously, however, two last characteristics are annotated only for the whole video. This makes it impossible to develop a system able to evaluate the conversational characteristics' in real-time for small human groups.

That is why we have developed our own multi-modal corpus DyCoDa with remote online collaborations. It is able to fill in gaps that have arisen in other datasets, while it also increases the available amount of data for the analysis of multi-party human-human intensive remote interactions.

3   Corpus Design

3.1   Participants and Privacy

Overall, 30 participants (21 male, 9 female) have taken part in the DyCoDa experiment, making up 10 groups of three people each. They were recruited in Otto von Guericke University located in Magdeburg, Germany. All the informants are native German speakers. All participants were the students, therefore the mean age is 21.97 years (standard deviation is 3.37). According to the self-reports filled in by the subjects before the experiment, 60% of them were familiar with their teammates, which could influence the way of interaction in such a sense that in these teams the participants are more willing to speak free and unbiased.

All participants were asked to sign a consent for participation, which includes an allowance to distribute recorded data for further use by the research community and for research purposes only. The possibility to block data for distribution at any time is also provided to the participant. The anonymity of each subject is ensured by giving him/her a unique ID generated right before the start of the experiment. Thus, during the experiment, each participant is associated only with the generated ID, while personal data is not recorded.

3.2   Questionnaires

Several self-defined and psychological questionnaires accompanied the experiment. While selecting questionnaires, we were focused on the information regarding dominance and engagement in group interactions, as well as role models in groups.

First of all, to identify personal characteristics of the participants, we have applied the following questionnaires:

– *Socio-demographic information.* This short questionnaire contains such information as sex, age, country of birth, nationality, level of education, employment, monthly income (if there is any).

- *Big Five Inventory (BFI-10).* This well-known questionnaire allows measuring roughly an individual personality structure of adult interviewees from the German-speaking general population [28].
- *Belbin Self-Perception Inventory (BTRI)* [2]. It denotes the function, position, or task that the team member usually has within a group. The success of a team depends on the right mix of different roles, and it can be assumed that a crisis team needs strong action-oriented roles [12].

In our experiments, we were interested in the group dynamics that emerge during the experiment. Apart from typically used external observers, which can rate the dynamics, the participants' self-assessments of group events that happened during the experiment are also important and can provide valuable information about past processes in the group. Therefore, we have included the following questionnaires in the experiment:

- *User Engagement Scale Short Form (UES-SF)* [26]. This questionnaire allows measuring the engagement of the participant (user) in a specific context such as, for example, game setting or task-completing setting. To not bother participants with many questions, we have used a short version of the UES-SF. As it is recommended by the authors of this questionnaire, we have modified the wording of the UES-SF so that its content fits our experiment.
- *Perceived dominance questionnaire (PDQ).* To measure the participant dominance shown during the experiment, we have implemented the PDQ based on the ideas presented in [33]. The PDQ consists of two main items: one asks to rank all participants in terms of dominance (including the performing participant) via constructing the list of participants (the more left a participant is placed in the list, the more dominant is he/she), while another one asks to distribute 10 points of perceived dominance among all three participants.
- *Simplified System for the Multiple Level Observation of Groups (S-SYMLOG)* [3]. Despite the fact that this questionnaire is more about personal identity, we listed it here, because it directly refers to the participants' behavior within the group of people. S-SYMLOG allows measuring participant's social interaction within the group in three dimensions: Up-Down (dominant vs submissive), Positive-Negative (cold vs friendly), Forward-Backward (emotionally inexpressive vs expressive).

3.3 Procedure

General description. Every session requires a group of three participants. We have formed the groups randomly from a pool of registered students. The entire experiment divides into three phases, schematically depicted in Fig. 1.

Every phase serves for different data acquisition task.

Pre-experimental Phase. Before the experiment, the participants have been told a goal and a short description of the experiment. They have also signed consent for participation, giving the possibility to distribute recorded data within the research community. In addition, the participants should fill in questionnaires

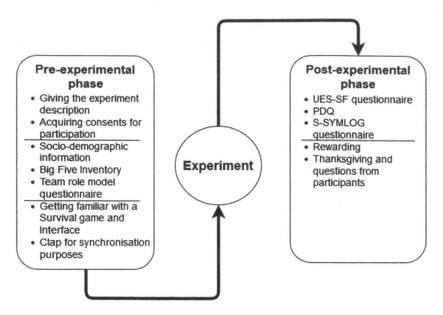

Fig. 1. Pipeline of the experimental procedure.

about their personalities. At the end of this phase, the experimenter introduces the Survival Game and interface, through which the interaction will take place. The pre-experimental phase takes around 20 min to complete.

Interaction Experiment "Survival Game". The experiment itself is a winter variant of "Survival Game", which is supposed to induce rich discussions (debates) among participants due to the task's nature. We have allocated the description of a scenario of this game in the Sect. 3.4 due to formatting reasons. The procedure of the Interaction Experiment was as follows:

The participants were sitting in front of a computer. Video, audio, depth, and infrared signals were captured by Microsoft Azure Kinect, while another one audio signal was recorded by a headset. We have ensured the audio-visual interaction among participants via Zoom[1] application. Moreover, for the task completion goal, participants were able to interact via a shared whiteboard. For this, we have used the Miro[2] application. To give an example of it, we have depicted the whiteboard participants have exploited in Fig. 2.

On that whiteboard, participants were free to act as they want. The final ranking is done by allocating yellow stickers in the boxes with numbers, denoting the importance of each item. The participants were limited to 20 min for the discussions and task completion.

To make the interaction scheme clearer, we have depicted it in Fig. 3.

---

[1] https://zoom.us/.

[2] https://miro.com/.

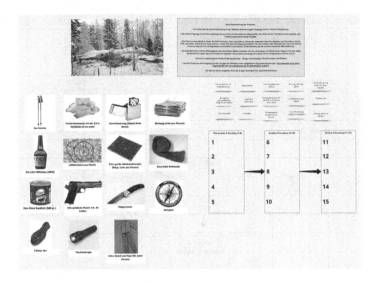

Fig. 2. Example of the online whiteboard used by the participants.

Post-experimental Phase. After the experiment, participants were asked to fill in questionnaires regarding their interaction and game experience. Afterwards, we gave rewards to participants and answered their questions if there were some.

3.4   Winter Survival Task Scenario

The Winter Survival Task and its variations are quite often used in research and as a social game to familiarize group members with each other, identify the personal identities of members, and elicit different implicit conversational attributes within the group. Originally, it was developed to examine the dynamics of team building and group decision-making during cooperative problem solving [17].

The idea of such a scenario is simple: the participants are given an imagined situation of crush-landing in a deep winter forest with cold weather, decently far from any human settlement. During the landing, only 15 items are saved from destruction. Participants should rank these items in terms of survival importance, giving them the numbers from 1 to 15, where 1 means the most important item and 15 denotes the least important. The ranking should be done mutually. This implies debates and shows rich affective information during the discussion.

Comparing the list of items provided by a participant with the one formed by an expert, the experimenter is able to evaluate the quality of the decision based on the difference between these two lists. In particular, for the Winter Survival Task, the more is a distinction between two lists, the more points are given to the performing team (0 points means the perfect solution). Based on the points earned, there are 4 possible outcomes of the game: all participants have "survived", participants got frostbite, only two participants have "survived", and all participants "passed away". To get more detailed information, the reader is kindly referred to [17] and to the example of Survival Task[3].

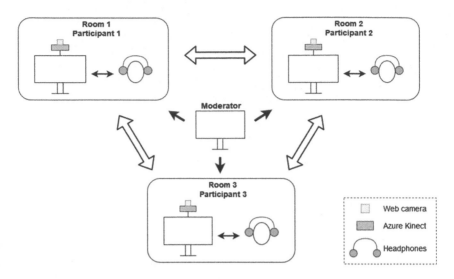

Fig. 3. Scheme of the Interaction Experiment "Survival Game". Participants are sitting alone in separate rooms and interact with each other via a computer interface. The moderator controls the experiment and intervenes only in case of technical problems.

3.5   Recording Setup

For simulation of online conversations, the experiments were conducted in three different rooms equipped with:

– *Personal Computer* required for task completion and data processing.
– *Microsoft Azure Kinect* required for recording audio, video, depth, and infrared signals.
– *Headset (Creative Chat 3,5-mm-Stereo-Headset)* for audio playback, while the head microphone is used additionally for high quality voice recording.
– *Web camera (Logitech C920s PRO HD Webcam)* for ensuring video interaction among participants via Zoom application (as a separate channel).

An example of the recording setup is presented in Fig. 4. We combined the Azure Kinect device with the Web camera and located them in front of the participant (behind the monitor) so that it would be possible to observe all gestures and upper body postures of the participant. Both the Azure Kinect and Web camera were placed so that it models typical places for office (home) workplace setups. While participants were interacting with group members via Zoom, the headset was on all the time. The screen was divided into two zones: (1) two-thirds of the space for the Miro application, (2) one-third for the Zoom.

---

[3] https://ed.fnal.gov/arise/guide.html.

Fig. 4. Example of the data collection setup.

The participants were randomly distributed among the experiment's rooms after the experimenter gave an introduction and briefing. For the questionnaires, we used the SoSci survey [21] to collect the data in a secure manner.

4   Collected Data

In this work, the audio, video, depth, and infrared signals were recorded. We have summarized the dataset characteristics in Table 1. Apart from the standard audio and video data, we provide the information from the depth and infrared channels. Regarding the audio, there are two audio sources extracted from every participant: (1) attached to the headset microphone, which allows getting a high-quality recording of the participant's speech, and (2) the microphone array, which captures all sounds in the room, including speech.

All channels are synchronised. The synchronisation of audio with video data was carried out manually, while the depth and infrared channels are synchronised with the video channel by default. In addition, the results of questionnaires, socio-demographic information, and group performance scores are also included in the distributing data.

5   Annotations

To provide a good basis for analysis of conversations, we have decided to annotate several attributes of conversation, which compose the structure and success of the discussion. The affective state (*Emotions*) of every participant is an essential part of any human-human conversation, which influences the discussions in many ways. The *Dominance* helps to understand the established structure in the group, formed social roles, and information flow among the participants. The *Engagement* can provide the cues of efficiency and involvement in the group activity of a particular participant and the whole group, opening the opportunity to predict the productivity of the group.

Table 1. DyCoDa dataset characteristics.

Participants	30
Group interactions	10
Males/females	21/9
Age mean (std)	21.97 (3.37)
Language	German
Total recorded data	10 h
Session length mean (std)	20.0 min (0.0 min)
Data	
Audio (headset)	1xMono, 32 Bit, 44.1 kHz
Audio (Azure Kinect)	7xMono, 32 Bit, 44.1 kHz
Video (Azure Kinect)	RGB 1920 × 1080 px, 30 FPS
Depth (Azure Kinect)	320 × 288 px, 30 FPS
Infrared (Azure Kinect)	1024 × 1024 px, 30 FPS

The *Emotion, Dominance,* and *Engagement* are subjective terms and can greatly vary based on the experience of the rater. Therefore, following the experience of other authors [18,31], we have applied a crowdsourcing platform for the annotation process, relying on the "wisdom-of-the-crowd" approach. Such a technique allows getting annotations with good quality, while the number of raters is measured in tens or even hundreds of people, giving good distributed opinions for every annotation segment. We used the Amazon Mechanical Turk[4].

5.1 Main Annotations

We have asked all workers (raters) of the Amazon Mechanical Turk to annotate three various characteristics. Since the annotation process of every characteristic is different, we have divided the annotation into three sub-tasks:

- *Emotions.* Every video file was split into 1-second segments. This type of partitioning allows reducing annotations costs, while keeps the annotation frequency high. As a reference for annotation of every segment, we have used six (universal) emotion categories defined by P. Ekman [10] plus neutral state. Overall, we got 36 000 1-second segments, which is being annotated by three raters at least.
- *Dominance.* For the Dominance annotation, most researchers have used the timescale with four minutes on average [1,16] or whole recordings of meetings [33]. However, as a compromise between the context length and annotation frequency, we have chosen a period of 60 s for the *Dominance* evaluation. This allows us to have more data for machine learning models. Following the technique presented in [1,16], we asked the raters to distribute 10 points

---

[4] https://www.mturk.com/.

among participants so that the more points a participant has, the more dominant he/she seemed. Moreover, we have provided an additional 5-point Likert scale to note the *annotation confidence*, because some segments could be poor on signals conveyed by participants, causing ambiguity in the annotation process. The whole number of 60-s segments is 200, while each segment is being annotated by five raters.

– *Engagement.* For the *Engagement* annotation, several timescales were used [30,36]. Moreover, the classification granularity varies from binary to 10 classes [14,25,30]. We have applied the engagement scale with four classes as it is used in [13,36]. Such scale forces the rater to choose between low and high observed engagement levels, eliminating the problem of gravitating to the middle class in case of a sense of uncertainty [13]. Thus, we have chosen a timescale of 10 s, while the classes have been {*No engagement, Moderate engagement, High engagement, Very high engagement*}. We have added the fifth option as well, to note that the video segment does not contain a person or no visual and audio cues have been shown. To alleviate the annotation task, we have provided a clear definition for each class with typical visual and audio cues, which arise during a certain level of engagement.
The whole number of 10-s video segments is 3 600. Each segment is being annotated by three raters.

Every annotation sub-task is delivered as follows: before the beginning, the precise description of the phenomenon to be annotated, typical cues for presented categories, and the description of the annotation interface are given to the rater. After reading provided explanation, to learn the procedure of the annotation process, the raters are given three samples of sub-task - these are training examples with predefined answers. Finally, the annotation process itself starts. The rater can get done as many sub-tasks as he/she wants to. Besides, to reduce the number of malicious or low-performing raters, the special video segments (honeypots) with known in advance answers (or annotations) for all the sub-tasks were prepared. If a rater does not answer rightly on at least two honeypots, his/her annotations are not approved.
We have summarized characteristics of all main annotations in Table 2.

Table 2. Characteristics of main annotations. VS - video sequence.

Descriptor	VS length (seconds)	Total # VS	Raters/VS	Categories
Emotions	1	36 000	3	7 emotion categories
Dominance	60	200	10	10 distributed points
Engagement	10	3 600	3	4 classes

5.2 Complement Annotations

In addition to the main annotations presented above, we provide the following low-level annotations and features:

- *Transcripts.* We provide the transcriptions of every audio file. The transcription is done utilizing the Google Speech-to-Text API.
- *Speech regions.*
- *Acoustic features.* As acoustic features, we take a set of features presented in ComParE 2016 Emotion Recognition Challenge [34]. We have used the OpenSMILE toolkit [11] to extract them from the raw audio files.
- *Face bounding boxes and Deep features.* For every video frame, we provide the coordinates of faces and pre-calculated deep embeddings. The face detection is done utilizing the RetinaFace model [7], while deep embeddings are extracted using the VGGFace2 [6].

6   Availability

The DyCoDa corpus is available for research purposes only. The data is being distributed upon request. We welcome the collaborative research using DyCoDa in such domains as automatic analysis and evaluation of group dynamics, affective computing, conversational user interfaces, and assistive technologies. A general description of the database and future annotation can be found on GitHub[5].

7   Conclusion

In this paper, we have introduced a novel multi-party multi-modal dataset on dynamic conversations of small groups. The focus of this dataset is on the rich affective group interactions among members involved in gamified task completion. Within the course of the experiment, participants need to provide a mutual solution to the cooperative task called the Winter Survival Task. The set time limit allows getting plentiful and intensive polylogs with different manifestations of emotions, engagement, dominance, and other conversational characteristics.

We provide the audio, video, depth, and infrared data recorded by the Microsoft Azure Kinect and headset devices. Furthermore, the participants' socio-demographic characteristics, as well as self-assessment of the interaction and their personalities, were gathered via questionnaires.

In total, 30 subjects (10 groups) took part in the experiment. The mean length of all sessions is 20 min, resulting in 10 h of recorded material.

Having rich emotional and intensive interactions among a group of three people, we believe that the collected data can be valuable for analysis of natural human-human conversations, development of efficient systems for automatic evaluation of group dynamics and emotional states, and in general, bringing computer systems to a more natural human-computer interaction.

We note that although the annotation process has not been completed yet (it is in process on Amazon Mechanical Turk), all data and annotations will be available soon on request.

---

[5] https://github.com/DresvyanskiyDenis/DyCoDa.

References

1. Aran, O., Hung, H., Gatica-Perez, D.: A multimodal corpus for studying dominance in small group conversations. In: LREC workshop on Multimodal Corpora: Advances in Capturing, Coding and Analyzing Multimodality, vol. 22 (2010)
2. Belbin, R.M.: Management Teams: Why They Succeed or Fail. Elsevier Science & Technology Books, Amsterdam (1981)
3. Blumberg, H.H.: A simplified version of the SYMLOG® trait rating form. Psychol. Rep. **99**(1), 46–50 (2006)
4. Braley, M., Murray, G.: The group affect and performance (GAP) corpus. In: Proceedings of the Group Interaction Frontiers in Technology, GIFT 2018. Association for Computing Machinery, New York (2018)
5. Cafaro, A., et al.: The NoXi database: multimodal recordings of mediated novice-expert interactions. In: Proceedings of the 19th ACM International Conference on Multimodal Interaction, ICMI 2017, pp. 350–359. Association for Computing Machinery (2017)
6. Cao, Q., Shen, L., Xie, W., Parkhi, O.M., Zisserman, A.: VGGFace2:: a dataset for recognising faces across pose and age. In: 2018 13th IEEE International Conference on Automatic Face and Gesture Recognition (FG 2018), pp. 67–74 (2018)
7. Deng, J., Guo, J., Ververas, E., Kotsia, I., Zafeiriou, S.: RetinaFace: single-shot multi-level face localisation in the wild. In: Proceedings of the IEEE/CVF Conference on Computer Vision and Pattern Recognition, pp. 5202–5211, June 2020
8. Doherty, K., Doherty, G.: Engagement in HCI: conception, theory and measurement. ACM Comput. Surv. **51**(5), 1–39 (2018)
9. Eberhard, K., Nicholson, H., Kübler, S., Gundersen, S., Scheutz, M.: The Indiana "cooperative remote search task" (CReST) corpus. In: Proceedings of the Seventh International Conference on Language Resources and Evaluation (LREC 2010) (2010)
10. Ekman, P., Friesen, W.V.: Constants across cultures in the face and emotion. J. Pers. Soc. Psychol. **17**(2), 124 (1971)
11. Eyben, F., Wöllmer, M., Schuller, B.: OpenSMILE: the Munich versatile and fast open-source audio feature extractor. In: Proceedings of the 18th ACM International Conference on Multimedia, MM 2010, pp. 1459–1462. Association for Computing Machinery, New York (2010)
12. Fisher, S.G., Hunter, T.A., Macrosson, K.W.D.: The structure of Belbin's team roles. J. Occup. Organ. Psychol. **71**, 283–288 (1998)
13. Gupta, A., D'Cunha, A., Awasthi, K., Balasubramanian, V.: DAiSEE: towards user engagement recognition in the wild. arXiv preprint arXiv:1609.01885 (2016)
14. Huang, Y., Gilmartin, E., Campbell, N.: Conversational engagement recognition using auditory and visual cues. In: Proceedings of Interspeech 2016, pp. 590–594 (2016)
15. Hung, H., Chittaranjan, G.: The Idiap Wolf corpus: exploring group behaviour in a competitive role-playing game. In: Proceedings of the 18th ACM International Conference on Multimedia, MM 2010, pp. 879–882. Association for Computing Machinery, New York (2010)
16. Jayagopi, D.B., Hung, H., Yeo, C., Gatica-Perez, D.: Modeling dominance in group conversations using nonverbal activity cues. IEEE Trans. Audio Speech Lang. Process. **17**(3), 501–513 (2009)
17. Johnson, D.W., Johnson, F.P.: Joining Together: Group Theory and Group Skills. Prentice-Hall, Inc., Englewood Cliffs (1991)

18. Kamath, A., Biswas, A., Balasubramanian, V.: A crowdsourced approach to student engagement recognition in e-learning environments. In: 2016 IEEE Winter Conference on Applications of Computer Vision (WACV), pp. 1–9 (2016)
19. Koutsombogera, M., Vogel, C.: Modeling collaborative multimodal behavior in group dialogues: the MULTISIMO corpus. In: Proceedings of the Eleventh International Conference on Language Resources and Evaluation (LREC 2018), Miyazaki, Japan. European Language Resources Association (ELRA), May 2018
20. Latulipe, C., Carroll, E.A., Lottridge, D.: Love, hate, arousal and engagement: exploring audience responses to performing arts. In: Proceedings of the SIGCHI Conference on Human Factors in Computing Systems, CHI 2011, pp. 1845–1854. Association for Computing Machinery, New York (2011)
21. Leiner, D.J.: SoSci Survey (version 3.1.06) (2019). https://www.soscisurvey.de
22. Lieberman, A., Schroeder, J.: Two social lives: how differences between online and offline interaction influence social outcomes. Curr. Opin. Psychol. 31, 16–21 (2020)
23. McCowan, I., et al.: The AMI meeting corpus. In: Noldus, L., Grieco, F., Loijens, L., Zimmerman, P. (eds.) Proceedings of Measuring Behavior 2005, 5th International Conference on Methods and Techniques in Behavioral Research, pp. 137–140. Noldus Information Technology, August 2005
24. Mehrabian, A.: Nonverbal Communication. Aldine-Atherton, Chicago (1972)
25. Oertel, C., Scherer, S., Campbell, N.: On the use of multimodal cues for the prediction of degrees of involvement in spontaneous conversation. In: Proceedings of Interspeech 2011, pp. 1541–1544 (2011)
26. O'Brien, H.L., Cairns, P., Hall, M.: A practical approach to measuring user engagement with the refined user engagement scale (UES) and new UES short form. Int. J. Hum. Comput. Stud. 112, 28–39 (2018)
27. Pianesi, F., Zancanaro, M., Lepri, B., Cappelletti, A.: A multimodal annotated corpus of consensus decision making meetings. Lang. Resour. Eval. 41(3), 409–429 (2007)
28. Rammstedt, B., Kemper, C.J., Klein, M.C., Beierlein, C., Kovaleva, A.: Big five inventory (BFI-10). Zusammenstellung sozialwissenschaftlicher Items und Skalen (ZIS) (2014)
29. Ringeval, F., Sonderegger, A., Sauer, J., Lalanne, D.: Introducing the RECOLA multimodal corpus of remote collaborative and affective interactions. In: 10th IEEE International Conference and Workshops on Automatic Face and Gesture Recognition (FG 2013), pp. 1–8 (2013)
30. Salam, H., Chetouani, M.: Engagement detection based on multi-party cues for human robot interaction. In: 2015 International Conference on Affective Computing and Intelligent Interaction (ACII), pp. 341–347 (2015)
31. Salam, H., Çeliktutan, O., Hupont, I., Gunes, H., Chetouani, M.: Fully automatic analysis of engagement and its relationship to personality in human-robot interactions. IEEE Access 5, 705–721 (2017)
32. Sanchez-Cortes, D., Aran, O., Mast, M.S., Gatica-Perez, D.: Identifying emergent leadership in small groups using nonverbal communicative cues. In: International Conference on Multimodal Interfaces and the Workshop on Machine Learning for Multimodal Interaction, ICMI-MLMI 2010. Association for Computing Machinery, New York (2010)
33. Sanchez-Cortes, D., Aran, O., Mast, M.S., Gatica-Perez, D.: A nonverbal behavior approach to identify emergent leaders in small groups. IEEE Trans. Multimedia 14(3), 816–832 (2012)

34. Schuller, B., et al.: The INTERSPEECH 2016 computational paralinguistics challenge: Deception, sincerity & native language. In: 17th Annual Conference of the International Speech Communication Association (Interspeech 2016), pp. 2001–2005. ISCA (2016)
35. Siegert, I., Niebuhr, O.: Case report: women, be aware that your vocal charisma can dwindle in remote meetings. Front. Commun. **5**, 611555 (2021)
36. Whitehill, J., Serpell, Z., Lin, Y.C., Foster, A., Movellan, J.R.: The faces of engagement: automatic recognition of student engagement from facial expressions. IEEE Trans. Affect. Comput. **5**(1), 86–98 (2014)
37. Zhao, J., Li, R., Chen, S., Jin, Q.: Multi-modal multi-cultural dimensional continues emotion recognition in dyadic interactions. In: Proceedings of the 2018 on Audio/Visual Emotion Challenge and Workshop, AVEC 2018, pp. 65–72. Association for Computing Machinery, New York (2018)

On the Use of Ensemble X-Vector Embeddings for Improved Sleepiness Detection

José Vicente Egas-López[1(✉)], Róbert Busa-Fekete[3], and Gábor Gosztolya[1,2]

[1] Institute of Informatics, University of Szeged, Szeged, Hungary
egasj@inf.u-szeged.hu
[2] MTA-SZTE Research Group on Artificial Intelligence, Szeged, Hungary
[3] Google Research, New York, NY, USA

Abstract. The state-of-the-art in speaker recognition, called x-vectors, has been adopted in several computational paralinguistic tasks, as they were shown to extract embeddings that could be efficiently utilized as features in the subsequent classification or regression step. Nevertheless, similarly to all neural networks, x-vectors might also prove to be sensitive to several training meta-parameters such as the number of hidden layers and neurons, or the number of training epochs. In this study we experimentally demonstrate that the performance of x-vector embeddings is also affected by the random seed of the initial weight initialization step before training. We also show that, by training an ensemble learning method by repeating x-vector DNN training, we can make the utterance-level predictions more robust, leading to notable improvements in the performance on the test set. We perform our experiments on the publicly available Dusseldorf Sleepy Language Corpus, for estimating the degree of sleepiness. Improving upon our previous results, we present the highest Spearman's correlation coefficient on this dataset that was achieved by a single method.

Keywords: Human-computer interaction · Computational paralinguistics · X-vectors · Ensemble learning · Sleepiness detection

1 Introduction

Excessive daytime sleepiness (EDS) is usually considered to be caused by sleep deprivation, sleep disorders (e.g. apnea, which is the cessation of breathing), or by insomnia (the inability to fall asleep) [11]. Instant identification of the levels of sleepiness for a subject might be crucial for preventing accidents, analyzing when to recommend a break, or even minimizing the mortality risk caused by sleep deprivation. Moreover, as EDS is catalogued as a symptom rather than a condition, it could also be caused by latent neurological or psychiatric disorders [12,13,20]. In that case, the early diagnosis of EDS could be helpful for diminishing the effects of an underlying problem in a subject. Patients with sleep disorders often show symptoms of tiredness and fatigue, which, amongst other things, might affect the way they produce their speech. This modality – that

© Springer Nature Switzerland AG 2022
S. R. M. Prasanna et al. (Eds.): SPECOM 2022, LNAI 13721, pp. 178–187, 2022.
https://doi.org/10.1007/978-3-031-20980-2_16

is, the speech – could be a non-intrusive and economic way of controlling and monitoring the degree of sleepiness of the subjects.

A key problem in computational paralinguistic tasks is the choice of the features extracted from the audio utterances. Besides developing task-dependant attributes, a significant direction of research is to apply general-purpose attributes in paralinguistic tasks. Such an attribute set is the 'ComParE functionals', developed by Schuller et al. [19], consisting of utterance-level statisticals (e.g. mean, standard deviation, 1st and 99th percentiles) of frame-level features. Other frequently applied features are the i-vectors [2], originally developed for speaker recognition, which were applied in various paralinguistic tasks such as determining the cognitive load of the speaker [21], or estimating the speaker's age [7]. The current state-of-the-art technique for speaker recognition is the so-called *x-vector* approach [24], which employs a Deep Neural Network to map variable-length utterances to fixed-dimensional embeddings. A handful of previous studies exploited x-vector embeddings in computational paralinguistic tasks; for instance, to classify emotion from the speech of subjects [14], and to screen neuro-degenerative diseases like Alzheimer's Disease [28], and Parkinson's Disease [10]. In previous studies, x-vectors were applied for sleepiness detection as well [3,9].

Since the x-vector feature extractors are neural networks, they might prove to be sensitive to several training meta-parameters such as number of hidden layers and neurons, learning rate, and number of training epochs. Furthermore, since it is common to train a DNN from scratch by initializing the weights randomly (although, of course, from a specific distribution, following e.g. the initialization strategy of Glorot and Bengio [5] or He et al. [8]), the performance of a neural network might even be dependent on the random seed of this weight initialization step. This might also hold for x-vectors, even if they are used only for feature extraction, followed by a machine learning method (e.g. SVM). Perhaps because x-vectors are a relatively recent technique, earlier studies did not consider this stochastic behaviour as a potential source of suboptimal classification performance. In fact, we found no study at all that investigated the effect of randomness for the x-vector encodings.

Our study has two key results. Firstly, we demonstrate experimentally that paralinguistic classification is indeed adversely affected by the random noise introduced by the x-vector representation. Then, in the second step, we also demonstrate that by training an *ensemble* learning method (by repeating the x-vector DNN training process several times), we can make the utterance-level prediction process more robust, leading to notable improvements in the performance on the test set.

2   The Dusseldorf Sleepy Language Corpus

We performed our experiments on the SLEEP (Dusseldorf Sleepy Language) Corpus. It was created by the Institute of Psychophysiology, Duesseldorf, and the Institute of Safety Technology, University of Wuppertal, Germany. The corpus comprises the recordings of 915 German speakers (364 females and 551 males), from 12 to 84 years of age (mean age was 27.6 years). The subjects were asked to read passages and to speak about specific topics, such as their last weekend or to describe a picture, which resulted in spontaneous narrative speech. It contains 5564, 5328 and 5570 utterances, training, development and test sets, respectively; all three subsets contain recordings of slightly less than six hours, leading to 17 h and 35 min of speech overall. After recording, the utterances were converted to a 16 kHz sampling rate with a quantisation of 16 bits.

The degree of sleepiness of the subjects was assessed using the Karolinska Sleepiness Scale (KSS, [22]). Each subject reported their sleepiness level on the Karolinska Sleepiness Scale (KSS): from 1 (extremely alert) to 9 (very sleepy). At the same time, two observers assigned posthoc observer KSS ratings. The average of both scores was the reference sleepiness value [18]. Later, this corpus was included in the Interspeech Computational Paralinguistic Challenge (ComParE) in 2019 [18]. Studies using this corpus found that, instead of opting for classification, it is beneficial to treat this task as a regression one, and round the predictions to integer values on the scale $1, \ldots, 9$ later (see e.g. [6,18,26,27]). We will follow the same strategy in our experiments.

In the ComParE Challenge, the participants applied several techniques like attention networks and adversarial augmentation [27], end-to-end CNNs [4] and Fisher vectors [6,26]. The performance of the methods was measured with Spearman's Correlation Coefficient (CC); the results lay in the range of 0.290 and 0.373 for the development set, and between 0.325 and 0.387 on the test set. Most of the better-performing approaches were combinations of two or more methods.

3   X-Vector Embeddings

The x-vector approach is a neural network-based feature extraction method that provides fixed-dimensional embeddings for variable-length utterances. This system can be viewed as a feed-forward Deep Neural Network that computes such embeddings.

3.1   DNN Architecture

The lower, *frame-level* layers of the network have a time-delay architecture. Following the frame-level layers, the *statistics pooling* layer gets the frame-level activations of the last frame-level layer, aggregates over the input segment, and computes the mean and the standard deviation. These vectors are concatenated and used as input for the next, *segment-level* layer, which is followed by one (or possibly more) additional segment-level layers. The *x-vectors* embeddings can be extracted from any of *segment* layers [23,24]. Instead of predicting frames, the DNN is trained to predict speakers from variable-length utterances. Namely, it is trained to classify speakers present in the train set utilizing a multi-class cross entropy objective function (for more details, see [23]). Therefore, the output softmax layer has as many neurons as there are speakers in the training set. Notice that, to calculate the embeddings, this output layer is not required any more, so it can be discarded after training.

The (utterance-level) embeddings produced by this network capture information from the speakers over the whole audio-signal. These embeddings are called *x-vectors* and they can be extracted from any *segment* layer.

4   Ensemble X-Vectors

Next, we introduce ensemble learning in general, and then we describe the proposed 'Ensemble x-vectors approach' in detail.

4.1   Ensemble Learning

The basic principle of ensemble learning is to train several different, but similar machine learning models, and combine their outputs in some way. Perhaps the best-known such techniques are *bagging* and *boosting*. Bagging carries out the training of such similar models by randomly selecting *subsets* of the training data [1]. Boosting, in contrast, trains the next individual classifier model by focusing on training instances which were mis-classified by previous models (e.g. by using larger weights for these examples [17]). *Stacking*, another ensemble learning technique, is basically a two-step learning scheme, where the outputs of different classifier models (e.g. different algorithms) are combined via another machine learning method [25].

4.2   The Ensemble X-Vector Model

In this study we propose to build an ensemble model based on the x-vector feature extractors. Notice that this approach differs substantially from the above-listed ensemble approaches in the sense that those trained the classification models on the same features; the difference between the models came from a different training subset selection or from utilizing a different machine learning technique. In contrast, we seek to train our classifier or regressor models on the whole training data, and on similar (albeit different) features.

That is, in this study we propose training several x-vector neural network models on the same data, but each time applying a different random seed. By calculating the embeddings with each of them, we get a number of different representations of the same training data. Although in theory concatenating these feature vectors and training only one classifier model might lead to a more robust performance than relying on any of the individual representations, we would end up with unfeasibly huge feature vectors. Therefore we chose to train separate machine learning (e.g. SVR) models on these x-vector representations in the next step. To make the predictions more robust (and hence, make hyperparameter selection more reliable), we suggest simply averaging out the predictions scores got after evaluation in an unweighted manner. Formally, we calculate the posterior estimate provided by the ensemble model as

$$f_e(X) = \frac{1}{m} \sum_{j=1}^{m} f_j(X) = \frac{1}{m} \sum_{j=1}^{m} f_j(H^j), \tag{1}$$

where X denotes the frame-level feature sequence of the actual utterance, H^j is the utterance-level representation (i.e. embedding) of X calculated by the jth x-vector model, and the f_j value is the individual prediction provided by the jth SVR model. According to our hypothesis, the unweighted average of the predictions should improve the robustness of the combined model, provided that the predictions of the individual models are noisy. We call this approach the 'Ensemble x-vector approach'. In our experiments, the number of models in the ensemble (m) was set to 10.

5   Experimental Setup

Next, we describe our experimental setup: how our x-vectors were trained, how we trained our Support Vector Regression methods, and how we evaluated model performance.

5.1   X-Vector Training

Following the results of our previous experiments, we trained our x-vector DNN models (i.e. extractors) on the combined training and development sets of the SLEEP corpus (10892 utterances, 11 h and 39 mins). We employed the Kaldi framework [16] to do this. The *segment6* layer of the DNN is used to compute the 512-dimensional neural network embeddings (i.e. *x-vectors*). As is common in x-vector extraction, we used 23 MFCCs and log-energy as frame-level features; these were also extracted by Kaldi. Although it is standard practice to employ additive noise and reverberation both to increase training data size and to improve the noise robustness of the model, in our earlier experimental results we found that for this particular corpus this process does not assist regression performance [3]; therefore, in our actual experiments we did not employ these techniques during x-vector training.

5.2   Regression and Evaluation

Support Vector Regression (SVR) was used to estimate the degree of sleepiness of the speakers. DNN embeddings were standardized by removing the mean and scaling to unit variance before training the model; transformation parameters were set on the training set. We relied on the scikit-learn implementation [15] with a linear kernel (nu-SVR method); the C complexity parameter was set in the range $10^{-6}, \ldots, 10^1$, based on the performance on the development set; we trained a new SVR model with the best complexity value on the training and development sets combined to obtain predictions for the test set. Before rounding to the nearest integer in the $1 \ldots 9$ scale, first we linearly transformed the predictions to have the same mean and standard deviation as those of the labels of the training set; transformation parameters were set on the development set. Since no parameter setting of this transformation involved the test set, and in the end all scores were integers in the range $1 \ldots 9$, the presented results are directly comparable to those found in the literature (e.g. [4, 26, 27]).

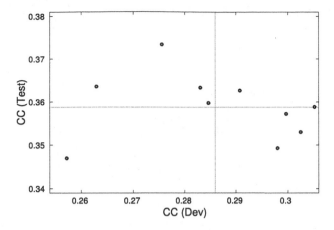

Fig. 1. Spearman's Correlation Coefficients of the individual x-vector models on the development and on the test set; the dotted lines show the average performance of the ten models.

6   Experimental Results

6.1   Model Stochasticity

First, we focused on measuring the amount of stochasticity of predictions when using x-vectors as features. That is, we experimented with training 10 individual x-vector models with the same parameters (i.e. following Sect. 5.1), only with different random seeds used during DNN weight initialization. SVR complexity C was set individually, based on development set performance (although it turned out to be 10^{-4} in all ten cases). Figure 1 shows the measured Spearman's Correlation Coefficients for the ten models for the development and for the test set. (The average CCs of the ten models are shown as dotted lines.) Note that the CC values for the test set are most likely higher than those for the development set because more data used to train the SVR models (as test predictions were obtained by training on both the training and the development sets).

We can also clearly see that the performance on the two sets is only loosely related: the model with the highest performance on the development set just achieved average scores on the test set, while the x-vector model which led to the highest CC on the test set had a CC score below average on dev. As expected, the scores also have a low correlation value (-0.130), which also indicates only a slight (practically none) connection between the performance of the models on the different sets.

Table 1 lists the exact value of some more important cases. This summarizes our previous findings: using just the x-vector model with the first random seed, which is standard practice when employing x-vectors (case 'x-vectors, single'), gave a good performance on the development set (CC = 0.300), but on the test set it scored slightly below average (CC = 0.357). The SVR model with the best performance on the development set produced an average performance on the

Table 1. Spearman's CC scores obtained for some more important x-vector-based approaches.

Regression approach	Correlation	
	Dev	Test
x-vectors, single	0.300	0.357
x-vectors, average	0.286	0.359
x-vectors, best (dev)	0.305	0.359
x-vectors, best (test)	0.276	0.373
x-vectors, ensemble (proposed)	0.298	0.370

test set (CC = 0.359), while the SVR model with the best test set performance (CC = 0.373) had a quite low (and also sub-average) Spearman's correlation coefficient on the development set (0.276).

We would like to emphasize that the differences among the ten models (that is, 0.257...0.305 and 0.347...0.373, development and test sets, respectively) are usually viewed as significant on this particular corpus. In our opinion, these experimental results indicate that the x-vectors are sensitive to random DNN weight initialization, and that this stochastic behaviour affects the subsequent, classification or regression step as well. In our opinion, these differences also justify our approach for building an ensemble of the x-vector models, as we can expect the combined model (following Sect. 4.2) to be more robust than the individual x-vector feature extractors.

6.2   Ensemble X-Vectors

Table 1 also shows the CC values for the proposed ensemble x-vector approach. We can readily see that, by training independent SVR models on the ten different x-vector representations, we obtained Spearman's Correlation Coefficient values that exceed the average CCs of the individual models, both on the development and on the test sets. On the test set the proposed method was actually better than 9 out of the 10 models, while its predictions were better than 6 models on the development set. Interestingly though, among the four individual SVR models which were able to match or surpass the performance of the ensemble on the development set, none of them could exceed even the average Correlation Coefficient value of the ten models on the test set.

By using this approach, we improved on our previous results, where we used a single x-vector model for feature extraction [3]. Therefore, the Spearman's correlation coefficient score of 0.370 achieved by the ensemble x-vector model is the highest value which was obtained via a standalone (single) method for this particular task, and it exceeds most studies which employed some kind of fusion as well (with the sole exception of [6]). Of course, the predictions of the ensemble x-vector model could have been combined with some other methods (e.g. ComParE functionals, Bag-of-Audio-Words, Fisher vectors etc.), but this was outside the scope of the current study.

7 Conclusions and Discussion

In this study we focused on the task of sleepiness detection from the speech of the subjects. To do this, we used the public Dusseldorf Sleepy Language Corpus, which contains the speech of 915 subjects, and the ratings of their sleepiness on the Karolinska Sleepiness Scale, on the range $1, \ldots, 9$. Following our previous study, we employed Support Vector Regression (SVR) and used x-vectors as features. For this, we trained custom x-vector extractor models on the training set of the Dusseldorf Sleepy Language Corpus.

X-vectors are extracted by a Deep Neural Network with a special structure, where a pooling layer allows the mapping of variable-length utterances into a fixed-dimensional feature space; the x-vector embeddings are the activations of a specific layer in the network. Of course, like all neural networks, x-vectors might prove to be sensitive to various training meta-parameters. In this study our first research question was whether they are sensitive to the *random seed* used at the weight initialization step. In particular, we were interested in the differences we might find in the performance of the classifier (or in this case, regressor) Support Vector model, which uses the x-vector embeddings directly as features.

To this end, we trained ten x-vector extractor DNNs, which just differed in their random seed, and then trained individual SVR models on each of them. In our first experiment we found that the measured Spearman's Correlation Coefficients differed significantly: they appeared in the range $0.257 \ldots 0.305$ for the development set and $0.347 \ldots 0.373$ for the test set. More importantly, the CC values for the two sets were pretty much independent (we measured a correlation coefficient of -0.130 for the two metric vectors). Then, in our second experiment we built an ensemble x-vector classifier by taking the average of the predictions of the ten SVR models. According to our experimental results, the ensemble was able to notably outperform the average performance of the individual models on the development set and, more importantly, on the test set as well.

Of course, there were several approaches which gave similar (or even higher) CC values on the development set as the proposed ensemble x-vectors did; besides other studies (e.g. [4,6,26], such an approach is our "baseline", the 'x-vectors, single' approach in Table 1). However, we would like to stress that the role of the development set is to support *model selection*; that is, to help to find a machine learning model that produces good-quality predictions on the unseen examples (which is simulated by the elements of the test set). Therefore, even if the ensemble had just produced average CC scores on the development set, we would consider it as a useful approach, because it reduces model stochasticity (and hence it improves model robustness). In our opinion, this would be advantageous even if it would only gave slight improvements on the test set (or even none at all), compared to the average classifier model. Of course, in our case the ensemble x-vector approach led to an improvement; overall, we achieved a Spearman's Correlation Coefficient of 0.370 on the test set, which is the highest value reported so far that was obtained with a standalone method on this corpus.

Acknowledgements. This research was supported by the NRDI Office of the Hungarian Ministry of Innovation and Technology (grants no. K-124413, NKFIH-1279-2/2020 and TKP2021-NVA-09), and within the framework of the Artificial Intelligence National Laboratory Program (MILAB, RRF-2.3.1-21-2022-00004). G. Gosztolya was also funded by the János Bolyai Scholarship of the Hungarian Academy of Sciences and by the Hungarian Ministry of Innovation and Technology New National Excellence Program ÚNKP-21-5-SZTE.

References

1. Breiman, L.: Bagging predictors. Mach. Learn. **24**(2), 123–140 (1996)
2. Dehak, N., Kenny, P.J., Dehak, R., Dumouchel, P., Ouellet, P.: Front-end factor analysis for speaker verification. IEEE Trans. Audio Speech Lang. Process. **19**(4), 788–798 (2011)
3. Egas-López, J.V., Gosztolya, G.: Deep Neural Network embeddings for the estimation of the degree of sleepiness. In: Proceedings of ICASSP, Toronto, Canada, June 2021 (2021, accepted)
4. Fritsch, J., Dubagunta, S., Magimai-Doss, M.: Estimating the degree of sleepiness by integrating articulatory feature knowledge in raw waveform based CNNs. In: Proceedings of ICASSP, pp. 6534–6538 (2020)
5. Glorot, X., Bengio, Y.: Understanding the difficulty of training deep feedforward neural networks. In: Machine Learning Research, pp. 249–256 (2010)
6. Gosztolya, G.: Using Fisher Vector and Bag-of-Audio-Words representations to identify Styrian dialects, sleepiness, baby & orca sounds. In: Proceedings of Interspeech, Graz, Austria, pp. 2413–2417, September 2019
7. Grzybowska, J., Kacprzak, S.: Speaker age classification and regression using i-vectors. In: Proceedings of Interspeech, San Francisco, CA, pp. 1402–1406, September 2016
8. He, K., Zhang, X., Ren, S., Sun, J.: Delving deep into rectifiers: surpassing human-level performance on ImageNet classification. In: Proceedings of ICCV, Santiago, Chile, pp. 1026–1034, December 2015
9. Huckvale, M., Beke, A., Ikushima, M.: Prediction of sleepiness ratings from voice by man and machine. In: Proceedings of Interspeech, Shanghai, China, pp. 4571–4575, October 2020
10. Jeancolas, L., et al.: X-vectors: new quantitative biomarkers for early Parkinson's Disease detection from speech. arXiv preprint arXiv:2007.03599 (2020)
11. Johns, M.: Daytime sleepiness, snoring, and obstructive sleep apnea: the Epworth Sleepiness Scale. Chest **103**(1), 30–36 (1993)
12. Murray, B.: A practical approach to Excessive Daytime Sleepiness: a focused review. Can. Respir. J. **2016**, 4215938 (2016)
13. Pagel, J.: Excessive daytime sleepiness. Am. Fam. Phys. **79**(5), 391–396 (2009)
14. Pappagari, R., Wang, T., Villalba, J., Chen, N., Dehak, N.: X-vectors meet emotions: a study on dependencies between emotion and speaker verification. In: Proceedings of ICASSP, Barcelona, Spain, pp. 7169–7173, May 2020
15. Pedregosa, F., et al.: Scikit-learn: machine learning in Python. J. Mach. Learn. Res. **12**, 2825–2830 (2011)
16. Povey, D., et al.: The Kaldi speech recognition toolkit. In: Proceedings of ASRU, Big Island, HI, USA, December 2011
17. Schapire, R.E., Singer, Y.: Improved boosting algorithms using confidence-rated predictions. Mach. Learn. **37**(3), 297–336 (1999)

18. Schuller, B.W., et al.: The INTERSPEECH 2019 computational paralinguistics challenge: styrian dialects, continuous sleepiness, baby sounds & orca activity. In: Proceedings of Interspeech, Graz, Austria, pp. 2378–2382, September 2019
19. Schuller, B.W., et al.: The interspeech 2013 computational paralinguistics challenge: social signals, conflict, emotion, autism. In: Proceedings of Interspeech, Lyon, France, pp. 148–152, September 2013
20. Schwartz, J.R., Roth, T., Hirshkowitz, M., Wright, K.P., Jr.: Recognition and management of excessive sleepiness in the primary care setting. Prim. Care Companion J. Clin. Psychiatry 11(5), 197 (2009)
21. Segbroeck, M.V., et al.: Classification of cognitive load from speech using an i-vector framework. In: Proceedings of Interspeech, Singapore, pp. 751–755, September 2014
22. Shahid, A., Wilkinson, K., Marcu, S., Shapiro, C.M.: Karolinska sleepiness scale (KSS). In: Shahid, A., Wilkinson, K., Marcu, S., Shapiro, C. (eds.) STOP, THAT and One Hundred Other Sleep Scales, pp. 209–210. Springer, New York (2011). https://doi.org/10.1007/978-1-4419-9893-4_47
23. Snyder, D., Garcia-Romero, D., Povey, D., Khudanpur, S.: Deep Neural Network embeddings for text-independent speaker verification. In: Proceedings of Interspeech, Stockholm, Sweden, pp. 999–1003, August 2017
24. Snyder, D., Garcia-Romero, D., Sell, G., Povey, D., Khudanpur, S.: X-vectors: robust DNN embeddings for speaker verification. In: Proceedings of ICASSP, Calgary, Canada, pp. 5329–5333, September 2018
25. Wolpert, D.H.: Stacked generalization. Neural Netw. 5(2), 241–259 (1992)
26. Wu, H., Wang, W., Li, M.: The DKU-LENOVO systems for the INTERSPEECH 2019 computational paralinguistic challenge. In: Proceedings of Interspeech, Graz, Austria, pp. 2433–2437, September 2019
27. Yeh, S., et al.: Using Attention Networks and adversarial augmentation for Styrian dialect, continuous sleepiness and baby sound recognition. In: Proceedings of Interspeech, Graz, Austria, pp. 2398–2402, September 2019
28. Zargarbashi, S., Babaali, B.: A multi-modal feature embedding approach to diagnose Alzheimer's disease from spoken language. arXiv preprint arXiv:1910.00330 (2019)

Multiresolution Decomposition Analysis via Wavelet Transforms for Audio Deepfake Detection

Abderrahim Fathan, Jahangir Alam$^{(\boxtimes)}$, and Woohyun Kang

Computer Research Institute of Montreal, Montreal, (Quebec) H3N 1M3, Canada
{abderrahim.fathan,jahangir.alam,woohyun.kang}@crim.ca
https://www.crim.ca/en/

Abstract. Voice and face recognition are becoming omnipresent, and the need for secure biometric technologies increases as technologies like deepfake are making it increasingly harder to spot fake generated content. To improve current audio spoofing detection, we propose a curated selection of wavelet transforms based-models where, instead of the widely employed acoustic features, the Mel-spectrogram image features are decomposed through multiresolution decomposition analysis to better handle spectral information. For that, we adopt the use of median-filtering harmonic percussive source separation (HPSS), and perform a large-scale study on the application of several recent state-of-the-art computer vision models on audio anti-spoofing detection. These wavelet transforms are experimentally found to be very useful and lead to a notable performance of 4.8% EER on the ASVspoof2019 challenge logical access (LA) evaluation set. Finally, a more adversarialy robust WaveletCNN-based model is proposed.

Keywords: Deepfake detection · Audio anti-spoofing · Wavelet CNNs · Wavelet transform

1 Introduction

Automatic speaker verification (ASV) consists of using the voiceprint of a speaker to verify their identity. ASV is one of the most convenient means of biometric recognition. Unfortunately, as is the case for every biometric, spoofing is a major threat to the security offered by ASV systems. With the development of new technologies like deepfakes [31] and sophisticated spoof generation processes (e.g., voice conversion, speech synthesis), it is getting tricky to identify spoofed data since the created images, videos and audios are becoming more credible. As the quality of generative algorithms increases, the challenge of detecting them increases, thus the need for more effective technologies that can automatically and reliably evaluate the integrity of those media.

Because of the rapid development of better generative algorithms, the threat of spoofing is a moving target. Indeed, a security system needs to defend against

© Springer Nature Switzerland AG 2022
S. R. M. Prasanna et al. (Eds.): SPECOM 2022, LNAI 13721, pp. 188–200, 2022.
https://doi.org/10.1007/978-3-031-20980-2_17

every attack while the attacker only needs to succeed once. That means the system also needs to be able to defend against types of spoofing attacks and strategies it has not seen before. The latter try to obscure the malicious/anomalous artefacts, hence confusing the spoof detection system. One important factor slowing the development of anti-spoofing algorithms is the continuous need of large labeled datasets for the latest types of attacks or the absence of labeled data in the case of unknown attacks. Moreover, data distribution mismatch can make the task even more challenging using current deep learning models.

To tackle practical spoofing scenarios, the ASVspoof2019 challenge [43], aims to develop countermeasures to detect spoofed audio involving text-to-speech (TTS), voice conversion (VC), and replayed attacks. TTS and VC attacks are used in the scenario referred to as Logical Access (LA), where Replay attacks are referred to as Physical Access (PA). They provide a common method to evaluate solutions and a dataset consisting of both legitimate (bonafide) and spoofed speech.

Most conventional spoof detection systems and speech processing tasks (e.g., speaker recognition, speech recognition) extract the cepstral feature from the speech and use it as an input representation. Since the cepstral coefficient represents the decorrelated frequency components, this makes it easy to analyze the effect of speech-dependent attributes disentangled from the redundant information. Although this can be very useful for speech processing, we suspect that such decorrelation can limit the performance when it comes to spoof detection. As the spoof generative algorithms introduce different types of artefacts on various frequency bins, analyzing the local frequency correlation may be beneficial in terms of detecting the spoof attacks.

In light of this, in this work we propose to take not only the time dependency, but also the frequency dependency into consideration when building end-to-end spoof detection systems. To achieve this, we used the mel-spectrogram as input and adopted several various recent state-of-the-art (SOTA) computer vision models. These are various architectures based exclusively or on hybrid combinations of 2D-convolution neural networks (CNNs), attention-based networks, or multi-layer perceptrons (MLPs), often used for image classification and object detection [36]. As these architectures are optimized for capturing the spatial correlation, we believe that this will help detecting the local time-frequency artefacts from the input mel-spectrogram, in particular, with the use of median-filtering harmonic percussive source separation (HPSS) that enables us to analyse the audio signal at different levels that have different structures. Furthermore, in order to analyze the spectral attributes in more detail, we have also adopted the WaveletCNN architecture [13], which introduces multi-resolution analysis to the convolutional layers via wavelet transform.

Moreover, we have investigated the effect of different types of wavelet transforms on the performance of spoof detection. The contributions of this paper are as follows:

- Explore various recent computer vision architectures, and study their generalization to unseen spoofing attacks. In particular, based on the DenseNet and

WaveletCNN architectures, in conjunction with additive margin softmax loss, our models showed high ability to learn efficient acoustic representations and a considerably higher classification performance and generalizability compared to the presented baselines.

- Instead of the conventional acoustic features, we experimented with several spectrogram image-based spoof detection systems trained with strictly the original train set.
- We propose to use Median-filtering harmonic percussive source separation (HPSS) to extract more efficient and robust features against spoofing attacks, as clearly demonstrated throughout our experiments.
- Investigate the effect of different types of wavelet transforms on the performance of spoof detection.
- Propose to incorporate a simple, yet effective improvement to the original WaveletCNN model by employing Lasso regression as an adversarial defence to improve the model's robustness[1]

2 Related Work

Since CNNs effectiveness has been proven for image classification, works like [14] showed that deep learning models such as CNNs and RNNs are able to outperform previous models on audio classification. However, they showed that performance is highly dependent on large, labeled datasets, and they tend to overfit easily on smaller ones [5]. Unfortunately, large, labeled, audio datasets are less common than images and texts.

While we can find that multiple solutions were proposed for audio spoofing detection, such as residual neural networks, light-CNN, inception and densely connected convolutional networks [1,4,19], or by employing short and long-term linear prediction error of the input speech signals [17], or ensemble-based approaches combining both LA and PA tasks [30], only a handful of acoustic features such as Constant Q Cepstral Coefficient (CQCC) [39], Inverted Mel-Frequency Cepstral Coefficients (IMFCC), Joint Gram [3], Group Delay Gram (GD Gram) [41], and RawNet2 [37] have been proved to be useful for anti-spoofing. Unconventionally, this work studies and adopts Mel-spectrogram image features as input to our models and explores improvements to both features and model architectures. To this aim, we explore various SOTA models that embed most of the existing components in deep computer vision processing, several are very recent and, to our knowledge, have never been explored yet for speech applications: VGG16 [36], NASNetMobile and NASNetLarge [46], Squeeze-and-Excitation (SE)-based SE-ResNet18 [15], aggregated transformations-based SE-ResNext50 [44], shorter intra-layers-connections-based DenseNet121 [16], convolu-tion-less Vision Transformer [8], hierarchical ConvNet priors-based Swin Transformer [27], ResNet-based modernized ConvNeXt [28], parameters-efficient EfficientNetV2 [38], and the all-MLP MLP-Mixer architecture [40].

---

[1] Models and full code of our experiments are available at: https://github.com/fathana/ARWaveletCNN.

3   End-to-End Spoof Detection Systems Based on Computer Vision Architectures

Although the information contained in cepstral features such as MFCC or PLP is usually enough to recognize phonemes, it is often beneficial to let your model learn complex representations directly from the Mel-spectrogram and not impose them with cepstral features. Indeed, the latter are more compressed and decorrelarated and not very robust to noise. Also, Mel-spectrogram can be an effective tool to extract hidden features from audio and to represent the details of frequency composition of the audio signal over time, similar to what a human would perceive [33]. With lots of data and strong deep models, mel-spectrogram can often perform better. Moreover, features such as MFCC remove fine spectral structure that is less informative about speech from audio and are thus generally considered unusable for speech synthesis [18]. We believe that this discarded micro-structure could carry information about artefacts essential to detect spoofed or synthesized audio.

In order to fully exploit the spectral attributes, we have adopted various computer vision architectures based exclusively or on hybrid combinations of 3 main components, namely: 2D-CNNs, Multi-head Attention-based networks, and MLPs. We used mel-spectrogram(s) as input, and we mainly study the architectures influence on performance by restricting training to only the official train set, and omitting the use of augmentations to compensate for the variability of spoofing artefacts (although data augmentation can help to fully utilize the models power because of problems such as over-parameterization, etc.). Since these architectures were proposed for image recognition, they use 2D-CNN layers to capture the spatial correlations within the input images and construct informative features by fusing both spatial and channel-wise information within local receptive fields, multiple attention heads for attending differently to parts of the images, and fully connected MLPs as universal function approximators. Therefore, we expect at least some of these architectures to extract relevant information for spoof detection taking, for instance, into account both time- and frequency-correlations when considering the mel-spectrogram feature as a 2D-image, by learning to focus on the small but important anomalous parts of the spectrogram via attention mechanisms depending on the context, and/or through adaptive recalibration of channel-wise feature responses via Squeeze-and-Excitation blocks that explicitly model interdependencies between our HPSS-based channels.

3.1   WaveletCNN Architecture

To better handle our spectrogram image features, we additionally adopt the special WaveletCNN architecture [13], which was originally applied on texture classification and image annotation. The WaveletCNN combines a multi-resolution analysis and CNNs into one model, using wavelet transform [29]. It utilizes spectral information which is mostly lost in conventional CNNs but is very useful for our spectrogram-based approach. Indeed, wavelet transform is often an ideal method to process/zoom details of signals, as it provides a time-frequency window which can capture higher and lower resolution of details of signals. The wavelet representation in this case can be interpreted as a decomposition of the original signal into a set of independent orientation selective frequency channels [29]. We believe that the WaveletCNN architecture is especially very suitable for our anti-spoofing task. To achieve this goal, WaveletCNN architecture reformulates convolution and pooling layers in CNNs into a more generalized form of filtering and downsampling. It is based on VGG16 architecture, and embeds dense connections and projection shortcuts. As performed in the original paper [13], we include VGG16 architecture into our ablation study.

For ablation studies, and to compare the use of 1-channel spectrogram-image inputs versus 3-channels Median-filtering HPSS-based features, we slightly modify its architecture to adapt to 1-channel 2D inputs instead of originally handling 3 channels. WaveletCNN architecture led to better results in the ASVspoof2019 challenge and proved to be more stable and consistent during training and more robust in handling new spoofing attacks during evaluation.

Additionally, we explore two wavelet transform-based architectures that were designed for noise-robust image classification, and tasks such as image denoising and image artefacts removal. Multi-level wavelet CNN (MWCNN) model [24] was proposed as an improvement to dilated filtering and as a generalization of average pooling. This is because naive pooling can cause information loss and introduce effects that are detrimental to effective features extraction and analysis. On the other hand, Wavelet Integrated CNNs (WaveCNets) [22] also replaces max- and average-pooling, and strided-convolution layers with Discrete Wavelet Transform (DWT) where low- (main structural information) and high-frequency (e.g., data noise) components are extracted from feature maps and noisy features are dropped to enhance noise-robustness. This allows to perform downsampling without information loss and preserve details in image features thanks to the good time-frequency localization property of DWT. We study both architectures using several types of wavelets (e.g., Haar, Daubechies, etc.).

3.2 Adversarially Robust WaveletCNN

Following the work of [34] on defenses against adversarial attacks, we incorporate two suggested techniques, namely the use of Lasso regression ($l1$ regularization) to promote weight sparsity which can lead to a more robust neural network, and the random noising mechanism (RSE) [26] that adds a noise layer before each convolution layer in both training and testing phases, and ensembles the prediction results. In our case, Gaussian noise layers are only employed during training to robustify the model by introducing noise to defend against adversarial perturbations to input features, and are omitted during evaluation.

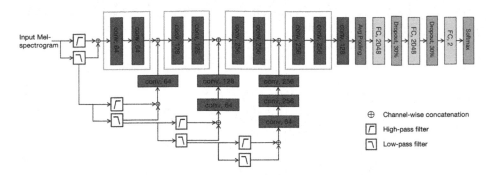

Fig. 1. Block diagram of our adversarially robust WaveletCNN (ARWaveletCNN) model architecture.

Lasso regularization works by shrinking the less important features to zero thus, removes some features altogether and only the most salient features remain. This works particularly well for features selection in the presence of a large number of input features, as is our case. The architecture of our Adversarially Robust WaveletCNN (ARWaveletCNN) model is depicted in Fig. 1.

3.3 Median-filtering Harmonic Percussive Source Separation (HPSS)

To better detect anomalous artefacts in audio spectrograms and increase robustness, we follow the work of [9,12] to separate the harmonic and percussive parts of an audio signal. Using median filtering at the spectrogram level across both successive frames and frequency bins, this allows us to analyse the original signal at different levels that have different structures (e.g, horizontal vs. vertical). Here, we extract 3 Mel-spectrograms from the original audio and its harmonic and percussive parts respectively, and concatenate them into a single 3-channels image-feature. The choice to apply the same operations on top of the 3 different, but homogeneous, audio signals helps parameter sharing of CNN kernels across the 3 channels, and showed the best performance among other experimented features.

3.4 Additive Margin Softmax Loss

In order to improve performance on previously unseen data and to generalize to out-of-domain spoofed speech samples, we use the additive margin softmax loss (AM Softmax) [42] for training. Indeed, softmax suffers from several drawbacks such as that (1) its computation of inter-class margin is intractable [10] and (2) the learned projections are not guaranteed equi-spaced. Indeed, the projection vectors for majority classes occupy more angular space compared to minority

Table 1. Details of the training, dev and eval partitions of the logical access (LA) dataset of ASVspoof2019 challenge.

	#Speakers	#Recordings	
		bonafide	Spoof
Train	20	2580	22800
Development	10	2548	22296
Evaluation	48	7355	63882

classes [25]. To solve these problems, AM Softmax loss applies an additive margin constraint in the angular space to the softmax loss for maximizing inter-class variance and minimizing intra-class variance.

4   Experiments and Results

In this section, we describe the various experiments conducted. Following the official ASVspoof2019 LA track metrics, the results are reported in terms of equal error rate (EER).

Throughout our experiments, models were trained on the Mel-spectrogram(s) images created from strictly the official train set. They are trained with Adam optimizer using cross-entropy loss with a batch size of 128 and initial learning rate of 0.001. We first extract 128-dimensional Mel filterbank integrated DFT (discrete Fourier transform) spectrogram (denoted as Mel-spectrogram) per frame, then plot the Mel-spectrogram in an 224×224 feature image as a heat map for each audio file separately. The generated images are then fed as inputs to our classification algorithms. We use global min-max data normalization, followed by mean-standard deviation normalization. All models are trained for 1200 epochs, except 1-channel models which we train for 500 epochs. We also employ cosine decay learning rate schedule. Since there are 9 times as many spoofed samples as bonafide ones, we do a weighted sampling from the dataset to balance batches by training on an equal number of spoofed and bonafide samples. Models were developed with Keras library using TensorFlow backend.

Additionally, we include a comparison analysis of several families of discrete wavelet transforms by using the python-based PyWavelets library [21]: the Haar wavelet (Haar), the Daubechies wavelets (db2, db3, db4, db5, db6), the Symlets wavelet (sym2), the Coiflets wavelet (coif2), the Biorthogonal wavelet (bior2.2), the reverse biorthogonal wavelet (rbio2.2), and the discrete FIR approximation of Meyer wavelet (dmey). Where the difference between these wavelets lies in their number of vanishing moments, degree of symmetry, the usage or not and frequency of overlapping windows, scaling coefficients, and their smoothness.

Table 2. Ablation experiments of different incremental improvements on the original WaveletCNN architecture. A Gaussian Noise layer is applied before the second convolutional layer of each block (4 noise layers in total). When applied, Lasso regression is included into all model's layers, except the output softmax layer.

Mel-spectrogram	RSE	Lasso regression	Freeze layers	EER (%)
original	✗	✗	✗	7.5
audio	✓	✓	✗	8.0
(1 channel)	✗	✓	✗	6.6
HPSS	✗	✗	✗	7.1
decomposition	✗	✓	✗	4.8
(3 channels)	✗	✓	✓	4.7

4.1   ASVspoof 2019 Logical Access (LA) Dataset

The ASVspoof 2019 database was derived from the Voice Cloning Toolkit (VCTK) corpus [45] and is comprised of both logical access (LA) and physical access (PA) datasets. In this work, we focus on the LA task.

The ASVspoof2019 LA dataset [43] includes bonafide spoof signals generated with recent speech synthesis and voice conversion algorithms such as Tacotron2 [35] and Wavenet [32]. All audio files are in the flac format, stored in 16-bit. The sampling rate is 16 kHz. Access and further details about the dataset can be found in [43]. The ASVspoof2019 LA dataset include 20 training speakers in the training set, 10 target and 10 non-target speakers in the development test set, and 48 target and 19 non-target speakers in the evaluation test set. The training and development partitions contain known spoofing attacks whereas the evaluation set contains 2 known attacks and 11 unknown attacks i.e., attacks that are not seen in the training and development sets. Therefore, the evaluation test set is more challenging than the train or dev sets, as it consists of new speakers and unseen spoofing attacks. Table 1 summarizes the partitions of the LA dataset.

4.2   Adversarially Robust WaveletCNN (ARWaveletCNN)

Following the suggested enhancements to the original Wavelet-CNN model, we perform an ablation study in Table 2 to investigate which techniques are effective for spoof detection.

In particular, we find Lasso regression to be the most effective at spotting spoof artefacts. Since this task is all about learning spoof artefacts present in the spectrograms, this pushes the model to focus on detecting/keeping those anomalous artefacts and to remove normal bonafide artefacts since they are less relevant for further decisions (absence of spoof artefacts at the end of the model is equivalent to a bonafide audio in hand). Additionally, we found median-filtering

HPSS-based features to lead to further performance gains across different configurations, which allowed us to achieve a notable 4.8% EER performance, gaining 46% improvement over the best official baseline model in Table 3, and achieving very competitive results compared to other existing single systems.

Table 3. Results of our best performing vision models versus the GMM official baselines on the ASVspoof2019 Eval set, and other selected single-system benchmarks.

Model	EER (%)
GMM (CQCC features) [6]	9.6
GMM (LFCC features) [6]	8.1
CNNTL (Mel-spectrogram features) [2]	5.32
LRADF (eCQCC features) [7]	11.08
SHNU (logspec features) [11]	5.82
STC (FFT spectrum features) [20]	4.53
ARWaveletCNN	**4.8**
DenseNet121	**4.4**

Table 4. Experiments using 1-channel Mel filterbank integrated DFT Mel-spectrogram versus 3-channels Mel-spectrograms of the original audio and its harmonic and percussive parts.

Model	Mel-spectrogram	**EER (%)**
WaveletCNN	Original audio (1 channel)	6.6
VGG16		9.5
ConvNeXt		7.8
EfficientNetV2S		11.2
WaveletCNN	HPSS decomposition (3 channels)	4.8
VGG16		8.9
ConvNeXt		7.3
EfficientNetV2S		8.9

We further study the usefulness of HPSS decomposition for spoof detection in Table 4. We compare the performance of 3 additional SOTA models on our proposed HPSS-based features. Results confirm that these features are very useful across the 3 architectures, suggesting that they should be considered for adoption in spoof detection tasks. Finally, experiment freezing one random layer during each training epoch to improve robustness, helped to slightly improve the results to 4.7% EER (due to the big differences between the various architectures, and to keep comparison simple, layers freezing is not used in remaining experiments).

4.3 Performance Study of Computer Vision Models

Table 5 shows the results of our suggested selection of various good performing SOTA computer vision architectures on the ASVSpoof2019 Evaluation set, using HPSS-based features.

First, results show that performance varies greatly depending on both the model's architecture and the type of wavelet transform. In particular, DenseNet-121, ARWaveletCNN and WaveCNets performed the best, achieving a notable 4.4% EER performance for DenseNet121, and 4.8% EER performance for ARWaveletCNN. This shows that dense and shorter intra-layers connections, which encourage features reuse, are crucial to learn generalizable robust feature-maps and to strengthen the propagation of anomalous features throughout the layers without critical information loss.

Table 5. Comparison study of various SOTA architectures versus our proposed ARWaveletCNN model on ASVspoof2019 LA Eval set, in terms of percentage of equal error rate (EER). Wavelet type is mentioned in brackets. DWTP refers to the additional use of DWT Pooling before CNN layers and no pooling strides, as performed in the WaveCNets model.

Model	EER	Model	EER	Model	EER	Model	EER
NASNetMobile	12.6	Swin transformer	11.3	WaveCNets [Haar]	7.1	ARWaveletCNN [sym2]	10.8
VGG16	8.9	Vision transformer (ViT)	6.7	WaveCNets [bior2.2]	8.3	ARWaveletCNN [db2]	8.3
SE-ResNext50	7.4	ARWaveletCNN+ViT [2]	8.5	WaveCNets [db3]	8.2	ARWaveletCNN [bior2.2]	9.8
ResNet50	7.3	MWCNN [Haar]	7.4	WaveCNets [db5]	6.3	ARWaveletCNN [db5]	11.4
InceptionResNetV2	6.6	MLP-Mixer (Relu based)	8.0	WaveCNets [db4]	12.2	ARWaveletCNN [Haar DWTP]	7.1
NASNetLarge	9.8	WaveCNets [sym2]	10.8	WaveCNets [db6]	10.9	ARWaveletCNN [sym2 DWTP]	10.0
SE-ResNet18	6.8	WaveCNets [dmey]	9.8	WaveCNets (Max Pooling)	6.2	ARWaveletCNN [coif2 DWTP]	7.8
DenseNet121	**4.4**	WaveCNets [coif2]	12.9	ARWaveletCNN [Haar]	**4.8**	ARWaveletCNN (2x wider)	6.2
ConvNeXt	7.3	WaveCNets [rbio2.4]	15.3	ARWaveletCNN [db6]	10.0		
EfficientNetV2S	8.9	WaveCNets [db2]	9.7	ARWaveletCNN [rbio2.4]	8.8		

[2] ARWaveletCNN+ViT stands for the fusion of both ARWaveletCNN and Vision Transformer architectures.

Interestingly, ViT which has few locality biases, is able to generalize very well without using any convolutional operation (compared to the hierarchical CNN-based Swin Transformer) despite the relatively small train data size and the difficulty of the spoof detection task, suggesting that CNNs are not that necessary. Compared to the benchmarked VGG16 architecture, we see that introducing multi-resolution analysis to the convolutional layers via wavelet transform is very useful to preserve features details at multiple scales of time and space. This prevents anomalous information loss, which is crucial for spoof detection decision. This result is further confirmed by replacing the use of Discrete Wavelet Transform (DWT) with max-pooling in the original WaveCNets architecture, which achieved 6.2% EER, outperforming the use of DWT pooling, which suggests that multi-resolution analysis via wavelet transform is key to good performance. Similarly, introducing DWT pooling to our ARWaveletCNN architecture degraded the performance and did not seem to help.

In particular, Haar transform, which resembles a step function and is less complex than the other types of wavelets (no overlapping windows, and only two scaling and wavelet function coefficients), stands out via its ability to analyze the localized features of signals, especially those with sudden transitions, which we believe helps in our anomalies detection case [23]. Indeed, the simple Haar discrete wavelet transform captures not only a notion of the frequency content of the input, by examining it at different scales, but also temporal content, i.e. the times at which these frequencies occur. Finally, increasing the width of our ARWaveletCNN model by doubling the number of output filters in the convolutional layers, or by fusing both the ARWaveletCNN and the Vision Transformer architectures through the concatenation of their extracted features before final classification (in order to benefit from the complementarity between them) slightly degraded performance, suggesting some over-parameterization issues due to the limited size of the dataset.

5   Conclusion

In this work, we provided a study of a selection of various wavelet transforms-based models where the Mel-spectrogram image features are decomposed through multiresolution decomposition analysis. We proposed to adopt the use of median-filtering harmonic percussive source separation (HPSS) to better handle spectral information in audio deepfake detection by analysing the audio signal at different levels that have distinct structures, and proposed an adversarialy robust model (ARWaveletCNN) against spoofing attacks. Our suggested ARWaveletCNN and DenseNet121 models largely outpermed all baselines and other studied models.

Acknowledgments. The authors wish to acknowledge the funding from the Natural Sciences and Engineering Research Council of Canada (NSERC) through grant RGPIN-2019-05381 and Ministry of Economy and Innovation (MEI) of the Government of Quebec for the continued support.

References

1. Alzantot, M., Wang, Z., et al.: Deep residual neural networks for audio spoofing detection. arXiv preprint arXiv:1907.00501 (2019)
2. Aravind, P., Nechiyil, U., Paramparambath, N., et al.: Audio spoofing verification using deep convolutional neural networks by transfer learning. arXiv preprint arXiv:2008.03464 (2020)
3. Cai, W., et al.: The DKU replay detection system for the asvspoof 2019 challenge: on data augmentation, feature representation, classification, and fusion. arXiv preprint arXiv:1907.02663 (2019)
4. Chang, S.Y., et al.: Transfer-representation learning for detecting spoofing attacks with converted and synthesized speech in automatic speaker verification system. Transfer **51**, 2 (2019)

5. Chiu, C.C., et al.: State-of-the-art speech recognition with sequence-to-sequence models. CoRR abs/1712.01769 (2017). http://arxiv.org/abs/1712.01769

6. Consortium, A.: ASVspoof 2019: Automatic Speaker Verification Spoofing and Countermeasures Challenge Evaluation Plan (2019). https://www.asvspoof.org/asvspoof2019/asvspoof2019_evaluation_plan.pdf

7. Das, R.K., Yang, J., Li, H.: Long range acoustic and deep features perspective on asvspoof 2019. In: 2019 IEEE Automatic Speech Recognition and Understanding Workshop (ASRU), pp. 1018–1025. IEEE (2019)

8. Dosovitskiy, A., Beyer, L., Kolesnikov, A., Weissenborn, D., Zhai, X., et al.: An image is worth 16 × 16 words: transformers for image recognition at scale. arXiv preprint arXiv:2010.11929 (2020)

9. Driedger, J., Müller, M., Disch, S.: Extending harmonic-percussive separation of audio signals. In: ISMIR, pp. 611–616 (2014)

10. Elsayed, G.F., et al.: Large margin deep networks for classification. Adv. Neural Inf. Process. Syst. **32** (2018)

11. Feng, Z., Tong, Q., Long, Y., Wei, S., Yang, C., Zhang, Q.: SHNU anti-spoofing systems for asvspoof 2019 challenge. In: 2019 Asia-Pacific Signal and Information Processing Association Annual Summit and Conference (APSIPA ASC), pp. 548–552. IEEE (2019)

12. Fitzgerald, D.: Harmonic/percussive separation using median filtering. In: Proceedings of the International Conference on DAFx, vol. 13 (2010)

13. Fujieda, S., et al.: Wavelet convolutional neural networks. arXiv preprint arXiv:1805.08620 (2018)

14. Hershey, S., et al.: CNN architectures for large-scale audio classification. CoRR abs/1609.09430 (2016). http://arxiv.org/abs/1609.09430

15. Hu, J., Shen, L., Sun, G.: Squeeze-and-excitation networks. In: Proceedings of the IEEE conference on CVPR, pp. 7132–7141 (2018)

16. Huang, G., Liu, Z., Van Der Maaten, L., Weinberger, K.Q.: Densely connected convolutional networks. In: Proceedings of the IEEE Conference on CVPR, pp. 4700–4708 (2017)

17. Janicki, A.: Increasing anti-spoofing protection in speaker verification using linear prediction. Multimedia Tools Appl. **76**(6), pp. 9017–9032 (2017)

18. Juvela, L., et al.: Speech waveform synthesis from MFCC sequences with generative adversarial networks. In: Proceedings of the IEEE ICASSP, pp. 5679–5683. IEEE (2018)

19. Lai, C.I., et al.: Assert: anti-spoofing with squeeze-excitation and residual networks. arXiv preprint arXiv:1904.01120 (2019)

20. Lavrentyeva, G., Novoselov, S., Tseren, A., Volkova, M., Gorlanov, A., Kozlov, A.: STC antispoofing systems for the asvspoof2019 challenge. arXiv preprint arXiv:1904.05576 (2019)

21. Lee, G., Gommers, R., Waselewski, F., Wohlfahrt, K., O'Leary, A.: Pywavelets: a python package for wavelet analysis. J. Open Sour. Softw. **4**(36), 1237 (2019)

22. Li, Q., Shen, L., et al.: Wavelet integrated CNNS for noise-robust image classification. In: Proceedings of the IEEE/CVF Conference on CVPR, pp. 7245–7254 (2020)

23. Liu, J.W., Zuo, F.L., Guo, Y.X., Li, T.Y., Chen, J.M.: Research on improved wavelet convolutional wavelet neural networks. Appl. Intell. **51**(6), 4106–4126 (2021)

24. Liu, P., et al.: Multi-level wavelet convolutional neural networks. IEEE Access **7**, 74973–74985 (2019)

25. Liu, W., Wen, Y., et al.: Large-margin softmax loss for convolutional neural networks. In: ICML, vol. 2 (2016)
26. Liu, X., Cheng, M., Zhang, H., Hsieh, C.J.: Towards robust neural networks via random self-ensemble. In: Proceedings of the ECCV, pp. 369–385 (2018)
27. Liu, Z., Lin, Y., Cao, Y., Hu, H., et al.: Swin transformer: hierarchical vision transformer using shifted windows. In: Proceedings of the IEEE/CVF International Conference on Computer Vision, pp. 10012–10022 (2021)
28. Liu, Z., Mao, H., Wu, C.Y., Feichtenhofer, C., Darrell, T., Xie, S.: A convnet for the 2020s. arXiv preprint arXiv:2201.03545 (2022)
29. Mallat, S.G.: A theory for multiresolution signal decomposition: the wavelet representation. In: Fundamental Papers in Wavelet Theory, pp. 494–513. Princeton University Press (2009)
30. Monteiro, J., et al.: An ensemble based approach for generalized detection of spoofing attacks to automatic speaker recognizers. In: Proceedings of the ICASSP, pp. 6599–6603. IEEE (2020)
31. Nguyen, T.T., et al.: Deep learning for deepfakes creation and detection: a survey (2020)
32. Oord, A.V.D., et al.: Wavenet: a generative model for raw audio. CoRR abs/1609.03499 (2016). http://arxiv.org/abs/1609.03499
33. Prahallad, K.: Spectrogram, cepstrum and mel-frequency analysis (2015)
34. Ren, K., Zheng, T., Qin, Z., Liu, X.: Adversarial attacks and defenses in deep learning. Engineering 6(3), 346–360 (2020)
35. Shen, J., et al.: Natural TTS synthesis by conditioning wavenet on mel spectrogram predictions. CoRR abs/1712.05884 (2017). http://arxiv.org/abs/1712.05884
36. Simonyan, K., Zisserman, A.: Very deep convolutional networks for large-scale image recognition. arXiv preprint arXiv:1409.1556 (2014)
37. Tak, H., et al.: End-to-end anti-spoofing with rawnet2. In: Proceedings of the ICASSP, pp. 6369–6373. IEEE (2021)
38. Tan, M., Le, Q.: Efficientnetv2: smaller models and faster training. In: Proceedings of ICML, pp. 10096–10106. PMLR (2021)
39. Todisco, M., et al.: A new feature for automatic speaker verification anti-spoofing: constant q cepstral coefficients. In: Odyssey, vol. 2016, pp. 283–290 (2016)
40. Tolstikhin, I.O., Houlsby, N., Kolesnikov, A., Beyer, L., et al.: Mlp-mixer: An all-mlp architecture for vision. Adva. Neural Inf. Process. Syst. 34 (2021)
41. Tom, F., et al.: End-to-end audio replay attack detection using deep convolutional networks with attention. In: Interspeech, pp. 681–685 (2018)
42. Wang, F., et al.: Additive margin softmax for face verification. IEEE Sign. Process. Lett. 25(7), 926–930 (2018)
43. Wang, X., et al.: Asvspoof 2019: a large-scale public database of synthesized, converted and replayed speech. Comput. Speech Lang. 64, 101114 (2020)
44. Xie, S., Girshick, R., Dollár, P., Tu, Z., He, K.: Aggregated residual transformations for deep neural networks. In: Proceedings of the IEEE Conference on CVPR, pp. 1492–1500 (2017)
45. Yamagishi, J., Veaux, C., MacDonald, K.: CSTR VCTK corpus: English multi-speaker corpus for CSTR voice cloning toolkit (version 0.92) (2019). https://doi.org/10.7488/ds/2645
46. Zoph, B., Vasudevan, V., Shlens, J., Le, Q.V.: Learning transferable architectures for scalable image recognition. In: Proceedings of the IEEE Conference on CVPR, pp. 8697–8710 (2018)

Automatic Rhythm and Speech Rate Analysis of Mising Spontaneous Speech

Parismita Gogoi[1,3](✉) ⓘ, Priyankoo Sarmah[1] ⓘ, and S. R. M. Prasanna[2] ⓘ

[1] Indian Institute of Technology Guwahati, Guwahati 781039, India
{parismitagogoi,priyankoo}@iitg.ac.in
[2] Indian Institute of Technology Dharwad, Dharwad 580011, India
prasanna@iitdh.ac.in
[3] DUIET, Dibrugarh University, Dibrugarh 786004, India

Abstract. The objective of this current study is to analyse rhythm measures and speech rate of Mising, a low resource language spoken in the NE region of India. In this work, two Mising dialects - Pagru and Delu - are considered, along with Assamese to study their rhythmic characteristics in the case of spontaneous speech. Rhythm metric measures are generally computed from the annotated speech regions. However, for spontaneous speech, hand-annotation may be difficult and time-consuming. Therefore, this work explores the vowel onset point and offset point detection algorithm to automate the rhythm measure calculation process. Results show that Mising varieties are stressed-timed as compared to mora-timed Assamese language. Finally, automatically computed rhythm measures and speech rate are explored for classifying Assamese and Mising using machine learning models.

Keywords: Rhythm · Speech rate · SVM · Random forest · Mising

1 Introduction

Over the years, linguistic rhythm research has been focused on the idea that acoustic measures of duration of vowels and consonants can be assessed in order to classify languages according to rhythmic templates. Based on the rhythm class hypothesis, languages can be classified as syllable-timed, stress-timed, and mora-timed [1,7,18,21,22]. Rhythm metrics are defined as the formulas that quantify vocalic and consonantal variability used for topological studies in classifying languages rhythmically. The stress-, syllable- and mora-timing distinction in languages is quantified based on vowels and consonants duration, rather than syllables or stress feet. It is reported that Spanish (syllable-timed) has less complex consonant clusters and less vowel reduction as compared to English (stress-timed) [5]. Low et al. demonstrated that identification of vowel/consonant boundaries is rather straightforward compared to syllabification rules that differ in world languages [16].

In 1999, Ramus et al. carried out a preliminary attempt to quantify consonantal and vocalic variability by proposing the standard deviation of vocalic and

ⓒ Springer Nature Switzerland AG 2022
S. R. M. Prasanna et al. (Eds.): SPECOM 2022, LNAI 13721, pp. 201–213, 2022.
https://doi.org/10.1007/978-3-031-20980-2_18

consonantal interval duration ('ΔV' and 'ΔC' respectively) [25]. The percentage of utterance duration that is vocalic rather than consonantal is termed as (%V). Rhythm classification in increasing %V order was performed on previously classified languages (Dutch/English/Polish, Catalan/French/Italian/Spanish, and Japanese) to reflect statistically in the rhythm continuum, using a combination of ΔC and %V. The pairwise variability indices nPVI and rPVI (pairwise comparisons of successive vocalic and intervocalic intervals) were later introduced by Grabe and Low [11,16]. PVIs capture syntagmatic distinction over an utterance by averaging vocalic/consonantal durational differences [19]. Low et al. identified a Singaporean and a British dialect of English based on PVI-based measures [16]. Speech rate (SR) tends to show a high correlation with interval duration measures based on variance. It is reported that with a slower rate, lengthening of intervals takes place [6]. Coefficients of variation for consonantal intervals (VarcoC: [6]) and vocalic intervals (VarcoV: [9]) are also explored to implement speech rate normalization. At best, metrics such as VarcoV and %V are approximate indicators of broad phonetic and phonotactic patterns [6].

Using normalized PVI (nPVI)-based metrics, interval durations were normalized to understand speech rate variation also [16]. Speech rate tends to show high correlation with interval duration measures based on variance. It is reported that with slower rate, lengthening of intervals take place [6]. Many authors presented with newer methods of quantifying rhythmic distinctions [15,27]. Coefficients of variation for consonantal intervals (VarcoC: [6]) and vocalic intervals (VarcoV: [9]) are also explored to implement speech rate normalization. At best, metrics such as VarcoV and %V are approximate indicators of broad phonetic and phonotactic patterns [6].

1.1   Previous Work

The major limitation of working with large speech file sizes and the mixture of elicitation methods such as story reading, spontaneous speech, and reading a set of sentences is the laborious nature of the manual measurement of segment duration. Also, there lie some language-specific biases in applying segmentation criteria [17]. The biases are also subjected to the annotator's expertise in the language. Several measures for rhythm analysis are conventionally derived by annotating each phonetic unit with time-stamps and interval durations using a speech tool, such as Praat [3], which may be time-consuming and cumbersome. Previously, automated approaches were adopted for calculating segment durations using data-trained models for the recognition and forced alignment [30]. However, such methods are not very successful as forced alignment is available only for a few languages and they address purely acoustic-based automatic annotation of speech files [17]. A completely automated sonority estimation technique based on spectrogram was employed [10], which mapped spans of the speech file indicated by the entropy from one time-stamp to the next. This method also required pre-labeling the acoustic signal as Cs and Vs before final measurements. This method of automatic sonority estimation could rhythmically classify eight languages (English, Dutch, Spanish, Italian, French, Catalan, Italian, and

Japanese) with results that were comparable to Ramus et al. (1999) [25]. In an approach, using the knowledge of loudness and periodicity, annotations of acoustic waveforms were carried out for calculating units relevant for rhythmic identification [17]. Fifteen Rhythm metrics, including %V, ΔC, and PVIs, were measured to rhythmically classify Russian, Greek, and Taiwan Mandarin, Southern British English, French languages. The accuracy rates were found to be in the range of 34% to 43% above chance. Another method utilized an automatic vowel detection algorithm [27], originally applied in a language identification task [8]. The methodology could classify the vowel and non-vowel portions and parse the utterance string into pseudo syllables. Another work has been reported to demonstrate a rhythm metric-based LID approach, using GMM based learning [14] for a multi-lingual system. Total consonant cluster duration, total vowel duration, and complexity of the consonantal cluster (i.e., number of the consonants in the cluster) were computed from each pseudo-syllable. Then, 7 languages (English, German, Mandarin. French, Italian, Spanish, and Japanese) were classified with mean correct rhythmic accuracy from 80% for mora-timed to 92% for stress-timed languages using Gaussian Mixture Models (GMM). Another work has been reported to demonstrate a rhythm metric-based LID approach, using GMM based learning [14] for a multi-lingual system.

1.2 Motivation and Contribution

Our current work aims at exploring rhythmic variability in the Mising language of the Eastern Tani sub-group of the Tibeto-Burman language family in North-East India [24]. Most of the Tibeto-Burman (TB) languages are yet to be fully documented or scientifically described. Eight Mising dialects are traditionally recognized: Pagro, Delu, Sayang, Oyan, Moying, Dambuk, Somuwa, and Samuguria [28]. Despite having a large number of native speakers of different dialects, the phonetics of prosody in Mising has not previously been investigated by researchers. There is next to no work on Mising speakers' rhythm analysis in dialectal data. And therefore, rhythmic characteristics and its difference among the dialects are largely unknown.

We focus on identifying the rhythm class of Mising as per the rhythm class hypothesis in our preliminary attempt, using automatic computation of rhythm measures. This investigation will shed light on many questions on the stress, rhythm, and prosodic behavior of Tibeto-Burman languages, which are still important and open to understanding. Considering the limitations pointed out earlier regarding the manual assessment of rhythm measures, we employ an automated method of vowel onset (VOP) and offset points (VEP) detection from acoustic signals for measuring the interval durations and utilize these values to compute rhythm measures [23]. The rhythm measures are calculated from consonantal and vocalic intervals derived from the VOP and VEP detection method. This automated method will be helpful compared to transcription-based forced alignment techniques, where linguistic knowledge is a must for processing the

Table 1. Database details.

Language/Dialect	Gender		Age ($\mu \pm \sigma$bf)	#tokens
	M	F		
Assamese (A)	3	6	22.55 ± 1.25	392
Mising - Pagro (P)	4	6	34.31 ± 7.69	193
Mising - Delu (D)	2	7	30.07 ± 11.14	209
Total	**9**	**19**	**28 (Total speaker)**	**794**

audio files. An LID approach is proposed between Mising and Assamese languages using the speech rhythm measures and speech rate as a feature set. This work studies the rhythm characteristics of two Mising dialects, namely Pagro and Delu, using spontaneous speech data. Assamese, spoken by about 15 million people in the state of Assam, is an Indo-European language. Assamese data is also considered for language identification tasks with Mising. The rhythm measures of Assamese are comparable to that of the mora-timed languages, such as Japanese [7].

To summarize, the following are the contributions of the present paper-

1. Classification of Mising is conducted as per rhythm class hypothesis, which is hitherto un-analyzed for rhythm.
2. Automatic annotation based on VOP and VEP is carried out for calculating interval durations in rhythm measure calculation.
3. Language identification of two under-resourced languages viz. Mising vs. Assamese has been conducted using rhythm measures and speech rate.

2 Database Preparation

In order to study the rhythm of Mising, spontaneous speech of native speakers of Pagro (P) and Delu speakers (D) were recorded in a noiseless environment. In this work, Assamese spontaneous speech has been collected from Assamese (A) speakers residing in the upper Assam region. The recordings were done in a noiseless environment using a Zoom H1n recorder. The sampling frequency was kept at 44.1 kHz and 16 bit in .wav format. The data recorded was segmented into short utterances in Praat 6.0.35 [3].

2.1 Speakers

In this work, a speech database is prepared from a total of 28 speakers belonging to the Assamese (A), Pagro (P), and Delu (D) groups. Data has been collected from ten Pagro Mising speakers who reside mostly near to Jonai area of the Dhemaji district. Delu Mising speakers are residing near the banks of the Burhidihing river in Rajabari area of Sivasagar district. The recordings were completed during the months of Jan.- Dec. 2020. Assamese speech has been collected from

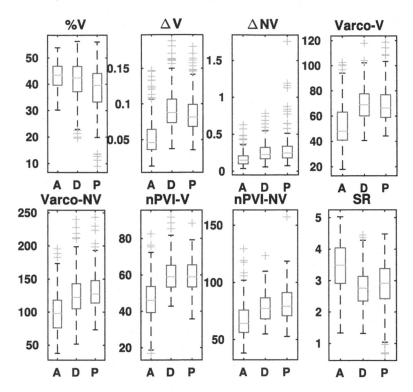

Fig. 1. Box plots of the rhythm measures for two dialects of Mising and Assamese.

nine Assamese (A) speakers. Assamese has been explored as the control language to understand the prosody of two broad categories of language, namely Indo-European and Tibeto-Burman language (Mising), respectively. None of the 28 speakers reported any speech disorders during the recording. A detailed description of the database can be found in Table 1.

2.2   Materials

The principal elicitation method used in this study is spontaneous speech. Five topics were provided to the speakers of both languages for recording. The topics were mainly related to their daily livelihoods and ethnocultural practices of the Assamese and Mising communities, respectively. The five topics for Assamese were- Bihu festival, introduction to own village, weaving methods of Assamese dresses, Assamese community, and ethnic food preparation methods. The five topics in Mising were- Ali-Aye-Ligang festival, introduction to own village, weaving methods of Mising dresses, Mising community, and ethnic food preparation methods. The duration of the spontaneous speech recordings ranged from 1 min to 4 mins.

Table 2. Overall rhythm measures for Assamese (A), Pagro (P) and Delu (D).

Rhythm measures	A $(\mu \pm \sigma)$	P $(\mu \pm \sigma)$	D $(\mu \pm \sigma)$
%V	43.04 ± 7.15	38.37 ± 8.21	41.51 ± 8.13
ΔV	0.05 ± 0.02	0.086 ± 0.02	0.093 ± 0.029
ΔNV	0.17 ± 0.08	0.292 ± 0.20	0.26 ± 0.14
Varco-V	52.25 ± 16.30	68.86 ± 14.10	70.12 ± 13.79
Varco-NV	98.61 ± 28.66	132.55 ± 29.25	126.06 ± 31.49
nPVI-V	46.19 ± 10.48	59.34 ± 8.96	59.86 ± 9.20
nPVI-NV	66.58 ± 14.63	81.10 ± 14.55	78.02 ± 12.96
SR	3.45 ± 0.72	2.89 ± 0.74	2.75 ± 0.63

3 Methodology

This section discusses the methodology to automatically derive the rhythm measures, by segmenting the vowel (V) regions and non-vowel (NV) regions. Here, V-region includes the vowels present in the speech signal, whereas, NV corresponds to the consonants and pauses. The segmentation of V and NV regions are performed using an algorithm proposed in [23]. This method uses excitation source information, such as zero-frequency filtered signal and Hilbert envelope of the linear prediction residual to locate the VOP and VEP in a speech signal [23]. We have considered speech region from one VOP to adjacent VEP as the V-region, whereas, one VEP to adjacent VOP is considered as the NV-region. For more detailed description interested reader can refer to the original paper [23]. The steps to derive the rhythm measures automatically are summarized as given below.

- Detection of VLRs (V) and non-VLRs (NV) in the speech signal.
- Compute the duration of each VLR and non-VLR.
- Compute the rhythm measure and speech rate using rhythm metric formulas.

To analyze rhythm, five interval measures, namely, %V, ΔV, ΔNV, Varco-V and Varco-NV are calculated. %V is the percentage of V-regions in an utterance. ΔNV is the standard deviation of the duration of NV-regions, and ΔV is the standard deviation of the duration of V-regions [25]. Varco-NV is defined as the percentage of the standard deviation of NV interval duration (ΔNV) of the average duration of V-regions (mean NV). Similarly, Varco-V is calculated from the V-regions. Two Pairwise Variability Index measures, nPVI-V and nPVI-NV are evaluated following [19]. nPVI-V is the rate normalized measure of the durational variation of two consecutive V-regions, and nPVI-NV is the rate normalized measure of the durational variation of two consecutive NV-regions.

4 Experiments and Results

4.1 Rhythm Metrics

Figure 1 shows the box plots of the eight rhythm measures and SR for two dialects of Mising and Assamese. Table 2 shows values of the rhythm measures calculated for spontaneous speech for Assamese (A), Pagro (P), and Delu (D). %V and ΔNV are directly related to the syllabic structure. A higher ΔNV means a greater variability in the number of consonants, referring to a language that may instantiate more syllable types. From the table, we can see that Mising having more syllable types, shows lower %V and higher ΔNV. Higher value of ΔV for Mising can be interpreted due to the combination of several phonological factors present in the language. Contrastive vowel length, vowel lengthening in specific contexts and long vowels, influence the vocalic interval variability. We have plotted the %V and nPVI-V values obtained from Assamese speakers and two varieties of Mising speakers. In order to compare them with prototypical syllable-timed, stress-timed and mora-timed languages, we have plotted the measures from British English, Spanish and Japanese, obtained from previous observations [11,12,29]. Figure 2 shows the distribution of languages on a %V and nPVI-V plane, supporting the notion of stress-, syllable- and mora-timed languages. Languages like Spanish do not show such type of phonological phenomenon, and hence show a lesser value of ΔV [5]. Syllable-timed languages typically have a higher standard deviation of C-intervals (ΔNV) and a lower percentage of time over which speech is vocalic (%V) than stress-timed languages.

As observed from the figure, the Assamese gets clustered closer to the Japanese. This result is in agreement with a previous study, where authors have used

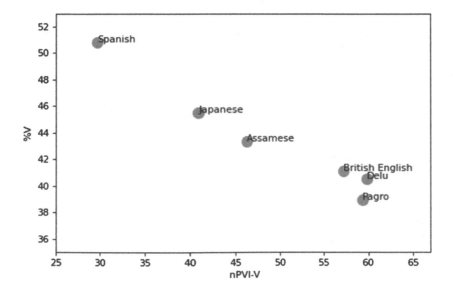

Fig. 2. Distribution of languages over the (%V, nPVI-V) plane.

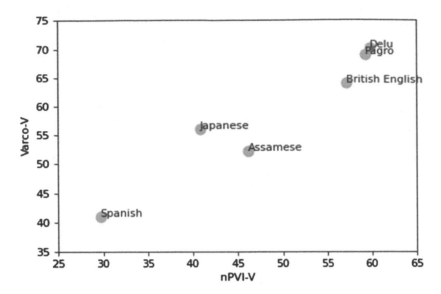

Fig. 3. Distribution of languages over the (Varco-V, nPVI-V) plane.

manual annotation-based computation for five Assamese varieties [7]. Pagro and Delu are placed closer to British English. From this plot, stress- timing is found to be dominant in two varieties of Mising. It is believed that in stressed timed languages, codas and consonant clusters contribute to a greater consonantal portion of the signal [26]. In Mising, seven long and seven short vowels are present, which is a marker of rhythm [28]. Additionally, diphthongization is more robust on long vowels [20] and the presence of long vowels in a language is connected with greater durational variability. Greater durational variability is reported in stress timed language due to vowel reduction, which is measured from metrics PVI, DeltaV, Varco-V. Mora timed languages generally exhibit a simpler syllable structure. Researchers have provided significant attention in the possibility of an interaction between suprasegmental rhythm and vocabulary systems. Many works have been concentrated on criteria of segmental phonology to link to rhythm class hypothesis [26].

In the process of capturing hypothesized rhythm class in language continuum, rate normalized metrics based on vowels, Varco-V and nPVI-V are found to be most reliable. Hence, Varco-V values are plotted on the vertical axis against nPVI-V values on the horizontal axis, as shown in Fig. 3. The PVI profiles depict acoustic evidence for rhythmic differences between English, Mising (Pagro, Delu) on the one hand, and Spanish on the other. Mora- timed Japanese and Assamese are patterned between the stress-timed and syllable-timed language. Stressed time language is said to exhibit more vocalic variability (high vocalic nPVI-V) than syllable-timed languages related to vowel quality.

The findings of the present method seem to be consistent with the previous method reported in [7]. In Fig. 4, RM values computed using proposed

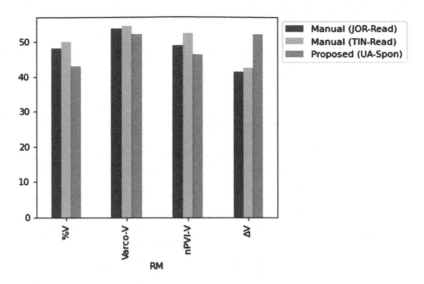

Fig. 4. Comparison of Rhythm measure (RM) values computed using proposed automatic method for spontaneous speech recorded speakers from Upper Assam (Proposed (UA-Spon)) and Praat-based manual annotation (Manual (JOR-Read) and Manual (TIN-Read)) reported in [7] for read speech recorded from speakers from Jorhat and Tinsukia, two district from Upper Assam region.

automatic method are compared with Praat-based manual annotation method reported in [7]. The proposed automatic method is applied in spontaneous speech recorded speakers from Upper Assam (Proposed (UA-Spon)). And Praat-based syllable level manual annotation (Manual (JOR-Read) and Manual (TIN-Read)) is applied in read speech recorded from speakers from Jorhat and Tinsukia, two major districts from Upper Assam region [7]. We have considered RMs obtained from vowel duration statistics, such as %V, Varco-V, nPVI-V, and ΔV for comparison. The plots depict that RM values are comparable in both the approaches.

4.2   Statistical Analysis

To find if the computed rhythm measures and speech rate are different across the two varieties of Mising and Assamese, we perform the Linear Mixed Effects (LME) model [2] based statistical analysis. In the LME model, we have considered rhythm measures as the dependent variable, whereas gender and language are the fixed factors. Speaker information is the random factor in our model. Finally, we perform the Wald χ^2 to see the effect of language and gender effect on the rhythm measures. Table 3 summarized the results of the LME-based statistical tests for Mising vs. Assamese. The table shows that except for the %V, all the rhythm measures and speech rate show significant p-values (<0.001). However, gender has no effect on the rhythm measures. Also, we have found no significant difference between the rhythm and speech rate values of the Mising varieties considered.

Table 3. Wald χ^2 tests on LME models for rhythm measures (RM) and speech rate (SR) for Assamese and Mising.

Measures	Mixed factor	χ^2	p-value
%V	Language	0.43	0.51
	Gender	0.3	0.57
	Language:gender	1.12	0.28
ΔV	Language	33.23	8.1E-09
	Gender	3.87	0.04
	Language:gender	3.64	0.05
ΔNV	Language	14.19	0.000165
	Gender	1.58	0.2
	Language:Gender	1.83	0.17
Varco-V	Language	11.58	0.00066
	Gender	0.31	0.57
	Language:Gender	4.21	0.04
Varco-NV	Language	17.01	0.0000371
	Gender	1.79	0.18
	Language:Gender	0.4	0.52
nPVI-V	Language	45.58	1.46E-11
	Gender	1.53	0.21
	Language:Gender	3.51	0.06
nPVI-NV	Language	22.2	0.00000245
	Gender	0.07	0.79
	Language:Gender	0.69	0.4
SR	Language	22.28	0.00000234
	Gender	0.67	0.41
	Language:Gender	2.57	0.1

4.3   Automatic Language Identification Using Speech Rhythm Features and Speech Rate

This work explores two machine learning models, viz. SVM and RF to investigate the effectiveness of automatically computed Rhythm measures and speech rate for classifying Mising (Pagro and Delu combined) and Assamese language. The SVM maps the input features into high dimensional space so that features can be linearly separable [4]. RF is an ensemble of decision trees, and its prediction for input will be the class voted by most trees [13].

The models are trained using the 4-fold cross-validation and in a speaker-independent manner. In each iteration, speech data from three folds (approx. 80% of total data) are used for training, and the remaining one fold is used to evaluate the performance. The training set is further divided into the actual training set, which is used to train the model, and a development set, which is used to optimize the model's hyperparameters. Thus, the models are evaluated four times, and at each fold, accuracy and F1-score on the test set are considered as evaluation metrics. We use the grid-search method to tune the hyperparameters of SVM, such as C and γ, and RF, such as the number of trees. The results

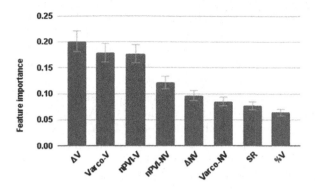

Fig. 5. Feature importance computed from RF using the 4 fold cross-validation.

Table 4. Classification results of the 4-fold cross validation for Assamese and Mising.

Classifier		SVM (RBF Kernel)		RF	
Features	Dimension	Accuracy ($\mu \pm \sigma$)	F1-Score ($\mu \pm \sigma$)	Accuracy ($\mu \pm \sigma$)	F1-Score ($\mu \pm \sigma$)
RM	7	81.48 ± 7.30	81.08 ± 8.90	81.12 ± 7.17	80.94 ± 9.43
RM + SR	8	82.53 ± 7.62	81.96 ± 9.24	81.73 ± 7.70	81.27 ± 9.23
RM+ SR (except %V)	7	83.10 ± 7.85	82.34 ± 9.21	81.55 ± 7.64	81.14 ± 9.95

are noted in terms of mean (μ), standard deviation (σ) accuracy, and the F1-score of the four-folds. The speakers in the train set are not included in the test set in each fold. Hence, the classification results are reported in a speaker-independent manner. The classification results of the 4-fold cross-validation are mentioned in Table 4. The models are developed for three different combinations of features, such as RM, RM and SR, and RM and SR excluding %V. The average accuracy of 81.48% and average F1-score of 81.12% are observed in the case of the RM-based SVM model. And similar performance can also be seen for the RF classifier. Inclusion of SR with the RM provides around a 1% improvement for the SVM. However, it is found that excluding the %V features improves the SVM-based system performance. The table shows that RM and SR computed automatically using the VOP and VEP detection can be utilized in classifying Mising and Assamese. Figure 5 shows the contribution of each feature in classifying Mising and Assamese. Rhythm measures related to the vowel regions (except %V) are very important in the classification. Further investigation needs to be carried to identify the possible cause of this trend.

5   Conclusion and Future Directions

This paper discusses a methodology for computing the rhythm measures and speech rate by automatically locating VOP and VEP from spontaneous speech. This automated method relies on acoustic information alone, which is beneficial compared to labour-consuming manual annotation and forced alignment methods. We have analyzed the rhythm measures of Mising, a low resource language spoken in Assam, and performed a comparative study with Assamese, the official language of Assam. From the analysis, it is found that Mising is more stress-timed on the language continuum. And Assamese falls in the mora-timed language category, which has been validated as per previous studies [7]. A significant difference is observed between Mising and Assamese for all the measures, except %V. However, between the two dialects of Mising, no statistical significance difference is noted, which can be seen from the eight feature boxplots between Pagro and Delu types. LID systems are designed using machine learning models such as SVM and RF, considering combinations of rhythm measures and speech rate. SVM-based system with 7- dimensional feature set seems to provide the best accuracy of 83.10% and 82.34% F1-score.

We have observed significantly large values for the Varco-NV in Assamese and two Mising varieties. The value of the Varco-NV for Assamese is found to be high as compared to [7]. One possible reason may be due to the inclusion of the silence region in the NV region. Future work is planned to further investigate this measure in more detail. Moreover, current work only considers two Mising dialects; hence, rhythm analysis of other Mising dialects is also planned in future research to investigate between- and within-speaker rhythmic variability.

References

1. Abercrombie, D.: Elements of General Phonetics. Edinburgh University Press, Edinburgh, Scotland (1980)
2. Bates, D., Mächler, M., Bolker, B., Walker, S.: Fitting linear mixed-effects models using lme4. J. Stat. Softw. **67**(1), 1–48 (2015)
3. Boersma, P., Weenink, D.: Praat: doing phonetics by computer (version 5.1.13) (2009). http://www.praat.org
4. Cortes, C., Vapnik, V.: Support-vector networks. Mach. Learn. **20**(3), 273–297 (1995)
5. Dauer, R.M.: Stress-timing and syllable-timing reanalyzed. J. Phonet. **11**(1), 51–62 (1983)
6. Dellwo, V., Wagner, P., Solé, M., Recasens, D., Romero, J.: Relations between language rhythm and speech rate (2003)
7. Dihingia, L., Sarmah, P.: Rhythm and speaking rate in assamese varieties. In: Proceedings of 10th International Conference on Speech Prosody 2020, pp. 561–565 (2020)
8. Farinas, J., Pellegrino, F.: Automatic rhythm modeling for language identification. In: Seventh European Conference on Speech Communication and Technology (2001)
9. Ferragne, E., Pellegrino, F.: Rhythm in read British English: interdialect variability. In: Eighth International Conference on Spoken Language Processing (2004)
10. Galves, A., Garcia, J., Duarte, D., Galves, C.: Sonority as a basis for rhythmic class discrimination. In: Speech Prosody 2002, International Conference (2002)
11. Grabe, E., Low, E.L.: Durational Variability in Speech and the Rhythm Class Hypothesis, pp. 515–546. De Gruyter Mouton (2008)

12. Grenon, I., White, L.: Acquiring rhythm: a comparison of l1 and l2 speakers of Canadian English and Japanese. In: Proceedings of the 32nd Boston University Conference on Language Development, pp. 155–166. Citeseer (2008)

13. Ho, T.K.: Random decision forests. In: Proceedings of 3rd International Conference on Document Analysis and Recognition, vol. 1, pp. 278–282. IEEE (1995)

14. Kim, H., Park, J.S.: Automatic language identification using speech rhythm features for multi-lingual speech recognition. Appl. Sci. **10**(7) (2020). https://doi.org/10.3390/app10072225, https://www.mdpi.com/2076-3417/10/7/2225

15. Lee, C.S., Todd, N.P.M.: Towards an auditory account of speech rhythm: application of a model of the auditory 'primal sketch'to two multi-language corpora. Cognition **93**(3), 225–254 (2004)

16. Ling, L.E., Grabe, E., Nolan, F.: Quantitative characterizations of speech rhythm: syllable-timing in Singapore English. Lang. Speech **43**(4), 377–401 (2000). https://doi.org/10.1177/00238309000430040301, pMID: 11419223

17. Loukina, A., Kochanski, G., Rosner, B., Keane, E., Shih, C.: Rhythm measures and dimensions of durational variation in speech. J. Acoust. Soc. Am.**129**(5), 3258–3270 (2011). https://doi.org/10.1121/1.3559709

18. Murty, L., Otake, T., Cutler, A.: Perceptual tests of rhythmic similarity: I. mora rhythm. Lang. Speech **50**(1), 77–99 (2007)

19. Nolan, F., Asu, E.L.: The pairwise variability index and coexisting rhythms in language. Phonetica **66**(1–2), 64–77 (2009)

20. Pegu, J.: Morpho-syntactic variation in the pagro and sa:jan dialects of the mising community. North East Indian Linguist. **3**, 155–170 (2011)

21. Pike, K.: The Intonation of American English. University of Michigan Press, Ann Arbor, MI, USA (1945)

22. Port, R.F., Dalby, J., O'Dell, M.: Evidence for mora timing in Japanese. J. Acoust. Soc. Am. **81**(5), 1574–1585 (1987)

23. Pradhan, G., Prasanna, S.R.M.: Speaker verification by vowel and nonvowel like segmentation. IEEE Trans. Audio Speech Lang. Process. **21**(4), 854–867 (2013)

24. Prasad, B.: Mising grammar. Mysore, Central Institute of Indian languages (CIIL) Eds: Sastry and Abraham (1991)

25. Ramus, F., Nespor, M., Mehler, J.: Correlates of linguistic rhythm in the speech signal. Cognition **75**(1), AD3-AD30 (2000)

26. Rathcke, T.V., Smith, R.H.: Speech timing and linguistic rhythm: on the acoustic bases of rhythm typologies. J. Acoust. Soc. Am. **137**(5), 2834–2845 (2015). https://doi.org/10.1121/1.4919322

27. Rouas, J.L., Farinas, J., Pellegrino, F., André-Obrecht, R.: Rhythmic unit extraction and modelling for automatic language identification. Speech Commun. **47**(4), 436–456 (2005)

28. Taid, T.: A short note on mising phonology. Linguistics of the Tibeto-Burman Area 10.1 (1987)

29. White, L., Mattys, S.: Rhythmic Typology and Variation in First and Second Languages, pp. 237–257 (2007). https://doi.org/10.1075/cilt.282.16whi

30. Wiget, L., White, L., Schuppler, B., Grenon, I., Rauch, O., Mattys, S.L.: How stable are acoustic metrics of contrastive speech rhythm? J. Acoust. Soc. Am. **127**(3), 1559–1569 (2010)

An Electroglottographic Method for Assessing the Emotional State of the Speaker

Aleksey Grigorev$^{(\boxtimes)}$ (iD), Anna Kurazhova(iD), Egor Kleshnev(iD),
Aleksandr Nikolaev(iD), Olga Frolova(iD), and Elena Lyakso(iD)

The Child Speech Research Group, St. Petersburg State University, St. Petersburg
199034, Russia
a.s.grigoriev89@gmail.com

Abstract. The purpose of the study is to determine the shape of the electroglottographic (EGG) wave, the values of the closed quotient (CQ) coefficient and
the pitch values (F0) of speech uttered in emotional states of joy, sadness, fear,
anger and in a neutral (calm) state. Two methods were used: EGG and spectrographic analysis. The object of the study was electroglottograms and speech (F0
and duration of phrases) of 12 healthy speakers (6 men and 6 women, age 25.3
± 4.5 and 24.5 ± 4.8 years, respectively). It was found that the values of the CQ
coefficient in men are maximal in the neutral (calm) state – 0.98; in women – in
a state of sadness – 0.97. The minimal values of the CQ coefficient for men are
shown for the state of fear – 0.81, for women – for the state of joy – 0.69. In men,
the states of anger and joy are characterized by significantly higher pitch values
than the neutral (calm) state; in women, the pitch values are significantly higher
in the states of fear, anger, and joy vs the state of sadness and the neutral state.
Significant differences in the pitch values between the states of fear, anger, joy; a
neutral state and a state of sadness were not revealed.

Keywords: Electroglottography (EGG) · Emotions · Pitch frequency

1 Introduction

Electroglottography is an extralaryngeal non-invasive method for recording true vocal
fold oscillations during phonation [1]. The electroglottogram (EGG) reflects the phase
of opening of the glottis, the phase of its maximum opening, the phase of closure and
the phase of complete closure of the true vocal folds. The main indicator is the closed
quotient (CQ) – the percentage of oscillatory cycles in which the glottis closes completely
when pronouncing speech material [2, 3]. EGG can be administered non-invasively
method has a surprisingly large scope of applications, encompassing, among others [1]:
basic voice science, voice production physiology, phonetics, speech processing, speech
signal analysis and classification, singing, speech and language therapy, clinical work
(including swallowing, psychology, and hearing).

The EGG method is proposed to be used for more accurate identification of emotions
by voice [4]. EGG data allows you to get directly "clean" information about the work

© Springer Nature Switzerland AG 2022
S. R. M. Prasanna et al. (Eds.): SPECOM 2022, LNAI 13721, pp. 214–225, 2022.
https://doi.org/10.1007/978-3-031-20980-2_19

of the vocal folds [5], avoiding the noise of the speech signal. It has been shown that the emotional state of the speaker affects the shape of the EGG wave [6] and the pitch values [7]. When recognizing emotions from speech, the following characteristics are taken into account [8]: excitation of the vocal cords (voice pitch), which reflects the frequency of vocal fold vibrations; intonation structure (change in Intonation contour) and speech rate [9]; the energy of the voice perceived as intensity. It is used because of its correlation with the valence of the emotion; the frequency spectrum containing information about the excitation of the vocal voice source and the modulating processes in the vocal tract. A change in the emotional state of the speaker leads to a change in the characteristics of the excitation of the vocal cords and the modulation of sound in the vocal tract. For example, when speakers are more active, the pressure in the lungs increases accordingly, resulting in faster vibration of the vocal folds. At the same time, the spectral information in the vocal tract also changes [10].

When considering the relationship between emotions, it can be noted that some emotions are more similar to each other, such as sadness and a neutral state, anger, surprise and joy. This can be explained in terms of the characteristics of different emotions. For example, from spatial structure theories [11], sadness and neutrality show low activation, while anger, surprise, and happiness show high activation. Different levels of activation largely correspond to the average pitch frequency [12]. The data available in the literature on changes and the correlation between EGG parameters and speaker characteristics, such as gender, age, and his emotional state, are contradictory. The work [13] showed that EGG parameters depend on the nature of the spoken material, but no such relationship was found in other works [14, 15]. A study in Australian English [16] shows that CQ values increase with age in women, but decrease in men, as confirmed by work in Chinese [17]. However, there are opposite data on an increase in CQ values in men and a decrease in women [18] or an increase in this parameter in both genders, but more pronounced in men [19] (based on the German language).

The purpose of our study is to determine the shape of the EGG wave, the values of CQ coefficient and the pitch values of speech uttered in emotional states of joy, sadness, fear, anger and in a neutral state.

2   Materials and Methods

The Study Participants were 12 native Russian speakers (6 men and 6 women, age 25.3 ± 4.5 and 24.5 ± 4.8 years, respectively), the object of the study was their electroglottograms and speech. EGG was recorded using electroglottograph (Model 7050A, VoceVista, Netherlands). During the study, speakers were asked to simulate emotions when pronouncing: words, phrases, and a meaningless text – the first quatrain of "Jabberwocky", the poem by Lewis Carroll [20], and the meaningless (sentence) by L.V. Shcherba "glokaya kuzdra" (1930) [21] in emotional states of joy, sadness, fear, anger and in a neutral state. All speakers were not professional actors and had no acting education. All tasks were completed by reading the proposed tasks. For each subject, 20 EGGs were recorded – 4 for each of the 5 emotional states. The EGG was used to determine the values of the CQ coefficient, the pitch frequency and the shape of the electroglottographic wave using the VoceVista 3.2 software. The threshold level for determining the CQ coefficient is 20%, because it was this level that made it possible to analyze all electroglottograms.

The speaker's facial expressions were video recorded using a Sony Handycam FDR-AX700 4K HDR camcorder paralell with the EGG recordings. All video recordings of facial expressions obtained during the experiment were processed in the software for analyzing facial expressions FaceReader v. 8.0 (Noldus, the Netherlands) to determine the emotional state of the informants using the built-in algorithms for processing the results.

Previously, we have identified 4 forms of EGG waves [22]: an even wave with no vibrations with a sharp increase in the leading front of the wave (form 1); a wave with insignificant vibrations with a rather sharp increase in the leading front of the wave (form 2); a wave with an increased (2–3) number of peaks (form 3); a wave with a very large number of additional vibrations (noise) (form 4) (Fig. 1).

The recordings of speech of participants were made by the "Marantz PMD660" recorder with external microphone "SENNHEIZER e835S" with the following settings: the sampling rate was set to 16,000 Hz and the mono audio channel was used in all the recording sessions.

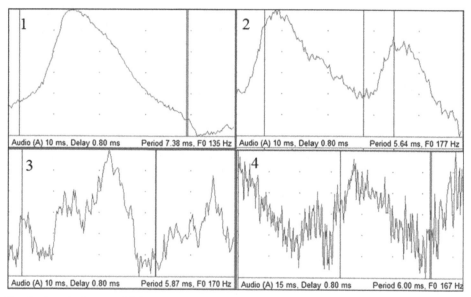

Fig. 1. 4 main forms of EGG waves: 1 – an even wave with no vibrations; 2 – a wave with insignificant vibrations; 3 – a wave with an increased (2–3) number of peaks; 4 – a wave with a very large number of additional vibrations (noise) [22].

Instrumental Analysis of the speech material was carried out in the Cool Edit Pro sound editor. For all speech samples, the pitch values (F0, Hz) – average, F0 max, F0 min, intensity values E (dB), the duration (ms) of a phrase, and duration of pauses were determined. F0 is the main characteristic of the voice, resulting from the swaying of vocal folds. F0 statistics are one of the most important features that correlate with emotional vocal expressions. A higher and wider range of F0 and energy (intensity) are usually associated with high-arousal emotions compared to neutral speech [23]. For each utterance, the range of F0 was calculated by subtracting the minimum F0 from the maximum F0 values: F0 range = F0max-F0min. The rate of speech was determined as the number of phonemes per second (s).

Statistical Data analysis was carried out using non-parametric tests: Mann-Whitney U-test, correlation (Spearman, $p < 0.05$), regression analysis in STATISTICA 10 software.

All procedures were approved by the Health and Human Research Ethics Committee of Saint Petersburg State University.

3 Results

3.1 EGG and Speech Features in Different Emotional States

A neutral emotional state is characterized by high values of the CQ coefficient (for men – 0.98; for women – 0.89, hereinafter – the median). The predominant form of the EGG wave is form 2 (a wave with insignificant vibrations with a rather sharp increase in the leading front of the wave) – 45% of records in men and 88% of records in women. In men, there is a direct wave (form 1) – 40% of the records and a wave with additional peaks (form 3) – 15% of the records. In women, in addition to form 2, form 4 and form 1 occur (8% and 4% of records, respectively) (Fig. 2).

When registering an electroglottogram, it was found that in a neutral state, men have minimal F0 – 114.3 ± 17.5 Hz, compared with the states of joy, sadness, fear and anger. In women in the neutral state, the F0 are 200.3 ± 26.1 Hz. According to the results of instrumental analysis, it was found that in the neutral state in men, the F0 average for the phrase are 150.2 ± 18.8 Hz, the F0 max are 178.2 ± 38 Hz, the F0 min are 103 ± 18.9 Hz; the pitch range is 75.2 ± 25.7 Hz. The average duration of a phrase is 4128 ± 968 ms, the average duration of pauses is 180 ms. The average rate of speech is 12.1 ± 2.4 phonemes per s. In women in the neutral state, the F0 average for the phrase are 218.7 ± 23.7 Hz, the F0 max are 265.3 ± 24.2 Hz, the F0 min are 187.5 ± 0.8 Hz; the pitch range is 77.8 ± 23.5 Hz. The average duration of an utterance is 4429 ± 782 ms, the average duration of pauses is 73 ms. The average rate of speech is 11.1 ± 1.9 phonemes per s.

The emotional state of sadness is characterized in men by rather high values of the CQ coefficient (0.88), in women – by the maximal values (0.97). The predominant form of the EGG wave is form 2 – 50% of records in men and 88% in women. Also, in men and women, other waveforms are observed (except for the 4th form in men): form 1 (45% and 4%, respectively), form 3 (5% and 4%), and form 4 (4% in women) (Fig. 2). F0 in men is 122.6 ± 22.0 Hz, in women it is 197.8 ± 33.7 Hz. The F0 average for a phrase in men are 148.6 ± 35.2 Hz, the F0 max for a phrase are 172 ± 38 Hz, the F0 min are 109.5 ± 24 Hz; the pitch range is 62.5 ± 24 Hz. The average duration of an utterance is 4391 ± 571 ms, the average duration of pauses is 258.8 ms, the average speech rate is 11.1 ± 1.4 phonemes per s. In women in a state of sadness, the F0 average for the phrase are 226.3 ± 18.8 Hz, the F0 max are 288.8 ± 54.9 Hz, the F0 min are 187.5 ± 0.8 Hz; the pitch range is 101.3 ± 54.7 Hz. The average duration of an utterance is 4795 ± 997.7 ms, the average duration of pauses is 399.2 ms, the average speech rate is 10.3 ± 1.8 phonemes per s.

The emotional state of fear in men is characterized by the minimum values of the CQ coefficient – 0.81, in women – 0.87. The predominant form of the EGG wave in men is form 1 – 55% of records, in women – form 2 (75%). In men, waveforms are observed – form 2 (40% of records), form 3 (5%). In women, in addition to form 2, form 1 is observed – 25% of the records, forms 3 and 4 are absent in women in a state of sadness (Fig. 2). F0 in men is 123.7 ± 36.2 Hz, in women it is 235.9 ± 46.8 Hz. The F0 average for the phrase in men are 150.2 ± 19.3 Hz, the F0 max are 168.8 ± 39.1 Hz, the F0 min are 103.2 ± 19.3 Hz, the pitch range is 65.6 ± 24 Hz. The average utterance duration is 4005 ± 384 ms, the average duration of pauses is 354 ms, the average speech rate is 12.1 ± 1.3 phonemes per s. The F0 average for the phrase in women are 257.5 ± 57.6 Hz, the F0 max are 304.5 ± 64.8 Hz, the F0 min are 195.5 ± 18.9 Hz, the pitch range is 109 ± 48.9 Hz. The average utterance duration is 4434 ± 633 ms, there are no pauses, the average speech rate is 11 ± 1.6 phonemes per s.

The emotional state of anger is characterized by high CQ values – 0.94 for men and 0.97 for women. The predominant form of the EGG wave in men are forms 1 and 2 (45% each), in women – form 2 (83%). Also in men there is form 3 (10%); in women, form 1 (17%), forms 3 and 4 are absent (Fig. 2). F0 in men is 129.8 ± 24.9 Hz, in women it is 240.1 ± 53.2 Hz. The F0 average for a phrase in men are 156.3 ± 38 Hz, the F0 max are 187.3 ± 41.6 Hz, the F0 min are 109.5 ± 24 Hz, the pitch range is 77.8 ± 37.9 Hz. The average utterance duration is 3951 ± 625 ms, the duration of pauses is 219 ms, the average speech rate is 12.4 ± 1.7 phonemes per s. The F0 average in women are 249.8 ± 64 Hz, the F0 max are 312.3 ± 56.9 Hz, the F0 min are 187.5 ± 29.4 Hz, the pitch range is 124.8 ± 48.3 Hz. The average duration of the utterance is 4321 ± 273 ms, the duration of pauses is 94 ms, the rate of speech is 11.1 ± 0.7 phonemes per s.

The emotional state of joy is characterized in men by rather high values of the CQ coefficient (0.91), in women – by the minimum values of the coefficient (0.69). The predominant wave form in men and women is form 2 (57% and 75%, respectively). Men also have form 1 (43% of records), and forms 3 and 4 do not occur. In women, waveform 1 is present in 25% of the records, waveforms 3 and 4 are absent (Fig. 2). F0 in men is 135.5 ± 31.1 Hz, in women it is 245.5 ± 38.5 Hz. The F0 average for a phrase in men are 159.6 ± 24 Hz, the F0 max are 206.2 ± 23.9 Hz, the F0 min are 103 ± 18.9 Hz, the pitch range is 103.2 ± 35.2 Hz. The average utterance duration is 3764 ± 333 ms, the average duration of pauses is 90 ms, the average speech rate is 12.8 ± 1.1 phonemes per s. In women, the F0 average for the phrase in a state of joy is 249.8 ± 64 Hz, the F0 max are 366.8 ± 80.4 Hz, the F0 min are 180 ± 19 Hz, the pitch range is 186.8 ± 72.2 Hz. The average duration of utterances is 4383 ± 444 ms, the duration of pauses is 125 ms, the rate of speech is 11.0 ± 1.2 phonemes per s.

3.2   Comparison of EGG Parameters of Male and Female Subjects

The values of the CQ coefficient in men are maximum in the neutral state – 0.98; in women, the maximum in a state of sadness is 0.97. The minimum values of the CQ

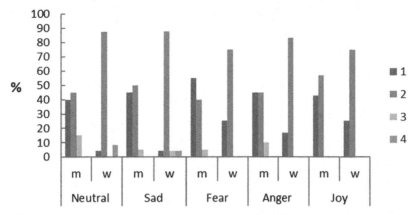

Fig. 2. Forms of the electroglottographic wave occurring in different emotional states. Numbers 1, 2, 3, 4 are the corresponding forms of the electroglottographic wave, m – the data for men, w – for women. On the horizontal axis – emotional states, on the vertical axis – % of records.

coefficient in men are shown for the state of fear – 0.81, in women – for the state of joy – 0.69 (Fig. 3). Indicators of the CQ coefficient do not differ significantly in men and women, do not differ in different emotional states. The predominant wave form in men in a neutral state, a state of sadness and joy is form 2, for a state of anger – forms 1 and 2, for a state of fear – form 1. In men, in all emotional states, form 4 of the wave is not found, in a state of joy there is no form 3. The predominant waveform in women for all emotional states is form 2, in all emotional states form 1 occurs, in the neutral state and in the state of sadness form 4 occurs (a large amount of noise), form 3 occurs only in the state of sadness.

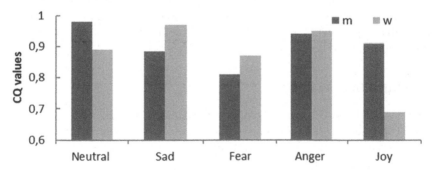

Fig. 3. The median values of the CQ coefficient in men and women when pronouncing speech material in different emotional states. m – data for man, w – data for women. On the horizontal axis – emotional states, on the vertical axis – coefficient values.

According to the results of the analysis of the pitch frequency, obtained during the registration of EGG, it was found that in men, the states of anger ($p < 0.05$) and joy ($p < 0.01$) are characterized by significantly higher values of pitch than the neutral state; no significant differences were found for other states. In women, the F0 are significantly higher in the states of fear (p < 0.01), anger (p < 0.01) and joy (p < 0.001) than in the states of sadness and the neutral state, while the F0 values between the states of fear, anger and joy, as well as between a neutral emotional state and a state of sadness, do not differ significantly (Fig. 4).

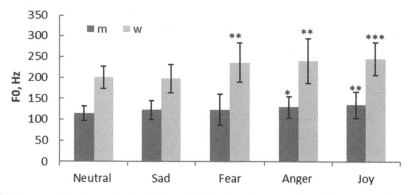

Fig. 4. Average F0 values obtained during EGG registration. m – data for men, w – for women. On the horizontal axis – emotional states, on the vertical axis – the values of F0, Hz.

According to the results of instrumental analysis, it was found that in men the rate of speech in an emotional state of joy is significantly higher than in a state of sadness, the duration of statements in a state of joy is significantly lower than in a state of sadness. No significant differences between emotional states in terms of the average F0 values for the phrase, the minimum and maximum F0 values, and pitch range values were found.

In women, the F0 maximum values in the state of joy are significantly higher than in the neutral state, the difference between the maximum and minimum F0 values is higher in the state of joy than in the neutral state. There were no statistically significant differences in the parameters of average F0 values, minimal F0 values, utterance duration, and pause duration and speech rate.

3.3 Statistical Data Analysis

Correlations are shown between the gender of the subjects and the F0 values (r = 0.79, p < 0.0001), the average F0 values for the phrase (r = 0.86, p < 0.0001), the maximum F0 values (r = 0.36, p = 0.0047), the pitch range values (r = 0.34, p = 0.0084); the intensity values of the average F0 (r = 0.43, p = 0.0007) and the intensity values of the maximum F0 (r = 0.36, p = 0.0047), the duration of the utterance (r = 0.34, p = 0.0079). The age of the subjects is associated with the values of F0 (r = −0.40, p = 0.0014), intensity F0 average (r = -0.41, p = 0.0012) and intensity F0 max (r = −0.38, p = 0.025). The emotional state is associated with the values intensity F0 average (r = 0.40, p = 0.0014) and intensity F0 max for a phrase (r = 0.30, p = 0.022). The values of the CQ coefficient are associated with the F0 values obtained during the EGG registration (r = −0.26, p = 0.047), the values of the intensity F0 average (r = −0.28, p = 0.031) and intensity F0 maximum (r = -0.26, p = 0.043). At the trend level, the relationship between the emotional state and the shape of the EGG wave, between the shape of the EGG wave and CQ is shown.

4 Discussion

In the study, we described the values of the CQ parameter and electroglottographic waveforms, as well as the F0 parameters obtained during EGG registration. Based on the instrumental analysis of the speech material, the pitch values and the duration of meaningless phrases in different emotional states are described. It was shown that the F0 values obtained during the registration of EGG significantly differ depending on the emotional state in both genders. Based on the material of German and Tamil languages, it is shown that the emotional state of anger is characterized by the highest F0 values, the minimum values of F0 on the material of German are shown for the state of boredom and the neutral state, on the material of Tamil – for the state of sadness [7]. The results obtained in our study on significant differences in the pitch values obtained during the registration of EGG in different emotional states correlate with these results. It has previously been shown that in a neutral emotional state, the initial characteristics of voice waves show significant variation in terms of the number of voice cycles, amplitude, and shape compared to other emotions [7]. The use of F0 data obtained using EGG improves the results of automatic emotion recognition in, comparison with the use of F0 values determined only from the audio recording of a speech [7].

A study [4] used an electroglottograph as an emotion recognition system by measuring pitch differences. Our data are consistent with results [4] that in the state of joy, the F0 values recorded using EGG are significantly higher than in the state of sadness and the neutral state. In this study, it was shown that the F0 values of the neutral state and the sad state often overlap, but the F0 values of the sad state are lower than in the neutral state. In our work, the values of F0 in the neutral state and the state of sadness do not differ significantly.

Our study found an inverse correlation between CQ values and F0 and intensity values: highly activated emotions are characterized by higher F0 values and lower CQ values. This can be explained by the fact that emotions that have a high activation are often characterized by a louder voice, its pitch and timbre change, but sometimes, on the contrary, a decrease in the strength of the voice can occur. A change in the emotional state leads to the activation of the autonomic nervous system, which leads to a change in breathing, heartbeat, sensation of trembling, feeling of dryness in the throat, etc. All this can affect CQ values. In our work, CQ values in the state of anger in men and women turned out to be high and did not differ from the neutral state. This can be explained by the fact that the study participants were not professional actors, and the display of vivid negative emotions is traditionally not welcomed in public places.

In a study that included 50 Indian young people (25 men and women each, average age 21 years), the influence on the EGG parameters of the character of the spoken material (vowels /a/, /u/, /i/), pronunciation register (modal or vocal) and speaker gender [15] were revealed. It is shown that the values of the CQ coefficient are significantly higher in both men and women during vocal pronunciation, compared with modal. It is also shown that the values of the CQ coefficient in men are significantly higher than in women in any pronunciation variant, but do not differ when pronouncing different vowels. In our study, there were no significant differences in the parameters of the CQ coefficient between men and women.

It has been shown that the values of the CQ coefficient differ in children and adult men, in men and women [24], and in this work it was found that the electroglottographic wave visually differs in children and adults. Based on the material of the Finnish language, it is shown that when singing in the normal frequency range of female speech, the values of the CQ coefficient vary from 0.25 to 0.62, however, there are no data on the value of the CQ coefficient in the simple pronunciation of speech sounds [25].

On the material of the Finnish language, when professional actors and actresses depict emotional states when pronouncing individual vowel sounds, it is shown that in men the maximum values of CQ are observed in a state of joy, then, in decreasing order, the states of fear, anger, surprise, sadness, disgust, neutral state and interest. In women, the maximum values of the CQ coefficient are observed in the state of anger, then, in decreasing order, the states of disgust, surprise, fear, sadness, joy, interest, and the neutral state follow [26]. Our data differ from these results – in men, the maximum values of CQ were found in the neutral state, the minimum – in the state of fear; in women, the maximum in a state of sadness, and the minimum – in a state of joy. These differences can be explained by the fact that our study involved subjects who were not professional actors and the degree of severity of their emotional state differs from that of professionals. The second feature of our study was the speech material that the subjects had to pronounce, demonstrating different emotions – meaningless texts. Since there was no preliminary training of the subjects, each subject puts his own meaning into the spoken phrases, and, accordingly, the degree of expression of the emotional state was different. In our study, EGG was recorded when pronouncing speech material, and in the study [26], when pronouncing isolated vowel sounds. Data on the dependence of EGG parameters on the type of spoken material are contradictory: it has been shown that EGG parameters depend on the nature of the spoken material [13], but no such relationship has been found in other studies [14, 15].

Two studies [27, 28] analyzed various parameters of the electroglottogram while singing one vowel [a] in different emotional states. Such as glottal cycle length, fundamental frequency, closed quotient, contacting quotient (contact time of the vocal folds divided by cycle duration), max. Velocity of contact, max. Negative velocity at opening, acceleration of contact, speed quotient, normalized closing time (closing time divided by cycle length), normalized opening time (approximate opening time divided by cycle length) and others were calculated. At the same time, it was shown that in order to distinguish between different emotions, it is preferable to use different indicators, for example, joy is better separated from neutral using contacting quotient as opposed to closed quotient. Normalized closing quotient did not provide clear separation of the emotions and was highest for anger. Our study is a pilot one, since we assume the possibility of express discrimination of emotions, using the parameters already embedded in the electroglottograph, without using further data transformations, so we used only the pitch frequency and CQ. Adult speakers took part in this study. In the future we plan to conduct a study with children. In order to study the parameters of the electroglottogram, obtained when registering in children in real conditions, it is extremely important for us to understand the applicability of the electroglottography method when pronouncing whole utterances, and not individual vowels, as in some other works [26–28].

EGG parameters can be influenced by the speaker's age – with age, women experience a decrease in F0 values and an increase in CQ values [17] (on the material of Mandarin Chinese), which is confirmed by a study [16], in which CQ values have been shown to increase with age in women but decrease in men (Australian English speakers). However, there are conflicting data on the increase in CQ values in men and decrease in women [18] or the increase in this parameter in both genders, but more pronounced in men [19] (based on German). In all these studies, the difference in age between the subjects was significant (for example, groups of subjects aged 18–30 and 60–82 years [19]), in our study, the subjects belonged to the same age group, so the effects of age on CQ parameters were not identified.

The main difference between our study and other works devoted to the problem of analyzing changes in EGG parameters in different emotional states is that speakers in our study were not professional actors, so changes in their EGG will apparently be observed when registering EGG in natural recording conditions.

5   Conclusion

On the material of the Russian language, for the first time the parameters of the electroglotogram of a person are described when pronouncing speech material in various emotional states. The predominant forms of the electroglottographic wave and the values of the CQ coefficient are described, significant differences between different emotional states are determined by the values of the pitch. It is shown that emotions with high activation are characterized by higher values of F0 and lower values of the CQ coefficient.

The study showed the promise of using the EGG method to assess the work of the voice source in the emotional state of the speaker.

Acknowledgements. This study is financially supported by the Russian Science Foundation (project 22-45-02007).

References

1. Herbst, C.T.: Electroglottography – an update. J. Voice **34**(4), 503–526 (2020)
2. Kankare, E., Laukkanen, A.M., Ilomäki, I., Miettinen, A., Pylkkänen, T.: Electroglottographic contact quotient in different phonation types using different amplitude threshold levels. Logoped. Phoniatr. Vocol. **37**(3), 127–132 (2012)
3. Lyakso, E., Grigorev, A., Frolova, O., Nikolaev, A.: Using spectrographic and electroglottographic methods to determine the values of the pitch frequency. In: Proceedings of the All-Russian Acoustic Conference, Proceedings of the III All-Russian Conference, pp. 713–717 (2020). (in Russian)
4. Lu, H., Liu Hui, T., Lan See, S., Chan, P.Y.: Use of electroglottograph (EGG) to find a relationship between pitch. Emot. Pers. Procedia Manuf. **3**, 1926–1931 (2015)
5. Chen, P., Chen, L., Mao, X.: Content classification with electroglottograph. J. Phys.: Conf. Ser. **1544**, 012191 (2020)

6. Cummings, K.E., Clements, M.A.: Analysis of glottal waveforms across stress styles. In: International Conference on Acoustics, Speech, and Signal Processing, vol. 1, pp. 369-372 (1990)
7. Pravena, D., Govind, D.: Significance of incorporating excitation source parameters for improved emotion recognition from speech and electroglottographic signals. Int. J. Speech Technol. **20**(4), 787–797 (2017). https://doi.org/10.1007/s10772-017-9445-x
8. Chen, L., Mao, X., Wei, P., Compare, A.: Speech emotional features extraction based on electroglottograph. Neural Comput. **25**(12), 3294–3317 (2013)
9. Fujisaki, H.: Information, prosody, and modeling—with emphasis on tonal features of speech. In: Proceedings of Speech Prosody, pp. 1–10 (2004)
10. Ververidis, D., Kotropoulos, C.: Emotional speech recognition: resources, features, and methods. Speech Commun. **48**, 1162–1181 (2006)
11. Russell, J.A., Barrett, F.L.: Core affect, prototypical emotional episodes, and other things called emotion: dissecting the elephant. J. Personal. Soc. Psychol. **76**, 805–819 (1999)
12. Chen, L., Ren, J., Mao, X., Zhao, Q.: Electroglottograph-based speech emotion recognition via cross-modal distillation. Appl. Sci. **12**, 4338 (2022)
13. Higgins, M.B., Netsell, R., Schulte, L.: Vowel-related differences in laryngeal articulatory and phonatory function. J. Speech Lang. Hear. Res. **41**(4), 712–714 (1998)
14. Chen, Y., Robb, M.P., Gilbert, H.R.: Electroglottographic evaluation of gender and vowel effects during modal and vocal fry phonation. J. Speech Lang. Hear. Res. **45**(5), 821–829 (2002)
15. Paul, N., Kumar, S., Chatterjee, I., Mukherjee, B.: Electroglottographic parameterization of the effects of gender, vowel and phonatory registers on vocal fold vibratory patterns: an indian perspective. Indian J. Otolaryngol. Head Neck Surg. **63**(1), 27–31 (2011)
16. Ma, E.P.-M., Love, A.L.: Electroglottographic evaluation of age and gender effects during sustained phonation and connected speech. J. Voice **24**(2), 146–152 (2010)
17. Ning, L.H.: The effects of age and pitch level on electroglottographic measures during sustained phonation. J. Acoust. Soc. Am. **146**(1), 640–648 (2019)
18. Higgins, M.B., Saxman, J.H.: A comparison of selected phonatory behaviors of healthy aged and young adults. J. Speech Lang. Hear. Res. **34**(5), 1000–1010 (1991)
19. Winkler, R., Sendlmeier, W.: EGG open quotient in aging voices—changes with increasing chronological age and its perception. Logoped. Phoniatr. Vocol. **31**(2), 51–56 (2006)
20. Carrol, L.: Through the Looking-Glass and What Alice Found There. Macmillan and Co, London (1872)
21. http://languagehat.com/glokaya-kuzdr (2019). Accessed 30 July 2022
22. Grigorev, A.S., Lyakso, E.E.: Analysis of the shape of the electroglottographic wave in patients before and after thyroid surgery. In: VI IEEE International Conference "Video and Audio Signal Processing in the Context of Neurotechnologies" SPCN – 2021, St.-Petersburg, Russia (2021)
23. Lyakso, E., Frolova, O., Ruban, N., Mekala, A.M.: Child's emotional speech classification by human across two languages: russian & tamil. In: Karpov, A., Potapova, R. (eds.) SPECOM 2021. LNCS (LNAI), vol. 12997, pp. 384–396. Springer, Cham (2021). https://doi.org/10.1007/978-3-030-87802-3_35
24. Patel, R.R., Ternström, S.: Quantitative and qualitative electroglottographic wave shape differences in children and adults using voice map-based analysis. J. Speech Lang. Hear. Res. **64**(8), 2977–2995 (2021)
25. Ong Tan, K.G.: Contact quotient of female singers singing four pitches for five vowels in normal and pressed phonations. J. Voice **31**(5), 645.e15-645.e22 (2017)
26. Waaramaa, T., Kankare, E.: Acoustic and EGG analyses of emotional utterances. Logoped. Phoniatr. Vocol. **38**(1), 11–18 (2013)

27. Murphy, P.J., Laukkanen, A.-M.: Electroglottogram analysis of emotionally styled phonation. In: Esposito, A., Hussain, A., Marinaro, M., Martone, R. (eds.) Multimodal signals: Cognitive and algorithmic issues. LNCS (LNAI), vol. 5398, pp. 264–270. Springer, Heidelberg (2009). https://doi.org/10.1007/978-3-642-00525-1_27

28. Murphy, P.J., Laukkanen, A.-M.: Analysis of emotional voice using electroglottogram-based temporal measures of vocal fold opening. In: Esposito, A., Campbell, N., Vogel, C., Hussain, A., Nijholt, A. (eds.) Development of multimodal interfaces: active listening and synchrony. LNCS, vol. 5967, pp. 286–293. Springer, Heidelberg (2010). https://doi.org/10.1007/978-3-642-12397-9_24

Significance of Distance on Pop Noise for Voice Liveness Detection

Priyanka Gupta$^{(\boxtimes)}$ⓘ and Hemant A. Patilⓘ

Speech Research Lab, DA-IICT, Gandhinagar 382007, Gujarat, India
{priyanka_gupta,hemant_patil}@daiict.ac.in

Abstract. Voice Liveness Detection (VLD) systems are used to distinguish a live speech utterance from spoofed speech. Such systems are known to use *pop noise* as the discriminating cue for detection of live speech. In this work, we propose an algorithm based on Morlet wavelet, to capture pop noise energy. The proposed algorithm is tested to analyse the effect of variability of speaker-microphone distance on the strength of pop noise. Furthermore, the type of phoneme uttered also plays an important role, when dealing with pop noise. Therefore, in this work, we have analysed the variability of pop noise strength with distance, for each of the phoneme types. Our analysis shows that phoneme types such as liquids and nasals have the least amount of pop noise, and are also the least affected by increasing distance of the speaker from the microphone. It is also observed that the phoneme types such as plosives and fricatives have the highest pop noise and the most affected when distance is varied.

Keywords: Continuous wavelet transform · Morlet wavelet · Voice liveness detection · Scalogram · Pop noise

1 Introduction

Machine-based authentication of individuals using speech signals is done with the help of voice biometric systems, also known as Automatic Speaker Verification (ASV) systems [7]. They have wide range of applications in areas, which require access to classified information, such as banking transactions. However, ASV systems can undergo spoofing attacks, such as impersonation, Voice Conversion (VC), Speech Synthesis (SS), and replay. To that effect, various ASVSpoof challenge campaigns were organized during INTERSPEECH in 2015, 2017, 2019, and 2021, w.r.t. the development of countermeasure systems, which can detect whether a speech signal is spoofed or not [2,5,8,24,25]. However, most of the existing countermeasure systems have been designed w.r.t. a particular type of attack only. An attacker can use any type of attack (*known* attack as well as *unknown* attack). Therefore, it is important to detect whether a speech is live or not.

In VLD systems, *pop noise* is used as the discriminating acoustic cue to detect live speech which is present in live speech and is diminished or even

S. R. M. Prasanna et al. (Eds.): SPECOM 2022, LNAI 13721, pp. 226–237, 2022.
https://doi.org/10.1007/978-3-031-20980-2_20

absent in spoofed speech. Pop noise is a distortion caused due to close proximity of a speaker's mouth with the microphone. Pop noise is generated when a live speaker is speaking, which results in a burst of air striking the microphone. The burst of air captured on the microphone is called as pop noise [13]. Spoofed speech signals, such as synthetic speech and replayed speech, fail to reproduce the pop noise as strongly as a live speech signal [1,18].

Initial studies for VLD used techniques such as low frequency-based single channel detection and subtraction in [19], and phoneme-based pop noise detection in [14]. Moreover, to the best of the authors' knowledge, POCO dataset is the first and the only publicly available corpus for VLD research. The release of POCO dataset also released the baseline system which is based on Short-Time Fourier Transform (STFT)-based features for liveness detection [1]. It was found that pop noise is predominantly found in lower frequency regions (i.e., ≤ 40 Hz) [1]. Recent research w.r.t. pop noise detection has been carried out using various techniques, such as spectral root smoothing [21], Modified Group Delay Cepstral Coefficients (MGDCC) [20], STFT [22], Constant Q-Transform (CQT) [9], and wavelet-based features [15–17]. In particular, the approach of using Continuous Wavelet Transform (CWT) was first proposed in [17], wherein a bump wavelet was used for VLD task.

Our work in this paper demonstrates that pop noise is an important acoustic cue for VLD task in the context of voice biometrics. In particular, we demonstrate that the pop noise energy decreases as the distance between the microphone and the speaker's mouth increases. Its significance lies greatly and importantly in the scenario of a replay spoof attack, where an attacker discreetly records the live speech from a distance. The distance is large enough for pop noise to be *absent* in replayed speech. This work is an extension of our recent work reported in [15], wherein we had proposed Morlet wavelet-based features for VLD task. We extend this work, by the additional contributions as follows:

- Analytic behaviour (i.e., causality in the frequency-domain) of the Morlet wavelet is observed for its two variants, i.e., one case where Morlet wavelet does not follow analytic properties, and a second case where it obeys analytic characteristics.
- To that effect, Morlet wavelet-based algorithm is proposed for pop noise energy estimation.
- Effect of distance variability on pop noise energy is analysed using the proposed algorithm.
- Experimental results are shown w.r.t. effect of pop noise strength on the type of phoneme, with varying distances between the microphone and the speaker.
- Finally, our distance-based analysis of pop noise also corroborates with the state-of-the-art results reported for VLD task in [15].

The rest of the paper is organized as follows: Sect. 2 describes the proposed algorithm. Sect. 3 includes the experimental setup details, followed by Sect. 4, which contains the experimental results. Lastly, the Sect. 5 summarizes and brings out conclusions and future research directions from this work.

2   Proposed Work

2.1   Motivation And Analysis For Morlet Wavelet

Sudden high energy in low-frequency regions indicates the presence of pop noise in a speech signal. To that effect, time-frequency representations, such as STFT have been used in the literature [19, 23]. Given that we already know that pop noise energy is present in low-frequency regions, typically ≤ 40 Hz, we take advantage of the excellent frequency resolution of Morlet wavelet-based CWT in the lower frequency regions. To that effect, this sub-Section discusses the basics of CWT.

A mother wavelet is known to be a wave of short duration that has zero average, and is mathematically defined as [11]:

$$\psi_{s,b}(t) = \frac{1}{\sqrt{s}} \psi\left(\frac{t - b}{s}\right), \qquad a \in R^+, b \in R, \tag{1}$$

where b is called the *translation* (position), and s is called the *dilation* (scale) coefficient. We choose the famous Morlet wavelet in this work because it is said to be closely related to the human perception process (for both hearing and vision) [12]. Moreover, CWT is also related to constant-Q filtering, which is a short-time analysis performed by the peripheral auditory system. In particular, as per original investigations by Flanagan in [4], the wavelet function for the mechanical spectral analysis performed by the Basilar membrane in the cochlea of human ear is given by $\psi(t) = (t\omega)^2 e^{-t\omega/2}$. Furthermore, Morlet wavelet is the first wavelet (named in honour of its first formal inventor Jean Morlet, even though originally Haar wavelets were formally invented by Haar in 1910) of its kind in formal historical developments of wavelets in the geophysics literature for the detection of transients and improving the joint time-frequency resolution of seismic signals [3]. Mathematically, Morlet wavelet is a modulated Gaussian, and it is defined as [6, 11]:

$$\psi(t) = e^{j\omega_0 t} e^{-t^2/2}, \tag{2}$$

where ω_0 is 5 Hz for a standard Morlet wavelet. This is also because of the analysis shown in Fig. 1. It can be observed that the Morlet wavelet exhibits analytic behaviour when $\omega_0 = 5$, i.e., its spectral content is strictly in the positive frequency region (as observed in Fig. 1 (d)). However, it shows *spectral leakage* when $\omega_0 = 1.5$ (as observed in Fig. 1 (c)). Therefore, to exploit the strictly analytic properties of the wavelet, we take $\omega_0 = 5$ in this work.

2.2   Proposed Algorithm

The CWT of signal $f(t)$ is mathematically expressed as:

$$\begin{aligned} Wf(s,b) &= <f(t), \psi_{s,b}(t)>, \\ &= \frac{1}{\sqrt{s}} \int_{-\infty}^{\infty} f(t)\psi^*\left(\frac{t - b}{s}\right) dt, \end{aligned} \tag{3}$$

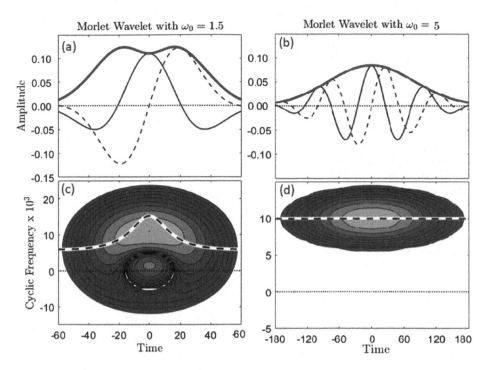

Fig. 1. Variations of analytic behaviour of the Morlet wavelet with varying ω_0 values. (a) and (b) represent the Morlet wavelet in time-domain, and (c) and (d) represent the corresponding Wigner-Ville distributions. After [10].

where $< \cdot, \cdot >$ indicates inner product operation to compute wavelet coefficients, and $*$ denotes the complex conjugate operation. The proposed algorithm (shown as Algorithm 1) uses CWT coefficients corresponding to lower frequency regions, so that the pop noise event is detected efficiently. To that effect, we extract CWT coefficients from the speech data of POCO corpus by taking Morlet as the mother wavelet. CWT coefficients are found for frequencies ≤ 40 Hz. The absolute square of the CWT coefficient for a particular frequency bin gives us the energy of the signal for that particular frequency bin (denoted as *Pop_energy*). Furthermore, to quantify the pop noise energy cumulatively for all the frequency bins below 40 Hz, the mean of all the energies is taken, resulting in *E_mean*. It should be noted that our selection of patch from the scalogram (corresponding to <40 Hz region) is based on the fact that the energy of the underlying speech signal is concentrated (i.e., present) in the time-frequency domain similar to Parseval's energy equivalence for Fourier transform, which in turn is a manifestation of the energy conservation principle in physics (See Appendix A.1).

Algorithm 1: Proposed Algorithm for Pop Noise Energy Estimation Using Morlet Wavelet for VLD.

Input: Speech signal $f(t)$
Output: Emean

1 w_name='amor'   // Taking Morlet wavelet
2 [cwt_coeffs, F] ← cwt(f(t), w_name)
   /* Finding CWT coefficients for low frequencies   */
3 Low_F ← find $(0 < F \leq 40$ Hz$)$
   Low_coeffs ← cwt_coeffs (Low_F)
4 Pop_energy = abs (Low_coeffs)^2
5 [r,c]=size(Pop_energy)
6 **for** $i \leftarrow 0$ **to** r **do**
7 ⌊ E_LF(i)=sum(Pop_energy(i,:))

   /* Each row of E_LF has energy for 1 frequency bin   */
8 Emean=mean(E_LF)   // mean of energy for $1 < F \leq 40$ Hz

---

2.3   Distance-Based Analysis

In this sub-Section, we show the effect of distance variability on the strength of pop noise. To that effect, Fig. 2 shows 3 cases, where the distance between a speaker's mouth and the microphone is varied as 5 cm, 10.78 cm, and 20.48 cm, as Panel-I, II, and III, respectively. The word spoken is *'pink'* taken from the POCO dataset. It can be observed that in time-domain representation of the signal, the pop noise is dominantly visible in Panel-I, where the speaker's mouth is the closest to the microphone (i.e., 5 cm). Similar observation can be made from its CWT-based full-frequency as well as low-frequency scalogram representations, where pop noise energy is highlighted in red boxes. Next, Panel-II shows when the speaker's mouth is at a distance of 10.78 cm from the microphone. One can observe from Panel-II that the pop noise is not visible dominantly in the time-domain representation. On the other hand, the scalogram-based time-frequency representation is able to capture the pop noise energy in the low-frequency regions. However, the strength of pop noise energy is degraded as compared to Panel-I. Lastly, Panel-III shows the case, when the speaker's mouth is at the farthest distance from the microphone, i.e., 20.40 cm. One can observe the lowest strength of pop noise energy in this case, for time-domain representation, as well as the scalogram-based representations. For analysis purposes, in this sub-Section, we considered a particular word 'pink' as an example to show the effect of distance. However, it should be noted that the word 'pink' contains plosives predominantly. Apart from the distance, the strength of pop noise captured also depends on the type of phonemes present in the word uttered in front of the microphone. To that effect, the experimental setup and the results pertaining to the phoneme type and distance as presented in Sect. 3 and Sect. 4, respectively.

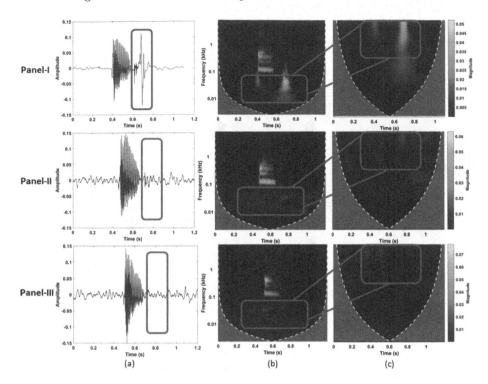

Fig. 2. Panel I, Panel II, and Panel-III represent the varying distance of the speaker from the microphone, i.e., 5 cm, 10.78 cm, and 20.40 cm, respectively, for (a) time-domain signal for the word *'pink'*, (b) corresponding scalogram, and (c) corresponding low-frequency (0 − 40 Hz) scalogram. Solid boxes in red indicate the presence of pop noise. (Color figure online)

3   Experimental Setup

3.1   Dataset Used

The dataset used is the POp noise COrpus (POCO) with speech data sampled at 22.05 kHz [1]. The POCO dataset consists of 3 parts, which are described briefly as below:

Genuine Utterances with Microphone-A (RC-A): In this set, only one microphone (Audio-Technica AT4040) is used. The distance between the speaker and the mic is kept fixed as 10 cm. The utterances in RC-A correspond to genuine utterances, as they have pop noise.

Genuine Utterances with Microphone Array (RC-B): This set contains only genuine utterances. These utterances are captured with a microphone array comprising 15 microphones (Audio-Technica AT9903 microphones), labelled from $M1$ to $M15$ in this work. There are three configurations in this set, each corresponding to a fixed distance between the speaker and $M7$ of each configuration. The 3 distances are 5 cm, 10 cm, and 20 cm.

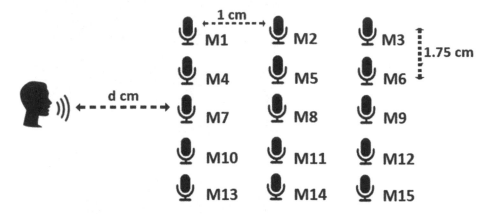

Fig. 3. The microphone array consists of 15 Audio-techinica AT9903 microphones (M1 to M15) without pop filter. Speaker's mouth is positioned in front of mic M7 at a distance of d cm from the mic M7. After [1].

Replay Utterances with Microphone-A (RP-A): Like the RC-A set, this set also contains utterances corresponding to one microphone and the distance between the speaker and the microphone is 10 cm. However, a TASCAM TM-AG1 pop filter is used between the speaker's mouth and the microphone. Given the use of pop-filter in this case, this set is emulated and considered to be spoofed and specifically designed for pop noise detection. Therefore, the utterances in RP-A correspond to spoof utterances, as they have pop noise.

3.2   Phoneme-wise Categorization

There are 44 words in POCO dataset and their corresponding International Phonetic Alphabet (IPA) have been mentioned in [1]. Given that, a word can

Table 1. 44 words of the POCO dataset divided into phoneme categories. After [1,15,17].

Phoneme	Associated words in the dataset
Plosive	Paw, Tip, Pink, Open, Pay, Pin, Sit, Spider, Be, Kit, Bird, End, Dad, Steer, Quick, About, Tourist, Bug, Honest
Fricative	Wolf, Laugh, Five, Funny, Fat, Live, Shout, Chair, Sham, Leather, Thong, Busy
Whisper	Who, Hop, You, His
Nasal	Arm, Monkey, Summer
Liquids	Run, Gun
Affricate	Chip, Join, Exaggerate, Division

have multiple phonemes in it, only the most *prominent* phoneme in the word is taken into consideration. The 44 words of the POCO dataset are categorized into various phoneme classes as shown in Table 1.

4   Experimental Results

This Section presents the distance-wise analysis using the proposed Morlet wavelet-based algorithm. To that effect, Fig. 4 shows the various cases of phoneme categories and the effect of distance on the strength of the pop noise. For this analysis, the RC-B subset of the POCO dataset is used in this work.

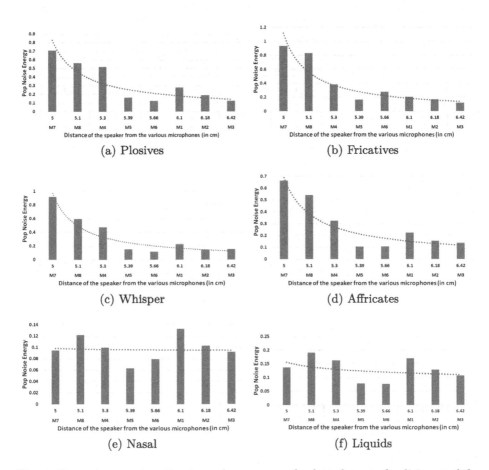

(a) Plosives   (b) Fricatives

(c) Whisper   (d) Affricates

(e) Nasal   (f) Liquids

Fig. 4. Pop noise energies of various phoneme sounds plotted w.r.t. the distance of the speaker from various microphones for the case when the speaker is at a distance of 5 cm from Mic 7. The pop noise energies are obtained using the proposed Algorithm 1. The dotted curve in each of the sub-figures indicates that the energy of pop noise decreases with the distance of the speaker's mouth from the microphone.

The trend of pop noise energy is shown with the help of the dotted line. In particular, we observe a somewhat similar trend for four of the phoneme categories, namely, plosives, fricatives, whisper, and affricates. However, for nasal and liquids, we see an almost constant-like trendline, which shows that the distance does not affect the pop noise energies in nasals and liquids categories of phonemes.

Furthermore, the existing results (in the form of % classification accuracy for VLD task) in the literature as shown in Table 2, also show that the best performance is achieved using the Morlet wavelet-based scalogram approach. In particular, for *all* the phoneme classes, the proposed system shows relatively the best performance. Furthermore, it should also be noted that the lowest accuracies of 80.77% and 79.49% are obtained on nasal and liquid sounds. A similar observation can be made by the analysis done in Fig. 4, wherein the nasal and liquids have the *least* pop noise energies (as shown in Fig. 4 (e) and (f)). In addition to this, the trendlines show that these two classes of phonemes are the *least* affected by the distance of the microphone from the speaker. Thus, our results and analysis presented via Fig. 4 are in strong agreement with the recent results reported on VLD task in [15].

Table 2. Average accuracy (in %) of different phoneme types. after [15].

Phoneme type	Handcrafted morlet wavelet-based (CNN) (Proposed)	Handcrafted morlet scalogram (CNN) (Proposed)
Freq. range	**0–40 Hz**	**0–40 Hz**
Plosive	79.35	**89.07**
Fricatives	79.27	**87.61**
Whisper	79.48	**86.21**
Nasal	71.36	**80.77**
Liquids	65.38	**79.49**
Affricates	74.35	**85.26**

5   Summary and Conclusion

In this work, we exploited the effectively improved resolution of CWT in lower frequency regions to capture pop noise event effectively. Pop noise is an important acoustic cue for VLD task. However, the strength of pop noise also determined by the distance of the speaker from the microphone. To that effect, we propose an algorithm to compute pop noise energy using Morlet wavelet transform, which we further use to show the effect of distance on the pop noise energies for various phoneme categories. Given that the strength of pop noise also depends on the phonemes in the word, we observe that the nasals, and the liquids phonemes are the least affected by the distance variability. In the future, upon availability of the corresponding spoofed utterances, the performance of VLD system w.r.t. each of the distance configurations can be evaluated. One of the limitations of the present work is that the Morlet wavelet is found to suffer from the problem of *spectral leakage* in the negative frequencies, i.e., it is *not always* analytic. To alleviate this issue, our future research efforts will be directed to employ Generalized Morse Wavelets (GMWs) for analysis of pop noise event, and subsequently for VLD task.

Acknowledgments. The authors would like to thank the Ministry of Electronics and Information Technology (MeitY), New Delhi, Govt. of India, for sponsoring the consortium project titled 'Speech Technologies in Indian Languages' under 'National Language Translation Mission (NLTM): BHASHINI', subtitled 'Building Assistive Speech Technologies for the Challenged' (Grant ID: 11(1)2022-HCC (TDIL)). We also thank the consortium leaders Prof. Hema A. Murthy, Prof. S. Umesh of IIT Madras, and the authorities of DA-IICT Gandhinagar, India for their support and cooperation to carry out this research work.

Appendix A.1. Energy Conservation in CWT

The inverse wavelet formula reconstructs the analytic part of a signal x as:

$$x_a(t) = \frac{1}{C_\psi} \int_0^\infty \int_{-\infty}^\infty W x_a(u, s) \psi_s(t - u) \frac{ds}{s^2} du. \tag{4}$$

Applying the Plancherel formula for energy conservation for the analytic part of x_a given by

$$\int_{-\infty}^{+\infty} |x_a(t)|^2 dt = \frac{1}{C_\psi} \int_0^{+\infty} \int_{-\infty}^{+\infty} |W_a x(u, s)|^2 du \frac{ds}{s^2}. \tag{5}$$

Since $W x_a(u, s)$ is $2W x(u, s)$ and $||x_a||^2$ is $2||x||^2$. If x is real, and the variable change ζ is $\frac{1}{s}$ in energy conservation demonstrates that

$$||x||^2 = \frac{2}{C_\psi} \int_0^\infty \int_{-\infty}^\infty P_w x(u, \zeta) du d\zeta. \tag{6}$$

It reinforces the notion that a scalogram represents a time-frequency energy density.

References

1. Akimoto, K., Liew, S.P., Mishima, S., Mizushima, R., Lee, K.A.: POCO: a voice spoofing and liveness detection corpus based on pop noise. In: INTERSPEECH, pp. 1081–1085. Shanghai, China (2020)
2. Das, R.K., Yang, J., Li, H.: Long range acoustic and deep features perspective on ASVSpoof 2019. In: IEEE Automatic Speech Recognition and Understanding (ASRU) Workshop, Singapore, pp. 1018–1025 (2019)

3. Daubechies, I.: Where do wavelets come from? a personal point of view. Proceedings IEEE **84**(4), 510–513 (1996)
4. Flanagan, J.L.: Speech Analysis Synthesis and Perception, vol. 3. Springer Science & Business Media (2013)
5. Font, R., Espín, J.M., Cano, M.J.: Experimental analysis of features for replay attack detection-results on the ASVS2017 challenge. In: INTERSPEECH, pp. 7–11. Stockholm, Sweden, 20–24 August 2017
6. Grossmann, A., Morlet, J.: Decomposition of hardy functions into square integrable wavelets of constant shape. SIAM J. Math. Anal. **15**(4), 723–736 (1984)
7. Hansen, J.H.L., Taufiq, H.: Speaker recognition by machines and humans: a tutorial review. IEEE Sign. Process. Mag. **32**(6), 74–99 (2015)
8. Jung, J.W., Shim, H.J., Heo, H.S., Yu, H.J.: Replay attack detection with complementary high-resolution information using end-to-end DNN for the ASVSpoof 2019 challenge. arXiv preprint arXiv:1904.10134 (2019). Accessed 31 Jan 2020
9. Khoria, K., Ankur, T., Patil, Patil, H.A.: Significance of constant-Q transform for voice liveness detection. In: 29th European Signal Processing Conference (EUSIPCO). Dublin, Ireland, 23–27 August 2021
10. Lilly, J.M., Olhede, S.C.: Higher-order properties of analytic wavelets. IEEE Trans. Sign. Process. **57**(1), 146–160 (2008)
11. Mallat, S.: A Wavelet Tour of Signal Processing, 2nd Ed. Elsevier (1999)
12. Mallat, S.G., Zhang, Z.: Matching pursuits with time-frequency dictionaries. IEEE Trans. Sign. Process. **41**(12), 3397–3415 (1993)
13. Mochizuki, S., Shiota, S., Kiya, H.: Voice livness detection based on pop-noise detector with phoneme information for speaker verification. J. Acoust. Soc. Amer. (JASA) **140**(4), 3060–3060 (2016)
14. Mochizuki, S., Shiota, S., Kiya, H.: Voice liveness detection using phoneme-based pop-noise detector for speaker verification. In: Odyssey 2018 the Speaker and Language Recognition Workshop. ISCA, pp. 233–239 (2018)
15. Gupta, P., Chodingala, P.K., Patil, H.A.: Morlet wavelet-based voice liveness detection using convolutional neural network. In: in European Signal Processing Conference (EUSIPCO) (2022)
16. Gupta, P., Chodingala, P.K., Patil, H.A.: Morse wavelet features for pop noise detection. In: IEEE International Conference on Signal Processing and Communication (SPCOM) (2022)
17. Gupta, P., Gupta, S., Patil, H.A.: Voice liveness detection using bump wavelet with CNN. In: International Conference on Pattern Recognition and Machine Intelligence. Springer, ISI Kolkata, India. (2021)
18. Sahidullah, M., Thomsen, D.A.L., Hautamäki, R.G., Kinnunen, T., Tan, Z.H., Parts, R., Pitkänen, M.: Robust voice liveness detection and speaker verification using throat microphones. IEEE/ACM Trans. Audio Speech Lang. Process. **26**(1), 44–56 (2017)
19. Shiota, S., Villavicencio, F., Yamagishi, J., Ono, N., Echizen, I., Matsui, T.: Voice liveness detection algorithms based on pop noise caused by human breath for automatic speaker verification. In: INTERSPEECH, pp. 2047–2051. Dresden, Germany (2015)
20. Singh, S., Khoria, K., Patil, H.A.: Modified group delay cepstral coefficients for voice liveness detection. In: 2021 29th European Signal Processing Conference (EUSIPCO), pp. 146–150. IEEE (2021)
21. Singh, S., Khoria, K., Patil, H.A.: Modified group delay function using different spectral smoothing techniques for voice liveness detection. In: Karpov, A.,

Potapova, R. (eds.) SPECOM 2021. LNCS (LNAI), vol. 12997, pp. 649–659. Springer, Cham (2021). https://doi.org/10.1007/978-3-030-87802-3_58

22. Gupta, S., Khoria, K., Patil, A.T., Patil, H.A.: Deep convolutional neural network for voice liveness detection. In: Speech and Computer International Conference (SPECOM). Springer (2021)

23. Wang, Q., et al.: Voicepop: a pop noise based anti-spoofing system for voice authentication on smartphones. In: IEEE Conference on Computer Communications, pp. 2062–2070 (2019)

24. Witkowski, M., et. al.: Audio replay attack detection using high-frequency features. In: INTERSPEECH, pp. 27–31. Stockholm, Sweden (2017)

25. Zhizheng, W., et. al.: ASVSpoof 2015: the first automatic speaker verification spoofing and countermeasures challenge. In: INTERSPEECH, pp. 2037–2041. Dresden, Germany (2015)

CRIM's Speech Recognition System for OpenASR21 Evaluation with Conformer and Voice Activity Detector Embeddings

Vishwa Gupta[✉] and Gilles Boulianne

Centre de Recherche Informatique de Montréal (CRIM), Quebec, Canada
{vishwa.gupta,gilles.boulianne}@crim.ca

Abstract. CRIM participated in all the 15 low resource languages and the three languages with case sensitive scoring in OpenASR21 for the constrained condition. For acoustic modeling, we developed both hybrid DNN-HMM systems and a conformer based system. We trained three different multi-stream acoustic models for decoding: with MFCC + i-vector features, with combined MFCC, i-vector and conformer embeddings, and with combined MFCC, i-vector and VAD (voice activity detector) embeddings. For final submission, we used two different VADs for segmenting the evaluation audio: GMM-HMM based and TDNN based. For language model text, we used the training text from LDC corpora when available. We also found significant amount of text over the internet. In the past, using this downloaded text for language modeling increased the word error rate significantly for the development set containing conversational speech. So we used sentence selection to filter this text in order to use it effectively to reduce word error rates (WER). For most languages, we were able to reduce WER with this strongly filtered text. Our best results combined six decodes: two different VAD based segments, and three different acoustic models. In the final evaluation, we ranked second in Tamil, third in Farsi and Javanese, and fourth in seven other languages. Since then, we have reduced the WER for all the languages significantly. Major contributing factors for this additional WER reduction were the intelligent use of MUSAN noise for data augmentation, and further tuning of acoustic models.

Keywords: OpenASR21 · Low resource · Speech recognition · Conformer embedding · Voice activity detector embedding

1 Introduction

The OpenASR21 (Open Automatic Speech Recognition 2021) Challenge set out to assess the state of the art of ASR technologies under low-resource language constraints. The task consisted of performing ASR on audio datasets in up to 15 different low-resource languages and 3 languages with case sensitive scoring, to produce the recognized text. Ten languages were carried over from the OpenASR20 challenge [20], and five new languages were added. A case sensitive scoring was added for three of these languages: Kazakh, Swahili and Tagalog.

© Springer Nature Switzerland AG 2022
S. R. M. Prasanna et al. (Eds.): SPECOM 2022, LNAI 13721, pp. 238–251, 2022.
https://doi.org/10.1007/978-3-031-20980-2_21

The low resource transcription and keyword spotting effort received a strong impetus from the IARPA Babel program[1]. The main goal of the program was to improve keyword search on languages with very little transcribed data (low-resource languages). Data from 26 languages was collected with certain languages held out as *surprise* languages to test the ability of the teams to rapidly build a system for a new language[2]. Many different DNN training algorithms have been experimented with within the Babel program [3,7,14,15,26,28]. In [7] they experiment with both DNN and tandem systems and get token error rates (TER) between 60% and 77% with limited language packs (10 h of training audio), depending on the language and training algorithms. They also experiment with data augmentation by automatically labeling untranscribed data.

In [14], the authors experiment with multilingual DNN models by keeping the senones separate for each language in the softmax layer, while sharing the hidden layers across language. In [27], the authors experiment with two different ways of generating multilingual phone sets: keep phones for each language separate, or merge phones that have the same IPA symbols across different languages.

In [16], the authors experiment with three different ways of modeling multilingual phone sets in order to generate good universal phone set with good coverage across many low resource languages: private (separate phones for each language), shared (pooling phones with the same IPA symbol across languages), and allosaurus (predict over a shared phone inventory, then map into language-specific phonemes with an allophone layer).

In [4], the authors present a cross-lingual speech representation (XLSR) system which learns cross-lingual speech representations by pretraining a single model from 53k h of raw waveform of speech in multiple languages. On the Common Voice benchmark, XLSR leads to significant reduction in phoneme error rate. On Babel also, the XLSR system shows significant reduction in word error rate.

CRIM took part in the OpenASR21 **constrained condition** for all the 15 languages and the 3 languages with case sensitive scoring. In the constrained condition, only a 10-hour audio in the Build dataset for that language can be used for training acoustic models. **Multilingual training by pooling audio from multiple languages was not allowed.** Additional text data, either from the Build dataset or publicly available resources, can be used for training the language model in the constrained condition. Any such additional training text must be specified in detail in the system description.

For OpenASR20, two teams achieved very good results [1,29]. They used larger training text and lexicon from Linguistic Data Consortium (LDC) corpora for training language models (LM). These LMs reduced the word error rate (WER) significantly for each language. However, they were not able to reduce WER with additional text from the internet. For 13 of the 15 languages in OpenASR21, CRIM downloaded training text from LDC to augment the LM training text and the lexicon. This additional text reduced the development

---

[1] https://www.iarpa.gov/index.php/research-programs/babel.
[2] https://www.ldc.upenn.edu/sites/www.ldc.upenn.edu/files/harper.pdf.

set WER significantly. We also downloaded significant amounts of text for all the languages from the internet, but as found in OpenASR20, using all the downloaded text for language modeling increases WER. We had to heavily filter this text with sentence selection to match conversations in the training text. Adding filtered text to the language model text lead to significant reduction in WER for some languages.

For acoustic modeling, we experimented with factored TDNN models with multi-stream architecture [13,18]. We optimized this architecture to get significantly lower WER than the single-stream TDNN-F architecture: reduce three streams to two, reduce the number of hidden layers in each stream, and reduce their dimensions. One of our contributions in this paper is to show that optimized multi-stream TDNN-F models give significantly lower WER even for small training sets containing 10 h of audio. We also evaluated models with 2 and 3 streams of MFCC and i-vector features, conformer embeddings, and VAD embeddings, which all reduced WER significantly when their results are combined.

After the evaluation, we experimented with adding MUSAN noise [25] to the training data. MUSAN noise consists of reverberation noise, music from several genres, speech from twelve languages, and a wide assortment of technical and non-technical noises. The usual data augmentation is to add each of these noises to each audio file resulting in a 4-fold increase in the training audio [1,12]. This strategy was not able to reduce WER for a single decode. We changed it to add only one of these noises to each audio file randomly just like SpecAugment [19] leading to only doubling the training data. This data augmentation with MUSAN noise together with the improved model architecture reduced the WER after ROVER [6] from 1.4% to 2.4% absolute on 15 of the 18 eval sets (compared to our evaluation results), resulting in getting the lowest WER for Tamil, and 2nd best WER for 10 other languages.

2   Dataset and Preprocessing

In the constrained condition, for acoustic model training, we only used the 10-hour Build dataset provided by NIST for the language being processed, with the corresponding transcripts in UTF-8 encoding. The evaluation conditions[3] did not allow any other audio to be used for acoustic modeling. Also, training of multilingual acoustic models from multiple languages was not allowed. The idea was to see how well one can do with limited amount of audio for acoustic modeling. However, any publicly available text could be used for language modeling.

Training and development audio were segmented and transcribed. But the evaluation audio was not segmented and the transcripts were not released. So we did not use the provided segments for the development set, just the complete transcripts for the audio. We used the same voice activity detectors (VADs) to segment the development and evaluation audio. These VADs were trained from the 10 h of training audio.

---

[3] https://www.nist.gov/system/files/documents/2021/08/31/OpenASR21_ EvalPlan_v1_3_1.pdf.

Training and development lexicons (with word to phoneme sequences) were also provided by NIST. For the 13 languages with LDC packs, we used the expanded lexicon and training transcripts (for language modeling) from the larger training set provided in those packs.

3   ASR Approach

Our system is a hybrid HMM-DNN based on WFSTs (Weighted Finite-State Transducers) and trained with the Kaldi toolkit [22]. These DNN-HMM systems need alignments between the acoustic data and the training transcripts. We generated these alignments with a GMM-HMM based system trained using the Kaldi recipe in babel egs[4], separately on each language, using only the 10 h Build dataset provided for each. This recipe uses 13-dim PLP features, except for Cantonese and Vietnamese. For Cantonese and Vietnamese, we add 3 additional pitch features for a total of 16 features.

3.1   Voice Activity Detectors

For removing noise segments from development and evaluation sets, we trained three different voice activity detectors from the training set audio: one GMM-HMM based VAD, and two different TDNN based VAD.

1. *VAD-GMM-HMM*: we used the recipe in the babel egs of Kaldi to train GMM/HMM for segmentation. This GMM-HMM system is trained from complete audio, including noise/silence segments between speech segments. This allows the silence phone to be trained with a lot more data. First, a 3-gram phone language model (LM) is trained from the aligned phone sequence for the training set. This 3-gram LM is then used to decode the dev and eval sets. Silence segments longer than a second are labeled as silence. The dev and eval audio after voice activity detection are then decoded. When listening to the resulting speech and noise/silence segments, beginning or end of a speech segment is sometimes classified as the adjoining silence segment. From this perspective, the resulting segments are aggressive in removing noise segments, as compared to the ones generated by TDNN-based voice activity detector (VAD) described below:

2. *VAD-TDNN*: TDNN as outlined in Chime6 track2 speech activity detection[5] : 40-dim MFCC features, 5 TDNN layers and 2 layers of statistics pooling [9]. We added a 40-dim bottleneck layer before the last hidden layer to generate embeddings. This TDNN is trained from the OpenASR21 training set separately for each language. For Cantonese and Vietnamese, we added 3 pitch features to represent the tones in these languages.

3. *VAD-TDNN with specAugment layer*: We add a specAugment layer [19] after the input layer in the VAD-TDNN above. This VAD-TDNN gave lower WER than the VAD-TDNN without specAugment, so VAD-TDNN with

---

[4] https://github.com/kaldi-asr/kaldi/tree/master/egs/babel/s5d.
[5] https://chimechallenge.github.io/chime6/track2software.html.

specAugment was used for final segmentation of dev and eval sets for decoding. This VAD-TDNN gave lower WER than GMM-HMM based VAD for 10 out of 18 languages for dev set, and 12 out of 18 languages for eval set. Some example WER differences are shown in Table 1 for the dev set. Even though the WER differences are small, the speech segments for the two VAD's are quite different. For VAD-TDNN, both the begin and end of each speech segment includes some silent segments, so VAD-TDNN is less aggressive in removing silent segments as compared to VAD-GMM-HMM. Because of these differences, we used outputs of both the VAD-GMM-HMM and VAD-TDNN (with specAugment) for voice activity detection on the eval set for final decoding. Combining the multiple decodes of the eval set resulted in significant reduction in WER.

Table 1. WER for VAD-GMM-HMM versus VAD-TDNN with specAugment.

Language	VAD-GMM-HMM	VAD-TDNN with specAugment
Amharic	39.7%	39.2%
Cantonese	47.9%	48.6%
Farsi	53.8%	53.5%
Mongolian	50.1%	49.1%

3.2 Acoustic Models

For each language, we trained three different acoustic models based on a multi-stream convolutional neural net (CNN) architecture [13,18] shown in Fig. 1 of [18]. We varied this architecture and added new features (or embeddings) as another stream to get the lowest possible WER for three different features for each language: 40-dim MFCC's + 100-dim i-vectors, 40-dim MFCC + i-vectors + 40-dim conformer embeddings from an end-to-end conformer model, and 40 dim MFCC + i-vectors + 40-dim embeddings from the VAD-TDNN with specAugment layer. The surprising part was that the multi-stream architecture gave lower WER than the single stream architecture even with only 10 h of audio for training (the multi-stream architecture was initially used with 960 h of libri-speech audio for training).

Multi-stream Acoustic Models with MFCCs and I-Vectors. In the multi-stream CNN architecture that gave state-of-the-art results on librispeech [13], input features (MFCC + i-vectors) are processed by 5 CNN layers in a single stream. This stream is branched out into 3 streams with 17 TDNN-F layers in each stream and different dilation rates (or time strides). MFCC features are first converted into filter-bank features by IDCT (inverse-discrete cosine transform), followed by SpecAugment, combined with i-vectors and then processed by 5 2D-CNN layers. We did not change this CNN stream. The optimal time strides for the 3 TDNN-F streams for 960 h of librispeech data [13] are 6, 9 and 12. The acoustic data in OpenASR21 is only 10 h. So we experimented with one, two or three streams, and with the number of TDNN-F layers in each stream. We compared this multi-stream architecture with the 17 layer TDNN-F architecture in the librispeech egs[6] [21] (lines 1 and 2 in Table 2). From Table 2, the best multi-stream model has 2 streams (time strides 6 and 9), and 12 TDNN-F layers per stream (line 9). This architecture worked well for all the languages.

Table 2. WER for Amharic dev set for TDNN-F and multi-stream architectures (with a 3-gram LM from OpenASR21 build).

Architecture	# of parameters	WER
1. TDNN-F (17 layers)	4.84 M	57.5%
2. TDNN-F in (1) with specAugment layer	4.84 M	54.2%
3. 1-stream of multi-stream CNN(time stride 6)	4.79 M	52.4%
4. Reduce output layer dim by half in (3)	3.92 M	52.3%
5. Reduce 17 TDNN-F layers to 12 in (4)	3.76 M	52.26%
6. Reduce TDNN-F layer dimensions by half in (5)	2.85 M	54.0%
7. Add 2 streams in (6) with time strides 9, 12	4.09 M	52.8%
8. Add 2 streams in (5) with time strides 9, 12	6.34 M	52.17%
9. Add 1 stream in (5) with time stride 9	5.05 M	**51.94%**

Conformer Embeddings. To generate the conformer embeddings used in the following subsection, we used a Conformer model [10], a transformer-based architecture augmented with convolutional input layers that we trained from scratch on each language, with a LF-MMI criterion [23]. We based our implementation on the snowfall k2-fsa[7] version. Features were filterbanks with 80 mel bins. Default model sizes were reduced to 6 encoder layers, 4 attention heads, and the bottleneck and hidden layers to an embedding dimension of 40. We performed data augmentation with 5 speed perturbation values $[0.8, 0.9, 1.0, 1.1, 1.2]$ but no other augmentation such as SpecAugment or noise/music/reverberation. We trained for 50 epochs for all languages, with 3000 warmup steps, except for Cantonese for which the latest epoch was 15. We average models over the last 5 epochs. The mean development set WER over the 18 training languages was 72%, when no LM is used, compared to 56% for the baseline TDNN-F with a 3g LM trained from the build set text only. These embeddings were then used in a multi-stream TDNN-F architecture as follows.

Multi-stream Acoustic Models With MFCCs, I-Vectors and 40-dimensional Conformer Embeddings. Conformers give very competitive results in end-to-end speech recognition [10]. The idea behind using conformer embeddings was to see if, together with MFCCs and i-vectors, they will contribute to reducing the WER for the dev and eval sets. We experimented with

---

[6] https://github.com/kaldi-asr/kaldi/egs/librispeech/s5/local/chain/run_tdnn.sh.
[7] https://github.com/k2-fsa/snowfall.

many different acoustic model architectures to get lowest possible WER with conformer embeddings. We tried embeddings from the conformer model alone, and with MFCC + i-vector features. The best model has a 2-stream architecture for MFCCs + i-vectors (line 9 Table 2) and a third stream (with time stride 6) for 40-dim conformer embeddings (see Fig. 1). Conformer embeddings are computed every 40 msec, so we duplicate each conformer embedding 4 times. We varied the number of TDNN-F layers in the third stream (Table 3), and 6 TDNN-F layers worked the best. We use this architecture (Fig. 1) for all the languages.

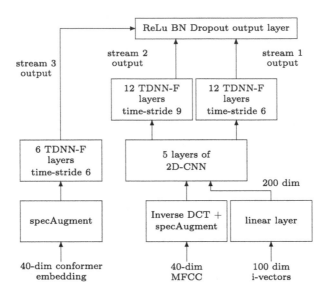

Fig. 1. Multi-stream model with MFCC and conformer embeddings as input.

Table 3 uses a 4-gram LM from larger LDC build text, so the WERs are lower than in Table 2 that uses a 3-gram LM from OpenASR21 build text. Even though MFCCs+i-vectors+conformer embeddings did not give lower WER than MFCCs+i-vectors alone (45.04% versus 40.4% for Amharic), combining the results from different features reduced the WER significantly.

Table 3. WER for Amharic dev set for different numbers of TDNN-F layers in the third stream for conformer embeddings. (decoding uses 4-gram LM from LDC build).

Architecture	WER
1. 1 TDNN-F layer in 3rd stream	48.55%
2. 6 TDNN-F layers in 3rd stream	**45.04%**
3. 12 TDNN-F layers in 3rd stream	45.83%

Multi-stream Acoustic Models with MFCCs, I-Vectors and VAD-TDNN Embeddings. We trained acoustic models with MFCCs + i-vectors + 40-dim embeddings from *VAD-TDNN with specAugment layer* in Sect. 3.1. The idea is that VAD embeddings will provide a gradual transition from silence frames to voiced frames and may lead to better results, specially for noisy utterances. The same 3-stream model is used as for MFCC + i-vector + conformer embeddings: the third stream has VAD instead of conformer embeddings as input (see Fig. 1). Comparison between MFCC + i-vectors versus MFCC + i-vector + VAD features are shown in Table 4 for some languages. For Farsi, the VAD embeddings reduce WER by 0.4% absolute. MFCCs + i-vectors + VAD embeddings gave competitive results with MFCCs + i-vectors alone, and contributed to significant reduction in WER when combined with other results.

Table 4. Dev set WER for MFCC + i-vector versus MFCC + i-vector + VAD embedding (with 4-gram LM from LDC build).

Language	MFCC + i-vector	MFCC + i-vector + VAD embeddings
Amharic	39.7%	39.85%
Cantonese	47.9%	48.54%
Farsi	53.8%	53.38%
Javanese	54.0%	54.19%

4 Language Model

For language modeling (LM) in the constrained condition, we could use any text publicly available over the internet. For 13 of the 15 languages, we used the LDC IARPA Babel language packs from 2016 to 2020. Farsi and Somali did not have a Babel language pack. The larger LDC text together with the larger lexicon reduced the WER for the 13 languages (the OpenASR21 build is a subset of the LDC build). This LDC text is from conversational speech, and the LSP (language specific peculiarities) file in the LDC build contains details about dialects of speakers, any special handling of spelling, character set used for orthographic transcription, romanization scheme, word boundary detection, where the transcribers are from, etc. So the text is probably quite consistent in transcription and using the training text for language model training reduces the WER for the dev set significantly (see Table 5).

Table 5. Comparative dev set WER for language model (LM) from OpenASR21 build versus LM from LDC build.

Language	OpenASR21 build	LDC build
Amharic	51.7%	39.7%
Georgian	53.4%	41.2%
Guarani	52.5%	42.8%

We used two other sources of publicly available text, collected for machine translation research: Monolingual NewsCrawls[8] [2] extracted from online newspapers, and CommonCrawl[9] [5] from web pages. The amount of text in NewsCrawls (NC) and CommonCrawl (CC) for some languages (to save space) is shown in Table 6. We found additional text relevant to our data: 22M words for Amharic in DKE[10] [8] and 230k words in the Hong Kong Cantonese corpus[11] [17].

If we take Amharic as an example, if we add any new text from NewsCrawls to the LM training text, the perplexity on the dev set goes up: from 296 to 725 with only 3 years of news, with larger texts the perplexity gets even worse. Probably for the same reason neither [1] nor [29] used any downloaded text for language modeling in OpenASR20 evaluation. Authors in [1] used the downloaded text in Somali only for a larger dictionary.

To reduce domain mismatch between conversational speech and news sources, we used sentence selection [24]. This method selects a set of sentences from out-of-domain texts so that the distribution is similar to the overall in-domain distribution, rather than just match its peak. We tried sentence selection using acoustic training text as the in-domain data and news text as out-of-domain; perplexity on dev set is better but still worse than using the original acoustic training text (315 with our best combination of sentence selection hyper-parameters).

We get slightly smaller degradation of perplexity for Amharic when adding sentences selected with the larger LDC training text as the in-domain text. We finally selected 233K words of text from NewsCrawls and DKE text for Amharic through sentence selection. This additional text reduced WER from 38.46% (using LDC text) to 37.8% (using LDC + 233k words) after LSTM LM rescoring of decoded lattices (forward LSTM LM rescoring followed by backward LSTM LM rescoring). The WER reduction is good enough that we used LSTM LM generated from this augmented text for our final submissions.

Advantage of larger text for language modeling is that it improves training of LSTM language models, and results in lower WER after lattice rescoring. We trained 2-layer LSTM language models with the larger text using the recipe in Kaldi swbd egs[12] with reduced cell and embedding dimension of 256.

---

[8] http://data.statmt.org/news-crawl.

[9] http://data.statmt.org/cc-100/.

[10] https://wwwiti.cs.uni-magdeburg.de/iti_dke/Datasets.

[11] http://compling.hss.ntu.edu.sg/hkcancor.

[12] https://github.com/kaldi-asr/kaldi/egs/swbd/s5c/local/rnnlm/run_tdnn_lstm.sh.

Table 6. Text (in millions of words) in NewCrawls (NC) and CommonCrawl (CC).

Language	NC	CC	Language	NC	CC	Language	NC	CC
Amharic	8.1	67.4	Guarani	0.0	1.0	Javanese	0.0	23.4
Cantonese	24.6	0.0	Kazakh	34.9	471.1	Kurmanji-kurdish	0.0	65.9
Farsi	61.1	0.0	Pashto	17.9	95.7	Somali	13.2	62.6
Georgian	0.0	460.1	Swahili	18.2	272.0	Tagalog	6.1	562.3

Total text through sentence selection for some of the languages (to save space) is shown in Table 7. The WER after rescoring decoded lattices with these LM are shown in Table 8. For nine languages, and 3 case sensitive scoring languages, we reduced the WER. For all case sensitive scoring languages, we reduced WER significantly since they include broadcast news.

5   Combining Multiple Decodes

In the past, we have found that combining multiple ctm files with ROVER [6] leads to lower WER than combining two lattices and doing MBR decoding [11]. So we generated 6 different ctm files[13] using two different voice activity detec-

Table 7. Words (in thousands) selected from each source, and total used in language model.

Language	ASR21	LDC	NC	CC	Total	Lang	LDC	Total
Amharic	80	238	150	83[a]	550	Guarani	261	462
Cantonese	123	844	307	20[b]	1293	Javanese	263	665
Farsi	77	0	124	0	201	Kazakh	235	665
Georgian	86	259	0	810	1154	Kurmanji	285	960

[a]For Amharic, this is selected from the DKE corpus.
[b]For Cantonese, from the Hong Kong Cantonese corpus.

Table 8. Dev set WER after rescoring with LSTM LM trained with LDC text versus total text after sentence selection. css = case sensitive scoring.

Language	LSTM LM LDC text	LSTM LM LDC+NC+CC text	Lang	LSTM LM LDC text	LSTM LM LDC+NC+CC text
Amharic	38.46%	37.8%	Tamil	60.67%	60.51%
Cantonese	46.47%	45.97%	Guarani	41.84%	41.73%
Georgian	40.27%	40.42%	Kurmanji	64.88%	64.91%
Swahili css	50.21%	47.55%	Pashto	47.14%	46.98%
Mongolian	47.88%	47.73%	Swahili	36.06%	35.95%

---

[13] ctm files contain the time marked word sequence of decoded audio.

tors (GMM-HMM VAD and TDNN VAD), and three different acoustic models: MFCC + i-vectors input to 2-stream CNN, MFCC + i-vector + conformer embedding input to 3-stream acoustic models, and MFCC + i-vector + VAD embedding input to 3-stream acoustic models. The 6 decoded ctm files are combined using ROVER. The results on all the evaluation sets are shown in Table 9. In the evaluation, CRIM came second in tamil, third in farsi and javanese, and fourth in 7 other languages.

6   Post Evaluation Improvements

After the evaluation, we reduced the WER significantly for all the languages by further optimizing the acoustic models. During evaluation, the two MFCC streams (see Fig. 1) had time strides of 6 and 9, and embedding streams a time stride of 6. By changing MFCC streams to time-strides of 3 and 6 and embedding stream to time-stride 3 for all the acoustic models results in over 1% drop in WER for all the models. This results in 6 more ctm files for the eval set (eval set processed by 2 different VADs X 3 different acoustic models). We also trained acoustic models by adding MUSAN noise [25] randomly to each audio file at low amplitude (30 dB SNR). MUSAN noise consists of reverberation noise, music from several genres, speech from twelve languages, and a wide assortment of noises. The usual data augmentation with MUSAN noise is to add each of these noises to each audio file resulting in a 4-fold increase in the training audio [1,12]. The noises we added randomly here included music, babble and noise. Only one of these noise files is picked randomly to add to the training wav file. So the total audio files after speed perturbation were doubled (we added MUSAN noise to both speed perturbed and unperturbed audio files). The idea of adding MUSAN noise randomly was to mimic specAugment. However, specAugment applies random perturbation for each epoch of training, while here, the MUSAN noise choice was the same for every epoch. Training with MUSAN noise reduced WER for 6 languages, increased for 4 languages, and was similar for other languages. This is the first time we have been able to reduce WER for a single decode after adding MUSAN noise.

After combination with ROVER, we reduced the WER significantly for the eval set for all the languages. Combining with ROVER the 14 ctm files (6 from old models, 6 from new models and 2 from acoustic models trained with MUSAN noise) results in 1.4% to 2.4% absolute reduction in WER for 15 of 18 languages (compared to WER after ROVER of 6 decodes) (Table 9 columns 3 versus 6). In the NIST eval leaderboard, our latest eval set WER's will result in CRIM coming first for Tamil, and second for 10 other languages.

Table 9. WER for eval sets after final submission (rover 6) and after new results (rover 14). Best decode is best single decode followed by rescoring with LSTM LM. Best WER is the lowest WER on the eval leaderboard. css = case sensitive scoring.

Language	Best decode	Rover 6	Best 2021	Rank CRIM	Rover 14	New rank CRIM	Text source
Amharic	44.1	43.1	39.9	4	40.9	2	ldc+nc+dke
Cantonese	44.1	42.8	37.6	5	41.2	4	ldc+nc+cc
Farsi	80.4	79.3	68.0	3	79.0	3	ASR21+nc
Georgian	44.6	42.55	39.2	4	40.8	2	ldc
Guarani	47.7	46.0	42.6	5	44.0	2	ldc+nc+cc
Javanese	53.7	52.0	48.1	3	49.8	2	ldc
Kazakh	57.8	56.9	50.0	5	54.9	5	ldc
kazakh css	59.0	58.6	49.8	3	56.8	3	ldc+nc+cc
Kurmanji-kurdish	67.2	65.7	61.7	4	63.3	2	ldc
Mongolian	47.8	46.0	41.0	7	43.6	4	ldc+nc+cc
Pashto	49.1	47.2	43.2	4	45.1	2	ldc+nc+cc
Somali	61.0	59.2	55.6	5	57.5	2	ASR21
Swahili	36.4	35.0	32.4	4	32.9	2	ldc+nc+cc
Swahili css	50.7	48.5	43.5	3	47.9	3	ldc+nc+cc
Tagalog	45.2	43.2	40.4	4	41.2	2	ldc
Tagalog css	54.8	53.2	46.2	3	52.6	3	ldc+nc+cc
Tamil	65.0	63.8	62.3	2	62.0	1	ldc+nc+cc
Vietnamese	46.1	44.0	40.3	4	42.6	2	ldc

7 Conclusion

CRIM participated in all the 15 low resource languages and the three languages with case sensitive scoring in the OpenASR21 Challenge for the constrained condition. We improved both the acoustic and language models significantly.

For acoustic modeling, specAugment made a significant difference in all scenarios: whether we added it after MFCC features, after MFCC features transformed by inverse discrete cosine transform, after conformer embeddings, after embeddings from VAD, and even for VAD models. Multi-stream acoustic models outperformed the single stream acoustic models even with only 10 h of training audio, and optimization of time strides, number of TDNN layers and their dimensions in each stream reduced word error rate (WER) significantly. The best DNN architecture for Amharic gave similar reduction in WER for other languages, showing that this optimisation is not language specific.

In the final submission, we used two different voice activity detectors for segmenting the evaluation audio: one based on a GMM-HMM system, and another one based on a TDNN system. GMM-HMM based VAD is much more aggressive (classifies ends of some speech segments as silence) than the TDNN-based VAD (which includes some silent segments at the ends of speech segments). Decoded outputs from the two VADs when combined reduced the WER significantly.

For the previous OpenASR20 evaluation, there are no published papers that improve language models by adding text from outside LDC. We improved our language models by downloading text from internet and filtering it drastically with sentence selection to match the filtered text to conversations in the training text. For example, this filtering reduced the downloaded text for Amharic from over 75 million words to 233k words. Adding these 233k words of filtered text to the language model text lead to significant reduction in WER.

All the above improvements led to CRIM's final submission ranking second in Tamil, third in Farsi and Javanese, and fourth in seven other languages for the constrained condition. After the evaluation, we tuned the multi-stream acoustic models even further, reducing the WER for the eval set by 1.4% to 2.4% absolute for 15 out of the 18 languages. On the eval leaderboard, this tuning would rank us first in Tamil and second in 10 other languages.

Acknowledgments. The authors would like to thank Ministry of Economy and Innovation (MEI) of the Government of Quebec for the continued support.

References

1. Alumäe, T., Kong, J.: Combining hybrid and end-to-end approaches for the openASR20 challenge. In: Proceedings of Interspeech, pp. 4349–4353 (2021)
2. Birch, A., et al.: Global under-resourced media translation (GoURMET). In: Proceedings of Machine Translation Summit XVII, vol. 2, pp. 122–122 (2019)
3. Chen, G., Khudanpur, S., Povey, D., Trmal, J., Yarowsky, D., Yilmaz, O.: Quantifying the value of pronunciation lexicons for keyword search in low resource languages. In: Proceedings of ICASSP, pp. 8560–8564 (2013)
4. Conneau, A., Baevski, A., Collobert, R., Mohamed, A., Auli, M.: Unsupervised Cross-lingual Representation Learning for Speech Recognition. arXiv eprint arXiv:2006.13979 (2020)
5. Conneau, A., et al.: Unsupervised cross-lingual representation learning at scale. In: Proceedings of ACL, pp. 8440–8451 (2020)
6. Fiscus, J.G.: A post-processing system to yield reduced word error rates: recognizer output voting error reduction (ROVER). In: Proceedings of ASRU, pp. 347–352 (1997)
7. Gales, M.J.F., Knill, K.M., Ragni, A., Rath, S.P.: Speech recognition and keyword spotting for low resource languages: BABEL project research at CUED. In: Proceedings of SLTU, pp. 14–16 (2014)
8. Gezmu, A.M., Seyoum, B.E., Gasser, M., Nürnberger, A.: Contemporary amharic corpus: automatically morpho-syntactically tagged amharic corpus. In: Proceedings of the First Workshop on Linguistic Resources for Natural Language Processing, pp. 65–70 (2018)
9. Ghahremani, P., Manohar, V., Povey, D., Khudanpur, S.: Acoustic modelling from the signal domain using CNNs. In: Proceedings of Interspeech, pp. 3434–3438 (2016)

10. Gulati, A., et al.: Conformer: convolution-augmented transformer for speech recognition. In: Proceedings of Interspeech, pp. 5036–5040 (2020)
11. Gupta, V., Boulianne, G.: CRIM's system for the MGB-3 English multi-genre broadcast media transcription. In: Proceedings of Interspeech 2018, pp. 2653–2657 (2018)
12. Gupta, V., Rebout, L., Boulianne, G., Ménard, P.A., Alam, J.: Crim's speech transcription and call sign detection system for the ATC airbus challenge task. In: Proceedings of Interspeech, pp. 3018–3022 (2019)
13. Han, K.J., Pan, J., Tadala, V.K.N., Ma, T., Povey, D.: Multistream CNN for robust acoustic modeling. In: Proceedings of ICASSP, pp. 6873–6877 (2021)
14. Huang, J.T., Li, J., Yu, D., Deng, L., Gong, Y.: Cross-language knowledge transfer using multilingual deep neural network with shared hidden layers. In: Proceedings of ICASSP, pp. 7304–7308 (2013)
15. Knill, K.M., Gales, M.J., Ragni, A., Rath, S.P.: Language independent and unsupervised acoustic models for speech recognition and keyword spotting. In: Proceedings of Interspeech, pp. 16–20 (2014)
16. Li, X., et al.: Universal phone recognition with a multilingual allophone system. arXiv eprint arXiv:2002.11800v1 (2020)
17. Luke, K.K., Wong, M.L.Y.: The Hong Kong Cantonese corpus: design and uses. J. Chin. Linguist. **25**(2015), 309–330 (2015)
18. Pan, J., Shapiro, J., Wohlwend, J., Han, K.J., Lei, T., Ma, T.: ASAPP-ASR: Multistream CNN and self-attentive SRU for SOTA speech recognition. arXiv preprint arXiv:2005.10469 (2020)
19. Park, D.S., et al.: SpecAugment: a simple data augmentation method for automatic speech recognition. In: Proceedings of Interspeech, pp. 2613–2617 (2019)
20. Peterson, K., Tong, A., Yu, Y.: OpenASR20: an open challenge for automatic speech recognition of conversational telephone speech in low-resource languages. In: Proceedings of Interspeech, pp. 4324–4328 (2021)
21. Povey, D., et al.: Semi-orthogonal low-rank matrix factorization for deep neural networks. In: Proceedings of Interspeech, pp. 3743–3747 (2018)
22. Povey, D., et al.: The Kaldi speech recognition toolkit. In: Proceedings of ASRU (2011)
23. Povey, D., et al.: Purely sequence-trained neural networks for ASR based on lattice-free MMI. In: Proceedings of Interspeech, pp. 2751–2755 (2016)
24. Sethy, A., Georgiou, P.G., Ramabhadran, B., Narayanan, S.: An iterative relative entropy minimization-based data selection approach for n-gram model adaptation. IEEE Trans. Audio Speech Lang. Process. **17**(1), 13–23 (2009)
25. Snyder, D., Chen, G., Povey, D.: Musan: a music, speech, and noise corpus. arXiv preprint arXiv:1510.08484 (2015)
26. Trmal, J., et al.: A keyword search system using open source software. In: Proceedings of SLT Workshop, pp. 530–535 (2014)
27. Vu, N., Povey, D., Motlicek, P., Schultz, T., Bourlard, H.: Multilingual deep neural network based acoustic modeling for rapid language adaptation. In: Proceedings of ICASSP, pp. 7689–7693 (2014)
28. Zhang, X., Trmal, J., Povey, D., Khudanpur, S.: Improving deep neural network acoustic models using generalized maxout networks. In: Proceedings of ICASSP, pp. 215–219 (2014)
29. Zhao, J., et al.: The TNT team system descriptions of cantonese and mongolian for IARPA OpenASR20. In: Proceedings of Interspeech, pp. 4344–4348 (2021)

Joint Changes in First and Second Formants of /a/, /i/, /u/ Vowels in Babble Noise - a New Statistical Approach

Alisa P. Gvozdeva[1]([✉]), Alexander M. Lunichkin[1], Larisa G. Zaytseva[1], Elena A. Ogorodnikova[1,2], and Irina G. Andreeva[1]

[1] Sechenov Institute of Evolutionary Physiology and Biochemistry, Russian Academy of Sciences (IEPhB RAS), St. Petersburg, Russia
alisap.gvozdeva@gmail.com
[2] Pavlov Institute of Physiology, Russian Academy of Sciences, St. Petersburg, Russia
https://www.iephb.ru/en/, https://www.infran.ru

Abstract. In this paper we propose a new statistical approach to description of changes in vowels formants under influence of surrounding noise. The approach consists in presenting changes of first (F1) and second (F2) formants as vectors in ΔF1-ΔF2 coordinates and further plotting of polar histograms reflecting probabilities to find the vectors in twelve 30°-sectors of the coordinate space for every vowel. To illustrate this approach we performed audio recordings of several words with basic vowels /a/, /i/ and /u/ in stressed positions pronounced by 17 adult native Russian speakers (7 men, 10 women) in silence and on the background of 60 dB (A) babble noise. The noise was presented via headphones and an auditory feedback was provided to compensate for dampening effect of headphones' cushions. Group polar histograms reflecting changes in F1 and F2 of vowels /a/, /i/ and /u/ in babble noise had specific shapes with 2–3 dominant petals and were significantly different from each other ($p < 0.0001$, Watson's U2 test). This indicates that there are relatively stable and distinctive patterns characterizing joint changes in F1 and F2 for each of the studied vowels. The data can be used to account for changes in the formant structure of vowels in noise to improve performance of automatic speech recognition systems and also for planning and assessment of speech rehabilitation process.

Keywords: Vowel articulation · Lombard effect · Formants · Babble noise · Polar histograms

1 Introduction

Speech perception by human listeners and automatic speech recognition tasks are often performed in noise. In everyday communication situations babble noise of moderate levels (up to 60–70 dB) is the most common type of interference, which is known to effectively mask speech signals [1]. To overcome the masking effect and improve signal-to-noise ratio in noisy environments speakers modify parameters of their voice:

© Springer Nature Switzerland AG 2022
S. R. M. Prasanna et al. (Eds.): SPECOM 2022, LNAI 13721, pp. 252–264, 2022.
https://doi.org/10.1007/978-3-031-20980-2_22

they increase its intensity and change spectral characteristics, and also duration of speech sounds [2]. The modifications of voice parameters in noise are called the Lombard effect, and Lombard speech is shown to have higher intelligibility rates for human listeners than normal speech [3, 4]. One of the most noticeable manifestations of Lombard effect is the change of vowels' formant structure. It has been shown that speakers increase their fundamental frequency (F0) and first formant (F1) in noise and may both increase and decrease second formant (F2), depending on the particular vowel sound [2, 5]. It is known that vowels increase their duration in Lombard speech, while consonants, in contrast, are shortened [2]. The increase in vowels' steady-state segment duration facilitates estimation of F1 and F2.

Since automatic speech recognition systems widely use algorithms of vowels' formant structure extraction [6], modification of the structure in Lombard speech, if not taken into account, may be the source of speech recognition errors. The first two formants are known to carry essential information which allows distinguishing between different vowels. We hypothesized that in spite of inter-individual differences in F1 and F2, distributions of their joint changes probabilities in noise compared to silence for a given vowel should be quite close for all speakers.

In current paper we suggest a new statistical approach to assess and visualize joint changes in F1 and F2. According to this approach the changes are presented as vectors in $\Delta F1$–$\Delta F2$ coordinate space, i.e. they converted from rectangular to polar coordinates. Angles of the vectors are used for plotting polar histograms, reflecting probabilities to find vectors with certain directions. Thus, by using the method one can determine the most probable directions of joint changes in F1 and F2 in noise compared to silence for different vowels. To illustrate this approach we performed audio recordings of several nouns, containing vowels /a/, /i/ and /u/ (representing the apexes of formant triangle of vowels) in stressed positions, pronounced in silence and in noise by adult native Russian speakers.

2 Methods

Experiments were conducted with 17 participants (10 women, 7 men) who were native Russian speakers and ranged in their age from 18 to 35 years (mean age 23 ± 5 years). All the speakers had normal hearing according to results of audiometric examination and had no speech defects. Speakers were familiarized in detail with the experimental procedure and signed an informed consent to participate in the experiment. All experiments performed in this study were approved by the Committee of Ethics of Sechenov Institute of Evolutionary Physiology and Biochemistry and were carried out in accordance with The World Medical Association's Declaration of Helsinki for experiments involving humans.

Nine Russian words were used for speech recordings. Nouns "rUchka" (a pen), "posUda" (dishes), "shalUn" (a varmint), "mIna" (a mien), "malIna" (raspberry), "kredIt" (a credit), "Armiya" (an army), "bumAga" (paper), "strokA" (a line) were chosen to meet the following criterion: each vowel which forms an apex of the formant triangle (/a/, /i/, /u/) appears in stressed position in the beginning, in the middle and in the end of a word.

Noise signal represented babble noise, which was artificially created by mixing down pre-recorded words, pronounced by two male and two female speakers, who did not take part in this work. The mixing procedure, voice characteristics of the speakers and temporal parameters of the recordings are described in detail in our earlier paper [7]. Noise signal was 40 s long with linear rise and fall times of 1 s each. When presented to speakers via headphones it had sound pressure level of 60 dB (A) considering the binaural growth of loudness [8]. Amplitude-frequency spectrum of babble noise signal is presented in Fig. 1.

Experiments were conducted in an anechoic soundproof chamber (dimensions: 5 × 5 × 2.5 m). We performed voice recordings using Rode NT-USB condenser microphone with built-in digital-to-analog converter (44100 Hz, 16 Bit). The microphone was connected to ASUS Sonic Master laptop with Adobe Audition 1.6 software. The software allowed simultaneous playback of the noise signal and speaker's voice recording. The noise signal was played back via closed circum-aural headphones Sennheiser HD-380-Pro. Sound pressure level (SPL) of the noise signal was measured monaurally by a sound meter RFT 00014 using A-weighted mode. Then a recalculation of SPL was performed taking into account the binaural growth of loudness [8].

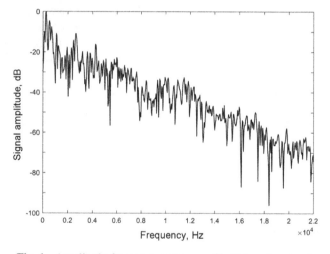

Fig. 1. Amplitude-frequency spectrum of babble noise signal.

During all recordings real-time auditory feedback was provided for speakers in order to compensate for dampening effect of headphones' cushions. Auditory feedback level was adjusted by the speaker themselves before the beginning of the experiment: the speaker had to set up feedback level in such a way that perceived loudness of their voice was close to that without headphones. Feedback level did not change throughout the experiment and did not affect level of the noise signal.

Voice recordings and adjustments of the auditory feedback were performed in the same acoustic conditions (i.e. in the anechoic chamber) with the headphones put on. The speaker sat in an armchair with a headrest and was instructed to maintain the back of their head pressed to the headrest and not to tilt or rotate the head. The microphone was fixed on a floor stand in such a way that the distance between the speaker's lips and the microphone amounted to approximately 20 cm. Speakers always addressed their words to an experimenter, who sat in front of them at 1 m distance. The experiment included three consecutive recording sessions. During one session three of nine words were recorded (3 sessions × 3 words = 9 words). Each session consisted of two recording periods. In the first period the speaker pronounced words under silent condition, in the second period – on the background of 60 dB (A) babble noise presented via headphones. In every session the speaker pronounced three words one-by-one four times for each period. In the end of each session the recording was saved by the experimenter as a file with extension.wav. Wav files were analyzed using PRAAT software.

For each recorded word the stressed vowel steady-state segment was selected manually and listings for first (F1) and second (F2) formants were obtained (sampling rate 300 Hz). Total number of analyzed vowel samples amounted to 1092 (546 vowels pronounced in silence and the same number – pronounced in noise). In rare cases the listings could not be obtained due to the absence of the steady-state segment for a particular vowel sample or inability to detect F1 or F2 in the sample. For the vast majority of analyzed vowels' samples listings were obtained successfully and F1 and F2 mean values were calculated for each stressed vowel. Values of F1 and F2 were converted into Barks by the following formula [9]:

$$F_{Bark} = 13 \cdot arctg\left(\frac{0.76F_{Hz}}{1000}\right) + 3.5 \cdot arctg\left(\left(\frac{F_{Hz}}{7500}\right)^2\right) \tag{1}$$

where F_{Bark} – frequency in Barks, F_{Hz} – frequency in Hz.

Then we calculated ΔF1 and ΔF2 – changes of F1 and F2 in babble noise compared to silence:

$$\begin{aligned} \Delta F1 &= F1_{noise} - F1_{silence} \\ \Delta F2 &= F2_{noise} - F2_{silence}, \end{aligned} \tag{2}$$

where $F1_{noise}$ and $F1_{silence}$ – are first formants in noise and in silence for the same speaker, vowel (/a/, /i/ or /u/), vowel position (beginning, middle or end of the word) and repetition (first, second, third or fourth). The same applies to $F2_{noise}$ and $F2_{silence}$.

Thus, 36 or less pairs of ΔF1 and ΔF2 values were calculated for each speaker (3 vowels × 3 positions × 4 repetitions). Each pair of ΔF1 and ΔF2 was presented as a vector in ΔF1–ΔF2 coordinates and the vector was labeled as $\overrightarrow{\Delta F12}$. The vector always began in [0, 0] point and ended in the point with [ΔF1, ΔF2] coordinates (for example see Fig. 2A). Previously described procedure of converting F1 and F2 into Bark scale allowed us to standardize changes in F1 and F2 so that they had equal influence on a resulting angle of the vector (∠F12). The angle of each vector was calculated in degrees by using the following rules:

$$\left[\begin{array}{l} if\ \Delta F1 > 0\ \&\ \Delta F2 > 0 \Rightarrow \angle F12 = arctg\left(\dfrac{\Delta F2}{\Delta F1}\right) \\[3mm] if\ \Delta F1 < 0\ and\ \Delta F2 > 0\ or\ \Delta F1 < 0\ and\ \Delta F2 < 0 \Rightarrow \angle F12 = 180° + arctg\left(\dfrac{\Delta F2}{\Delta F1}\right) \\[3mm] if\ \Delta F1 > 0\ and\ \Delta F2 < 0 \Rightarrow \angle F12 = 360° + arctg\left(\dfrac{\Delta F2}{\Delta F1}\right) \end{array}\right.$$

(3)

Then the histograms were plotted representing probabilities to find the vector in each of twelve 30°-sectors (30° × 12 = 360°) for a specific vowel, its position or repetition, or for a specific vowel pronounced by male or female speakers (Fig. 2B). Thus, the histograms demonstrated distribution of directions of $\overrightarrow{\Delta F12}$ for different vowels under various conditions.

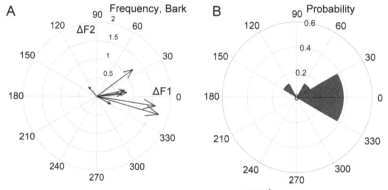

Fig. 2. Example of plotting a polar histogram for vectors $\overrightarrow{\Delta F12}$. A – a set of vectors, reflecting hypothetical $\overrightarrow{\Delta F12}$ for a certain condition in $\Delta F1$-$\Delta F2$ coordinate space. Number of vectors in sectors: 3 (0–30°), 1 (30–60°), 1 (120–150°), 3 (330–0°). B – probability polar histogram created on the basis of the vectors' set. Height of the histogram's petals reflects probability of finding $\overrightarrow{\Delta F12}$ in each of twelve 30°-sectors, i.e. in the current case 0.375 (0–30°), 0.125 (30–60°), 0.125 (120-150°), 0.375 (330–0°). Thus, the histogram reflects only directions of $\overrightarrow{\Delta F12}$, but not the length of the vectors.

Comparisons of distributions (i.e. histograms) between different repetitions, positions and speakers' genders for the same vowel and comparison of distributions for different vowels were performed by Watson's U2 test [10]. P-values were calculated by using a permutation test [11]. For each pair of compared distributions 10000 permutations were performed and equal number of U2-statistics was calculated. Each p-value was determined as a proportion of calculated U2-statistics for permuted data which exceeded the value of U2-statistic for original data. To reduce the risk of type I errors for multiple comparisons a false discovery rate control procedure was used [12]. All calculations, statistical analysis and data visualization were performed in Matlab 2017b.

3 Results

Individual $\overrightarrow{\Delta F12}$ when speaking in 60 dB (A) babble noise compared to silence were quite similar for all speakers for the same vowel. In Fig. 3 twelve individual polar histograms for vowels /a/, /i/ and /u/ are presented, which illustrate distributions of directions of $\overrightarrow{\Delta F12}$ in two male and two female speakers. In case of vowel /a/ the histograms' petals were mostly in I quadrant and partly in IV quadrant, indicating that in general there was an increase in F1 accompanied by an increase or slight decrease in F2. Cases when histograms' petals for vowel /a/ were situated in II or III quadrants were quite rare. For vowel /i/ in the majority of cases we observed an increase in F1 accompanied by a decrease in F2, which resulted in corresponding histograms' petals to be found mostly in IV quadrant and much rarely in I-III quadrants. $\overrightarrow{\Delta F12}$ for vowel /u/ in noise compared to silence resembled those for vowel /a/. However, more prominent increase in F2 was observed for vowel /u/ which resulted in more vertical position of histograms' petals in I quadrant. Rarely petals of /u/ histogram could be found in III and IV quadrants. Thus, individual polar histograms evidenced that there were relatively stable and distinctive patterns which reflected changes in F1 and F2 in noise compared to silence for each of the analyzed vowels.

Histograms reflecting distribution of $\overrightarrow{\Delta F12}$ in babble noise compared to silence for the whole group of speakers resembled visually the corresponding individual polar histograms described above (Fig. 4). In case of vowel /a/ the most probable directions of $\overrightarrow{\Delta F12}$ were 0–30° (probability 0.30), 330–0° (0.21) and 30–60° (0.15). In other sectors the probabilities did not exceed 0.08. For vowel /i/ $\overrightarrow{\Delta F12}$ were predominately in 300–330° and 330–0° sectors with probabilities of 0.27 and 0.22, respectively. For remaining sectors the probabilities did not exceed 0.12. The most probable directions of $\overrightarrow{\Delta F12}$ in case of vowel /u/ were between 60 and 90° (0.23), 0 and 30° (0.18), and 30 and 60° (0.17). Probabilities for other directions (sectors) were 0.12 or less.

To evaluate differences between probabilities' distributions of $\overrightarrow{\Delta F12}$ for different vowels, Watson's U2 test was performed. It also allowed comparing distributions for different repetitions, vowel's positions and speakers' genders for the same vowel. Results of the analysis are presented in Table 1. The comparisons revealed that differences between distributions of $\overrightarrow{\Delta F12}$ for vowels /a/, /i/ and /u/ were statistically significant ($p < 0.0001$ for all vowels' combinations, Watson's U2 test). Additionally, statistically significant differences were found between $\overrightarrow{\Delta F12}$ distributions for male and female speakers in case of vowel /a/ ($p < 0.05$) (Fig. 5 A).

The distribution of $\overrightarrow{\Delta F12}$ when pronouncing vowel /a/ in female speakers was predominately in I quadrant indicating increase in both F1 and F2 in noise. Male speakers also increased F1, but F2 could increase and decrease with equal probability, resulting in more horizontal position of the histogram's petals. A significant difference between distributions of $\overrightarrow{\Delta F12}$ was also revealed for vowel /i/ when pronounced in the beginning and in the end of the word ($p < 0.0001$). Histograms in Fig. 5 B evidence that $\overrightarrow{\Delta F12}$ for vowel /i/ in the end of the word were less variable than the corresponding $\overrightarrow{\Delta F12}$ in the beginning of the word: the first histogram had one dominant petal (300-330°,

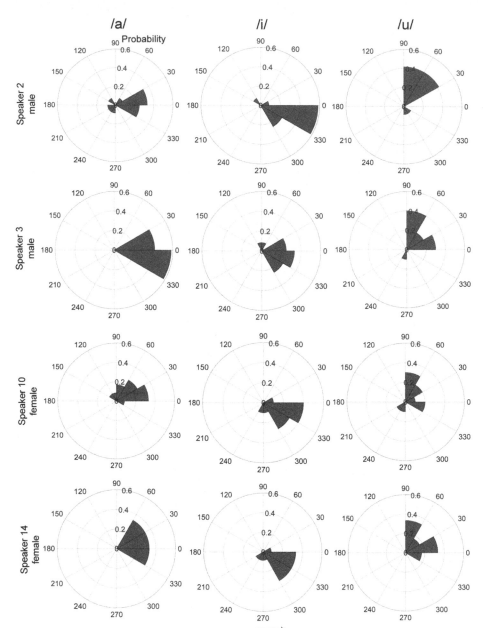

Fig. 3. Individual probabilities' distributions for $\overrightarrow{\Delta F12}$ in 60 dB (A) babble noise compared to silence for vowels /a/, /i/, /u/ spoken by two male and two female speakers. Height of the histograms' petals shows probability to find $\overrightarrow{\Delta F12}$ in each of twelve 30°-sectors. Corresponding angles of the vectors were calculated using Eq. (3). Number of vectors used to plot each individual histogram for vowels /a/, /i/ and /u/, respectively: 12, 12 and 12 (speaker 2); 12, 12 and 10 (speaker 3); 12, 10 and 10 (speaker 11); 12, 12 and 12 (speaker 14).

probability 0.4) while the second histogram was less sharp. Other comparisons did not reveal statistically significant differences between studied conditions (see Table 1).

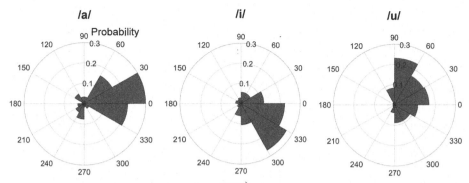

Fig. 4. Group probabilities' distributions for $\overrightarrow{\Delta F12}$ in 60 dB (A) babble noise compared to silence for vowels /a/, /i/, /u/ (N = 17). Summarized data for all three vowel positions (beginning, middle and end). Height of the histograms' petals shows probability to find $\overrightarrow{\Delta F12}$ in each of twelve 30°-sectors. Corresponding angles of the $\overrightarrow{\Delta F12}$ were calculated using Eq. (3). N = 184 (/a/), N = 180 (/i/), N = 182 (/u/).

Table 1. The results of Watson's U^2 test for probabilities' distributions of $\overrightarrow{\Delta F12}$ in case of different vowels, speakers' genders, vowel positions and words repetitions (rep). P-values were calculated by using a permutation test.

Compared conditions	U^2	d.f	p observed	p adjusted
/a/, /i/, /u/				
/a/ - /i/	1.511	184, 180	< 0.0001	**< 0.0001[a,b]**
/a/ - /u/	0.881	184, 182	< 0.0001	**< 0.0001**
/i/ - /u/	1.289	180, 182	< 0.0001	**< 0.0001**
/a/				
Male - female	0.320	79, 105	0.003	**0.022**
Beginning – middle	0.143	68, 62	0.110	0.289
Beginning – end	0.195	68, 54	0.043	0.179
Middle – end	0.146	62, 54	0.114	0.289
Rep 1 – rep 2	0.126	47, 47	0.169	0.340
Rep 1 – rep 3	0.120	47, 45	0.185	0.340
Rep 1 – rep 4	0.093	47, 45	0.326	0.504
Rep 2 – rep 3	0.040	47, 45	0.843	0.927

(*continued*)

Table 1. (*continued*)

Compared conditions	U^2	d.f	p observed	p adjusted
Rep 2 – rep 4	0.368	47, 45	0.873	0.929
Rep 3 – rep 4	0.041	45, 45	0.826	0.927
/i/				
Male – female	0.213	82, 98	0.027	0.149
Beginning – middle	0.184	58, 61	0.054	0.199
Beginning – end	0.611	58, 61	< 0.0001	**< 0.0001**
Middle – end	0.124	61, 61	0.181	0.340
Rep 1 – rep 2	0.031	46, 44	0.931	0.931
Rep 1 – rep 3	0.058	46, 45	0.628	0.829
Rep 1 – rep 4	0.122	46, 45	0.184	0.340
Rep 2 – rep 3	0.035	44, 45	0.905	0.931
Rep 2 – rep 4	0.046	44, 45	0.777	0.916
Rep 3 – rep 4	0.057	45, 45	0.654	0.830
/u/				
Male – female	0.208	68, 114	0.034	0.162
Beginning – middle	0.167	63, 60	0.072	0.236
Beginning – end	0.111	63, 59	0.230	0.380
Middle – end	0.131	60, 59	0.151	0.340
Rep 1 – rep 2	0.067	46, 46	0.540	0.743
Rep 1 – rep 3	0.075	46, 45	0.471	0.675
Rep 1 – rep 4	0.052	46, 45	0.711	0.869
Rep 2 – rep 3	0.092	46, 45	0.336	0.504
Rep 2 – rep 4	0.162	46, 45	0.080	0.239
Rep 3 – rep 4	0.114	45, 45	0.208	0.362

[a]Statistically significant differences are marked by bold font.
[b]p-Values of less than 0.0001 indicate that in the test, which consisted of 10000 permutations there were no U^2-statistics for permuted data exceeding U^2-statistics for original data.

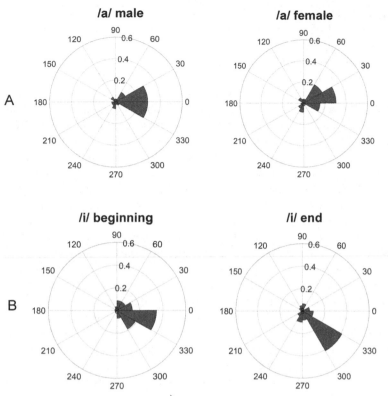

Fig. 5. Probabilities' distributions for $\overrightarrow{\Delta F12}$ in 60 dB (A) babble noise compared to silence: A – vowel /a/ in male and female speakers, B – vowel /i/ in the beginning and in the end of the word. Height of the histograms' petals shows probability to find $\overrightarrow{\Delta F12}$ in each of twelve 30°-sectors. Corresponding angles of the vectors were calculated using Eq. (3). N (/a/ – male speakers) = 79; N (/a/ – female speakers) = 105; N (/i/ – beginning) = 58; N (/i/ – end) = 61.

4   Discussion

The new statistical approach to description of formants' modifications when speaking in babble noise confirms the hypothesis on the resemblance between probabilities' distributions of $\overrightarrow{\Delta F12}$ for different speakers in case of the same vowel (Fig. 3). Accordingly, for the whole group of speakers stable patterns characterizing probabilities' distributions of $\overrightarrow{\Delta F12}$ are received for vowels /a/, /i/ and /u/ (Fig. 4). Individual and group data evidence that the voice forcing which takes place on the background of babble noise induces typical changes in F1 and F2. The relations between these changes are quite stable for each of the studied vowels.

Vowels /a/, /i/ and /u/ were chosen by us as the basic ones which form apexes of the so-called formant triangle. The formant triangle limits the area of possible positions for all vowels in F1-F2 coordinate space. Changes in the positions of formant triangle apexes, i.e. the in the formant structure of basic vowels, under influence of noise have been analyzed in several languages [13]. This allows juxtaposing our results with data of previous studies based on the traditional non-vector approach to description of vowels modifications in Lombard speech. We consider such comparison of the results as an important control procedure.

In our paper we explored the effect of moderate level babble noise – 60 dB (A), on the formant structure of stressed Russian vowels in elicited speech. This level of noise is common for moderately noisy public places [14, 15], and it is known to induce noticeable Lombard effect [16]. To compare data obtained in our study with the results of previous research we will look firstly at separate changes in F1 and F2 in noise. Regardless of the studied vowel, in the vast majority of cases we observed increase in F1, which was in a good agreement with results of previous studies of Lombard effect [4, 17]. Cases of F1 decrease in our work were relatively rare for all vowels and could be due to articulation errors. Presence of F1 decrease cases could also be explained by natural variability in formant structure of vowels during speech production. In paper of DiCanio and colleagues [18] the largest standard deviations of F1 were found for vowel /a/ in both spontaneous and elicited speech, which may be responsible for the highest probability of F1 decrease for sound /a/ amongst all vowels in our study. F2 changes for vowels /a/, /i/ and /u/ revealed by us were not as clear as F1 changes: for all three vowels both increase and decrease in F2 could be observed. Other studies have also described changes in F2, but the descriptions were mostly qualitative. For example, in the paper of Kirchhuebel [19] changes in F2 in babble-noise were characterized as "very variable and complex", which matches our result. Thus, we can conclude that changes in F1 and F2 in babble noise, revealed in current work, were in a good agreement with the data on Lombard effect from other studies.

Statistically significant differences between probabilities' distributions of $\overrightarrow{\Delta F12}$ were found not only between different vowels, but also for vowel /a/ between male and female speakers – the latter tended to increase F2 in noise more often the former (Fig. 5A). This result confirms observations from the paper [20], where tendency to increase F2 in noise was more prominent for female speakers. As one can see from Table 1, comparisons of probabilities distributions between male and female speakers for two other vowels – /i/ and /u/, revealed smallest of adjusted non-significant p-values (0.149 and 0.162, respectively). This may indicate presence of slight differences between strategies used by female and male speakers for formants' modification in noise.

We also found statistically significant difference between probabilities' distributions of $\overrightarrow{\Delta F12}$ for vowel /i/ when it was pronounced in the beginning and in the end of the word (Fig. 5B). In the latter case the changes were less scattered within the IV quadrant and were mostly concentrated in 300-330° sector, indicating an increase in F1 and a proportional decrease in F2. These data may evidence higher stability of formant modifications in noise compared to silence for vowel /i/ in the end of the word.

5   Conclusion

Vowels' formant structure change when speaking in noise, which can affect both human communication and automatic speech recognition processes. The approach suggested by us allows revealing the most probable directions of changes in F1 and F2 under influence of background babble noise. The information may be useful for improvement of speech recognition rates in automatic systems, for speech rehabilitation process planning and assessment of its effectiveness. The revealed directions of formants changes are fairly stable relative to vowel position, gender differences of voices and individual variability of formants values in case of multiple words repetitions. At the same time, the suggested approach is relatively simple and allows reduction of the data dimensionality. We hope that it will be useful and can be applied in a wide range of research and practical tasks concerned with the reduced auditory feedback control of speech production.

Acknowledgments. This research is supported by the Russian Science Foundation (project No. 22-25-00068).

References

1. Wang, X., Xu, L.: Speech perception in noise: masking and unmasking. J. Otol. **16**(2), 109–119 (2021)
2. Garnier, M., Henrich, N.: Speaking in noise: How does the Lombard effect improve acoustic contrasts between speech and ambient noise? Comput. Speech Lang. **28**(2), 580–597 (2014)
3. Lane, H., Tranel, B.: The Lombard sign and the role of hearing in speech. J. Speech Lang. Hear. Res. **14**(4), 677–709 (1971)
4. Junqua, J.-C.: The influence of acoustics on speech production: a noise-induced stress phenomenon known as the Lombard reflex. Speech Commun. **20**(1–2), 13–22 (1996)
5. Lunichkin, A.M., Gvozdeva, A.P., Zaytseva L.G., Ogorodnikova E.A., Andreeva I.G.: Spectral changes of Russian vowels pronounced in babble noise, Virtual conference. In: 8th International Symposium on Auditory and Audiological Research ISAAR 2021 "The Auditory System Throughout Life – Models, Mechanisms, and Interventions" (2021)
6. Anusuya, M.A., Katti, S.K.: Front end analysis of speech recognition: a review. Int. J. Speech Technol. **14**(2), 99–145 (2011)
7. Andreeva, I.G., Dymnikowa, M., Gvozdeva, A.P., Ogorodnikova, E.A., Pak, S.P.: Spatial separation benefit for speech detection in multi-talker babble-noise with different egocentric distances. Acta Acust. Acust. **105**(3), 484–491 (2019)
8. Marks, L.E.: Binaural summation of loudness: noise and two-tone complexes. Percept. Psychophys. **27**(6), 489–498 (1980)
9. Zwicker, E., Terhardt, E.: Analytical expressions for critical-band rate and critical bandwidth as a function of frequency. J. Acoust. Soc. Am. **68**(5), 1523–1525 (1980). https://doi.org/10.1121/1.385079
10. Zar, J.H.: Biostatistical Analysis, 5th edn. Prentice-Hall/Pearson, Upper Saddle River (2010)
11. Berry, K.J., Mielke, P.W., Jr., Johnston, J.E.: Permutation Statistical Methods: An Integrated Approach. Springer, Heidelberg (2016)
12. Benjamini, Y., Hochberg, Y.: Controlling the false discovery rate: a practical and powerful approach to multiple testing. J. Roy. Stat. Soc.: Ser. B (Methodol.) **57**(1), 289–300 (1995)
13. Uma Maheswari, S., Shahina, A., Nayeemulla Khan, A.: Understanding Lombard speech: a review of compensation techniques towards improving speech based recognition systems. Artif. Intell. Rev. **54**(4), 2495–2523 (2020). https://doi.org/10.1007/s10462-020-09907-5
14. Zemke, D.M., Hertzman, J.L., Raab, C., Singh, D.: A little more noise and a little less conversation? ambient noise in restaurants. J. Foodserv. Bus. Res. **14**(3), 256–271 (2011)
15. Busch-Vishniac, I.J., West, J.E., Barnhill, C., Hunter, T., Orellana, D., Chivukula, R.: Noise levels in Johns Hopkins Hospital. The J. Acoust. Soc. Am. **118**(6), 3629–3645 (2005)

16. Garnier, M., Henrich, N., Dubois, D.: Influence of sound immersion and communicative interaction on the lombard effect. J. Speech Lang. Hear. Res. **53**(3), 588 (2010)
17. Garnier, M., Bailly, L., Dohen, M., Welby, P., Lœvenbruck, H.: An acoustic and articulatory study of Lombard speech: Global effects on the utterance. In: Ninth International Conference on Spoken Language Processing (2006)
18. DiCanio, C., Nam, H., Amith, J.D., García, R.C., Whalen, D.H.: Vowel variability in elicited versus spontaneous speech: evidence from Mixtec. J. Phon. **48**, 45–59 (2015)
19. Kirchhuebel, C.: The effects of Lombard speech on vowel formant measurements. São Paulo School of Advanced Studies in Speech Dynamics SPSASSD 2010 Accepted Papers, vol. 38 (2010)
20. Junqua, J. C., & Anglade, Y. Acoustic and perceptual studies of Lombard speech: Application to isolated-words automatic speech recognition. In: International conference on acoustics, speech, and signal processing IEEE, pp. 841–844 (1990)

Comparing NLP Solutions for the Disambiguation of French Heterophonic Homographs for End-to-End TTS Systems

Maria-Loulou Hajj⬤, Martin Lenglet⬤, Olivier Perrotin⬤, and Gérard Bailly$^{(\boxtimes)}$⬤

Grenoble -Alps Univ, GIPSA-Lab, 11, rue des Mathématiques, St Martin d'Hères, France
{maria.hajj,martin.lenglet,olivier.perrotin,gerard.bailly}@gipsa-lab.fr

Abstract. This paper presents a study on different NLP solutions for French homographs disambiguation for text-to-speech systems. Solutions are compared using a home-made corpus of 8137 sentences extracted from the Web, comprising roughly one hundred instances of each of 34 pairs of prototypical words. A disambiguation system based on per-case Linear Discriminant Analysis (LDA) classifiers using contextual word embeddings as input features achieves state-of-the-art F-scores superior to 0.96.

Keywords: End-to-end text-to-speech · Letter-to-sound · Heterophonic homographs

1 Introduction

English and French are considered to have the most opaque orthographies among languages with alphabetic (as opposed to logographic or syllabary) writing systems: fluent reading of French requires a visual attention span (VAS = the number of distinct visual elements that can be processed simultaneously at a glance) [3] of up-to 5 to 6 characters (see Fig. 1). Note that this VAS is highly structured: the whole span is not screened and processed for all characters. On the other hand, some words may require a larger span (and likely several saccades and fixations through the text) to get properly pronounced, such as homographs. An heterophonic homograph is 'one of two or more words spelled alike but different in meaning or pronunciation' (such as 'mon fils' my son vs. 'des fils' which is the plural of 'fil', a thread or wire). The correct classification of a homograph has always been an issue for natural language processing when it comes to text-to-speech (TTS) systems and the analysis of texts. And so, using a word that has homographs, can change the meaning and context of a text if read or analyzed

© Springer Nature Switzerland AG 2022
S. R. M. Prasanna et al. (Eds.): SPECOM 2022, LNAI 13721, pp. 265–278, 2022.
https://doi.org/10.1007/978-3-031-20980-2_23

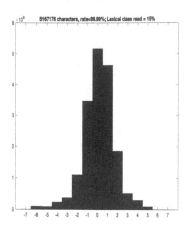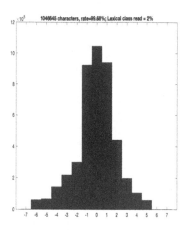

Fig. 1. Histograms of the distance of context characters left and right from the current character a minimum-length decision tree [2] has to question to pronounce it correctly. Minimum length training of these isolated words is very efficient. Left: French (using entries from the Robert dictionary); Right: English (using CMUDICT). Word entries are augmented with POS tags. On these datasets, French uses much more this information than English. Weighted means are 0.15 vs. −0.07: French seems to use a bit more look-ahead context. Note however that these data depend on the grapheme-to-phoneme alignments. Both writings need an attention span of more than 10 letters.

by a machine. Moreover, French has a significant amount of homographs[1] which are usually not well analyzed [4].

In this study, we will try to get the best results possible generating the pronunciation of homographs, using different approaches and methods. We will first show that popular end-to-end neural TTS systems with text input such as Tacotron2 can be trained to perform a rather performative letter-to-sound (LTS) alignment and mapping, using both aligned and non-aligned acoustic corpora as well a pronunciation dictionary. We also tested the performance of a part-of-speech (POS) tagging transformer to bias this LTS mapping. We finally compared these models with homograph classification models also built on FlauBERT; a French version of BERT. Classification is performed by Linear Discriminant Analysis (LDA) trained on a corpus of 8137 homographs observed in context.

2   State of the Art

Early solutions for letter-to-sound conversion consisted in storing orthography/ pronunciation pairs of a finite list of words in a lexicon enriched with lexical, syntactic or semantic information that condition the retrieval of the right pronunciation given orthography and information provided by POS taggers or homograph

---

[1] https://fr.wiktionary.org/wiki/Categorie:Homographes_non_homophones_en_ francais

disambiguators [5]. Statistical LTS models have then been introduced to generalize LTS mapping to out-of-vocabulary words: neural sequence-to-sequence models are the current state of the art [1,16].

The first generation of end-to-end (E2E) neural TTS such as Tacotron2 [13] or Deep Voice [11] proposed to generalise from character input to acoustic output from fairly large sets of parallel text and speech audio data, implicitly learning LTS mappings. Taylor and Richmond [15] showed that this implicit LTS models underperformed explicit LTS. Reported LTS errors (close to 10%) were quite alarming. Latest generation of E2E models now opt for a phonetic input [12]. Note that phonological variations (ways of words are pronounced) depend on linguistic context – hopefully captured by the text encoder – but also on speaking style and speaker components that usually bias embeddings computed by the phonetic encoder of current E2E neural TTS. An external component should thus restore the covariation between these segmental and suprasegemental components. With implicit LTS models, speaker and expressivity components can implicitely modulate the phonological variations at all levels in a more ecological framework. Experiments comparing explicit and implicit LTS have not yet been confirmed on French. Our experience with implicit LTS on French is rather more positive, given appropriate supervision (see below).

Concerning the processing of specific LTS mappings by E2E TTS, Taylor et al. [15] compared explicit vs. implicit LTS results focusing on French liaisons. They show that Tacotron2 over-inserts liaison sounds, leading to a significant preference for an explicit LTS control.

Nicolis et al. [10] describe an explicit heterophonic homograph disambiguation system for English based on per-case classifiers using contextual word embeddings as input features. They report an accuracy of 0.991 with as little as 100 sentences of training material.

The current paper builds on these experiments. Our main contributions are:

- Enhanced implicit LTS for E2E TTS using grapheme-to-phoneme alignments gathered during pre-training the TTS system with both orthographic and phonetic input. Implicit LTS for general text input (more than 100 h of read speech) achieves an accuracy of 0.989 for all input characters and 0.999 when considering only word characters.
- Homograph-specific LDA classifiers using contextual word embeddings using a similar approach as proposed by [10] achieves good performance
- Performance and generalization can be improved by clustering homographs into groups

3   Dataset and Models

We collected 8137 sentences comprising at least one heterophonic homograph. The samples were collected from various sources: articles from various journals, google searches, etc. Most sentences are kept in their original phrasing, in-between punctuation marks. We nevertheless cleaned (removing lists of proper

Table 1. Multispeaker audio data used to train the Tacotron2.

Speaker	Sex	Type	#Utts		#Duration	
			All	Aligned	All	Aligned
NEB[a]	F	Audiobooks	83021	45099	71:16	34:30
DG	M	Audiobooks	20179	7749	17:16	6:31
RO	F	Read sentences	9371	0	0:00	9:57
IZ	F	Scripted dialogs	11073	386	9:28	0:17
AD	F	Read sentences	6476	2853	5:05	2:14
Total			130105	56102	112:59	43:35

[a] Part of this data is available at https://zenodo.org/record/4580406.

nouns, dates, etc) and shortened part of them (removing unnecessary clauses, inserts, etc). Since some homographs occur frequently (e.g. we have 1373 occurrences of the auxiliary "est" in the homograph dataset), we end-up with 9997 homographs.

3.1 Our Baseline: End-to-End TTS Augmented with Phone Prediction

Using Multidimensional Scaling, we analyzed the latent space computed by the output of the text encoder of a Tacotron2 [13] trained on 113 h of a multi-speaker French data (see Table 1). Speaker embeddings are simply added to the output of the text encoder. This baseline model was trained for 250 Epochs, a batchsize of 128 and a learning rate of $4e^{-5}$. We used the HPC facilities provided by the Jean-Zay supercomputer in Paris.

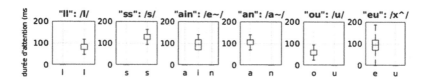

Fig. 2. Distributions of durations of activation (ms) of 6 character sequences: when one phoneme is encoded by two letters, the second character gets mostly activated in double consonants, while the first is activated for vowels.

The text encoder was trained using both text and phonetic input when hand-checked (38% of the utterances): while this representation mixing has been shown to improve spectrogram estimation [6], it also provides a letter-to-sound alignment [1] as a by-product of the Tacotron2 attention map: using activation patterns (see sample statistics in Fig. 2) and joint projection of input phones and characters embeddings into a common latent space (see Fig. 3) using Multidimensional Scaling (MDS), we obtain a lawful correspondence between phones and characters [9], including pauses and spaces/punctuations.

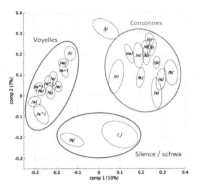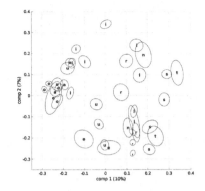

Fig. 3. Projection of the embeddings of the 25 most frequent phones (left) and the 15 most frequent characters (right) at the output of the text encoder. The projection is performed on the first factorial plane of Multidimensional Scaling (MDS) of the embeddings of all input symbols of 10% of the training data. A Gaussian mixture model clusters scattered distributions of each character. As an example, "s" has four clusters, one overlapping the phone /s/, one on /z/ and two on the silence /_/, reflecting the pronunciation of "sot", "asie" vs. "tu es bien"; "o" has five clusters, overlapping the phones /u/, /o/, /oˆ/ (/ɔ/), /xˆ/ (/ʃ/), and /o˜/ (/ɔ̃/), reflecting the pronunciation of "loup", "dos", "cor", "coeur" and "long".

We thus enriched the original Tacotron2 with an additional task: phone prediction from the text encoder's output. This prediction is simply performed by a full-connected layer with softmax. This model is named TC2 in the following. The set of target phonemes comprises the input phoneme inventory augmented with a "silent" symbol and several diphones such as /k&s/, /i&j/, /d&zˆ/ (/dʒ/) ... paired with single characters such as "x" (in "six"), "y" (in "appuyer") or "j" (as in "jazz"). We also have symbols for hiatus, syntactic vs. breath pauses, often paired with punctuations and sometimes with spaces.

For aligned utterances, two input/output patterns are thus provided: the output pattern for orthographic input has "silent" symbols and diphones, while that for phonetic input has one-to-one correspondence except for spaces and punctuations that may be associated with "silent" symbols or pauses. Of course, both utterances are associated with the same spectrogram. Please find an excerpt of our corpus below (note that the name of the audiofile and the timestamps have been removed):

```
sans l'imp\'{e}rieuse exigence,|s a˜ _ _ _ l _ e˜ _ p e r j x _ z _ _ e˜ g&z i z^ a˜ _ s _ __
{s a˜} {l e˜ p e r j x z} {e^ g z i z^ a˜ s},|s a˜ _ l e˜ p e r j x z _ e^ g z i z^ a˜ s __
```

Note that TC2 was only exposed to the homographs used in the audiobooks (plus one exemplar per homograph from the Robert lexicon, see below). The column #obs/Audio of Table 2 gives the number of occurrences of each homograph in the 113 h corpus: This distribution is very uneven: the auxiliary verb "est" occurs more than 10000 times whereas the homographs "adoptions", "détections", "négligent", "somnolent" and "pressent" occur less than once.

The resulting letter-to-sound mapping is quite accurate (see Fig. 4). The accuracy of phonetic predictions of 4771684 word characters is superior to 99.9% and close to 98.9% when considering punctuations and other special characters.

Note that this mapping opens up the possibility to improve pronunciation accuracy for words not present in the audiobooks (modern terms[2], loan or rare words, etc). We thus performed the letter-to-sound alignment of the pronunciation input from the Robert dictionary (1995 version) and also include some conjugated forms. We thus added one exemplar of each homograph given in minimal context (adding sufficient grammatical words for disambiguisation, e.g. "Ils convient." vs "Il convient"). When training TC2 speaker embeddings, these additional "normative" out-of-context 104332 entries are set for all speakers with no dialectal nor style variation.

The final parametrization of TC2 was trained in two steps: 10 epochs for training the phone prediction layer from the frozen baseline, then 40 epochs for fine-tuning the whole model.

While not having observed so many homographs (see column "audio" in Table 2), the pronunciation accuracy of homographs is quite good (see F-scores in Table 2). Some scores ("convient", "minerai", etc) are not so high for several reasons: large asymmetry of the empirical distributions (frequency of appearance of each homograph is highly imbalanced: "est" as auxiliary is twenty times more frequent than "est" as noun, the use of "minerai" or "violent" as conjugated verbs

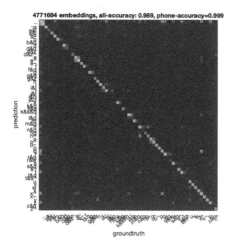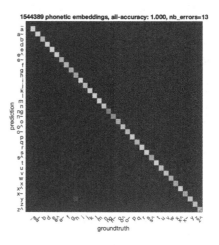

Fig. 4. Confusion matrix of phonetic prediction for orthographic (left) vs. phonetic (right) input. On average, we have three characters per phone. Trained with phonetic alignments, the output of Tacotron2 text encoder actually embeds quite precise phonetic representations.

---

[2] e.g. the root "techniqu" is only used 5 times in our audiobook database: with no additional patterns from a pronunciation lexicon, "ch" will likely be mispronounced with the post-alveolar fricative ʃ.

in our audiobooks are never encountered), limited amount of training material and detection capabilities of the text encoder, etc.

3.2 Part-of-Speech (POS) Tagging

Most homographs can be solved using POS Tagging. The few of them with identical POS require computation of grammatical variables (such as "convient" or "os") or semantic analysis (such as "fils"). POS Tagging has been shown to improve pronunciation accuracy, phrasing and prosody [14]. In this paper, we used the *Hugging Face* French POS tagger trained on the free French-treebank dataset[3].

The pronunciation accuracy of homographs given this POS prediction (see F-scores in Table 2 is rather disappointing: probably because of the asymmetrical distributions of the homographs in the French-treebank dataset: this largely explains the poor tagging of "content", "couvent" and "parent" as verbs. It also could be due to the tag inventory that could not be appropriate to homograph disambiguation: as an example, infinitives are either classified as verbs or infinitives, adjectives may be confused with nouns or past participes.

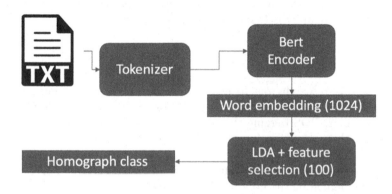

Fig. 5. Combining BERT word embeddings (using a tokenizer with a vocabulary of 68729 words and sub-word units) with feature selection and Linear Discriminant Analysis.

3.3 Linear Discriminant Analysis of BERT Embeddings

Self-supervised NLP models such as Bidirectional Encoder Representations from Transformers (BERT) use "auxiliary" or "pre-training" task – such as predicting masked words, next words in an utterance, sentence order, etc. – to learn latent representations that are further used for downstream supervised tasks [7]. Word embeddings computed by the last transformer before the final softmax layer are often used has representation vectors for the supervised tasks.

---

[3] https://huggingface.co/gilf/french-postag-model.

Since our task consists in separating two classes (no words with more than two pronunciations in French), we combined feature selection and linear discriminant analysis (LDA) on the BERT embeddings for each pair of homographs (see Fig. 5).

We used FlauBERT, which stands for "French Language Understanding via Bidirectional Encoder Representations from Transformers", one of the few pre-trained French version of BERT [8]. From the original 1024 embedding dimensions of the Flaubert large-cased model, we iteratively select the 110 dimensions that are the most relevant for the LDA classification.

We explored two different ways of grouping homographs:

Embeddings of word pairs (B-wrd) builds a model for each homograph. An example of this method is found in Appendix A.1.

Embeddings of class pairs (B-grp) builds a model specific to each class of homograph. Some classes are quite large such as homographs ending with "ions" or "ent"; some are word-specfific and equivalent to B-wrd such as "fils" or "plus". This method allows us to build more general models, trained on larger groups, that can be further applied on words not seen or trained before (or homographs that are rather difficult to observe in context). Example of this method on a poetry paragraph from a Facebook post complaining opacity of French orthography is found in Appendix A.2.

4   Results

The goal of this research was to evaluate performance and accuracy of each of four NLP methods, which were applied for the disambiguation of French homographs: TC2, POS tagging, B-wrd and B-grp. The results of F1-scores for each homograph after each solution are found in Table 2.

Amongst these solutions, the POS tagging performed the worst, with a mean F1-score of .67, when POS tags are sufficient for disambiguation. This low score is likely to be explained by the poor and unbalanced representation of homographs in the French-treebank. It also shows that the use of BERT embeddings is highly dependent of the targeted task: the POS ambiguities of the rare homographs are outliers when considering the empiral distribution of word tokens.

TC2, with a mean F1-score of .8, has rather good results distributed across all homographs compared to the POS tagging method. Especially for the homographs where POS tagging performed poorly, TC2 had much higher scores. Rare homographs requiring calculation of grammatical variables such as number get low scores, like "convient", "os". More detailed results about the phonetics generated for some homographs by TC2 are given in Fig. 6.

Both methods of LDA from FlauBERT embeddings, B-wrd and B-grp, got the highest and best scores distributed across all homographs but also compared to POS tagging and Tacotron2. Both performed very well, but with minor differences.

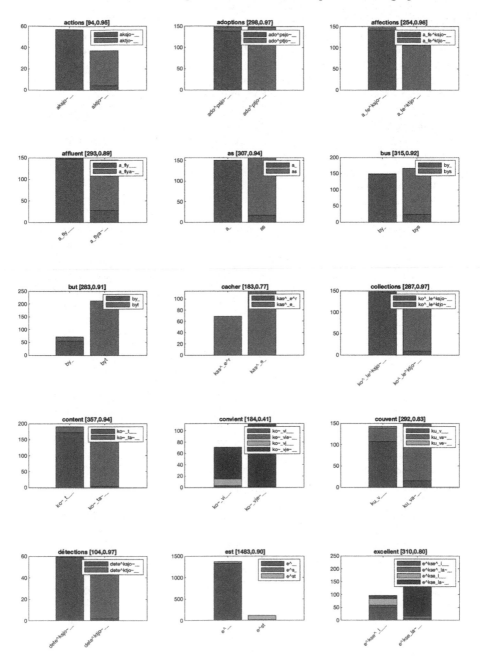

Fig. 6. Average F1-score of the first 15 homographs processed by our Tacotron2 end-to-end system augmented with phone prediction. Phonological variations of homographs are aggregated.

Table 2. Results of F1-Score for each homograph after the different methods used. Number of observations in the 113 hours of read speech and in the 8137 sentences are given in colmuns Audio (word count) and Homo (for each homograph). Abbreviations for POS tags: Ns/Np=Noun singular/plural; Vs/Vp/Inf=Verb singular/plural/Infinitive; A/Pps=Adjective/Past Participle; Pas=Negation. No errors are scored .999. F-scores below .25 and .50 are enlighten in red and blue.

Homograph	POS	Sounds	#obs		F1-Score			
			Audio	Homo	POS	TC2	B-wrd	B-grp
Actions	Np/Vp	[aksjɔ̃]/[aktjɔ̃]	38	44/37	.22	.95	.991	.995
Adoptions	Np/Vp	[adɔpsjɔ̃]/[adɔptjɔ̃]	0	149/149	.92	.97	.993	.993
Affections	Np/Vp	[afɛksjɔ̃]/[afɛktjɔ̃]	10	148/106	.99	.98	.999	.999
Collections	Np/Vp	[kɔlɛksjɔ̃]/[kɔlɛktjɔ̃]	11	145/139	.04	.97	.978	.989
Détections	Np/Vp	[detɛksjɔ̃]/[detɛktjɔ̃]	0	58/44	.99	.97	.967	.989
Intentions	Np/Vp	[ɛ̃tɑ̃sjɔ̃]/[ɛ̃tɑ̃tjɔ̃]	13	101/40	.27	.91	.950	.987
Options	Np/Vp	[ɔpsjɔ̃]/[ɔptjɔ̃]	6	80/38	.80	.69	.843	.999
Portions	Np/Vp	[pɔʁsjɔ̃]/[pɔʁtjɔ̃]	12	93/52	.80	.73	.972	.999
Affluent	Ns/Vp	[aflyɑ̃]/[afly]	4	143/148	.98	.89	.999	.999
Couvent	Ns/Vp	[kuvɑ̃]/[kuv]	13	149/142	.04	.83	.976	.989
Ferment	Ns/Vp	[fɛʁmɑ̃]/[fɛʁm]	7	102/104	.68	.84	.995	.995
Parent	Ns/Vp	[paʁɑ̃]/[paʁ]	9	140/153	.08	.94	.987	.997
Résident[a]	Ns/Vp	[rezidɑ̃]/[rezid]	0	101/99	.95	.62	–	.990
As	N/Vs	[as]/[a]	342	157/141	.95	.94	.995	.999
Bus	N/Vs	[bys]/[by]	4	163/149	.15	.92	.993	.993
But	Ns/Vs	[byt]/[by]	88	125/149	.50	.91	.993	.993
Sens	N/Vs	[sɑ̃s]/[sɑ̃]	213	208/155	.99	.95	.997	.997
Vis	N/Vs	[vis]/[vi]	128	120/99	.98	.94	.990	.999
Content	A/Vp	[kɔ̃tɑ̃]/[kɔ̃t]	56	167/190	.04	.94	.997	.999
Excellent	A/Vp	[ɛksɛlɑ̃]/[ɛksɛl]	60	213/96	.56	.80	.979	.999
Négligent	A/Vp	[negliʒɑ̃]/[negliʒ]	1	106/108	.92	.79	.978	.981
Somnolent	A/Vp	[sɔmnɔlɑ̃]/[sɔmnɔl]	1	77/56	.97	.56	.978	.999
Urgent	A/Vp	[yʁʒɑ̃]/[yʁʒ]	16	166/114	.98	.94	.975	.978
Violent	A/Vp	[vjɔlɑ̃]/[vjɔl]	48	248/110	.86	.75	.991	.999
Convient	Vs/Vp	[kɔ̃vjɛ̃]/[kɔ̃vi]	40	108/71	–	.41	.962	.965
Pressent	Vs/Vp	[presɑ̃]/[pres]	1	64/84	–	.73	.976	.994
Est	Ns/Vs	[est]/[ɛ]	10624	114/116	.94	.90	.957	.965
Minerai	Ns/Vs	[minəʁɛ]/[minəʁe]	4	36/17	.97	.48	.962	.970
Cacher	A/Inf	[kaʃɛʁ]/[kaʃe]	56	69/112	.83	.77	.987	.991
Fier	A/Inf	[fjɛʁ]/[fje]	35	217/148	.11	.94	.992	.997
Fils	Ns/Np	[fis]/[fil]	270	158/105	–	.85	.995	
Os	Ns/Np	[ɔs]/[o]	38	91/72	-	.32	.966	
Plus	A/Pas	[plys]/[ply]	5307	219/404	–	.71	.967	
Reporter	Ns/Inf	[ʁəpɔʁtɛʁ]/[ʁəpɔʁte]	107	59/84	.75	.58	.994	.995
Supporter	Ns/Inf	[sypɔʁtɛʁ]/[sypɔʁte]	42	89/105	.91	.70	.982	.986

[a] As an example, this homograph was not included in the training dataset. The B-wrd model nevertheless scores .999.

For B-wrd, the F1-score ranges from 0.843 to 0.999, making it the second-best approach applied in our research.

Finally, for B-grp, the F1-score ranges from 0.957 to 0.997. Its results are always higher than the minimum of B-wrd's results.

5   Comments

We tried to populate the corpus of different French homographs with a balanced set of utterances in their respective contexts, in order to unbias homograph recognition. Several solutions were applied for the disambiguation of French homographs. We worked on POS, Tacotron2, LDA/BERT models and trained the model to get more accurate results using four different methods:

- **POS** is very accurate for most homographs but its performance heavily depends on empirical distributions of the underlying BERT model and the corpus with TAG labels used for supervised training. Hence, the extremely low scores especially below .25 (highlighted in red) are probably due to underrepresented homophones (e.g. "collections", "intentions", "couvent" or "parent" as verbs. It is our low anchor.
- **Tacotron2** performed quite well on average. Compared to POS tagging, it has full coverage of homographs and its text encoder seems to be able to perform some semantic calculations to solve complex cases such as "fils" or "plus". Poor performance for "minerai", "reporter", "convient" and "os" are largely explained by the empirical distribution of the examplars in the 113 speech data: all "minerai" and "reporter" are nouns, the 40 "convient" are all from "convenir" (none from "convier") and only 1 "os" is singular.
- **B-wrd** works on the embeddings of words pairs of the homograph extracted from balanced corpora. Unlike both previously mentioned solutions, this one is very accurate, with almost perfect scores.
- **B-grp** groups homographs according to the proximity of POS tags and grammatical variables involved in the disambiguation: the prediction of the pronunciation and meaning of the homograph would depend on the group it belongs. The two advantages of this model are: (a) its generalisation capabilities (see performance on the unseen homograph "résident" in Table 2), (b) its robustness, since LDA works on bigger samples.

6   Conclusions and Perspectives

We extend the work performed by Nicolis et al. [10] on English. We collected a significant database of heterophonic homographs for French. We show that the grouping of homographs into grammatical cases offers generalization and robustness. Some groupings are not so successful: "est" and "minerai" should certainly be treated separately. More generally, grouping should be automatized, in particular when considering other rare homographs (e.g. "bis", "helas", "sus"). We did not consider here the problem of phonological variation: some homographs could be pronounced with optional liaisons, mute-es, schwas, depending on numerous factors such as speed, context or speaker's style. One possibility is to use representation mixing and only overwrite parts of the words that are ambiguous: "fils" when used as "thread/wire" could be rewriten as {fil}s, "est" when used as the auxiliary "is" as {e^}t, etc. The idea is to combine the B-grp precision for solving rare heterophonic homographs with the TC2 flexibility for handling implicit LTS. First results are encouraging but the interaction with other components should be analyzed.

We also show that text encoders of current end-to-end TTS are capable of performing quite impressive LTS mapping, given proper LTS alignment and mixed input training. Augmenting training material with homographs in context – and not only entries in isolation provided by the text/phonetic alignment data – will certainly improve performance of LTS mapping while keeping the flexibility of orthographic input for phonological variation.

We are currently exploring the impact of multi-speaker training on LTS mapping, in particular phonological variations and phrasing. Building TTS with orthographic input is a prerequisite for shaping latent spaces that can capture segmental and suprasegmental variations in the same embeddings.

Acknowledgments. Supported by the ANR 19-P3IA-0003 MIAI. This work was performed using HPC/AI resources from GENCI-IDRIS (Grant AD011011542).

A Appendices

A.1 Example of Embeddings of Word Pairs (B-wrd)

For example, processing two sentences using the word "as" by the LDA from FlauBERT embeddings of "as":

```
% do_traite_homographes_heterophones.py
>>Les as.
['Les</w>', 'as</w>', '.</w>']
Les {a s}.
>>Tu les as mangés.
['Tu</w>', 'les</w>', 'as</w>', 'mangés</w>', '.</w>']
Tu les {a} mangés.
```

A.2 Example of Embeddings of Class Pairs (B-grp)

Phonetization of heterophone homographes of a FaceBook post of French poetry with no errors:

```
Nous {p o^ r t j o~} les {p o^ r s j o~}.
Les poules du {k u v a~} {k u v}.
Mes {f i s} ont cassé mes {f i l}.
Il {e^} à l'{e^ s t}.
```

Je {v i} ces {v i s}.
Cet homme {eˆ} {f j eˆ r}. Peut-on s'y {f j e}?
Avant, nous {e d i t j o˜} de belles {e d i s j o˜}.
Je suis {k o˜ t a˜} qu'ils {k o˜ t} ces histoires.
Il { k o˜ v j e˜} qu'ils {k o˜ v i} leurs amis.
Ils ont un caractère {v j oˆ l a˜}: ils {v j oˆ l} leurs promesses.
Nos {e˜ t a˜ s j o˜} sont que nous {e˜ t a˜ t j o˜} ce procès.
Ils {n e g l i z˜} leurs devoirs, je suis moins {n e g l i zˆ a˜} qu'eux.
Ils {r e z i d} à Paris chez le {r e z i d a˜} d'une nation étrangère.
Les cuisiniers {e k s eˆ l} à faire ce mets {e k s e l a˜}.
Les poissons {a f l y} à un {a f l y a˜}.

References

1. Bisani, M., Ney, H.: Joint-sequence models for grapheme-to-phoneme conversion. Speech Commun. **50**(5), 434–451 (2008)
2. Black, A.W., Lenzo, K., Pagel, V.: Issues in building general letter to sound rules. In: The Third ESCA/COCOSDA Workshop (ETRW) on Speech Synthesis. Jenolan Caves House, Blue Mountains, Australia (1998)
3. Bosse, M.L., Tainturier, M.J., Valdois, S.: Developmental dyslexia: the visual attention span deficit hypothesis. Cognition **104**(2), 198–230 (2007)
4. Goldman, J.P., Laenzlinger, C., Wehrli, E.: La phonétisation de plus, tous et de certains nombres: une analyse phono-syntaxique. Actes de TALN99, Cargese, Corse, pp. 165–174 (1999)
5. Gorman, K., Mazovetskiy, G., Nikolaev, V.: Improving homograph disambiguation with supervised machine learning. In: Proceedings of the Eleventh International Conference on Language Resources and Evaluation (LREC 2018) (2018)
6. Kastner, K., Santos, J.F., Bengio, Y., Courville, A.: Representation mixing for TTS synthesis. In: ICASSP 2019–2019 IEEE International Conference on Acoustics, Speech and Signal Processing (ICASSP), pp. 5906–5910. IEEE (2019)
7. Kumar, A.: NLP pre-trained models explained with examples (2021)
8. Le, H., et al.: Flaubert: unsupervised language model pre-training for French (2019). https://arxiv.org/abs/1912.05372
9. Lenglet, M., Perrotin, O., Bailly, G.: Modélisation de la parole avec tacotron2: analyse acoustique et phonétique des plongements de caractère. In: 34e Journées d'Études sur la Parole (JEP), pp. 845–854. Noirmoutier, France (2022)
10. Nicolis, M., Klimkov, V.: Homograph disambiguation with contextual word embeddings for TTS systems. In: ISCA Speech Synthesis Workshop (SSW), pp. 222–226 (2021). https://doi.org/10.21437/SSW.2021-39
11. Ping, W., et al.: Deep voice 3: scaling text-to-speech with convolutional sequence learning. arXiv preprint arXiv:1710.07654 (2017)
12. Ren, Y., et al.: Fastspeech: fast, robust and controllable text to speech. Adv. Neural Inf. Process. Syst. **32** (2019)
13. Shen, J., et al.: Natural TTS synthesis by conditioning wavenet on mel spectrogram predictions (2018). https://arxiv.org/abs/1712.05884
14. Sun, M., Bellegarda, J.R.: Improved pos tagging for text-to-speech synthesis. In: 2011 IEEE International Conference on Acoustics, Speech and Signal Processing (ICASSP), pp. 5384–5387. IEEE (2011)

15. Taylor, J., Richmond, K.: Analysis of pronunciation learning in end-to-end speech synthesis. In: INTERSPEECH, pp. 2070–2074 (2019)
16. Yao, K., Zweig, G.: Sequence-to-sequence neural net models for grapheme-to-phoneme conversion. arXiv preprint arXiv:1506.00196 (2015)

Detection of Speech Related Disorders by Pre-trained Embedding Models Extracted Biomarkers

Attila Zoltán Jenei, Gábor Kiss, and Dávid Sztahó$^{(\boxtimes)}$

Budapest University of Technology and Economics, Magyar tudósok körútja 2, Budapest 1117, Hungary

jeneia@edu.bme.hu, {kiss.gabor,sztaho.david}@vik.bme.hu

Abstract. Several research studies are conducted to support the diagnosis of certain disorders. Depression, Parkinson's disease and dysphonia are such disorders which can manifest in speech. This provides a non-invasive and rapid method to support/confirm the diagnosis. Knowledge-based acoustic features are heavily researched for each disorder. However, the importance and quantity of these features are still open questions. Moreover, this feature-engineering procedure can be time-consuming and may require more effort for analysis. Therefore, it is a state-of-art approach to use the feature extraction part of an out-of-domain speech recognition system for feature extraction. In our research, x-vector and ECAPA pre-trained models were used to derive feature vectors. Binary and multiclass classification were conducted using Support Vector Machines. Nested cross validation method was applied for cost and gamma parameter selection. Our results pointed out that disorders can be recognized with similar accuracy using pre-trained feature extractors as with knowledge-based features in the case of binary classification. This highlights the opportunity to omit feature engineering for every disorder but use the same out-of-domain feature extractor for classification. On the other hand, with four-class classification better results were achieved than in our previous research where knowledge-based features were used. This supports the idea of robust discrimination between disorders.

Keywords: Biomarkers · Speech · Machine learning · Deep learning · X-Vector · ECAPA · Depression · Parkinson · Pathological speech

1 Introduction

Several studies report speech as a possible biomarker in the recognition of certain disorders. As these disorders disrupt the voice/speech formation system, they may appear in the speech product. Using these acoustic features in the recognition of disorders is an intensive research field [1, 2].

Many modes of speech product can be analyzed for different research purposes: sustained vowels, rapid repetition of syllables, reading or announcing short sentences or texts. For certain disorders (for example depression), the use of longer running text can provide more detailed analysis and more accurate recognition performance [3–5].

© Springer Nature Switzerland AG 2022
S. R. M. Prasanna et al. (Eds.): SPECOM 2022, LNAI 13721, pp. 279–289, 2022.
https://doi.org/10.1007/978-3-031-20980-2_24

Different disorders alter speech in different ways. This research examines depression, Parkinson's disease and dysphonia, which are briefly presented in the followings. Depression is one of the most common psychiatric illnesses. The most typical symptoms are sadness, hopelessness, self-blame and lack of interest [6]. Parkinson's disease is the second most common neurological disease, which is characterized by the death of dopamine-producing cells. Its main symptoms are resting limb tremor, bradykinesia, muscle rigidity and posture abnormalities [7]. Dysphonia is a larger collective term that includes disorders related to changes in the voice-producing system. It can be divided into two large groups following Mathieson: behavioural (hyperfunctional, psychogenic) and organic (e.g. neurogenic or endocrine) dysphonia [8].

Our recent research presented 74.9% [9] and 77.6% [10] accuracy with the above-mentioned disorders using multi-class classification applying time-shift correlation matrices of acoustic features. Experimenting with multi-class classification with all datasets separately, a top 84.7% accuracy was resulted with radial basis function (rbf) based Support Vector Machine (SVM) using several acoustic features [11]. Using Long short-term memory (LSTM) and Autoencoder based binary classification (disorder vs healthy), 85% (Parkinson's disease), 86% (Dysphonia) and 90% (Depression) accuracy were achieved on the test datasets [12]. These achievements going to be compared with the results shown in this study due to the similar database.

Many acoustic features have already been explored to recognize the above-mentioned three disorders as accurately as possible. However, it is still unclear which speech characteristics are necessary and sufficient for the correct classification [13–16].

Therefore, a reasonable approach is to use a general-purpose speaker recognition system trained on hundreds/thousands of speakers for feature extraction (transfer learning for feature extraction). These speech characteristics presumably contain all important information for a given person (and are not limited to certain acoustic/phonetic features). So, they may be applicable for the recognition of speech-related disorders [17].

Botelho and her colleagues examined i-vector and x-vector pre-trained algorithms to recognize Parkinson's disease and obstructive sleep apnea. In their results, they pointed out that the results achieved with traditional features (knowledge-based features) can be overperformed with i-vector and x-vector technologies [18]. Egas-López and his colleagues performed depression recognition using their own and pre-trained x-vectors. They highlighted that better results can be achieved with a self-trained custom x-vector extractor classifier compared to an out-of-domain pre-trained model [19]. Jeancolas and her colleagues also investigated the recognition of Parkinson's disease using x-vector feature extraction. Their studies were compared to the standard Mel-Frequency Cepstral Coefficients - Gaussian Mixture Model (MFCC-GMM). Several experiments were carried out: they examined the quality of the microphone, the length of the recordings and the role of gender in recognition. In their results, they concluded, that the x-vector outperforms the traditional GMM model for text-independent tasks [20].

Currently, there is no clear indication of which approach is more effective. Furthermore, the comparison depends on how the feature-extractor unit was trained, and with which traditional technology it is compared. However, it has the advantage that the researcher does not have to deal with the selection of knowledge-based features.

In this research, feature extraction is carried out with x-vector and ECAPA Time Delay Neural Network (TDNN) models pre-trained on the VoxCeleb [29] dataset. These feature vectors are used to train Support Vector Machines in cross-validation method. Further split is performed for parameter optimization.

In the second Section, we present the scientific methods in detail. The third Section describe the speech databases for each disorder class. The fourth Section illustrates the results of binary classifications. Finally, the fifth Section summarize and highlights the research findings.

2 Methods

2.1 Embedding Models

In this study, we investigate two deep learning based feature extractors for the applicability as a biomarker for disease detection. The deep learning based feature extraction method called x-vector was developed primarily for speaker verification [21]. It is based on a multiple layered DNN architecture (with fully connected layers) with different temporal context at each layer (which they call 'frames'). Due to the wider temporal context, the architecture is called time-delay NN (TDNN). The TDNN embedding architecture can be seen in Fig. 1 and Table 1.

Table 1. The x-vector DNN layer architecture [21]. It contains the layers, contexts and the input, output dimensions.

Layer	Layer context	Total context	Input × Output
Frame1	$[t - 2, t + 2]$	5	120×512
Frame2	$\{t - 2, t, t + 2\}$	9	1536×512
Frame3	$\{t - 3, t, t + 3\}$	15	1536×512
Frame4	$\{t\}$	15	512×512
Frame5	$\{t\}$	15	512×1500
Stats pooling	$[0, T\}$	T	$1500T \times 3000$
Segment6	$\{0\}$	T	3000×512
Segment7	$\{0\}$	T	512×512
Softmax	$\{0\}$	T	$512 \times N$

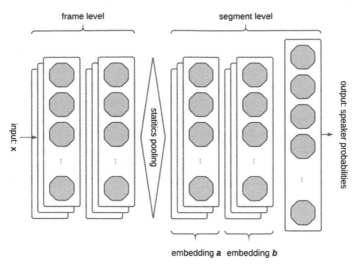

Fig. 1. The x-vector DNN embedding architecture in [21]. The two parts: frame level (with the 5 frame layers) and segment level (with segment6, segment7 and softmax).

The first five layers operate on speech frames, with small temporal context centered at the current frame t. For example, the frame indexed as 3 sees a total of 15 frames, due to the temporal context of the earlier layers. After training with disease types as target vectors, the output of layer *segment6* ('x-vector') is used as input to a classifier. The dimension of the x-vectors was set to 512.

The ECAPA-TDNN model is the extension of the x-vector model architecture in three ways [22]: channel- and context-dependent statistics pooling, 1-Dimensional Squeeze-Excitation Res2Blocks (1D SE-Res2Block) and multi-layer feature aggregation and summation. The channel- and context-dependent statistics pooling enables the network to focus more on speaker characteristics that do not activate on identical or similar time instances, e.g. speaker-specific properties of vowels versus speaker-specific properties of consonants. Using the SE-Res2Block (taken from the field of computer vision), the limited frame context of the x-vector (15) is extended to global properties of the recording. The multi-layer feature aggregation means that not only the activation of the selected deep layer is used as a feature map (as in x-vector), but the shallower layers (here: SE-Res2Blocks) are also concatenated, because they also hold information about the speaker identity. The architecture is shown in Fig. 2. The dimension of the extracted embedding vector was 192. Both models pre-trained on the VoxCeleb dataset (VoxCeleb1 + Voxceleb2) were downloaded from Huggingface (https://huggingface.co/speechbrain/spkrec-ecapa-voxceleb and https://huggingface.co/speechbrain/spkrec-xvect-voxceleb).

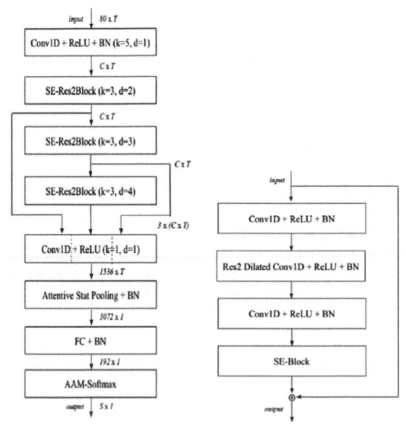

Fig. 2. The ECAPA-TDNN layer architecture (left) and its SE-Res2Block (right).

2.2 Classification

SVM [23] was chosen as the learning method for classification. The LibSVM [24] implementation was used with rbf and linear kernels.

The SVM models were trained and tested with 10-fold cross-validation. The accuracy of SVM is highly dependent on the proper choice of hyperparameters (cost and gamma). Thus, we also implemented the optimization of the models using 10-fold cross-validation on the selected training data set. This double cross-validation is called nested loop [25]. The advantage of the method is that the train, development and test sets are completely independent of each other, thus minimizing the possibility of overfitting, and gives a realistic overview of the accuracy and generalizability of the given method. The hyperparameters (cost and gamma) were optimized using the grid search method, where powers of 2 were tried between -10 and $+10$. All the calculated features were included in the feature vector, where the feature values were normalized between -1 and $+1$.

We created classification models with two classes, separating subjects with a given disorder and control subjects (one disorder vs healthy), and multiple classes, separating subjects with all the examined disorders and healthy subjects (all disorders vs healthy).

2.3 Evaluation Metrics

Since the individual data sets were not the same size, we chose UAR (un-weighted average recall) as the primary evaluation metric. Moreover, the accuracy was also calculated. In addition to the results achieved on test sets, we provide the results obtained during the optimization (by averaging the results of the inner cross-validation), which is marked with an asterisk.

3   Evaluation Datasets

The biomarkers were evaluated on three disorder types separately from which speech samples were available: (1) depression (DE), (2) Parkinson's disease (PD) and (3) organic and functional voice disorders (VD). For each dataset, healthy speakers are included as a control population. All speakers read the approximately one-minute-long tale 'The North Wind and the Sun'. Table 2 shows the descriptive statistics of the disease categories. For the sake of completeness (explicitly not used in the study), the severity statistics are also shown. The severity levels are measured with the BDI scale [26], Hoehn & Jahr scale [27] and the RBH scale [28] for depression, PD and VD, respectively. All recordings were resampled to 16 kHz sampling rate and 16-bit quantization. All speakers gave their signed consent to record their voice and use it for research purposes.

Table 2. Descriptive statistics of the disease categories and healthy class.

Category	Gender	Number of samples	Mean and standard deviation of age	Mean and standard deviation of severity
Depression	Female	85	37.7 ± 13.4	27.7 ± 8.9
	Male	46	40.1 ± 13.5	25.8 ± 7.9
Parkinson's disease	Female	40	65.4 ± 9.4	2.7 ± 1.1
	Male	45	64.0 ± 9.5	2.7 ± 1.1
Organic and functional voice disorder	Female	159	57.3 ± 14.8	1.7 ± 0.8
	Male	103	53.7 ± 15.1	2.0 ± 0.8
Healthy control	Female	133	48.5 ± 14.7	–
	Male	95	47.6 ± 19.9	–

4   Results

Table 3 contains the results of two-class classification experiments. "UAR*" and "Accuracy*" show the results achieved in the inner cross-validation, i.e. the estimated goodness of the model based on optimization.

Table 3. Results of two-class classification for each disorder

Examined disorder	Embedding method	Kernel	UAR	Accuracy	UAR*	Accuracy*
Depression	ECAPA	Linear	71%	74%	72%	75%
		rbf	72%	75%	73%	75%
	x-Vector	Linear	84%	86%	85%	87%
		rbf	**84%**	**86%**	**86%**	**88%**
Parkinson's disease	ECAPA	Linear	85%	89%	86%	90%
		rbf	85%	90%	86%	91%
	x-Vector	Linear	91%	94%	92%	94%
		rbf	**91%**	**94%**	**93%**	**95%**
Organic and functional voice disorder	ECAPA	Linear	92%	92%	93%	93%
		rbf	92%	92%	93%	93%
	x-Vector	Linear	92%	92%	93%	93%
		rbf	**93%**	**92%**	**93%**	**93%**

Examining the results (Table 3), it can be concluded that there was no overfitting, since the difference between the estimated (*) and the test results is not significant. Using the RBF kernel, we generally obtained better or the same results as using the linear kernel, however, the difference was within 1%, i.e., not significant either. The most significant difference was found between the embedding methods, where x-vector performed better in the case of depression and Parkinson's disease. In these cases, the relative reduction of the error was around 40%, while in the case of organic and functional voice disorder the performance of two embedding methods was similar.

Table 4. Results of four-class classification

Embedding method	Kernel	UAR	Accuracy	UAR*	Accuracy*
ECAPA	Linear	70%	75%	71%	75%
	rbf	70%	75%	72%	76%
x-vector	Linear	80%	83%	82%	84%
	rbf	**81%**	**84%**	**82%**	**85%**

In the case of the 4-class classification (Table 4), the same phenomena can be observed as in the case of the 2-class classification, that is, the most significant difference is between the use of x-vector or ECAPA, where x-vector performed better in this case as well. In the case of multi-class classification, it is also worth checking the confusion matrix, since neither the UAR nor the accuracy adequately shows how accurately the individual classes were recognized. Table 5 shows the confusion matrix of the four-class classification experiment using x-vector and rbf kernel.

Table 5. Confusion matrix of four-class classification

		True class				
		Depression	Organic and functional voice disordered	Healthy control	Parkinson's disease	Class precisions
Predicted class	Depression	**94**	3	13	5	82%
	Organic and functional voice disordered	2	**231**	10	2	94%
	Healthy control	27	27	**202**	14	75%
	Parkinson's disease	8	1	3	**64**	84%
	Class recalls	72%	88%	89%	75%	

In the case of the healthy control group and the organic and functional voice disorder classes, we got 89–88% for recall, while in the case of depression and Parkinson's disease, we got only 72–75% for recall (Table 5). On the other hand, in the case of precision, the lowest value was obtained for the healthy control group (75%), thus, it can be stated that in the case of a given disorder, the model did not wrongly decide on another disorder, but instead decided on the healthy control group.

5   Discussion

The obtained results show that the applied features indeed hold information about the voice disorder types. The binary classification experiments show different performance for the voice disorders investigated in the present study. The best classified disorder were Parkinson's disease and organic and structural voice disorders (91% and 93% UAR). The UAR of depression was a bit lower (84%). This can be due to the nature of the deep learning based features. They are developed mostly for speaker recognition and generally meant to capture the spectrum (and its short time variation) of the speaker. Because speech features related to intonation play a great role in depression, this information may not be captured by TDNN-based features.

The four-class classification experiments show that the derived features can distinguish the given voice disorders. It is a very important factor, because it is always an argument against speech-based biomarkers that implementing binary classification scenarios (a disorder against the healthy population) doesn't ensure that the trained model will not predict a sample as disordered for a sample affected by a completely different disease. The four-class results show the applied features have distinctive power (between the disorders used here).

Binary classifications provided about the same results as we achieved previously with knowledge-based acoustic features. Depression was classified with 4% lower accuracy here (in absolute), but Parkinson's disease and Dysphonia reached 9% and 6% higher accuracy (in absolute) in this study than before, respectively. Furthermore, four-class classification appeared more robust and discriminative with out-of-domain deep learning feature extractor as with the use of acoustic features (6.4% accuracy difference).

An interesting observation is that the x-vector outperforms the newer ECAPA-TDNN models. One should expect the ECAPA-TDNN performs better, because it is superior in speaker recognition. This was not the case here when it is applied to a different domain. The x-vector was clearly superior, even with the original vector size and no dimension reduction (such as PCA or LDA, which are commonly used in speaker recognition).

The confusion matrix of the four-class experiment (Table 5) shows that there is little misclassification between the voice disorder categories. If a sample is classified into a wrong class, it is mostly categorized as healthy. It can be a good behavior of a possible diagnostic support tool. To control the recall and precision (also sensitivity and specificity) metrics, the decision threshold can be calibrated for a given class. However, binary models can be more suitable for a decision support tool, because in a multi-class scenario many questions arise: how to control unseen disease categories, how to control imbalanced datasets.

These observations make the x-vector based features proper biomarkers for detecting diseases from speech and to build a diagnostic support tool. The calculation of the features (once the models are trained offline) are fast and doesn't need much computation power. Also, they show robust performance in various diseases. The possible extension of the current study is to extend the data with multi-lingual recording to see the language dependency of the given features, experiment with dimension reduction methods for x-vector and apply multiple classification techniques besides SVM.

Acknowledgements. The work was funded by project no. K128568 that has been implemented with the support provided from the National Research, Development and Innovation Fund of Hungary, financed under the K_18 funding scheme.

References

1. Robin, J., Harrison, J.E., Kaufman, L.D., Rudzicz, F., Simpson, W., Yancheva, M.: Evaluation of speech-based digital biomarkers: review and recommendations. Digital Biomarkers **4**(3), 99–108 (2020). https://doi.org/10.1159/000510820
2. Ramanarayanan, V., Lammert, A.C., Rowe, H.P., Quatieri, T.F., Green, J.R.: Speech as a biomarker: opportunities, interpretability, and challenges. Perspect. ASHA Spec. Interest Groups **7**(1), 276–283 (2022)
3. Pompili, A., et al.: Automatic detection of parkinson's disease: an experimental analysis of common speech production tasks used for diagnosis. In: Ekštein, K., Matoušek, V. (eds.) TSD 2017. LNCS (LNAI), vol. 10415, pp. 411–419. Springer, Cham (2017). https://doi.org/10.1007/978-3-319-64206-2_46
4. Liu, Y., Lee, T., Ching, P.C., Law, T.K., Lee, K.Y.: Acoustic assessment of disordered voice with continuous speech based on utterance-level ASR posterior features. IEEE/ACM Trans. Audio, Speech, Lang. Process. **27**(6), 1047–1059 (2019)

5. Vadovsky, M., Paralic, J.: Parkinson's disease patients classification based on the speech signals. In: 2017 IEEE 15th International Symposium on Applied Machine Intelligence and Informatics (SAMI), pp. 321–326. Herl'any, Slovakia (2017)
6. Rejaibi, E., Komaty, A., Meriaudeau, F., Agrebi, S., Othmani, A.: MFCC-based recurrent neural network for automatic clinical depression recognition and assessment from speech. Biomed. Signal Process. Control **71**, 103107 (2022). https://doi.org/10.1016/j.bspc.2021.103107
7. Balestrino, R., Schapira, A.H.V.: Parkinson disease. Eur. J. Neurol. **27**(1), 27–42 (2020). https://doi.org/10.1111/ene.14108
8. Mathieson, L.: Green and Mathieson's the Voice & its Disorders. Whurr Publishers (2001)
9. Jenei, A.Z., Kiss, G., Tulics, M.G., Sztahó, D.: Separation of several illnesses using correlation structures with convolutional neural networks. Acta Polytech. Hung. **18**(7), 47–66 (2021). https://doi.org/10.12700/APH.18.7.2021.7.3
10. Sztahó, D., et al.: Automatic separation of various disease types by correlation structure of time shifted speech features. In: 2018 41st International Conference on Telecommunications and Signal Processing (TSP). IEEE, pp. 1–4. Greece, Athens (2018)
11. Sztahó, D., Kiss, G., Tulics, M. G., Vicsi, K.: Automatic discrimination of several types of speech pathologies. In: 2019 International Conference on Speech Technology and Human-Computer Dialogue (SpeD), pp. 1–6. IEEE, Timisoara, Romania (2019)
12. Sztahó, D., Gábor, K., Miklós, G.T.: Deep learning solution for pathological voice detection using LSTM-based autoencoder hybrid with multi-task learning. In: 14th International Conference on Bio-Inspired Systems and Signal Processing (BIOSIGNALS), pp. 135–141. Vienna, Austria (2021)
13. Patil, M., Wadhai, V.: Selection of classifiers for depression detection using acoustic features. In: 2021 International Conference on Computational Intelligence and Computing Applications (ICCICA), pp. 1–4. Nagpur, India (2021)
14. Verde, L., et al.: A lightweight machine learning approach to detect depression from speech analysis. In: 2021 IEEE 33rd International Conference on Tools with Artificial Intelligence (ICTAI), pp. 330–335. Washington, DC, USA (2021)
15. Braga, D., Madureira, A.M., Coelho, L., Ajith, R.: Automatic detection of Parkinson's disease based on acoustic analysis of speech. Eng. Appl. Artif. Intell. **7**, 148–158 (2019)
16. Umapathy, S., Rachel, S., Thulasi, R.: Automated speech signal analysis based on feature extraction and classification of spasmodic dysphonia: a performance comparison of different classifiers. Int. J. Speech Technol. **21**(1), 9–18 (2017). https://doi.org/10.1007/s10772-017-9471-8
17. Harati, A., et al.: Speech-based depression prediction using encoder-weight-only transfer learning and a large corpus. In: 2021 IEEE International Conference on Acoustics. Speech and Signal Processing (ICASSP), pp. 7273–7277. ON, Canada, Toronto (2021)
18. Botelho, C., Teixeira, F., Rolland, T., Abad, A., Trancoso, I.: Pathological speech detection using x-vector embeddings. arXiv preprint arXiv:2003.00864 (2020)
19. Egas-López, J.V., Kiss, G., Sztahó, D., Gosztolya, G.: Automatic assessment of the degree of clinical depression from speech using X-vectors. In: 2022 IEEE International Conference on Acoustics, Speech and Signal Processing (ICASSP), pp. 8502–8506. Singapore (2022)
20. Jeancolas, L., et al.: X-Vectors: new quantitative biomarkers for early Parkinson's disease detection from speech. Front. Neuroinform. **15**, 578369 (2021)
21. Snyder, D., Garcia-Romero, D., Povey, D., Khudanpur, S.: Deep neural network embeddings for text-independent speaker verification. In: Interspeech 2017, pp. 999–1003. Stockholm, Sweden (2017)
22. Desplanques, B., Thienpondt, J., Demuynck, K.: Ecapa-tdnn: Emphasized channel attention, propagation and aggregation in tdnn based speaker verification. arXiv preprint arXiv:2005.07143. (2020)

23. Cortes, C., Vapnik, V.: Support vector networks. Mach. Learn. **20**(3), 273–297 (1995)
24. Chang, C.-C., Lin, C.-J.: LIBSVM: a library for support vector machines. ACM Trans. Intel. Syst. Technol. (TIST) **2**(3), 1–27 (2011)
25. Gosztolya, G., Vincze, V., Tóth, L., Pákáski, M., Kálmán, J., Hoffmann, I.: Identifying mild cognitive impairment and mild Alzheimer's disease based on spontaneous speech using ASR and linguistic features. Comput. Speech Lang. **53**, 181–197 (2019)
26. Beck, A.T., Steer, R.A., Ball, R., Ranieri, W.F.: Comparison of beck depression inventories -IA and -II in psychiatric outpatients. J. Pers. Assess. **67**(3), 588–597 (1996)
27. Hoehn, M., Yahr, M.D.: Parkinsonism onset, progression, and mortality. Neurology **17**(5), 427–442 (1967)
28. Gaber, A.G.H., Liang, F.-Y., Yang, J.-S., Wang, Y.-J., Zheng, Y.-Q.: Correlation among the dysphonia severity index (DSI), the RBH voice perceptual evaluation, and minimum glottal area in female patients with vocal fold nodules. J. Voice **28**(1), 20–23 (2014)
29. Chung, J. S., Nagrani, A., Zisserman, A.: VoxCeleb2: deep speaker recognition. In: Proceedings of the Interspeech 2018, pp. 1086–1090. Hyderabad, India (2018)

Multi-label Dysfluency Classification

Melanie Jouaiti[✉] and Kerstin Dautenhahn

Electrical and Computer Engineering Department, University of Waterloo,
200 University Ave, Waterloo, ON N2L3G1, Canada
{mjouaiti,kerstin.dautenhahn}@uwaterloo.ca

Abstract. Stuttering is a neuro-developmental disorder represented in 1% of the population. Dysfluency classification is still an open research question, with concerns of which feature representation or which classifier to use. Another issue, which has been neglected so far, is how to deal with audio samples that contain more than one type of dysfluency. Research has mostly preferred considering only single-labels problems, in part due to the lack of substantial multi-labels datasets. However, the FluencyBank and SEP-28K datasets are now available and contain multi-label data, which should pave the way for more research taking this aspect into account.

In this paper, we give an overview of different ways to handle multi-label classification and compare them, while fine-tuning the ResNet50 network to perform multi-label dysfluency classification. We show that, fine-tuning the ResNet50, independently of the label representation, performs better than current state of the art results.

Keywords: Dysfluency classification · Transfer learning · Multi-label classification

1 Introduction

Stuttering is a neuro-developmental disorder represented in 1% of the population. It can be identified by anomalies of speech such as pauses, repetition, prolongation of words or sounds and the use of interjections as filler words ("hum"). Automatic dysfluency classification would be an invaluable tool, especially in the context of speech therapy, so that therapists can track patients' progress but also as an integral part of technology-assisted speech therapy.

An important and still open problem of speech classification and generally of sound classification, is to find an appropriate feature representation. Most works consider the frequency domain, using features such as modulation spectrum [24], FFT [28,29], spectrograms [11,12], MFFCs [2,16,19,22,25]. Others tried to use some biological data (heart-rate, respiratory air volume and air flow) [30] or some speech analysis features (pitch, linguistic, duration, gestural, speech rate) [9,9,33], or even demographics (age, gender) [4].

In this work, we will use a spectrogram representation. While CNNs are now the go-to solution for image classification tasks, LSTMs are usually used

© Springer Nature Switzerland AG 2022
S. R. M. Prasanna et al. (Eds.): SPECOM 2022, LNAI 13721, pp. 290–301, 2022.
https://doi.org/10.1007/978-3-031-20980-2_25

for speech tasks. There are, however, a great many more works on image classification than in speech classification, so using a spectrogram representation (considering it as an image) allows us to harness the power of computer vision for our dysfluency classification task. Deep learning methods are growing in popularity but deep learning requires a very large amount of labeled data, which is a problem in the stuttering community as there are few datasets and most of them have few data. A popular and effective way to circumvent this issue consists in fine-tuning a pre-trained network.

Moreover, dysfluency classification has mostly been approached, so far, from the easier perspective of single label classification but even in single label datasets, such as the UCLASS dataset [8], there is an overlap for some audio clips so, some of the data is actually multi-label. Single labels may, therefore, not reflect the data accurately. This oversight was probably due to the lack of truly multi-label datasets, however, recently Lea et al. curated two multi-label datasets: FleuncyBank and SEP-28K [15]. To our knowledge, only Lea et al. attempted multi-label classification so far, though they did not provide detailed information on how they handled it.

In this paper, we undertake multi-label dysfluency classification by fine-tuning a ResNet using the spectrogram amplitude of the audio clip as an image for our input features and test our system on the FluencyBank and SEP-28K datasets. We compare performance using different label representations.

2   Related Work

Transfer learning in speech processing has become increasingly popular in the last few years (See [31, 32] for reviews). One favoured applications with significant performance improvements is Speech Emotion Recognition in cross-language or cross-corpus contexts [3, 14]. It has also been used for several Automatic Speech Recognition (ASR) tasks, such as generalizing English ASR to German ASR, when memory and lack of data were an issue [13], transferring knowledge learned from adults' voices to children's voices [27], or for multi-lingual DNN to generalize between native languages and learnt languages [18].

More specifically, using a pre-trained ResNet, transfer learning is a suitable approach for Speech Emotion Recognition, with several works using the mel-spectrogram of the audio as an input [6, 20]. Extracting features from mel-spectrograms with a ResNet has also been applied to speech intelligibility prediction [17] and spoofing attacks detection [1].

While, stuttering detection and dysfluency classification have been tackled from different angles (See [11, 26] for reviews), some methods work on text transcripts [5, 34], while others focus on the audio data, and more accurately on finding a suitable representation of speech. The most popular input feature remains the mel-frequency cepstral coefficients (MFCCs). However, obtained results have been overall underwhelming and it has mostly been used for binary detection: detect syllable repetitions using perceptron and dynamic time warping [23] or classify prolongation versus repetition with K-nearest neighbours and Linear Discriminant Analysis [2].

Machine learning and deep learning methods have also been investigated and have recently become increasingly popular. Using a deep neural network, Oue et al. detected repetitions in dysarthric speech, using MFCCs and linear predictive cepstral coefficients [19]. StutterNet, a neural network based on Time Delay Neural Networks and using MFCCs as well, has also been proposed to classify dysfluency from the UCLASS datasets [25]. Recurrent neural networks (RNN) have surprisingly been underused, despite the temporal nature of speech data. Recently, a LSTM-based network has been put forward to classify dysfluency and tested on the FluencyBank and SEP-28K datasets, with good results, using a combination of speech features, such as mel-filterbank energy features, pitch information and articulatory features [15]. Combining a ResNet and BiLSTM also yielded very good results on 25 files of the UCLASS dataset when applied on audio spectrograms [11].

3   Method

3.1   Datasets

In this paper, we performed a comparison of performance using different label representations on two different multi-label datasets. First, we used the FluencyBank dataset [21], which contains recordings from 32 adults who stutter. We used the dataset re-annotated by [15], due to inaccuracies in temporal alignments for the original annotations. We discarded files where the annotations were labelled as "unsure". Second, we also employed the SEP-28K dataset. This dataset, manually curated by [15], contains 28 177 clips extracted from publicly available podcasts. We also removed all files where the annotations were labelled as "unsure". Both datasets are labelled with 12 classes which can be combined into eight main classes: silence, music, fluent, word-repetitions (wordrep), sound-repetitions (soundrep), prolongations, interjections and blocks. In both datasets, audio clips can belong to more than one class and the number of occurrences of each class in an audio clip can be more than one. As both datasets are very imbalanced, we set class weights appropriately. There are no samples annotated as music or silence in the FluencyBank dataset.

We had approval from the University of Waterloo's Research Ethics Board to process those datasets.

3.2   Transfer Learning

Transfer learning is often motivated by "Learning to Learn", i.e. try to generalize past experience to new tasks, as opposed to learning from scratch, which is often time-consuming or limited. It consists in re-training a network on new data, thus transferring the knowledge already learned by the network to a new task. Transfer learning is particularly relevant when computational resources or data are lacking.

In this work, we used a ResNet50 pre-trained on ImageNet [7]. ResNet50 is a 50-layers residual network that tries to solve the vanishing gradient and degradation problems. This kind of network attempts to learn residuals instead of features. It has been extensively used in image classification and recognition tasks with good results.

To fine-tune ResNet50, we removed the classification layer and appended a Dropout (0.8) layer and a fully connected layer with l2-regularization (0.001). We fine-tuned the entire network for 100 epochs with a batch size of 4, using the Adam optimizer, with a learning rate of $1e^{-4}$ and with early-stopping (patience = 5). To rigorously test the fine-tuned model, we employed 10-fold cross validation where each audio file is randomly assigned to one fold. We conducted 10 experiments where the networks learns on 90% of the data and tests on the remaining 10%. The reported results represent the average of the 10 test experiments. For each tested method, the data is split in the same way to ensure that each model is tested in the same conditions. We ran our experiments on a GeForce RTX 2060 GPU.

3.3 Input Features

ResNet50 expects a RGB image of size $(224, 224)$ as the input. We therefore use the spectrogram amplitude of the audio-clip (257×188), resized to the expected size as the input feature (See Fig. 1 for examples of audio clips and their image representation). Due to memory limitations, the audio clip is first downsampled to 8 kHz and padded with 0 if it is shorter than 3 s. The audio is then converted to a spectrogram image and we reduced its brightness and increase its contrast before normalizing it between 0 and 1. The audio processing is performed with the librosa library.

$$\text{img} = log(1 + \text{amplitude\_of\_spectrogram}(\text{stft}(\text{audio}))) \tag{1}$$

3.4 Label Representation

Multi-label problems can be approached in several different ways:

- Transform the multi-label problem into a single label problem, so that we can use a hard one-hot label. To compute the new label, we convert to base 10 a binary representation of the labels where the 6 bits are, respectively, *fluent, wordrep, soundrep, prolongation, interjection, block*. We now have labels between 0 and 63. *Music* and *silence* are classes 64 and 65. This thus yields 66 very unbalanced classes (See Fig. 2). The activation of the classification layer is softmax and the loss is categorical cross-entropy.
- Use boolean multi-labels where each value in the label arrays being 0 or 1. The activation of the classification layer is sigmoid and the loss is binary cross-entropy, so that each class is handled independently.
- Use soft labels, by normalizing the label arrays. The activation of the classification layer is sigmoid and the loss is binary cross-entropy.

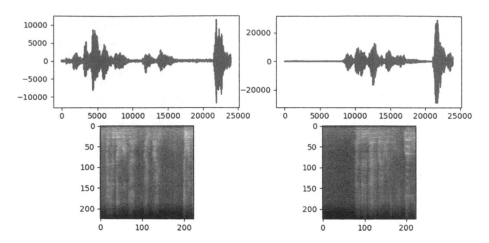

Fig. 1. Examples of audio clips and their corresponding image. On the left: example of word repetition, on the right: exàmple of fluent speech.

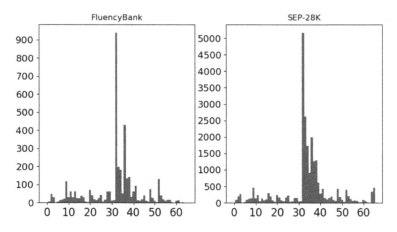

Fig. 2. Histogram of the distribution of samples in each class for the one-hot 66 classes representation. We can see that both datasets are very imbalanced.

3.5   Metrics

We will use several metrics to evaluate performance in this work: accuracy, recall, F1-score. However, these are not suitable to evaluate performance in the case of soft labels and are not giving an accurate view of performance for multi-label classification. We are therefore also using the Hamming score and the Exact Match Ratio which are more suitable for multi-label classification. We are also reporting results with the Kullback-Leibler KL-divergence, Jensen-Shannon JS-divergence and Mean Square Error, which are appropriate for soft labels.

The Hamming score is a forgiving way to compute accuracy in multi-labels problems as it considers partially correct predictions:

$$Hamming(T, P) = \frac{1}{n} \sum_{k}^{n} \frac{T[k] \&\& P[k]}{T[k] || P[k]} \tag{2}$$

with n the number of samples, $P[k]$ and $T[k]$ the predicted and expected label for sample k.

Table 1. Results on the FluencyBank and SEP-28K datasets.

FluencyBank	Accuracy	Hamming	KL	JS	MSE	Recall	F1	EMR
One-hot	53.79 (21.16)	48.74 (20.45)	3.88 (2.48)	0.45 (0.2)	**0.01 (0.005)**	53.78 (21.16)	55.86 (20.5)	48.74 (20.45)
Soft-label	NA	NA	**0.72 (0.24)**	**0.15 (0.07)**	0.019 (0.007)	NA	NA	NA
Multi-label	**66.49 (14.83)**	**80.01 (8.31)**	1.48 (0.82)	0.33 (0.15)	0.06 (0.03)	**56.78 (8.49)**	**65.83 (6.62)**	**66.49 (14.83)**
SEP-28K	Accuracy	Hamming	KL	JS	MSE	Recall	F1	EMR
One-hot	57.5 (11.86)	38.96 (4.73)	2.81 (0.38)	0.46 (0.05)	**0.009 (0.001)**	55.5 (6.86)	59.03(6.4)	38.63 (4.8)
Soft-label	NA	NA	**0.7 (0.3)**	**0.1 (0.04)**	0.015 (0.006)	NA	NA	NA
Multi-label	**72.95 (10.71)**	**84.44 (6.6)**	1.9 (0.77)	0.24 (0.1)	0.056 (0.02)	**56.37 (5.76)**	**66.6 (4.64)**	**72.95 (10.71)**

The Exact Match Ratio (EMR) is an evaluation metric to compute the accuracy of a multi-label classification problem. The EMR metrics is strict as it does not account for partially correct labels:

$$EMR(T, P) = \frac{1}{n} \sum_{k}^{n} I(T[k] == P[k]) \tag{3}$$

where I is the indicator function.

The KL-divergence is usually used for soft-labels problems and computes the difference between the expected and predicted probability distributions:

$$KL(T, P) = \sum_{k}^{n} T[k] \cdot log_2(T[k]/P[k]) \tag{4}$$

The JS-divergence provides a smoothed symmetrical version of KL-divergence:

$$JS(T, P) = 0.5 \cdot KL(T, M) + 0.5 \cdot KL(P, M) \tag{5}$$

with $M = 0.5 \cdot (P + T)$

Moreover, the Mean Squared Error (MSE) is also often used to evaluate soft-labels classification:

$$MSE(T, P) = \frac{1}{n} \sum_{k}^{n} (T[k] - P[k])^2 \tag{6}$$

4   Results

Table 1 gives an overview of the results. The one-hot encoding leads to lower MSE than the other representations (See Fig. 3 for the confusion matrix).

The soft-label representation (See Fig. 4 for the ROC curves), however, yields lower KL- and JS-divergence than the other two label representations. Finally the boolean multi-label representation (See Fig. 5 and 6 for the confusion matrix of the each dataset and Fig. 7 for the ROC curves) achieved a higher recall, accuracy, F1-score, Hamming score and EMR. Those results are consistent across both datasets. The only discrepancy appears for the accuracy which is highest for the one-hot encoding in the case of FluencyBank but highest for the boolean multi-label representation for the SEP-28K dataset.

Besides, to our knowledge, only Lea et al. attempted multi-label classification previously [15]. They reported classification results for each class, by considering each class independently. That is, if a clip belongs to the *fluent* and the *interjection* class and the network classifies it as *interjection* only, the clip will be considered as correctly classified for the *interjection* class and incorrectly for the *fluent* class. We therefore also report those results for the boolean multi-label representation and compare our results with theirs (See Table 2). Our results by fine-tuning are consistently better than their reported results, by a large margin.

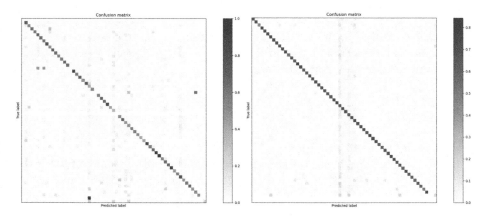

Fig. 3. Confusion matrix for the one-hot representation. Left: FluencyBank, Right: SEP-28K.

5   Discussion

The main limitation of the one-hot encoding, is that it creates classes with very few samples or even none. This strongly biases the metrics when computed with macro average, we therefore reported weighted average results in this paper.

Moreover, it is harder to accurately compare the soft-label representation with the other ones as the accuracy, Hamming, EMR, recall, and F1-scores are not available for soft labels.

Furthermore, the UCLASS dataset [8] is another popular dataset, available as a single label dataset. However, there is some overlap of audio clips, in the case of a sentence with multiple dysfluencies. Indeed, they extracted several audio clips, each centred around one dysfluency, thus sometimes the difference between two audio clips is as small as several milliseconds. So this dataset should probably be re-labeled to take this into account.

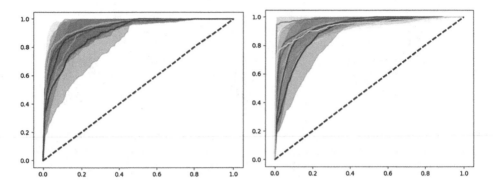

Fig. 4. Mean ROC curves and standard deviation for the soft labels. Left: FluencyBank; right: SEP-28K(blue: fluent, green: wordrep, red: soundrep, orange: prolongation, cyan: interjection, purple: block, grey: music, yellow: silence). (Color figure online)

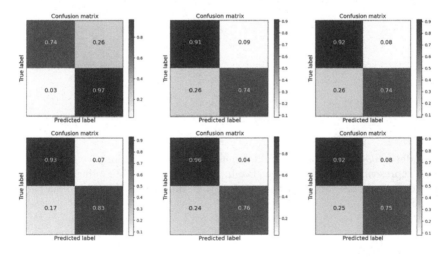

Fig. 5. Confusion matrices for the multi-label boolean representation in the Fluency-Bank dataset. The matrices represent one-over-rest performance for each class (respectively fluent, word repetition, sound repetition, interjection, prolongation and block).

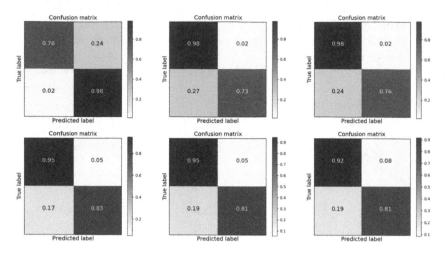

Fig. 6. Confusion matrices for the multi-label boolean representation in the SEP-28K dataset. The matrices represent one-over-rest performance for each class (respectively fluent, word repetition, sound repetition, interjection, prolongation and block).

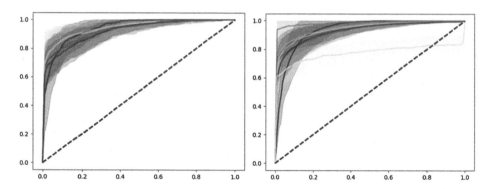

Fig. 7. Mean ROC curves and standard deviation (shaded region) for the multi-label boolean representation. Left: FluencyBank; right: SEP-28K (blue: fluent, green: wordrep, red: soundrep, orange: prolongation, cyan: interjection, purple: block). (Color figure online)

Besides, fine-tuning a ResNet lead to a very good performance, though this type of network is usually associated to images. This leads us to believe that fine-tuning a network that already learned a good representation of speech, such as a speech transformer, could lead to even better results.

Table 2. Results of the boolean multi-label classification when considering the 8 classes by themselves.

FluencyBank	Accuracy	Recall	F1	F1 [15]
Fluent	91.18	85.49	87.44	NA
WordRep	87.42	82.66	**83.04**	59.3
SoundRep	87.54	83.16	**83.7**	74.3
Interjection	88.96	88.04	**88.37**	71.3
Prolongation	91.29	86.02	**86.91**	67.9
Block	86.12	83.08	**83.74**	56.8
SEP-28K	Accuracy	Recall	F1	F1 [15]
Fluent	94.19	86.97	89.4	NA
WordRep	93.72	85.51	**87.72**	60.4
SoundRep	94.17	86.83	**89.06**	63.2
Interjection	90.73	88.85	**89.54**	71.3
Prolongation	90.37	87.66	**88.35**	68.5
Block	87.17	86.07	**88.86**	55.9
Music	99.77	96.17	96.16	NA
Silence	98.59	78.04	83.15	NA

6   Conclusion

In multi-label classification, the different ways of encoding the labels have a strong influence over the performance. In this paper, we fine-tuned a ResNet50, using different label representations and compared their performance, in terms of accuracy, recall, F1-score, Hamming score, EMR, KL-divergence and JS-divergence. Encoding the labels into a Boolean representation appears to yield the best performance. Moreover, fine-tuning the ResNet for any type of label encoding performs better than current state of the art reported results [10]. We hope that these results will contribute to the development of high-quality, automatic dysfluency classification as a automatic evaluation and monitoring tool to be used in the context of speech therapy. In future works, we will try to improve generalization.

Acknowledgments. This research was undertaken, in part, thanks to funding from the Canada 150 Research Chairs Program.

References

1. Aravind, P., Nechiyil, U., Paramparambath, N., et al.: Audio spoofing verification using deep convolutional neural networks by transfer learning. arXiv preprint arXiv:2008.03464 (2020)

2. Chee, L.S., Ai, O.C., Hariharan, M., Yaacob, S.: MFCC based recognition of repetitions and prolongations in stuttered speech using k-NN and LDA. In: 2009 IEEE Student Conference on Research and Development (SCOReD), pp. 146–149. IEEE (2009)
3. Deng, J., Zhang, Z., Marchi, E., Schuller, B.: Sparse autoencoder-based feature transfer learning for speech emotion recognition. In: 2013 Humaine Association Conference on Affective Computing and Intelligent Interaction, pp. 511–516. IEEE (2013)
4. Geetha, Y., Pratibha, K., Ashok, R., Ravindra, S.K.: Classification of childhood disfluencies using neural networks. J. Fluen. Disord. **25**(2), 99–117 (2000)
5. Georgila, K.: Using integer linear programming for detecting speech disfluencies. In: Proceedings of Human Language Technologies: The 2009 Annual Conference of the North American Chapter of the Association for Computational Linguistics, Companion Volume: Short Papers, pp. 109–112 (2009)
6. Gerczuk, M., Amiriparian, S., Ottl, S., Schuller, B.W.: EmoNet: a transfer learning framework for multi-corpus speech emotion recognition. IEEE Trans. Affect. Comput. (2021)
7. He, K., Zhang, X., Ren, S., Sun, J.: Deep residual learning for image recognition. In: Proceedings of the IEEE Conference on Computer Vision and Pattern Recognition, pp. 770–778 (2016)
8. Howell, P., Davis, S., Bartrip, J.: The university college London archive of stuttered speech (UCLASS) (2009)
9. Howell, P., Sackin, S., Glenn, K.: Development of a two-stage procedure for the automatic recognition of dysfluencies in the speech of children who stutter: I. Psychometric procedures appropriate for selection of training material for lexical dysfluency classifiers. J. Speech Lang. Hear. Res. **40**(5), 1073–1084 (1997)
10. Jouaiti, M., Dautenhahn, K.: Dysfluency classification in stuttered speech using deep learning for real-time applications. In: ICASSP 2022–2022 IEEE International Conference on Acoustics, Speech and Signal Processing (ICASSP), pp. 6482–6486 (2022). https://doi.org/10.1109/ICASSP43922.2022.9746638
11. Kourkounakis, T., Hajavi, A., Etemad, A.: Detecting multiple speech disfluencies using a deep residual network with bidirectional long short-term memory. In: ICASSP 2020–2020 IEEE International Conference on Acoustics, Speech and Signal Processing (ICASSP), pp. 6089–6093. IEEE (2020)
12. Kourkounakis, T., Hajavi, A., Etemad, A.: FluentNet: end-to-end detection of speech disfluency with deep learning. arXiv preprint arXiv:2009.11394 (2020)
13. Kunze, J., Kirsch, L., Kurenkov, I., Krug, A., Johannsmeier, J., Stober, S.: Transfer learning for speech recognition on a budget. arXiv preprint arXiv:1706.00290 (2017)
14. Latif, S., Rana, R., Younis, S., Qadir, J., Epps, J.: Transfer learning for improving speech emotion classification accuracy. arXiv preprint arXiv:1801.06353 (2018)
15. Lea, C., Mitra, V., Joshi, A., Kajarekar, S., Bigham, J.P.: Sep-28k: a dataset for stuttering event detection from podcasts with people who stutter. In: ICASSP 2021–2021 IEEE International Conference on Acoustics, Speech and Signal Processing (ICASSP), pp. 6798–6802. IEEE (2021)
16. Mahesha, P., Vinod, D.S.: Classification of speech dysfluencies using speech parameterization techniques and multiclass SVM. In: Singh, K., Awasthi, A.K. (eds.) QShine 2013. LNICST, vol. 115, pp. 298–308. Springer, Heidelberg (2013). https://doi.org/10.1007/978-3-642-37949-9_26
17. Marcinek, L., Stone, M., Millman, R., Gaydecki, P.: N-MTTL SI model: non-intrusive multi-task transfer learning-based speech intelligibility prediction model with scenery classification. In: Interspeech (2021)

18. Matassoni, M., Gretter, R., Falavigna, D., Giuliani, D.: Non-native children speech recognition through transfer learning. In: 2018 IEEE International Conference on Acoustics, Speech and Signal Processing (ICASSP), pp. 6229–6233. IEEE (2018)
19. Oue, S., Marxer, R., Rudzicz, F.: Automatic dysfluency detection in dysarthric speech using deep belief networks. In: Proceedings of SLPAT 2015: 6th Workshop on Speech and Language Processing for Assistive Technologies, pp. 60–64 (2015)
20. Padi, S., Sadjadi, S.O., Sriram, R.D., Manocha, D.: Improved speech emotion recognition using transfer learning and spectrogram augmentation. In: Proceedings of the 2021 International Conference on Multimodal Interaction, pp. 645–652 (2021)
21. Ratner, N.B., MacWhinney, B.: Fluency bank: a new resource for fluency research and practice. J. Fluen. Disord. **56**, 69–80 (2018)
22. Ravikumar, K., Rajagopal, R., Nagaraj, H.: An approach for objective assessment of stuttered speech using MFCC. In: The International Congress for Global Science and Technology, p. 19 (2009)
23. Ravikumar, K., Reddy, B., Rajagopal, R., Nagaraj, H.: Automatic detection of syllable repetition in read speech for objective assessment of stuttered disfluencies. Proc. World Acad. Sci. Eng. Technol. **36**, 270–273 (2008)
24. Santoso, J., Yamada, T., Makino, S.: Categorizing error causes related to utterance characteristics in speech recognition. Proc. NCSP **19**, 514–517 (2019)
25. Sheikh, S.A., Sahidullah, M., Hirsch, F., Ouni, S.: StutterNet: stuttering detection using time delay neural network. arXiv preprint arXiv:2105.05599 (2021)
26. Sheikh, S.A., Sahidullah, M., Hirsch, F., Ouni, S.: Machine learning for stuttering identification: review, challenges & future directions. arXiv preprint arXiv:2107.04057 (2021)
27. Shivakumar, P.G., Georgiou, P.: Transfer learning from adult to children for speech recognition: evaluation, analysis and recommendations. Comput. Speech Lang. **63**, 101077 (2020)
28. Suszyński, W., Kuniszyk-Jóźkowiak, W., Smołka, E., Dzieńkowski, M.: Prolongation detection with application of fuzzy logic. Ann. Universitatis Mariae Curie-Sklodowska Sectio AI-Informatica **1**(1), 1–8 (2015)
29. Szczurowska, I., Kuniszyk-Jóźkowiak, W., Smołka, E.: The application of Kohonen and multilayer perceptron networks in the speech nonfluency analysis. Arch. Acoust. **31**(4(S)), 205–210 (2014)
30. Villegas, B., Flores, K.M., Acuña, K.J., Pacheco-Barrios, K., Elias, D.: A novel stuttering disfluency classification system based on respiratory biosignals. In: 2019 41st Annual International Conference of the IEEE Engineering in Medicine and Biology Society (EMBC), pp. 4660–4663. IEEE (2019)
31. Wang, D., Zheng, T.F.: Transfer learning for speech and language processing. In: 2015 Asia-Pacific Signal and Information Processing Association Annual Summit and Conference (APSIPA), pp. 1225–1237. IEEE (2015)
32. Weiss, K., Khoshgoftaar, T.M., Wang, D.D.: A survey of transfer learning. J. Big Data **3**(1), 1–40 (2016). https://doi.org/10.1186/s40537-016-0043-6
33. Yildirim, S., Narayanan, S.: Automatic detection of disfluency boundaries in spontaneous speech of children using audio-visual information. IEEE Trans. Audio Speech Lang. Process. **17**(1), 2–12 (2009)
34. Zayats, V., Ostendorf, M., Hajishirzi, H.: Disfluency detection using a bidirectional LSTM. arXiv preprint arXiv:1604.03209 (2016)

Harnessing Uncertainty - Multi-label Dysfluency Classification with Uncertain Labels

Melanie Jouaiti[✉] and Kerstin Dautenhahn

Electrical and Computer Engineering Department, University of Waterloo,
200 University Ave, Waterloo, ON N2L3G1, Canada
{mjouaiti,kerstin.dautenhahn}@uwaterloo.ca

Abstract. Manually labelled datasets inherently contain errors or uncertain/imprecise labelling as sometimes experts cannot agree or are not sure. This issue is even more prominent in multi-label datasets as some labels may be missing. However, discarding samples with high uncertainty may lead to the loss of valuable data.

In this paper, we study two datasets where the uncertainty is explicit in the expert annotations. We give an overview of the different approaches available to deal with uncertainty and evaluate them on two dysfluency datasets. Our results show that adopting methods that embrace uncertainty leads to better results than using only labels with high certainty and performs better than current state of the art results.

Keywords: Dysfluency classification · Transfer learning · Uncertainty

1 Introduction

While benchmark datasets strive to be error-free and clean, most real-world datasets cannot provide any guarantee that the data is perfectly labelled [2]. This is especially true for dysfluency datasets as the data has to be labelled by experts to be reliable. However, this task is extremely expensive, labor-intensive and time-consuming which inevitably leads to annotation mistakes. Imprecise labels are a critical problem of machine learning as neural networks are able to fit random labels [22], which leads to degraded performance as the network learns from wrong annotations.

As this has been a rising concern, the research community has endeavoured to design solutions, so that the consequence of uncertain data is minimized. However, most research on the topic take datasets with hard labels and introduce artificial noise. In this work, we will focus on dysfluency classification and test three of those approaches with stuttering datasets that already encompass uncertainty as some of the data is labelled as *unsure*.

Stuttering is a neuro-developmental disorder represented in 1% of the population. It is characterized by anomalies of speech, including pauses, repetition,

© Springer Nature Switzerland AG 2022
S. R. M. Prasanna et al. (Eds.): SPECOM 2022, LNAI 13721, pp. 302–311, 2022.
https://doi.org/10.1007/978-3-031-20980-2_26

prolongation of words or sounds and interjections (filler words: "hum", "huh"). Robust automatic dysfluency classification is still an open research problem and would be a useful addition in the context of speech therapy, to track patients' progress but also to advance progress in technology-assisted speech therapy to alleviate the work-load of speech therapists. Our long-term goal is not to replace therapists but to provide a valuable tool that they can use.

In this work, we tackle this speech classification problem from a computer vision perspective, employing the popular method of fine-tuning. Indeed, while deep learning approaches remain increasingly popular, they require significant amounts of data, which is an ongoing issue for stuttering. A way to circumvent this issue consists in fine-tuning a pre-trained network. CNN are now the go-to solution for image classification tasks, so converting the audio data allows us to take advantage of the widely available computer vision resources and methods, such as fine-tuning pre-trained deep neural networks.

We will consider two multi-label datasets: FluencyBank and SEP-28K, curated by Lea et al. [9]. To our knowledge, only Lea et al. reported results on multi-label dysfluency classification so far, so this problematic has been mostly neglected, while research focused on single-label classification tasks. Besides, in those datasets, the samples are also labelled in terms of how sure/unsure the experts were about the assigned labels.

In this paper, we undertake multi-label dysfluency classification by fine-tuning a ResNet50 using the spectrogram amplitude of the audio clip as an image for our input features and test our system on the FluencyBank and SEP-28K datasets. We present different methods to harness the power of uncertainty and show that taking uncertainty into account improves the performance of the model.

2   Related Work

One approach for dealing with uncertain labels consists in performing knowledge distillation [18]. Knowledge distillation consists in training a network on hard labels with unambiguous data, getting soft label predictions for the uncertain data and retraining the network on all the data. Tachika et al. compared knowledge distillation with two kinds of loss: sequence-level distillation and sequence-level interpolation. They also compared performance for a noisy ASR task and a large vocabulary continuous ASR task.

Moreover, it has also been shown that classifiers trained on fuzzy labels are more resilient than classifiers trained on hard labels [19], though in a single label classification task with artificially added noise.

Another proposed method focuses on handling samples depending on their loss, as the loss is an insight into the difficulty and confidence of each sample. On the one hand, some prioritize (higher sample weight) samples with high loss to accelerate training, which has been known to work well in datasets with a small proportion of noise [10,17]. On the other hand, recently research took the opposite approach of prioritizing easy samples with low loss [1,3,6]. Shin et al. proposed to prioritize samples with low loss and high uncertainty and validated their approach on three benchmark datasets injected with symmetric and asymmetric synthetic noise [16].

Besides, Younes et al. employed the EML-kNN [20] method, applied to several classification tasks with artificially introduced imprecision [21]. They achieved better results that usual classifiers. EML-kNN is a multi-label variation of kNN that integrates the Dempster-Shafer theory of belief functions [13] that can classify imperfect instances based on their k nearest neighbors.

Stuttering detection and dysfluency classification are still an open research question and have been tackled from different angles, using various kinds of input features and classification methods (See [8,15] for reviews).

Recently, some deep learning approaches have been proposed. Oue et al. detected repetitions in dysarthric speech with a deep neural network using MFCCs and linear predictive cepstral coefficients as inputs [11]. Also using MFCCs, Sheikh et al. designed StutterNet, a network based on Time Delay Neural Networks to classify dysfluency from the UCLASS dataset [14]. Exploiting the temporal aspect of speech, there have also been a few attempts using recurrent neural networks (RNN). Combining a ResNet and BiLSTM network yielded an average accuracy of 91.15% on 25 files of UCLASS using audio spectrograms [8]. A LSTM-based network applied to a combination of features, such as mel-filterbank energy features, pitch information and articulatory features yielded F1-scores of 66.8 and 80.8 on the SEP-28K and FluencyBank datasets [9].

3   Method

3.1   Datasets

In this work, we compare classification performance when dealing with uncertainty in multi-label dysfluency datasets. We selected two datasets which contain multi-label annotations but also a sure/unsure label, as such datasets are scarce. First, we used the FluencyBank dataset [12], which contains recordings from 32 adults who stutter. We used the dataset re-annotated by [9], due to inaccuracies in temporal alignments for the original annotations. It contains 5.5% of samples labelled as unsure. Second, we also used the SEP-28K dataset. This dataset, also manually labelled by [9], contains 28 177 3-seconds clips extracted from publicly available podcasts. It contains 2.9% of samples labelled as unsure. Both datasets are labelled with 12 classes which can be combined into eight main classes: silence, music, fluent, word-repetitions (wordrep), sound-repetitions (soundrep), prolongations, interjections and blocks. The FluencyBank dataset has no occurrence of music or silence class. In both datasets, audio clips can belong to more than one class and the number of occurrences of each class can be more than one for each sample. As both datasets are very imbalanced, we set class weights appropriately. We had approval from the University of Waterloo's Research Ethics Board to process those datasets.

3.2   Transfer Learning

Transfer learning consists in training a base network on a base dataset and then the features learned from this first network can be transferred to train a second network on another dataset. This is very useful as deep networks such as ResNet [4] require weeks of training and very large datasets but transfer learning is a lot faster and still achieves very good results, even in the case of smaller datasets.

Here, we used a ResNet50 pre-trained on ImageNet [4]. ResNet50 is a 50-layers residual network that tries to solve the vanishing gradient and degradation problems. This kind of network attempts to learn residuals instead of features. It has been extensively used in image classification and recognition tasks with good results.

To fine-tune the ResNet50, we removed the classification layer and appended a Dropout (0.8) layer and a fully connected layer with l2-regularization (0.001), in order to avoid overfitting. We fine-tuned the entire network for 100 epochs with a batch size of 4 with an early-stopping criteria of patience=5. We also used the Adam optimizer with a learning rate of $1e^{-5}$. To rigorously test the fine-tuned model, we employed 10-fold cross validation where each audio file is randomly assigned to one fold. We conducted 10 experiments where the networks learns on 90% of the data and tests on the remaining 10%. The reported results represent the average of the 10 test experiments. We ran our experiments on a GeForce RTX 2060 GPU.

3.3   Input Features

Since ResNet50 expects a RGB image as an input, we use the spectrogram amplitude of the audio-clip, resized to the expected size of $(224, 224)$ as the input feature for the network (Fig. 1). First, we downsample the audio clip from 16 kHz to 8 kHz to obtain a vector of size (24000, 1) and pad it with 0 if necessary. This vector is then converted to a spectrogram and its brightness is decreased and its contrast increased before normalizing it between 0 and 1. All the audio processing are performed with the librosa library.

$$img = \log(1 + \text{amplitude\_of\_spectrogram}(\text{stft}(audio))) \qquad (1)$$

3.4   Dealing with Uncertainty

The uncertainty in our multi-label problem can be approached from different angles:

- Our baseline approach will consist in using Boolean multi-labels with each value in the label arrays being 0 or 1, thus not discriminating between sure and unsure labels.
- Fuzzy multi-labels with each value in the label arrays between 0 or 1. For labels where the experts were certain, we give the value 0.9 to labels that

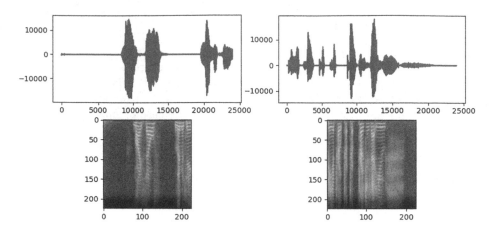

Fig. 1. Examples of audio clips and their corresponding spectrogram from the SEP-28K dataset. On the left: example of fluent speech, on the right: example of sound repetition.

are positive and 0.1 to negative labels. For labels where the experts were uncertain, we give the value 0.7 to positive labels and 0.3 to negative labels. This is different from soft labels as we are not forcing the sum of the labels to be 1.

- Low-loss prioritization [16]: Use Boolean multi-labels with low-loss and high uncertainty prioritization. Samples with a low-loss and high uncertainty are assigned a higher sample weight, i.e. samples with a loss value in the 70th percentile and predictions certainty inferior to 0.5, will be assigned a weight of 0.7. All the other samples are assigned a weight of 0.3.
- Knowledge distillation [18]: We first train on labels that are labelled as *sure* with Boolean multi-labels, get soft predictions for the uncertain data, then train the network again on all the data.

For each method, the activation of the classification layer is a sigmoid and the loss is binary cross-entropy, so that each class is handled independently.

3.5   Metrics

We will report results using several metrics to evaluate classification performance: recall, F1-score. However, these handle each class independently and are therefore forgiving when not all the belonging classes are predicted. To get a more accurate and strict evaluation of performance, we also report the Hamming score and the Exact Match Ratio (EMR).

The Hamming score is a forgiving way to compute accuracy in multi-labels problems as it considers partially correct predictions:

$$Hamming(y_{true}, y_{pred}) = \frac{1}{n} \sum_{k}^{n} \frac{y_{true,k} \,\&\& \, y_{pred,k}}{y_{true,k} || y_{pred,k}} \qquad (2)$$

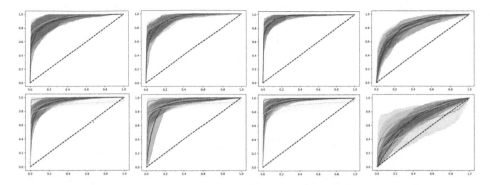

Fig. 2. Mean ROC curves and standard deviation (shaded region) for each method (Boolean labels, fuzzy labels, knowledge distillation, low-loss prioritization) and each dataset. Top: FluencyBank, Bottom: SEP-28K (blue: fluent, green: wordrep, red: soundrep, orange: prolongation, cyan: interjection, purple: block, grey: music, yellow: silence). (Color figure online)

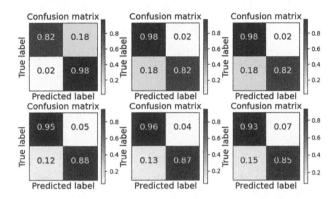

Fig. 3. Confusion matrix for the SEP-28K dataset with knowledge distillation (respectively fluent, word repetition, sound repetition, interjection, prolongation and block).

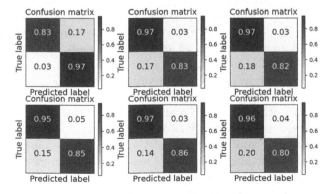

Fig. 4. Confusion matrix for the FluencyBank dataset with knowledge distillation (respectively fluent, word repetition, sound repetition, interjection, prolongation and block).

Table 1. Results on the FluencyBank and SEP-28K datasets.

FluencyBank	Hamming	Recall	F1	EMR
Bool labels	80.86 (10.65)	83.75 (6.78)	84.47 (8.1)	69.93 (17.49)
Fuzzy labels	83.42 (6.98)	82.57 (6.41)	86.0 (5.9)	75.61 (10.6)
Distillation	88.84 (6.39)	88.98 (6.39)	90.75 (5.49)	82.35 (10.65)
Low-loss	59.37 (5.26)	71.92 (5.82)	70.5 (4.11)	31.96 (7.58)
SEP-28K	Hamming	Recall	F1	EMR
Bool labels	84.71 (6.53)	87.15 (5.98)	88.34 (5.16)	73.81 (10.78)
Fuzzy labels	84.55 (6.84)	86.48 (6.15)	88.16 (5.46)	74.18 (10.95)
Distillation	87.69 (6.39)	89.72 (5.55)	90.75 (4.94)	78.06 (10.89)
Low-loss	46.79 (8.38)	60.19 (6.7)	59.36 (6.93)	16.82 (8.08)

The Exact Match Ratio (EMR) is an evaluation metric to compute the accuracy of a multi-label classification problem. The EMR metrics is strict as is does not account for partially correct labels:

$$EMR(y_{true}, y_{pred}) = \frac{1}{n} \sum_{k}^{n} I(y_{true}[k] == y_{pred}[k]) \tag{3}$$

where I is the indicator function.

4   Results

Table 1 gives an overview of the results for each approach and Table 2 reports the F1-scores when considering each class independently. See also Fig. 2 for the ROC curves. While, the distillation method consistently yields better results than the other methods (See Fig. 3 and Fig. 4 for the confusion matrices of each dataset), the low-loss prioritization approach consistently fares worse than the others, with a very low EMR score, though still obtaining better results than those reported by [9], in terms of individual class F1-score. Using fuzzy labels, also improves performance, compared to Boolean labels for the FluencyBank dataset but lead to similar results for the SEP-28K dataset.

To our knowledge, only Lea et al. attempted multi-label classification previously [9]. They reported classification results for each class, by considering each class independently. That is, if a clip belongs to the *fluent* and the *interjection* class and the network classifies it as *interjection* only, the clip will be considered as correctly classified for the *interjection* class and incorrectly for the *fluent* class. We therefore also report those results and compare our results with theirs (See Table 2). Fine-tuning with a knowledge distillation approach leads to significantly better results for each class than those reported by [9].

Table 2. Results of the multi-label classification for each approach, when considering the 8 classes by themselves.

FluencyBank	F1-bool	F1-fuzzy	F1-dis	F1-llp	F1- [9]
Fluent	89.44	90.54	**94.55**	76.86	NA
WordRep	88.69	91.3	**94.33**	77.87	59.3
SoundRep	87.99	89.75	**93.66**	78.7	74.3
Interjection	88.0	88.79	**91.95**	75.07	71.3
Prolongation	91.1	93.41	**95.41**	82.05	67.9
Block	86.18	87.52	**91.34**	74.91	56.8
SEP-28K	F1-bool	F1-fuzzy	F1-dis	F1-llp	F1- [9]
Fluent	93.46	93.14	**95.62**	63.57	NA
WordRep	93.42	93.74	**95.4**	73.45	60.4
SoundRep	93.17	93.16	**95.14**	71.19	63.2
Interjection	90.64	90.23	**93.02**	68.67	71.3
Prolongation	91.22	91.10	**93.41**	76.63	68.5
Block	87.44	87.22	**93.56**	63.73	55.9
Music	99.79	99.78	**99.82**	97.34	NA
Silence	98.41	98.63	**98.73**	95.12	NA

5   Discussion

The low-loss prioritization approach is the only one which performed worse than our baseline. We tried to replicate the approach described in [16], which extracts the uncertainty of each sample from the predictions that the model outputs. This approach, however, ignores the uncertainty label assigned to each sample. In our case, maybe a hybrid approach that considers both the uncertainty from the expert and the uncertainty from the model would yield better results.

Moreover, surprisingly, for the SEP-28K dataset, fuzzy and Boolean labels yielded similar results, contrary to the FluencyBank dataset where fuzzy labels improved performance. This can perhaps be explained by the amount of uncertain labels, as FluencyBank has 5.5% of uncertain labels and SEP-28K only has 2.9%. However, the knowledge distillation approach lead to improved metrics for both datasets.

Another popular dataset is the UCLASS dataset [5], which contains speech of children. This dataset is single label and does not encompass a measure of uncertainty for each sample. We also fine-tuned a ResNet50 on one split of this dataset, using Boolean (one-hot in this case) and fuzzy (all 0.9 or 0.1) labels. The overall performance of those two label encodings was similar: (Boolean F1: 92%, Fuzzy F1: 93%). However, using fuzzy labels improved individual classes scores for the interjection class: **Boolean F1** for fluent speech (95%), word repetitions (89%), sound repetitions (87%), interjections (60%) and prolongations (77%);

Fuzzy F1 for fluent speech (95%), word repetitions (89%), sound repetitions (86%), interjections (66%) and prolongations (77%).

6 Conclusion

Uncertainty is inherent to manually labeled datasets and it becomes a valuable information when label uncertainty is documented in the dataset, as the neural network can make use of this additional information to learn a more robust representation. In this paper, presented and tested four different approaches of dealing with uncertainty on two datasets which explicitly contain an uncertainty measure for each sample. Results when fine-tuning a ResNet50 showed that knowledge distillation yields the best performance for both datasets. This approach outperforms previously reported results on those datasets, using only the hard label data [7]. Using fuzzy labels that encode the uncertainty also fares better than our baseline approach of using Boolean labels. Our future goal is to contribute to the development of tools that speech therapists can use in their daily practice for automatic monitoring and evaluation of children's progress.

Acknowledgments. This research was undertaken, in part, thanks to funding from the Canada 150 Research Chairs Program.

References

1. Chen, P., Liao, B.B., Chen, G., Zhang, S.: Understanding and utilizing deep neural networks trained with noisy labels. In: International Conference on Machine Learning, pp. 1062–1070. PMLR (2019)
2. Frénay, B., Verleysen, M.: Classification in the presence of label noise: a survey. IEEE Trans. Neural Netw. Learn. Syst. **25**(5), 845–869 (2013)
3. Han, B., et al.: Co-teaching: robust training of deep neural networks with extremely noisy labels. In: Advances in Neural Information Processing Systems, vol. 31 (2018)
4. He, K., Zhang, X., Ren, S., Sun, J.: Deep residual learning for image recognition. In: Proceedings of the IEEE Conference on Computer Vision and Pattern Recognition, pp. 770–778 (2016)
5. Howell, P., Davis, S., Bartrip, J.: The university college London archive of stuttered speech (UCLASS) (2009)
6. Huang, J., Qu, L., Jia, R., Zhao, B.: O2U-Net: a simple noisy label detection approach for deep neural networks. In: Proceedings of the IEEE/CVF International Conference on Computer Vision, pp. 3326–3334 (2019)
7. Jouaiti, M., Dautenhahn, K.: Dysfluency classification in stuttered speech using deep learning for real-time applications. In: ICASSP 2022–2022 IEEE International Conference on Acoustics, Speech and Signal Processing (ICASSP), pp. 6482–6486 (2022). https://doi.org/10.1109/ICASSP43922.2022.9746638
8. Kourkounakis, T., Hajavi, A., Etemad, A.: Detecting multiple speech disfluencies using a deep residual network with bidirectional long short-term memory. In: ICASSP 2020–2020 IEEE International Conference on Acoustics, Speech and Signal Processing (ICASSP), pp. 6089–6093. IEEE (2020)

9. Lea, C., Mitra, V., Joshi, A., Kajarekar, S., Bigham, J.P.: SEP-28k: a dataset for stuttering event detection from podcasts with people who stutter. In: ICASSP 2021–2021 IEEE International Conference on Acoustics, Speech and Signal Processing (ICASSP), pp. 6798–6802. IEEE (2021)

10. Malisiewicz, T., Gupta, A., Efros, A.A.: Ensemble of exemplar-SVMs for object detection and beyond. In: 2011 International Conference on Computer Vision, pp. 89–96. IEEE (2011)

11. Oue, S., Marxer, R., Rudzicz, F.: Automatic dysfluency detection in dysarthric speech using deep belief networks. In: Proceedings of SLPAT 2015: 6th Workshop on Speech and Language Processing for Assistive Technologies, pp. 60–64 (2015)

12. Ratner, N.B., MacWhinney, B.: Fluency bank: a new resource for fluency research and practice. J. Fluen. Disord. **56**, 69–80 (2018)

13. Shafer, G.: Dempster-Shafer theory. Encycl. Artif. Intell. **1**, 330–331 (1992)

14. Sheikh, S.A., Sahidullah, M., Hirsch, F., Ouni, S.: StutterNet: stuttering detection using time delay neural network. arXiv preprint arXiv:2105.05599 (2021)

15. Sheikh, S.A., Sahidullah, M., Hirsch, F., Ouni, S.: Machine learning for stuttering identification: review, challenges & future directions. arXiv preprint arXiv:2107.04057 (2021)

16. Shin, W., Ha, J.W., Li, S., Cho, Y., Song, H., Kwon, S.: Which strategies matter for noisy label classification? Insight into loss and uncertainty. arXiv preprint arXiv:2008.06218 (2020)

17. Shrivastava, A., Gupta, A., Girshick, R.: Training region-based object detectors with online hard example mining. In: Proceedings of the IEEE Conference on Computer Vision and Pattern Recognition, pp. 761–769 (2016)

18. Tachioka, Y.: Knowledge distillation using soft and hard labels and annealing for acoustic model training. In: 2019 IEEE 8th Global Conference on Consumer Electronics (GCCE), pp. 689–690. IEEE (2019)

19. Thiel, C.: Classification on soft labels is robust against label noise. In: Lovrek, I., Howlett, R.J., Jain, L.C. (eds.) KES 2008. LNCS (LNAI), vol. 5177, pp. 65–73. Springer, Heidelberg (2008). https://doi.org/10.1007/978-3-540-85563-7_14

20. Younes, Z., Abdallah, F., Denœux, T.: An evidence-theoretic k-nearest neighbor rule for multi-label classification. In: Godo, L., Pugliese, A. (eds.) SUM 2009. LNCS (LNAI), vol. 5785, pp. 297–308. Springer, Heidelberg (2009). https://doi.org/10.1007/978-3-642-04388-8_23

21. Younes, Z., abdallah, F., Denœux, T.: Evidential multi-label classification approach to learning from data with imprecise labels. In: Hüllermeier, E., Kruse, R., Hoffmann, F. (eds.) IPMU 2010. LNCS (LNAI), vol. 6178, pp. 119–128. Springer, Heidelberg (2010). https://doi.org/10.1007/978-3-642-14049-5_13

22. Zhang, C., Bengio, S., Hardt, M., Recht, B., Vinyals, O.: Understanding deep learning (still) requires rethinking generalization. Commun. ACM **64**(3), 107–115 (2021)

Continuous Wavelet Transform for Severity-Level Classification of Dysarthria

Aastha Kachhi[(✉)], Anand Therattil, Priyanka Gupta[ID],
and Hemant A. Patil[ID]

Speech Research Lab, DA -IICT, Gandhinagar 382007, Gujarat, India
{aastha_kachhi,anand_therattil,priyanka_gupta,hemant_patil}@daiict.ac.in

Abstract. Dysarthria is a neuro-motor speech defect that causes speech to be unintelligible and is largely unnoticeable to humans at various severity-levels. Dysarthric speech classification is used as a diagnostic method to assess the progression of a patient's severity of the condition, as well as to aid with automatic dysarthric speech recognition systems (an important assistive speech technology). This study investigates the significance of Generalized Morse Wavelet (GMW)-based scalogram features for capturing the discriminative acoustic cues of dysarthric severity-level classification for low-frequency regions, using Convolutional Neural Network (CNN). The performance of scalogram-based features is compared with Short-Time Fourier Transform (STFT)-based features, and Mel spectrogram-based features. Compared to the STFT-based baseline features with a classification accuracy of 91.76%, the proposed Continuous Wavelet Transform (CWT)-based scalogram features achieve significantly improved classification accuracy of 95.17% on standard and statistically meaningful UA-Speech corpus. The remarkably improved results signify that for better dysarthric severity-level classification, the information in the low-frequency regions is more discriminative, as the proposed CWT-based time-frequency representation (scalogram) has a high-frequency resolution in the lower frequencies. On the other hand, STFT-based representations have *constant* resolution across all the frequency bands and therefore, are not as better suited for dysarthric severity-level classification, as the proposed Morse wavelet-based CWT features. In addition, we also perform experiments on the Mel spectrogram to demonstrate that even though the Mel spectrogram also has a high frequency resolution in the lower frequencies with a classification accuracy of 92.65%, the proposed system is better suited. We see an increase of 3.41% and 2.52% in classification accuracy of the proposed system to STFT and Mel spectrogram respectively. To that effect, the performance of the STFT, Mel spectrogram, and scalogram are analyzed using $F1$-Score, Matthew's Correlation Coefficients (MCC), Jaccard Index, Hamming Loss, and Linear Discriminant Analysis (LDA) scatter plots.

Keywords: Wavelet transform · Dysarthria · UA-Speech corpus · Morse wavelet · CNN

© Springer Nature Switzerland AG 2022
S. R. M. Prasanna et al. (Eds.): SPECOM 2022, LNAI 13721, pp. 312–324, 2022.
https://doi.org/10.1007/978-3-031-20980-2_27

1   Introduction

Proper coordination between brain and speech-producing muscles is required for the production of speech sounds [15]. Lack of this coordination leads to speech disorders, such as aparaxia, dysarthria, and stuttering. These disorders affect a person's ability to produce speech sounds. They are further categorized as neurological or neurodegenerative diseases, such as cerebral palsy or Parkinson's disease. The severity-level of these diseases might be mild or severe, depending upon the impact on the area of the brain. In the case of mild severity, the patient may mispronounce a few words, whereas, in high severity, the patient lacks the ability to produce intelligible speech. Among these speech disorders, dysarthria is a relatively common speech disorder [24]. Dysarthria is a neuro-motor speech disorder. The muscles that produce speech are weak in people with this disorder. Dynamic movements of articulators, such as lips, tongue, throat, and upper respiratory tract system are also affected due to brain damage. Apart from brain damage, cerebral palsy, muscular dystrophy, and stroke are also some of the other factors, which can cause dysarthria [19].

Severity-level of dysarthria depends on the impact and damage to the area of neurological injury, which is diagnosed using a brain and nerve test. The type, underlying cause, severity-level, and its symptoms, all influence the manner in which it is treated [4]. Due to this uncertainty in treatment, researchers are motivated to develop speech assistive tools for dysarthric intelligibility categorization.

In the literature, dysarthria severity-level classification has been exploited extensively using Short-Time Fourier Transform (STFT) [9], and various acoustical features [1]. State-of-the-art feature sets, such as Mel Frequency Cepstral Coefficients (MFCC) feature set was employed in [12] due to its capacity of capturing global spectral envelope properties. In addition to a perceptually-motivated state-of-the-art feature set, glottal excitation source parameters derived from the quasi-periodic sampling of the vocal tract system were implemented in [8]. In the signal processing framework, due to the wide and dynamic range of multiple frequency components in short-time spectra, speech signals are considered to be non-stationary signals. Due to the dynamic movements of articulators, the frequency spectrum varies instantaneously.

In this work, we demonstrate the capability of Continuous Wavelet Transform (CWT)-based representation (i.e., scalogram) for dysarthric severity-level classification. According to study in [5], wavelet transform has better frequency resolution in the low frequency regions, as compared to the STFT. In the literature, for acoustical research problems, wavelet-based features have been successfully implemented as in [3,22]. To that effect, the motivation of utilizing CWT for this study is the improved frequency resolution of CWT-based scalograms at lower frequencies as compared to the STFT-based and Mel spectrogram-based techniques. To the best of the authors' knowledge and belief, the use of CWT has been explored to Model Articulation Impairments in Patients with Parkinson's Disease [23]. However the use of CWT to capture discriminative acoustic cues for dysarthric severity-level classification is being proposed for the first time in this study. Results are presented on standard Universal Access (UA)-Speech Corpus.

The rest of paper is organized as follows: Sect. 2 discusses the motivation of using scalogram-based approach over a spectrogram. Section 3 describes the proposed approach of Morse wavelet-based dysarthric severity level classification. Furthermore, experimental setup is described in Sect. 4, followed by experimental results in Sect. 5. The Sect. 6 concludes the paper along with potential future research directions.

2   Spectrogram and Scalogram

STFT-based spectrograms are made up of windows of equal and fixed lengths that run across the length of the signal. As a result, in a spectrogram, the spread in time, as well as frequency-domains, remains constant throughout the time-frequency plane (i.e., constant time and frequency resolution). On the other hand, we can achieve *variable* time-frequency resolution by employing CWT-based representation (also known as scalogram). The time-frequency spread of the wavelet atoms $\psi_{u,s}$ determines the time-frequency resolution of scalogram. A Heisenberg box is defined by the spread in time multiplied by the spread in frequency in a time-frequency representation. In a scalogram, for low frequency regions, the spread in frequency is less, leading to a better frequency resolution, as shown by the boxes in Fig. 1. Furthermore, CWT can be computed using the wavelet $\psi_{u,s}(t)$, which has its Fourier transform denoted by $\hat{\psi}_{u,s}(\omega)$ [20]

Given that the center frequency of $\hat{\psi}(\omega)$ is indicated by η, the wavelet $\psi_{u,s}$ has a center frequency at $\frac{\eta}{s}$. The wavelet $\psi_{u,s}$ has an energy spread about the center frequency of $\psi_{u,s}$, which is given by [20]:

$$\frac{1}{2\pi} \int_0^{+\infty} \left(\omega - \frac{\eta}{s}\right)^2 |\hat{\psi}_{u,s}(\omega)|^2 d\omega = \frac{\sigma_\omega^2}{s^2}, \tag{1}$$

where,

$$\sigma_\omega^2 = \frac{1}{2\pi} \int_0^{+\infty} (\omega - \eta)^2 |\hat{\psi}(\omega)|^2 d\omega. \tag{2}$$

Furthermore, the energy density in local time-frequency plane is denoted $P_W f$, given by:

$$P_W f(u, \xi) = \left| W f(u, s) \right|^2 = \left| W f\left(u, \frac{\eta}{\xi}\right) \right|^2. \tag{3}$$

The Eq. (3) is nothing but a scalogram with scaled time-frequency resolution.

Figure 1 shows the motivation behind choosing CWT-based approach over STFT. Energy conservation in STFT is [20]:

$$\int_{-\infty}^{+\infty} |f(t)|^2 dt = \frac{1}{2\pi} \int_{-\infty}^{+\infty} \int_{-\infty}^{+\infty} |Sf(u, \varsigma)|^2 d\varsigma \, du. \tag{4}$$

Energy conservation is preserved in analytic WT as well [20].

$$\int_{-\infty}^{+\infty} |f_a(t)|^2 dt = \frac{1}{C_\psi} \int_0^{+\infty} \int_{-\infty}^{+\infty} |Wf(u,s)|^2 du \frac{ds}{s^2}. \tag{5}$$

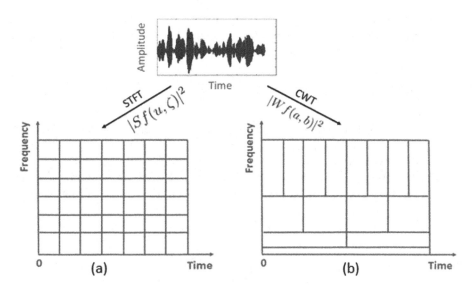

Fig. 1. Tilings of the time-frequency plane for (a) STFT and (b) CWT.

3   Proposed Work

3.1   Continuous Wavelet Transform (CWT)

Due to lack of co-ordination between brain and articulators, the speech produced by dysarthric patients have change in energy. To analyse this energy change in different severity-levels, recent investigations using spectrogram are made in [9]. However, to get better insight of energy spread in time-frequency representation, we propose CWT-based scalogram approach through this study. The key idea for employing CWT-based scalogram approach for dysarthric severity-level classification is to exploit the energy spread in the low frequency regions for different severity-levels in time-frequency distributions. A wavelet is a waveform with a zero-average and an effectively restricted duration, i.e., it is wave for a short duration and hence the name wavelet. It is defined as [17]:

$$\psi_{u,s}(t) = \frac{1}{\sqrt{s}} \psi^* \left(\frac{t-u}{s} \right), s \in R^+, u \in R, \tag{6}$$

where the dilation (scaling) parameter is denoted by s and the translational (positional) parameter is denoted by u. The CWT of a signal $f(t)$ is

$$
\begin{aligned}
W_f(u, s) &= <f(t), \psi_{u,s}(t)>, \\
&= \frac{1}{\sqrt{s}} \int_{-\infty}^{\infty} f(t) \psi^* \left(\frac{t-u}{s} \right) dt,
\end{aligned}
\tag{7}
$$

where $<\cdot, \cdot>$ indicates inner product operation to compute wavelet coefficients, and $*$ denotes complex conjugate. The scalogram is defined as the square of absolute of the CWT coefficients, i.e., $|W_f(u, s)|^2$.

3.2 Exploiting Morse Wavelet for CWT

There are various types of analytic wavelets in the literature, such as Cauchy, complex Shannon, lognormal, Derivative of Gaussian, and Morlet wavelets [10, 13, 20]. However, due to the existence of various types of wavelets, choosing an appropriate wavelet for a particular task becomes an issue. Generalized Morse Wavelets (GMWs) is considered as a superfamily of analytic wavelets that are causal in the frequency-domain. In frequency-domain, the Morse wavelet is given by [16]:

$$
\hat{\psi}_{\beta,\gamma}(\omega) = \int_{-\infty}^{\infty} \psi_{\beta,\gamma}(t) e^{-i\omega t} dt = U(\omega) a_{\beta,\gamma} \omega^{\beta} e^{-\omega^{\gamma}},
\tag{8}
$$

where β and γ are the two parameters of the Morse wavelet, which control the *shape* and *size*, respectively, of the wavelet and $U(\omega)$ is unit-step function due to causality in the frequency-domain. The parameter β is called as the *order* and the parameter γ represents the *family* of wavelets. With each value of γ, one can get a family of wavelets from the Morse wavelet representation as shown in Eq. (8) [16]. The amplitude of the wavelet is normalized by a real-valued constant factor given by $\alpha_{\beta\gamma}$. The value of the constant scaling factor $\alpha_{\beta\gamma}$ is given by [17]:

$$
\alpha_{\beta\gamma} \equiv 2 \left(\frac{e\gamma}{\beta} \right)^{\frac{\beta}{\gamma}}.
\tag{9}
$$

Furthermore, the "*wavelet duration*" denoted by $P_{\beta,\gamma}^2$ is given by the 2nd order derivative of Morse wavelet. Mathematically, $P_{\beta,\gamma}^2$ can be defined as [17]:

$$
P_{\beta,\gamma}^2 \equiv -\frac{\omega_{\beta,\gamma}^2 \hat{\psi}_{\beta,\gamma}''(\omega_{\beta,\gamma})}{\hat{\psi}_{\beta,\gamma}(\omega_{\beta,\gamma})} = \beta\gamma.
\tag{10}
$$

The number of peak frequency oscillations that may be fitted in the central window of a wavelet in the time-domain is given by $\frac{P_{\beta,\gamma}^2}{2\pi}$. The Morse wavelet with parameter $\gamma = 3$ (also known as 'Airy family') is used in this study. The optimum Heisenberg area $A_{\beta,\gamma}$, reached at $\gamma = 3$ even for a small wavelet duration (as shown in Fig. 2), justifies our choice of $\gamma = 3$. For a Morse wavelet, $A_{\beta,\gamma}$ is given by [5, 18]:

$$
A_{\beta,\gamma} \equiv \sigma_t \sigma_\omega,
\tag{11}
$$

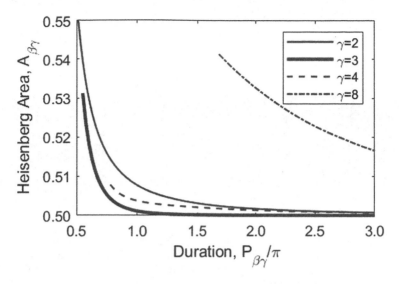

Fig. 2. Effect of γ parameter on the time-frequency Heisenberg area $A_{\beta,\gamma}$ w.r.t. wavelet duration $P_{\beta,\gamma}/\pi$. After [16].

where time spread σ_t^2 and frequency spread σ_ω^2 of wavelet atom representation are given by [17]:

$$\sigma_t^2 = \omega_\psi^2 \frac{\int t^2 |\psi(t)|^2 dt}{\int |\psi(t)|^2 dt} \quad \text{and,} \tag{12}$$

$$\sigma_\omega^2 = \frac{1}{\omega_\psi^2} \frac{\int (\omega - \tilde{\omega}_\psi)^2 |\psi(\omega)|^2 d\omega}{\int |\psi(\omega)|^2 d\omega}, \tag{13}$$

where $\tilde{\omega}_\psi$ represents the energy frequency of the Morse wavelet (which is also the mean of $|\Psi(\omega)|^2$) [17]. The study, reported in [16] shows that all the Morse wavelets attain the information concentration of $A_{\beta,\gamma} = 1/2$. For $\gamma = 3$, degree of concentration of information, i.e., $A_{\beta,\gamma}$ is the highest even for a small value of wavelet duration, $P_{\beta,\gamma}/\pi$, as shown in Fig. 2. To that effect, in this work, scalogram images were extracted using MATLAB with $\gamma = 3$ and $\beta = 20$ (i.e., $P_{\beta,\gamma}^2 = 60$) as the default parameter setting for Morse wavelet-based scalogram for full frequency band upto 8 kHz (since sampling frequency $F_s = 16$ kHz). Each scalogram image extracted is of $512 \times 512 \times 3$ dimension. These scalogram-based features are then fed as input to the CNN classifier. The experimental setup is explained in the following Section.

4   Experimental Setup

4.1   Dataset Used

The Universal Access dysarthric Speech (UA-Speech) corpus [25] is used to evaluate the proposed CWT-based approach. In this study, a dataset configuration

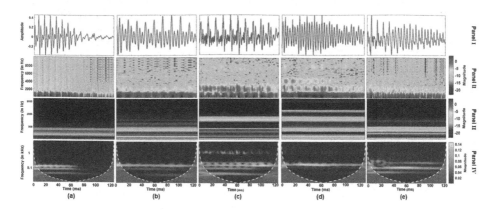

Fig. 3. Dysarthic speech utterance (for vowel /e/) for male speaker with various dysarthic severity-level (Panel I), corresponding STFT (Panel II), corresponding Mel spectrogram (Panel III), and corresponding Morse Wavelet Scalogram (Panel IV) for (a) normal, dysarthic speech with severity-level as (b) very low, (c) low, (d) medium, and (e) high. Best viewed in color. (Color figure online)

identical to that described in [9] is used. It has 8 speakers, out of which 4 are male and 4 are female speakers. Furthermore, 90% of the dataset is dedicated to training set and the remaining 10% is dedicated to the testing partition.

4.2   Feature Details

In this study, the energy capturing capabilities of scalogram at low frequencies are compared with the baseline spectrogram and Mel spectrogram. As mentioned in [9], the STFT was applied to generate a time-frequency representation with a window size of 2 ms, and window overlap of 0.5 ms. Furthermore, the performance of scalogram was also compared with Mel spectrogram, which are generated with a window of size 2 ms and overlap of 0.5 ms. The dimensions of the generated Mel spectrogram are $512 \times 512 \times 3$. As discussed in Sect. 3, the scalograms of dimension $512 \times 512 \times 3$ were generated with $\gamma = 3$, and $\beta = 20$ (i.e., $P_{\beta,\gamma} = 60$) as the default parameter setting.

4.3   Classifier Details

Based on the experiments presented in [12], the Convolutional Neural Network (CNN) is used as a classifier in this study. According to a study reported in [12], CNN gives comparable results with the other deep neural network (DNN)-based classifiers for the UA-Speech corpus. For this study, the CNN model was trained employing the Adam optimizer algorithm, four convolutional layers with kernel size of 5×5, and one Fully-Connected (FC) layer [14]. Mel spectrograms and scalograms, both of size 512×512, were used in these investigations. A max-pool layer and Rectified Linear Activation (ReLU) are utilised. For loss estimation, a learning rate of 0.001 and cross-entropy loss are chosen.

4.4   Performance Evaluation

F1-Score. It is a widely used statistical parameter for analyzing the performance of the model. As stated in [7], it is calculated as the harmonic mean of the model's precision and recall. Its value ranges from 0 to 1, with a score closer to 1 indicating higher performance.

MCC. It shows the degree of correlation between the expected and actual class [21]. For model comparison, it is typically regarded as a balanced measure. It is in the range of -1 to 1.

Jaccard Index. The Jaccard index is a metric for determining how similar and different the two classes are. It is in the range of 0 to 1. It is described as [2]:

$$\text{Jaccard Index} = \frac{TP}{TP + FP + FN}, \tag{14}$$

where TP, FP, and FN, represent True Positive, False Positive, and False Negative, respectively.

Hamming Loss. It considers class labels that were predicted wrongly. The prediction error (prediction of an incorrect label), and the missing error (prediction of a relevant label) are normalized across all the classes and test data. The following formula can be used to determine Hamming loss [6]:

$$\text{Hamming Loss} = \frac{1}{nL} \sum_{i=1}^{n} \sum_{j=1}^{L} I(y_i^j \neq \hat{y}_i^j), \tag{15}$$

where y_i^j and $\hat{y}_i^j$ are the actual and predicted labels, and I is an indicator function. The more it is close to 0, the better the performance of the algorithm.

5   Experimental Results

5.1   Spectrographic Analysis

Panel I of the Fig. 3 show the speech segment of vowel /e/. Panel II, III, and IV shows the spectrogram, Mel spectrogram, and scalogram, respectively, for (a) normal, (b) very low, (c) low, (d) medium, and (e) high dysarthric severity-level for the same speech segment. It can be observed from Fig. 4 that the scalogram-based features can capture energy-based discriminative acoustic cues for dysarthric severity-levels more accurately than the STFT and Mel spectrogram-based features. Furthermore, from scalogram, it can be observed that as the dysarthtic severity-level increases, patients struggle to speak the prolonged vowel, /e/. This may be due to the lack of coordination between articulators and the brain. Due to this, the energy spread is seen over the entire time-axis. However, the utterance of vowel /e/ is of short duration for medium and high dysarthtic severity-levels.

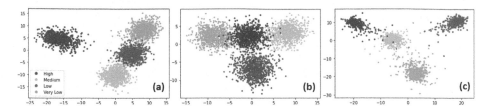

Fig. 4. Scatter plot obtained using LDA for (a) STFT, (b) Mel spectrogram, and (c) Scalogram. After [11]. Best viewed in color.

Table 1. Results in (% classification accuracy) for CNN classifier.

Feature set	CNN
STFT	91.76
Mel-spectrogram	92.65
Scalogram	**95.17**

5.2   Performance Evaluation

The performance evaluation for various feature sets is done *via* % classification accuracy (as shown in Table 1). On CNN, the scalogram performs relatively better with a classification accuracy of 95.17% than the baseline STFT, and Mel spectrogram. The analyses in the following sub-Section and the % classification accuracy obtained through the CNN classifier, show the capabilities of the scalogram in capturing the energy spread generated during the speech production mechanism for various dysarthric severity-level. Furthermore, Table 2 shows the confusion matrix of the STFT, Mel spectrogram, and scalogram for CNN model. It can be observed that the scalogram reduces the false prediction error, which indicates the better performance of the scalogram *w.r.t* the baseline STFT, and Mel spectrogram. Additionally, Table 3 shows the comparison between statistical measures using the F-1 score, Jaccard index, MCC, and Hamming loss for various feature sets. It can be observed from Table 3 that scalogram performs relatively better than the baseline STFT and Mel spectrogram.

5.3   Visualization of Various Features Using Linear Discriminant Analysis (LDA)

The capabilities of scalogram for the classification of the dysarthic severity-level is also validated by LDA scatter plots due to it's higher image resolution and better projection of the given higher-dimensional feature space to lower-dimensional than the scatter plots obtained using t-sne plots [11]. Here, the LDA plot of STFT, Mel spectrogram, and scalogram are projected onto 2-D feature space, and represented using the scatter plot shown in Fig. 4 (a), Fig. 4 (b), and Fig. 4 (c), respectively. From Fig. 4, it can be observed that wavelet-based scalogram

Table 2. Confusion matrix obtained for STFT, Mel-spectrogram, and scalogram.

Feature Set	Severity	High	Medium	Low	Very Low
STFT	High	63	6	3	3
	Medium	10	79	3	1
	Low	3	4	79	7
	Very Low	1	2	1	89
Mel-Spectrogram	High	69	1	3	2
	Medium	5	81	4	3
	Low	4	1	91	0
	Very Low	4	0	2	89
Scalogram (Morse Wavelet)	High	69	5	1	0
	Medium	3	89	1	0
	Low	1	1	90	1
	Very Low	3	0	1	89

Table 3. Various statistical measures of STFT, Mel spectrogram, and scalogram.

Feature set	F1-score	MCC	Jaccard index	Hamming loss
STFT	0.87	0.83	0.776	0.124
Mel spectrogram	0.92	0.90	0.86	0.073
Scalogram	**0.95**	**0.91**	**0.94**	**0.05**

has low intra-class variance and high inter-class variance, which increases the distance between the clusters $w.r.t$ baseline STFT, and Mel spectrogram, thereby better classification performance by the Morse wavelet.

6   Summary and Conclusion

In this study, we investigated CWT, in particular, the Morse wavelet, to achieve improved resolution in time and frequency representation for various dysarthric severity levels. The low-frequency resolution of Morse wavelet-based scalogram is higher than the resolution of STFT and Mel spectrogram. Therefore, the energy spread corresponding to the dysarthric severity in low-frequency region is better visualized in the scalogram. Hence, the low-frequency discriminative cues are better classified using a scalogram. This can also be observed with the significant increase in % classification accuracy as compared to the STFT and Mel spectrogram. Furthermore, it was also observed that as the severity-level increases, due to difficulty for patients to utter the complete word, the energy spreading is more in frequency representation over the entire time-axis. The performance of the scalogram is also analyzed using various statistical performance parameters, such as $F1$-Score, MCC, Jaccard Index, Hamming Loss, and LDA scatter plots. Other dysarthric speech corpora, such as TORGO and Homeservice, will be used to further validate this work in the future. Our future efforts will focus on extending and validating this work on other dysarthric speech corpora, such as TORGO and Home service.

Acknowledgments. The authors would like to thank the Ministry of Electronics and Information Technology (MeitY), New Delhi, Govt. of India, for sponsoring the consortium project titled 'Speech Technologies in Indian Languages' under 'National Language Translation Mission (NLTM): BHASHINI', subtitled 'Building Assistive Speech Technologies for the Challenged' (Grant ID: 11(1)2022-HCC (TDIL)). We also thank the consortium leaders Prof. Hema A. Murthy, Prof. S. Umesh of IIT Madras, and the authorities of DA-IICT Gandhinagar, India for their support and cooperation to carry out this research work.

Appendix

A.1. Energy Conservation in STFT

The energy conservation in STFT for any signal $f(t) \in L^2(R)$ is given by

$$\int_{-\infty}^{+\infty} |f(t)|^2 dt = \frac{1}{2\pi} \int_{-\infty}^{+\infty} \int_{-\infty}^{+\infty} |Sf(u,\varsigma)|^2 d\varsigma du, \tag{16}$$

Here, u and ς indicate the time-frequency indices that vary across R and hence, covers the entire time-frequency plane. The reconstruction of signal can then be given by

$$f(t) = \frac{1}{2\pi} \int_{-\infty}^{+\infty} \int_{-\infty}^{+\infty} Sf(u,\varsigma)g(t-u)e^{i\varsigma t} d\varsigma du. \tag{17}$$

Applying Parseval's formula to Eq. (17) w.r.t. to the integration in u, we get

$$Sf(u,\varsigma) = e^{-iu\varsigma} f * g_\varsigma(u), \tag{18}$$

Here, $g_\varsigma(t) = g(t)e^{i\varsigma t}$. Hence, Fourier Transform of $Sf(u,\varsigma)$ is $\hat{f}(\omega_\varsigma)\hat{g}(\omega)$. Furthermore, after applying the Plancherel's formula to Eq. (16) gives

$$\frac{1}{2\pi} \int_{-\infty}^{+\infty} \int_{-\infty}^{+\infty} |Sf(u,\varsigma)|^2 dud\varsigma = \frac{1}{2\pi} \int_{-\infty}^{+\infty} \frac{1}{2\pi} \int_{-\infty}^{+\infty} |\hat{f}(\omega+\varsigma)\hat{g}(\omega)|^2 d\omega d\varsigma. \tag{19}$$

Finally, the Plancheral formula and the Fubini theorem result in $\frac{1}{2\pi} \int_{-\infty}^{+\infty} |\hat{f}(\omega+\varsigma)|^2 d\varsigma = ||f||^2$, which validates STFT's energy conservation as demonstrated in Eq. (16), It explains why the overall signal energy is the same as the time-frequency sum of the STFT.

A.2. Energy Conservation in CWT

Using the same derivations as in the discussion of Eq. 17, one can verify that the inverse wavelet formula reconstructs the analytic part of f :

$$f_a(t) = \frac{1}{C_\psi} \int_0^{+\infty} \int_{-\infty}^{+\infty} W f_a(u, s)\psi_s(t - u)\frac{ds}{s^2}du. \tag{20}$$

Applying the Plancherel formula for energy conservation for the analytic part of f_a given by

$$\int_{-\infty}^{+\infty} |f_a(t)|^2 dt = \frac{1}{C_\psi} \int_0^{+\infty} \int_{-\infty}^{+\infty} |W_a f(u, s)|^2 du \frac{ds}{s^2}. \tag{21}$$

Since $W f_a(u, s) = 2W f(u, s)$ and $||f_a||^2 = 2||f||^2$. If f is real, and the variable change $\zeta = \frac{1}{s}$ in energy conservation denotes that

$$||f||^2 = \frac{2}{C_\psi} \int_0^{+\infty} \int_{-\infty}^{+\infty} P_w f(u, \zeta)dud\zeta. \tag{22}$$

It reinforces the notion that a scalogram represents a time-frequency energy density.

References

1. Al-Qatab, B.A., Mustafa, M.B.: Classification of dysarthric speech according to the severity of impairment: an analysis of acoustic features. IEEE Access **9**, 18183–18194 (2021)
2. Bouchard, M., Jousselme, A.L., Doré, P.E.: A proof for the positive definiteness of the Jaccard index matrix. Int. J. Approx. Reason. **54**(5), 615–626 (2013)
3. Chen, H., Zhang, P., Bai, H., Yuan, Q., Bao, X., Yan, Y.: Deep convolutional neural network with scalogram for audio scene modeling. In: INTERSPEECH, Hyderabad India, pp. 3304–3308 (2018)
4. Darley, F.L., Aronson, A.E., Brown, J.R.: Differential diagnostic patterns of dysarthria. J. Speech Hear. Res. (JSLHR) **12**(2), 246–269 (1969)
5. Daubechies, I.: The wavelet transform, time-frequency localization and signal analysis. IEEE Trans. Inf. Theory **36**(5), 961–1005 (1990)
6. Dembczyński, K., Waegeman, W., Cheng, W., Hüllermeier, E.: Regret analysis for performance metrics in multi-label classification: the case of hamming and subset zero-one loss. In: Balcázar, J.L., Bonchi, F., Gionis, A., Sebag, M. (eds.) ECML PKDD 2010. LNCS (LNAI), vol. 6321, pp. 280–295. Springer, Heidelberg (2010). https://doi.org/10.1007/978-3-642-15880-3_24
7. Fawcett, T.: An introduction to ROC analysis. Pattern Recognit. Lett. **27**(8), 861–874 (2006)
8. Gillespie, S., Logan, Y.Y., Moore, E., Laures-Gore, J., Russell, S., Patel, R.: Cross-database models for the classification of dysarthria presence. In: INTERSPEECH, Stockholm, Sweden, pp. 3127–31 (2017)
9. Gupta et al., S.: Residual neural network precisely quantifies dysarthria severity-level based on short-duration speech segments. Neural Netw. **139**, 105–117 (2021)
10. Holschneider, M.: Wavelets. An analysis tool (1995)

11. Izenman, A.J.: Linear discriminant analysis. In: Izenman, A.J. (ed.) Modern Multivariate Statistical Techniques. Springer Texts in Statistics, pp. 237–280. Springer, New York (2013). https://doi.org/10.1007/978-0-387-78189-1_8

12. Joshy, A.A., Rajan, R.: Automated dysarthria severity classification using deep learning frameworks. In: 28th European Signal Processing Conference (EUSIPCO), Amsterdam, Netherlands, pp. 116–120 (2021)

13. Knutsson, H., Westin, C.F., Granlund, G.: Local multiscale frequency and bandwidth estimation. In: Proceedings of 1st International Conference on Image Processing, Austin, TX, USA, vol. 1, pp. 36–40, 13–16 November 1994

14. LeCun, Y., Kavukcuoglu, K., Farabet, C.: Convolutional networks and applications in vision. In: Proceedings of 2010 IEEE International Symposium on Circuits and Systems, Paris, France, pp. 253–256 (2010)

15. Lieberman, P.: Primate vocalizations and human linguistic ability. J. Acoust. Soci. Am. (JASA) 44(6), 1574–1584 (1968)

16. Lilly, J.M., Olhede, S.C.: Generalized Morse wavelets as a superfamily of analytic wavelets. IEEE Trans. Signal Process. 60(11), 6036–6041 (2012)

17. Lilly, J.M., Olhede, S.C.: Higher-order properties of analytic wavelets. IEEE Trans. Signal Process. 57(1), 146–160 (2008)

18. Lilly, J.M., Olhede, S.C.: On the analytic wavelet transform. IEEE Trans. Inf. Theory 56(8), 4135–4156 (2010)

19. Mackenzie, C., Lowit, A.: Behavioural intervention effects in dysarthria following stroke: communication effectiveness, intelligibility and dysarthria impact. Int. J. Lang. Commun. Disord. 42(2), 131–153 (2007)

20. Mallat, S.: A Wavelet Tour of Signal Processing, 2nd edn. Elsevier, Amsterdam (1999)

21. Matthews, B.W.: Comparison of the predicted and observed secondary structure of T4 phage lysozyme. Biochimica et Biophysica Acta (BBA) Prot. Struct. 405(2), 442–451 (1975)

22. Ren, Z., Qian, K., Zhang, Z., Pandit, V., Baird, A., Schuller, B.: Deep scalogram representations for acoustic scene classification. IEEE/CAA J. Automatica Sinica 5(3), 662–669 (2018)

23. Vásquez-Correa, J.C., Orozco-Arroyave, J.R., Nöth, E.: Convolutional neural network to model articulation impairments in patients with Parkinson's disease. In: INTERSPEECH, Stockholm, pp. 314–318 (2017)

24. Young, V., Mihailidis, A.: Difficulties in automatic speech recognition of dysarthric speakers and implications for speech-based applications used by the elderly: A literature review. Assist. Technol. 22(2), 99–112 (2010)

25. Yu, J., et al.: Development of the CUHK dysarthric speech recognition system for the UA speech corpus. In: INTERSPEECH, Hyderabad, India, pp. 2938–2942 (2018)

Significance of Energy Features for Severity Classification of Dysarthria

Aastha Kachhi[1]([✉]), Anand Therattil[1], Ankur T. Patil[1], Hardik B. Sailor[2], and Hemant A. Patil[1]

[1] Speech Research Lab, DAIICT, Gandhinagar, India
{aastha_kachhi,anand_therattil,ankur_patil,hemant_patil}@daiict.ac.in
[2] Samsung R&D Bangalore, Bengaluru, India

Abstract. Dysarthria is a neuro-motor speech disorder that affects the intelligibility of speech, which is often imperceptible depending on its severity-level. Patients' advancement in the dysarthric severity-level are diagnosed using the classification system, which also aids in automatic dysarthric speech recognition (an important assistive speech technology). This study investigates presence of the linear *vs.* non-linear components in the dysarthic speech for severity-level classification using the Squared Energy Cepstral Coefficients (SECC) and Teager Energy Cepstral Coefficients (TECC), which captures the linear and non-linear production features of the speech signal, respectively. The comparison of the TECC and SECC is presented *w.r.t* the baseline STFT and MFCC features using three deep learning architectures, namely, Convolutional Neural Network (CNN), Light-CNN (LCNN), and Residual Neural Network (ResNet) as pattern classifiers. SECC gave improved classification accuracy by 6.28% (7.89%/3.60%) than baseline STFT system, 1.7% (4.23%/0.99%) than MFCC and 0.1.41% (0.56%/0.28%) than TECC on CNN (LCNN/ResNet) classifier systems, respectively. Finally, the analysis of feature discrimination power is presented using Linear Discriminant Analysis (LDA), Jaccard index, Matthew's Correlation Coefficient (MCC), F1-score, and Hamming loss followed by analysis of latency period in order to investigate practical significance of proposed approach.

Keywords: Dysarthria · UA-Speech corpus · TEO profiles · TECC · Squared energy · SEO profiles

1 Introduction

Speech production requires proper coordination between speech producing muscles and brain [17]. Speech disorders, such as aparaxia, dysarthria, and stuttering are caused by a lack of this coordination. These conditions affect a person's capacity to produce speech sounds. These disorders are categorized as neurological or

This work was done when Dr. Hardik B. Sailor was at Samsung Research Institute, Bangalore, India in collaboration with DA-IICT, Gandhinagar.

© Springer Nature Switzerland AG 2022
S. R. M. Prasanna et al. (Eds.): SPECOM 2022, LNAI 13721, pp. 325–337, 2022.
https://doi.org/10.1007/978-3-031-20980-2_28

neurodegenerative disorders. These disorders might be mild or severe, depending on the impact and damage done on the area of brain. Amongst these disorders, dysarthria is the most common disorder [28]. Dysarthria is a neuro-motor disorder, which weakens the muscles that are responsible for speech production. Apart from the muscles, articulators such as lips, tongue, throat, and upper respiratory tract system of a patient are also affected. Severity of dysarthria depends on intensity of damage done to neurological area, and its treatment also depends on the cause and symptoms [2]. These factors have inspired researchers to create a diagnostic aid for the enhancement of speech intelligibility for dysarthic speech.

Extensive study for this problem has been explored in the literature. These studies employed state-of-the-art Mel Frequency Cepstral Coefficients (MFCC) because of their ability to capture *global* spectral envelope for a perceptually-motivated audio classification tasks [11]. Moreover, studies based on glottal source parameters derived from quasi-periodic sampling of vocal tract systems are also explored in [6]. The mismatch in vocal fold vibration between dysarthric and normal speech production, as indicated in [20], cannot be explained merely by the rate of vibration (i.e., excitation source information); rather the *mode* of vibration (oscillations) of vocal folds is also influenced. As a result, information generated by the waveform of acoustic speech excitation and glottal flow may have useful information. Moreover, there is difference in non-linearities in speech production for normal *vs.* dysarthric speech. Hence, the speech signal energies could not be estimated accurately using linear filter theory [26]. Hence, to capture the non-linearities present during the speech production mechanism, Teager Energy Operator (TEO) was proposed in 1990 [19]. Many recent studies reveal that feature representation using TEO are useful for anti-spoofing task [4]. To that effect, the key objective of this study is to explore and analyse the difference in non-linearities present in normal and various severity-level dysarthric speech using Teager Energy Cepstral Coefficients (TECC) [4,7], and Squared Energy Cepstral Coefficients (SECC).

To validate this hypothesis, we compare the performance of SECC with TECC. The Short-Time Fourier Transform (STFT) is used as baseline for this study as in [11]. The features extracted from the word utterances spoken by speakers from standard UA-Speech corpus were used to train CNN, LCNN, and ResNet models. Dysarthric speech is enhanced using speech enhancer designed for formants [12] and hence, this study also investigates the proposition by analysing the TEO profile and Squared Energy Operator (SEO) around 1st formant frequency for vowel, $/i/$, and $/e/$.

The rest of the paper is organized as follows: Sect. 2 presents the TEO *vs.* SEO analysis alaong with feature extraction process whereas Sect. 3 gives the Experimental setup. Section 4 gives the detailed experimental results and analysis. Finally Sect. 5 concludes the paper along with potential future direction.

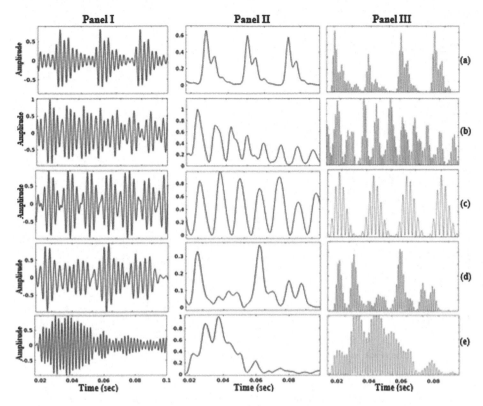

Fig. 1. Subband filtered signal (for vowel /i/) for male speakers around $1^{st} formant F_1 = 500$ Hz (Panel I), corresponding TEO profile (Panel II), and corresponding $|.|^2$ (i.e., SEO profile) envelope (Panel III) for (a) normal, dysarthic speech with severity-level as (b) very low, (c) low, (d) medium, and (e) high. After [19].

2   TEO *vs.* SEO

2.1   Analysis of SEO and TEO Profile

In the signal processing literature, the energy of the speech signal $x(t)$ is estimated by calculating the integral of square of absolute operation across the entire signal under consideration, i.e., estimating the squared energy of the signal, referred to as SEO [21]. This energy estimation method is based on linear filtering theory (specifically, Parseval's energy equivalence, the total energy of a signal, i.e., squared energy is conserved in the frequency-domain and this is also the condition of existence of inverse for several *linear* transforms, such as Fourier, Gabor, and Wavelet transforms), which can only represent the linear components of the speech generation process [19]. However, in particular consider a discrete-time speech signal $x(n)$. The parseval's energy equivalence in Discrete-Time Fourier Transform (DTFT) framework is given by [25]:

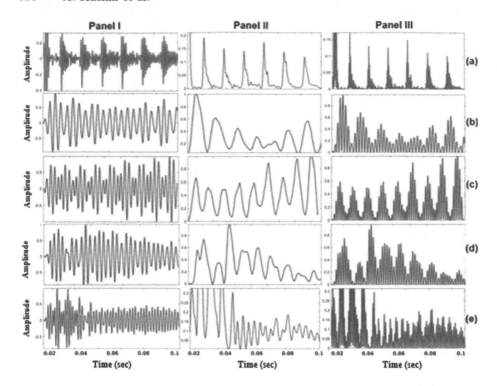

Fig. 2. Subband filtered signal (for vowel /e/) for male speakers around 1st formant $F_1 = 500$ Hz (Panel I), corresponding TEO profile (Panel II), and corresponding $|.|^2$ (i.e., SEO profile) envelope (Panel III) for (a) normal, dysarthic speech with severity-level as (b) very low, (c) low, (d) medium, and (e) high. After [19].

$$\sum_{n=-\infty}^{\infty} x(n).x^*(n) = \frac{1}{2\pi} \int_{-\infty}^{\infty} X(e^{j\omega}).X^*(e^{j\omega}) \, d\omega \tag{1}$$

where $*$ denotes the complex conjugate operation, and $X(e^{j\omega})$ represents DTFT of $x(n)$. From the Eq. (1), it can be inferred that

$$<x(n), x(n)> = \frac{1}{2\pi}<X(e^{j\omega}), X(j\omega)> \tag{2}$$

where $<,>$ indicates inner product operator. Equation 2 can be represented as

$$x(n) * \bar{x}(n) = \frac{1}{2\pi}<X(e^{j\omega}), X(e^{j\omega})>, \tag{3}$$

where $\bar{x}(n) = x^*(-n)$, and in Eq. (3) $*$ is convolutional operator $w.r.t.$ LTI operator. Thus it can be observed that the square of the L^2 norm, (i.e.), energy of a signal imposes an inner product structure on the speech signal and this in turn imposes linear structure on the data through convolution operation.

The energy of the speech wave could not be properly approximated using linear filter theory because the true speech production mechanism is non-linear [26]. Hence, TEO was developed to alleviate this issue [13]. It is defined as a nonlinear differential operator that can represent the speech production mechanism as well as the features of the airflow pattern in the vocal tract system during speech production [21,23]. The TEO for a discrete-time signal $x(n)$ with amplitude A and monocomponent angular frequency ω is obtained by approximating the derivative operation in continuous-time with backward difference in discrete-time [13]. In particular,

$$\Psi\{x(n)\} = x^2(n) - x(n-1)x(n+1) \approx A^2\Omega_m^2. \tag{4}$$

Here, we analyse the TEO profiles around the 1st formant frequency (i.e., $F_1 = 500$ Hz) for the utterance /i/ and /e/ for normal vs. different dysarthric severity-levels. Panel I of Fig. 1 and Fig. 2 shows the subband filtered signal around 1st formant (F_1) frequency using a linearly-spaced Gabor filter, and Panel II shows corresponding TEO profiles. Figure 1 and Fig. 2(a), Fig. 1 and Fig. 2(b), Fig. 1 and Fig. 2(c), Fig. 1 and Fig. 2(d), and Fig. 1 and Fig. 2(e) shows the analysis for normal, very low, low, medium, and high severity-levels, respectively. The high energy pulses shown in the TEO profiles are around GCIs. The *sudden* closure of glottis provides the impulse-like excitation to vocal tract. TEO, by virtue of it's property, captures the high energy strength due to sudden closure of glottis and airflow through the glottis. The region around the sudden closure point also has relatively high energy [22]. As observed from Fig. 1(a) and Fig. 2(a) the TEO profiles shows the non decaying function with *bumps* within glottal cycle. Therefore, the presence of bumps within the glottal cycle indicates that the speech production process is not linear only due to the linear model, but also includes a significant contribution from nonlinear effects (captured through the TEO profile, which may not be well captured through the linear model alone). We refer to this contribution as the aeroacoustic contribution [13,19,23]. It can be observed that TEO profile for normal speech shows *bumps* within two consecutive Glottal Closure Instants (GCIs), which are known to indicate non-linearities in the speech production mechanism [23]. Furthermore, it can also be observed that the quasi-periodicity in glottal excitation source decreases with increase in severity-level (as observed via aperiodic TEO profile) indicating *disruption* in the rhythmic quasi-periodic movements of vocal folds due to dysarthria. Moreover, it is all the more significant in high severity dysarthric condition. Furthermore, as the severity-level increases, the neuro-motor impairment also increase, which leads to increased disruption in vocal fold closure and loosing *structural* periodicity. From Panel III of Fig. 1 and Fig. 2, which shows the SEO profiles around 1st formant frequency for vowel /i/ and /e/ respectively, it can be observed that the SEO is capable of maintaining the periodicity in the speech produced by dysarthric speaker, which are not captured by TEO due to possible decrease in non-linearities. Hence, it can be said that as the dysarthric severity-level increases, the linearities (i.e., linear component) in speech signal increases.

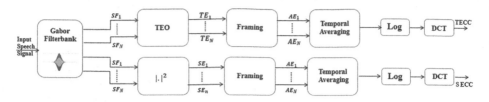

Fig. 3. Functional block diagram of the proposed TECC and SECC feature sets. (SF: Subband filtered signal, SE: Squared linear energies, TE: Teager energies, AE: Averaged energies over frames). After [4].

2.2   SECC and TECC Feature Extraction

TEO was originally derived to find the running estimate of the signal's energy for a monocomponent signal [13]. However, speech signal consists of the frequency range varying from low frequency to the Nyquist frequency. Hence, to obtain the monocomponent approximation of the signal, the speech signal is passed through the filterbank, which consists of several subband filters with appropriate center frequency and bandwidth. The subband filtered signals are narrowband signals, which are supposed to approximate the monotone signals and hence, TEO can be applied on these subband filtered signals. In this work, Gabor filterbank with linearly-spaced subband filters are utilized for subband filtering. We chose Gabor filters due to their *optimal* time and frequency resolution in the context of Heisenberg's uncertainty principle in signal processing framework [19]. TEO is applied on each subband filtered signal to accurately estimate the signal's energy. Furthermore, these narrowband energies are segmented into the frames of 20 ms duration with overlapping of 10 ms. Then, temporal average for each frame is estimated to produce N-dimensional (D feature vector) *subband Teager energy representations (subband-TE)*. Discrete Cosine Transform (DCT) is applied on *subband Teager energy representations* to obtain the TECC feature vector.

For SECC extraction, these narrowband output signals from Gabor filterbank are squared to estimate corresponding energies. Next, these narrowband energies are segmented with similar number of frames and window overlap. Temporal averaging for each frame is estimated (i.e., squared energy of each subband signal) to get N-D *subband Squared Energy representation (subband-SE)*. DCT is applied on *subband Squared energy representations* to obtain the SECC. The functional block diagram representation of TECC and SECC feature vectors are shown in Fig. 3. Throughout this paper, TECC and SECC features extracted using linear frequency scale and for both the feature vectors, DCT does the job of feature decorrelation, energy compaction, and dimensionality reduction.

3   Experimental Setup

3.1   Dataset Used

The proposed technique is validated using standard Universal Access dysarthric speech (UA-Speech) Corpus [29]. Table 1 shows the statistics of UA Speech

Corpus. In our experiments, we have used data of 8 speakers, i.e., 4 males, namely, $M01$, $M05$, $M07$, and $M09$ and 4 females, namely, $F02$, $F03$, $F04$, and $F05$. From 765 word utterances, 465 utterances per speaker as mentioned in [8] was used. For training and testing, we used 90% and 10% of the data, respectively.

Table 1. Class-wise patient details. After [29].

	Female	Male
High	F03	M01, M04, M12
Medium	F02	M07, M16
Low	F04	M05, M11
Very Low	F05	M08, M09, M10, M14

3.2 Details of Feature Sets

In this study, performance of SECC is analysed against three baseline systems, namely, STFT, TECC, and MFCC [8,24]. The STFT features are extracted using a 2 ms window length and 0.5 ms TECC feature set is extracted as mentioned in Subsect. 2.2. The DCT applied on *subband-TE* gives 120-D TECC feature vector which, consists of 40-D static, Δ, and $\Delta\Delta$ coefficients, each. MFCC feature set is extracted by applying STFT on the speech signal. The weighted sum is performed on each Mel scale subband filtered signals and as a result, we get Mel filterbank coefficients. Thereafter, log and DCT are applied to obtain MFCC feature vector of 120-D including 40-D of each, static, Δ, and $\Delta\Delta$ coefficients.

3.3 Classifier Details

Convolutional Neural Network (CNN). Based on the experiments reported in [11], CNN performs comparable $w.r.t$ the other deep neural network (DNN)-based classifiers for UA-Speech corpus. Hence, we employed CNN classifier in this study. CNN model was trained using Adam optimizer algorithm and 3 convolutional layers each with kernel size 5×5, and 1 Fully-Connected (FC) layer [16]. The input feature is made of uniform size of $D \times 300$, where D is the dimension of the feature vector. Rectified Linear Activation (ReLU) and a max-pool layer are used. Learning rate of 0.001 and cross-entropy loss is selected for loss estimation.

Light-CNN. The LCNN architecture was also implemented, since it is one of the most successful designs for anti-spoofing tasks [14,15,27]. The experiments were performed on the uniform $D \times 300$ features. LCNN architecture uses Max-Feature-Map (MFM) activation operation, for learning with a small number of parameters [27].

Residual Neural Network (ResNet). ResNets are one of the popular DNN classifiers and introduced to take the advantage of more DNN by integrating the high/mid/low-level features. ResNets are introduced to alleviate the issue of vanishing/exploding gradients of more DNNs. It utilizes the identity mapping as explained in [9], which allows stacking more number of layers without introducing the vanishing/exploding gradients and permits the possibility of smooth convergence. The increase in layers of DNN allow learning high-level features and thus, improving the classification performance of the system. We have utilized ResNet architecture having 22 layers.

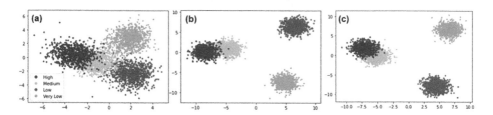

Fig. 4. Scatter plots obtained using LDA for (a) MFCC, (b) TECC, and (c) SECC. After [10]. Best viewed in colour. (Color figure online)

3.4 Performance Evaluation

Performance of SECC is compared *w.r.t.* TECC and MFCC using various statistical measures, such as $F1$-Score, Matthew's Correlation Coefficient (MCC), Jaccard's Index, and Hamming Loss.

F1-Score. It is an extensively used statistical measure to analyse the performance of the model. It is the harmonic mean of the precision and recall of the model, as in [5]. It ranges between 0 and 1, where model with score closer to 1 indicated better performance.

MCC. It gives the correlation degree between predicted and actual class [18]. It is generally considered balanced measure for model comparison. It ranges between -1 and 1.

Jaccard Index. Jaccard Index is a parameter for calculating similarity and dissimilarity between given classes. It ranges between 0 and 1. It is defined as [1]:

$$\text{Jaccard Index} = \frac{TP}{TP + FP + FN},\tag{5}$$

where TP, FP, and FN, represents True Positive, False Positive, and False Negative, respectively.

Hamming Loss. It takes into account class labels that were incorrectly predicted. The prediction error (i.e., prediction of an inaccurate label) and missing error (prediction of a relevant label) are normalised over the total number of classes and test data. Hamming loss can be calculated using the following formula [3]:

$$\text{Hamming Loss} = \frac{1}{nL}\sum_{i=1}^{n}\sum_{j=1}^{L}I(y_i^j \neq \hat{y}_i^j), \tag{6}$$

where y_i^j and $\hat{y}_i^j$ are the actual and predicted labels, and I is an indicator function. The more it is close to 0, the better is the performance of the algorithm.

4   Experimental Results

4.1   Performance Evaluation

The results obtained as % classification accuracy using various feature sets are reported in Table 2. It can be observed that SECC performs absolute relative performance than the baseline STFT, MFCC, and TECC with classification accuracy of 6.28% (7.89%/3.6%) than baseline STFT, 1.7% (4.23%/0.99%) than MFCC and 0.1.41% (0.56%/0.28%) than TECC on CNN (LCNN/ResNet) classifier systems, respectively. Furthermore, SECC performs better than the baseline MFCC explored in [11]. The analysis in the subsequent Section, along with the classification accuracy obtained using various classifiers, indicate that the linearities in speech production mechanism increases with increase in dysarthric severity-level.

Furthermore, Table 3 shows the confusion matrices for MFCC, TECC, and SECC for ResNet model. It can be observed that SECC reduces the misclassification errors corresponding to the different severity-levels, indicating the better performance of SECC *w.r.t.* TECC and MFCC. Furthermore, performance of SECC *w.r.t.* TECC and MFCC is also analysed using $F1$-Score, MCC, Jaccard Index, and Hamming Loss as shown in Table 4. It can be observed from Table 4 that SECC performs better than the TECC for the dysarthic severity-level classification.

Table 2. Confusion matrix obtained for STFT, MFCC, TECC, and SECC.

Feature set	% Classification accuracy		
	CNN	LCNN	ResNet
STFT	91.76	88.43	95.32
MFCC	96.32	92.09	95.33
TECC	96.61	95.76	96.04
SECC	**98.02**	**96.32**	**98.92**

Table 3. Confusion matrix for MFCC, TECC, and SECC using CNN.

Feature	Severity	High	Medium	Low	Very Low
MFCC	High	67	4	3	1
	Medium	2	90	0	0
	Low	1	1	91	0
	Very Low	1	0	0	92
TECC	High	72	1	2	0
	Medium	2	90	0	0
	Low	1	1	91	0
	Very Low	0	0	0	93
SECC	High	74	1	0	0
	Medium	2	90	0	0
	Low	1	0	92	0
	Very Low	0	0	0	93

Table 4. Various statistical measures of MFCC, TECC, and SECC.

Feature set	F1-score	MCC	Jaccard index	Hamming loss
MFCC	0.96	0.95	0.82	0.036
TECC	0.97	0.96	0.95	0.025
SECC	**0.98**	**0.97**	**0.96**	**0.019**

4.2 Visualization of Various Features Using Linear Discriminant Analysis (LDA)

Capability of SECC to classify severity-level is also validated by LDA scatter plots due to it's higher image resolution and better projection of the given higher-dimensional feature space to lower-dimensional than the scatter plots obtained using t-sne plots [10]. Here MFCC, TECC, and SECC features are projected to the 2-D space to get the scatter plots for various severity-levels of dysarthria. Figure 4(a), Fig. 4(b), and Fig. 4(c) shows the LDA plots of MFCC, TECC, and SECC, respectively. From the Fig. 4, it can be observed that for SECC, the variance of each severity-level clusters is less resulting in relatively better performance of SECC, which increases the interclass distance between the clusters than the baselines STFT, MFCC, and TECC.

4.3 Latency Analysis

Latency period for SECC *w.r.t.* TECC and MFCC were also analysed as shown in Fig. 5. Latency period was calculated using the % classification accuracy on varying test utterance. The utterance was varied from 50 ms to 300 ms. To that

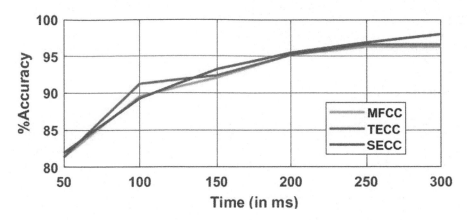

Fig. 5. Latency period *vs.* % classification accuracy comparison between MFCC, TECC, and SECC. Best viewed in colour. (Color figure online)

effect, experiments were performed on $x86\_64$ 32 bit, INTEL(R) Core(TM) i5-2400 CPU at 3.10 GHz. For short speech segments, the better performing model should produce higher accuracy in terms of relatively lower latency period. From the Fig. 5, it can be observed that SECC gives consistent and relatively better classification accuracy in short duration of time as 60 ms. Furthermore, TECC and MFCC gives increased classification accuracy for speech segment of 100 ms and 250 ms, respectively. Hence, these results signifies the practical suitability of SECC in dysarthric speech severity-level classification.

5   Summary and Conclusion

In this study, we analysed the effect of the linear *vs.* non-linear energy operator for the analysis and classification of the severity-level of the dysarthric speech. The squared energy operator is analysed against TEO to validate the effect of non-linearity w.r.t. severity-level in dysarthric speech. The bumps which characterizes the non-linearities in the speech production mechanism were observed in the TEO profile of normal speech signal. Whereas, this bumpy structure was found to be reduced w.r.t. increase in the severity-level. Hence, we believe that the squared energy operator seems to be more suitable for dysarthric speech analysis as SEO is known to impose linear structure on the speech data and have help in capturing linear components in speech production. These hypotheses are tested by performing the experiments using CNN, LCNN, and ResNet classifiers. The experimental results showed that the squared energy operator is more suitable over nonlinear operator, such as TEO for dysarthric speech analysis and classification. The observation were validated using various statistical measures, such as $F1$-score, MCC, Jaccard Index, Hamming Loss, LDA, and analysis of latency period. Our future efforts will be directed to extend and validate this work on the other dysarthic speech corpora, such as TORGO, and Home service.

Acknowledgments. The authors sincerely thank the PRISM team at Samsung R&D Institute, Bangalore (SRI-B), India. We would also like to thank the authorities of DA-IICT Gandhinagar for kind support and cooperation to carry out this research work.

References

1. Bouchard, M., Jousselme, A.L., Doré, P.E.: A proof for the positive definiteness of the Jaccard index matrix. Int. J. Approx. Reason. **54**(5), 615–626 (2013)
2. Darley, F.L., Aronson, A.E., Brown, J.R.: Differential diagnostic patterns of dysarthria. J. Speech Hear. Res. (JSLHR) **12**(2), 246–269 (1969)
3. Dembczyński, K., Waegeman, W., Cheng, W., Hüllermeier, E.: Regret analysis for performance metrics in multi-label classification: the case of hamming and subset zero-one loss. In: Balcázar, J.L., Bonchi, F., Gionis, A., Sebag, M. (eds.) ECML PKDD 2010. LNCS (LNAI), vol. 6321, pp. 280–295. Springer, Heidelberg (2010). https://doi.org/10.1007/978-3-642-15880-3_24
4. Dimitriadis, D., Maragos, P., Potamianos, A.: Auditory Teager energy cepstrum coefficients for robust speech recognition. In: INTERSPEECH, Lisbon, Portugal, pp. 3013–3016, September 2005
5. Fawcett, T.: An introduction to ROC analysis. Pattern Recognit. Lett. **27**(8), 861–874 (2006)
6. Gillespie, S., Logan, Y.Y., Moore, E., Laures-Gore, J., Russell, S., Patel, R.: Cross-database models for the classification of dysarthria presence. In: INTERSPEECH, Stockholm, Sweden, pp. 3127–31 (2017)
7. Grozdic, D.T., Jovicic, S.T.: Whispered speech recognition using deep denoising autoencoder and inverse filtering. IEEE/ACM Trans. Audio Speech Lang. Process. (TASLP) **25**(12), 2313–2322 (2017)
8. Gupta et al., S.: Residual neural network precisely quantifies dysarthria severity-level based on short-duration speech segments. Neural Netw. **139**, 105–117 (2021)
9. He, K., Zhang, X., Ren, S., Sun, J.: Deep residual learning for image recognition. In: Proceedings of the IEEE Conference on Computer Vision and Pattern Recognition (CVPR), LV, Nevada, USA, pp. 770–778 (2016)
10. Izenman, A.J.: Linear discriminant analysis. In: Izenman, A.J. (ed.) Modern Multivariate Statistical Techniques, pp. 237–280. Springer Texts in Statistics. Springer, New York (2013). https://doi.org/10.1007/978-0-387-78189-1_8
11. Joshy, A.A., Rajan, R.: Automated dysarthria severity classification using deep learning frameworks. In: 28th European Signal Processing Conference (EUSIPCO), Amsterdam, Netherlands, pp. 116–120 (2021)
12. Kain, A.B., Hosom, J.P., Niu, X., Van Santen, J.P., Fried-Oken, M., Staehely, J.: Improving the intelligibility of dysarthric speech. Speech Commun. **49**(9), 743–759 (2007)
13. Kaiser, J.F.: On a simple algorithm to calculate the energy of a signal. In: International Conference on Acoustics. Speech, and Signal Processing (ICASSP), New Mexico, USA, pp. 381–384 (1990)
14. Lavrentyeva, G., Novoselov, S., Malykh, E., Kozlov, A., Kudashev, O., Shchemelinin, V.: Audio replay attack detection with deep learning frameworks. In: INTERSPEECH, Stockholm, Sweden, pp. 82–86, August 2017
15. Lavrentyeva, G., Novoselov, S., Tseren, A., Volkova, M., Gorlanov, A., Kozlov, A.: STC Antispoofing systems for the ASVSpoof2019 challenge. In: INTERSPEECH, Graz, Austria, pp. 1033–37, September 2019

16. LeCun, Y., Kavukcuoglu, K., Farabet, C.: Convolutional networks and applications in vision. In: Proceedings of 2010 IEEE International Symposium on Circuits and Systems, Paris, France, pp. 253–256 (2010)
17. Lieberman, P.: Primate vocalizations and human linguistic ability. J. Acoust. Soc. Am. (JASA) **44**(6), 1574–1584 (1968)
18. Matthews, B.W.: Comparison of the predicted and observed secondary structure of T4 phage lysozyme. Biochimica et Biophysica Acta (BBA) Protein Struct. **405**(2), 442–451 (1975)
19. Teager, H.M., Teager, S.M.: Evidence for nonlinear sound production mechanisms in the vocal tract. In: Hardcastle, W.J., Marchal, A. (eds.) Speech Production and Speech Modelling. NATO ASI Series, vol. 55, pp. 241–261. Springer, Dordrecht (1990). https://doi.org/10.1007/978-94-009-2037-8_10
20. Narendra, N., Alku, P.: Dysarthric speech classification using glottal features computed from non-words, words, and sentences. In: INTERSPEECH, Hyderabad, India, pp. 3403–3407 (2018)
21. Oppenheim, A.V., Willsky, A.S., Nawab, S.H., Hernández, G.M., et al.: Signals & Systems, 1st edn. Pearson Educación (1997)
22. Patil, H.A., Parhi, K.K.: Development of TEO phase for speaker recognition. In: 2010 International Conference on Signal Processing and Communications (SPCOM), pp. 1–5. IEEE (2010)
23. Quatieri, T.F.: Discrete-Time Speech Signal Processing: Principles and Practice, 3rd edn. Pearson Education, India (2006)
24. Strand, O.M., Egeberg, A.: Cepstral mean and variance normalization in the model domain. In: COST278 and ISCA Tutorial and Research Workshop (ITRW) on Robustness Issues in Conversational Interaction, Norwich, United Kingdom, pp. 30–31, August 2004
25. Szeliski, R.: Computer Vision: Algorithms and Applications. Springer, London (2010). https://doi.org/10.1007/978-1-84882-935-0
26. Teager, H.M.: Some observations on oral air flow during phonation. IEEE Trans. Acoust. Speech Signal Process. **28**(5), 599–601 (1980)
27. Wu, X., He, R., Sun, Z., Tan, T.: A light CNN for deep face representation with noisy labels. IEEE Trans. Inf. Forensics Secur. **13**(11), 2884–2896 (2018)
28. Young, V., Mihailidis, A.: Difficulties in automatic speech recognition of dysarthric speakers and implications for speech-based applications used by the elderly: a literature review. Assist. Technol. **22**(2), 99–112 (2010)
29. Yu, J., et al.: Development of the CUHK dysarthric speech recognition system for the UA speech corpus, In: INTERSPEECH, Hyderabad, India, pp. 2938–2942 (2018)

An Analytic Study on Clustering-Based Pseudo-labels for Self-supervised Deep Speaker Verification

Woo Hyun Kang, Jahangir Alam$^{(\boxtimes)}$, and Abderrahim Fathan

Computer Research Institute of Montreal (CRIM), Montreal, QC, Canada
{woohyun.kang,jahangir.alam,abderrahim.fathan}@crim.ca

Abstract. One of the most widely used self-supervised methods to train a speaker verification system is to generate the pseudo-labels using unsupervised clustering algorithms and train the speaker embedding network using the pseudo-labels in a discriminative fashion. Although the pseudo-label-based self-supervised speaker embedding extraction scheme have shown impressive performance, not much exploration was done regarding the pseudo-label generation process. In this paper, we have conducted a set of experiments using several clustering algorithms to analyze the impact of different clustering configurations for the pseudo-label-based self-supervised speaker verification system training strategy. From the experimental results, we observe that the performance of the self-supervised speaker embedding system heavily depends on the accuracy of the pseudo-labels, and the performance can be severely degraded when overfitting to the inaccurately generated pseudo-labels.

Keywords: Self-supervised speaker verification · Speech representation learning · VoxSRC 2021 · Clustering

1 Introduction

Attributed to the widespread deployment of smart devices, speaker verification has become a key technology for personal authentication in many commercial, forensics, and law enforcement applications [11]. Commonly, utterance-level fixed-dimensional vectors (i.e., embedding vectors) are extracted from the enrollment and test speech samples and then fed into a scoring algorithm (e.g., cosine distance, probabilistic linear discriminant analysis) to measure their similarity or likelihood of being spoken by the same speaker. Classically, the i-vector framework has been one of the most dominant approaches for speech embedding [6,14]. The widespread popularity of the i-vector framework in the speaker verification field was mainly due to its ability to summarize the distributive pattern of the speech with a relatively small amount of training data in an unsupervised manner.

© Springer Nature Switzerland AG 2022
S. R. M. Prasanna et al. (Eds.): SPECOM 2022, LNAI 13721, pp. 338–348, 2022.
https://doi.org/10.1007/978-3-031-20980-2_29

In recent years, various methods have been proposed utilizing deep learning architectures for extracting embedding vectors and have shown better performance than the i-vector framework when a large amount of training data with sufficient number of speakers is available [23]. In [22,23], a speaker recognition model consisting of a time-delay neural network (TDNN)-based frame-level network and a segment-level network was trained and the hidden layer activation of the segment-level network denoted as x-vector, was extracted as the embedding vector. In [8], an ECAPA-TDNN architecture was proposed, which has shown state-of-the-art performance by introducing residual and squeeze-and-excitation (SE) components to the widely used TDNN-based embedding system. Moreover in [2], a hybrid framework was proposed, which exploits the complementarity of different network modules to extract the speaker-dependent information from short- and long-context of speech. Although the deep embedding methods have outperformed the i-vector framework in various speaker verification benchmarks, since most of these models are trained in a fully supervised fashion, they require a large amount of speaker labeled dataset for optimization. But there are many challenges to extend this supervised strategy to every application or target domain as the cost of annotating a new dataset for every task domain can be very expensive and time-consuming. On the other hand, there are many resources that can be used to learn representations, but have not been used due to the lack of annotations.

To overcome this limitation and to leverage the available abundant unlabeled data, a number of self-supervised embedding learning methods for deep speaker verification were proposed over the past couple of years [3,9,13,16,24–26]. One of the most widely adopted strategies for self-supervised embedding learning is to create a pseudo-label using clustering algorithms [3,24,25]. Since the clustering algorithm focuses on grouping different samples together depending on their distance, one can assume that samples within the same clusters are likely to have the same or similar speaker identity. Therefore, once the pseudo-labels are created, the embedding network can be trained using the same pipeline with the supervised scenario. Although this pseudo-label-based strategy has shown impressive performance in self-supervised speaker verification task, its performance is highly dependent on the clustering algorithms' performance and can show unstable performance in certain training conditions. Regardless of the wide adoption of the pseudo-label-based self-supervised speaker embedding extractor training scheme, not many researches have investigated on this issue.

In light of this, we explore the effect of different configurations in the pseudo-label-based self-supervised speaker verification system. To analyze the performance, we have experimented with multiple speaker embedding architectures and pseudo-labels generated via different clustering algorithms and configurations. The contributions of this paper are as follows:

- We experimented with pseudo-labels created using GMMs with different configurations (e.g., number of clusters).
- We compared the performance of pseudo-labels created using different clustering algorithms (e.g., K-means [12], BIRCH [27], CURE [10], AHC [5]).

– We analyzed the training behaviour with pseudo-labels generated from different configurations and its limitation.
– We compared the pseudo-label-based training strategy on different embedding network architectures (e.g., ECAPA-TDNN [8], Hybrid [2]).

2 Self-supervised Speaker Embedding Extraction System

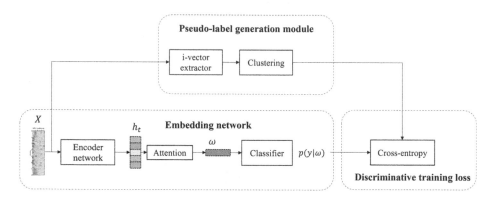

Fig. 1. General process for the clustering generated pseudo-label-based self-supervised speaker embedding network training.

2.1 Speaker Embedding Network

Generally a typical speaker embedding extraction system is composed of 2 networks: an encoder network and a classifier network. In the encoder network, given a speech utterance $\mathbf{X}$ with T frames, a sequence of frame-level acoustic features $\{\mathbf{x}_1, ..., \mathbf{x}_T\}$ extracted from $\mathbf{X}$ is fed into the frame-level network. Once the frame-level outputs $\{\mathbf{h}_1, ..., \mathbf{h}_T\}$ are obtained, they are aggregated to obtain an utterance-level embedding ω. The embedding is then fed into the classifier network, which is usually composed of feed-forward layers and outputs the probabilities $p(y|\omega)$, where y is the training class identity (e.g., speaker identity for supervised training, pseudo-label cluster identity for self-supervised training). After training the encoder and classifier networks, usually the classifier network is discarded and the encoder network is used for extracting the embedding vectors.

In our research, we have experimented with two types of encoder architectures which have shown good performance in speaker verification:

– Hybrid [2]: a CNN-LSTM-TDNN hybrid architecture with multi-level global-local statistics pooling, which has demonstrated good performance in various speaker verification tasks.

– ECAPA-TDNN [8]: an architecture that achieved state-of-the-art performance in text-independent speaker recognition. The ECAPA-TDNN uses squeeze-and-excitation as in the SE-ResNet, but also employs channel- and context-dependent statistics pooling and multi-layer aggregation.

The encoder network takes the acoustic feature as input and outputs the frame-level representations.

The ECAPA-TDNN outputs are aggregated via self-attention pooling, which computes the weighted average of the frame-level representations to obtain an utterance-level fixed dimensional embedding vector. On the other hand, in the Hybrid system, the statistics from the last layers of CNN, LSTM and TDNN blocks aggregated in order to capture speaker specific information from different spaces and learn more discriminative utterance level representations by bagging complementarity available in CNN, LSTM and TDNN networks. Moreover, the Hybrid architecture extracts the statistics not only globally, but also locally to exploit the short-durational correlation, where each modules (i.e., TDNN, LSTM) takes both the frame-level outputs from the previous model, and the local statistics extracted from them as input. Interested readers are referred to [2] for detailed information about the Hybrid embedding system.

2.2 Self-supervised Angular Additive Margin Softmax (AAMSoftmax) Objective

The angular additive margin softmax (AAMSoftmax) objective is one of the most popular methods for training a speaker embedding network [7]. The AAMSoftmax objective is formulated as follows:

$$L_{AAMSoftmax} = -\frac{1}{N}\sum_{i=1}^{N}log(\frac{e^{s(cos(\theta_{y_i,i}+m))}}{K_1}), \tag{1}$$

where $K_1 = e^{s(cos(\theta_{y_i,i}+m))} + \sum_{j=1,j\neq i}^{c}e^{scos\theta_{j,i}}$, N is the batch size, c is the number of classes, y_i corresponds to label index, $\theta_{j,i}$ represents the angle between the column vector of weight matrix W_j and the i-th embedding ω_i, where both W_j and ω_i are normalized. The scale factor s is used to make sure the gradient is not too small during the training and m is a hyperparameter that encourages the similarity of correct classes to be greater than that of incorrect classes by a margin m.

Although the AAMSoftmax has shown impressive performance in various speaker verification tasks, it cannot be directly used for self-supervised speaker embedding learning as the AAMSoftmax objective requires speaker labels for training. Therefore, in order to use the AAMSoftmax for training the embedding network in a self-supervised scenario, we have to create a pseudo-label using unsupervised methods, such as clustering [25].

2.3 Clustering-Based Pseudo-label Generation

To generate the pseudo-labels, we have extracted i-vector [6,14], which is a statistical unsupervised fixed-dimensional representation from each training utterance and performed clustering on top of them. After training the clustering algorithms, we selected the aligned cluster for each utterance and used the cluster-id as pseudo-label. With the clustering-based pseudo-labels, we can train the embedding network via softmax-based objectives (e.g., Eq. 1), analogous to the supervised learning scenario. The general framework for the clustering generated pseudo-label-based self-supervised speaker embedding network training is depicted in Fig. 1.

3   Experiments

3.1   Experimental Setup

In order to evaluate the performance of the proposed technique for self-supervised speaker verification, we conducted a set of experiments based on the VoxCeleb2 dataset [4]. For training the embedding networks, we used the *development* subset of the VoxCeleb2 dataset, consisting of 1,092,009 utterances collected from 5,994 speakers. The evaluation was performed according to the original Vox-Celeb1 trial list [17], which consists of 4,874 utterances spoken by 40 speakers. In addition, we have also conducted experiments on the VoxCeleb Speaker Recognition Challenge (VoxSRC) 2021 validation set, which consists of more challenging trials [1].

The acoustic features used in the experiments were 40-dimensional Mel-frequency cepstral coefficients (MFCCs) extracted at every 10 ms, using a 25 ms Hamming window via Kaldi toolkit [21]. The embedding networks are trained with segments consisting of 180 frames, using the ADAM optimization technique [15]. Moreover, we have used waveform-level data augmentations including additive noise and room impulse response (RIR) simulation [23]. In addition to the waveform-level augmentations, for the ECAPA-TDNN systems, we have also applied augmentation over the extracted MFCCs feature, analogous to the specaugment scheme [18]. For the Hybrid systems, we have applied specaugment to the spectrogram of the input speech.

For extracting the pseudo-labels, we first extracted the i-vectors using the Kaldi toolkit [21]. On the i-vectors extracted from the VoxCeleb2 development set, we have trained multiple GMMs with different number of clusters. In this paper, we report the results from 3 GMMs with the best performance, where each model consists of 3500, 5000 and 6000 clusters. The GMM training was done via scikit-learn toolkit [20].

The Hybrid embedding system was trained using the Kaldi toolkit [21]. All the other experimented networks were implemented via PyTorch [19], based on the voxceleb-unsupervised open-source project [13][1]. The networks were trained with initial learning rate 0.001 decayed with ratio 0.95 for 150 epochs, and the models from the best performing checkpoint were selected. The batch size for training was set to be 200. With the ECAPA-TDNN systems, Cosine similarity was used for computing the verification scores in the experiments. For the

---

[1] https://github.com/joonson/voxceleb_unsupervised.

hybrid networks, probabilistic linear discriminant analysis (PLDA), trained on VoxCeleb2 development set with pseudo labels, was used for verification scoring.

3.2   Experimental Results

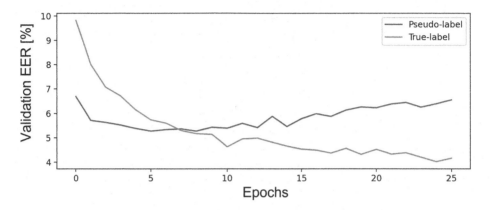

Fig. 2. EER (%) performance of speaker embedding systems trained with pseudo-labels and true labels on different training epochs.

Training Analysis on the Pseudo-label-Based Self-supervised Speaker Embedding. In this section, we analyze the training behaviour of the self-supervised speaker embedding system. Figure 2 shows the VoxCeleb1-O equal error rate (EER) performance of the ECAPA-TDNN systems trained with true speaker labels and GMM pseudo labels on different training epochs. As shown in the figure, when training an embedding system on true speaker labels (i.e., supervised training), the verification performance improves as the training proceeds. However, when training on the pseudo-labels, the EER performance improves until epoch 5, but slowly degrades afterward. This may be attributed to the fact that the pseudo-labels are not an accurate representation of the speakers. Therefore in a strong discriminative objective such as AAMSoftmax, overfitting to an incorrect label can lead to severe performance degradation. Hence from this result, we could see that it is important to either generate an accurate pseudo-label or to monitor the validation performance while training to ensure optimal performance in terms of self-supervised speaker verification.

Speaker Verification Performance Comparison Between Systems Trained with Different GMM Pseudo-label Configurations. In this section, we compare the self-supervised systems with different architectures and pseudo-labels. As depicted in Table 1, it could be noticed that training the embedding networks with pseudo-labels can achieve impressive performance.

Table 1. EER (%) comparison between the embedding networks trained with different GMM pseudo-label and objective configurations on the VoxCeleb1-O trial set.

Encoder	Objective	EER [%]
Human benchmark [13]		15.77
i-vector + Cosine [13]		15.28
i-vector + LDA + PLDA (Supervised)		5.55
i-vector + LDA + PLDA (5000 GMM)		8.30
i-vector + LDA + PLDA (6000 GMM)		8.73
Hybrid	Softmax (Supervised)	1.55
	Softmax (3500 GMM)	5.09
	Softmax (5000 GMM)	4.88
	Softmax (6000 GMM)	5.71
ECAPA-TDNN	AAMSoftmax (Supervised)	1.82
	AAMSoftmax (3500 GMM)	5.61
	AAMSoftmax (5000 GMM)	5.28
	AAMSoftmax (6000 GMM)	6.00

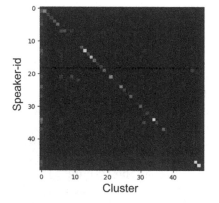 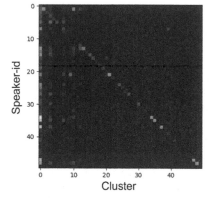

(a) Contingency matrix of 50 speakers and 50 clusters from the 5000 GMM pseudo-labels.

(b) Contingency matrix of 50 speakers and 50 clusters from the 6000 GMM pseudo-labels.

Fig. 3. Contingency matrix between the speaker labels and the pseudo-labels.

Although the pseudo-label-based deep embedding systems showed worse performance than the systems trained on true labels (i.e., Supervised), they were able to outperform the human benchmark performance [13] and even the conventional i-vectors with unsupervised (i.e., Cosine) self-supervised (i.e., 5000 GMM, 6000 GMM PLDA) and supervised (i.e., Supervised PLDA) backends. Among the self-supervised systems (e.g., 3500 GMM, 5000 GMM, 6000 GMM), the best performance was achieved by the Hybrid system trained on 5000 mixture GMM, which achieved a relative improvement of 69.04% in terms of EER over the human benchmark reported in [13].

One interesting observation is that in both Hybrid and ECAPA-TDNN systems, pseudo-labels generated from 5000 mixture GMM yielded better performance than the 6000 mixture GMM. Although the 6000 mixture is much closer to the actual number of speakers within the training set (i.e., 5994 speakers), since GMM clustering is done without any context about the speaker, the resulting clusters are not guaranteed to represent the accurate speaker identity. Therefore, training on pseudo-labels with high mixture numbers may lead the embedding network to learn non-speaker attributes which can influence the distance on the i-vector space (e.g., language, emotion, recording environment), and result in the inclusion of features/components that are less relevant to the downstream task. This can be seen from the contingency matrix depicted in Fig. 3, which shows the number of samples assigned to each speaker and cluster pairs. Ideally, each cluster should be aligned to distinct speaker in order to maximize the embedding networks speaker discriminability. However it could be seen that in both 5000 GMM and 6000 GMM, the clusters are not exactly aligned to the speakers. Moreover as suspected from the results in Table 3, we could observe that the pseudo-labels from the 5000 GMM were better aligned than the ones from 6000 GMM. This observation is also apparent in the performance gap between the systems trained on pseudo-labels (i.e., 3500 GMM, 5000 GMM, 6000 GMM) and the true labels (i.e., Supervised), which indicates that the pseudo-labels do not necessarily represent the speaker identity.

Similarly, using a GMM with low number of mixtures (i.e., 3500 GMM) has also decreased the performance. This may be due to the fact that when using a small number of clusters, each cluster is likely to consist of multiple overlapping speakers within it. Thus, when training the network with this pseudo-label, the resulting embeddings may have high similarity even if they are from different speakers.

Speaker Verification Performance Comparison Between Systems Trained with Pseudo-labels Generated via Different Clustering Algorithms. In this section, we compare the performance of the self-supervised systems trained with pseudo-labels generated via different clustering algorithms. More specifically, in addition to the GMM pseudo-label, we have generated pseudo-labels with 5000 classes using K-means [12], BIRCH [27], CURE [10], and agglomerative hierarchical clustering (AHC) [5] algorithms. As shown in Table 2, it could be observed that the performance of the system varies heavily depending on the algorithm used for pseudo-label generation. Especially on the ECAPA-TDNN system, the AHC pseudo-label outperformed the K-means pseudo-label with a relative improvement of 71.51% in terms of EER. This further substantiates our assumption that the performance of the pseudo-label-based self-supervised speaker verification system is crucially dependent on the quality of the clustering model. The best performance was observed from the Hybrid system trained with the AHC pseudo-labels, which yielded 3.07% EER.

Table 2. EER (%) comparison between the embedding networks trained with pseudo-labels generated via different clustering algorithms on the VoxCeleb1-O trial set.

Encoder	Objective	EER [%]
Hybrid	Softmax (Supervised)	1.55
	Softmax (5000 GMM)	4.88
	Softmax (5000 AHC)	3.07
ECAPA-TDNN	AAMSoftmax (Supervised)	1.82
	AAMSoftmax (5000 K-means)	13.06
	AAMSoftmax (5000 BIRCH)	5.56
	AAMSoftmax (5000 CURE)	6.99
	AAMSoftmax (5000 GMM)	5.28
	AAMSoftmax (5000 AHC)	3.72

Table 3. EER (%) comparison between the embedding networks trained with different pseudo-labels on the VoxSRC2021 validation set.

Encoder	Objective	EER [%]
i-vector + LDA + PLDA (Supervised)		14.29
i-vector + LDA + PLDA (5000 GMM)		17.49
Hybrid	Softmax (5000 GMM)	12.91
	Softmax (5000 AHC)	10.91
ECAPA-TDNN	AAMSoftmax (5000 GMM)	14.46
	AAMSoftmax (5000 AHC)	11.36

The same performance behaviour can be found in the VoxSRC2021 validation set, which can be seen in Table 3.

4   Conclusion

In this paper, we investigated the effect of different configurations for generating the pseudo-labels on the self-supervised speaker verification task. In order to achieve this, we conducted several experiments using different neural speaker network architectures and pseudo-labels generated from different clustering algorithms. Our results showed that the pseudo-label-based self-supervised speaker embedding systems can show comparable performance to the supervised embedding systems and even outperform the human benchmark performance and the conventional i-vector framework. Also, from our results, we could see that the performance of the pseudo-label-based self-supervised speaker embedding systems heavily depends on the accuracy of the pseudo-labels. Moreover, we observed that the speaker verification performance can be severely degraded when overfitting to the inaccurately generated pseudo-labels.

Acknowledgments. The authors wish to acknowledge the funding from the Government of Canada's New Frontiers in Research Fund (NFRF) through grant NFRFR-2021-00338 and Ministry of Economy and Innovation (MEI) of the Government of Quebec for the continued support.

References

1. The voxceleb speaker recognition challenge 2021 (voxsrc-21). https://www.robots.ox.ac.uk/~vgg/data/voxceleb/competition2021.html
2. Alam, J., Fathan, A., Kang, W.H.: Text-independent speaker verification employing CNN-LSTM-TDNN hybrid networks. In: Karpov, A., Potapova, R. (eds.) SPECOM 2021. LNCS (LNAI), vol. 12997, pp. 1–13. Springer, Cham (2021). https://doi.org/10.1007/978-3-030-87802-3_1
3. Cai, D., Li, M.: The DKU-DukeECE system for the self-supervision speaker verification task of the 2021 voxceleb speaker recognition challenge (2021)
4. Chung, J.S., Nagrani, A., Zisserman, A.: VoxCeleb2: deep speaker recognition. In: INTERSPEECH (2018)
5. Day, W.H.E., Edelsbrunner, H.: Efficient algorithms for agglomerative hierarchical clustering methods. J. Classif. **1**, 7–24 (1984)
6. Dehak, N., Kenny, P.J., Dehak, R., Dumouchel, P., Ouellet, P.: Front-end factor analysis for speaker verification. IEEE Trans. Audio Speech Lang. Process. **19**(4), 788–798 (2011). https://doi.org/10.1109/TASL.2010.2064307
7. Deng, J., Guo, J., Yang, J., Xue, N., Cotsia, I., Zafeiriou, S.P.: ArcFace: additive angular margin loss for deep face recognition. IEEE Trans. Pattern Anal. Mach. Intell., 1 (2021). https://doi.org/10.1109/TPAMI.2021.3087709
8. Desplanques, B., Thienpondt, J., Demuynck, K.: ECAPA-TDNN: emphasized channel attention, propagation and aggregation in TDNN based speaker verification. In: Meng, H., Xu, B., Zheng, T.F. (eds.) Interspeech 2020, pp. 3830–3834. ISCA (2020)
9. Ding, K., He, X., Wan, G.: Learning speaker embedding with momentum contrast (2020)
10. Guha, S., Rastogi, R., Shim, K.: CURE: an efficient clustering algorithm for large databases. SIGMOD Rec. **27**(2), 73–84 (1998). https://doi.org/10.1145/276305.276312
11. Hansen, J.H., Hasan, T.: Speaker recognition by machines and humans: a tutorial review. IEEE Signal Process. Mag. **32**(6), 74–99 (2015). https://doi.org/10.1109/MSP.2015.2462851
12. Hartigan, J.A., Wong, M.A.: A k-means clustering algorithm. JSTOR Appl. Stat. **28**(1), 100–108 (1979)
13. Huh, J., Heo, H.S., Kang, J., Watanabe, S., Chung, J.S.: Augmentation adversarial training for unsupervised speaker recognition. In: Workshop on Self-Supervised Learning for Speech and Audio Processing, NeurIPS (2020)
14. Kenny, P.: A small footprint i-vector extractor. In: Odyssey (2012)
15. Kingma, D.P., Ba, J.: Adam: A method for stochastic optimization. In: Bengio, Y., LeCun, Y. (eds.) 3rd International Conference on Learning Representations, ICLR 2015, San Diego, CA, USA, May 7–9, 2015, Conference Track Proceedings (2015). http://arxiv.org/abs/1412.6980
16. Mun, S.H., Kang, W.H., Han, M.H., Kim, N.S.: Unsupervised representation learning for speaker recognition via contrastive equilibrium learning (2020)

17. Nagrani, A., Chung, J.S., Zisserman, A.: VoxCeleb: a large-scale speaker identification dataset. In: INTERSPEECH (2017)
18. Park, D.S., et al.: SpecAugment: a simple data augmentation method for automatic speech recognition. In: Interspeech 2019, pp. 2613–2617 (2019)
19. Paszke, A., et al.: PyTorch: an imperative style, high-performance deep learning library. In: Wallach, H., Larochelle, H., Beygelzimer, A., d' Alché-Buc, F., Fox, E., Garnett, R. (eds.) Advances in Neural Information Processing Systems 32, pp. 8024–8035. Curran Associates, Inc. (2019)
20. Pedregosa, F., et al.: Scikit-learn: machine learning in Python. J. Mach. Learn. Res. **12**, 2825–2830 (2011)
21. Povey, D., et al.: The Kaldi speech recognition toolkit. In: IEEE 2011 workshop (2011)
22. Snyder, D., Garcia-Romero, D., Povey, D., Khudanpur, S.: Deep neural network embeddings for text-independent speaker verification. In: INTERSPEECH (2017)
23. Snyder, D., Garcia-Romero, D., Sell, G., Povey, D., Khudanpur, S.: X-vectors: Robust DNN embeddings for speaker recognition. In: 2018 IEEE International Conference on Acoustics, Speech and Signal Processing (ICASSP), pp. 5329–5333 (2018). https://doi.org/10.1109/ICASSP.2018.8461375
24. Tao, R., Lee, K.A., Das, R.K., Hautamäki, V., Li, H.: Self-supervised speaker recognition with loss-gated learning (2021)
25. Thienpondt, J., Desplanques, B., Demuynck, K.: The IDLAB VoxCeleb speaker recognition challenge 2020 system description (2020)
26. Zhang, H., Zou, Y., Wang, H.: Contrastive self-supervised learning for text-independent speaker verification. In: ICASSP 2021–2021 IEEE International Conference on Acoustics, Speech and Signal Processing (ICASSP), pp. 6713–6717 (2021). https://doi.org/10.1109/ICASSP39728.2021.9413351
27. Zhang, T., Ramakrishnan, R., Livny, M.: BIRCH: a new data clustering algorithm and its applications. Data Min. Knowl. Discov. **1**(2), 141–182 (1997)

Investigation of Transfer Learning for End-to-End Russian Speech Recognition

Irina Kipyatkova$^{(\boxtimes)}$ (iD)

St. Petersburg Federal Research Center of the Russian
Academy of Sciences (SPC RAS), St. Petersburg, Russia
`kipyatkova@iias.spb.su`

Abstract. End-to-end speech recognition systems reduce the speech decoding time and required amount of memory comparing to standard systems. However they need much more data for training, which complicates creation of such systems for low-resourced languages. One way to improve performance of end-to-end low-resourced speech recognition system is model's pre-training by transfer learning, that is training the model on the non-target data and then transferring the trained parameters to the target model. The aim of the current research was to investigate application of transfer learning to the training of the end-to-end Russian speech recognition system in low-resourced conditions. We used several speech corpora of different languages for pre-training. Then end-to-end model was fine-tuned on a small Russian speech corpus of 60 h. We conducted experiments on application of transfer learning in different parts of the model (feature extraction block, encoder, and attention mechanism) as well as on freezing of the lower layers. We have achieved 24.53% relative word error rate reduction comparing to the baseline system trained without transfer learning.

Keywords: End-to-end speech recognition · Transfer learning · Encoder-decoder · Russian speech

1 Introduction

In recent years, developing of end-to-end systems became the main trend in researches on automatic speech recognition (ASR). End-to-end ASR systems transform an input speech signal to a sequence of letters using single deep neural network (DNN). This results in reducing the processing time and required amount of memory comparing to standard ASR systems consisting of independent components. However, training the end-to-end system requires much more data than standard system. This drawback makes it difficult to create an end-to-end ASR system for low-resourced languages. One way to overcome this drawback is to use transfer learning methods.

Transfer learning consists in transferring the knowledge obtained on one or several initial tasks to be used for improving the training on target task. There are several ways of application of transfer learning. The most common of them are [1, 2]: (1) instances-based (instances of non-target domain are added to target train dataset with appropriate

© Springer Nature Switzerland AG 2022
S. R. M. Prasanna et al. (Eds.): SPECOM 2022, LNAI 13721, pp. 349–357, 2022.
https://doi.org/10.1007/978-3-031-20980-2_30

weight); (2) feature-based, which can be asymmetric (original features are transformed to match the target features) and symmetric (source and target features are transformed into a new feature representation); (3) mapping-based (instances from target and non-target domains are mapped into a new data space with better similarity); (4) network-based (the pre-trained network including its structure and parameters is transferred to target domain with its subsequent fine-tuning on the target data); (5) adversarial-based (the adversarial technology is used to find transferable features that are both suitable for two domains).

Transfer learning is very effective at training DNNs. In the view of speech recognition, the idea of transfer learning is based on the fact that features learned by lower layers of DNN do not depend on language while language specific features are learned by higher layers [3]. At creating the end-to-end ASR for under-resourced language, transfer learning is mostly performed by pre-training the model on data of non-target language and then fine-tuning the model on data of the target language. The parameters of low layers of DNN can be frozen that means that they are not updated during fine-tuning. The transfer learning scheme is presented on Fig. 1.

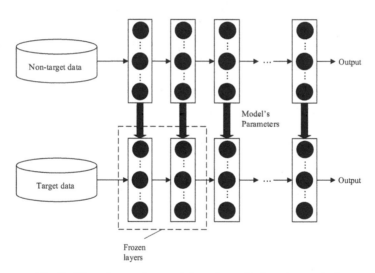

Fig. 1. The scheme of network-based transfer learning method.

The aim of this research was to explore transfer learning method for training the end-to-end Russian speech recognition system in low-resourced conditions. We have tried several languages for pre-training the model and we have investigated influence of low layer freezing on speech recognition results. The rest of the paper is organized as follows. In Sect. 2 we give a brief survey of the researches in which transfer learning was used for the training of the ASR system, in Sect. 3 we describe our end-to-end Russian speech recognition system with transfer learning, the experimental results are given in Sect. 4, in Sect. 5 we make a conclusion to our work.

2 Related Work

There are many scientific researches on application of transfer learning for training the ASR systems. One of the earliest methods of transfer learning in ASR is a tandem approach [4]. In the tandem approach, at first DNN with bottleneck is trained and then the parameters of bottleneck output are used in standard Hidden Markov model (HMM) based system or hybrid DNN/HMM system [5].

Recently, transfer learning is mostly used for training the hybrid HMM/DNN and end-to-end systems. For example, transfer learning was applied to train the acoustic models for two Tibetan dialects with usage of Mandarin as non-target language in [6]. In [7], German ASR system based on convolutional neural network was trained using transfer learning from the model of English speech trained on Librispeech corpus, with the lower layers of the network being frozen. The influence of freezing of low layer parameters on results of end-to-end speech recognition was researched in [8]. The authors performed experiments on German and Swiss German, with English being used for pre-training. The experiments have shown that freezing of the low layers results in increasing of speech recognition accuracy and reduction of training time. Significant improvement of the accuracy was achieved when the first layer was frozen. The freezing of the higher layers did not lead to recognition accuracy increasing.

The research on training of the hybrid DNN/HMM children speech recognition system using transfer learning was presented in [9]. The adult speech database was used for pre-training. The authors obtained 16.5% relative reduction of WER comparing to the baseline system with Speaker Adaptive Training technique.

In the paper [10], feature transfer learning was performed. At first, the encoder's lower layers predicting spectral features on the raw waveform were trained. Then trained parameters were transferred to the attention-based encoder-decoder model.

In [11], the transfer learning method called teacher-student was used for initialization of parameters of online speech recognition system by parameters obtained at training of the large offline end-to-end system. The teacher-student learning is an approach to transfer the knowledge from a large deep ("teacher") network to shallower model [12]. The student neural network is trained to minimize difference between its own output distributions and teacher network's distributions.

It also should be noted that transfer learning can also be realized as multi-task learning in a multilingual system. Such approach was realized, for example in [13, 14]. In [15] a technique for DNN-based acoustic model adaptation to specific domain in multilingual system was proposed. It performs adaptation of low-resourced language system trained for one source domain into a target domain using adaptation data of high-resourced language.

In the current paper we consider the training of monolingual ASR system in low-resourced condition.

3 End-to-End Speech Recognition Model with Transfer Learning

3.1 Architecture of the End-to-End Speech Recognition Model

We used joint CTC-attention based encoder-decoder model similar to the model proposed in [16]. Our model was described in detail in [17]. Encoder was Bidirectional Long

Short-Term Memory (BLSTM) network contained five layers with 512 cells in each with highway connections [18]. Decoder was Long Short-Term Memory (LSTM) network contained two layers with 512 cells in each. Location-aware [19] attention mechanism was used in decoder. Before the encoder, there was a feature extraction block that was VGG [20] model with residual connection (ResNet). At the training stage, the CTC weight was equal to 0.3. Filter banks features were used as input.

At the decoding stage, we additionally used LSTM-based language model (LM), which was trained on text corpus of about 350M words. The text corpus was collected from online Russian newspapers. LSTM contained one layer with 512 cells. The vocabulary consisted of 150K most frequent word-forms from the training text corpus.

For training and testing the end-to-end Russian speech recognition model we used ESPnet toolkit [21] with a PyTorch as a back-end part.

3.2 Application of Transfer Learning at Model's Training

Transfer learning was carried out by pre-training the model on non-target speech data, transferring the trained parameters of neural network to the target model and the following training the model on Russian speech data.

The first step was to choose speech corpora for pre-training. The main criteria for selection the speech corpora were the following: (1) speech data duration of more than 100 hours; (2) sentence-level segmentation; (3) availability of transcripts. We chose five speech corpora of non-target languages which are presented in Table 1. Among these corpora there is a corpus of Ukrainian speech which does not meet the require-ment of duration. However, we decided to use this corpus as well because Ukrainian language is related to Russian, so we hypothesized that pre-training on these speech data may be useful.

Table 1. Characteristics of speech corpora used for pre-training.

Language	Speech corpus	Duration	Description
English	LibriSpeech (clean) [22]	360 h	Read audiobooks
Italian	TEDx [23]	107 h	Recordings of TEDx talks
Catalan	ParlamentParla v1.0 [24]	320 h	Recordings of the Catalan Parliament plenary sessions
German	M-AILABS German Corpus [25]	237 h 22 m	Read audiobooks
Ukrainian	M-AILABS Ukrainian Corpus [26]	87 h 08 m	Read audiobooks

The weights obtained from the model trained on non-target data were used for initialization of weights of the feature extraction block, encoder, and attention mechanism. Then, we conducted experiments on freezing parameters of low layers at transfer learning. Architecture of our end-to-end model with transfer learning is presented on Fig. 2.

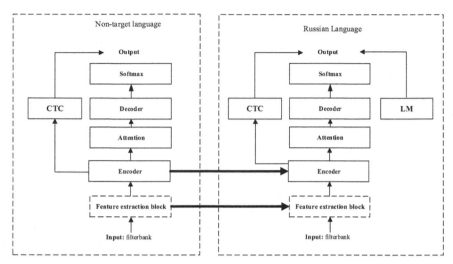

Fig. 2. Architecture of end-to-end speech recognition model with transfer learning.

The end-to-end model was trained on Russian speech data composed from the speech corpus collected at SPC RAS [17] as well as free speech corpora Voxforge [26] and M-AILABS [25]. The corpus collected at SPC RAS consists of the recordings of phonetically rich and meaningful phrases and texts, also it includes commands for the MIDAS information kiosk [27] and 7–digits telephone numbers. As a result we had 60.6 h of speech data. This speech dataset was splitted into validation and trains parts with sizes of 5% and 95%.

4 Experiments

Experiments on continuous Russian speech recognition were performed on our test speech corpus consisting of 500 phrases pronounced by 5 speakers. The phrases were taken from online newspaper which was not used for LM training. During experiments we used beam search pruning method similar to the approach proposed in [28] and substituted softmax with gumbel-softmax [29]. The decoding setup is described in [30].

We have obtained CER = 14.9% and WER = 37.1% without usage of transfer learning. The results obtained after application of transfer learning using different languages for pre-training are presented in Table 2. In the table, "Init." means that pretrained parameters were used only for initialization of the parameters of the model's block without their freezing.

Table 2. Experimental results on Russian speech recognition using different non-target languages for transfer learning (%).

Non-target language	Transfer learning scheme						Experimental results	
	Feature extraction			Encoder		Attention		
	Init	1 layer frozen	2 layer frozen	Init	1 layer frozen	Init	CER, %	WER, %
No transferring (baseline)	−	−	−	−	−	−	14.9	37.1
English	+	−	−	−	−	−	13.9	34.5
	+	+	−	−	−	−	13.9	35.7
	−	−	−	+	−	−	13.2	34.8
	+	−	−	+	−	−	10.5	**28.0**
	+	−	−	+	+	−	11.3	30.0
	+	−	−	+	−	+	**10.2**	28.6
Italian	+	−	−	−	−	−	14.2	35.0
	+	+	−	−	−	−	12.5	32.1
	+	+	+	−	−	−	14.7	36.6
	−	−	−	+	−	−	12.6	**29.5**
	+	+	−	+	−	−	12.7	31.2
	+	+	−	+	+	−	12.8	31.8
	+	+	−	+	−	+	**12.4**	30.3
Catalan	+	−	−	−	−	−	14.8	38.5
	+	+	−	−	−	−	14.0	36.9
	+	+	+	−	−	−	14.4	37.4
	−	−	−	+	−	−	13.5	32.9
	+	+	−	+	−	−	12.1	32.3
	+	+	−	+	+	−	12.9	32.5
	+	+	−	+	−	+	**11.4**	**31.0**
German	+	−	−	−	−	−	14.8	38.2
	+	+	−	−	−	−	15.3	36.6
	+	+	+	−	−	−	14.4	37.0
	−	−	−	+	−	−	13.6	33.0
	+	+	−	+	−	−	**13.4**	**31.2**
	+	+	−	+	+	−	13.9	35.0

(*continued*)

Table 2. (*continued*)

Non-target language	Transfer learning scheme						Experimental results	
	Feature extraction			Encoder		Attention		
	Init	1 layer frozen	2 layer frozen	Init	1 layer frozen	Init	CER, %	WER, %
	+	+	−	+	−	+	13.4	33.6
Ukrainian	+	−	−	−	−	−	15.7	37.4
	+	+	−	−	−	−	15.9	37.9
	−	−	−	+	−	−	14.3	34.8
	+	−	−	+	−	−	12.2	31.9
	+	−	−	+	+	−	13.3	32.9
	+	−	−	+	−	+	**12.1**	**29.9**

We conducted a series of experiments on application of transfer learning in different parts of the model. Transferring neural network parameters from non-target model for initialization of feature extraction block only slightly decreased recognition error and in some cases even slightly increased it that can be connected with statistic fluctuation. Freezing of first layer of feature extraction block resulted in reduction of CER and WER when Italian, Catalan, and German languages were used. Freezing higher layers did not lead to a decrease in recognition error. Application of transfer learning for initialization of encoder's parameters decreased recognition error in all cases. Then we conducted experiments on transfer parameters of both encoder and feature extraction block, with first layer of feature extraction block being frozen when transferring from language with which freezing gave better result than just initialization. Freezing the first layer of encoder increased recognition error, therefore we did not perform experiments on freezing the higher layers. Then transfer learning was carried out in attention mechanism. In most cases (except English) application of transfer learning for initialization of parameters in attention mechanism in addition to encoder and feature extraction block gave additional improvement of the result.

The best result (WER = 28.0) was achieved when English was used as non-target language and transfer learning was applied for initialization of parameters of both feature extraction block and encoder. This may be due to the fact that the English corpus was the largest that we used for pre-training. It should also be noted that usage of Ukrainian language gave us the result comparable to usage of other non-target languages although the size of the Ukrainian corpus was significantly smaller. This can be due to the fact that Russian and Ukrainian are related languages. Therefore we can draw a conclusion that in low-resourced condition the usage of other low-resourced language related to the target language can improve speech recognition result.

5 Conclusions and Future Work

In the paper, we have investigated the application of speech data of different non-target languages for pre-training of the end-to-end Russian speech recognition system. The best results were achieved when parameters were transferred from the model pre-trained on English speech for initialization of parameters of the feature extraction block and encoder. In this case relative reduction of WER was 24.53%. The further researches will be connected with enlarging the training data and experimenting with other architectures of neural network for Russian end-to-end speech recognition, for example, Transformer.

Acknowledgements. This research was supported by the state research № FFZF-2022-0005.

References

1. Tan, C., Sun, F., Kong, T., Zhang, W., Yang, C., Liu, C.: A survey on deep transfer learning. In: Kůrková, V., Manolopoulos, Y., Hammer, B., Iliadis, L., Maglogiannis, I. (eds.) ICANN 2018. LNCS, vol. 11141, pp. 270–279. Springer, Cham (2018). https://doi.org/10.1007/978-3-030-01424-7_27
2. Zhuang, F., et al.: A comprehensive survey on transfer learning. Proc. IEEE **109**(1), 43–76 (2020)
3. Wang, D., Zheng, T.F.: Transfer learning for speech and language processing. In: Proceedings of Asia-Pacific Signal and Information Processing Association Annual Summit and Conference (APSIPA), pp. 1225–1237 (2015)
4. Grézl, F., Karafiát, M., Kontár, S., Cernocky, J.: Probabilistic and bottle-neck features for LVCSR of meetings. In: Proceedings of IEEE International Conference on Acoustics, Speech and Signal Processing (ICASSP-2007), pp. IV-757–IV-760 (2007)
5. Yan, Z.J., Huo, Q., Xu, J.: A scalable approach to using DNN-derived features in GMM-HMM based acoustic modeling for LVCSR. In: Proceedings of Interspeech-2013, pp. 104–108 (2013)
6. Yan, J., Lv, Z., Huang, S., Yu, H.: Low-resource tibetan dialect acoustic modeling based on transfer learning. In: Proceedings of SLTU. pp. 6–10 (2018)
7. Kunze, J., Kirsch, L., Kurenkov, I., Krug, A., Johannsmeier, J., Stober, S.: Transfer learning for speech recognition on a budget. ArXiv preprint arXiv:1706.00290 (2017). https://arxiv.org/abs/1706.00290
8. Eberhard, O., Zesch, T.: Effects of layer freezing on transferring a speech recognition system to under-resourced languages. In: Proceedings of the 17th Conference on Natural Language Processing (KONVENS 2021), pp. 208–212 (2021)
9. Shivakumar, P.G., Georgiou, P.: Transfer learning from adult to children for speech recognition: evaluation, analysis and recommendations. Comput. Speech Lang. **63**, 101077 (2020)
10. Tjandra, A., Sakti, S., Nakamura, S.: Attention-based wav2text with feature transfer learning In: Proceedings of Automatic Speech Recognition and Understanding Workshop (ASRU), pp. 309–315 (2017)
11. Kim, S., Seltzer, M.L., Li, J., Zhao, R.: Improved training for online end-to-end speech recognition systems. In: Proceedings of Interspeech-2018, pp. 2913–2917 (2018)
12. Li, J., Zhao, R., Huang, J.-T., Gong Y.: Learning small-size DNN with output-distribution-based criteria. In: Proceedings of Interspeech-2014, pp. 1910–1914 (2014)

13. Tachbelie, M.Y., Abate, S.T., Schultz, T.: Multilingual speech recognition for GlobalPhone languages. Speech Commun. **140**, 71–86 (2022)
14. Qin, C.-X., Qu, D., Zhang, L.-H.: Towards end-to-end speech recognition with transfer learning. EURASIP J. Audio, Speech, Music Process. **2018**(1), 1–9 (2018). https://doi.org/10.1186/s13636-018-0141-9
15. Abad, A., Bell, P., Carmantini, A., Renais, S.: Cross lingual transfer learning for zero-resource domain adaptation. In: Proceedings of IEEE International Conference on Acoustics, Speech and Signal Processing (ICASSP-2020), pp. 6909–6913 (2020)
16. Kim, S., Hori, T., Watanabe, S.: Joint ctc-attention based end-to-end speech recognition using multi-task learning. In: Proceedings of IEEE International Conference on Acoustics, Speech and Signal Processing (ICASSP-2017), pp. 4835–4839 (2017)
17. Kipyatkova, I., Markovnikov, N.: Experimenting with attention mechanisms in Joint CTC-attention models for Russian speech recognition. In: Karpov, A., Potapova, R. (eds.) SPECOM 2020. LNCS (LNAI), vol. 12335, pp. 214–222. Springer, Cham (2020). https://doi.org/10.1007/978-3-030-60276-5_22
18. Srivastava, R.K., Greff, K., Schmidhuber, J.: Highway networks. arXiv preprint arXiv:1505.00387 (2015). https://arxiv.org/abs/1505.00387
19. Chorowski, J.K., Bahdanau, D., Serdyuk, D., Cho, K., Bengio, Y.: Attention-based models for speech recognition. Adv. Neural. Inf. Process. Syst. **28**, 577–585 (2015)
20. Simonyan, K., Zisserman, A.: Very deep convolutional networks for large-scale image recognition. ArXiv preprint arXiv:1409.1556 (2014). https://arxiv.org/abs/1409.1556
21. Watanabe, S., et al.: Espnet: End-to-end speech processing toolkit. In: INTERSPEECH-2018, pp. 2207–2211 (2018)
22. Panayotov, V., Chen, G., Povey, D., Khudanpur, S.: Librispeech: an ASR corpus based on public domain audio books. In: IEEE International Conference on Acoustics, Speech and Signal Processing (ICASSP-2015), pp. 5206–5210 (2015)
23. Salesky, E., et al.: The multilingual TEDx corpus for speech recognition and translation. In: Proceedings of Interspeech-2021, pp. 3655–3659 (2021)
24. Külebi, B., Armentano-Oller, C., Rodríguez-Penagos, C., Villegas, M.: ParlamentParla: A speech corpus of catalan parliamentary sessions. In: Workshop on Creating, Enriching and Using Parliamentary Corpora, pp. 125–130 (2022)
25. The m-ailabs speech dataset. https://www.caito.de/2019/01/the-m-ailabs-speech-dataset/. Accessed 30 Jun 2022
26. VoxForge. http://www.voxforge.org/. Accessed 30 Jun 2022
27. Karpov, A.A., Ronzhin, A.L.: Information enquiry kiosk with multimodal user interface. Pattern Recogn. Image Anal. **19**(3), 546–558 (2009)
28. Freitag, M., Al-Onaizan, Y.: Beam search strategies for neural machine translation. ArXiv preprint arXiv:1702.01806 (2017). https://arxiv.org/abs/1702.01806
29. Jang, E., Gu, S., Poole, B.: Categorical reparameterization with gumbel-softmax. ArXiv preprint arXiv:1611.01144 (2016). https://arxiv.org/abs/1611.01144
30. Markovnikov, N., Kipyatkova, I.: Investigating joint CTC-attention models for end-to-end russian speech recognition. In: Salah, A.A., Karpov, A., Potapova, R. (eds.) SPECOM 2019. LNCS (LNAI), vol. 11658, pp. 337–347. Springer, Cham (2019). https://doi.org/10.1007/978-3-030-26061-3_35

Prosodic Features of Verbal Irony in Russian and French: Universal vs. Language-Specific

Uliana Kochetkova(✉) ⓘ, Pavel Skrelin ⓘ, Rada German ⓘ, and Daria Novoselova ⓘ

Saint Petersburg State University, Saint Petersburg 199034, Russia
{u.kochetkova,p.skrelin}@spbu.ru, {st067973,
st065112}@student.spbu.ru

Abstract. This study investigates acoustic features of irony in Russian and French languages. Two series of experiments were conducted. First, homonymous ironic and non-ironic stimuli were read by two native French speakers (man and woman) and two native Russian speakers (man and woman) and then presented for perceptual evaluation. Acoustic and statistical analysis of the reliably recognized stimuli (correctly defined by more than 60% of listeners) showed that acoustic characteristics differ significantly in ironic and non-ironic phrases in both French and Russian. Changes in the speech rate, increase of the stressed vowel and syllable duration, as well as the intensity level and average pitch augmentation were used by both Russian and French speakers while expressing irony. In order to verify these observations various modifications of the original stimuli were carried out. Second series of listening perceptual experiments with the modified stimuli showed the role of various prosodic parameters and their combinations in irony perception in two languages.

Keywords: Irony · Prosodic features · Acoustic analysis · Russian linguistics · French linguistics · Listening perceptual experiments · Signal processing

1 Introduction

Nowadays, one can observe an increased interest in studying phonetic properties of verbal irony in various languages [1–4, 6, 7, 10–13, 18], conditioned by the actual need of such information in automatic speech recognition and synthesis systems, widely used in human-machine communication. Yet, the data obtained don't provide a complete view of the acoustic cues of irony, nor are they convergent. Besides the diversity of languages, these incongruences can be attributed to a variety of factors: the type of irony taken into consideration in the concrete study, the research methodology, the type of approach, i.e., the linguistic analysis vs. the use of machine learning and automatic identification of features of emotional speech and ironic speech notably, the intra- and inter-speaker variability, the communication situation, etc. At the same time, adding such a factor as irony acoustic cues would improve speech recognition process and notably prosodic models, which cannot be otherwise robust enough in cases of syntactic homonymy.

© Springer Nature Switzerland AG 2022
S. R. M. Prasanna et al. (Eds.): SPECOM 2022, LNAI 13721, pp. 358–371, 2022.
https://doi.org/10.1007/978-3-031-20980-2_31

In our previous studies on acoustic characteristics of irony in Russian language, we found that both increase and decrease of the prosodic parameters (in comparison with neutral utterances) may indicate that the utterance is ironic and should be understood as opposite to its direct meaning [9, 14–16]. However, the increase occurred more frequently, the most important prosodic features of ironic meaning were the stressed vowel lengthening, the intensity level augmentation and the pitch range widening.

In order to test the cross-language significance of these parameters and their role in irony implementation in two languages with different accentual and rhythmic structures, we carried out two series of pilot experiments on the basis of Russian and French languages using the methodology we developed in our previous works [9, 14–16]. First, the original recorded stimuli were presented to listeners and then analyzed. Second, various parameters of the original stimuli were modified according to the results of the acoustic analysis and then presented to listeners.

Thus, the aim of the current paper is to establish the cross-linguistic or language-specific character of acoustic parameters of irony in Russian and French, as well as to evaluate the procedure of the modification of these parameters in two different languages. In our study we consider only one type of irony – antiphrasis or ironic negation (treated by some authors as sarcasm [12]), which is crucial for the communication effectiveness in case when there is no context, so that the interlocutor is forced to interpret the message relying on its phonetic characteristics only. As this situation is frequent in telephonic human-machine communication, detecting acoustic cues of antiphrasis becomes a highly important task for the development of the artificial intelligence (AI) systems. In most of cases the focus of irony was the lexical item, then the intonation center of the phrase was the stressed syllable of this lexical item. In most cases, the intonation center was the last word in the phrase. When the focus of irony was the whole statement, several lexical items, besides the last word, could be stressed and were considered as words with additional prosodic prominence. We considered the intonation phrase as the minimal target fragment, in which all the parameters were analyzed.

2   Experiments with Original Stimuli

The main goal of this series of experiments was not to fully describe the language standards of and idiolects in irony expression in Russian and French, but to find the perceptually relevant phonetic properties of irony, i.e., those few characteristics that will ensure the high percentage of the correct understanding of the ironic meaning by listeners without any other context.

2.1   Material and Methods

Reading Task and Recording Procedure. At the first stage, two sets of target utterances were composed in Russian and French respectively. Each of these sets included six declarative utterances, six general (yes or no) questions with the direct word order, which were homonymous to the declarative utterances, and four exclamatory utterances with interrogative words (see Table 1). These target utterances were inserted into contexts clearly suggesting ironic or non-ironic interpretation, which resulted in a total of

32 Target utterances for each language. The contexts represented mini-texts that were composed in a way to be read by the speaker along with the target utterances themselves. The obtained contexts including target fragments were randomized, printed on paper and then read by one male and one female native speaker of each of the languages. The recording was conducted in a sound-proof studio at the Department of Phonetics of Saint Petersburg State University. The speaker was allowed to give as many variants as she/he could do or to reread the context in case of an error.

Table 1. List of the target utterances.

Sentence type	French	Russian
Declarative/ Interrogative	C'est à vous *(That's yours)* Tu es venu très tôt *(You came too early)* Elle a oublié *(She forgot)* Il est fatigué *(He's tired)* Le téléphone n'a pas sonné *(The phone didn't ring)* Génial *(Brilliant)*	Хорошо *(Well)* Печальная история *(It's a sad story)* Это мой сосед *(He's my neighbour)* И это конец *(And this is the end)* Раньше нельзя было это сделать *(It was impossible to do this before)* Гениально *(Brilliant)*
Exclamatory	Comme c'est gentil! *(How nice!)* Qu'il est sympa! *(What a nice person!)* Que c'est beau ! *(How beautiful it is!)* Quelle horreur! *(What a horror!)*	Как это мило! *(How nice!)* Какой молодец! *(Well done!)* Да ты что! *(Come on!)* Какой позор!*(What a shame!)*

Listening Perceptual Experiments. A series of listening perceptual experiments were conducted in order to find the acoustic cues of irony in the data obtained. Homonymous target stimuli were manually extracted from the ironic and non-ironic contexts; any marker of or explicit remarks on the ironic or non-ironic meaning were excluded from these snippets. The listeners were suggested to assign the stimulus they heard with one of the contexts (ironic or non-ironic) presented on the screen, from which this stimulus seemed to be extracted.

In total, eight experiments were conducted (two surveys per speaker) using the SoSciSurvey platform. On average, 20 subjects participated in each survey. Each questionnaire consisted of 25 questions, three questions were asked in order to collect the personal data of the informants (their gender, age and level of proficiency in Russian or French language).

Most of Russian and French stimuli were correctly recognized by the majority of native listeners of the Russian and French languages respectively (more than 85% stimuli in Russian and more than 73% in French). Non-ironic phrases were better recognized than ironic ones in French (the difference was 4% in male speech and 9% in female speech). In Russian this difference was insignificant. At the same time, the Russian ironic stimuli had 12% higher identification and non-ironic stimuli – 6% higher identification than the French stimuli of the same type.

Only the pairs of homonymous ironic and non-ironic stimuli pronounced by the same speaker, in which both types of stimuli were correctly recognized by more than 60% of the listeners were selected for further acoustic analysis. A pairwise comparison of the reliably identified target phrases allowed us to make some conclusions and observations.

Acoustic Analysis. Using the Praat software, reliably identified target stimuli were annotated at the following levels: phrase, stressed vowel, stressed syllable, pre-stressed vowel.

In French material the stressed syllable was the final syllable of the target fragment. If the speaker pronounced the phrase such as "Tu es venu très tôt" *(You came too early)* with another stress on the last syllable of the word "venu", both stressed syllables were analyzed. In most Russian phrases the stressed syllable in the last word was the intonation center (focus). In seven phrases out of ten the last syllable was the stressed one, for example, in phrase "Хорошо" *(Well)*. Nevertheless, the intonation center (focus) could be moved to another word, as in the phrase "Печальная история" *(It's a sad story)*, where the second syllable of the word "печальная" was stressed and became the intonation center.

The duration and intensity of the units listed above were measured. Speech rate was also calculated by dividing the number of syllables in the target fragment by its duration. The calculation of pitch was done automatically via the Wave Assistant program, followed by a manual adjustment (both in Hertz and semitones). The following melodic characteristics were considered: average pitch level, pitch range, pitch interval between pre-stressed and stressed vowels. Melodic patterns were obtained through the Prosogram software.

Statistical Analysis. The data were tested using the Student's t-test to establish the statistical significance of the differences in the mean values. Statistical analysis was carried out in the Excel program. It confirmed the existence of reliable differences in the following acoustic characteristics between ironic and non-ironic stimuli within the language: duration of the stressed vowel and syllable, intensity of the stressed vowel and syllable, average pitch and pitch range. Only statistically approved results are presented below.

2.2 Results

Speech Rate. Both Russian and French speakers used a slower speech rate in ironic utterances (see Table 2). On average, in ironic phrases that were reliably recognized, the speech rate decreased by one or two syllable per second, i.e., by 18% – 34% comparing to the speech rate in the non-ironic utterances. As this parameter is related to the duration of various units within the phrase, we compared their duration in ironic and non-ironic utterances.

Table 2. Average speech rate in homonymous ironic and non-ironic utterances

Speakers	Neutral utterances (syllables per second)	Ironic utterances (syllables per second)	Difference in speech rate between ironic and non-ironic utterances (syllables per second; %)
French male speaker	6	5	↓1 (18%)
French female speaker	5	4	↓1 (9%)
Russian male speaker	6	5	↓1 (23%)
Russian female speaker	7	5	↓2 (34%)

Duration. As it can be seen from Table 3, Russian speakers and the French male speaker lengthened the stressed vowel and syllable in most of the ironic utterances correctly recognized by native listeners (in comparison with the homonymous non-ironic utterances). Only the French female speaker used both strategies: lengthening and reduction depending on the sentence type and lexical structure, yet the latter type of duration changes occurred less frequently. Thus, we can suppose that the increase of the duration may be used in both languages to indicate the ironic meaning. At the same time, the comparison of the stressed vowel and syllable shows that the increase of duration is implemented through the stressed vowel lengthening.

Table 3. Changes in stressed vowel and syllable duration in ironic utterances compared to the homonymous non-ironic utterances.

Speakers	Stressed vowel		Stressed syllable	
	Increase of duration in ironic phrases (ms, %)	The frequency of lengthening in ironic phrases	Increase of duration in ironic phrases (ms, %)	The frequency of lengthening in ironic phrases
French male speaker	115 (123%)	69%	111 (48%)	92%
French female speaker	112 (66%) ↓ - 231 (37%)	50% ↓ 21%	135 (48%) ↓- 169 (24%)	50% ↓36%
Russian male speaker	67 (78%)	70%	90 (40%)	67%
Russian female speaker	82 (93%)	77%	112 (48%)	86%

Intensity Level. Table 4 demonstrates that the intensity level of the stressed vowel and syllable in ironic utterances may change in both directions. Although two Russian speakers and French female speaker increased intensity in most of the ironic utterances, French male speaker preferred decreasing intensity, and still the ironic meaning was well recognized by the listeners.

Table 4. Changes in intensity level of the stressed vowel and syllable in ironic utterances compared to the homonymous non-ironic utterances.

Speakers	Stressed vowel				Stressed syllable			
	Intensity increase		Intensity reduction		Intensity increase		Intensity reduction	
	dB	Frequency of occurrence	dB	Frequency of occurrence	dB	Frequency of occurrence	dB	Frequency of occurrence
French male speaker	13	46%	−11	54%	13	38%	−9	62%
French female Speaker	6	79%	−2	14%	6	71%	−2	21%
Russian male speaker	5	63%	−5	30%	5	67%	−3	30%
Russian female speaker	7	82%	−2	14%	6	91%	−3	9%

Pitch. As shown in Table 5, all four speakers demonstrated an increase of the average F0 in most of ironic phrases. However, different trends for the Russian and French languages exist in the pitch range change. An increase of the pitch range was typical for the Russian speakers, while for the French speakers, on the contrary, its decrease prevailed.

Table 5. Changes in the pitch characteristics in ironic utterances compared to the homonymous non-ironic utterances.

Speakers	Average pitch			Pitch range					
	Increase			Increase			Decrease		
	Hz	St	Frequency of occurrence	Hz	St	Frequency of occurrence	Hz	St	Frequency of occurrence
French male speaker	23	2	69%	44	4	38%	−19	−2	62%
French female speaker	27	1,5	71%	65	3	36%	−48	−3	64%

(*continued*)

Table 5. (*continued*)

| Speakers | Average pitch | | | Pitch range | | | | | |
| | Increase | | | Increase | | | Decrease | | |
	Hz	St	Frequency of occurrence	Hz	St	Frequency of occurrence	Hz	St	Frequency of occurrence
Russian male speaker	22	2	67%	30	4	67%	−17	−3	30%
Russian female speaker	66	4	73%	94	5	86%	−8	−1	14%

Intonation Patterns. Although the detailed acoustic and statistical analysis of intonation patterns was not the goal of our study, a number of observations were done along with the calculation of particular prosodic parameters. Thus, below we give an overview of the most illustrative cases for each sentence type.

Declarative Sentences. The typical examples of melodic patterns for ironic and non-ironic declarative utterances in Russian and French are given below (see Figs. 1 and 2)

Fig. 1. Intonation curve for non-ironic (left) and ironic (right) declarative Russian phrases.

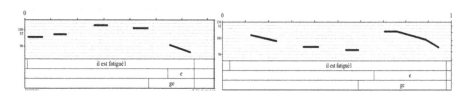

Fig. 2. Intonation curve for non-ironic (left) and ironic (right) declarative French phrases.

The pitch curve resembles a descending line that corresponds to IP1 in the system of Russian intonation patterns suggested by E. Bryzgunova (the falling tone) [8, 17] for the Russian language and the intonation pattern of finality in the system suggested for the French language by P. Delattre [5]. Comparing the non-ironic and ironic curves, we can notice the same trend for Russian and French. The descending contour is preserved in these examples, but the pitch interval between the pre-stressed and the stressed element of the utterance increases, the stressed vowel starts falling from a much higher level than in non-ironic phrases. In the French ironic utterance we can also observe the change in the pitch movement direction in the pre-nuclear part.

Questions. Figures 3 and 4 show the representative melodic contours of interrogative phrases in the studied material. Each curve has an ascending line corresponding to IP3 in the model of intonation patterns by E. Bryzgunova (the rising tone with subsequent fall) and the intonation pattern of a question in the model of P. Delattre [5]. When comparing non-ironic and ironic melodic curves, it can be noticed that in both Russian and French, in ironic utterances the intonation contour starts higher, descends almost to the level of the beginning of the non-ironic phrase, and then continues its upward movement (as in non-ironic variants). It results in the "broken" melodic patterns both in Russian and French.

Fig. 3. Intonation curve for non-ironic (left) and ironic (right) interrogative Russian phrases.

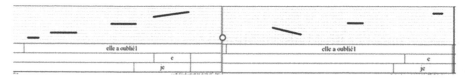

Fig. 4. Intonation curve for non-ironic (left) and ironic (right) interrogative French phrases.

Exclamatory Sentences. The typical pitch curves for exclamatory utterances in both languages represent the decrease of the prosodic parameters, indicated as less frequent characteristic of irony expression (see Figs. 5 and 6). It may be related to the syntactical and grammatical construction of these utterances, though we didn't carry out such analysis in the frame of the current study. The melodic contours correspond to IP5 according to E. Bryzgunova (combination of the rising, flat and falling tones) [8, 17] and an exclamatory intonation pattern with an additional emphasis on the first syllable according to P. Delattre [5]. The curve is ascending at the beginning of the utterance and descending at the end. The pitch range and the duration are reduced in ironic utterances compared to the non-ironic ones.

Fig. 5. Intonation curve for non-ironic (left) and ironic (right) exclamatory Russian phrases.

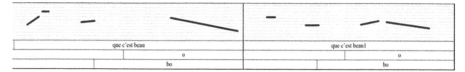

Fig. 6. Intonation curve for non-ironic (left) and ironic (right) exclamatory French phrases.

2.3 Interim Conclusions

The results of these pilot experiments carried out on the basis of the comparable material in Russian and French, using the same methodology, allowed us to suppose that there are some common prosodic features of irony expression in both languages, such as: a slower speech rate, the increase of the duration and intensity level of the stressed vowel and syllable, the increase of the average pitch in a phrase.

In order to evaluate the role of the common features established in the first series of pilot experiments, we carried out another series of experiments, in which these parameters were modified.

3 Experiments with Modified Stimuli

3.1 Method

This series of experiments was based on imposing acoustic characteristics of ironic target phrases (duration and intensity of the stressed vowel, as well as the pitch contour) and their combinations onto homonymous non-ironic stimuli, the similar method was used in [7]. Thus, seven types of modifications were carried out: 1) manipulation of the stressed vowel duration; 2) manipulation of the stressed vowel intensity; 3) manipulation of the pitch contour of the target stimulus; 4) a combination of changes in the stressed vowel duration and intensity; 5) a combination of changes in the stressed vowel duration and the pitch contour of the stimulus; 6) a combination of changes in the pitch contour of the target phrase and the intensity of the stressed vowel; 7) a combination of changes in the stressed vowel duration, intensity and the pitch contour of the stimulus.

Duration. The duration of the stressed vowel was shown to be an important acoustic parameter for identifying irony in the previous series of experiment. Modification of this acoustic feature was performed using the Wave Assistant sound processing software. After semi-automatic pitch-marking, the stressed vowel duration of a non-ironic target phrase was adjusted to match that of the homonymous ironic utterances. It was done by adding or subtracting a necessary amount of wave cycles of the sound.

Pitch. In order to manipulate pitch characteristics of the stimuli a method of prosody transplantation was employed whereby the melodic contour from target ironic phrases was superimposed on homonymous non-ironic phrases produced by the same speaker. Thus, non-ironic fragments with a pitch contour transplanted from the corresponding ironic stimuli were obtained. The procedure of pitch transplantation was as follows. Pitch marks of the target phrases were manually labeled using the Wave Assistant sound processing software and then exported to a Praat file with the pitchtier format. After that, the resulting contour was manually imposed onto the corresponding segment based on the key points of local minimum and maximum of the pitch frequency using the Praat software. This allowed to preserve the original dynamic, temporal and voice quality characteristics while changing the melodic contour of the utterances.

Intensity. Manipulation of intensity was carried out using the Wave Assistant software feature that allows to change the amplitude of a sound by multiplying it by a constant. The stressed vowel amplitude of a non-ironic target phrase was adjusted so that it would have the same mean intensity as the stressed vowel from the corresponding ironic stimulus.

Combination of Manipulations. Based on the 3 types of manipulations described above, 4 types of their combinations were also carried out. These combinations include altering the stressed vowel duration and intensity, changing the stressed vowel duration with a subsequent pitch contour manipulation of the target phrase, altering the pitch contour followed by a change of the stressed vowel intensity and finally combining all three parameters together: manipulating the stressed vowel duration, modification of the pitch contour and change of the stressed vowel intensity.

Only reliably identified non-ironic stimuli with reliably identified corresponding homonymous ironic stimuli (both correctly identified by more than 85% of the informants) were modified and then presented to the listeners in the next series of auditory experiments. French male and female speakers produced 4 and 6 adequate stimuli respectively, whereas Russian male and female speakers provided 8 and 10 such stimuli. This resulted in a total of 70 modified fragments for French speakers and 126 modified fragments for Russian speakers. These fragments together with the original non-ironic stimuli were presented to French and Russian listeners for further evaluation.

Listening Perceptual Experiments. The modified snippets obtained were presented for perceptual experiments. Their organization based on the modified fragments was generally very similar to the methodology applied to the previous surveys: the participants were instructed to listen to the recording and determine from which sentence it was extracted. The participants had to fill out a personal data form as well. The informants could only choose one response option. An effort was made to avoid any direct indication of the purpose of the survey: the response options did not contain explicit ironic remarks and the listeners were unaware of the purpose of the study. The survey was published on the SoSci Survey online platform.

A total of 5 surveys were conducted (on average 20 subjects participated in each survey): 3 surveys for native speakers of Russian (each survey contained 48 questions) and 2 surveys for native speakers of French (each survey contained 40 questions).

3.2   Results

French Language. As we can see from Fig. 7, the most important modification of the original stimuli of both French native speakers was the simultaneous modification of the three parameters: duration, intensity level and pitch contour. The second most important modification that allowed listeners to perceive the phrase as ironic was the combination of the duration and pitch modifications. The third combination also included pitch contour modification, but coupled with intensity level increase.

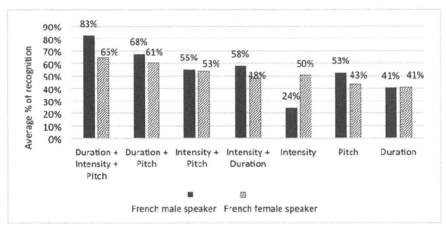

Fig. 7. The average percentage of recognition of phrases as ironic according to various types of modifications on the basis of the original stimuli produced by French speakers.

It seems that pitch pattern plays an important role, but always in pair with another parameter. Modified separately from other prosodic parameters it doesn't create a reliable perception of irony by the French native listeners. The worst recognized stimuli were those in which only intensity or duration were modified.

Russian Language. Perceptual experiments based on the Russian material showed slightly different results (see Fig. 8). As shown in the diagram, the results differ depending on the speaker, whose original stimuli were modified. However, the first three types of modifications that provide the best recognition of irony by native listeners stay the same that for the French material: combination of duration, intensity and pitch contour changes (yet with a less successful recognition by listeners), as well as the combination of duration and pitch. The third combination – intensity modification along with pitch changes – gives even better recognition than in French. The pitch contour also seems to play an important role in irony perception, even when modified alone.

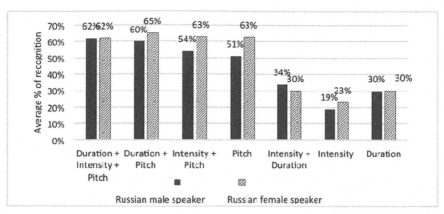

Fig. 8. The average percentage of recognition of phrases as ironic according to various types of modifications on the basis of the original stimuli produced by Russian speakers.

3.3 Interim Conclusions

After analyzing the data obtained, it was possible to establish the most effective sets of modifications that contribute to the creation of an ironic phrase for both languages:

- Duration + Intensity + Pitch.
- Duration + Pitch.
- Intensity + Pitch.

In all the modifications that turned out to be significant for the recognition of the phrase as ironic, both in French and Russian languages, one of the components was necessarily the pitch parameter. And the phrases in which only one type of modification was presented were the worst recognized, especially those phrases, in which only the duration or intensity were changed.

4 Discussion and Conclusion

Results obtained in the current study showed that there are several prosodic character-istics that can be supposed as common or universal means of expressing verbal irony in two languages with the different accentual and rhythmic structure, such as Russian and French. Although the previous study on irony implementation in Russian showed the importance of changes in the stressed vowel duration, intensity level, as well as in the pitch range, it was of interest to study the role of these parameters in the French language. The results of the experiments with the original stimuli allowed us to consider the following parameters as possibly common for two languages:

- Slower speech rate in the phrase;
- Increase of the duration and intensity level of the stressed vowel and syllable,
- Increase of the average pitch in a phrase.

According to the observations on the intonation patterns, possible common feature of irony expression may also be:

- Higher number of melodic peaks resulting in "broken" intonation patterns,
- Change of the pitch movement direction in the pre-nuclear part of the phrase,
- Reduction of the prosodic parameters, notably of the pitch range, in exclamatory sentences with interrogative words.

Other characteristics seem to be language-specific: the increase of the melodic interval from the pre-stressed vowel to the stressed one, reduction of the melodic range in various sentence types is more typical for the French language, while for the Russian language such typical feature would be the increase of the pitch range (except the exclamatory utterances).

The second series of experiments, in which the modified stimuli were suggested to listeners, provided new results on the role of various prosodic parameters in Russian and partially approved the results obtained previously on the material of the French language [7]. The combinations of changes in duration, intensity level and pitch gave the most successful recognition; the second combination was also duration modification coupled with pitch modification. However, the new result of the current study is the suggestion of the cross-linguistic character of such changes, providing irony perception. Also the significance of pitch characteristics seems to be higher in Russian, than in French, according to the results of the two series of experiments. There were noticeable differences in realization and perception of irony in male and female speech, but to explain these differences another study should be conducted. Despite the limitations in the volume of material, caused by the pandemic and geopolitical situation, the data obtained provide new information not only on the possible acoustic cues of irony, but also on their possible hierarchy in irony perception.

Acknowledgements. This research was supported by the RFBR grant No 20–012-00552 and by the grant of Saint Petersburg State University, ID 97183094.

References

1. Akimoto, Y., Sugiura, M., Yomogida, Y., Miyauchi, C.M., Miyazawa, S., Kawashima, R.: Irony comprehension: social conceptual knowledge and emotional response. Hum. Brain Mapp. **35**(4), 1167–1178 (2014)
2. Attardo, S.: The Routledge Handbook of Language and Humor, 1st edn. Routledge, New York (2017)
3. Braun, A., Schmiedel, A.: The phonetics of ambiguity: a study on verbal irony. In: Cultures and Traditions of Wordplay and Wordplay Research, pp. 111–136. De Gruyter, Berlin (2018)
4. Clark, H., Gerrig, R.: On the pretense theory of irony. J. Exp. Psychol. **113**(1), 121–126 (1984)
5. Delattre, P.: Les dix intonations de base du français. French review **40**, 1–14 (1966)
6. Gibbs, R.: Irony in language and thought: A cognitive science reader. Erlbaum, New York, NY (2007)

7. González-Fuente, S., Prieto, P., Noveck, I.: A fine-grained analysis of the acoustic cues involved in verbal irony recognition in French. In: Barnes, J., Brugos, A., Shattuck-Hufnagel, S., Veilleux, N. (eds.) Speech Prosody 2016, pp. 902–906. International Speech Communication Association (ISCA), Boston (2016)
8. Kachkovskaia, T., Kocharov, D., Skrelin, P., Volskaya, N.: CoRuSS-a new prosodically annotated corpus of Russian spontaneous speech. In: Proceedings of the 10th International Conference on Language Resources and Evaluation (LREC'16), pp. 1949–1954. European Language Resources Association (ELRA), Portorož (2016)
9. Kochetkova, U., Skrelin, P., Evdokimova, V., Novoselova, D.: The Speech Corpus for Studying Phonetic Properties of Irony. In: Chernigovskaya, T., Eismont, P., Petrova, T. (eds.) Language, Music and Gesture: Informational Crossroads, pp. 203–214. Springer, Singapore (2021). https://doi.org/10.1007/978-981-16-3742-1_16
10. Kodzasov, S.V.: Studying Russian prosody [Issledovanija v oblasti russkoj prosodii]. Iazyki slavjanskikh kultur, Moscow (2009)
11. Li, S., Gu, W.: Prosodic profiles of the mandarin speech conveying ironic compliment. In: 12th International Symposium on Chinese Spoken Language Processing (ISCSLP 2021), pp. 1–5. Institute of Electrical and Electronic Engineers (IEEE), Hong Kong (2021)
12. Lœvenbruck, H., Jannet, M., D'Imperio, M., Spini, M., Champagne-Lavau, M.: Prosodic cues of sarcastic speech in French: slower, higher, wider. In: Proceedings of the 14th Annual Conference of the International Speech Communication Association (Interspeech 2013), pp. 3537–3541. International Speech Communication Association (ISCA), Lyon (2013)
13. Ré, A.D., Hirsch, F., Dodane, C.: L'ironie dans le discours: des premières productions enfantines aux productions des adultes. Cah. Praxém. **70**, 1–24 (2018)
14. Skrelin, P., Kochetkova, U., Evdokimova, V., Novoselova, D.: Can We Detect Irony in Speech Using Phonetic Characteristics Only? – Looking for a Methodology of Analysis. In: Karpov, A., Potapova, R. (eds.) SPECOM 2020. LNCS (LNAI), vol. 12335, pp. 544–553. Springer, Cham (2020). https://doi.org/10.1007/978-3-030-60276-5_52
15. Skrelin, P., Kochetkova, U., Evdokimova, V., Novoselova, D.: On collecting material for creating a database of ironic speech [Osobennosti sbora materiala dlja sozdanija bazy dannykh ironicheskoj rechi]. In: Proceedings of International conference on sciences and humanities (Science SPbU–2020), pp. 1588–1590. Skifia-print, Saint Petersburg (2020)
16. Skrelin, P., Kochetkova, U., Evdokimova, V., Novoselova, D., German, R.: Prosodic characteristics of ironic utterances in Russian and French [Prosodicheskije kharakteristiki ironicheskikh vyskazyvanij v russkom i frantsuzkom jazykakh]. In: Kocharov, D., Skrelin, P. (eds.) Analysis of the Russian colloquial speech 2021, pp. 81–86. Skifia-print, Saint Petersburg (2021)
17. Volskaya, N., Kachkovskaia, T.: Prosodic annotation in the new corpus of Russian spontaneous speech CoRuSS. In: Barnes, J., Brugos, A., Shattuck-Hufnagel, S., Veilleux, N. (eds.) Speech Prosody 2016, pp. 917–921. International Speech Communication Association (ISCA), Boston (2016)
18. Wilson, D., Sperber, D.: Meaning and Relevance – Explaining irony. Cambridge University Press, Cambridge (2012)

Categorization of Threatening Speech Acts

Liliya Komalova[1,2](✉) [iD] and Lyubov Kalyuzhnaya[2] [iD]

[1] Institute of Scientific Information for Social Sciences of the Russian Academy of Sciences, 51/21, Nakhimovsky Prospect, 117418 Moscow, Russia
komalova@inion.ru
[2] Moscow State Linguistic University, 38, Ostozhenka Street, 119034 Moscow, Russia

Abstract. The paper explores the notion of threatening speech act which is defined as an intentional speech action aimed at suppressing the will of other people and deterioration of their mental state. Based on semantic and pragmatic features of threatening speech acts described in the literature we build a dataset out of randomly collected messages containing verbalized threats presented open access on different Internet social networks sites, Internet forums and Internet messengers. A total number of 68 messages dated from 2015 to 2021 in Russian language are manually processed using contextual analysis and methods of Forensic Linguistics. Categorization method based on (1) type of addressor's intention, (2) direction of threatening speech act, and (3) type of threatening speech act gave a matrix proving our research hypothesis, that among the analyzed messages the most frequent type of threatening speech acts are threats-punishments towards addressees aiming at harming their lives or health. At the same time the prevalent communicative intention of the addressor in such threatening speech acts is the realization of psycho-emotional affect in the form of a threat and the desire to demonstrate the "power" in communication.

Keywords: Threatening speech act · Pragmatics · Corpus linguistics · Forensic linguistics · Perception · Communicative intention · Internet communication

1 Introduction

The scientific research on threatening acts in written speech is of high topicality as these acts represent confrontation strategy in communication and, within the framework of digitalizing world such speech practices gain more popularity every day through digital gadgets and via different types of Internet interfaces.

The fact of threats verbalization in digital environments testifies against abusive behavior of communicants [20] which is a socially unacceptable form of interaction [14]. A verbalized threat is considered to be an intentional speech action [15, 18, 23]. Threatening acts are aimed at suppressing the will of other people and deterioration of their mental state [16, 25]. Such destructive form of communication, containing threatening speech acts, provokes a series of negative emotional states and feelings (emotions of fear, despair, anxiety etc.), and in the future may result in a strong emotional outcome and even in a serious psychological trauma [6]. The long-term consequences of threatening influence could be low self-esteem, anxiety, depression and suicidal tendencies [21].

S. R. M. Prasanna et al. (Eds.): SPECOM 2022, LNAI 13721, pp. 372–381, 2022.
https://doi.org/10.1007/978-3-031-20980-2_32

From morality and law stance, speech behavior containing threatening speech acts is being censored and criticized because it restrains the freedom and rights of other people, the possibility to make decisions and use their resources without any external pressure [6].

The semantics of threatening speech acts contain two components identifying them: (1) threatening speech acts motivate an addressee to act for the interest of the addressor, and (2) threatening speech acts suppose the promise to impose negative sanctions in case the addressor's request is not executed [17].

The pragmatic components of threatening speech acts are the following [4, 5, 19, 22, 24]:

1. The addressee is interested in not fall under any sanctions of the addressor.
2. The addressor knows about this concern of the addressee.
3. The addressor is really possible to implement the sanctions.
4. The addressor is interested in the addressee doing certain actions.
5. The addressor is committed to realize the action declared in the threatening speech act.

Generalizing on the typology of threatening speech acts, A.N. Baranov defines two types of threatening speech acts [2, 3].

1. Threats-punishments are verbalized when the addressee made something that the addressor does not accept and is warning the addressee about the sanction that will be soon realized against the addressee. This way the addressor negatively assesses the actions of the addressee. Threats-punishments do not stimulate the addressee to fulfill the addressor's will, but they have a negative emotional effect on the addressee (or a third party) by implication of consequent harm in form of sanctions. The main goal of a threat-punishment is to make the addressee dread punishment as a sanction for the addressee's action [3, p. 34]. The communicative intention of threats-punishments is to make a commitment to realize sanction against the addressee for he/she made something unpleasant to the addressor [ibid., p. 140].
2. Threats-warnings are used when the addressor understands that the addressee may (or may not) do something the addressor considers as undesirable for the addressor (or associated individuals) and is trying to avoid it. The communicative intention of threats-warnings is to get the appropriate behavior (action or omission) of the addressee so that it (the behavior) does not lead to an event undesirable for the addressor [ibid].

2 Methodology

Due to the fact that over the past seven years, Digital Civility index of Russian language resources on the Internet has not been increased [7], it can be stated that existing legislative tools do not cover the entire variety of destructive behavior realized on Internet sites or mediated by the Internet. Therefore, there is a need for the development of mechanisms for detecting facts of destructive speech behavior, based on the laws of morality and the subjective modal of such behavior, based on the ideas of naive native speakers.

In particular, existing works in the field of Forensic Linguistics and research of phenomena, which are included in the objective base of Forensic Linguistics (such as conflict generative texts, extremist statements, speech provocation, speech threats, etc.), are deprived of the harmonious classification and criteria base of the destructive speech behavior. Within this framework the question is how to ensure safe communication between Internet users in cases where destructive speech behavior, in particular verbalized threats, does not fall under legal grounds, but are perceived as harmful to the human psychological health?

The *research question* that motivates this study is: How does the form of threat verbalization correlate with the desire that the addressor seeks to satisfy with this threat?

The *research hypothesis* consists in the assumption that, as a rule, in the form of a direct verbalized threat on the Internet towards addressee's life/health the addressor strives to realize the desire to externalize his/her negative emotional and psychological state and to build the image of the person endowed with the power.

Categorization of threatening speech acts as a potentially procedural legal notion of conflictive type is required in classification tasks for elaboration of automated systems of Internet content filtration (e.g. on SNS, Internet forums, etc.) and for elaboration of professional software for Forensic Linguistics' purposes. As a whole, it serves to ensure digital security within Internet communication. Scientific researches provide applicable solutions to achieve in this way (see, for example [9–12]).

We suppose that threatening speech act category identification would provide opportunity to produce effective solutions on how to neutralize or/and punish for it implementation in speech practice. In reference to this, we hypothesize that within Internet communication the most frequent type of threatening speech acts in messaging are threats-punishments towards addressees aiming at harming their lives or health. At the same time we suppose that the communicative intention of the addressor in such threatening speech acts is the realization of psycho-emotional affect in the form of a threat.

To prove this hypothesis we completed the dataset out of the messages (written text posts, comments, and declarations) in Russian language retrieved from open Internet sources such as social network sites (SNS), Internet sites and forums, Internet messengers (open sources at VKontakte, Instagram, WhatsApp, Viber, Odnoklassniki, Twitter). We retrieved those messages that contained verbalized threatening speech acts. We selected the research dataset by continuum sampling method based on qualitative parameters and features of threatening speech acts described in the literature and briefly presented in the Introduction section of the present paper.

During the empirical study we applied contextual[1], conceptual and syntax-stylistics types of analysis, distributive analysis, comparing and systematization of empirical and theoretical data, methods of Forensic Linguistics.[2]

---

[1] Contextual analysis is based on the idea that the statement gets meaning in a situational and social context and is the function of this context [1, p. 46–49].

[2] When analyzing a disputed text through Forensic Linguistic procedure an expert uses general scientific methods such as analysis and synthesis, and specific linguistic methods such as semantic-syntactic, lexical-semantic, functional-stylistic, grammatical, functional-pragmatic types of analysis, analysis of the communicative structure of text organization, analysis of

The collected dataset consisted of 65 messages dated from 2015 to 2021. Three of the analyzed responses of the addressees contained three threatening speech acts, that is why the final dataset consists out of 68 messages.

3 Results

Dataset analysis revealed that threats-punishments are the dominant (76,47%) type of the messages, for example:

*I have to do what I conceived, **for**, you insulted me*[3] (an adverbial clause of reason)	*Ya obyazan sdelat togo chego vzdumal, **ibo**, ty oskorbil menya*

Threats-warnings are presented in a smaller proportion (23,53%), for example:

*You have 2 weeks to fall apart from Russia, **otherwise** you will meet her. In hell* (an adverbial clause of result)	*U tebya 2 nedeli, chtoby svalit iz Rossii, **inache** ty vstretish Elenu Grigorievny. V adu*

We managed to combine all messages in the dataset into three groups:

- threats towards the **addressee's** life/health/reputation/social status (88,24%), for example:

*I will find **you you** will pray for the death*	*Ya naidu **tebya ty** molit budesh o smerti budesh;*
*Silence do not dare I will find **you** on IP and **you** are a dead man*	*Molchi ne smei ya **tebya** po ip naidu a **tebe** khana*

- threats towards life/health/reputation/social status of **other people associated with the addressee** (10,29%), for example:

*Consider, I have your address, the data of **your father and mother**, your personal tax id. Watch somebody would not has slaughtered **them***	*Schitai adres, dannye **tvoego** otsa, materi i tvoj INN uzhe u menya. Sledi, chtoby **ikh** ne zarezali*

---

presuppositions, analysis of propositions, component analysis, content analysis, contextual analysis [13].

[3] Translation from Russian into English is made by the authors of this paper. We tried to convey the author style of writing in punctuation marks, but failed to convey all the syntax and lexical peculiarities presented in original messages in Russian language.

- threats towards **the addressee's property**[4] (1,47%), for example:

*Look, creature, **your dogs** would better not have got in my hands. Will smash **them** together with you*	*Smotri, tvar, chtoby **tvoi sobake** ko mne ne popali. Razmazhu vmeste s toboj*

The analysis of threats-punishments and threats-warnings revealed the following trends.

- The leading intention (51,47% of all cases) of the addressor to verbalize threatening speech acts is his/her affective psycho-emotional state: speech behavior of the addressor is driven by the desire to realize negative emotional states (e.g., anger, disgust), to show the intention to take revenge on the addressee, for example:

I will find you and cut your heart out	*Ya naidu tebya i vyrezhu tebe serdtse*
You are not a tenant on the earth !!!!! Call the police and your term of the arrival on this land will be reduced faster!!!!	*Ty ne zhilets na belom svete!!!!! Obratishsya v politsiyu tvoj srok prebyvaniya na etoj zemle sokratitsya bystrej!!!!*

- Another frequent type of intention (39,71% of all cases) for threatening speech act verbalization is the desire to assert oneself through demonstration of "power", for example:

*Listen here, a kid, if **I show you who I am in the real life**, you will piss to death. And will shudder... From every knock at the door. Not every woman on the NET is stupid...*	*Sluchaj syuda, patsan, **esli ya tebe pokazhu kto ya v reale**, ssat budesh do smerti. I boyatsya ... kazhdogo zvonka v dver. V nete ne vse prostushki sidyat, no i...*
I'm chatting with you on the relaxes, I can give you all day. And you are scared, you are angry, you are nervous. Yes, I logged in to slaughter you, oh you are my lactose!	*Ya na rasslabonchikakh bazaryu, mogu ves den tebe udelit. A ty boishsya, zlishsya, nervnichaesh. Da ya zabajtilsya chtoby zarezat tebya, akh ty moya laktoza!*

- In some messages (5,88% of all cases) threatening speech act was used to blackmail the addressee: the addressor's speech behavior was motivated by the desire to get (money) benefits, not to sanction against the addressee, for example:

---

[4] According to Article 137 "Animals" of the Civil Code of the Russian Federation, «the general rules about the property are applied to animals since other laws or other legal acts are not established» [8].

| Now you **owe** my bank **a big money,** and you have a week or my guys will come for you | Ty teper moemu banku **realnye dengi torchish** i u tebya nedelya ili moi rebyata pridut za toboj |
| Doggie rough find me **10 000 rubles or I will** put you on a skewer | Pes brodyaga **najdi mne 10.000 rublej** ili na shampur |

- Sometimes (2,94% of all cases) the addressees themselves verbalized threats in response to the addressors' threatening speech acts. Such reactions were motivated by the desire to explain what sanction the addressor would meet in case his/her threat would be realized, for example:

| You know, **the threats on the Internet are now being pursued by law** [explanation] and tomorrow loath as I am to take this correspondence to the police [threat in response] | A vot **ugrozy v internete sejchas presleduyutsya po zakonu** i ya ne polenyus i zavtra s etoj perepiskoj obraschus v militsiyu |

Next we analyzed the combination of type of threatening speech act (Table 1) and type of intention motivating the addressor to verbalize threat (Table 2).

Table 1. Type of threatening speech acts.

Direction of threatening speech act	%
Towards addressee's life/health (affect)	41,19
Towards addressee's life/health (power)	29,41
Towards addressee's life/health (blackmail)	4,41
Towards addressee's reputation/social status (power)	8,82
Towards addressee's reputation/social status (affect)	1,47
Towards addressee's reputation/social status (blackmail)	1,47
Towards addressee's reputation/social status (explanation)	1,47
Towards life/health of the people associated with the addressee (affect)	7,35
Towards life/health of the people associated with the addressee (blackmail)	1,47
Towards life/health of the people associated with the addressee (explanation)	1,47
Towards addressee's property (affect)	1,47

Results obtained (Table 3) confirm the hypothesis that among the analyzed messages the most frequent type of threatening speech acts are threats-punishments towards addressees aiming at harming their lives or health. At the same time the prevalent communicative intention of the addressor in such threatening speech acts is the realization of psycho-emotional affect in the form of a threat (35,29%) and the desire to demonstrate the "power" (25%).

Table 2. Type of motivation to verbalize threats.

Type of addressor's intention	%
Affected speech behavior	**51,47**
Verbalized demonstration of "power"	**38,23**
Blackmail	7,35
Explanation	2,94

Table 3. Complex description of threatening messages.

Type of addressor's intention	Direction of threatening speech act	Type of threatening speech act (in %)	
		Threats-punishments	Threats-warnings
Affected speech behavior	Towards addressee's life/health	**35,29**	5,88
	Towards addressee's reputation/social status	1,47	0
	Towards life/health of the people associated with the addressee	7,35	0
	Towards addressee's property	0	1,47
Verbalized demonstration of "power"	Towards addressee's life/health	**25**	4,41
	Towards addressee's reputation/social status	4,41	4,41
Blackmail	Towards addressee's life/health	1,47	2,95
	Towards addressee's reputation/social status	0	1,47
	Towards life/health of the people associated with the addressee	1,47	0
Explanation	Towards addressee's reputation/social status	0	1,47
	Towards life/health of the people associated with the addressee	0	1,47

4   Conclusion

The results obtained in the empirical research speak for the hypothesis confirming that (within the analyzed messages) threatening speech acts are mostly affective actions – rude form of expressing negative emotional states of the addressor, and the addressee is only a trigger to activate them. Even if these actions do not have the potential to be implemented on the addressee, they are perceived as real threats, as they are aimed at life/health of people.

This research was performed within the framework of qualitative analysis of verbalization of 68 direct threatening speech acts extracted from the contexts of real interactions between internet-interlocutors. The prognostic potential of this research results is limited to the dataset volume, since it is impossible to build a general prognostic model of speech behavior of an average internet-user verbalizing threats based on the quantitative results obtained in this research.

However, the qualitative results obtained, namely, the types of addressor's intentions, the direction of threatening speech acts in combination with the existing classification of the types of threatening speech acts allow to indicate the categories of verbalized threats that can be used to determine the addressor's desire. We believe that decoding this desire motivating the addressor to verbalize threats will make it possible to understand what really he/she requires by the threatening speech act: whether to attract attention to his/her person, to receive acknowledgement, to initiate or stop somebody's action, to get something declared in the threat, to proceed keeping the addressee in fear, or something else. This knowledge will reduce the destructive potential of threatening speech acts.

Further investigation is needed to find out, in what way such threatening speech acts influence mental health of people. And if they have any influence, should such acts be regulated by, for example, the owner of an Internet social network site or needs state legislation.

Acknowledgements. The research is carried out within the framework of the state assignment to the Federal State Budgetary Educational Institution «Moscow State Linguistic University», project No FSFU-2020-0020 «Perspective technologies of Government's informational function realization and maintenance of digital sovereignty».

References

1. Arnold, I.V.: Osnovy nauchnykh issledovanyj v lingvistike. Vysshaya shkola, Moscow (1991).(in Russian)
2. Baranov, A.N.: Semantika ugrozy v lingvisticheskoj ekspertize (Semantics of threat in Forensic Linguistics). In: Computernaya lingvistika i intellektualnye tekhnologii. Po materialam ezhegodnoj Mezhdunarodnoj konferentsii "Dialog" (Computational Linguistics and Intellectual Technologies. International conference "Dialogue"), vol. 12(19), issue 1, pp. 72–82. Moscow (2013). https://www.dialog-21.ru/media/1223/baranovan.pdf (in Russian)
3. Baranov, A.N.: Ugroza v kriminal'nom diskurse (semantika i pragmatika) (Threat in criminal discourse (semantics and pragmatics)). Azbukovnik, Moscow (2021).(in Russian)
4. Brinev, K.I.: Sudebnaja lingvisticheskaja jekspertiza po delam, svjazannym s ugrozoj (Forensic linguistic expertise on threatening cases). Theor. Pract. Aspects Speech Act. **4**, 43–49 (2009). (in Russian)

5. Brinev, K.I.: Teoreticheskaja lingvistika i sudebnaja lingvisticheskaja jekspertiza (Theoretical linguistics and forensic linguistic expertise). AltGPA, Barnaul. http://os.x-pdf.ru/20k ulturologiya/519346-1-ki-brinev-teoreticheskaya-lingvistika-sudebnaya-lingvisticheskaya-eks.php (2009). (in Russian)
6. Dayshutov, M.M., Dineka, V.I., Denisenko, M.V.: Mental abuse in criminal law. Vestnik Moscovskogo Universiteta MVD Rossii **3**, 77–81 (2019). https://elibrary.ru/item.asp?id=385 81612 (in Russian)
7. Digital civility index – 2021 report (2021). https://www.microsoft.com/en-us/online-safety/digital-civility#coreui-banner-q42zgbu
8. Grazhdanskij kodeks Rossijskoj Federacii (Civil Code of the Russian Federation) (2022). http://www.consultant.ru/document/cons_doc_LAW_5142/fd6980fe6d3f891c65ca0 0040c9d100eeb2ef3ee/. (in Russian)
9. Komalova, L., Glazkova, A., Morozov, D., Epifanov, R., Motovskikh, L., Mayorova, E.: Automated classification of potentially insulting speech acts on social network sites. In: Alexandrov, D.A., et al. (eds.) DTGS 2021. CCIS, vol. 1503, pp. 365–374. Springer, Cham (2022). https://doi.org/10.1007/978-3-030-93715-7_26
10. Komalova, L., Goloshchapova, T.: Differentiated analysis of the "insult" speech genre based on messages from a social network Internet sites. RUDN J. Lang. Stud. Semiot. Seman. **12**(3), 619–631 (2021). https://doi.org/10.22363/2313-2299-2021-12-3-619-631. (in Russian)
11. Komalova, L., Kulagina, D.: Perceiving speech aggression with and without textual context on twitter social network site. In: Karpov, A., Potapova, R. (eds.) SPECOM 2021. LNCS (LNAI), vol. 12997, pp. 348–359. Springer, Cham (2021). https://doi.org/10.1007/978-3-030-87802-3_32
12. Komalova, L., Sadova, E.: Pragmatic vector of verbalized aggression within internet mediated communication: textual context dimension. Vestn. Volgogr. Gos. Univ.. Ser. 2 Jazykozn. **3**, 77–89 (2022). https://doi.org/10.15688/jvolsu2.2022.3.7. (in Russian)
13. Kukushkina, O.V.: Methods used in Forensic Linguistic analysis. Theory Pract. Forensic Sci. **1**, 118–126 (2016). https://doi.org/10.30764/64/1819-2785-2016-1-118-126. (in Russian)
14. Ljubešić, N., Fišer, D., Erjavec, T.: The FRENK datasets of socially unacceptable discourse in Slovene and English. In: Ekštein, K. (ed.) TSD 2019. LNCS (LNAI), vol. 11697, pp. 103–114. Springer, Cham (2019). https://doi.org/10.1007/978-3-030-27947-9_9
15. Nick, I.M.: In the wake of hate: a mixed-method analysis of anonymous threatening communications sent during the 2016 US presidential election. Nord. J. Linguist. **41**(2), 183–203 (2018). https://doi.org/10.1017/S0332586518000148
16. Novozhenova, Z.L., Probst, N.A.: On the speech-act nature of the verbal threat. Vestnik IKBFU. Philology, Pedagogy, and Psychol. **4**, 31–36 (2019). https://elibrary.ru/item.asp?id= 41424254 (in Russian)
17. Plotnikova, A.M.: Linguistic creativity in threat speech and its mechanisms. Ural Philological Herald. Series Language. System. Pers.: The Linguistics Creativity **2**, 81–88 (2017). https://elibrary.ru/item.asp?id=29246424 (in Russian)
18. Probst, N., Shkapenko, T., Tkachenko, A., Chernyakov, A.: Speech act of threat in everyday conflict discourse: production and perception. Lege Artis **3**(2), 204–250 (2018). https://doi.org/10.2478/lart-2018-0019
19. Shelinger, T.N.: Netradicionno vydeljaemye kommunikativnye edinicy sovremennogo anglijskogo jazyka (Non-traditionally allocated communicative units of modern English). PhD Dissertation. A.A. Zhdanov Leningrad State University, Leningrad (1986) (in Russian)
20. Simrat, K., Sarbjeet, S., Sakshi, K.: Abusive content detection in online user-generated data: a survey. Procedia Comput. Sci. **189**, 274–281 (2021). https://doi.org/10.1016/j.procs.2021.05.098
21. Sourander, A., et al.: Psychosocial risk factors associated with cyberbullying among adolescents: a population-based study. Arch. Gen. Psychiatry **67**(7), 720–728 (2010)

22. Walton, D.: Speech acts and indirect threats in ad baculum arguments: a reply to Budzynska and Witek. Argumentation **28**(3), 317–324 (2014). https://scholar.uwindsor.ca/crrarpub/14
23. Watt, D., Kelly, S., Llamas, C.: Inference of threat from neutrally-worded utterances in familiar and unfamiliar language. York Pap. Linguist. Ser. **2**(13), 99–120 (2013)
24. Wierzbicka, A.: Speech genders. Speech Genders **1**, 99–111 (1997). https://www.elibrary.ru/item.asp?id=36422407 (in Russian)
25. Zlokazov, K.V., Kolmykova, T.I., Rybyakova, E.A., Stepanov, R.I.: Perception of threat in infosphere by the reader: experimental research results. Political Linguistics **2**, 131–138 (2017). https://elibrary.ru/item.asp?id=29115157 (in Russian)

Assessment of Speech Quality During Speech Rehabilitation Based on the Solution of the Classification Problem

Evgeny Kostyuchenko[1]([✉]) [iD], Ivan Rakhmanenko[1] [iD], and Lidiya Balatskaya[1,2] [iD]

[1] Tomsk State University of Control Systems and Radioelectronics, Lenina Str. 40, 634050 Tomsk, Russia
key@keva.tusur.ru, nii@oncology.tomsk.ru
[2] Tomsk Cancer Research Institute, Kooperativniy Av. 5, 634050 Tomsk, Russia
http://www.tusur.ru, http://www.oncology.tomsk.ru/

Abstract. The article considers an approach to the problem of assessing the quality of speech during speech rehabilitation as a classification problem. For this, a classifier is built on the basis of an LSTM neural network for dividing speech signals into two classes: before the operation and immediately after. At the same time, speech before the operation is the standard to which it is necessary to approach in the process of rehabilitation. The metric of belonging of the evaluated signal to the reference class acts as an assessment of speech. An experimental assessment of rehabilitation sessions and a comparison of the resulting assessments with expert assessments of phrasal intelligibility were carried out.

Keywords: Speech rehabilitation · Speech quality assessment · LSTM

1 Introduction

The problem of oncological diseases of the organs of the speech-forming tract is urgent. According to statistical studies [1], for the period from 2009 to 2019, there has been a steady increase in such indicators for the localization of the lip, oral cavity, pharynx, as the incidence per 100,000 people, the overall incidence, and the cumulative risk of this type of disease in the age category 0–74 years old. At the same time, the proportion of tumors of the organs of the speech-forming tract in the total number of oncological diseases remains practically unchanged due to a decrease in the proportion of diseases of the lips. These trends are graphically presented in Fig. 1. These quantitative values determine the relevance of research related to oncological diseases of the organs of the vocal tract.

Another feature of this localization of diseases is the influence of its treatment on the quality of life. Surgical treatment requires re-learning to speak. This requires a speech rehabilitation procedure. The particular importance of this procedure is due to the fact that the bulk of the sick are of working age, and the lack of speech function significantly reduces the quality of life, preventing most of the communicative functions from being performed both at work and at home. Based on these facts, it can be concluded

S. R. M. Prasanna et al. (Eds.): SPECOM 2022, LNAI 13721, pp. 382–390, 2022.
https://doi.org/10.1007/978-3-031-20980-2_33

that developments in the field of increasing the effectiveness of speech rehabilitation are relevant. One of the subspecies of such studies is obtaining objective quantitative assessments of speech quality, which this work is devoted to.

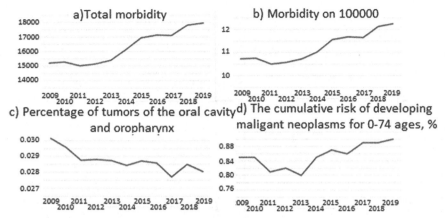

Fig. 1. Dynamics of the incidence of oncological diseases of the organs of the speech-forming tract (lips, oral cavity, pharynx). a) morbidity per 100,000 people, b) newly detected cases of diseases, c) the proportion of diseases in the studied localization, d) The cumulative risk of developing malignant neoplasms for 0–74 ages, %

2   Existing Approaches to Assessing Speech Quality

If we consider the general structure of methods for assessing the quality of speech (Fig. 2), then they can be divided into 2 categories: objective and subjective. Sub-jective assessment methods are based on research and assessment of pronounced units by experts. At the same time, the units themselves can differ significantly: indi-vidual phonemes, syllables, phrases. The most striking example of this category is the assessment based on GOST R 50840-95 [2]. For rehabilitation tasks, this standard allows one to obtain estimates of syllable and phrasal intelligibility [3].

Objective assessment methods, in turn, can be divided into 2 classes: they work on the basis of comparison of the same signal before and after transmission and use different signal realizations for assessment. At the same time, the use of the former for the tasks of speech rehabilitation is extremely problematic, since the recordings of the patients' speech before and after the operation are not the same signal before/after exposure. In the second category, many assessment methods have been developed with input from our team. It is possible to distinguish assessment approaches based on the normalization of signals and their subsequent comparison [4, 5] and the use of recognition tools for assessment as a substitute for an expert in the GOST method [6, 7].

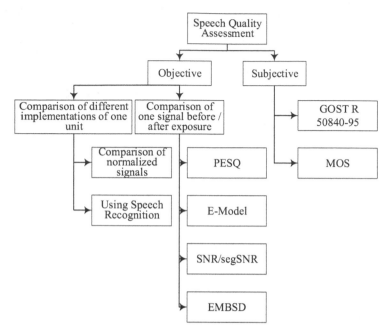

Fig. 2. Classification of methods for assessing speech quality

However, the limited number of assessment methods and their incomplete coincidence with the GOST reference method in terms of the accuracy of the estimates obtained and their interpretability, suggests the relevance of the search for new approaches to obtaining such estimates.

In this paper, we propose to consider a new class of such methods - based on the application of machine learning methods to obtain an estimate of the speech quality as a result of solving the classification problem.

3   Speech Quality Assessment Based on the Classification Problem

The main idea of the proposed approach is easy to understand. At the time of the visit to the clinic, the patient, despite the presence of the disease, practically does not disturb the intelligibility of speech. The resulting grades of phrasal intelligibility are almost always equal to 1, and the grades of syllabic intelligibility are close to 1 (differences may arise more due to incorrect reading of syllables than due to their incorrect pronunciation). This fact allows us to speak about the possibility of using the notes before the operation as a standard of speech for a particular patient. This approach allows us to take into account the presence of speech features and individual defects in the patient, because further comparison will go exactly with the speech of a particular patient.

After the operation, speech intelligibility is significantly reduced. The final value depends on the volume and localization of the surgical intervention, however, syllabic intelligibility in some cases may fall below 0.1.

In fact, we can say that we have 2 classes of records: before and after surgery. Within the framework of the proposed approach, it is proposed to build a machine learning system that solves the problem of determining whether the presented record is a record before or after the operation. If you train such a system to solve the described problem, then there is an opportunity to present it with the notes made during the rehabilitation process and use the metric of belonging to the reference class as an assessment of the quality of pronouncing the phrase.

The next section describes the experimental study of the proposed approach and the establishment of its applicability.

4 Experiment

4.1 Dataset

During the experiment, we used a previously collected set of recorded phrases from GOST. Made 25 records of phrases in one session. The number of patients with two sessions (before and after surgery) is 24, with three sessions - 18, with four sessions - 7. The total number of records is 3250. The sampling rate is 12000 Hz. The number of pairs of sessions suitable for constructing the classifier was 49. To construct the classifier, 80% of the sets were selected into the training set, the remaining 20% into the test set.

During processing, each signal was converted into a spectral form using the Fourier transform, block length 64 ms, 50% overlap. After that, the obtained spectrograms were transferred to the input of the classifier. This approach to constructing inputs is basic [8] and is suitable as the first iteration in constructing a classifier.

4.2 Neural Network

A neural network was chosen as a machine learning method for constructing the classifier. The use of such networks is typical for solving a variety of speech analysis problems, such as speech recognition [9, 10], authentication [11, 12], sentiment determination [13], and others. For this reason, it was decided to use this particular type of city when constructing the classifier.

Considering the small amount of data and examples of using these networks for speech analysis tasks [14], a neural network based on LSTM was chosen [15].

To combat overfitting, regularization, dropout and batch normalization were applied. The architecture of this neural network is shown in Table 1.

Table 1. Neural network architecture.

Layer (type)	Output shape	Param #
lstm_1 (LSTM)	(None, 16, 128)	328704
Batchnormalization_1(Batch)	(None, 16, 128)	64

(continued)

Table 1. (*continued*)

Layer (type)	Output shape	Param #
lstm_2 (LSTM)	(None, 64)	49408
dropoutl (Dropout)	(None, 64)	0
dense_l (Dense)	(None, 64)	4160
activation_l(Activation)	(None, 64)	0
dense_2 (Dense)	(None, 16)	1040
activation_2(Activation)	(None, 16)	0
dense_3 (Dense)	(None, 1)	17
activation_3(Activation)	(None, 1)	0
Total params: 383,393		
Trainable params: 383,361		
Non-trainable params: 32		

4.3 All-User Training and Personalized Training

Training was carried out according to two methods: for all users and a separate one only for the user of interest. The second training is based on a limited set of data, but the output is a classifier designed to work with a specific patient. A system trained on all users is more capable of generalizing data, however, due to the lack of focus on working with an individual user, it is likely to show less accurate results in the final assessment. Graphs of changes in accuracy and loss-function depending on the iteration number are presented in Figs. 3 and 4.

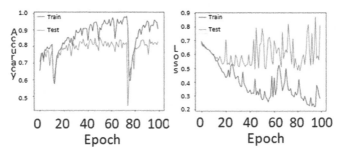

Fig. 3. Precision and lost-function for learning on all users

It can be seen that it is possible to train the neural network without retraining for one user. The final accuracy for the case without separation of users was 0.8, and there are signs of overfitting.

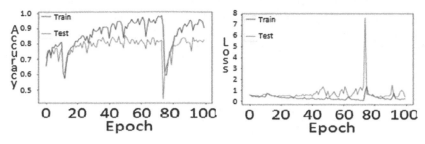

Fig. 4. Precision and lost-function for learning on one user

4.4   Obtaining Final Speech Quality Scores

After constructing a ready-made classifier, the signals were processed during the rehabilitation process, their quality was assessed and the resulting estimate was compared with the estimate obtained by an expert. Thus, values were obtained for 32 sessions. For all considered methods, estimates are obtained from the range [0; 1]. The obtained values are presented in Table 2.

Table 2. Speech quality estimates obtained using the basic expert method and the proposed classification approach.

No. seans	Expert	Class all	Class one	No. seans	Expert	Class all	Class one
1	0.84	0.42	0.73	17	0.84	0.46	0.71
2	0.68	0.87	0.52	18	0.56	0.12	0.27
3	0.88	0.68	0.66	19	0.92	0.90	0.68
4	0.96	0.24	0.94	20	0.68	0.84	0.55
5	0.78	0.46	0.50	21	0.84	0.46	0.60
6	1.00	0.32	0.75	22	0.92	0.12	0.88
7	0.96	0.92	0.84	23	0.84	0.76	0.84
8	1.00	0.95	0.91	24	0.92	0.46	0.90
9	0.96	0.54	0.68	25	0.84	0.14	0.75
10	0.96	0.42	0.79	26	0.76	0.86	0.59
11	0.56	0.64	0.45	27	0.84	0.42	0.69
12	0.96	0.96	0.90	28	0.92	0.18	0.74
13	0.70	0.28	0.63	29	1.00	0.28	0.83
14	0.96	0.18	0.74	30	0.96	0.92	0.96
15	0.96	0.94	0.95	31	0.92	0.84	0.63
16	0.88	0.82	0.75	32	0.84	0.50	0.55

For greater clarity, we can sort the obtained values in ascending order and plot all the obtained values of quality assessments on a diagram. The result is shown in Fig. 5. After that, there is a strong relationship between the expert assessment and the one proposed based on the classification for one user.

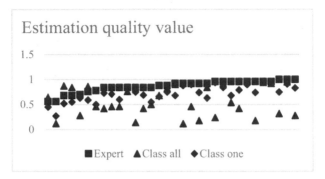

Fig. 5. Estimation values after sorting in ascending of expert rating order

After the expected receipt of quality assessments, you can proceed to the analysis of the results obtained.

5   Discussion

To assess the results obtained, we will find the correlation coefficient between them and check its statistical significance. The calculation will be carried out using Spearman's rank correlation coefficients. The calculation was carried out in the SPSS program.

The obtained values and the level of their significance are presented in Table 3.

Table 3. Assessment of the significance of the correlation coefficient. **. Correlation is significant at the 0.01 level (two-tailed).

			Expert	ClassAll	ClassOne
Rho Spearman	Expert	Correlation coefficient	1.000	0.115	0.772**
		Mean. (double-sided)		0.532	0.000
		N	32	32	32
	ClassAll	Correlation coefficient	0.115	1.000	0.116
		Mean. (double-sided)	0.532		0.526
		N	32	32	32
	ClassOne	Correlation coefficient	0.772**	0.116	1.000
		Mean. (double-sided)	0.000	0.526	
		N	32	32	32

The results show that the results obtained for one user are consistent, which allows us to speak about the absence of obvious contradictions between the considered assessment method. For estimates based on all users, more significant discrepancies are visible and the correlation coefficient turns out to be statistically insignificant. This is due to the fact that during the training all users were united in one class, regardless of the volume and localization of the surgical intervention. Thus, the previous assumption about the best applicability of the method when working with one user is experimentally confirmed.

6 Conclusion

The experiment carried out has shown the potential applicability of the proposed approach based on the application of the classification. The efficiency in solving the problem of dividing speech into classes before/after the operation is shown. The applicability of this approach is shown when constructing a classifier for a specific patient. Spearman's correlation coefficient for estimates obtained by this method and estimates obtained by an expert way is 0.772 and is statistically significant. In the future, it is planned to analyze the applicability of the proposed approach when grouping patients into groups (gender, location and volume of surgery).

Acknowledgements. This research was funded by the Ministry of Science and Higher Education of the Russian Federation within the framework of scientific projects carried out by teams of research laboratories of educational institutions of higher education subordinate to the Ministry of Science and Higher Education of the Russian Federation, project number FEWM-2020-0042. The authors would like to thank the Irkutsk Supercomputer Center of SB RAS for providing access to the HPC-cluster «Akademik V.M. Matrosov» [16].

References

1. Kaprin, A., Starinskiy, A., Petrova, G.: Malignant neoplasm in Russia in 2019 (morbidity and mortality). P. A. Hertsen Moscow Oncology Research Center - Branch of FSBI NMRRCof the Ministry of Helth of Russia, Moscow (2020)
2. Standard GOST R 50840-95: Voice over paths of communication. Methods for assessing the quality, legibility and recognition. Publishing Standards, Moscow, 234 p. (1995)
3. Balatskaya, L.N., Choinzonov, E.L., Chizevskaya, S.Y., Kostyuchenko, E.U., Meshcheryakov, R.V.: Software for assessing voice quality in rehabilitation of patients after surgical treatment of cancer of oral cavity, oropharynx and upper jaw. In: Železný, M., Habernal, I., Ronzhin, A. (eds.) SPECOM 2013. LNCS, vol. 8113, pp. 294–301. Springer, Cham (2013). https://doi.org/10.1007/978-3-319-01931-4_39
4. Kostyuchenko, E., Meshcheryakov, R., Ignatieva, D., Pyatkov, A., Choynzonov, E., Balatskaya, L.: Correlation normalization of syllables and comparative evaluation of pronunciation quality in speech rehabilitation. In: Karpov, A., Potapova, R., Mporas, I. (eds.) SPECOM 2017, pp. 262–271. LNCS, vol. 10458. Springer, Cham (2017). https://doi.org/10.1007/978-3-319-66429-3_25
5. Meschryakov, R.V., et al.: Speech quality measurement automation for patients with cancer of the oral cavity and oropharynx. In: 2016 International Siberian Conference on Control and Communications (SIBCON), pp. 1–5. IEEE, May 2016

6. Nikolaev, A.N.: Mathematical models and a set of programs for automatic assessment of the quality of a speech signal. The dissertation for the degree of candidate of technical sciences, specialty 05.13.18 - Mathematical modeling, numerical methods and program complexes, Ekaterinburg (2002)
7. Kostuchenko, E., et al.: The evaluation process automation of phrase and word intelligibility using speech recognition systems. In: Salah, A., Karpov, A., Potapova, R. (eds.) SPECOM 2019. LNCS, vol. 11658, pp. 237–246. Springer, Cham (2019). https://doi.org/10.1007/978-3-030-26061-3_25
8. Rippel, O., Snoek, J., Adams, R.P.: Spectral representations for convolutional neural networks. arXiv preprint arXiv:1506.03767 (2015)
9. Kipyatkova, I.S., Karpov, A.A.: Variants of deep artificial neural networks for speech recognition systems. Trudy SPIIRAN **49**, 80–103 (2016)
10. Graves, A., Mohamed, A., Hinton, G.: Speech recognition with deep recurrent neural networks. In: 2013 IEEE International Conference on Acoustics, Speech and Signal Processing. IEEE (2013)
11. Lim, C.P., Woo, S.C., Loh, A.S., Osman, R.: Speech recognition using artificial neural networks. In: Proceedings of the First International Conference on Web Information Systems Engineering, vol. 1, pp. 419–423. IEEE, June 2000
12. Shukla, A., Tiwari, R.: A novel approach of speaker authentication by fusion of speech and image features using Artificial Neural Networks. Int. J. Inf. Commun. Technol. 1(2), 159–170 (2008)
13. Kaya, H., Karpov, A.A.: Efficient and effective strategies for cross-corpus acoustic emotion recognition. Neurocomputing **275**, 1028–1034 (2018)
14. Graves, A., Jaitly, N., Mohamed, A.R.: Hybrid speech recognition with deep bidirectional LSTM. In: 2013 IEEE Workshop on Automatic Speech Recognition and Understanding, pp. 273–278. IEEE, December 2013
15. Gers, F.A., Schmidhuber, J., Cummins, F.: Learning to forget: continual prediction with LSTM. Neural Comput. **12**(10), 2451–2471 (2000)
16. Irkutsk Supercomputer Center SB RAS. http://hpc.icc.ru/en/. Accessed 15 July 2022

Multi-level Fusion of Fisher Vector Encoded BERT and Wav2vec 2.0 Embeddings for Native Language Identification

Dani Krebbers[1], Heysem Kaya[1(✉)], and Alexey Karpov[2]

[1] Department of Information and Computing Sciences, Utrecht University, Utrecht, The Netherlands
h.kaya@uu.nl
[2] St. Petersburg Federal Research Center of the Russian Academy of Sciences, St. Petersburg, Russia
karpov@iias.spb.su

Abstract. Native Language Identification is a prominent paralinguistic study with applications ranging from biometric analysis to speaker adaptation. Former studies on this task have benefited from alternative acoustic feature representations and pre-trained neural networks. In this work, we explore the Native Language Identification performance of contextual acoustic (wav2vec 2.0) and linguistic (BERT) embeddings as state-of-the-art feature representations and combine them with acoustic features at different levels. We encode acoustic and linguistic features using Fisher Vectors, applying Fisher Vector encoding on BERT word embeddings and wav2vec 2.0 for the first time for a paralinguistic task. We compare this approach with conventional functional summarization. In line with our former study using only acoustic modality, the results indicate the superiority of Fisher Vectors encoding over the traditional techniques. Moreover, we show the efficacy of combining alternative representations now in both acoustic and linguistic modalities. Results indicate a notable contribution of the transformer-based contextual auditory and linguistic feature representations to bimodal Native Language Identification systems.

Keywords: Computational Paralinguistics · Native Language Identification · BERT · Wav2vec 2.0 · Fisher Vector

1 Introduction

Native Language Identification (NLI) is a field related to Natural Language Processing (NLP) that focuses on deriving someone's native language (L1) based on speech or writing in a later learned language (L2). Studies in this field mainly focus on non-native English speakers, where we address the task as a classification problem. The assumption, that motivates this research area, is that a

© Springer Nature Switzerland AG 2022
S. R. M. Prasanna et al. (Eds.): SPECOM 2022, LNAI 13721, pp. 391–403, 2022.
https://doi.org/10.1007/978-3-031-20980-2_34

speaker's L1 influences his/her L2. Therefore, by deriving characteristics from someone's L2, their L1 can be determined.

Motives to explore this domain are manifold. First, we can apply it to computer linguistics, mainly used for authorship profiling [22]. Second, it is helpful for the automated personalization of educational applications. Adapting facets of a system, such as feedback, based on their native language, is beneficial for the learning process [27]. Third, it can be used for spoken language applications, where automatic speech recognition (ASR) systems are customized to specific L1s. Finally, it can help with second language acquisition research [19,20]. Medical spheres that relate to treatment of speech disorders are possible as well.

NLI is closely related to the overarching topic of language identification, and dialect identification [3], given that those topics cover classification tasks based on acoustic and linguistic information as well. Nativeness is another closely related topic, as covered in [28]. It defines the degree of someone's L2 capabilities. This degree is measured on a continuous scale and is determined by expert decisions. This subjective measure is in contrast with NLI, where there is an objective truth for someone's L1. This more objective performance measure for NLI makes it a more sound research domain, less prone to subjective influences.

In this study, we propose a bimodal approach using classical and state-of-the-art acoustic and linguistic feature representations extending our contribution [15] to ComParE INTERSPEECH 2016 Computational Paralinguistics Challenge (ComParE) [29] - Native Language Identification Sub-challenge (NLI SC). This sub-challenge features an 11-class NLI task. The contributions of this work are manifold. First, we apply Fisher Vector (FV) representation on BERT and wav2vec embeddings for the first time, as opposed to applying functionals (e.g., averaging) to these state-of-the-art contextual representations. We propose a bimodal system for the NLI task, comparing alternative fusion strategies at feature and decision levels. We carry out extensive experiments on different acoustic feature representations, FV hyperparameters, and summarize the best performances per feature representation.

2   Background and Related Work

2.1   Transformer-Based Linguistic Features

Given the performance and generalizability of pre-trained transformer-based models, we use BERT to capture the linguistic contents of utterances [5]. While models like BERT are often used in an end-to-end fashion being fine-tuned on specific tasks [9], we extract contextual word embeddings using only the pre-trained model. In [5], the authors found that using a weighted sum of the last four hidden layers to obtain embeddings resulted in the best performance, therefore we adopt this in our system as well.

The 2016 ComParE NLI Sub-challenge corpus did not include any textual data. Therefore, we used Google Cloud's speech-to-text[1] services to obtain transcripts of the audio. Valuable linguistic content can be captured using ASR services even though their performance is not perfect. The ASR errors can even be

---

[1] https://cloud.google.com/speech-to-text.

used to distinguish different speaker classes according to Shivakumar et al. [31], since "an ASR transcript will contain consistent errors based on consistent mispronunciations resulting from L1 specific phonemic confusability".

2.2 Transformer-Based Acoustic Features

In recent years, transformer-based models have been successfully used on various NLP tasks. While they are often used on linguistic content, acoustic input-based models have been implemented as well. The most well-known audio input-based system in this category is wav2vec 2.0 [2]. As seen in Fig. 1, it consists of two main components: a Convolutional Neural Network (CNN) based feature encoder, and a transformer to contextualize the representations. While wav2vec 2.0 is often used in an end-to-end classification fashion, it can also produce vector representations, as the name suggests. Wav2vec 2.0 has been pretrained in a self-supervised manner on large amounts of data. It is often fine-tuned for specific tasks such as speech recognition [4], emotion recognition [21], speaker verification and language identification [7]. Here, we use the wav2vec2-base-960h pretrained model from[2] without further self-supervised training or supervised fine-tuning, extracting embeddings as the low-level descriptors (LLDs) to form the basis for more elaborate feature representations. In [26], the authors showed that aggregating wav2vec 2.0 embeddings outperforms supervised counterparts, and they show aggregation is suitable for extracting phonotactic constraints. In [21], the authors showed the effectiveness of using different layers from the pretrained wav2vec model on emotion recognition tasks. They also showed that wav2vec embeddings improved results in combination with features from other modalities, in their case prosodic. This suggests that using wav2vec embeddings is complementary to other feature representations.

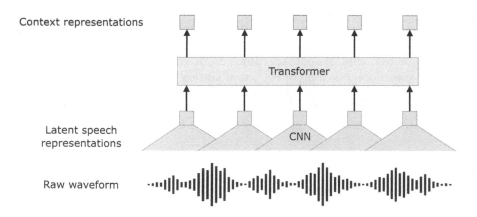

Fig. 1. Framework for wav2vec 2.0, adapted from [2].

---

[2] https://huggingface.co/facebook/wav2vec2-base-960h.

2.3 Fisher Vector Encoding

With Fisher Vector encoding [23] we can create fixed-length utterance-level features over an arbitrarily long sequence of LLDs. Our proposed system applies FV to the acoustic LLDs as well as the linguistic representations. While FV encoding has been applied to Word2vec word embeddings in the past [24], to our knowledge, we are the first to use FV encoding on contextualized BERT and wav2vec embeddings.

FV encoding takes a background probability model, usually a Gaussian Mixture Model (GMM) with diagonal covariances, and quantifies the change in the GMM parameters needed to fit the new incoming data (e.g., the LLDs of an utterance). We measure both first (mean) and second-order (variance) statistics for the combination of each mixture component and each descriptor. This results in a $2*d*K$ dimensional supervector, where d is the number of dimensions in the data, and K is the number of GMM components. To efficiently learn the diagonal covariance GMM, the data needs to be decorrelated. We apply Principal Component Analysis (PCA) for this purpose, as well as for dimensionality reduction. To reduce computational costs, we use every k-th frame for the acoustic LLDs before learning PCA and the GMM, where initially k is set to 4. However, we apply the fitted PCA model and FV encoding to all frames from an utterance.

2.4 Kernel Extreme Learning Machines

In our fusion scheme, we use Kernel Extreme Learning Machine (KELM) [12] to model high-dimensional feature vectors, motivated by its fast and accurate learning capability and state-of-the-art results on paralinguistic challenge corpora [15,16,32]. We obtain kernels from the dataset and use them in KELM, optimizing the hyper-parameters on the development set.

ELM was initially proposed as an alternative to back-propagation: a fast learning method for Single Hidden Layer Feed-forward Networks (SLFN) [13]. In this approach, the input layer weights are randomly generated and then orthogonalized, while the second layer weights are optimized via (regularized) least squares. The Kernel ELM approach, however, does not benefit from random hidden layer generation but from direct use of kernels for regularized least-squares-based learning. Here, a hyper-parameter C is introduced for regularization of the kernel. Given a kernel $\mathbf{K}$ and the label vector[3] $\mathbf{T} \in \mathbb{R}^{N \times 1}$, where N denotes the number of instances, the projection vector β is learned as follows [12]:

$$\beta = (\frac{\mathbf{I}}{C} + \mathbf{K})^{-1}\mathbf{T}. \tag{1}$$

In order to prevent parameter over-fitting, we use the linear kernel $\mathbf{K}(x, y) = x^T y$, where x and y are the (normalized) feature vectors. With this approach, the only parameter of our model is the regularization coefficient C, which we optimize on the development set.

---

[3] In case of classification, $\mathbf{T}$ represents the one-hot-encoding matrix of the training set class labels.

3   Proposed NLI Framework

The pipeline of the proposed NLI system is illustrated in Fig. 2. In the framework, the upper pipe that combines reduced baseline openSMILE features with FV encoded MFCC+RASTA-PLPC features, extending the best performing approach used in our contribution to the challenge [15]. In our former paper, due to computational limitations, only Mel-Frequency Cepstral Coefficients (MFCC) features were used in FV encoding, while the fused acoustic representations were modeled with both Kernel ELM used here and Kernel Partial Least Squares Regression-based classifier for subsequent weighted decision fusion [33]. The research question tackled in this work investigates the contribution of transformer-based state-of-the-art acoustic and linguistic embeddings and the suitability of the FV encoding of these embeddings. For the final predictions, we use weighted score fusion on the individual classifier scores.

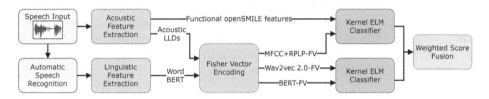

Fig. 2. The pipeline of the proposed bimodal NLI system. RPLP is short for RASTA-PLPC.

3.1   Extracting Conventional Acoustic LLDs

In line with our former work on the same task [15], we extract MFCCs 0-24 and RASTA-style Perceptual Linear Prediction Cepstral Coefficients (RASTA-PLPC) [10,11] using 12th order linear prediction as low-level descriptors. Both of these LLDs are extracted from 25 ms windows with 10 ms steps and are augmented with their first and second-order delta coefficients yielding LLD-vectors of length 75 (3×25) and 39 (3×13) for MFCC and RASTA-PLPC, respectively. For a direct comparison with the openSMILE-based challenge baseline feature set, we also extract LLDs with openSMILE [6] using INTERSPEECH 2013 configuration [30], which has been used in the ComParE series since then.

3.2   Fusion Schemes

Based on our experience with former audio and video signal processing challenges [14,15,32], in this work we propose a stacking framework, where we use feature level fusion followed by a decision level fusion using simple weighted score fusion(SF), where the classifier confidence scores S^A and S^B are fused using the weight $\gamma \in [0,1]$:

$$S^{fusion} = \gamma * S^A + (1 - \gamma) * S^B. \tag{2}$$

In the pipeline, FV representations of state-of-the-art transformer-based contextual acoustic and linguistic embeddings are fused at feature level on one pipe, and classical acoustic features that are used in our contribution to ComParE 2016 [15] on the other pipe. We further compare the stacking approach with class-based weighted score fusion where we replace γ with a vector Γ containing the weights for each of L classes. This vector contains bounded normal distribution values (mean=0.5 and variance=0.1) where $\Gamma \in [0,1]^L$ and is found by random sampling. A third score fusion method we apply is by using Random Forest (RF) classification applied to the individual classifier scores.

4   Experimental Results

We conducted unimodal and bimodal experiments to showcase the contribution of the proposed transformer-based acoustic and linguistic features with FV encoding. To this end, we also compare the classical functional summarization-based approach with FV representation on acoustic and linguistic representations. In all experiments, we apply a cascaded normalization, composed of feature level z-normalization, value level (signed) power normalization, and feature vector-level L_2 normalization, respectively, as in [15,17]. Below we briefly revisit the dataset and subsequently introduce our results.

4.1   ComParE 2016 Native Language Corpus

As shown in Table 1, in total there are eleven different native languages in the dataset. The complete dataset has around 45 s of speech from each of the 5,132 distinct speakers, all in non-native English. The training partition for all different classes consists of 300 instances, making the class distributions equal. Overall, the classes are distributed fairly equally when we include the development and test set.

Table 1. ETS corpus of non-native spoken English with ComParE 2016 challenge split.

#	Train	Dev	Test	Σ
Arabic	300	86	80	466
Chinese	300	84	74	458
French	300	80	78	458
German	300	85	75	460
Hindi	300	83	82	465
Italian	300	94	68	462
Japanese	300	85	75	460
Korean	300	90	80	470
Spanish	300	100	77	477
Telugu	300	83	88	471
Turkish	300	95	90	485
Σ	3300	965	867	5132

4.2 Comparative Experiments with Unimodal Features

The FV extraction with MFCC+RASTA-PLPC LLD combination, we experimented with P = {90, 100, 110} PCA dimensions and K = {64, 128, 200, 256} GMM components. For a better insight in comparison with the challenge baseline features, we extract the same set of openSMILE (OS13 - openSMILE feature set with INTERSPEECH 2013 configuration) LLDs as the challenge paper [29], apply both functionals, and FV encoding for utterance representation, in addition to the original set of acoustic features. We use 10 functionals that include mean, standard deviation, min (+ its relative location), max (+ its relative location), zero-crossing rate, coefficients of the first (slope, offset) and second-order (curvature) polynomials fit to the LLD contours.

BERT and wav2vec 2.0 output 768 dimensional embeddings and hence we use P = {350, 400, 450, 500} PCA dimensions with K = {64, 128} GMM components. BERT provides word-level embeddings, while wav2vec 2.0 provides an embedding for 25 ms windows of the speech signal with 20 ms steps. To alleviate the computational issues and obtain quasi-phoneme level information, we summarize wav2vec over consecutive 5 frames. The summary of best development set performances in terms of the Unweighted Average Recall (UAR) for each utterance feature representation is given in Table 2. Here, we have multiple observations. The first observation is that FV representation dramatically boosts the performance compared to a simple use of 10 functionals both with proposed MFCC+RASTA-PLPC and with openSMILE LLDs. The second observation is that wav2vec embedding with FV representation outperforms the best conventional LLDs-based FV model, reaching 73.65% UAR on the development set. Third, while a simple mean averaging of BERT outperforms classical acoustic features summarized with 10 functionals, FV encoding of these acoustic features outperforms BERT-FV by 13% to 20% absolute difference.

In line with [15], we apply feature selection using the Canonical Correlation Analysis-based approach [18] and retain the top 5300 features out of the original 6373. This selection improves the Kernel ELM performance of the baseline set to 52.1%. A feature-level combination of the reduced openSMILE set and Ac2 in Table 2 gives a development set UAR score of 72.43%.

4.3 Proposed Bimodal System and Ablation Studies

The test set performances of the bimodal system in comparison with the works presented in the challenge and the state-of-the-art system presented after the challenge are presented in Table 3. The proposed system reaches a test set UAR performance of 83.89%, outperforming the challenge-winning system (UAR 81.30%), while remaining below the current state-of-the-art work of Qian et al. [25] that employs a pre-trained Time-Delayed Deep Neural Network (TDNN)-based i-vector approach using Probabilistic Linear Discriminant Analysis (PLDA) as a classifier.

Of the constituent models, feature fusion of selected openSMILE features with MFCC+RASTA-PLPC FV gives a test set UAR score of 73.44%, while the

Table 2. Unimodal development set UAR (%) performances of the constituent feature representations of the proposed framework. RPLP: RASTA-PLPC, NFun: Summarization using N functionals. P_{PCA} and K_{GMM} represent the number of PCA dimensions and GMM components, respectively.

SysID	LLD	Utterance rep.	Notes	UAR
Ac1	MFCC+RPLP	10Fun		34.05
Ac2	MFCC+RPLP	FV	$P_{PCA} = 110$, $K_{GMM} = 200$	70.95
Ac3	OS13	10Fun		37.59
Ac4	OS13	54Fun	Baseline set [29]	51.17
Ac5	OS13	FV	$P_{PCA} = 130$, $K_{GMM} = 200$	63.31
Ac6	wav2vec 2.0	FV	$P_{PCA} = 400$, $K_{GMM} = 128$	73.65
Lin1	BERT	Mean		40.20
Lin2	BERT	FV	$P_{PCA} = 400$, $K_{GMM} = 64$	50.67

combination of FV representations of wav2vec 2.0 and BERT reaches a test set UAR of 76.52%. We obtain the best performance when we use simple weighted score fusion, resulting in 83.89% UAR on the test set. Removing the wav2vec features from the proposed system decreases the performance to 77.93%. Further removal of the selected openSMILE features (leaving us with BERT FV and MFCC+RASTA-PLPC FV pipes) results in 76.10% UAR on the test set.

Table 3. UAR (%) Performance comparison of the proposed system with literature on ComParE 2016 NLI sub-challenge. The first part reports the performances in the official challenge, the second part reports the performance after the challenge.

Work	Dev.	Test
Baseline paper [29]	45.10	47.50
Gosztolya et al. [8]	70.70	70.10
Kaya and Karpov [15]	67.60	71.50
Shivakumar et al. [31]	78.60	80.13
Abad et al. [1]	84.60	**81.30**
Our system	82.52	83.89
Qian et al. [25]	87.10	**87.20**

Figure 3 illustrates the test set confusion matrix corresponding to the predictions giving 83.89% UAR. Interestingly, results of the current and past research on the dataset have shown that Hindi and Telugu often give the highest confusion. Both languages are used in India, and share similarities in pronunciation, which could be correlated to this higher level of confusion. French, Italian and Spanish share the same language family (Indo-European Romance), while

Japanese, Korean and Turkish are Ural-Altaic languages. Being in the same language families partly explains the relatively higher confusion observed in the former works and the present work for these language subsets. Although Chinese (Sino-Tibetan) is not under the same language family as Japanese and Korean, its tonal nature and geographic proximity to these countries are thought to influence the (mis)classification in this group. Moreover, the confusions within language families (e.g. Indo-European Romance) and among those languages spoken in geographical proximity (such as Hindi & Telugu, as well as Japanese & Korean) can be used to generate groups of languages for a two-stage hierarchical classification in a future work.

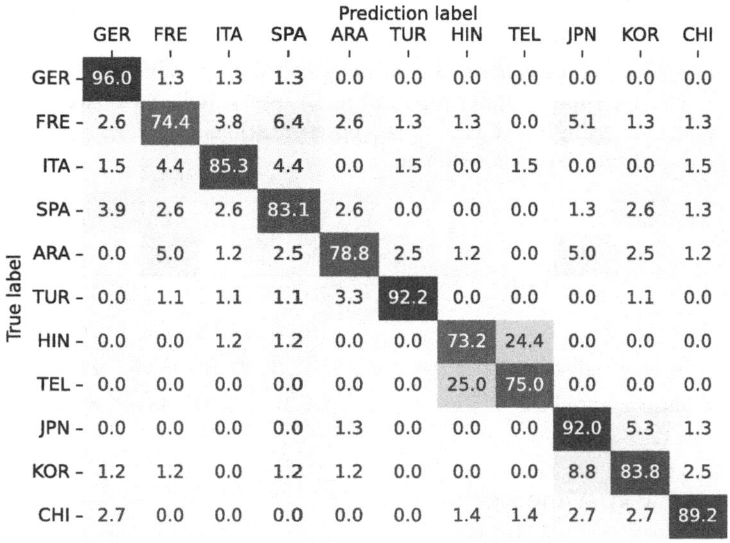
Prediction label
GER FRE ITA SPA ARA TUR HIN TEL JPN KOR CHI
True label
GER 96.0 1.3 1.3 1.3 0.0 0.0 0.0 0.0 0.0 0.0 0.0
FRE 2.6 74.4 3.8 6.4 2.6 1.3 1.3 0.0 5.1 1.3 1.3
ITA 1.5 4.4 85.3 4.4 0.0 1.5 0.0 1.5 0.0 0.0 1.5
SPA 3.9 2.6 2.6 83.1 2.6 0.0 0.0 0.0 1.3 2.6 1.3
ARA 0.0 5.0 1.2 2.5 78.8 2.5 1.2 0.0 5.0 2.5 1.2
TUR 0.0 1.1 1.1 1.1 3.3 92.2 0.0 0.0 0.0 1.1 0.0
HIN 0.0 0.0 1.2 1.2 0.0 0.0 73.2 24.4 0.0 0.0 0.0
TEL 0.0 0.0 0.0 0.0 0.0 0.0 25.0 75.0 0.0 0.0 0.0
JPN 0.0 0.0 0.0 0.0 1.3 0.0 0.0 0.0 92.0 5.3 1.3
KOR 1.2 1.2 0.0 1.2 1.2 0.0 0.0 0.0 8.8 83.8 2.5
CHI 2.7 0.0 0.0 0.0 0.0 0.0 1.4 1.4 2.7 2.7 89.2

Fig. 3. The test set confusion matrix (in %) of the proposed system yielding 83.89% UAR.

4.4 Effect of Design Choices on the Proposed Pipeline

To test the robustness of the proposed pipeline, we test for alternative pipeline components. Simple weighted score fusion is substituted by the individual class-weighted score fusion technique. In this approach, we randomly generate fusion weights for each class independently, and check the fusion UAR performance for a pool of such generated fusion vectors. Using a pool of 50K randomly generated fusion vectors, on the same feature fusion pipelines, this results in 83.50% UAR on the test set, obtaining slightly lower performance compared to the current best pipeline. Stacking the classifier scores to RF results in 80.60% on the test set. This shows that the simple weighted score fusion method is the best option out of these three methods for the task, both regarding performance and simplicity.

The current approach applies L_2 normalization as a final step of the normalization process, followed by calculating a linear kernel as the first step of the classification process. This two-step process essentially results in a cosine kernel. Alternatively, we remove the L_2 normalization and replace the linear kernel with an RBF kernel, since non-linear kernels usually can fit the data better. However, we see a performance drop of around 3% UAR, justifying the use of the simpler cosine kernel approach.

By only retaining the first-order statistics (means) from FV, we reduce the dimensionality by half of the initial size. The resulting feature vector is in line with the Vectors of Locally Aggregated Descriptors (VLAD) representation, even though K-means is more commonly used as a background probability model. Interestingly, as Table 4 shows, we find only minimal performance differences between FV and VLAD.

Table 4. Development and test set UAR (%) performances of the two pipes and the proposed pipeline using alternative clustering-based feature representations and score fusion (SF) methods. Pipe 1 (upper pipe in Fig. 2) uses classical acoustic features with functional and clustering-based utterance representations. Pipe 2 uses transformer-based acoustic and linguistic embeddings.

System	VLAD		FV	
	Dev.	Test	Dev.	Test
Pipe 1	70.55	71.22	72.43	73.44
Pipe 2	76.50	78.45	75.51	76.52
Simple weighted SF of Pipe 1 & 2	83.23	**83.80**	82.52	**83.89**
Class-weighted SF of Pipe 1 & 2	84.37	**83.91**	83.88	83.50

4.5 Further Experiments

Since the FV features consist of large dimensions, we try several feature reduction techniques to further improve the performance by removing redundant information. Instead of single-column feature reduction techniques, we reduce features GMM component-wise. We apply the first method, Permutation Feature Importance (PFI), per section of the whole FV encoding. While results improved marginally during testing (an increase of $< 0.5\%$), we decide the dramatically increased computational costs do not weigh up against this marginal improvement.

We apply PCA after obtaining the FV encodings in a similar fashion as PFI. Different approaches for retaining a considerable amount of explained variance in the data 85%, 95%, 99% did not yield improved results. Furthermore, Linear Discriminant Analysis (LDA) for feature reduction, applied in the same GMM component-wise style, did not improve results either.

5   Conclusions and Future Work

In this paper, we employ transformer-based acoustic and linguistic embeddings as LLDs and model them via Fisher Vector over the utterance for NLI tasks.

Without any further self-supervised pre-training or task-dependent fine-tuning, the transformer-based acoustic and linguistic embeddings modeled with FV provide a marked contribution to the traditional acoustic features for the NLI task. The ablation studies show the overall robustness and preference for simpler versions of pipeline components. Thus, future works may benefit from a simplistic approach with clustering-based modeling using GMM, probably comparing the performances of FV and VLAD earlier, in a preliminary set of experiments. Other future works include task-based fine-tuning of the transformer networks and further prosodic modeling for NLI tasks. Furthermore, a two-level hierarchical classification approach can be exploited to minimize the confusion among highly confused L1 classes.

Acknowledgments. Work of A. Karpov is supported by the RSF (project No. 22-11-00321). We also thank the data donors and challenge organizers for making this research possible.

References

1. Abad, A., Ribeiro, E., Kepler, F., Astudillo, R., Trancoso, I.: Exploiting phone log-likelihood ratio features for the detection of the native language of non-native English speakers. In: Proceedings of Interspeech 2016, pp. 2413–2417 (2016). https://doi.org/10.21437/Interspeech.2016-1491
2. Baevski, A., Zhou, Y., Mohamed, A., Auli, M.: wav2vec 2.0: a framework for self-supervised learning of speech representations. Adv. Neural Inf. Process. Syst. **33**, 12449–12460 (2020)
3. Chowdhury, S.A., Ali, A., Shon, S., Glass, J.: What does an end-to-end dialect identification model learn about non-dialectal information? In: Proceedings of Interspeech 2020, pp. 462–466 (2020). https://doi.org/10.21437/Interspeech.2020-2235
4. Conneau, A., Baevski, A., Collobert, R., Mohamed, A., Auli, M.: Unsupervised cross-lingual representation learning for speech recognition. arXiv preprint arXiv:2006.13979 (2020)
5. Devlin, J., Chang, M.W., Lee, K., Toutanova, K.: Bert: pre-training of deep bidirectional transformers for language understanding. arXiv preprint arXiv:1810.04805 (2019)
6. Eyben, F., Weninger, F., Groß, F., Schuller, B.: Recent developments in opensmile, the Munich open-source multimedia feature extractor. In: Proceedings of the 21st ACM International Conference on Multimedia, pp. 835–838. ACM (2013)
7. Fan, Z., Li, M., Zhou, S., Xu, B.: Exploring wav2vec 2.0 on speaker verification and language identification. In: Proceedings of Interspeech 2021, pp. 1509–1513 (2021). https://doi.org/10.21437/Interspeech.2021-1280
8. Gosztolya, G., Grósz, T., Busa-Fekete, R., Tóth, L.: Determining native language and deception using phonetic features and classifier combination. In: Proceedings of Interspeech 2016, pp. 2418–2422 (2016). https://doi.org/10.21437/Interspeech.2016-962
9. Hao, Y., Dong, L., Wei, F., Xu, K.: Visualizing and understanding the effectiveness of bert. arXiv preprint arXiv:1908.05620 (2019)
10. Hermansky, H.: Perceptual linear predictive (PLP) analysis of speech. the J. Acoust. Soc. Am. **87**(4), 1738–1752 (1990)

11. Hermansky, H., Morgan, N.: Rasta processing of speech. IEEE Trans. Speech Audio Process. **2**(4), 578–589 (1994)
12. Huang, G.B., Zhou, H., Ding, X., Zhang, R.: Extreme learning machine for regression and multiclass classification. IEEE Trans. Syst. Man Cybern. Part B Cybern. **42**(2), 513–529 (2012)
13. Huang, G.B., Zhu, Q.Y., Siew, C.K.: Extreme learning machine: theory and applications. Neurocomputing **70**(1), 489–501 (2006)
14. Kaya, H., Gurpinar, F., Ali Salah, A.: Multi-modal score fusion and decision trees for explainable automatic job candidate screening from video CVS. In: Proceedings of the IEEE Conference on Computer Vision and Pattern Recognition (CVPR) Workshops, pp. 1–9, July 2017
15. Kaya, H., Karpov, A.A.: Fusing acoustic feature representations for computational paralinguistics tasks. In: Proceedings of Interspeech 2016, pp. 2046–2050 (2016). https://doi.org/10.21437/Interspeech.2016-995
16. Kaya, H., Karpov, A.A.: Introducing weighted kernel classifiers for handling imbalanced paralinguistic corpora: snoring, addressee and cold. In: Proceedings of Interspeech 2017, pp. 3527–3531 (2017). https://doi.org/10.21437/Interspeech.2017-653
17. Kaya, H., Karpov, A.A., Salah, A.A.: Robust acoustic emotion recognition based on cascaded normalization and extreme learning machines. In: Cheng, L., Liu, Q., Ronzhin, A. (eds.) ISNN 2016. LNCS, vol. 9719, pp. 115–123. Springer, Cham (2016). https://doi.org/10.1007/978-3-319-40663-3_14
18. Kaya, H., Özkaptan, T., Salah, A.A., Gürgen, F.: Random discriminative projection based feature selection with application to conflict recognition. IEEE Sig. Process. Lett. **22**(6), 671–675 (2015). https://doi.org/10.1109/LSP.2014.2365393
19. Malmasi, S., Dras, M.: Language transfer hypotheses with linear SVM weights. In: Proceedings of the 2014 Conference on Empirical Methods in Natural Language Processing (EMNLP), pp. 1385–1390 (2014)
20. Malmasi, S., et al.: A report on the 2017 native language identification shared task. In: Proceedings of the 12th Workshop on Innovative Use of NLP for Building Educational Applications, pp. 62–75 (2017)
21. Pepino, L., Riera, P., Ferrer, L.: Emotion recognition from speech using wav2vec 2.0 embeddings. arXiv preprint arXiv:2104.03502 (2021)
22. Perkins, R.: Native language identification (NLID) for forensic authorship analysis of weblogs. In: New threats and Countermeasures in Digital Crime and Cyber Terrorism, pp. 213–234. IGI Global (2015)
23. Perronnin, F., Dance, C.: Fisher kernels on visual vocabularies for image categorization. In: 2007 IEEE Conference on Computer Vision and Pattern Recognition, pp. 1–8. IEEE (2007)
24. Plummer, B.A., Kordas, P., Kiapour, M.H., Zheng, S., Piramuthu, R., Lazebnik, S.: Conditional image-text embedding networks. In: Proceedings of the European Conference on Computer Vision (ECCV), pp. 249–264 (2018)
25. Qian, Y., et al.: Improving sub-phone modeling for better native language identification with non-native English speech. In: Proceedings of Interspeech 2017, pp. 2586–2590 (2017). https://doi.org/10.21437/Interspeech.2017-245
26. Ramesh, G., Kumar, C.S., Murty, K.S.R.: Self-supervised phonotactic representations for language identification. In: Proceedings of Interspeech 2021, pp. 1514–1518 (2021). https://doi.org/10.21437/Interspeech.2021-1310
27. Rozovskaya, A., Roth, D.: Algorithm selection and model adaptation for ESL correction tasks. In: Proceedings of the 49th Annual Meeting of the Association for Computational Linguistics: Human Language Technologies, pp. 924–933 (2011)

28. Schuller, B., et al.: The interspeech 2015 computational paralinguistics challenge: Nativeness, parkinson's & eating condition. In: Proceedings of Interspeech 2015, pp. 478–482 (2015). https://doi.org/10.21437/Interspeech.2015-179
29. Schuller, B., et al.: The interspeech 2016 computational paralinguistics challenge: deception, sincerity & native language. In: Proceedings of Interspeech 2016, pp. 2001–2005 (2016). https://doi.org/10.21437/Interspeech.2016-129
30. Schuller, B., et al.: The interspeech 2013 computational paralinguistics challenge: Social signals, conflict, emotion, autism. In: Proceedings of Interspeech 2013, pp. 148–152 (2013). https://doi.org/10.21437/Interspeech.2013-56
31. Shivakumar, P.G., Chakravarthula, S.N., Georgiou, P.: Multimodal fusion of multirate acoustic, prosodic, and lexical speaker characteristics for native language identification. In: Proceedings of Interspeech 2016, pp. 2408–2412 (2016). https://doi.org/10.21437/Interspeech.2016-1312
32. Soğancıoğlu, G., et al.: Is everything fine, grandma? acoustic and linguistic modeling for robust elderly speech emotion recognition. In: Proceedings of Interspeech 2020, pp. 2097–2101 (2020). https://doi.org/10.21437/Interspeech.2020-3160
33. Wold, H.: Partial least squares. In: Kotz, S., Johnson, N.L. (eds.) Encyclopedia of Statistical Sciences, pp. 581–591. Wiley, New York (1985)

Fake Speech Detection Using OpenSMILE Features

Devesh Kumar, Pavan Kumar V. Patil, Ayush Agarwal$^{(\boxtimes)}$,
and S. R. Mahadeva Prasanna

Department of Electrical Engineering, Indian Institute of Technology Dharwad,
Dharwad 580011, India
{200030017,200030041,201081001,prasanna}@iitdh.ac.in

Abstract. With the advancement of technology in deep learning, we
have developed methods that generate fake speech, which is impossible
to differentiate from a natural speech by an ordinary person perceptually.
Fake speech can be used maliciously to harm society or a person (impersonation, fake news spreading, etc.), so we need to develop methods to
detect fake speech. Several features have been proposed in the literature
that can identify fake speech. Each of those features has different contributions to the detection task. In this work, we propose to use the most
common speech features together for fake speech detection. openSMILE
toolkit is an open-source library that extracts the most common speech
features and stores them in the vector of 88 dimensions. We use these
features over machine learning models to detect fake speech. To check the
robustness of the proposed method, we test it over various datasets that
contain session, gender, domain, and synthesizer variability. The experimental results on the different variabilities showed that the openSMILE
features were able to detect the fake speech in session, gender and synthesizer variability with high performance, whereas the performance is
low with the domain variability conditions.

Keywords: Fake speech · OpenSMILE features · Feature selection

1 Introduction

Among the various authentication modes like fingerprint, iris, face, and speech,
speech has the advantage of remote authentication. However, this added advantage draws the attention of people with malicious intent and introduces threats
to the speaker verification systems [1,2]. The advancements in deep learning-
based speech technologies like voice conversion and speech synthesis have made
it possible for the machines to produce fake speech that has the speaker's identity
indistinguishable from the real one. The zero-shot voice conversion and speech
synthesis systems can accurately generate the speech with only one utterance
of the speaker's speech [5,15]. With the publicly available data and the ease
of recording the speaker's voice, it is easy to generate fake speech and hence

© Springer Nature Switzerland AG 2022
S. R. M. Prasanna et al. (Eds.): SPECOM 2022, LNAI 13721, pp. 404–415, 2022.
https://doi.org/10.1007/978-3-031-20980-2_35

has imposed a severe threat on the automatic speaker verification (ASV) system. Therefore this has dragged the community's attention to propose several features and methods to identify fake speech.

Various works are done in the literature to identify fake speech. Series of challenges are organised like ASVSpoof2015 [20], ASVSpoof2017 [8], ASVSpoof2019 [18]. The ASVSpoof2015 challenge gave the countermeasures for developing text-to-speech (TTS) and voice conversion (VC) attacks. ASVSpoof2017 challenge focused on record and replay attacks, and ASVSpoof2019 focused on developing countermeasures for physical and logical access [18].

Various features, countermeasures, and methods were proposed to identify the fake speech. Mel frequency cepstral coefficient (MFCC) features along with support vector machine (SVM) was used to detect the spoofed speech in [4]. In [21] MFCC and Modified Group Delay Cepstral Coefficients (MGDCC) features extracted from magnitude and phase spectrogram and used as a feature on Gaussian Mixture Model (GMM) to identify the synthetic speech. In [16], bispectral and MFCC features are used to capture the high frequency features present in the synthetic speech. Constant Q Cepstral Coefficient (CQCC) features have been extensively used for spoof detection. These features capture the high resolution of the low frequencies that are not addressed in MFCC [17].

Linear Prediction (LP) analysis-based LP residual features like Residual MFCC (RMFCC) features along with MFCC have also proven to work as a strong countermeasure for replay attacks [12]. Long-term features like pitch variation are used along with CQCC to detect fake speech [13]. Fundamental frequency contour combined with the strength of excitation is used in [14] as a countermeasure to detect spoofed speech. Features like jitter and shimmer are used in [19] to identify the spoofed signal.

In the literature survey listed above, we can see a wide variety of speech features. Every feature contributes in some way to detecting fake speech. This motivated us to combine these features for the fake speech detection task. In this work, we propose using openSMILE features [6] that extract speech features and form a vector of 88 dimensions. openSMILE is an open-source toolkit that extracts important speech features like signal energy, loudness, Mel spectra, MFCC, Perceptual Linear Prediction (PLP), PLP-Cepstral Coefficient (PLPCC), pitch, jitter, shimmer, formants, Linear Predictive Coding (LPC), line spectra from the speech signal (for more details refer to Sect. 2).

Also, the previous methods have mainly focused on developing countermeasures that are more specific to a dataset or the generation process of fake speech. In this work, we have shown the working of the openSMILE on the diversity of datasets that contains session, gender, domain, and synthesizer variability. We hypothesize that since the openSMILE features include a wide variety of speech-related features, they can give a robust performance to detect fake speech in diverse conditions.

The chronological order of the paper are as follows: Sect. 2 explains the openSMILE features, Sect. 3 gives the experimental setup, Sect. 4 shows the experimental results, Sect. 5 discusses the results, and in Sect. 6 we conclude and give the future work.

2   OpenSMILE Features for Fake Speech Detection

2.1   OpenSMILE Features

openSMILE [6] is an open source-available software for automatic extraction of features from audio signals and for classification of speech and music signals. "**SMILE**" stands for "Speech and Music Interpretation by Large-space Extraction". Speech related features extracted from openSMILE are signal energy, loudness , Mel-/Bark-/Octave-spectra, MFCC (Mel-frequency cepstral coefficients), PLPCC (perceptual linear prediction cepstral coefficient), pitch, voice quality (jitter and shimmer), formants, LPC (linear predictive coding), Line Spectral Pairs (LSP), Spectral shape descriptors. After data processing and applying statistical functions on above speech related features openSMILE generates totally 88 features which are listed in the following drive [1].

3   Experimental Setup

This work classifies the real and fake speech using openSMILE features under the diverse conditions. The variabilities present in the dataset are as follows:

3.1   Variabilities

- **Session variability:** Session variability is when the speech of a particular speaker is recorded at different instants of time. The purpose is to capture the variations in the vocal tract of a speaker at different points in time.
- **Gender variability:** Gender variability is due to the variability of male and female speakers present in the dataset. The differences in the fundamental frequency of male (85 155 Hz) and female (165 255 Hz) is the cause of gender variability.
- **Domain variability:** Domain variability is due to the variations in the recording conditions of the speech. These variations can be due to different recording environments, changes in the background noise, the use of different sensors like microphones, mobile, tablets for recording, and the bit resolution.
- **Synthesizer variability:** Due to advancements in deep learning, a lot of speech synthesis methods are proposed. Synthesizer variability is when the dataset contains the speech generated from various speech synthesizers. The purpose is to check the robustness of the proposed method in detecting the synthesized speech irrespective of its source of generation.

---

[1] https://docs.google.com/spreadsheets/d/16_7RUgXKOty4s4MkD_db0EKmvqtqoTUg/edit#gid=1002269497.

3.2   Dataset Description

The fake speech detection task is performed on the CMU-arctic [9], LibreTTS [23], and LJ Speech dataset [7]. Each dataset consisted of 50% real speech files and 50% fake speech files (corresponding to the real speech files) for both testing and training. For testing the *session variation* all three datasets can be used. In the CMU-arctic dataset every speaker has 2 sessions. Similarly, LibreTTS contains the session variations. LJ Speech contains the session variation as it is the speech recording of the same speaker recorded in different intervals of time. For performing the *gender variation*, the male and female speaker from CMU-arctic and LibreTTS speaker is taken and cross-gender training and testing is performed. For *domain variability*, the training data belongs from any of the three datasets, and testing is done on other data. All the data that contains session, gender, and domain variability are synthesized using parallel WaveGAN [22]

To check the robustness of the proposed method in the synthesizer variability the speech is synthesized with various speech-to-text synthesizers like Parallel WaveGAN, MelGAN [11], MelGAN Large [11] and, HifiGAN [10]. The dataset used for experiments are publically available in the following drive[2].

3.3   Feature Selection

Out of the 88 speech-related features of the openSMILE we select the most prominent features by following a feature selection strategy. The motivation behind the feature selection is explained by Fig. 1. In Fig. 1, accuracy is plotted

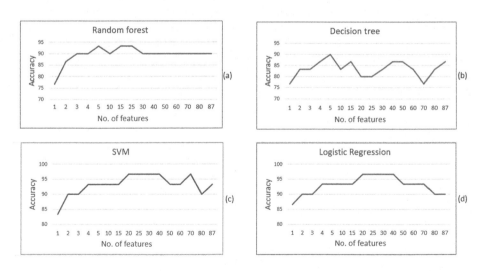

Fig. 1. The figure consists of accuracy(in percentage) vs no. of features for different machine learning models, where (a) random forest, (b) decision tree, (c) SVM, and (d) logistic regression over a single speaker from the CMU-arctic dataset.

---

[2] https://drive.google.com/drive/folders/1sd_QzcUNnbiaWq7L0ykMP7Xmk-zOuxTi?usp=sharing.

with respect to the top $'N'$ significant features where $'N'$ varies from $1, 2, ..., 88$. In this work, the selection of top $'N'$ features is done using the extra-tree classifier [3]. From the figure, it can be seen that after the top 5 features the accuracy starts to saturate in all the 4 classifier cases. Therefore all further experiments will be carried out using the top 5 features.

For the same dataset, we observed that the set of top 5 features was not common in every execution. Out of 5 features, 3–4 features would be the same while the other(s) would vary. The variation in the 4th and/or 5th feature is due to the feature selection strategy of the extra tree classifier. For this work we used this strategy and in future we will use a better feature selection method to get the consistent set of top features.

3.4   System Description

The speech signal is passed through the openSMILE toolkit to extract the features. The extracted features are of 88 dimensions that contain the commonly used speech features. Out of these 88 features, the top 5 features are selected using the features selection strategy mentioned in Sect. 3.3. Fake speech is detected using these selected features. These top 5 features are taken, and machine learning models are trained individually. Random forest (RF), decision tree (DT), support vector machine (SVM), and logistic regression (LR) models are trained.

While testing, top 5 features are extracted, and each model's probabilistic score is computed. Here the probabilistic score is the amount of resembling the feature has with real/fake speech when a particular classifier is used. It varies in the range of $0 - 1$. A score level combination is performed from every classifier's probabilistic output according to Eq. 1. In the equation, S represents the combined score, and S_{RF}, S_{DT}, S_{SVM} and S_{LR} represent the score of random forest, decision tree, SVM, and logistic regression. The combined score (S) is used for decision-making/classification based on the threshold. In the current work, the threshold is chosen to be 0.5.

$$S = (S_{RF} + S_{DT} + S_{SVM} + S_{LR})/4 \qquad (1)$$

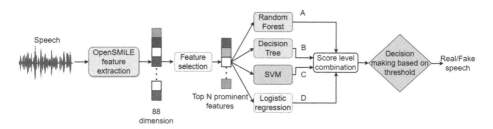

Fig. 2. Process of fake speech detection using openSMILE features. Top N dimensions are selected from the 88 dimension openSMILE features. The probabilistic score is computed using random forest, decision tree, SVM, and logistic regression. Further score level combination is done for the scores and a decision is made to perform the classification.

4   Results

The results reported for training and testing are performed for the features obtained by the feature selection from the extra-tree classifier. We have tabulated the accuracy score in the five cases: Same speaker case when both train and test set are from the session, gender, domain, and synthesizer variability (Fig. 2).

4.1   Train and Test on the Same Conditions

In this case, the train and test data belong to identical recording conditions. Since the train and test set belong to the same conditions the accuracy reported, in this case, is said to be the baseline. The closer the performance is to this accuracy better is the classification. Table 1 shows the result for 2 sessions of LJ Speech,

Table 1. The table contains the accuracy obtained in the classification of fake and original speech by using score probability combination on the four classifiers Random Forest, Decision Tree, SVM, and Logistic Regression. Each row contains the train and test data of a single speaker and is recorded in a single session. Here A, B, C, and D are weights for the random forest, decision tree, SVM, and logistic regression respectively.

Data set	Gender	Train set size	Test set size	Top 5 features				
				Weightage				Accuracy
				A	B	C	D	
LJ speech(session 49)	Female	400	44	100%	0%	0%	0%	97%
				0%	100%	0%	0%	97%
				0%	0%	100%	0%	97%
				0%	0%	0%	100%	97%
				10%	**10%**	**70%**	**10%**	**97.7%**
LJ speech(session 50)	Female	502	54	100%	0%	0%	0%	100%
				0%	100%	0%	0%	100%
				0%	0%	100%	0%	100%
				0%	0%	0%	100%	100%
				10%	**10%**	**70%**	**10%**	**100%**
CMU arctic (ksp)	Male	370	30	100%	0%	0%	0%	73.3%
				0%	100%	0%	0%	73.3%
				0%	0%	100%	0%	76%
				0%	0%	0%	100%	70%
				10%	**10%**	**70%**	**10%**	**80%**
CMU arctic (slt)	Female	370	30	100%	0%	0%	0%	97%
				0%	100%	0%	0%	96.6%
				0%	0%	100%	0%	97%
				0%	0%	0%	100%	98.8%
				10%	**10%**	**70%**	**10%**	**100%**
LibreTTS - 84	Female	374	42	100%	0%	0%	0%	90.4%
				0%	100%	0%	0%	83.3%
				0%	0%	100%	0%	87.6%
				0%	0%	0%	100%	89.1%
				10%	**30%**	**10%**	**50%**	**95.2%**
LibreTTS - 251	Male	384	42	100%	0%	0%	0%	80%
				0%	100%	0%	0%	80.4%
				0%	0%	100%	0%	87%
				0%	0%	0%	100%	86.6%
				80%	**0%**	**10%**	**10%**	**88.1%**

and 2 speakers of CMU-arctic (ksp and slt) and LibreTTS (84 and 251). For every case 5 accuracy score is reported. One for every model and the other for the score level combination according to Eq. 1. It can be seen from the table, that in most of the cases the accuracy is greater than 95%. Also, the score level combination from all the models gives the highest accuracy (highlighted) in all the cases. These scores will be taken as a baseline comparison for further studies.

4.2   Session Variability

The Table 2 shows the session variability study on LJ speech, CMU-arctic and LibreTTS dataset. In LJ speech the 49th is used for training and the 50th session is used for testing and vice versa. Every speaker of the CMU-arctic dataset has

Table 2. Session Variability: This table contains the accuracy obtained in the classification of fake and original speech by using score probability combination on the four classifiers Random Forest, Decision Tree, SVM, and Logistic Regression. Each row contains the train and test data of a single speaker and recorded in different sessions. Here A, B, C, and D are weights of Random Forest, Decision Tree, SVM, and Logistic Regression respectively.

Training data			Testing data			Weightage				Accuracy
Data set	Gender	Count	Data set	Gender	Count	A	B	C	D	
L.J speech 49	Female	400	L.J speech 50	Female	54	100%	0%	0%	0%	100%
						0%	100%	0%	0%	100%
						0%	0%	100%	0%	100%
						0%	0%	0%	100%	100%
						10%	**10%**	**40%**	**40%**	**100%**
L.J speech 50	Female	502	L.J speech 49	Female	44	100%	0%	0%	0%	95.4%
						0%	100%	0%	0%	95.4%
						0%	0%	100%	0%	97.7%
						0%	0%	0%	100%	97.7%
						10%	**0%**	**70%**	**20%**	**97.7%**
CMU-arctic (session a)	Female	370	CMU-arctic (session b)	Female	30	100%	0%	0%	0%	86.6%
						0%	100%	0%	0%	86.6%
						0%	0%	100%	0%	80%
						0%	0%	0%	100%	80%
						40%	**30%**	**0%**	**30%**	**90%**
CMU-arctic (session b)	Female	370	CMU-arctic (session a)	Female	30	100%	0%	0%	0%	90%
						0%	100%	0%	0%	90%
						0%	0%	100%	0%	93.33%
						0%	0%	0%	100%	93.33%
						0%	**40%**	**50%**	**10%**	**93.33%**
LibreTTS-84 {121123}	Female	121	LibreTTS-84 {12 1550}	Female	30	100%	0%	0%	0%	87.33%
						0%	100%	0%	0%	86.66%
						0%	0%	100%	0%	93.33%
						0%	0%	0%	100%	93.33%
						0%	**0%**	**50%**	**50%**	**93.33%**
LibreTTS-84 {12150}	Female	244	LibreTTS-84 {121123}	Female	20	100%	0%	0%	0%	79.33%
						0%	100%	0%	0%	61.33%
						0%	0%	100%	0%	73.33%
						0%	0%	0%	100%	72.66%
						60%	**0%**	**0%**	**40%**	**80%**

two sessions (a and b). Here we train the system with one session and test it with another session. Similarly, we perform for the LibreTTS dataset. From the accuracy score, we can see that in session variability conditions the openSMILE features are able to classify fake and real speech.

4.3   Gender Variability

In this case, we check the robustness of the proposed method when train and test data belong to different genders. The variability is mainly because of the difference in the fundamental frequency of the male and female speakers. Gender variations are present in the CMU-arctic and LibreTTS dataset and the accuracy is reported in Table 3. From the table, we can see that for most of the cases the accuracy is close to the baseline performance. Therefore we can say that the proposed approach is able to detect fake speech in the gender variation conditions.

Table 3. Gender Variability: This table contains the accuracy obtained in the classification of fake and original speech by using score probability combination on the four classifiers Random Forest, Decision Tree, SVM, and Logistic Regression. Each row contains the train and test data of a different speaker mainly male and female genders. Here A, B, C, and D are weights of Random Forest, Decision Tree, SVM, and Logistic Regression respectively.

Training data			Testing data			Weightage				Accuracy
Data set	Gender	Count	Data set	Gender	Count	A	B	C	D	
CMU-arctic (ksp)	Male	370	CMU-arctic (slt)	Female	30	100%	0%	0%	0%	70%
						0%	100%	0%	0%	66.66%
						0%	0%	100%	0%	80%
						0%	0%	0%	100%	80%
						0%	40%	50%	10%	**83.3%**
CMU-arctic (slt)	Female	370	CMU-arctic (ksp)	Male	30	100%	0%	0%	0%	73.33%
						0%	100%	0%	0%	63.33%
						0%	0%	100%	0%	66.66%
						0%	0%	0%	100%	66.66%
						0%	0%	50%	50%	**73.33%**
Libre-TTS (84)	Female	374	Libre-TTS (251)	Male	42	100%	0%	0%	0%	77.11%
						0%	100%	0%	0%	71.11%
						0%	0%	100%	0%	75.55%
						0%	0%	0%	100%	78.44%
						70%	**0%**	**0%**	**30%**	**78.57%**
Libre-TTS (251)	Male	374	Libre-TTS (84)	Female	42	100%	0%	0%	0%	83.33%
						0%	100%	0%	0%	83.33%
						0%	0%	100%	0%	81.33%
						0%	0%	0%	100%	83.33%
						0%	50%	0%	50%	**83.33%**

4.4 Domain Variability

Domain variability is when the train and test data belong to different recording conditions. The difference can be either in environmental conditions, sampling frequency, and recording devices. LJ speech, CMU-arctic, and LibreTTS contain all these recording condition variations. From Table 4, we can see that training has been done in one of the datasets, and testing is done in another dataset. The results show that the proposed openSMILE-based method is unable to classify real and fake speech when there is domain variability is present in the dataset.

Table 4. Domain Variability: This table contains the accuracy obtained in the classification of fake and original speech by using score probability combination on the four classifiers Random Forest, Decision Tree, SVM, and Logistic Regression. Each row contains the train and test data of different speakers recorded in different domains. Here A, B, C, and D are weights of Random Forest, Decision Tree, SVM, and Logistic Regression respectively.

Training data		Testing data		Weightage				Accuracy
Data set	Count	Data set	Count	A	B	C	D	
LJ speech	902	CMU-arctic data	30	100%	0%	0%	0%	50%
				0%	100%	0%	0%	50%
				0%	0%	100%	0%	50%
				0%	0%	0%	100%	50%
				10%	20%	30%	40%	50%
CMU-arctic data	370	LJ speech	98	100%	0%	0%	0%	50%
				0%	100%	0%	0%	50%
				0%	0%	100%	0%	50%
				0%	0%	0%	100%	50%
				40%	30%	0%	30%	50%
CMU arctic data	370	LibreTTS	42	100%	0%	0%	0%	50%
				0%	100%	0%	0%	50%
				0%	0%	100%	0%	50%
				0%	0%	0%	100%	50%
				0%	0%	50%	50%	50%
LibreTTS	187	CMU-arctic data	30	100%	0%	0%	0%	50%
				0%	100%	0%	0%	50%
				0%	0%	100%	0%	50%
				0%	0%	0%	100%	50%
				60%	0%	0%	40%	50%
LibreTTS	187	LJ speech	30	100%	0%	0%	0%	50%
				0%	100%	0%	0%	50%
				0%	0%	100%	0%	50%
				0%	0%	0%	100%	50%
				10%	30%	20%	40%	50%
LJ speech	902	LibreTTS	30	100%	0%	0%	0%	50%
				0%	100%	0%	0%	50%
				0%	0%	100%	0%	50%
				0%	0%	0%	100%	50%
				10%	20%	30%	40%	50%

4.5   Synthesizer Variability

In this experiment, we check the robustness of the proposed approach to detect fake speech irrespective of its source of generation. Speech synthesized from text-to-speech (TTS) synthesizers like Parallel-waveGAN, MelGAN, HifiGAN, and MelGAN Large are used for the experiment. From Table 5 we can see that other than Parallel WaveGAN, for all the other synthesizers the proposed method is able to give around 80% accuracy when trained and tested in cross synthesizer conditions. Cross synthesizer condition is when training is done in with the data from one model and testing from the other model.

Table 5. Synthesizer Variability: This table contains the accuracy obtained in the classification of fake and original speech by using score probability combinations on the four classifiers Random Forest, Decision Tree, SVM, and Logistic Regression. The training and testing dataset of a row consists of a fake speech generated using different methods.

Train	Test			
	Parallel WaveGAN	MelGAN	HifiGAN	MelGAN Large
Parallel WaveGAN	97.72%	50%	50%	50%
MelGAN	70.4%	77.2%	72.7%	72.72%
HifiGAN	88.6%	81.8%	90.9%	84.09%
MelGAN Large	79.5%	70.4%	72.72%	79.5%

5   Discussion

Based on results obtained we can infer that when the model is tested in the domain variability case, it gives low accuracy while classifying due to change in a larger number of factors as compared to the other cases.

In case of gender variability even after the difference in the frequencies of the training and testing data the proposed method gave good accuracy while classifying fake and real speech which matched to the claimed hypothesis. For session variability and speaker variability the proposed method is able to classify fake and real audio close to the baseline (same train and test conditions) because of lesser number of variable factors.

6   Conclusion and Future Work

In this work, we proposed an openSMILE-based fake speech detection approach. We saw from the literature survey that each and every speech feature has its own contribution to detecting fake speech. Motivated by that, we proposed the use of openSMILE feature which contains the most commonly used speech feature. We checked the robustness of the proposed method under various variabilities like session, gender, domain, and synthesizer variability. The results from various experiments showed that the proposed approach is able the detect fake speech in session, gender, and synthesizer variability with good accuracy but fails to perform in domain variability conditions.

This work has opened several avenues for future work. The feature selection strategy used here is an extra tree classifier. We can use some better feature selection methods to improve the performance. The degradation in the domain variability case needs to be addressed. Machine learning models have been able to show good classification accuracy in most cases but to get improved and generalized performance we will use the deep learning algorithms with the openSMILE features.

Acknowledgments. This work is funded by Ministry of Electronics and Information Technology (MeitY), Govt. of India under the project title "Fake Speech detection using Deep Learning Framework".

References

1. Agarwal, A., Swain, A., Mishra, J., Prasanna, S.M.: Significance of prosody modification in privacy preservation on speaker verification. In: 2022 National Conference on Communications (NCC), pp. 245–249. IEEE (2022)
2. Agarwal, A., Swain, A., Prasanna, S.M.: Speaker anonymization for machines using sinusoidal model. In: 2022 IEEE International Conference on Signal Processing and Communications (SPCOM), pp. 1–5. IEEE (2022)
3. Baby, D., Devaraj, S.J., Hemanth, J., et al.: Leukocyte classification based on feature selection using extra trees classifier: atransfer learning approach. Turkish J. Electr. Eng. Comput. Sci. **29**(8), 2742–2757 (2021)
4. Bhangale, K.B., Titare, P., Pawar, R., Bhavsar, S.: Synthetic speech spoofing detection using MFCC and radial basis function SVM. IOSR J. Eng. (IOSRJEN) **8**(6), 55–62 (2018)
5. Cooper, E., et al.: Zero-shot multi-speaker text-to-speech with state-of-the-art neural speaker embeddings. In: ICASSP 2020–2020 IEEE International Conference on Acoustics, Speech and Signal Processing (ICASSP), pp. 6184–6188. IEEE (2020)
6. Eyben, F., et al.: The Geneva minimalistic acoustic parameter set (GeMAPS) for voice research and affective computing. IEEE Trans. Affect. Comput. **7**(2), 190–202 (2016). https://doi.org/10.1109/TAFFC.2015.2457417
7. Ito, K., Johnson, L.: The lj speech dataset. https://keithito.com/LJ-Speech-Dataset/ (2017)
8. Kinnunen, T., et al.: The ASVspoof 2017 challenge: assessing the limits of replay spoofing attack detection (2017)
9. Kominek, J., Black, A.W., Ver, V.: CMU arctic databases for speech synthesis. Technical Report (2003)
10. Kong, J., Kim, J., Bae, J.: HiFi-GAN: generative adversarial networks for efficient and high fidelity speech synthesis. Adv. Neural Inf. Process. Syst. **33**, 17022–17033 (2020)
11. Kumar, K., et al.: Melgan: Generative adversarial networks for conditional waveform synthesis. In: Advances in Neural Information Processing Systems, vol. 32 (2019)

12. Mishra, J., Singh, M., Pati, D.: Processing linear prediction residual signal to counter replay attacks. In: 2018 International Conference on Signal Processing and Communications (SPCOM), pp. 95–99. IEEE (2018)
13. Pal, M., Paul, D., Saha, G.: Synthetic speech detection using fundamental frequency variation and spectral features. Comput. Speech Lang. **48**, 31–50 (2018)
14. Patel, T.B., Patil, H.A.: Effectiveness of fundamental frequency (f 0) and strength of excitation (SOE) for spoofed speech detection. In: 2016 IEEE International Conference on Acoustics, Speech and Signal Processing (ICASSP), pp. 5105–5109. IEEE (2016)
15. Qian, K., Zhang, Y., Chang, S., Yang, X., Hasegawa-Johnson, M.: AutoVC: zero-shot voice style transfer with only autoencoder loss. In: International Conference on Machine Learning, pp. 5210–5219. PMLR (2019)
16. Singh, A.K., Singh, P.: Detection of AI-synthesized speech using cepstral & bispectral statistics. In: 2021 IEEE 4th International Conference on Multimedia Information Processing and Retrieval (MIPR), pp. 412–417. IEEE (2021)
17. Todisco, M., Delgado, H., Evans, N.: Constant q cepstral coefficients: a spoofing countermeasure for automatic speaker verification. Comput. Speech Lang. **45**, 516–535 (2017)
18. Todisco, M., et al.: ASVspoof 2019: future horizons in spoofed and fake audio detection. arXiv preprint arXiv:1904.05441 (2019)
19. Woubie, A., Bäckström, T.: Voice-quality features for replay attack detection (2022)
20. Wu, Z., et al.: ASVspoof 2015: the first automatic speaker verification spoofing and countermeasures challenge. In: Sixteenth Annual Conference of the International Speech Communication Association (2015)
21. Wu, Z., Xiao, X., Chng, E.S., Li, H.: Synthetic speech detection using temporal modulation feature. In: 2013 IEEE International Conference on Acoustics, Speech and Signal Processing, pp. 7234–7238. IEEE (2013)
22. Yamamoto, R., Song, E., Kim, J.M.: Parallel WaveGAN: a fast waveform generation model based on generative adversarial networks with multi-resolution spectrogram. In: ICASSP 2020–2020 IEEE International Conference on Acoustics, Speech and Signal Processing (ICASSP), pp. 6199–6203. IEEE (2020)
23. Zen, H., et al.: Libritts: a corpus derived from librispeech for text-to-speech. In: Interspeech (2019). https://arxiv.org/abs/1904.02882

Nonverbal Constituents of Argumentative Discourse: Gesture and Prosody Interaction

Anna Leonteva and Tatiana Sokoreva(✉)

Moscow State Linguistic University, 38 Ostozhenka Street, Moscow 119034, Russian Federation
jey-t@yandex.ru

Abstract. The present paper explores the correlation between prosodic characteristics (pitch accents) and manual gestures in argumentative court speech. The analysis of tone configuration regarding its accompanying gestures and their types in defense and prosecution opening statements revealed specific nonverbal characteristics of speech aimed at convincing the jury and contributing to the general impression of definite, categorical, confident and highly convincing utterance. The research results proved the prevailing use of falling intonation contours in both defense and prosecution with non-final level tones being typical of the former as well as the dominant usage of recurrent gestures combined with falling configurations across all the speakers.

Keywords: Argumentative discourse · Opening statement · Prosecution · Defense · Prosody · Intonation · Tone · Gesture

1 Introduction

Argumentation is a necessary part of our everyday life and it has been studied since the Ancient Greece. A court hearing is regarded as an exemplary case of argumentation, as it is competitive and persuasive by its nature [1]. If we represent a court schematically, we will see how x, an active participant of the trial (lawyers, the defendant, witness, plaintiff) is trying to convince y, a passive participant of the trial (judge(s) or jurors) that z (the speaker's point of view). In order to convince the listeners and to persuade them to choose their side, the speakers use argumentation on verbal and nonverbal levels. The current article studies the nonverbal means, hand gestures and prosody, used by lawyers in criminal trials during the very first step, opening statements.

Court discourse is an institutional, ritualized type of discourse. These two features are reflected in the order of the trial. A court hearing in the US consists consequently of three stages: opening statements, cross-examination and closing arguments. The first stage is regarded as a roadmap for the whole trial. The opening statement is used to influence the jury and their position from the very beginning. During the statement the speaker, prosecution or defense, narrates a story of what happened from their point of view and instructs the jury. The opening statement should characterize past events without any explicit evaluation. Thus, the opening statement can be regarded as a case of narrated argumentation, because the story is used to win the jury over.

© Springer Nature Switzerland AG 2022
S. R. M. Prasanna et al. (Eds.): SPECOM 2022, LNAI 13721, pp. 416–425, 2022.
https://doi.org/10.1007/978-3-031-20980-2_36

One of the major functions of the opening statement is to help jurors and to guide them through the process by explaining the basic facts and evidence, as they are ordinary people without any legal experience [2]. All the legal terms are explained and commented on by the judge, whose main role is to maintain the order and logic of the process.

As it has been already mentioned, the argumentation in courts is presented on all language level, thus, it is multimodal. The hand gestures, used in courts, can be of several types. We distinguish the following types: representational, recurrent and pointing.

The first type, representational or iconic gestures, are used to describe an object, action or event. They are based on the idea of similarity between the gesture and its referent [3, 4]. There are different approaches to classifying this type of gestures (see [5–7]). In this article we distinguish the following 6 types: holding, molding, embodying, touching, tracing and acting.

Holding gestures are static, can be performed with one or two hands and usually have the idea of the metaphoric "container". These gestures can be used when describing both abstract or concrete notions. Molding gestures are non-static and performed with the help of the hand movement reminding of the process of working with clay. Embodying in gestures is aimed at representing the referent through the process of nonverbal substitution. As a result, the hand becomes the object in question. Touching gestures are used to represent some objects by locating them in space. The gesture is performed with the help of the tips of fingers and can be done with one or more fingers. Tracing gestures are also created with the tips of fingers or the palm of the hand by outlining some objects in space.

The second type, recurrent gestures, have various forms, but their semantic, structural and functional features are similar in different contexts [8–11]. These gestures have pragmatic and discourse functions. Pragmatic gestures are used to express the opinion about some object, notion or event. They can also be used to qualify them by sharing some information. Discourse gestures can be distinguished into 3 types according to their functions: emphatic, structuring and referential.

Emphatic gestures are used to highlight some parts of the speech and they have no additional functions, e. g. representational or pragmatic. These gestures can be rhythmical and go together with the stress in speech (also known as batons or beats, see [12]).

Discourse structuring gestures are used to help the audience to follow the speaker and to perceive a great amount of information presented to them. These gestures are based on the division of space around the speaker with the palms and hands. The idea of the structuring is based on the opposition of the location of hands in space, their shift, e. g. from left to right or from up to down.

Discourse presenting gestures are different from representational gestures mentioned above as they are used to prove some statements with the help of metaphorical representation of discourse as some object [12]. These gestures usually take the form of palm(s) up open hand, palm(s) down and palms opposite each other.

Pointing gestures have deictic properties and are used to locate objects, abstract or concrete, and events in space. They have a form of the index or big finger extended. Sometimes the index and the small fingers are used together to point at something. These gestures are indexical and unite some object in space, the referent, and the speaker [13,

14]. The referent can be located in or out of sight of the speaker and the listeners. It helps to create a visibility of the object/event and focus the attention of the audience.

Undoubtedly possessing communicative value, gestures are inseparably connected with linguistic means of communication. The problem of interaction of gestures and prosody represents one of the most intensively developed issues in this area.

Prosodic and nonverbal characteristics of the utterance demonstrate parallelism and consistency not only in terms of time alignment, but also in terms of the modal meanings associated with them, which makes it possible to recognize coexistence of prosodic and nonverbal means of communication. Such coherence is part of a complex cognitive-communicative mechanism for the linguistic and paralinguistic means formation that serves to enhance the impact of speech [15].

The presence of nonverbal labeling acts as a communicatively useful sign, reinforcing the modal meaning and ensuring its better perception by the listener/viewer. Thus, in the audiovisual speech study the assessment of the modal and lexical content of the utterance should go together with nonverbal and prosodic characteristics analysis.

The aim of the present research is to establish the correlation between prosody (pitch accent in particular) and manual gestures in argumentative court discourse specifying gesture characteristics and prosodic modifications in the speech of American trial lawyers in order to identify the distinctions in prosodic and non-verbal organization of discourse between two groups of participants – prosecution and defense representatives.

2 Research Material

The study is based on the authentic video material taken from the Internet resource YouTube. The research material incudes four opening statements in the US court (2 criminal cases), given by both prosecution and defense. The total amount of the corpus is over one hour of speech. The general length of each video is approximately 20–25 min. The speakers are professional lawyers, men (M) and women (F) of more than 35 years.

The two criminal cases under study are: the Caronna case (prosecution (P1)[1], defense (D1)[2]), in which Joseph Caronna was accused of killing his wife and the Creato case (prosecution (P2)[3], defense (D2)[4]) in which David Creato was accused of killing his son.

3 Methodology

The first stage of analysis included video material annotation for gestures and specifying their types by means of ELAN program [16]. Gesture types comprise representational, recurrent and pointing groups described above. The gesture annotation was performed by two researchers. To measure the degree of the agreement between the coders, Cohen's

---

[1] https://www.youtube.com/watch?v=YNIGhIoF8g0.

[2] https://www.youtube.com/watch?v=JGR2fnlbHqI.

[3] https://www.youtube.com/watch?v=dINEq4oMdEY&t=7s.

[4] https://www.youtube.com/watch?v=vMve4nje8hw&t=345s.

Cappa statistical coefficient [17] was used. The agreement coefficient showed a high degree of agreement, i.e. 93.27%.

The prosodic analysis implied the video material transformation into audio files in order to rely strictly on the acoustic signal. Conducted with the help of PRAAT computer program [18], the prosodic analysis includes the identification of IPs, their boundaries and the place and configuration of pitch accents. While specifying the pitch accents in speech samples the British system of intonation annotation was used which is based on the assumption that the melodic form of an utterance is a unity of functionally independent configurations the main one being the nuclear tone (or terminal tone) that is used to mark the word which is of most importance for the meaning [19]. The system was worked out by such famous phoneticians as H. Sweet, D. Jones, H. E. Palmer, L. Armstrong, I. C. Ward, J. D. O'Connor and others.

The analysis comprised the identification of the following nuclear tones in speech samples: the falling tone (Fall), including falling and rising-falling tones and their configurations; the level tone (Level); the rising tone (Rise), including rising and falling-rising tones and their configurations. The total number of tones under analysis is 1900 items.

The prosodic annotation for pitch accents was performed by two annotators (agreement 92.38%) in PRAAT computer program: identifying F0 curve values (Hz) and configurations enabled the authors to differentiate between falling, level, rising and other types of into-nation contours. The next stage of analysis included inserting PRAAT Textgrid files into ELAN program to establish the pitch accent-gesture correspondence. The words containing pitch accents were attributed to hand gestures (comprising their start, hold and end) in case they run parallel or their durations intersect by at least 50%.

The received data were subject to statistical analysis in PAWS Statistics where the results were cross tabulated and tested by Chi-Square and Cramer's V criteria. The choice of the criteria was determined by the variable type and the lack of variance equality. Chi-Square was employed to analyse the conjugacy tables presented as the frequency of nominal data in order to study the joint influence of a factor on the outcome. Being the most resistant to the table size, the Cramer's criterion (V) was used to measure the association between the two nominal variables.

4   Results

4.1   Tones

Table 1 provides the descriptive statistics over the analyzed speech samples that last over one hour of time and contain 1900 tones.

The results of the quantitative analysis showed that the defense used more nuclear tones than the prosecution (506 vs 354) in the first trial but the second trial is characterized by the opposite values (477 vs 563 tones in defense and prosecution speech respectively). The falling tones are the most frequent, as they constitute 50% and above of the total number of tones in speeches of both prosecution and defense and even reach 68% in P2. The defense tends to use more level tones than prosecution (34% and 29% in D1 and D2 vs 16% and 23% in P1 and P2). The rising tones are distributed differently in two trials: the larger percentage has P1 and D2 (25% and 20% respectively) compared to the values of D1 (8%) and P2 (7%). The amount of fall-rises and rise-falls is insufficient to form

Table 1. The descriptive statistics of tone distribution over four speech samples.

	D1(M)	P1(F)	D2(M)	P2(F)
Total number of tones	506	354	477	563
– Fall	276 (55%)	180 (51%)	237 (50%)	384 (68%)
– Level	173 (34%)	57 (16%)	139 (29%)	126 (23%)
– Rise	41 (8%)	88 (25%)	95 (20%)	39 (7%)
– Fall-Rise	16 (3%)	25 (7%)	4 (1%)	13 (2%)
– Rise-Fall	0	4 (1%)	2 (0,4%)	1 (0,2%)
Number of tones accompanied by gestures	282 out of 506 (**56%**)	262 out of 354 (**74%**)	319 out of 477 (**67%**)	148 out of 563 (**26%**)
Number of gestures with tones	189 out of 237 (**80%**)	147 out of 162 (**91%**)	181 out of 214 (**85%**)	121 out of 181 (**67%**)
Number of gestures without tones	48 (**20%**)	15 (**9%**)	33 (**15%**)	60 (**33%**)
One tone for two gestures	14 (**5%**)	5 (**2%**)	0	1 (**0,7%**)
One gesture for several tones (from 2 to 9 tones)	68 (**36%**)	67 (**46%**)	83 (**46%**)	20 (**17%**)

separate groups, therefore, in further analysis they were added to the rising and falling tones accordingly as fall-rise and rise and rise-fall and fall belong to the non-final and final categories of tones respectively.

The number of tones accompanied by gestures counts 56% in D1, 74% in P1, 67% in D2 and 26% in P2. Thus, in all cases, except P2, over a half of all tones in speech are accompanied by gestures which reinforce the linguistic message of the speakers and provide an intended impact on the listener.

The proportion of gestures that go together with tones is rather high in all speakers (80%, 91%, 85% and 67% in D1, M1, D2 and P2 respectively) and demonstrates the tendency of using gestures and tones together.

The gestures that were not accompanied by nuclear tones in speech comprise from 9% to 33% of all gestures and were not included in further analysis.

The tokens when one tone was employed with two gestures are not numerous, by contrast the cases when one gesture was extended for several tones (up to nine tones in a row) comprise the greater part and reach 46% in P1. The category of multiple tones accompanied by a single gesture is marked 'multi' in graphs and figures. Both categories of tone-gesture relationship were included in further analysis.

4.2 Tones with Gestures

The distribution of tone configuration occurring along with gestures in four opening statements is provided in Fig. 1. The rise-falls and fall-rises are added to the falling and rising groups of tones respectively, the 'Multi' set consists of cases with multiple tones accompanied by a single gesture.

The values show the prevalence of falling and multiple groups of tones in all the speech samples, the level and rising tones being fewer in quantity. The distribution of different types of tones in groups comprising multiple tones revealed the predominance of falling configurations in prosecution speech compared to defense statements (57% and 47% respectively), the level tones prevail in defense (33%) compared to prosecution (16%) and the percentage of rises is higher in prosecution samples (27% to 20% in defense).

All the tone configurations employed by defense and prosecution representatives irrespective of the quantity of gestures accompanying them is displayed in Fig. 2.

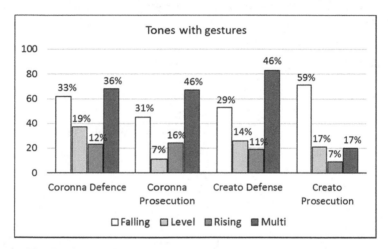

Fig. 1. The distribution of tones accompanied by gestures across four speech samples.

The statistical analysis of tone configurations regarding the type of opening statement (defense and prosecution) revealed the significant difference in tone usage (p < .05). Thus, the results confirm the larger amount of falls in prosecution speech (60%) compared to defense speech (49%), the fewer level tones in prosecution (16%) compared to defense (33%) and 27% and 20% of rises in prosecution and defense statements respectively.

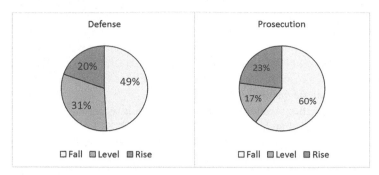

Fig. 2. Distribution of tone configuration in defense and prosecution opening statements where groups of multiple tones are represented by their constituents.

4.3 Tones and Gesture Types

Table 2 contains cross tabulated results of tone configuration with corresponding gestures of three types.

Table 2. The number and percentage of tone configurations in three gesture types.

Tone * Gesture type crosstabulation

			Gesture type			Total
			Pointing	Representational	Recurrent	
Tone	Fall	Count	36	62	125	223
		% within tone	16,1%	27,8%	56,1%	100,0%
		% within gesture type	32,4%	32,1%	38,9%	35,7%
		% of total	5,8%	9,9%	20,0%	35,7%
	Level	Count	24	31	40	95
		% within tone	25,3%	32,6%	42,1%	100,0%
		% within gesture type	21,6%	16,1%	12,5%	15,2%
		% of total	3,8%	5,0%	6,4%	15,2%
	Rise	Count	11	18	43	72
		% within tone	15,3%	25,0%	59,7%	100,0%
		% within gesture type	9,9%	9,3%	13,4%	11,5%
		% of total	1,8%	2,9%	6,9%	11,5%
	Multi	Count	40	82	113	235
		% within tone	17,0%	34,9%	48,1%	100,0%
		% within gesture type	36,0%	42,5%	35,2%	37,6%
		% of total	6,4%	13,1%	18,1%	37,6%

(*continued*)

Table 2. (*continued*)

Tone * Gesture type crosstabulation

		Gesture type			Total
		Pointing	Representational	Recurrent	
Total	Count	111	193	321	625
	% within tone	17,8%	30,9%	51,4%	100,0%
	% within gesture type	100,0%	100,0%	100,0%	100,0%
	% of total	17,8%	30,9%	51,4%	100,0%

The most frequent gestures are recurrent gestures (321 cases, 51,4%). The next mostly used type is representational (193 cases, 30,9%) and the least used is pointing gestures (111 cases, 17,8%). Recurrent gestures were mainly accompanied by falling (38,9%) and multiple (35,2%) tones, representational by multiple (42,5%) and falling tones (32,1%) and pointing by multiple (36%) and falling (32,4%) tones as well. The least frequently employed tones are level (12,5%) in recurrent gestures and rising in representational (9,3%) and pointing (9,9%) ones.

5 Discussion

The research results revealed the predominance of falling intonation contours in both defense and prosecution samples which might indicate that most utterances of both parties at trial are supposed to be categorical, accurate, convincing and unequivocal which is generally achieved by the usage of final (falling) intonation configurations [20]. We believe that each discourse type is characterized by a combination of features including intonation specificities which are not always identical (e. g. 'uptalk' or level speech of youngsters) and depends on the audience, setting, social characteristics of speakers and other factors. The judicial type of discourse, as well as the narrative-argumentative speech, we assume, influence the choice of intonation patterns and can be characterized by certain pitch contours that comprise predominant falling configurations.

The speech of prosecution proved to show a tendency of appealing to the public as the prosecutors use more rising tones in their statements than the defense representatives. The latter employ twice as many level tones as the former which may weaken their performance as this tone is non-final and non-categoric in character, is frequently used to express hesitation and uncertainty or to search for words [21].

In terms of gesture type, the research analysis proved that the most frequent combination in trial discourse is recurrent gestures accompanied by falling intonation contour. Recurrent gestures, used to express opinion, to share information, to highlight certain parts of the speech, to help the audience to follow the speaker, bear no implication and indefiniteness that is why they are mostly combined with falling intonation in the lawyers' speech that is supposed to be categoric, definite, obvious and highly convincing.

Representational gestures, used to describe an object, action or event, are more often accompanied by a combination of tones with falling tone prevailing. The same tendency of using multiple tones within a single gesture is traced in pointing gestures. Thus, the trial speech manner imposes certain restrictions on lawyers as they need to sound definite and persuasive in order to win the case. Hence, the opening statements contain far fewer level and rising tones as they express indefiniteness, incompleteness and non-finality [20].

6   Conclusion

Court hearing as an example of argumentative discourse is characterized by specific multimodal communication. In order to convince the audience and the jury and to persuade them to choose their side, the speakers in court use argumentation on verbal and nonverbal levels. The present research attempted to dwell on the issue of interaction of hand gestures and prosodic organization in the form of pitch accent configuration in lawyers' speech at criminal trials during the very first stage, i. e. the opening statements. The results of the analysis conducted on trial speech samples revealed a strong connection and a certain relationship of intonation configurations and gesture characteristics in court discourse. Both prosody and gestures reinforce the linguistic component of communication contributing to achieving the set aim of winning the trial by engaging the nonverbal constituents in the process of court interaction.

Further research on other prosodic components such as duration, intensity, voice quality as well as the correlation with other gestural features is needed to confirm the received results and expand the scope of characteristics of polymodal communication in argumentative discourse.

References

1. Cicero: Dialogues: About government; about laws. AST, Moscow (1994). (in Russian)
2. Heffer, C.: The Language of Jury Trial. A Corpus-Aided Analysis of Legal-Lay Discourse. Palgrave Macmillan (2005)
3. Ekman, P., et al.: The repertoire of nonverbal behavior: categories, origins, usage, and coding. Semiotica 1(1), 49–98 (1969)
4. Streeck, J.: Depicting by gesture. Gesture 8(3), 285–301 (2008)
5. Kendon, A.: Gesture: Visible Action as Utterance. Cambridge University Press, Cambridge (2004)
6. Sowa, T.: Understanding coverbal iconic gestures in shape descriptions. Dissertation, University of Bielefeld (2006)
7. Müller, C.: Gestural modes of representation as techniques of depiction. In: Müller, C., Cienki, A., Fricke, E., Ladewig, S.H., McNeill, D., Teßendorf, S. (eds.) Body – Language – Communication: An International Handbook on Multimodality in Human Interaction, vol. 2, pp. 1687–1702. Mouton de Gruyter, Berlin/Boston (2014)
8. Ladewig, S.H.: Beschreiben, suchen und auffordern - Varianten einer rekurrenten Geste. Sprache und Literatur 41(1), 89–111 (2010)
9. Ladewig, S.: Putting the cyclic gesture on a cognitive basis. CogniTextes, vol. 6 (2011). https://doi.org/10.4000/cognitextes.406
10. Muller, C.: Forms and uses of the palm open hand: a case of a gesture family. In: The Semantics and Pragmatics of Everyday Gestures. Weidler Buchverlag, Berlin (2004)

11. Müller, C.: Wie Gesten bedeuten. Eine kognitiv-linguistische und sequenzanalytische Perspektive. Sprache und Literatur **41**(1), 37–68 (2010)

12. McNeill, D.: Hand and Mind: What Gestures Reveal About Thought. The University of Chicago Press, Chicago (1992)

13. Clark, H.: Pointing and placing. Pointing: Where Language, Culture and Cognition Meet. Lawrence Erlbaum Associates Publishers, Mahwah, New Jersey, London (2003)

14. Cienki, A.: Ten lectures on Spoken language and Gesture from Perspective of Cognitive Linguistics. Issues of Dynamicity and Multimodality, pp. 24–44. Brill, Leiden, Boston (2017)

15. Nizhivinskaya, O.V.: Prosodic and nonverbal means of transmitting the utterance modal content (experimental study based on the material of the English-language media discourse). Ph.D. Minsk (2022). (in Russian)

16. ELAN (Version 5.8) [Computer software]. Max Planck Institute for Psycholinguistics, The Language Archive, Nijmegen (2019). https://archive.mpi.nl/tla/elan

17. Landis, J.R., Koch, G.G.: The measurement of observer agreement for categorical data. Biometrics **33**(1), 159–174 (1977)

18. Boersma, P., Weenink, D.: Praat: doing phonetics by computer [Computer program]. Version 5.3.80 (2015). http://www.praat.org/. Accessed 05 Apr 2015

19. Buraya, E.A., Galochkina, I.E., Shevchenko, T.I.: Phonetics of Contemporary English. Academia, Moscow (2014). (in Russian)

20. O'Connor, J.D., Arnold, G.F.: Intonation of colloquial English. Longman Group Ltd., Bristol (1973)

21. Vassyliev, V.A.: English Phonetics. A Practical Course. HSPH, Moscow (2009)

Classifying Mahout and Social Interactions of Asian Elephants Based on Trumpet Calls

Seema Lokhandwala$^{(\boxtimes)}$, Priyankoo Sarmah , and Rohit Sinha

Centre for Linguistic Science and Technology, Indian Institute of Technology
Guwahati, Guwahati 781039, India
{seema176155001,priyankoo,rsinha}@iitg.ac.in

Abstract. This paper explores the possibility of classifying elephant vocalizations as per their associated contexts. While elephants produce a variety of calls, trumpet calls only were explored to distinguish between two contexts: interaction with other elephants and interaction with their human caretakers (mahouts). For this study, we collected task-specific elephant vocalization data through fieldwork. A support vector machine based classifier is developed on openSMILE features for the said classification. The classification accuracy in categorizing elephant directed and human directed trumpet calls was found to be 81.43%. A detailed analysis of the employed acoustic features revealed that loudness, the spectral slope of 500–1500 Hz band, and spectral flux were found to be maximally contributing to the said categorization.

Keywords: Bioacoustics · Elephant acoustics · Trumpet calls · Mahout interactions · Social interactions · Sound classification

1 Introduction

Animal behaviour is the scientific study of how animals interact with their environment, other living creatures, and each other. Ability to classify elephant vocalizations based on behavioural context is a crucial part of understanding the elephant communication system which can help in making better-informed decisions for improvement in animal welfare. Asian elephants *(Elephas maximus)* are highly social but spatially dispersed species [3,23]. Therefore, acoustic communication over short and long distances is crucial for mating as well as group cohesion and coordination [8,11,16]. Asian elephants produce a wide range of calls, from low-frequency rumble and growl to high-frequency trumpet, chirp, roar, bark as well as a range of imitation and combination calls [8,10,16,21].

Studies have related the acoustic structure of elephant vocalizations to be a reflection of an individual's arousal or motivational state. For example, Berg et al., in a pioneering study, examined elephant calls and divided them into ten call types [1]. Comparing these call types with their associated behaviors, they observed that elephants emitted high frequency calls (e.g. trumpets) during

© Springer Nature Switzerland AG 2022
S. R. M. Prasanna et al. (Eds.): SPECOM 2022, LNAI 13721, pp. 426–437, 2022.
https://doi.org/10.1007/978-3-031-20980-2_37

periods of emotional arousal, usually related to aggression or mating (high social excitement) and produced low frequency calls (e.g., rumbles, and growls) during periods of more relaxed social contexts (low excitement). Soltis *et al.* [18] showed that emotional arousal in individuals is reflected in the acoustic details of rumbles. They studied rumble calls in "tense" and "calm" social contexts, where a "tense" social context was defined as when subordinate animals were in proximity to dominant animals, and "calm" social context as when subordinate animals were not in proximity to dominant animals. They showed rumbles recorded in the "tense" social context had lower cepstral coefficients, compared with the rumbles in the "calm" social context. In contrast to rumbles associated with feeding and resting, Wood *et al.* demonstrated that rumbles are also associated with socialising and agitation [25]. These rumbles were characterised by increased and more variable fundamental frequencies, as well as a decrease in duration. Wesolek *et al.* measured rumbles of infant elephants associated with affiliate social interactions and after cessation of nursing from adult females. They showed that infant elephants produced rumbles with more energy in higher frequencies after nursing cessations, compared with rumbles of infant elephants produced in other contexts [24]. Recently, Stoeger *et al.* showed that African savannah *(Loxodonta africana)* elephants are capable of producing different call types such as trumpets, snorts and rumbles in response to verbal cues by trainer (mahout). Her research also demonstrated that rumbles produced while elephants were associating with other conspecifics had a different acoustic structure from rumbles produced when trainer cues were used to elicit rumble responses from elephants [20].

The majority of elephant vocal communication studies have focused on the low-frequency "rumble". The trumpet, for example, is a more characteristic elephant call that has received less attention. However, a thorough knowledge of the elephant vocal system necessitates a detailed examination of other types of vocalisations and their functions. In recent years, a few studies have looked into the trumpet call modulation in diverse contexts. Sharma *et al.* studied whether wild Asian elephants modulate their vocalizations (rumbles and trumpets) when disturbed. They showed that rumbles produced in disturbed conditions had lower mean F0 and mean positions of F1 and F2 also decreased compared with the undisturbed conditions. However, the trumpet calls showed no significant difference under disturbed conditions, except for a little decreased duration [14]. Similarly, Fuchs *et al.* showed that trumpets convey the information content of individual identity, but found no evidence of trumpet call modulation in the context of greeting versus disturbance [5]. In the disturbed context, trumpets in response to disturbance through dogs, cars, or mahout (elephant caretaker) commands were included, and to induce the greeting context, elephants were separated and then brought back together in a social separation experiment. Since manipulative experiments were performed to achieve acoustic and behavioural responses, it is possible that these experiments did not mimic natural responses. Therefore, no effects on call modulation were observed.

Motivated by findings from the above-mentioned studies, we inferred that the structure of specific elephant call types differs in a context-dependent manner.

These context-specific structures could reflect the emotional state of elephants in their vocalizations. Langbauer *et al.* divided the emotional state of African elephant callers into two trumpet sub-types depending on the narrower context of fear vs social excitement [6]. In the current study, we aim to investigate mahout interactions (mahout interacting with elephants) and social interactions (elephants interacting with other elephants) based on trumpet calls in Asian elephants. A study on mahout-elephant interactions showed that in certain scenarios, when the mahout commanded, the elephants exhibited a fearful response by vocalizing [19]. These interactions which induced fear may be reflected in the acoustic structure of elephant vocalizations.

Considering the lack of studies focusing on trumpet calls associated with elephant behaviour, in this study, we investigate the possibility of classification of mahout interactions and social interactions based on trumpet calls. We reviewed publicly available datasets to investigate this question and found only one dataset available online [15]. However, as that database was of calls from wild or free-ranging elephants, there was no mahout interaction involved. As a result of that, we decided to create our own dataset by means of field data collection, to carry out the intended study.

The rest of the paper is organized as follows. Section 2 describes the details of created elephant vocalization database. The trumpet call based classification of mahout and social interactions is presented in Sect. 3. Section 4 describes the findings and discussions, followed by conclusions in Sect. 5.

2   Database

2.1   Study Site and Subjects

The elephant vocalization data was collected at Kaziranaga National Park and Tiger Reserve (called KNP henceforth), which is a World Heritage Site located in the northeast Indian state of Assam, spread across the floodplains of the Brahmaputra river. The KNP hosts approximately 60 semi-captive Asian elephants utilized for various purposes such as patrolling, anti-poaching activities, conducting census and tourism. These animals have been assigned at least one mahout, who takes care of their feeding, bathing, dusting, and other daily needs. Every evening, these animals are given a bath by their mahouts and are frequently allowed to interact socially in larger groups at these bathing and browsing locations. Most of the time, the elephants are allowed to freely browse in open grassland and woodland areas. All elephants are accustomed to the presence of humans. For this study, 25 elephants were selected based on their location within the KNP. Their age group ranges from 1 year to 60 years; broadly classified into four major age classes: calf (<1 year), juvenile (1–5 years), sub-adult (5–15 years), and adult (15 years and above) as reported in [22]. The sex and age classifications of the studied individuals are given in Table 1.

Table 1. Distribution of age-class and sex of the studied subjects for the elephant vocalization data.

Age-Class	Female	Male
Calf (<1 year)	0	1
Juvenile (1 to 5 years)	1	0
Sub-Adult (5 to 15 years)	4	4
Adult (15 years and above)	9	6

2.2 Recording Context

Recording sessions were conducted in various areas of the field site, including bathing areas, browsing areas, and locations where elephants are tethered for the night. In these recording sessions, no manipulative experiments were performed to induce elephant responses. The recording sessions were conducted in a round-robin manner. Each studied subject is monitored for an average of 4 h and its behaviour is recorded every 30 s for a minimum of 15 min to an hour per session. We classified elephant behaviour into broad categories such as Self-Directed, Handler (Mahout) Interaction, Locomotion, Social, Comfort, Foraging, and Other behaviour [9,13].

The vocalizations were recorded in two separate contexts for this study. In the first context, we recorded vocalizations of the subjects when mahouts were interacting with their elephants by commanding them to walk, sit or lie down, etc. In response to the directives from mahouts, the elephants' immediate responses were elevated tail, J-shaped trunk, lying down or walking, etc. However, mahouts did not provide the elephants any cues to get them to vocalise or respond. The "Mahout" class data refers to the behaviour and vocalizations of elephant observed during these interactions. In the second context, referred to as social interactions, we recorded elephants interacting with conspecifics. Elephants exhibited S-shaped trunks (periscope trunks), walking or running towards one another, or remaining still. The callers were not in the proximity of their mahouts. The "Social" class data refers to the behaviour and vocalizations of elephants noticed during these interactions.

2.3 Acoustic Data Collection and Categorization

The data was recorded during daytime between 8 a.m. and 6 p.m. from February to April 2021. This yielded a total of 47 days and 103 h of acoustic recordings. For each recorded vocalization the behaviour, the context, the identity of the caller and approximate recording distance were noted. All vocalizations were recorded using an Earthworks QTC-40 microphone (frequency 3 Hz to 40 kHz) connected to a Sound Devices MixPre-3 II audio recorder at the sampling rate of 48 kHz and distance ranging from 5–100 m. The loudness levels of varying distance recording were normalised using the adjustable gain function available in the audio recorder. For capturing the elephant behaviour, the video recordings were done using two digital single-lens reflex cameras (Cannon 1200-D and Nikon D5100) interchangeably.

All vocalizations were identified using field notes, listening, and visual inspection of spectrograms. Based on the findings in these studies [1,8,16], we categorized vocalizations into four major call types and combination calls. Our fieldwork yielded a total of 401 elephant calls, spanning all age groups and sex. A combination call is a call with two different call types with no temporal overlap and no intervening silence emitted by the very individual. Trumpet-Roar, Roar-Rumble as well as Chirp-Rumble are the three combinations that were recorded in combination calls. In our dataset, Rumbles, which are the only low-frequency call in elephants, were found to be the most common followed by Chirps and Trumpets respectively. Rumbles constituted 53.86% of total calls recorded, out of which Adult females emitted 87.5% of calls (Table 2).

Table 2. Sex-wise breakup of the vocalization recordings in the database.

Male subjects				
Call type	Calf	Sub-Adult	Adult	Total
Combination calls	0	1	1	2
Chirp	0	0	13	13
Roar	1	4	1	6
Rumble	1	16	10	27
Trumpet	0	4	16	20
Total	2	25	41	68
Female Subjects				
Call type	Juvenile	Sub-Adult	Adult	Total
Combination calls	5	0	3	8
Chirp	6	18	45	69
Roar	10	3	9	22
Rumble	2	23	164	189
Trumpet	0	23	22	45
Total	23	67	243	333

Comparing the calls across two sex, 83.04% of the calls were recorded from female subjects while only 16.96% of the calls were recorded from male subjects. These observations are consistent with the findings reported in the literature [6, 7,12], that male subjects produce fewer calls than females. The separation of male and female social systems is a typical explanation for these discrepancies.

3   Mahout and Social Interaction Classification

From the above-mentioned data set, trumpet calls were used to classify the mahout and social interactions as trumpet call type in Asian elephants is not

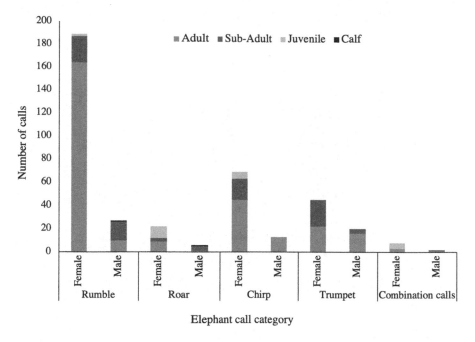

Fig. 1. Age-class and sex-wise distribution of different call types in the elephant vocalization database.

widely studied [5]. Based on the quality of the recordings and the context of the calls, 52 trumpet calls from the sub-adult and adult age groups were selected for this analysis. Twenty-seven of the 52 trumpet calls were recorded in the "Mahout" class, while the rest were recorded in the "Social" class (Fig. 1).

3.1 Pre-processing

Each acoustic recording was first visually examined using PRAAT 6.2.03 [2] software based on field notes and listening. Trumpets were then located in the raw data and then calls were marked and trimmed from start to end for extraction of relevant information for further analysis. The mean duration of trumpets in "Social" class is 0.99 s (SD = 0.64) and in "Mahout" class is 0.74 s (SD = 0.28). Trumpets were then down-sampled to 16 kHz and high-pass filters were applied with 200 Hz cutoff to reduce wind noise.

3.2 Experimental Setup

The open-source feature extraction toolkit openSMILE toolkit [4] in python was used to extract features. In the openSMIlE toolkit, extended Geneva Minimalistic Acoustic Parameter Set (eGeMAPS) was used to extract the feature set which is a basic standard acoustic parameter set for various areas of automatic voice analysis. We extracted 25 low-level descriptors (LLD) and 88 functionals.

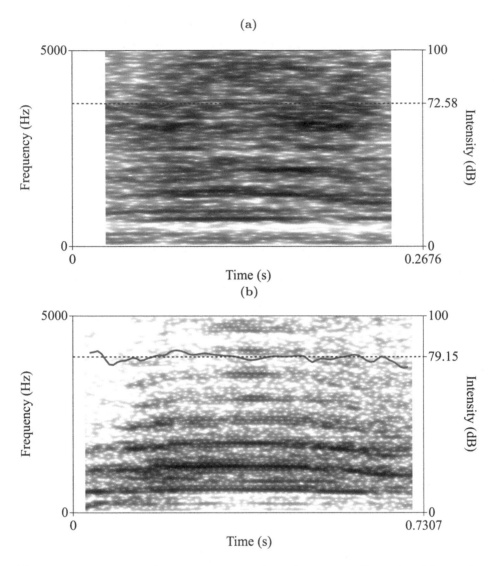

Fig. 2. Spectrograms and intensity contour plots of trumpet calls produced by a sub-adult Asian male elephant in two contexts: (a) social interaction and (b) mahout interaction. In each case, the dotted line indicates the mean value of the intensity and the red line indicates the intensity contour. The mean intensity was observed to be higher during the mahout interaction contexts compared to social interaction contexts. (Color figure online)

The 25 LLDs consist of spectral features (e.g. Spectral flux), voicing features (e.g. F0semitoneFrom 27.5 Hz, Jitter), energy features (e.g. F1 amplitudeLogF0, Loudness), and cepstral features (e.g. mfcc). Statistics such as arithmetic mean, percentiles, variances, and standard deviations, of the LLDs are calculated which results in 88 functionals. These LLDs were extracted every 10 ms from 25 ms frames (Fig. 2).

For training and classification, three combinations of the above feature set were used. These three combination sets are LLD feature set which consists of only all LLD, Functionals feature set which consists of only all functionals, and LLD +Functionals feature set which consists of both LLD and Functionals. We used the k-fold validation methodology to evaluate the performance of the model for LLD, Functionals, and LLD +Functionals. Due to small size of the database, we set k = 5. The subsets were created such that the set of utterances are mutually exclusive in these 5 subsets. Specifically, subsets 1, 2, 3, 4, and 5 consist of data of 13 test utterances such that each subset consists of 25% testing set.

The classification model was developed using support vector machine (SVM) as a classifier with a linear kernel. We have chosen SVM as a classifier because SVMs can generate robust models even from a small size of training set, cope well with asymmetric class distribution and is computationally efficient.

4   Results and Discussion

The classification model was created using three separate feature set combinations as described in Sect. 3. For each fold of k-fold evaluation, separate SVM model was trained using the respective training set. Here, the performance of the classification model is measured in terms of Accuracy and F-score, defined as

$$Accuracy(\%) = 100 * \frac{TP + TN}{TP + FP + TN + FN} \tag{1}$$

$$\text{F-score} = \frac{TP}{TP + \frac{1}{2}(FP + FN)} \tag{2}$$

where TP is the number of true positives, TN is the number of true negatives, FP is the number of false positives and FN is the number of false negatives. The average accuracy (%) and average F-score of the 5-fold data were calculated and are shown in Table 3.

The averaged accuracies (%) of LLD, Functionals, and LLD +Functionals are 79.57, 84.62, and 81.43, respectively. For the sake of reference, the fold-wise accuracies obtained in the 5-fold experiments are shown in Table 4.

Using the Functionals feature set, we obtained higher F-score compared to LLD and LLD +Functionals feature set. However, when we compared the 95% confidence interval of the accuracy between Functionals and LLD +Functionals, we observed that the 95% CI of the accuracy of LLD +Functionals was much narrower than that of Functionals. This effect could be due to the low number of

Table 3. 5-fold averaged percentage accuracy and F-score obtained of the "Mahout" and "Social" classification for different groups of features sets.

Feature set	Average accuracy (%)	Average F-score
LLD	79.57	0.79
Functionals	84.62	0.85
LLD +Functionals	81.43	0.78

utterances in the testing set for Functionals. Hence, combining all performance parameters, using the LLD +Functionals technique with a full set of all LLD and all functionals to classify the elephant vocalization dataset into mahout and social classes is the best approach. Reduction from LLD +Functionals feature set to only the LLD feature set led to a degradation in the performance of the SVM classifier.

Table 4. Fold-wise classification accuracy for reference purposes.

Feature set	Accuracy (%)				
	Fold 1	Fold 2	Fold 3	Fold 4	Fold 5
LLD	68.89	91.25	71.25	83.46	83.00
Functionals	76.92	92.31	84.62	76.92	92.31
LLD +Functionals	80.61	88.99	81.26	64.51	91.80

To find the contribution of each of the LLD features in the classification, we trained single-feature SVMs and evaluated them. On rank-ordering, the resulting performances, the top three features contributing to categorization are found to be "slope 500–1500", "spectral flux", and "loudness". The mean "spectral flux" and "loudness" were observed to be higher in mahout class compared to social class, while the mean "slope 500–1500" was found to be higher in social class than in mahout class. The 3-D scatterplot of mahout and social class data with respect to those dominant features is shown in Fig. 3.

Based on trumpet calls, we could distinguish between mahout and social interactions. We inferred that the classification was achieved because mahout interactions incited fear, which was reflected in elephant vocalizations [19]. However, there is a limitation to this study. In the social context, a subordinate may be calling because of dominant interactions, which may have caused elephants to become fearful and modulate their vocalisations. Hence, in future dominance interactions between elephant pairs will need to be investigated. Soltis *et al.* showed that the acoustic structure of rumbles in elephants varied between "negative" (i.e., dominance interactions), "positive" (i.e., social excitement), and "neutral" interactions (i.e., minimal social activity). Rumbles in negative interactions exhibited an increase in maximum amplitude and range of amplitude [17]. These

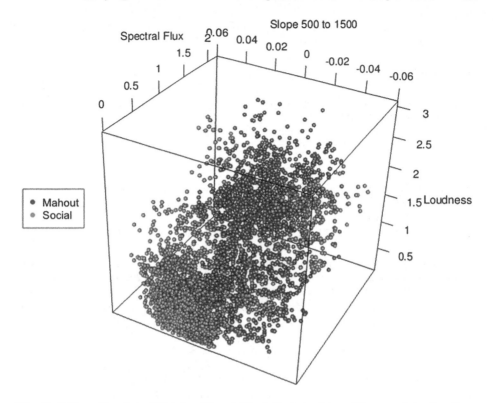

Fig. 3. 3-D scatterplot of "Mahout" and "Social" class data with respect to the three dominant LLD features.

findings are comparable to what we noticed that loudness, an estimate of perceived signal intensity from an auditory spectrum, is a predominant feature in the classifier. In the future, an in-depth study of each feature within the feature set is required to understand the modulation of trumpet calls.

5   Conclusion

In the current work, we made an attempt to classify the trumpet calls of semi-captive Asian elephants based on two scenarios. We attempted to classify the trumpet calls made in response to the mahout interactions versus in response to other conspecifics interactions. As with the previous studies conducted on elephant calls, it was shown that the calls produced in negative interactions have higher intensity compared with calls produced in neutral and positive interactions. These findings are similar to our findings too, in which loudness is one of the dominant aspects aiding the said classification. Our findings suggest that acoustics of trumpets are context-specific, a trend that maybe extended to other call types. We intend to look into other call types in the future. Another issue that we would be interested in pursuing is the estimation of physiological factors to determine stress levels through elephant vocalizations.

Acknowledgments. The authors thank the Assam Forest Department for their permission to collect the data. The first author would also like to thank all the forest guards and elephant handlers in Kaziranga National Park and Tiger Reserve for their help in conducting the fieldwork.

References

1. Berg, J.K.: Vocalizations and associated behaviors of the African elephant (Loxodonta africana) in captivity. Zeitschrift für Tierpsychologie (J. Comp. Ethol.) **63**, 63–79 (1983). https://doi.org/10.1111/j.1439-0310.1983.tb00741.x
2. Boersma, P., Weenink, D.: PRAAT: doing phonetics by computer (version 5.1.13) (2009). http://www.praat.org
3. Calabrese, A., et al.: Conservation status of Asian elephants: the influence of habitat and governance. Biodivers. Conserv. **26**(9), 2067–2081 (2017). https://doi.org/10.1007/s10531-017-1345-5
4. Eyben, F., Wöllmer, M., Schuller, B.: openSMILE - the Munich versatile and fast open-sourceaudio feature extractor. In: ACM Multimedia (MM), pp. 1459–1462 (2010)
5. Fuchs, E., Beeck, V.C., Baotic, A., Stoeger, A.S.: Acoustic structure and information content of trumpets in female Asian elephants (Elephas maximus). PLoS ONE **16**, 1–19 (2021). https://doi.org/10.1371/journal.pone.0260284
6. Langbauer, W.R.: Elephant communication. Zoo Biol. **19**, 425–445 (2000). https://doi.org/10.1002/1098-2361(2000)19:5<425::AID-ZOO11>3.0.CO;2-A
7. Leong, K.M., Ortolani, A., Burks, K.D., Mellen, J.D., Savage, A.: Quantifying acoustic and temporal characteristics of vocalizations for a group of captive African elephants Loxodonta Africana. Bioacoustics **13**, 213–231 (2003). https://doi.org/10.1080/09524622.2003.9753499
8. Nair, S., Balakrishnan, R., Seelamantula, C.S., Sukumar, R.: Vocalizations of wild Asian elephants (Elephas maximus): structural classification and social context. J. Acoust. Soc. Am. **126**, 2768–2778 (2009). https://doi.org/10.1121/1.3224717. http://asa.scitation.org/doi/10.1121/1.3224717
9. Olson, D.: Ethogram of Elephant Behaviors: Elephant Husbandry Resource Guide, American Zoo and Aquarium Association Elephant Taxon Group, United States, pp. 103–121 (2004)
10. Pardo, M.A., et al.: Differences in combinatorial calls among the 3 elephant species cannot be explained by phylogeny. Behav. Ecol., 1–12 (2019). https://doi.org/10.1093/beheco/arz018
11. Poole, J.H., Payne, K., Langbauer, W., Moss, C.: The social contexts of some very low-frequency calls of African elephants. Behav. Ecol. Sociobiol. **22**, 385–392 (1988). https://doi.org/10.1007/BF00294975
12. Poole, J.: Sex differences in the behaviour of African elephants. The differences between the sexes, pp. 331–346 (1994)
13. Rees, P.A.: Activity budgets and the relationship between feeding and stereotypic behaviors in Asian elephants (Elephas maximus) in a zoo. Zoo Biol. **28**, 79–97 (2009)

14. Sharma, N., Kohshima, S., Sukumar, R.: Asian elephants modulate their vocalizations when disturbed. Animal Behav. **160**, 99–111 (2020). https://doi.org/10.1016/j.anbehav.2019.12.004

15. Silva, S.: Asian Elephant Vocalizations LDC2010S05. Web Download. Linguistic Data Consortium, Philadelphia (2010)

16. Silva, S.D.: Acoustic communication in the Asian elephant, elephas maximus maximus. Behaviour **147**, 825–852 (2010). https://doi.org/10.1163/000579510X495762

17. Soltis, J., Blowers, T.E., Savage, A.: Measuring positive and negative affect in the voiced sounds of African elephants (Loxodonta Africana). J. Acoust. Soc. Am. **129**, 1059–1066 (2011). https://doi.org/10.1121/1.3531798. http://asa.scitation.org/doi/10.1121/1.3531798

18. Soltis, J., Leong, K., Savage, A.: African elephant vocal communication II: rumble variation reflects the individual identity and emotional state of callers. Anim. Behav. **70**, 589–599 (2005). https://doi.org/10.1016/j.anbehav.2004.11.016

19. Srinivasaiah, N., Varma, S., Sukumar, R.: Documenting Indigenous Traditional Knowledge of the Asian Elephant in Captivity. Asian Nature Conservation Foundation (ANCF), c/o Centre for Ecological Sciences, Indian Institute of Science, Bangalore 560012, India (2014)

20. Stoeger, A.S., Baotic, A.: Operant control and call usage learning in African elephants. Philos. Trans. R. Soc. B **376**(1836), 20200254 (2021)

21. Stoeger, A.S., et al.: An Asian elephant imitates human speech. Curr. Biol. **22**, 2144–2148 (2012). https://doi.org/10.1016/j.cub.2012.09.022

22. Varma, S., Baskaran, N., Sukumar, R.: Field Key for Elephant Population Estimation and Age and Sex Classification. Resource material for synchronized elephant population count using block count, line transect dung count method and waterhole count. Asian Nature Conservation Foundation, Innovation Centre, Indian Institute of Science, Bangalore - 560 012, Karnataka and Centre for Ecological Sciences, Indian Institute of Science, Bangalore, 560 012 (2012)

23. Vidya, T.N., Sukumar, R.: Social organization of the Asian elephant (Elephas maximus) in Southern India inferred from microsatellite DNA. J. Ethol. **23**, 205–210 (2005). https://doi.org/10.1007/s10164-005-0144-8

24. Wesolek, C.M., Soltis, J., Leighty, K.A., Savage, A.: Infant African elephant rumble vocalizations vary according to social interactions with adult females. Bioacoustics **18**, 227–239 (2009). https://doi.org/10.1080/09524622.2009.9753603

25. Wood, J.D., McCowan, B., Langbauer, W.R., Viljoen, J.J., Hart, L.A.: Classification of African elephant Loxodonta Africana rumbles using acoustic parameters and cluster analysis. Bioacoustics **15**, 143–161 (2005). https://doi.org/10.1080/09524622.2005.9753544

Recognition of the Emotional State of Children with Down Syndrome by Video, Audio and Text Modalities: Human and Automatic

Elena Lyakso[1]([✉]) [iD], Olga Frolova[1] [iD], Anton Matveev[1] [iD], Yuri Matveev[1] [iD], Aleksey Grigorev[1] [iD], Olesia Makhnytkina[2] [iD], and Nersisson Ruban[3] [iD]

[1] The Child Speech Research Group, St. Petersburg State University, St. Petersburg, Russia
lyakso@gmail.com
[2] ITMO University, Saint Petersburg 197101, Russia
[3] School of Electrical Engineering, Vellore Institute of Technology, Vellore, India

Abstract. The paper presents the results of perceptual experiments (by humans) and automatic recognition of the emotional states of children with Down syndrome (DS) by video, audio and text modalities. The participants of the study were 35 children with DS aged 5–16 years, and 30 adults – the participants of the perceptual experiment. Automatic analysis of facial expression by video was performed using FaceReader software runs on the Microsoft Azure cloud platform and convolutional neural network. Automatic recognition of the emotional states of children by speech was carried out using a recurrent neural network. Specifically for this project, we did not apply any additional transfer learning or fine-tuning as our goal was to investigate how the generic models perform for children with DS. The results of perceptual experiments showed that adults recognize the emotional states of children with DS by video better than by audio. Automatic classification of children's emotional states by facial expression revealed better results for joy and neutral states than for sadness and anger; by audio the best results were shown for the neutral state, by the texts of children's speech - for joy, the state of sadness was not recognized automatically. The study revealed the possibility of using the available software for classifying the neutral state and the state of joy, i.e. states with neutral and positive valence, and the need to develop an approach to determine the state of sadness and anger.

Keywords: Emotional state · Perceptual and automatic recognition · Child with down syndrome · Video · Audio · Text modalities

1 Introduction

In recent decades, various aspects of child development, including the emotional sphere, are widely studied considering the age and neurological state of a child. The results of these studies are used in medical practice as additional diagnostic technique, and in the field of artificial intelligence to create systems of assistive and alternative communication. Many works are devoted to study the recognition of emotions by adults and

S. R. M. Prasanna et al. (Eds.): SPECOM 2022, LNAI 13721, pp. 438–450, 2022.
https://doi.org/10.1007/978-3-031-20980-2_38

children with Down syndrome (DS) by facial expression [1–9] and by facial expression and vocalizations [4]. Studies on the manifestation of emotional states by children with DS are few [10–14] that to a certain extent may be due to traditional views. People with DS are characterized as friendly and very sociable, charming personalities with a positive mood [15–17]. However, the extensive symptoms of the disease may include a violation of the emotional sphere [18].

The study of the reflection of emotional states by children with DS and the correct recognition of these states by adults is necessary as a basis for the automatic recognition systems creating. Conversational agents, virtual assistants and educational robots are developed for adults and children with autism spectrum disorders [19–21] and intellectual disabilities [22], but they are rare for children with DS [23–25]. Educational programs and virtual assistants, as a rule, are based on multimodal interaction, relying primarily on visual and acoustic information in recognizing the emotional states of children. The present study is aimed at recognizing the emotional state of children with DS according to separate modalities: the visual channel based on the analysis of facial expression and auditory channel - recognition by voice, speech and text.

The aim of the study was to reveal the specificity of human recognition of the emotional state of children with DS by their facial expressions and speech, and to test the possibility of automatic recognition using existing programs and developed algorithms.

2 Methods

2.1 Participants of the Study

The participants of the study were 35 children with DS aged 5–16 years (10.3 ± 2.8 years - mean ± standard deviation) - 21 boys, 14 girls, and 30 adults – the participants of the perceptual experiment. 15 adults, the research team of the Child Speech Research Group of Saint Petersburg University (experts, age 39.9 ± 19.6 years) viewed the video test. 15 adults of different specialties - in the field of information technology, psychophysiology, speech therapy, with experience in working with child speech (listeners, age 36.7 ± 11.1 years) listened to the audio test.

2.2 Data Collection

Video and audio recordings of facial expression, behavior and speech of children were made in the child center of the public organization "Down Center" (St. Petersburg) in a natural situation of interaction of a child with parents and the experimenter. The situation included a conversation on topics suggested by parents, playing with toys, describing pictures in a book.

For video recording of facial expression of children, a SONY HDR-CX560 video camera (maximum resolution 1920 × 1080 at 50 frames per second) was used, which was located at a distance of 1 m from the child's face. To record children's speech, Marantz PMD660 tape recorder with a SENNHEIZER e835S external microphone was used. The microphone was set at a distance of 30–50 cm from the child's face. Audio files were saved in.wav format, 48000 Hz, 16 bits. The total recording time for each child did not exceed 30–40 min. All details concerning the features of the child's behavior were recorded in a detailed protocol.

The parents of the children participating in the study signed an informed consent approved by the Ethics Committee of St. Petersburg State University.

2.3 Perceptual Study

Video recordings of facial expressions were annotated into 4 emotional states of children: neutral (calm), joy, anger, sadness. The annotation was made by two specialists with professional experience in the area of child development, based on the analysis of the video and the recording protocol. The specialists selected video fragments during which the child demonstrates facial expressions corresponding to one of the four emotional states (neutral, joy, anger, sadness), chose only the video fragments when the child's face and the whole head were completely in the frame and were not covered by hands or toys. The requirements for the selection of material are determined by the further analysis of video in the FaceReader program. If the opinions of two specialists were consistent, the video fragment was attributed to a certain emotional state and used for further analysis. 50 video fragments were selected. The duration of the fragments was from 4 to 31 s (1–2 fragments for each child). Video and audio tests were created for the perceptual experiment.

The video test included 50 fragments, mixed in a random order. Before each video fragment, the number was inserted. The pause between the fragments was 10 s. Each of the video fragments was included in the test once. The duration of the test was 20 min. The video test was presented to a group of adults (experts) without sound from a monitor of a personal computer. The experts were in a classroom with an area of 25 m². Before the experiment, in the questionnaire, the experts indicated their gender and age. Watching the test, experts noted the emotional state of the children, choosing one of the four proposed categories: neutral, joy, sadness, anger.

The audio test contained children's speech corresponding to video fragments. Each speech signal was repeated once in the test, the pause between speech signals was 5 s. The audio test was presented to adults (listeners) in an open field. There was no preliminary training of experts and listeners.

The video and audio tests were used for automatic analysis.

Confusion matrixes for perceptual experiments were prepared. We calculated recall, precision, F-1 score for each emotion, Unweighted Average Recall (UAR) - for all emotions [26]. Agreement between experts and listeners is assessed using the Cohen kappa statistic (k) [27, 28]. Relative strength of agreement was associated with kappa statistics: slight (0.00–0.20), fair (0.21–0.40), moderate (0.41–0.60), substantial (0.61–0.80), and almost perfect (0.81–1.00) [29].

2.4 Automatic Analysis of Facial Expression and Emotional Speech of Children with DS

Analysis of Facial Expression in FaceReader Program. Analysis of facial expression was performed in the FaceReader v.8.0 program (Noldus Information Technology,

Netherlands). FaceReader software runs on the Microsoft Azure cloud platform. The program automatically highlights six basic emotions "joy – sadness – anger – surprise – fear - disgust", and a neutral state [30]. Each of the emotions is associated with a genetically determined program of facial muscle movement. Special settings working with the analysis of facial expressions of adults and children over four years old. Over 10,000 expert-marked images have been used to train emotional expression classifiers, achieving a classification accuracy of 89% [31]. Recognition accuracy varies in different versions of FaceReader.

Based on the algorithms embedded in the program, the following parameters are determined: the time during which the child demonstrates a certain emotional state in facial expression (as a percentage of the time of the video fragment), and the valence of the emotions. The data obtained from the automatic analysis of children's facial expression were compared with the results of a perceptual experiment.

Analysis of Facial Expression Using Convolutional Neural Network. For preprocessing, the video records were split into series of frames (static images) with FFmpeg [32], a free and open-source software project consisting of a suite of libraries and programs for handling video, audio, and other multimedia files and streams, and then each frame was processed with Multi-task Cascaded Convolutional Networks (MTCNN) via Deepface [33], a lightweight face recognition and facial attribute analysis framework. Since the video segments with a single child contained only a small number of frames without a detected face, we applied a sliding window to filter out the empty frames, timestamped the segments, and mapped them to the labels. For the face emotion detection, we used a simple convolutional neural network with five convolutional, three pooling, and two fully-connected layers trained on the FER2013 dataset from the Kaggle facial expression recognition challenge in 2013 [34].

Analysis of Emotional Speech Using Recurrent Neural Network (RNN). For the audio records, the segments with utterances of a single child were manually clipped via Audacity [35], a free and open-source digital audio editor and mapped to the labels. For the speech emotion detection, we used a simple recurrent neural network with two recurrent and two fully-connected layers with 128 RNN and dense units each trained on a combination of The Ryerson Audio-Visual Database of Emotional Speech and Song (RAVDESS), Toronto Emotional Speech Set (TESS), and Berlin Database of Emotional Speech (EMO-DB) datasets with Mel-frequency cepstral coefficients (MFCC), Chromagram, and MEL Spectrogram Frequency features.

Specifically for this project, we did not apply any additional transfer learning or fine-tuning as our goal was to investigate how the generic models perform for children with DS.

Automatic Analysis of the Text of CHILD's Speech. Two specialists transcribed the speech of children from the fragments of the video tests manually. Then the graphematic text analysis was conducted automatically - the number of sentences, the number of unfinished words, and the average number of tokens were counted in the child's speech. Morphological text analysis was made using the morphological analyzer pymorphy2 [36], and the relative frequencies of the use of different parts of speech for each child were calculated. The assessment of the use of positive and negative words was carried out using the LinisCrowd 2015 tone dictionary [37].

Statistical analysis was made in the program "Statistica", the Mann-Whitney test, Spearman correlation ($p < 0.05$) and Regression analysis were used.

3   Results

3.1   Perceptual Experiment

Recognition of the Emotional State by Facial Expression of Children. An analysis of the results of the perceptual experiment showed that by video fragments of children experts recognize the neutral state and joy better than sadness and anger (Table 1). The Unweighted Average Recall was 0.66.

Table 1. Confusion matrix for recognition by experts of the emotional states of children by video (% of answers).

	joy	neutral	sad	anger
joy	72	24	1	3
neutral	1	78	15	6
sad	0	32	64	4
anger	11	26	12	51
Recall	0.72	0.78	0.64	0.51
Precision	0.86	0.49	0.70	0.80
F1-score	0.78	0.60	0.67	0.62
UAR 0.66				

Significant differences in the number of experts' correct answers between emotional states: sadness and joy ($p < 0.05$ - Mann-Whitney test), anger and joy ($p < 0.01$), anger and neutral ($p < 0.01$), anger and sadness ($p < 0.05$) were revealed. Experts demonstrated moderate agreement in recognizing all emotional states. For the state of joy, the agreement between experts was substantial, for the states of sadness and anger - moderate, for the neutral state - fair (Table 2).

Table 2. Agreement between experts when recognizing the emotional state of children by video tests (Cohen's kappa coefficient).

Emotional state	joy	neutral	sad	anger	all states
Cohen's kappa coefficient	0.632	0.375	0.407	0.492	0.455

The high recall and low precision values for the neutral state indicate that experts select this state more often than other emotions. The high value of accuracy and Cohen's kappa for the joy indicates a significant specificity in the manifestation of this emotion.

Recognition of the Emotional State by the Speech of Children. The listeners recognize anger and a neutral state better than sadness and joy (Table 3). The UAR was 0.61. Significant differences in the number of correct listeners' answers between emotional states: anger and sadness ($p < 0.05$ - Mann-Whitney test), anger and joy ($p < 0.001$), neutral state and joy ($p < 0.001$) were found.

Table 3. Confusion matrix for recognition by listeners of emotional states by speech of children (% of answers).

	joy	neutral	sad	anger
joy	45	34	4	17
neutral	11	69	16	4
sad	0	42	58	0
anger	7	10	10	73
Recall	0.45	0.69	0.58	0.73
Precision	0.71	0.45	0.66	0.78
F1-score	0.55	0.54	0.62	0.75
UAR 0.61				

The agreement of the listeners for all emotional states was weak, for joy, anger it was moderate, and for neutral state and sadness – weak (Table 4).

Table 4. Agreement between listeners when recognizing the emotional state of children by audio tests (Cohen's kappa coefficient).

Emotional state	joy	neutral	sad	anger	all states
Cohen's kappa coefficient	0.406	0.360	0.280	0.503	0.388

The accuracy for video test was higher than for audio test ($p < 0.01$ - significant differences in the number of correct adult's answers, Mann-Whitney test). The state of joy was recognized better by video fragments ($p < 0.001$), the state of anger ($p < 0.05$) - by the speech of children.

Factors Affecting Recognition of the Emotional State of Children. The duration of video fragments did not significantly affect the recognition accuracy. When watching video tests, experts recognized better the emotional state of girls than the emotional state of boys (p < 0.05 - Mann-Whitney test). The gender of the experts influences the recognition of the state of anger: $F(1.13) = 7.186$ p < 0.05 ($R^2 = 0.356$ $\beta = 0.597$) – according to the regression analysis, women recognized anger better than men. Older adults recognized the emotional states of children worse than younger ($r = -0.53$, p < 0.05 - Spearman correlation). When listening to audio test, listeners classified the speech of boys as anger more often than the speech of girls (p < 0.01).

3.2 Automatic Analysis of Facial Expression

FaceReader Program. Automatic analysis of children's facial expressions in the FaceReader 8.0 program showed that children's facial expressions corresponded mainly to a neutral state (Table 5).

The neutral state and joy were recognized better, than sadness and anger (Table 5).

Table 5. Facial expression of children, % of the time of the video test (FaceReader 8.0).

Emotional state	joy	neutral	sad	anger	fear	surprise	disgust	other
joy	26.49	47.33	3.29	1.52	0.39	13.13	1.45	6.40
neutral	2.11	57.72	8.40	7.07	4.27	13.81	0.79	5.83
sad	0.00	55.66	12.27	6.53	5.10	9.77	4.60	6.07
anger	6.19	52.87	10.64	0.80	4.80	11.13	6.59	6.98

Note: Rows correspond to real emotional states; columns correspond to emotional states highlighted by the FaceReader 8.0 program

The facial expression of children in a state of joy is characterized by positive valence (0.17); state of sadness (-0.16), anger (-0.11) and neutral state (-0.12) - by negative values.

Analysis Using Convolutional Neural Network. Classifying video fragments on 7 categories (corresponding 6 basic emotional states and neutral state) we revealed that the state of joy and neutral state are classified better than the state of anger. Anger confused with sadness, neutral state, and fear (Table 6).

Table 6. The cumulative probabilities for the automatic classification of emotions via static images of facial expression of children, %.

Emotional state	joy	neutral	sad	anger	fear	surprise	disgust
joy	35	18	21	9	14	3	0
neutral	5	32	25	8	18	12	0
sad	17	16	29	23	15	0	0
anger	10	22	24	18	21	5	0

For the video, the joy and neutral state were classified better than anger and sad (Table 7). We obtained the overall precision of 0.46, the total recall of 0.43, and the overall F1-score of 0.42. The performance is above chance level.

Table 7. Confusion matrix for automatic classification of emotional state of children by video fragments, %.

	joy	neutral	sad	anger
joy	**68**	9	18	5
neutral	6	**50**	31	13
sad	33	0	**33**	34
anger	11	33	34	**22**
Recall	0.68	0.5	0.33	0.22
Precision	0.83	0.62	0.08	0.33
F1-score	0.75	0.55	0.13	0.27
UAR 0.43				

The approaches used for automatic classification of emotions by facial expression allows to determine the state of joy and the neutral state better than the state of sadness and anger, with best recognition of joy using convolutional neural network.

3.3   Automatic Analysis of Child Speech

Analysis Using Recurrent Neural Network. For the audio, neutral state was classified better than joy, anger and especially sad state (Table 8). We obtained the total precision of 0.31, the total recall of 0.32, and the total F1-score of 0.275. The performance is lower than for video, but is above chance.

Analysis of the Text of the Speech. Using AdaBoostClassifier to predict class labels (emotional states) achieved an accuracy of 0.58. For the text, we obtained the weighted-averaged precision of 0.61, the weighted-averaged recall of 0.58, and the weighted-averaged F1-score of 0.55. The performance is above chance. For the text, joy was classified better than anger, neutral state and especially sad state (Table 9).

Table 8. Confusion matrix for automatic classification of emotional state of children by audio.

	joy	neutral	sad	anger
joy	**23**	64	0	13
neutral	13	**81**	0	6
sad	0	100	**0**	0
anger	22	56	0	**22**
Recall	0.23	0.81	0	0.22
Precision	0.56	0.37	0	0.33
F1-score	0.32	0.51	0	0.27
UAR 0.32				

Table 9. Classification results (text of children's speech).

	joy	neutral	sad	anger
joy	**86**	14	0	0
neutral	56	**33**	11	0
sad	67	33	**0**	0
anger	60	0	0	**40**
Recall	0.86	0.33	0	0.40
Precision	0.58	0.43	0	1.00
F1-score	0.69	0.38	0	0.57
UAR 0.40				

4 Discussion

The study showed the possibility of using the method of perceptual experiment and automatic recognition of the emotional states for children with DS by visual, audio modalities and text. The specificity of recognition was revealed depending on the applied method, modality and the type of emotions.

The results of the study indicated that the state of joy is classified by the facial expression of children with DS and by the text of children's speech better than the states of sadness and anger. By the audio, anger was recognized by listeners with high accuracy and neutral state was classified automatically better than other emotional states.

Expert agreement was maximal for recognition of joy by the facial expressions of children. This finding is correspond to the data obtained in the study of the emotions' manifestation in infants with DS [12]. The authors of this study conclude that in infants with DS, facial expressions should be a specific feature used by adults to identify affective states [12]. In our study, the recognition of the emotional state of children with DS by video was better than by audio. This allows us to conclude that facial manifestations in children with DS are more vivid than vocal ones.

The appearance features of people with DS are characterized by a flat and wide face and nose, slanted eyes [38]. The facial soft tissue structures of people with DS differ from typically developing people of the same age, sex, and ethnic group: a reduced facial size and global anomalous relationship between individual measurements (three-dimensional coordinates of soft tissue facial landmarks obtained using a computerized digitizer) are revealed [39]. These facial features may complicate the human perception and automatic classification of facial expression in children with DS, but they are considered as the basis for creating automatic methods for identifying people suffering from Down syndrome [40, 41].

The results of an auditory perceptual experiment showed that listeners recognized the state of anger with high probability, which confirms the data about better recognition of the discomfort state in speech and vocalizations of children with DS compared with comfort and the neutral states [13]. At the same time, the state of anger is defined worse than joy by the text of children's replies. Perhaps, in a perceptual experiment, listeners rely more on the voice features, but not on the verbal component. The speech of children with DS is characterized by low intelligibility [42]. For children with DS, a number of features in the structure of the speech apparatus are inherent: a small mouth, lowered chin, large fissured tongue, and high-vaulted palate, all of which lead to a more distinct nasal voice, relatively short vocal tract, poor muscle tone. Most of the children with DS have open bite where the top teeth and bottom teeth do not come together or bite in the correct position and more narrow than usual upper jaw [43]. The anatomical and physiological features of the speech apparatus and the specificity of the manifestation of emotional states in the voice and speech of children with DS complicate the task of recognition and, possibly, lead to confusion.

Worse recognition of children's emotional states was demonstrated in automatic classification of emotional states by audio fragments. It is important to note that in our study, we did not apply any additional transfer learning or fine-tuning and used generic models for emotions classification in children with DS. Wrong classifications often correlate with disagreements between expert labels. Another significant point is that while the specialists was labeling the video and the audio simultaneously, the automatic classification was conducted separately for each modality, which points us in the direction of utilizing cross-modal models in further research. This approach turns us to natural human multimodal perception and may be of interest for automatic classification in order to improve recognition accuracy.

However, this study was conducted to test the possibility of recognizing the emotional state of children with DS using only one modality, which is important, in view of the behavior of children - their activity, the inability to maintain static postures for a long time, which is necessary for the analysis of facial expression. We assumed that the automatic analysis of the emotional voice and speech could provide the information about emotional state of child, but the results of the study did not confirm this. Therefore, we plan future work in the following areas: cross-modal classification models, development of the approach for determining the state of sadness and anger, and improving the accuracy of classification especially for emotional speech of children with DS. The most prominent way to solve the problem is to use deep learning techniques.

5 Conclusion

Adults recognize the emotional states of children with DS by video better than by audio. The accuracy and agreement between adults are maximal when recognizing the state of joy by video and the state of anger by speech of children with DS.

Automatic classification of the emotional states of children by facial expression using the convolutional neural network and the algorithms of the FaceReader program, revealed better results for joy and the neutral state than for sadness and anger. Automatic classification of the emotional states of children by audio revealed better results for the neutral state, by the texts of child speech – for joy; the state of sadness was not recognized automatically.

The results of the study showed the possibility of using the available software for classifying the neutral state and the state of joy, i.e. states with neutral and positive valence, and the need to develop an approach to determine the state of sadness and anger.

Acknowledgements. This study is financially supported by the Russian Science Foundation (project 22-45-02007) for Russian researches and Department of Science and Technology (DST) (INTRUSRFBR382) - for Indian researchers.

References

1. Hippolyte, L., Barisnikov, K., Van der Linden, M.: Face processing and facial emotion recognition in adults with Down syndrome. Am. J. Ment. Retard. 113(4), 292–306 (2008)
2. Carvajal, F., Fernández-Alcaraz, C., Rueda, M., Sarrión, L.: Processing of facial expressions of emotions by adults with Down syndrome and moderate intellectual disability. Res. Dev. Disabil. 33(3), 783–790 (2012)
3. Virji-Babul, N., Watt, K., Nathoo, F., Johnson, P.: Recognition of facial expressions of emotion in adults with Down syndrome. Phys. Occup. Ther. Pediatr. 32(3), 333–343 (2012)
4. Pochon, R., Declercq, C.: Emotion recognition by children with Down syndrome: a longitudinal study. J. Intellect. Dev. Disabil. 38(4), 332–343 (2013)
5. Cebula, K.R., Wishart, J.G., Willis, D.S., Pitcairn, T.K.: Emotion recognition in children with Down syndrome: influence of emotion label and expression intensity. Am. J. Intellect. Dev. Disabil. 22(2), 138–155 (2017)
6. Barisnikov, K., Thomasson, M., Stutzmann, J., Lejeune, F.: Relation between processing facial identity and emotional expression in typically developing school-age children and those with Down syndrome. Appl. Neuropsychol. Child 9(2), 179–192 (2020)
7. Barisnikov, K., Theurel, A., Lejeune, F.: Emotion knowledge in neurotypical children and in those with down syndrome. Appl. Neuropsychol. Child 11(3), 197–211 (2022)
8. Pochon, R., Touchet, C., Ibernon, L.: Recognition of basic emotions with and without the use of emotional vocabulary by adolescents with down syndrome. Behav. Sci. 12(6), 167 (2022). https://doi.org/10.3390/bs12060167

9. Roch, M., Pesciarelli, F., Leo, I.: How individuals with down syndrome process faces and words conveying emotions? Evidence from a priming paradigm. Front. Psychol. **11**, 692 (2020)

10. Sorce, J.F., Emde, R.N.: The meaning of infant emotional expressions: regularities in caregiving responses in normal and Down's syndrome infants. J. Child Psychol. Psychiatry **23**(2), 145–158 (1982)

11. Berger, J., Cunningham, C.C.: Aspects of early social smiling by infants with Down's syndrome. Child Care Health Dev. **12**(1), 13–24 (1986)

12. Carvajal, F., Iglesias, J.: Judgements of facial and vocal signs of emotion in infants with Down syndrome. Dev. Psychobiol. **48**(8), 644–652 (2006)

13. Lyakso, E., Frolova, O., Gorodniy, V., Grigovev, A., Nikolaev, A., Matveev, Y.: Re-flection of the emotional state in the characteristics of voice and speech of children with Down syndrome. In: Proceedings SpeD 2019, 10th IEEE International Conference on Speech Technology and Human-Computer Dialogue, Timisoara, Romania, pp. 1–6 (2019)

14. Lyakso, E.E., Frolova, O.V., Matveev, Y.N.: Facial expression: psychophysiological study. In: Joseph, R.A.N., Mahesh, V.G.V., Nersisson, R. (eds.) Handbook of Research on Deep Learning-Based Image Analysis under Constrained and Unconstrained Environments, Hershey, PA, pp. 266–289. IGI Global (2021)

15. Dykens, E., Hodapp, R.M., Evans, D.W.: Profiles and development of adaptive behavior in children with Down syndrome. Am. J. Ment. Retard. **98**(5), 580–587 (1994)

16. Carr, J.: Down's Syndrome: Children Growing Up. Cambridge University Press, Cambridge (1995)

17. Fidler, D.J.: The emerging Down syndrome behavioral phenotype in early childhood implications for practice. Infants Young Child. **18**(2), 86–103 (2005)

18. Izard, C.E., Youngstrom, E.A., Fine, S.E., Mostow, A.J., Trentacosta, C.J.: Emotions and developmental psychopathology. In: Cicchetti, D., Cohen, D.J. (eds.) Developmental psychopathology, pp. 244–292. Wiley, New York (2006)

19. Kim, E.S., Paul, R., Shic, F., Scassellati, B.: Bridging the research gap: making HRI useful to individuals with autism. J. Hum.-Robot Interact. **1**, 26–54 (2012)

20. Garg, R., et al.: The last decade of HCI research on children and voice-based conversational agents. In: Proceedings of the 2022 CHI Conference on Human Factors in Computing Systems (CHI 2022), pp. 1–19. Association for Computing Machinery, New York (2022). Article: 149

21. Scassellati, B., et al.: Improving social skills in children with ASD using a long-term, in-home social robot. Sci. Robot. **3**(21), eaat7544, 1–9 (2018)

22. Tsai, Y.T., Lin, W.A.: Design of an intelligent cognition assistant for people with cognitive impairment. In: IEEE 20th International Conference on High Performance Computing and Communications, 16th International Conference on Smart City and 4th International Conference on Data Science and Systems, HPCC/SmartCity/DSS 2018, Exeter, UK, pp. 1207–1212. IEEE (2018)

23. Bargagna, S., et al.: Educational robotics in down syndrome: a feasibility study. Technol. Knowl. Learn. **24**(2), 315–323 (2018). https://doi.org/10.1007/s10758-018-9366-z

24. González-González, C.S., et al.: Computational thinking and down syndrome: an exploratory study using the KIBO robot. Informatics **6**(25), 1–20 (2019). https://doi.org/10.3390/informatics6020025

25. Alemi, M., Bahramipour, S.: An innovative approach of incorporating a humanoid robot into teaching EFL learners with intellectual disabilities. Asian-Pac. J. Second Foreign Lang. Educ. **4**, 10 (2019). https://doi.org/10.1186/s40862-019-0075-5

26. Dalianis, H.: Evaluation metrics and evaluation. In: Dalianis, H. (ed.) Clinical Text Mining, pp. 45–53. Springer, Cham (2018). https://doi.org/10.1007/978-3-319-78503-5_6

27. Juremi, N.R.M., Zulkifley, M.A., Hussain, A., Zaki, W.M.D.: Inter-rater reliability of actual tagged emotion categories validation using Cohen's Kappa coefficient. J. Theor. Appl. Inf. Technol. **95**, 259–264 (2017)
28. Bobicev, V., Sokolova, M.: Inter-annotator agreement in sentiment analysis: machine learning perspective. In: Recent Advances in Natural Language Processing Meet Deep Learning, Varna, Bulgaria, pp. 97–102 (2017)
29. Landis, J.R., Koch, G.G.: The measurement of observer agreement for categorical data. Biometrics **33**(1), 159–174 (1977)
30. Ekman, P.: Basic emotions. In: Dalgleish, T., Power, M.J. (eds.) Handbook of cognition and emotion, pp. 45–60. Wiley, Hoboken (1999)
31. Terzis, V., Moridis, C.N., Economides, A.A.: Measuring instant emotions during a self-assessment test: the use of FaceReader. In: 7th International Conference on Methods and Techniques in Behavioral Research, Eindhoven, The Netherlands, pp. 192–195 (2010)
32. FFmpeg. https://ffmpeg.org. Accessed 31 July 2022
33. Multi-task Cascaded Convolutional Networks (MTCNN) via Deepface. https://github.com/serengil/deepface. Accessed 31 July 2022
34. Kaggle facial expression recognition challenge in 2013. https://www.kaggle.com/c/challenges-in-representation-learning-facial-expression-recognition-challenge. Accessed 31 July 2022
35. Audacity. https://www.audacityteam.org. Accessed 31 July 2022
36. Korobov, M.: Morphological analyzer and generator for Russian and Ukrainian languages. In: Khachay, M.Y., Konstantinova, N., Panchenko, A., Ignatov, D.I., Labunets, V.G. (eds.) AIST 2015. CCIS, vol. 542, pp. 320–332. Springer, Cham (2015). https://doi.org/10.1007/978-3-319-26123-2_31
37. LinisCrowd 2015 tone dictionary. http://linis-crowd.org/. Accessed 31 July 2022
38. Kumin, L.: Early Communication Skills for Children with Down Syndrome: A Guide for Parents and Professionals. Woodbine House, Bethesda (2003)
39. Sforza, C., Dellavia, C., Dolci, C., Donetti, E., Ferrario, V.F.: A quantitative three-dimensional assessment of abnormal variations in the facial soft tissues of individuals with Down syndrome. Cleft Palate-Craniofac. J. **42**(4), 410–416 (2005)
40. Zhao, Q., et al.: Automated Down syndrome detection using facial photographs. In: 35th Annual International Conference of the IEEE Engineering in Medicine and Biology Society (EMBC), Osaka, Japan. IEEE Engineering in Medicine and Biology Society, pp. 3670–3673. IEEE (2013)
41. Mittal, A., Gaur, H., Mishra, M.: Detection of Down syndrome using deep facial recognition. In: Chaudhuri, B.B., Nakagawa, M., Khanna, P., Kumar, S. (eds.) Proceedings of 3rd International Conference on Computer Vision and Image Processing. AISC, vol. 1022, pp. 119–130. Springer, Singapore (2020). https://doi.org/10.1007/978-981-32-9088-4_11
42. Kent, R.D., Vorperian, H.K.: Speech impairment in Down syndrome: a review. J. Speech Lang. Hear. Res. **56**(1), 178–210 (2013)
43. Kanamori, G., Witter, M., Brown, J., Williams-Smith, L.: Otolaryngologic manifestations of Down syndrome. Otolaryngol. Clin. North Am. **33**(6), 1285–1292 (2000)

Fake Speech Detection Using Modulation Spectrogram

Raghav Magazine, Ayush Agarwal[✉], Anand Hedge,
and S. R. Mahadeva Prasanna

Department of Electrical Engineering, Indian Institute of Technology Dharwad,
Dharwad 580011, India
{200010042,201081001,200020007,prasanna}@iitdh.ac.in

Abstract. Nowadays, speech technology like automatic speaker verification (ASV) systems can accurately verify the speaker's identity, and hence they are extensively used in biometrics and banks. With the advancements in deep learning, deepFake has become the primary threat to these ASV systems. The researchers keep proposing methods to generate speech with characteristics indistinguishable from the original speech. Various techniques exist that perform fake speech detection, but these methods are oriented toward a specific dataset or the source of the generation of fake speech. In this work, we propose a modulation spectrogram-based fake speech detection. We show the ability of the modulation spectrogram to classify when there is speaker, session, gender, domain, and source of generation variation. The proposed approach is evaluated on CMU-arctic, LJ Speech, and LibreTTS datasets, and classification accuracy is reported. The accuracy score shows that the proposed approach can classify fake speech.

Keywords: Fake speech · Modulation spectrogram · Spectrogram

1 Introduction

Fake speech refers to the speech generated by a human impersonator or automatic impersonation methods like speech synthesis or voice conversion/cloning [5]. Fake speech detection (FSD) focuses on studying the nature of real and impersonated speech signals to identify their differences. Nowadays, deepFake artificial intelligence (AI) technology enables replacing one person's voice with someone else's. It is a great asset in the digital world, but if used maliciously to generate fake audio, it can have a strong and negative social impact [1,2]. For instance, fraudulent users may generate fake speech and try to gain access to systems that need voice-based authentication or service. Also, generate voice messages and spread the same on social networks to create confusion or unrest in society. This poses a challenge for the community to develop countermeasures.

Most of the work in the literature aims to develop an FSD system as a countermeasure. In this direction concerning the generation source, fake speech is

© Springer Nature Switzerland AG 2022
S. R. M. Prasanna et al. (Eds.): SPECOM 2022, LNAI 13721, pp. 451–463, 2022.
https://doi.org/10.1007/978-3-031-20980-2_39

divided into two subgroups: physical access (PA) and logical access (LA) [15]. The fake speech generated through record and replay comes under the physical access category. The fake speech generated through text-to-speech synthesis (TTS), voice conversion (VC), and adversarial framework are termed logical access. To develop the FSD system, the community organized a series of challenges: ASVSpoof2015 [16], ASVSpoof2017 [11], and ASVSpoof2019 [9,15]. In ASVSpoof2015, the challenge focused on developing countermeasures for TTS and VC attacks. ASVSpoof2017 focused on detecting record and replay attacks. In ASVSpoof2019, the focus was on developing countermeasures for physical and logical attacks.

One of the primary goals is to protect automatic speaker verification (ASV) systems from fake speech. Therefore ASVSpoof2021 and ASVSpoof2022 focused on developing ASV systems along with FSD. The challenge summary shows that the proposed countermeasures use either feature-level or model-level exploration to develop FSD systems [4]. Alternatively, in spoof detection, the focus was more on developing countermeasures to PA and LA cases and not going into the details of inherent characteristics of the speech signal to understand how a natural speech is different from that of a spoofed one. The limitation of such an approach is the overfitting of proposed methods for specific datasets [4].

The main objective of this work is to differentiate between real and fake speech without being influenced by any specific type of impersonation and dataset. The nature of the speech signal characteristics is exploited to classify fake and real speech. The earlier work reported in [4] focused on using features like aperiodic parameters (AP), spectral envelope (SP), Mel frequency cepstral coefficient (MFCC), constant Q cepstral coefficients (CQCC), and spectrogram for the detection of fake speech. The synthesized speech using the current deep learning algorithms is accurate enough to generate fake speech like real speech. In Fig. 2 we can see that the speech signal and its corresponding spectrogram are the same for both real and fake speech. Therefore it is challenging to classify real and fake speech using them as the features.

In [17], it has been shown that the phase modulation spectrum can detect the synthesized speech generated from the STRAIGHT [10] algorithm. The motivation was to capture the long-term temporal artefacts in the synthesized speech. In that approach, they created the super vector by concatenating all the frames and then performed principal component analysis (PCA) to reduce the dimension of the super vector. The drawback of this method is that much important information gets lost when the dimensionality is reduced. From Fig. 2 we can see some visible differences in the high modulation frequency ranges. The dimensionality reduction may miss this information and hence give poor detection. In this work, we have used a modulation spectrogram as the feature for the classification task. The primary goal is to classify the fake and real speech generated by the state-of-the-art classifiers. We hypothesize that the modulation spectrogram shows a much better difference than the time-frequency spectrogram as it captures the long-term information. Further, the robustness of the modulation spectrogram feature is tested under various diverse conditions of the dataset. The diversity of the dataset contains session variability, speaker variability, gender variability, domain variability, and synthesizer variability (refer to Sect. 3.1).

The chronological order of the paper are as follows. Section 2 explains the modulation spectrogram extraction process and its motivation to use in fake speech classification. In Sect. 3 we give the experimental setup. Section 4 reports the results for the experiments carried out and in Sect. 5 these results are discussed. Finally we conclude in Sect. 6.

2   Modulation Spectrogram and Motivation

2.1   Generation of Modulation Spectrogram

A modulation spectrogram encodes a signal in terms of the distribution of slow modulations across time and frequency. It is computed in critical-band-wide channels to match the frequency resolution of the auditory system and emphasize spectro-temporal peaks. It represents modulation frequencies in the range of 0–8 Hz, with a peak sensitivity 4 Hz.

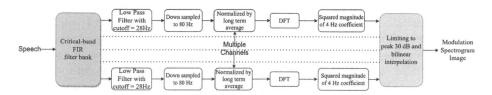

Fig. 1. Block diagram to generate the modulation spectrogram.

Figure 1 explains the steps to generate the modulation spectrogram. The input signal is sampled at 8000 Hz Hz to compute the modulation spectrogram. A finite impulse response (FIR) filter bank is used to analyze critical band-wide channels. The filters are trapezoidal with minimal overlap between adjacent channels. The signal envelope is derived by half-wave rectification and low-pass filtering within each channel. Each channel is down-sampled 80 Hz and normalized by the average envelope level in that channel. The squared magnitudes 4 Hz coefficients of the fast Fourier transform (FFT) are plotted in spectrographic format. The colour encodes the log energy. The effective filter response for 4 Hz component is down by 10 dB at 0 8 Hz. A threshold is used in energy colour mapping. 30 dB is set as the peak of the colour axis, and levels more than 30 dB below the global peak are mapped to the colour of −30 dB. Finally, bilinear smoothing is used to produce the final image [6]. Figure 2 shows the plots of signal and modulation spectrogram of fake and real speech.

2.2   Motivation to Use Modulation Spectrogram for Fake Speech Detection

The modulation spectrogram captures the long-term temporal artefacts in the fake speech. This property was used in [17] to classify the speech generated from the STRAIGHT synthesizer. In that approach, they created the super vector by concatenating all the frames and then performed a principal component analysis (PCA) to reduce the dimension of the super vector. The drawback of this method is that much important information gets lost when the dimensionality is reduced. Figure 2 shows visible differences in the high-frequency regions between the modulation spectrogram of real and fake speech. When dimensionality reduction is applied to the modulation spectrogram, this information might be missed. Therefore, the entire modulation spectrogram information should be used for the classification task.

The spectrogram captures the time-frequency variation of the speech signal. Figure 2 shows the spectrogram plot of real and fake speech. It can be seen that both spectrograms are very similar, and there are no visible differences between them. The structural similarity index measure (SSIM) score is computed to find if there is any difference at the pixel level [8]. SSIM is a measure that compares two images based on luminescence, contrast, and structure. The SSIM measure varies in the range of 0–1. The higher the score is towards 1, the better the similarity. The comparison of spectrogram and modulation spectrogram of real and fake speech is tabulated in Table refSSIM. From the table, we can see that the SSIM score of the modulation spectrogram is very low compared to that of the spectrogram. This shows that the modulation spectrogram carries differences in real and fake speech and can be used for the classification task. In this work, the ability of the modulation spectrogram to classify the real and fake speech under various variations in the dataset is done. These variations are session variability, speaker variability, gender variability, domain variability, and synthesizer variability. The detailed experiments on these variabilities are given in the next section (Table 1).

Table 1. Structural Similarity Index Measure (SSIM) between the spectrogram and modulation spectrogram of real and fake speech.

Feature extractor	Spectrogram	Modulation spectrogram
Similarity index	0.97	0.69

3   Experimental Setup

This work classifies the real and fake speech using modulation spectrogram as the features under various variability present in the dataset. These variabilities are explained below:

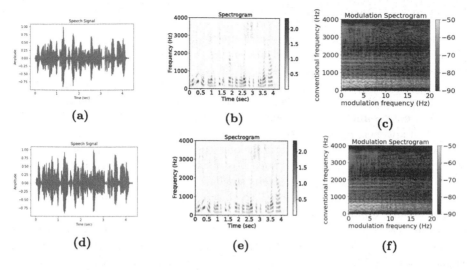

Fig. 2. The comparison between the speech signal ((a) and (d)), spectrogram ((b) and (e)) and modulation spectrogram ((c) and (f)) of real and fake speech. The region in the red block of real speech has difference with that of fake speech. (Color figure online)

3.1 Variabilities

- **Speaker variability:** Speaker variability occurs within speech files of different speakers of the same gender. The cause of variability is the biological uniqueness of the vocal tract of each individual.
- **Session variability:** Session variability occurs when the same speaker is speaking in a different session, i.e., the same person's speech is recorded in two different intervals of time, under similar conditions. The cause of variability is the difference in the state of a person's vocal tract at different points in time.
- **Gender variability:** This variability arises in speech files of speakers of a different gender. Speaker's utterances have unique features like pitch and vocal tract length that might be gender-specific. These gender-specific traits in speech are the cause of variability.
- **Domain variability:** This variability occurs across various speech datasets. It is caused due to differences in recording conditions (background noise, recording sensor, etc.), speakers, and other features which are unique to a certain dataset and absent in other datasets. The cause of variability is the difference in the curation of datasets.
- **Synthesizer Variability:** This variability is present across synthetically generated speech datasets due to the difference in the synthesizer used to generate synthetic speech from the same real speech. The cause of variability is the difference in the technique each text-to-speech (TTS) system uses to generate the synthetic speech.

3.2 Dataset Description

The choice of the dataset for the fake speech detection task is made so that all the five variabilities described above can be introduced. The combination of CMU-Arctic [3], LJ Speech [14], and LibreTTS [20] data in the test set are used to introduce these variabilities. The subset of CMU-Arctic, LJ Speech, and LibreTTS datasets are taken to introduce the domain variability as the recording environment of all three datasets are different. CMU arctic dataset consists of speaker, gender, and session variations. For every speaker, there are 1150 utterances, out of which half belong to one session, and the other half belongs to a different session. LJ speech is a single speaker dataset in which the speaker reads fiction books in various sessions. The LJ speech dataset consists of the session variation. The LibreTTS dataset is the multi-speaker dataset of both male and female gender. This data consists of speaker, gender, and session variations. Table 2 gives the summary of the variabilities in the three datasets. To generate the corresponding fake speech of the datasets mentioned above, a parallel-waveGAN-based text-to-speech (TTS) system is used.

The fake speech is generated from various deep learning-based text-to-speech (TTS) synthesizers to introduce the synthesizer variation. The TTS used for this work are Parallel wave GAN [18], MelGAN [13], MelGAN Large [13], Multi-band MelGAN [19], and HifiGAN [12]. The dataset is publicly available in the following drive[1].

Table 2. Variabilities present in CMU-arctic, LibreTTS, LJ Speech.

Variabilites → Dataset ↓	Speaker	Session	Gender
CMU-arctic	✓	✓	✓
LibreTTS	✓	✓	✓
LJ Speech	✗	✓	✗

3.3 System Description

Modulation spectrogram is extracted from the speech as described in Sect. 2.1. The extracted modulation spectrogram is used as a feature. Resnet-34 is used to perform the classification task. It is a 34-layer convolutional neural network divided into 5 main sections. These sections are further divided into blocks. The block structure is essential for accommodating skip connections. Skip connections are present which connect the input and output of each block. The sections are conv1, conv2_x, conv3_x, conv4_x and conv5_x. The conv1 section has 64 filters with a kernel size of 7×7, and the stride is set to 2, which has the same

---

[1] Fake Speech Dataset.

value in the next layers. Next is the conv2_x section, which has a 3×3 max pooling layer followed by a block containing 2 convolutional layers with 64 filters and a kernel size of 3×3. This block is repeated 3 times. Conv3_x, conv4_x, and conv5_x have similar blocks with 128, 256, and 512 filters, respectively. Also, the blocks are repeated 4, 6, and 3 times respectively. The final layer has average pooling and softmax function. Also, ReLU activation function is used at the end [7] (Fig. 3).

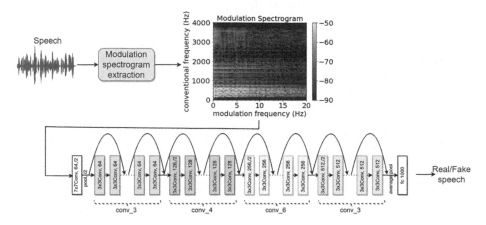

Fig. 3. Real and fake speech classification with modulation spectrogram feature using Resnet-34.

3.4 Training Details

We have conducted the experiments using modulation spectrogram and spectrogram as features. We have done a 90:10 split in the datasets to get the training and testing sets. We have then again split the training data into training and validation sets in the ratio 80:20. We then train the Resnet-34 on these datasets with spectrogram and modulation spectrogram as features. We have set the batch size to be 8. We have trained the Resnet-34 model for 15 epochs and noted the results. We have chosen accuracy as a measure as the data is not skewed.

4 Results

Various levels of experiments based on the variations mentioned in Sect. 3.1 are done and results are reported.

4.1 Trained and Tested on the Same Condition

In this case, the training and testing conditions are kept identical. The train and test set have the same speaker, session, and recording conditions. Spectrogram and modulation spectrogram are used as features, and a comparison between them is shown in Table 3. 2 speakers of the same session of the CMU-arctic and LibreTTS dataset and the same speaker of 2 different sessions of LJ speech are used for experiments. In all the cases, it can be seen that the modulation spectrogram outperforms the spectrogram features. Modulation spectrogram gives good results on LJ Speech, whereas spectrogram gives a chance performance (around 50% accuracy). Since all the variabilities are kept identical in the train and test set, the performance of Table 3 will be used as the baseline. The closer the classification accuracy to the baseline values better the classification.

Table 3. The classification accuracy when the speech utterances in the train and test set belong to the same conditions, i.e. speaker, recording session and recording environment are identical. Spectrogram and modulation-spectrogram are used as features.

Dataset	Training set size	Test set size	Spectrogram	Modulation spectrogram
CMU-arctic (slt speaker)	370	30	93%	96%
CMU-arctic (ksp speaker)	360	40	75%	85%
LJ Speech (LJ049 session)	400	44	50%	100%
LJ Speech (LJ050 session)	502	54	49%	100%
LibriTTS (84 speaker)	171	19	100%	100%
LibriTTS (1462 speaker)	231	27	96%	100%

4.2 Session Variability

Table 4. The classification accuracy for session variation in train and test data using spectrogram and modulation-spectrogram. The performance is shown for 49th and 50th session of LJ speech and the session a and b of CMU arctic dataset.

Feature extractor	Spectrogram		Modulation spectrogram	
Train set	Test set			
	LJ049	LJ050	LJ049	LJ050
LJ049	50%	52%	100%	100%
LJ050	51%	49%	96%	100%
Train set	Test set			
	CMU-arctic(A)	CMU-arctic(B)	CMU-arctic(A)	CMU-arctic(B)
CMU-arctic (A)	95%	80%	100%	100%
CMU-arctic (B)	75%	90%	100%	96%

In this experiment, we trained the model on the data from one of the sessions in the dataset and then tested the data from the other session by the same speaker. This would tell whether the model is vulnerable to the variations in the state of a person's vocal tract when speech is recorded at different points. The results in Table 4 are shown for 2 sessions of the same speaker of LJ speech and CMU-arctic dataset. The results for cross sessions are also shown in which the training and testing data belong to different sessions. It can be seen that the modulation spectrogram has performed better than the spectrogram, even in cross-session conditions.

4.3   Speaker and Gender Variability

The speaker variability experiments are performed to check the ability of the feature and model to classify the fake and real speech in the speaker-independent-/variable case. The speaker independent/variable cases are when the model is trained and tested on different speakers. Two different speakers of the same gender from the LibreTTS dataset (speaker label 84 and 1462) are chosen to perform the experiments. From Table 5 it can be seen that modulation spectrogram can classify in both the cross-speaker conditions whereas spectrogram gives chance level performance when trained for speaker 1462 and tested for 84.

Table 5. The classification accuracy for speaker variability using spectrogram and modulation-spectrogram. Two different speakers of same gender from LibreTTS dataset are chosen to perform the experiments.

Feature extractor	Spectrogram		Modulation spectrogram	
Train set	Test set			
	LibriTTS (84)	LibriTTS (1462)	LibriTTS (84)	LibriTTS (1462)
LibriTTS (84)	100%	88.4%	100%	89.4%
LibriTTS (1462)	50%	96%	100%	100%

Table 6. The classification accuracy for gender variability using spectrogram and modulation-spectrogram. Experiments were performed on the male (ksp) and female (slt) speakers of the CMU-arctic dataset.

Feature extractor	Spectrogram		Modulation spectrogram	
Train set	Test set			
	CMU-arctic (slt)	CMU-arctic (ksp)	CMU-arctic (slt)	CMU-arctic (ksp)
CMU-arctic (slt)	93%	70%	96%	85%
CMU-arctic (ksp)	55%	75%	82.5%	85%

When we vary the gender, a significant drop in the performance for both the features can be seen in Table 6. Experiments were performed on the male (ksp) and female (slt) speakers of the CMU-arctic dataset. These results give us an estimate of how vulnerable these features are to the variations in the pitch frequencies. The degradation can be interpreted as the model looking at some specific frequencies present in the spectrogram/modulation-spectrogram to perform classification. Since the train and test set contains the features of different pitch frequencies, there is degradation in performance.

4.4 Domain Variability

For domain variability analysis, the train and test speech files belong to different datasets. This analysis is done to evaluate whether the features and model performance is independent of the recording conditions. Table 7 shows the result on CMU-arctic, LibreTTS, and LJ Speech datasets. These data are recorded in different environments and have domain variability. The result in the table shows that there is a degradation in performance to classify when there is a change in recording conditions across the dataset.

Table 7. The classification accuracy for domain variability using spectrogram and modulation-spectrogram. Experiments were performed on the CMU-arctic, LibreTTS, and LJ Speech recorded in different recording conditions.

Feature extractor	Spectrogram			Modulation spectrogram		
Train set	Test set					
	CMU-arctic	LibriTTS	LJ Speech	CMU-arctic	LibriTTS	LJ Speech
CMU-arctic	80%	59%	55%	90%	53%	50%
LibriTTS	65%	82%	61%	83%	100%	72%
LJ Speech	52%	49%	53%	56%	67%	100%

4.5 Synthesizer Variability

In the synthesizer variability scenario, we want to study if the model and feature can distinguish equally well between real speech and fake speech when the train and test set have fake speech generated from different synthesizers. The purpose is to evaluate the system's ability to classify irrespective of the source of generation of the fake speech.

From comparing Tables 8 and 9 is can be seen that modulation-spectrogram outperforms the spectrogram. When the variability is introduced for the spectrogram, it begins to give a chance level performance with an accuracy of around 50%-60% for most cases. However, the modulation spectrogram performs better with accuracy predominantly in the range 70%-80%. This shows that the modulation spectrogram can extract features that are less vulnerable to synthesizer variability as compared to the spectrogram.

Table 8. The classification accuracy for synthesizer variability using spectrogram. Fake speech was generated using Parallel WaveGAN, MelGAN, MelGAN Large, Multi-band MelGAN, and HifiGAN for 49th session of LJ Speech.

Feature extractor	Spectrogram				
Train set	Test set				
	Parallel wave GAN	Mel GAN	Mel GAN large	Multi-band Mel GAN	Hifi GAN
Parallel wave GAN	50%	50.0%	50.0%	50.0%	50.0%
Mel GAN	50.0%	97.7%	95.45%	52.27%	47.72%
Mel GAN large	51.5%	69.5%	100%	50.0%	50.5%
Multi-band Mel GAN	61.36%	50.0%	52.27%	68.18%	45.45%
Hifi GAN	56.81%	59.09%	56.81%	43.18%	52.27%

Table 9. The classification accuracy for synthesizer variability using modulation spectrogram. Fake speech was generated using Parallel WaveGAN, MelGAN, MelGAN Large, Multi-band MelGAN, and HifiGAN for 49th session of LJ Speech.

Feature extractor	Modulation spectrogram				
Train set	Test set				
	Parallel wave GAN	Mel GAN	Mel GAN large	Multi-band Mel GAN	Hifi GAN
Parallel wave GAN	100%	65%	70%	60%	65%
Mel GAN	70%	96%	75%	72%	80%
Mel GAN large	75%	72%	95%	71%	75%
Multi-band Mel GAN	72%	80%	82%	96%	74%
Hifi GAN	77%	82%	80%	79%	100%

5 Discussion

As we can see from the results, Resnet-34 is performing well using modulation spectrogram, as an input feature, across gender, session, and speaker variability. Domain variability poses a challenge to the fake speech detection models. Though the model is able to efficiently distinguish between fake and real speech within a certain domain, it fails to replicate the same in a different domain. This is true for both modulation spectrogram and spectrogram. The modulation spectrogram proves to be a better feature from speech as compared to a spectrogram in the case of synthesizer variations. This is probably due to the extra data preprocessing steps that are carried out while computing the modulation spectrogram, before feeding it into the Resnet-34-based classifier.

6 Conclusion and Future Work

In this work, we identified the shortcoming of the existing modulation spectrogram-based fake speech classifier. The existing method has three drawbacks: (1) It performs dimensionality reduction of modulation spectrogram, and this may miss important information present at higher frequencies (2) The previous methods were not tested with the variations present in the datasets and (3) The previous methods are not general, as they were dependent towards the source of generation of fake speech. To solve the dimensionality reduction issue, we propose to use the entire modulation spectrogram as features on a Resnet-34-based CNN. We have tested the system on various variabilities like the speaker, session, gender, and domain. It was found that the proposed method was able to classify for speaker, session, and gender variations but showed some degradation in domain variation. The classification ability of the proposed method in the source/synthesizer independent scenario is done. The modulation spectrogram feature could classify the fake speech from most synthesizers.

This study has opened several avenues for future work. The degradation in the performance due to domain variability has to be addressed. The source independence is only tested when fake speech is generated from text-to-speech synthesizers. In the future, we will also test the performance when fake speech is generated from a voice conversion system. Due to the success of the Resnet-34-based classifier in speaker and language identification tasks, we have used it for fake speech classification in this work. In the future, we will implement other CNN architectures and improve the accuracy. In the current work, we have used accuracy as the feature. In further experiments, we intend to test the robustness of the proposed feature over the automatic speaker verification (ASV) system such that the ASV system does not get fooled by malicious attacks.

Acknowledgments. This work is funded by Ministry of Electronics and Information Technology (MeitY), Govt. of India under the project title "Fake Speech detection using Deep Learning Framework".

References

1. Agarwal, A., Swain, A., Prasanna, S.R.M.: Speaker anonymization for machines using sinusoidal model. In: 2022 IEEE International Conference on Signal Processing and Communications (SPCOM). IEEE (2022)
2. Agarwal, A., et al.: Significance of prosody modification in privacy preservation on speaker verification. In: 2022 National Conference on Communications (NCC). IEEE (2022)
3. Black, A.W.: CMU wilderness multilingual speech dataset. In: ICASSP 2019–2019 IEEE International Conference on Acoustics, Speech and Signal Processing (ICASSP). IEEE (2019)
4. Balamurali, B.T., et al.: Toward robust audio spoofing detection: a detailed comparison of traditional and learned features. IEEE Access **7**, 84229–84241 (2019)
5. Gao, Y., et al.: Detection and evaluation of human and machine generated speech in spoofing attacks on automatic speaker verification systems. In: 2021 IEEE Spoken Language Technology Workshop (SLT). IEEE (2021)
6. Greenberg, S., Kingsbury, B.E.D.: The modulation spectrogram: in pursuit of an invariant representation of speech. In: 1997 IEEE International Conference on Acoustics, Speech, and Signal Processing, vol. 3. IEEE (1997)
7. He, K., et al.: Deep residual learning for image recognition. In: Proceedings of the IEEE Conference on Computer Vision and Pattern Recognition (2016)
8. Hore, A., Ziou, D.: Image quality metrics: PSNR vs. SSIM. In: 2010 20th International Conference on Pattern Recognition. IEEE (2010)
9. Jung, J., et al.: SASV challenge 2022: a spoofing aware speaker verification challenge evaluation plan. arXiv preprint arXiv:2201.10283 (2022)
10. Kawahara, H.: Speech representation and transformation using adaptive interpolation of weighted spectrum: vocoder revisited. In: 1997 IEEE International Conference on Acoustics, Speech, and Signal Processing, vol. 2. IEEE (1997)
11. Kinnunen, T., et al.: The ASVspoof 2017 challenge: assessing the limits of replay spoofing attack detection (2017)
12. Kong, J., Kim, J., Bae, J.: HIFI-GAN: generative adversarial networks for efficient and high fidelity speech synthesis. Adv. Neural. Inf. Process. Syst. **33**, 17022–17033 (2020)

13. Kumar, K., et al.: MelGAN: generative adversarial networks for conditional wave-form synthesis. In: Advances in Neural Information Processing Systems,vol. 32 (2019)
14. Ito, K.: The LJ speech dataset (2017). https://keithito.com/LJ-Speech-Dataset/
15. Todisco, M., et al.: ASVspoof 2019: future horizons in spoofed and fake audio detection. arXiv preprint arXiv:1904.05441 (2019)
16. Wu, Z., et al.: ASVspoof 2015: the first automatic speaker verification spoofing and countermeasures challenge. In: Sixteenth Annual Conference of the International Speech Communication Association (2015)
17. Wu, Z., et al.: Synthetic speech detection using temporal modulation feature. In: 2013 IEEE International Conference on Acoustics, Speech and Signal Processing. IEEE (2013)
18. Yamamoto, R., Song, E., Kim, J.-M.: Parallel WaveGAN: a fast waveform genera-tion model based on generative adversarial networks with multi-resolution spectro-gram. In: ICASSP 2020–2020 IEEE International Conference on Acoustics, Speech and Signal Processing (ICASSP). IEEE (2020)
19. Yang, G., et al.: Multi-band MelGAN: faster waveform generation for high-quality text-to-speech. In: 2021 IEEE Spoken Language Technology Workshop (SLT). IEEE (2021)
20. Zen, H., et al.: LibriTTS: a corpus derived from LibriSpeech for text-to-speech. arXiv preprint arXiv:1904.02882 (2019)

Self-Configuring Genetic Programming Feature Generation in Affect Recognition Tasks

Danila Mamontov[1,2]($\boxtimes$), Wolfgang Minker[1], and Alexey Karpov[3]

[1] Ulm University, Ulm, Germany
{danila.mamontov,wolfgang.minker}@uni-ulm.de
[2] ITMO, Saint-Peterburg, Russia
[3] St. Petersburg Institute for Informatics and Automation of the Russian Academy of Sciences, St. Petersburg Federal Research Center of the Russian Academy of Sciences (SPC RAS), St. Petersburg, Russia
karpov@iias.spb.su

Abstract. Feature extraction is one of the main parts of Machine Learning. Regardless of the nature of solving tasks, developers either need to use standard sets of features for a certain problem or try to generate their own features from raw data. In this paper, we present the genetic programming (GP) algorithm for feature generation issues in affect recognition tasks. We tested this approach in human affect recognition tasks on two corpora the WESAD and the RECOLA. We also used classical methods for feature space reduction Principal Component Analysis (PCA) and Independent Component Analysis (ICA). The results show the effectiveness of the GP approach in comparison with PCA and ICA and its capability to significantly reduce the feature space saving a high performance of classifiers in affect recognition tasks.

Keywords: Evolutionary algorithms · Feature space reduction · Heart rate variability · Low-level descriptors

1 Introduction

In the field of Machine Learning (ML), on the one hand, there are end-to-end systems with raw signals as an output, we obtain a final solution for a problem. On the other hand, classical algorithms operate on pre-extracted features. For some issues, end-to-end approaches are preferable, but there are situations when it is not possible to use such systems due to the lack of explainability of the given solution [6]. An example is a neural network (NN), which is essentially a black-box model. A weak point of black-box models is that we cannot explain exactly due to their complexity why the model made a particular decision. While for certain issues, the importance of understanding how the model works is paramount. Example tasks are related to healthcare, where we must clearly understand how and why machine learning models draw certain medical

© Springer Nature Switzerland AG 2022
S. R. M. Prasanna et al. (Eds.): SPECOM 2022, LNAI 13721, pp. 464–476, 2022.
https://doi.org/10.1007/978-3-031-20980-2_40

conclusions [10]. Another important factor is the amount of data needed to train and operate the models. In the modern world, the number of tasks resolving by ML algorithms is growing rapidly and the necessity for adequate use, collection, and storage of data are increasing. As an example, we may consider human affect recognition. In some cases, this problem is successfully solved when analyzing audio-video modalities using deep neural networks, but if we set the task of affect recognition in real conditions when a human does ordinary life being at home, at work, or in a car, the usage of such modalities becomes more difficult. We are forced to reduce the amount of collected and stored data and to use other modalities like physiological signals from wearable devices. One way to minimize the necessity for collecting and storing large amounts of data is to reduce the feature space while at the same time saving a high performance of models. This can be done by selecting features or generating new ones by projecting them into a smaller space.

In this paper, we suggest a feature generation approach based on genetic programming (GP) with a modified fitness function. Affect recognition tasks from the WESAD and the RECOLA corpora [17,20] are used to test the proposed method. This paper is organized as follows. In Sect. 2, we describe related works. In Sect. 3, we introduce a genetic programming feature generation algorithm and explain it in detail. Experimental results and discussion are given in Sect. 4. In Sect. 5, we provide conclusion and further plans.

2   Related Work

Previously, there were researches on the possibility of the application of evolutionary algorithms for automatic feature generation, particularly genetic programming. Gue et al. in [8] applied this to the issue of mechanical fault classification and showed the ability of GP to generate features from an original data set. Smith and Bull investigated GP not only for feature generation problems but also for feature selection [22]. More recently, Tran et al. researched the GP approach for the feature generation on high-dimensional data [23,24]. At the same time, the capabilities of GP are not limited to the generation of features, a special way of the solution encoding in GP allows us to search for structures of any kind. For example, structures of neural networks [14] or completely composite models [15]. In general, feature extraction and representation are important aspects of data mining, so there are many types of research. For example, Kaya et al. suggested using Fischer vectors to encode the low-level descriptors (LLD) for paralinguistic analysis, and in combination with cascaded normalization, they significantly improved the previously achieved performance for this task [9]. In turn, Lopez et al. successfully applied Fischer vectors to encode Mel Frequency Cepstral Coefficients (MFCC) of a speech signal for assessing Parkinson's disease [2]. There is also another popular technique for audio feature representation called Bag-of-Audio-Words (BoAW). Although BoAW is less effective than Fisher vector since BoAW is a particular case of Fisher vectors, it has been used in plenty of studies [1,7,16,19]. Meanwhile, in this paper, we take the classical Principal

Component Analysis (PCA) and the Independent Component Analysis (ICA) methods and compare their effectiveness with our proposed GP-based feature generation technique.

3   Method

In this section, we cover the genetic programming algorithm description as well as its application for feature generation when solving classification issues. Then we describe two corpora that have been used for testing our approach, including the process of preprocessing and task definitions.

3.1   Genetic Programming

The genetic programming algorithm was introduced by Koza in 1992 in [12]. GP is a stochastic optimization algorithm and belongs to the class of Evolutionary Algorithms (EAs), which are based on Charles Darwin's ideas about natural selection. In GP the solution of an optimization task is encoded by a tree. Each of the trees represents an individual and many such individuals form a population. The search for a solution is carried out using the selection, crossing, and mutation operators. Each individual is characterized by fitness, individuals with greater fitness are more likely to become a parent of the next generation. The selection operator selects individuals as parents for crossing and produces a new generation, according to their fitness. It is one of the most important stages of GP, which to a high extent determines the efficiency of the entire algorithm. Crossover is the operator by which the genetic information of the parents is mixed. The mutation is an operator that allows us to add diversity to existing genetic information or restore lost information. The higher the probability of mutation, the greater the spread of points in the search space. Regularly we should select parameters of operators manually, but in the scope of this work, we used the self-configured genetic programming modification proposed in [21].

As we previously mentioned the usual way for solution encoding is using trees and they can contain $n - ary$ functions which take n arguments. In our research we use binary and unary functions, thus our trees have binary and unary nodes. In Fig. 1 we can see how a tree represents a solution obtained by GP using an example of a formula generated for a classification task on the RECOLA corpus. Equation 4 is its decoded representation.

Feature Generation Using GP. Figure 2 shows a detailed description of a GP application for a feature generation problem. In the first stage, we need to extract features from raw data using already known formulas for each specific task. For example, heart rate variability (HRV) indicators for heart rate signals or spectral characteristics for an audio signal. Then we split the whole data into three parts train, test, and development. The development part is used by genetic programming for searching for new formulas which are non-linear combinations of previously extracted features. Then we apply these formulas and generate new

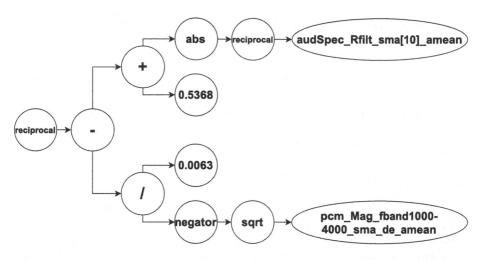

Fig. 1. An example of a tree encoding a formula obtained by GP. This representation corresponds to a formula obtained on the two-classes RECOLA task.

features from train and test sets. We named them GP Train and GP Test. In the end, we train our models on Train and GP Train sets and test them respectively on Test and GP Test sets.

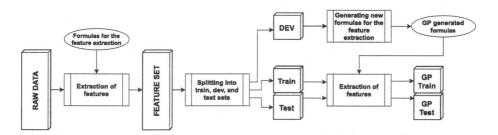

Fig. 2. The pipeline of an application of Genetic Programming for the feature generation problem.

Fitness Function. The fitness function controls and navigates the evolution process in genetic programming. It is a crucial aspect of the algorithm. Therefore, we should construct it accurately to gain desirable results. In our case, we want to generate features that can distance the centers of classes, as well as reduce their intersection. Thus, we take the Fisher criterion and calculate it for any two i and j classes as follows:

$$\overrightarrow{fisher_{ij}} = \frac{\left|\widehat{X}_i - \widehat{X}_j\right|}{\sqrt{\sigma_i^2 + \sigma_j^2}}, \; where \; i \neq j \tag{1}$$

Having the vector of fisher criteria for all pairwise classes, we define the fitness function as the sum of the minimum and mean values of this vector, but taking into account that the minimum value will contribute more to the fitness:

$$Fitness = min(\overrightarrow{fisher_{ij}}) + 0.01 * mean(\overrightarrow{fisher_{ij}}) \qquad (2)$$

In [8] Guo et al. defined the fitness function through Fisher criteria as well.

Therefore, using such a fitness function allows us to obtain from GP a solution that theoretically increases distances among all classes. But what if we need to generate more than one solution, several features in our case? Just running GP several times could provide us with solutions that are strongly correlated to each other and do not add additional value to the final solution. Hence, we need to take into account solutions generated from previous GP runs during evaluating fitnesses when running GP for the second and further times. We calculate the Pearson correlation between a current solution and all previously obtained by GP features and incorporate it into Eq. 1 as follows:

$$Fitness = min(\overrightarrow{fisher_{ij}}) + 0.01 * mean(\overrightarrow{fisher_{ij}}) - max(|\overrightarrow{pearson_{ij}}|) + 1 \quad (3)$$

We also added +1 to the fitness to avoid the situation when it becomes negative.

Terminal and Functional Sets. The functional set consists of the following functions:

$+, -, /, *, power\ of\ 2, sqrt, cos, sin, ln, reciprocal, abs, negator, sigmoid, tanh, hyperb.$

The Terminal set consists of variables that represent original features, and random numbers from -1 to 1.

3.2 WESAD Corpus Description

The Multimodal Dataset for Wearable Stress and Affect Detection (WESAD) dataset is collected in Germany in 2018 [20]. The experiment involves the data from 15 graduated students and the goal is to investigate the possibility of using physiological signals to detect affective states. The WESAD contains three types of them (amusement, neutral, and stress). The authors use well-known the Trier Social Stress Test (TSST) to make participants feel stress [11]. For the amusement stage, several funny videos are used. The baseline (neutral) state was recorded, while subjects are sitting or standing and reading magazines. This corpus contains signals of various modalities: Photoplethysmography (PPG), Electrodermal Activity (EDA), Acceleration (ACC), and Temperature. We used only the first of them. We extracted a classical set of HRV features from a raw PPG signal recorded by the Empatica E4 smart wristband. Then we split the whole data into three parts. The first part of development consists of samples from six participants and it has been used for the feature generation by GP. The rest nine participants are used for training and testing parts. We followed the same procedure as the corpus's authors performed, therefore, we did Leave-One-Subject-Out Cross-Validation (LOSO CV). In more detail, all indicators are described in [13]. Following the author's definition, we distinguish two tasks on the WESAD. The first one we call the three-classes WESAD task. The goal is to predict one amusement, neutral, or stress class. For the second task amusement and neutral classes are merged into one class. Further, we call this the two-classes WESAD task.

Baseline Feature Set Description. We used the most common way for feature extraction in the case of heart rate signal processing. We extracted Heart Rate Variability (HRV) indicators in time, frequency, and geometrical domains from the PPG signal using Python Heart Rate Analysis Toolkit (HeartPy) [4,5]. Time-domain features include: beats per minute (BPM), inter-beat interval (IBI), the standard deviation of RR intervals (SDNN), the standard deviation of successive differences (SDSD), root mean square of successive differences (RMSSD), the proportion of successive differences above 20 ms (pNN20), the proportion of successive differences above 50 ms (pNN50), median absolute deviation of RR intervals (MAD). Frequency domain features consist of a low-frequency, frequency spectrum between 0.05 and 0.15 Hz (LF); a high-frequency, frequency spectrum between 0.15 and 0.5 Hz (HF); and the ratio of high frequency to low frequency (HF/LF). A function that takes peak-peak intervals and computes Poincare parameters: standard deviation perpendicular to identity line (SD1), standard deviation along identity line (SD2), area of ellipse described by SD1 and SD2, SD1/SD2 ratio. In more detail, all indicators are described in [13].

To compare our results with a baseline from [20] in the most accurate way, all features are extracted using the rolling window with a width of 1 min and an overlap of 25 ms. Extracted features are standardized with zero mean and unit variance.

3.3 RECOLA Corpus Description

The RECOLA corpus is multimodal and includes such modalities as Video, Audio, Electrocardiograms (ECG), and EDA [17]. The total duration of recordings is about three hours and fifty minutes. All of the participants are French native speakers and their behavior is spontaneous due to the nature of the experiment. Originally the authors labeled the data using a circumplex model of affect [18]. For further investigation, we moved to a categorical description and defined two classification tasks. The first one is the two-classes RECOLA task where we set the low arousal class for $arousal < 0$ and the high arousal class for $arousal >= 0$. For the second task we took valence labels as well and defined four quadrants from the arousal valence space as classes (ex. $arousal > 0$ and $valence > 0$ is the high arousal high valence class). Further, we call this task simply the four-classes RECOLA task. For both tasks, we split the corpus into three parts as well. Each part consists of six participants. In contrast to the WESAD tasks, we did not perform LOSO CV, since there are no baseline results with the same task definition as we did on the RECOLA corpus. Hence, the train and test parts are fixed from the beginning.

Baseline Feature Set Description. We exploit only the audio modality of the RECOLA and used a baseline acoustic feature set of 130 attributes named "ComParE 2013" with the low-level descriptors from the 2013 INTERSPEECH challenge. Features are extracted from raw audio signals with a frequency 25 Hz. This is made via the openSMILE toolkit [3]. All features are standardized to mean and unit variance.

4   Results and Discussion

Standard machine learning algorithms such as Decision Tree (DT), Random Forest (RF), AdaBoost(AB), Linear Discriminant Analysis (LDA), and K-Nearest Neighbors (KNN) are used as classifiers. Tests are performed on complete feature sets, feature sets generated by GP, and finally on features obtained from PCA and ICA which are the most popular ways for feature space reduction. As we previously mentioned, we use the self-configuration for GP and are not required to specify GP parameters except for the size of the population, the number of generations, and the maximal depth of trees. Therefore, we set them at 400, 500, and 5 respectively.

The WESAD Corpus. Before the evaluation of GP feature generation effectiveness we compared the baseline results from [20] and our results on the complete HRV feature set without splitting the data into parts, but using LOSO CV. Table 1 presents the achieved performance for two and three-classes WESAD tasks. As we can note, the achieved efficiency of the classifiers on extracted features is higher in comparison to the baseline. The difference can be explained by differences in feature sets, because of using different tools for the extraction.

Further, we move to our previously defined tasks. We reduced the feature space using PCA and ICA to only one feature and also with PCA to seven or eight features saving 95% of the initial variance depending on LOSO CV folds. Then we compressed the feature space to one feature by GP for both tasks. The following equations $-ibi + sin(pnn20)$ and $ibi - sin(pnn50)$, which are non-linear representations of original features, are generated by GP for the two-classes WESAD task and the three-classes WESAD task, respectively. Table 2 contains averaged LOSO CV scores on all feature sets. The results indicate that classifiers gain a higher macro-f1 score on WESAD tasks operating GP-generated feature sets than using PCA or ICA feature sets in all cases. In both tasks, LDA with GP features achieved the highest performance among all classifiers.

The RECOLA Corpus. On the RECOLA corpus, we tested several options. We reduced the feature space to one, three, and five dimensions for both tasks applying PCA and GP, since using only one feature did not provide comparable

Table 1. Comparison of the classifier's efficiency in the macro-f1 score when using the complete set of extracted features by us and baseline results from the authors of the WESAD corpus.

The two-classes WESAD task						
Name	Number of Features	DT	RF	AB	LDA	KNN
Baseline	20	78.27	81.35	81.23	**83.08***	78.94
Our	16	83.38	83.65	83.97	**84.69**	83.72
The three-classes WESAD task						
Name	Number of Features	DT	RF	AB	LDA	KNN
Baseline	20	51.15	53.83	53.29	**54.72**	50.97
Our	16	54.48	**56.60**	52.40	53.68	55.94

*Bold values are the highest among all with the same number of features.

performance with the baseline. Also, we applied PCA saving 95% of the initial variance that gave us 54 features. Table 3 contains achieved results for all sets of features.

As we can see from Table 3 the best score is achieved on baseline feature sets for both tasks. Nevertheless, GP generated feature sets that allow us to gain almost the same high score as baseline results, exploiting only five features. At the same time, PCA provides worse performance if we take five features. Moreover, even if we save 95% of the initial variance with the reduction to 54 attributes in the four-classes RECOLA task applying PCA the performance is lower than with the five features generated by GP. It is the same for the two-classes RECOLA task and the best result with only one feature generated by GP is higher than the best score on 54 attributes from PCA.

We do not provide all generated features on the RECOLA, because of space limitations, but we do it for cases of reduction to one feature. For the two-classes RECOLA task, the following feature is obtained:

$$feature = \frac{1}{\frac{-\sqrt{x102}}{0.0063} - (\left|\frac{1}{x20}\right| + 0.5368)} \tag{4}$$

In Eq. 4 the variable $x102$ is $pcm\_Mag\_fband1000 - 4000\_sma\_de\_amean$ and $x20$ is $audSpec\_Rfilt\_sma[10]\_amean$. For the four-classes RECOLA task, the obtained feature is:

$$feature = (sigmoid(\frac{0.0666}{x17}) * hyperb(sigmoid(hyperb(x6))))^2 \tag{5}$$

$x17$ is the attribute named $audSpec\_Rfilt\_sma[7]\_ameannumeric$ and $x6$ is $audspec\_lengthL1norm\_sma\_amean$ numeric. The variable numbers are the same as their sequence number in the feature set from the OpenSMILE toolkit.

Table 2. Comparison of the classifier's efficiency in the macro-f1 score when using features generated by genetic programming and features obtained by PCA on the WESAD corpus.

The two-classes WESAD task						
Name	Number of Features	DT	RF	AB	LDA	KNN
Our	16	83.34	84.21	**84.55***	83.47	84.06
PCA (95%)	7–8	81.49	81.85	82.18	**83.00**	82.13
PCA	1	68.85	68.36	70.38	70.31	70.37
ICA	1	67.37	67.87	76.42	70.31	70.33
GP	1	83.01	81.78	83.06	**86.71**	82.80
The three-classes WESAD task						
Name	Number of Features	DT	RF	AB	LDA	KNN
Our	16	53.05	**54.46**	54.96	52.76	54.88
PCA (95%)	7–8	53.20	53.40	54.16	52.63	**54.19**
PCA	1	46.00	45.68	45.99	46.96	46.08
ICA	1	45.20	45.45	46.84	46.96	46.43
GP	1	54.17	53.89	54.15	**55.02**	54.26

*Bold values are the highest among all with the same number of features.

Including such functions as *sigmoid*, *tanh*, *hyperb* into the functional set of GP, brings our approach closer to generating neural network structures, since these functions are used in NNs as activation ones. Any NNs are also a nonlinear transformation of the input. The usage of embeddings from the last layers can also be called a reduction of the feature space. But unlike GP, NNs do not allow us to visualize these transformations in the form of simple equations. In cases where the original set of features contains a lot of redundant indicators, GP simply does not include them in generated formulas, while in NN, even if the feature is superfluous, it must be presented in the data set when the trained NN is used further.

If we look at Table 2 and Table 3 we can note that Linear Discriminant Analysis achieves in all cases better performance than other classifiers on features generated by GP. Arguably, this can happen, because LDA is a generalization of the Fisher linear discriminant. If we define the fitness function for GP through Fisher criteria, we use the same Fisher Discriminant Analysis Optimization.

Table 3. Comparison of the classifier's efficiency in the macro-recall score when using features generated by genetic programming and features obtained by PCA on the RECOLA corpus.

The two-classes RECOLA task						
Name	Number of Features	DT	RF	AB	LDA	KNN
Baseline	130	62.18	**73.22** *	72.56	70.70	68.13
PCA (95%)	54	61.48	**70.87**	70.05	68.45	68.20
PCA	1	54.17	54.19	50.00	50.00	55.02
ICA	1	54.73	54.15	49.99	50.00	55.02
GP	1	61.14	61.16	**71.93**	71.79	65.88
PCA	3	59.88	65.46	63.13	49.89	64.38
ICA	3	59.88	65.64	68.94	49.89	64.55
GP	3	59.92	65.90	70.42	**72.21**	63.90
PCA	5	61.29	68.61	64.68	49.99	66.97
ICA	5	61.62	68.60	66.88	49.99	66.98
GP	5	62.84	71.79	72.71	**72.73**	68.35
The four-classes RECOLA task						
Name	Number of Features	DT	RF	AB	LDA	KNN
Baseline	130	31.28	**36.82**	36.30	34.52	33.37
PCA (95%)	54	31.02	34.31	**34.38**	33.67	33.50
PCA	1	26.86	26.87	25.00	25.00	27.00
ICA	1	26.68	26.94	25.00	25.00	27.00
GP	1	29.26	29.26	32.01	**33.25**	30.20
PCA	3	29.53	32.43	31.26	24.97	31.35
ICA	3	30.57	32.33	33.36	24.97	31.36
GP	3	29.61	32.24	33.78	**34.15**	31.49
PCA	5	31.16	34.12	34.44	24.99	32.66
ICA	5	31.08	33.91	32.65	24.99	32.68
GP	5	30.91	34.54	36.10	**36.77**	32.63

*Bold values are the highest among all with the same number of features.

5   Conclusion

In this study, we proposed a method for automatic feature generation based on genetic programming. In particular, we modified the fitness function so that it is possible to generate non-correlating features after several GP launches. The results indicate superior performance of the proposed method over the features obtained by PCA and ICA. On the WESAD corpus, GP-generated features outperformed the baseline feature set for both tasks. We plan to continue experiments taking in the scope of work more corpora for affect recognition issues. Also, we expect to improve the approach by adjusting the fitness function and the procedure of generation of several features, which is done now only by adding the Pearson correlation coefficient.

Acknowledgments. Work of A. Karpov is supported by the RSF (project No. 22-11-00321).

References

1. Cummins, N., Amiriparian, S., Ottl, S., Gerczuk, M., Schmitt, M., Schuller, B.: Multimodal bag-of-words for cross domains sentiment analysis. In: ICASSP, IEEE International Conference on Acoustics, Speech and Signal Processing - Proceedings. vol. 2018-April, pp. 4954–4958. Institute of Electrical and Electronics Engineers Inc. (sep 2018). https://doi.org/10.1109/ICASSP.2018.8462660
2. Egas López, J.V., Orozco-Arroyave, J.R., Gosztolya, G.: Assessing Parkinson's disease from speech using fisher vectors. In: Proceedings of the Annual Conference of the International Speech Communication Association, INTERSPEECH. vol. 2019-Septe, pp. 3063–3067. International Speech Communication Association (2019). https://doi.org/10.21437/Interspeech. 2019–2217
3. Eyben, F., Wöllmer, M., Schuller, B.: OpenSMILE - The Munich versatile and fast open-source audio feature extractor. In: MM'10 - Proceedings of the ACM Multimedia 2010 International Conference. pp. 1459–1462 (2010). https://doi.org/10.1145/1873951.1874246
4. van Gent, P., Farah, H., van Nes, N., van Arem, B.: Analysing noisy driver physiology real-time using off-the-shelf sensors: Heart rate analysis software from the taking the fast lane project. Journal of Open Research Software 7(1), – (oct 2019). https://doi.org/10.5334/jors.241, https://doi.org/10.5334/jors.241
5. van Gent, P., Farah, H., van Nes, N., van Arem, B.: HeartPy: A novel heart rate algorithm for the analysis of noisy signals. Transportation Research Part F: Traffic Psychology and Behaviour 66, 368–378 (oct 2019). https://doi.org/10.1016/j.trf.2019.09.015
6. Glasmachers, T.: Limits of End-to-End Learning. In: Zhang, M.L., Noh, Y.K. (eds.) Proceedings of the Ninth Asian Conference on Machine Learning. Proceedings of Machine Learning Research, vol. 77, pp. 17–32. PMLR (2017), http://proceedings.mlr.press/v77/glasmachers17a.html
7. Gosztolya, G.: Using Fisher Vector and Bag-of-Audio-Words representations to identify Styrian dialects, sleepiness, baby & orca sounds (2019)
8. Guo, H., Jack, L.B., Nandi, A.K.: Feature generation using genetic programming with application to fault classification. IEEE Transactions on Systems, Man, and Cybernetics, Part B: Cybernetics 35(1), 89–99 (feb 2005). https://doi.org/10.1109/TSMCB.2004.841426, https://ieeexplore.ieee.org/document/1386429
9. Kaya, H., Karpov, A.A., Salah, A.A.: Fisher vectors with cascaded normalization for paralinguistic analysis. In: Proceedings of the Annual Conference of the International Speech Communication Association, INTERSPEECH. vol. 2015-Janua, pp. 909–913 (2015). https://doi.org/10.21437/interspeech.2015-193
10. Khedkar, S., Gandhi, P., Shinde, G., Subramanian, V.: Deep Learning and Explainable AI in Healthcare Using EHR. pp. 129–148. Springer, Cham (2020). https://doi.org/10.1007/978-3-030-33966-1_7, https://link.springer.com/chapter/10.1007/978-3-030-33966-1_7

11. Kirschbaum, C., Pirke, K.M., Hellhammer, D.H.: The 'Trier social stress test' - A tool for investigating psychobiological stress responses in a laboratory setting. In: Neuropsychobiology. vol. 28, pp. 76–81. Karger Publishers (1993). https://doi.org/10.1159/000119004, https://www.karger.com/Article/FullText/119004

12. Koza, J.R., Koza, J.R.: Genetic programming: on the programming of computers by means of natural selection, vol. 1. MIT press (1992)

13. Malik, M., John Camm, A., Thomas Bigger, J., Breithardt, G., Cerutti, S., Cohen, R.J., Coumel, P., Fallen, E.L., Kennedy, H.L., Kleiger, R.E., Lombardi, F., Malliani, A., Moss, A.J., Rottman, J.N., Schmidt, G., Schwartz, P.J., Singer, D.H.: Heart rate variability: Standards of measurement, physiological interpretation, and clinical use. Circulation **93**(5), 1043–1065 (mar 1996). https://doi.org/10.1161/01.cir.93.5.1043, https://www.ahajournals.org/doi/abs/10.1161/01.CIR.93.5.1043

14. Mamontov, D., Polonskaia, I., Skorokhod, A., Semenkin, E., Kessler, V., Schwenker, F.: Evolutionary Algorithms for the Design of Neural Network Classifiers for the Classification of Pain Intensity. In: Lecture Notes in Computer Science (including subseries Lecture Notes in Artificial Intelligence and Lecture Notes in Bioinformatics), vol. 11377 LNAI, pp. 84–100 (2019). https://doi.org/10.1007/978-3-030-20984-1_8, http://link.springer.com/10.1007/978-3-030-20984-1_8

15. Nikitin, N.O., Polonskaia, I.S., Vychuzhanin, P., Barabanova, I.V., Kalyuzhnaya, A.V.: Structural Evolutionary Learning for Composite Classification Models. In: Procedia Computer Science. vol. 178, pp. 414–423. Elsevier B.V. (2020). https://doi.org/10.1016/j.procs.2020.11.043

16. Pokorny, F.B., Graf, F., Pernkopf, F., Schuller, B.W.: Detection of negative emotions in speech signals using bags-of-audio-words. In: 2015 International Conference on Affective Computing and Intelligent Interaction, ACII 2015. pp. 879–884. Institute of Electrical and Electronics Engineers Inc. (dec 2015). https://doi.org/10.1109/ACII.2015.7344678

17. Ringeval, F., Sonderegger, A., Sauer, J., Lalanne, D.: Introducing the RECOLA multimodal corpus of remote collaborative and affective interactions. In: 2013 10th IEEE International Conference and Workshops on Automatic Face and Gesture Recognition, FG 2013 (2013). https://doi.org/10.1109/FG.2013.6553805

18. Russell, J.A.: A circumplex model of affect. Journal of Personality and Social Psychology **39**(6), 1161–1178 (dec 1980). https://doi.org/10.1037/h0077714, /record/1981-25062-001

19. Sánchez, J., Perronnin, F., Mensink, T., Verbeek, J.: Image classification with the fisher vector: Theory and practice. International Journal of Computer Vision **105**(3), 222–245 (dec 2013). https://doi.org/10.1007/s11263-013-0636-x

20. Schmidt, P., Reiss, A., Duerichen, R., Marberger, C., Van Laerhoven, K.: Introducing WESAD, a Multimodal Dataset for Wearable Stress and Affect Detection. In: Proceedings of the 20th ACM International Conference on Multimodal Interaction. pp. 400–408. ACM, New York, NY, USA (2018), https://doi.org/10.1145/3242969.3242985

21. Semenkin, E., Semenkina, M.: Self-configuring genetic programming algorithm with modified uniform crossover. In: 2012 IEEE Congress on Evolutionary Computation, CEC 2012 (2012). https://doi.org/10.1109/CEC.2012.6256587

22. Smith, M.G., BULL LarryBull, L.: Genetic Programming with a Genetic Algorithm for Feature Construction and Selection. Genetic Programming and Evolvable Machines **6**, 265–281 (2005). https://doi.org/10.1007/s10710-005-2988-7, http://www.ics.uci.edu/

23. Tran, B., Xue, B., Zhang, M.: Genetic programming for feature construction and selection in classification on high-dimensional data. Memetic Computing **8**(1), 3–15 (2015). https://doi.org/10.1007/s12293-015-0173-y
24. Tran, B., Xue, B., Zhang, M.: Genetic programming for multiple-feature construction on high-dimensional classification. Pattern Recognition 93, 404–417 (sep 2019). https://doi.org/10.1016/j.patcog.2019.05.006

A Multi-modal Approach to Mining Intent from Code-Mixed Hindi-English Calls in the Hyperlocal-Delivery Domain

Jose Mathew[1]([✉]), Pranjal Sahu[1,2], Bhavuk Singhal[1,3], Aniket Joshi[1,4], Krishna Reddy Medikonda[1], and Jairaj Sathyanarayana[1]

[1] Swiggy, Bengaluru, India
{jose.matthew,jairaj.s}@swiggy.in
[2] IIIT, Sri City, India
[3] B.I.E.T, Jhansi, India
[4] IIIT, Hyderabad, India

Abstract. In this work we outline an approach to mine insights from calls between delivery partners (DP) and customers involved in hyperlocal food delivery in India. Incorrect addresses/ locations or other impediments prompt the DPs to call customers leading to suboptimal experiences like breaches in the promised arrival-time, cancellation, fraud, etc. We demonstrate an end-to-end system that utilizes a multi-modal approach where we combine data across speech, text and geospatial domains to extract the intent behind these calls. To transcribe calls to text, we develop an Automatic Speech Recognition (ASR) engine that works in the Indian context where the calls are typically highly code-mixed (in our case Hindi and English) along with variations in dialects and pronunciations. Additionally in the hyperlocal delivery space, the calls are also corrupted by high levels of background noise due to the nature of the business. Starting with Wav2Vec2.0 as the base we carried out a series of data and model based experiments to progressively reduce the WER from 85.30% to 31.17%. The transcripts from the ASR engine are encoded into embeddings by adapting an IndicBERT based model. Features extracted from the geospatial markers of calls are concatenated with the embeddings and passed through an XGBoost classification head to classify calls into one of three intents. Through ablation studies we show incremental improvements attributable to signals from different modalities. The winning multi-modal model has a macro average precision of 68.33% which is a 29.3pp lift over the baseline not utilizing all the modalities.

Keywords: Automatic speech recognition · Wav2Vec2.0 · Multi-modal models

P. Sahu, B. Singhal, A. Joshi, and K. Reddy Medikonda—Work done while at Swiggy.

S. R. M. Prasanna et al. (Eds.): SPECOM 2022, LNAI 13721, pp. 477–493, 2022.
https://doi.org/10.1007/978-3-031-20980-2_41

1 Introduction

In recent years there has been an explosion of progress in the field of automatic speech recognition (ASR). Models like Wav2Vec2.0 [3], NEMO [20] and lighter Conformer [14] architectures have been at the forefront of this. Outputs from ASR systems enable at-scale understanding of millions of calls leading to intelligence like sentiment analysis, extracting customer pain points, identifying lapses in processes and repeated patterns that can be used to inform new product development ideas, insights for coaching customer-service agents, fixing loopholes to name a few.

While most of the above-mentioned models work out of the box for single/ code-mixed Western languages in relatively less noisy environments, there is a dearth of openly available research on adapting these for Indian languages and environments. As a company that operates in the hyperlocal convenience-delivery space in India, a majority of our calls occur in code-mixed Indian and English languages in highly noisy environments like traffic-congested roads, spoken while wearing a helmet, in the presence of a variety of background noises, varying levels of call clarity, etc. These conditions often result in conversations being muffled, mixed with cross-talk and/or ambient noise from natural (like rain, wind, kids, etc.) and artificial sources (like traffic, TV, etc.). This is especially the case with calls that occur between our delivery partners (DP) and customers. The intents behind these calls largely fall into three, equi-distributed categories—from (1) confirming directions ('should I take a left turn on the 4th Main?') or asking for directions to reach the exact customer location after reaching the address (say, an apartment within a large apartment complex with intricate layouts and road-use rules) to (2) asking for how to deliver the order ('should I leave the order with the Security at Gate B of Tower 4?') to (3) simply checking if the customer would be available at the specified address. The first two categories are somewhat unique to India (and possibly other non-Western markets) due to non-standard address and location systems. There are also scenarios where DPs potentially make calls (sometimes an excessive number of them) with an intent to defraud the customer or the platform and/or other deviations from protocols. We bucket (3) and fraud scenarios into a catch-all 'Others' bucket for the rest of this paper. Note that while each of these three intents can be further broken down into granular sub-intents for an even more nuanced understanding, we propose that as a future research direction and limit our current scope.

In all of the above cases, several key customer-experience metrics are breached. As a result, it is imperative to understand what's being said in these calls and use that information to build products and processes to improve existing systems. ASR systems are central to enabling this when dealing with millions of calls on any given day. Additionally, since most of what transpires in these calls is related to addresses and directions, utilizing geospatial signals can add valuable side information. Hence an end-to-end system that takes a multi-modal approach where data across speech, text and geospatial domains are combined to mine intent from these calls, can be powerful.

In this paper we describe our journey and lessons learned in building an end to end ASR system for calls with code-mixing between English and Hindi (also called Hinglish), with high levels of background noise. We start with the off-the-shelf Wav2Vec2.0 fine-tuned using an hour of our data, as the baseline with a word-error rate (WER) of 85.30%. We then describe a suite of experiments ranging from data augmentation to denoising to decoder choices to chunk sizes to language models to reduce the WER to 31.17% for a 54.13pp improvement.

We then describe a classification pipeline with XGBoost as the discriminator that classifies calls into the above-mentioned categories. The baseline uses Fast-Text embeddings learned on ASR transcripts, as features. We then experiment with the baseline by using transformers pretrained on Indic languages as feature encoders. We also show that adding features extracted from the geospatial markers of calls (for example, 'distance between the DP and the customer', 'time elapsed since beginning the last-mile of the trip', etc.) significantly improves the classification accuracy. Through ablation studies we show that the winning pipeline which utilizes the multi-modal approach combining data across speech, text and geospatial domain, achieves a 29.3pp improvement in macro average precision from 39.00% to 68.33%, vs. the baseline.

The rest of the paper is organized as follows. Section 3 reviews related work in the fields of ASR and intent detection. To the best of our knowledge, there is no one work that marries ASR for intent detection in the hyperlocal delivery space. Section 4 provides an overview of the dataset involved. Section 5, through its various subsections, describes our experiments with the ASR pipeline culminating in the inference flow. Section 6 showcases the experiments around generating embeddings from the ASR transcripts leading to Sect. 7 with a summary of results. We end with potential future research directions in Sect. 8.

2 Related Work

While research into ASR systems dates back to the 1950s s at Bell Labs [9], it was only in the 1970s s that Hidden Markov Models (HMM) were applied to this problem [18]. Audio data broken down to phonemes which are then inferred by HMMs to be finally mapped to legible text using n-gram based language models is how most traditional ASR systems worked [22]. The exploration towards feed-forward neural network acoustic models began around two decades back [6]. The recent explosion in deep learning has led to a flurry of end-to-end ASR models which have continually improved the state of the art (SOTA). It has now become possible to merge separate acoustic, pronunciation and language models (AM, PM, LM) of a conventional ASR system into a single neural network. Existing literature suggests that recurrent neural networks (RNNs) have been in one of the most prominent choices for building ASR [8] due to their ability of learning temporal dependencies in audio data [12]. Convolutional neural networks (CNNs) based architectures have also been successful for ASR [23] as they can learn local context through several convolution layers. The learned features through these convolution layers are then classified by a softmax layer at the end.

Recently, the introduction of transformers has strengthened the abilities of ML models in various fields like ASR, speech synthesis, machine translation, computer vision, and so on. Transformer was first introduced in the area of ASR in 2018 [11] where the authors minimally modify the architecture by adding CNN layers before passing the features to the input layers. Although the results were not SOTA this work confirmed that transformers can indeed be successfully used in speech recognition. Further improvements in speech-transformers can be observed in [29] where researchers suggested techniques for integrating the CTC loss along with the language models and proposed methods for transducer-based solutions. The transducer approach can be used to build real-time/ streamable ASR systems due to its immediate response mechanism. However, for the ASR to be streamable it is necessary for the model itself to be able to process audio sequentially and not the entire audio in one shot. This idea of feeding input as segments or chunks can be seen in [28]. Later studies show that the transformer-based architectures have found success in constructing better latent representations when pretrained with thousands of hours of unlabeled data [26]. Especially, in Wav2Vec2.0, the authors show that pretraining with a large corpus of unlabeled data can yield better results on fine-tuning even with a few minutes of labeled data. IndicWav2Vec [16] is an adaptation of a Wav2Vec2.0 for Indic languages, pre-trained on thousands of hours of Indic audio data. As we discover in the subsequent sections, no off-the-shelf model is able to perform at accuracies needed for user-facing actions, without significant domain adaptation.

Developing an ASR system with a high enough quality level is only one (albeit a significant one) part of the problem. To derive intelligence out of the ASR transcripts at a scale of millions, we need high quality representations that can be fed to downstream classification tasks. To this end, quite a few pre-trained word embeddings can be found for many Indian languages leveraging limited corpora [21]. The Polyglot [2] and FastText [5] projects provide embeddings trained on Wikipedia and/or CommonCrawl corpora. However, these embeddings typically haven't been used in multi-lingual/code-mixed downstream tasks. Here again, transformers come to our rescue having gained widespread adoption due to their efficacy in dealing with multilingual, code-mixed text and with out-of-vocabulary (OOV) words. Embeddings learned thusly have been shown to work well in downstream tasks like sentence classification. IndicBERT [19] is a pre-trained multilingual model trained on 12 Indian languages. This model handles code-mixing between these languages as well as with English. Additionally it can handle data in native as well as Latin scripts for writing these languages.

3   Overview of Data

3.1   Training Data for ASR

On a given day, well over 1.5 million calls happen on our platform between the various entities (namely, customer, DP, restaurant, customer-care (CC) agent), with a majority happening between the customer and the CC agent and the customer and the DP. Most of these calls are highly code mixed and typically happen in noisy environments such as in traffic, with the TV on, kids screaming in the background, etc. Most off-the-shelf SOTA ASR systems cannot be directly used to get the transcripts from these calls as these audio samples are recorded in a very different environment when compared to the audio data using which the SOTA models were trained. Hence, there is no single pretrained ASR which works for our use cases and thus there was a need to train our own ASR model using the audio data from our context. To do this, we required labeled data (audio files and its corresponding transcriptions) which is typically a time-consuming and cumbersome task. We engaged with an external vendor to annotate a sample of calls provided by us. The annotation was made more difficult by the fact that we store calls in mono format and it is not easy (or sometimes even impossible) to disambiguate who is speaking when. Through this process we got ~180 h of labeled speech data featuring calls in Hindi, English and Hinglish (Hindi and English code-mixed). The annotated dataset was divided into two subsets, ~170 h for training (Dataset A) and ~5 h for validation (Dataset B). We also procured an out-of-time, out-of-sample labeled data of ~5 h for testing (Dataset C) which is used to report all final metrics.

We augmented this in-house data with labeled data sourced from the AI4Bharat [1] group at IIT Madras. We call this dataset the IITM Dataset and is ~21 h. This dataset differs from our domain in the sense that it is almost entirely noise-free and each call is about a single speaker (male or female) speaking in a single Indian language. There is also the nuance of a native speaker of one language speaking in another language (for example, native Hindi speaker speaking in English).

3.2   Training Data for Intent Classification

We manually tagged 4,800 ASR transcripts into three intents, namely, 'Asking for directions to reach (class 2)', 'Reached the location and calling for further instructions (class 1)', and 'Others (class 0)'. As mentioned previously, the 'Others' class is a catch-all for sundry intents and scenarios like incomplete calls, extremely noisy transcripts, etc. We split this dataset in 80–20 proportions for training (3,800 samples) and validation (960 samples) respectively. Apart from these annotated text samples, we also use structured geospatial information from the calls and DP journeys. These features are (1) DP_CX_DISTANCE: the distance (in km) between the customer and DP at the time of the call, (2) 'TIME_DIFF': Time difference (in seconds) between the call start and when we received the DP's location from their phone. This difference is normally a few seconds but egregious differences indicate that something might be off (and hence provides useful information to the model), (3) 'DE_DISTANCE_FROM_START': the distance traveled by the DP since the start of last-mile trip. Additionally, we also use two one-hot features that indicate whether a given transcript contains certain keywords, one for each intent. For example, if the transcript contains class-1 related words like 'location', 'पर', 'gate', 'खड़ा', 'floor', the first one-hot feature is turned on while the second one-hot feature lights up for words like 'road', 'गली', 'अंदर', 'side', 'left', which are related to class-2.

4 Developing the ASR System

4.1 Wav2vec2.0

Wav2vec2.0 has the potential to yield better ASR systems for many languages and domains using a relatively smaller amount of annotated data by leveraging self-supervised learning. It can be finetuned using a few hours of domain-specific, labeled data to solve a particular use case for a specific language or a set of languages. For some languages, even the un-annotated data is limited and therefore the authors pre-trained the model on multiple languages in a combined manner which resulted in better pretrained representations for low-resource languages.

Model Architecture: The architecture of Wav2vec 2.0 mainly consists of three parts: (1) a feature encoder that encodes raw audio input into a sequence of T latent representations. It is a multilayered CNN that takes raw audio signal as input and outputs a sequence of frames $Z = z_1, z_2, \ldots, z_T$ where T is the number of timesteps and $z_i \in R^d$., (2) a transformer-based context network that takes the output generated by the feature encoder as an input and computes a contextualized representation for each of the T units in the input as $C = c_1, c_2, \ldots, c_T$, where c_i is the contextual representation for the i-th input (i.e., z_i), and (3) a quantizer which takes Z as input and discretizes it to a finite set of representations using product quantization [17] which helps in setting the target for self-supervised learning. The output of the quantizer is a sequence of representations $Q = q_1, q_2, \ldots, q_T$ where q_i is the quantized representation for the i-th input (i.e., z_i).

We use the LARGE version of the Wav2Vec2.0 model (pretrained on ~53K hours of unlabeled data) as the base for our experiments. This model contains 24 transformer blocks with a model dimension of 1024, inner dimension of 4096, and 16 attention heads.

4.2 Developing the ASR

Fine-tuning Wav2vec 2.0: To finetune the model for our use-case, we add a randomly initialized output layer on top of the transformer-based context network which maps each d dimensional output of the context network into a C dimensional output where C is the size of the vocabulary (97 in our case). The softmax function is then used to compute the distribution over the characters. The model was fine-tuned using standard CTC loss function [13]. The training data (Dataset A + IITM Dataset) was augmented using a modified version of SpecAugment [24] as mentioned in [3]. We set the masking probability to 0.05 and LayerDrop rate to 0.1 for the augmentation strategy. We used the Adam optimizer with a learning rate of 1e-4 with regularization handled by setting the dropout rate to 0.1 for both hidden and attention units. For the other hyperparameters, default values were retained.

Since it is generally difficult and time-consuming to get labeled training data for ASR tasks, especially for Indian languages, we wanted to achieve the best model performance with as little training data as possible. Our choice of

Wav2Vec2.0 is primarily driven by this promise of needing very little training data. We experimented with different amounts of training data for fine-tuning the Wav2Vec2.0 model starting from 1 h of data from Dataset A (this serves as our baseline). It can be seen that WER improves dramatically with increase in the amount of data in the beginning but plateaus out at around 100 h (Table 1). As expected, the lowest WER occurs when fine-tuned on the full 170 h of data. The experiments were conducted on GPUs ranging from g4.dn.xlarge (for 1 h of data) to g4.dn.12xlarge (for 170 h of data).

Table 1. Impact of training data size on WER.

Training data size (in h) from dataset A	WER on dataset B
1	80.01
5	65.71
10	60.43
25	53.83
50	52.58
100	49.54
Full 170 h	48.81

While this was good progress, a WER of 48+ is not acceptable for user-facing applications. Since the WER plateaued out with in-house data, we experimented with adding out-of-domain data. We did this by the IITM Dataset to Dataset A resulting in ~191 h (say, Dataset D). However, this only led to a modest 0.78pp improvement in WER from 48.81 to 48.03, indicating that more data was not necessarily helping. This (i.e., inferencing the best model so far) translated to a WER of 50.84 on the holdout Dataset C.

Conversion Dictionary: To inform our next set of experiments (using Dataset D for training), we did a sample-level error analysis to understand where the model was failing and what kind of words were being deleted or substituted. For example, were the words being deleted really important ones or could we afford to skip them without loss of interpretability? Or were the substituted words primarily of a particular type? We discovered that most of the substituted/deleted words were fairly short but commonly occurring Hindi words like 'nahi' (नहीं), 'hai' (है), 'aap' (आप), 'toh' (तो), etc. Additionally, a lot of the substitutions were also due to the way we were converting the code-mixed output from the ASR into the English transcript (in Latin script). For example, our code converted the Hindi word नहीं to 'nahin', whereas in the ground-truth annotations it was written as 'nahi'. This is a common issue when phonetic Indian languages are transliterated in English and does not really constitute an error in the real-world sense.

We solved this by introducing a dictionary we call the conversion dictionary that maps the most frequently occurring variants (and hence the errors) of

Hindi words to their correctly-assigned (as in ground-truth compliant) spellings. Applying this dictionary to remove the spelling 'mistakes' helped improve the WER from 48.03 to 42.22. This translated to a WER of 41.95 on the holdout Dataset C.

Training with Less Noisy Data: As mentioned in the previous sections, our call data is fairly noisy and we observed that the model was not able to transcribe such calls well. This led us to experiment with denoising using a variety of off-the-shelf libraries like Facebook Denoiser [10], noisereduce [25], Speech Enhancement [4], DLTN [30] and NSNet2 [7]. While we qualitatively observed that Facebook Denoiser achieved better noise reduction, it did not translate to improvement in WER. Upon investigation we found that while the denoiser was able to fully remove background noise, since our data is mono-aural, the amplitude was being compressed for one of the speakers while all data was being lost for the other speaker(s). As a result, the model was not able to retrieve all of the words being spoken in a call resulting in WER loss. We propose developing a diarization model as a future direction.

Since denoising was too important to be abandoned, we experimented with an alternative method to obtain less noisy data. We did this by inferencing the best model so far (the one with 42.22 WER) on Dataset A and computing the WER for each call in this training set. We subsetted this data into all calls with a WER of 40 or less (an empirical threshold given the performance thus far) resulting in a dataset of 134 h (say, Dataset A'). We appended the IITM Dataset (21 h) to Dataset A' to construct a new training set of 155 h. We call this Dataset D' and it was used for all subsequent experiments. Repeating the full cycle of train and test on this dataset resulted in WER reducing from 42.22 to 41.85. Note that this does not constitute peeking because the holdout set Dataset C is untouched and translated to a WER of 41.47 on it.

Decoding: It is empirically understood that the choice of decoder could have a bearing on the WER. Following this track, we experimented with using the PyCTC [27] decoder instead of the default Wav2vec2.0 decoder. After iterations we found the beam width of 100 to be optimal while retaining default values for all other hyperparameters of this decoder. This experiment gave us roughly 1pp improvement in WER bringing it down from 41.85 to 40.89. This translated to a WER of 40.53 on the holdout Dataset C.

Inference-chunk Size: The experiments described so far were with a chunk size of 100,000 which corresponds to about 6.2 s of audio given our sampling rate of 16 KHz. However since the real world datasets could have audio clips of longer (or any) duration, we hypothesized that the chunk size of input data could impact the WER. We experimented with dividing the audio into different chunk lengths before passing it through the model. The transcripts generated from all of these chunks were concatenated to get the final transcript.

We observed that increasing chunk size lowers the WER and the model generates better transcripts with lesser spelling mistakes and word joins. For example, doubling the chunk size to 200,000 with no other changes improved the WER to 36.9 from 40.89. The gain was maximal at a chunk size of 900,000 yielding a WER of 33.94 as shown in Fig 1. Beyond this, the results plateaued and the ROI was not justified in terms of increased computing cost. Table 2 shows a comparison of predictions (on Dataset B) made by models with 100,000 and 900,000 chunk sizes. The three examples shown in the table highlights the benefit of increased chuck size which enables a) proper separation of english and hindi words (e.g. separation of 'almost' and hindi word 'hoon' in example 1, b) identification of words missing from the 100K chunk size model and c) changing the meaning of entire sentence due to insertion of word keywords like 'nahi' (translated to 'no' in english) in the last example. The results clearly show that using a bigger chunk size helped the model to predict more accurately. Using the 'winning' chunk size of 900,000 translated to a WER of 35.57 on the holdout Dataset C.

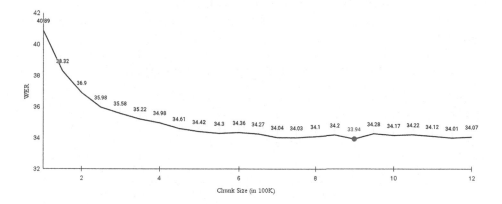

Fig. 1. Impact of chunk size.

Table 2. Impact of chunk size on quality of predictions.

Prediction using 100K chunk size	Prediction using 900K chunk size
kar sakta **hoonalmost** twenty five minutes	kar sakta **hoon sir almost** twenty five minute
service ke **lieinconvenience**	service ke **liye jo inconvenience**
address confirm karne ke **lieaesi** problem pehle toh kabhi **haii**	address confirm karne ke **liye mere paas aisi** problem pehle toh kabhi **aahi nahi hai**

Language Model (LM): In this experiment, instead of directly decoding the output using the PyCTC-based decoder using the maximum logit at each timestamp, we use a beam search-based decoding combined with an LM. In this way, we take the probabilities of all possible characters into account and apply a beam search while also leveraging the probabilities of next characters in the sequence as emitted by an n-gram based LM. We chose an n-gram based LM over the transformer based model due to significantly lower computational costs (the n-gram based LM queries a lookup table for retrieving the next word given the previous (n-1) words whereas a transformer based LM would require a full forward pass to get the next word probabilities).

We chose KenLM library [15] for building our n-gram based language model for its speed, efficiency, and simplicity. We experimented with multiple values of n and observed that the 3-gram based LM performed the best (on Dataset B), moving the WER from 33.94 to 30.54. This translated to a WER of 31.5 on the holdout Dataset C.

A sample of transcripts predicted with and without the above LM is shown in Table 3. We can see that the LM is able to correct spelling mistakes (e.g. 'order', 'minute', 'delivered' in the three respective examples) which most likely happened due to the background noise suppressing the acoustic input. The language model also enables separation of asr transcripts that are fused together (e.g. 'pick up tell me the order' in example 1) thus imparting more meaning to the sentences.

Table 3. Impact of LM on quality of predictions.

Prediction without LM	Prediction with LM
how may i assist you thn our back ok pick **uptel mis** back **theodei** can see his **notet** picked up **o**	how may i assist you back ok pick **up tell me the order** i can see is **not** picked up **ok**
he **tol** me that he will be delivering the order **netto** fifteen **milute** yes just now he has picked up your order from that **o ono**	he **told** me that he will be delivering the **orderfifteen** minutes yes just now he has picked up your order from that **no no**
i **ha** just ordered chicken biryani from **lucki** biryani ok ok n i would **deliverd** some some other biryani some chicken biryani from another **outlit** ok so i **clited** on help and i was talking to this guy he is talking **bulchik woth** me e no you know **wat** he is telling me	i **have** just ordered chicken biryani from **lucky** biryani ok ok i would **delivered** some some other biryani some chicken biryani from another **outlet** ok so i **clicked** on help and i was talking to this guy he is talking **bullshit with me no** you know **what** he is telling me

Probabilistic Splitting: This final experiment was motivated by the observation that many of the words were being incorrectly joined while transcribing. For example, 'biryaniokay', 'arrivedat', 'feedbackthis', 'orderक्योंकि', 'करdelivery', etc. We handled these by introducing heuristics like (1) splitting the word at the junction of the Hindi and English characters, (2) probabilistic splitting where we find the correct split by finding the subword with maximal occurrence in the training data. Applying these post-processing helped reduce WER from 30.54 to 29.85. This translated to a WER of 31.17 on the holdout Dataset C.

To summarize, our experiments improved the WER from an initial 80+ to less than 30 by systematically hypothesizing and analyzing the data and the outputs from each step of the ASR process.

4.3   Final Inferencing Flow for ASR

The final inference flow after all the experiments is shown in Fig. 2. Audio is given as an input to the best model from Sect. 5.2. The emissions from the last layer are decoded by a word-level 3-gram KenLM language model (trained on our text data) along with the PyCTC decoder with a beam width of 100. The outputs are post-processed via a conversion dictionary and probabilistic-splitting heuristics to produce the final transcripts.

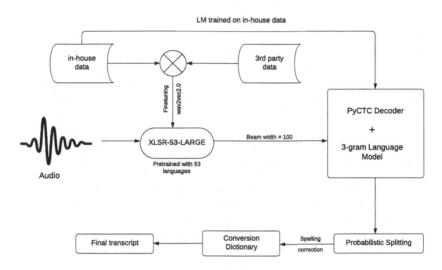

Fig. 2. The ASR pipeline.

Having obtained reasonably-accurate transcription of calls, the next steps are to extract useful intelligence from this textual data. In the upcoming sections, we describe the experiments and the pipeline to achieve intent recognition and classification from transcripts.

5   Intent Detection Through Transcripts

In this section, we detail our approach to deriving insights from the calls between the DP and the customer. The first step is to use the above-described ASR model to convert calls into text transcripts. Next we convert this text into lower dimensional embeddings using a variety of techniques. We augment these with geospatial and other categorical features before running through an XGBoost discriminator to classify each call into one of three intents. The subsequent sections explain the different embedding approaches and the classifier fine-tuning in detail.

5.1   Text Embeddings

We experimented with multiple embedding techniques ranging from Word2Vec, FastText to BERT-based ones. We quickly ruled out Word2Vec because it can not handle OOV cases which could be (and are) a major part of the ASR outputs wherein, a word has a slightly different spelling than its accepted form.

FastText: To handle this, we switched to FastText which generates embeddings (we experimented with 100, 300 and 500 dimensions) at character n-grams level and is robust against OOV cases. However, to obtain the vector representation of an entire sentence, we need a way to 'roll up' n-gram level embeddings. A simple but naive approach to this is to calculate the mean of all the embeddings across a dimension. This poses an issue wherein the embeddings of longer transcripts tend to be ambiguous since the embeddings tend to have higher values when averaged over long sequences. This can be countered by weighting the embeddings of words by their TF-IDF scores, using the scaled dot product of the embeddings. Our baseline is the 100-dimension version with naive (i.e., non-TF-IDF) weighting.

IndicBERT: This is a pretrained multilingual model based on the ALBERT architecture. This was trained on 11 major Indian languages and tested on the IndicGlue benchmark. We chose to generate the embeddings by pooling the last four layers of outputs in the hidden states. These pooled embeddings are then multiplied with the attention vector and scaled across dimensions. The end result is a 768-dimensional vector representation of the text.

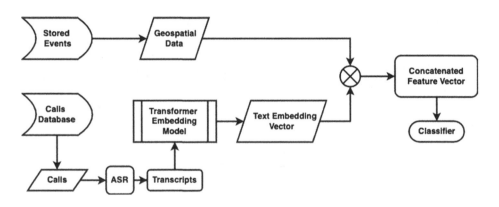

Fig. 3. Feature generation pipeline.

Classification of Transcripts. Once the transcripts are encoded as features, the next task is to classify them into respective intents as described in Sect. 3. With XGBoost as the classification head, we experimented with various inputs while noting precision and recall for each variant. Note that it is trivial to replace this discriminator with a neural network or a logistic regression or any other algorithm, XGBoost is a just convenient and pragmatic choice. Figure 3 above shows the end to end classification pipeline

6   Results and Analysis

The progress and development of the classification process are summarised in Table 4. The XGBOOST model shown in the first row, built entirely on categorical and geospatial features has the lowest macro average precision (39%) and recall (38.7%) across all classes, compared to all other variants where ASR inputs are introduced. The Fast Text (100-dimension) + XGBOOST model which takes embeddings of the ASR transcripts provides higher lift in performance (macro average precision of 61.3% and macro averaged recall of 56.3%) across all classes. As the Fast Text embedding dimension is increased from 100 to 500, there is a corresponding lift in both the macro averaged precision(66.7%) and recall (63.7%) numbers. It is easy to see that the variants using information from ASR perform significantly better than those that do not. There is a slight drop in both macro averaged precision(64.7%) and recall(61.7%) in moving to 500-dimensional Fast Text embeddings obtained by TF-IDF weighting. Augmenting the Fast Text embedding with geospatial features improves the macro average precision to 67%. Further introducing IndicBERT-extracted embeddings (768-dimension) improves the macro precision metric to 67.00% and recall to 63.3%. Finally, augmenting with geospatial and categorical features (775 total dimensions) produces the winning model with a macro average precision of 68.33% and a recall of 63%. Thus a multi-modal approach of using textual embeddings from audio transcripts and augmenting with geospatial and categorical features enables us to extract insights from audio calls in the hyperlocal delivery domain.

Table 4. Metrics on the test-set using different embedding models and features. *All the points in bold indicate the highest number in that particular column.*

Approach	Specifics	Classwise Precision				Classwise Recall				Classwise F-1 Score		
		0	1	2	Macro Avg	0	1	2	Macro Avg	0	1	2
	Feature size : 3	29.0	48.0	40.0	39.00	12.0	58.0	46.0	38.67	17.0	52.0	43.0
XGBoost (only geospatial/categorial features, no ASR features)	Feature size : 5 (geo + categorical)	58.0	56.0	57.0	57.00	39.0	59.0	65.0	54.33	47.0	58.0	61.0
	Vector Size: 100	65.0	58.0	61.0	61.33	45.0	61.0	63.0	56.33	53.2	59.5	61.98
FastText + XGBoost	Vector Size: 300	67.0	62.0	61.0	63.33	51.0	63.0	67.0	60.33	57.9	62.5	63.86
	Vector Size: 500	73.0	63.0	64.0	66.67	**55.0**	66.0	70.0	**63.67**	62.7	64.5	66.87
TF-IDF-weighted FastText + XGBoost	Vector Size: 500	72.0	61.0	61.0	64.67	53.0	64.0	68.0	61.67	61.1	62.5	64.31
FastText + XGBoost (with geospatial features)	Vector Size: 500	74.0	62.0	65.0	67.00	47.0	69.0	72.0	62.67	57.5	65.3	68.32
IndicBERT + XGBoost (without geospatial features)	Vector Size: 768. Feature size: 772	74.0	64.0	63.0	67.00	48.0	70.0	72.0	63.33	58.2	66.9	67.20
IndicBERT + XGBoost (with geospatial features)	**Vector Size : 768, Feature Size: 775**	**76.0**	**65.0**	64.0	**68.33**	45.0	70.0	**74.0**	63.00	56.5	**67.4**	**68.64**

From the examples in Table 5 it can be seen that the calls pertaining to the 'Asking for directions to reach' intent are rather long and most of the calls corresponding to 'Reached the location' are shorter (DPs typically informing the customers that they have reached the location, a relatively short conversation). The sentence embeddings created using FastText by averaging each token embeddings would produce higher numbers for sentences with more tokens (long sentences) making them ambiguous. The pooled embeddings along with the attention vectors in IndicBERT however produce more reasonable vectors for individual sentences reducing the ambiguity for the classification model. Some of the unclear/incomplete transcripts also correspond to ambiguous geospatial data and are correctly identified by the model and clubbed as "Others", also seen in the last example in Table 5.

In the same Table 5, the first example depicts a typical short conversation scenario wherein the DP called the customer to inform "Hello, yes sir I have reached the location" and the corresponding DE_CX_DISTANCE is roughly 11 m. The second example "haan boliye station...", however, is a rather lengthy conversation which is typical of scenarios where the DPs are requesting guidance to reach customer locations. The corresponding DE_CX_DISTANCE is over 702 m which further verifies the label. The third conversation is somewhere between the two, the call transcript does not make a lot of sense indicative of either an incomplete conversation or a noisy call causing the ASR to fail, thus the argumentative label of 'Others' is justified. On the other hand, the Table 6 shows a few instances where the geospatial and categorical features helped improve the accuracy of the model, especially for cases where ASR transcription was ambiguous.

Table 5. Example predictions depicting the usefulness of the geospatial feature: DE_CX_DISTANCE.

Call Transcript	DE_CX_ **DISTANCE** (In KMs)	Correctly predicted intent
hello hello haan sir main location pe pahunchehoon	0.011	Reached Location
haan boliye station vale road pe toh yahaan entry gate pe aaee hai lobby mein aayi hai lenge theek hai mujhe haan woh lobby mein aapko aane denge aap lobby entry gate se aa jaiye woh lobby mein aapko aane denge theek hai mam aap lobby mein aaj ke mujhe call kariye mam main toh bas yahi kiya do minute aa raha hoon theek hai aap ji main bhi ek minute mein meri allo	0.702	Directions to Reach
nahi aaya hoga hello yeh location pe hoon aapki hello ya location pe hoon na jo chij mngaee tho mili kya nahi nahi pane ki bottle bhi nahi mili nahi are theek hai nahi main	0.002	Others

Table 6. Qualitative analysis of results- before and after adding the geospatial features.

Call Transcript	DE CX DIST. (in KMs)	DE DIST. FROM START (in KMs)	Prediction without the geospatial features	Prediction with geospatial features	Ground truth
yeh valene andar aana na theek andar aa jo baar kha raha dikhta ok ek mint kiye ka theek request	0.9100	1.734	"Reached the Location"	"Directions to Reach"	"Direction to Reach"
ji ji ji bhai yeh na location abhi sahi number pehle ki aaee andar man bahar khare ji ki aliz house number do sau bhaiyya gurdoarali lunch line sakta location andar tooti aa rahe tooti jaa rahe haipichhle paas aa gaya bahar gaya na usse na ji o body gali t nahi jana na gali gali di jana theek do baar aari sidhi gali kar da re aa rahi ghari market itni gali aa rahi nahi woh theek ji par location mujhe meri ek minute mat dedication dekh ji ji is li gali khare ji di ko duvari the khudi der ji kyunki phir side mode mode ji location bataa do na naye bhi aur lag nahi ki door lagaa di gali chali ji six	0.5900	2.771	"Direction To Reach"	"Others"	"Others"
dont worry indra nagar right han ek one second one second india mila aapko veg nahi nahi kuch khula india nahi mila nahi bola ok nahi mila aage bhaiyya niche aa jao aap five thirty one na ji five thirty one bahar right bhaiyya aap ji one eat second are bhaiyya ek chu raha	0.0019	4.358	"Direction To Reach"	"Reached the Location"	"Reached the Location"

7   Conclusion and Future Work

In this work, we documented our learnings from building an in-house ASR model using Wav2Vec2.0 as the base. We showed through experiments on various stages of the ASR process that we could improve the WER from over 80 to around 30. We further showed that IndicBERT worked well as a feature encoder for extracting embeddings from call transcripts. Further incorporating a few geospatial features resulted in improved performance in the final task of intent classification. This has unlocked the ability to transcribe and mine intent from millions of calls per day at a fraction of the cost of third-party providers, which is significant at our scale. This intelligence enables a variety of product and process improvements which would not have been possible before.

In terms of future work, we see at least three directions. One would be around mining more granular intents, especially double-clicking on the 'Others' category to find fraud instances. We plan to employ weak supervision techniques like Snorkel to generate/augment intent-data at a larger scale. Secondly we intend to expand to more downstream tasks like keyword-spotting (for example, knowing how many times a keyword like 'cancel' or 'failed' is uttered in a call can be informative), sentiment analysis, identifying lapses in standard operating procedures (for example, missed greetings), to name a few. With the ASR engine in place, collecting annotated data for more downstream tasks is relatively straightforward and less time consuming. Lastly, given that our calls are stored in mono for cost purposes, we intend to build a diarization model to accurately classify who is talking when which can help improve ASR's accuracy. We also plan to experiment with iterative pseudo labeling techniques to augment training data for ASR.

References

1. Ai4bharat group. https://ai4bharat.org/
2. Al-Rfou', R., Perozzi, B., Skiena, S.: Polyglot: Distributed word representations for multilingual NLP. In: Proceedings of the Seventeenth Conference on Computational Natural Language Learning, pp. 183–192. Association for Computational Linguistics, Sofia, Bulgaria (2013). https://aclanthology.org/W13-3520 ¡error l="305" c="Invalid ¡error l="303" c="Invalid command: paragraph not started." /¿ command: paragraph not started." /¿
3. Baevski, A., Zhou, Y., Mohamed, A., Auli, M.: wav2vec 2.0: a framework for self-supervised learning of speech representations. Advances in Neural Information Processing Systems, vol. 33, pp. 12449–12460 (2020)
4. blenz, V.: Speech enhancement with deep learning (2020). https://github.com/vbelz/Speech-enhancement/tree/b6056c6ac745f88b00779d1083eceddfda1efb43
5. Bojanowski, P., Grave, E., Joulin, A., Mikolov, T.: Enriching word vectors with subword information (2016), CoRR abs/ arXiv:1607.04606
6. Bourlard, H.A., Morgan, N.: Connectionist Speech Recognition: A Hybrid Approach, vol. 247. Springer Science & Business Media, Berlin (2012)
7. Braun, S., Tashev, I.: Data augmentation and loss normalization for deep noise suppression. In: International Conference on Speech and Computer, pp. 79–86. Springer (2020)
8. Chiu, C.C., Sainath, T.N., Wu, Y., Prabhavalkar, R., Nguyen, P., Chen, Z., Kannan, A., Weiss, R.J., Rao, K., Gonina, E., et al.: State-of-the-art speech recognition with sequence-to-sequence models. In: 2018 IEEE International Conference on Acoustics, Speech and Signal Processing (ICASSP), pp. 4774–4778. IEEE (2018)
9. Davis, K.H., Biddulph, R., Balashek, S.: Automatic recognition of spoken digits. J. Acoust. Soc. Am. **24**(6), 637–642 (1952)
10. Défossez, A., Usunier, N., Bottou, L., Bach, F.: Music source separation in the waveform domain (2019). arXiv preprint arXiv:1911.13254
11. Dong, L., Xu, S., Xu, B.: Speech-transformer: a no-recurrence sequence-to-sequence model for speech recognition. In: 2018 IEEE International Conference on Acoustics, Speech and Signal Processing (ICASSP), pp. 5884–5888. IEEE (2018)
12. Graves, A.: Sequence transduction with recurrent neural networks (2012). arXiv preprint arXiv:1211.3711
13. Graves, A., Fernández, S., Gomez, F., Schmidhuber, J.: Connectionist temporal classification: labelling unsegmented sequence data with recurrent neural networks. In: Proceedings of the 23rd International Conference on Machine Learning, pp. 369–376 (2006)
14. Gulati, A., Qin, J., Chiu, C.C., Parmar, N., Zhang, Y., Yu, J., Han, W., Wang, S., Zhang, Z., Wu, Y., et al.: Conformer: Convolution-augmented transformer for speech recognition (2020). arXiv preprint arXiv:2005.08100
15. Heafield, K.: Kenlm (2021). https://github.com/kpu/kenlm
16. Javed, T., Doddapaneni, S., Raman, A., Bhogale, K.S., Ramesh, G., Kunchukuttan, A., Kumar, P., Khapra, M.M.: Towards building asr systems for the next billion users. In: Proceedings of the AAAI Conference on Artificial Intelligence, vol. 36, pp. 10813–10821 (2022)
17. Jegou, H., Douze, M., Schmid, C.: Product quantization for nearest neighbor search. IEEE Trans. Pattern Anal. Mach. Intell. **33**(1), 117–128 (2010)
18. Jelinek, F.: Continuous speech recognition by statistical methods. Proc. IEEE **64**(4), 532–556 (1976)

19. Kakwani, D., Kunchukuttan, A., Golla, S., N.C., G., Bhattacharyya, A., Khapra, M.M., Kumar, P.: IndicNLPSuite: Monolingual corpora, evaluation benchmarks and pre-trained multilingual language models for Indian languages. In: Findings of EMNLP (2020)

20. Kuchaiev, O., Li, J., Nguyen, H., Hrinchuk, O., Leary, R., Ginsburg, B., Kriman, S., Beliaev, S., Lavrukhin, V., Cook, J., et al.: Nemo: a toolkit for building ai applications using neural modules(2019). arXiv preprint arXiv:1909.09577

21. Kunchukuttan, A., Kakwani, D., Golla, S., N.C., G., Bhattacharyya, A., Khapra, M.M., Kumar, P.: Ai4bharat-indicnlp corpus: Monolingual corpora and word embeddings for indic languages (2020). arXiv preprint arXiv:2005.00085

22. Levinson, S.E., Rabiner, L.R., Sondhi, M.M.: An introduction to the application of the theory of probabilistic functions of a Markov process to automatic speech recognition. Bell Syst. Tech. J. **62**(4), 1035–1074 (1983)

23. Li, J., Lavrukhin, V., Ginsburg, B., Leary, R., Kuchaiev, O., Cohen, J.M., Nguyen, H., Gadde, R.T.: Jasper: An end-to-end convolutional neural acoustic model (2019). arXiv preprint arXiv:1904.03288

24. Park, D.S., Zhang, Y., Chiu, C.C., Chen, Y., Li, B., Chan, W., Le, Q.V., Wu, Y.: Specaugment on large scale datasets. In: ICASSP 2020–2020 IEEE International Conference on Acoustics, Speech and Signal Processing (ICASSP), pp. 6879–6883. IEEE (2020)

25. Sainburg, T., Thielk, M., Gentner, T.Q.: Finding, visualizing, and quantifying latent structure across diverse animal vocal repertoires. PLoS Comput. Biol. **16**(10), e1008228 (2020)

26. Song, X., Wang, G., Wu, Z., Huang, Y., Su, D., Yu, D., Meng, H.: Speech-xlnet: unsupervised acoustic model pretraining for self-attention networks (2019). arXiv preprint arXiv:1910.10387

27. Technologies, K.: Pyctc decoder (2021). https://github.com/kensho-technologies/pyctcdecode

28. Tian, Z., Yi, J., Bai, Y., Tao, J., Zhang, S., Wen, Z.: Synchronous transformers for end-to-end speech recognition. In: ICASSP 2020–2020 IEEE International Conference on Acoustics, Speech and Signal Processing (ICASSP), pp. 7884–7888. IEEE (2020)

29. Wang, Y., Mohamed, A., Le, D., Liu, C., Xiao, A., Mahadeokar, J., Huang, H., Tjandra, A., Zhang, X., Zhang, F., et al.: Transformer-based acoustic modeling for hybrid speech recognition. In: ICASSP 2020–2020 IEEE International Conference on Acoustics, Speech and Signal Processing (ICASSP), pp. 6874–6878. IEEE (2020)

30. Westhausen, N.L., Meyer, B.T.: Dual-Signal Transformation LSTM Network for Real-Time Noise Suppression. In: Proceedings of Interspeech 2020, pp. 2477–2481 (2020). https://doi.org/10.21437/Interspeech. 2020-2631

Importance of Supra-Segmental Information and Self-Supervised Framework for Spoken Language Diarization Task

Jagabandhu Mishra[✉] and S. R. Mahadeva Prasanna

Department of Electrical Engineering, Indian Institute of Technology (IIT) Dharwad, Dharwad 580011, India
{jagabandhu.mishra.18,prasanna}@iitdh.ac.in

Abstract. Spoken language diarization (LD) is a task of automatically extracting the monolingual segments present in a given code-switched utterance. Generally in the bilingual code-switched scenario, when a single speaker spokes both the languages, mostly the phoneme production of the secondary language is biased towards the primary, leading to acoustic similarity. It is also noticed that the turn duration of the primary language is significant over the secondary, leading to data imbalance. Due to the acoustic similarity and data imbalance, the performance of the available work is biased toward the primary language. The influence of acoustic similarity can be minimized by capturing the supra-segmental language specific information. Similarly, the influence of data imbalance can be suppressed, by prior capturing the language specific information through a pre-training framework. Therefore, this work proposes a wav2vec2 based self-supervised pre-training framework to capture the supra-segmental language specific information. The obtained results show that the proposed framework provides a relative improvement of 33.4% in terms of Jaccard error rate (JER), over the available baseline deep-speech2 based approach. The improvement in JER suggests that the proposed approach can be able to resolve the performance bias issue to some extent.

Keywords: Spoken language diarization (LD) · Supra-segmental evidence · Self-supervised framework · Diarization error rate (DER) · Jaccard error rate (JER)

1 Introduction

Spoken language diarization (LD) is a task of automatically segmenting and labeling the monolingual segments present in a given code-switched (CS) utterance. The basic block diagram of the LD system is shown in Fig. 1. Figure 1a shows a CS speech utterance given as input to the LD system. The LD system provides a file having time annotated language labels, called a rich transcription

© Springer Nature Switzerland AG 2022
S. R. M. Prasanna et al. (Eds.): SPECOM 2022, LNAI 13721, pp. 494–507, 2022.
https://doi.org/10.1007/978-3-031-20980-2_42

time marked (RTTM) file. After that, the time annotations are used to extract the monolingual segments, as depicted in Fig. 1b.

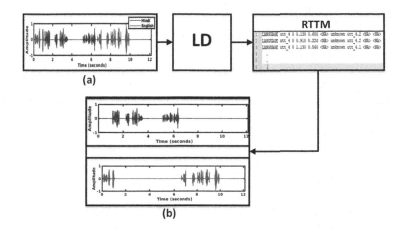

(a)

(b)

Fig. 1. LD task: **a** Multilingual code-switched utterance and **b** Extracted monolingual utterances, RTTM: Rich transcription time marked.

The deployment of speech based applications in a multilingual environment demands the development of the LD system [11,23]. Till today, the related works available in this direction are very few. Like language identification (LID), LD can also be developed in two ways: (1) acoustic-phonetic and (2) phonotactic approach [11–13,15,25]. Most of the works available uses the latter approach, which requires transcribed speech data. However, in a country like India, most of the speakers spoke more than two languages while having a conversation, and the primary languages spoken by them generally have low resources [6,15,24]. Hence, it is difficult to use the phonotactic approach in the Indian scenario. Therefore, we have developed the LD system using the acoustic-phonetic approach as it does not require any transcribed speech data.

In literature, few related works are reported to use acoustic-phonetic approaches, which are not actual LD systems. The approaches are developed to perform sub-utterance level language identification (SLID) and CS point detection task [11,16,22]. However, the SLID can be viewed as a first-level LD system as it predicts the language ID at the sub-utterance level. But the performance of the SLID systems is biased towards the primary language [4]. Generally, in a CS utterance, a single speaker speaks both languages, and phonemes of the secondary language are produced by adapting the phoneme production mechanism of the primary language (i.e. mother tongue language). From this, it can be hypothesized that the acoustic features extracted in sub-segmental (one glottal cycle) and segmental (10−30 ms) levels may be biased towards the primary language. This issue can be termed acoustic similarity and may cause false predictions of primary language. But this can be resolved by capturing the temporal dynamics at supra-segmental ($> 100\,\text{ms}$) level as the grammatical rules vary with language. Furthermore, in a code-switched bilingual scenario, the turn duration of the primary language is significant over the secondary. This leads to a data imbalance problem and poses a challenge for the training of machine learning and deep learning (ML/DL) models, but can be resolved to some extent by using a pre-trained transfer learning based framework [2,8,10]. Therefore, this work proposes a self-supervised framework (known as wav2vec2 [3,7]), that learns the language independent supra-segmental evidence during pre-training and language discriminative information during the fine-tuning stage.

The available approaches mostly use frame error rate (FER), equal error rate (ERR), and identification accuracy (IDA) for evaluating the performance [11,13, 22]. But, these measures are more suitable for identification/verification tasks. On the other hand for the diarization task, the evaluation matrix like diarization error rate (DER) and Jaccard error rate (JER) is more appropriate [19]. Hence this work uses DER and JER with suitable modifications for evaluating the performance.

The rest of the paper is organized as follows: Sect. 2 describes the nature of CS bilingual data and the motivation of the proposed approach. Section 3 describes the working principle of the proposed approach and in Sect. 4, the experimental setup, and the obtained results are discussed. Finally, the conclusion and the future directions of the work have been discussed in Sect. 5.

2   Analysis of Bilingual Code-Switched Data

The CS utterances generally consist of speech samples from multiple languages. But in these utterances, the turn duration of the primary language is significant over the secondary. Again, the acoustic characteristic of the utterances at the sub-segmental and segmental levels is also biased towards the primary language. The detailed analysis of the claim is reported in the following subsections.

2.1   Data Imbalance

For enhancing the research on CS speech, Microsoft organized a challenge on CS utterance detection in Interspeech 2021 [22]. In the challenge, the team shared the spontaneous speech recordings of the three CS language pairs: (1) Gujarati-English (GUE), (2) Tamil-English (TAE), and (3) Telugu-English (TEE). The average turn duration and the percentage of the total duration of each primary and secondary language pair are depicted in Fig. 2.

Figure 2a, b show the average turn duration of the primary and secondary language in the training and development partition respectively. From the figure, it can be observed that the average turn duration of the primary language is approximately three times greater than the turn duration of the secondary. This leads to the data imbalance in both training and development partition, which can be observed from Fig. 2c, d respectively.

2.2   Acoustic Similarity

After carefully listening to the CS utterances, it can be inferred that the second language is somewhat biased towards the primary language and it is almost impossible to detect the change if the person has not been exposed to any of the languages present in the utterance. This hypothesizes that human cognition may use higher level information (like phonotactic, prosodic and lexical) to locate the language change.

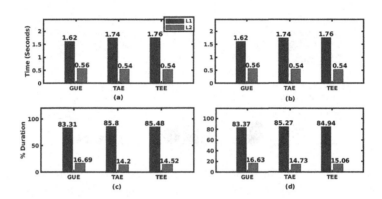

Fig. 2. Duration statistics, **a** average turn duration of training data, **b** average turn duration of development data, **c** % duration of training data, and **d** % duration of development data, L1 and L2 referred to primary and secondary language respectively.

For validating the hypothesis, we have extracted the acoustic information on three different levels: sub-segmental, segmental, and supra-segmental. It is assumed that the sub-segmental and segmental features mostly encapsulate the phoneme production characteristic, whereas the supra-segmental features capture the higher level features by observing the phonemic temporal flow. For a given code-switched utterance, all three levels of representation are depicted in Fig. 3. Figure 3a shows a Hindi-English CS speech utterance having one language switching point. An utterance is passed on a glottal activity detector and the resultant signal is represented in Fig. 3b [1]. The resultant signal is used to compute the linear prediction (LP) residual signal and depicted in Fig. 3c [20]. The Hilbert envelope of the residual signal is depicted in Fig. 3d. The spectrogram of the CS utterance in the glottal activity region is shown in Fig. 3e. The pitch contour at each syllable region (vowel-like region) of the utterance is depicted in Fig. 3f. From the signal level representations, it can be observed that it is difficult to discriminate between the languages. Hence to validate the claim, a feature distribution based analysis is carried out for discriminating the language.

The Hilbert envelope signal is parameterized as peak-to-side-lobe-ratio (PSR) and represents information present in sub-segmental level [9]. The 39 dimensional Mel frequency cepstral co-efficients with their time derivatives (MFCC+Δ + $\Delta\Delta$) are computed from the short time Fourier transform (STFT) of the CS

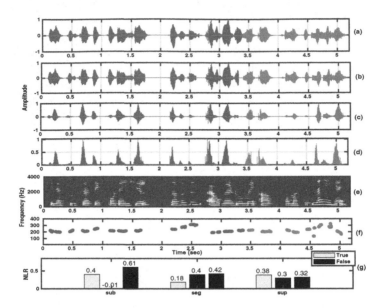

Fig. 3. Acoustic similarity, **a** CS speech signal, **b** glottal activity detected signal, **c** LP residual signal, **d** Hilbert envelope signal, **e** spectrogram, **f** pitch contour on glottal activity region, **g** NLR.

utterance to represent the segmental feature. Similarly, the seven-dimensional prosodic features have been computed from the vowel-like regions to represent the supra-segmental feature [14]. After that, the extracted features are segmented for the true and false change points (denoted as A and B), and a normalized generalized likelihood measure (NLR) has been used to estimate the confidence of the feature for discriminating the language pair. The true change point is the actual ground truth change point and the false change point is the mid-point of the mono-lingual segments present in an utterance (detailed procedure can be found in [17]). The NLR score for the true/false change points is computed as given in Eq. 1, where P and S define the primary and secondary language respectively. $G(P, S)$ is the generalized likelihood ratio (GLR) between the segments around the true change point, and $G(P, P)$ and $G(S, S)$ is the GLR around the false change point of primary and secondary language respectively. The GLR measures the degree of confidence between two distributions coming from two different class [18]. The GLR is computed around the true/false change point as in Eq. 2, where $C = \{A, B\}$. The obtained NLR corresponding to the true and false change points are depicted in Fig. 3g.

$$NLR(P, S) = \frac{G(P, S)}{G(P, S) + G(P, P) + G(S, S)} \tag{1}$$

$$G(A, B) = \frac{P(A|\mathcal{N}_A)P(B|\mathcal{N}_B)}{P(C|\mathcal{N}_C)} \tag{2}$$

Ideally, the NLR around the true change point should be higher than the false. But, it can be observed that the NLR value of the false change point is higher than the true case, with the sub-segmental and segmental features. However, in the supra-segmental scenario, the NLR value is higher around the true change point than the false. This justifies the hypothesis that the phoneme production characteristics (mostly attributed to the sub-segmental and segmental features) are biased towards primary language, whereas the higher level prosodic information (the temporal flow of phonemes) can provide the discrimination. To further strengthen the claim, the experiment is extended with 15 randomly chosen utterances. The language discrimination is predicted if $NLR(P, S) > NLR(P, P)$ and $NLR(P, S) > NLR(S, S)$ is satisfied. From the analysis, it is observed that the language change is successfully predicted in 46% of the utterances using supra-segmental features followed by 26% and 26% using segmental and sub-segmental features. Therefore, this study concludes that the acoustic similarity between languages can be reduced by considering supra-segmental evidence.

3 Proposed Self-Supervised Framework

The analysis of CS utterances suggests that there have two kinds of challenges that need to be resolved for developing a reliable LD system. The issues with acoustic similarity can be resolved to some extent by capturing supra-segmental language specific evidence. From the literature, it has been observed that the data imbalance based issue can be resolved using pre-trained transfer learning based framework [2, 10]. This motivates the use of a self-supervised pre-trained wav2vec2 framework.

The use of wav2vec2 based framework will benefit us in two ways. Firstly, the framework during pre-training does not require language labeled speech data [3]. Generally, if the DL frameworks use language labeled speech data then it fails to generalize and suffers from domain mismatch [5]. Secondly, if the speech data from multiple languages are used to train the pre-training framework with masking duration greater than 200 ms (by considering $M \geq 10$), then it captures essentially the phonemic temporal flow pattern (mostly within a syllable) in the supra-segmental level. Therefore it is hypothesized that the multi-lingual pre-training of wav2vec2 architecture will resolve both issues to some extent. The details of the pre-training and fine-tuning architecture are depicted in Fig. 4 and discussed in the following sub-sections.

3.1 Pre-training

The pre-training stage consists of four operations: (1) feature extraction using convolutional neural networks (CNN), (2) quantization using product quantization, (3) sequence learning using transformers, and (4) computing the contrastive and divergence loss. Zero mean and amplitude normalized speech samples (X) of 25 msec duration (i.e. 400 samples) with a shift of 20 msec are given as input to the CNN filters to learn the latent representation (Z). The latent representation

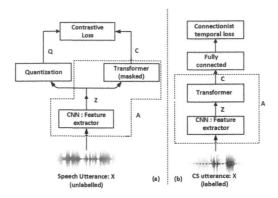

Fig. 4. Wav2vec2 Architecture, **a** pretraining and **b** finetuning.

Z is given as input to the quantization block, where a product quantizer is used to quantize using G codebooks and each having V number of d/G dimension quantization vectors. After that, for a given $z \in Z$, Gumbel softmax is used to choose the nearest quantization vector from each codebook and then concatenate to give a d dimensional quantized representation ($q \in Q$) [3]. The latent representations (Z) are also passed through the transformer layer with random masking to obtain the contextualized representation (C). Then the output of the contextualized vectors (c_m) and quantized vectors (q_m) belong to the masked latent representations (z_t) are compared with k distractor's contextualized (c') and quantization (q') vectors to obtain the contrastive loss (L_c) (as given in Eq. 3), where sim refers to the cosine similarity function. To ensure each of the quantized vectors contributes equally, an entropy-based divergence loss (L_d) is also computed using Eq. 4, where $\bar{p}_{g,v}$ is the mean probability of the latent representations of the batched utterances belonging to the specific (g, v) quantized vector.

$$L_c = -log \frac{e^{sim(c_m, q_m)/k}}{\sum_{q' \in Q'} e^{sim(c', q')/k}} \qquad (3)$$

$$L_d = \frac{1}{GV} \sum_{g=1}^{G} \sum_{v=1}^{V} \bar{p}_{g,v} \log(\bar{p}_{g,v}) \qquad (4)$$

The addition of both the contrastive and divergence loss ($L_c + \alpha L_d$) are used to optimize the parameters of the architecture. In this case, α is a hyperparameter. The architecture and the signal flow of the pre-training stage are shown in Fig. 4a. Since, this work focuses on the LD task on Indian bilingual CS utterances, the pre-training model that has been trained on 23 Indian languages with 10000 hrs of speech data (proposed for automatic speech recognition (ASR) task and available in [7]), is used here.

3.2   Fine-Tuning

It is assumed that during pre-training the model learns to predict the syllables of the global language set (23 Indian languages) and thereafter the language specific finetuning will help, the model to learn the language specific syllable level information for discriminating the primary and secondary language. Therefore, the pre-training model's CNN and transformer layers along with their trained parameters are taken and, a fully connected layer with softmax is added to it, to obtain the fine-tuning framework (shown in Fig. 4b). The softmax output will provide the language prediction at each 20 msec duration. But the ground truth label sequences are available at each 200 msec. This makes the task seen as the best language sequence prediction task. Hence, this work use CTC loss instead of categorical cross-entropy loss for finetuning.

4   Experimental Setup and Results

4.1   Database Details

This work uses the Microsoft code-switched task-B(MSCWTB) dataset for performing the experiments [22]. The dataset consists of three language pairs. These are GUE, TAE, and TEE. The speech data from each language pair have been partitioned for the training and development set. In this work, the training partition is used to train the models, and the development partition is used for testing purposes.

4.2   Experimental Setup

For validating the significance of the proposed wav2vec2 based framework, the performance is initially compared with the available baselines for the sub-utterance level LID (SLID) task. After that, the evaluation is extended for the LD task, and the performance is evaluated in terms of DER and JER.

The framework based on deepspeech2 (DS2) is available for SLID task in [22], and deepspeech2 with secondary language masking technique (DS2-LM) in [21] is used as the baselines systems for comparison. For validating the claim of primary language bias, the quoted results of the baselines in their respective work are reproduced and then compared with the proposed approach. The hyperparameters and the architecture of the baselines are kept identical, as mentioned in [22] and [21]. The architecture and the used hyperparameters of the proposed wav2vec2 architecture are reported in the following subsection. For all the approaches the best language sequences are predicted using a beam decoder with a beam width of 10 frames. Furthermore, for each case, the training is stopped by observing the training and development set's identification accuracy in the consecutive epochs. Accordingly, the DS2 and DS2-LM architecture are trained for 80 and 100 epochs respectively.

4.3   Wav2vec2

The pre-trained model of wav2vec2 that was developed and open-sourced by the Vakyansh team is being used here [7]. For training, the model uses 23 Indian languages and has approximately 10000 h of speech data. The network has seven 1D-CNN layers and twelve transformer layers. All the 1D-CNN layers have 512 convolution filters and have filter size of $(10, 3, 3, 3, 3, 2, 2)$ and stride of $(5, 2, 2, 2, 2, 2, 2)$ respectively. The receptive field of the CNN embeddings is 25 msec and computed in each 20 msec duration. The output of the CNN embedding is masked with $M = 10$ (approximately 200 msec) and processed through the transformer layers to predict the masked embeddings. The masked embeddings and the quantized CNN embeddings are compared using contrastive and divergence loss to train the model. The details of the training and the chosen hyperparameters can be found in [7].

On the pre-training model, a fully connected layer with softmax activation is added with random parameter initialization to obtain the fine-tuned model. The training set of each language pair is used to fine-tune the architecture with CTC loss. For each language pair, the architecture is fine-tuned with 900 epochs.

4.4   Performance Measure

Till now, as per our knowledge, true LD systems are not attempted. However, the SLID task (somewhat similar to the LD task) has been reported in the literature. Mostly, the SLID tasks are evaluated in terms of Identification accuracy (IDA) and equal error rate (ERR) [11,22]. But, as discussed in Sect. 2.1, the CS utterances have more than 80% of the duration from the primary language. Hence it can be inferred that, even if the system is not able to predict the secondary language, the performance of 80% IDA can be achieved. This provides a miss interpretation of performance. A similar interpretation can also be inferred for the EER measure as it is also computed by considering the total number of ground truth language tags as base [22]. Therefore, there is a need to come up with a performance measure, which can represent the system performance in a better way. Initially, the confusion matrix is taken to compare the performance.

Generally, for speaker diarization (SD) tasks, DER and JER have been widely used. The DER can be computed using Eq. 5, where FA and M represent the false acceptance and miss voiced segment duration, LE is the duration of the language error and T is the total utterance duration. If we consider voice activity detection (VAD) is performed ideally by the machine, the DER will be mostly influenced by LE/T. The LE/T will mostly reflect the primary language error, as the duration of the primary language segment is comparatively higher than the secondary. Hence provide a miss interpretation of the obtained overall performance.

$$DER = \frac{FA + M + LE}{T} \tag{5}$$

The JER can be computed, as mentioned in Eq. 6, where N_r is the number of reference language, FA_i and M_i is the false acceptance and miss duration of ith language. T_i is the union of the ith language duration in the reference and predicted. From the Eq. 6, it can be inferred that the measure is giving equal importance to each language present in an utterance. Therefore, as per the nature of the CS utterance, JER better fits the LD system performance evaluation.

$$JER = \frac{1}{N_r} \sum_{i=1}^{N_r} \frac{FA_i + M_i}{T_i} \tag{6}$$

The SD task generally uses a collar (i.e. discard x duration around the boundary from the score computation) during evaluation. But for LD, the average secondary language segment duration is around 0.5 sec, hence for DER and JER computation, this work assumes the collar is equal to zero.

4.5   Results and Discussion

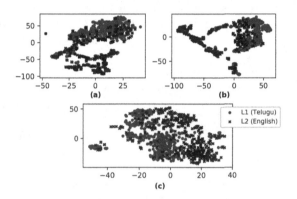

Fig. 5. t-SNE distribution of **a** DS2 **b** DS2-LM and **c** wav2vec2 for TEE, CS bilingual utterances.

Initially, the proposed approach is compared with the baselines for SLID task. The performance of the SLID task is evaluated in terms of IDA and EER, and depicted in Fig. 6. From the figure, it can be observed that irrespective of the language pair, the performance of the proposed wav2vec2 approach is much better than the baseline in terms of both IDA and EER. This is because the proposed approach can resolve the acoustic similarity and data imbalance issue to some extent. To further compare the primary language bias the embeddings of both the baselines and the proposed approach are projected in a 2D plane using t-SNE distribution and depicted in Fig. 5. From the figure, it can be noticed that the separation between the primary and secondary language is better in the case of the proposed approach than in the baselines. This shows the primary language bias is reduced to some extent, as compared to the baselines. To further

Table 1. Comparison between available and proposed approaches using confusion Matrix. The percentage values are averaged across all three language pairs. L1 and L2 represent the primary and secondary languages respectively.

Model	Actual/Predicted	L1	L2	Silence
DS2	L1	85.2	6.7	8
	L2	62.1	**30.4**	7.4
	Silence	31.9	4.5	63.5
DS2 - LM	L1	90.6	1.3	7.9
	L2	79.9	**12.3**	7.6
	Silence	29.1	1.3	69.3
Wav2vec2	L1	90.9	3.8	5.1
	L2	31.3	**63.9**	4.6
	Silence	23	4.6	72.3

validate the fact, the confusion matrix (averaged across language pairs) of all the three systems is tabulated in Table 1. For the DS2 approach, the primary (L1) is predicted as L1 and secondary (L2) with 85.2% and 6.7% of times respectively. The L2 is predicted as L1 and L2 with 62.1% and 30.4% respectively. This demonstrates the bias of the L2 language towards L1. This may be due to the DS2 model is not able to capture the language specific discrimination and providing biased performance. In the case of DS2-LM, though in terms of IDA and EER the performance is better than the DS2, the t-SNE distribution and confusion matrix contradicts. It can be observed from the t-SNE and confusion matrix that the bias of the DS2-LM is more than the DS2. The bias of DS2-LM is because of the augmentation of utterances using secondary language masking. This indirectly increases the data imbalance and the system predicts L1 dominantly. At the same time, the proposed approach can reduce the primary language bias by predicting L2 to L2 63.9% and L1 31.3%. Similarly, the proposed approach predicts L1 to L1 90.9% and L2 3.8%.

After discussing the significance of the proposed framework for SLID task, the work has been extended for the LD task. From the predicted best language sequence, each language Id's duration is assumed as 200 msec, and the predicted RTTM files are generated using that. Similarly, the ground truth RTTM is generated using the available ground truth language Id's. After that, the DER and JER are computed by comparing the predicted and ground truth RTTM files. The computed DER and JER values are depicted in Fig. 6c, d, and also tabulated in Table 2. The figure shows that irrespective of the measure, the performance of the wav2vec2 based approach is better than the baselines. The wav2vec2 approach provides a relative improvement of 17.86%, 17.51% and 22.98% (average 19.45%) in terms of DER and 36.3%, 33.3% and 30.72% (average 33.4%) in terms of JER from the baselines for GUE, TAE and TEE language pairs respectively. The figure also demonstrates the JER is the appropriate measure of the LD

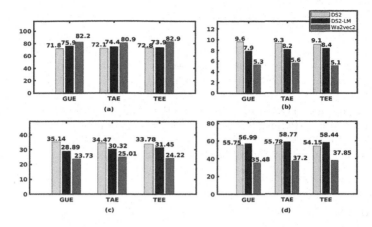

Fig. 6. Performance statistics: **a** IDA, **b** EER, **c** DER, **d** JER.

task. The bias of the DS2-LM is higher than the DS2 approach, which has been well reflected in the JER measure, whereas the other standard measure fails to capture. Hence JER is a better measure for the LD task, than the rest.

Table 2. Performance comparison in terms of DER and JER.

Model/CS	GUE		TAE		TEE	
	DER	JER	DER	JER	DER	JER
DS2	35.14	55.75	34.47	55.78	33.78	54.15
DS2-LM	28.89	56.99	30.32	58.77	31.45	58.44
Wav2vec2	**23.73**	**35.48**	**25.01**	**37.20**	**24.22**	**37.85**

5   Conclusion and Future Work

The analysis of bilingual CS data suggests that the occurrence of the primary language is more significant than the secondary. Additionally, the phoneme production of the secondary language is biased towards the phoneme production of the primary language. These two properties of the CS utterance lead to data imbalance and acoustic similarity, which pose a challenge for the machine learning models to discriminate between the primary and secondary language, and end with biased performance towards the primary language. Hence to resolve the issue, a wav2vec2 based self-supervised framework is proposed for capturing the supra-segmental temporal phoneme flow in the pre-training stage. It is expected that, during language specific finetuning, the supra-segmental information is used to predict the best language sequences. From the experimental results, it has been observed that the proposed approach can reduce the primary language bias to some extent. Furthermore, it has also been observed that the JER provides a better performance inference (as it gives equal weights to the languages present in an utterance) than the other available measures. As the fine-tuning data is still imbalanced, the performance can be further improved by employing data augmentation on secondary language or following some weighted loss during fine-tuning. Therefore in the future, we will explore the approaches related to augmentation and weighted optimization to further improve the performance.

Acknowledgments. The authors like to acknowledge "Anatganak", high performance computation (HPC) facility, IIT Dharwad, for enabling us to perform our experiments. And Ministry of Electronics and Information Technology (MeitY), Govt. of India, for supporting us through "Bhashini: Speech technologies in Indian languages" project.

References

1. Adiga, N., Prasanna, S.R.M.: Detection of glottal activity using different attributes of source information. IEEE Signal Process. Lett. **22**(11), 2107–2111 (2015)
2. Al-Stouhi, S., Reddy, C.K.: Transfer learning for class imbalance problems with inadequate data. Knowl. Inf. Syst. **48**(1), 201–228 (2016)
3. Baevski, A., Zhou, Y., Mohamed, A., Auli, M.: wav2vec 2.0: A framework for self-supervised learning of speech representations. Advances in Neural Information Processing Systems, vol. 33, pp. 12449–12460 (2020)
4. Barras, C., Le, V.B., Gauvain, J.L.: Vocapia-limsi system for 2020 shared task on code-switched spoken language identification. In: The First Workshop on Speech Technologies for Code-Switching in Multilingual Communities (2020)
5. Dey, S., Saha, G., Sahidullah, M.: Cross-corpora language recognition: A preliminary investigation with Indian languages. In: 2021 29th European Signal Processing Conference (EUSIPCO), pp. 546–550. IEEE (2021)
6. Diwan, A., Vaideeswaran, R., Shah, S., Singh, A., Raghavan, S., Khare, S., Unni, V., Vyas, S., Rajpuria, A., Yarra, C., Mittal, A., Ghosh, P.K., Jyothi, P., Bali, K., Seshadri, V., Sitaram, S., Bharadwaj, S., Nanavati, J., Nanavati, R., Sankaranarayanan, K., Seeram, T., Abraham, B.: Multilingual and code-switching asr challenges for low resource Indian languages. In: Proceedings of Interspeech (2021)
7. Gupta, A., Chadha, H.S., Shah, P., Chimmwal, N., Dhuriya, A., Gaur, R., Raghavan, V.: Clsril-23: cross lingual speech representations for indic languages (2021). arXiv preprint arXiv:2107.07402
8. Jati, A., Georgiou, P.: Neural predictive coding using convolutional neural networks toward unsupervised learning of speaker characteristics. IEEE/ACM Trans. Audio, Speech, Lang. Process. **27**(10), 1577–1589 (2019)
9. Jelil, S., Das, R.K., Prasanna, S.R.M., Sinha, R.: Spoof detection using source, instantaneous frequency and cepstral features. In: Interspeech, pp. 22–26 (2017)
10. Krawczyk, B.: Learning from imbalanced data: open challenges and future directions. Prog. Artif. Intell. **5**(4), 221–232 (2016). https://doi.org/10.1007/s13748-016-0094-0
11. bibitemch42liu2021end Liu, H., Perera, L.P.G., Zhang, X., Dauwels, J., Khong, A.W., Khudanpur, S., Styles, S.J.: End-to-end language diarization for bilingual code-switching speech. In: 22nd Annual Conference of the International Speech Communication Association, INTERSPEECH 2021, vol. 2. International Speech Communication Association (2021)

12. Lyu, D.C., Chng, E.S., Li, H.: Language diarization for code-switch conversational speech. In: 2013 IEEE International Conference on Acoustics, Speech and Signal Processing (ICASSP), pp. 7314–7318. IEEE (2013)
13. Lyu, D.C., Chng, E.S., Li, H.: Language diarization for conversational code-switch speech with pronunciation dictionary adaptation. In: 2013 IEEE China Summit and International Conference on Signal and Information Processing (ChinaSIP), pp. 147–150. IEEE (2013)
14. Mary, L., Yegnanarayana, B.: Extraction and representation of prosodic features for language and speaker recognition. Speech Commun. **50**(10), 782–796 (2008)
15. Mishra, J., Agarwal, A., Prasanna, S.R.M.: Spoken language diarization using an attention based neural network. In: 2021 National Conference on Communications (NCC), pp. 1–6. IEEE (2021)
16. Mishra, J., Gandra, J., Patil, V., Prasanna, S.M.: Issues in sub-utterance level language identification in a code switched bilingual scenario. In: 2022 IEEE International Conference on Signal Processing and Communications (SPCOM), pp. 1–5. IEEE (2022)
17. Mishra, J., Prasanna, S.R.M.: Language vs speaker change: a comparative study (2022). arXiv preprint arXiv:2203.02680
18. Mori, K., Nakagawa, S.: Speaker change detection and speaker clustering using vq distortion for broadcast news speech recognition. In: 2001 IEEE International Conference on Acoustics, Speech, and Signal Processing. Proceedings (Cat. No. 01CH37221), vol. 1, pp. 413–416. IEEE (2001)
19. Park, T.J., Kanda, N., Dimitriadis, D., Han, K.J., Watanabe, S., Narayanan, S.: A review of speaker diarization: recent advances with deep learning. Comput. Speech & Lang. **72**, 101317 (2022)
20. Prasanna, S.R.M., Gupta, C.S., Yegnanarayana, B.: Extraction of speaker-specific excitation information from linear prediction residual of speech. Speech Commun. **48**(10), 1243–1261 (2006)
21. Rangan, P., Teki, S., Misra, H.: Exploiting spectral augmentation for code-switched spoken language identification (2020). arXiv preprint arXiv:2010.07130 . arXiv preprint arXiv:2010.07130
22. Shah, S., Sitaram, S., Mehta, R.: First workshop on speech processing for code-switching in multilingual communities: shared task on code-switched spoken language identification. WSTCSMC **2020**, 24 (2020)
23. Sitaram, S., Chandu, K.R., Rallabandi, S.K., Black, A.W.: A survey of code switching speech and language processing (2019). arXiv:1904.00784 [cs.CL]
24. Spoorthy, V., Thenkanidiyoor, V., Dinesh, D.A.: SVM Based Language Diarization for Code-Switched Bilingual Indian Speech Using Bottleneck Features. In: Proceedings of the 6th International Workshop on Spoken Language Technologies for Under-Resourced Languages, pp. 132–136 (2018). https://doi.org/10.21437/SLTU.2018-28
25. Yilmaz, E., McLaren, M., van den Heuvel, H., van Leeuwen, D.A.: Language diarization for semi-supervised bilingual acoustic model training. In: 2017 IEEE Automatic Speech Recognition and Understanding Workshop (ASRU), pp. 91–96. IEEE (2017)

Low-Resource Emotional Speech Synthesis: Transfer Learning and Data Requirements

Anton Nesterenko[1,2], Ruslan Akhmerov[2], Yulia Matveeva[3(✉)],
Anna Goremykina[2], Dmitry Astankov[2], Evgeniy Shuranov[4],
and Alexandra Shirshova[3]

[1] Ivanovo State University of Chemistry and Technology, Ivanovo, Russia
`imdxdd@gmail.com`
[2] Big Data Academy MADE by VK, Saint Petersburg, Russia
`akhmerov.r.h@yandex.ru`, `anyagoremykina@gmail.com`,
`astankov.dmitry@gmail.com`
[3] Huawei Saint-Petersburg Research Center, Saint Petersburg, Russia
`matveeva.yulia@huawei.com`, `alexandra.sh.spb@gmail.com`
[4] ITMO University, Saint Petersburg, Russia
`evgeniy.v.shuranov@gmail.com`

Abstract. Recently, a number of solutions were proposed that improved on ways of adding an emotional aspect to speech synthesis. Combined with core neural text-to-speech architectures that reach high naturalness scores, these models are capable of producing natural human-like speech with well discernible emotions and even model their intensities. To successfully synthesize emotions the models are trained on hours of emotional data. In practice however, it is often difficult and rather expensive to collect a lot of emotional speech data per speaker. In this article, we inquire upon the minimal data requirements of expressive text-to-speech solutions to be applied in practical scenarios and also find an optimal architecture for low-resource training. In particular, a different number of training speakers and a different amount of data per emotion are considered. Frequently occurring situations are considered when there is a large multi-speaker dataset with neutral records and a large single-speaker emotional dataset, but there is little emotional data for the remaining speakers. On top of that we study the effect of several architecture modifications and training procedures (namely adversarial training and transfer learning from speaker verification) on the quality of the models as well as their data avidity. Our results show that transfer learning may lower data requirements from 15 min per speaker per emotion to just 2.5–7 min maintaining non-significant changes in voice naturalness and giving high emotion recognition rates. We also show how the data requirements change from one emotion to another. A demo page illustrating the main findings of this work is available at: https://diparty. github.io/projects/tts/emo/nat.

Keywords: Emotional speech synthesis · Expressive speech synthesis · Data requirements · Low-resource text-to-speech · Adversarial training · Transfer learning from speaker verification

S. R. M. Prasanna et al. (Eds.): SPECOM 2022, LNAI 13721, pp. 508–521, 2022.
https://doi.org/10.1007/978-3-031-20980-2_43

1   Introduction

Recently there has been rapid progress in the field of neural speech synthesis [11,17,18,20,21]. Current approaches reach human-level voice quality in terms of naturalness, prosody and clarity. While these advances mostly refer to the neutral speech synthesis, there has been a lot of promising research in the area of style and emotions modeling. Categorical-label based approaches require all training data to be labeled for emotions, which requires both expensive annotator work and has the problem of being subjective, thus potentially creating a certain level of incoherence in training data. To circumvent this and some other problems multiple studies have developed approaches based on reference-audio encoding, which do not require emotional labeling of training data but instead are trained to extract an abstract style representation from a sample audio. One of the recently popular architectures allowing for such style encoding is Global Style Tokens (GST) [28]. In this paper we consider a GST-Tacotron multi-speaker architecture of the text-to-speech backend and investigate its training-data requirements by using different amounts of emotional data for training in an attempt to form some practical advice on training-data collection. In addition we study the effect of transfer learning from speaker verification on the efficacy and data avidity of such models, as well as several types of additional losses helping to disentangle speaker information from emotional prosody encoding.

In Sect. 2 we give an overview of related works. In Sect. 3 we describe the model architecture studied in this work as well as the training procedure. In Sect. 4 we give a description of how we filtered and validated the training data. Section 5 gives a more detailed description of model hyper-parameters for better reproducibility. Section 6 gives a description of the evaluation procedures we used. Section 7 summarizes the experiments results. Finally, we conclude in Sect. 8.

2   Related Work

2.1   Data Requirements of Emotional TTS Systems

In [25] a GST-Tacotron based model was trained on 3.79 h of data representing happy, sad, angry and neutral emotions. Another GST-based emotional TTS model [2] used the dataset IEMOCAP containing 12.5 h for the neutral, angry, sad, happy and excited emotions. A reinforcement learning GST + Tacotron based framework [14] used the English subset of the ESD dataset consisting of 13 h of multispeaker emotional recordings for happy, angry, neutral, sad and surprise emotions. The approach in [13] uses 14 h of single-speaker recordings for neutral, happy, angry, disgust, fear, surprise and sadness emotions, with 6000 sentences in the neutral category and 620 sentences for each of the remaining ones.

An important practical question arises, namely, how much reference data per emotion is enough for successfully synthesizing this emotion. To our knowledge, not much work has been done in this direction. However, this question was also raised in [24], where authors studied the quality of emotional synthesis from a Deep Convolutional TTS (DCTTS) [23] model that was first pretrained on the single-speaker LJSpeech dataset [6] and then fine-tuned on the English part of the EmoV-DB emotional dataset [1]. In the end, the authors had access to a varied number of minutes of emotional data ranging from 15 to 36 per emotion.

2.2 Adversarial Training in Text-to-Speech

Adversarial training was first introduced in [5] in which it was defined as a two-player mini-max game with the discriminator attempting to guess the information that the generator is trying to hide or obscure from the discriminator. In particular, in the original paper the information to hide was the answer to the question whether a sample was synthesized by the generator or came from the pool of ground truth samples. In this setting the generator learned to mimic the distribution of original data. For this purpose two separate optimizers were used and two separate losses: one for the discriminator and a different one for the generator. Later in [4] a new technique for adversarial training based on gradient reversal was proposed. In this case a single common loss is computed and gradients are also computed only once for both the generator and the discriminator, however the sign of the gradients is flipped for the generator.

In text-to-speech the approach [5] is mainly used in vocoders [7,11,12,30]. The approach introduced in [4] is meanwhile widely used in various text-to-speech and voice conversion models for better disentanglement of intermediate learned representations. Thus, for example, in [31] speaker-adversarial loss with gradient reversal is applied to the text-encoder outputs to make sure that text representations remain speaker-independent. The gradient reversal technique is particularly popular in emotional speech synthesis. In [27] the authors aim at disentangling separate speech representations, namely content, timbre, rhythm and pitch to allow for independent control over each of these speech aspects at inference time. To achieve this goal they use a special type of mask-and-predict (MAP) adversarial approach: the MAP network is trained to predict masked speech characteristics from the unmasked ones, while the speech representation encoders use reverse gradient on the MAP loss in order to minimize correlations between these representations. In [32], similar to [31], a speaker adversarial and an emotion adversarial loss with gradient reversal [4] is applied to the text encoder. In [19] as well as in [15] a speaker-adversarial loss with gradient reversal is applied to the prosody encoder. As the authors of [15] work on Chinese speech synthesis they additionally apply tone-adversarial loss on the style encoder.

In our work we have decided to use the approach introduced in [5]. We assume here that better disentanglement may lead to better overall emotional synthesis quality, because we force the GST module to have richer encodings of speaker-independent emotion-relevant prosodic dimension instead of duplicating the information already present in the speaker encoder. Furthermore this kind of information separation may be beneficial for potential style-control capability (changing the style without changing the speaker identity).

2.3 Transfer Learning from Speaker Verification in Text-to-Speech

In our paper we also study how transfer learning from speaker verification affects training data requirements of emotional speech synthesis systems. To our knowledge this particular question was not yet well studied in the literature, however the idea of using pretrained voice-print models as speaker encoders in a TTS system is certainly not new. In [9] voiceprint speaker embeddings were used to build a multispeaker text-to-speech model capable of zero-shot voice cloning. The authors have specifically mentioned that transfer learning from a speaker verification task significantly lowers the requirements for multispeaker TTS training, however experiments were conducted with neutral speech only (VCTK and LibriSpeech datasets). In [3] these speaker embeddings were used for the same purpose, plus an additional loss was imposed on the predicted mel-spectrograms, which compared the speaker-encoder outputs on the original and the predicted spectrograms, thus leading to a claimed improvement of speaker similarity in the voice cloning task. The datasets used were again VCTK and LibriSpeech with no emotional data.

3   Methods

The backend of our text-to-speech system is a Non-Attentive Tacotron [20] architecture with a standard Global-Style-Token (GST) reference-audio encoder [28] and a speaker embedding. Two types of speaker embeddings are used in different experiments. In one set of experiments lookup embeddings are used, which are trained from scratch with the rest of the model. In the other experiments transfer learning from speaker verification is being leveraged by having a pretrained voiceprint model generate speaker embeddings (as proposed in [3,9]).

Following [28], the style embedding as well as the speaker embedding are upsampled to match the length of the input sequence and concatenated with encoder outputs. We then use a HiFiGAN vocoder [11] which recovers the waveform from the predicted mel spectrum.

We have chosen to feed phonemized texts to the backend model. Phonemisation (conversion of text in the form of a sequence of graphemes to a sequence of phonemes) as well as phoneme-to-audio alignment are performed using the Montreal Forced Aligner (MFA) [16]. At inference a proprietary phonemizer is used to perform the first task.

For training the HiFi-GAN vocoder we use the NVIDIA repository [10] and take the pretrained multi-speaker model which the authors have called Universal in that repository. We then finetune it on outputs predicted by our Tacotron-based backend model. For each backend model the vocoder was separately finetuned on the predicted mel spectrum and then the vocoder checkpoint was chosen individually by one independent annotator. We have noticed that unlike Tacotron and its variations, HiFiGAN training may be non-monotonic in quality on the evaluation set, thus it is not always true that the last checkpoint is the best.

The implementation of the non-attentive Tacotron architecture with all the mentioned modifications can be found in the following open-source repository: https://github.com/IMDxD/emotts.

We train the GST module along with the whole network, however we choose to introduce an additional discriminator layer D consisting of a single linear hidden layer with leaky ReLU activation followed by a linear layer with softmax activation that is supposed to try to recognize the speaker from the style information. We then introduce an adversarial loss intended to prevent the style encoder from retaining speaker information (so as to leave more expressive capacity for speaker-independent prosodic information). This creates a mini-max game between the discriminator layer D and the style encoder. This adversarial objective is implemented in the following way. We optimize two separate cross-entropy losses (inspired by the methodology described in [5]):

$$\min_{D_w} L_D = \mathcal{L}\Big(D(G(x_i)), y_i\Big), \ \min_{\bar{D}_w} L_G = \mathcal{L}\Big([1 - D(G(x_i))], y_i\Big) \qquad (1)$$

where
$$\mathcal{L}(p, y) = -\log(p) * y. \qquad (2)$$

with x denoting the input to the style encoder (a normalized reference mel-spectrogram in our case) and $G(x)$ referring to the GST style embedding, D_w being the set of weights of the discriminator network and $\bar{D}_w$—the weights of the rest of the network without the discriminator. Note that in this setting the different parts of the network are basically iteratively learning from each other's outputs (much like in most generative adversarial networks), so that the style-encoder uses the outputs from the currently trained discriminator in order to be penalized for all the correct answers the latter could get at this stage.

4   Training Data

All experiments have been carried out on opensource datasets, namely vctk [29] (English neutral speech dataset, 108 speakers, 37 h (without speakers p315 and p280)) and subsets of the English part of ESD [33] (parallel expressive-speech dataset, 10 speakers, 5 emotions, 12.5 h). The ESD emotions are: neutral, happy, angry, sad and surprise.

Our team of linguists has additionally verified the English part of the ESD dataset for audio deficiencies and transcript-audio mismatches. We have concluded that dataset quality is at a rather high level, no transcript-audio mismatches were found except rare cases of definite/indefinite article substitutions or other small grammatical words which from our experience do not affect the quality of the trained TTS systems greatly. However there might be a problem with speaker labeling as speaker-label 0019 happens to appear for two very different voice timbres, presumably male and female. This latter speaker was excluded from all experiments.

4.1   Emotional Data Validation and Subset Choice

When it comes to emotions, the task of emotion generation and recognition can be tough not only for machines, but also for people. Different actors happen to play out the same emotion in different ways, not to mention the fact that a mere consensus on what each emotion label should mean might often be a matter of debate. To take this fact into consideration we first asked the annotators to label emotions in a subset of the training dataset, so as to score the original recordings before analyzing the trained models. These scores should serve as a reference for the interpretation of the scores for the synthesized speech, since in our setting we cannot expect the model to express the emotions a lot better than the actors who provided the training data.

In our experiments we had 6 annotators that participated in emotion recognition tests. The first two annotators got all 9 speakers (numbers 11 to 18 and 20, excluding speaker 19 as discussed above). From the feedback of these two annotators only five (subjectively) most expressive speakers (12, 14, 16, 17, 20) were chosen for all the following model tests (their synthesized samples were included in the human evaluation procedures), while seven or less were used for training. Following this logic, we have eliminated the speakers that had the lowest emotion recognition annotator precision and annotator F-score rates on the original recordings (lowest precision (below 0.6) or highest standard deviation between annotators for speakers 11, 13, 15 and 18 respectively). The 4 best-scoring speakers were chosen to be the "base" speakers (numbers 15–18), that were then used to train the emotion encoder with full data (15 min per emotion per speaker) in all experiments, plus 5 more "test" speakers (numbers 11–14 and 20) had their training datasets gradually reduced from 15 min to 7, 2.5 and 1 per emotion per speaker.

Table 1 and Fig. 1 present the emotion recognition rates for all the speakers' original recordings.

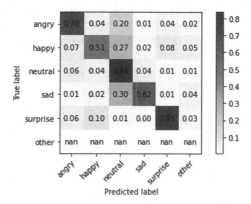

Fig. 1. Normalized confusion matrix (recall) of human-annotator results: emotion recognition for original English recordings in the ESD dataset. True labels are taken from the dataset, predicted labels were given by our team of annotators.

Table 1. Emotion recognition rates (macro-averaging) for original recordings of the English actors in the ESD dataset.

	Precision	Recall	F-score
speaker_20	0.721	0.644	0.651
base_speaker_18	0.696	0.633	0.646
base_speaker_17	0.679	0.633	0.646
base_speaker_16	0.667	0.621	0.631
base_speaker_15	0.632	0.561	0.539
speaker_14	0.602	0.553	0.568
speaker_11	0.599	0.473	0.462
speaker_12	0.595	0.543	0.547
speaker_13	0.573	0.506	0.484

5   Model Hyper-Parameters

As was mentioned earlier, the core architecture of all the speech synthesis models in this paper is based on non-attentive Tacotron [20]. All backend models take ARPABET phonemes as input, which are then encoded using a lookup embedding table of size 512. The encoder block starts with 3 convolutional layers with 512-channel kernels and 5×1 filters. Both the encoder and decoder have 3 (Bi)LSTM layers with 512 hidden units each, the duration and range predictors have LSTM's with 2 layers and 256 hidden units each. The post-net consists of 5 convolutional layers, first 3 having 512 channels and the last one having 128. Each decoder step predicts 3 mel-spectrogram frames at a time. The style encoder is implemented as a Global-Style-Tokens block [28] with multi-head attention having 8 heads, the style embedding having size 128 and the number of style tokens being 10. The speaker embedding is of size 256 in all models and is either trained with the whole model as a lookup-table or is taken from a pretrained voiceprint encoder (explained in more detail in Sect. 7.1).

We take audios 22050 Hz sample rate and use a short time Fourier transform (STFT) using 1024-sample frame size, 256-sample hop size and a Hann window function to compute the linear spectrogram, then a mel filterbank with 80 channels is applied. The mel spectrogram is what is predicted by the backend models. We first trained all models for 500000 steps with batch size 16 on a big neutral dataset (VCTK) and after that fine-tuned them for 360000 steps with batch size 16 on an emotional dataset (ESD). Learning rate was set to 1e-3, L2-regularization weight to 1e-6. Learning rate was scheduled with linear ramp-up for 4000 steps and then a half-decay every 50000 steps. Adam was used as the optimizer, with betas equal to 0.9 and 0.999, and a 1e-6 term added to the denominator to improve numerical stability (the epsilon parameter). The loss consisted of two parts: a mixed mel-spectrum loss (MSE + MAE) is used with a weight of 1.0 and a duration loss with weight 2.0. When the GST module has its own adversarial loss, its weight is fixed to 0.1.

All the backend models' encoder, decoder and duration predictor are first pre-trained on the neutral VCTK dataset, then the text-encoder gets frozen, the style encoder is added to the architecture and the rest is trained on the chosen subset of the emotional ESD dataset.

All systems used the same pretrained HiFiGAN vocoder model [10] further fine-tuned on VCTK + ESD with batch size 16 for 500 epochs to generate speech waveforms from mel spectrum. All HiFiGAN parameters except for scheduler and optimizer were inherited from the base universal model downloaded from the aforementioned repo [10].

6   Evaluation Metrics

For comparing the models we have chosen to do two types of subjective tests. First was traditional mean opinion score (MOS). However for a deeper understanding of model quality we split the MOS metrics into 3 different aspects: voice quality (human-like nature of the voice itself, whether it sounds robotic, unnatural or distorted in any way), voice prosody (intonation) and clarity (how hard it is to understand the linguistic contents + the phonetic correctness of pronunciation). The second test was an emotion recognition test: each annotator had 5 emotions to choose from for each audio (neutral, surprise, happy, angry, sad) with an ability to put the label "other" instead, if he/she heard a distinct non-neutral emotion that could not be identified with any of the five from the list.

7   Experiments

7.1   Transfer Learning from Speaker Verification and Data Requirements of Emotional TTS

In the next set of experiments we have taken 4 emotional speakers with 15 min per emotion and 5 emotions in total each. We call them "base" training speakers. For the remaining 5 speakers the amount of data per emotion was gradually reduced from 15, to 7, to 2.5 and finally to 1 min (they are encoded as 15, 7, 2 and 1 in model names respectively). The 1- and 2.5- min training subsets were manually hand-picked from the dataset by the annotators, choosing the most expressive and clean audios. The rest were randomly sampled from the full dataset as an addition to these 2.5. The goal was to find the minimum amount of training data sufficient to train the emotional text-to-speech systems under consideration.

On top of that we have compared two types of speaker embeddings: (lkp) lookup speaker embeddings trained from scratch with the rest of the Emotional TTS system and (vp) Voiceprint embeddings taken from a pretrained speaker encoder originally trained for the task of speaker verification. The size of the speaker embedding is 256 in both cases. A recurrent speaker encoder, introduced in [26], was used. We have taken its implementation and the pretrained English model from the github repository [8]. All these models used adversarial training with loss (1).

We have found out that the optimal choice (best subjective scores and least data requirements) is to use pretrained voiceprint embeddings, to have at least 4 emotional training speakers with at least 15 min of audios per emotion, then it is possible to have just 2.5 min of training data per speaker per emotion for the rest of the speakers to get decent voice naturalness and expressiveness.

We have then fixed the amount of data per so called "test" speakers to 2.5 min each and proceeded to reducing the number of "base" speakers (those are speakers that get the highest emotion recognition scores on original recordings and who have 15 min per emotion in the training dataset). In this series of experiments the decrease in the number of base speakers from 4 to 2 and then to 1 gave significant model quality degradation, so the general advice would be that low-resource emotional text-to-speech system with the chosen architecture requires at least 4 emotional speakers for training the model (training the global style tokens and fine-tuning the decoder).

Mean Opinion Scores for Speech Naturalness. Note that in MOS tests emotions were disregarded when evaluating for any of the aspects, the only concern was whether it sounded human-like and whether the sound was clean.

Table 2. Dependence of MOS on dataset size and speaker embedding type (generated emotional speech for five emotions, three test speakers).

model	Clarity	Prosody	Voice quality	MOS mean
vp_15_advloss	4.891	4.831	4.368	4.697
lkp_15_advloss	4.870	4.742	4.611	4.741
vp_7_advloss	4.919	4.808	4.347	4.691
lkp_7_advloss	4.878	4.753	4.559	4.730
vp_2_advloss	4.914	4.840	4.346	4.700
lkp_2_advloss	4.795	4.616	4.323	4.578
vp_1_advloss	4.867	4.811	4.150	4.609
lkp_1_advloss	4.784	4.650	4.266	4.567

Table 3. Dependence of MOS on the number of "base" speakers (generated emotional speech for five emotions, three test speakers).

model	Clarity	Prosody	Voice quality	MOS mean
vp_2_4bs_advloss	4.914	4.840	4.346	4.700
vp_2_2bs_advloss	4.926	4.831	4.338	4.698
vp_2_1bs_advloss	4.919	4.858	4.384	4.721

We have further executed several pair-wise dependent t-tests [22] to compare the naturalness scores given to the models. As we can conclude from the mean scores and the statistical tests, in a low-resource setting (1–2.5 min) the approach using voiceprint speaker embeddings gives significantly better results given the same amount of training data (p-value $< 1e-5$) than the lookup-embedding approach. Moreover the voiceprint-based models prove to be significantly less data-hungry: for **vp** models the mean MOS scores differ significantly (p-value $< 1e-10$) only between 1 and 2.5 min of training data, while further increase in training dataset size does not give significant improvements (p-value > 0.4).

When it comes to the lookup-embedding approach, 1 and 2.5 min of training data give roughly the same mean MOS scores (p-value > 0.3) as do 7 and 15 min. The only significant change was noticed when going from 2.5 min to 7 (p-value $< 1e-30$).

In all the models the most distinct changes affected by training data size was the "quality of the voice" aspect of naturalness, rather than the clarity of pronunciation or the prosody (intonation) naturalness. For voiceprint models neither clarity nor prosody naturalness changed for any of the training-data sizes at a significance level of 0.01. For lookup speaker-embedding models all the aspects taken separately improve significantly when increasing dataset size to 7 min per speaker per emotion.

Once the optimal architecture and the optimal number of minutes for "test" speakers was obtained, we went further to reducing the number of the so-called "base" speakers. In these experiments we basically model the hypothetical situation in which there is a budget for more data (15 min per emotion in our case) for a limited number of professional actors (our top scoring speakers in this case), which are needed to be at the core of training the style encoder and the emotional synthesis. Then other speakers may be added to the model with fewer data (we call these test speakers). We have chosen 4 speakers (15, 16, 17, 18) from the ESD dataset that got highest mean emotion recognition scores on the original recordings to be the base speakers.

In Table 3 you can see the subjective scores for models with 4 base speakers (model **vp_2_4bs_advloss**), with 2 base speakers (model **vp_2_2bs_advloss**, speakers 17 and 18) and a single base speaker (model **vp_2_1bs_advloss**, speaker 18). The conclusion is somewhat not as intuitive as in the previous experiments: the model with only one base speaker beats the others (with 2 and 4 base speakers) in terms of MOS naturalness. We can assume that the quality of the dataset in this case is more important than its size. However as will be seen from the emotion recognition scores, this is not the case for the model's capacity to produce recognizable emotions, where more than one speaker in the training dataset is strictly preferred.

Expressivity of Speech and Emotion Recognition Scores. Here we present the results of blind emotion-recognition tests, in which all the synthesis results from all the models were presented in random order and the annotators were asked to pick the most appropriate emotion tag for each audio.

Table 4. Dependence of emotion recognition rates (macro-averaging) on dataset size and speaker-embedding type (generated emotional speech for five emotions, three test speakers).

model	Precision	Recall	F-score
ground_truth_all	0.628	0.577	0.589
ground_truth_base	0.666	0.617	0.628
ground_truth_test	0.636	0.580	0.592
vp_15_advloss	0.543	0.506	0.507
lkp_15_advloss	0.474	0.444	0.449
vp_7_advloss	0.547	0.523	0.527
lkp_7_advloss	0.299	0.303	0.296
vp_2_advloss	0.481	0.455	0.455
lkp_2_advloss	0.208	0.193	0.192
vp_1_advloss	0.325	0.321	0.316
lkp_1_advloss	0.147	0.147	0.143

Table 5. Dependence of emotion recognition rates (macro-averaging) on the number of "base" speakers (generated emotional speech for five emotions, three test speakers).

	Precision	Recall	F-score
ground_truth_4bs	0.628	0.577	0.589
vp_2_4bs_advloss	0.481	0.455	0.455
ground_truth_2bs	0.680	0.633	0.648
vp_2_2bs_advloss	0.261	0.283	0.262
ground_truth_1bs	0.696	0.633	0.646
vp_2_1bs_advloss	0.255	0.256	0.250

As can be concluded from Table 4 the approach with transfer learning from speaker verification steadily beats the approach with lookup speaker embeddings on any given training dataset size. The quality of emotion expression by the model (as modelled by human emotion recognition) changes significantly with the growing dataset size up until 7 min of data. Increasing from then on does not seem to give a significant profit. If the "test speakers" come with very few data (2.5 min), then it seems advisable to have no less than 4 "base" emotional training speakers in the dataset (results shown in the Table 5), because otherwise the model does not learn to express the emotions for the low-resource speakers well (with F-scores below 30%).

Lastly we should note that the aforementioned conclusions on the sufficiency of data and the optimality of architectures are valid for the set of all the emotions together. However we have noticed that in different models different emotions have varying data requirements. A more detailed vision may be obtained from Tables 6 and 7 (here the true label is the desired emotion intended for synthesis and the predicted emotion is the one given by the annotators after listening to the synthesized audio). The "sad" emotion is the simplest to model for both approaches (mainly expressed by a slowdown in speech speed), the "angry" emotion seems harder to model and requires more data (7 min being enough for **vp** approach and 15 for **lkp**). The "surprise" emotion (mostly expressed via a pitch-variation towards the end of the sentence) seems to be best encoded by the voiceprint embedding which allows for a very low-resource training of this emotion (just 1 min is enough to have a human recognition rate higher than 55%).

Table 6. Emotion recognition recall from annotator results on audios synthesized from the model with lookup speaker embeddings.

	Angry	Happy	Neutral	Sad	Surprise
1_advloss	0.22	0.09	0.26	0.26	0.07
2_advloss	0.28	0.13	0.32	0.30	0.16
7_advloss	0.26	0.20	0.47	0.66	0.25
15_advloss	0.69	0.25	0.61	0.70	0.46

Table 7. Emotion recognition recall from annotator results on audios synthesized from the models with voiceprint speaker embeddings.

Angry	Happy	Neutral	Sad	Surprise
0.38	0.10	0.46	0.40	0.59
0.44	0.30	0.63	0.79	0.57
0.65	0.34	0.57	0.81	0.76
0.61	0.30	0.74	0.87	0.51

8   Conclusion

In this work we have shown that transfer learning from speaker verification is capable of drastically improving the quality of a low-resource emotional speech synthesis system, both in terms of voice naturalness and the capacity to express emotions. We have established an optimal amount of emotional training data to be 4 "base" emotional speakers with at least 15 min of data per emotion, after which for low-resource speakers it may suffice to use from 2.5 to 7 min of audio per emotion. We have also established that the amount of data for low-resource speakers seems to affect the voice quality of synthesized speech most of all (rather than noisiness of the audio or the human-like nature of the prosody) and the emotion expressivity of this model. We have also shown that different emotions differ in data size requirements.

Our next step is to study the speaker-independent style-control capability of the model and to work on further extensions allowing for this functionality.

References

1. Adigwe, A., Tits, N., El Haddad, K., Ostadabbas, S., Dutoit, T.: The emotional voices database: towards controlling the emotion dimension in voice generation systems 06 (2018)
2. Cai, X., Dai, D., Wu, Z., Li, X., Li, J., Meng, H.: Emotion controllable speech synthesis using emotion-unlabeled dataset with the assistance of cross-domain speech emotion recognition. In: ICASSP 2021 IEEE International Conference on Acoustics, Speech and Signal Processing (ICASSP) (2020). arXiv:abs/2011.08679
3. Cai, Z., Zhang, C., Li, M.: From speaker verification to multispeaker speech synthesis, deep transfer with feedback constraint 08, 1032 (2020). https://doi.org/10.21437/Interspeech
4. Ganin, Y., Ustinova, E., Ajakan, H., Germain, P., Larochelle, H., Laviolette, F., March, M., Lempitsky, V.: Domain-adversarial training of neural networks. J. Mach. Learn. Res. **17**(59), 1–35 (2016). https://jmlr.org/papers/v17/15-239.html
5. Goodfellow, I., Pouget-Abadie, J., Mirza, M., Xu, B., Warde-Farley, D., Ozair, S., Courville, A., Bengio, Y.: Generative adversarial nets. In: Ghahramani, Z., Welling, M., Cortes, C., Lawrence, N., Weinberger, K.Q.

(eds.) Advances in Neural Information Processing Systems, vol. 27. Curran Associates, Inc. (2014). https://proceedings.neurips.cc/paper/2014/file/5ca3e9b122f61f8f06494c97b1afccf3-Paper.pdf

6. Ito, K., Johnson, L.: The LJ speech dataset (2017). https://keithito.com/LJ-Speech-Dataset/

7. Jang, W., Lim, D., Yoon, J.: Universal MelGAN: a robust neural vocoder for high-fidelity waveform generation in multiple domains (2020). https://doi.org/10.48550/ARXIV.2011.09631, arXiv:abs/2011.09631

8. Jemine, C., et al.: Real time voice cloning (2021). https://github.com/CorentinJ/Real-Time-Voice-Cloning

9. Jia, Y., et al.: Transfer learning from speaker verification to multispeaker text-to-speech synthesis. In: Proceedings of the 32nd International Conference on Neural Information Processing Systems, pp. 4485–4495. NIPS'18, Curran Associates Inc., Red Hook, NY, USA (2018)

10. Kong, J., Casanova, E.: Hifi-gan (2013). https://github.com/jik876/hifi-gan

11. Kong, J., Kim, J., Bae, J.: Hifi-gan: generative adversarial networks for efficient and high fidelity speech synthesis (2020). arXiv:abs/2010.05646

12. Kumar, K., Kumar, R., de Boissiere, T., Gestin, L., Teoh, W.Z., Sotelo, J., de Brébisson, A., Bengio, Y., Courville, A.C.: MelGAN: generative adversarial networks for conditional waveform synthesis. In: Wallach, H., Larochelle, H., Beygelzimer, A., d'Alché-Buc, F., Fox, E., Garnett, R. (eds.) Advances in Neural Information Processing Systems 32 (NeurIPS 2019), vol. 32. Curran Associates, Inc. (2019)

13. Li, T., Yang, S., Xue, L., Xie, L.: Controllable emotion transfer for end-to-end speech synthesis (2020). arXiv:abs/2011.08679

14. Liu, R., Sisman, B., Li, H.: Reinforcement learning for emotional text-to-speech synthesis with improved emotion discriminability (2021). arXiv:abs/2104.01408

15. Lu, C., Wen, X., Liu, R., Chen, X.: Multi-speaker emotional speech synthesis with fine-grained prosody modeling. In: ICASSP 2021–2021 IEEE International Conference on Acoustics, Speech and Signal Processing (ICASSP), pp. 5729–5733 (2021). https://doi.org/10.1109/ICASSP39728.2021.9413398

16. McAuliffe, M., Socolof, M., Mihuc, S., Wagner, M., Sonderegger, M.: Montreal forced aligner: trainable text-speech alignment using kaldi. In: INTERSPEECH (2017)

17. Ren, Y., Hu, C., Tan, X., Qin, T., Zhao, S., Zhao, Z., Liu, T.Y.: Fastspeech 2: fast and high-quality end-to-end text to speech. In: International Conference on Learning Representations (2021)

18. Ren, Y., Ruan, Y., Tan, X., Qin, T., Zhao, S., Zhao, Z., Liu, T.Y.: Fastspeech: Fast, robust and controllable text to speech. In: Wallach, H., Larochelle, H., Beygelzimer, A., dÁlché-Buc, F., Fox, E., Garnett, R. (eds.) Advances in Neural Information Processing Systems, vol. 32. Curran Associates, Inc. (2019)

19. Shang, Z., Huang, Z., Zhang, H., Zhang, P., Yan, Y.: Incorporating cross-speaker style transfer for multi-language text-to-speech. In: Proceedings of the Interspeech 2021, pp. 1619–1623 (2021). https://doi.org/10.21437/Interspeech.2021-1265

20. Shen, J., Jia, Y., Chrzanowski, M., Zhang, Y., Elias, I., Zen, H., Wu, Y.: Non-attentive tacotron: robust and controllable neural TTS synthesis including unsupervised duration modeling (2020). arXiv:abs/2010.04301

21. Shen, J., Pang, R., Weiss, R.J., Schuster, M., Jaitly, N., Yang, Z., Chen, Z., Zhang, Y., Wang, Y., Skerry-Ryan, R.J., Saurous, R.A., Agiomyrgiannakis, Y., Wu, Y.: Natural TTS synthesis by conditioning wavenet on mel spectrogram predictions (2017). arXiv:abs/1712.05884

22. Student: the probable error of a mean. Biometrika **6**(1), 1–25 (1908). http://www. jstor.org/stable/2331554

23. Tachibana, H., Uenoyama, K., Aihara, S.: Efficiently trainable text-to-speech system based on deep convolutional networks with guided attention (2017). arXiv:abs/1710.08969

24. Tits, N., Haddad, K.E., Dutoit, T.: Exploring transfer learning for low resource emotional TTS (2019). arXiv:abs/1901.04276

25. Um, S.Y., Oh, S., Byun, K., Jang, I., Ahn, C., Kang, H.G.: Emotional speech synthesis with rich and granularized control. In: ICASSP 2020–2020 IEEE International Conference on Acoustics, Speech and Signal Processing (ICASSP), pp. 7254–7258 (2020). https://doi.org/10.1109/ICASSP40776.2020.9053732

26. Wan, L., Wang, Q., Papir, A., Moreno, I.L.: Generalized end-to-end loss for speaker verification. In: 2018 IEEE International Conference on Acoustics, Speech and Signal Processing (ICASSP), pp. 4879–4883 (2018). https://doi.org/10.1109/ICASSP. 2018.8462665

27. Wang, J., Li, J., Zhao, X., Wu, Z., Kang, S., Meng, H.: Adversarially learning disentangled speech representations for robust multi-factor voice conversion. In: Proceedings of the Interspeech 2021, pp. 846–850 (2021). https://doi.org/10.21437/ Interspeech

28. Wang, Y., Stanton, D., Zhang, Y., Skerry-Ryan, R.J., Battenberg, E., Shor, J., Xiao, Y., Ren, F., Jia, Y., Saurous, R.A.: Style tokens: unsupervised style modeling, control and transfer in end-to-end speech synthesis (2018). arXiv:abs/1803.09017

29. Yamagishi, J., Veaux, C., MacDonald, K.: CSTR VCTK corpus: english multi-speaker corpus for CSTR voice cloning toolkit (version 0.92) (2019)

30. Yamamoto, R., Song, E., Kim, J.M.: Parallel wavegan: a fast waveform generation model based on generative adversarial networks with multi-resolution spectrogram. In: ICASSP 2020 IEEE International Conference on Acoustics, Speech and Signal Processing (ICASSP), pp. 6199–6203 (2020). https://doi.org/10.1109/ ICASSP40776.2020.9053795

31. Zhang, Y., Weiss, R.J., Zen, H., Wu, Y., Chen, Z., Skerry-Ryan, R., Jia, Y., Rosenberg, A., Ramabhadran, B.: Learning to speak fluently in a foreign language: multilingual speech synthesis and cross-language voice cloning. In: Proceeding of the Interspeech 2019, pp. 2080–2084 (2019). https://doi.org/10.21437/Interspeech

32. Zhou, K., Sisman, B., Li, H.: Limited data emotional voice conversion leveraging text-to-speech: two-stage sequence-to-sequence training. In: Proceeding of the Interspeech 2021, pp. 811–815 (2021). https://doi.org/10.21437/Interspeech

33. Zhou, K., Sisman, B., Liu, R., Li, H.: Emotional voice conversion: theory, databases and ESD (2021). arXiv:abs/2105.14762

Fuzzy Classifier for Speech Assessment in Speech Rehabilitation

Dariya Novokhrestova$^{(\boxtimes)}$ ⓘ, Ilya Hodashinsky ⓘ, Evgeny Kostyuchenko ⓘ,
Konstantin Sarin ⓘ, and Marina Bardamova ⓘ

Systems and Radioelectronics, Tomsk State University of Control, Lenina Str. 40, 634050
Tomsk, Russia
ndi@fb.tusur.ru

Abstract. The article describes the use of a fuzzy classifier as a mechanism for combining the values calculated from three metrics to obtain a quantitative assessment of the intelligibility of the syllable pronunciation. The resulting assessment is used to assess speech in speech rehabilitation after the treatment of the oral cavity and oropharynx oncology. The evaluation is based on the calculation of the distance as the similarity degree between the syllable pronunciation in the estimated recording (the patient's speech in the process of rehabilitation) and the syllable pronunciation in the reference recording (the patient's speech before surgery). It is proposed to use a fuzzy classifier with the genetic optimization algorithm NSGA II. The training datasets are quantitative and expert estimates of a set of syllable pronunciation recordings provided by the Cancer Research Institute Tomsk NRMC. Three datasets were used: 1020 recordings for each of the problematic phonemes [k], [s], [t]. Separate fuzzy classifiers were trained for each of the datasets. Classification accuracies are shown on the initial datasets and rebalanced datasets. The NeighborhoodCleaningRule and SMOTEENN algorithms were used for rebalancing the data. It was concluded that it is possible to use a fuzzy classifier as a combination mechanism to obtain the intelligibility assessment of the syllable pronunciation.

Keywords: Speech assessment · Syllable intelligibility · Fuzzy classifier ·
Genetic algorithms · Speech rehabilitation

1 Introduction

An important step in speech rehabilitation is to assess the quality of speech. Cancer of the speech organs is one of the types of diseases, the treatment of which requires speech rehabilitation. In 2020, more than 20,000 new cases of detection of the oral cavity and oropharynx tumors were registered, the average annual growth rate is 2.5% [1, 2]. The slight decrease in the total number of diagnoses is due to the global health situation, namely Covid-19. At the same time, the proportion of cases of more severe stages of the disease (stages III and IV) has increased significantly. In the Cancer Research Institute Tomsk NRMC, a combined treatment of oncology of the oral cavity and oropharynx is carried out. It includes chemoradiotherapy and surgical intervention in various

S. R. M. Prasanna et al. (Eds.): SPECOM 2022, LNAI 13721, pp. 522–532, 2022.
https://doi.org/10.1007/978-3-031-20980-2_44

sequences, the surgical stage remains the leading component of the treatment. The amount of surgical intervention depends on the stage of the disease and the location of the neoplasm. The surgery is performed on the articulatory organs, which leads to a violation of the function of speech and the mechanisms of sound production. Previously, speech assessment in speech rehabilitation occurred using a subjective assessment method. The patient pronounced a set of syllables, then the expert evaluated the recordings of one of two ratings: 1 - the syllable was pronounced legibly, 0 - the syllable was pronounced illegible. This approach is based on the method for assessing the intelligibility of speech during transmission over communication channels, described in [3]. The approach has significant drawbacks, such as the significant influence of the expert's opinion, the large time costs and the impossibility of building an individualized evaluation algorithm. The current research is devoted to the development of methods and algorithms for speech analysis, which will solve the task of automated assessment of the syllable pronunciation quality.

The approach proposed in the study is based on a quantitative assessment of the similarity of pronunciation at the current stage of speech rehabilitation with some reference pronunciation. The presence of neoplasms on the organs of the speech apparatus can lead to distortions in the patient's speech. However, due to the impossibility of obtaining records of the patient's speech before the onset of the disease, preoperative speech is used as a reference point for speech rehabilitation. Therefore, recordings of the patient's speech before surgery are used as a reference. This will consider the initial features of the patient's speech. Using the recordings of another speaker as a reference, even if he has perfect pronunciation, leads to an underestimation of the obtained estimates. However, such a situation is possible (for example, if it is impossible to record speech before surgery), but it requires more attention from a speech therapist who interprets the results.

The algorithm for obtaining a quantitative estimate consists in: 1) representing speech signals in the form of sequences of numeric values, bringing them to a single length using the dynamic time warping (DTW) algorithm [4], 2) calculating values for three selected metrics (DTW distance [4], correlation coefficient [5] and Minkowski distance [6]), and 3) obtaining a final quantitative estimate by combining the calculated values by metrics. In [7] the analysis of the values calculated by the metrics, obtained using the developed algorithm, and their pairwise comparison with expert estimates are described. The comparison was made due to the binarization of the obtained values. The DTW-distance metric has the highest agreement with the expert estimates and the least number of errors (84.2% of matches, 161 errors for 1020 records). The disadvantage of the approach described in [7] is the manual selection of the binarization parameter, which leads to the impossibility of its practical application in the process of speech rehabilitation. This paper proposes the use of a fuzzy classifier as a mechanism for combining values calculated by metrics to obtain a final quantitative estimate.

The aim of the work is to improve the quality of speech assessment in speech rehabilitation by developing a new hybrid measure for assessing the syllable pronunciation based on interpretable fuzzy classifiers. The use of these classifiers makes it possible to explain the result of the assessment using the production rules base of the IF-THEN type. The scientific novelty of the work is in the development of a hybrid measure for assessing the syllable pronunciation quality, based on a fuzzy classifier.

Experts' assessments of the quality of syllables suggest only two possible meanings: "the pronunciation of the syllable is illegible" and "the pronunciation of the syllable is legible". This binary version of the assessment does not allow assessing the progress in the rehabilitation process. The calculation of the quantitative value of the assessment would solve this problem. The fuzzy classifier returns the degrees of membership in the sets "unintelligible pronunciation" and "intelligible pronunciation", which take values in the range [0, ..., 1]. In this work, the degree of membership in the set "pronunciation of the syllable is legible" is used as such a quantitative assessment of quality.

2   Experiment

2.1   Data Description

By analogy with [7], sound files were taken for the experiment, which were recorded in the process of speech rehabilitation after the treatment of oncological diseases of the vocal tract, carried out at the Cancer Research Institute Tomsk NRMC. Recordings of 15 patients were selected. The recordings are combined into sessions, each session was recorded at a certain point of the treatment (before surgery, after surgery and before rehabilitation, during rehabilitation). 4 patients had 4 sessions; 11 patients had 3 sessions. The first session for each patient is a reference, that is, it is with the recordings of this session that the corresponding records from the remaining sessions will be compared. Thus, 34 sessions will be used to calculate estimates.

The list of syllables for recording contains syllables with the most problematic phonemes [k], [s], [t]. The most problematic phonemes are the phonemes that most often undergo changes in pronunciation after surgical treatment of oncology of the oral cavity and oropharynx. Examples of syllables are taken from the tables of syllables in Appendix B of GOST [3]. The list consists of 90 syllables, 30 syllables for each of the problematic phonemes. There are 90 syllables in the list. These 30 syllables for each phoneme are selected in such a way that there are 5 examples for all possible phoneme locations in a syllable (at the beginning, in the middle and at the end). Since the features of the change in each of the problematic phonemes differ, the study of estimates, and, accordingly, the training of fuzzy classifiers was carried out for each of the phonemes separately.

All selected recordings were evaluated in two ways. The first way is a subjective assessment of speech according to the method based on GOST [3]. The speech therapist gave a binary score: 1 if the syllable was pronounced correctly, 0 otherwise.

The second way: obtaining three values by metrics using the developed algorithm for automated speech quality assessment. The algorithm receives two sound files as input: an estimated recording and a reference recording. For time normalization, the DTW algorithm was used in the estimation algorithm. Calculated metrics: DTW – distance, Pearson correlation coefficient, Minkowski distance (the optimal value of the parameter is 3 for the problem being solved [6]).

For each of the problematic phonemes denote expert estimates as a set of values $X = \{X_1, X_2, ..., X_{1020}\}$, estimates obtained using the DTW distance metric as $Y = \{Y_1,$

$Y_2, ..., Y_{1020}$}, estimates obtained using the correlation coefficient as $Z = \{Z_1, Z_2, ..., Z_{1020}\}$ and estimates obtained using the Minkowski distance metric as $W = \{W_1, W_2, ..., W_{1020}\}$.

2.2 Fuzzy Classifier

In essence, the speech therapist performs the task of classification. In the evaluation process, he assigns a score of 1 or 0, thereby dividing the set of audio recordings into two classes: if the score is 1, then the audio recording belongs to class C1 "the pronunciation of the syllable in the audio recording is fully intelligible", if the score is 0, then the audio recording belongs to class C0 "the pronunciation of a syllable in an audio recording is unintelligible." Therefore, the use of a fuzzy classifier is proposed as a combination mechanism in a hybrid evaluation measure.

The basis of the fuzzy classifier is the base of production rules that evaluate the value of the features of the object $\mathbf{x} = (x_1, x_2, ..., x_n)$ by fuzzy terms [8, 9]. The rules have the following form:

$$R_j: \text{IF } x_1 = T_{1j} \text{ AND } x_2 = T_{2j} \text{ AND } ..., \text{ AND } x_n = T_{nj}, \text{ THEN class} = c_j, \quad (1)$$

where T_{ij} – fuzzy set (terms) characterizing the i-th features in the rule $R_j, j = 1, ..., r$, r – the number of rules; c_j – the class index of the j-th rule

The definition of the object class $\mathbf{x}$ is carried out using a fuzzy inference procedure using the rule base and the value of the object's features. As a result of this procedure, the membership degrees of the object $\mathbf{x}$ to each class are determined:

$$\beta_k(\mathbf{x}) = \max_{j \,|\, c_j = k} \left(\prod_{i=1}^{n} \mu_{T_{ij}}(x_i) \right), \quad (2)$$

where $\beta_k(\mathbf{x})$ – the membership degree of the object $\mathbf{x}$ to class k ($k = 1, ..., M$, M – the number of classes), $\mu_{T_{ij}}(x_i)$ – the membership degree of the feature x_i to fuzzy term T_{ij}. The class of an object is determined by the class to which $\mathbf{x}$ has the highest membership degree:

$$\text{class} = \arg \max_{k=1,...,M} (\beta_k). \quad (3)$$

In the current study, the authors use genetic fuzzy classifiers [10]. These classifiers are created using a genetic algorithm, and in this work the construction was applied, according to the approach of the scientific group led by H. Ishibuchu [11, 12]. In their work, the group used multiobjective optimization for learning, providing a compromise between the interpretability and accuracy of the resulting classifiers.

A chromosome (individual) in a population represents a separate fuzzy classifier. Each chromosome gene encodes the membership function of a particular rule with an integer value; the number of possible variants of this value depends on the fuzzy partitioning (granulation) of the variable change space. For example, if the space is divided into three fuzzy sets (see Fig. 1) that are associated with linguistic granules (terms) "Small", "Medium" and "Large", then the value of the gene can be selected

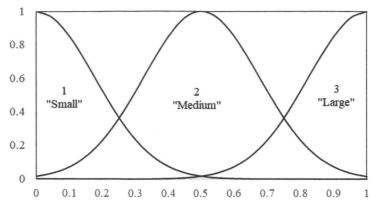

Fig. 1. Membership function variants in a fuzzy classifier

from the set {0, 1, 2, 3}, where 0 denotes the absence of a membership function, the remaining values encode the corresponding functions.

The rule class is not encoded because it can be determined based on the membership functions of the rules and training data. To do this, the sums of belongings for each class instances to the fuzzy set formed by the antecedent part of the rule are found, and the class with the largest value is selected.

In this work, we use the multiobjective genetic algorithm NSGA II (Nondominated Sorting Genetic Algorithm II) [13]. The optimization criteria are: classification error, the number of terms in the entire rule base, the number of fuzzy rules. All obtained criteria values should be minimized. The algorithm returns a population of classifiers that are on the Pareto front of the given criteria. On the resulting Pareto front, the solution for the classifier with the smallest classification error is selected.

Figure 2 shows one of the rule bases obtained during the experiment for determining the correct pronunciation of a syllable with the phoneme [k]. The last column on Fig. 2 defines the rule class label.

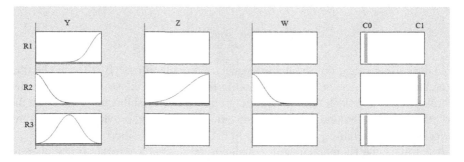

Fig. 2. Fuzzy classifier rule base for determining the intelligibility of the phoneme [k]

The extracted rules are interpreted as follows.

Rule 1 (R1). IF the value of the DTW distance (Y) is "Large" THEN the syllable pronunciation is illegible (C0).

Rule 2 (R2). IF the value of the DTW distance (Y) is "Small" AND the correlation coefficient value (Z) is "Large" AND the Minkowski distance value (W) is "Small" THEN the syllable pronunciation is legible (C1).

Rule 3 (R3). IF the value of the DTW distance (Y) is "Medium" IF the syllable pronunciation is illegible (C0).

The distance value means the calculated value of the metric between the reference and the estimated recordings.

The classifier receives three values Y, Z, W as an input. The output is a value of class C0 or C1. A set of X values is used to train the classifier.

2.3 Rebalancing Data

The presence of noise and imbalanced data distribution can have a significant impact on the classifier construction process. When there is a large difference in the number of instances of different classes, classifiers tend to overtrain on the classes with the highest representation, leading to a decrease in the recognition accuracy of rarer instances. However, the simplest random sampling reduction leads to the loss of important information. Modern rebalancing algorithms aim not only at obtaining a sample with equal class representation, but also at correcting related data weaknesses. Thus, the algorithms for reducing the number of samples of the largest classes (under-sampling) first remove instances that can be treated as outliers and that are too far from the decision-making border. Advanced algorithms for generating artificial data (over-sampling) are directed at generating new instances near the decision boundary, but in such a way that overlapping areas of different classes are avoided as much as possible. One of the most effective ways to rebalance is to apply an integrated approach that combines both over- and under-sampling [14].

Two algorithms from an open-source library for the python programming language "imbalanced learn" were used in this work [15]. The NeighbourhoodCleaningRule algorithm is designed to reduce noise instances. In the "majority" mode used, it removes a sample of the largest class if among its k nearest neighbours the majority belongs to a contrary class. In addition, if among a group of neighbours all mistakenly belong to an opposite class by the k-nearest neighbors classifier, they are also excluded. The second tool, the hybrid algorithm SMOTEENN, was directly responsible for rebalancing. The first step of the algorithm is to generate instances of the smallest class. A set of k nearest neighbours is determined for a randomly chosen instance of the smallest class, and an artificial instance with some deviation between them is created. This step is repeated until the number of instances of the different classes is equal. In the second step the number of samples is reduced. If among the k nearest neighbours of an instance the majority belongs to the opposite class, the observed instance is removed. For both algorithms, the default number of neighbours k was three. For SMOTEENN the desired ratio of the number of samples of different classes has been set as one to one, but this ratio may not always be achieved due to the specific distribution of the data. Table 1 provides information on the number of instances of the data studied before and after the application of rebalancing. Since a separate classifier is built for each phoneme, there is no need to maintain equality of instances between sets for different phonemes. The significant decrease in the size of the data set for the phoneme [k] is the result of the rebalancing algorithms and indicates the presence of a large amount of noise in the data corresponding to this phoneme.

Table 1. Volume of data sets before and after rebalancing.

Phoneme	[k]		[s]		[t]	
	Initial set	After rebalancing the data	Initial set	After rebalancing the data	Initial set	After rebalancing the data
The total volume of the data set	1020	528	1020	830	1020	776
Number of instances of the class C0	379	279	212	469	196	449
Number of instances of the class C1	641	249	808	361	824	327

3   Results

Classifiers were trained using 10-fold cross-validation. Table 2 shows the accuracy values on the test samples for the initial sets of values (before applying data rebalancing methods). Here and below, the following notation is used: Acc is the value of accuracy on the test sample, Acc C1 is the proportion of correctly assigned class labels for instances of class C1, Acc C0 is the proportion of correctly assigned class labels for instances of class C0. Despite the rather high values of the overall accuracy, it can be seen that these values were achieved due to the predominance of the class C1 instances, while the instances of the class C0 were not correctly defined in most cases. This is especially noticeable in results for dataset for the phoneme [s], where data imbalance was initially greater. If we consider the dataset for the phoneme [t], the trained classifier assigned the class label C1 to the entire test sample, and instances of the class C0 were not defined at all. Therefore, the datasets were rebalanced and the classifiers were retrained.

The classifier testing methodology must match the actual working conditions. In particular, it is assumed that there may be no instances of spoken syllables of the tested patient in the training data. Therefore, in our study, patients who spoke syllables for training and test data do not overlap.

Table 2. Values of classification accuracy on test samples: general and by classes.

Phoneme	[k]			[s]			[t]		
	Acc	Acc C1	Acc C0	Acc	Acc C1	Acc C0	Acc	Acc C1	Acc C0
1	0.7157	0.984	0.263	0.7941	1	0.045	0.8039	1	0
2	0.7255	1	0.263	0.7941	1	0.045	0.8039	1	0
3	0.667	0.906	0.263	0.7941	0.988	0.048	0.8137	1	0
4	0.7157	1	0.267	0.8039	0.988	0.095	0.8039	1	0
5	0.7157	0.953	0.316	0.8333	0.988	0.238	0.8039	1	0
6	0.6471	0.875	0.263	0.7941	1	0	0.8039	1	0
7	0.6863	0.922	0.289	0.8137	1	0.095	0.8137	1	0
8	0.6961	0.922	0.316	0.8235	0.951	0.333	0.8039	1	0
9	0.7353	0.922	0.421	0.7941	1	0	0.8137	1	0
10	0.7059	0.969	0.243	0.7941	0.975	0.095	0.8137	1	0
Average	0.701			0.8039			0.8078		

Table 3 presents classification accuracies for test samples on rebalanced datasets. It can be noted that after applying the rebalancing methods, the accuracy of the determination for each of the classes is approximately at the same level. The average classification accuracy for the [k] phoneme dataset is 0.89, for the [s] phoneme dataset it is 0.84, and for the [t] phoneme dataset it is 0.8.

Table 3. Values of classification accuracy on test samples after rebalancing: general and by classes.

Phoneme	[k]			[s]			[t]		
	Acc	Acc C1	Acc C0	Acc	Acc C1	Acc C0	Acc	Acc C1	Acc C0
1	0.9057	0.88	0.929	0.8072	0.861	0.766	0.7949	0.788	0.8
2	0.8113	0.84	0.789	0.8313	0.75	0.894	0.7179	0.697	0.733
3	0.9434	0.88	1	0.8072	0.694	0.894	0.7564	0.697	0.8
4	0.8491	0.76	0.929	0.8313	0.889	0.787	0.8077	0.788	0.822
5	0.9057	0.88	0.929	0.8795	0.944	0.83	0.8462	0.758	0.911
6	0.8868	0.84	0.929	0.8554	0.861	0.851	0.8718	0.788	0.933
7	0.8491	0.76	0.929	0.8675	0.917	0.83	0.7273	0.688	0.756
8	0.9434	0.96	0.929	0.8434	0.861	0.83	0.8182	0.875	0.778
9	0.9039	0.875	0.929	0.8313	0.889	0.787	0.7792	0.813	0.756
10	0.8654	0.84	0.889	0.8072	0.838	0.783	0.8831	0.848	0.909
Average	0.8864			0.8361			0.8003		

If we consider the question of the sufficiency of the obtained accuracy values for the conclusion about the possibility of using such an approach, we can note the presence of small but significant differences between the expert and automated approaches to scoring. In expert assessment, if the entire syllable is mispronounced, and if only one phoneme in the syllable is mispronounced, the score will be the same and equal to 0. When calculating the values from the metrics, it is obvious that in the above cases the values will differ and may differ significantly. Therefore, in this work, the purpose of the study was not to build a classifier, whose results will completely coincide with the expert opinion. The purpose was to develop an assessment system based on existing expert assessments.

4 Conclusion

As a result of the analysis of the obtained data, it can be concluded that the fuzzy classifier can be used as a mechanism for combining the values calculated from the metrics to obtain a final quantitative assessment of the syllables pronunciation. The average share of coincidence of estimates obtained by the algorithm using a fuzzy classifier and expert estimates by the previously used method is 84%. Using a hybrid measure based on a fuzzy classifier allows to get accuracy at the same level as using separate metrics to calculate a quantitative estimate [7]. However, proposed in this paper the hybrid measure does not have the disadvantage of requiring manual selection of the binarization parameter for comparison with expert ones. The algorithm with a fuzzy classifier will be included in the software for use in the process of speech rehabilitation at the Cancer Research Institute Tomsk NRMC. The application of this algorithm makes it possible to obtain interpretable quantitative estimates of the similarity of two different recordings with the same phonetic unit. Based on the estimates obtained, it is possible to build reinforcing stimuli within the framework of the biofeedback implementation in the process of speech rehabilitation.

The use of a fuzzy classifier to assess the quality of the syllable pronunciation made it possible to achieve the following results: 1) quantitative estimates of the quality of the pronunciation of syllables were obtained, which will be used to assess the recovery of the patient's speech during the rehabilitation process; 2) an accuracy of 0.84 was achieved in determining the intelligibility of the pronunciation of syllables in coincidences with expert estimates; 3) a base of production rules of the IF-THEN type was obtained, which makes it possible to explain the result of the classifier. Rule bases contain fuzzy terms used in diagnostics, which allows interpreting them into expert knowledge.

A possible direction for further research may be the task of selecting the optimal parameters of a fuzzy classifier, which may improve the accuracy of data classification. Also, one of the tasks to be solved can be the development of a mechanism for regularly updating the training data for the classifier to take into account new recordings and patients.

Acknowledgments. This research was funded by the Ministry of Science and Higher Education of the Russian Federation within the framework of scientific projects carried out by teams of research laboratories of educational institutions of higher education subordinate to the Ministry of Science and Higher Education of the Russian Federation, project number FEWM-2020-0042.

The authors would like to thank the Irkutsk Supercomputer Center of SB RAS for providing access to the HPC-cluster «Akademik V.M. Matrosov» [16].

References

1. Kaprin, A.D., Starinskiy, V.V., Shahzadova, A.O.: Malignancies in Russia in 2020 (morbidity and mortality), 252 p. MNIOI name of P.A. Herzen, Moscow (2021)
2. Kaprin, A.D., Starinskiy, V.V., Shahzadova, A.O.: The state of oncological care for the population of Russia in 2020, 239 p. MNIOI name of P.A. Herzen, Moscow (2021)
3. Standard GOST R 50840-95 voice over paths of communication. Methods for assessing the quality, legibility and recognition, 234 p. Publishing Standards, Moscow (1995)
4. Salvador, S.: FastDTW: toward accurate dynamic time warping in linear time and space. In: Salvador, S., Chan, P. (eds.) Workshop on Mining Temporal and Sequential Data, Seattle, pp. 70–80 (2004)
5. Kostyuchenko, E., Meshcheryakov, R., Ignatieva, D., Pyatkov, A., Choynzonov, E., Balatskaya, L.: Correlation criterion in assessment of speech quality in process of oncological patients rehabilitation after surgical treatment of the speech-producing tract. In: Bhatia, S.K., Tiwari, S., Mishra, K.K., Trivedi, M.C. (eds.) Advances in Computer Communication and Computational Sciences. AISC, vol. 759, pp. 209–216. Springer, Singapore (2019). https://doi.org/10.1007/978-981-13-0341-8_19
6. Kostyuchenko, E., Roman, M., Ignatieva, D., Pyatkov, A., Choynzonov, E., Balatskaya, L.: Evaluation of the speech quality during rehabilitation after surgical treatment of the cancer of oral cavity and oropharynx based on a comparison of the Fourier spectra. In: Ronzhin, A., Potapova, R., Németh, G. (eds.) SPECOM 2016. LNCS (LNAI), vol. 9811, pp. 287–295. Springer, Cham (2016). https://doi.org/10.1007/978-3-319-43958-7_34
7. Novokhrestova, D., Kostuchenko, E., Hodashinsky, I., Balatskaya, L.: Experimental analysis of expert and quantitative estimates of syllable recordings in the process of speech rehabilitation. In: Karpov, A., Potapova, R. (eds.) SPECOM 2021. LNCS (LNAI), vol. 12997, pp. 483–491. Springer, Cham (2021). https://doi.org/10.1007/978-3-030-87802-3_44
8. Sarin, K.S., Hodashinsky, I.A.: Bagged ensemble of fuzzy classifiers and feature selection for handwritten signature verification. Comput. Opt. **43**(5), 833–845 (2019)
9. Lavygina, A., Hodashinsky, I.: Hybrid algorithm for fuzzy model parameter estimation based on genetic algorithm and derivative based methods. In: ECTA 2011 and FCTA 2011 - Proceedings of the International Conference on Evolutionary Computation Theory and Applications and International Conference on Fuzzy Computation Theory and Applications, pp. 513–515 (2011)
10. Georgieva, P.: Genetic fuzzy system for financial management. Cybern. Inf. Technol. **18**(2), 20–35 (2018)
11. Omozaki, Y., Masuyama, N., Nojima, Y., Ishibuchi, H.: Multiobjective fuzzy genetics-based machine learning for multi-label classification. In: 2020 IEEE International Conference on Fuzzy Systems, pp. 1–8 (2020)
12. Nishihara, A., Masuyama, N., Nojima, Y., Ishibuchi, H.: Michigan-style fuzzy genetics-based machine learning for class imbalance data. J. Jpn. Soc. Fuzzy Theory Intell. Inform. **33**(1), 525–530 (2021)
13. Deb, K., Agrawal, S., Pratap, A., Meyarivan, T.: A fast and elitist multiobjective genetic algorithm: NSGA-II. IEEE Trans. Evol. Comput. **6**(2), 182–197 (2002)
14. Lemnaru, C., Potolea, R.: Imbalanced classification problems: systematic study, issues and best practices. In: Zhang, R., Zhang, J., Zhang, Z., Filipe, J., Cordeiro, J. (eds.) ICEIS 2011. LNBIP, vol. 102, pp. 35–50. Springer, Heidelberg (2012). https://doi.org/10.1007/978-3-642-29958-2_3

15. Imbalanced-learn documentation, 10 April 2022. https://imbalanced-learn.org/stable/introduction.html
16. Irkutsk Supercomputer Center SB RAS. http://hpc.icc.ru/en/. Accessed 16 Jan 2021

Analysis-By-Synthesis Modeling of Bengali Intonation

Moumita Pakrashi[1](✉) ⓘ and Shakuntala Mahanta[2] ⓘ

[1] Centre for Linguistic Science and Technology, IIT Guwahati, Assam, India
moumi176155103@iitg.ac.in
[2] Department of Humanities and Social Sciences, IIT Guwahati, Assam, India
smahanta@iitg.ac.in

Abstract. The main concern behind deriving natural sounding synthesized speech lies in the objective mapping of the relation between formal and functional representations of prosody in human speech. Besides stress, rhythm, and duration, intonation is the most vital part of prosody that contributes to the naturalness of any synthetic speech. Latest prosodic studies of Bengali and their application have been carried out using Autosegmental-Metrical and Fujisaki models, but there remains much scope for improving naturalness of synthetic speech in existing TTS systems. In this paper, we study Bengali intonation patterns with a language-independent, hybrid phonetic-phonological model of Momel-INTSINT. Analysis-by-synthesis paradigm involves automatic symbolic coding of the prosodic form by INTSINT (INternational Transcription System for INTonation) that has been derived from the Momel (Modelling Melody) algorithm by stylizing the raw F0 curve to reduce the complex acoustic data to a simplified model. This symbolic representation then becomes the input to the ProZed tool for generating synthetic speech. Our study is based on the prosodically representative sentence set of Bengali speech developed by CDAC-Kolkata. The automatic labeling framework of INTSINT tones helps in precise modeling of intonation patterns within hierarchical prosodic units of accentual, intermediate, and intonation phrases in Bengali utterances.

Keywords: Speech synthesis · Intonation model · Analysis by synthesis · Momel–INTSINT · Prosodic hierarchy

1 Introduction

Intonation along with temporal properties of speech exercises the most prominent influence on enhancing naturalness of synthetic speech. Despite long term research in developing comprehensive theories to describe prosodic variations across languages, there remain many conflicts among experts as to what approach is most suitable and precise enough to describe prosodic units [1]. Some recent encouraging works in developing synthetic speech has been carried out during the Blizzard challenge 2015 to synthesize six Indian languages including Bengali. Even so, there remains a lot of scope for improving the naturalness of such synthetic speech. Therefore, if prosodic information representing the necessary contrasts between prosodic forms are derived from a model

© Springer Nature Switzerland AG 2022
S. R. M. Prasanna et al. (Eds.): SPECOM 2022, LNAI 13721, pp. 533–544, 2022.
https://doi.org/10.1007/978-3-031-20980-2_45

and given as input to a synthesis system, then the resulting synthetic speech will also be able to incorporate them appropriately.

In this paper, we adopt the application of the analysis by synthesis paradigm of the MOMEL model and a narrow transcription system INTSINT to study and model Bengali intonation contours. In his works, Daniel Hirst argues for the need for explicit, predictive and unified features in a prosodic model [2]. Therefore, Hirst's analysis by synthesis paradigm attempts to achieve such an explicit predictive model. In order to be explicit, a model must be able to derive a simple and abstract underlying representation from the complex and raw acoustic data; and to be predictive the model must be reversible and thus be able to synthesis acoustic data from the underlying representation [3] (Fig. 1).

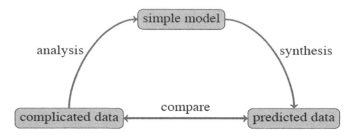

Fig. 1. The analysis by synthesis paradigm [2].

Intonation models can be broadly classified into two categories of phonological and phonetic models. A phonological model creates a phonological representation of the F0 contour by using abstract phonological categories, each of which have their own linguistic function. Autosegmental Metrical (AM) model is a typical phonological model, which uses a discrete set of tones to mark different types of accents and phrasal boundaries and Tone and Break Indices (ToBI) is its corresponding tonal transcription system [4]. Latest extensive work in Bengali based on this approach of a broad transcription of intonation is the implementation of B-ToBI by Khan (2008) [5]. On the other hand, a phonetic model such as the Fujisaki command response model, creates a close approximation of the F0 contour that is usually a superimposition of two factored out curves of the word intonation and sentence intonation curve [6]. Such an analysis has been carried out for development of Bengali TTS system by the application of Fujisaki model [7]. Yet the synthetic speech derived through this TTS application on Bengali, is far from being natural. In our study, we have adopted the hybrid model of Momel and a narrow transcription system for intonation INTSINT developed by Hirst & Di Cristo (1998) for the purpose of our prosodic analysis [8]. The automatic analysis and annotation (few manual corrections done later) of the large speech corpus was easily carried out using this model, thus avoiding time-consuming, manual analysis required using a phonological model. Also, the re-synthesis of F0 contour could be done more accurately because the tonal labels applied here bore quantitative values.

Hirst posits a theory-friendly nature of this model in that it can be used in conjunction with other intonational theories by stressing on the need for a cumulative nature of building knowledge [2]. Therefore, in this paper we build upon the existing prosodic analysis of Bengali speech, and adopt the prosodic hierarchies of phrases to describe the prominence and boundary tones. Additionally, we also study the influences of syllable duration segments that were automatically predicted by the model through ProZed plugin in Praat software [9, 10].

2 Data Analysis Using Momel-INTSINT Algorithm and ProZed

The algorithm of Momel (abbreviated for Modelling Melody) has been implemented in our analysis by using the openly accessible Praat plugin [9]. The plugin can be easily incorporated into the Praat analysis software, [11] which then stylizes the F0 contour by detecting some prominent pitch targets and finally coding those detected points with the automatic transcription system of INTSINT (International Transcription System for INTonation).

2.1 Corpus

In this paper we analyze the prosodic representative data set of Bengali language, developed by C-DAC (Centre for Development of Advanced Computing) Kolkata. This corpus approximately contains 900 sentences. Speech data has been recorded of both male and female informants (5 each) belonging to the age group 20 to above 40, who speak Standard Colloquial Bengali (SCB). Prosodic patterns that have been represented in this data are guided largely on three factors here; types of sentences, mode of speaking (reading and conversational speech) and on the gender and age of informants. On the basis of these characteristics, following types of sentences have been particularly addressed in this corpus:

Simple (with verb and without verb); Simple, negative; Complex affirmative; Complex negative; Compound affirmative; Compound negative; Passive; Imperative; Exclamatory; Interrogative (Yes/No and Wh-questions) and Continuous dialogues.

A large number of sentences in varied word and phrase combinations with various functions and structures have been collected from written sources that use colloquial Bengali language. The sources used are popular fictions of contemporary writers, children's books, newspaper reports and articles, etc. A process of random selection has been used to select a sentence from a source. More than two thousand sentences have been selected initially. For the C-DAC corpus, an experienced linguist, who is also a native speaker of Bengali selected 880 sentences covering all the aforesaid category of sentences. These sentences primarily represent the prosodic structure in text reading mode. The speech data consisted of the audio files, their corresponding transcription in Bengali and the tag files containing their phoneme, syllable and word boundary information. We incorporated the tag files in PRAAT using a Perl script.

2.2 The Momel Algorithm

A raw fundamental frequency (F0) curve is basically a product of two components: a global macroprosodic component representing the underlying intonation pattern of the utterance, and a local microprosodic component determined by the individual phoneme segments that usually creates the visible discontinuities of the F0 contour. The Momel algorithm models the underlying macroprosodic component as a smooth and continuous curve using a quadratic spline function (Fig. 2).

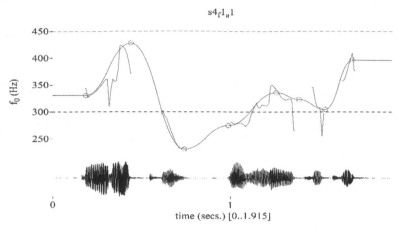

Fig. 2. Momel curve for an interrogative utterance [ke likʰlo tɐhole e ʧitʰi] "Then who wrote this letter?", where the raw and discontinuous F0 curve (green) is modelled as the smooth F0 curve (red)along with pitch targets (black circles). (Color figure online)

2.3 INTSINT Coding

INTSINT symbolic coding implements 8 alphabets as symbols to describe pitch contrasts in the surface phonological level. The tonal symbols are of three types:

The **absolute tones** Top (**T**), Mid (**M**) and Bottom (**B**), are calculated from a speaker's pitch range. Pitch range is defined by the two parameters of key (Hz) and span (octave); where key is the central point of a speaker's pitch range and the span can be defined as the maximum and minimum pitch values.

The **relative tones** Higher (**H**), Same (**S**), and Lower (**L**) are defined locally with respect to their immediately preceding tones.

The **iterative relative tones** Upstepped (**U**), and Downstepped (**D**) generally occurring in sequences are also similar to the relative tones, but they indicate even smaller pitch change in the contour.

2.4 ProZed

ProZed can be integrated with Praat as a plugin and it uses the Mbrola program for the purpose of re-synthesis [10]. It allows for the multilingual integration of the analysis by synthesis of speech prosody [15]. The language independent prosodic parameters that can be represented in ProZed are F0 and segmental duration. With these parameters we were able to re-synthesis the utterances, after the automatic analysis and annotation. The re-synthesis step basically allows us to verify the correctness of the INTSINT annotation of the pitch contour, by listening and comparing the perceptual similarity of the original and the synthesized utterances (Fig. 3).

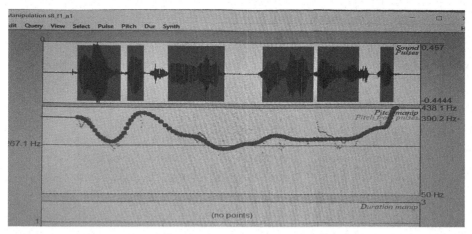

Fig. 3. Screenshot of the quadratic interpolation of a re-synthesized pitch contour in PRAAT window.

2.5 Application of Momel on Bengali Speech Data

The Momel plugin algorithm functions in a step-by-step manner to carry out the final automated annotation [9]. The data to be analyzed should be kept in a working directory. With the initiation of the algorithm in PRAAT, each speech file of the data is then automatically placed with an individual file with its name on it. The subsequent files generated from each of the step below is placed in that same file with the speech file's name and their corresponding extension.

Calculation of Max and Min F0. Since the correct F0 detection is the most vital function, the Momel plugin automatically provides the appropriate maximum and minimum values for pitch for that particular speaker. This is especially helpful for big speech corpus. Corresponding files are saved as.Pitch files.

Momel Target Detection. From these.Pitch files, the sequence of Momel pitch targets are generated by a quadratic spline function, and are subsequently saved as.PitchTier files. This results in the generation of a smooth, continuous pitch contour.

INTSINT Coding. The automatically generated target points of Momel are then coded using the INTSINT alphabets.

Momel and INTSINT Manipulation. This step reverses the INTSINT codes into a Momel targets, that enables to generate the re-synthesized pitch curve and allows for comparison with the original curve.

Manual Correction of Momel Targets. Finally, some Momel target corrections were done manually and the erroneous pitch points were removed. Such erroneous pitch points were detected in a few cases. Primarily, those tones which created a significant disruption in generating semblance to the re-synthesized contours were removed; such as a sudden spike in pitch caused in the silent part of a pitch contour by a T/H tone, mostly due to a following sibilant or aspirated segment.

We carried out a statistical analysis to determine how successfully the algorithm could automatically generate the Momel targets for Bengali speech and how much of it had to be corrected manually. The F-measure showed an efficiency of about 96.58%, which makes it quite suitable for analysis and synthesis of Bengali speech (Table 1).

Table 1. Statistical evaluation of Momel algorithm application on Bengali speech.

Number of points			Evaluation		
Detected	Added	Deleted	Recall	Precision	F-measure
6367	132	297	97.87	95.33	96.58

3 Bengali Prosodic Structure

Bengali is an Indo-Aryan language that originates from the Indo-European group of languages. It is the official language of the Indian state of West Bengal and the national language of Bangladesh. It is also spoken in some parts of the adjacent states of Assam, Tripura and so on. Here the prosodic analysis has been carried out on standard colloquial Bengali that is spoken mostly in south-eastern part of West Bengal and specifically in and around Kolkata [12].

Most of the prosodic studies of Bengali suggest that it is primarily a stress-accent language and words usually bear stress on the initial syllable. Nonetheless most studies suggest that this stress is phonologically significant and not phonetically. Studies on Bengali prosody began with the exhaustive analysis of Chatterjee (1921) [13], followed by Ferguson & Chowdhury (1960), Ray, Hai & Ray (1966). But majority of the later day prosodic analysis of Bengali was done using Autosegmental – Metrical (AM) model of intonation in the works of Hayes & Lahiri (1991), Lahiri & Fitzpatrick-Cole (1999), Michaels & Nelson (2004), Jun (2005), Selkirk (2006) and Khan (2008). The first ToBI transcription system of Bengali known as B-ToBI was proposed in Michaels & Nelson's (2004) model. In B-ToBI analysis of Bengali, all the pitch accents and boundary tones are defined by two tones High (H) and Low (L) and even with bitonal tones such as HL or LH. The tones are mostly guided by Obligatory Contour Principle (OCP) constraints, which dictate that consecutive tones must be opposite tonal targets (H or L) and not same [14].

Recent works on Bengali intonational phonology [5] classify its prosodic hierarchy as having three basic units, Accentual Phrase (AP), Intermediate Phrase (ip) and Intonation Phrases (IP). The IP being the largest unit usually make up an utterance and can consist of one or more ips. An ip which roughly equals syntactic phrases can consist of one or more AP. In the current study we use Momel – INTSINT analysis system to carry out the prosodic analysis of Bengali narrative speech, which has not yet been explored for analyzing Indian languages.

4   Analysis of Bengali Intonation Patterns

For the analysis of Bengali prosodic structure, we analyze different types of sentences and observe some recurring intonation patterns for the three types of AP, ip, and IP phrases and the focus elements. Within the larger phrases, nuclear tones can be identified and distinguished from prenuclear tones. Different prosodic phrases have been manually marked in separate tiers of a Praat textgrid file, to analyse and identify the recurring patterns of INTSINT tones which have been automatically generated by the algorithm.

4.1   Accentual Phrase (AP)

Bengali is a language with a word initial accent. Therefore, the first syllable is usually the unmarked position for its accentual phrase prominence. Accentual phrases mostly comprise of a single word, with the exception of complex verbs like *[dije dao]* "give away". Also, when a content word is preceded or followed by a function word, they may group together to form a single AP.

Nuclear Accentual Phrase. Within a basic unemphatic utterance, the last accentual phrase is the nuclear AP. Usually the rightmost accented syllable is marked as the nuclear unit of an utterance. This nucleus is usually indicated with a single relative tone of L for declaratives and exclamations; and a H tone for interrogatives. These relative tones are usually followed by one of the global tones M/B or T to demarcate the utterance boundary tone, and sometimes maybe with a local falling tone L in case of interrupted utterances.

Pre-Nuclear Accentual Phrase. All the accentual phrases preceding the nuclear unit are prenuclear accentual phrases. Iterative relative tones are used along with relative tones to indicate these AP accents. The prenuclear accents can be marked as low with L followed by a boundary tone U, or a rising accent tone of H or UU followed by a boundary tone L.

Obligatory Contour Principle (OCP). The OCP constraint can be very clearly observed in all types of sentence patterns. When there are two consecutive relative tones (H/L), they are always of the pattern H followed by L or vice-versa. But when one relative tone (H/L) is followed by iterative relative tones (U/D), there may be a sequence of UU or DD tones after an L or H respectively. This is essentially because the iterative relative tones occur within very small pitch ranges and may occur in pairs in order to focus the small, local pitch changes indicating a smooth valley or peak on the pitch contour (Fig. 4).

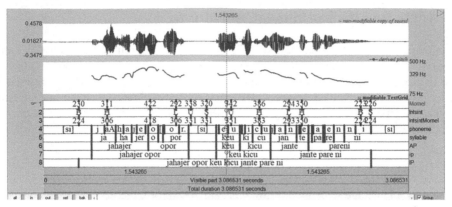

Fig. 4. The OCP illustrated in this simple negative statement [ʤɐhɐʤer opor keu kiʈʰu ʤɐnte pɐreni] "Nobody on the ship's deck came to know anything". The 3 ips indicate repeated local tones of L-H patterns interspersed by iterative relative tones UU.

4.2 Intermediate Phrase (Ip)

The intermediate phrase (ip) usually consists of one or more than one AP. This phrase may coincide with a syntactic group such as a noun phrase, postpositional or adverbial phrase (eg. [kolkɐtɐ ʃɔhorer dokkʰine] "southern part of the city of Kolkata") in Fig. 6. The predominant tone occurring in an ip boundary is usually high indicated as H or high rising indicated by duplicate iterative relative tones such as UU or LH or DU. Occasionally though a low tone as L or DD may occur. But the final syllable of an ip is usually lengthened to mark its boundary.

4.3 Intonation Phrase (IP)

The Intonation Phrase (IP)/Intonation Unit (IU) is equivalent to an utterance and is the largest phrasal unit marked by intonation. The INTSINT tones demarcate the global contour of an IP by the absolute tones of M (Mid), T (Top) and B (Bottom).

An initial IP boundary tone is usually marked as M/B to indicate an utterance beginning after a certain amount of pause since the preceding utterance.

The final IP boundary tone depends on the type of sentence like declaratives, interrogatives or imperatives. Declarative (both affirmative and negative) and imperative utterances can be identified with a B tone on its right boundary to indicate a falling/low final tone. While the interrogatives both Wh and Yes-no questions end with either a T or H tone as seen in Fig. 5. Increased duration of final IP syllable acts as a cue to its end.

The IP tones are superimposed on the pitch contour of an utterance, which gives the overall intonation pattern. The final boundary tone may override the final AP/ip boundary tone but not always. This is because even after the appearance of an absolute tone (T/B/M), there can be a relative tone (H/L/U/D) marking the final AP/ip boundary tones.

A significant distinction found between the current and the previous prosodic studies of Bengali [5, 14] is that, unlike the manually marked B-ToBI boundary tones, it has

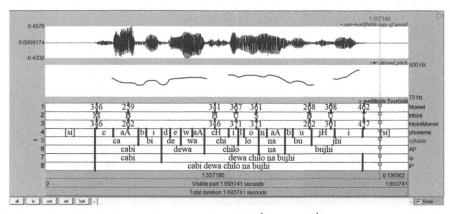

Fig. 5. An interrogative Yes/No utterance [tʃʰɐbi deʋɐ tʃʰilo nɐ budʒʰi] "Was it not locked? ending with a final global tone T in the IP phrase boundary position, while beginning with the global tones M-B.

been quite difficult to determine the Accentual phrase boundary tones with INTSINT. While there is a distinct prominence marking tone for each AP, the following tones are either an upstepping or downstepping sequence or no tone at all.

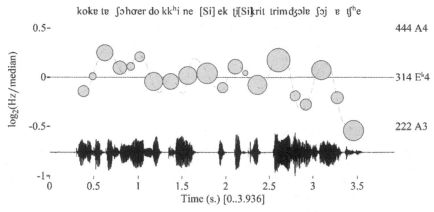

Fig. 6. A sample ProZed output with the green line indicating the smooth and continuous Momel curve and the yellow circles showing the syllable durations of the declarative utterance [kolkɐtɐ ʃɔhorer dokkʰine ekʈi krittrim dʒɔleʃɔj ɐtʃʰe] "There is an artificial water body in the southern part of the city of Kolkata".

A comparative analysis was done using the ProZed segmental durations to see how the syllable final durations help to mark the phrase terminal or non-terminal boundaries. As shown below in Fig. 7, higher level phrase final syllables are longer than the lower ones.

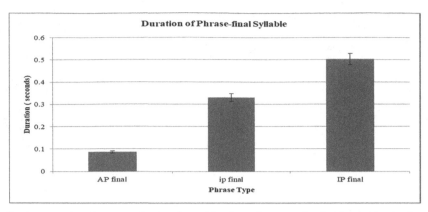

Fig. 7. A comparison between the duration of the three phrase final syllables, indicating how the higher-level phrases are demarcated by their final syllable lengthening.

4.4 Focus Tones

Focus tones are those that stand out as the most prominent one in an intonation contour. In Bengali the focused tones are not very much phonetically realized, but they can be perceived as stressed ones. Focus can occur in many contexts in Bengali speech. It can be indicated through the revealing of a new information in an utterance, or as an encliticised element (by addition of –ei or –eo at the end of the word) marked with an L tone. In Surprise statements, a focused constituent as [naki] is marked with a H tone. In passive constructions, when the subject needs special attention, the noun phrase stands out as a T tone.

5   Conclusions

In this paper we have tried to identify the major intonation patterns for Bengali based on this hybrid model. Apart from the automatic annotation of large speech corpus, the mapping of prosodic form and function in this model makes it quite unique. The automatic annotations create inter speaker differences for the same sentence. Therefore, a more improved algorithm might to able to account better for these discrepancies and capture inter or intra speaker differences more efficiently. The analysis by synthesis algorithm of Momel-INTSINT clearly identifies pitch accent tones much easily than the boundary tones of the lower-level prosodic units. The analysis by synthesis algorithm of Momel-INTSINT has been used to study many languages such as English, French, Spanish, Russian, Italian, Korean, Chinese, Arabic, isiZulu [8, 16–20]. Hopefully with more studies and analysis of Indian languages, this model could be optimized to adapt more language variations. Future research would entail optimizing better automatic intonation models to help predict suitable prosodic units by extracting more functional information from speech.

Acknowledgements. We would like to thank C-DAC (Centre for Development of Advanced Computing) for providing us with the Bengali speech data; special thanks to Speech Processing

Lab, C-DAC Kolkata for developing such a prosodically enriched Bengali speech database, which is definitely a valuable resource for different speech researches.

References

1. Xu, Y.: Speech prosody: a methodological review. J. Speech Sci. 1(1), 85–115 (2011). https://doi.org/10.20396/joss.v1i1.15014
2. Hirst, D.J.: The analysis by synthesis of speech melody: from data to models. J. Speech Sci. 1(1), 55–83 (2011). https://doi.org/10.20396/joss.v1i1.15011
3. Hirst, D., Di Cristo, A., Espesser, R.: Levels of representation and levels of analysis for the description of intonation systems. In: Horne, M. (ed.) Prosody: Theory and Experiment, pp. 51–87. Springer Netherlands, Dordrecht (2000). https://doi.org/10.1007/978-94-015-9413-4_4
4. Pierrehumbert, J.B.: The Phonology and Phonetics of English Intonation. Ph.D. Dissertation. MIT, Cambridge, MA (1980)
5. Khan, S.: Intonational Phonology and Focus Prosody of Bengali. Ph.D. Thesis (2008)
6. Fujisaki, H.: Analysis and modeling of voice fundamental frequency contours for declarative sentences of Japanese. J. Acoust. Soc. Japan 5, 640–657 (1984). https://doi.org/10.1250/ast.5.233
7. Das Mandal, S.K., Saha, A., Sarkar I., Datta, A.K.: Phonological, international & prosodic aspects of concatenative speech synthesizer development for Bangla. In: Proceedings of SIMPLE 05, pp. 56–60 (2005)
8. Hirst, D.J., Di Cristo, A. (eds.) Intonation Systems. A survey of Twenty Languages. Cambridge University Press, Cambridge (1998). https://doi.org/10.2307/417674
9. Hirst, D.J.: A Praat plugin for Momel and INTSINT with improved algorithms for modeling and coding intonation. In: Proceedings of the 16th International Congress of Phonetic Sciences, pp. 1233–1236 (2007)
10. Hirst, D.J.: ProZed: a speech prosody editor for linguists, using analysis-by-synthesis. In: 6th International Conference on Speech Prosody. Shanghai, China (2012)
11. Boersma, P., Weenink, D.: Praat: a system for doing phonetics by computer. http://www.praat.org (Version 6.2.01)
12. Bhattacharya, K.: Bengali phonetic reader. Central Institute of Indian Languages (1999). https://doi.org/10.1017/S0035869X00082319
13. Chatterji, S.K.: Bengali phonetics. Bull. Sch. Orient. Afr. Stud. 2, 1–25 (1921). https://doi.org/10.1017/S0041977X0010179X
14. Hayes, B., Lahiri, A.: Bengali intonational phonology. Nat. Lang. Linguist. Theory 9, 47–96 (1991). https://doi.org/10.1007/BF00133326
15. Hirst, D.J., Auran, C.: Analysis by synthesis of speech prosody: the ProZed environment. In: 9th European Conference on Speech Communication and Technology. Lisbon, Portugal (Sep 2005)
16. Zhi, N., Hirst, D.J., Bertinetto, P.: Automatic analysis of the intonation of a tone language. Applying the Momel algorithm to spontaneous Standard Chinese (Beijing). In: 11th Annual Conference of the International Speech Communication Association. Makuhari, Chiba, Japan (Sep 2010)
17. Wang, T., Hongwei, D., Qiuwu, M., Hirst, D.J.: Automatic analysis of emotional prosody in mandarin Chinese: applying the Momel algorithm. In: International Conference on Speech Prosody, vol. 7. Dublin, Ireland (May 2014). https://doi.org/10.21437/SpeechProsody.2014-12

18. Zhi, N., Hirst, D.J., Bertinetto, P., Li, A., Jia, Y.: An analysis-by-synthesis study of Mandarin Speech Prosody. International Conference on Speech Prosody (2016). https://doi.org/10.21437/SpeechProsody.2016-22
19. Ali, S., Hirst, D.J.: Analysis by synthesis of English intonation patterns: generalising from form to function. In: Proceedings of the 16th International Congress of Phonetic Sciences, pp. 1205–1208 (Aug 2007)
20. Louw, J.A., Barnard, E.: Automatic intonation modeling with INTSINT. In: Proceedings of the 15th Annual Symposium of the Pattern Recognition Association of South Africa, Grabouw, pp. 107–111 (2004)

Neural Network Based Curve Fitting to Enhance the Intelligibility of Dysarthric Speech

K. S. Pavithra[1]([✉]), H. M. Chandrashekar[2], and Veena Karjigi[3]

[1] Department of ECE, Atria Institute of Technology, Bengaluru, India
pavithra.ks2104@gmail.com
[2] Department of ETE, Siddaganga Institute of Technology, Tumakuru, India
[3] Department of ECE, Siddaganga Institute of Technology, Tumakuru, India

Abstract. Dysarthria is a motor speech disorder resulting from disturbance in neuromuscular control. The speech produced by people with dysarthria is distorted speech, whose intelligibility is poor compared to the normal speakers. This work attempts to increase the intelligibility of dysarthric speech by using a fitting function neural network transformation model created by Levenberg-Marquardt algorithm and Bayesian Regularization algorithm. The Linear Predictive coefficients from dysarthric speech signal and normal speech signal are taken as input and target for the fitting model respectively. The modified LP coefficients are obtained for the test dysarthric speech signal using transformation model and modified speech signal is reconstructed using LP synthesis followed by Overlap and Add method. It is observed that the mean opinion score is increased from 1.24 to 1.37 and 1.32 after modification for given set of dysarthric speech signals with Levenberg-Marquardt algorithm and Bayesian Regularization algorithm respectively.

Keywords: Dysarthria · Intelligibility · Curve fitting · Neural network · Synthesis

1 Introduction

State-of-the-art automatic speech recognizers are being used in a number of applications. However, a class of people with disordered speech still can't enjoy these devices. The reason being the large difference between the characteristics of normal and disordered speech. Stroke is the common cause for speech disorders. Dysarthria is a speech disorder where the intelligibility of the speech produced by the affected person is low compared to the controlled speech. Stroke results in weakness in hands also. As a result, the effected person finds it difficult to communicate through gestures. Enhancing the intelligibility of dysarthric speech helps others to decode the message in the dysarthric speech.

Speech therapy and rehabilitation help in regaining the intelligibility in early diagnosed persons. In the most affected case augmentative and alternate communication (AAC) is used in severely affected cases. AAC serves the basic needs of a person. In moderate affected persons, a ray of hope for improved communication is by improving the intelligibility by signal processing.

© Springer Nature Switzerland AG 2022
S. R. M. Prasanna et al. (Eds.): SPECOM 2022, LNAI 13721, pp. 545–553, 2022.
https://doi.org/10.1007/978-3-031-20980-2_46

Intelligibility of dysarthric speech can be enhanced by processing the dysarthric and control signal and understanding the similarities and differences. Intelligibility of the dysarthric speech can be improved in two ways. First is by performing acoustic transformation where distortions in dysarthric speech are identified and modified [1–10]. Second is by creating the transformation model (conversion model) using dysarthric and control speech signal (features). The modifications can be done at the signal level or feature level [11–13].

In this work, we are using linear prediction coefficients from dysarthric speech and control speech signal to create a transformation model using Levenberg-Marquardt algorithm and Bayesian Regularization algorithm for curve fitting in neural network. For learning the transformation model LPCs of dysarthric speech signal are the inputs and LPCs of control speech signal are the targets. Dynamic Time Warping (DTW) is used to make the dimension of the input and target feature matrix same. The trans-formation model is built using neural network curve fitting. The transformation mod-el gives the modified LP coefficients for a given test dysarthric speech LPCs. These modified LP coefficients and LP residual of the dysarthric speaker are used to synthesis the modified speech signal using Overlap and Add method.

In all, the objectives of the proposed work are: 1. To modify the features of the dysarthric speech to resemble those of controlled speech thereby improving the intel-ligibility of dysarthric speech. 2. To synthesize the intelligibility improved speech by liner prediction synthesis.

The related work in the field of increasing the intelligibility of dysarthric speech by modifying the speech in signal level or feature level, the features used to enhance the intelligibility, methods used to create the transformation model and synthesis the modified speech are discussed in Sect. 2. Section 3 describes the proposed methodology. Database used in this work and Objective Evaluation of Model Performance are provided in Sect. 4 followed by conclusion in Sect. 5.

2 Related Work

The distortions in dysarthric speech are speaker specific. Few authors identified these distortions and modified at the signal level. Intelligibility can be improved by locating and replacing the poorly uttered phonemes from the utterance of a dysarthric speaker with that of the normal speaker's speech signal [6]. The wrongly uttered phonemes in the dysarthric speech are corrected by using concatenating algorithm and a grafting technique. The concatenating algorithm is used to choose the units such that at least one vowel is present in it, the wrongly uttered sound units following or preceding the vowel are replaced by the grafting algorithm from a normal speaker [3]. Devoicing of voiced stops in which, the phonemes /b, d, g/ are pronounced as /p, t, k/ respectively will affect the intelligibility of the speech. This problem can be solved by inserting a voice bar of low frequency before the burst onset [7]. In fricative distortion, the weak fricatives /th/ and /dh/ sounds like strong fricative /s/. This distortion is modified by identifying the land marks of fricatives and removing the extended fricative portion [8]. In the above methods, the modifications are done at the signal level.

Intelligibility of dysarthric speech can be enhanced by performing modifications at the feature level and synthesizing the speech from the modified features. The features formants and energies are extracted from dysarthric speech and modified to desired normal speech features. The transformed speech is obtained by formant synthesizer with using modified features [2, 4]. The increase in phone duration due to elongation of vowels in dysarthric speech is corrected by using Dynamic Time Warping (DTW) algorithm to compare the similarity between MFCC features of dysarthric and corresponding normal speech. In this, the frames in dysarthric speech are deleted when the slope of the DTW path is zero for a specific number of frames [9]. The feature level transformation techniques based on LP coefficient mapping and frequency warping of LPC poles can be used to enhance the intelligibility of dysarthric speech [10].

To improve the intelligibility of dysarthric speech, a conversion model is created by learning (training) a model with direct dysarthric speech as input and normal speech as target or dysarthric speech features as input and normal speech features as target. The features for the learning model may be Pitch, energy and spectral features [1], Wideband spectrograms of dysarthric and normal speech signals obtained by STFT, Phonetic Posteriorgrams (PPGs) features [11]. Even, Linear Predictive Coding (LPC) and MFCC features can also provide as input and target for the learning model. The learning model can be simple ANN, Convolution Neural Network (CNN), Gated Convolutional Neural Network (Gated CNN) or bidirectional long short-term memory (BLSTM) [11]. Recently, a model for dysarthric to normal speech conversion is created using cycle-consistent GAN (Generative Adversarial Networks) and Discover GAN (DiscoGAN) [12, 13].

To synthesis (reconstruct) the speech signal from its features specific method will be used based on the feature. WaveRNN vocoder can be used to synthesis the speech from Phonetic Posteriorgrams (PPGs) features [11]. Griffin and Lim algorithm is used synthesis the speech signal from the spectrograms by using the STFT magnitude [12]. Overlap and add method can be used to synthesis the speech from LPC features.

3 Methodology

The intelligibility of the dysarthric speech signal can be improved by transforming the dysarthric speech signal features to control speech signal features. In this work we used LP coefficients to transform the dysarthric speech. LPC is a commonly used technique for speech analysis and synthesis [14]. It accurately models the human vocal tract parameters. The LPC analysis involves finding a linear all-Pole (IIR) filter having the system transfer function:

$$H(z) = \frac{1}{1 - \sum a_k z^{-k}} \tag{1}$$

where a_k is the filter coefficient.

The 10th order LP coefficients are extracted for dysarthric speech signal ($\vec{x}$) and Control speech signal ($\vec{y}$) by taking frame size of 30 ms and frame shift of 15 ms. Let 'M' be number of frames in $\vec{x}$ and 'N' be number of frames in $\vec{y}$. The length of dysarthric speech signal is greater than that of control speech signal, therefore M > N.

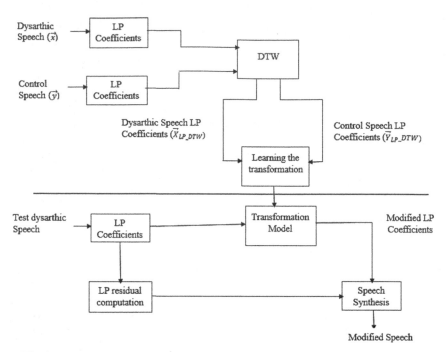

Fig. 1. Schematic representation of dysarthric to control speech conversion system.

Let $\vec{X}_{LP} = \begin{bmatrix} 1 & 1 & & 1 \\ x_{LP11} & x_{LP21} & & x_{LPM1} \\ x_{LP12} & x_{LP22} & & x_{LPM2} \\ \cdot & \cdot & & \cdot \\ \cdot & \cdot & \cdots & \cdot \\ x_{LP1k} & x_{LP2k} & & x_{LPMk} \end{bmatrix}$ represents the LP coefficient matrix of $\vec{x}$,

where $k = 10$, the order LPC coefficient. This is $((k + 1) \times M)$ matrix.

and $\vec{Y}_{LP} = \begin{bmatrix} 1 & 1 & & 1 \\ y_{LP11} & y_{LP21} & & y_{LPN1} \\ y_{LP12} & y_{LP22} & & y_{LPN2} \\ \cdot & \cdot & & \cdot \\ \cdot & \cdot & \cdots & \cdot \\ y_{LP1k} & y_{LP2k} & & y_{LPNk} \end{bmatrix}$ represents the LP coefficient matrix of $\vec{y}$. .

This is $((k + 1) \times N)$ matrix.

DTW technique is used to make the dimension of LP coefficient matrix of $\vec{x}$ and LP coefficient matrix of $\vec{y}$ same. DTW [15] is a technique used to provide timing variations and facilitate feature wise comparison between dysarthric and control speech LP coefficients. After DTW the new LP coefficient matrices are:

$$\vec{X}_{LP\_DTW} = \begin{bmatrix} 1 & 1 & & 1 \\ x_{LP11} & x_{LP21} & & x_{LPM1} \\ x_{LP12} & x_{LP22} & & x_{LPM2} \\ . & . & & . \\ . & . & \cdots & . \\ x_{LP1k} & x_{LP2k} & & x_{LPMk} \end{bmatrix} \text{ and } \vec{Y}_{LP\_DTW} = \begin{bmatrix} 1 & 1 & & 1 \\ y_{LP11} & y_{LP21} & & y_{LPM1} \\ y_{LP12} & y_{LP22} & & y_{LPM2} \\ . & . & & . \\ . & . & \cdots & . \\ y_{LP1k} & y_{LP2k} & & y_{LPMk} \end{bmatrix}$$

Now the dimension of both the matrices will be $((k + 1) \times M)$. To create a transformation model that map the dysarthric speech LP coefficients to control speech LP coefficients a fitting neural network is used.

3.1 Learning the Transformation

The curve fitting is the process of creating a curve, or mathematical function, that has the best fit of a given dataset. Regression Analysis is the related area in Machine Learning. Regression involves predicting a real value for each input data. Commonly used functions for curve fitting are power, exponential, logarithmic. Spline interpolation is also used for curve fitting. Combination of sinewaves like Fourier series is another option. However, instead of these handpicked curve fitting methods, use of neural network can model complex patterns [16]. Capturing the complex patterns helps in accurate modeling.

In this work, we train a feedforward neural network using back propagation algorithms like Levenberg–Marquardt and Bayesian regularization. The Levenberg–Marquardt algorithm [17], provides numerical solution to the problem of minimizing a nonlinear function. It converges quickly. Bayesian regularization automates the learning process by pruning the unnecessary weights of a feed-forward neural network [17].

The neural network comprises of input and output layers along with one hidden layer. There are 11 nodes in both the input and output layers, whereas the number of nodes in the hidden layer is 10. The neural network uses sigmoid hidden neurons and linear output neurons. This configuration is suitable for regression tasks.

Frame-wise LP coefficients computed for controlled and dysarthric speakers are aligned using dynamic time warping. The dysarthric speech LP coefficients $(\vec{X}_{LP\_DTW})$ and control speech LP coefficients $\left(\vec{Y}_{LP_{DTW}}\right)$ are applied to fitting neural network and transformation model is obtained after fitting. Figure 2 and Fig. 3 shows the regression plots obtained using Levenberg-Marquardt algorithm and Bayesian Regularization algorithm respectively. The correlation between the inputs and the targets are shown by R values in regression plot. R value tending to '1' shows a close relationship between both parameters. For our dataset we got almost same R values in both the algorithms. In this work we used linear regression model as it is easier to use and simpler to interpret. Nonlinear regression can fit many more types of curves, but it can require more effort to find the best fit and to interpret the role of the independent variables.

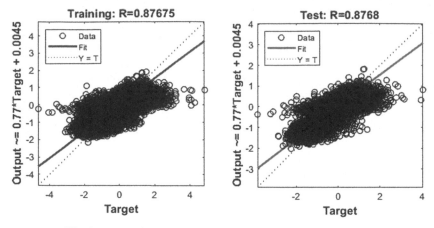

Fig. 2. Regression Plots using Levenberg-Marquardt algorithm.

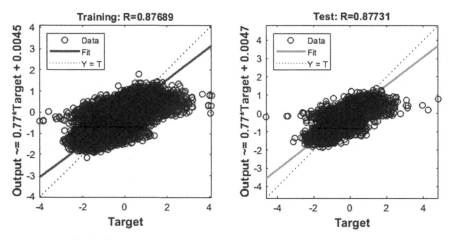

Fig. 3. Regression Plots using Bayesian Regularization algorithm.

3.2 Transformation and Synthesis

In this stage, LP coefficients are extracted for test dysarthric speech signal and applied to transformation model as input to obtain transformed LP coefficients. LP residual for the test dysarthric speech signal is obtained by passing the dysarthric speech through all zero filter with LP coefficients. To get the natural quality in synthesized speech, LP residual of test dysarthric speech along with transformed LP coefficients are used to synthesis the modified speech frame-wise and complete utterance is derived using overlap and add method. The complete schematic representation of dysarthric to control speech conversion system is depicted in Fig. 1. Figure 4 shows the LPC Spectrograms for the word 'Command' obtained using Levenberg-Marquardt algorithm and Bayesian Regularization algorithm for Control speech, Dysarthric speech and Modified speech signals. It can be observed from Fig. 4 that formant tracks are continuous in case of controlled speech compared to that of the dysarthric speech.

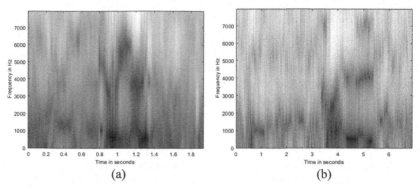

(a)   (b)

Fig. 4. LPC Spectrograms for the word 'Command': (a) Control speech (b) Dysarthric speech.

4 Database

The work uses the Universal Access (UA) database developed and analyzed at the University of Illinois [18]. It is composed of speech materials such as digits, computer commands, a radio alphabet and common words recorded from dysarthric speakers as well as controlled speakers. The speech data was recorded using array of eight microphones with 16 kHz sampling rate. In total, there are 765 isolated words per speaker are recorded: 300 distinct uncommon words, 3 repetitions of common words, radio alphabets, and computer commands.

In this work, we used 2 repetitions of 153 words ($2 \times 153 = 306$) from dysarthric speaker F02 and same set of words from control speaker CF02 in learning the transformation. The size of input and target feature matrix is 11×83277. That is, we considered 83277 frames of dysarthric and control speech in total. Seven repetitions of 19 computer commands ($7 \times 19 = 133$) from the same dysarthric speaker are used for testing.

5 Objective Evaluation of Model Performance

Speech data from dysarthric speaker is used to test a system for improving dysarthric speech intelligibility using LP coefficient mapping. Intelligibility can be estimated accurately and reliably through subjective tests. These tests, however, take a lot of time and are expensive. As a result, objective measures are straightforward, easy, and only factor in the speech signal to evaluate the quality of speech [19]. In order to assess objective speech quality, perceptual evaluation of speech quality (PESQ) can be used [20]. Based on the results of the PESQ, mean opinion scores (MOS) range from 1 (minimal value) to 5 (maximum value). The MOS value for 133 test dysarthric signal before modification is 1.24 and after modification the MOS value is increased to 1.37 in case of Levenberg-Marquard algorithm and to 1.32 in case of Bayesian Regularization algorithm.

6 Conclusion

The intelligibility of the dysarthric speech signal is improved by transforming the dysarthric speech signal features to control speech signal features. In this work we used LP coefficients from dysarthric speech and control speech signal to create a function fitting neural network transformation model. The LP coefficients from 306 dysarthric Normal-paired speech signals are used to created transformation model. The transformation model gives the modified LP coefficients for a given test dysarthric speech LP coefficients. These modified LP coefficients and LP residual of the dysarthric speaker are used to synthesis the modified speech signal using Overlap and Add method. The proposed work resulted in improvement of intelligibility of dysarthric speech in terms of MOS.

The work can be extended by using advance signal processing methods at signal or feature level. Generative Adversarial Network can be used to create acoustic transformation models. Use of ASR for performance evaluation will be explored. Robustness of the system can be improved by increasing the data size.

References

1. Hosom, J.P., Kain, A.B., Mishra, T., Santen, J.P.H., Fried Oken, M., Staehely, J.: Intelligibility of modifications to dysarthric speech. In: Proc. IEEE International Conference on Acoustic, Speech and Signal Processing (ICASSP), pp. 924–927. Hong-Kong (2003)
2. Young, V., Mihailids, A.: Difficulties in automatic speech recognition of dysarthric speakers and implications for speech-based applications used by the elderly: a literature review. Assistive Technology: The official Journal of RESNA 22(2), 99–112 (2010)
3. Yakoub, M.S., Selouani, S.-A., O'Shaughnessy, D.: Improving dysarthric speech intelligibility through re-synthesized and grafted units. In: Proc. IEEE Canadian Conference on Electrical and Computer Engineering, pp. 1523–1226. Canada (2008)
4. Tolba, H., Torgoman, A.S.E.: Towards the improvement of automatic recognition of dysarthric speech. In: Proc. 2nd IEEE International Conference on Computer Science and Information Technology, pp. 277–281. Beijing (2009)
5. Saranya, M., Vijayalakshmi, P., Thangavelu, N.: Improving the intelligibility of dysarthric speech by modifying system parameters, retaining speaker's identity. In: Proc. IEEE International Conference on Recent Trends in Information Technology, pp. 60–65. Tamil Nadu (2012)
6. Rudzicz, F.: Adjusting dysarthric speech signals to be more intelligible. Comput. Speech Lang. 27(6), 1163–1177 (2013)
7. Shilpa, C., Swathi, V., Pavithra, K.S., Sultana, S., Karjigi, V.: Landmark based modification to correct distortions in dysarthric speech. In: IEEE Twenty Second National Conference on Communication (NCC), pp. 1–6 (2016)
8. Sultana, S., Pavithra, K.S., Karjigi, V., Madhusudhana, R.D., Real time detection of fricative landmarks to modify distortion in dysarthric speech using TMS320C6713 DSK. IEEE Conference on Advances in Signal Processing (CASP), Cummins College of Engineering for Women, Pune, Jun 9–11 (2016)
9. Prakash, A., Reddy, M.R., Murthy, H.A.: Improvement of continuous dysarthric speech quality. Workshop on Speech and Language Processing for Assistive Technologies (2016)
10. Kumar, S.A., Kumar, C.S.: Improving the intelligibility of dysarthric speechtowards enhancing the effectiveness of speech therapy. In: International Conference on Advances in Computing, Communications and Informatics (ICACCI), Sept. 21–24, Jaipur, India (2016)

11. Chen, C.-Y., Zheng, W.-Z., Wang, Y.S.-S., Tsao, P.-C.L., Lai, Y.-H.: Enhancing Intelligibility of Dysarthric Speech Using Gated Convolutional-based Voice Conversion System. INTERSPEECH, Shanghai, China (2020)
12. Yang, S.H., Chung, M.: Improving dysarthric speech intelligibility using cycle-consistent adversarial training. Audio and Speech Processing; Computation and Language (2020)
13. Purohit, M., et al.: intelligibility improvement of dysarthric speech using MMSE DiscoGAN. In: IEEE International Conference on Signal Processing and Communications (SPCOM), Bangalore, India, 19–24 July 2020
14. Rabiner, L.R., Schafer, R.W.: Digital Processing of Speech Signals. Prentice Hall (1978)
15. Rabiner, L.R., Juang, B.-H.: Fundamentals of speech recognition (1993)
16. Gonzalez-Diaz, E.R., Mainar, E.P.-H., Rubio, B.: Neural-network-based curve fitting using totally positive rational bases. Mathematics **8**(12), 2197 (2020). https://doi.org/10.3390/math8122197
17. Ekong, E.E., Adewale, A.A., Ben-Obaje, A., Alalade, A.M., Ndujiuba, C.N.: Performance comparison of ANN training algorithms for hysteresis determination in LTE networks. J. Phys. Conf. Ser. **1378**(4), 042094 (2019). https://doi.org/10.1088/1742-6596/1378/4/042094
18. Kim, H., et al.: Dysarthric speech database for universal access research .In: Proc. International Conference on Speech and Language Processing, pp. 1741–1744. Australia (2008)
19. Loizou, P.C.: Speech quality assessment. In: Lin, W., Tao, D., Kacprzyk, J., Li, Z., Izquierdo, E., Wang, H. (eds.) Multimedia Analysis, Processing and Communications, pp. 623–654. Springer Berlin Heidelberg, Berlin, Heidelberg (2011). https://doi.org/10.1007/978-3-642-19551-8_23
20. Gu, L., Harris, J.G., Shrivastav, R., Sapienza, C.: Disordered speech evaluation using objective quality measures. In: ICASSP, pp. 321–324 (2005)

Personalizing Retrieval-Based Dialogue Agents

Pavel Posokhov[ID], Anastasia Matveeva[ID], Olesia Makhnytkina[(✉)][ID],
Anton Matveev[ID], and Yuri Matveev[ID]

ITMO University, Saint Petersburg, Russia
makhnytkina@itmo.ru

Abstract. The development of various kinds of interactive assistants at present is highly in demand. In this field, one critical problem is the personalization of these dialog assistants seeking to increase user loyalty and involvement in a conversation, which may be a competitive advantage for enterprises employing them. This paper presents a study of retrieve models for a personalized dialogue agent. To train models the Persona Chat and Toloka Persona Chat Rus datasets are used. The study found the most effective models among the retrieval models, learning strategies. Also, to solve one of the major limitations of the personalization of dialogue assistants—the lack of large data sets with dialogues containing person characteristics—a text data augmentation method was developed that preserves individual speech patterns and vocabulary.

Keywords: Personalized dialogue systems · Retrieve models · Text augmentation

1 Introduction

Currently, due to the promising prospects for the practical use of dialogue systems in various fields, their development has become one of the most relevant tasks in NLP. Conversational systems, also known as chatbots, are in a high demand in industry and everyday life. According to a study by Business Insider, the chatbot market will grow from $2.6 billion in 2021 to $9.4 billion by 2024 at a compound annual growth rate (CAGR) of 29.7%.

Currently, depending on the tasks being solved, it is common to separate goal-oriented models, the purpose of interaction with which is strictly defined and aimed at solving a specific problem: ordering movie tickets, booking a hotel room, etc., usually the dialogue in this case is constricted to one subject area, which greatly simplifies the interaction between the chatbot and a person and open-domain models which can operate in various subject areas, the goals of communication in this case can be different, including phatic (idle-domestic). The latter are of the greatest interest due to their versatility, since fine-tuning open-domain chatbots is more optimal than developing a new model to solve a specific problem. Also, it is clear that the construction of these types of models

S. R. M. Prasanna et al. (Eds.): SPECOM 2022, LNAI 13721, pp. 554–566, 2022.
https://doi.org/10.1007/978-3-031-20980-2_47

is an important step necessary to create a strong AI. In addition, the task of open-domain communication, that is, without a strict goal-setting of a dialogue, on free topics, is also relevant, for example, less than five percent of Twitter posts are specific questions, while about 80 percent contain statements about a personal emotional state, thoughts or actions, represented by the so-called 'Me'-forms.

Like all systems, open-domain systems have several disadvantages. For example, despite the rapid development of natural language processing, and the presence of numerous dialogue studies in particular, caused by the success of the application of modern deep learning techniques to computational linguistics problems, modern dialogue systems are at the initial stage of their development. Human interactions with such models indicate the existence of numerous problems, such as lack of a coherent personality, lack of explicit long-term memory, a tendency to give vague and meaningless answers, these factors are the main reason for the decrease in the motivation of the second participant (human) to continue the communicative act. Often these problems are caused by the lack of direct information about the person and learning from the aggregate sample of dialogues of various people, which leads to the model adhering to a general, average personality, which can often lead to factual errors, inconsistency or superficiality of the narrative. It is possible to avoid such behavior of the model by creating personalized dialogue agents trained on datasets of people's dialogues, extended by personality characteristics.

Retrieval architectures, generative models, and hybrid models combining the first two types in varied sequences are commonly used for the development of dialogue agents. This article proposes an approach to developing a personalized dialogue agent using retrieval models.

Currently, the field of natural language processing is actively developing in the direction of improving the quality of solving problems via the emergence of more complex and deep architectures of neural networks that require large datasets for training. The use of pre-trained models and additional fine-tuning on target datasets also relies on the amount of data available. To increase the volume, data often are collected from multiple sources. This approach has significant drawbacks for the development of virtual assistants, smart speakers, interactive robots, etc. since the data contains the speech of multiple people, each with its personal characteristics, which leads to a lack of cohesion in the responses, views, judgments, and style of communication. For handling this issue, augmentation of text data preserving individual speech patterns and vocabulary that is unique to the original text is relevant. This article presents a study on the influence of the use of augmentation methods that preserve style and vocabulary distinctive for a person on the performance of models for the automatic generation of replicas of a personalized dialogue agent.

For producing high-quality models, it is critical to have large datasets. It is possible to increase the volume using successful dialogues between a bot and a user [10]. However, at the stage of training neural networks, this approach is not applicable and the use of data augmentation methods is suggested.

2 Related Work

For building open-domain dialog systems, it is common to distinguish two types
of architectures [18, 20]: retrieval search models which are based on the principle
of ranking: choosing the most relevant answers to the input context from the
selection of possible answers, and refine models which are generator models that
produce a system response token by token, based on the input context and,
optionally, additional data necessary for generation, and also hybrid ensembles of
those models, based on various strategies for their interaction. Non-goal-oriented
dialogue systems have several features, including:

1. Models tend to produce generic, low-content answers. This problem is more
   characteristic of generative models, however, with a sufficient variety of candidates in the data for retrieval models, this problem also occurs. The main
   reason for that is the lack of extensive extralinguistic knowledge of the model,
   which is why it produces answers containing as little factual information as
   possible, thus reducing the likelihood of making a mistake.
2. The conversational agents are not consistent in their responses which is
   reflected in contradictory statements following one another (for example, to
   the question "What do you like?" the model may answer "winter", but the
   next answer to "What do you not like?" might be "cold and snow"). The main
   reason for that is the lack of an explicit logical apparatus and reliance on a
   consistent personality of the agent, which, without additional personification,
   is represented by an average set of all personalities in the training sample.
3. Dialogue models are not fully capable of grasping the context, primarily due
   to the lack of extralinguistic knowledge and the inability to personalize communication.

One of the main approaches to solving these problems is the personalization
and personification of dialogue agents. Personalization is changing or modifying
the responses of the model according to the information about another participant of the dialogue, passed to the model as an additional metadata vector. Some
researchers find this method unethical in certain cases, however, personalization
is more applicable to goal-oriented dialogue systems and is not included in this
study. Personification involves full-fledged modeling of responses by the model
in the context of the information about the persona of the sender. Person metadata can include various facts about the person (e.g., gender, age, hobbies, etc.)
enabling a direct or indirect communication on behalf of the described person.

Recent studies of retrieval models [5] show that the use of pre-trained BERT
type transformer models as an embedding component of NLP models significantly increases their efficiency in solving a wide range of problems, including
solving ranking problems as encoders, which was also confirmed in the first phase
of our study. Bidirectional Encoder Representations from Transformers (BERT)
is the coding part of the transformer architecture, it uses the self-attention mechanism and multi-head attention to represent words, positional coding of tokens,
which allows to achieve the effect of a contextual representation of words. The
effectiveness of this approach is largely attributed to pre-training BERT on a

large dataset with auto-labeling (MLM—masked word prediction, next sentence prediction, etc.), with the possibility of further fine-tuning on the target dataset to improve the representation of the lexical meaning of words in the context of the problem under consideration.

1. Bi-Encoder [12] architecture is represented by a pair of independent BERT base models, which are initialized with the same parameters before the training starts. Models receive context and candidate vectors as inputs, encoded using the WordPiece tokenizer, and process them independently. Dotprod is used to calculate an error. Negative sampling, where the distance value for distractors can be partially masked, can also be used during training.

2. Cross-Encoder [12]—the architecture for ranking tasks which employs one instance of BERT, the input of which is a concatenated vector of context and candidates separated by a special token. The resulting vector is then compacted by weighted summation through a linear layer to obtain a scalar value that can be interpreted as the similarity between the candidate vector and the context. This approach allows the internal attention of the model to encode both vectors, which significantly increases the efficiency of their representation, though significantly increases the operating time and memory resources consumed.

3. Poly-Encoder [12]—the architecture that utilizes a pair of BERT embedders to represent contexts and candidates, similar to the Bi-Encoder model, but for the calculation of the similarity of the candidate and context vectors, the latter passes through an attention block that has a collection of representations of the context initialized randomly and optimized during training, where the candidate vector is the query. Then the distance between the context and the candidates is calculated by multiplying their vectors. This approach allows to obtain contextual representations that are dependent both on the context and on the candidates, similar to how it happens in the Cross-Encoder architecture and improves the performance of the model.

4. Co-Encoder [30] similar to the Poly-Encoder architecture has two independent context and candidate representation blocks, but instead of the standard attention mechanism, it processes several stages of co-attention. This approach also produces extended views of the context. Additionally, the diffusion of information in this case extends to the representation of candidates, and the use of co-attention allows for incorporation of additional metadata vectors which are also used to expand the views.

Generative architectures of conversational agents generate responses token by token using language modeling. Among the modern approaches to training generative models of personalized dialogue agents are:

1. GPT [7] is a Transformer-based architecture and training procedure for natural language processing tasks. Training follows a two-stage procedure. First, a language modeling objective is used on the unlabeled data to learn the initial parameters of a neural network model. These parameters are adapted to a target task using the corresponding supervised objective.

2. Blenderbot [21] is a model created by the Facebook AI development team. It is built according to the standard architecture of the Seq2Seq transformer model. It is created for user interaction but can also be used for many other text generation tasks.
3. Seq2Seq [16, 24, 28] is a tandem of two recurrent neural networks: encoder and decoder. These models can consist of several encoder and decoder blocks and a variable number of parameters. Also, such models employ an attention mechanism that solves the issue that the influence of previous block states on the current one decreases exponentially with the distance between words. The layer of this mechanism is often implemented by a single-layer neural network that receives the hidden state of the encoder block and the context, which is represented by the previous hidden state of the decoder block, as input.

A tremendous advantage of retrieval models over generative ones is the high volume of relevant content in the answers, allowing the dialogue to appear more meaningful and realistic. Moreover, retrieval models have an objective advantage over generative ones since the former are evaluated by simple and effective metrics such as top-k, which reflects the probability of finding the correct answer in the first k ranks, R-precision k (equivalent to the value of recall for the k-th position), mrr (the reciprocal of the rank of the target response), etc. However, since automated evaluation metrics may not adequately reflect the quality of the dialogue system, it is critical to evaluate the performance of the model by a person; as the study of dialogue systems shows, retrieval models are superior to generative ones in this respect as well. Taking all of that into account, in this study, we focus on retrieval models.

Also for producing high-quality models it is critical to have large datasets. It is possible to increase the volume using successful dialogues between a bot and a user [10], however, at the stage of training neural networks this approach is not applicable and the use of data augmentation methods is suggested.

A set of the basic augmentation techniques is presented in the EDA algorithm [25], which consists of four operations: synonym replacement, random insertion, random permutation, and random deletion. When augmenting textual data, it is important to preserve the meaning of the text; various dictionaries, for example, WordNet [8, 25] or pre-trained language models such as BERT [26], GPT2 [15], Word2Vec [19], Glove [8], etc. are commonly used to replace words with synonyms.

Work [19] considers several augmentation techniques similar to those in [8]: interpolation method, extrapolation method, adding random noise. The difference was the use of a pre-trained Word2Vec language model, unlike Glove in the previous work. The experiments were conducted for the problem of extracting types of contract elements from a text [3].

Various techniques for adding noise to word vector representations obtained using the Word2Vec model were reviewed in [29]: Gaussian noise, Bernoulli noise, Adversarial Noise, etc. Studies of adding noise to vector representations of words [8, 19, 29], in general, showed favorable results, however, the use of such augmentation methods involves embeddings of non-existing words, which can potentially lead to a mismatch in message class labels.

Work [14] proposes a contextual augmentation approach based on the assumption that sentences are natural even if words in sentences are replaced by other words with paradigmatic relations.

An alternative to generation of paraphrases is reverse translation. Reference [6] has studied the quality of reverse translation using deep neural networks, showing positive results.

A study in [2] reviews the GECA (Good-Enough Compositional Data Augmentation) method, which is based on the idea that if two entities appear in a common environment, then any additional environment where one of the entities appears independently is also valid for another entity.

Another non-trivial augmentation technique is presented in [9] where the augmentation is performed via text shuffling using a neural network.

Unfortunately, none of the methods above preserve the style and the vocabulary unique to the original message which is one of the most important issues for various applications such as the development of dialog assistants [17] since the personalization of dialog assistants is key to user loyalty.

The method using the generative model LAMBADA [1] showed particular efficiency in text data augmentation. One of the main traits of this method is a phase for filtering augmented data using the BERT classifier. Also, this method is noteworthy for its supposed ability to preserve the speech characteristic of a person. A significant drawback of this method is the high demand for computing resources. Additionally, data from intermediate stages can not be immediately discarded due to the specifics of the algorithm, which leads to an increased usage of permanent (physical) memory.

When modifying text data, transformations can lead to distortions in the text making it grammatically or semantically incorrect or stylistically distinct from the original text and it demands for techniques that can augment text preserving the style, vocabulary while maintaining syntactic integrity.

There are also more advanced augmentation methods that have the ability to preserve the styles and vocabulary of a text, for example, Paraphrases generator based on syntax trees transformation [4]. This method involves modifying a text by transforming the syntax tree based on syntactic grammars. Text augmentation via syntax trees with the generation of new data based on syntactic templates was also considered in [23, 27].

3   Methods

3.1   Models

In the study, we consider retrieval and refine models approaches for creation of personalized dialogue agents.

Retrieval Models. Numerous studies show that it is possible to improve the performance of nlp models in solving a wide range of tasks, including ranking tasks, by using pre-trained BERT-type transformer models as an embedding component. Bidirectional Encoder Representations from Transformers (BERT) is the encoding part of the transformer architecture. A self-attention mechanism, multi-head attention, and positional coding of tokens are employed for representing words in BERT, which allows obtaining of contextual representation of words. Pre-training BERT on a large dataset with auto-labeling (MLM—masked word prediction, next sentence prediction, etc.) is one of the main reasons for the effectiveness of the method. As part of the study, we performed fine-tuning of BERT models on target datasets to improve the representation of the lexical meaning of words within the scope of the problem under consideration.

Within the scope of this study, we consider the following architectures based on BERT base models—Simple Bi-Encoder, Bi-Encoder with Coattention [11]. Text preprocessing includes only tokenization based on the Wordpiece [22] method. The following metrics are used to evaluate the performance of the models:

(1) $R@k$—an interpretation of the recall for the ranking problem. The number of relevant responses from the k highest ranks divided by the total number of relevant responses. In the traditional form, the value k must match the number of relevant responses, thus $R@k = acc(topk)/k$, however, the number of highest ranks considered can be changed independently. Computing $R@k$ requires knowledge of all documents relevant to the query (in the case of a dialog system, $k = 1$), then $R@1 = acc(topk)$. The sensitivity of the model can be analyzed by varying the number of ranks.

(2) MRR or inverse rank, calculated by the formula $MRR = 1/r$, where r is the rank of the correct answer. This is a statistical measure for evaluating models that return responses sorted by probability of correctness. Unlike $R@1$, MRR can only be applied in the case of a single correct answer, and the metric itself is multiplicatively inverse.

3.2   Augmentation

In this work, we present a new augmentation method that preserves the distinctive characteristics of a person's speech (see Fig. 1). The idea for this augmentation method derives from the adapted data augmentation scheme shown in [4]. The proposed method also includes the stage of extracting syntax trees. The stage of transformation and generation of paraphrased data in this method is executed in a single process.

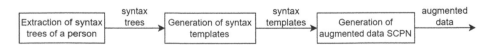

Fig. 1. Schematic diagram of the augmentation process.

Syntax tree extraction—in this stage, syntax trees are extracted for each replica using Stanford Core Nlp for the English language and SyntaxNet for the Russian language producing syntax trees of all replicas used by each person.

```
(ROOT
  (SQ
    (VP (VB have)
      (NP
        (NP (DT any) (NNS pets))
        (PP (IN at)
          (NP (NN home)))))
    (?)))
```

The example of a syntax tree is produced from the original message "Do you have any pets at home?". Creation of syntactic templates—the syntactic trees obtained at the previous stage are transformed to a uniform format by removing all the words of the original sentence from them and leaving only syntactic structural units. Further, duplicates and similar ones are removed from the set of obtained syntactic structures, and n most frequently used ones are selected from the remaining ones. An example of a template is represented by formula (1).

$$(ROOT(SQ(VP(VB)(NP(NP(DT)(NNS))(PP(IN)(NP(NN)))))(?))) \quad (1)$$

where $ROOT$ is the root of the sentence; SQ—inverted yes/no question, or main clause of a wh-question, following the wh-phrase in $SBARQ$; VP—verb phrase; VB—verb, base form; NP—noun phrase; DT—determiner; NNS—noun, common, plural; PP—prepositional phrase; IN—preposition or subordinating conjunction; To these sets of templates obtained for each person we add common for OpenAttacker EOS line endings. Then, together with the original replica of the person, they are sent to the Syntactically Controlled Paraphrase Network (SCPN—encoder-decoder model for syntactically controlled generation of paraphrases) from the OpenAttaker framework [13] to generate augmented data. This way, each replica can be transformed in n different ways. Since only syntactic structures characteristic of a person are used for data augmentation, the syntactic features of a person's speech are preserved. Vocabulary and style are preserved since they remain almost unchanged as augmentation is based on transformation of the syntax tree. If any of the parts of speech is not present in the original replica, SCPN adds the necessary parts of speech (conjunctions, prepositions, particles) to maintain the syntactic coherence of the augmented replicas. If the remaining parts of speech are missing, they are added using a word generating LSTM.

4 Experiments

4.1 Datasets

1. PERSONA-CHAT is an English-language corpus of dialogues between two participants, reproducing artificial personas modeled based on 3–5 sentences

with a description (e.g. "I like to sk, "I am an artist", "I eat sardines for breakfast daily"). This dataset consists of 8939 completed conversations and 955 persons as a training set, 1000 dialogues and 100 persons for validation, and 968 dialogues and 100 persons for testing. To prevent word overlapping, information about persons after the collection of dialogues was reworked, using paraphrasing, generalization, and concretization.

2. Toloka Persona Chat Rus is a dataset compiled at the Laboratory of Neural Systems and Deep Learning at the Moscow Institute of Physics and Technology by each participant in the study modeling a certain specified person in dialogues. This dataset is packaged in two files: profile.tsv containing lines with characteristics of 1505 different persons, represented by 5 sentences such as "I draw", "I live abroad", or "I have a snake"; dialogues.tsv containing 10,013 dialogues in Russian between study participants. Russian.

4.2 Retrieval Models Results

In this study, we chose the most optimal configurations of ranking: Simple Bi-Encoder and CoBERT. In addition, for the modules, we employed a modified training method which involves the preliminary training of Siamese architectures, when the encoders of context and candidates are trained synchronously and then are separated and trained separately. One key condition for such learning method is to prevent a complete optimization of the weights at the pre-learning stage because, having reached the clear minima of the error function, the Siamese encoders, when separated, will find themselves in local minima, the escape from which will require unreasonably large values of the learning step, which negates the benefit of pre-learning. A comparison of the selected methods applied to the English Persona Chat dataset is presented in Table 1.

Table 1. Performance of retrieval models Persona Chat.

Strategy	Model	Persona	Valid loss	Valid acc	Valid r1	Valid r5	Valid r10	Valid MRR
15/0	Cobert	Mean	0.898	0.535	0.535	0.714	0.971	0.653
	Cobert	Concat	0.892	0.512	0.512	0.680	0.968	0.634
	Simple	Mean	0.911	0.509	0.509	0.686	0.963	0.629
	Simple	Concat	0.919	0.522	0.521	0.694	0.952	0.638
0/15	Cobert	Mean	1.220	0.259	0.260	0.484	0.929	0.425
	Cobert	Concat	0.932	0.257	0.257	0.467	0.870	0.412
	Simple	Mean	1.298	0.253	0.254	0.474	0.919	0.418
	Simple	Concat	0.921	0.352	0.352	0.490	0.949	0.489
5/10	cobert	mean	0.874	0.539	0.539	0.716	0.972	0.656
	Cobert	Concat	0.890	0.533	0.533	0.712	0.970	0.653
	Simple	Mean	0.900	0.519	0.519	0.696	0.964	0.638
	Simple	Concat	0.995	0.519	0.519	0.699	0.962	0.642

According to the results of the comparison, the best result was achieved with the training with five epochs trained together and ten separately. With this approach to training, the most effective was the CoBERT model.

The performance results when using the Russian-language Toloka Persona Chat Rus dataset are presented in Table 2.

Table 2. Performance of retrieval models Toloka Persona Chat Rus.

Strategy	Model	Persona	Valid loss	Valid acc	Valid r1	Valid r5	Valid r10	Valid r10
15/0	Cobert	Mean	0.9	0.53	0.53	0.71	0.97	0.65
	Cobert	Concat	0.89	0.51	0.51	0.68	0.97	0.63
	Simple	Mean	0.91	0.51	0.51	0.69	0.96	0.63
	Simple	Concat	0.92	0.52	0.52	0.69	0.95	0.64
0/15	Cobert	Mean	1.22	0.26	0.26	0.48	0.93	0.43
	Cobert	Concat	0.93	0.26	0.26	0.47	0.87	0.41
	Simple	Mean	1.3	0.25	0.25	0.47	0.92	0.42
	Simple	Concat	0.92	0.35	0.35	0.49	0.95	0.49
5/10	Cobert	Mean	0.87	0.55	0.54	0.72	0.97	0.66
	Cobert	Concat	0.89	0.53	0.53	0.71	0.97	0.65
	Simple	Mean	0.9	0.52	0.52	0.7	0.96	0.44
	Simple	Concat	0.99	0.52	0.52	0.7	0.96	0.44

With Russian-language data, the best performance was achieved by the CoBERT and the 5/10 training approach.

4.3   Augmentation Results

Examples of data augmented with syntactic paraphrasing are presented in Table 3.

Table 3. Examples of data augmented with syntactic paraphrasing.

Source text	Dataset	Result
No I am not found a new girl at a wedding last week	PERSONA-CHAT	i didn't find a girl at the wedding.
Люблю животных, просто обо- жаю, как и свою работу). Я фан-Rustастику люблю	Toloka Persona Chat Rus	Люблю животных, просто люблю свою работу и фан- тастику.

Training of retrieval models (simple Bi-encoder, CoBERT) was performed with three different setups for data augmentation. The option $aug - prob = 0.0$ corresponds to training without augmentations. With $aug - prob = 1.0$, each statement is replaced by augmentation. The option $augprob = 0.5$ where half of the statements are replaced by augmentation. Results of the experiments are presented in Table 4.

Table 4. Performance of retrievel models with augmentation.

Augment Prob	Language	Model	Valid acc	Valid r1	Valid r5	Valid r10	Valid MRR
0.0	En	Cobert	0.455	0.456	0.652	0.945	0.585
	En	Simple	0.405	0.406	0.6860	0.943	0.537
1.0	En	Cobert	0.234	0.234	0.428	0.788	0.340
	En	Simple	0.290	0.290	0.522	0.874	0.407
0.5	En	Cobert	0.463	0.463	0.655	0.942	0.593
	En	Simple	0.425	0.425	0.702	0.950	0.554
0.0	Ru	Cobert	0.516	0.517	0.694	0.965	0.636
	Ru	Simple	0.520	0.520	0.699	0.959	0.440
1.0	Ru	Cobert	0.234	0.234	0.429	0.765	0.338
	Ru	Simple	0.283	0.284	0.507	0.857	0.401
0.5	Ru	Cobert	0.645	0.645	0.795	0.967	0.739
	Ru	Simple	0.629	0.629	0.785	0.967	0.728

5   Discussion and Conclusion

Within the scope of this study, we analysed the modern types and architectures of dialogue systems, among which we identified the most efficient type, namely, retrieval models. Among them, the best performance metrics were achieved by the CoBERT architecture when training five epochs together and ten others separately. Also in this paper, we propose a text data augmentation method that preserves individual speech patterns and vocabulary. We find that data augmentation with the presented method produces an increase in performance at values of $aug - prob < 1.0$ because in this case there is a chance that the original message remains unchanged. We observe a performance increase for different models up to 12%.

Acknowledgments. The research was financially supported the Russian Science Foundations (project 22-11-00128).

References

1. Anaby-Tavor, A., Carmeli, B., Goldbraich, E., Kantor, A., Kour, G., Shlomov, S., Tepper, N., Zwerdling, N.: Not enough data? deep learning to the rescue! (2019). http://arxiv.org/abs/1911.03118
2. Andreas, J.: Good-enough compositional data augmentation (2019). http://arxiv.org/abs/1904.09545
3. Chalkidis, I., Androutsopoulos, I., Michos, A.: Extracting contract elements. In: Proceedings of the 16th Edition of the International Conference on Artical Intelligence and Law, pp. 19–28. ICAIL '17, Association for Computing Machinery, New York, NY, USA (2017). https://doi.org/10.1145/3086512.3086515
4. Coulombe, C.: Text data augmentation made simple by leveraging NLP cloud apis (2018). http://arxiv.org/abs/1812.04718

5. Devlin, J., Chang, M.W., Lee, K., Toutanova, K.: BERT: pre-training of deep bidirectional transformers for language understanding. In: Proceedings of the 2019 Conference of the North American Chapter of the Association for Computational Linguistics: Human Language Technologies, vol.1 (Long and Short Papers), pp. 4171–4186. Association for Computational Linguistics, Minneapolis, Minnesota (2019). https://doi.org/10.18653/v1/N19-1423, https://aclanthology.org/N19-1423

6. Edunov, S., Ott, M., Auli, M., Grangier, D.: Understanding back-translation at scale. In: Proceedings of the 2018 Conference on Empirical Methods in Natural Language Processing, pp. 489–500. Association for Computational Linguistics, Brussels, Belgium (2018). https://doi.org/10.18653/v1/D18-1045, https://aclanthology.org/D18-1045

7. Floridi, L., Chiriatti, M.: GPT-3: its nature, scope, limits, and consequences. Mind. Mach. **30**(4), 681–694 (2020). https://doi.org/10.1007/s11023-020-09548-1

8. Giridhara, P.K.B., Mishra, C., Venkataramana, R.K.M., Bukhari, S.S., Dengel, A.R.: A study of various text augmentation techniques for relation classification in free text. In: ICPRAM (2019)

9. Guo, H., Mao, Y., Zhang, R.: Augmenting data with mixup for sentence classification: an empirical study (2019). arXiv:abs/1905.08941

10. Hancock, B., Bordes, A., Mazare, P.E., Weston, J.: Learning from dialogue after deployment: feed yourself, chatbot! pp. 3667–3684 (2019). https://doi.org/10.18653/v1/P19-1358

11. Humeau, S., Shuster, K., Lachaux, M., Weston, J.: Real-time inference in multi-sentence tasks with deep pretrained transformers (2019). http://arxiv.org/abs/1905.01969

12. Humeau, S., Shuster, K., Lachaux, M.A., Weston, J.: Poly-encoders: architectures and pre-training strategies for fast and accurate multi-sentence scoring. In: International Conference on Learning Representations (2020). https://openreview.net/forum?id=SkxgnnNFvH

13. Iyyer, M., Wieting, J., Gimpel, K., Zettlemoyer, L.: Adversarial example generation with syntactically controlled paraphrase networks. In: Proceedings of the 2018 Conference of the North American Chapter of the Association for Computational Linguistics: Human Language Technologies, vol. 1 (Long Papers), pp. 1875–1885. Association for Computational Linguistics, New Orleans, Louisiana (2018). https://doi.org/10.18653/v1/N18-1170, https://aclanthology.org/N18-1170

14. Kobayashi, S.: Contextual augmentation: data augmentation by words with paradigmatic relations (2018). arXiv:abs/1805.06201

15. Kumar, V., Choudhary, A., Cho, E.: Data augmentation using pre-trained transformer models (2020). arXiv:abs/2003.02245

16. Lin, Z., Liu, Z., Winata, G.I., Cahyawijaya, S., Madotto, A., Bang, Y., Ishii, E., Fung, P.: XPersona: evaluating multilingual personalized chatbot. In: Proceedings of the 3rd Workshop on Natural Language Processing for Conversational AI. pp. 102–112. Association for Computational Linguistics, Online (2021). https://doi.org/10.18653/v1/2021.nlp4convai-1.10, https://aclanthology.org/2021.nlp4convai-1.10

17. Matveev, A., Makhnytkina, O., Matveev, Y., Svischev, A., Korobova, P., Rybin, A., Akulov, A.: Virtual dialogue assistant for remote exams. Mathematics **9**(18) (2021). https://doi.org/10.3390/math9182229, https://www.mdpi.com/2227-7390/9/18/2229

18. Ni, J., Young, T., Pandelea, V., Xue, F., Adiga, V., Cambria, E.: Recent advances in deep learning-based dialogue systems (2021)

19. Papadaki, M., Chalkidis, I., Michos, A.: Data augmentation techniques for legal text analytics (2017)
20. Posokhov, P., Apanasovich, K., Matveeva, A., Makhnytkina, O., Matveev, A.: Personalizing dialogue agents for Russian: retrieve and refine, vol. 2022, pp. 245–252 (2022). https://doi.org/10.23919/FRUCT54823.2022.9770895
21. Roller, S., Dinan, E., Goyal, N., Ju, D., Williamson, M., Liu, Y., Xu, J., Ott, M., Smith, E.M., Boureau, Y.L., Weston, J.: Recipes for building an open-domain chatbot. In: Proceedings of the 16th Conference of the European Chapter of the Association for Computational Linguistics: Main Volume, pp. 300–325. Association for Computational Linguistics, Online (2021). https://doi.org/10.18653/v1/2021.eacl-main.24, https://aclanthology.org/2021.eacl-main.24
22. Sennrich, R., Haddow, B., Birch, A.: Neural machine translation of rare words with subword units. CoRR abs/1508.07909 (2015), http://arxiv.org/abs/1508.07909
23. Shen, T., Lei, T., Barzilay, R., Jaakkola, T.S.: Style transfer from non-parallel text by cross-alignment (2017). arXiv:abs/1705.09655
24. Sugiyama, H., Mizukami, M., Arimoto, T., Narimatsu, H., Chiba, Y., Nakajima, H., Meguro, T.: Empirical analysis of training strategies of transformer-based Japanese chit-chat systems (2021). arXiv:abs/2109.05217
25. Wei, J.W., Zou, K.: EDA: easy data augmentation techniques for boosting performance on text classification tasks (2019). arXiv:abs/1901.11196
26. Wu, X., Xia, Y., Zhu, J., Wu, L., Xie, S., Fan, Y., Qin, T.: Mixseq: a simple data augmentation method for neural machine translation, pp. 192–197 (2021). https://doi.org/10.18653/v1/2021.iwslt-1.23
27. Yang, Z., Hu, Z., Dyer, C., Xing, E.P., Berg-Kirkpatrick, T.: Unsupervised text style transfer using language models as discriminators (2018). arXiv:abs/1805.11749
28. Zhang, S., Dinan, E., Urbanek, J., Szlam, A., Kiela, D., Weston, J.: Personalizing dialogue agents: I have a dog, do you have pets too? In: Proceedings of the 56th Annual Meeting of the Association for Computational Linguistics (vol. 1: Long Papers), pp. 2204–2213. Association for Computational Linguistics, Melbourne, Australia (2018). https://doi.org/10.18653/v1/P18-1205, https://aclanthology.org/P18-1205
29. Zhang, Z., Zweigenbaum, P.: Gneg: graph-based negative sampling for word2vec (2018). https://doi.org/10.18653/v1/P18-2090
30. Zhong, P., Sun, Y., Liu, Y., Zhang, C., Wang, H., Nie, Z., Miao, C.: Endowing empathetic dialogue systems with personas (2020). arXiv:abs/2004.12316

Forensic Identification of Foreign-Language Speakers by the Method of Structural-Melodic Analysis of Phonograms

Rodmonga Potapova[1] , Vsevolod Potapov[2] , and Irina Kuryanova[3,4(✉)]

[1] Institute of Applied and Mathematical Linguistics, Moscow State Linguistic University, 38 Ostozhenka Street, Moscow 119034, Russia
[2] Centre of New Technologies for Humanities, Lomonosov Moscow State University, Leninskije Gory 1, 119991 Moscow, Russia
[3] Experimental Phonetic Laboratory of Criminalistics for Speech Translation, Institute of Applied and Mathematical Linguistics, Moscow State Linguistic University, 38 Ostozhenka Street, Moscow 119034, Russia
ivkuryanova@mail.ru
[4] Department of Forensic Linguistics, Moscow Research Center, 5 Nizhnyaya Syromyatnicheskaya Street, Moscow 105120, Russia

Abstract. The crime rate observed in any country in the world necessitates the study of the parameters of speech signal in terms of foreign speech in order to carry out phonoscopic examinations in an ethnic language (for example, gypsy). This study is of pragmalinguistic nature and is not intended to be a typological study and comparison of the languages under consideration. The need for an expert who is not a native speaker of the language under study to determine the key prosodic characteristics of foreign language speech, taking into account the perceptual-auditory and acoustic types of analysis of phonograms in order to identify a foreign-language speaker, poses a number of qualitatively new tasks for computer linguistics. Prosody plays a special role in personality identification as a fundamental paraverbal means of spoken speech communication. This paper describes a technique for identifying foreign-language speakers in Tajik and Gypsy languages by an expert who is a native speaker of the Russian language, by studying the prosodic organization of an utterance using perceptual-auditory and acoustic types of analysis based on the identification module as part of a specialized sound editor SIS II (developed by LLC Speech Technology Center, St. Petersburg), a universal acoustic-linguistic platform for the study of voice and speech, designed to automate the process of speaker identification.

Keywords: Prosody · Identification of foreign-language speakers by voice and spoken speech · Structural and melodic analysis of phonograms · Prosodic identification parameters of spontaneous foreign language speech

S. R. M. Prasanna et al. (Eds.): SPECOM 2022, LNAI 13721, pp. 567–578, 2022.
https://doi.org/10.1007/978-3-031-20980-2_48

1   Introduction

Technological progress and social changes in the modern world, related to the use of high tech solutions in all spheres of society, cover not only political, economic and socio-cultural aspects, but also the criminal sphere, causing transnational crimes committed in recent decades [1–3]. The high level of technical equipment makes it possible for members of modern transnational groups to ensure clandestine secrecy: using a mobile phone, the masterminds control the commission of crimes from anywhere in the world [4]. The main difficulty in investigating such crimes was the impossibility of identifying a foreign-language speaker by an expert who is not a native speaker of this language [1, 4]. This has led to the particular relevance of expert studies aimed at solving the problem of identifying a foreign-language speaker by computer methods by an expert who is native speaker of another language.

In order to solve the tasks set, a number of studies were conducted on the possibility of recognizing a foreign-language speaker by ear. In particular, such experiments were performed in Germany and Great Britain, which, on the basis of the German language, highlighted the issues of the interference of the native language of the auditor, who perceives foreign language speech in the process of identification [11–20]. The first fundamental studies of the foreign speech perception features in Russia were carried out by R.K. Potapova on the material of the English, German and French languages (for example, [5, 8–10]). In the course of the experiments, it was found that prosody as a fundamental paraverbal means of spoken speech communication plays a paramount role in the perception of foreign language speech for the purpose of subsequent identification of the speaker. When perceiving unfamiliar speech, when the meaning of words cannot be understood by the recipient, prosody is an operational unit of perception, since it has such informative features that help the auditor segment speech into syntactic blocks [4].

2   Method

The main challenge of assessing and selecting identification-significant stable features of foreign speech was the need to attract a highly qualified linguist who knows the basics of forensic identification of a person by voice and speech and has a command of the national language under study. This task was especially complicated in the study of languages that were little studied in terms of their linguistic structure, in particular, gypsy. In this regard, the most promising area of activity was the search for new complex language-independent automatic and automated methods that make it possible to study the segmental and suprasegmental parameters of a speech signal by an expert who does not know the language spoken by the suspect.

To this end, as part of scientific, technical and experimental design work, the scientific team of LLC Speech Technology Center (St. Petersburg) took on the task of collecting speech databases in Tajik, Gypsy, Uzbek and Azerbaijani languages, taking into account their existing dialects; and in 2013, a universal acoustic-linguistic tool for the study of voice and speech for forensic purposes was created that uses both fully automatic and automated identification methods (SIS II). The SIS II special software for the forensic investigation of phonograms is part of the IKAR-Lab hardware-software complex (LLC

Speech Technology Center, St. Petersburg) and contains identification modules as part of a specialized sound editor [4]. The identification algorithms presented in SIS II formed the basis of the unified methodology for studying the speech signal "Typical identification by voice and speech" [21], which provides a unified scientific and practical approach in performing forensic activities.

2.1 Informative Prosodic Characteristics of Unprepared Speech, Used in the Structural-Melodic Analysis of Phonograms

The proposed structure for describing the melodic contour of the syntagma was developed on the basis of approaches and methods used both in national [22–25] and foreign intonology [26, 27]. The melodic contour is traditionally understood as the trajectory of the change in the voice pitch frequency (VPF), which is realized in a certain speech segment [22–25, 27].

Syntagma. In this research method, in relation to foreign language speech, a syntagma is understood as the shortest interpause group of a phrase, intonationally designed, having a pronounced direction of the voice pitch frequency movement (F_0 in time), united by syntagmatic (phrasal) stress [4]. Depending on the direction of the melodic curve, a "syntagma" can be realized with three main subtypes: a syntagma with a falling or rising accent, as well as a syntagma with a level tone of the fundamental pitch of various levels. The figure below shows an example of a syntagma with a rising accent (Fig. 1).

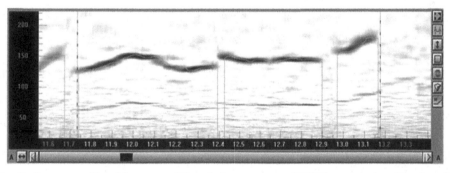

Fig. 1. Syntagma with a rising accent "Tu az kujo zang mezany?" ("Where are you calling from?"; translation from Tajik).

The melodic contour of the syntagma is heterogeneous in its structure. Within these subtypes, syntagmas can have various melodic patterns. Also, various parts of the syntagma have different significance in the transfer of communicative meanings [6]. Traditionally, taking into account the melodic pattern, the syntagma is divided into the following parts: the nuclear part (or measure, center), the pre-nuclear part (or pre-measure, pre-center), the post-nuclear part (or anacrusis, post-center).

Nuclear and Nuclear-Post-Nuclear Segment. The most significant and the only obligatory element in the composition of the syntagma contour is the nucleus, the main stressed
syllable of the most accentuated word of the syntagma. The nucleus has a number of
characteristics that experts should rely on for macro- and micro-segmentation of spoken
speech in a language unfamiliar to the expert. All sounds of the nuclear syllable are
pronounced with more discrete word intelligibility in relation to other sounds; therefore, in perceptual-auditory identification, the nucleus is the most distinct and accentuated syllable of the most intonationally marked word of the syntagma [4]. An estimate
of the signal energy in order to isolate the nuclear segment of the syntagma can be
calculated automatically on the SIS II module when plotting the standard deviation
(root-mean-square-deviation, RMSD) (see Fig. 2).

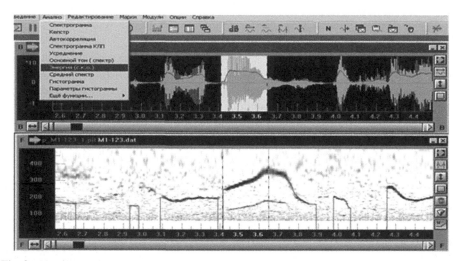

Fig. 2. Plotting RMSD energy in the oscillograph record window. Isolation of the nuclear syllable
by the RMSD energy.

The nuclear segment of the syntagma is an independent substratum in the structure
of the melodic contour, which can be studied both independently and as a structural
cluster of the VFP envelope integrated with the nuclear segment [4, 28, 29].

Pre-nuclear Segment. This segment has some isolation in the contour structure due to a
certain variability of parameters that are not directly related to the type of melodies realized in the nuclear segment [3, 4]. In the composition of the pre-nuclear segment, when
analyzing the VFP envelope (melodic contour of the syntagma), a scale is traditionally
distinguished, that is, a segment from the first stressed syllable of the syntagma to the
nucleus, and a pre-scale, that is, unstressed syllables that precede the scale or directly
the nucleus (in the absence of a scale) [22, 27, 29]. Depending on the direction of voice
frequency pitch movement (VFP envelope) in the pre-nuclear segment, two subtypes
of the scale are distinguished: falling and rising; the types of pre-scale used are high
and low [27, 29]. Pre-scales are analyzed by the values of the minimum, maximum and
average frequency.

2.2   Description Parameters for Melodic Contour Types/Subtypes

The method of structural-melodic analysis in the SIS II module consists in identification of melodic structures of the same type in the studied phonograms [4, 30]. For each selected element of the melodic contour, a certain set of parameters is calculated in the SIS II module. The used set of elements (types and subtypes) of the melodic contour and the parameters of their description are presented in Table 1.

Table 1. Types, subtypes and parameters for describing the elements of a melodic contour.

No	Type	Subtype	Parameters used	List of parameters
1	Nuclear syllable	Rising	1–11, 15	1. Initial VFP value (Hz)
2		Falling	1–5, 7–11, 15	2. Final VFP value (Hz)
3		Rising - falling	1–13, 15	3. Maximum VFP value (Hz)
4		Falling - falling	1–15	
5	Nuclear-post-nuclear segment	Rising	1–15	4. Peak time (%)
6		Falling	1–5, 7–15	5. Minimum VFP value (Hz)
7		Rising - falling	2–5, 8, 10–15	6. Minimum time (%) -
8		Falling - rising	1–5, 7, 8, 10–15	7, 8. Interval: the difference between the maximum and
9	Scale	Falling	1–8, 14	minimum VFP values
10		Rising	1–8, 10, 14	(Hz; PT)
11	Pre-scale	Low	3, 5, 10	9. Half frequency time (%)
12		High	3, 10	10. Average VFP value (Hz)
13	Syntagma	Falling tone	2–6, 8, 14	11. Rate of change of VFP values (PT/sec)
14		Rising tone	2–6, 8, 14	12. Shift (asymmetry)
15	Long speech fragment		3, 5, 7, 8, 10–14	13. Kurtosis
16	Hesitation pause		3, 5, 10	14. Unevenness factor of the VFP envelope
17	Pre-nuclear syllable + nucleus	Rising	1–10, 12–15	15. Duration of the selected fragment (ms)
18		Falling	1–4, 6–8, 10, 12–15	

It has been established that the maximum and minimum VFP values in the rising and falling nuclear segments are characterized by sufficient stability and regularity of manifestation [31]. The average VFP value is traditionally considered an essential feature in the identification study of speech [7, 15, 27, 32]. Based on the material of Tajik and Gypsy speech, it was found that the most stable and promising for identification comparison are the so-called "physical" parameters associated with the VFP values (first of all, the minimum VFP value of the nuclear rising and nuclear falling tones, as well as the values of the average, initial and final VFPs) [4].

2.3   Principles of Phonogram Comparison by the Method of Structural-Melodic Analysis

The purpose of structural-melodic analysis is to identify melodic structures of the same type in the studied phonograms and compare their characteristics to establish the degree of proximity of the melodic contours parameters (VFP envelope) [4, 30]. This objective is accomplished by sequential selection of several realizations of reference fragments for each type/subtype of the melodic contour in the compared phonograms. For each pair of compared values, the SIS II module automatically calculates the difference of values, which is then compared with the corresponding threshold [4, 30]. Each parameter has its own weight coefficient, which determines its contribution in the overall assessment of the degree of similarity/difference for each of the involved types/subtypes of the VFP envelope. Weight coefficients are assigned to prosodic parameters with regard to the degree of their realization stability, on the one hand, and their distinctive function, on the other [4, 30].

To make a generalized decision, the SIS II identification module introduces the concept of likelihood ratio (LR-estimates, LR - Likelihood Ratio) [4]. The principle of forming a decision on the similarity or difference of persons on the compared phonograms is based on a formula showing the ratio of the probability of coincidence to the probability of difference:

$$LR = FR/FA,$$

where LR is the likelihood ratio (LR-estimate); FR (falserejection) is the probability of false rejection of the "speaker"; FA (falseacceptance) is the probability of false acceptance of the "speaker". If the value of the LR-estimate is greater than one, then the probability of coincidence of "speakers" on the phonograms under study exceeds the probability of their difference. If the value of the LR-estimate is less than one, then the difference between "speakers" becomes more probable [4].

The FR and FA values are presented as a graph of the distribution of these values, showing the dependence of the speaker false rejection error probability (FR, the curve located on the left part of the plane relative to the EER intersection point) and speaker false acceptance error probability (FA, the curve located on the right part of the plane relative to the EER intersection point) on the distance between the feature vectors of the studied signals (the parameter responsible for the similarity/difference of phonograms) for the comparison method used [4, 30]. On the graph below, the position corresponding to the result of the comparison is marked; the corresponding FR and FA values are found (see Fig. 3). If this position falls into the area where the FR value exceeds the FA value, then the identification result is considered positive. If the result of the comparison of phonograms falls into the area where the FA value exceeds the FR value, then the identification decision is negative. If the position falls into the area bounded by pink vertical lines (near the EER value – a measure of the reliability of the decision made with this method, – the equiprobable error of this method for this type of comparison), then the identification result is considered uncertain.

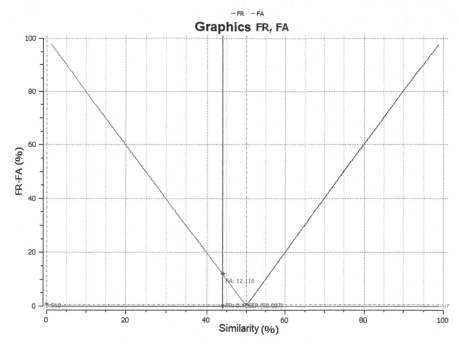

Fig. 3. Graph of distribution for FR and FA values.

The method of structural-melodic voice analysis (automated speaker identification method in the SIS II module) based on the use of procedures for comparing VFP statistics is one of the most resistant to the quality of phonograms. This is due to the fact that not the entire spectrum of the phonogram speech signal is used for identification, but only one of its components, namely, the sequence of VFP values [4].

3 Results

The automated identification method based on the comparison of the same type of melodic structures in the SIS II identification module is universal for the studied languages, makes it possible to study the features of inter-speaker and intra-speaker variability inherent in speech in Tajik and Gypsy languages, and to identify foreign-language "speakers" who speak these languages.

Statistical analysis of temporal characteristics consisted in the study of the rate of utterance of the structural components of the syntagma (pre-scales, scales and nuclear syllables). The temporal features of speech among the representatives of the studied language groups consist in varying degrees of differentiation in the rate of utterance in terms of syllables. Thus, in the Gypsy language, the rate of utterance of the nuclear syllable is approximately equal to the rate of utterance of the post-nuclear segment and is opposed to the scale and pre-scale, while the stressed and unstressed syllables of the scale and pre-scale do not differ from each other virtually. Tajik "speakers" when pronouncing nuclear syllables demonstrate the same tendency as "speakers" speaking the Gypsy language; however, unlike the Gypsy speakers, the former have more clearly differentiated stressed and unstressed syllables of the scale and pre-scale, as well as the nuclear-post-nuclear segment [3, 4]. The average value of the rate of utterance of syllables for the mentioned languages is presented in Table 2 and on the graph shown in Fig. 4.

Table 2. Average rate of utterance for syllables (ms).

structure under study	Tajik speech	Gypsy speech
pre-scale (unstressed syllable)	268.03	86.05
scale (stressed syllable)	388.06	90.08
nuclear syllable	511.06	229.08
post-nuclear segment	304.06	200.01

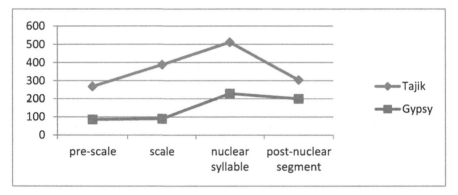

Fig. 4. Graph of distribution for average values of rate of utterance for syllables (ms).

The graph shows a difference in the dispersion of the rate of utterance for sylla-bles in different languages: for "speakers", the duration of the nuclear syllable almost doubles compared to the beginning and end of the syntagma; Gypsy "speakers" pro-nounce syllables in the nuclear-post-nuclear segment at approximately the same rate of utterance.

Analysis of the filling of hesitation pauses made it possible to establish the following. It is typical for Tajik speakers to fill hesitation pauses by stretching the final vowel; [a]-like, [er]-like, [erm]-like filling; while all Tajik speakers are characterized by a uniform pattern of filling and using such pauses: filling (100% of the duration of the entire pause) → the beginning of communication. Hesitation pauses occur both at the beginning and in the middle of a phrase [3, 4]. Gypsy speakers have a more varied filling of hesitation pauses; for them, as well as for Tajik speakers, [a]-like, [er]-like, [erm]-like filling is characteristic; there were also frequent cases of filling hesitation pauses with smacking, tongue clicking, noisy inhalation or exhalation, laughter or creaking sounds. The schemes for filling and using pauses are also diverse; the most frequent are two of them: 1) filling (100% of the duration of the entire pause) → the beginning of communication; 2) filling (30%-40% of the duration of the entire pause) → silence (10%-20% of the duration of the entire pause) → filling (50%) → the beginning of communication [3, 4].

In addition to the actual comparison of the same-type elements of the melodic contour, useful information was obtained from the analysis of the distribution of certain parameters of the VFP envelope in the speech of a particular "speaker". Thus, there is a good reason to consider the following characteristics of the speech of a foreign-language speaker as informative ones [4]:

– preferred models of the melodic pattern of the main communicative types (for example, completeness, incompleteness, general question, special question);
– features in the nature of the syntagma (for example, the predominant use of rising or, conversely, falling completion when listing a sequence of events; or a falling-rising direction of the VFP curve movement, such as IK-4 according to E.A. Bryzgunova, etc.);
– the occurrence of filled hesitation pauses, their frequency and nature of filling.

Preferences of this kind are part of the individual specifics of intonation, so taking them into account, of course, increases the reliability of expert analysis.

The study also made it possible to formulate criteria for the suitability of phonograms for research by analyzing the melodic contour of syntagmas:

– in order to achieve the reliability of an identification decision when comparing phonograms by this method, it is not the duration itself that is important, but the representativeness of the sound recording, that is, the representation in the phonogram of target structures for analysis, that is, nuclear tones, pre-scales, scales, hesitation pauses, etc.;
– depending on the speech tempo, on the accent-rhythmic structure and segment composition, the sufficient duration of a speaker's speech on the phonogram can vary from 30–40 s to several minutes. The recommended number of selected fragments of each type is 5–10;
– technically, differences in the recording channel do not have a significant effect on the values of the VFP parameters; the important factors are the signal-to-noise ratio (at least 10–15 dB) and the absence of reverberation on both phonograms.

4 Conclusion

This study confirmed the applicability of these methods of analysis for the identification of foreign-language "speakers" by trained (experienced) experts [33]. The established differential features that characterize the prosodic structure of speech are manifested in a specific distribution in the syntagma and in the phrase as a whole and are significant when identifying foreign-language speakers by an expert who does not speak the language under study. At the same time, prosodic parameters and their characteristics have varying degrees of informativeness for the formation of a conclusion about the identity/difference of the voice and speech of persons speaking national languages.

The experimental study on a group of subjects and analysis of their identification reports performed by the method of structural-melodic analysis of utterances, revealed a direct relationship between the experience of expert work of the subject and the comprehensiveness and correctness of the expertise, in particular, the completeness and accuracy of identifying types/subtypes of the VFP envelope fragments [4, 33]. To achieve a reliable identification result by melodic contour analysis in a language unfamiliar to an expert, certain conditions shall be met. Comparison of phonograms by this method shall be preceded by a thorough analysis of the available speech material. Before starting a comparative analysis, the compared phonograms are subject to assessment for their general comparability in terms of speech style, emotional and modal intensity, etc.; this ensures the optimal approach for each specific case, that is, the types and composition of the melodic contour segments within the syntagma that will be compared. In the perception of foreign speech by an expert who does not know the language under study, the prosodic characteristics of the voice are an essential factor. Prosody is an operational unit of perception in relation to foreign-language speech. The results of the experimental study of the perception of the voice and speech of Tajik and Gypsy "speakers" by different auditors suggest it is possible to obtain a correct perceptual-auditory assessment of voice and foreign-language speech by trained experts with experience in the field of forensic identification by voice and speech. The correctness of perception of foreign-language speech at the suprasegmental level depends on the auditors' perceptual standards (prosodic models); and this interdependence decreases if the auditor has experience in perceiving and analyzing speech segments by ear.

The approach proposed in this paper for the study of spoken speech by assessing prosodic parameters (an instrumental method for analyzing VFP parameters on various melodic structures), based on perceptual-auditory analysis, makes it possible to provide a holistic analysis of a speech signal both acoustically (VFP parameters) and linguistically (intonation, timbre, tempo, pauses, etc.).

Acknowledgments. This research was supported by the Russian Science Foundation (RSF) according to the research project № 22–28-01050.

References

1. Goloschapova, T.I.: Advanced directions of forensic research of sound recordings in ethnic languages. In: Kirin, V.I. Materials of the international conference "Informatization and information security of law enforcement agencies". Moscow, Administration Academy of the Ministry of Internal Affairs of Russia, pp. 337–341 (2009), (in Russian)
2. Kuryanova, I.V.: Ethnic stereotypes of foreign-language speech perception. In: edited by Kirin, V.I.. Materials of the international conference "Informatization and information security of law enforcement agencies". Moscow, Administration Academy of the Ministry of Internal Affairs of Russia, pp. 367–372 (2010), (in Russian)
3. Kuryanova, I.V.: Possibilities of identification of foreign-language speakers by expert methods. Bulletin of the Volgograd State University. Series Linguistics **17**(3), 60–69 (2018), (in Russian)
4. Kuryanova, I.V.: Identification features of foreign-language speakers (forensic aspect). Ph. Diss.: 10.02.21. Moscow (2020), (in Russian)

5. Potapova, R.K., Potapov, V.V.: Language, Speech, Personality. Languages of Slavic culture, Moscow (2006).(in Russian)
6. Potapova, R.K., Potapov, V.V.: Speech Communication: From Sound to Utterance. Languages of Slavic cultures, Moscow (2012), (in Russian)
7. Potapova, R.K., Potapov, V.V., Lebedeva, N.N., Agibalova, T.V.: Interdisciplinarity in the Research of Speech Polyinformativity. Languages of the Slavic Cultures, Moscow (2015), (in Russian)
8. Potapova, R.K., Potapov, V.V.: Auditory Perception of Speech by Non-Native Speakers. The Phonetician – CL–78, 6–12 (1998)
9. Potapova, R.K., Potapov, V.V.: Perceptual-auditory features of the identification of a foreign-language speaker. Bulletin of the Moscow State Linguistic University. Series Humanities 3(771), 80–92 (2017), (in Russian)
10. Potapova, R.K.: Subject-oriented perception of foreign-language speech. Questions of linguistics, No.2, 46–65 (2005), (in Russian)
11. Antaki, Ch., Condor, S., Levine, M.: Social identities in talk: speakers' own orientations. British Journal of Social Psychology, pp. 473–492. Printed in Great Britain (1996). http://journals.eecs.gub.ac.uk/BPS/BGSP/1996/Vol35Pt4/SP0435a/html. Accessed 12 May 2022
12. Yarmey, A.D.: Earwitness descriptions and speaker identification. Forensic linguistics 8(1), pp. 113–122. University of Birmingham Press (2001)
13. Cappe, O.: Etat actuel de la recherché en reconnaissance du locuteur et des applications en criminalistique. Ecole Nationale Superieure des Telecommunications, department Signal (1995)
14. Nolan, F.: Speaker recognition and forensic phonetics. In: Gibbons, J. (ed.) A handbook of phonetic sciences, pp. 744–767. Blackwell, Oxford (1997)
15. Nolan, F.: Intonation in speaker identification: an experiment on pitch alignment features. Forensic Linguistics. The international Journal of Speech language and the law 9(1), 1–21. University of Birmingham Press (2002)
16. Moosmüller, S.: The influence of creaky voice on formant frequency changes. Forensic linguistics 8(1), 100–112. University of Birmingham Press (2001)
17. Künzel, H.J.: Beware of the 'telephone effect': the influence of telephone transmission on the measurement of formant frequencies. Forensic Linguistics 8(1), 80–99. University of Birmingham Press (2001)
18. Hollien, H., Schwartz, R.: Aural-perceptual speaker identification: problems with noncontemporary samples. Forensic Linguistics 7(2), 199–211. University of Birmingham Press (2000)
19. Klasmeyer, G., Sedlmeier, W.F.: The classification of different phonation types in emotional and neutral speech. Forensic Linguistics 4(1), 105–124. University of Birmingham Press (1997)
20. Schiller, N.O., Köster, O., Duckworth, M.: The effect of removing linguistic information upon identifying speakers of a foreign language. Forensic Linguistics The Journal of Speech Language and the Law 4(1), 1–18. The university of Birmingham (1997)
21. Goloshchapova, T.I., Kochetov, N.A., Voropaeva, O.V., Devyatova, M.A., Krasovskaya, E.A.: Type identification by voice and speech, DCN "TIGR": guidelines. Moscow, Federal Drug Control Service of the Russian Federation Directorate of Criminal Expertise (2015), (in Russian)
22. Kodzasov, S.V.: Research in the Field of Russian Prosody. Languages of Slavic cultures, Moscow (2009). (in Russian)

23. Potapova, R.K.: Acoustic-linguistic decoding of a speech signal as a basic component of phonoscopic analysis in forensic science. In: edited by Kirin, V.I.. Materials of the international conference "Informatization and information security of law enforcement agencies". Moscow, Administration Academy of the Ministry of Internal Affairs of Russia, 34–335 (1994), (in Russian)
24. Potapova, R.K.: Theoretical and applied aspects of speech segmentology. Issues of phonetics II. Moscow, Russian Language Institute, 7–20 (1995), (in Russian)
25. Potapova, R.K.: Speech. Communication. Information. Cybernetics. Moscow, Radio and Communications (1997), (in Russian)
26. Atal, B.: Automatic Recognition of Speakers from Their Voices.Proceedings of the IEEE **64**, 460–475 (1976). https://www.researchgate.net/publication/2994391_Automatic_Recognition_of_Speakers_From_Their_Voices. Accessed 2 Jume 2022
27. Ladd, D.R.: Intonational Phonology. Cambridge University Press, Cambridge (1996)
28. Smirnova, N.S.: Identification of speakers based on comparison of the realization parameters of melodic contours of utterances. Computational Linguistics and Intelligent Technologies: Proceedings of the International Conference "Dialogue 2007". Moscow, Russian State University for the Humanities, 502–507 (2007), (in Russian)
29. Hart, J., Collier, R., Cohen, A.A.: Perceptual Study of Intonation: An experimental-phonetic approach to speech melody.Cambridge: Cambridge University Press. https://www.researchgate.net/publication/271084306_A_Perceptual_Study_of_Intonation_An_Experimental-Phonetic_Approach_to_Speech_Melody. Accessed 21 June 2022
30. Kuryanova, I.V., Yelemeshina, Y.A.: Analysis of the melodic contour of utterances in the identification of foreign-language speakers. Bulletin of the Moscow State Linguistic University. Applied and Experimental Linguistics: Issues, Solutions **13**(646), 85–94 (2012), (in Russian)
31. Grandstrom, A., Léon, P.: L'intonation des questions en Français Standart. Interrogation et Intonation, Didier, Paris **8**, 19-51 (1973)
32. Potapova, R.K., Mikhailov, V.G.: Fundamentals of speech acoustics: a textbook. Moscow, Moscow State Linguistic University "Rema" (2012), (in Russian)
33. Potapova, R., Potapov, V., Kuryanova, I.: Acoustic correlates of the native language speaker identity / Moscow State University Bulletin. Series 9. Philology, No. **4,** 32–43 (2022)

Logistics Translator. Concept Vision on Future Interlanguage Computer Assisted Translation

Rodmonga Potapova[1] ⓘ, Vsevolod Potapov[2] ⓘ, and Oleg Kuzmin[1](✉)

[1] Institute of Applied and Mathematical Linguistics, Moscow State Linguistic University, 38 Ostozhenka Street, Moscow 119034, Russia
rkpotapova@yandex.ru, oleg.kuzmin.999@mail.ru
[2] Centre of New Technologies for Humanities, Lomonosov Moscow State University, Leninskije Gory 1, 119991 Moscow, Russia
volikpotapov@gmail.com

Abstract. The computer translation task is ambiguous and before starting the process it occurs many difficulties and questions to be solved. The simple texts on general topics can be fast translated by using the modern machine translation systems based on cloud exchange algorithms. In this regard it should be noted that the main problem exists by translation of specialized texts including terms, abbreviations and linguistics items related to the particular sublanguage. The issue of post-editing can be solved manually, but taking into account the volume of texts, it has been risen a strong demand to automatize the process by development and implementation a professional tool that can proceed the semi-automatic translation of sublanguages. In this regard it was researched the modern computer assisted translation programs, the main mechanism of their functioning, advantages and disadvantages and based on them it was developed the advanced web tool with friendly-user interface based on the main mistakes of the machine translation systems. This program is unique due to the wide range of tools that are aimed to the implementation of practical tasks and without any exaggeration, it can change the idea of computer translation due to the new approach to the interlanguage perception. For realizing not only translation task, but providing a complex professional solution, it was added some additional functions as translation memory (MT), Natural Language Toolkit (NLTK) and some other features aimed at performing special linguistic tasks. The using of the program and first conducted tests based on preselected multilingual corpora can only prove the practical value of this development. The conducted survey of received feedbacks only maintain and prove the necessity of further continuation of research aimed to creation the advanced computer assisted translation tool that could complete professional linguistic tasks, in particular as the main task to perform the high-quality translation of sublanguages.

Keywords: Translation studies · Sublanguages · Computer-assisted translation · Machine translation · Parallel corpora · Translation memory

S. R. M. Prasanna et al. (Eds.): SPECOM 2022, LNAI 13721, pp. 579–589, 2022.
https://doi.org/10.1007/978-3-031-20980-2_49

1 Introduction

Machine translation (MT) is a very useful digital tool based on computer algorithms that can perform a good quality automated translation of texts from one language into another. For many years of its practical use, it has undoubtedly proved its efficiency [7].

With one click of the mouse, we will know what is happening on the other side of the world and it is not necessary to spend time for learning foreign languages. The search output will be provided quickly and the content will be quite understandable to the average user. One cannot underestimate the importance of such technology for the global world.

It should be noted that machine translation is used in those areas where speed is required in the first place. These include short news digests, for instance, internet sites with short and simple text fragments. Recent studies have proven the effectiveness of machine translation of scientific texts, texts on international relations and politics that include words and phrases on general topics. Algorithms are trained on a huge amount of internet texts and articles. This made it possible to quickly achieve the ideal level of quality that can be compared with human manual translation.

The machine translation process consists of two stages: input and output. All actions and internal calculations are performed without human intervention based on a hybrid approach (statistical and neural). The algorithms are trained on big data of the entire language model that include a wide range of unclassified texts. The quality of the output depends entirely on the sample size.

Despite the fact that machine translation is a very popular and useful tool, it has some disadvantages that shall be taken into account. The correct translation of the text parts made by MT is a rare phenomenon and no doubt it cannot be used in official regulatory documents in foreign languages due to various factors, including the peculiarities of each individual language.

Besides not only language difference can influence on machine translation. Sublanguages include a wide range of special terms that need to be appropriately classified and structured to prevent some possible translation errors and inaccuracies. Machine translation algorithms based either on statistics or on neural approaches cannot be focused only on the particular sublanguage, as they are trained on the entire range of language texts. As a result, it can lead to a complete confusion of meanings, deteriorate overall comprehension of the translated text and affect the quality of the final output [5].

The only way to avoid the misinterpretation is to create special linguistic databases that will make it possible to collect meanings of words and recommend them more accurately. This particular task can be implemented with the help of the popular technology of translation memory (TM) [8]. Pre-selected linguistic models are trained and stored in memory, and in case of a match of words in the text, program modules based on computer codes will predict the context, correct the grammar in automatic mode, suggest correction of translated words or phrases depending on the subject field.

2 Method

The aim of the work was search and analytical work aimed at identifying and comprehensive linguistic description of errors made by automated translation systems, as well as an attempt to implement a software solution that allows the user to offer options for more accurate contextual translation depending on the subject area.

The research materials were specially selected texts and working documents of transport companies in foreign languages, printed and digital versions of magazines and publishers that cover the events of the transport and logistics market, using the appropriate terminology of this industry. Based on the inconsistencies between the original texts in a foreign language and the translation texts, a linguistic study was conducted and, based on its results, a database of machine translation errors in the subject area "logistics" was compiled.

As a result, it was created the digital database of the sublanguage included words (glossary), bilingual phrases and sentences, overall, more than thousand entities. With the use of self-engineered software product, it was realized the translation of a preselected texts related to this sublanguage. The translated segments were evaluated by the quality and compared with machine translation. The use of the program with the specialized tools allow not only to simplify the computer translation process, in particular by implement neural algorithms aimed to attract attention to the segments that were translated incorrectly manually or by using machine translation and provide some examples for correct them or translate another way according to the related sublanguage. The feedbacks gained maintain the programs efficiency by performing demanded tasks and its advantages over existing computer-assisted translation programs.

2.1 Brief Outlook on Modern Computer-Assisted Translation Programs (Main Tasks, Functions and Areas of Application)

The CAT programs provide a complete product solution with a variety of special tools aimed at solving the tasks set, in particular to correct and improve the quality of machine or manual translation of sentences. To achieve the goal, special software tools are used to interfere with the translation process and influence the quality of the output. As for software solutions, the following tools can be distinguished: quality control, search and detection of errors (spelling and punctuation), development and integration of digital glossaries, as well as translation memory modules.

Automatic translation is used when translating professional texts of sublanguages and subject areas where the quality of the final result is required. The scope of application also includes texts of technical documentation, where ambiguity and complex grammatical constructions are of frequent occurrence. In this case, machine translation cannot guarantee the accuracy of the translated terminology.

Taking into account the popularity of the considered issues related to automatic translation systems and the creation of digital linguistic databases, it is important to note some scientific projects [14, 15].

The creation of special translation system is a demanding task because of the increasing num- ber of bilingual parallel texts on the internet [11]. The creation of databases can be implemented with the use of parsing. Parsing could be done in two ways: manually (by collecting special items) or automatically (by using tags and other settings). This is the process of collecting data with subsequent processing and analysis. This method is used when a large amount of unsorted information has to be processed, which is difficult to handle manually. The program that collects information is called parser. With it, one can simplify the task of searching content for one's own resource and complete it in a short time.

Today the most popular computer assisted translation programs are SmartCAT, Mate-Cat and Trados. They are widely use by the translators because of the functions and free access via web browser. The most features that they provide for the user are translation memory, automatic correction of machine translation within the existing bilingual corpora, the possibility to work collectively on the same document making amendments and automatic correction of text input. The main advantage of such an approach is the technical possibility to enable/disable functions or tools you need for your work making the translation process more interactive [8].

Despite the wide range of useful functions, the programs don't include very necessary natural language processing tools that should be mentioned. The algorithms could only approve the percentage match of the entire entities by comparing with the original text. They don't provide any user recommendations based on bag-of-words model or any synonyms, phrases based on pretrained word samples, tokenization, lemmatization and search of them by N-grams [3].

The words prediction function like it is realized in Microsoft Visual Studio or web browsers search engines based on word2vec algorithms uses a neural network is very demanded in performing computer translation tasks and necessary to be integrated in the future computer-assisted translation programs [9].

2.2 Reason for Creation of a Computer-Assisted Translator for the "Logistics" Sublanguage

Experience with popular online machine translation tools such as Google Translate, Yandex.Translate and PROMT revealed the following problems associated with errors in the translation of professional words, terms and phrases of the logistics sublanguage. With a large number of bilingual texts and the task of their rapid translation without loss of quality, we faced an urgent need to create a special software application capable of not only translating, but also making corrections and explanations of some terms in related languages. In order to optimize the routine work and avoid divergence in interpretation, an at-tempt was made to digitalize and unify multilingual units and find the right software solution for them.

At the preparatory stage, the following tasks were formulated for the project:

1. Collection of language examples with errors and correct translations;
2. Identification of qualitative relationship between manual and machine translation of sublanguage sentences;
3. Formation of digital databases in the three languages;
4. Study of the principles of operation and functionality of CAT programs;
5. Learning how to integrate CAT tools into the program;
6. Creation of a web interface using Python add-ons and other repositories;
7. Testing of pre-trained samples on specific examples;
8. Monitoring the results and planning the prospects of further development of the topic.

In accordance with professional and education tasks closely related to written translation, it was necessary to translate sentences related to a particular sublanguage from one language to another. Due to the huge variability and complexity of some language units as well as impossibility of correctly translating them, it was decided to use additional tools that could help in the process of disambiguating words, making it more automated.

Taking into account the demand in high quality translation of texts related to the "logistics" sublanguage, it was used some computer assisted programs that are based on cloud technology and include special tools for improving translation quality.

Because the used CAT programs didn't include all the needed functions for automated translation and it was decided to create a program with a friendly and intuitive interface for the end user. Therefore, some efforts have been made to develop and implement such a program.

2.3 Logistics Translator – a Professional Program for Computer Assisted Translation of Sublanguages. Operation Principle and Main Functions

The Logistics Translator is assumed to be the first web-based program that can provide a special approach to the issue of translation. It includes a machine translation algorithm, as well as an additional translation memory (TM) field, that is why it is more sublanguage-oriented and per- forms professional language tasks.

The program is developed on the HTML web interface and includes additional Python tools that allow performing tasks of machine translation of texts, as well as translation using special databases. As a unique feature, a term interpreter (professional glossary) has been implemented that makes it possible to understand the meanings of important language units.

All project codes and other related program information are placed in the demonstration mode and are available on GitHub [6].

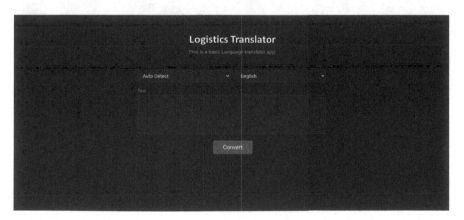

Fig. 1. Interface of the Logistics Translator main window.

The main window of the program (Fig. 1) provides the user with the following features:

- a field for entering the text to be translated with language autodetection;
- after clicking convert it will translate the text into another language.

The field includes also special program additions and improvements:

- machine translation with Python algorithms based on API cloud libraries;
- translation memory (TM) algorithms. It includes all bilingual parallel sentence matches in the three languages.

All the tools that are used in the program are basically parts of natural language processing (NLP). They are widely used and developed using the Python language [2, 9].

One of the tasks set for the project was the collection of data necessary for the research, that is, bilingual parallel sentences (corpora), in which there are verbal errors (the use of words that do not correspond to the context or have a different meaning) [16]. Thus, the main objective was to identify sematic errors made by machine translation of the logistics sublanguage, in particular phrases that have a special interpretation only in the sublanguage context. With the help of the developed program, they were precluded proactively.

The program operation principle includes some text preprocessing techniques as tokenization, stop words, stemming, lemmatization and others. To implement them it was used the TextBlob – simplified text processing tool for python that is based on natural language processing principles.

The alternative is the Natural Language Toolkit (NLTK) that has the same functions as TextBlob, but is more specialized and adopted for processing of bilingual words and phrases (Fig. 2).

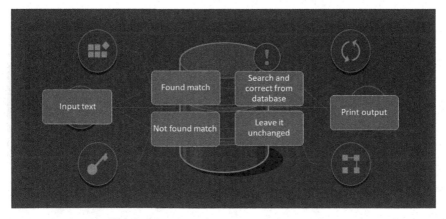

Fig. 2. Linguistic database operation principle.

At first the database was created in the Excel format. A special server written in golang programming language is used to storage the database.

The text required for translation is entered in the special field. Further it is translated by Textblob translation modules using Google Translate API into the demanded language.

The python algorithms analyze the incoming sequences and, in case of a match, replaces a word or phrase with a more appropriate one from the database.

After loading the text into the database and checking matches from the database, it is decided whether correct the input text or leave it unchanged.

The corrected phrases or text parts are highlighted with the color to facilitate the process of text analysis.

The database size is planned to be over thousand professional multilingual sentences, including special terminology and it will be timely updated with new linguistic items.

3   First Tests and Quality Evaluations. Practical Importance of the Conducted Research

The conducted work that involved collection of linguistic units, identification of errors and development of a special program aimed at improving the quality of machine translation was confirmed by a number of test experiments.

Due to the huge variety of the linguistics items included in the database and diversity of text required for translation, it should be evaluated by the quality. The first tests consisted of evaluating the quality of translated sentences using the Logistics Translator databases. The experiment consisted of software testing by professional translators working with some sublanguage areas. A total of 40 people were selected: 10 random people with little knowledge of foreign languages; 10 people who have to make translations in their everyday work; 10 university students who study at least two foreign

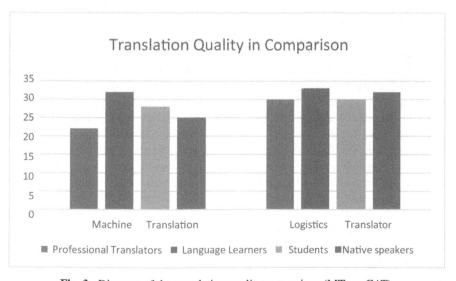

Fig. 3. Diagram of the translation quality comparison (MT vs. CAT).

languages; and 10 native speakers. It was proposed to translate 50 pre-selected sentences from one language to another (from English into Russian) using the Logistic Translator and evaluate the quality of the translation on a scale from 1 to 10 points. The results were visualized in the following diagram (Fig. 3):

The main indicators reflect the improved quality of translated sentences noted by native speakers and professional translators. The results are expected and predictable. A group of people who are deeply involved in studying foreign languages understand better what a correctly translated text should be.

Though the subject sample for the experiment was not as large as planned, it demonstrates key factors that can be proven in future research on the topic. The overall number of points reflects the need to use the program for translation of sublanguages and this preliminary result can serve as a basis for improving the efficiency of the program and involving additional subjects for further experiments.

Moreover, the usability of the program and the capability to compare two translation versions within the same web interface were additionally noted. The glossary of terms can expand language knowledge and perform educational functions [7].

4   Results

To sum up all the conducted work in the field of linguistics and software implementation, some points and achievements of the project can be highlighted.

In the course of the research described in the article, it was possible to create a digital database of texts related to the "logistics" sublanguage based on Python algorithms, to design a special Computer-Assisted Translation (CAT) program ("Logistic Translator") that can start translating pre-selected sublanguage sentences, and to create an additional special glossary with language units and definitions of their words.

The "Logistics Translator" program has proven its effectiveness, and the first tests have demonstrated the practical significance of the research. Unique approaches to the problem of digital translation may be implemented in further Natural Language Processing (NLP) projects.

The elements used in the development of the program have already been created and exist within some projects carried out at the Institute of Applied and Mathematical Linguistics.

Due to the limited sample and number of subjects involved in the test research, it was not possible to take into account all the linguistic features related to a particular sublanguage. However, the main criterion for evaluating digital translation was identified, specified and clarified; it can now be used in order to improve the quality and effectiveness of machine translation and used as guideline for development of future computer-assisted translation programs.

Using the example of previous successful research projects, it is clear that in order to obtain the most objective results, it is important for a scientist to have a large diverse collection of data and effective tools for its analysis (in this case, bilingual parallel text corpora and a digital programming approach) in his arsenal. The testing of the program was completed successfully (the goals were achieved and confirmed by the results of the sample). With the help of the program, an attempt was also made to eliminate lexical ambiguity.

It is assumed that the developed software will become a good tool for automatic translation and will find its application in future research projects.

5   Conclusion

Computer-Assisted Translation (CAT) systems and, in particular, CAT tools are convenient software solutions that make it possible to work with texts, process information and improve the final result of translation. The timeliness of such systems is beyond all question due to their wide application potential [1]. Taking into account the wide functionality of these systems, as well as the capability of their customization, it is possible to predict their further development in the future and widespread implementation in a number of large international companies, where accurate and professional translation is required. While Computer-Assisted Translation (CAT) is gaining the most popularity in the commercial realm of society, these systems can also be of great assistance in linguistic research.

The developed program "Logistics Translator" is an example of future specialized expert systems for professional tasks. Although the database is not yet complete, it shows the main difference between machine translation and the professional translation of a sublanguage. The general purpose of the linguistic research conducted using the developed program is to show alternative ways of digital translation, in particular, those related to sublanguages. The results achieved have made it possible to change the simple concept of the translation task.

Using the example of previous scientific projects conducted at the Institute of Applied and Experimental Linguistics (Moscow State Linguistic University), it can be seen that in order to obtain the most objective results, it is important for a scientist to have a large diversified sample and effective tools for its analysis in their arsenal (in this case, bilingual parallel texts and digital software approach) [4, 12, 13]. The program implementation attempt was successfully completed (goals achieved and confirmed by the sample results). With the help of the program, an attempt was also made to eliminate ambiguity.

It is assumed that the software developed will become a good tool for automated translation and will find its application in future research projects at the Institute of Applied and Mathematical Linguistics.

Speaking about future prospects it should be noted that the developed program needs to be finalized and modified according to the feedback received from the subjects of the conducted tests.

In particular, it was proposed to upgrade or integrate the following functions:

- Expand the database (increase the number of sentences and terms);
- Add an algorithm for incomplete matching of sentences from translation memory databases (phrases, N-grams etc.);
- Add an algorithm for automatic spelling correction;
- Add a field for self-translation with the capability to copy it with a button or save in document format (.docx);

- Add the program function to upload/download a database and provide cloud navigation through it;
- Upgrade a digital engine to search for machine translation errors;
- Develop a digital algorithm for comparing the results of machine translation and translation made using the program databases;
- Add other languages.

Further development of such programs is to minimize the human impact on the post-editing processes [4]. They will include a specific set of tips, hints and recommendations for translating documents. Automated translation programs will acquire the features of expert systems and will not only partially replace a translation specialist, but will also provide the user with search or reference information necessary for solving applied tasks [10].

Thanks to the widespread use of artificial intelligence technologies, it will be possible to achieve almost maximum automation of the translation process. In the future, Artificial Intelli- gence (AI) will analyze the source text, select the appropriate supporting materials and resources (translation memories, term databases, machine translation systems), as well as select translators and editors for a specific project.

The use of which in studying the problem of machine translation could make con-tribution to the future development of computer-assisted translation (CAT) products, specifically, with regard to sublanguages (for example, logistics).

However, it is important to conclude that language is a human tool and creation of the man- kind. A machine based on binary algorithms will never reach human parity and will not be able to understand any language as well as a human can. "There is a human behind every program" – this statement remains unchanged forever.

Acknowledgments. We thank programmer Leonid Motovskikh (Moscow State Linguistic University) for providing technical assistance in the development of the program.

References

1. Bing, X., Hongmei, G., Xiaoli, G.: Computer-aided translation tools in the 21st century. Shandong Foreign Languages Teaching J. **4**, 79–86 (2007)
2. Bird, S., Klein, E., Loper, E.: Natural Language Processing with Python. O'Reilly Media., Sebastopol, CA (2009)
3. Bolshakova, E.I., Klyshinskij, E.S., Lande, D.V., Noskov, A.A., Peskova, O.V., Yagunova, E.V.: Avtomaticheskaya obrabotka tekstov na estestvennom yazyke i kompyuternaya lingvis-tika : ucheb. Posobie — M.: MIEM, p. 272 (2011)
4. Borisova, I.A.: Some Observations on Machine Translation (Russian-English Direction) Postediting (Comparison of Online Translators GOOGLE and PROMPT). Vestnik of Moscow State Linguistic University **13**(699), 53–59 (2014, in Russian)
5. Borisova, I.: Automatic text processing in cross-language computer communication. In: Fako-takis, N., Ronzhin, A., Potapova, R. (eds.): SPECOM 2015. Proceedings, vol. II. University of Patras (Greece), pp. 19–27 (2015)
6. GitHub https://github.com/LarsFox/logistics-translator

7. Hutchins, W.J.: Machine Translation: Past, Present. Future. Ellis Horwood; Halsted Press, Chichester, New York (1986)
8. Ivleva, M.A., Melekhina, E.A.: Cloud platform SmartCAT in teaching future translators. In: Filchenko, A., Anikina, Z. (eds.) LKTI 2017. AISC, vol. 677, pp. 155–160. Springer, Cham (2018). https://doi.org/10.1007/978-3-319-67843-6_19
9. Mikolov, T., Chen, K., Corrado, G., Dean, J.: Efficient estimation of word representations in vector space. In: Proceedings of Workshop at ICLR (2013a)
10. Omar, M., Choi, S., Nyang, D., Mohaisen, D.: Robust Natural Language Processing: Recent Advances, Challenges, and Future Directions. arXiv preprint arXiv:2201.00768v1 (2022)
11. Peng, H.: The impact of machine translation and computer-aided translation on translators. In: IOP Conference Series: Materials Science and Engineering. **322**, 052024 (2018). https://doi.org/10.1088/1757-899X/322/5/052024
12. Potapov, V.V.: Linguistic and cognitive approach to the creation of an automated translation system based on specialized parallel terminological databases (Review). Social and human sciences. Domestic and foreign literature. Series 6: Linguistics. Abstract Journal **2**, 37–43 (2022, in Russian)
13. Potapova, R.K. (ed.): Speech Communication in Information Space. URSS, Moscow (2017).(in Russian)
14. Potapova, R.K.: New Information Technologies and Linguistics, 7th edn. URSS, Moscow (2021).(in Russian)
15. Potapova, R.K., Bobrov, N.V.: Versatile linguistic databases annotation: practical issues and a new flexible approach. In: Fakotakis, N., Ronzhin, A., Potapova, R. (eds.): SPECOM 2015. Proceedings, vol. II. University of Patras (Greece), pp. 45–53 (2015)
16. Potapova, R.K., Potapov, V.V.: Some elaboration methods for written and spoken multilingual databases. Moscow University Philology Bulletin **3**, 71–91 (2019)

Analysis of Time-Averaged Feature Extraction Techniques on Infant Cry Classification

Aditya Pusuluri[✉], Aastha Kachhi, and Hemant A. Patil

Speech Research Lab, DA-IICT Gandhinagar Gujarat, Gandhinagar, India
{aditya_pss,aastha_k,hemant_patil}@daiict.ac.in

Abstract. Classification of infant cry into normal and pathological cries is a socially relevant research problem for a long time. Crying is the *only* means that an infant use for communication. The state-of-the-art feature vectors, such as Short-Time Fourier Transform (STFT) representations and Mel Frequency Cepstral Coefficients (MFCC) have been earlier reported for this task. However, *quasi-periodic* sampling of vocal tract spectrum by high pitch-source harmonics of infant cry results in poor spectral resolution in STFT based spectrum and hence, these feature vectors could not produce satisfactory performance. In this work, we compare the performance of various time-averaged feature extraction techniques of window sizes 20, and 55 ms with three different classifiers, namely, Support Vector Machine (SVM), K-Nearest Neighbor (KNN), and Random Forest (RF). The experiments in this work are performed using the *10*-fold stratified cross-validation on standard and statistically meaningful *Baby Chillanto* dataset using various state-of-the-art features vectors. It was observed that the time-averaged dynamic MFCC feature vector gives a classification accuracy of 98.48%. Furthermore, the performance of the proposed feature vectors was also studied using the confusion matrix and found to be better than other features, such as LFCC and CC.

Keywords: Infant cry classification · MFCC · LFCC · Cepstral coefficients · Time average · KNN · Random forest · SVM

1 Introduction

Crying is the only mode of communication for an infant to convey information to the parents or caregivers. The cry of an infant can be meant for many reasons, which indicate the emotional, physical, and pathological needs of infants. The exact reasoning behind the infant's cry is difficult to understand for inexperienced mothers and caregivers. Hence, the infant cry classification system can be used for the early detection and diagnosis of the infant's condition. Research has found that there is a typical pattern associated with various kinds of crying and hence, the infant cry classification problem can also be seen as a pattern classification problem. Fingerprint-based biometrics [9] were developed apart from

© Springer Nature Switzerland AG 2022
S. R. M. Prasanna et al. (Eds.): SPECOM 2022, LNAI 13721, pp. 590–603, 2022.
https://doi.org/10.1007/978-3-031-20980-2_50

cry-based identification [17] to prevent the infant mortality rate due to vaccine-preventable diseases and malnutrition.

The initial work on the infant cry started in the 1940s [10,13]. Later, in the 1960s, four types of infant cries were identified [22]. Ten distinct cry modes were identified based on the variation of fundamental frequency (F_0) and its harmonics from the narrowband spectrogram by Xie et al. [24]. This study was extended from normal infant cry to pathological infant cry, where *dysphonation* and *hyperphonation* cry modes were found to be correlated with the pathological cry [18]. Despite the interest in the prospects offered by the study of infant cry in the early diagnosis, scientific work was not restricted to this area alone. There has been research on categorizing the cry since the 1960s [23]. While the previous works were based on a manual study by experts and doctors, recent advances in automation and machine learning have opened the doors for automating the detection of any discomfort in the infant's cry. State-of-the-art cepstral features, such as Mel Frequency Cepstral Coefficients (MFCC) are also recently used for cry classification tasks using a Gaussian Mixture Model (GMM) classifier [1,14], using fuzzy logic based classifier [20], decision tree, Support Vector Machine, boosted tree [16], feedforward network [11]. Another state-of-the-art feature vector, namely, Linear Frequency Cepstral Coefficients (LFCC) is also used for the classification task with the k-Nearest Neighbors classifier [7,8]. However, there hasn't been a lot of work done on a comparative study of normal *versus* pathological cry classification among MFCC, LFCC, and Cepstral Coefficients feature extraction techniques.

In this work, we present a comparative study among multiple feature extraction techniques, such as MFCC, LFCC, and CC on different window sizes combined with various classifiers, namely, k-Nearest Neighbor (KNN), Random Forest (RF), and Support Vector Machine (SVM). MFCC being the state-of-the-art feature vector replicates the hearing mechanism of the human ear, i.e., inducing non-linear characteristics in tone perception. LFCC is a feature extraction technique similar to the MFCC, where the Mel filterbank is replaced by a linear filterbank. The LFCC is found to capture information at higher frequencies better than the MFCC [8]. It is observed that the performance of the classifier with the MFCC feature vector is better than the LFCC and CC [8]. We have used various classification algorithms, namely, SVM, RF, and KNN. Instead of using the MFCC, LFCC, and CC features as it is, we averaged the feature matrix across the time-axis as most of the cepstral information of the sound wave is captured in the first 13–14 indexes of coefficient values.

The rest of this paper is organized as follows. Section 2 presents the proposed work on time averaging feature extraction. Section 3 describes the standard and statistically meaningful Baby Chillanto database. The experimental results and the analysis of the results are presented in Sect. 4. Finally, Sect. 5 concludes the paper along with potential future research work.

2 Proposed Work

In this work, we analyze multiple combinations of feature extraction techniques and classifiers. We also compare different feature extraction techniques and the effect of averaging of feature extraction matrix on the classification accuracy. The work is done considering 2 window sizes for the feature extraction technique: 20 and 55 ms. The 20 ms is the default window size for the STFT function and 55 ms is the default window size for the MFCC function using the Librosa toolkit. Apart from the above explanation, 20 and 55 ms are selected as this reflects the clear differences in the effect of increasing the window size on the classifiers.

2.1   Mel Frequency Cepstral Coefficients (MFCC)

MFCC is one of the state-of-the-art feature extraction techniques. The speech signal is a time-varying signal and hence, when analyzed for a short-time period, it acts as a stationary signal. One way of short-time signal analysis is by employing MFCC, which aims to develop segmental features from audio signals. The procedure for obtaining MFCC is shown in Fig. 1. The feature vector obtained after the MFCC feature extraction technique for an audio file is a 2-D array or a matrix. To perform a short-term analysis, we frame block the audio signal into different segments called *frames* with each segment having a 20 ms length with an overlap of 10 ms in general. In order to avoid the introduction of noise at higher frequency stages, we use windowing after framing to eliminate the abrupt chopping of the signal. In general, Hamming or Hanning windows are used as they result in reasonable side lobes widths with the desired main lobe width [2]. Next, Fast Fourier Transform (FFT) is used to convert the signal in the time-domain to the frequency-domain. The results are then passed through the Mel filterbank to change the frequency into the Mel scale. The conversion of frequency into the Mel scale is done by [12]:

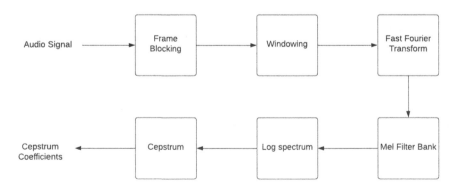

Fig. 1. Block Diagram of MFCC feature extraction [6].

$$Mel(f) = 2595 * log(1 + f/700).$$

The Mel scale filterbank is a bandpass triangular filterbank followed by a logarithmic function. This decreases the resolution at the higher frequencies and improves the resolution at lower frequencies. Later, the spectrum is passed through the DCT block to convert the spectrum to cepstrum and to decorrelate the sub-band energies from the frequency filterbank. After obtaining the coefficients, these coefficients are termed *static* MFCC feature vectors. Later, upon applying the first-order and second-order difference (i.e., numerical approximation to the derivative operator) on the static feature vector, we get a dynamic MFCC feature vector. The dynamic features track the rate of change in features (in particular, cepstral trajectory) w.r.t time. These dynamic features can be useful, however, also redundant sometimes.

In the static MFCC feature extraction technique, 13 coefficients are considered, a window length of 20 and 55 ms, a hop length of 10 and 15 ms respectively, a minimum frequency 100 Hz, and a maximum frequency of sampling rate/2. In dynamic MFCC, 39 coefficients are considered, a window length of 20 and 55 ms, a hop length of 10 and 15 ms, a minimum frequency 100 Hz, and a maximum frequency of sampling rate/2.

2.2 Linear Frequency Cepstral Coefficients (LFCC)

LFCCs are another state-of-the-art feature extraction technique widely used. The procedure is similar to that of MFCC, here the Mel filterbank is replaced with a linear filterbank. Due to the presence of a linear frequency filterbank, the resolution is better at higher frequencies compared to the MFCC as here the spacing is not logarithmic but is linear. Hence, it captures details better at higher frequencies compared to MFCC. Further, for both MFCC and LFCC, DCT does the job of feature decorrelation, energy compaction, and dimensionality reduction of the feature vector.

Here, 13 coefficients are considered, a window length of 20 and 55 ms, a hop length of 10 and 15 ms, a minimum frequency 100 Hz, and a maximum frequency of sampling rate/2.

2.3 Cepstral Coefficients (CC)

In this technique, there is no application of any filterbank and extract the features skipping the filterbank procedure present in the MFCC and LFCC feature sets.

13 coefficients are considered, a window length of 20 and 55 ms, a hop length of 10 and 15 ms, a minimum frequency 100 Hz, and a maximum frequency of sampling rate/2.

2.4 Time Averaging of Features

The sound files of normal *versus* pathology infant cry classification are recordings of cries and they don't contain any time-specific information and our the is to classify the infant cry but not detect the infant cry. Hence, the temporal axis in the extracted features of MFCC, LFCC, and CC doesn't contain much information, and averaging them doesn't lead to information loss, which can be proved from the classification results obtained. This time-averaging technique helps to overcome the computational complexity while obtaining a good classification accuracy. Another explanation to justify the averaging of feature vectors across time is that as the window size is increased in the feature extraction technique, the time resolution decreases and the frequency resolution increases, and the average classification accuracy increased for every feature extraction technique. This implies that for the infant cry classification, the information across the frequency axis of the matrix obtained from the feature extraction technique is more informative than the information obtained from the time-axis.

3   Experimental Setup

3.1   Dataset Used

Baby Chillanto dataset is used in this work. It was developed by the recordings conducted by medical doctors, which is a property of NIAOE-CONACYT, Mexico [21]. Each cry signal was segmented into one-second duration (which represents one sample), and is grouped into five categories. Two groups were formed for binary classification of healthy *versus* pathology. Healthy cry signals include three categories, namely, normal, hungry, and pain resulting in 1049 cry samples. Pathology cry signals include two categories, namely, asphyxia and deaf resulting in 1219 cry samples. Table 1 shows the statistics of Baby Chilanto database. The normal class consists of 1038 samples and the pathology class consists of 1229 samples. 70% of the data is used for training, and 30% of the data is used for testing.

Table 1. Statistics of the Baby Chillanto dataset used [21].

Class	Category	# Utterances
Healthy	Normal	507
	Hungry	350
	Pain	192
Pathology	Asphyxia	340
	Deaf	879

3.2   Classifier Parameters

Support Vector Machines (SVM): It is a non-probabilistic binary linear classifier as it assigns any new data sample directly to one of the classes. The SVM is based on discriminative training and it gives an optimal hyperplane in the higher-dimensional feature space than the dimension of the original feature vector, given labeled training samples that categorize new examples [3]. In particular, SVM is based on Cover's theorem on the separability of patterns, i.e., the patterns that are nonlinearly separable in low-dimensional feature space become linearly separable in the high-dimensional feature space by using a suitable kernel function [5]. Here the classification is done using a decision boundary. Table 2 specifies the best parameters obtained for SVM with a linear kernel using grid search algorithm.

Table 2. Parameter tuning for SVM using grid search method for a window size of 55 ms.

Parameter	Static MFCC	Dynamic MFCC	LFCC	CC
C	0.1	1	10	100

K Nearest Neighbours (KNN): KNN is a well-known pattern recognition method that helps to classify binary or multiple classes which are having its own label vectors. KNN classifier determines the class based on the concept of majority voting of the nearest neighbors. The nearest neighbors are measured using a distance metric. The Euclidean distance metric is one of the most commonly used distances [3]. Here the classification is done using the concept of clustering. Table 3 specifies the best parameters obtained for KNN using grid search algorithm.

Table 3. Parameter tuning for KNN using grid search method.

Parameter	Static MFCC	Dynamic MFCC	LFCC	CC
Neighbors	3	3	3	3

Random Forest (RF) Classifier: This classifier consists of a large number of uncorrelated decision trees that work as an ensemble. Each individual tree in the random forest spits out a class prediction and the class with the most votes becomes our model's prediction [3]. It uses the concept of bagging and feature randomness while building the decision trees. Here the classification is done using the concept of majority voting. Table 4 specifies the best parameters obtained for RF using grid search algorithm.

3.3   Evaluation Metric and Procedure

Repeated Stratified K-Fold Valuation: A single run k-fold evaluation can result in a noisy estimation of model performance. The repeated k-fold validation repeated the cross-validation specified number of times which means that instead of increasing the k value to decrease the noise in the evaluation, the number of times the k-fold runs can be increased. The result which we consider is the mean result of all the runs. The term stratified indicates that the proportion of positive and negative classes in the train data and the test data is split equally.

Table 4. Parameter tuning for RF using grid search method.

Parameter	Static MFCC	Dynamic MFCC	LFCC	CC
Maximum depth	20	50	10	50
Samples leaf	1	1	1	1
Estimators	300	150	300	150

Accuracy: Accuracy is a metric that describes how well a model is performing in all the classes. It is used when the dataset is balanced. It is calculated by considering the ratio between TP+TN and TP+TN+FP+FN.

4   Results and Analysis

4.1   Spectrographic Analysis

In Fig. 2, Panel-I and Panel-II represent the spectrographic analysis generated using Librosa [15] for randomly sampled normal and pathological cry signals, respectively. In particular, we took Fourier transform of obtained cepstral features i.e., MFCC, LFCC, and CC. This is indeed a valid representation of log magnitude spectrum as Fourier transform of cepstrum [18]. Figure 2a represents the Static MFCC representations, Fig. 2b represents the dynamic MFCC representations, Fig. 2c represents the LFCC representations, and Fig. 2d represents the cepstral coefficient representations. It can be observed from Fig. 2a and b that there is a difference in the pattern formed by F_0 and its harmonics for normal *versus* pathological cry signals. These differences in the pattern are also visible for LFCC representation as shown in Fig. 2c. However, these differences are more vivid for dynamic MFCC representations as shown in Fig. 2b compared to the static MFCC and LFCC spectrogram. It might be because of the fact that dynamic MFCC can accurately estimate the discriminative acoustic cues of the signal over the entire frequency band considering non-linear aspects of the speech production mechanism and also properties of airflow pattern in the vocal tract system [19]. Furthermore, the results obtained using *10*-fold cross-validation also validate that the dynamic MFCC gives the maximum classification accuracy in this work. On the other hand, the dynamic MFCC is also containing redundant information as seen in the spectrogram compared to the static MFCC, Hence, the average accuracy of static MFCC is greater than that of dynamic MFCC. The features captured by CC are not sufficiently discriminative. Hence, the classifiers are finding it difficult to classify using the features obtained using Cepstral Coefficients.

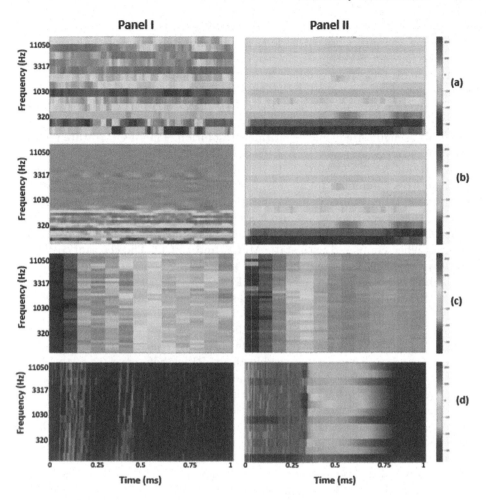

Fig. 2. Panel-I and Panel-II represent the spectrographic analysis (log-magnitude spectrum) of cepstral based features for normal *versus* pathological cry samples, respectively. Figure 2a represents the Static MFCC feature set, Fig. 2b represents the dynamic MFCC representations, Fig. 2c represents the LFCC representations, and Fig. 2d represents the cepstral coefficient representations.

4.2 Performance Evaluation

The performance analysis of various classifiers is done using *3*-repeat *10*-fold stratified cross-validation. The static coefficients of MFCC and dynamic coefficients of MFCC performed similarly resulting in an average fold accuracy across all the classifiers of 95.22 and 93.71%. The features provided by the dynamic MFCC can be redundant features in some cases meaning it degrades the performance of some classifiers, like SVM with a soft margin [4]. In general, the dynamic MFCC represent the trajectory of MFCCs over time by using differential (delta) and accelerated (delta-delta) coefficients. Hence, even though we are considering 39 coefficients with additional features delta and delta-delta, we are not receiving any additional information other than the information obtained from static MFCC. Hence, the features of the dynamic MFCC feature vector act as *redundant* features reducing the performance of classifiers.

The average repeated *10*-fold accuracy of LFCCs is 94.17%. LFCCs have a linear filterbank meaning that the resolution is better in higher frequencies than the MFCC's higher frequency logarithmic resolution. The LFCC feature vector is having an average accuracy across all the classifiers higher than dynamic MFCC but less than the static MFCC. This indicates that the amount of information obtained from the higher frequencies is significant and cannot be neglected, but at the same time, the average classification accuracy of static MFCC is higher showing that lower frequencies also contain significant crucial information. This comparison also shows the effect of redundancy on the accuracy of dynamic features, when compared with static MFCC and LFCC. The cepstral coefficient feature vector has the worst classification accuracy since it doesn't have any filterbanks as in the case of MFCC and LFCC feature sets.

Coming to the classifiers, all three classifiers handle the redundant data differently as the classification technique of all the 3 classifiers vary. The SVM classifier uses a decision boundary of the linear kernel to classify among the classes. While the KNN classifier uses the clustering concept and assigns a label based on the majority voting of neighbors, the RF classifier assigns a label based on the majority voting on the output of all the decision trees. Hence, we can see a decrease in the performance of some classifiers, when we go from static MFCC to dynamic MFCC feature vector; while the others remain unaffected. The SVM-linear kernel performs better only when the feature extraction is done well else the classification results are poor, and the SVM classifier is affected by the redundant data. The KNN classifier, on the other hand, is a pattern recognition algorithm, which is also another algorithm that is highly dependent on features extracted, it works using the concept of clustering for classification. Hence, when the feature extraction is done properly, the performance of KNN is better than the linear SVM due to the clustering classification technique and the classification with a linear decision boundary is ineffective; which can be observed from the results. The Random Forest classifier tries to outperform both these classifiers (i.e., SVM and KNN) in all the feature extraction techniques. In the RF classifier, the classification accuracy is better compared to the other classifiers across all the feature vectors because the classifier combines many uncorrelated decision trees, as the number of decision trees increases the chances of correct prediction also increase. The RF classifier fails to handle redundant data as the importance score misleads the model.

The average classification accuracy of KNN across all the feature extraction techniques is 89.42%. The number of neighbors parameter for the KNN classifier is obtained using the grid search algorithm and the KNN performed best when the number of neighbors is 3. The average classification accuracy of the Random Forest classifier across all the feature extraction techniques is 90.29%.

The parameters maximum depth, minimum sample leaf, and several estimators are tuned using a grid search algorithm and set to 20, 1, and 300, respectively to obtain the best result of 98.27%. The average classification accuracy of SVM with the linear kernel is 78.82%. The parameter C is tuned using a grid search algorithm and set to 10 for the best result of 87.75%.

From Tables 5, and 6, we can see the effect of window size (20 and 55 ms) on the classification accuracy. The last column of Tables 5 and 6 represents the average performance of various classifiers. The last row of Tables 5 and 6 represents the average accuracy of using various feature extraction techniques. As the window size is increased in any feature extraction technique, the time resolution decreases, and the frequency resolution increases. So, when we increased the window size from 20 to 55 ms, we can see an increase in accuracy across the classifiers indicating that the temporal information can be neglected. The Fig. 3 shows the multi-bar plot of various feature sets for a window size of 55 ms using various classifiers.

Table 5. % Fold accuracy for multiple time-averaged feature vectors with a window size of 20 ms.

Model	Static MFCC	Dynamic MFCC	LFCC	CC	Average acc.
KNN	97.98	98.38	96.74	61.28	88.59
RF	97.66	96.49	96.78	67.98	89.72
SVM linear	86.91	86.99	87.67	58.30	79.96
Average acc.	94.18	93.95	93.73	62.52	

Table 6. % Fold accuracy for multiple time-averaged feature vectors with a window size of 55 ms.

Model	Static MFCC	Dynamic MFCC	LFCC	CC	Average acc.
KNN	98.42	**98.48**	97.50	63.30	89.42
RF	97.92	96.61	97.27	69.37	90.29
SVM linear	85.44	86.07	87.75	56.05	78.82
Average acc.	93.92	93.72	94.17	62.90	

Since temporal information is not very important in the classification of normal *versus* pathological cry, we averaged the temporal-axis of the matrix obtained from the feature extraction technique and converted it into a *1*-D vector. The results show that there is not much loss of information as the maximum stratified *10*-fold accuracy obtained is 98.48% (Table 6). This also reduces the computational complexity while feeding the features into the classifiers or deep learning architectures.

The secondary goal is to keep the false positive count to a minimum so that the misclassification of pathology cry as normal is less which is very important in

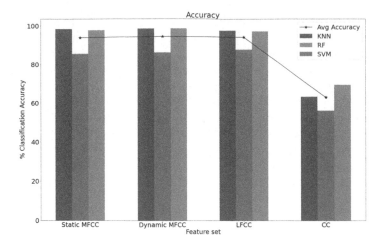

Fig. 3. % Classification accuracy of various feature vectors of window size 55 ms with various classifiers.

realistic scenarios. This is consistently achieved in static MFCC feature vectors across all three classifiers and the best results are seen using dynamic MFCC feature extraction with KNN and RF as classifiers as shown in Fig. 4 and Table 7.

Table 7. Confusion Matrix for Dynamic MFCC using various classifiers.

Classifier	Class	Normal	Pathology
KNN	Normal	**300**	4
	Pathology	5	**370**
RF	Normal	**290**	15
	Pathology	2	**380**
SVM	Normal	**260**	43
	Pathology	61	**320**

The results obtained apparently gave counterintuitive analysis, i.e., dynamic MFCC performed better than static MFCC for a few classifiers. This might be because of the fact that each classifier selected has a different method of deciding the classification boundary, hence the additional data obtained using dynamic MFCC affects the classifiers uniquely. However, it should be noted that the gradient time-averaged feature vector implicitly captures dynamic information, as it is the concatenation of static features, delta features, and delta-delta features.

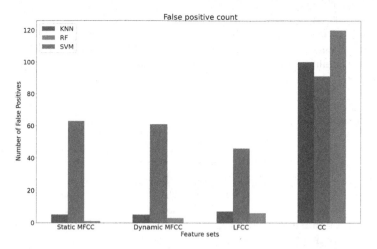

Fig. 4. False positive count of various feature vectors of window size 55 ms with various classifiers.

5   Summary and Conclusion

In this work, we presented a comparative study of various time-averaged feature extraction techniques such as MFCC, LFCC, and Cepstral Coefficients. The effect of different window sizes was also studied in this work. It was found that the dynamic MFCC feature vector with a window size of 55 ms along with the KNN classifier results in the best relative classification accuracy of 98.48% with 5 false positives. It was also observed that there was an increase in the classification accuracy of about 0.5% on KNN and RF classifiers with static MFCC, however, there was a minor change in the classification accuracy by using dynamic MFCC. Hence, it can be concluded that the infant's cries contain discriminative cues in the spatial or the frequency plane rather than the temporal or time plane. Hence, the feature extraction techniques are averaged across the time-axis reducing a 2-D array into a 1-D array for each audio file. It was also observed that the amount of information in lower frequencies is slightly higher than in the higher frequencies. However, the linear kernel SVM failed to perform well enough compared to the other classifiers. To that effect, our future work will be directed toward exploring non-linear kernels, such as Radial Basis Functions (RBF), and polynomial kernels for SVM. Furthermore, Deep learning architectures like Convolutional Neural Network (CNN) and Light CNN (LCNN) along with data augmentation can be explored for the classification task across various feature extraction techniques.

Acknowledgments. The authors sincerely thank the organizers the National Institute of Astrophysics and Optical Electronics, CONACYT Mexico for the statistically meaningful Baby Chilanto database, the Ministry of Electronics and Information Technology (MeitY), New Delhi, Govt. of India, for sponsoring a consortium project titled 'Speech Technologies in Indian Languages' under 'National Language Translation

Mission (NLTM): BHASHINI', subtitled 'Building Assistive Speech Technologies for the Challenged' (Grant ID: 11(1)2022-HCC (TDIL)). We also thank the consortium leaders Prof. Hema A. Murthy and Prof. S. Umesh of IIT Madras, and the authorities of DA-IICT Gandhinagar, India for their support and cooperation to carry out this research work.

References

1. Alaie, H.F., Abou-Abbas, L., Tadj, C.: Cry-based infant pathology classification using GMMs. Speech Commun. **77**, 28–52 (2016)
2. Bakshi, A., Kopparapu, S.K., Pawar, S., Nema, S.: Novel windowing technique of MFCC for speaker identification with modified polynomial classifiers. In: 2014 5th International Conference—Confluence The Next Generation Information Technology Summit (Confluence), pp. 292–297 (2014). https://doi.org/10.1109/CONFLUENCE.2014.6949342, Accessed: 15 Aug 2022
3. Bishop, C.M.: Pattern Recognition and Machine Learning. Springer, Berlin (2006)
4. Cohen, G., Hilario, M., Sax, H., Hugonnet, S., Geissbuhler, A.: Learning from imbalanced data in surveillance of nosocomial infection. Artif. Intell. Med. **37**(1), 7–18 (2006)
5. Cover, T.M.: Geometrical and statistical properties of systems of linear inequalities with applications in pattern recognition. IEEE Trans. Electron. Comput. **3**, 326–334 (1965)
6. Davis, S., Mermelstein, P.: Comparison of parametric representations for monosyllabic word recognition in continuously spoken sentences. IEEE Trans. Acoust. Speech Signal Process. **28**(4), 357–366 (1980)
7. Dewi, S.P., Prasasti, A.L., Irawan, B.: Analysis of LFCC feature extraction in baby crying classification using KNN. In: 2019 IEEE International Conference on Internet of Things and Intelligence System (IoTaIS), pp. 86–91. IEEE (2019)
8. Dewi, S.P., Prasasti, A.L., Irawan, B.: The study of baby crying analysis using MFCC and LFCC in different classification methods. In: 2019 IEEE International Conference on Signals and Systems (ICSigSys), pp. 18–23. IEEE (2019)
9. Engelsma, J.J., Deb, D., Cao, K., Bhatnagar, A., Sudhish, P.S., Jain, A.K.: Infant-id: fingerprints for global good. IEEE Trans. Pattern Anal. Mach. Intell. **44**, 3543–3559 (2021)
10. Fairbanks, G., Wiley, J.H., Lassman, F.M.: An acoustical study of vocal pitch in seven- and eight-year-old boys. Child Dev. **20**(2), 63–69 (1949). https://www.jstor.org/stable/1125607. Accessed 15 Aug 2022
11. Garcia, J.O., Garcia, C.R.: Mel-frequency cepstrum coefficients extraction from infant cry for classification of normal and pathological cry with feed-forward neural networks. In: Proceedings of the International Joint Conference on Neural Networks, vol. 4, pp. 3140–3145. IEEE (2003)
12. Hossan, M.A., Memon, S., Gregory, M.A.: A novel approach for MFCC feature extraction. In: 2010 4th International Conference on Signal Processing and Communication Systems, pp. 1–5 (2010). https://doi.org/10.1109/ICSPCS.2010.5709752. Accessed 11 Aug 2022
13. Irwin, O.C., Curry, T.: Vowel elements in the crying vocalization of infants under ten days of age. Child Dev. **12**(2), 99–109 (1941). https://www.jstor.org/stable/1125343. Accessed 12 Aug 2022

14. Ji, C., Mudiyanselage, T.B., Gao, Y., Pan, Y.: A review of infant cry analysis and classification. EURASIP J. Audio, Speech, Music. Process. **2021**(1), 1–17 (2021). https://doi.org/10.1186/s13636-021-00197-5

15. McFee, B., Raffel, C., Liang, D., Ellis, D.P., McVicar, M., Battenberg, E., Nieto, O.: librosa: audio and music signal analysis in python. In: Proceedings of the 14th Python in Science Conference, vol. 8, pp. 18–25. Citeseer (2015)

16. Osmani, A., Hamidi, M., Chibani, A.: Platform for assessment and monitoring of infant comfort. In: AAAI Fall Symposium Series, p. 2017. Virginia, Arlington (2017)

17. Patil, H.A.: Infant identification from their cry. In: 2009 Seventh International Conference on Advances in Pattern Recognition, pp. 107–110. IEEE (2009)

18. Patil, H.A.: Cry baby: using spectrographic analysis to assess neonatal health status from an infant's cry. In: Newtein, A. (ed.) Advances in Speech Recognition, pp. 323–348. Springer, Berlin (2010)

19. Quatieri, T.F.: Discrete-Time Speech Signal Processing: Principles and Practice. 1st edn, Pearson Education India (2015)

20. Rosales-Pérez, A., Reyes-García, C.A., Gonzalez, J.A., Arch-Tirado, E.: Infant cry classification using genetic selection of a fuzzy model. In: Iberoamerican Congress on Pattern Recognition, pp. 212–219. Springer, Berlin (2012)

21. Rosales-Pérez, A., Reyes-García, C.A., Gonzalez, J.A., Reyes-Galaviz, O.F., Escalante, H.J., Orlandi, S.: Classifying infant cry patterns by the genetic selection of a fuzzy model. Biomed. Signal Process. Control **17**, 38–46 (2015)

22. Wasz-Höckert, O., Partanen, T., Vuorenkoski, V., Michelsson, K., Valanne, E.: The identification of some specific meanings in infant vocalization. Experientia **20**(3), 154–154 (1964)

23. Wasz-Hockert, O., Valanne, E., Vuorenkoski, V., Michelsson, K., Sovijarvi, A.: Analysis of some types of vocalization in the newborn and in early infancy. In: Annales Paediatriae Fenniae, vol. 9, pp. 1–10 (1963)

24. Xie, Q., Ward, R.K., Laszlo, C.A.: Automatic assessment of infants' levels-of-distress from the cry signals. IEEE Trans. Speech Audio Process. **4**(4), 253 (1996)

Should We Believe Our Eyes or Our Ears? Processing Incongruent Audiovisual Stimuli by Russian Listeners

Elena Riekhakaynen[(✉)] [iD] and Elena Zatevalova[iD]

Saint-Petersburg State University, Universitetskaya Emb. 7/9, 199034 St. Petersburg, Russia
e.riehakajnen@spbu.ru

Abstract. In this paper, we describe the pilot study aimed at finding out those combinations of auditory syllables and lip movements for which the misinterpretation of auditory information because of the incongruent visual one would be the strongest for Russian listeners. We conducted an experiment where 60 schoolchildren and 60 adults processed congruent and incongruent audiovisual stimuli (the syllables containing one of six Russian consonants /t/, /d/, /p/, /b/, /f/, /v/ and the vowel /a/ pronounced by one female speaker). Most often we observed the visual dominance in the pairs "labial stop consonant in the auditory channel – labiodental fricative in the visual channel", i.e., baVA and paFA. The labial stops were most often substituted in responses to other sounds. Audiovisual integration was more prominent in adults than in schoolchildren, although the average number of mistakes did not differ much. We did not observe the effect of the preferred perceptual modality on the recognition of auditory stimuli which supports the previous findings in the field. Further studies can include the experiments with the data from several speakers and with other Russian consonants. The results of the study contribute to better understanding of multichannel processing and can be presumably taken into account in automatic audiovisual recognition.

Keywords: Audiovisual integration · McGurk effect · Russian

1 Introduction

When perceiving speech in a situation of direct contact with a speaker, we not only use auditory information, but also process the gestures and facial expressions of the speaker and correlate them with what we hear. The interaction of different modalities is often discussed in studies that focus on learning [1, 2, etc.]. Many of these studies draw on the Cognitive Theory of Multimedia Learning (CTML) [3]. This theory, among other things, postulates the existence of two independent channels of information processing – auditory and visual. Both channels have limited bandwidth. Apparently, due to this limitation, in the process of natural communication, we try to combine the information coming through these two channels. This process is called a multimodal association – a synergistic use of information received from different modalities. The term can refer to any stage of the integration process where there is a combination of different sources

© Springer Nature Switzerland AG 2022
S. R. M. Prasanna et al. (Eds.): SPECOM 2022, LNAI 13721, pp. 604–615, 2022.
https://doi.org/10.1007/978-3-031-20980-2_51

of information. In recent studies carried out on the material of the Russian language, it was shown that a multimodal text that combines auditory text and its written summary is perceived better than only auditory or only written one [4, 5]. It is believed that cross-modal merging increases the reliability of the system (both a cognitive and an automatic one) in case of an error or failure [6].

Moreover, the interaction of auditory and visual modalities can occur not only at high levels of perception (such as text or word processing), but also at lower ones. In particular, it has been shown that visual information about the articulation of sounds affects their auditory perception. This influence is called audiovisual integration. The nature of this phenomenon is not fully understood (see [7] for the overview). For instance, it is not clear what factors can enhance or weaken audiovisual integration: whether it depends on specific sounds, as well as on the individual characteristics of the speaker and listener. Recent studies of the McGurk effect have shown that this effect is not automatic. Thus, the "two-stage model of audiovisual fusion" is developed which includes the binding stage that is followed by the fusion one [8]. The binding is believed to be highly contextual [9].

The problem of audiovisual integration is crucial not only for cognitive studies, but also for automatic speech synthesis [10–12] and recognition [13] as well as for such practical issue as dubbing. We believe that the experimental evidence on how auditory and visual information are interconnected at low levels (i.e., individual sounds and their articulation) can be used to improve automatic audiovisual speech recognition systems, and also be taken into account in audiovisual synthesis. For example, for audiovisual synthesis, information about whether all native speakers equally rely on both auditory and visual information while perceiving speech is useful. Speech recognition systems based on articulation can possibly benefit from the data about the most perceptually stable articulations, which determine the interpretation of what is heard, even if the auditory signal does not match the visual information.

2 Previous Experimental Studies of the Incongruent Audiovisual Stimuli Processing

Much of the experimental research that considers the interaction of auditory and visual information at low linguistic levels is based on the McGurk effect [14]. If this effect occurs, the listener cannot correctly determine what he/she hears if the movements of the speaker's lips do not correspond to the auditory signal. In the original experiment by McGurk and McDonald, participants interpreted the syllable /ba/ as /da/ if the articulation in the video they were shown along with the sound corresponded to the syllable /ga/. Later studies [15] have shown that participants in the experiment proposed one more interpretation – /gba/, i.e., a syllable that includes both the consonant that was pronounced and the one that was articulated.

Many studies were conducted in English [16], but more recently there have been experiments in Chinese [17, 18, etc.], Japanese [19, 20, etc.], Dutch [21, 22, etc.], Swedish [23], and other languages, some of which have been part of cross-linguistic studies of the McGurk effect. In most studies, the effect is tested on the material of con-sonants, but there is evidence that it can also appear on vowels (for example, in Swedish

[23] and Dutch [24]), as well as on the tones of the Chinese language [25]. When consonants are analyzed, they are most often presented in a syllable with the vowel /a/ (as was done in [14]). However, it was shown in [26] that the McGurk effect is most prominent in syllables with the /i/ vowel, and weakest in syllables with the /u/ vowel. As for the consonants used, they are usually bilabial, alveolar, and velar stops, i.e. consonants that coincide in the manner of articulation, but differ in the place of articulation.

This effect has been used in certain studies aimed at describing neural mechanisms of auditory and visual speech information processing [18, 27, 28, etc.]. The aim of quite numerous cross-linguistic studies was, first of all, to answer the question of whether the interaction of visual and auditory information in the processing of auditory speech is universal or language specific. In the future, the results of such studies should allow a better understanding of the cognitive mechanisms of information processing. A separate area of research, which is addressed in a number of papers, is the comparison of how stimuli based on the McGurk effect are processed by different groups of recipients. There is evidence that the effect of visual information on the perception of auditory information is the weakest in 4- to 6-year-old preschool children, while it is quite pronounced in older informants, as well as in infants under similar conditions (for review, see [29]). It can be also assumed that different people rely on information coming through different channels of perception not in one and the same way. There are those for whom auditory modality is more crucial and those who prefer visual information. This assumption has been thoroughly discussed within the theory of cognitive/learning styles. The current experimental studies, however, claim that there is not a great difference between so called verbal learners and visual learners [30] and that "none of the four learning styles (visual, auditory, read/write, or kinesthetic) predicted students' retention of the material" [31]. The study of the McGurk effect can provide new evidence on the role of cognitive styles and preferred perceptual modalities in audiovisual processing.

Despite a fairly large number of experimental studies conducted on the material of various languages, there is almost no experimental evidence for the McGurk effect in Russian listeners. Perhaps the only exception is [29], which describes the methodology of a cross-linguistic study using Russian-language material. However, the author does not present the results of the study, but only discusses what they could be. Thus, it seems promising to use the McGurk effect to study the processing of information coming simultaneously through the auditory and visual channels. Since there is no experimental data for the Russian language on how this effect manifests itself, in the pilot experiment that will be described in this paper, we tried to find out those combinations of audio and visual stimuli that will cause the most errors in the perception of auditory information, i.e. demonstrate the highest audiovisual integration.

3   Our Experiment

3.1   Goal

The main goal of our study is to find out those combinations of auditory syllables and lip movements for which the misinterpretation of auditory information because of the incongruent visual one would be the strongest for Russian listeners. At the same time, we tried to take into account the recipient factor and check whether the results would differ depending on the individual characteristics of the participants: on the preferred perceptual modality and on age group.

3.2 Stimuli

Audiovisual stimuli were created specifically for this experiment. We asked a 20-year-old Russian native speaker to pronounce six syllables of the Russian language /ta/, /da/, /pa/, /ba/, /fa/ and /va/. The speaker is female. She is a linguist, but she is not a professional speaker. She does not have any pronunciation disorders. As our study was a pilot one, we used the data from only one speaker, although we understand that it is probably the most crucial limitation of the study.

In contrast to the classic experiments aimed at studying the McGurk effect, which use only stop consonants, we decided to choose consonants that are close in place of articulation and, at the same time, those whose articulation is easy to distinguish by the listener when he/she looks at the speaker. Therefore, in our experiment, we included bilabial stop consonants, labio-dental fricative consonants, and alveolar stop consonants. We used the syllables with the /a/ vowel as this vowel was used in the majority of previous studies of the McGurk effect.

The speaker repeated each syllable five times. The pronunciation of the syllables was recorded on video. Then, we compiled stimuli from the original videos, some of which were supposed to provoke the participants to experience an effect close to the McGurk effect, namely, to lead to misinterpretation of what they heard. To do this, the sound track of one syllable was combined with the video of another. The synchronization process was performed manually by one of the experimenters and then checked by the other. Records with voiceless consonants were combined only with voiceless consonants, and voiced ones – only with voiced ones. A total of 18 combinations were obtained: six initial ones, in which the auditory and visual information coincided (these were control stimuli) and 12 stimuli that were supposed to provoke audiovisual integration – six each for voiceless and voiced consonants.

3.3 Procedure

The experiment was conducted on the Google Forms platform. It consisted of two parts. Participants had to read the instructions for the experiment, provide consent to take part in it and some personal information (gender, age, year of study (for schoolchildren)). After that, participants had to choose one of four questionnaire options, which differed from each other only in the sequence of stimuli (thus, pseudo-randomization was achieved in order to reduce the influence of the order of stimuli presentation on the participants' answers).

In the first part of the experiment, participants had to carefully look and listen to each of the 18 stimuli and note what the speaker said, choosing one of the six proposed answers or writing down their own. It is the forced-choice paradigm that is used in most studies of the McGurk effect (see [29] for review), so we also chose it. But at the same time, we left the participants the opportunity to write their own answer if they believed that none of the proposed options was suitable. All 6 syllables that were used in the experiment appeared as suggested answers for all stimuli.

The second part of the Google form contained a questionnaire aimed at determining the preferred modality of perception. For this, a questionnaire by S. Efremtsev was used, consisting of 48 questions that must be answered "yes" or "no". This questionnaire is said to determine how strongly a person has expressed preferences for each of the three following modalities of perception: auditory, visual and kinesthetic. There are 16 questions for each modality in questionnaire. The more "yes" answers the participant gives to questions from the corresponding block, the greater the role for him/her in the process of perception plays precisely this channel of information transmission.

The experiment was conducted in accordance with the Declaration of Helsinki and the existing Russian and international regulations concerning ethics in research. It took participants around 10 min to pass the experiment. The experiment can be found at the link: https://forms.gle/riGhH1smjiPzchWdA At the end of the experiment, participants could leave their email address to get results of the Efremtsev's questionnaire.

3.4 Participants

Two groups of respondents took part in the experiment: schoolchildren from 14 to 17 years old and adults from 18 to 50 years old. Initially, there were 70 people in each group. We decided to analyze the results of schoolchildren (teenagers) separately, since the problem of learning and cognitive styles is often referred to school education.

3.5 The Principles of Data Analysis

We calculated the number of "correct" responses of each participant to each stimulus, which, within the framework of the study, were those answers that corresponded to the auditory token in the stimulus, regardless of the visual token. In further sections of the paper, we refer to the answers that did not corresponded to the auditory tokens as errors or the cases of audiovisual integration. The responses of those participants who made at least one error in their responses to control stimuli (where the audio and video corresponded to the same sound), were excluded from the analysis. The responses of those participants who, after completing the experiment, reported that they had problems with video playback, were also excluded. As a result, we analyzed the data from 60 schoolchildren (Me = 16.0; M = 15.9; SD = 0.9; 49 females) and 60 participants from 18 to 50 years old (Me = 20.5; M = 23.5; SD = 7.3; 46 females).

Using the chi-squared test, we compared the number of correct answers for different syllables. Using the Mann-Whitney test, the chi-squared test with continuity correction and the Spearman's rank correlation coefficient we compared the data obtained on schoolchildren and adults. Correlation analysis was also used to test the hypothesis about the dependence of the number of correct answers on the participant's preferences for one or another modality of perception. Only responses to target stimuli were taken into account, i.e., to those in which the sound of the stimulus did not coincide with the articulation in the video. Free software JASP (https://jasp-stats.org/) was used for statistical processing.

3.6 Results: Schoolchildren vs. Adults

We observed the influence of the group factor. Audiovisual integration was more prominent in adults than in schoolchildren: schoolchildren, on average, made significantly fewer mistakes than adults, although the average number of correct answers did not differ much (10.5 and 9.8 respectively, W = 1414, p = 0.037; see Fig. 1).

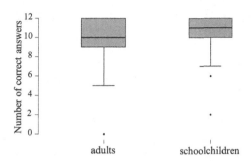

Fig. 1. The number of correct answers in two groups of participants.

The total number of incorrect answers among schoolchildren is significantly less than in the group of adults (91 (12.6%) and 135 (18.8%), respectively, for 720 answers in each of the groups; $X^2 = 9.704$; p = 0.002). The smallest number of correct answers given by one participant in the group of schoolchildren is 2 out of 12. In the adult group, two participants did not give a single correct response to the target stimuli (while they correctly identified all control stimuli). We decided not to exclude such participants from the sample because we were interested, among other things, in the influence of individual factors (in particular, the preferred perceptual modality) on the perception of target stimuli.

We also tested the hypothesis that the number of correct answers decreases with age. A significant weak negative correlation was found (Spearman's rho = −0.222; p = 0.015), but it should be noted that not the oldest participants in the experiment did not give a single correct answer, but two girls, whose age was 21 years old.

In the following sections, we will describe the results of recognition of all stimuli. The data will be given as a whole for all 120 participants, because all the trends that will be discussed below were the same for both groups of participants.

3.7 Results: Quantitative Analysis of Audiovisual Integration

A total of 1214 correct responses and 226 incorrect responses were received for 12 target stimuli. There is no significant difference in the number of correct answers between voiceless and voiced sounds ($X^2 = 0.635$; p = 0.426): participants made 119 errors in voiced consonant pairs and 107 errors in voiceless ones.

We found the influence on the number of errors both of the syllable that sounded ($X^2 = 91.240$; df = 5; p =< 0.001), the syllable that was articulated ($X^2 = 49.042$; df = 5; p =< 0.001), and the combination of spoken and articulated syllables ($X^2 = 196.987$; df = 11; p =< 0.001).

Most often, the audiovisual integration occurred when the participants heard the syllables /ba/ (76 errors) and /pa/ (60 errors). The integration was the greatest when the speaker articulated the syllables /va/ (65 errors) and /fa/ (51 errors) in the video. These results indicate that bilabial stop consonants are the most vulnerable to the impact of contradictory visual information (which was confirmed by statistical analysis: $X^2 = 87.052$; df $= 2$; p $=< 0.001$; see Table 1).

Table 1. The number of errors and correct answers to different types of auditory tokens.

Answer	Type of the sound (auditory token)			
	Alveolar	Labial	Labiodental	Total
AV integration	47	136	43	226
Correct	433	344	437	1214

And vice versa: the greatest number of errors in the perception of auditory tokens was provoked by the articulation of labiodental consonants in the video ($X_2 = 44.381$; df $= 2$; p $=< 0.001$; see Table 2).

Table 2. The number of errors and correct answers to different types of visual tokens.

Answer	Type of the articulation (visual token)			
	Alveolar	Labial	Labiodental	Total
AV integration	42	68	116	226
Correct	438	412	364	1214

As for the combinations of auditory and visual tokens, the most common errors were found when the syllable /ba/ sounded, while the speaker articulated /va/ in the video (57 errors (47%)), and when /pa/ sounded, while in the video the speaker pronounced /fa/ (48 errors (40%)) (see Table 3; the first two small letters in each stimulus correspond to what was heard (auditory token), whereas two big letters show what was articulated (visual token)). The least common errors occurred when /ta/ was pronounced and the video had /fa/ (3 errors) and vice versa (6 errors), as well as when /va/ sounded and the video had /da/ (5 errors; in the opposite combination, 8 errors were made).

Table 3. The number of different types of audiovisual integration for all the stimuli.

	Total	Visual dominance	Audiovisual serialization: two consonants in the answer	Audiovisual fusion: substitutions for another sound	Substitutions for the voiceless / voiced pair of the auditory token
baDA	19	4	4	11	0
baVA	57	50	7	0	0
daBA	14	6	8	0	0
daVA	8	3	4	1	0
faPA	16	13	2	0	1
faTA	6	1	4	1	0
paFA	48	43	5	0	0
paTA	12	2	3	7	0
taFA	3	3	0	0	0
taPA	22	6	15	0	1
vaBA	16	10	6	0	0
vaDA	5	1	0	3	1

3.8 Results: Qualitative Analysis of Audiovisual Integration

All the errors that were made by the participants in the experiment can be divided into four groups: 1) visual dominance: answers with the consonant, the articulation of which was in the video (or with its voiced/voiceless pair); 2) audiovisual serialization – answers in which two consonants occur: the one that sounded and the one that was in the video (in this case, different options are possible: *ba-da-ba-da-ba* or *bda-bda-bda-bda-bda* for the **baDA** stimulus), or a combination of one of the consonants from the stimulus with some other consonant (for example, *ba-va-ba-va-ba* for the **baDA** stimulus); 3) audiovisual fusion: answers containing only one consonant, which does not match either the one that sounded or the one that was in the video (for example, *va-va-va-va-va* for **baDA**); 4) responses containing a voiced/voiceless pair consonant to the consonant that sounded in the stimulus (for example, *va-va-va-va-va* for the **faPA** stimulus). The distribution of responses to each stimulus is presented in Table 3.

For the stimuli with the highest number of incorrect responses (**baVA** and **paFA**), we observed mostly visual dominance (substitutions for the sound shown in the video). Interestingly, the cases of audiovisual serialization (when there are two or more consonants in the response) were observed for almost all stimuli (except for **vaDA** and **taFA**, for which the smallest number of errors occurred). The largest number of responses containing a consonant that does not match either the one that sounded or the one that was in the video was obtained for the pairs **baDA** and **paTA**: in both cases, these were consonants, whose place of articulation is between the place of articulation of the auditory and visual tokens from the stimulus: /v/ and /f/ respectively.

3.9 Results: The Influence of the Preferred Perceptual Modality

Correlation analysis using Spearman's test did not reveal a relationship between the number of correct responses to target stimuli and a greater preference for any of the modalities of perception (according to Efremtsev's questionnaire), neither for all participants in general, nor separately for schoolchildren and adults (see Table 4).

Table 4. The results of the Spearman's rank correlation test for the number of correct answers and the number of answers "yes" to each of three perceptual modalities

Modality	All participants	Schoolchildren	Adults
Auditory	rho = −0.028 p = 0.759	rho = 0.012 p = 0.929	rho =−0.133 p = 0.311
Visual	rho = 0.012 p = 0.893	rho = 0.014 p = 0.916	rho = 0.077 p = 0.558
Kinesthetic	rho = −0.051 p = 0.583	rho = −0.019 p = 0.888	rho = −0.060 p = 0.649

4   Discussion and Conclusions

The experiment showed that the greatest audiovisual integration is in pairs "labial stop consonant in the auditory channel - labiodental fricative in the visual channel" (i.e., **baVA** and **paFA**) where we observed visual dominance. Such cases, strictly speaking, do not indicate the emergence of the McGurk effect, but they show that the labiodental articulation of Russian consonants is quite clear and even can lead to the misinterpretation of what was pronounced. The labial stops are the most vulnerable from the point of view of auditory perception: they were most often substituted in responses to other sounds.

Examples of the manifestation of the McGurk effect can be considered the answers with the combination of several consonants (primarily those that were presented in the stimulus, as reported in [15]), as well as those cases when the sound in the answer is the one articulated between the sounded consonant and the one that was in video (these are examples with the responses to **baDA** and **paTA** stimuli, see Sect. 3.8).

The fact that there is no difference in the processing of voiceless and voiced consonants in the experiment shows that in further similar studies with the participation of native speakers of the Russian language, both stimuli with voiced and voiceless consonants can be used.

The influence of the factor of the group of participants was revealed: schoolchildren gave more correct answers than those who had already graduated from school. At the same time, we understand that in our study the boundary between the two groups of participants is largely conditional: in the group of adult participants, there were 1st year University students, i.e., those who are 18 years old, and the average age of the adult group is 23.5 years. Therefore, the question of the influence of the age of participants on the results of the study requires further study. Perhaps the greater number of correct answers in the group of schoolchildren is due to the fact that, on the whole, because of their habit of completing school assignments, they were more attentive and responsible in completing the experimental task.

The fact that we did not find the effect of the preferred modality of perception on the recognition of auditory stimuli can be explained by various reasons. For example, this may support the previous findings [30, 31] that people cannot be easily divided into auditory, visual and kinesthetic groups and cognitive styles are not that crucial for audiovisual interaction while processing speech. Or it can indicate the imperfection of the questionnaire that was chosen to identify these groups, although it is this questionnaire that is most often used to determine the preferred perceptual modality in the studies with Russian-speaking informants. In any case, this aspect of the study requires further development. Perhaps, in the future, it makes sense to test the hypothesis about the influence of the preferred modality of perception on multimodal processing only using the stimuli for which audiovisual integration is high in Russian speakers, but involving a larger number of speakers. An increase in the number of speakers is also necessary in order to make sure that the results obtained are not due to the individual articulatory characteristics of a particular speaker.

The experiment that we conducted included only six consonants, the articulation of which we considered the most obvious (noticeable) for the listener. In the future, we can expand the experiment to include other consonants (in particular, velar stops, as in most classic experiments on the McGurk effect). We believe that our further studies of the McGurk effect in Russian speakers will contribute to the discussion of the theoretical problem of audiovisual binding and audiovisual integration in general.

Acknowledgements. The study is supported by the research grant #21–18-00429 from the Russian Science Foundation.

References

1. Griban, O.N.: Application of educational presentations in the educational process: types, stages and structure of presentations. Historical Pedagogical Readings **20**(3), 23–32 (2016). (In Russian)
2. Svärdemo Åberg, E., Åkerfeldt, A.: Design and recognition of multimodal texts: selection of digital tools and modes on the basis of social and material premises? J. Computers Educ. **4**(3), 283–306 (2017). https://doi.org/10.1007/s40692-017-0088-3
3. Mayer, R.E.: Principles for managing essential processing in multimedia learning: Segmenting, pretraining, and modality principles. In: The Cambridge Handbook of Multimedia Learning. Cambridge University Press, Cambridge, pp. 169–182 (2005). http://dx.doi.org/https://doi.org/10.1017/cbo9780511816819.012
4. Petrova, T.E.: Text presentation and information processing in Russian In: ExLing 2021. 12th International Conference of Experimental Linguistics. In: International Society of Experimental Linguistics, pp, 164–167 (2021)
5. Riekhakaynen, E., Skorobagatko, L.: Written, not spoken or too much to read: How to present information more effectively? In: Neurobiology of Speech and Language. Proceedings of the 5th International Conference. Saint Petersburg, pp. 15–16 (2021)

6. Ivanko, D.V., Kipyatkova, I.S., Robzhin, A.L., Karpov, A.A.: Analysis of methods for multimodal information combination for audiovisual speech recognition // scientific and technical bulletin of information technologies. Mechanics and Optics **16**(3), 387–401 (2016). (In Russian)

7. Brown, V.A., Strand, J.F.: "Paying" attention to audiovisual speech: do incongruent stimuli incur greater costs? Atten. Percept. Psychophys. **81**(6), 1743–1756 (2019). https://doi.org/10.3758/s13414-019-01772-x

8. Berthommier, F.: A phonetically neutral model of the low-level audio-visual interaction. Speech Commun **44**(1–4), 31–41 (2004). https://doi.org/10.1016/j.specom.2004.10.003

9. Ganesh, A., Berthommier, F., Schwartz, J.-L.: Audiovisual binding for speech perception in noise and in aging. Lang. Learn. **68**(S1), 193–220 (2018). https://doi.org/10.1111/lang.12271

10. Lobanov, B.M., Tsyrulnik, L.I., Zhelezny, M., Krnoul, Z., Ronzhin, A., Karpov, A.: System of audiovisual synthesis of Russian speech. Informatics **4**(20), 67–78 (2008). (In Russian)

11. Thézé, R., Gadiri, M.A., Albert, L., Provost, A., Giraud, A.L., Mégevand, P.: Animated virtual characters to explore audio-visual speech in controlled and naturalistic environments. Sci. Rep. **10**(1), 1–12 (2020)

12. Almeida, N., Cunha, D., Silva, S., Teixeira, A.: Designing and deploying an interaction modality for articulatory-based audiovisual speech synthesis. In: Karpov, A., Potapova, R. (eds.) SPECOM 2021. LNCS (LNAI), vol. 12997, pp. 36–49. Springer, Cham (2021). https://doi.org/10.1007/978-3-030-87802-3_4

13. Ivanko, D., Ryumin, D., Axyonov, A., Kashevnik, A.: Speaker-dependent visual command recognition in vehicle cabin: methodology and evaluation. In: Karpov, A., Potapova, R. (eds.) SPECOM 2021. LNCS (LNAI), vol. 12997, pp. 291–302. Springer, Cham (2021). https://doi.org/10.1007/978-3-030-87802-3_27

14. McGurk, H., MacDonald, J.: Hearing lips and seeing voices. Nature **264**, 746–748 (1976). https://doi.org/10.1038/264746a0

15. Green, K.P., Gerdeman, A.: Cross-Modal discrepancies in coarticulation and the integration of speech information: the McGurk effect with mismatched vowels. J. Experiment Psychology: Human Perception Performance **21**(6), 1409–1426 (1995). https://doi.org/10.1037/0096-1523.21.6.1409

16. Summerfield, Q.: Some preliminaries to a comprehensive account of audiovisual speech perception. In: Dodd, B., Campbell, R. (eds.) Hearing by eye: Psychology of lipreading Hillsdale, pp. 3–51. Erlbaum, NJ (1987)

17. Sekiyama, K.: Cultural and linguistic factors in audiovisual speech processing: the McGurk effect in Chinese subjects. Percept. Psychophys. **59**(1), 73–80 (1997). https://doi.org/10.3758/BF03206849

18. Wu, J.: Speech perception and the McGurk effect: A cross cultural study using event-related potentials. Electronic Theses and Dissertations. Paper 1597 (2009). https://doi.org/10.18297/etd/1597

19. Sekiyama, K., Burnham, D.: Impact of language on development of auditoryvisual speech perception. Dev. Sci. **11**(2), 306–320 (2008). https://doi.org/10.1111/j.1467-7687.2008.00677.x

20. Sekiyama, K., Tohkura, Y.I.: Inter-language differences in the influence of visual cues in speech perception. J. Phon. **21**(4), 427–444 (1993). https://doi.org/10.1016/S0095-4470(19)30229-3de

21. de Gelder, B., Bertelson, P., Vroomen, J., Chen, H.C.: Inter-language differences in the McGurk effects for Dutch and Cantonese listeners. In: Eurospeech 1995: Proceedings of the Fourth European Conference on Speech Communication and Technology, Madrid, Spain, September 18–21, pp. 1699–1702 (1995)

22. Massaro, D.W., Cohen, M.M., Smeele, P.M.: Cross-linguistic comparisons in the integration of visual and auditory speech. Mem. Cognit. **23**(1), 113–131 (1995). https://doi.org/10.3758/BF03210561

23. Traunmüller, H., Öhrström, N.: Audiovisual perception of openness and lip rounding in front vowels. J. Phon. **35**(2), 244–258 (2007). https://doi.org/10.1016/j.wocn.2006.03.002

24. Valkenier, B., Duyne, J.Y., Andringa, T.C., Baskent, D.: Audiovisual perception of congruent and incongruent Dutch front vowels. J. Speech Lang. Hear. Res. **55**(6), 1788–1801 (2012). https://doi.org/10.1044/1092-4388(2012/11-0227)

25. Wang, R.: Audiovisual perception of Mandarin lexical tones. Doctoral dissertation, Bournemouth University (2018)

26. Shigeno, S.: Influence of vowel context on the audio-visual speech perception of voiced stop consonants. Jpn. Psychol. Res. **42**(3), 155–167 (2000). https://doi.org/10.1111/1468-5884.00141

27. Besle, J., Caclin, A., Mayet, R., Bauchet, F., Delpuech, C., Giard, M.H., et al.: Audiovisual events in sensory memory. J. Psychophysiol. **21**, 231–238 (2007). https://doi.org/10.1027/0269-8803.21.34.231

28. Kelly, S.D., Kravitz, C., Hopkins, M.: Neural correlates of bimodal speech and gesture comprehension. Brain Lang **89**(1), 253–260 (2004)

29. Yang, Z.: A cross-linguistic examination on the McGurk effect in different developmental states. Research Master's Thesis in Linguistics, Utrecht University (2021)

30. Massa, L.J., Mayer, R.E.: Testing the ATI hypothesis: should multimedia instruction accommodate verbalizer-visualizer cognitive style? Learn. Individ. Differ. **16**(4), 321–335 (2006). https://doi.org/10.1016/j.lindif.2006.10.001

31. Cuevas, J., Dawson, B.L.: A test of two alternative cognitive processing models: learning styles and dual coding. Theory Res. Educ. **16**(1), 40–64 (2018). https://doi.org/10.1177/1477878517731450

Emotional Speech Recognition Based on Lip-Reading

Elena Ryumina(ID) and Denis Ivanko(✉)(ID)

St. Petersburg Federal Research Center of the Russian Academy
of Sciences, St. Petersburg 199178, Russia
ryumina_ev@mail.ru, ivanko.d@iias.spb.su

Abstract. Automatic speech recognition and emotion recognition have been research hotspots in the field of human-computer interaction over the last years. However, despite significant recent advances, the problem of robust recognition of emotional speech remains unresolved. In this research we try to fill this gap by looking into the multimodality of speech and starting to use visual information to increase both recognition accuracy and robustness. We present extensive experimental investigation of how different emotions (anger, disgust, fear, happy, neutral, and sad) affect automatic lip-reading. We train the 3D ResNet-18 model on the CREMA-D emotional speech database by experimentation with different parameters of the model. To the best of our knowledge, this is the first research investigating the influence of human emotions on automatic lip-reading. Our results demonstrate that speech with the emotion of disgust is the most difficult to recognize correctly. This is due to the fact that a person significantly curves his lips and articulation is distorted. We have experimentally confirmed that the accuracy of models trained on all types of emotions (mean UAR 94.04%) significantly exceeds the accuracy of recognition of models trained only on a neutral emotion (mean UAR 65.81%), or on any other separate emotion (mean UAR from 54.82% to 68.62% with the emotion of disgust and sadness respectively). We have carefully analyzed the visual manifestations of various emotions and assessed their impact on the accuracy of automatic lip-reading. Current research is the first step in the creation of emotion-robust speech recognition systems.

Keywords: Automated lip-reading · Emotional speech · Visual speech recognition · Machine learning · End-to-end

1 Introduction

Automatic speech recognition systems (ASR) based on processing audio and visual information gaining popularity in the last decade. They are actively used in our daily lives, e.g. in assistive systems, voice search, voice control, etc. [1–3] However, the efficiency of state-of-the-art ASRs is significantly deteriorating due to a number of factors, one of which is the speaker's emotions [4]. Depending on the speaker's emotion, it changes: (1) timbre, pitch and loudness of the voice, (2) duration of sounds, (3) duration of pauses, (4) articulation.

© Springer Nature Switzerland AG 2022
S. R. M. Prasanna et al. (Eds.): SPECOM 2022, LNAI 13721, pp. 616–625, 2022.
https://doi.org/10.1007/978-3-031-20980-2_52

Speech changes can be observed both in audio and video information. E.g., with emotions "happy" and "anger", words are pronounced with a more open mouth than with emotions "neutral" and "sad", in addition with the emotion "anger" the pauses between words are shorter than with the emotion "sadness" [5, 6]. The observed temporal shift of frames is due to the fact that during the emotion of "anger" the speaker tries to express his thoughts faster, while the pauses between words are reduced. These changes lead to the fact that speech is not recognized by ASR, although it is often very important for a person to be understood in the emotional state by his/her devices.

Nowadays, automatic speech recognition systems based on audio and video information are being actively researched and developed all over the world [7, 8]. At the same time, scientific studies aimed at analyzing the influence of the speaker's emotional state on automatic speech recognition and lip-reading have not been conducted. In this regard, the relevance of this research topic cannot be overestimated and requires detailed study. In this paper, we investigate the influence of 6 main emotional states, namely anger, disgust, fear, happy, neutral, and sad, on the accuracy of speech recognition based on processing video information.

2   Related Work

Emotional state (emotions/affect) is a psychophysical process that reflects the inner intentions of a person. In the scientific literature, two models for describing emotions are known: categorical and spatial (continuous). The categorical model is based on a fixed unit, a discrete category that separates one emotion category from others. Paul Ekman in [9] proposed division of emotions into 6 basic categories. These categories of emotions appear almost identically in people from all over the world, regardless of race and social affiliation. Another view of the theory of emotion is a spatial model (for example, Russell's model [10]), which considers emotion as a numerical value in two or three dimensions, rather than as separate categories. Knowledge of both categorical and spatial emotions allows to more accurately determine the emotional state of a person.

Nowadays there are various emotional databases, that are collected for different purposes and with different means [11, 12] (mainly for emotions recognition). At the same time, there are many audio-visual (AV) speech datasets [13–15]. However, at the moment there are almost no combined emotional audio-visual speech databases suitable for models training in the scope of modern machine learning approaches. In order to develop emotion-robust automatic speech recognition systems, high-quality training and testing corpora are crucial. In addition to the emotional states (the number of emotions and intensity levels) that corpora contain, they also differ from each other in the number of speakers, recordings, phrases, etc.

Despite the variety of existing emotional datasets, we found only 4 that are suitable for solving the audio-visual emotional speech recognition problem: CREMA-D [16], RAVDESS [17], SAVEE [18], eNTERFACE'05 [19]. Among them, CREMA-D is more promising, since 91 speakers in the age range from 20 to 74 years old took part in the assembly of the corpus. In addition, it contains 12 common (for each emotional state) phrases, which significantly exceeds the total number of phrases in three other corpora. We expect that a more accurate analysis of the influence of the emotional state on automatic lip-reading will be obtained.

The RAVDESS corpus is also suitable for phrase recognition, depending on the style of speech. Using the SAVEE corpus, phrases and words can be recognized depending on the speaker's emotion. The eNTERFACE'05 corpus is less suitable than others for analyzing phrase recognition depending on the emotional state of the speaker, since the phrases in the corpus are isolated for each specific emotion.

Research on audio-visual speech recognition has a long history [20]. In the recent years, with the rapid developments of machine learning approaches and artificial intelligence, deep neural networks were introduced to this area. With these impressive methods, state-of-the-art visual speech recognition accuracy has been raised from 61.1% [21] to 88.5% [22] on the English dataset LRW during the last five years.

According to the design of the front-end network, the current state-of-the-art visual speech recognition methods can be divided into three main categories: 2-dimensional (2D) convolutional neural networks (CNN), such in [23], 3-dimensional convolutional neural networks (3D CNNs), such in [24], or a combination of 2D and 3D convolutions, which inherit the advantages of both [25]. Recently, methods of the third type have become widely used in visual speech recognition due to its ability to simultaneously capture temporal dynamics of lips movements and extract discriminative features. The first end-to-end sentence lip-reading model LipNet was proposed by researchers in [26].

The combination of state-of-the-art deep learning approaches and large-scale audio-visual datasets has been highly successful, achieving significant recognition accuracy results and even surpassing human performance. However, there is still a long journey for practical visual speech recognition systems to meet the performance requirements of real-life scenarios and deal with various emotional states of the speakers.

3   Dataset

In current research we use the CREMA-D [14] dataset, presented in Table 1.

Table 1. CREMA-D dataset emotions examples (left) and spoken phrases (right).

Emotions			Phrases
(a) Fear	(b) Happy	(c) Anger	"IEO": "It's eleven o'clock"
			"TIE": "That is exactly what happened"
			"IOM": "I'm on my way to the meeting"
			"IWW": "I wonder what this is about"
			"TAI": "The airplane is almost full"
			"MTI": "Maybe tomorrow it will be cold"
			"IWL": "I would like a new alarm clock"
			"ITH": "I think I have a doctor's appointment"
			"DFA": "Don't forget a jacket"
			"ITS": "I think I've seen this before"
			"TSI": "The surface is slick"
(d) Disgust	(e) Sad	(f) Neutral	"WSI": "We'll stop in a couple of minutes"

It contains around 7500 audio-visual clips from 91 speakers. These clips were recorded by 48 male and 43 female actors aged between 20 and 60 +. The database contains people of different races and ethnicities (African American, Asian, Caucasian, etc.). Speakers uttered from a selection of 12 sentences. The sentences were pronounced using one of six different emotions (anger, disgust, fear, happy, neutral, and ad). The average duration of one phrase is 2.5 s - approximately 75 frames.

4 Methodology

In this section, we describe the strategy used to build a state-of-the-art lip-reading system and train the models, making best use of the limited amount of data available. We divided the CREMA-D database into training, validation and test sets in the ratios of 70, 10 and 20, respectively, considering speaker independence, gender and age. On average, in each training set there are 63 instances per class, for the IEO class there are always three times more instances (with the exception of the Neu training set), because this class reproduces an emotion with different levels of intensity.

We used the Mediapipe open-source library [27] to detect lips areas. To train the models, a window size of 30/60 frames with a step two times smaller than the specified window size was used. Frames were selected sequentially from the video without thinning.

Since there is no out-of-the-box solution to process emotional speech, in current research we use the well-known 3D ResNet-18 [28] to tackle emotional speech recognition. 3D ResNet is a type of model for video that employs 3D convolutions. The general architecture and layers dimensions of the model are shown in Table 2 (with the dimension of the input data $60 \times 88 \times 88 \times 3$). ResNet includes 17 3D convolutional layers that make it relatively easy to increase accuracy by increasing depth, which is more difficult to achieve with other networks.

Table 2. Emotional speech lip-reading model architecture.

Layer Name	3D ResNet-18	Repeat	Output Size
Conv1	$3 \times 3 \times 3$, 64, stride 2	1	$30 \times 44 \times 44 \times 64$
Max Pool	$3 \times 3 \times 3$, stride 2	1	$14 \times 21 \times 21 \times 64$
ResBlock 1	$3 \times 3 \times 3$, 64, stride 1 $3 \times 3 \times 3$, 64, stride 1	2	$14 \times 21 \times 21 \times 64$
ResBlock 2	$3 \times 3 \times 3$, 128, stride 2 $3 \times 3 \times 3$, 128, stride 1	2	$7 \times 11 \times 11 \times 128$
ResBlock 3	$3 \times 3 \times 3$, 256, stride 2 $3 \times 3 \times 3$, 256, stride 1	2	$4 \times 6 \times 6 \times 256$
ResBlock 4	$3 \times 3 \times 3$, 512, stride 2 $3 \times 3 \times 3$, 512, stride 1	2	$2 \times 3 \times 3 \times 512$
Global Average Pool	$2 \times 3 \times 3$	1	512
Fully connected	512×12	1	12

Table 3. Selection of model parameters based on the validation set.

Model	Image size, pixels	Channels	Sequence len	UAR (Valid)	UAR (Test)
3D ResNet-18	**88 × 88**	**3**	30	59.62	64.63
			60	**66.51**	**65.67**
		1		64.20	61.04
	44 × 44	3		64.23	65.34
	112 × 112			62.38	62.21

The input of the CNN is an image that passes through the first 3D convolution layer and the pooling layer, then 4 residual blocks with 3D convolution layers follow, each of which is re-peated 2. The global average pooling layer is next, and a fully connected layer of 12 neurons completes the CNN. The last fully connected layer determines the most probable hypothesis from 12 recognition classes. As a further improvement of the model can be applied recurrent neural networks, such in [29].

We divide the training set into 6 parts according to emotions. At first, we train the model only on records with neutral emotions. We do not divide the validation and test sets according to emotions. Initially, we trained the model on neutral emotions. We fine-tuned the training parameters, such as: sequence length, image size, batch size, number of image channels, prior to training the model on other emotions (Table 3).

Then, according to the best parameters, we train the model on phrases related to other emotions. Based on experimental results, it was revealed that the highest UAR value for recognizing 12 phrases is achieved when: 1) the image size is 88 × 88 × 3, where 3 is the number of channels; 2) sequence length equals 60.

5   Evaluation Experiments

In this section we evaluate and compare the proposed architecture on different emotions. Table 4 shows the UAR results of 7 lip-reading models (6 models trained on separate emotions plus 1 model trained on all emotions simultaneously) on the test set.

Table 4. Dependence of lip-reading accuracy on various emotions.

Training emotion	Recognition accuracy on the test set						
	NEU	ANG	DIS	FEA	HAP	SAD	mean UAR
NEU	**78.95**	68.27	53.36	64.33	63.16	66.81	65.81
ANG	63.16	**78.36**	47.81	60.23	54.09	52.92	59.43
DIS	56.58	**56.87**	50.15	55.70	53.65	55.99	54.82

(*continued*)

Table 4. (*continued*)

Training emotion	Recognition accuracy on the test set						
	NEU	ANG	DIS	FEA	HAP	SAD	mean UAR
FEA	66.23	74.42	54.82	**78.51**	65.50	61.26	66.79
HAP	54.39	56.58	49.12	62.13	**78.22**	53.80	59.04
SAD	72.37	70.91	59.21	73.10	60.67	**75.44**	68.62
mean UAR	73.32	67.49	57.31	64.45	57.15	61.21	-
All	94.30	94.74	93.42	95.76	95.76	94.59	94.04

The training was carried out on 100 epochs, the learning rate is 0.001 and it is constant throughout the training process; the optimizer is SGD. Training stops if UAR does not increase during 6 epochs on validation. We chose the unweighted average recall (UAR) metric because it is better suited for unbalanced classes, e.g. we have IEO class three times larger than the others.

E.g., when the model is trained on the emotion of disgust (DIS) and we try to recognize other types of emotional speech, we get only from 50.15 to 56.87 percent of recognition accuracy (with a mean UAR of 54.82%). It turned out that the best solo-emotional model training on which gives the highest recognition accuracy on other emotions is sadness (SAD) with a mean UAR of 68.62%.

Additionally, as expected, the best recognition accuracy on the test set was achieved for the emotions on which the model was trained. Except the emotion of disgust (DIS). This is explained by the fact that the disgust emotion significantly distorts the lips and articulation of the speaker. Also, speakers tend to express the emotion of disgust visually quite differently. For other emotions, consistency is preserved.

At the same time, despite type of emotion used for model training, the test recognition accuracy is higher for phrases uttered with the emotion of anger (mean UAR 67.49), least of all - with the emotion of happiness (mean UAR 57.15), if not considering the neutral (NEU) emotion.

Another point is that a huge gain in accuracy between models trained on individual emotions and the last model ("All") is mainly caused by 7-times larger training set in the latter case. The additional frank comparison of models with identical size of the training sets was performed for that case. We divided our training set into 6 parts in a way that in each there are instances of 63 speakers, of different gender and age, all 6 emotions and 13 phrases, so that all instances are as uniform as possible. Table 5 shows the UAR results for that case.

According to the obtained results, we can conclude that if we use all emotions, then the UAR is higher than for training only on the emotions "anger", "happiness", "disgust". In addition, we can see that if we train on all emotions, then the UAR value for phrases pronounced with the emotion "happiness" increased from 57.15% to 63.77%, the value of UAR for phrases pronounced with the emotion "angry" or "fear", also increased.

Table 5. Additional frank comparison results.

Training emotion	Recognition accuracy on the test set						
	NEU	ANG	DIS	FEA	HAP	SAD	mean UAR
train 1	**73.25**	72.81	53.65	**70.47**	**70.03**	**66.52**	**67.79**
train 2	65.35	68.27	45.76	60.38	62.13	55.26	59.53
train 3	66.23	69.01	50.00	66.23	64.47	57.75	62.28
train 4	66.67	70.76	52.78	65.35	61.55	59.94	62.84
train 5	62.28	63.89	**56.14**	66.52	58.19	61.55	61.43
train 6	69.74	**73.68**	53.65	66.81	66.23	60.23	65.06
mean UAR	67.25	69.74	52.00	65.96	63.77	60.21	63.15
Std	3.79	3.55	3.64	3.25	4.11	3.80	3.69

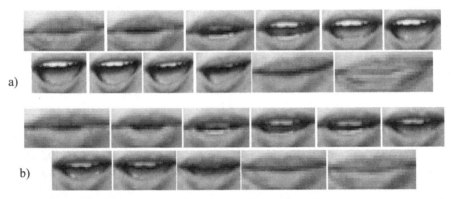

Fig. 1. An example of changing the articulation of the lips depending on the speaker's emotion: a) the "anger" emotion (frames 50 to 61), b) the "sadness" emotion (frames 84 to 95).

Figure 1 shows an example of changing the articulation of the lips depending on the speaker's emotion. A comparison of two examples of changes in the articulation of the lips for one phrase with different emotions of the speaker shows that: 1) with the emotion "anger", the activity of the mouth area is higher than with the emotion "sadness"; 2) with the emotion "anger", the beginning of the movement of the lips begins from frame 50, while with the emotion "sadness" from frame 84. The observed temporal shift of frames is characteristic of the fact that during the emotion of "anger" the speaker tries to express his thoughts faster, while the pauses between words are reduced.

A similar picture is observed for other types of emotions, and the numerical expression of the influence of various emotions on the accuracy of speech recognition is shown in Table 4. It should be noted, that despite the highest mean UAR values is achieved for models trained with the emotion Sadness (68.62), the highest absolute values were achieved on neutral (NEU) emotion (78.95) and fear (FEA) emotion (78.51).

6 Conclusions

In this paper, we present experimental investigation of how different emotions, namely anger, disgust, fear, happy, neutral, and sad affect automatic lip-reading. We train the 3D ResNet-18 model on the CREMA-D emotional speech database by experimentation with different parameters of the model. To the best of our knowledge, the results obtained in this research work are the first study of the effect of emotional speech on the accuracy of lip-reading in scientific literature.

Additionally, in this research we analyze existing emotional speech databases suitable for training state-of-the-art lip-reading models, develop and fine-tune ResNet-18-based architecture for automatic lip-reading.

We have experimentally confirmed that the accuracy of models trained on all types of emotions (mean UAR 94.04%) significantly exceeds the accuracy of recognition of models trained only on a neutral emotion (mean UAR 65.81%), or on any other separate emotion (mean UAR from 54.82% to 68.62% with the emotion of disgust and sadness respectively).

We have discovered that despite the type of emotion used for model training, the test recognition accuracy is higher for phrases uttered with the emotion of anger (mean UAR 67.49), least of all - with the emotion of happiness (mean UAR 57.15), not taking into account the neutral (NEU) emotion. We have carefully analyzed the visual manifestations of various emotions and assessed their impact on the accuracy of automated lip-reading. Current research is the first step in the creation of emotion-robust speech recognition systems and leaves open a wide field for further research.

Acknowledgments. This research is financially supported by the Russian Science Foundation (project No. 22–11-00321). Section 5 is supported by the Grant No. MK-42.2022.4.

References

1. Zhou, P., Yang, W., Chen, W., et al.: Modality attention for end-to-end audio-visual speech recognition. In: IEEE International Conference on Acoustics, Speech and Signal Processing (ICASSP), pp. 6565–6569 (2018)
2. Ivanko, D., Ryumin, D., Kashevnik, A., et al.: DAVIS: Driver's Audio-Visual Speech Recognition. In: ISCA Annual Conference Interspeech, pp. 1141–1142 (2022)
3. Kim, M., Hong, J., Park, S.J., et al.: Multi-modality associative bridging through memory: Speech sound recollected from face video. In: IEEE/CVF International Conference on Computer Vision, pp. 296–306 (2021)
4. Ryumina, E., Verkholyak, O., Karpov, A.: Annotation Confidence vs. Training Sample Size: Trade-off Solution for Partially-Continuous Categorical Emotion Recognition. In: ISCA Annual Conference Interspeech, pp. 3690–3694 (2021)
5. Erickson, D., Zhu, C., Kawahara, S.: Articulation, acoustics and perception of Mandarin Chinese emotional speech. Open Linguistics **2**, 620–635 (2016)
6. Dresvyanskiy, D., Ryumina, E., Kaya, H., et al.: End-to-end modeling and transfer learning for audiovisual emotion recognition in-the-wild. Multimodal Technologies and Interaction **6**(2), 11 (2022)

7. Afouras, T., Chung, J. S., Senior, A., et al.: Deep audio-visual speech recognition. In: IEEE Transactions on Pattern Analysis and Machine Intelligence, pp. 1–13 (2018)

8. Ivanko, D.: Audio-Visual Russian Speech Recognition. PhD thesis, 404 (2022)

9. Ekman, P.: Are there basic emotions? Psychol Rev. **99**(3), 550–553 (1992)

10. Russel, J.: A circumplex model of affect. J. Pers. Soc. Psychol. **39**(6), 1161–1178 (1980)

11. Poria, S., Majumder, N., Mihalcea, R., et al.: Emotion recognition in conversation: research challenges, datasets, and recent advances. IEEE Access **7**, 100943–100953 (2018)

12. Kashevnik, A., Lashkov, I., Axyonov, A., et al.: Multimodal corpus design for audio-visual speech recognition in vehicle cabin. IEEE Access **9**, 34986–35003 (2021)

13. Ivanko, D., Ryumin, D., Axyonov, et al.: Multi-speaker audio-visual corpus rusavic: Russian audio-visual speech in cars. In: LREC, pp. 1555–1559 (2022)

14. Fernandez-Lopez, A., Sukno, F.M.: Survey on automatic lip-reading in the era of deep learning. Image Vis. Comput. **78**, 53–72 (2018)

15. Afouras, T., Chung, J.S., Zisserman, A.: LRS3-TED: a large-scale dataset for visual speech recognition. arXiv preprint arXiv:1809.00496 (2018)

16. Cao, H., Cooper, D.G., Keutmann, M.K., et al.: CREMA-D: Crowd-sourced emotional multimodal actors dataset. In: IEEE Transactions on Affective Computing **5**(4), 377–390 (2014)

17. Livingstone, S.R., Russo, F.A.: The Ryerson Audio-Visual Database of Emotional Speech and Song (RAVDESS): a dynamic, multimodal set of facial and vocal expressions in North American English. PloS one **13**(5), e0196391 (2018)

18. Haq, S., Jackson, P.J., Edge, J.: Audio-visual feature selection and reduction for emotion classification. In: International Conference on Auditory-Visual Speech Processing (AVSP'08), pp. 185–190 (2008)

19. Martin, O., Kotsia, I., Macq, B., Pitas, I.: The eNTERFACE'05 audio-visual emotion database. In: IEEE International Conference on Data Engineering Workshops (ICDEW'06), pp. 1–8 (2006)

20. Ivanko, D., Ryumin, D., Axyonov, A., Kashevnik, A.: Speaker-dependent visual command recognition in vehicle cabin: methodology and evaluation. In: Karpov, A., Potapova, R. (eds.) SPECOM 2021. LNCS (LNAI), vol. 12997, pp. 291–302. Springer, Cham (2021). https://doi.org/10.1007/978-3-030-87802-3_27

21. Chung, J.S., Zisserman, A.: Lip reading in the wild. In: Asian Conference on Computer Vision, pp. 87–103 (2016)

22. Ma, P., Martinez, B., Petridis, S., et al.: Towards practical lipreading with distilled and efficient models. In: IEEE International Conference on Acoustics, Speech and Signal Processing (ICASSP), pp. 7608–7612 (2021)

23. Petridis, S., Stafylakis, T., Ma, P., et al.: End-to-end audiovisual speech recognition. In: IEEE International Conference on Acoustics, Speech and Signal Processing (ICASSP), pp. 6548–6552 (2018)

24. Ivanko, D., Ryumin, D., Karpov, A.: Automatic Lip-Reading of Hearing Impaired People. In: International Archives of the Photogrammetry, Remote Sensing & Spatial Information Sciences, vol. XLII-2/W12, pp. 97–101 (2019)

25. Zhu, H., Luo, M.D., Wang, R., et al.: Deep audio-visual learning: a survey. Int. J. Automation Comput. **18**(3), 351–376 (2021)

26. Assael, Y.M., Shillingford, B., Whiteson, S., et al.: Lipnet: End-to-end sentence-level lipreading. arXiv preprint arXiv:1611.01599 (2016)

27. Grishchenko, I., Ablavatski, A., Kartynnik, Y., et al.: Attention mesh: High-fidelity face mesh prediction in real-time. In: CVPRW on Computer Vision for Augmented and Virtual Reality, pp. 1–4 (2020)

28. Ivanko, D., Ryumin, D., Kashevnik, A., et al.: Visual Speech Recognition in a Driver Assistance System. In: EURASIP 30th European Signal Processing Conference (EUSIPCO), pp. 1131–1135 (2022)
29. Zhao, X., Yang, S., Shan, S., et al.: Mutual information maximization for effective lip reading. In: IEEE International Conference on Automatic Face and Gesture Recognition, pp. 420–427 (2020)

Exploring the Use of Machine Learning for Resume Recommendations

Anna Shestakova[1] and Andrea Corradini[2(✉)]

[1] University of Liverpool, Liverpool, UK
olashest@liverpool.ac.uk
[2] Copenhagen School of Design and Technology, Copenhagen, Denmark
andc@kea.dk

Abstract. Typically, career recommendation systems use content-based and collaborative filtering techniques to create a personalized list of vacancies that a candidate might be interested in. These techniques individually have both advantages and disadvantages. Content-based filtering has a high classification accuracy since it is based on data from the user's resume. Collaborative filtering gives the best predictable result, but it is necessary to collect data on the user's interests for such a model to work correctly.

This study explores the applicability of hybrid filtering to improve the quality of recommendations and the possible solution to the cold start problem. The cold start problem occurs when the system is unable to form any relation between users and items for which it has insufficient data [1]. While hybrid filtering may help solve the problem of information overload, we also considered the use of skillset vectors to tackle the issue of data sparseness that has also plagued recommender systems. We analyze the applicability and quality of the DistilBERT and BERT models for use in a career recommender system.

A comparative analysis of the results obtained from the online evaluation (user testing) and offline evaluation of the ML model quality is given.

Keywords: Machine learning · Resume · Career recommendation · BERT · DistilBERT · Filtering

1 Introduction

When companies hire hundreds of employees every month and receive thousands of responses for each job, they use automated resume review systems to screen candidates. These systems match jobseeker profiles to open positions based on keywords in the resume and filter out inappropriate resumes [2]. Thus, a CV of a good specialist may not pass such a check due to incorrect design or the use of wrong terms. This problem is especially relevant, for example, for professionals in a specific area who may not know the terms used within the domain or organization they are applying to [3] or do not know that their skills are suitable for other positions within the same organization.

Nowadays industries are starting to develop areas they have never been involved in before. For example, banks can develop a taxi service, telecommunications companies

© Springer Nature Switzerland AG 2022
S. R. M. Prasanna et al. (Eds.): SPECOM 2022, LNAI 13721, pp. 626–640, 2022.
https://doi.org/10.1007/978-3-031-20980-2_53

create trading platforms and other ecosystems [4]. And now these companies are look-ing for people with specific skills they've never hired before. Meanwhile, a candidate experienced in forwarding services may, for example, find a position with a bank which is developing retail sales area. New specifications are being required to the candidates and one need to keep an eye on a huge number of new vacancies in order to have an understanding of what skills the industries are looking for.

Modern machine learning (ML) methods make it possible to analyze various data, extract valuable information and make recommendations [5, 6]. In [2] it is argued that the task of using machine learning methods to validate an applicant's resume requires further development, as well as the creation of a recommender system. [7] also note that referral systems are underutilized on job posting sites; or after processing user feedback, the accuracy of the recommendations is still low [8].

In this paper, we focus on the application of machine learning techniques for recom-mender systems to career counseling. Developing an automated resume review system based on machine learning techniques, including a performance recommender system, can help companies to check whether job seekers are a good match for positions they applied for in the first place as well as for other open vacancies that fit the applicants' skills.

This paper is aimed at investigating the following questions:

- Which machine learning model is optimal for natural language recognition in automatic resume and recommendation systems?
- How to determine the accuracy of the ML model used for the vacancy recommender system based on the candidates' resumes?

The rest of this article is organized as follows. Section 2 briefly describes the modern approach to career recommender systems. Section 3 describes the ML algorithms that we used for our study, as well as the reason for this choice and a brief description of the criteria for evaluating the effectiveness of the recommendations. Section 4 describes the developed prototype of our career recommendation system. Eventually, in Sect. 5 we describe the results we obtained after evaluating our system.

2   State of the Art

Collaborative filtering is the most common technique used to build recommender sys-tems. The most common implementations of collaborative filtering algorithms are based on a few main methods such as the memory-based method, the model-based method and a hybrid combination of techniques [9]. Memory-based techniques make use of the available data set to establish correlations between users in order to recommend a spe-cific item to a user that was not encountered before. The recommendation is calculated on the basis of user ratings to determine the similarity between users or items. Thus, this approach relies on a similarity measure to cluster users or items together. By storing ratings in the cells of a two-dimensional matrix where users are represented along one dimension and items along the other one, such a similarity measure can be calculated based on the rows or columns of the matrix.

Model-based techniques generate models using several data mining and machine learning algorithms to predict users' rating of unrated items. Usually, dimensionality reduction is carried out as complementary technique of this approach. In this way, instead of having to deal with large sparse datasets, the recommender system can handle with a much smaller matrix in a lower-dimensional space. Therefore, the problem of sparsity in the matrix originally used in memory-based approaches can be tackled more efficiently.

A large amount of literature exists especially for the identification of friends for social recommendation. A probabilistic matrix factorization method for adding social network users to the user-item rating matrix was proposed in [10]. The same authors also proposed a social trust ensemble method that interprets the ratings in the user-item matrix as a mixed representation of the user's taste and the ratings of the item by the user's trusted friends [11].

In [12] a regularization method that posits that the feature vector of users should be close to the average of their social relations is proposed. To account for the fact that a user's trusted neighbors do not necessarily have the same ratings and preferences, an approach where the preference similarity between users and their social ties is determined by the similarity of their past rating patterns was put forward in [13]. Other studies focus on modeling influence of first-order and higher-order neighbors in social recommendation [14, 15]. Since explicit social relations are not always available, researchers have also explored implicit social relations [16, 17]. A system that models the explicit and implicit influence for social recommendation is presented in [18].

Creating effective career recommender system covering several different functional areas and job openings is a challenging research task that involves data mining, natural language processing (NLP), and other machine learning techniques [19]. For the development of a recommender system, several approaches have been suggested. Recommender systems for online stores and streaming services use the approach when a user wants to find a certain product or movie that does not fully fit the query or is not on sale, then the recommender system can recommend another product or movie if the product is not available, or the desired product is not good enough, or the customer has viewed different similar products or movies before. We suggest that a similar approach could be used in career recommendations. The applicant may be recommended for vacancies in a different career area but corresponding to their skill set. Thus, the main task of the study is to issue recommendations from different career areas regarding the list of user skills, which is formed from the resume text. Also, the user is offered information about how his skills correspond to the proposed vacancies and what skills are required. Thus, the user can expand the search area, consider vacancies in unexpected areas that were not originally considered and find a suitable job in a new area [20].

Another goal of the research is to improve the accuracy of such recommendations and user satisfaction with the recommendations received, and the ability to focus on suitable vacancies, rather than random recommendations [21].

Information about the required skills is highlighted from the list of vacancies and, in the same way, from the user's CV. Further, the received sets are cleared of insignificant information, duplicates, and rare skills, and then recommendations are given to the user based on the received list of skills.

To improve recommendations, we use a hybrid recommendation algorithm that combines joint collaborative filtering and content-based filtering models [22]. This approach provides more accurate recommendations and avoids some of the well-known shortcomings of recommender systems [23] such as cold start issues, and the issue of storing data from the applicant's resume.

After issuing initial recommendations, the user evaluates how suitable the recommended vacancy is for them in terms of career area and list of skills, and then a second recommendation is issued, adjusted according to the user's feedback. Online and offline experiments was evaluated to assess the quality of the career recommender system. The online evaluation presents the recommendation resulting from the feed-back from human users who interacted with the system. In offline mode, we evaluate the quality of the ML model.

3   Methodology and Evaluation Criteria

3.1   Theory

Recommender systems are a set of algorithms and models, applications, and services to predict content that may interest a user. Such predictions are based on information about the user.

Based on the assumption made by [22] in a review of the applied approaches and methods in developing career recommendation, it is assumed that the quality of predictions can be improved by using hybrid filtering. This approach combines two ML models: content-based filtering which improves classification accuracy based on content, and collaborative filtering which gives the best predictable result.

Thus, two types of filtering are used in this study to obtain more accurate career recommendations. Initial recommendations are given using content-based filtering, since there is information from the resume, but there is no information about grades. After an applicant receives a list of recommended vacancies and assesses the compliance with the proposed options, collaborative filtering are additionally used to improve the quality of recommendations [24].

3.2   Data Collection and Data Preparation

The preliminary stage of preparation is data collection and data preparation. [25] notes that the quality of the preparation of the dataset for content filtering has a significant impact on the efficiency of the model and the quality of the recommendations. Thus, the task of finding a qualitative dataset is one of the main tasks of this study.

A dataset of skills and job profiles was compiled from a public dataset in Kaggle with anonymous personal data. The first step is to prepare a set of skills data required from applicants for relevant job profiles in various fields.

Content filtering is most commonly used for datasets that represent an unstructured description of the subject of a recommendation [26], such as articles and books. Thus, this model can be used to work with job descriptions and resume texts. The signs (skills) in this case are keywords from the job description.

Unstructured features of textual information can be described using the vector-space model [27], where each element of the vector is an attribute, potentially characterizing the main skills required in a particular professional area, and the user's profile with his/her skill set is a vector in the same space. This is how the vector of skills for the vacancy and the vector of the applicant's skills are formed.

In the next step we use the k-means algorithm to find the k-nearest neighbors [28], which will represent the recommended vacancies. Not all the values are equally significant for defining skills, e.g. toponyms, name of months, and proper nouns are obviously of no importance. This is why it is necessary to start weighing the elements according to their importance and delete some elements with minimum weights. Therefore, the matching elements in two vectors will be more accurate. To do this, we use NLP methods to analyze a set of resumes from different career areas, and to extract a matrix of skills.

In our system, we store the skill vector as a string of 30 values. In this case, the weight of the skill is not stored, but it is used when calculating the values that fall into the vector. The first stage in the preparation of the job profiles matrix is the selection of elements from the resume corpus, which are the key skills of a particular job profile. The task of determining the weight of elements can be solved using the TF-IDF transform, which assigns more weight to frequently used skills. Further, the vector of a certain user's interest is calculated in the same way.

The proximity of the two vectors (A,B) and hence the identity of the job profile and user skills, can be calculated using the cosine distance (Pearson correlation). In scientific notation it could be represented by equation:

$$\text{similarity}(A, B) = \cos(\theta) = \frac{A \cdot B}{\|A\| \|B\|} = \frac{\sum_{i=1}^{n} A_i B_i}{\sqrt{\sum_{i=1}^{n} A_i^2} \sqrt{\sum_{i=1}^{n} B_i^2}} \tag{1}$$

The metric values range from 0 to 1. If two vectors are aligned, then the angle between them equals zero, hence the cosine of that angle is 1. Thus, the closer the similarity value to one, the more similar the profile of user interest and vacancy, i.e. have a large number of matching elements (skills).

3.3   Provision of Recommendations

The next step is to display a list of recommended vacancies to the user. After the user reads the recommendations and rates them, the vector of the user interests should be updated, but only for those elements (skills) that have changed. At the same time, new assessments of elements (skills) may have more weight, since they express the user is currently interested in, and not information from the resume, which may be irrelevant.

The weight of elements (skills) is updated using the collaborative filtering (user-based approach) method. The collaborative filtering approach is shown Fig. 1. The principle of operation of the algorithm is as follows: the set of elements of the vector space is divided into a given number of clusters k.

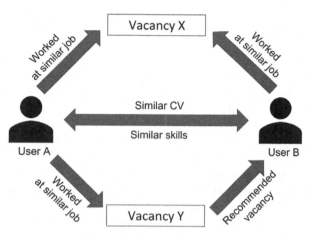

Fig. 1. Collaborative filtering.

Next, the algorithm minimizes the standard deviation at the points of each cluster. In this case, the center of mass for each cluster will be recalculated at each next iteration. Further, depending on which of the new centers was closer in the chosen metric, the vectors are again divided into clusters. The operation of the algorithm ends at an iteration after which no cluster changes occurred.

For the tasks of the study, this means that for each user skill, it is necessary to find the k skills most similar to it in the job profile and supplement the vector of user interests with new data. Another approach to updating the recommendation is based on the following user ratings.

Assessment of the recommendation against the expected career area:

- Meets Expectations: the system will show other suitable vacancies from this field. With the same match rate, vacancies from priority areas will be shown.
- Partially Compliant: with the same matching rate, jobs from priority areas or jobs that have not yet been shown to the user will be shown.
- Does not meet expectations: jobs from this area will no longer show up in recommendations.

Assessment of the recommendation for compliance with the expected vacancy:

- Meets Expectations: this vacancy will remain on the reissued referral list as expected.
- Partially Compliant: with the same matching rate, jobs from priority areas or jobs that have not yet been shown to the user will be shown.

- Does not meet expectations: this vacancy will no longer appear in recommendations, but other vacancies from this field may be shown.

After updating the vector of interest, as well as filtering categories in relation to user ratings, recommendations for vacancies will be re-issued.

3.4 Quality Assessment

The general goal of research on recommender systems is to improve the accuracy of the classification of forecasts. In the context of this study, information on what profession to recommend to the applicant based on his/her skill set. To assess the effective-ness of the methods used to achieve the goal of the study, you can use various indica-tors. But only with the help of a combination of methods of analysis of indicators, it is possible to assess the results of the study. Thus, in the study, two approaches used to assess the quality of the prototype recommender system.

Online evaluation: The most preferred way to assess the quality of a recommender system is through direct user validation in the context of business metrics. After issuing recommendations, users must complete a survey in which it is necessary to evaluate resulted elements. Online evaluation should be considered the main one since the result represents the feedback of real users who interacted with the system.

Offline evaluation: No user participation is required for offline evaluation. Some of the data that was used to train the algorithm was used to check the predictions. To assess the quality of a career recommender system, it is necessary to define a metric for evaluating the model, that is, to measure how correct vacancies the system offers to the user. As such a measure, root-mean-square deviation (RMSD) was used.

Ideally, when the given recommendations met the user's expectations, the root-mean-square error would be zero. Thus, the lower this value, the higher the quality of the recommendations.

4   Models

4.1 Data Preprocessing Module

For the task of a recommender system, collecting and cleaning a dataset is the primary process. The full data preprocessing process schema is shown Fig. 2. An anonymized set of resumes, structured by career areas, was uploaded for this study, consisting of 2506 PDF files. Each file contains data on the title of the position held, description of tasks, and required skills. Additionally, some resumes may contain information about education and hobbies and various images (for example, medals and certificates). It is necessary to collect a dataset of the form:

- ID - line number in order,
- Career area - data is grouped into 24 professional areas for the issuance of recommendations from the professional area that does not belong to the user's interests.

- Job title - info about the job title that will be provided to the IT Artifact user,
- Skills is a string of built-in 30 skills extracted from the resume corpus.

Next, it is required to filter the text from stop words, such as "a", "an", "the", "of", "in", etc. Such words are found in almost every sentence and do not have an informative load, being noise for subsequent deep learning.

For the ML tasks, bringing words to one form (remove word endings) is necessary to reduce the dimension. The method of lemmatization is used to bring to the initial form. The difference between stemming and lemmatization is that lemmatization takes context into account and transforms a word into its meaningful base formula, while stemming removes a few characters at the end of a word, leading to misspellings and mistranslated words.

For example, the word "care" will be transformed into "car" using stemming. Considering the above, we will carry out a morphological analysis of the word and reveal its initial form. But with a simple lemmatization, the words "waiting", "waits", "waited" are not transformed into "wait" as expected. For this, we provide the parts of speech (POS) tag as an argument to the lemmatize() function. But sometimes, a word can have several lemmas, depending on the meaning or context. Therefore, we need to find the correct POS tag for each word. This will build a set of skill words in their initial form.

Using the algorithm for finding the similarity of vectors by cosine, you can find similar words and suggest them to the user. Values for this metric range from 0 to 1.

To calculate the cosine position, we need to translate words into numbers. For this, we apply tokenization algorithm, which forms a dictionary in which each word corresponds to a sequence number. In the process of tokenization, words are replaced by numbers, and a word vector of up to 512 characters is formed. The numbers reflect the interaction of words with each other, taking into account the order of the words relative to the importance of the skill, since in the process of tokenization, the sentence is broken down into words regarding the importance of each word in relation to the sentence.

The study uses the DistilBERT transform model to classify tasks and create embeddings. DistilBERT is a derivative of the BERT model, which has 40% fewer parameters and is 60% faster but still retains more than 95% of the performance of the original BERT model [29]. It is the optimal choice for the tasks of this study. The maximum length of the mask is set, an attention mask is created for each marked-up set of words and reduced to a single set length. The DistilBERT model translates the tokenized set of words into an embedding. The results obtained are saved as a matrix in an XLSX file for future use in the career recommender module.

4.2 Career Recommender Module

The process of reading the user's resume file and its preliminary analysis is performed identically to the algorithm described in Sect. 4.1. Full Career recommender process schema is shown Fig. 3.

After primary preparation, 30 user skills will be found. The correlation coefficient calculation is one of the most commonly used methods for finding the similarity of objects if they have the same set of metrics. A set of metrics (numerical characteristics of skills) is a vector. For example, if it is required to find occupations with a skill set

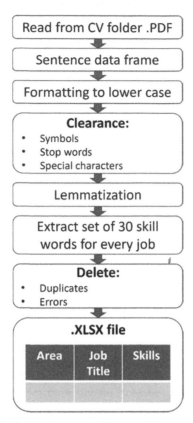

Fig. 2. Data preprocessing module process.

similar to that of the user, the skill set and weight are com-pared. Let's consider a pre-prepared test skill set. Each row of the table is a job profile - a vector with numerical characteristics.

Since the dataset is presented in a tabular form, the calculation of the similarity of vectors can be implemented using the method, which calculates the Pearson correlation coefficient.

The convenience of the method also lies in the fact that it can compare vectors with missing data. Thus, the similarity of two pairs of objects is calculated: the data collected from the user's resume and the i-th row in the skills matrix. Only those values are selected where the cosine distance from the sample is less than 15%, or the cosine similarity is greater than or equal to 85%. Thus, we read all the matrix rows in a loop, save the obtained values of the correlation coefficient, and sort them in descending order. The user is given the vacancies' recommendations with the highest coefficient of three different career directions.

After the user evaluates the quality of the recommendations, three updated vacan-cies will be issued, selected according to the user's ratings. Thus, a professional area or vacancy with a score of less than 5 points will no longer be shown to the user.

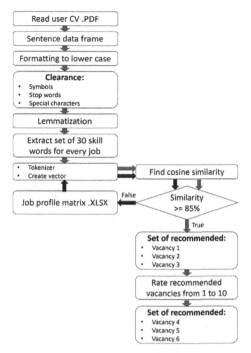

Fig. 3. Job recommender module process.

Profession-al areas and vacancies that receive six or more points in the user assessment are prioritized.

5 Results

The section provides information on the results obtained using the IT Artifact developed during the study. The results of the application work, the assessment of the effective-ness of the applied ML models [27, 28], and the results of a survey of the application users are given. The study researches the impact of ML model selection and the accuracy of recommendations for the use in career recommender systems.

To achieve the research goals, a test dataset with job vacancies was generated using the data collection module. 2506 anonymized resumes from 24 professional fields were automatically processed. The resulting dataset was automatically cleared of erroneous records and duplicate vacancies. Additionally, a manual check was carried out, and some records were deleted. As a result, the career recommender system test dataset contains the skillset for 479 unique jobs.

Seventeen people took part in the testing of the career recommendation module. Test participants belong to the following professional areas: Information Technology (developers, testers, UX designers), Marketing, Translation, and Art Each test participant ran the recommender system at least once and completed the participants' questionnaire based on the results. The results of the user survey and offline evaluation of the quality of the ML model were processed and analyzed. From the results shown in Fig. 4, we can see that the offline evaluation in the columns DistilBERT and BERT have fairly high accuracy scores for the ML model. Columns REC1 and REC2 show the results of a user survey after the first and second issuance of recommended vacancies. As it can be seen, these results have a larger spread in accuracy scores.

	DISTILBERT	BERT	REC1	REC2
USER1	77,3	82,3	70	73,33
USER2	81,5	85,1	63,33	80
USER3	83	87,9	23,33	66,67
USER4	83,4	91,2	23,33	80
USER5	88,1	93,7	70	86,67
USER6	79,3	83,1	16,67	20
USER7	87,1	86,6	43,33	80
USER8	79,9	85,5	50	73,33
USER9	83,6	88,3	56,67	76,67
USER10	81,2	84,7	70	86,67
USER11	84,1	89,5	50	80
USER12	83,5	85	43,33	76,67
USER13	88,6	89,3	73,33	86,67
USER14	87,3	90,7	43,33	80
USER15	79,5	84,9	93,33	86,67
USER16	88,6	94,1	70	76,67
USER17	82,6	87,2	53,33	76,67

Fig. 4. Model's testing results.

Although in the research, a recommender system prototype was developed, which has several limitations, the study confirms the high potential for continuing the study of the applicability of ML models for career recommender systems [30]. The concept of using a matrix structure for storing skills data for recommendations was tested. But with an in-crease in the number of different professional areas, the necessary skills in which do not intersect, the matrix greatly increased in size and became too sparse. Only 30 skills were selected for each vacancy, respectively, and skills related to other professions remained unfilled. Based on the results of the initial testing of the model, it was decided to forgo this concept in favor of a vector representation of the skill set.

Also, in the course of research and testing of the prototype, it was found that DistilBERT model accuracy for recommendations based on resume text analysis averages 83.44%. Testing the BERT model showed a higher accuracy of 87.59%. Detailed results of model's tests are shown in Fig. 4. Testing was carried out using the RMSE calculation. The test dataset contained 20% of the records from the complete dataset. DistilBERT and BERT models can be further trained with fine-tuning that updates the model weights for the type of text. This is the way a better performance in classifying skills in resume text and job descriptions can presumably be achieved.

	IRV1	IRV2	IRV3	URV1	URV2	URV3
USER1	8	6	4	8	9	8
USER2	8	8	5	9	8	9
USER3	1	1	5	5	7	8
USER4	1	5	6	8	6	7
USER5	3	3	3	8	8	9
USER6	1	1	1	1	2	3
USER7	5	5	7	8	1	8
USER8	4	4	5	6	7	9
USER9	4	5	8	9	7	5
USER10	6	6	7	8	9	8
USER11	2	2	5	7	8	9
USER12	4	4	5	7	8	8
USER13	6	6	6	8	9	10
USER14	1	1	4	7	8	9
USER15	10	10	9	9	9	8
USER16	4	4	4	6	8	9
USER17	4	5	7	6	8	9

Fig. 5. User's survey results.

As a result of testing the artifact, it was found that the use of the Hybrid filtration approach is more effective in terms of user satisfaction, because after receiving an assessment, the quality of recommendations increases, since information about the user's interests becomes available, which can be more efficiently used in filtering recommendations. Thus, the factors that positively influenced users' satisfaction from working with the prototype of the recommender system were identified.

The results of the survey shows that users noted that the accuracy of determining the list of skills averaged 84.7%. It is to be noted that at the first issuance of recommendations, users were most often dissatisfied with the proposed options, and the average result was 59.8% for the professional field and 53.7% for vacancies. After scoring and refining recommendations, users were on average 75.6% satisfied with the result, an average of 21.9% higher than the results of the first recommendation. The assessment of satisfaction results based on the survey is shown Fig. 5, where IRV – Initial Recommendations Vacancy, URV – Updated Recommendations Vacancy.

A new list of vacancies was recommended based on the users feedback, depending on the ratings received after the first issue. According to [31], even if the accuracy of the recommender system is high, user satisfaction is reduced if the service recommends the same product every time, or, in the case of a career recommender system, the same vacancy or a vacancy from a professional field that the user does not like.

It should be noted that it was not the vacancies corresponding to the user's skillset that were recommended but the vacancies that could arouse interest, regardless of the skill-set. Therefore, during user testing, not the accuracy of the model was assessed but the degree of user satisfaction.

6 Conclusion

The choice of an ML model for use in career recommender systems should take into account the size of the dataset and its diversity. The accuracy of the recommendations can be improved using a hybrid filtering approach, where the recommendations can be improved after processing the user's feedback.

In conclusion, we note that the study offers a new look at the recommender system, built on the principle used in the recommendation of texts (for example, articles and books), rather than searching for a direct match to a set of skills. This approach allows the user to recommend unexpected vacancies from other professional fields, assuming that such a vacancy may be of interest to the user, regardless of whether he has the necessary skillset. Such recommendations are especially interesting for people who would like to change their field of activity.

In our study, we did not touch upon such topics as scalability of our approach (for example, working with data in multiple languages, issuing recommendations from any career field, etc.), questions of datasets, such as obtaining descriptions and recommending real vacancies from relevant hiring sites, dependence from the size of the dataset for initial analysis, cold start issues, and the issue of storing data from the applicant's resume Thus, the most popular approach to recommender systems was applied to implement the prototype.

The choice of algorithms is also of great importance, but at the same time, complex modern algorithms will not always be more efficient than classical ML models. Also, a specific algorithm can be effective in recognizing textual information from news, but at the same time, it does not work well with structured information, such as a resume text or instructions for use.

In the research was studied what factors influence the choice of the ML model and what effect this has on user satisfaction. The results were obtained through a series of experiments with publicly available datasets, user testing, and questionnaires, which are widely used to assess the performance of recommender systems.

References

1. Schein, A.I., Popescul, A., Ungar, L.H., Pennock, D.M.: Methods and metrics for cold-start recommendations. In: Proceedings of the 25th International ACM SIGIR Conference on Research and Development in Information Retrieval, New York, USA, pp. 253–260 (2002)
2. Roy, P., Chowdhary, S., Bhatia, R.: A machine learning approach for automation of resume recommendation system. In: International Conference on Computational Intelligence and Data Science, Procedia Computer Science 2020 (2020)
3. Axelrod, J.: A robot reading your resume? 10 tips for vets to beat job screening software (2019). https://www.militarytimes.com/veterans/2019/03/28/a-robot-reading-your-resume-10-tips-for-vets-to-beat-job-screening-software/ Accessed 16 Sep 2022

4. Hawkins, A.J.: Uber unveils new products for business travellers, wedding parties, and EVs (2022). https://www.theverge.com/2022/5/16/23071034/uber-product-travel-wedding-eats-av-ev-delivery-features Accessed 18 Sep 2022
5. Choy, M.: What Netflix's Recommendation Systems Can Teach Us About the Computing Challenges of the Near Future (2021). https://www.forbes.com/sites/forbestechcouncil/2021/02/19/what-netflixs-recommendation-systems-can-teach-us-about-the-computing-challenges-of-the-near-future/?sh=271173c87489 Accessed 18 Sep 2022
6. Lin, Y., Lei, H., Addo, P., Li, X.: Machine Learned Resume-Job Matching Solution (2016). https://arxiv.org/abs/1607.07657. Accessed 18 Sep 2022
7. Shalaby, W., et al.: Help me find a job: A graph-based approach for job recommendation at scale. In: Proceedings of the IEEE International Conference on Big Data, 1544–1553 (2017)
8. McNee, S., Riedl, J., Konstan, J.: Being accurate is not enough: How accuracy metrics have hurt recommender systems. CHI'06, pp. 1097–1101 (2006)
9. Geetha, S., Fancy, C., Saranya, D.A.: Hybrid approach using collaborative filtering and content based filtering for recommender system. In: Journal of Physics: Conference Series, Volume 1000, National Conference on Mathematical Techniques and its Applications, Kattankulathur, India, 5–6 January 2018 (2018)
10. Ghazanfar, M.A.: Robust, scalable, and practical algorithms for recommender systems. University of Southampton, Faculty of Physical and Applied Science, Doctoral Thesis (2012)
11. Hao, M., et al.: Sorec: social recommendation using probabilistic matrix factorization. In: Proceedings of the 17th ACM Conference on Information and Knowledge Management, CIKM 2008, Napa Valley, CA, USA, October 26–30 (2008)
12. Hao, M., King, I., Lyu, M.R.: Learning to recommend with social trust ensemble. In: Proceedings of the 32nd Annual International ACM SIGIR Conference on Research and Development in Information Retrieval, Boston, MA, USA, July 19–23, (2009)
13. Jamali, M., Ester, M.: A matrix factorization technique with trust propagation for recommendation in social networks. In: ACM Conference on Recommender Systems (2010)
14. Hao, M., et al.: Recommender systems with social regularization. In: Proceedings of the 4th International Conference on Web Search and Web Data Mining, Hong Kong, China (2011)
15. Ying, R., et al.: Graph Convolutional Neural Networks for Web-Scale Recommender Systems. ACM (2018)
16. Wu, L., et al.: DiffNet++: A Neural Influence and Interest Diffusion Network for Social Recommendation (2020)
17. Sun, Y., et al.: PathSim: meta path-based Top-K similarity search in heterogeneous information networks. In Proceedings of the Vldb Endowment 4(11), 992–1003 (2011)
18. Fu, T.Y., Lee, W.C., Lei, Z.: HIN2Vec: Explore Meta-paths in Heterogeneous Information Networks for Representation Learning (2017)
19. Song, C., et al.: Social recommendation with implicit social influence. In: Proceedings of the 44th International ACM SIGIR Conference on Research and Development in Information Retrieval (2021)
20. Ferrari Dacrema, M., Cremonesi, P., Jannach, D.: Are we really making much progress? a worrying analysis of recent neural recommendation approaches. In: Proceedings of the 13th ACM Conference on Recommender Systems (RecSys'19). Association for Computing Machinery, New York, NY, USA, 101–109 (2019)
21. Ahmed, S., Hasan, M., Hoq, M.N., Adnan, M.A.: User interaction analysis to recommend suitable jobs in career-oriented social networking sites. In: 2016 IEEE International Conference on Data and Software Engineering, pp. 1–6 (2016)
22. Jiang, M., Fang, Y., Xie, H., Chong, J., Meng, M.: User click prediction for personalized job recommendation. World Wide Web 22(1), 325–345 (2018)

23. Ravita, M., Sheetal, R.: Efficient and Scalable Job Recommender System Using Collaborative Filtering. https://doi.org/10.1007/978-981-15-1420-3_91. ICDSMLA 2019, pp. 842–856 (2020)
24. Al-bashiri, H., Abdulgabber, M., Romli, A., Hujainah, F.: Collaborative Filtering Recommender System: Overview and Challenges. Advanced Science Letters (2017)
25. Yadalam, T.V., Gowda, V.M., Kumar, V.S., Girish, D.: Career recommendation systems using content based filtering. In: 5th International Conference on Communication and Electronics Systems (ICCES), 2020, pp. 660–665 (2020)
26. Ghidini, C.: The Semantic Web - ISWC 2019: 18th International Semantic Web Conference: Auckland, New Zealand, October 26–30, (2019)
27. Dan, M.: Vector space model for document representation in information retrieval. Annals of Dunarea de Jos. (2007)
28. Chen, S.: K-Nearest Neighbor Algorithm Optimization in Text Categorization. IOP Conference Series: Earth and Environmental Science. 108 (2018)
29. Sanh, V., Debut, L., Chaumond, J., Wolf, T.: DistilBERT, a distilled version of BERT: smaller, faster, cheaper and lighter. arXiv preprint https://arxiv.org/abs/1910.01108 (2019)
30. Parida, B., Kumar Patra, P., Mohanty, S.: Prediction of recommendations for employment utilizing machine learning procedures and geoarea-based recommender framework. Sustainable Operations and Computers 3(2022), 83–92 (2022)
31. Wojciechowski, J., Wandresen, R.R., Mantovani Fontana, R., Marynowski, J.E., Kutzke, A.R.: Is products recommendation good? an experiment on user satisfaction. In: Proceedings of the 19th International Conference on Enterprise Information Systems, Volume 2, pp. 713–720 (2017)

The Role of Pause in Interaction: A Case of Polylogue

Tatiana Sokoreva$^{(\boxtimes)}$ (iD) and Tatiana Shevchenko (iD)

Moscow State Linguistic University, 38 Ostozhenka Street, Moscow 119034, Russian Federation
jey-t@yandex.ru

Abstract. The paper gives a brief account of the role of pause in verbal interaction and presents new corpus data on communication strategies of 40 American English speakers engaged in ten everyday polylogues. We distinguish pause as a natural phenomenon in speech production which provides for breathing and cognitive planning from pause as a tool in acting and other forms of public speaking utilized as a rhetorical device. We hold that silence may speak, and the role of pause in verbal interaction is underestimated, as our research testified. Personality traits expressed by means of silent and filled pauses may receive an entirely new interpretation when viewed as a way of manipulating audiences, making an impact, regulating other participants' speaking time, i.e. considered in the situation of talk-in-interaction. In polylogues we found that by discriminating the length of between-turns-pauses from pauses within turns one speaker managed to achieve dominance, while others, who failed to do it, consciously or unconsciously, turned out to be passive participants in the interaction. We also specified gender roles in coordinating participants' speaking time by overlaps and interruptions.

Keywords: Polylogue · American english · Turn-taking · Pause · Gender · Conversation strategy

1 Introduction

Being a speech component, pauses perform several functions: first, they are essential for respiration in the process of speech production. Second, pauses contribute to the cognitive task of planning, since during pauses the person thinks about what he/she will say next. Regarding this, the more difficult the task ahead, the longer the pause will be. The utterance planning and pause duration, therefore, are related to the complexity of the upcoming remark. The third function of pause is associated with the implementation of the interaction of interlocutors in a conversation [1]. For example, according to Couper-Kuhlen's theory of conversational analysis, a pause in the speech of the second interlocutor, following a request, suggestion or invitation in the phrase of the first speaker, may indicate a refusal on the part of the second participant of the conversation [2].

Pauses split into filled and unfilled, and both are classified by duration. Pauses also correlate with syntactic boundaries in the utterance and, from the point of view of

© Springer Nature Switzerland AG 2022
S. R. M. Prasanna et al. (Eds.): SPECOM 2022, LNAI 13721, pp. 641–650, 2022.
https://doi.org/10.1007/978-3-031-20980-2_54

intonation segmentation, correspond to the boundaries of intonation phrases (IPs), the longest pauses occurring at the end of the so-called speech paragraphs, or super-phrasal units. In a spontaneous conversation, the longest pauses correlate with a topic change. The results of the study by Wennerstorm and Siegel indicate that short (less than 500 ms) and long (1.5 s) pauses occur between separate utterances, and only medium-long pauses occur within utterances [3]. These results confirm earlier studies by Jefferson [4] and Wilson and Zimmerman [5]. However, the present work indicates the presence of other pause tendencies in conversation.

According to the results of the study by Shevchenko T. I. and Gorbyleva A.V., most of the utterances in the coordinated friendly dialogue hold a very short pause, lasting up to about one syllable, meaning that this pause is barely felt, since on average it lasts up to 200 ms [6]. This transition from one remark to another is smooth, but there exist other pause categories. Thus, the corpus analysis of American speech dialogues revealed the mechanisms of regulating the speaking time of two participants, manifested in the fact that some of the utterances were interrupted by overlapping and speaking together in case of exceeding the speaking time by one participant [6].

In addition to duration and filled/unfilled categories, pauses can be defined as stable or unstable. The degree of pause stability can characterize a human personality. Psycholinguists believe that the abundance of pauses in a conversation is a sign of a speech malfunction or psychological instability of the talking person [7]. For instance, a large quantity of hesitation pauses means that the speaker doubts, and the malfunction occurring in his/her conversation, leads to a speech smoothness violation [8, pp. 269–270].

The above-mentioned phenomenon can characterize a single speaker, as well as it can classify the whole language, since the distribution of pauses in different languages may vary. For example, when comparing English and French, it was found that the French are more likely to make respiratory pauses while speaking compared to the English, but the inter-pausal sound speech segments of French speakers are 1.5 times longer than those of the English.

Thus, the degree of pause stability in speech (including speech failures) can be a characteristic of a personality and his/her psycholinguistic features, can characterize individual languages and, finally, the very presence of pauses can indicate a speech style.

The parameter of the total pause duration also plays an important role in speech. And in this respect, the phonation - pause ratio in different speech styles also turns out to be diversified. Lecturers, politicians and other public figures, for example, are able to manipulate pauses, using them for rhetorical purposes. Thus, pauses may increase or decrease in duration, may be stable or unstable, which is usually due to the prominence of the part of the utterance that follows the pause. Sometimes a pause is inserted after a very important part of a statement in order to produce an effect on the audience.

Recently pause as a subject of manipulation has appeared in the mass media, as today the technical possibilities of pause adjustment are unlimited, and radio and television time is restricted and expensive. Studying the ratio of phonation to pause in the speech of American TV presenters, Shevchenko and Uglova revealed that when reading the news and weather forecast the above-mentioned ratio counts 12:1 and 14:1 respectively [9]. While in usual reading of an English fable, the same ratio is 3:1 or 4:1. Obviously, since these types of broadcasts are prepared in advance, such figures can be accounted for by the technical processing. Hoping that the consumer would focus mainly on the TV picture, the editors significantly reduced the pause time, and therefore added to the impression of very fast speech, even if in fact the presenter speaks at a normal pace. Consequently, the pauses were cut off, because both in the case of news and in the case of a weather forecast, it is assumed that viewers rely mainly on a video picture, that is, audio information is compensated by a visual channel, and the message itself is multimodal in nature. It should be noted that when checking the perception of information, the authors found that viewers retain only one third of verbal information, and they are able to retell only one third of the message, while the overall impression is created by the visual channel [9].

Regarding the phenomenon of pause stability and its cognitive function, it is vital to mention the study by Sokoreva, Shevchenko, Chyrvonaya, where Chinese students, when reading in Mandarin, English and Russian, had pauses of almost the same duration. The complexity of this cognitive task, which consisted in a sequential transition from one language to another when reading, was manifested in other parameters: when switching from Mandarin to Russian, Chinese speakers, as well as when switching from Russian to Mandarin, Russian speakers sharply increased the quantity of pauses and the overall time of pausing and reading [10].

Attempting to show the psycholinguistic characteristics of a person, Ramsey studied the speech samples of actors who played extroverts and introverts, depicting the difference between the psychotypes of extroverts and introverts in terms of pause variation. According to the research results, the speech of introverts is characterized by longer pauses: they are in no hurry to speak, they make less contact. However, in the extroverts' talk, especially in the process of persuasion or in an excited state, an increase or decrease in the duration of pauses was stated. By slowing down or speeding up speech tempo due to pause alteration, the extrovert may exert pressure on his interlocutor. Thus, pause length between utterances correlates with the personality factor of extraversion-introversion [11].

A person's pause characteristics can be influenced by the age factor. As the study showed, the average duration of syllable in speech increases with age, as well as the contrast between the average duration of stressed and unstressed syllables, but at the same time pause duration grows with age as well [12], which adds to the age-related psycholinguistic characteristics of a particular person.

Pauses perform the function of influencing the interlocutor and contribute to the making of a certain impression. Certain linguists argue that the result of the message perception depends not so much on the articulation rate, as on the presence of pauses between intonation phrases. Thus, with the help of pauses that determine the pace of message presentation, it is possible to regulate the nature of the impact on the listener: for example, by removing all pauses from the text or shortening them, the impression of an accelerated tempo is achieved [13].

Hence, on the one hand, pause making is a natural process, though this parameter will still be dependent on individual personality, the psychotype and psycholinguistic characteristics of a person, as well as on the situation and style of communication. On the other hand, the deliberate modification of pause in speech is a matter of art and manipulation. There is also a well-known technique of "not finishing" the phrase, pronouncing a pause before the very end of the utterance, which allows the interlocutor to finish the phrase himself/herself, since the speaker does not want to pronounce these words and tries to bring the second participant of the conversation to this idea.

Studying pausation (pause and resumption) in human-human dialogues where the participants could rely only on the acoustic signal, Edlund and his colleagues revealed a significant difference in speaker response times [14]: it was proved that the speaker stops as fast as possible if the interruption occurs in the middle of the phrase but when the speaker is close to the end of the remark he/she considers it preferable to finish talking and not to stop immediately. The speaker response time, according to Strömbergsson and her co-authors [15], also depends on question type, response type and the topic of the conversation. Studying the human-human dialogue data, the researchers found that positive responses came earlier than negative answers, and special and open questions had significantly longer response times than general and alternative questions.

The interaction in polylogues regarding speech overlaps was described in the work by Laskowski, Heldner and Edlund [16]. Analysing the speech samples in meetings, they found that the simultaneous talk in a multi-party conversation tends to end concurrently less frequently than it begins simultaneously. The issue of overlapping and turn-taking in human-robot interaction in conversation-al systems is extensively covered in [17].

The authors of the present paper are also aware of the results of the research on pausation and its dependence on discourse and social characteristics of speakers as well as the effect of extra-linguistic features on the verbal interaction of interlocutors by Vered Silber-Varod [18], Oliver Niebuhr [19] and other researchers.

2 Methodology

The goal of the present study is to explore the turn-taking phenomenon regarding pause characteristics in American English friendly talks. The research material includes ten conversations of American English speakers (n = 40), residents of different US regions (14 men and 26 women): the West Coast (5 polylogues – 18 people in total), the Southwest (2 polylogues – 9 people in total), and the Northeast (3 polylogues – 13 people in total). The speech samples are part of Santa Barbara University Corpus [20], provided with socio-demographic data for each participant and with typescripts made by native speakers of English. The duration of each talk is normalized at 5 min, the total duration of the analyzed corpus is 50 min.

In order to determine the leader among the interlocutors and establish the nature of turn-taking in a friendly multi-party conversation, 10 polylogues were analyzed with PRAAT computer program used to calculate the quantity and duration of pauses as well as evaluate the manner of turn-taking in each conversation.

The analyzed duration of pauses includes the time between the turns of the interlocutors, as well as the time within the turns of the speakers: both the internal pauses (within the turn of the interlocutor) as well as the external pauses (between the turns of the interlocutors) were tested. Pauses were classified into three groups: no pause or very short pause (from 0 to 200 ms), short pause or unit pause (from 200 to 800 ms) and long pause (from 800 to 1000 ms).

The manner of turn-taking comprises three variants of interaction among the participants of polylogues: smooth transition, when no one interrupts the other interlocutor's speech; overlaps and backchannels with positive result (when the first speaker completes his/her turn); and overlaps with interruptions (when the first speaker gives up without completing one's turn).

The statistical analysis was employed to compare the median values of pause quantity and pause duration of interlocutors as well as the amount of three types of turn-taking in each of the polylogues and find the significant difference in the analyzed parameters (Kruskal-Wallis test). The Mann-Whitney test was used to check the gender-related distinctions in speech characteristics under analysis. The above-mentioned statistical criteria represent non-parametrical tests that require no special distributional assumptions and can be applied to scale and nominal variables (in which the non-normal distribution was testified by Shapiro-Wilk criterion) [21, p. 188].

3   Results

The results of the study of speakers' interaction in the polylogue revealed the following: as in a dialogue, one leader is always identified in a polylogue. The leading speaker is distinguished by the total conversation time – the leader of the participants in the polylogue is the one who spoke longer in time. As a rule, the leader takes twice as long as the other participant, the ratio of the leader's speaking time to the speech of the second interlocutor is approximately 2:1.

However, it is interesting to note that in the polylogue, a longer speaking time of the leader is formed due to a larger number of pauses inside his/her utterances. For example, in polylogue 4 the female speaker makes more very short pauses or doesn't make them at all, as well as more long pauses, unlike the other participants of the conversation (see Fig. 1).

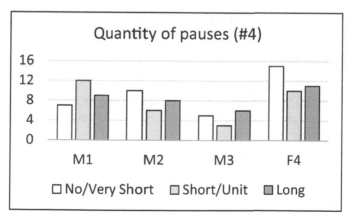

Fig. 1. The quantity of pauses in the speech of four interlocutors in polylogue 4.

Similar results were found for female leading speakers in polylogues 1, 4, 8 and male leading speakers in polylogue 2. In certain conversations the leading speakers are characterized by a larger number of all pauses compared to the same value in the other participants' speech (female speakers in polylogues 3, 7, 9, 10) or a larger number of *no pause* or *very short pause* speech components (female speakers in polylogue 6). In polylogue 5 the received values showed insignificant difference, thus in terms of leadership all the three participants of the conversation are equal.

The significant gender-related distinctions in pause quantity parameter were not registered.

It turned out that in the polylogue, leaders quickly enter a conversation, and at the same time, the turn-taking occurs either with a very short pause (up to 200 ms), or without any pauses at all. After the leaders have taken the floor, they begin to speak slowly, making long pauses, including hesitation pauses. That is, having received the right to speak, the leaders continue to think about what they are going to say, while all the other participants of the conversation patiently wait while the leading speaker reflects and select the right phrases. In polylogue 7, for instance, the female speaker and the second male speaker pronounce longer pauses within the turns than between the remarks with other interlocutors. Similar results were found in the speech of females and males in polylogues 1, 3, 5, 6, 9, 10 (Fig. 2).

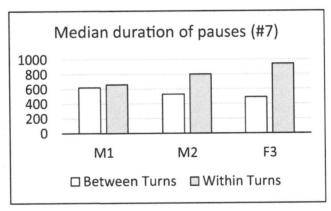

Fig. 2. The median duration of pauses (ms) in the speech of three interlocutors in polylogue 7.

Therefore, the leader's speech is characterized by long statements with rather long pauses that turn out to be inside their utterances. By formulating their thoughts and statements, the leader of the conversation, thus, capture the listeners' attention and, holding the opportunity to speak, take up most of the time in the polylogue.

Unlike leaders, the "non-leaders" strategy is characterized by other pausing features. Those people who do not want to speak out, but want to be seen participating in the conversation, make long extensive pauses between their remarks when they are addressed or when their reaction is expected (see female speaker 4 in Fig. 3). Similar results were found in male and female speech in polylogues 1, 3, 4, 6, 8, 9, 10.

The "guided" participants of the polylogue make rather long pauses, including filled ones, so everyone understands that they are pondering or formulating their statement, or they are not ready to answer. Consequently, such interlocutors are not addressed next

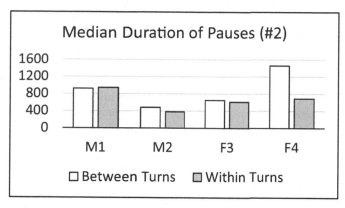

Fig. 3. The median duration of pauses (ms) in the speech of three interlocutors in polylogue 2.

time, because they participate very modestly in the conversation and do not seek to master the situation and the attention of the audience, and as a result, the duration of their speaking time remains insignificant.

These two manners of participation in the polylogue represent two speech strategies, strategies of people with leadership qualities and people who modestly participate in the general conversation, but do not seek self-disclosure in the conversation.

Studying the gender variation in pause characteristics revealed the insignificant difference in pause length both between (p = .630) and within turns (p = .736) (see Fig. 4).

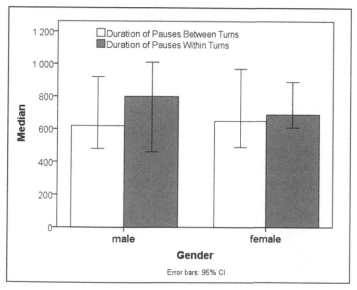

Fig. 4. The duration of pause between and within turns in male and female speakers.

Though there is a slight tendency of larger duration of internal pauses compared to external ones illustrated in Fig. 4.

The significant results in the analysis of turn-taking manner include the type distinctions that is the relevant difference in the way the speakers take their turn. The research proved the significantly larger number of overlaps and backchannels with positive results compared to smooth transitions and overlaps with interruptions (p < .000) (see Fig. 5). The gender difference in the manner of turn-taking was not confirmed in the study (p = .985).

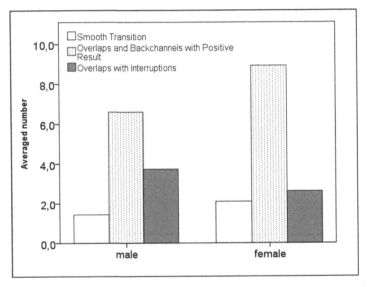

Fig. 5. The average number of turn-taking types in male and female speech.

4   Conclusions

Pauses, as a natural phenomenon contributing primarily to breathing during speech production and to cognitive speech planning, can characterize the speaker's personality in terms of his cognitive potential and his ability to participate in the conversation, as well as the speaker's psychophysiological state, which is represented in pause characteristics related to breathing and cognitive planning.

The controlled pauses perform the function of influencing the listener. The employment of these pauses is an oratorical art and presents a rhetorical device used in public speech by actors and public figures who work with the audience. To take dramatic pause, to pause before an important message, to pause without finishing your statement are skills not subject to everyone. These rhetorical techniques were tested in the experiment, when the impression of rapid speech tempo was achieved by removing a certain number of pauses. This is especially evident in the mass media communication, namely on television, when oral information perception is compensated with the help of other multimodal means, particularly the visual channel.

And finally, pausing contributes to interaction, which is also very important in discourse. The function of interaction plays a primary role in dialogues, still there are cases of joint speaking when several remarks match in time, which is a violation that has both a negative and a positive effect. Nevertheless, initially, the main type of turn-taking in the dialogue of mutually agreed friendly people are namely pauses.

In the case of polylogue, as the research results revealed, we found that by discriminating the length of between-turns-pauses from pauses within turns one speaker managed to achieve dominance, while others, who failed to do it, consciously or unconsciously, turned out to be passive participants in the interaction. The speech strategy of the polylogue's leader lies in achieving the opportunity to enter a conversation almost without pause or with the help of a short pause, and then, using his dominant position, employing both filled and unfilled pauses of sufficiently long duration. The speech strategy of passive participants of the polylogue consists in usage of long pauses between remarks and thus not getting involved too much in the conversation and sometimes thereby losing the right to speak.

Regarding the manner of turn-taking in polylogues we proved a much larger amount of cases where there are overlaps and backchannels with positive result, i. e. when the first speaker completes his/her turn anyway despite a slight overlap, which contributes to politeness strategy of the speakers.

The research results, however, are limited by the analyzed linguistic corpus, thus, further study is needed to verify the received outcome on other American English datasets. The work will also benefit from further perceptual research on the subjective impression about the leaders perceived by other participants of the conversation. As an alternative to our method of calculating pause quantity, we could also look at the relative frequency of pauses, i. e. occurrence of pauses per unit of time. Finally, the individual differences and cultural distinctions of the speakers have to be taken into account in the course of future studies as well.

References

1. Fletcher, J.: The prosody of speech: timing and rhythm. In: Hardcastle, W.J., Laver, J., Gibbon, F.E. (eds.) The Handbook of Phonetic Sciences, 2nd edn., pp. 523–602. Wiley-Blackwell, Oxford/Maiden, MA (2010)
2. Couper-Kuhlen, E.: English Speech Rhythm: Form and Function in Everyday Verbal Interaction. John Benjamins, Philadelphia, PA (1993)
3. Wennerstrom, A., Siegel, A.F.: Keeping the floor in multiparty conversations: intonation, syntax, and pause. Discourse Process **36**, 77–107 (2003)
4. Jefferson, G.: Notes on a possible metric which provides for a "standard maximum" silence of approximately one second in conversation. In: Roger, D., Bull, P. (eds.) Conversation: An Interdisciplinary Perspective, pp. 166–196. Multilingual Matters, Clevedon, UK (1988)
5. Wilson, T., Zimmerman, D.: The structure of silence between turns in two-party conversation. Discourse Process **9**, 375–390 (1986)
6. Shevchenko, T., Gorbyleva, A.: Temporal concord in speech interaction: overlaps and interruptions in spoken American english. In: Karpov, A., Potapova, R. (eds.) SPECOM 2020.

LNCS (LNAI), vol. 12335, pp. 490–499. Springer, Cham (2020). https://doi.org/10.1007/978-3-030-60276-5_47

7. Kess, J.F.: Psycholinguistics: Psychology, Linguistics, and the Study of Natural Language. John Benjamins Publishing Company, Amsterdam/Philadelphia (1992)

8. Fedorova, O.V.: Experimental Discourse Analysis. Languages of Slavic cultures, Moscow (2014). (in Russian)

9. Shevchenko, T., Uglova, N.: Temporal features in TV news and weather forecasts. J. Acoust. Soc. Am. **117**(4), 2544 (2005). https://doi.org/10.1121/1.4788459

10. Sokoreva, T., Shevchenko, T., Chyrvonaya, M.: Complex rhythm adjustments in multilingual code-switching across Mandarin, English and Russian. In: Karpov, A., Potapova, R. (eds.) SPECOM 2021. LNCS (LNAI), vol. 12997, pp. 660–669. Springer, Cham (2021). https://doi.org/10.1007/978-3-030-87802-3_59

11. Ramsey, R.W.: Speech patterns and personality. Lang. Speech **2**(1), 54–63 (1968)

12. Sokoreva, T.V.: Age-related changes in speech rhythm: an experimental phonetic study of US dialogue corpus. PhD Moscow (2018). (in Russian)

13. Nadeina, T.M.: Phrasal Prosody as a Factor of Speech Influence. RAN Institute of Linguistics, Moscow (2003)

14. Edlund, J., Edelstam, F., Gustafson, J.: Human pause and resume behaviours for unobtrusive humanlike in-car spoken dialogue systems. In: Proceedings of the of the EACL 2014 Workshop on Dialogue in Motion (DM), pp. 73–77. Gothenburg, Sweden (2014)

15. Strömbergsson, S., Hjalmarsson, A., Edlund, J., House, D.: Timing responses to questions in dialogue. In: Proceedings of the Interspeech 2013, pp. 2584–2588 (2013). https://doi.org/10.21437/Interspeech.2013-581

16. Laskowski, K., Heldner, M., Edlund, J.: On the dynamics of overlap in multi-party conversation. In: Proceedings of the Interspeech 2012, pp. 847–850 (2012). https://doi.org/10.21437/Interspeech.2012-191

17. Skantze, G.: Turn-taking in Conversational Systems and Human-Robot Interaction: A Review. Comput. Speech & Lang. **67**, 101178 (2021). https://doi.org/10.1016/j.csl.2020.101178

18. Silber-Varod, V., Alfon, E., Amir, N.: Perception of the strength of prosodic breaks in three conditions: explicit pause, implicit pause, and no pause. In: Proceedings of the Speech Prosody 2022, pp. 475–479 (2022). https://doi.org/10.21437/SpeechProsody.2022-97

19. Barnes, J., Mixdorff, H., Niebuhr, O.: Phonetic variation in tone and intonation systems. In: Gussenhoven, C., Chen, A. (eds.) The Oxford Handbook of Language Prosody, pp. 125–149. Oxford University Press, Oxford (2020)

20. Du Bois, J.W., et al.: Santa Barbara Corpus of Spoken American English, Parts 1–4. Linguistic Data Consortium, Philadelphia (2005)

21. Woods, A., Fletcher, P., Hughes, A.: Statistics in Language Learning. Cambridge University Press, Cambridge (1986)

Dictionary with the Evaluation of Positivity/Negativity Degree of the Russian Words

Valery Solovyev$^{(\boxtimes)}$, Musa Islamov , and Venera Bayrasheva

Kazan Federal University, 420008 Kazan, Russia
Maki.solovyev@mail.ru

Abstract. The article describes the Russian Dictionary containing a numerical evaluation of the positivity/negativity degree of words. It includes more than 25 thousand frequency words from the main parts of speech – nouns, verbs, and adjectives. Scores were obtained for 1000 words by crowdsourcing of respondents through Yandex. Toloka service with manual quality control of answers. For the remaining 24 thousand words, the evaluation was obtained by extrapolating the available ones using the BERT model. A dictionary with the evaluation of positivity/negativity degree is built using neural networks for the Russian language for the first time. It is shown that the Dictionary developed with the help of such methodology can be used to replenish the RuSentiLex. Another obtained result was the verification for the hypothesis existing in the Russian language concerning the predominant use of positive vocabulary. The hypothesis was confirmed basing on the sub-corpus of the Russian National Corpus. The results obtained are compared with the data of investigations of the English language. Finally, the article manifests the opportunity to use the Dictionary for analyzing of fiction.

Keywords: Dictionary · Valence · BERT · Russian language · Sentiment analysis · Pollyanna hypothesis

1 Introduction

Affective evaluation of words turns to be essential in many psychological studies [37]. Affective toning of words possesses 3 main parameters – dominance (strong/weak), arousal (active/passive) and valence (pleasant/unpleasant or positive/negative) [26, 37], complying with Osgood's potency, activity and evaluation [25]. The valence parameter, the one this article is devoted to, attracts perhaps the greatest attention. There are three main lines of research and application of this parameter, which can be highlighted here: psychology, computer linguistics, cognitive science.

Valence evaluation of words is important for automatic sentiment analysis of texts. It is a popular line of research in computer linguistics having important application. In particular, for sentiment analysis of user reviews stored in recommendation services [19], monitoring that tracks positive and negative feedback about a company and its

© Springer Nature Switzerland AG 2022
S. R. M. Prasanna et al. (Eds.): SPECOM 2022, LNAI 13721, pp. 651–664, 2022.
https://doi.org/10.1007/978-3-031-20980-2_55

products [32]. Recent reviews of the research can be found in [20, 30] for application in the Russian language.

Interesting results concerning sentiment evaluations of the entire language were mainly obtained in the works [10, 14]. The so-called Pollyanna hypothesis was put forward earlier, in the work [5], according to which people use positively toned words more often than negatively toned ones. This phenomenon is also known as Positive bias. In the work [14] the hypothesis was confirmed basing on 4 large corpuses of the English language, and in the work [10] – basing on 24 corpuses of 10 languages of different cultures.

To support all of the above studies, a number of dictionaries (databases) have been created with word evaluations made by people. Conventionally, two types of such dictionaries can be distinguished. Evaluative words, expressing a positive/negative attitude to something [16], are important for sentiment analysis of texts. Such dictionaries usually include only a small number of neutral words. They are often based on previously selected vocabulary with positive/negative connotations. Other types of dictionaries include a continuous sample of words (for example, all high-frequency ones). Evaluation of words in these dictionaries, made by people, reflects their positive/negative connotations. Of course, we do not have a strict definition of positive/negative words, experiments reflect the average intuitive understanding of words by people.

The first dictionary of this type is the dictionary [6], which contains only a little over 1 thousand words of the English language. It was noted in the work [37] that this number of words with scores is not enough for carrying out large-scale mega-studies. Then the dictionary was created, which involves almost 14 thousand words [37], including all the well-known high-frequency content words of the English language. The surveys were based on the 9-point scale. Each word received 20 scores. Thereafter other databases were created, including the one basing on 20 thousand words [28], which is in free access at http://saifmohammad.com/WebPages/nrc-vad.html. An overview of English dictionaries can be found in the work [16]. Databases with evaluations made by people have been created for other languages as well: Danish [24], Spanish [35], German [36], Finnish [31], and Chinese [38].

We should mention the work [15] made on the basis of the Russian language, describing the LinisCrowd dictionary for almost 10 thousand words, created using the crowdsourcing method (http://linis-crowd.org/). The dictionary is developed on the basis of 26771 word scores. That means there are on average less than 3 scores for a word. The work [10] presents a dictionary also constructed by the crowdsourcing method on the basis of 10 thousand words. The work [8] describes the multilingual dictionary SenticNet, created by way of translation. Its Russian part includes almost 25 thousand words. Recent and highly detailed reviews of the Russian language dictionaries can be found in the works [16, 20].

The need for large dictionaries with scores (based on tens of thousands of words) was marked in a number of works [13, 37]. However, their creation by the survey method is extremely labor-intensive. In this respect, it was proposed to use computer methods for extrapolating scores made by people to the words still missing such evaluations.

Various extrapolation options were considered, based, ultimately, on distributive semantics [4]. The quality of the obtained computer evaluations was assessed by comparing them with those made by people. As a standard, the existing set of words with human evaluations could be divided into parts in a ratio of 90/10, 90% of the words – the training sample – are used to train extrapolation algorithms, and for the remaining 10% – the test sample – the correlation coefficient between human and the machine evaluations is considered. This is usually the Pearson or Spearman correlation coefficient.

Most of the research is carried out for the English language. In work [3], evaluations of 1000 words from the work [6] were extended to 17 thousand words. This work uses a vector space model and the distance calculation from the target word to the words with the known human evaluations. The correlation coefficient of the obtained computer evaluations with human ones comprised 0.71. The compatibility vectors in the article [27] were created from the words included in the bigrams with the analyzed ones. Further, the method of the nearest neighbors was applied. The obtained correlation coefficient turned to be 0.74, slightly improving the previous results.

The next improvement is presented in the work [29]. Here the semantic space is built using the word2vec model, after which the clustering method is applied, which was proposed in the article. As a result, it becomes possible to obtain dictionaries with a correlation coefficient of 0.768 for English and slightly lower indicators for Spanish and Danish.

The article [13] uses a skip-gram vector model and applies Backwards stepwise regression with the Akaike information criterion. The acquired result is 0.786. The deep learning neural networks were obviously applied for the first time in the work [7]. It was a feed-forward neural network, with the fastText vectors of the Common Crawl model fed to its input. Significant improvement of results has been achieved: 0.870. Scores extrapolation was carried out for some other languages. Thus, for the German language the score of 0.798 was obtained in the work [23]. Another idea is to transfer ratings from one language to another with linear regression. In the work [38], in the process of transfer from English to Chinese, a correlation coefficient of 0.852 was obtained.

A completely different approach to computation of dictionaries of positive/negative words (of evaluative character) generation has been developed in [21]. This work describes a number of local contexts (patterns) with characteristic words and syntactic constructions typical of positive and negative words. These patterns are automatically selected in a large corpus of news texts; and the corresponding words are marked as positive, negative, neutral or mixed (in different senses, different evaluations) with subsequent expert correction. An accurate numerical evaluation of the degree of positivity/negativity is not assumed with this approach. As a result, the RuSentiLex dictionary was generated (https://www.labinform.ru/pub/rusentilex/index.htm) containing more than 12 thousand words and phrases.

The main goals of the study are the following. 1. To build a large dictionary with evaluation of positivity/negativity degree for the Russian language. 2. To check the Pollyanna hypothesis about the predominance of positive words over negative ones for the Russian language.

During the research, a number of noteworthy differences were found, which are discussed in detail in the paper. These are differences between our human and machine dictionaries, between results for the Russian and English languages, between the scores for different texts.

In Sect. 2, we describe a methodology for building a vocabulary using crowdsourcing and machine learning methods. Section 3 provides statistics on various types of texts and discusses The Pollyanna hypothesis. Other possible uses of the created dictionary are indicated. The last fourth section provides a detailed comparison of our dictionary with other dictionaries with evaluation of positivity/negativity degree for the Russian language, discusses the results obtained and indicates the research perspectives.

2   Dictionary Structure

Like most positivity/negativity dictionaries basing on the Russian language, we limit ourselves to separate words, not involving phrases. We have created two dictionaries of the Russian language with numerical evaluation of positivity/negativity. One of them was generated by the method of controlled crowdsourcing, which involves attracting a large number of respondents online with the subsequent screening out of careless ones. It includes 1000 words, in equal proportions of nouns, adjectives, verbs. The most frequent words in the dictionary [22] were taken for each part of speech. Another vocabulary is generated through extrapolating of available human scores using machine learning methods. For this dictionary, words with a frequency of more than 1 per million (ipm) were also selected from the dictionary [22] in equal proportions for the main parts of speech. It includes an additional 24466 words. For creation of both dictionaries we used a methodology described below, previously used for the English and other languages.

The first dictionary was created using the Yandex.Toloka service. We imposed certain and rather strict requirements to the qualification of the respondents. Requirements for participation included: (1) age – no younger than 30 y.o, (2) native speakers of Russian, (3) higher education, (4) top 10% of performance activity (only 10% of Toloka performers in terms of speed/quality correlation).

The survey participants were given questionnaires of 50 words and were asked to score words on a 9-point scale, from 1 – the most negative to 9 – the most positive. The most frequent words were taken for the rating process from the frequency dictionary of the Russian language by O. Lyashevskaya, S. Sharova [22] (http://dict.ruslang.ru/freq.php). The main parts of speech – nouns, verbs, adjectives – were taken in equal parts. 65 scores were obtained for each word; it was noticeably larger than in all previous dictionaries for any languages. The questionnaires were checked manually and the answers of careless respondents were screened out. There were about 10–15% of such answers. This applies to cases when all the scores were the same for all words of the questionnaire, or some obviously positive words were given negative evaluations, and vice versa. Thus, each word obtained at least 50 scores. Earlier, a similar approach to screening out low-quality questionnaires was applied in other works [18]. Additional information on the methodology for generating a dictionary is given in [2].

The Fig. 1 shows the distribution of the evaluation rating of the words in the dictionary. The average value is 6.20. The median value is 6.34. Words with a value of less than 5 comprise 14.6%. The histogram clearly shows a bias to the right, while there are more positive words there. The word with the lowest score is *война* (*war*) – 1.19, the word with the highest score is *мама* (*mother*) – 8.92.

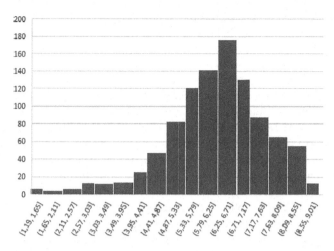

Fig. 1. The histogram of the word ratings for the human dictionary.

Positive or negative orientation of the texts is usually being assessed in the context of the Pollyanna hypothesis verification [14]. However, there is a possibility in this aspect to evaluate the lexicon of the language itself. Until now, no such assessments have been carried out. Judging from the above data, we can see that our vocabulary has an obviously positive bias. For comparison, we present a similar data from the dictionary in free access based on the Russian language described in [11] with a distribution of scores histogram in Fig. 2.

The number of words is 9943. The average score is 5.33. Number of words with a score of less than 5 is 22.3%. The median is 5.38. The same is for the English language [37]: the number of words is 13915, the average score is 5.06, the median is 5.20, the number of words with a score of less than 5 is 42.7%. Thus, the Pollyanna hypothesis is confirmed on the material of the examined dictionaries.

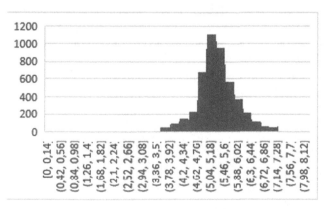

Fig. 2. The histogram of the dictionary from https://hedonometer.org/words/labMT-ru-v2/.

If you need to generate a large size dictionary, it turns out that crowdsourcing, especially controlled, will be extremely labor intensive. Therefore, the machine learning approach described in the introduction has been applied for obtaining a large positivity/negativity dictionary. An machine dictionary was generated containing more than 24 thousand words based on deep learning technology, the BERT model [9]. This is the first time this approach has been applied for the Russian language. We used the standard BERT version, pre-trained in the Russian corpus. RuBERT (Russian, cased, 12-layer, 768-hidden, 12-heads, 180M parameters) was trained on the Russian part of Wikipedia and News data. We used this training data to build a vocabulary of Russian subtokens and took a multilingual version of BERT-base as an initialization for RuBERT.

For fine-tuning, we used the human vocabulary described above. Fine-tuning was made with the help of Hugging Face Trainer class which, in fact, provides training and eval loop for PyTorch, optimized for Hugging Face Transformers (Transformers provides APIs and tools to easily download and train state-of-the-art pretrained models). The network input receives the words equipped with a number as a label. Therefore, in fine-tuning, we use positive/negative rating prediction as a numeric output. We use mean squared error as a loss function. Training sets was scaled in the following manner: ratings from the dictionary are linearly transformed from a range [1, 9] to a range between 0.0 and 1.0. During fine-tuning we use typical settings for learning rate ($2 * 10 - 5$). Selected hyper parameter values are: num_train_epochs = 10, per_device_train_batch_size = 64 (batch size per device during training), per_device_eval_batch_size = 64 (batch size per device during evaluation). The most frequent words were taken for the dictionary from the Frequency dictionary of the Russian language, mentioned above, as well as the words from RuSentiLex.

For evaluation of the selected model quality, it was trained on 900 words from the human vocabulary, generated scores for the remaining 100 words, and only then the Pearson correlation coefficient was calculated between human and machine evaluations basing on these 100 words. The coefficient turned out to be 0.707, which is below the best correlation coefficients for the English language. The distribution of neural network scores is shown in Fig. 3. The average value is 0.57. The median value is 0.59. The share

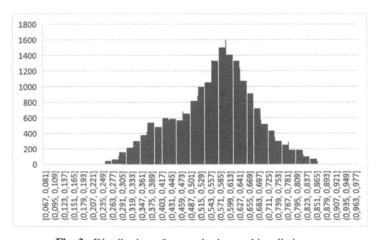

Fig. 3. Distribution of scores in the machine dictionary.

of words with values less than 0.5 is equal to 25.17%; that means almost exactly a quarter in total values. The median value turns out to have a bias to the right, but less significantly than in the human vocabulary. Thus, the Pollyanna hypothesis is confirmed by the machine dictionary as well. The lowest score is for the word *погибнуть* (*perish*), it is 0.067; the highest is for the word *миленький* (*lovely*) – 0.976.

We have developed the unified dictionary – the human dictionary together with the machine one. All dictionaries are in free access on the site of the project https://kpfu.ru/tehnologiya-sozdaniya-semanticheskih-elektronnyh.html.

3 Application of the Dictionaries

The main application is related to the verification of the Pollyanna hypothesis for the Russian language. Above, we have already checked it on a dictionary, but this is usually done on texts [14]. For texts, frequencies of use of words with different positivity ratings are calculated. I.e., unlike the dictionary of the whole language, each word is counted as many times as it occurs in the text.

The part of the Russian National Corpus, which is in free access (https://ruscorpora.ru/new/, hereinafter RNC), was taken for this purpose. It includes 1 million words. All texts are divided into sections: fiction, science, public, speech, and blogs. The texts underwent preprocessing: the accent marks were removed, the tokens were highlighted, and words were brought back to their original form. Texts within the section were combined into one text. After that, each word may be selected in the combined dictionary; and if it is found in it, it is replaced with the corresponding number, otherwise it is ignored.

Table 1 summarizes the basic statistics for 5 sub-corpuses. As you can see, a positive bias is recorded in all types of texts. The spread in the values of the parameters Median and Average is small; it does not exceed 5%. The share of negative words (with a score of less than 0.5) is the smallest in scientific texts, which is quite natural for the academic style of presentation. If we compare the share of negative words in English texts, it will be much higher. According to [14], Twitter scores 28.00% of negative words, Google Books collection – 21.20%, New York Times – 21.62%, and Music lyrics collection – 35.86%.

Table 1. Statistic parameters of sub-corpuses in the Russian National Corpus.

Subcorpora	Volume	Mean value	Median	Share of words scored ≤ 0.5
Public	145268	0.620	0.636	12.86%
Science	119908	0.630	0.631	9.25%
Speech	103018	0.636	0.648	11.43%
Blogs	26318	0.650	0.658	10.92%
Fiction	110117	0.624	0.636	14.72%

We analyzed several specific fiction pieces of different styles and genres. The statistical data is shown in Table 2.

Table 2. Statistic parameters of the selected fiction texts.

Fiction text	Volume	Mean value	Median	Share of words scored ≤ 0.5	Share of words scored ≤ 0.2	Share of words scored ≥ 0.8
The resurrection	60573	0.620	0.633	15.80	0.32	5.71
The mystery of Edwin Drood	35614	0.631	0.622	12.85	0.19	6.71
Roadside picnic	120861	0.624	0.634	12.69	0.21	5.21
Martin Eden	49889	0.638	0.650	12.66	0.20	8.09
Crime and punishment	63291	0.609	0.625	14.45	0.54	5.78

And again, the hypothesis of a positive bias has been confirmed. This effect is not particularly influenced by the genre, time of the work creation, or its original or translated variant. Thus, the modern science fiction novel by Arkady and Boris Strugatsky "Roadside Picnic" has practically the same parameter values as "Martin Eden", the classical novel by Jack London. Thus we see that a positive bias is manifested in texts of different types and is a very stable phenomenon. It is characteristic that a positive bias could be traced even in such a gloomy work as "Crime and Punishment", although quite expectedly it is less than in other works.

Table 2 shows data on sections of the texts' lexicon with different positivity degree. It can be seen that the median and mean vary slightly, reflecting the fact that the bulk of the words in all pieces belong to vocabulary, which close to neutral. The differences between the pieces become more significant when considering the tails on the histograms - the shares of strictly negative (index ≤ 0.2) and strictly positive (index ≥ 0.8) vocabulary. For example, the share of strictly negative vocabulary in "Crime and Punishment" is more than 2.5 times higher than the share of such words in "Martin Eden". Thus, our dictionary provides literary researchers a new quantitative tool for analyzing fiction.

In terms of these goals, our dictionary has advantages over other existing dictionaries. RuSentiLex was created on the basis of a corpus of news texts and, as will be shown below, does not contain a number of words that are very likely in literary texts. The dictionaries of works [10, 15] are much smaller in volume.

A program for calculating the measure of positivity/negativity of texts is available at https://filology-web.herokuapp.com/. When entering text in txt format, it returns an excel file with the ratings of all the words in the text.

Let us point out other promising possibilities of using our dictionary. One obvious application of the created dictionaries is to use the obtained data for replenishing of other digital dictionaries. A larger volume of the dictionary will allow for a more complete sentiment analysis of texts. Consider, for example, the popular RuSentiLex resource. Here is a list of the 10 most negative words missing from RuSentiLex:

умереть, мертвый, расстрелять, расстреливать, сбитый, умирать, застрелить, бунтовать, виселица, смертный (die, dead, shoot, shoot down, knocked down, die, shoot dead, riot, gallows, mortal). 10 most positive words missing from RuSentiLex: миленький, милая, милочка, слава, любознательный, солнце, ласка, любимая, великодушие, мама (lovely, honey, darling, glory, inquisitive, sun, caress, beloved, generosity, mother). Probably, these words did not appear in the news corpus, on the basis of which RuSentiLex was generated.

Another difference between our vocabulary and RuSentiLex is in the attitude to the neutral words. RuSentiLex contains a small number of neutral words, to be more precise, the words with one of the neutral meanings. Note, that some dictionaries, for example [15], discard neutral words altogether. If we select all such words and calculate the average score for them according to our dictionary, we get 0.58. That means, these words do have slight positive connotations. For example, RuSentiLex records only a neutral meaning for the word экзотика (exotics), which is nevertheless perceived rather as positive. It seems that neutral words with slightly positive connotations can make a certain contribution to the sentiment analysis of texts.

4 Discussion

The article describes the dictionary with numerical scores of the positivity/negativity degree of words in the Russian language. The technologies for developing the vocabulary – both human and machine – correspond to those previously applied for generation of the vocabulary of words with scores of concreteness/abstractness [33, 34]. The main salient features of our human vocabulary are as follows:

- word scores in the interval [0, 1]
- crowdsourcing
- manual control of the answers and screening out of careless respondents
- a record number of scores for each word
- most of all high-frequency content words are included
- phrases are not included.

A prominent feature of our machine vocabulary is the application of the BERT model to extrapolate human scores. Let us briefly compare our dictionary with the four most precisely machine dictionaries for Russian.

Ternary characterization of words as positive, neutral or negative (with the ability to have several evaluations) is contained in such well-known resource as RuSentiLex. The differences between our dictionary and RuSentiLex are as follows: 1. Our dictionary (machine version) contains much more words. 2. Our dictionary does not contain phrases. 3. Our dictionary contains only one score for each word, while RuSentiLex highlights different meanings of words which may have different scores. 4. Our dictionary contains scores from a continuous interval, while RuSentiLex contains only 3 discrete scores (with the possibility of combining them). Thus, these two dictionaries have significant differences, leading to different application possibilities. In comparison with the latest version of the KartaSlovSent dictionary [17] and in comparison with the dictionary in the work [10], our dictionary has been generated by the method of controlled crowdsourcing with manual quality control of respondents' answers. Compared to the LinisCrowd dictionary [15], we received by an order more scores for each word.

One of the research work types, which can be carried out using our dictionary, is the study of positive bias in the Russian language. Positive bias can be considered both in relation to the dictionary and in relation to texts. Positive bias is found both for human and machine dictionaries. At the same time, it is noticeably larger for the human dictionary – its median equals 0.634 versus 0.590 for machine dictionary. The following explanation for this difference can be proposed. BERT is context sensitive. Perhaps words that are intuitively perceived as essentially positive (negative) occur in less positive (negative) contexts, and this is what BERT detects. So, our data allow us to put forward a hypothesis about the discrepancy between the degree of intuitively perceived positivity/negativity of the word and the degree of positivity/negativity of the contexts in which it is used. Of course, serious additional diverse studies are required to confirm or refute this hypothesis.

Note that some previously developed dictionaries show negative bias. The RuSentiLex dictionary contains 9499 negative meanings versus 3339 positive ones; the dictionary [15] contains 25% of negative and 11.6% of positive words, while the rest of the words are neutral. The KartaSlovSent dictionary [17] also contains more negative words: 25.7% versus 13.5% positive ones. At the same time, the SenticNet_Ru dictionary shows a large positive bias – 14 650 positive words against 10 115 negative ones. The crowdsourcing dictionary shows similar results [10]. It contains 16.8% of words with a score of more than 6 (as usual, a score in the range from 1 to 9), and only 6.3% of words with a score of less than 4. This discrepancy can be attributed to a number of factors.

Firstly, to the difference in the selection of vocabulary for dictionaries and the difference in the selection of corpuses and contexts, related to the purposes of creating the dictionary. Thus, in the RuSentiLex dictionary, 35 patterns for negative words and only 20 for positive words have been developed to extract positive and negative evaluative words from the corpus of texts. Usually, such dictionaries tend to include evaluative emotively toned vocabulary, which provides a negative bias. It is well known that there are more words in languages denoting negative emotions than those denoting positive emotions. We in our research work were processing a continuous sample of words from the frequency dictionary containing a large number of words, which do not have a pronounced evaluative toning, but demonstrate a small positive bias.

Secondly, they differ by the volume of the dictionary. The Russian-language part of the SenticNet dictionary, which has almost exactly the same number of words as our dictionary, shows a similar positive bias. According to the review [16], the largest three dictionaries based on the English language have a positive bias.

Thirdly, one should also take into account the nature of the data collection, which may have an impact on the results obtained. In the works [10, 15, 17], crowdsourcing is not controlled, the screening out procedure of careless answers from respondents is not described. Whereas such screening out was carried out at generating of our dictionary. The prior instruction of the respondents is important at dictionary generating with crowdsourcing method application. However, not all publications describe this instruction, which does not allow accurate comparison of different dictionaries made under controlled conditions.

The dictionary is used to analyze the phenomenon of positive bias in various types of texts, the same way as it is done for the English language [14]. Calculations carried out on texts from the RNC and several large fiction forms confirm the presence of this phenomenon in the Russian language as well. You can pay attention to the following general patterns. The positive bias in the texts turned out to be higher than in the vocabulary. In other words, not only are there more positive words in the language, but positive words are used more often than negative ones. The average value and the median of word scores are approximately the same for all considered types of texts from the RNC – fiction, science, public, speech, blogs, and within fiction pieces – with different authors. As compared with the English language, a somewhat unexpected phenomenon has been revealed in the Russian language – negative vocabulary is used much less in Russian than in English. However, the research has been carried out on different types of texts, which may affect the results. The most commensurable in terms of content are the collections of Google Books for English and fiction + science for Russian language. In Google Books, the share of negative words is 21.20%, and in the indicated Russian collections – 14.72% and 9.25%. Also comparable are the New York Times, with a share of negative words of 21.62% and the collection Public with a share of 12.86%.

A possible explanation for this is related to the volume of dictionaries used in the compared works. In [14], where the data for the English language collections was taken from, calculations were carried out only for 5 thousand of the most high-frequency words. While we used 25 thousand words. As noted above, larger dictionaries usually show a bigger positive shift. However, it is possible that some other factors affect the result: the differences in the psychology of the authors of the texts on the Russian and English languages, or just some unclear differences in the research methodology, for example, the selection of respondents.

5   Conclusion

The article describes the dictionary of the Russian language with ratings of positivity/negativity of words. At the moment, this is the largest dictionary containing more than 25 thousand words. The dictionary was created using deep learning technology. The article provides a detailed comparison of it with other similar dictionaries created by various methods. When compared with a dictionary with expert ratings of words, the Spearman correlation coefficient was obtained – 0.707. According to the Chaddock scale, this level of correlation is considered high. In similar studies, a higher correlation coefficient was obtained for the English language. The likely reason for this is that the BERT model for English is better pre-trained on a larger body of texts than RuBERT for Russian.

The article demonstrates two possibilities of using the created dictionary. Firstly, to replenish other dictionaries, and secondly, to test the Pollyanna hypothesis about the predominant use of positive words.

One of the further possible applications of the generated dictionary is a detailed analysis of fictions for positive/negative bias, including from the point of view of the dynamics of the narrative in the spirit of the work [12]. The created dictionary can also be recommended for automatic sentiment analysis, including for building narrower domain-specific dictionaries.

Acknowledgements. This research was supported by the Kazan Federal University Strategic Academic Leadership (Priority 2030).

References

1. Adelman, J.S., Estes, Z.: Emotion and memory: a recognition advantage for positive and negative words independent of arousal. Cognition **129**, 530–535 (2013)
2. Andreeva, M.I.: Negativnye/pozitivnye slova: ocenka, slovar. Mezhdunarodnyj zhurnal gumanitarnyh i estestvennyh nauk, 12 (2021). (in Russian)
3. Bestgen, Y., Vincze, N.: Checking and bootstrapping lexical norms by means of word similarity indexes. Behav. Res. Methods **44**(4), 998–1006 (2012). https://doi.org/10.3758/s13428-012-0195-z
4. Bhatia, S., Richie, R., Zou, W.: Distributed semantic representations for modeling human judgment. Curr. Opin. Behav. Sci. **29**, 31–36 (2019). https://doi.org/10.1016/j.cobeha.2019.01.020
5. Boucher, J., Osgood, C.E.: The pollyanna hypothesis. J. Verbal Learn. Verbal Behav. **8**, 1–8 (1969)
6. Bradley, M.M., Lang, P.J.: Affective norms for English words (ANEW): stimuli, instruction manual and affective ratings (Technical Report No. C-1). FL: University of Florida, NIMH Center for Research in Psychophysiology, Gainesville (1999)
7. Buechel, S., Hahn, U.: Word emotion induction for multiple languages as a deep multi-task learning problem. In: Proceedings of NAACL-HLT 2018, pp. 1907–1918 (2018)
8. Cambria, E., Poria, S., Hazarika, D., Kwok, K.: SenticNet 5: discovering conceptual primitives for sentiment analysis by means of context embeddings. In: Proceedings of the Thirty-Second AAAI Conference on Artificial Intelligence (AAAI-18), pp. 1795–1802 (2018)
9. Devlin, J., Ming-Wei, Ch., Kenton, L., Kristina, T.: BERT: Pre-training of Deep Bidirectional Transformers for Language Understanding. arXiv preprint arXiv:1810.04805 (2018)
10. Dodds, P.S., Clark, E.M., Desu, S., et al.: Human language reveals a universal positivity bias. Proc. Natl. Acad. Sci. **112**(8), 2389–2394 (2015)
11. Dodds, P.S., Harris, K.D., Kloumann, I.M., Bliss, C.A., Danforth, C.: Temporal patterns of happiness and information in a global-scale social network: hedonometrics and Twitter. PLoS ONE **6**, e26752 (2011)
12. Enrique, A., Corujo, A., Gonzalo, J., Meij, E., Rijke, M.: Overview of RepLab. 2012: Evaluating Online Reputation Management Systems. CLEF-2012 Working Notes (2012). http://ceur-ws.org/Vol-1178/CLEF2012wn-RepLabAmigoEt2012.pdf
13. Hollis, G., Westbury, C., Lefsrud, L.: Extrapolating human judgments from skip-gram vector representations of word meaning. Q. J. Exp. Psychol. **70**(8), 1603–1619 (2017). https://doi.org/10.1080/17470218.2016.1195417
14. Kloumann, I.M., Danforth, C.M., Harris, K.D., Bliss, C.A., Dodds, P.S.: Positivity of the English language. PLoS ONE **7**(1), e29484 (2012). https://doi.org/10.1371/journal.pone.0029484

15. Koltsova, O.Y., Alexeeva, S.V., Kolcov, S.N.: An opinion word lexicon and a training dataset for russian sentiment analysis of social media. In: Komp'yuternaia Lingvistika i Intellektual'nye Tekhnologii: Trudy Mezhdunarodnoj Konferentsii "Dialog", pp. 277–287 (2016)

16. Kotel'nikov, E.V., et al.: Sovremennye slovari ocenochnoj leksiki dlya analiza mnenij na russkom i anglijskom yazykah (analiticheskij obzor). Nauchno-tekhnicheskaya informaciya. Seriya 2: Informacionnye processy i sistemy **12**, 16–33 (2020). (in Russian)

17. Kulagin, D.I.: Publicly available sentiment dictionary for the Russian language KartaSlovSent. In: Computational Linguistics and Intellectual Technologies: Proceedings of the International Conference "Dialog" [Komp'yuternaia Lingvistika i Intellektual'nye Tekhnologii: Trudy Mezhdunarodnoj Konferentsii "Dialog"] (20), pp. 1106–1119 (2021)

18. Kuperman, V., Estes, Z., Brysbaert, M., Warriner, A.B.: Emotion and language: valence and arousal affect word recognition. J. Exp. Psychol. Gen. **143**(3), 1065–1081 (2014). https://doi.org/10.1037/a0035669

19. Liu, B.: Sentiment analysis and opinion mining. Morgan & Claypool, San Rafael, CA (2012)

20. Loukachevitch, N.: Automatic sentiment analysis of texts: the case of Russian. In: Gritsenko, D., Wijermars, M., Kopotev, M. (eds.) The Palgrave Handbook of Digital Russia Studies, pp. 501–516. Springer, Cham (2021). https://doi.org/10.1007/978-3-030-42855-6_28

21. Loukachevitch, N., Levchik, A.: Creating a general russian sentiment lexicon. In: Proceedings of Language Resources and Evaluation Conference LREC-2016 (2016)

22. Lyashevskaya, O.N., Sharoff, C.A.: Chastotnyj slovar' sovremennogo russkogo yazyka (na materialah Nacional'nogo korpusa russkogo yazyka). Azbukovnik, M. (2009). (in Russian)

23. Koper, M., Im Walde, S.S.: Automatically generated affective norms of abstractness, arousal, imageability and valence for 350000 German lemmas. In: LREC 2016 — Proceedings of the 10th International Conference on Language Resources and Evaluation, pp. 2595–2598 (2016)

24. Moors, A., et al.: Norms of valence, arousal, dominance, and age of acquisition for 4,300 Dutch words. Behav. Res. Methods **45**(1), 169–177 (2012). https://doi.org/10.3758/s13428-012-0243-8

25. Osgood, C.E., Suci, G., Tannenbaum, P.: The Measurement of Meaning. University of Illinois Press, Urbana, IL (1957)

26. Russell, J.A.: Core affect and the psychological construction of emotion. Psychol. Rev. **110**(1), 145–172 (2003)

27. Recchia, G., Louwerse, M.M.: Reproducing affective norms with lexical co-occurrence statistics: predicting valence, arousal, and dominance. Q. J. Exp. Psychol. **68**(8), 1584–1598 (2015)

28. Saif, M.M.: Obtaining reliable human ratings of valence, arousal, and dominance for 20,000 English words. In: Proceedings of the 56th Annual Meeting of the Association for Computational Linguistics, pp. 174–184 (2018)

29. Sedoc, J., Preotiuc-Pietro, D., Ungar, L.: Predicting emotional word ratings using distributional representations and signed clustering. In: Proceedings of the 15th Conference of the European Chapter of the Association for Computational Linguistics, vol. 2, pp. 564–571 (2017)

30. Smetanin, S.: The applications of sentiment analysis for russian language texts: current challenges and future perspectives. IEEE Access **8**, 110693–110719 (2020). https://doi.org/10.1109/ACCESS.2020.3002215

31. Söderholm, C., Häyry, E., Laine, M., Karrasch, M.: Valence and arousal ratings for 420 Finnish nouns by age and gender. PLoS ONE **8**(8), e72859 (2013)

32. Solovyev, V., Ivanov, V.: Dictionary-based problem phrase extraction from user reviews. In: Sojka, P., Horák, A., Kopeček, I., Pala, K. (eds.) TSD 2014. LNCS (LNAI), vol. 8655, pp. 225–232. Springer, Cham (2014). https://doi.org/10.1007/978-3-319-10816-2_28

33. Solovyev, V., Ivanov, V.: Automated compilation of a corpus-based dictionary and computing concreteness ratings of Russian. In: Karpov, A., Potapova, R. (eds.) SPECOM 2020. LNCS (LNAI), vol. 12335, pp. 554–561. Springer, Cham (2020). https://doi.org/10.1007/978-3-030-60276-5_53

34. Solovyev, V.D., Volskaya, Y.A., Andreeva, M.I., Zaikin, A.A.: Russian dictionary with concreteness/abstractness ratings. Russ. J. Linguist. **26**(2), 515–549 (2022). https://doi.org/10.22363/2687-0088-29475

35. Stadthagen-Gonzalez, H., Imbault, C., Pérez Sánchez, M.A., Brysbaert, M.: Norms of valence and arousal for 14,031 Spanish words. Behav. Res. Methods **49**(1), 111–123 (2016). https://doi.org/10.3758/s13428-015-0700-2

36. Vo, M., Conrad, M., Kuchinke, L., Urton, K., Hofmann, M., Jacobs, A.: The berlin affective word list reloaded (bawl-r). Behav. Res. Methods **41**(2), 534–538 (2009)

37. Warriner, A.B., Kuperman, V., Brysbaert, M.: Norms of valence, arousal, and dominance for 13,915 English lemmas. Behav. Res. Methods **45**(4), 1191–1207 (2013). https://doi.org/10.3758/s13428-012-0314-x

38. Yao, Z., Wu, J., Zhang, Y., Wang, Z.: Norms of valence, arousal, concreteness, familiarity, imageability, and context availability for 1,100 Chinese words. Behav. Res. Methods **49**(4), 1374–1385 (2016). https://doi.org/10.3758/s13428-016-0793-2

Effects of Depth of Field on Focus Using a Virtual Reality Escape Room

Nikolaos Tsiftsis, Konstantinos Moustakas$^{(\boxtimes)}$, and Nikolaos Fakotakis

Electrical and Computer Engineering Department, University of Patras, Patras, Greece
moustakas@upatras.gr

Abstract. Depth of Field (DOF) is an effect that can be found in every single optical camera. Nowadays DOF is a common effect even for virtual cameras and it is used for more realistic rendering. In this work, an Escape Room is constructed and it is equipped with a post-process DOF effect to help the players navigate through the game. The DOF is independent from the player's vision direction. It is designed to highlight the objects that are important to progress towards the end of the game and not the ones the player is looking at. It is desired to shift the attention of the user subconsciously and make him move more efficiently. If an object becomes important during the game it gets highlighted too and if one is no longer useful the DOF stops focusing on it. Finally, an experiment took place to test if the DOF is making the players navigate more effectively inside the game, and check for possible side effects, like frustration and motion sickness. The analysis results suggest that the DOF can be used as a hint system.

Keywords: Depth of field · Virtual reality · Immersive game · Escape Room

1 Introduction

Virtual reality applications are starting to be considered mainstream and they become more popular day by day. Many of these applications like [2], [18], [19], [16] and [1] have to manage the user's focus so they can be at their maximum potential. The DOF of the human eye is a function of optical parameters (pupil size, optical aberrations, etc.) but is also affected by retinal, neural and more complex psycho-physical factors [17]. It is accepted that the DOF does not depend exclusively on the optical parameters and it can be mimicked using maths and graphics. For cameras that can only focus on one object at a time, depth of field is the distance between the nearest and the farthest objects that are in acceptably sharp focus. Acceptably sharp focus is defined using a property called the circle of confusion. The depth of field can be determined by the focal length, aperture, distance to subject and the acceptable circle of confusion size. There are various techniques to simulate DOF. One of these was used on the Escape Room which was developed with Unity Engine. In the application

© Springer Nature Switzerland AG 2022
S. R. M. Prasanna et al. (Eds.): SPECOM 2022, LNAI 13721, pp. 665–675, 2022.
https://doi.org/10.1007/978-3-031-20980-2_56

the effect's main purpose is to shift the interest of the users wherever the game requires for its completion, without them noticing the help.

2 Related Work

2.1 Escape Rooms

Observation is an important factor for problem solving inside an escape room. Previous research works suggest that an escape room can be used as an applied game in favor of training and education [11] [6]. This is the reason why it was decided to use one as DOF tester. The first part of the project is the game development. Ideas were inspired from other escape rooms and got enriched. The present escape room has no educational character but is a tool used to prove that depth of field can redirect the user's attention.

2.2 Motion Sickness

A major side effect of virtual reality application is motion sickness. [9] It is proven that when the virtual environment is not rotating according to our head's rotation we develop nausea. To avoid this, users are advised to use actual head rotation as much as possible and use controller joystick (right controller's joystick can be used to rotate around yourself) only when necessary. Another important factor, that causes motion sickness, is the speed of movement and rotation, which was taken into consideration during the game development.

2.3 Depth of Field Usage in Virtual Reality Applications

DOF is used for Virtual Reality applications in previous works. Its main goal is a more realistic graphic environment and therefore bigger immersion. [14] Record shows that DOF is not enjoyable from all the players and it decreases accuracy. Therefore no task that have to do with aiming were included. We understand that DOF can be used alongside other post-process effects to have a more realistic and better depth precise image [8] but that is not the direction that our work aims. We decided to have a different approach and use it as a tool to give hints for better and more effective navigation. The hint should not be obvious to the user but subconsciously manipulate his vision direction and object of interest. A similar approach can be found on prior research, [3] it experiment with different kind of image modulations to draw the visual attention of the observer. Even though the techniques used differ from the DOF there is a lot of overlapped space and useful information. Subtle gaze direction study was extended to immersive environments and [12] suggest that gaze guidance can be achieved.

2.4 Questionnaire

The questionnaire, that is created, has its core based on already existing ones. Most of the questions are inspired from other papers [15] [22] [4] and are slightly altered wherever it is needed. Also, new questions are added for the evaluation of our hypothesis. It should not be ignored that during the evaluation the learning curve, inside virtual environments, of younger adults is significantly faster than the older ones [10].

2.5 Contribution

In summary, the work presented in this paper builds on previous research to explore how the depth of field effect in virtual reality applications can be related to user's in-app decisions. While earlier work is primarily focused on the creation of a more realistic vision, this project focuses on how the DOF affects the decisions of the user. This hypothesis is examined through a small scale experiment with user-testing inside an escape room game.

3 Methods

3.1 Game Development

Unity and the XR-Toolkit Asset were used to develop the escape room. The headset that was used for development and user testing is Oculus Quest. A 2 by 2 meters free space was available for the real life movement. The game development was not rushed since the game itself played a major role for the project. The physics were built to be as realistic as possible and the modeling targeted on real life objects. No sci-fi or futuristic concepts were used at all. After the rooms were designed, the creation of the storytelling followed. The series of events for the game's completion were set and the main objects of each event were chosen. The primary objects were pointed by the DOF. When an event occurred, its main objects went back to being unfocused, and the focus was set on the items of the next desired event. To trigger an event information from the previous ones is needed, but sometimes out of the box thinking or luck can help skip some minor events. The escape room is designed with dimensions close to 5 by 5 meters. Therefore, regardless of the position of the player, for most of the time it is possible to look at the focused objects. The virtual rooms are bigger than the given real life free space, so players have to use a joystick from the controllers to move around the room. In-game movement not corresponding to real-life movement along with the realistic environment added some undesired nausea, but it could not be avoided. The length of the game was taken into consideration because the longer the game goes the intenser the motion sickness becomes. [9] It is important to eliminate other nausea factors as much as possible due to the fact that they add noise to the measurements of the unwanted dizziness of the DOF.

The main part of the game is divided into two Rooms. The necessity of the two rooms derives from the better-player factor. No matter the help you get, someone who is better at the game will be faster. Therefore it is important to be able to compare the results of every person with himself. That is the reason why most players played only one of the rooms with the DOF active. This way the time needed to accomplish the room with the DOF enabled can be compared with the total game length.

A training room was developed so the player would get comfortable with the mechanics of the game before he moved on to the actual game. The importance of the training room emerges from the learning factor. The fact that some users learn faster than others would affect the time measurements, which is undesired. Training contains an example for every kind of interaction you might come across during the game. Also, it is necessary for anyone inexperienced with virtual reality headsets to get familiar with the unique feeling of movement inside the virtual reality [7].

In order to analyze the impact of the DOF, an experiment was carried out with 35 participants. After the game was finished, the players answered the questionnaire. Most of the attention was given to the time the players needed to finish the game. Motion sickness after using the virtual reality devices and if the DOF was noticed during the game were also taken into consideration. The results suggested that the DOF helped the users find the solution path, with little to no side effects.

3.2   Depth of Field Construction

After the Escape Room was complete the construction of the DOF effect followed. Unity's Universal Render Pipeline has a Post-Process component. The Post-Process at the camera component was enabled and the right Volume Mask was selected. A volume at the correct layer (the same with the Volume Mask) was created and a Depth of Field override was added. The parameters were adjusted to get the desired result. Then the depth of the objects of interest had to be chosen. This created a problem because the depth could not be changed dynamically according to the position of one object due to two reasons. First, there were more than one objects of interest and secondly if the objects were not close the right effect could not be acquired by choosing any depth between theirs. One solution was to change the design to always have a single object of interest but this would decrease the number of cases the effect could be used on and it also had some undesired effects. The most serious was that if the object was too close or too far away from the Headset-Camera the blur effect would become extremely strong. To avoid these problems a multi-camera solution was adopted. One camera renders perfectly the focused objects and the other render the rest with a slight out of focus filter. The technique that was used for the DOF is the built-in post-process volume override from the Universal Render Pipeline of Unity Engine. The properties that we gave are Mode:Bokeh, Focus Distance:1, Focal Length:17 , Aperture:1.1, Blade Count:5, Blade Curvature:1 and Blade Rotation:0. The Bokeh Depth of Field mode closely imitates the effect of a real-life camera. For this reason, the settings are based on real-life camera settings, and offer a number of properties to adjust the diaphragm blades on the camera.

4   Experiment

4.1   Alpha Testing

First of all the game quality had to be improved [20]. When the game was ready to be played, some people were needed in order to test the game for major

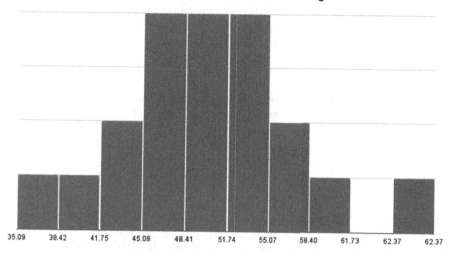

Fig. 1. Time percentage histogram.

issues. The target was to gain some feedback from the first few testers and improve the mechanics of the game. Also its difficulty was adjusted in order to have the time that it required to be completed within 25 minutes duration. This phase was important due to the fact that the possibility of errors and bugs was decreased for the Beta Testing and the measurements. Even though it is almost impossible to create a bugless game, some minor graphic glitches or other minor unintentional behaviour will not impact the measurements if they do not disturb or delay the player.

4.2   Questionnaire Construction

Before getting to the actual testing it was important to have a solid questionnaire that would provide us with all the information that would be needed later. The first section of the questionnaire was filled out by us and contained the time measurements and details about which rooms had the DOF effect. The second section was filled out by the participants. They were asked about their Virtual Reality experience in total and their thoughts on it. Also in this section some data were gathered about the DOF effect and the possible side effects [15].

4.3   Beta Testing

During the Beta Testing people were invited to play the game. The participants were equally distributed between males and females. The age varied from 18 to 30 years old. After they played a sort training(each person stayed at the training room as long as they needed to get used to the controls), they proceeded to the two main rooms of the Escape Room. They played both, none or one of the

Rooms with the DOF effect enabled. Total and separate times for each room were measured. After the completion of the game they were asked to answer the questionnaire. To be sure that no bug would affect the measurements the progress of the players was being monitored during the game and if a serious bug occurred the results were not kept but fortunately no such event took place.

Experiment Precautions. Before any player testing, the experiment was approved by the ethics committee. There were no personal data collected at all. Additionally every single step of the process was executed with respect to the hygiene measures and suggestions of the World Organization of Health.

5 Results

5.1 Effectiveness Improvement

One of the most important questions is which room the participants found easier. For the Group-A of the participants the DOF effect was used in either both rooms or none of them. In all of the answers the first room was chosen as easier. We knew in advance that the first room was easier due to the design and users of Group-A confirmed it. This means that from an objective point of view the first one was easier. The Group-B of the participants, that had the DOF effect enabled at the first room and disabled at the second, followed the objective opinion and answered that the first room was easier with only a single exception. The most of the Group-C participants, that had the DOF effect enabled at the second room and disabled at the first disagreed to the objective opinion and answered that the second room was easier. So Group-C deviated from the popular and more objective opinion on a high percentage of 70%. The pattern was recognised and it suggested that the DOF made the riddles simpler and the solution path more clear on the room that it was enabled.

The time that players needed to complete the game varied from 11 minutes and 4 s to 23 minutes and 14 s. Taking into consideration only the participants that had the DOF effect enabled at one of the rooms (Group-B and Group-C) it is easy to notice that the room with the DOF effect enabled was the quickest for the vast majority, regardless of it being room one or two. The percentage-A comes from the time that the first room needed to be completed divided by the total time (as total time we refer to the sum of the time of the first and the second room together). This percentage was selected for various tests due to the fact that it is free of the better-player factor and also it provides the opportunity to compare two measurements no matter their difference in time length. When the participants get sorted by ascending order on the percentage-A , it is obvious that the result is also sorted by group by its own. So a clear link can be seen between the 2 variables. This link suggests that if the DOF effect is enabled only in one room, a smaller percentage of the total game time is needed compared to the same percentage if DOF effect was enabled on the other room. It is possible that in larger samples the separation will not be 100 percent clear and a small mix might appear in the middle of the sorted data.

While observing the histogram of the percentage-A (It is already declared where the percentage-A refers to) it can be noticed that the distribution is approaching the normal distribution. Running the data trough SPSS software statistics that support our previous observation can be obtained. A normalized distribution is assumed and this way means of Percentage-A can be compare using as separation variable the Group. Using a T-test a p value of 0.76 is given and also a clear deference between the 2 means with 44.99% for Group-B and 55.16% for Group-C. The data were also clustered with K-means algorithm into 2 clusters using as our variable the Percentage-A. The second cluster contained every single Group-C participant and 2 Group-B participants while the first one contained the rest of the Group-B participants. Some assumptions were made to run the tests but the results were clear and therefore trustworthy [5]. For the statistical review the Group-A was completely ignored because it contained users that played the whole game with the effect either ON or OFF and there were no switching between them.

5.2   Side Effects

Almost every single user that played at least one room with DOF active noticed a "blur" effect with a single exception. The DOF caused some frustration to the players but its levels remained around the low value 3. The scale was from 1-"Almost Unnoticed" to 9-"Disturbing" and the higher value, that was acquired as an answer, was 6. Even though the frustration levels were expected to be someway linked with the motion sickness the results showed no such relationship. Motion sickness stayed at very low levels and peaked at value 1. The scale was from 1-"Unnoticed" to 9-"Too Heavy Dizziness". Only one participant deviated from the norm and experienced intense dizziness. As a result she did not manage to finish the game. She mentioned that the headset could not fit well at her head and we suppose that this was the reason of the motion sickness.

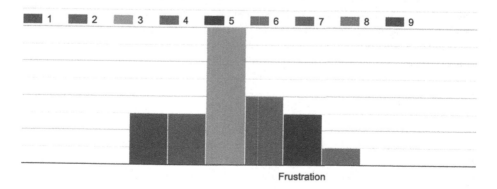

Fig. 2. Frustration level.

(Her times and some of the questionnaire answers could not be included in the final analysis). Some of the users believed that the "blur" was disturbing but a pretty small amount of motion sickness was noticed, which suggests that DOF did not increase it or at least not for a noticeable amount. Therefore the disturbance mentioned above possibly refers to a more aesthetic point of view.

6   Discussion

6.1   Limitation

Depth of Field Intensity. The goal was to test different intensities but the number of participants did not make this possible. During the experiment 3 participants became aware of the effect and used it as a game mechanic. They were scanning the room for "high quality" objects and after spotting them they used them without any critical thinking. This way the DOF was not a subconscious hint but an obvious way to "cheat" and find the solution. Although their times and answers agreed with the desired results, these participants were not taken into consideration for the analysis. If there were more than one intensities the perfect intensity could be found that would provide a helping effect without the previously mentioned "cheating" opportunity. The idea of a growing intensity as long as the user made no progress with a top limit that would reset after any progress would also be an interesting test case but due to the large amount of participants it requires to check its effectiveness there was no capability to run it.

Game Development. Unfortunately there was a containment to only two rooms in order not to prolong the game. Maybe more rooms could give us some information about the virtual environment where the DOF have the biggest impact and the ones that affect the least. Already it was noticed that the second room needed a sharper DOF effect to make the eye sight similar to the first one. Eye tracking is an addition that could offer a lot to the experiment, but hardware limitation did not make that possible. Eye tracking would provide an even better idea about the desired effect. The hypothesis was that DOF effect could draw the visual attention of the user, but the escape room's test measurements inform us about actions and not about vision direction. So the eye tracking would present useful data for analysis and new concepts of testing.

6.2   Observations

Linear Solution. During the experiment the participants were being watched for safety reasons but also to collect some data through observation. The DOF effect pushed the players towards more linear solutions. The DOF helped players go through the events with the same order they were designed to. Even though some minor events could be skipped because they were not necessary (they were only providing information in order to help the player complete the main events), they could be triggered later. As a result some players would get a little confused if they received information about an accomplished mission and would waste time on objects that had no further use. So, following the designed solution path may not be obligatory but it certainly is useful.

Realism and Aesthetics. Despite the fact that the DOF usually makes the game more realistic [13], [21] this effect was not achieved. The way our approach used the DOF did not contribute to the realism of the game and probably worked the other way around. The constant "blur" effect on the most of the objects downgraded the image quality therefore it made the scenes less beautiful and less attractive.

6.3 Future Work

The most of the participants had no previous Virtual Reality experience. Despite their lack of previous experience in the small period of 20-30 minutes that they used the training room and played the Escape Room they got pretty excited. In addition some of them believe that they developed the following skills:

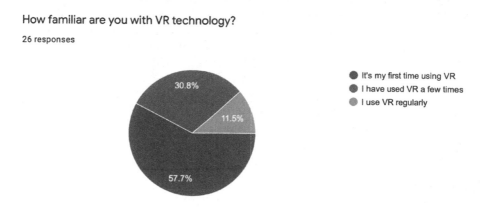

Fig. 3. The Chart represents the familiarity of participants with the Virtual Reality Technology.

Moreover they were positive that virtual reality technology can be used for professional training. The positive attitude towards the virtual technology opens new possibilities at training. it offers the opportunity to inexperienced staff and amateurs to participate in tasks that may be dangerous or too expensive to risk trying in real life. Especially if the task is standardized the recreation on a virtual environment is usually pretty simple. Even though access could be given by many different types of applications , Virtual Reality may be the most interactive and fun way. Adding a DOF effect to the equation can improve the speed and the effectiveness of the training. It is important to take into account that some people are more and some less sensitive to motion sickness.

Do you believe you developed some of the following skills?

15 responses

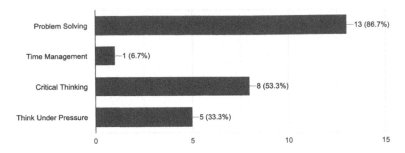

Fig. 4. The percentages does not include the 11 empty responses that had none of the skills checked.

7   Conclusion

After the analysis of the experiment we strongly believe that Depth of Field can be used as a hint assist. Further experiments are needed to verify our results. Despite the amount of participants, the results are convincing and go along our hypothesis. No matter the type of the application (educational,professional or entertainment), if the user needs to navigate through space or find an observation based solution, this depth of field effect approach can assist. All the virtual environments were indoor, so we do not have knowledge about larger scale space.

Conflict of Interest. The authors declare that the research was conducted in the absence of any commercial or financial relationships that could be construed as a potential conflict of interest.

References

1. Abdul Rahim, E., et al.: A desktop virtual reality application for chemical and process engineering education. In: Proceedings of the 24th Australian Computer-Human Interaction Conference, pp. 1–8 (2012)
2. Argyropoulos, S., et al.: Multimodal user interface for the communication of the disabled. J. Multimodal User Interfaces **2**(2), 105–116 (2008)
3. Bailey, R., McNamara, A., Sudarsanam, N., Grimm, C.: Subtle gaze direction. ACM Trans. Graph. (TOG) **28**(4), 1–14 (2009)
4. Beck, D.: Augmented and virtual reality in education: immersive learning research. J. Educ. Comput. Res. **57**(7), 1619–1625 (2019)
5. Boneau, C.A.: The effects of violations of assumptions underlying the t test. Psychol. Bull. **57**(1), 49 (1960)
6. Brown, N., Darby, W., Coronel, H.: An escape room as a simulation teaching strategy. Clin. Simul. Nurs. **30**, 1–6 (2019)
7. David, D., Arman, E., Chandra, N., Nadia, N., et al.: Development of escape room game using vr technology. Procedia Comput. Sci. **157**, 646–652 (2019)

8. Deering, M.: High resolution virtual reality. In: Proceedings of the 19th Annual Conference on Computer Graphics and Interactive Techniques, pp. 195–202 (1992)
9. Dichgans, J., Brandt, T.: Optokinetic motion sickness and pseudo-coriolis effects induced by moving visual stimuli. Acta Otolaryngol. **76**(1–6), 339–348 (1973)
10. Dobrowolski, P., Skorko, M., Pochwatko, G., Myśliwiec, M., Grabowski, A.: Immersive virtual reality and complex skill learning: transfer effects after training in younger and older adults. Front. Virtual Real. **1**, 40 (2020)
11. Eukel, H.N., Frenzel, J.E., Cernusca, D.: Educational gaming for pharmacy students-design and evaluation of a diabetes-themed escape room. Am. J. Pharm. Edu. **81**(7), 6265 (2017)
12. Grogorick, S., Stengel, M., Eisemann, E., Magnor, M.: Subtle gaze guidance for immersive environments. In: Proceedings of the ACM Symposium on Applied Perception, pp. 1–7 (2017)
13. Hillaire, S., Lecuyer, A., Cozot, R., Casiez, G.: Using an eye-tracking system to improve camera motions and depth-of-field blur effects in virtual environments. In: 2008 IEEE Virtual Reality Conference, pp. 47–50 (2008). https://doi.org/10.1109/VR.2008.4480749
14. Hillaire, S., Lécuyer, A., Cozot, R., Casiez, G.: Depth-of-field blur effects for first-person navigation in virtual environments. IEEE Comput. Graphics Appl. **28**(6), 47–55 (2008). https://doi.org/10.1109/MCG.2008.113
15. Kennedy, R.S., Lane, N.E., Berbaum, K.S., Lilienthal, M.G.: Simulator sickness questionnaire: an enhanced method for quantifying simulator sickness. Int. J. Aviat. Psychol. **3**(3), 203–220 (1993)
16. Li, L.: Application of virtual reality technology in clinical medicine. Am. J. Transl. Res. **9**(9), 3867 (2017)
17. Marcos, S., Moreno, E., Navarro, R.: The depth-of-field of the human eye from objective and subjective measurements. Vision. Res. **39**(12), 2039–2049 (1999)
18. Moustakas, K., Nikolakis, G., Tzovaras, D., Strintzis, M.G.: A geometry education haptic vr application based on a new virtual hand representation. In: IEEE Proceedings. VR 2005. Virtual Reality, 2005, pp. 249–252. IEEE (2005)
19. Moustakas, K., et al.: Masterpiece: physical interaction and 3d content-based search in vr applications. IEEE Multimedia **13**(3), 92–100 (2006)
20. Pendit, U.C., Mahzan, M.B., Fadzly Bin Mohd Basir, M.D., Bin Mahadzir, M., binti Musa, S.N.: Virtual reality escape room: the last breakout. In: 2017 2nd International Conference on Information Technology (INCIT), pp. 1–4 (2017). https://doi.org/10.1109/INCIT.2017.8257884
21. Rokita, P.: Generating depth of-field effects in virtual reality applications. IEEE Comput. Graphics Appl. **16**(2), 18–21 (1996)
22. Yeasmin, S., Albabtain, L.A.: Implementation of a virtual reality escape room game. In: 2020 IEEE Graphics and Multimedia (GAME), pp. 7–12 (2020). https://doi.org/10.1109/GAME50158.2020.9315039

Dynamics of Frequency Characteristics of Visually Evoked Potentials of Electroencephalography During the Work with Brain-Computer Interfaces

Yaroslav Turovsky⬤, Daniyar Wolf⬤, Roman Meshcheryakov⬤, and Anastasia Iskhakova⁽✉⁾ ⬤

V. A. Trapeznikov Institute of Control Sciences of Russian Academy of Sciences, Moscow, Russia
runsolar@mail.ru

Abstract. The paper verifies the hypothesis of time-dependent dynamics of steady-state visual evoked potentials during a short series of stimulations (15 s) simulating work with brain-computer interfaces. Using deep machine learning of a neural network with direct propagation and known methods of machine classification, the frequency characteristics of the visual evoked potentials of electroencephalography during the work with brain-computer interfaces are analyzed. It is shown that the temporal dynamics of steady-state visual evoked potentials even for such a short period of time can sufficiently change the parameters. It can potentially serve as an obstacle for work with this type of brain-computer interfaces for a number of users. The described approach allows us to confirm the hypothesis that over time the brain shows signs of fatigue, consisting in changes in the frequency-time characteristics of the registered signal. Thus, the human brain shows signs of fatigue during sessions of steady-state visual evoked potentials.

Keywords: Brain-computer interface · Steady-state visual evoked potentials · Machine learning · Electroencephalography

1 Introduction

Steady-state visual evoked potentials (SSVEPs) are signals generated by the brain in response to visual stimulation. When the retina is excited by flashes of frequency ranging from 3.5 to 75 Hz, the brain generates electrical activity with the frequency of the flashes [1, 2]. This potential has found wide application in the problems of development and further modification of the brain-computer interface (BCI) as one of well-detectable, reproducible, and in most cases not requiring special training of the operator phenomena of brain activity [3–5]. At the same time, as statistical material on the performance of this type of BCI is accumulated, it becomes obvious that the stability of this interface can vary quite widely even for the same user [6, 7]. One of the possible mechanisms of this variability is fatigue of the conductive and cortical parts of the visual analyzer, which

© Springer Nature Switzerland AG 2022
S. R. M. Prasanna et al. (Eds.): SPECOM 2022, LNAI 13721, pp. 676–687, 2022.
https://doi.org/10.1007/978-3-031-20980-2_57

may lead to a change in the character of signal generation serving as the basis for the BCI. In this case we mean fatigue of the central nervous system. Fatigue is understood here as a process of deterioration of excitability, conductivity, lability of nerve tissue, which occurs during prolonged work of the mentioned microsystems of neurons. The key differences from learning, which also occurs during work, are: total deterioration of the mentioned properties in all microsystems, as well as absence of local improvement of the mentioned properties.

Hypothesis. Presumably, during successive cycles of SSVEP generation over time, the brain shows signs of fatigue consisting in changes in the frequency-time characteristics of the registered signal, leading to the appearance of distinct patterns that differ from the photostimulation frequency.

2 Problematics of the Classification

For the study, a group of 30 subjects of both sexes aged 17 to 23 (12 women and 18 men) with no neurological or psychiatric pathology was formed. Before the experiment, the participants did not take any psychotropic drugs and had normal or corrected-to-normal vision. The electroencephalogram data were recorded with a Neuron-Spectr-4VP device (Neurosoft LLC, Russia) on O_1, O_2, O_z, P_3, P_4, and P_z leads with a sampling frequency of 5000 Hz, with the cutoff filter on and with the high- and low-frequency filter off [8, 9]. Photo stimulation was performed at the frequencies of 8 and 14 Hz. To collect and analyze the data we developed original software based on the SDK (software development kit) and API (application programming interface) provided by Neurosoft.

On the basis of the available input data set let us make an attempt to determine the dynamics of time-frequency characteristics of the SSVEP.

Let us assume that during the exposure to a stimulator of evoked potential lasting for 15 s three adaptation periods are formed for neuronal pools forming the SSVEP: during the first 5 s the human brain generates a stable pattern, which reflects in the absence of fatigue. And, conversely, suppose that during the last 5 s of the SSVEP session, there is adaptation, and possibly fatigue, of the groups of neurons forming the evoked potential, which may be reflected, for example, by less clear registration of the stimulation frequency, a decrease in the amplitude of the SSVEP, or the appearance of "parasitic" frequencies.

Figure 1 shows examples of electroencephalography (EEG) with SSVEP recorded from electrode "P_4" and "O_2". The graphs a, b, c, d show the changes in signal amplitudes over time (1 s.).

The results of the application of band-pass filtering with the Butterworth filter of the 6th order with passages of 2 (lowcut) and 35 (highcut) Hz, also do not give any obvious distinctive features when visually inspecting the signals [10].

Let us consider EEG with SSVEP in a time-frequency sweep, for example, for channels "P_4" and "O_2". (Fig. 2). For this purpose, we applied the short-time Fourier transform, pre-processing the signal with the above-mentioned Butterworth filter.

In graphs a, b, c and d (Fig. 2) we can observe the presence of the frequencies of the SSVEP. Also we can see that these frequencies are invariant over time. Since the

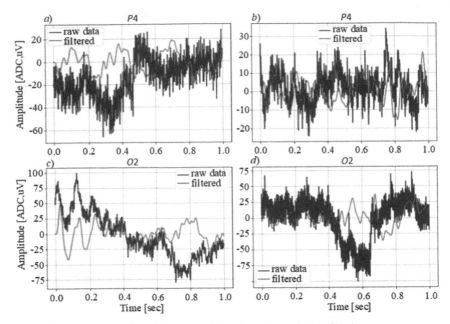

Fig. 1. Signals from the SSVEP before and after filtering.

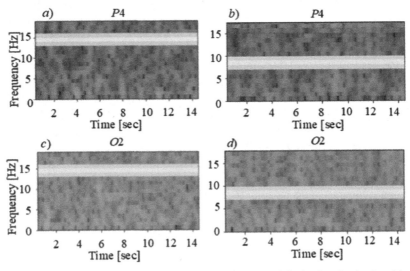

Fig. 2. Frequency spectrum with evoked steady-state potentials in the O_2 lead, with visual stimulation of 8 and 14 Hz – a and b, respectively.

pattern characteristic of the frequency-temporal restructuring estimated as fatigue is not known in advance, the amplitude power distribution on the frequency-time scale does not provide, as a first approximation, any information about the desired signal features. Let us search for possible fatigue patterns on the basis of machine learning.

Taking into account the stimulator frequency, let us group all signals from each test subject into the types: "O_1", "O_2", "O_z", "P_3", "P_4", "P_z".

As a result, taking into account the sampling rate of the signal, we obtain a matrix with dimension $N = 30 \times M = 75000 \times V = 6$ elements, where:

N – is the ordinal number of the subject (the total number of samples for a particular type of signal);

M – is the feature;

V – is the kind (type) of the signal.

If we select only the first and the last 25000 features, we can get two matrices containing information about signals for the first and the last 5 s.

However, this approach of data preparation for both machine learning and machine classification yields a very large vector of informative features – M, and a very small vector with samples for each signal (examples) – N. At a minimum, the high dimensionality of the features is associated with very high computational costs, and to a greater extent, a large number of trainable parameters can lead to a complex classification model which will have high variance and will not allow us to qualitatively identify the desired features.

Moreover, it is worth mentioning the individual psychophysical and psychoemotional features of each subject identified in a number of works [11–14], so there is no guarantee that the features are unambiguously separable in time for the entire group of subjects. In other words, someone's brain shows clear signs of fatigue already in the first seconds, and someone's much later, or signs may not show up at all at a given time of analysis.

To solve this problem, we applied deep machine learning to further machine classification based on classical methods [15].

3 Application of Deep Machine Learning to Compress Informative Features of Machine Classification

Let us make one more assumption: let us assume the same development of the patterns of SSVEP, in the DSP aspect, does not depend on the frequency of stimulation. In other words, the behavior of brain waves in the first 5 s of stimulation is different from the behavior of waves in the last 5 s. Thus, this allows us to abstract away from the stimulation frequency and focus on the appearance of possible fatigue patterns contained in the brain waves in its various zones.

Let us divide the first and the last 5 s of each signal into short time intervals of 0.2 s with an overlap of 0.1 s (50%) with the previous interval. This procedure does not differ from the usual procedure of signal preparation in the short-time Fourier transform. Taking into account the sampling rate of the initial signals, an interval of 0.2 s is comparable to a data array of 1024 elements, and each of the analysis epochs contains at least one period even for an oscillation evoked by low-frequency stimulation. Thus, from one subject, each signal yields 96 samples for the first and last 5 s. The total for each lead is 2880 samples. The first half of the samples will be classified as data that do not contain a sign of fatigue and the second half where the desired feature is present.

The result is a matrix with training data: $N = 2880 \times M = 1024 \times V = 6$.

To reduce the feature space M, we have developed a special encoder based on a deep neural network, which allows us to map the features with the dimension of 1024 elements into the features with the dimension of 24 elements. We have also estimated the relevance of the received features by means of a deep neural network in the part of the decoder which allows us to reconstruct the initial signal (see Fig. 3).

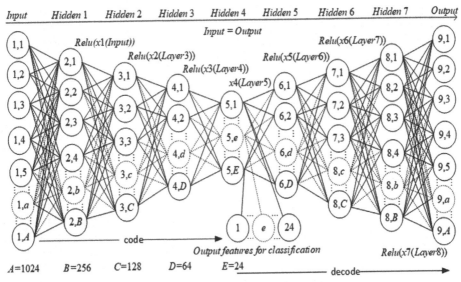

Fig. 3. Graph of a symmetric multilayered multi-adaptive feed-forward neuron providing the functions of an encoder and a decoder.

The architecture of the artificial neural network – "encoder-decoder" – is designed on the principle of an adversarial neural network and represents a symmetric multilayered multi-adaptive feed-forward neuron [16–18]. The task of deep machine learning is to match the input weighting coefficients of each neuron in such a way that the output signal approximates the input signal. The network consists of 9 layers of which 7 layers with perceptions are hidden (hidden1 – hidden7). The layers are multiply reduced to the 4th hidden layer (the 5th layer for the whole network) and also multiply increased towards the output layer, forming symmetric neural network architecture. Functionally, the left part of the network is the encoding part, and the right part is the decoding part. In the proposed architecture, the 4th hidden layer is the most interesting, because it is simultaneously an output for the encoder and an input for the decoder. Due to this fact, the neuron activation functions are not provided for this hidden layer. We will consider this layer of the network as non-core output features for classification.

Training of neuron weights is done by the backward-sweep method with the minimization of the network error distribution. The number of epochs for training is 800, and the batch selection from the general population is 64 samples.

As a result of deep machine learning, we have obtained a weight model of the artificial neural network which transforms the features from the space of 1024 output features for classification (in the initial sense, EEG signals with the duration of 0.2 s.) into the space of 24 features, with the further possibility of inverse transformation (restoration of the initial signal).

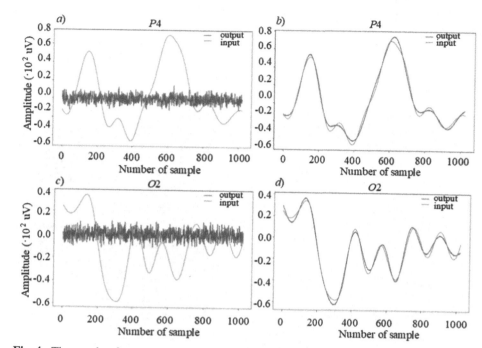

Fig. 4. The result of symmetric multilayered multi-adaptive neuron providing encoder and decoder functions for channels "P_4" and "O_2": before (*a, b*) and after deep machine learning (*c, d*).

Figure 4 shows the results of the proposed artificial neural network. When the network is not yet trained, there is random noise in the output (see Fig. 4a). After deep machine learning of the network, the output approximates the input (see Fig. 4b).

After running the data ($N = 2880 \times M = 1024 \times V = 6$) through the network, we received a machine classification dataset with the dimension of $N = 2880 \times M = 24 \times V = 6$.

At this stage, it is also not possible to give any interpretation to the resulting features, since the input of the 6th layer of the network is fed with encoded EEG values, with the specific layer coefficients. Otherwise, the signal recovery would not be possible.

4   Results of Machine Classification

Before performing machine classification, we evaluated for the presence of significant features in the resulting data set using a neural network. To evaluate the significant features, we used a random forest – the ensemble technique [19, 20]. Applying the random forest technique, we were able to estimate the importance of the features as an average reduction of "contamination" [20, 21] calculated from all decision trees in the forest. This allowed us to make no assumptions about whether or not the resulting data were linearly separable.

After training a forest of 500 trees on the resulting data set, we arranged 24 features in order of their relative importance (Fig. 5).

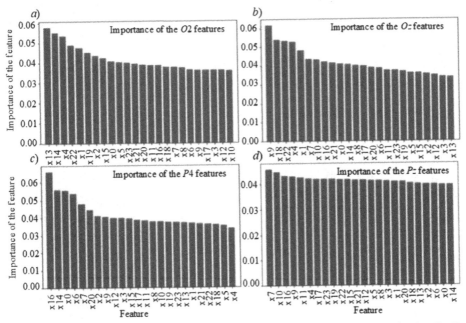

Fig. 5. Charts of the relative importance of the features in the SSVEP data set or the O_2, O_z, P_4, and P_z leads at 8 Hz stimulation.

Charts a, b, c in Fig. 5 clearly show some distinctive characteristics for some features of the leads: O_2, O_z, and P_4. It can be seen in chart d, that the significance of the features for the P_z lead does not differ significantly. A similar result was obtained for the O_1 and P_3 leads at stimulation at 8 Hz, and for the O_z and P_z leads at stimulation at 14 Hz. In these leads, the significance of the features has an almost equal distribution over the levels. This may serve as a marker that there are no differences between the signals as a result of machine classification for these regions.

It can be observed that for the selected group of subjects, the features x4 and x22 are present in the two leads O_2 and O_z, and the feature x16 is present in the leads P. Therefore, only these two features were used as an experiment for the leads O_2 and O_z, and for every other lead 4 of them were used.

For machine classification, we used the k-nearest neighbor algorithm [22]. We assigned the training samples for the first 5 s to the class "untired" – 0 (1440 samples), and the samples corresponding to the last 5 s to the class "tired" – 1 (the second half of N).

For the tests, 582 non-training samples were used (cross-validation was 20% of the training sample). Machine classification results for the test sample are shown in Tables 1, 2, 3, 4, 5, and 6.

Table 1. Results of machine classification of the first 5 s of encoded EEG with SSVEP using the k-means method. The stimulation frequency is 8 Hz.

Leads	Precision	Recall	f1-score	Support
O_1	0.53	0.52	0.52	289
O_2	0.62	0.64	0.63	285
O_z	0.63	0.71	0.67	303
P_3	0.50	0.51	0.51	290
P_4	0.65	0.74	0.70	290
P_z	0.50	0.62	0.56	293

Table 2. Results of machine classification of the last 5 s of encoded EEG with SSVEP using the k-means method. The stimulation frequency is 8 Hz.

Leads	Precision	Recall	f1-score	Support
O_1	0.55	0.54	0.54	293
O_2	0.64	0.62	0.63	297
O_z	0.64	0.55	0.59	279
P_3	0.50	0.48	0.49	292
P_4	0.71	0.61	0.65	292
P_z	0.50	0.37	0.43	289

Table 1 contains the estimates of the classifier's ability to distinguish the signal in the first 5 s of the SSVEP session from the last 5 s (8 Hz stimulation). Conversely, Table 2 shows the estimates distinguishing the last 5 s from the first. The estimation "precision" quantitatively indicates that. The estimation "recall" demonstrates how well the classification algorithm detects a series of the corresponding encoded EEG with SSVEP in general. The characteristic "f1-score" confirms the necessary average-harmonic balance between the estimations "precision" and "recall", especially since the classes are almost balanced. The parameter "support" indicates the number of test samples belonging to the first or second class when tested (in total, it is equal to 582). Table 3 indicates the overall recognition accuracy.

Table 3. Overall accuracy of the classification algorithm of the encoded EEG with SSVEP using the k-means method. The frequency of stimulation is 8 Hz.

Leads	Accuracy
O_1	0.53
O_2	0.63
O_z	0.63
P_3	0.50
P_4	0.68
P_z	0.50

The same types of estimates are given in Tables 4, 5 and 6, but for encoded EEG with SSVEP under stimulation of 14 Hz.

Table 4. Results of machine classification of the first 5 s of the encoded EEG with SSVEP using the k-means method. The stimulation frequency is 14 Hz.

Leads	Precision	Recall	f1-score	Support
O_1	0.59	0.62	0.60	289
O_2	0.58	0.58	0.58	283
O_z	0.55	0.54	0.55	292
P_3	0.69	0.59	0.63	283
P_4	0.67	0.61	0.64	289
P_z	0.56	0.55	0.56	296

Table 5. Results of machine classification of the last 5 s of encoded EEG with SSVEP using the k-means method. The stimulation frequency is 14 Hz.

Leads	Precision	Recall	f1-score	Support
O_1	0.60	0.58	0.59	293
O_2	0.60	0.60	0.60	299
O_z	0.55	0.56	0.55	290
P_3	0.66	0.75	0.70	299
P_4	0.65	0.70	0.67	293
P_z	0.54	0.55	0.55	286

The results in the tables show that in the total group of signals, there are signals that form a cluster between the first and last five seconds, and the probability of it is

Table 6. Overall accuracy of the classification algorithm of the encoded EEG with SSVEP using the k-means method. The frequency of stimulation is 14 Hz.

Leads	Accuracy
O_1	0.60
O_2	0.59
O_z	0.55
P_3	0.67
P_4	0.65
P_z	0.55

greater than 60%. Let us formulate a probabilistic answer to the hypothesis as follows: in 15-s SSVEP sessions the human brain exhibits changes in frequency-time patterns with a probability of more than 60%, which can be interpreted as signs of fatigue when working with BCI on SSVEP.

Also, from the obtained estimates we can assume that the human brain in the sessions of SSVEP is not subject to an unambiguous temporal rule of the occurrence of fatigue patterns on EEG leads. For example, fatigue may appear more pronounced in some brain areas in one session of SSVEP, and in the next session in other areas. This depends on the work of the group of brain neurons involved in the generation of evoked potential impulses in each particular case and under certain conditions. For example, for the P and P_z leads there are no distinctive features. Also, from the tables we can notice that at stimulation of 14 Hz, the differences between the first and the last 5 s are more pronounced. This may indicate that at 14 Hz stimulation, for the general group of subjects, the brain shows signs of fatigue faster than at 8 Hz.

5   Conclusion

The approach used in the article does not yield 99% accuracy in signal classification for determining human brain fatigue in the SSVEP sessions. Nevertheless, with a reasonably good probability, we can say that the approach described in the article allows us to confirm the initial hypothesis. In general, according to the results of our study, we can say that indeed in the process of SSVEP sessions the human brain shows signs of fatigue.

The model of the symmetric multilayered multi-adaptive feed-forward neuron providing functions of the encoder and decoder, proposed in the article, can find its application in solving problems related to the processing of EEG signals [23].

Acknowledgement. This work was supported by RFBR grant 19–29-01156 mk.

References

1. Tu, T., Xin, Y., Gao, X., Gao, S.: Chirp-modulated visual evoked potential as a generalization of steady state visual evoked potential. J. Neural Eng. **9**(1), 016008 (2012)

2. Kwak, N.S., Müller, K.R., Lee, S.W.: Toward exoskeleton control based on steady state visual evoked potentials. In: 2014 International Winter Workshop on Brain-Computer Interface (BCI), pp. 1–2. IEEE, Gangwon, Korea (South) (2014)

3. Balnytė, R., Ulozienė, I., Rastenytė, D., Vaitkus, A., Malcienė, L., Laučkaitė, K.: Diagnostic value of conventional visual evoked potentials applied to patients with multiple sclerosis. Medicina (Kaunas) **47**(5), 263–269 (2011)

4. Markand, O.: Visual evoked potentials. In: Clinical Evoked Potentials, pp. 83–137. Springer, Cham (2020).https://doi.org/10.1007/978-3-030-36955-2_3

5. Chaudhary, U., Birbaumer, N., Curado, M.R.: Brain-machine interface (BMI) in paralysis. Ann. Phys. Rehabil. Med. **58**(1), 9–13 (2015)

6. Dvoynikova, A., Verkholyak, O., Karpov, A.: Emotion recognition and sentiment analysis of extemporaneous speech transcriptions in Russian. In: Karpov, A., Potapova, R. (eds.) SPECOM 2020. LNCS (LNAI), vol. 12335, pp. 136–144. Springer, Cham (2020). https://doi.org/10.1007/978-3-030-60276-5_14

7. Dresvyanskiy, D., Minker, W., Karpov, A.: Deep learning based engagement recognition in highly imbalanced data. In: Karpov, A., Potapova, R. (eds.) SPECOM 2021. LNCS (LNAI), vol. 12997, pp. 166–178. Springer, Cham (2021). https://doi.org/10.1007/978-3-030-87802-3_16

8. NEURON-SPECTRUM-4/EPM 21-channel Upgradeable EEG System with EP Capabilities. https://neurosoft.com/en/catalog/eeg/neuron-spectrum-4epm

9. do Espírito-Santo, R.B., Dias, G.C.B., Bortoloti, R., Huziwara, E.M.: Effect of the number of training trials on the event-related potential correlates of equivalence relations. Learn. Behav. **48**, 221–233 (2020)

10. Mokhtar, S., Elmazeg, E.: Design and implementation of butterworth filter. Int. J. Innovative Res. Sci. Eng. Technol. **9**(9), 7975–7983 (2020)

11. Aminoff, M.J., Goodin, D.S.: Visual evoked potentials. J. Clin. Neurophysiol. Official Publ. Am. Electroencephalographic Soc. **11**(5), 493–499 (1994)

12. Taylor, M., McCulloch, D.: Visual evoked potentials in infants and children. J. Clin. Neurophysiol. Official Publ. Am. Electroencephalographic Soc. **9**, 357–372 (1992)

13. Liasis, A.: Visual evoked potentials. Acta Ophthalmol. **94**, S256 (2016)

14. Carter, J.: Visual evoked potentials. In: Clinical Neurophysiology, 4 edn., Contemporary Neurology Series, pp. 567–578. Oxford Academic, New York (2016)

15. Kwak, N.S., Müller, K.R., Lee, S.W.: A convolutional neural network for steady state visual evoked potential classification under ambulatory environment. PLoS ONE **12**(2), 1–20 (2017)

16. Nguyen, H., Bottone, S., Kim, K., Chiang, M., Poor, H.V.: Adversarial neural networks for error correcting codes. In: 2021 IEEE Global Communications Conference (GLOBECOM), 2021, pp. 1–6. IEEE, Madrid, Spain (2021)

17. Kose, U., Deperlioglu, O., Alzubi, J., Patrut, B.: Diagnosing Parkinson by using deep autoencoder neural network. In: Deep Learning for Medical Decision Support Systems. SCI, vol. 909, pp. 73–93. Springer, Singapore (2021). https://doi.org/10.1007/978-981-15-6325-6_5

18. Mirjalili, V., Raschka, S., Namboodiri, A., Ross, A.: Semi-adversarial networks: convolutional autoencoders for imparting privacy to face images. In: 2018 International Conference on Biometrics (ICB), pp. 82–89. IEEE, Gold Coast, QLD, Australia (2018)

19. Bicego, M., Escolano, F.: On learning random forests for random forest-clustering. In: 2020 25th International Conference on Pattern Recognition (ICPR), pp. 3451–3458. IEEE, Milan, Italy (2021)

20. Olson. M.: Essays on Random Forest Ensembles (PhD dissertation), p. 146 (2018)

21. Nayyar, A., Mahapatra, B.: Effective classification and handling of incoming data packets in mobile ad hoc networks (MANETs) using random forest ensemble technique (RF/ET). In: Sharma, N., Chakrabarti, A., Balas, V.E. (eds.) Data Management, Analytics and Innovation.

AISC, vol. 1016, pp. 431–444. Springer, Singapore (2020). https://doi.org/10.1007/978-981-13-9364-8_31

22. Fahim, A.: K and starting means for k-means algorithm. J. Comput. Sci. **55**, 101445 (2021)
23. Turovskiy, Y., Volf, D., Iskhakova, A., Iskhakov, A.: Neuro-computer interface control of cyber-physical systems. In: Jordan, V., Tarasov, I., Faerman, V. (eds.) HPCST 2021. CCIS, vol. 1526, pp. 338–353. Springer, Cham (2022). https://doi.org/10.1007/978-3-030-94141-3_27

Device Robust Acoustic Scene Classification Using Adaptive Noise Reduction and Convolutional Recurrent Attention Neural Network

Spoorthy Venkatesh$^{(\boxtimes)}$ ⓘ and Shashidhar G. Koolagudi

National Institute of Technology Karnataka, Surathkal, India
vspoorthy036@gmail.com, koolagudi@nitk.edu.in

Abstract. Acoustic Scene Classification (ASC) is the task of identifying a scene using sound cues and assigning a label to the identified scene. From the past two years, the datasets that are released for ASC consist of audio samples recorded with multiple devices bringing the problem closer to real-world scenarios. Therefore, we aim to develop a device robust ASC model consisting of audio samples recorded with three different devices. The dataset considered is DCASE 2019 ASC task 1a which consists of the primary recording device (Device A) and two mobile devices (Device B and C). This work introduces the Adaptive Noise Reduction (ANR) technique to reduce the device distortion present in devices B and C audio samples. Spectrograms are extracted from all audio samples and normalized to remove biased values in the input signal. The normalized features are fed to Light weight Convolutional Recurrent Attention Neural Network to perform ASC. The key contributions of this work are the reduction of device distortion in mismatched devices and the introduction of an attention layer in the Convolutional Recurrent Neural Network (CRANN). The results achieved from the proposed method have shown a considerable improvement in the accuracy related to mismatched device ASC.

Keywords: Device robust acoustic scene classification (ASC) · Device distortion · Adaptive noise reduction · Light weight convolutional recurrent attention neural network

1 Introduction

The task of characterizing environmental sounds as acoustic scenes by assigning a label based on the situation or location such as airport, metro, etc., is known as Acoustic Scene Classification (ASC) [2]. Several applications of ASC can be used in real-world issues like context-awareness in mobile devices [8], acoustic surveillance [18], smart homes [20], music genre classification [21], etc. Classifying acoustic scenes based on the sound events present in the scene can be an intriguing problem as the audio consists of a lot of information and rich content

© Springer Nature Switzerland AG 2022
S. R. M. Prasanna et al. (Eds.): SPECOM 2022, LNAI 13721, pp. 688–699, 2022.
https://doi.org/10.1007/978-3-031-20980-2_58

making the accurate scene prediction more difficult [7]. In the recent decade, the interest for ASC has increased, and benchmark data is made available by the Detection and Classification of Acoustic Scenes and Events (DCASE) challenge to encourage researchers to perform research in sound scene recognition and analyses [6].

In the recent trends, device robust ASC is more in focus. The most common challenge in the ASC is the mismatch in the recording devices. DCASE 2019 has released a dataset consisting of audio samples recorded from three different devices, and the focus is to draw attention to device invariant ASC without leveraging any device information. However, a huge data skewness was observed in the number of samples recorded with device A (main recording device), devices B and C. Also, another device D was included for the evaluation dataset, which made the problem similar to real-world conditions. Many solutions were proposed to deal with the issue of improving robustness in the ASC task. Most of the methods included ensemble models such as random forests [16], weight averaging ensemble methods [4], ensemble selection [12], averaging methods [5], etc. However, these solutions are computationally intensive and result in huge memory consumption. These models were trained on multiple features such as Constant Q Transform [14], mel-spectrograms with component separation [15], log-mel features [12], and so on.

1.1 Device Distortion Analysis

In the DCASE 2019 Task 1a [10] dataset, the acoustic scenes are recorded through high-quality recording devices, smartphones, and cameras. The audio signal consists of an original signal $s(n)$ which is convolved with an impulse response (IR) $h(n)$. The device distortion is present in the $h(n)$ of the signal [19]. The presence of device distortion in the audio signal can be illustrated using spectral analysis of the signal in the frequency domain. Therefore, audio samples of an acoustic scene 'Tram' are chosen from the dataset from three recording devices. The samples picked are recorded from the same location, 'Stockholm'. Three different spectral analysis characteristics are extracted from audio samples, namely, spectral flux, spectral rolloff, and spectral entropy. They are shown in Fig. 1 for perception.

The spectral flux is the measure of the variability of the spectrogram over time [17]. In Fig. 1(a), it can be observed that the flux of devices B and C has higher peaks than that of device A. The spectral rolloff point gives the audio signal bandwidth by determining the frequency bin in which a certain percentage of the overall energy is present [17]. The bandwidth of device B is higher as compared to devices A and C, as seen in Fig. 1(b). The final measure used is spectral entropy which measures the peakiness of the spectrogram or also known as the measure of disorder [11]. From Fig. 1(c), the entropy is very high for devices B and C. This measure gives a clear understanding of the distortion present in the audio signal, which is one of the significant factors affecting the performance of the ASC system.

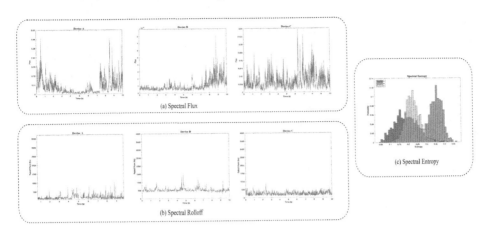

Fig. 1. Spectral feature analysis for multiple devices of DCASE 2019 Task 1a dataset.

In this work, the device distortion of audio samples is minimized by preprocessing the samples before performing the feature extraction step. Here, the audio samples recorded by mobile devices consist of higher distortion, and also the quality of the audio samples is low. Therefore, the device distortion is minimized by applying an adaptive noise reduction technique on these samples. Further, the feature extraction is carried out where log-Mel band energies are extracted from the preprocessed audio samples. In order to discard any more variability in the features, they are normalized. This technique helps in getting rid of any biased values in the spectrogram. The next step is to perform ASC, where the normalized features are fed to the Convolutional Recurrent Attention Neural Network (CRANN) and the newly introduced light-weight CRANN. In the light-weight CRANN architecture, the number of operations is reduced by making the network less complex. In the CRANN architecture, the attention layer is introduced to the Convolutional Recurrent Neural Network (CRNN) to enforce more weightage on misclassified samples.

Rest of the paper is organized as follows: Sect. 2 describes the working of the proposed method for device robust ASC. The experimental details are provided in Sect. 3. The performance achieved from the proposed ASC system is presented in Sect. 4. Finally, the summarization of the work is presented in Sect. 5.

2   Proposed Method

Block diagram of a device robust ASC system is shown in Fig. 2. The audio recordings can be recorded from any recording device, such as, high-quality recording devices, smartphones, cameras, etc. However, the recording quality can vary from device to device. In high-quality recording devices, noise cancellation techniques are in built in the devices, but that is not the case for smartphones or cameras. Hence, distortion may be present in the audio samples affecting the system's performance. Therefore, the input audio samples recorded with different devices need to be preprocessed to minimize device distortion. In this work, an adaptive noise reduction technique is applied to the audio samples before extracting features. In this technique, a High Pass Filter (HPF) is applied to the signal to attenuate the lower frequency components such as wind or idle noise. The additional noise that is not removed in the recording stage is discarded. In all the acoustic scenes, the wind and idle noise can be considered as the additional noises and can be attenuated without discarding the useful information in the scene. Similarly, the high-frequency components that are generated due to certain mics need to be attenuated. This is performed using the Infinite Impulse Response (IIR) Filter. The last step is to characterize the type of audio recording we need to achieve. This is performed using Dynamic Range Control (DRC). In DRC, the input signal is modified at four levels: makeup gain, compressor, noise gate, and limiter. Makeup gain is applied for middle-level signals to achieve a total gain. The compressor is used to attenuate the higher-level signals or to lessen the amplification of the signal. The noise gate is used when the signal is very low. The limiter is used only in a few cases where the compressor cannot catch some specific audio. These four components help remove noise and distortion in the audio samples of devices B and C in the DCASE 2019 Task 1a dataset.

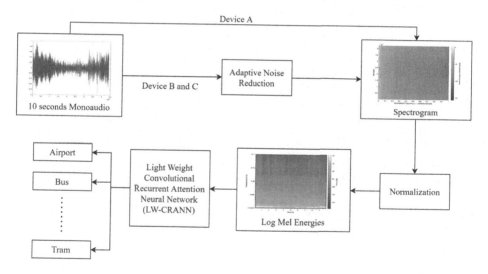

Fig. 2. Block diagram of the proposed device robust ASC system.

Once the audio samples are preprocessed, the spectrogram features are extracted. In order to avoid the biased values in the spectrogram, the zero mean and unit variance normalization method is applied to the spectrograms. For the classification of the acoustic scenes, light-weight Convolutional Recurrent Attention Neural Network (LW-CRANN) is proposed and shown in Fig. 3. The architecture is made light-weight/low complex to minimize the number of additions and multiplications in the computation of weights. The proposed method is efficient in terms of computation cost as the number of computations is reduced by 1/3 as compared to conventional CRANN. This is achieved by replacing the convolutions in the network with depthwise separable convolutions. Also, the addition of the attention layer on the architecture gives global attention to the features, and the information that is usually not given priority is also utilized. This reduces information loss in the network.

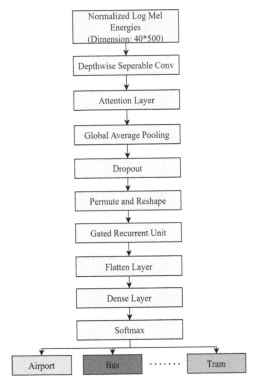

Fig. 3. Light weight Convolutional Recurrent Attention Neural Network (LW-CRANN) architecture.

The attention mechanism is added in the conventional CRNN architecture to handle the input with long and/or complex sequences. For cases with issues in dimensionality of the representation would be forced to be same for the shorter sequences [1]. In cases of acoustic scenes, the event activity in the audio lasts for only shorter span of time. Therefore, to capture this information adding attention layer to the network is advantageous. In this work, an attention layer is introduced in the CRANN architecture. The input fed to the CRANN is Normalized log Mel energies with a dimension of 40 * 500. The first layer of the network is depthwise convolution network. This layer learns the spatial information of the input features and the depthwise separable convolution layer uses less number of computations as compared to conventional convolution layer. This is followed by the attention layer. The attention layer uses a dropout score value of 0.2, i.e., 20% of the units of randomly dropped while training as it reduces the overfitting. The features that are learnt by the convolution layers are fed to embed the sequences and followed by the attention layer. The next layer is the pooling layer. The global average pooling layer captures the global information of the input feature as opposed to other pooling layers which pools small section of the input. The next layer includes the reshaping of the feature to feed into Gated Recurrent Layer (GRU). The features resulted by the GRU layer are flattened and fed to dense layer with softmax activation function for final acoustic scene label.

3   Experiments

3.1   Dataset Description

The dataset considered to evaluate the proposed device robust ASC system is DCASE 2019 Acoustic Scene Classification Task1a [10]. The audio samples in the dataset are recorded with three different devices. The dataset consists of a total of 10 acoustic scenes, and the data recordings from different devices are captured simultaneously. The devices the samples are recorded in are Soundman OKM II Klassik/studio A3, electret binaural microphone and a Zoom F8 audio recorder (Device A), Samsung Galaxy S7 (Device B), and iPhone SE (Device C). All the audio samples were recorded using a mono-aural channel set to a 48kHz sampling rate and 24-bit resolution. Device A consists of 40 h of data, and the rest of the devices are in smaller sizes. The number of audio samples present for each device is given in Table 1. The training and testing set consist of different audio samples and testing set's data are unseen data samples.

Table 1. Number of audio samples for three devices for train and test sets.

Device	Device A	Device B	Device C
Training	9185	540	540
Testing	4185	540	540

3.2   Signal Preprocessing

The audio samples in the dataset are of mismatched devices; the samples recorded from mobile devices (Devices B and C) can consist of device distortion. This may, in turn, lead to less performance for the ASC. Therefore, without discarding the necessary information from the signal, the distortion from the signal needs to be eliminated. This is performed using adaptive noise reduction, which is applied on audio samples of devices B and C. The attenuation of idle noise and distortion is performed by High Pass Filter (HPF) and an Infinite Impulse Response (IIR) filter. These filters remove the lower frequency components in the signal, such as wind, and the cutoff frequency is set 50 Hz. IIR is necessary because certain mics consist of high peak level frequencies that need to be attenuated to get a lesser distorted signal.

3.3   Feature Extraction

After the signal preprocessing step, feature extraction is performed on the audio samples. The audio segments are 10 s in length. Spectrogram features are extracted where the Short-Time Fourier Transform (STFT) uses the window function "hanning". The window length is set to 2048, and the hop size is set to 512. To increase the frequency resolution, the hop size is set smaller [13]. After extracting spectrogram features from the audio segments, the features are processed in the log-mel domain in 40 mel filters. Followed by this, the log-mel features are normalized using the zero mean and unit variance normalization technique in order to eliminate biased values in the feature matrix.

3.4   Neural Network Configuration

In this work, the ASC is performed with four different neural network architectures, namely, CRNN, Light-weight Convolutional Recurrent Neural Network (LW-CRNN), Convolutional Recurrent Attention Neural Network (CRANN), and Light-weight Convolutional Recurrent Attention Neural Network (LW-CRA NN). All the architectures are implemented using Keras 2.2.4 and Tensorflow 1.13.1 libraries in python. The common parameters set for these architectures are as follows: The learning rate of the Adam optimizer is set to 0.001, the loss function used for multi-class classification is Multi-Class Cross-Entropy Loss, the number of epochs the models are trained is set to 200 with early stopping criterion if the validation loss does not improve after ten epochs, and the batch size the samples are trained is set to 64. The CRNN architecture consists of both convolutional and recurrent layers, which capture the input's spatial and temporal information. In the LW-CRNN, the CRNN model is made low complex by replacing the convolution layers with depthwise separable convolution layers. In CRANN, the CRNN network is added with the Global Attention Layer. Like LW-CRNN, the model is made light-weight by replacing convolution layers with depthwise separable convolutions in LW-CRANN. All the models consist of Gated Recurrent Unit (GRU) layer after convolution layers. The last layers are dense.

4   Results and Discussion

The results achieved for the proposed device robust ASC system is presented in this section. In this work, adaptive noise reduction is performed. An illustration of this method is shown in Fig. 4. The analysis is presented for an audio sample chosen from DCASE 2019 Task 1a dataset (tram-stockholm-284-8593-c.wav). The figure illustrates the signal and its corresponding spectrogram before and after adaptive noise reduction.

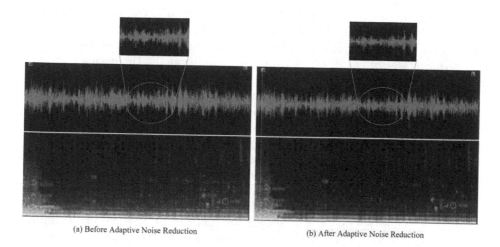

(a) Before Adaptive Noise Reduction   (b) After Adaptive Noise Reduction

Fig. 4. Illustration of an audio sample for adaptive noise reduction.

The proposed device robust ASC system is evaluated for two sets of features, log mel energies, and normalized log mel energies. The features are fed to four neural networks to analyze the performance of different deep learning models. The models are CRNN, LW-CRNN, CRANN, and LW-CRANN. By achieving this performance, the developed system will be more generalizable and can be used in real-world situations. The results achieved for proposed ASC system are given in Table 2.

Table 2. Results achieved for the proposed ASC system for different deep learning models.

Model	Noise reduction	Accuracy (in %)		
		A	B	C
CRNN	No	81.4	76.5	75.8
	Yes	82.0	76.9	76.1
LW-CRNN	No	81.8	77.3	75.6
	Yes	82.7	77.8	75.9
CRANN	No	85.1	78.7	77.9
	Yes	85.8	79.4	78.1
LW-CRANN	No	85.4	79.3	78.0
	Yes	**86.1**	**80.6**	**79.2**

The results obtained for the LW-CRANN with normalized log-mel energies resulted in the highest ASC performance and also the performance of devices B and C along with the performance of device A. The purpose of the proposed ASC was achieved. By comparing the performance of the devices, it can be observed that the gap between the performance of the three devices is reduced. The baseline system performance of ASC is 61.9%, 39.6%, and 43.1% for devices A, B, and C, respectively. In comparison with the baseline system, the performance of the proposed system is better in terms of accuracy and the gap between the performances of the device performance. Additionally, the normalization of the features has enhanced all network performances by at least +1%. From the obtained results, it can be stated that elimination of distortion from the audio signal can significantly improve the performance of the ASC system.

The class-wise performance analysis of the CRANN model is presented in Table 3. The results indicate that the performance obtained for the different classes is balanced across all the devices. The accuracy values of the different classes for devices A, B, and C is given in the table. The CRANN with normalization step resulted in highest accuracy for ASC task for all three devices. The performance of outdoor classes such as public square and street pedestrian resulted in lower accuracies. The reason for this can be the interclass similarity between the events present in these acoustic scenes. The highest results are achieved by the park and bus scenes.

Table 3. Class-wise performance of Devices A, B, and C for CRANN model.

Classes	Accuracy (in %)		
	A	B	C
Airport	78.5	71.2	70.3
Bus	96.2	86.4	88.7
Metro	89.9	80.3	84.2
Metro station	81.4	66.8	77.5
Park	96.4	97.5	95.5
Public square	68.0	61.2	66.2
Shopping mall	81.2	87.3	79.4
Street pedestrian	79.4	59.4	55.2
Street traffic	93.4	97.6	93.9
Tram	96.6	98.3	81.1
Average	**86.1**	**80.6**	**79.2**

The proposed ASC system is compared with the state-of-the-art systems in Table 4. DCASE 2019 Task 1(a) challenges' best results namely, McDonnell et al. [9] and Chen et al. [3] are used for comparing our results. These two are the top entries in the DCASE 2019 Task 1(a) challenge submissions. The comparison is done with respect to features, classifiers and accuracy of the system. Both state-of-the-art system used time frequency representations such as Mel-spectrograms, log-Mel spectrograms, and scalograms. In our proposed system, we have used Fisher feature vectors which are derived from the time frequency representations namely Mel-spectrograms and Gammatone Time Cepstral Cooefficients. Both [3,9] used deep learning based neural networks whose computation complexity is high compared to the CRANN performance in our work. Compared to the accuracies reported by the state-of-the-art works, our proposed approach has achieved an average accuracy of 86.1% which is an improvement of almost 1.1%.

Table 4. Comparison of performance of the proposed LW-CRANN network and other state-of-the-art ASC systems for DCASE 2019 Task 1(a) dataset.

Method	Accuracy (in %)
CNN with scalogram and Mel-filter bank features [3]	85
Deep residual networks [9]	82.3
Proposed LW-CRANN	**86.1**

5 Conclusion

This work proposes a device robust ASC system using adaptive noise reduction and low-complex deep learning methods. In a real-world scenario, the classification of acoustic scenes must be robust, which is, irrespective of the recording device, the ASC system must identify the scene, and the device characteristics should not affect the performance of the system. However, a significant performance decrease can be seen in real-time systems for the existing ASC systems. An adaptive noise reduction technique is introduced in this work to reduce the device distortion for audio samples recorded from mobile devices. A significant improvement in the performance of ASC is observed in mobile devices after the noise reduction technique is applied to these audio samples. The primary reason for improvement in the performance of ASC for mismatched devices is the elimination of the distortion and additional noises in the audio samples. The method for removal of the distortion has to be chosen carefully as in some cases critical audio information can also be discarded in the process. Once the pre-processing method is performed, feature extraction is carried out. Spectrograms are extracted for the audio samples, and to remove the biased values in the feature matrix, the normalization technique is applied. Later, the features are fed to four deep learning architectures. The key contributions of this work are the preprocessing of audio samples of mobile devices to attenuate device distortion and the use of light-weight CRANN deep learning architecture to perform the classification of acoustic scenes. From the results, it can be observed that eliminating distortion in the audio samples can increase the accuracy and decrease the loss of the ASC system without using any additional augmentation methods. Therefore in future work, more distortion removal techniques can be explored to improve the ASC performance in mismatched ASC audio recording datasets.

References

1. Bahdanau, D., Cho, K., Bengio, Y.: Neural machine translation by jointly learning to align and translate. arXiv preprint arXiv:1409.0473 (2014)
2. Barchiesi, D., Giannoulis, D., Stowell, D., Plumbley, M.D.: Acoustic scene classification: classifying environments from the sounds they produce. IEEE Signal Process. Mag. **32**(3), 16–34 (2015)
3. Chen, H., Liu, Z., Liu, Z., Zhang, P., Yan, Y.: Integrating the data augmentation scheme with various classifiers for acoustic scene modeling. Technical report, DCASE2019 Challenge (2019)
4. Dorfer, M., Lehner, B., Eghbal-zadeh, H., Christop, H., Fabian, P., Gerhard, W.: Acoustic scene classification with fully convolutional neural networks and i-vectors. DCASE2018 challenge (2018)
5. Eghbal-zadeh, H., Koutini, K., Widmer, G.: Acoustic scene classification and audio tagging with receptive-field-regularized CNNs. Technical Report, DCASE 2019 Challenge (2019)
6. Heittola, T., Mesaros, A., Virtanen, T.: Acoustic scene classification challenge: generalization across devices and low complexity solutions. In: Proceedings of the Detection and Classification of Acoustic Scenes and Events Workshop (DCASE2020), pp. 56–60 (2020)
7. Hu, H., et al.: Device-robust acoustic scene classification based on two-stage categorization and data augmentation. Technical report, DCASE2020 Challenge (2020)
8. Ma, L., Smith, D., Milner, B.: Environmental noise classification for context-aware applications. In: Mařík, V., Retschitzegger, W., Štěpánková, O. (eds.) DEXA 2003. LNCS, vol. 2736, pp. 360–370. Springer, Heidelberg (2003). https://doi.org/10.1007/978-3-540-45227-0_36
9. McDonnell, M.D., Gao, W.: Acoustic scene classification using deep residual networks with late fusion of separated high and low frequency paths. In: Proceedings of IEEE International Conference on Acoustics, Speech and Signal Processing (ICASSP), pp. 141–145 (2020)
10. Mesaros, A., Heittola, T., Virtanen, T.: A multi-device dataset for urban acoustic scene classification. In: Proceedings of the Detection and Classification of Acoustic Scenes and Events 2018 Workshop (DCASE2018), pp. 9–13 (2018)
11. Misra, H., Ikbal, S., Bourlard, H., Hermansky, H.: Spectral entropy based feature for robust ASR. In: 2004 IEEE International Conference on Acoustics, Speech, and Signal Processing, vol. 1, pp. I-193. IEEE (2004)
12. Nguyen, T., Pernkopf, F.: Acoustic scene classification using a convolutional neural network ensemble and nearest neighbor filters. In: Workshop on Detection and Classification of Acoustic Scenes and Events (2018)
13. Nguyen, T., Pernkopf, F., Kosmider, M.: Acoustic scene classification for mismatched recording devices using heated-up softmax and spectrum correction. In: ICASSP 2020–2020 IEEE International Conference on Acoustics, Speech and Signal Processing (ICASSP), pp. 126–130. IEEE (2020)
14. Pham, L.D., Mcloughlin, I., Phan, H.P., Palaniappan, R.: A multi-spectrogram deep neural network for acoustic scene classification technical report (2019)

15. Plata, M.: Deep neural networks with supported clusters preclassification procedure for acoustic scene recognition. Technical Report, DCASE2019 Challenge (2019)
16. Sakashita, Y.: Acoustic scene classification by ensemble of spectrograms based on adaptive temporal divisions. In: Technical Report, Detection and Classification of Acoustic Scenes and Events Challenge (2018)
17. Scheirer, E., Slaney, M.: Construction and evaluation of a robust multifeature speech/music discriminator. In: 1997 IEEE International Conference on Acoustics, Speech, and Signal Processing, vol. 2, pp. 1331–1334. IEEE (1997)
18. Sehili, M.A., et al.: Sound environment analysis in smart home. In: Paternò, F., de Ruyter, B., Markopoulos, P., Santoro, C., van Loenen, E., Luyten, K. (eds.) AmI 2012. LNCS, vol. 7683, pp. 208–223. Springer, Heidelberg (2012). https://doi.org/10.1007/978-3-642-34898-3_14
19. Song, H., Yang, H.: Feature enhancement for robust acoustic scene classification with device mismatch. Technical Report, DCASE2019 Challenge (2019)
20. Wang, D., Brown, G.J.: Computational Auditory Scene Analysis: Principles, Algorithms, and Applications. Wiley-IEEE press, Hoboken (2006)
21. Zieliński, S.K., Lee, H.: Automatic spatial audio scene classification in binaural recordings of music. Appl. Sci. 9(9), 1724 (2019)

Comparison of Word Embeddings of Unaligned Audio and Text Data Using Persistent Homology

Zhandos Yessenbayev$^{(\boxtimes)}$ ⓘ and Zhanibek Kozhirbayev$^{(\boxtimes)}$ ⓘ

National Laboratory Astana, Nur-Sultan, Kazakhstan
{zhyessenbayev,zhanibek.kozhirbayev}@nu.edu.kz

Abstract. We have performed preliminary work on topological analysis of audio and text data for unsupervised speech processing. The work is based on the assumption that phoneme frequencies and contextual relationships are similar in the acoustic and text domains for the same language. Accordingly, this allowed the creation of a mapping between these spaces that takes into account their geometric structure. As a first step, generative methods based on variational autoencoders were chosen to map audio and text data into two latent vector spaces. In the next stage, persistent homology methods are used to analyze the topological structure of two spaces. Although the results obtained support the idea of the similarity of the two spaces, further research is needed to correctly map acoustic and text spaces, as well as to evaluate the real effect of including topological information in the autoencoder training process.

Keywords: Unsupervised processing · Word embeddings · Topological data analysis · Persistent homology and diagram

1 Introduction

Topological data analysis (TDA) [1, 2] is a relatively new field of intelligent processing of unstructured data. It appeared as a result of computer implementation of algebraic topology methods [3]. Heuristically, the idea is to build a "shape" for a "point cloud" in spaces of not too high dimension. The forms are simplicial complexes, i.e. sets formed by vertices, edges, faces, tetrahedra, etc., obtained as a result of a filtering procedure: covering a cloud of points with balls of variable radius, or simply a proximity scale in an appropriate metric. A synchronous increase in the radii of the balls leads to their intersections, which are encoded by the elements of the complex: edges and faces. The complex allows calculating topological invariants - the so-called Betti numbers, which, roughly speaking, measure the number of k-dimensional holes. However, the topology obtained with the help of coverages depends significantly on the chosen spatial scale. The original solution was to evaluate the invariants on all scales simultaneously. Relationships between invariants on different scales are encoded by their lifetime in the filtering process in the form of a persistence diagram [4]. Roughly speaking, persistence is a metaphor for the lifetime, expressed in units of a distance scale, a topological pattern, for example, the appearance of a cycle and its transformation into a face. Nontrivial stability theorems

© Springer Nature Switzerland AG 2022
S. R. M. Prasanna et al. (Eds.): SPECOM 2022, LNAI 13721, pp. 700–711, 2022.
https://doi.org/10.1007/978-3-031-20980-2_59

for persistent diagrams with respect to perturbations were obtained [5], which made computational topology a universal non-metric apparatus for analyzing various objects [5–9].

2 Topological Data Analysis

2.1 Simplicial Complexes and Filtrations

Two points in the feature space are connected by an edge if the distance between them, in a suitable metric, does not exceed a given small number ε. In formal language, we are talking about the concept of the so-called ε-connected Cantor chain. This is the name of a sequence of non-equidistant points in which the number of linearly connected components depends on the chosen spatial resolution. In other words, we combine two components into one if our vision does not separate them separately on a scale $\leq \varepsilon$.

Chain proximity leads to the notion of a nerve of a topological covering of a point set. Let $S = \{v_i\}_{i=1}^{N}$ a finite set of points from R^2. Decorate each point with a disk $B(v_i, \varepsilon)$ centered at v_i and radius ε. Recall that a structure consisting of the simplest (simplicissima) elements - vertices, edges and triangular faces is called a simplicial complex if its adjacent elements intersect at a point or have a common edge. We will simultaneously increase the radii of the disks. The intersection of the resulting dilation elements leads to a simplicial complex, which is called the Cech complex [37]:

$$K(S, \varepsilon) = \bigcap_{i=1}^{N} B(v_i, \varepsilon) \tag{1}$$

To obtain the actual nerve, we connect adjacent points with an edge when the adjacent disks corresponding to them intersect. In addition, let us agree that the intersection of three adjacent disks generates a face, i.e. "shaded" triangle. As the radii increase, the complex becomes structurally simpler and turns into one "shaded" face (Fig. 1a). This process in algebraic topology is called filtration [10]. Recall that inflation or dilatation of the disk is one of the main operations in mathematical morphology - addition according to Minkowski, which is usually denoted as $B \oplus \varepsilon$ [7]. As before, we decorate each point of the set with a disk S of radius ε. The union of these disks is called a parallel body $S \oplus \varepsilon$ for S or a Minkowski covering. The nerve theorem states that the Cech complex (1) for a set S and its Minkowski covering $S \oplus \varepsilon$ are homotopic to each other [10]:

$$K(S, \varepsilon) \sim S \oplus \varepsilon \tag{2}$$

In other words, the union of disks for a Minkowski cover can be "compressed" by a continuous deformation to a simplicial Cech complex: note that the homotopy admits "sticking together" of points. On the other hand, the theorem allows one to compare two spaces, up to their approximation by combinatorial complexes loaded with integer topological invariants. Note that the essential elements of the complex are the number of separate ε-distinguishable components, which is measured by the so-called Betti number β_0, and the number of independent classes of unfilled holes, i.e., cycles formed by a closed chain of edges. Their number is measured by the Betty number β_1.

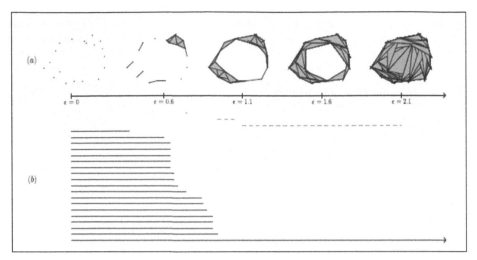

Fig. 1. Example: (a) filtrations (simplicial complexes for various ε) and (b) corresponding persistent barcodes built on the clouds of points.

In terms of pattern recognition, when constructing a filtering, we change our tolerance for determining the relationship between features from the smallest, when adjacent points do not intersect with their neighborhoods - disks, to the largest, when a point is related or similar to all points in the feature space, i.e. included in a single end face. It is obvious that in this procedure the lifetimes of each point, before it is included in the edge and each hole, until its disappearance (shading), are different. Lifespan or persistence can be measured by the interval of change in dilatation radii from the birth to the destruction of the rib or hole. Such differences are depicted by a set of horizontal segments - barcodes, parallel to the axis of radius change (Fig. 1b). It is more convenient to represent barcodes in the form of a persistence diagram, a cloud of points on a plane, the coordinates of each of which are the beginning and end of the barcode (Fig. 2). All points naturally lie above the diagonal, which corresponds to zero lifetime [4]. All of the above techniques relate to the calculation of persistent homologies by methods of computational topology. This is the name given to the computer version of algebraic topology, a science that has been actively developing in recent years [6, 11]. In the following section, we give a more formal definition of persistent homologies and diagrams.

2.2 Persistent Homology and Betti Numbers

Consider a simplicial complex K and a function $f : K \rightarrow R$ [5, pp. 150–152]. We require that f be monotonic, which means that it does not decrease along increasing chains of faces, that is, $f(\sigma) \leq f(\tau)$ if σ is a face of τ. Monotonicity means that the set of sublevels $K(a) = f^{-1}(-\infty, a]$ is a subcomplex of K for any $a \in R$. Let m be the number of simplices in K, we get $n+1 \leq m+1$ different subcomplexes, which we we arrange in the form of an increasing nested sequence of complexes: $\varnothing = K_0 \subseteq K_1 \subseteq \cdots \subseteq K_n = K$.

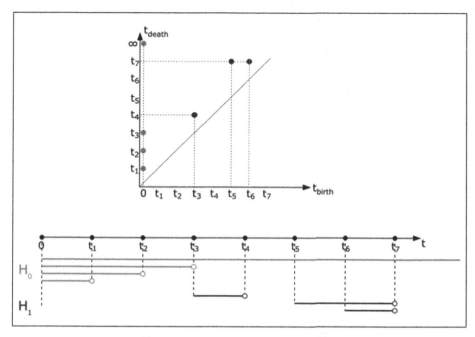

Fig. 2. Relationship between persistent barcodes and diagrams.

In other words, if $a_0 < a_1 < \ldots < a_n$ are the values of functions of simplices in K and $a_0 = -\infty$, then $K_i = K(a_i)$ for each i. We call this sequence of complexes the filtration f and perceive it as a construction that adds fragments of simplices in the process of their aggregation into a covering complex. We have already seen filtering examples before, namely the Cech complex. We are more interested in the topological evolution expressed by the corresponding sequence of homology groups. For every $i \leq j$ we have an inclusion map from the main space Ki to the space Kj and hence the induced homomorphism $f_p^{i,j} : H_p(K_i) \rightarrow H_p(K_j)$ for every dimension p. Thus, the filtration corresponds to a sequence of homology groups connected by homomorphisms:

$$0 = H_p(K_0) \rightarrow H_p(K_1) \rightarrow \ldots \rightarrow H_p(K_n) = H_p(K) \tag{3}$$

the same for each dimension p. As we move from K_{i-1} to K_i, we may get new homology classes and may lose some when they become trivial or merge with each other. We collect classes that are born at or before a certain threshold and die after another threshold in groups.

Definition. The p-th persistent homology groups are the images of the homomorphisms induced by the inclusion $H_p^{i,j} = imf_p^{i,j}$ for $0 \leq i \leq j \leq n$. The corresponding p-th persistent Betti numbers are the ranks of these groups, $\beta_p^{i,j} = rankH_p^{i,j}$.

Similarly, we define reduced persistent homology groups and reduced persistent Betti numbers. Note that $H_p^{i,j} = H_p(K_i)$. The persistent homology groups consist of the homology classes K_i that are still "alive" in K_j, or, more formally, $H_p^{i,j} =$

$Z_p(K_i)/(B_p(K_j)\cap Z_p(K_i))$. We have such a group for every dimension p and every pair of indices $i \leq j$. We can be more specific about the classes counted by persistent homology groups. Let γ be a class in $H_p(K_i)$, we say that it was born in K_i if $\gamma \notin H_p^{i-1,i}$. Further, if γ is born in K_i, then it dies, entering K_j, if it merges with an older class in the transition from K_{j-1} to K_j, that is, $f_p^{i,j-1}(\gamma) \notin H_p^{i-1,j-1}$, but $f_p^{i,j}(\gamma) \in H_p^{i-1,j}$ (Fig. 3). If γ is born in K_i and dies entering K_j, then we call the difference in function value persistence, $\mathrm{pers}(\gamma) = a_j - a_i$. If γ is born in K_i but never dies, then we set its persistence to infinity.

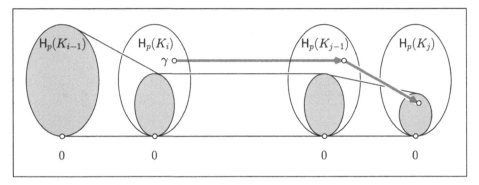

Fig. 3. Homology groups and homomorphisms [5].

2.3 Persistent Diagrams

Visualization of a set of persistent Betty numbers is carried out by drawing points in two dimensions [5, p.152]. Some of these points may have coordinates equal to infinity, and some may be the same, so we are really talking about a multiset of points in the extended real plane, $\overline{R}^2 = (R \cup \{\pm\infty\})^2$. Denoting $\mu_p^{i,j}$ as the number of independent p-dimensional classes that are born in K_i and die when entering K_j, we have:

$$\mu_p^{i,j} = \left(\beta_p^{i,j-1} - \beta_p^{i,j}\right) - \left(\beta_p^{i-1,j-1} - \beta_p^{i-1,j}\right), \tag{4}$$

for all $i < j$ and all p. Indeed, the first difference on the right-hand side counts the classes that were born on (or before) K_i and die on entering K_j, while the second difference counts the classes born on (or before) K_{i-1} and die on entering K_j. Drawing each point (a_i, a_j) with multiplicity $\mu_p^{i,j}$, we obtain the p-th persistence diagram of the given filtration, denoted as $\mathrm{Dgmp}(f)$. It represents the class as a point, the vertical distance to the diagonal of which is the persistence. Since the multiplicities are defined only for $i < j$, then all points lie above the diagonal. For technical reasons, we add points on the diagonal of the diagram with infinite multiplicity. Examples of persistence diagrams can be seen in Fig. 4. The persistent Betty numbers are easy to calculate. In particular, $\beta_p^{i,j}$ is the number of points in the upper left quadrant with the corner point (a_k, a_l). A class that was born in K_i and died in K_j is counted if and only if $a_i \leq a_k$ and $a_j > a_l$. Thus, the quadrant is closed on its vertical right side and open on its horizontal underside.

Fundamental Lemma on Persistent Homologies. Let $\varnothing = K_0 \subseteq K_1 \subseteq \cdots \subseteq K_n = K$ be a filtration. For each pair of indices $0 \leq k \leq l \leq n$ and each dimension p, the p-th persistent Betti number is $\beta_p^{i,j} = \sum_{i \leq k} \sum_{j > 1} \mu_p^{i,j}$.

This is an important property. It states that a persistence diagram encodes all information about persistent homologous groups.

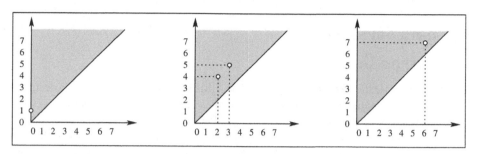

Fig. 4. Examples of the persistent diagrams [5].

3   Variational Autoencoders

Variation autoencoders (VAE) [12, 13] determine the probabilistic generative process between observing x and the latent variable z as follows $z \sim p_\theta(z)$ and $x \sim p_\theta(x|z)$, where $p_\theta(z)$ and $p_\theta(x|z)$ are the probability distribution functions parameterized with respect to θ. In an unsupervised learning setup, we are only given a data set $X = \{x_i\}$, but the true value of θ and the latent variable z for each observation x are not known. Often, we are interested in knowing the marginal probability of the data $p_\theta(x)$ or $p_\theta(z|x)$. However, both require the calculation of the intractable integral $\int p_\theta(z)\, p_\theta(x|z)dz$.

To solve this problem, VAE introduce the recognition model $q_\phi(z|x)$, which approximates the true probability $p_\theta(z|x)$. Therefore, we can rewrite the marginal likelihood as:

$$\text{Log } p_\theta(x) = D_{KL}(q_\phi(z|x)||p_\theta(z|x)) + L(\theta, \phi; x) \geq L(\theta, \phi; x) = -D_{KL}(q_\phi(z|x)||p_\theta(z)) + E_{q_\phi(z|x)}[\log p_\theta(x|z)] \tag{5}$$

where $L(\theta, \phi; x)$ is the variational lower bound (ELBO) we want to optimize with respect to θ and ϕ. Optimization of ELBO with respect to θ and ϕ is carried out using stochastic gradient variation Bayes (SGVB).

In the framework of VAE, we assume that the recognition model $q_\phi(z|x)$ and the generative model $p_\theta(x|z)$ are parameterized using diagonal Gaussian distributions in which the mean value and covariance are calculated using a neural network. It is also assumed that the a priori probability $p_\theta(z)$ is a centered isotropic multidimensional Gaussian, i.e. $p_\theta(z) = N(z, 0, \mathbf{I})$, which has no free parameters.

In practice, the expectation is approximated by sampling K samples from $z^k \sim q_\phi(z|x)$, and then calculating the equation $E_{q_\phi(z|x)}\left[\log p_\theta(x|z)\right] \approx \frac{1}{K}\sum_{k=1}^{K}\log p_\theta\left(x|z^k\right)$. To obtain a differentiable network after sampling, a reparametrization trick is used [13]. Suppose that $z = N(z; \mu_z, \sigma_z^2 I))$, then after reparameterization we have $z = \mu_z + \sigma_z \bullet \varepsilon$, where $\bullet$ denotes the element-wise product, and the vector ε is selected from $N(0; I)$ and is considered as an additional input.

4 Experiment Setup

4.1 TIMIT Dataset

As input, we chose the TIMIT dataset [14]. The TIMIT corpus of read speech is designed to provide speech data for acoustic-phonetic studies and for the development and evaluation of automatic speech recognition systems. TIMIT contains broadband recordings of 630 speakers of 8 major dialects of American English, each reading 10 phonetically rich sentences. The TIMIT corpus includes time-aligned orthographic, phonetic and word transcriptions as well as a 16-bit, 16 kHz speech waveform file for each utterance. Corpus design was a joint effort among the Massachusetts Institute of Technology (MIT), SRI International (SRI) and Texas Instruments, Inc. (TI). The speech was recorded at TI, transcribed at MIT and verified and prepared for CD-ROM production by the National Institute of Standards and Technology (NIST).

4.2 VAE Model

We use a variational autoencoder with convolutional layers, which were implemented in Keras. The model consists of an input layer, an encoder and decoder layers. The input shape has the dimension (256, 64, 1). To accommodate this, we reshape our audio and text data. In particular, for audio data we use two dimensional spectrograms where as for the text data we use two-dimensional word embeddings. The encoder and decoder have five convolutional layers each. We set the number of epochs to 150, and the batch size to 64. Figure 5 shows the VAE architecture with input and output parameters. Ultimately, we are interested in the intermediate vectors between the encoder and the decoder layers, i.e., those which have the dimension 128.

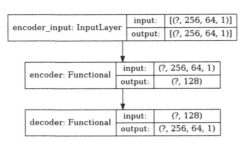

Fig. 5. VAE architecture with input and output parameters (question marks '?' correspond to the size of batches, which can be any number depending on the training settings).

4.3 Feature Extraction

To extract features from audio data, we need to do some preprocessing steps. Each audio file was divided into the words using the timestamps given in the annotations of TIMIT database. Then we performed signal padding and from these signals we extracted MFCC-spectrograms. For that, we used librosa [15], a music and audio pre-processing library. As a final step we normalized the vectors. All these steps were performed for each of the audio files in the dataset. These vectors were used for training of our VAE model and the extraction of the intermediate vectors. The Fig. 6 plots the training loss of the model. The Fig. 6 plots the training loss of the model.

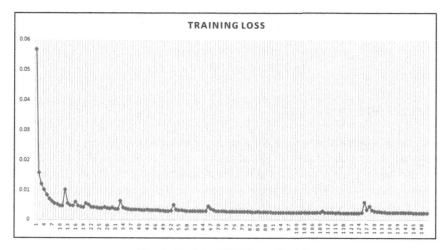

Fig. 6. Training VAE for audio data.

For the text data, we used Gensim library that supports the Word2Vec word embedding implementation for learning new word vectors from text. It also provides tools to download pre-trained word embeddings in multiple formats, and to use and query loaded embeddings [16]. Once the word embeddings were obtained, we then trained a VAE model and extracted the intermediate vectors. The Fig. 7 plots the training loss of the model.

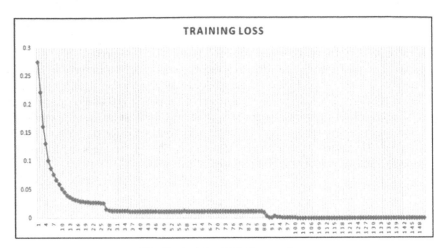

Fig. 7. Training VAE for text data.

5   Results and Discussion

Data for calculating persistent homology can be represented in different ways depending on the subject area under study - weighted graphs, images, and point clouds. In our case, we use the third type of audio and text data representation - point clouds, since the data has already been extracted in advance as a set of vectors corresponding to individual words. Thus, we have two 128-dimensional sets of vectors - for audio and text domains. Vectors are written line by line in a text file, and vector components are separated by commas. Here we assume that the vector space is equipped with the standard Euclidean metric. Table 1 shows statistics on the number of vectors for both types of data.

Table 1. Statistics of data.

Data type	Number of vectors	Vector size
Audio	54378	128
Text	6224	128

To construct the simplicial complexes (Vietoris–Rips) and persistent homology, we used the Ripser package [17], one of the best among other analogues in terms of computation speed and written in C++. The calculation process takes up to 3 h for audio data and up to 1.5 h for test data. The reason is that the volume of audio data is larger due to the repetition of individual words that are spoken several times, while in text data each word occurs only once. Finally, we built persistent diagrams shown in the Fig. 8 and 9. The red dots correspond to the Betti numbers $\beta = 0$, and the blue dots to $\beta = 1$.

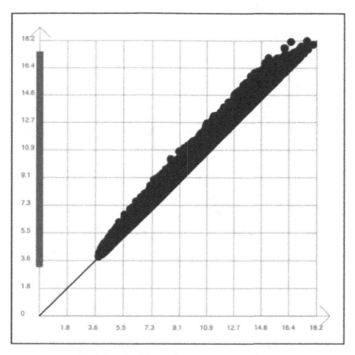

Fig. 8. Persistent diagram of audio data.

To analyze the distribution of persistent intervals, we constructed histograms of interval lengths for dimension 1 (Fig. 10). Histograms in both cases are similar to an exponential distribution, but with different parameters.

As can be seen from Fig. 8 and 9, the diagrams of audio and text data are very similar, i.e. have a similar topological structure, except that the blue dots are present to a lesser extent at the top of the graph. This may be due to the fact that the audio data for each word is repeated and, accordingly, forms more "holes" in space, which are closed at the later stages of filtration (at large ball radii).

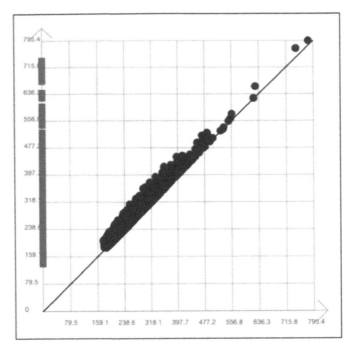

Fig. 9. Persistent diagram of text data.

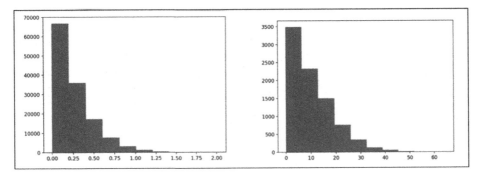

Fig. 10. Histograms for persistent intervals for audio (left) and text (right) at the dimension 1.

6 Conclusion

In this paper, we have presented our preliminary work on the analysis and visualization of audio and text data using persistent homology methods. As the results showed, the topological structure of both spaces is quite similar, which confirms the hypothesis about the similarity of audio and text spaces, and the research itself can be further developed. In particular, we plan to quantitively compare persistence diagrams using Riemannian or Wasserstein metrics. Furthermore, the information on topological similarity of both spaces can be used directly in course of training of the variational autoencoders and feature extraction.

Acknowledgements. The work is supported by the Ministry of Education and Science of the Republic of Kazakhstan under the grants No. AP13068635 and No. AP08053085.

We also thank Dr. Nikolay Makarenko from The Central Astronomical Observatory of the Russian Academy of Sciences at Pulkovo for his invaluable comments and lecture notes on the topic of topological data analysis.

References

1. Peikert, R., Hauser, H., Carr, H., Fuchs, R. (eds.): Topological Methods in Data Analysis and Visualization II: Theory, Algorithms, and Applications. Springer-Verlag, p. 299 (2012). https://doi.org/10.1007/978-3-642-23175-9
2. Carlsson, G.: Topology and data. Bulletin (New Series) of the Amer. Math. Soc. **46**, 255–308 (2009)
3. Zomorodian, A.J.: Topology for Computing. Cambridge University Press, p. 259 (2005)
4. Ghrist, R.: Barcodes: The Persistent Topology of Data. Bulletin (New Seires) of the Amer. Math. Soc. **45**, 61–75 (2008)
5. Edelsbrunner, H., Harer, J.: Computational Topology, An Introduction. American Mathematical Society, p. 241 (2010)
6. Kaczynski, T., Mischaikow, K., Mrozek, M.: Computational Homology, p. 480. Springer (2004). https://doi.org/10.1007/b97315
7. Carlsson, E., Carlsson, G., de Silva, V.: An algebraic topological method for feature identification. Int. J. Comput. Geom. Appl. **16**(4), 291–314 (2006)
8. Ferri, M., Frosini, P., Cerri, A., Di Fabio (eds.): Computational Topology in Image Context, p. 157. Springer (2012). https://doi.org/10.1007/978-3-642-30238-1
9. De Floriani, L., Spagnuolo, M.: Shape Analysis and Structuring, p. 296. Springer (2008). https://doi.org/10.1007/978-3-540-33265-7
10. Najman, L., Talbot, H.: Mathematical Morphology: From Theory to Applications, p. 503. John Wiley & Sons, Inc. (2010)
11. Edelsbrunner, H., Morozov, D.: Persistent homology: theory and practice. In: Proceedings of the European Congress of Mathematics, pp. 31–50 (2012)
12. Hsu, W., Zhang, Y., Glass, J.R.: Learning latent representations for speech generation and transformation (2017). arXiv:1704.04222, https://arxiv.org/abs/1704.04222
13. Kingma, D.P., Welling M.: Auto-encoding variational bayes (2013). arXiv:1312.6114, https://arxiv.org/abs/1312.6114
14. Garofolo, J.S., Lamel, L.F., Fisher, W.M., Fiscus, J.G., Pallett, D.S.: DARPA TIMIT acoustic-phonetic continous speech corpus. NIST speech disc 1–1.1. NASA STI/Recon technical report, 93, 27403 (1993)
15. McFee, B., Raffel, C., Liang, D., Ellis, D.P., McVicar, M., Battenberg, E., Nieto, O.: librosa: audio and music signal analysis in python. In: Proceedings of the 14th Python in Science Conference, vol. 8, pp. 18–25 (2015)
16. Srinivasa-Desikan, B.: Natural Language Processing and Computational Linguistics: A practical guide to text analysis with Python, Gensim, spaCy, and Keras. Packt Publishing Ltd (2018)
17. Bauer, U.: Ripser: efficient computation of Vietoris-Rips persistence barcodes. J. Appl. Comput. Topology **5**, 391–423 (2021)

Low-Cost Training of Speech Recognition System for Hindi ASR Challenge 2022

Alexander Zatvornitskiy$^{(\boxtimes)}$

Saint-Petersburg, Russia
al.zatv@gmail.com

Abstract. This paper describes the speech recognition system, developed for Gram Vaani ASR Challenge 2022. The acoustic modeling techniques included i-vectors-based speaker adaptation and a combination of convolutional and factored time-delayed neural networks, fine-tuned with state-level Minimum Bayes Risk criteria.

Experiments with text data augmentation and separation of different domains in test data are discussed.

Proposed system is quite competitive, as it was among the top four participants in the evaluation, and show best result among individual participants. Yet, it requires very low computation resources to build it, which can be important for developing countries.

Keywords: Gram vaani ASR challenge 2022 · Hindi · Low resource ASR

1 Introduction

It is now obvious that the greatest return on the efforts for researchers in ASR will be in low resource languages and dialects, especially the languages of the "next billion users of Internet". The main problem with ASR in these languages is that there is much less data for them. The second biggest problem is that researchers are less interested in these languages or have fewer resources.

As a result, while most researched languages have the quality of recognition rather high or even close to human level, in other languages it is still far from being adequate.

There are two main directions in the research of low-resource languages. The first one seeks to apply data from other languages and tasks, transferring them to a low resource language. The second focuses on the architecture of the system and the learning process, so that the available target data is sufficient for sustainable learning of the system. Of course, these directions are not mutually exclusive.

Employed by VK Company, Ltd. Proposed system and this paper were developed during vacation.

© Springer Nature Switzerland AG 2022
S. R. M. Prasanna et al. (Eds.): SPECOM 2022, LNAI 13721, pp. 712–718, 2022.
https://doi.org/10.1007/978-3-031-20980-2_60

As an example of the first approach, we can mention semi-supervised [8] and self-supervised [2,4] learning. Semi-supervised learning implies generating pseudo-labels for untranscribed data, using previously built "bootstrap model". This "bootstrap model" can be trained on small amount of manualy transcribed data, or it can be taken from other language.

Self-supervised learning approach tries to learn representations from unlabeled data, usually by predicting some properties of masked parts of audio from it's context. These representations are intended to be used in "upstream tasks". This paradigm promises fast and easy tuning of this – carefully pretrained – universal embedding extractors to solve tasks like speech recognition, speaker identification or verification, language detection, et cetera, with very little amount of manualy labeled data. This approach already show interesting results in natural language processing and computer vision, sometimes setting new state of the art.

But, as for speech recognition, such "foundational models" are not robust enought to domain or language discrepancy between pre-training and ASR finetuning. In other words, they are biased toward the domain and/or language from which the unlabelled data comes [5,6,20]. It means that they require massive amount of unlabeled data from similar language and/or domain, and big computational resources.

While these problems are waiting for new solutions, traditional approaches to low resource speech recognition problem are still competitive. They boils down to simplifying the task for the neural network so it can be trained robustly with a small amount of target data (hence, with little computational cost). It means that modeling of speech dynamics is taken out to a separately trained model, usualy Hidden Markov Models of Conditional Random Fields [14]. Same applies to pronunciation and language models, which often use additional sources of lingustic knowledge.

These methods dominates in closed tasks of low-resource speech recognition evaluations. For example, OpenKWS evaluation ([9], e.g. [7]) which was coordinated with DARPA's BABEL program, and OpenASR evaluation (including recent OpenASR21 [1], e.g. [21]) coordinated with DARPA MATERIAL program.

In this paper we apply this approach to Closed Track of Gram Vaani ASR Chalenge 2022. This challenge was organized around spontaneous telephone and broadcast speech, collected by Gram Vaani social technology enterprise. Corpus developers reports that it contains diverse regional variations of Hindi. Transcriptions are provided with varying degrees of accuracy due to crowd sourcing.

For Closed track, organizers had provided manualy labeled training and dev set (100h and 5h, respectively), and pronunciation lexicon. Participants must not use any pretrained models or additional data in this track.

As our computational resources are limited (3×1080Ti GPUs), our goal was to build system which requires small computational resources.

1.1 Our Contribution

This is a "system description" paper. It contributes a description of main decisions about structure and architecture of the competitive modern system for low
resource speech recognition, built with low training cost.

2 Data Description and Baseline System

The data set comprises of telephone quality speech data in different dialects of
Hindi. Organizers released approximately 1000 h of unlabelled data and 105 h of
labelled speech data through this challenge (5 h are hold out to development set)

Gram Vaani data has .mp3 files with mix of sampling rates from 8 KHz to
48 KHZ. They come from different sources (8 kHz data are phone calls, other
utterances are, probably, news from TV or radio). Here is the sampling rate
distribution in the Train set: 8 kHz – 60.87%, 16 kHz – 0.84%, 32 kHz – 0.25%,
44 kHz – 34.46%, 48 kHz – 3.56%. Development and evaluation sets have similar
sampling rate distribution.

Metadata is also available. It contains information about speakers' accent,
age, gender, and sentiment of the utterance.

There are 3 tracks in the challenge: closed, semi-supervised, and open. This
paper describes the system for closed track of the competition, where participants can use only the Gram Vaani 100 h Train dataset and 5 h Development
dataset for training models (both for acoustic and language models), and provided pronunciation lexicon.

Among the baselines provided by organizers, two strongest are Kaldi-based,
which we will call BL-TDNN-F and BL-CNN-TDNN-F. They mainly follows
Kaldi's [13] librispeech recipe. It assumes that system consist of separately
trained language, acoustic model, and pronunciation lexicon [14].

Acoustic model training involves initialization from flat-start with Gaussian
Mixture Models. They are iteratively trained, and used to provide lattice alignments and clustering of targets for neural networks.

Final acoustic models are trained on 40x mfcc features extracted from 3-
fold speed perturbed audio and concatenated with i-vectors [16], calculated by
separately trained extractor.

BL-TDNNF system consists of 12 layers of Factored Time-Delayed Neural
Network Layers (TDNNF, [12]). Final layer contain 7000 outputs. Each of them
is mapped to one of clustered left biphones with single state, as it is usual for
LF-MMI-trained DNN-HMM models. Total number of trainable parameters is
10816544, left and right contexts are 29 frames. This network is trained in 10
epochs with 8 GPU workers, in kaldi's "chain2" framework.

BL-CNN-TDNN-F system contains 12 TDNNF layers with CNN frontend, as
described in [3]. Final layer contains 6000 outputs. Total number of parameters
is 17389360, left and right contexts are 39 frames. This network is trained in 4
epochs with 16 GPU workers, in kaldi's "chain" framework. Organizers report
it achieves WER = 30.93% on dev set.

Baseline language model (LM) is a 3-gram Maximum Entropy LM [15,18] trained on 100h training set and tuned on official dev set.

Organizers report that BL-TDNNF and BL-CNN-TDNNF systems achieves 30.12% and 30.93% WER on dev set, respectively. Our results are little bit different (see Table 1), probably because of random initialization.

3   Acoustic Modeling

To receive maximum possible quality, it is common to build and fuse many single systems. If these systems make different mistakes, fusion procedure can benefit from their diversity.

It is often good idea to build as many systems as different as possible, and choose the combination which achieves best WER.

But, as one of our goals was to build a system using modest compute resources, we have to constrain our search. We decide to focus on diverse enought systems, which reuse as most of required prerequisites (like decision tree, alignments, features, etc.). So, we decide to use mfcc-based TDNN-F system trained with LF-MMI criteria, same system but fine-tuned with state-level Minimum Bayes Risk (sMBR) criteria [17], and CNN-TDNN-F LF-MMI system.

Also, to increase diversity of models, we decide to train one of these systems on audio downsampled to 8 kHz. As 60.87% of data set is 8 kHz spontaneous telephone speech, which is most difficult data source in proposed task, downsampling can help to train our compact Kaldi models.

To save computation time and ease fusion process, we use same alignments and same decision tree to train all of our systems. By series of experiments, which we leave outside of this paper, we find it optimal for this challenge to use decision tree with 8000 pdfs (as opposed to 6000 or 7000 used in CNN-TDNN-F and TDNN-F baselines), and train acoustic models in 4 or 6 epochs to save time (as opposed to 10 epochs in baseline). Data augmentation and i-vector adaptation scheme remains unchanged from the baseline system. Language model and acoustic models architectures are also inherited from baseline systems.

Table 1 gives a summary of performance for trained single systems.

Table 1. Performance of trained single systems.

ID	AM Topology	Freq.	WER, dev.
BL-TDNNF	Baseline TDNNF, 10 epochs, 8 GPUs)	16 kHz	30.23
BL-CNN-TDNNF	Baseline CNN-TDNNF (4 epochs, 16 GPUs)	16 kHz	30.75
tdnnf16a	TDNNF, 4 epochs, 3 GPUs	16 kHz	30.03
tdnnf16as	TDNNF tdnnf16a, fine-tuned with sMBR	16 kHz	28.97
tdnnf8b	TDNNF, 6 epochs, 3 GPUs	8 kHz	29.65
cnnt16c	CNN-TDNNF, 4 epochs, 3 GPUs	16 kHz	31.35
tdnnf16a-no-ivectors	As tdnnf16a, but no speaker adaptation	16 kHz	30.71
tdnnf16a-cmn	As tdnnf16a, but with CMN normalization	16 kHz	30.25

Table 2. Performance of systems combination.

#	IDs	WER
1	tdnnf16a(30.03%)+tdnnf8b(29.65%)	29.04
2	tdnnf16a(30.03%)+tdnnf8b(29.65%)+tdnnf16as(28.97%)	28.39
3	tdnnf16a(30.03%)+tdnnf8b(29.65%)+tdnnf16as(28.97%)+cnnt16c(31.35%)	28.23
4	tdnnf8b(29.65%)+tdnnf16a(30.03%))+cnnt16c(31.35%))	28.72
5	tdnnf8b(29.65%)+tdnnf16as(28.97%))+cnnt16c(31.35%))	28.13
6	tdnnf8b(29.65%)+tdnnf16as(28.97%))	28.30

To perform sequence training of $tdnnf16a$ system with sMBR criteria, we use 5000 iterations of training with effective learning rate $3 \cdot 10^{-8}$. Frame shifting, which is usual data augmentation technique for sMBR training in Kaldi, was not applied, to save GPU time.

It is also good to note that Cepstral Mean normalization (CMN) don't improve recognition. System without i-vector speaker adaptation is also worse than it's adapted counterpart.

4 Combination of Models

To build final system, we use minimum bayes risk (MBR) decoding with lattice combination technique [19]. The improvement is demonstrated in Table 2.

As we can see, system combination greatly improves individual results. The only notable exception is system #3, which can benefit from ellimination of $tdnnf16as$ (as we can see from performance of system #4 and #5).

Data processing and system combination pipeline for selected systems is presented at Fig. 1.

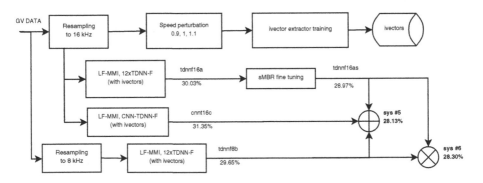

Fig. 1. Data processing and system combination pipeline for systems #5 and #6.

5   Discussion

System #6 from Table 2 was submitted to Gram Vaani ASR Challenge 2022 evaluation system. Reported WER on evaluation set is 27.3% (with CER = 14.35%). It was ranked #4. It is 0.35%abs. behind closest competitor (which is Samsung R&D Institute, Bangalore), and 3.56%abs. behind top system (Speech Technology Center, Ltd, Russia). It is highly likely that our system takes minimal computational resources to train (which is 3×1080Ti GPU with AMD Threadripper 1950 CPU), but it shows competitive results. We think that it is very important for developing countries, where access to computational resources is often limited.

As we can see from Table 2, it was wrong idea to include both LF-MMI and sMBR versions of the same model to system combination. Probably, it is better to fine-tune all systems with sMBR or other sequence training criteria.

We have left out of this article a large number of failed experiments with text data augmentation using neural language models. Such augmentation drastically reduce OOV rate [7,10,11]. This improves performance of systems with whole word dictionaries. In the proposed data, however, the OOV rate of dev set was close to zero. So, improvement in perplexity, achieved this way, did not lead to improvement in WER. As we don't know Hindi and it's writing system, it is unclear for us if it's a property of the language or property of the data. Anyway, for many low resource languages, dealing with text data sparsity is a very important process.

Also, outside of this article we made some experiments with adaptation to different parts of test set. Our motivation was as follows. Both dev and eval sets consists of data from different domains. They can be easily separated, thanks to different audio sample rate. So, in this challenge it is possible to build different models, tuned for, let say, 8kHz and 16+ kHz data. Our preliminary experiments shows that such separate sMBR fine tuning on top of common sMBR-trained model can provide more than 0.4%abs WER. These experiments lies in our main paradigm that we have to compensate data scarcity by using separately trained classifiers.

Acknowledgements. We want to thank the organizers of Gram Vaani ASR Challenge 2022 for interesting and important task, and for their work in collecting and open sourcing corpus of Hindi dialects.

References

1. OpenASR21 Homepage. https://sat.nist.gov/openasr21
2. Baevski, A., Zhou, Y., Mohamed, A., et al.: wav2vec 2.0: a framework for self-supervised learning of speech representations. Adv. Neural Inf. Process. Syst. **33**, 12449–12460 (2020)
3. Ghahremani, P., Manohar, V., Povey, D., et al.: Acoustic modelling from the signal domain using cnns. In: Interspeech, pp. 3434–3438 (2016)

4. Hsu, W.N., Bolte, B., Tsai, Y.H.H., et al.: Hubert: self-supervised speech representation learning by masked prediction of hidden units. IEEE/ACM Trans. Audio Speech Lang. Process. **29**, 3451–3460 (2021)
5. Hsu, W.N., Sriram, A., Baevski, A., et al.: Robust wav2vec 2.0: analyzing domain shift in self-supervised pre-training. In: Interspeech, pp. 721–725 (2021)
6. Javed, T., Doddapaneni, S., Raman, A., et al.: Towards building ASR systems for the next billion users. In: Proceedings of the AAAI Conference on Artificial Intelligence, vol. 36, pp. 10813–10821 (2022)
7. Khokhlov, Y.Y., Medennikov, I., Romanenko, A., et al.: The stc keyword search system for openkws 2016 evaluation. In: Interspeech, pp. 3602–3606 (2017)
8. Likhomanenko, T., Xu, Q., Kahn, J., et al.: slimIPL: language-model-free iterative pseudo-labeling. In: Interspeech, pp. 741–745 (2021)
9. Liu, J., Zhang, W.: Research progress on key technologies of low resource speech recognition. J. Data Acquisit. Process. **32**(2), 205–220 (2017)
10. Medennikov, I., Sorokin, I., Romanenko, A., et al.: The STC system for the CHiME 2018 challenge. In: CHiME5 Workshop (2018)
11. Medennikov, I., Khokhlov, Y.Y., Romanenko, A., et al.: The stc asr system for the voices from a distance challenge 2019. In: INTERSPEECH, pp. 2453–2457 (2019)
12. Povey, D., Cheng, G., Wang, Y., el al.: Semi-orthogonal low-rank matrix factorization for deep neural networks. In: Interspeech, pp. 3743–3747 (2018)
13. Povey, D., Ghoshal, A., Boulianne, G., et al.: The kaldi speech recognition toolkit. In: IEEE Workshop on Automatic Speech Recognition and Understanding. IEEE Signal Processing Society (2011)
14. Povey, D., Peddinti, V., Galvez, D., et al.: Purely sequence-trained neural networks for ASR based on lattice-free MMI. In: Interspeech, pp. 2751–2755 (2016)
15. Rosenfeld, R.: A maximum entropy approach to adaptive statistical language modeling. Comput. Speech Lang. **10**, 187–228 (1996)
16. Saon, G., Soltau, H., Nahamoo, D., et al.: Speaker adaptation of neural network acoustic models using i-vectors. In: IEEE Workshop on Automatic Speech Recognition and Understanding, pp. 55–59. IEEE (2013)
17. Veselý, K., Ghoshal, A., Burget, L., et al.: Sequence-discriminative training of deep neural networks. In: Proceedings of Interspeech, vol. 2013, pp. 2345–2349 (2013)
18. Wu, J., Khudanpur, S.: Efficient training methods for maximum entropy language modeling. In: Interspeech, pp. 114–118. Citeseer (2000)
19. Xu, H., Povey, D., Mangu, L., et al.: Minimum bayes risk decoding and system combination based on a recursion for edit distance. Comput. Speech Lang. **25**(4), 802–828 (2011)
20. Yang, S.W., Chi, P.H., Chuang, Y.S., et al.: SUPERB: speech processing universal PERformance benchmark. In: Interspeech, pp. 1194–1198 (2021)
21. Zhao, J., Wang, H., Li, J., et al.: The THUEE system description for the IARPA OpenASR21 challenge. In: Interspeech 2022, pp. 4855–4859 (2022)

Author Index

Printed in the United States
by Baker & Taylor Publisher Services